The Northern Standard
1839–1847

Birth, Marriage, and Death Notices,
with accounts of other
Auspicious and Adverse Events:
Transcripts, Extracts and Indexes.

Compiled and edited by
Alison Kilpatrick

The Armagh Guardian, 1844–1852:
Vol. I – Births, Marriages, and Deaths

The Niagara Courier Newspaper
Lockport, New York, 1828–1833
Transcripts, Extracts, and Indexes

THE NORTHERN STANDARD
1839 – 1847

BIRTH, MARRIAGE, AND DEATH NOTICES, WITH ACCOUNTS OF OTHER AUSPICIOUS AND ADVERSE EVENTS: TRANSCRIPTS, EXTRACTS, AND INDEXES

Transcripts and extracts, with surname, institution, and subject indexes; drawn from notices and articles published by Arthur Wellington Holmes in The Northern Standard newspaper, between January 12, 1839 – December 25, 1847, in the Town of Monaghan, county Monaghan.

compiled and edited by
Alison Kilpatrick

QUERCUS
ARBOREALIS

This volume consists of data that were: selected for transcription or extraction; entered, catalogued, indexed, and stored in a relational database created by the compiler; output, assembled, and articulated for publication as an historical reference and finding aid; and, supplemented by the editor with interpretive remarks, research notes, statistics, and annotations.

The compiler's database contains detailed fields for: publication references (date, page, column, type of notice); surnames, forenames, and titles; institutions and publications; cause of death*; occupations, including rank*; place names* (country, county, city or townland, and civic address, where stated). *Indexes not included in this volume.

For information regarding permissions, write to the publisher at:

Quercus Arborealis Publications
e-mail: editor@quercus-arborealis.ca
web: www.quercus-arborealis.ca

This book is for genealogists, local historians, and those who love reading stories from the past.

Some articles contain language and characterizations which may have been in common use at the time the articles or stories were written, but which are no longer acceptable. These articles do not reflect the opinions of the compiler, editor, or publisher of this book.

ISBN 978-0-9868873-3-8

First Edition

For Alice M'Mahon
of Carrickmacross
(1833–1843)

TABLE OF CONTENTS

1. INTRODUCTION

This book presents two related compilations: first, transcriptions of Birth, Marriage and Death (BMD) notices, and news accounts of other auspicious and adverse events, drawn from historic issues of *The Northern Standard* newspaper, published in Monaghan, Ireland between the years, 1839–1847; and second, various indexes to serve as finding aids for these articles.

Arthur Wellington Holmes, the first proprietor and editor of *The Northern Standard* commenced publication of his newspaper with the January 12, 1839 edition. Between 1839–1847, Mr. Holmes published 2,346 birth, marriage and death notices, as summarized in Table 1. This period of publication corresponds with such notable events in Irish history as the introduction of the Poor Law system, Daniel O'Connell's renewed campaign for Repeal of the Union, and the early years of the Great Famine. Queen Victoria had succeeded William IV just two years earlier, in 1837.

Table 1. Summary of notices of vital events by type.

Births	118
Marriages	890
Deaths	1,338
Total no. notices	2,346

Subjects—This volume also includes 1,557 transcripts and extracts of "other auspicious and adverse events." These articles contain references or allusions to a vital event, but were not reported in the BMD notices section of the newspaper. Examples of these related subject types, with the frequency of occurrence in this volume, are outlined in Table 2.

Table 2. Summary of notices and articles by subject, in rank order of frequency.

Subject	No.	Subject	No.
1. Death*	1,914	19. Wills, bequests	40
2. Marriage*	1,084	20. Famine	36
3. Accident	171	21. Memorials, testimonials	34
4. Obituary	160	22. Varieties (miscellaneous)	34
5. Disease, epidemic	145	23. Starvation	33
6. Legal, legislative	144	24. Estates	32
7. Inquest	135	25. Military	32
8. Birth*	134	26. Longevity	31
9. Religion	130	27. Titles and honours	29
10. Poem	100	28. Hospitals, dispensaries	27
11. Funeral	98	29. Weather, storms	23
12. Vacancy (post)	97	30. Alcohol and spirits	20
13. Notable (worthy of note)	89	31. Notices (other than BMD)	20
14. Marriage in high life	69	32. Fire	19
15. Marine, ships, harbours	63	33. Medicine, health	19
16. Suicide	59	34. Elopement	15
17. Sudden death	57	35. Bigamy	14
18. Illness	41	36. Census	13

* Includes the number of notices detailed in Table 1.

Other subjects that were classified in this work, but occurring less frequently than those outlined in the table above, include such diverse themes as entertainment and festivities, subscriptions (to raise funds), biographical notes, multiple births, bachelors and spinsters, divorce and separation, coroners, epitaphs, editorial remarks, and rumours.

A total of 3,903 BMD notices and related news articles have been transcribed, or extracted, and indexed for this volume.

Surnames—This series of BMD notices and articles contains 10,544 surname references. The surnames occurring most frequently were Johnson, Smith, Brown, Hamilton, Moore, Mitchell, Clark, Murray, Stewart, and Montgomery. Table 3 provides details of the distribution of the most oft-cited surnames, with spelling variants.

Table 3. Frequency of surnames reported in BMD notices & news articles, 1839–1847, in rank order.

Surname	No.	Surname	No.
1. Johnson, Johnston, Johnstone	119	38. Russell	32
2. Smith, Smyth, Smythe	101	39. Jones	31
3. Brown, Browne	76	40. William, Williams	31
4. Hamilton	70	41. Dawson	30
5. Moor, Moore	64	42. Foster	30
6. Mitchel, Mitchell	63	43. Read, Reade, Reed, Reid	30
7. Clark, Clarke	57	44. Coote	29
8. Murray, Murry	57	45. Kennedy	29
9. Stewart, Stuart	101	46. Boyd, Boyde	28
10. Montgomery	52	47. Leslie	28
11. Beresford, Berresford	51	48. O'Reilly, Reilly	28
12. Thompson, Thomson	51	49. Corry	27
13. Campbell	49	50. Dickson, Dixon	27
14. Graham	49	51. Fitz Gerald, Fitzgerald	27
15. Henry	44	52. Knox	27
16. Armstrong	43	53. Richardson	27
17. Irwin, Irwine	43	54. Evatt	26
18. Morphy, Murphy	43	55. White	26
19. Scott	43	56. Adams	25
20. Wilson	42	57. Hill	25
21. Wright	42	58. Holmes	25
22. King	40	59. Irvine	25
23. Robinson	40	60. M'Kee	25
24. Maffett, Moffet, Moffit, &c.	39	61. O'Connell	25
25. Crawford	39	62. Taylor	24
26. Kelly	36	63. Walsh, Walshe	23
27. Ross, Rosse	36	64. Bourke, Burke	22
28. Westenra	36	65. Lewis	22
29. Anketel, Anketell	35	66. Little, Lytle, Lyttle	22
30. Bell	34	67. Lloyd	22
31. Ker, Kerr	34	68. M'Guire, Maguire	22
32. Martin	34	69. Pratt	22
33. Mayne	34	70. Shirley	22
34. M'Mahon, Mahon	33	71. Walker	22
35. Millar, Miller	33	72. West	22
36. Atkinson	32	73. Duffey, Duffy	21
37. Jackson	32	74. Nixon	21

Place names—Tables 4 and 5 outline the number of articles in which the names of the various Irish counties and of foreign countries appear in this series of notices and news items.

Table 4. Ireland.—No. of articles.	
County	No.
Monaghan	798
Dublin	652
Down	361
Antrim	331
Armagh	324
Tyrone	262
Cavan	211
Fermanagh	187
Londonderry	135
Cork	126
Donegal	110
Louth	110
Tipperary	60
Limerick	57
King's (Offaly)	56
Roscommon	56
Galway	52
Meath	52
Sligo	47
Mayo	42
Waterford	42
Kerry	40
Leitrim	40
Kilkenny	37
Westmeath	30
Wexford	29
Kildare	28
Wicklow	27
Carlow	24
Queen's (Laois)	24
Clare	23
Longford	22

Table 5. Foreign Interest.—No. of Articles.	
Country or Region	No.
England	423
Scotland/North Britain	93
East Indies/India	57
France	39
United States of America	35
Italy	26
Canada	20
Wales	19
Spain	15
America/North America	13
Germany	12
Australia	7
Great Britain	7
Portugal	7
Belgium	6
China	6
Egypt	6
Europe	6
Jamaica	6
Lebanon	6
Afghanistan/Cabul	5
Guyana/British Guyana	5
Isle of Man	5
Africa	4
Antigua	4
Austria	4
Ceylon	4
Holland/the Netherlands	4
Switzerland	4
At Sea	3
Cape of Good Hope	3
Jersey	3

How to use this book:

Transcripts—One of the objectives in the production of this volume was to produce faithful transcriptions from the newspaper record. This work includes just a few exceptions to that rule: the insertion of the transcriber's notes and editorial remarks, which are enclosed within [square parentheses]; correction of spelling errors, and insertion of punctuation marks, particularly in run-on sentences; and, adjustments to layout, as discussed in a subsequent paragraph.

BMD notices are presented in Chapter 2, while Chapter 3 features the news accounts of "other auspicious and adverse events."

Each article has a serial number at the beginning of the transcript, and a reference number at the end of the transcript. This reference number is a unique identifier, which serves as a finding aid to the place in which the article would be found in the original publication. In **Chapter 2, *Birth, Marriage, and Death Notices***, this number appears in the following format:

(Date of issue: year-month-day; page & column numbers; type of notice: B, M, or D).

With respect to type of notice, the letter 'B' signifies a birth notice, 'M' a marriage, and 'D' a death. For example, the reference for article no. 1 in Chapter 2 is **(1839-01-12, 3:3, M)**—indicating that this notice announced a marriage that was published in the January 12, 1839 edition of the *Northern Standard* newspaper, on page 3, in column 3.

The references for transcripts and extracts in ***Chapter 3, Accounts of Auspicious and Adverse Events***, are similar, but omit the B, M, or D designation, that is:

(Date of issue:year-month-day; page & column numbers).

For example, the first article in Chapter 3 is no. 2347, with reference number, (1839-01-12, 2:3).

Indexes—A second objective in this work was to formulate convenient and useful finding aids, in the form of indexes, to assist readers in locating notices quickly and reliably. Three types of indexes have been compiled:

Chapter	Type of Index	BMDs or News Articles
4	Surname	Both
5	Institution and Publication	Both
6	Subject	News Articles

A wide array of institutions was indexed in this volume including churches, hospitals and dispensaries, societies, banks, government offices and boards, regiments of the British Army, workhouses, commercial enterprises, ships, religious denominations, schools, and other organizations. Publications that were indexed include books, journals, legislation, legal cases, newspapers, history texts, and poems.

For the news articles treating on "other auspicious and adverse events," (article numbers 2347 – 3903), subjects range from accidents, inquests, and suicide, to bigamy, elopement, and notices of errant wives whose abandoned husbands urge the public not to extend credit on his account! This volume also includes articles that describe such historic events as the Presbyterian Marriage Question, the early years of the Great Famine, and the deaths of the Earl of Caledon in 1839, and of the Liberator, Mr. Daniel O'Connell in 1847.

Please note that the numbers appearing in the indexes, i.e., in Chapters 4, 5, and 6, refer to Article numbers of the transcripts presented in **Chapters 2 and 3**, not to page numbers.

Editing and layout—Simplicity, ease of reference, and readability were the primary rules used to produce and format these transcripts and indexes. Generally, the layout[1] of the BMD

[1] Layout includes such considerations as typeface, capitalization, hyphenation, pagination, the width of the column, the number of words per line, the number of lines per notice, the number of columns per page, white space, margins and gutters, and so on.

notices and news articles, as rendered in the original newspaper record, has not been reproduced in this work. For example, while the original newspaper record contains occasional capitalization of surnames, this volume employs plain type for surnames throughout. In addition, this work italicizes the names of published works and of ships, a practice not always followed in the original newspaper record.

The compiler has exercised occasional editorial license, as indicated by the insertion of text [within square parentheses]. Examples include: the use of the editorial mark, [sic]; insertion of punctuation to improve readability (typically, in the form of a comma to separate the names of cities and counties); suggestions of alternative spellings; clarification of the meaning of the phrases "same date" and "same place"; and, [illegible] or [?] to indicate uncertainty about the spelling of a word where the original text was barely legible.

Extracts—A number of articles ran to several columns in the original text. In these instances, extracts have been prepared. Generally, an extract includes the first and final paragraphs; an extract further identifies the individuals, subjects, and place names included in the interim paragraphs of the original text, within [square brackets]. Examples of such extracts are article numbers 2815 and 3152, which reported on proceedings pertaining to the Presbyterian Marriage Question, and 3894, which described in detail—through nine columns in the original text—the judgment in a case adjudicated in the Court of Prerogative.

Errors and omissions—The vital events of only those who could afford to pay for a notice, or who were otherwise considered noteworthy, were recorded in *The Northern Standard* and other newspapers of the day. Thus, the BMD notices presented in this work are neither a complete survey nor a representative sample of all the vital events that occurred in county Monaghan and environs between the years 1839–1847.

Great care and every reasonable effort have been taken to produce a comprehensive and reliable set of transcripts and indexes, supported by useful research notes, statistics, and editorial annotations. However, because this work required analysis, interpretation and judgment, errors may have occurred, for which the compiler apologizes in advance. No matter how carefully designed and assembled, this book constitutes a secondary source. When in doubt, the original source record should be consulted as the final authority.

:: :: ::

Whether employed in the pursuit of family or local history research, or perused at leisure, may this book also serve as a tribute to the memory of the people who were born in the county Monaghan, in neighbouring counties, and in Ireland generally—and perhaps, especially—to the memory of the many Irish whose names were not immortalized in *The Northern Standard* or other contemporary newspapers.

ABBREVIATIONS AND ACRONYMS:

A.B.	Bachelor of Arts degree, *Artium Baccalaureus*
A.M.	Master of Arts degree, *Artium Magister*
ann.	annum (year)
B.A.	Bachelor of Arts degree, *Artium Baccalaureus*
Bart.	Baronet
Berks.	Berkshire
C.B.	Companion of the Bath
C.C.	Catholic Curate
C.C.P.	Court of Common Pleas
C.E.	Civil Engineer
Capt.	Captain
Co., or co.	County, county
Col.	Colonel
D.D.	Doctor of Divinity degree, *Doctor Divinitatis*
D.L.	Deputy Lieutenant
Esq.	Esquire
F.R.C.S.I.	Fellow of the Royal College of Surgeons of Ireland
F.T.C.D.	Fellow of Trinity College, Dublin
G.C.B.	Knight, or Dame, Grand Cross
Gen.	General
H.M.	Her Majesty, *or* Her Majesty's
H.M.S.	Her Majesty's Ship
H.P.	Half-Pay
Hon.	The Honourable
inst.	instant (this month)
J.P.	Justice of the Peace
K.C.B.	Knight Commander of the Bath
K.C.H.	Knight of the Royal Guelphic Order
Kt.	Knight
l.	pounds sterling
LL.D.	Doctor of Laws degree, *Legum Doctor*
L.R.C.S.	Licentiate of the Royal College of Surgeons
Lieut.	Lieutenant
Lieut.-Colonel	Lieutenant-Colonel
M.A.	Master of Arts degree, *Artium Magister*
M.D.	Medical Doctor, *Medicinae Doctor*
M.I.C.E.	Member of the Institution of Civil Engineers
M.N.I.	Madras Native Infantry
M.P.	Member of Parliament
M.R.C.S.	Member of the Royal College of Surgeons
Messrs.	Plural of *Mister*.
Mich.	Michael
N.B.	North Britain (Scotland)
N.I.	Native Infantry (India)
Nn.-Limavady	Newtownlimavady
P.P.	Parish Priest
Q.C.	Queen's Counsel
R.A.	Registered Architect
R.C.C.	Roman Catholic Curate
R.E.	Royal Engineers, Corps of
R.M.	Resident Magistrate
R.N.	Royal Navy
Regt.	Regiment

Abbreviations and acronyms, continued:

S.I.	Sub-Inspector (Constabulary)
S.T.C.D.	Student of Trinity College, Dublin
sic	a Latin adverb, meaning 'as written,' or 'intentionally so written'
T.C.D.	Trinity College, Dublin
Thos.	Thomas
ult.	ultimo (last month)
v.	versus
viz.	a Latin adverb, *videlicet*, meaning 'namely,' 'that is to say,'
Wm.	William

2. Birth, Marriage, and Death Notices

1. Jan. 5, in St. Mary's church, Cheltenham, by the Rev. Cooke Otway, M.A., the Rev. F.A. Murray Patten, of Eastham, in the county of Meath, to Elizabeth, eldest surviving daughter of the late Lieutenant-General Laye of the Royal Artillery. (1839-01-12, 3:3, M)

2. At Ballanascreen church, by the Rev. Holt Waring, the Rev. William Chichester, of Mallavilley, in the county of Armagh, to Henrietta, only daughter of the Hon. Mr. Justice Torrens. (1839-01-12, 3:3, M)

3. At St. Bride's, Liverpool, William Hobbs, Esq. of Cork, to Mary, eldest daughter, of the late Captain Joseph Martindale, of Northumberland. (1839-01-12, 3:3, M)

4. At Castlepollard, Robert Barrett, Esq., of Blessington-street, Dublin, to Catherine Sophia, eldest daughter of George Booker, Esq., of Rookbrook, county Westmeath. (1839-01-12, 3:3, M)

5. At St. Ann's church, Belfast, William Booker, Esq. of Belfast, to Margaret, second daughter of the late Joseph Dawson, Esq. of Lisnamorrow House, county Derry, for many years governor, &c., on the Western Coast of Africa. (1839-01-12, 3:3, M)

6. At Peter's church, John Hitchcock, of Antrim, Esq., to Kate, third daughter of Robert Hitchcock, of Pembroke-place, Esq., Barrister-at-Law. (1839-01-12, 3:3, M)

7. Jan. 8, at No. 6, Merrion-square, East, FitzPatrick FitzGerald Fox, third son of the Baron de Roebeck, aged four years and nine months. (1839-01-12, 3:3, D)

8. Jan. 4, at Rathmines, in his 37th year, Mr. John Newbold of Upper Merrion-street, Dublin. (1839-01-12, 3:3, D)

9. Jan. 6, of water on the brain, after three days' illness, Robert, youngest son of Joseph J. Stephens, Esq. of Lower Gardiner-street, Dublin, aged nine years. (1839-01-12, 3:3, D)

10. At Swansea, aged 75 years, Mrs. Hatton, only surviving sister of John Philip Kemble, Esq. and Mrs. Siddons. As "Ann of Swansea" she was well known in the literary world. (1839-01-12, 3:3, D)

11. William Ironside, Esq., of the 33d Regiment. (1839-01-12, 3:3, D)

12. January 6, aged 91 years, at Palace Anne, near Bandon, the seat of her son, Arthur Beamish Bernard, Esq., Elizabeth, daughter of the late Arthur Bernard, Esq. of the same place, and relict of the late Richard Beamish, Esq. of Raharoon. (1839-01-12, 3:3, D)

13. January 4, at her father's residence, in Cork, Sarah, youngest daughter of Captain Spread, R.N. (1839-01-12, 3:3, D)

14. On the 15th instant, in St. George's Church, Dublin, by the Rev. Frederick Bridge, Nathaniel, eldest son of the late Nathaniel Cook, of Cookemount, county Monaghan, Esq., to Rosamond Clare, third daughter of the late James Arthur Mayne, of Hardwick-place, Esq., in the city of Dublin. (1839-01-17, 3:5, M)

15. On Thursday, the 8th inst., in St. Nicholas's Church, Dundalk, by the Rev. E. Thackery, Mr. George Eyre, to Bessy, youngest daughter of I. Crowe, Esq., of Dundalk. (1839-01-17, 3:5, M)

16. In Ahoghill Church, on the 7th instant, by the Rev. George Kirkpatrick, Benjamin Humfrey, Esq., solicitor, Upper Temple-street, Dublin, to Harriet, youngest daughter of the late D. O'Rorke, of Ballybollan, county Antrim, Esq. deceased. (1839-01-17, 3:5, M)

17. On the 10th instant, by the Rev. Robert Morrison, of Markethill, Mr. George Scott, near Markethill, to Miss Jane Leeper, daughter of Mr. Wm. Leeper, of Ballylane. (1839-01-17, 3:5, M)

18. On the 31st ultimo, by the Rev. George Steen, A.M., Nn.-Limavady, Robert M'Leod, Esq., of Nn.-Limivady, to Jane Craig, daughter of the late Mr. Thomas Craig, of Falloward. (1839-01-17, 3:5, M)

19. On Friday, the 18th Inst., Mary, the beloved wife of Mr. Wm. Hanna, of Ballybay, after a lingering illness, which she bore with Christian fortitude. (1839-01-17, 3:5, D)

20. On Thursday last, Mr. John Scott, of Aughayest, near Ballybay. He was for many years an Elder in the 1st congregation in Ballybay. (1839-01-17, 3:5, D)

21. On the 7th instant, in the 87th year of her age, Anne Armstrong, wife of William Armstrong, Esq., of Drumchose, county Fermanagh. (1839-01-17, 3:5, D)

22. On the 4th instant, at Annahilt, near Hillsborough, Mr. James Jefferson, aged 43 years. (1839-01-17, 3:5, D)

23. Jan. 19, in London, the Right Hon. Lady Cottenham, of a daughter. (1839-01-26, 2:5, B)

24. Jan. 18, at Ardglass, the lady of Joseph Saunders, Esq., of a daughter. (1839-01-26, 2:5, B)

25. Jan. 12, at Omagh, the lady of Daniel Auchinleck, Esq., of a daughter. (1839-01-26, 2:5, B)

26. On the 17th, instant, Wm. A. M'Kenna, Esq., Solicitor, to Ellen, youngest daughter of the late Mr. Francis M'Kenna, Newry. (1839-01-26, 2:5, M)

27. Jan. 17, in St. Thomas's Church, Dublin, by the Rev. E. Leete, Samuel M'Clintock, Esq., of Newtown House, county Louth, to Dora, daughter of the late John Knox, Esq., of Summerhill in that city. (1839-01-26, 2:5, M)

28. At Drumcondra Church, by the Rev. Mr. Long, Robert Robinson, Esq., to Elizabeth, second daughter of Benjamin Eaton, Esq., Clitton Terrace, Monkstown. (1839-01-26, 2:5, M)

29. Jan. 17, at Strokestown Church, Godfrey Hogg, Esq., J.P., to Ellen, daughter of the late Rev. Thomas Knox, and niece to Colonel Knox, of Prehen, Londonderry. (1839-01-26, 2:5, M)

30. On the 20th inst. Eliza, the beloved wife of the Rev. Alexander Patterson, of Ballymena. She was enabled, by Divine grace, to bear a severe and unusually protracted illness with great submission to the will of her Heavenly Father, and died in the full assurance of eternal life, in humble, yet firm dependence on the merits and mediation of her Almighty Saviour. (1839-01-26, 2:5, D)

31. On Tuesday last, aged seven years, of water on the brain, Sarah, eldest daughter of Mr. James Swan, of Glasslough-street, in this town. (1839-01-26, 2:5, D)

32. On Tuesday last at his residence, Glenich, within four miles of this town, Mr. Wm. Riddle, aged 71 years. (1839-01-26, 2:5, D)

33. Jan. 10, at Downpatrick, James Rentoul, Esq., aged 55 years. (1839-01-26, 2:5, D)

34. At Larne, county of Antrim, Daniel Lanauze, Esq. (1839-01-26, 2:5, D)

35. Jan. 17, in Gardiner-street, Edward King, Esq., fourth son of the late Sir Robert King, Bart., of Charlestown, Drumsna, County Leitrim. (1839-01-26, 2:5, D)

36. Jan. 18, Margaret, relict of the late Rev. Joseph Crawford, of Cremorne. (1839-01-26, 2:5, D)

37. On the 14th instant, at Castleblayney, in the 44th year of his age, Mr. John Rooney. (1839-01-26, 2:5, D)

38. On the 15th inst. at Warrenpoint, of a protracted illness, which she bore with pious resignation, Anne, wife of Mr. Halligan, Hotel-keeper. (1839-01-26, 2:5, D)

39. On the 16th inst. after a protracted illness, which she bore with christian fortitude and pious resignation to the will of God, Anne, eldest daughter of Mr. Patrick Moore, organist, Boat-street, Newry. (1839-01-26, 2:5, D)

40. Jan. 8, perished, at Formby Banks, near Liverpool, from cold and hunger, in the rigging of the brig *Harvest Home*, outward bound to St. Thomas's, Henry Parker, College-street, Dublin, Esq.; and Mr. William Magrath, son of John Magrath, Killough, county Down, Esq., and nephew of John M'Dowal, North Frederick-street, Rutland-square, Dublin, Esq. (1839-01-26, 2:5, D)

41. At Portadown, on the 22d ult, the lady of John O. Woodhouse, Esq. of a daughter. (1839-02-02, 3:1, B)

42. On the 25th ultimo, at Elm Park in the county of Armagh, the lady of Thomas Knox Armstrong, Esq. of a daughter. (1839-02-02, 3:1, B)

43. On the 12th ult., at Omagh, the lady of Daniel Auchinleck, Esq. of a daughter. (1839-02-02, 3:1, B)

44. Jan. 29, in St. Ann's Church, by the Rev. Dr. Dickenson, Francis Brooke Norris, Esq., her Majesty's Surveyor-General in Ceylon, to Elizabeth Jane, daughter of T.S. Cooper, Esq., Comptroller-General of Stamps in Ireland. (1839-02-02, 3:1, M)

45. On the night of Saturday, the 26th ult., at Ballybay, of inflammation on the lungs, aged 48 years, Agnes, wife of Samuel Gray, Esq. In every relation of life, she was an example and pattern to her sex. As a wife, she displayed all those qualities which endear a woman to her husband; as a mother, she was gentle, kind, and affectionate, and as a friend, the best testimony to her merits is the wide circle of gloom which her decease has caused over a large list of acquaintances. Her remains were accompanied to the last recepticle of mortality by a long train of mourners, many of whom had experienced, during her life, her kindness and friendship. Throughout a protracted and painful illness, which she bore with Christian resignation, she was enabled to say, "Whom the Lord loveth he chasteneth." (1839-02-02, 3:1, D)

46. On the 5th inst., at Middletown Church, by the Rev. James Maulevere [sic], Thomas Edwards, Esq., of Clones, to Mary, only surviving daughter of the late Wm. Reynolds, Esq., of Feduff. (1839-02-16, 3:4, M)

47. On the 5th inst., in Thomas's Church, Dublin, Francis C. Annesley, Esq., of the King of Prussia's Life Guards, son of the Hon. Robert Annesley, late his Britannic Majesty's Consul at Antwerp, to Harriet, youngest daughter of the late John Bolton, Esq., of Mayne, in the county of Louth. (1839-02-16, 3:4, M)

48. On the 4th inst., in the church of Ardcarn, by the Ven. Archdeacon of Elphin, Arthur J.V. Lindsay, Esq., R.N., of Blackrock, in the county of Leitrim, to Jane, daughter of John Duckworth, Esq., J.P., of Mount Erris, in the county Roscommon. (1839-02-16, 3:4, M)

49. On the 11th inst., at Cavandish-row, Joseph Lynch, Esq., of Roebuck House, county Cavan, to Bellinda Jane, eldest daughter of John Breen, Esq., M.D. (1839-02-16, 3:4, M)

50. On the 9th inst., at Tallaght church, Wm. Hamilton Enery, Esq., only surviving son of John Enery, Esq., of Ballyconnoly house, county Cavan, to Isabella Alicia, daughter of Brook T. Ottley, Esq., of Delaford, in the county Dublin. (1839-02-16, 3:4, M)

51. On the 29th ult. at his residence, near Carrickfergus, Blayney Townley Walshe, Esq., late Lieutenant-Colonel Royal Artillery. (1839-02-16, 3:4, D)

52. On the 6th inst., Wm., son of John C. Boyd, Esq., of Jocelyn Cottage, Belfast. (1839-02-16, 3:4, D)

53. On the 10th inst., at Tramore, Mrs. Talbot, wife of Geo. Talbot, Esq. (1839-02-16, 3:4, D)

54. On the 17th inst., in Grosvenor-street, Frank Sotheron, Esq., Admiral of the White Squadron of her Majesty's Fleet, aged 73, formerly M.P. for the county of Nottingham. (1839-02-16, 3:4, D)

55. On the 10th at Lisheen, near Cashel, the residence of her husband, Sir John Judkin Fitzgerald, Bart., Lady Fitzgerald, of fever, taken after her accouchment. (1839-02-16, 3:4, D)

56. On Thursday, the 21st instant, at Corcreeny House, county of Tyrone, in Corthani church, county of Fermanagh, by the Rev. Allen Mitchell, vicar of Drumsnant, the Rev. Hugh Cunningham, chaplain of Omeath church, Diocese of Armagh, to Margaret, sixth daughter of the late John Reckins, Esq. of the county of Carlow. (1839-02-23, 3:3, M)

57. In Upper Canada, Colonel George Hamilton, of Hanksburry, third son of the late Charles Hamilton, of Hamwood, county Meath, Esq. (1839-02-23, 3:3, D)

58. On the 12th inst., in Waterford, Richard Barron, Esq., son of the late James Barron, Esq. of Sarahvill, county of Waterford, to Catherine, daughter of the late Richard Barron, Esq. of Durrow, county Waterford. (1839-02-23, 3:3, M)

59. On the 7th inst., in John-street, Belfast, Mr. Wm. John Matthews, aged 22 years. (1839-02-23, 3:3, D)

60. On the 7th inst. in Belfast, Hugh Walker, Esq. of Magherafelt, to Ann, second daughter of the late Samuel Hemphill, Esq., of Flowerfield. (1839-02-23, 3:3, M)

61. On Tuesday last, in Dundalk, the lady of Mr. Edward B. Cooper, of a son. (1839-03-02, 3:4, B)

62. At St. James's Church, London, Robert Richard Torrens, Esq., to Barbara Anson, widow to the late Lieut. George Anson, 11th Light Dragoons. (1839-03-02, 3:4, M)

63. On the 20th ult., in Tashinny church, by the Rev. F. Gregg, Thomas Richardson, Esq. son of the late Ralph Richardson, Esq., of Springfield, county of Down, to Alice Catherine, daughter of the Rev. Nicholas Gosselin, of Tashinny Glebe, county of Longford. (1839-03-02, 3:4, M)

64. On the 19th ult., the Rev. Robert Magill, A.M., Presbyterian Minister of Antrim. (1839-03-02, 3:4, D)

65. On the 19th ult., at Alwington House, Rear Admiral Sir John Ferris Devonshire, K.C.B., in the 65th year of his age. (1839-03-02, 3:4, D)

66. At Zarand, in Transylvania, Juan Graza, in his 120th Year, by accidentally falling on a scythe and mortally wounding himself. He left a son upwards of 100, and a grandson aged 80. (1839-03-02, 3:4, D)

67. On the 19th ult. at his house in Grafton-street, London, Lord St. Helens, in his 86th year. (1839-03-02, 3:4, D)

68. On the 24th ult., aged nine months, Francis, infant son of Francis Macdonogh, Esq., Barrister at law. (1839-03-02, 3:4, D)

69. On the 15th ult., Anna Maria Frances, eldest daughter of John Nunn, Esq., of Silverspring, county of Wexford. (1839-03-02, 3:4, D)

70. At Avon Lodge, near Armagh, John Knox, Esq., of Newry, to Sarah, eldest daughter of the late Norton Butler, Esq., J.P., of Grose Hall, county of Donegal. (1839-03-09, 3:4, M)

71. In this town, at his residence, in Dublin-street, after a short illness, Mr. Terence Murphy. (1839-03-09, 3:4, D)

72. In Tandragee, in this county [Armagh], on Sunday last, amid the regrets of his friends and acquaintances, at the age of 29 years, Wm. Acheson, Esq. It is a melancholy duty at any time to record the death of a fellow creature; but when youth, strength, benevolence, and the pride of manhood in its bloom is called from amongst us, the pang is doubly severe. Mr. Acheson was all that could be esteemed in a bosom friend, and his early fate has caused a vacant seat in the circle of his society that few can fill.—*sic transit gloria mundi*. (1839-03-09, 3:4, D)

73. On Monday Mr. Archibald Martin, after a few days' illness, aged 65. He was an ordained elder in the Ballybay Presbyterian congregation.(1839-03-09,3:4,D)

74. On the 2d instant, at Cullenswood, the Rev. J.G.F. Schultz, minister of the Dutch Lutheran Church, aged 76 years. (1839-03-09, 3:4, D)

75. In Calcutta, Lieutenant-Colonel Arthur Wade, commanding 3d Regiment Native Cavalry. (1839-03-09, 3:4, D)

76. February 27, at his residence, Clontarf, Captain Francis Dundas, H.P., of her Majesty's 81st regiment. (1839-03-09, 3:4, D)

77. On the 9th inst., at Lough Derry, county Monaghan, the lady of Henry L. Pendleton, Esq., of a daughter. (1839-03-16, 3:4, B)

78. On the 12th inst., at the parish church of Rossory, by the Rev. W. Ball, Rector, Miss Grace Larkin, of Willoughby-place, to John Thompson Carter, Esq., of Mount Caulfield, Newry. (1839-03-16, 3:4, M)

79. On the 11th inst., at Coleraine, by the Rev. Mr. Harvey, Rector, Henry Moore Cairnes, youngest son of the late J. Elliot Cairnes, Esq., of Saville Lodge, county Tyrone, to Emily Charlotte Louisa, third daughter of John Claudius Beresford, Esq. (1839-03-16, 3:4, M)

80. On the 10th inst., aged 17 years, Sarah, second daughter of the late Mr. Robert Murdock, of Glass-lough-street. (1839-03-16, 3:4, D)

81. On the evening of the 11th inst., of a rapid decline, in the 16th year of his age, John Thomas, eldest son of Michael Downey, of Newry. (1839-03-16, 3:4, D)

82. On the 5th inst., at Rostrevor, Sarah Anne, wife of the Rev. Charles Hamilton, vicar general of Dromore, and rector of Sligo. (1839-03-16, 3:4, D)

83. On the 15th inst., in St. Thomas's Church, by the Rev. Charles Evatt, Rector of Monaghan, Evelyn John Evatt, Esq., 66, Upper Gardener-street, Dublin, youngest son of the late Humphrey Evatt, of Mount Lewis, county of Monaghan, to Berri, youngest daughter of the late Captain Bayly, 5th Dragoon Guards. (1839-03-23, 3:4, M)

84. On the 16th inst., at Carrickmacross, in the 14th year of her age, Lucinda, the beloved daughter and only child of Mr.Thomas Robinson, head-constable of constabulary. She was a promising child, and her affectionate and engaging manners endeared her to all her acquaintances, and her parents who sensibly feel their loss are consoled by the pleasing reflection of her future resurrection to immortality and eternal life. (1839-03-23, 3:4, D)

85. On the 23d ult., the lady of Handcock Montgomery, Esq., of Bessmount Park, county Monaghan, of a son. (1839-04-06, 3:3, B)

86. On the 25th ult., at Armagh, the lady of Robert Turtle, Esq. of a son and heir. (1839-04-06, 3:3, B)

87. On the 23d ult., by the Rev. John Watson, Greyabbey, John Kelly, Esq., of Whinview, to Mary, only daughter of the late Andrew Kelly, Esq. of Mountstewart, County of Down. (1839-04-06, 3:3, M)

88. On the 19th ult., in the parish church of Innis-keen, Oliver Milling, Esq., of Shanliss, county of Louth, to Marianne, youngest daughter of the late John Steele, Esq., Castleblaney. (1839-04-06, 3:3, M)

89. On the 26th ult., in St. Peter's Church, Drogheda, by the Rev. Mr. Wall, Mr. Samuel Benson, of Stone-bridge, county Monaghan, to Mary Anne, second daughter of John Lloyd, Knockbollymore, county Fermanagh, Esq. (1839-04-06, 3:3, M)

90. On the 2d inst., at Malahide Church, Henry, only son of Arthur Baker, Esq. of Balheary House, county of Dublin, to Belinda, fourth daughter of the late Richard Sayers, Esq., of Greenmount, and niece to lord and lady Talbot de Malahide. (1839-04-06, 3:3, M)

91. On Wednesday last, in this town, in his 38th year, of inflammation of the throat, that caused a spasmodic affection which terminated existence, Mr. James Curran, proprietor of the Monaghan hotel. During his life Mr. Curran possessed the good will and friendship of all classes, and by his quiet and unassuming manners and respectful demeanor, won the esteem and patronage of the many. He has left behind him an inconsolable widow, and a young and helpless family to deplore his death. (1839-04-06, 3:3, D)

92. On the 27th inst., at his residence, Rockcorry, county Monaghan, Edward Calvert, Esq., aged 73 years. (1839-04-06, 3:3, D)

93. On the 31st ult., at the residence of his father, Ann-street, Belfast, in the 17th year of his age, Mr. James Ried [sic], printer. (1839-04-06, 3:3, D)

94. At the house of her brother, Mr. Foster Scott, Tattykeel, Omagh, Isabella, relict of the late Mr. John Christie, Derg-bridge. Although nearly 90 years old, she retained possession of all her faculties till within a few days of her dissolution. She died as she lived, a sincere Christian. (1839-04-06, 3:3, D)

95. In Omagh, on Sunday evening last, in the 52d year of his age, David Green, Esq. the much respected proprietor of the White Hart Hotel. (1839-04-06, 3:3, D)

96. On the 10th inst., at Tyholland Church, by the Rev. Henry Maffett, William M. Brice, Esq. of Cavan, to Anne, eldest daughter of the late A. Johnston, Esq., of this town. (1839-04-13, 3:3, M)

97. On the 9th inst., at the residence of Thomas Gilmore, Esq., High-street, in the 17th year of his age, Leslie Crawford, youngest son of John Leslie Crawford, Esq., Grange, Moy. (1839-04-13, 3:3, D)

98. On the 13th inst., at Clontibret Glebe, county of Monaghan, the lady of the Venerable the Archdeacon of Clogher, of twin daughters. (1839-04-20, 3:3, B)

99. On the 18th inst., at Monaghan, Dr. M'Carran, of Londonderry, to Anne, second daughter of the late Mr. John Duffy of this town. (1839-04-20, 3:3, M)

100. On the 2d instant, in St. George's Church, Dublin, by the Rev. Robert Daly, the Rev. Hugh Hamilton Madden, only son of the late Rev. Dodgson Madden, of Banefort [sic], county of Kilkenny, to Isabella, third daughter of Henry J. Monck Mason, Esq., LL.D., and grand-daughter of the late Sir Robert Langrishe, Bart. (1839-04-20, 3:3, M)

101. On the 15th instant, in St. Anne's Church, by the Rev. A.C. Macartney, Mr. Robert Gaffikin, of Belfast, to Sarah, third daughter of the late Mr. Wm. Trelford, Falls. (1839-04-20, 3:3, M)

102. On the 18th instant, in St. Mary's Church, by the Hon. and Venerable the Archdeacon of Kilmore, Robert Henry Cox, Esq., of Clonwilliam-place, eldest son of Captain Cox, of Carrick-on-Shannon, to Emily, second daughter of the late Wm. John Moor, Esq., of Rutland-square; and immediately afterwards, Russell Bedford Cameron, Esq., Sub-Inspector of county Leitrim Constabulary, only son of the late Major Allen Cameron, 20th Light Dragoons, to Helen, second daughter of Captain Cox. (1839-04-20, 3:3, M)

103. On the 9th instant, at the residence of his son, the Rev. Dr. M'Ardle, Catholic Rector of Clogher, Edward M'Ardle, Esq., late Castleblayney, county Monaghan, aged 85 years. (1839-04-20, 3:3, D)

104. On Sunday the 8th instant, aged 52 years, Mr. William Rainey, of Winetavern-street, Belfast, formerly of Randalstown. (1839-04-20, 3:3, D)

105. On the 15th instant, at Belfast, Mary Frances, the beloved wife of Walter Molony, Esq., resident Magistrate of police. (1839-04-20, 3:3, D)

106. At Downpatrick, on the 21st instant, by the Rev. Mr. Nelson, Mr. William Waring, of Hillsborough, to Miss Margaret Todd, of Downpatrick. (1839-04-27, 3:4, M)

107. April 17, in St. Mary's Church, Dublin, the Rev. Thos. U. Townsend, of Hilltown, county of Down, to Elizabeth, eldest daughter of Edward Carr, Esq., Arnestown, county of Wexford. (1839-04-27, 3:4, M)

108. April 22, in Omagh, Robert Wallace, Esq., for many years the Post-master, and latterly also the Manager of the Agricultural Bank there. (1839-04-27, 3:4, D)

109. At his residence, North-street, Belfast, on the 23d inst., after a very short illness, Mr. John Goodwin, aged 29. (1839-04-27, 3:4, D)

110. On the 15th instant, in his house, near Dromore, after a short illness, Mr. Richard Pantridge, aged 85 years. In his life he was a Christian, and in his death he had an undying hope of never-ending felicity. (1839-04-27, 3:4, D)

111. April 30, in Monkstown church, by the Rev. John St. George Williams, Robert Denny, Esq. eldest son of Capt. Denny, to Rebecca Sarah Deey, daughter of the late Captain Williams [sic] Irvine, of Gola, county of Fermanagh. (1839-05-04, 3:2, M)

112. May 1, in St. Peter's church, by the Rev. Dr. Singer, F.T.C.D., John Richardson, Esq., of Trinity College, Dublin, eldest son of Thomas Richardson, Esq., of Beech Park, in the county of Down, to Mary Catherine, eldest daughter of James Bessonnet, Esq., Q.C., of Leeson-street, Dublin. (1839-05-04, 3:2, M)

113. April 26, in the church of Castlebar, D. Kenny, Esq. M.D., of Claremorris, to Matilda, third daughter of Joint Smyth, Esq., late of Castlebar. (1839-05-04, 3:2, M)

114. On the 26th ult., by the Rev. G.S. Morrison, of Armagh, Mr. George Herron, to Miss Nancy Sloan, both of Armagh. (1839-05-04, 3:2, M)

115. On Wednesday evening last, by the Rev. H. Harrison, Mr. Isaac Murray, Malone, to Miss Ellen Eddis, of Shankhill. (1839-05-04, 3:2, M)

116. At his residence near this town, in his 88th year, Mr. Robert Harrison. (1839-05-04, 3:2, D)

117. April 23, at his residence Phippsborough House, John Birch, Esq., in the 71st year of his age. (1839-05-04, 3:2, D)

118. April 19, at Spring Vale, county of Down, George Matthews, Esq., J.P., formerly a Major in the Down-shire Militia, and subsequently collector of customs at the port of Newry. (1839-05-04, 3:2, D)

119. April 15, in Lisburn, in the 84th year of his age, Mr. Hamilton M'Cay, for many years, an Elder in the Presbyterian congregation of that place. (1839-05-04, 3:2, D)

120. April 24, at Ballyrath, near Armagh, William Scott Hutchinson, Esq., in the 39th year of his age. (1839-05-04, 3:2, D)

121. April 28, in Sligo, Malachy Donellan, Esq., a resident magistrate. (1839-05-04, 3:2, D)

122. In the church of Ballybay, on the 8th instant, by the Rev. Hercules Langrishe, Samuel Gray, Esq., of said town, to Amelia, daughter of Lieutenant Wymp, of Shircock, in the county Cavan. (1839-05-11, 3:2, M)

123. In Drumgoon church, county Cavan, on the 27th ult., by the Rev. James Adams, Richard Smerdan, Esq., officer of excise, Yorkshire, England, to the amiable and accomplished Miss M'Cabe, daughter of George M'Cabe, Esq., of Cootehill. (1839-05-11, 3:2, M)

124. On the 26th of October last, of fever, in the 21st year of his age, on board the schooner, *Rebecca*, of Baltimore, on his passage from Havannah, Mr. William Borlace, eldest son of Mr. Borlace, College of Health, Belfast. (1839-05-11, 3:2, D)

125. On the 3d instant, the lady of John Madden, Esq., of Hilton, county of Monaghan, of a son. (1839-05-18, 3:4, B)

126. May 15, in St. Peter's Church, Dublin, by the Rev. Richard Clarke, of Monivea, Francis Clarke, Esq., M.D., of Blackwater Town, county of Armagh, son of the late Rev. Richard Clarke, of Portarlington, Queen's County, to Rebecca, daughter of Jonathan David Clarke, of Merrion-square, South, Dublin, and La Bergerie, Portarlington. (1839-05-18, 3:4, M)

127. May 7, in Dublin, Pierce Newport Barron, Esq., second son of the late William Barron, Esq., of Castletown, county of Waterford, to Phebe Elizabeth, daughter of the late John Newell, Esq., of Kinghill, county of Down. (1839-05-18, 3:4, M)

128. May 14, in his 78th year, Mr. Gideon Ouseley, a zealous, laborious, and self-denying Minister of the Gospel of our Lord Jesus Christ. Throughout the United Kingdom, and during nearly half a century he was ceasely engaged in his Master's work—in Ireland especially, in towns, villages, fairs and markets, regardless of personal ease, fearless of danger, and uninfluenced by the temporising prudence of cowardly professors, he most persuasively called on men to repent and believe the Gospel. (1839-05-18, 3:4, D)

129. May 10, at Loughrea, Elizabeth Anne, relict of Major Persse O'Keeffe Boulger. (1839-05-18, 3:4, D)

130. May 11, in Queen-street, Cork, John Lecky, Esq., aged 74, the oldest merchant of that city, with the trade of which he was connected for upwards of 50 years; he was latterly the agent of the St. George Steam Packet Company. During his long life he earned the respect and esteem of all who knew him. (1839-05-18, 3:4, D)

131. May 7, at Cookstown, county of Tyrone, the Lady of the Rev. Alexander Fleming, of a son. (1839-05-25, 3:2, B)

132. Lately, the wife of Mr. F. Robinson, shoemaker, of Healy, near Mashom, of her twentieth child. This child was born on the twentieth anniversary of her marriage, and she is only 37 years of age. (1839-05-25, 3:2, B)

133. May 17, in Omagh church, by the Rev. James Hill, Mr. James Breen, of Church-street, Omagh, to Miss Isabella Stuart, of same place. (1839-05-25, 3:2, M)

134. May 21, in St. George's church, the Hon. and Rev. Francis Howard, Charles Cobbe, Esq., eldest son of Charles Cobbe, Esq., of Newbridge, in the county of Dublin, to Louisa Caroline, daughter of George Frederick Brook, Esq. (1839-05-25, 3:2, M)

135. May 14, Daniel M'Cartie, Esq., Ardnageeha, to Anne, eldest daughter of Roger O'Callaghan, Esq. Betteville, Mallow. (1839-05-25, 3:2, M)

136. On the 25th ult., by the Rev. Mr. Edmond, of Sandholes, Mr. Wm. James Shepherd, of Ballydonnell, near Magherafelt, to Ellen, eldest daughter of Alexander Ferguson, Esq. Ardtrea, near Cookstown, county Tyrone. (1839-05-25, 3:2, M)

137. On the 16th instant, at the church of Urney, by the Rev. Robert Home, Michael Head Burgoyne, Esq., son of the late Sir John J. Burgoyne, to Anne, eldest daughter of the late Galbraith Hamilton, Esq., of Ballyfatton, county Tyrone. (1839-05-25, 3:2, M)

138. On the 23d instant, at his residence in the Diamond of this town, George Bartley, Esq., aged 62 years. In him, society has lost an honourable and upright member, a consistent man and an humble christian. He for many years filled the office of Distributor of Stamps for this County, and his kind and obliging manners secured him the esteem of all with whom he had intercourse. As an elder he was, in health, a pattern to believers in the active duties of the Church and the family, and in his sore illness he submitted with a patience that was sustained by the consolations and cheered by the hopes of the Gospel. "Mark the perfect man, and behold the upright, for the end of that man is peace." (1839-05-25, 3:2, D)

139. In this town, on the 20th instant, William Barry Kempe, aged 32 years, son of the late Colonel John A. Kempe, of Cornwall, in England. (1839-05-25, 3:2, D)

140. At Pomeroy, county Tyrone, on the 13th instant, of fever, aged 17, Thomas, youngest son of Mr. James Trimble, of said place. Young in years, he was called to his eternal reward, leaving behind him many sorrowing friends and acquaintances to lament his premature decease. (1839-05-25, 3:2, D)

141. On Sunday, at the house of his brother, in Enniskillen, Charles Ferguson, of Donaghmore, county Tyrone. His death was very sudden, being seized of inflammation in the chest, caused by an incautious change from warmer to lighter clothing.(1839-05-25,3:2,D)

142. On the 16th instant, at the house of Mr. William Cowan, Belfast, aged 18 years, Joseph, son of Mr. John Blakeley, Board Mills. (1839-05-25, 3:2, D)

143. On the 14th instant, Robert Dickson, Esq., of Dromore, aged 73 years. (1839-05-25, 3:2, D)

144. On the 13th instant, after a long and painful illness, Miss Mary Mooney, youngest daughter of the late James Mooney, of Caragh, parish of Inch. (1839-05-25, 3:2, D)

145. On the 18th instant, after a short illness, aged four years and six months, Margaret, daughter of Mr. Francis Harrisson, Montgomery-street, Dublin. (1839-05-25, 3:2, D)

146. On the 19th instant, Edward, eldest son of Edmond Mooney, Solicitor, of Henrietta-street, Dublin. (1839-05-25, 3:2, D)

147. February 23, at Bombay, Captain J.S. Darby, of the 2d or Queen's Own Regiment. (1839-05-25, 3:2, D)

148. May 21, at the house of her brother, the Rev. W.R. Meade, Rector of Kinsale, Elizabeth, youngest daughter of the Rev. Robert Meade, Rector of Ballymony [sic]. (1839-05-25, 3:2, D)

149. At 12, Merrion-street, in the 73d year of his age, Michael Balfe, Esq., of South Park, county Roscommon. (1839-05-25, 3:2, D)

150. In Glasslough, on Tuesday, by the Rev. Mr. Armstrong, Wesleyan Minister, at the house of the lady's father, Mr. Samuel M'Kella, of Moy, in the county Armagh, to Anna, eldest daughter of Mr. Moses M'Mahon. (1839-06-01, 3:3, M)

151. May 28, at Newtownforbes, by the Rev. Samuel Forbes Auchmuty, Captain Henry Musters, third son of John Musters of Coolwick Hall, Nottinghamshire, to Margaret Domvile, only child of Thomas Gordon Auchmuty, Esq., of Brienstown county of Longford. (1839-06-01, 3:3, M)

152. May 27, at the residence of his mother, 4, Fitzwilliam-square, Dublin, George James, third son of James Woodwright, Esq., of Gola-House, in this county. Yesterday morning, his remains were attended by a large number of the respectable inhabitants of the neighbourhood, passed through Monaghan, on their way to the family burying place. (1839-06-01, 3:3, D)

153. At Crieve, county Tyrone, William Mazier, Esq., J.P., aged 83 years. (1839-06-01, 3:3, D)

154. On Friday, in Monaghan, at an advanced age, Jane, relict of the late Mr. James Wilson, an old and respectable inhabitant of Monaghan. (1839-06-01, 3:3, D)

155. May 26, at Newtownhamilton, aged 72 years, the Rev. W. Maclaughlin, Rector of Mount Talbot, county of Roscommon. (1839-06-01, 3:3, D)

156. On the 10th instant, at his residence in Coleraine, Benjamin Given, in his 73d year. (1839-06-01, 3:3, D)

157. May 23, at Killigar church, by the Rev. Robert Daly, the Rev. Henry O'Brien, youngest son of the late Sir Edward O'Brien, Bart., of Dromoland, to Harriet, eldest daughter of John Godley, Esq., of Killigar House, in the county of Leitrim. (1839-06-01, 3:3, M)

158. At Tullyvallen Glebe, Newtownhamilton, Sarah, relict of the late Rev. W. Maclaughlin, Rector of Mount Talbot, county Roscommon, and daughter of the late T. Willis [sic], Esq. of Willisgrove [sic], same county. (1839-06-01, 3:3, D)

159. This morning, Anne, eldest daughter of Robert Smyth, Esq., of Fitzwilliam-square. (1839-06-01, 3:3, D)

160. On Tuesday, the 4th inst., at the residence of the lady's brother, in Sligo, Mr. John Allen, near the city of Armagh, to Miss Allen, of Sligo. (1839-06-08, 3:1, M)

161. On Thursday last, at St. Mark's Church, Armagh, by the Rev. Colin Ivers, Colin Sym, bookbinder, to Ann Jane, third daughter of Mr. James Rea, Court-house, Armagh. (1839-06-08, 3:1, M)

162. May 27, in Newtownbarry Church, by the Rev. Walter Hore, the Hon. Frederick Savile, of the Royal Artillery, third son of the Earl of Mexborough, Methby [Methley] Hall, Yorkshire, and grandson of the late Earl of Hardwicke, formerly Lord Lieutenant of Ireland, to Antonia Leslie, youngest daughter of the Rev. William Archdall, of Tinteru, county of Wexford, and niece to the late Lord Lindores, the Earls of Melville and Lieven. (1839-06-08, 3:1, M)

163. On Friday, 21st ultimo, in the 44th year of her age, Jane Eliza, wife of Mr. George Harrison, stationer, Belfast. (1839-06-08, 3:1, D)

164. On Sunday, June 2, Harriet, wife of Benjamin Sadler, Esq., of Sandford-House, near Liverpool, and mother of J.G. Fenton, Esq., College-square, Belfast. (1839-06-08, 3:1, D)

165. On Saturday, Mr. William Bryson, of James's-street, Belfast, muslin manufacturer, in his 54th year. (1839-06-08, 3:1, D)

166. On the 4th inst., sincerely and deservedly regretted by her numerous family and a large circle of friends and acquaintances, Sarah, wife of the Rev. James Bridge, of Aughnacloy. (1839-06-08, 3:1, D)

167. On Monday morning last, the lady of Mr. Richard Ker, Newbliss, of a daughter. (1839-06-15, 3:4, B)

168. On the 4th instant, at Milton-on-Thames, John Edmund Jones, Esq., of Monaghan, Surgeon, to Mary Anne, eldest daughter of the late Francis Ayrest, Esq. of Brompton, Kent. (1839-06-15, 3:4, M)

169. On the 11th inst., at the Cathedral, Lisburn, by the Very Rev. the Dean of Ross, the Rev. Edward Sullivan, Lisburn, to Anna, second daughter of the late Robert Montgomery, Esq., Solicitor, Belfast. (1839-06-15, 3:4, M)

170. On the 30th ult., by the Rev. James Wilson, of Tandragee, Mr. John Henry, of Armagh, to Miss Pella Greenaway, Athol Cottage, near Tandragee. (1839-06-15, 3:4, M)

171. On Monday sen., by the Rev. J.A. Canning, Mr. J.E. Finlay, to Margaret eldest daughter of Mr. James Brazier, Downpatrick. (1839-06-15, 3:4, M)

172. By special license, on the 30th ult., the Hon. Richard Maxwell, M.P. for the county of Cavan, to Dorothea, youngest daughter of the Hon. Baron Pennefather. (1839-06-15, 3:4, M)

173. On the 2d instant, by the Rev. Mr. Lloyd, Ballyleeson, Mr. David Beatty M'Ilveen, Belfast, to Dilly Campbell, daughter of Mr. Edward Bell, of Ballycowan. (1839-06-15, 3:4, M)

174. This morning, in his 73d year, at his residence, Slaverow [Slieverow], between Monaghan and Ballybay, Hamilton Reed, Esq. Mr. Reed attained a good old age, with the respect and esteem of his neighbours, and died in the fullness of days, regretted by those who he taught to love him. After a long period of almost uninterrupted health, his life closed with illness, which, although painful, he bore without repining. (1839-06-15, 3:4, D)

175. At Mentrim, near Ardee, in the 50th year of his age, Mr. Henry Lisgow. (1839-06-15, 3:4, D)

176. On the 11th ult. in London, Frederick W. Macauley, Esq. solicitor, formerly of Antrim, and for some time, coroner for that county. (1839-06-15, 3:4, D)

177. After a short illness, on the 1st inst., Robert M'Ferran, Esq. of Refuge-hill, near Belfast. (1839-06-15, 3:4, D)

178. At Tyholland Church, on the 18th instant, by the Rev. Henry Maffett, Mr. Robert Moffett, merchant, Clones, to Bertha Elizabeth, only daughter of Mr. Robert Mitchell, Sub-Sheriff of this county. (1839-06-22, 3:3, M)

179. June 20, in Killeshandra Church, county Cavan, by the Rev. J.C. Martin, D.D., William Young, Esq., of Mountjoy-square, Dublin, to Mary, eldest daughter, of Richard Young, Esq., of Lakeville, in the county Cavan. (1839-06-22, 3:3, M)

180. On the 10th instant, by the Rev. Dr. Coyne, Dundalk, Mr. Dominick Daly, of Newry, merchant, to Catherine, third daughter of Mr. James Dolaghan, Barley-field. (1839-06-22, 3:3, M)

181. On the 13th instant, by the Rev. H.P. Dobbin, Brice Blair, M.D., of Ballymena, to Ellen, youngest daughter of the late Thomas Dunseath, of same place. (1839-06-22, 3:3, M)

182. June 13, at Crossgar, Mr. James Harper, jun., of Ardigon, to Eliza, only daughter of the late Rev. Thomas Walker of Saintfield, county Down. (1839-06-22, 3:3, M)

183. June 18, in St. George's Church, Belfast, by the Bishop of Down and Connor, Robert Wybrants, Esq., of Rutland-square, Dublin, to Maria, daughter of Cortland Macgregor Skinner, of Belfast. (1839-06-22, 3:3, M)

184. On the 13th inst., by the Rev. P. Shuldham Henry, at the residence of the lady's father, William Preston, Esq., of Loughhill, to Miss Sarah Jane, eldest daughter of John Turner, Esq., of the city of Armagh. (1839-06-22, 3:3, M)

185. On the 16th instant, in Stewartstown church, by the Rev. William John Knox, Mr. William Henry, of Charlemont, clerk, to Miss Caldwell, of Moy. (1839-06-22, 3:3, M)

186. On Wednesday, the 19th instant, at Derrylusk, in this county, in the 6th year of her age, Elizabeth, eldest daughter of the late John Ross, Esq., and grand-daughter of Alexander Fleming, Esq., of Gallana. (1839-06-22, 3:3, D)

187. On the 7th instant, at Duncarberry Lodge, Bundoran, Elizabeth, wife of the Rev. James Adams, of Cootehill, county Cavan. (1839-06-22, 3:3, D)

188. On the 4th instant, at Coolkeiragh House, the residence of his son-in-law, Richard Young, Esq., Dr. John Caldwell, aged 87, for many years an eminent physician in the city and county of Londonderry. (1839-06-22, 3:3, D)

189. On the 8th instant, in the 57th year of his age, Mr. Owen Henry, of Portadown. (1839-06-22, 3:3, D)

190. On the 9th instant, at Kingstown, of consumption, brought on by a severe cold, Charles O'Dogherty, Esq., solicitor, formerly of Derry, aged 38 years. (1839-06-22, 3:3, D)

191. On the 12th instant, in Belfast, William Clarke, Esq., the senior Magistrate on the Belfast Bench. (1839-06-22, 3:3, D)

192. On the 7th instant, at the residence of her father, James Denham, Esq., Bundoran, Mrs. Adams, wife of the Rev. James Adams, of Cootehill. (1839-06-22, 3:3, D)

193. In Dublin, on the 9th inst., in the 92d year of her age, Martha, relict of the late Samuel Hunter, Esq., formerly of Downpatrick. (1839-06-22, 3:3, D)

194. June 29, in St. George's, Hanover-square, London, Lieutenant-Colonel Henry A. Hankey, late of the 8th Hussars, to Caroline Maria, eldest daughter of Abraham W. Robarts, Esq., of Hill-street, Berkeley-square, London. (1839-07-06, 3:4, M)

195. On the 26th ult., by the Rev. Hugh Porter, of Tartaraghan, Mr. David Smyth, of Garvagh, to Miss Reid, of Rockcorry, near Loughgall. (1839-07-06, 3:4, M)

196. June 21, aged 67 years, at All Saints' Glebe, after a protracted illness, borne with singular patience and pious resignation to the will of God, William Ball, Esq., late of the city of Derry. (1839-07-06, 3:4, D)

197. June 24, at Kingstown, suddenly, aged 12 years, Stephen, fifth son of Sir Robert Bateson, Bart., M.P. (1839-07-06, 3:4, D)

198. July 2, at his father's residence, in Middle Gardiner-street, Dublin, James O'Connor, Esq. in the 23d year of his age. (1839-07-06, 3:4, D)

199. July 9th, at Dr. Geoghegan's in Kildare, the Lady of S. Robert B. Evatt, of Mt. Louise, county Monaghan, Esq., of a son and heir. (1839-07-13, 3:5, B)

200. On the 4th inst., at Armagh, Alexander Mackenzie Lyle, Esq., of Armagh, to Deboragh Frances, youngest daughter of the late John Winder, Esq., of Armagh. (1839-07-13, 3:5, M)

201. On the 25th ult., in St. Peter's Church, Dublin, by the Rev. H. Lloyd, Robert Clifford Lloyd, Esq., Captain in her Majesty's 76th Regiment, son of the late Provost, Trinity College, Dublin, to Anna Henrietta Jane, only child of the late George Savage, Esq., Captain of the 13th Light Dragoons, and of Balliloan, County Down. (1839-07-20, 3:3, M)

202. On Thursday, the 7th inst., at Auchnacloy, by the Rev. James Carter, Wesleyan Minister, the Rev. Thomas Hicker, Wesleyan Minister, to Margaret, sixth daughter of the late Mr. Beggs, of same place. (1839-07-20, 3:3, M)

203. In Enniskillen church, by the Rev. Mark Whittaker, on Friday, 12th inst., Mr. James Moffit, Primitive Wesleyan Preacher, to Mary, eldest daughter of Mr. Thomas Lowry, of that town. (1839-07-20, 3:3, M)

204. On the 15th inst., by the Rev. James Sheil, P.P., of Enniskillen, Edwin Francis, son of James Augustin Hardy, Esq., of Summer-hill Terrace, Birmingham, to Mary-Anne, second daughter of the late Thomas Maguire, Esq., of said town. (1839-07-20, 3:3, M)

205. On Saturday, the 13th inst., at Rocksavage, P. Plunkett Taafe, Esq., of Foxborough, county Roscommon, to Eliza, youngest daughter of N.W. Kenney, Esq., Rocksavage, county Monaghan. (1839-07-20, 3:3, M)

206. July 13, in St. George's Church, by the Rev. G. Black, Edward S. O'Reilly, Esq., of Mullagh, county Cavan, to Sarah Marshall, second daughter of the late Caleb Barnes, Esq., of Mahonstown, county Meath. (1839-07-20, 3:3, M)

207. On the 16th of May, in Jamaica, in the prime of life, greatly regretted by his brother officers, and to the inexpressible grief of his relatives and friends, Robert Atthill, Esq., Staff Assistant Surgeon, and second son of the Rev. Wm. Atthill, of Ardess, in the county Fermanagh. (1839-07-20, 3:3, D)

208. Yesterday, at Tyholland Church, Mr. Keckham, of this town, to Mrs. Goodwin, relict of the late Mr. Andrew Goodwin, of Monaghan. (1839-07-27, 3:2, M)

209. On Thursday evening, at his residence, Rathconnell [Raconnell], near this town, at the age of 76 years, Lieutenant Colonel Robert Lucas, of the York Rangers, in which corps he received the rank of Lieutenant Colonel, in 1811. The gallant veteran was for many years a deputy Lieutenant for the county of Monaghan, and was uncle to our esteemed representative, Edward Lucas, Esq., of Castleshane. He was a man distinguished for his urbanity, kindness to the poor, and although of late years, sickness had prevented him from going abroad among his friends, yet the most sincere regret is felt at his decease. (1839-07-27, 3:2, D)

210. On Saturday last, at his seat Mount Anketell, Roger Anketell, Esq., one of the oldest Magistrates in this County, and a highly esteemed and amiable man both in public and private life. (1839-07-27, 3:2, D)

211. In Derryisland, near Castleblayney, at the residence of his father, in the 34th year of his age, Hugh Henry, Surgeon, late of Glasslough, where he resided for some years. He bore a protracted illness with Christian submission. He possessed a highly cultivated mind; and the general estimation in which he was held was evinced by the large and respectable concourse of people, that accompanied his remains to the grave. (1839-07-27, 3:2, D)

212. This morning, at the residence of his brother-in-law, J. Nunn, Esq., in this town, at the age of 17 years, Alexander, son of the late Nathaniel Wright, Esq. This young gentleman has, for a long period, been suffering from a delicate constitution, but he bore his illness with much resignation to the will of the Most High. (1839-07-27, 3:2, D)

213. July 31, in Rathfarnham church, by the Rev. Henry Stewart, Rector of Loughgilly, in the county of Armagh, D.D., Arthur Mathew Downing, Esq., eldest son of the Rev. Samuel Downing, of Fenagh Glebe, in the county of Carlow, to Mary youngest daughter of the late Mathew Weld, Esq., Bagnalstown, in the county of Carlow. (1839-08-10, 3:2, M)

214. August 1, in St. Peter's church, Dublin, by the Rev. Henry Stewart, Rector of Loughgilly, in the county of Armagh, D.D., Lorenzo Weld, Esq., second son of the late Mathew Weld, Esq., of Bagnalstown, in the county of Carlow, to Elizabeth Charlotte Letablere, eldest daughter of Thomas Littleton, Esq., of Stephen's-green, Dublin. (1839-08-10, 3:2, M)

215. At Dromore, on the 23d ult., by the Rev. James Collins, A.M., Mr. Samuel Curry, of Dromore, merchant, to Martha, daughter of the late Mr. Wm. Scott. (1839-08-10, 3:2, M)

216. On the 29th ult., Desertcreight church, by the Rev. A.G. Stewart, Mr. William Charles, merchant, Cookstown, to Ellen, third daughter of Mr. Edward M'Crea of Donaghrisk, county Tyrone. (1839-08-10, 3:2, M)

217. July 27th, in London, aged 29 years, Eliza, the beloved wife of John Reed, Esq., of Rathans [sic], in the county of Monaghan, and youngest daughter of Sir Amyrald Dancer, Bart., of Modreeney, county of Tipperary. (1839-08-10, 3:2, D)

218. July 17, the Rev. Wm. Wilson, Presbyterian Secession Minister of Crossgar, near Coleraine, in the 71st year of his age, and 39th of his ministry. (1839-08-10, 3:2, D)

219. On Thursday, the 8th instant, by special license, by the Rev. Michael Homan, Rector of the Parish of Killymard, in the Diocese of Raphoe, at Killymard Church, John Chambers, of Upper Dorset-street, in the county of Dublin, Esq., Barrister-at-Law, third son of the late John Chambers, of Lifford, in the county of Donegal, Esq., to Jane, second daughter of the late Thomas Young, of Lough Esk, in same county, Esq. The bride was given away by her brother, Thomas Brooke, Esq. (1839-08-17, 3:1, M)

220. On the 12th inst., in the Church of Rathfriland, by the Rev. J. Cousins, Mr. Thomas Gilliam, of Newry, to Miss Jane Wilson, daughter of the late Mr. James Wilson, of Rathfriland. (1839-08-17, 3:1, M)

221. August 10, at Bannagher, by the Rev. Edward Gordon, Benjamin Bowen Brereton, Esq., Balliver Cottage, brother to Lieutenant-Colonel Brereton, late of Bristol, to Miss Jane Drew, Daughter of John Drew Coates, Esq. (1839-08-17, 3:1, M)

222. On the 6th inst., at Greenhill, in the county Donegal, the Rev. William Gamble, Reformed Presbyterian Minister, and Pastor of the joint Congregation of Milford, Ramelton, and Letterkenny, in the 77th year of his age and 54th of his ministry. (1839-08-17, 3:1, D)

223. August 8, after a tedious illness, which she bore with Christian piety and resignation, deservedly regretted by a large circle of friends and acquaintances, Mrs. Margaret Carolan, relict of the late Edward Carolan, Esq., Carrickmacross. (1839-08-17, 3:1, D)

224. August 11, at Carysfort Avenue, Blackrock, aged four years and a-half, William Henry Gilpin, elder son of Alexander Johnston, jun. (1839-08-17, 3:1, D)

225. On the 10th inst., aged 62 years, Mr. Henry Lowe, of Mountnorris. The demise of this kind-hearted and upright man must be long felt as a heavy bereavement to his family and friends, and a loss to the poor, to whom he was a steady benefactor. By a straightforward course of integrity and truth, he secured the confidence and esteem of all who knew him—of every class and creed. His funeral procession was the largest witnessed in the country for a long time. (1839-08-17, 3:1, D)

226. At Colombo, Ceylon, on the 1st May last, Sarah, wife of Lieutenant and Adjutant Rogers, 95th Regiment. (1839-08-17, 3:1, D)

227. In the Church of this town, on Wednesday morning, by the Rev. Henry Maffatt, Richard Mitchell, Esq., of Glasslough-street, Solicitor, to Elizabeth, eldest daughter of the late Mr. Henry Wright. After the ceremony was concluded and the party had partaken of a dejeune at the house of the lady's mother, the happy couple attended by the brides-maids, left for Kingstown, where they will pass the honeymoon. (1839-08-24, 3:2, M)

228. On the 15th instant, in the Chapel-of-Ease, by the Rev. Wm. Burton, Thomas Cholahan, Esq., of Ashgrove, in the King's County, to Alice, eldest daughter of the late Capt. C—h [*illegible*], 98th Regt., of Millfield, county of Donegal. (1839-08-24, 3:2, M)

229. On Thursday the 15th instant, at Lakefield, county Antrim, Louisa Richardson, youngest daughter of the late John Richardson, Esq., of Summerhill, Co. Fermanagh. (1839-08-24, 3:2, D)

230. In Drogheda, Richard Shegog, Esq. in his 64th[?] year. (1839-08-24, 3:2, D)

231. On the 13th instant, of pulmonary consumption, in the 49th year of his age, Doctor Joseph D. Dobbin, medical superintendent of the Newtownhamilton Dispensary for the last twenty-four years. (1839-08-24, 3:2, D)

232. At Glasslough, in the house of the Lady's father, Mr. John Wilson, of Caledon, to Maria, second daughter of Mr. Moses M'Mahon, of Glasslough. (1839-08-31, 3:5, M)

233. August 20, at St. Matthew's Ipswich, P. Frederick O'Malley, Esq., of the Middle Temple, Barrister-at-law, third son of Charles O'Malley, Esq., of Lodge, in the county of Mayo, to Emily, second daughter of William Rodwell, Esq., of the former place. (1839-08-31, 3:5, M)

234. August 22, at Kingsland House, county Roscommon, the seat of the lady's father, Darius John MacEgan, of Emonysky, county Tipperary, to Esmina, eldest daughter of John Conmee, Esq., J.P. (1839-08-31, 3:5, M)

235. August 23, at his residence in Castlebar, after a lingering illness, William Rowland, Esq., Solicitor. (1839-08-31, 3:5, D)

236. August 20, aged 20 years, Hugh, eldest son of William Wilson, Esq., of Belfast. (1839-08-31, 3:5, D)

237. August 23, at his residence at Sallymount, Thomas Knox Hill, Esq. (1839-08-31, 3:5, D)

238. August 15th, at Exeter, William Henry Proull, Esq., of Belfast, to Jane, daughter of the late Major R.B. Fulton, of the Bengal Artillery. (1839-09-07, 3:5, M)

239. Sept. 3, at Monkstown Church, by the Rev. Henry H.L. Wesby, Vicar of Oldcastle, George Pim, Esq. of Brenanstown House, county of Dublin, to Charlotte Henrietta, daughter of Lieutenant-Colonel Cash, of Belville, in the same county. (1839-09-07, 3:5, M)

240. On the 26th ult., at her house in Sandy's-street, Newry, aged 79, Mrs. Eleanor Kerr, daughter of the late Rev. William Campbell, D.D., Rector of Killeshell, and Vicar of Newry. (1839-09-07, 3:5, D)

241. On the 20th ult., at Toulouse, of consumption, aged 21, William Tennent Dillon Tennent, B.A., only son of Richard Dillon Tennent, Esq., and grandson of the late William Tennent, Esq., Belfast, deeply lamented. (1839-09-07, 3:5, D)

242. August 24, Deborah Harriet, eldest daughter of Charles Bigot, Esq., J.P., Kilcoursey House, King's County. (1839-09-07, 3:5, D)

243. August 23, in Dublin, Mr. William Carolan, newspaper reporter. (1839-09-07, 3:5, D)

244. September 1, at Belturbet, in the county Cavan, at an advanced age, Humphry Gumley, Esq., deeply regretted by all his acquaintances. (1839-09-07, 3:5, D)

245. August 27, at Newtownstuart, Mr. C. Ross, of Pubble, to Mrs. Hood, of Lisaratony. What makes it remarkable, is this, that it is the fifth time that the bridegroom has appeared at the alter [sic] of hymen, and the third time [for] the bride. Their joint ages amount to 185. (1839-09-14, 3:2, M)

246. By special license, at Dublin, Captain Sadlier, unattached, to Amelia, youngest daughter of the late Richard Campsie, Esq., of the county of Kildare. (1839-09-14, 3:2, M)

247. Isaac Newtown, Esq., of Oporto, merchant, to Maria, daughter of the late Captain Waldron Kelly, of the 40th Regiment, and barrack-master at Lucca and Montego Bay, Jamaica, and sister of Waldron Kelly, Esq., of Kildare. (1839-09-14, 3:2, M)

248. At Parsonstown, Daniel Shannon, Esq., to Martha, daughter of the late T. Dennison, Esq., of Enniscorthy. (1839-09-14, 3:2, M)

249. On the 24th ult., at Burton-on-Trent, Richard Fowler Butler, Esq. of Barton Hall, Staffordshire, to Agnes, eldest daughter of John Peel, Esq., of the Abbey, Burton-on-Trent. (1839-09-14, 3:2, M)

250. At Marlborough Church, Devon, George Howard Vyse, Esq., Captain, 2d Life Guards, to Lizzy, sixth daughter of the late Rear-Admiral Sir Michael Seymour, Bart., K.C.B. (1839-09-14, 3:2, M)

251. At St. George's, Hanover-square, London, the Right Hon. Lord Kilmaine, to Mary, daughter of the Hon. C. Ewen Law, M.P., Recorder of London. (1839-09-14, 3:2, M)

252. At St. Martin's-in-the-Fields, Captain Charles Stuart, Grenadier Guards, nephew of Lord Stewart de Rothsay, to Georgiana, eldest daughter of the late Vice-Admiral Sir John Gore, and Maid of Honor to the Queen Dowager. (1839-09-14, 3:2, M)

253. At Aughnaseda, county of Monaghan, William Henry, son of Mr. Edward Smith, Lower Sackville-street, Dublin. (1839-09-14, 3:2, D)

254. At Moygannon Cottage, Mrs. Pettigrew, aged 50, relict of the late William Pettigrew, of Crilly, county Tyrone, Esq. Also, her aunt, Miss M'Cright, formerly of Tandragee, at the advanced age of 83. (1839-09-14, 3:2, D)

255. On Tuesday, at Cork Barracks, John Moyneaux, Esq., Assistant-Surgeon, 61st Regiment. This is the third death that has taken place in the Medical Department of the Regiment within the last six months. (1839-09-14, 3:2, D)

256. Mrs. Rosanna Murray, of Stewartstown, county Tyrone. (1839-09-14, 3:2, D)

257. On Friday last, at Ballybay, by the Rev. Mark M'Dowell, Seceding Presbyterian Minister, Mr. Samuel Saunderson, of New Jersey, United States, America, to Margaret, eldest daughter of the late Mr. John Crawford, of Ballybay. (1839-09-21, 3:2, M)

258. On the 17th instant, by special license, by the Rev. Archibald Douglas, at Lyons, the seat of the Right Hon. Lord Cloncurry, the Hon. Edward Lawless, to Elizabeth, only daughter of John Kirwan, Esq., of Castle Hackett, county of Galway. (1839-09-21, 3:2, M)

259. At St. George's Church, Hanover-square, C.J. Tottenham, Esq., of the 2d Life Guards, eldest son of the Bishop of Clogher, to the Hon. Isabella Maude, daughter of Viscount Hawarden. (1839-09-21, 3:2, M)

260. At Ardtrea Church, Mr. John Hall, of Springhill, to Maria Louisa, daughter of Captain Robert Atkinson, late of the Monaghan Militia, and C.C.P. (1839-09-21, 3:2, M)

261. At her father's residence, Dawson-street, Mary Josephine Reilly, to M. M'Auliffe, merchant, of Dublin. (1839-09-21, 3:2, M)

262. At Vienna, Henry Eugene Perrin, Esq., merchant, in Dublin, to Isabella, daughter of the late Rev. Jas. Brown, Minister of Newbattle. (1839-09-21, 3:2, M)

263. On the 16th instant, at Newbliss, Mr. John Quinn, a Student of Belfast College, in his 21st year, after a protracted illness, (consumption) which he bore with Christian patience and resignation. His eyes were fixed on that celestial world, whose gates, it is humbly trusted, were just opening to receive his departing spirit into the Mansions of everlasting rest, prepared for him in his Father's house. He was borne to the grave by his fellow students, and there, in sorrow, they deposited the remains of their once loved friend. (1839-09-21, 3:2, D)

264. At Lisburn, on the 15th instant, in the 31st year of his age, Mr. John Griffith Rodgers. (1839-09-21, 3:2, D)

265. On the 14th instant, of fever, which he caught in the discharge of his duty, aged 34 years, the Rev. Jas. Rooney, P.P., of Glenish, near Enniskillen. (1839-09-21, 3:2, D)

266. In Limerick, aged 67 years, Stephen Dickson, Esq. He was one of the oldest Magistrates, and a Deputy Lieutenant for that county. (1839-09-21, 3:2, D)

267. On the 16th instant, at Leamington, the lady of James Hamilton, Esq., of Cornacassa, county of Monaghan, of a daughter. (1839-09-28, 3:3, B)

268. On the 19th instant, by the Rev. Anthony Cosslett, P.P., Captain M'Auley, of Belfast, to Mary, daughter of the late Mr. Edward Byrne, of Newtownbreda. (1839-09-28, 3:3, M)

269. In this town, on the 23d instant, Charlotte, eldest daughter of the late Joseph Mitchell, Esq., of Cappah Lodge, in this county, in the 24th year of her age. She lived esteemed and died regretted by a numerous circle of mourning friends, whose only consolation under this afflictive dispensation of divine Providence is, that she departed in possession of a lively faith in the all-atoning Saviour. (1839-09-28, 3:3, D)

270. At Derryhaw, near Tynan, on Saturday, the 31st ult., Mr. James Johnston, aged 77 years, 40 of which he was a regular and worthy member of the Masonic Society, No. 601, Tynan. Seldom has the death of so friendly a man been recorded, nor one more respected by all who had the pleasure of his acquaintance. Fully prepared by Divine grace, he calmly resigned his spirit, after a long illness, into the hands of his God and Saviour, realising that precious promise, "I will be thy guide even unto death, and afterwards receive thee into glory." (1839-09-28, 3:3, D)

271. On the 10th inst., at Hamilton-place, Belfast, aged 18, Mary Eleanor, daughter of the late James Fitzgerald, Esq. Clonavilla, county Monaghan. (1839-09-28, 3:3, D)

272. At Skibareen, Andrew M'Carthy, Esq. Attorney, to Anne, daughter of the late Luke Taylor, Esq. of Derry. (1839-10-19, 3:2, M)

273. At the Chapel of the British Embassy at Paris, Alexander Clotworthy Dawson, Esq., eldest son of the late Admiral Dawson, of Carrickfergus, to Elizabeth, daughter of Richard Gresley, Esq., late of Meriden, Warwick. (1839-10-19, 3:2, M)

274. Oct. 11, at his residence, Carnaveagh, county of Monaghan, Joseph Cunningham, Esq., deeply and deservedly regretted. (1839-10-19, 3:2, D)

275. On the 15th ult., by the Rev. David Stuart, of Dublin, John Dunn, of Cootehill, in the county of Cavan, druggist, to Jane Stuart, third daughter of James Stuart, General Inspector, of Naas, county Kildare. (1839-10-26, 3:2, M)

276. Oct. 22, by the Rev. David Stuart, D.D., Mr. John Lynch, to Miss Catherine D'Arcy, both of Dundalk. (1839-10-26, 3:2, M)

277. At the Cathedral, Quebec, William Young, Esq., to Eliza Ann, daughter of the late Blayney Winslow, Esq., of Mount Prospect, county Fermanagh. (1839-10-26, 3:2, M)

278. On the 19th instant, at Clonavilla, in this county, John Fitzgerald, Esq., aged 60 years. (1839-10-26, 3:2, D)

279. October 13, at his father's residence, Cootehill, of consumption, James, son of the Rev. William Lyttle, Presbyterian Secession Minister of that town. (1839-10-26, 3:2, D)

280. October 28, in Cavan Church, by the Rev. Thomas Carson, Mr. William Lee, to Anne, eldest daughter of Mr. George Chadwick, both of the town of Cavan. (1839-11-02, 2:5, M)

281. October 29, in Oranmore Church, Theobald Butler, Esq. of Ballygagan, only son of Captain Walter Butler, late of the 65th regiment, to Anna Maria Blake, second daughter of Andrew Blake, Esq., of Rocklands. (1839-11-02, 2:5, M)

282. In Malabrack Church, County of Armagh, the Rev. W.R. Williams, to Elizabeth Mary, daughter of Charles M'Anally, Esq., half-pay 90th Regiment. (1839-11-02, 2:5, M)

283. In St. Mary's Church, Newry, William Boyle Glenny, Esq., son of W. Glenny, Esq., to Anne, daughter of Archibald Little, Esq. (1839-11-02, 2:5, M)

284. At Ballinasloe, aged 25 years, Richard, son of Captain John Sutherland, of the Galway Militia. (1839-11-02, 2:5, D)

285. In Middleton, Dennis M'Carthy, Esq., M.D., aged 67 years. (1839-11-02, 2:5, D)

286. In Enniskillen, Mr. John Steel. While presenting himself before the Assistant-Barrister as a freeholder of the borough, he suddenly dropped dead, at the advanced age of 86. (1839-11-02, 2:5, D)

287. At her father's residence, on Saturday last, aged 19, Hannah, youngest daughter of Mr. Nathaniel Greacen, printer, of this town. Her decease is deeply felt and sincerely regretted by her friends and acquaintances. (1839-11-09, 3:2, D)

288. On the evening of the 31st ult., Mr. James O'Reilly, of Cootehill, aged 28 years, nephew to the late President O'Reilly, of Carrickmacross, and grand nephew to Dr. O'Reilly, Roman Catholic Bishop of Clogher. His death (which was awfully sudden, having been on his way to attend a nuptial party when it occurred) has left a vacuum amongst a large circle of friends which will not be soon filled up, on account of his affable disposition. (1839-11-09, 3:2, D)

289. On Sunday morning last, in this town, Francis Kennedy, of Donegal, Recruiting Serjeant of the 49th Regiment of Foot, after a few days' illness. (1839-11-09, 3:2, D)

290. At Monaghan, on the 9th instant, the lady of John Hatchell, Esq., of a daughter. (1839-11-16, 3:1, B)

291. In the Mall Preaching-house of Ballyshannon, Mr. John Lockhart, Lisahully, to Miss Margaret Keys, of same place. The bride is both deaf and dumb. (1839-11-16, 3:1, M)

292. Nov. 11, at his residence, near Stewartstown, the Rev. William Knox, eldest son of Samuel Knox, Esq., of Blessington-street, Dublin. (1839-11-16, 3:1, D)

293. On the 17th instant, the lady of George B. Clark, Boyne Lodge, Drogheda, Esq., of a son. (1839-11-23, 3:1, B)

294. On the 13th instant, at Foerboe-house, County Derry, the residence of the lady's mother, by the Rev. Mr. Dill, Mr. David Patterson, merchant, Downpatrick, to Miss Jane George. (1839-11-23, 3:1, M)

295. At Milverton, Warwickshire, the Rev. Arthur Buller, to Grace Bell Ward, second daughter of the late Chas. Lynd, Esq., of Mullantane, County Tyrone. (1839-11-23, 3:1, M)

296. On the 12th instant, at Moy, County Tyrone, at an advanced age, Elizabeth Hannah, relict of the late Edward Lysaght, Esq., Barrister-at-law. (1839-11-23, 3:1, D)

297. On the 11th instant, Mrs. Ovenden, the beloved wife of Charles Ovenden, Esq., of Enniskillen. (1839-11-23, 3:1, D)

298. On Saturday the 9th instant, after a short but painful illness, in the 37th year of his age, the Rev. John Sutcliffe, the beloved Pastor of the Moravian Congregation. (1839-11-23, 3:1, D)

299. On the 14th instant, at Whitehouse, Charlotte, daughter of Thomas Grimshaw, Esq. (1839-11-23, 3:1, D)

300. At Derryvalley House, the residence of T. M'Cullagh, Esq., the Lady of David Jackson, Esq., county Leitrim, of a son. (1839-11-30, 2:4, B)

301. November 22, in the Parish Church of Killyman, by the Rev. William Thompson, Henry Clindinning, of Wheatfield, in the county of Armagh, Esq., to Eliza, daughter of Samuel Davidson, of Union Place, Dungannon, in the co. of Tyrone, Esq. (1839-11-30, 2:4, M)

302. September 29, at Beyrout, in Syria, while travelling in the East, Alexander C. Downing Nesbitt, Esq., eldest son of John Downing Nesbitt, Esq., of Toberdaly, in the King's County, and Leixlip, in the county of Kildare. (1839-11-30, 2:4, D)

303. November 18, in Roscommon, Eleanor, wife of James Corr, Esq., and sister to John and Henry Mapother, Esqrs. of Kilteven-house, in that county. (1839-11-30, 2:4, D)

304. November 23, at Leamington, Mary Frances, wife of Lieut.-Col. Dixon, Scots Fusileer Guards. (1839-11-30, 2:4, D)

305. November 25, at his house, near Winkfield, Lieut.-Gen. the Hon. Sir Henry King, K.C.B. (1839-11-30, 2:4, D)

306. December 13, by proxy, at the residence of her mother, in Lower Sherrard-street, Dublin, Matilda Maria Clarke, youngest daughter of the late Edward Clarke, Esq., of Palmerstown, county Dublin, to Richard Meade, Esq., of the city of Guanajuato, Mexico. (1839-12-21, 3:5, M)

307. At Killead Church, Robert, son of the late Robert M'Naghten, Esq., of Mountjoy-square, Dublin, to Sarah Warren, daughter of James Moore, Esq., of Cloverhill, county Antrim. (1839-12-21, 3:5, M)

308. At Turnbridge [sic] Wells, William Sinclair, Esq., eldest son of James Sinclair, Esq., of Holy Hill, county Tyrone, to Sarah, daughter of James Cranbourne Strode, Esq., late of Shernfold Park, Sussex. (1839-12-21, 3:5, M)

309. In Merrion-street, Dublin, Archibald M'Fall Hull, Esq., only son of Mrs. Hull, of Abbeytown, Boyle. (1839-12-21, 3:5, D)

310. At Armagh, Elizabeth, wife of the Rev. Dr. Robinson. (1839-12-21, 3:5, D)

311. In Donaghmore, county Tyrone, at the advanced age of 106, Mrs. Millan. (1839-12-21, 3:5, D)

312. Of a lingering illness, the Rev. Mark Cassidy, of Newtownards, in the 72d year of his age. He was an upright and impartial magistrate. (1839-12-21, 3:5, D)

313. December 17, at her residence, 53, Old Dominick-street, aged 73, Mrs. Irvine, relict of the late Gerrard Irvine, of Rockfield, county Fermanagh, Esq. (1839-12-21, 3:5, D)

314. December 19, by special license, at Kilconly Church, by the Right Rev. the Lord Bishop of Tuam, James Wynne, Esq., of Rutland-square, Barrister-at-law, nephew to Owen Wynne, Esq., of Hazlewood, in the county Sligo, to Maria Elizabeth, second daughter of Edward Blake, Esq., D.L., of Castle Grove, county Galway. (1839-12-28, 3:2, M)

315. December 19, at St. John's Church, Westminister [sic], Geo. T.C. Fogarty, M.D., of the East India Company's service, to Mary Frances, eldest daughter of the late George Hodder, Esq., of the First Foot Guards. (1839-12-28, 3:2, M)

316. Dec. 21, in St. George's Church, Hanover-square, London, by the Rev. Mr. Dickinson, Charles F. Smyth, eldest son of Robert Smyth, Esq., of Stephen's-green, Dublin, to Ellen, only daughter of James Reynolds, Esq., of Boston, Lincolnshire. (1839-12-28, 3:2, M)

317. Dec. 20, by the Rev. Wm. Rossborough, Rathfriland, Mr. John Wiley, to Miss Sarah Heron. (1839-12-28, 3:2, M)

318. At Newtownstewart, Tyrone, Jones Crawford, Esq., J.P. (1839-12-28, 3:2, D)

319. Suddenly, at Newry, Mr. John Kennedy, woollen-draper. (1839-12-28, 3:2, D)

320. At Newtownards, county Down, the Rev. Mark Cassidy. (1839-12-28, 3:2, D)

321. In Newry, aged 81 years, Elizabeth, relict of Peter Quinn Kean, Esq., of Belfast. (1839-12-28, 3:2, D)

322. William Comerford Clarkson, Esq., of Doctor's Commons. (1839-12-28, 3:2, D)

323. On the 16th inst., at his residence, Rathbody, the Rev. Doctor Merron, P.P., of Tallenstown. This venerable clergyman had nearly completed the 80th year of his age and the 55th of his ministry. (1839-12-28, 3:2, D)

324. On the 16th inst., Eliza, the beloved wife of William Somerville, Esq., and second daughter of the late Lieut.-Colonel Bellingham, of Castlebellingham, county Louth. (1839-12-28, 3:2, D)

325. Dec. 17, aged 77 years, James M'Clelland, of Drumsnad, parish of Magheradroll, a steady Churchman, and well-tried. For many years he was the only Protestant in the townland; but, from the undeviating correctness and consistency of his character, he outlived all animosity. His neighbours (all of the Roman Catholic persuasion) vied with each other in unremitting attention during his illness, and to show their respect and regard, they insisted upon carry [sic] his remains to the church-yard, upwards of three miles, where the Vicar read the solemn funeral service, in which they seemed to take a deep interest, actually making their responses, &c. (1839-12-28, 3:2, D)

326. December 27, by special license, at St. Peter's Church, by the Rev. Doctor Porter, Walter Strickland, Esq., eldest son of the late George Strickland, Esq., of Newtown, Yorkshire, and grandson of the late Sir George Strickland, Bart., to Charlotte Augusta, daughter of John Carrol, of Fitzwilliam-square, Esq., Barrister-at-law. (1840-01-04, 3:2, M)

327. December 27, in St. Ann's Church, by the Rev. Mr. West, Richard Yoakley, Esq., Grafton-street, to Mary Anne, only daughter of the late John Irvine, Esq., Surgeon, R.N., Deerpark, county of Tyrone. (1840-01-04, 3:2, M)

328. December 27, by the Rev. James Shields, at the house of the Lady's uncle, Joseph Lyle, Esq., Canal-street, John Crothers, Esq., of Blackwatertown, to Margaret, eldest daughter of William Clarke, Esq., Buskhill, county of Down. (1840-01-04, 3:2, M)

329. December 26, at 2, Seville-place, by the Rev. Doctor Drummond, Mr. R.C. Dixon, of London, to Maria, youngest daughter of the late Mr. R.C. Wakefield, of Folkestone, Kent. (1840-01-04, 3:2, M)

330. December 30, at Termonfechin, county of Louth, the Rev. Stephen Lett, of Callan, to Harriet, second daughter of Gervas Gamson, Esq., of Buckingham, Notts. (1840-01-04, 3:2, M)

331. December 28, in Upper Pembroke-street, William, eldest son of the late Captain Christian, R.N. (1840-01-04, 3:2, D)

332. At Tenesee [sic], North America, William Graham, Esq., son of the late Andrew Graham, Esq., R.N., formerly of Cavanalee, near Strabane. (1840-01-04, 3:2, D)

333. October 18, on his passage from Africa, Doctor Robert Gosson, Surgeon, of the ship *Lady Stormont*, deeply regretted by the crew for his valuable services, and unremitting attention to their wants. (1840-01-04, 3:2, D)

334. December 26, at Cultra, in his 37th year, John Hughes Kennedy, late of the 14th Light Dragoons, eldest son of Hugh Kennedy, of Cultra, in the county of Down, Esq. (1840-01-04, 3:2, D)

335. December 20, at Paris, after a short illness, Major James Brown Horner, of Charlton, Kent, formerly of the 84th Regiment, aged 67 years; and within a few hours, his beloved wife, Helen C. Horner, aged 64. (1840-01-04, 3:2, D)

336. Of consumption, on Sunday, the 24th ultimo, in the 35th year of his age, after a long and protracted illness, borne with Christian piety and resignation, Mr. Harrington Dickson, of Ballygawley, fourth son of the late Mr. David Dickson, merchant, Dungannon. (1840-01-04, 3:2, D)

337. At his residence, Waterside, Coleraine, on the 28th ult., in the 62d year of his age, Mr. Thomas Dunlap, after a severe and protracted illness. (1840-01-04, 3:2, D)

338. On the 26th ult., by the Rev. George Steen, Newtownlimavady, James Hanson, Esq., Roe-Green, to Annie, second daughter of William Fleming, Esq., merchant, Nn-Limavady. (1840-01-11, 3:2, M)

339. At Carricklongfield, county Tyrone, by the Rev. J. M'Millan, Lyle-Hill, the Rev. H. Porter, Presbyterian Minister of Tartaraghan, to Mary, daughter of the late Mr. John M'Millan. (1840-01-11, 3:2, M)

340. On the 1st Jan., by the Rev. John M'Conaghey, Urney, near Strabane, Mr. Samuel Brown, to Jane, second daughter of Mr. John Etrican, Gortloher. (1840-01-11, 3:2, M)

341. December 27, in the parish church of St. Helier, in the island of Jersey, by the Very Rev. the Dean Askin Morrison, Esq., of Dublin, to Anne, youngest daughter of the late Hans Morrison, Esq., of Clonkeen, in the county of Tyrone. (1840-01-11, 3:2, M) *Note: The clergyman's, or the groom's, name is missing from this notice.*

342. On the 7th, suddenly, at his residence, Mount-Anketell, Thomas Anketell, Esq., aged 30 years, second son to the late Roger Anketell, Esq. Mount-Anketell. This young man is much and deservedly regretted by all who knew him. (1840-01-11, 3:2, D)

343. On the 16th instant, Mr. John Rankin, of Bishop-street, Derry, merchant, in the 46th year of his age. (1840-01-11, 3:2, D)

344. On Sunday, the 20th ultimo, aged 77 years, Mr. James M'Aleer, Moyle Cottage, near Newtown-stewart, county Tyrone. (1840-01-11, 3:2, D)

345. At Mobile, on the 23d September last, of yellow fever, after six days' illness, Mr. Ezekiel Anderson, fifth son of the late Mr. James Anderson, of Derry. (1840-01-11, 3:2, D)

346. On the 2d instant, at her residence, Donegall-place, Belfast, in the 88th year of her age, beloved by all who knew her, Elizabeth, relict of the late Thomas Bateson, Esq., and mother of Sir Robert Bateson, Bart., of Belvoir Park, M.P., for the county of Londonderry. (1840-01-11, 3:2, D)

347. At Coleraine, on the 17th ult., the Rev. John Dinnen, in the 86th year of his age, being one of the oldest ministers in the Wesleyan connexion. He was called to the Itinerant ministry in 1785, in which, during the space of 36 years, he labored with acceptance, and was signally owned of God in "turning many to righteousness." (1840-01-11, 3:2, D)

348. January 4, at his residence, at Monk-place, Fitz-borough, of a rapid decline, Robert N. M'Auley, Esq., for a long time connected with the reporting department of the *Morning Register*. (1840-01-11, 3:2, D)

349. Dec. 30, at his house 27, Grafton-street, deeply and deservedly regretted, Frederick Hodges, Esq. (1840-01-11, 3:2, D)

350. On the 13th instant, at St. George's Church, by the Rev. Thomas Nolan, A.M., of St. Peter's, Stockport, Isaac, eldest son of the late Trevor Corry, of Abbey-yard, Newry, Esq., to Eliza, youngest daughter of Henry Ryan, of Kiltera, county Kilkenny, and North Great George's-street, Dublin, Esq. (1840-01-18, 3:3, M)

351. In St. Mary's church, Newry, by the Rev. Dr. King, the Rev. George H. Ashe, Incumbent of St. Mark's church, Wilton, Blackburn, to Mary, second daughter of George Ogle, Esq., Marcus-square, Newry. (1840-01-18, 3:3, M)

352. January 6, after a protracted illness, Richard, son of the Bishop of Oxford and Lady Harriot Bagot, aged 10. (1840-01-18, 3:3, D)

353. January 1, at his residence, Woodside, Plymouth, Capt. Richard Dickinson, C.B., R.N., aged 55. (1840-01-18, 3:3, D)

354. January 4, at Abbey-View, county Sligo, the residence of her mother, Isabella, youngest daughter of the late William Philips, Esq. (1840-01-18, 3:3, D)

355. January 6, in Lower Grosvenor-street, London, in her 88th year, Madam d'Arblay, the author of *Evelina and Cecilla*, widow of the late, Lieutenant-General A. Piochard, Comte d'Arblay, and second daughter of the late Charles Burney, Mus.D. (1840-01-18, 3:3, D)

356. At his residence, Clanickney, near Glasslough, aged 58 years, after a few days' illness, Mr. William Armstrong, son of the late James Armstrong, Esq., of Old Deerpark, and brother to Mr. John Armstrong, of this town. He was a man whose good qualities gained him the esteem and friendship of all who knew him. He died in a sure hope of a glorious resurrection to a better world with his Redeemer. (1840-01-25, 3:3, D)

357. Jan. 18, suddenly, at his residence, 14, Charle-mont-street, John Holmes, Esq., in the 70th year of his age. (1840-01-25, 3:3, D)

358. Jan. 19, at Portadown, of brain fever, aged five years, Esther Elizabeth, only daughter of the Rev. Charles King Irwin. (1840-01-25, 3:3, D)

359. Rev. John Carroll, Rector of Clonlea, diocese of Killaloe. (1840-01-25, 3:3, D)

360. In Limerick, Ebenezer Wallace, Esq., Manager of the National Bank. (1840-01-25, 3:3, D)

361. Oct. 10, at Kurnaul, in the East Indies, H. Brougham, Esq., aged 28, of the 4th Cavalry, eldest son of the late J.W. Brougham, Esq., and nephew of Lord Brougham. (1840-01-25, 3:3, D)

362. Jan. 14, at Knocknagoney, in the 68th year of his age, Alexander Taggart, Esq., M.D., Surgeon of the Londonderry Militia. (1840-01-25, 3:3, D)

363. Jan. 18, at Belfast, Mrs. Bailie, relict of the late Robert Bailie, of Innisbargie [Innishargie], in the county Down, Esq., and daughter of the late Stephen Seed, Esq., of Belfast. (1840-01-25, 3:3, D)

364. Jan. 17, at Kinnaird, county of Roscommon, Barnwell Plunkett, Esq., aged 73. (1840-01-25, 3:3, D)

365. Jan. 23, at Stormanstown, of typhus fever, aged sixteen years, Alicia, youngest daughter of William Leslie Badham. (1840-02-01, 3:4, D)

366. January 21, at Dungannon, sincerely lamented, Eliza M'Cord, wife of the late Lieutenant M'Cord, of the 27th Regiment, who was killed at the siege of Badajos. (1840-02-01, 3:4, D)

367. January 20, at Aughnacloy, in the 78th year of his age, Edward Moore, Esq. For more than forty years, he held the office of Magistrate for the county of Tyrone. By his unflinching integrity in the discharge of his public duties, and his sterling worth in the various relations he was called to sustain, he endeared himself to a numerous circle of friends, who now deplore his loss. (1840-02-01, 3:4, D)

368. On Friday, the 31st ult., at the church of Clough, near Roslea, Mr. John M'Vittie, Aughlisabay, to Jane, only daughter of Richard Humphries, Esq., of Rock-vale, county Monaghan. (1840-02-08, 3:2, M)

369. Same day, Jan. 31, 1840, at the house of the father of the bride, Mr. Andrew Moorehead, of Raw, county Monaghan, to Catherine, second daughter of Mr. Henry M'Vittie of Aughlisabay. (1840-02-08, 3:2, M)

370. Feb. 4, at St. Thomas's Church, Dublin, Bessie Tynte Pratt, daughter of Lieutenant-Colonel Pratt, of Cabra Castle, to Robert Saunders, of Saunders's Grove, county Wicklow, Esq. (1840-02-08, 3:2, M)

371. On the 29th ult., by the Rev. Thomas Lloyd, Mr. James Henry, son of Mr. James Henry, of Camlough, County Armagh, to Ann, eldest daughter of Mr. Robert Beatty, of Tullyharnet. (1840-02-08, 3:2, M)

372. On the 30th ult., by the Rev. Thomas Boyd, Mr. Hugh Harrison, son of Thomas Harrison, Esq., of Drumakill, to Mary, youngest daughter of the late Mr. Thomas Wallace, of Tullycouragh. (1840-02-08, 3:2, M)

373. On Friday, the 31st ult., by the Rev. James Phillips, Mr. Arthur Little, of Toplish [Foglish], county Fermanagh, to Ann, daughter of Mr. Robert P. Hyde, Postmaster, Fivemiletown. (1840-02-08, 3:2, M)

374. Jan. 13, at Rome, whither he had gone for the benefit of his health, Thomas Knox Armstrong, Esq., of Elm Park, near Armagh. (1840-02-08, 3:2, D)

375. In Drogheda, Patrick Magrane, Esq. (1840-02-08, 3:2, D)

376. In Belfast, Richard Dobbs, Esq. of Castle Dobbs, county Antrim. (1840-02-08, 3:2, D)

377. In Tuam, Marcia, wife of Richard Rawson, Esq. (1840-02-08, 3:2, D)

378. Feb. 6 in Bangor Church, by the Rev. J. O'Hara, Matthew John, eldest son of William Anketell, Esq., Anketell Grove, county Monaghan, to Catherine Frances Anne, eldest daughter of David Ker, Esq., M.P., Portavo, county Down. (1840-02-15, 3:3, M)

379. Feb. 11, in St. Peter's Church, by the Rev. Henry Fitzalen M'Clintock, Vicar of Ballymodan, Bandon, Walter Hussey Burgh, Esq., of Donore House, county of Kildare, and of Dromkeen House, county of Limerick, to Hessie, daughter of the late Rev. Alexander M'Clintock, Rector of Newtownbarry and of Clonegal, in the diocese of Ferns. (1840-02-15, 3:3, M)

380. On the 8th instant, of typhus fever, at the house of her sister, in Castledawson, Anne, Widow of the late Hugh Hamill, Esq., of Ruskey, in the county of Monaghan. (1840-02-15, 3:3, D)

381. Feb. 13, at Clonakilty Church, Eliza Jane, eldest daughter of John Abbot, Esq., to Benjamin Wright, Esq., of Dunmanway. (1840-02-22, 3:2, M)

382. Feb. 15, in Lisburn, by the Very Rev. Dean of Ross, John L. Gaussen, Esq., M.D., Crumlin, to Anne, youngest daughter of Hercules Bradshaw, Esq., Culcavey Cottage, Hillsborough, county Down. (1840-02-22, 3:2, M)

383. Feb. 10, in Athy, James Allen Kelly, Esq., youngest son of John Kelly, Esq., of Stradbally, to Hannah, daughter of John Lord, Esq., of Athy Lodge, county Kildare. (1840-02-22, 3:2, M)

384. On Monday, the 10th instant, Mr. Thomas Mason, of Clover Lodge, county Leitrim, to Catherine Callen, niece to the Rev. P. O'Reilly, of Drang [Drung], and sister to the Rev. John Callen, Diocese of Dromore. (1840-02-22, 3:2, M)

385. Feb. 15, in Londonderry, by the Rev. Henry Wallan, William Black, Esq., of Cavan, to Hannah, second daughter of the late Samuel Peoples, Esq. (1840-02-22, 3:2, M)

386. Jan. 20, at Gretna-green, and on the 12th instant, in Manchester, William Clarke, Esq., of Bristol, to Louisa, second daughter of the Rev. J.F. Doreton, of Clifton, near Bristol. (1840-02-22, 3:2, M)

387. On the morning of the 18th of January last, at his residence in Armagh, Anna Maria, the eldest and dearly beloved daughter of Mr. William Johnston, aged three years and nine months. (1840-02-22, 3:2, D)

388. Feb. 14, Christopher Harman, Esq., of Middle Gardiner-street, Dublin, and Kilmacnoran, county Cavan. (1840-02-22, 3:2, D)

389. Feb. 5, at Hillsgrove, James Hogg, Esq., for many years a magistrate of the county Roscommon. (1840-02-22, 3:2, D)

390. On the 24th of November last, on his passage to Mobile, of inflammation, Mr. George Frazer, mate of the *England*, in the 21st year of his age. His death is greatly lamented by his employers, and a large circle of friends and acquaintances. (1840-02-22, 3:2, D)

391. On the 13th instant, at Busk-hill, his brother's residence, Mr. Wm. Marshall, of Margaret-st., Newry, aged 30 years. The large and respectable party who escorted his remains to the grave, told how the deceased was esteemed as an upright, honest man. (1840-02-22, 3:2, D)

392. On the 8th instant, suddenly, in the 69th year of his age, at his brother's house, in Newry, James Kidd, Esq., late of Millmount, Keady. (1840-02-22, 3:2, D)

393. February 25, at St. Thomas's Church, by the Rev. Mr. Handcock, Robert Galbraith, Esq., of Bally-bay, county of Monaghan, to Maria, only daughter of John Percy Howes, Esq., M.D., of Kilcock, in the county Kildare. (1840-02-29, 3:2, M)

394. At Bunnoe, Parish of Drung, county of Cavan, by the Rev. Peter Reilly, P.P., Mr. John Smith, of Cootehill, Innkeeper, and one of the Deputy High Constables for the Barony of Tullygarvery, in said county, to Miss Rosa Foy, of Bunnoe. (1840-02-29, 3:2, M)

395. On Tuesday, the 25th instant, by the Rev. Mr. Duffy, Mr. Samuel M'Murray, to Miss Mary M'Caffrey, both of Clones. (1840-02-29, 3:2, M)

396. February 24, in the church of Annaduff, county of Leitrim, by the Rev. George Shaw, Rector, the Rev. Richard S. Clifford, of Carrick-on-Shannon, to Hariet Young, eldest daughter of Captain Cox, J.P., Carrick-on-Shannon. (1840-02-29, 3:2, M)

397. At Portnelligan, Tynan, on the 22d ultimo, aged 67 years, Margarette Coote, wife of Alexander Cross, Esq., and daughter of the late Doctor Bond, of Bondville, county of Armagh. (1840-02-29, 3:2, D)

398. February 17, at his father's residence, aged 16 years, Samuel, eldest son of Thomas Saunders, of Rathmines, Esq., a youth of rare talents and acquirements. (1840-02-29, 3:2, D)

399. February 23, Maurice O'Connell, youngest son of C. Fitzsimon, Esq. (1840-02-29, 3:2, D)

400. Feb. 23, at Cookstown, Mrs. Irvine, relict of the late Major William Irvine, of the Royal Tyrone Regiment, in the 73d year of her age. (1840-02-29, 3:2, D)

401. Feb. 16, in Corporation-street, Jane, relict of the late John Chambers, Esq., Dundalk. (1840-02-29, 3:2, D)

402. On Tuesday, the 3d instant, at Drumsnat Church, by the Rev. Allan Mitchell, Mr. George Joseph Awe, printer, to Martha, eldest daughter of Mr. John Baxter, watch-maker, of this town. (1840-03-07, 3:3, M)

403. On Sunday, the 23d ult., in St. Michan's Church, by the Rev. Mr. M'Donnell, Mr. H. Browne, of Newbliss, to Mary, only daughter of Samuel Danby, Esq., of the City of York. (1840-03-07, 3:3, M)

404. On the 27th ult., by the Rev. Dr. Cooke, James Young, Esq., solicitor, to Miss Clara Kennedy, both of Belfast. (1840-03-07, 3:3, M)

405. On the 28th ult., by the Rev. Mr. Rutherford, Seceding Minister, Mr. John Hogg, Mountpleasant, near Gilford, to Mary, only daughter of the late Mr. John Spratt, Meadowvale, near Banbridge. (1840-03-07, 3:3, M)

406. On the 25th ult., at Tamlaght O'Crilly, Joseph Courtenay, of Tyanee, in the county of Derry, Esq., to Mary, fourth daughter of John M'Watters, of Laurel Lodge, in the county of Antrim, Esq. (1840-03-07, 3:3, M)

407. On the 20th ult., in Dublin, James Quin, Esq., of Newry, to Miss Ann White, of High-street, Dublin. (1840-03-07, 3:3, M)

408. At Rockcorry, on Thursday morning, the 27th ult., Jane, the beloved wife of Mr. Alexander Wilson. She was respected by all that knew her—during her sickness she was supported by faith in her Redeemer, and in her last moments committed herself into his covenant keeping, wholly depending on his "finished work," for salvation. The large and respectable concourse who escorted her remains to the grave told how she was respected and beloved. (1840-03-07, 3:3, D)

409. On the 12th instant, at Lismasheela, the Lady of John Jackson, Esq., of a son of an heir. (1840-03-14, 3:1, B)

410. March 11, in Molesworth-street, Dublin, the Lady of Richard Mayne, Esq., of Newbliss, county of Monaghan, of a son. (1840-03-14, 3:1, B)

411. On Friday, the 6th instant, in Lisnadill Church, by the Rev. Mr. Radcliff, Mr. Joseph M'Farland, Knockaneigh, Parish of Tynan, to Eliza, third daughter of Mr. James Jameson, of Ballymorran. (1840-03-14, 3:1, M)

412. At Leamington Spa, on the 2d instant, William Tenison, Esq., of Lough Bawn, county of Monaghan. (1840-03-14, 3:1, D)

413. March 17, in Anne's Church, Captain Hemphill, of the 29th Regiment, to Florinda, eldest daughter of the late Lieut.-Colonel Lucas, of Raconnell, county of Monaghan. (1840-03-21, 3:3, M)

414. March 17, at Termonfeekin, the Rev. Simon Foot, of Glenaghy, county of Armagh, to Frances Margaret, second daughter of the Rev. John Kerr, Rector of Termonfeekin, county of Louth. (1840-03-21, 3:3, M)

415. March 15, at Anketel Grove, in the 16th year of her age, Matilda Jane, youngest daughter of William Anketel, Esq. (1840-03-21, 3:3, D)

416. On the 10th instant, of consumption, Mr. John M'Culla, of Dundalk, aged 22 years. (1840-03-21, 3:3, D)

417. On the 3d instant, at Glenmore, Fanny Dorothea, the beloved child of Charles Styles, Esq.; a rapid consumption carried her off after a few months' illness, at the early age of 16, when her mental acquirements and enlighted piety gave hope of future satisfaction to family and friends. (1840-03-21, 3:3, D)

418. March 13, at Prospect Buildings, in the 29th year of her age, Marianne, eldest daughter of the late Andw. M'Math, Esq., of Thornford, county of Monaghan. (1840-03-21, 3:3, D)

419. At Banagher Church, the Rev. Edward French, to Mary, daughter of Michael King, Esq., of Dungiven, county of Londonderry. (1840-03-28, 3:4, M)

420. At Shinrone Church, James Charles, eldest son of James Blackwood, Esq., Strangford, county Down, to Ann Margaret, daughter of the late P.N. Savage, Esq. (1840-03-28, 3:4, M)

421. On the 18th instant, by the Rev. Richard Dill, Ballykelly, the Rev. William Simpson, of Stirling, Scotland, to Mary Ann, second daughter of the late Mr. Andw. Moody, of Farloe, county of Londonderry. (1840-03-28, 3:4, M)

422. At Castlegoy, on the 19th instant, by the Rev. Joseph Lytle, Presbyterian Minister of Letterkenny, Mathew Colhoun, of Rathdonnell House, Esq., to Miss Fanny Roulston, daughter of the late Robert Roulston, Esq., of Castlegoy [Cashelgay], near Kilmacrenan, county Donegal. (1840-03-28, 3:4, M)

423. At Corbrack, near Ballybay, on Monday, the 23d inst., aged 82 years, Mrs. Elizabeth Mitchell, wife of Mr. John Mitchell, of Corbrack. The survivor of this worthy couple has reached his 80th year, and they had spent 60 years of happiness together, and have reared a family of thirteen children. They have been highly respected during life, and the deceased has gone to her long home amid the regret of a numerous progeny, and of all who knew her. (1840-03-28, 3:4, D)

424. On the 15th instant, by the bursting of a blood-vessel, Mr. James Gillespie, printer, of Belfast, in the 33d year of his age. (1840-03-28, 3:4, D)

425. On Monday last, at her residence in this town, much and deservedly regretted, Mrs. Gass, relict of the late Mr. Charles Gass, printer. (1840-04-04, 3:3, D)

426. On Sunday, 22 March, Margaret, wife of Mr. Samuel Dixon, of Kinegad, county Westmeath, son to Mr. Thomas Dixon, of Drumgarley, county Monaghan. She was daughter of Mr. Murry, of Rathown, and she died of a rapid decline, leaving a husband and two small children to lament her loss. She bore her sickness with patience and resignation to the will of her Redeemer, resting her last hopes on his promise who saith, that all who come unto him, he will in no wise cast them out. (1840-04-04, 3:3, D)

427. At Middletown, county Armagh, James Johnston, Esq., aged 63 years. (1840-04-04, 3:3, D)

428. March 30th, at Lisorty Cottage, near Clones, much lamented, Thomas Welsh, Esq., late Lieutenant of the Leitrim Regiment. (1840-04-04, 3:3, D)

429. On the 8th inst., in Tullycorbet Church, county of Monaghan, by the Rev. Mr. Haire, Mr. Thomas Palmer, of Belturbet, Merchant, to Jane Edenid, only child of the late John E. Giddons, of Glasslough, Esq., M.D. (1840-04-11, 3:3, M)

430. At Derryheene Church, on the 25th ult., by the Rev. Mr. Mahon, Rector of the Parish of Urney, by special license, Mr. Samuel Sharpe, of Cootehill, to Sidney, relict of the late Mr. James Bredin, of Ennismore, Esq. (1840-04-11, 3:3, M)

431. April 4, at Johnstown House, county Dublin, Bernard Hughes, Esq., of Dungannon, county Tyrone, to Eliza Anne, eldest daughter of Arthur Anthony, Esq., of Ringville, county Waterford. (1840-04-11, 3:3, M)

432. April 4, in St. Andrew's Church, by the Rev. James Nevin, Charles Mathers, Esq., of Grafton-street, to Margaret, second daughter of J. Morrow, Esq., county of Tyrone. (1840-04-11, 3:3, M)

433. April 7, in St. Andrew's Church, by special license, by the Rev. James Nevin, Francis Smith Hamilton, Esq., Captain in the Royal Marines, to Margaret, second daughter of the late J. Foy, Esq., county of Fermanagh. (1840-04-11, 3:3, M)

434. At Rocksavage, county of Monaghan, by the Rev. Alexander Kindelan, Thomas Murphy, Esq., to Clara, eldest daughter of N.W. Kenny, Esq. (1840-04-11, 3:3, M)

435. March 30, at Ednaveses [Edenaveys] House, Armagh, in the 62d year of her age, Anne, the beloved wife of William Murray, Esq. (1840-04-11, 3:3, D)

436. At Fairy Mount, the residence of her bereaved and sorrowing parents, on Thursday, the 2d instant, after a short but violent attack of croup, Josephine, the beloved infant daughter of Francis R. Wallen, Esq. (1840-04-11, 3:3, D)

437. At Mullaghmore, near Omagh, on the 31st March, after a protracted illness, in her 49th year, Mary, the beloved wife of Mr. William Early. In every relation of life, she was generally esteemed, and her death is sincerely lamented. (1840-04-11, 3:3, D)

438. Of a fall from his horse, on Sunday last, the Rev. N. O'Kane, P.P., of Donoughmore. (1840-04-11, 3:3, D)

439. In the Parish Church of Tullamoone, by the Rev. John Lever, Rector, Mr. Thomas Mayne, Stonehouse, Plymouth, to Jane, eldest daughter of John Burgess, Esq., merchant, Tullamoone. (1840-04-18, 3:4, M)

440. April 10, by special license, the Right Hon. Henry Labouchere, M.P., to Frances, youngest daughter of Sir Thomas Baring, Bart., of Stratton Park. (1840-04-18, 3:4, M)

441. On Monday, the 13th inst., of apoplexy, aged 46, the Rev. Charles Evatt, Rector of Monaghan. His loss is deeply regretted by all, and his services for 27 years, as a zealous pastor, had so endeared him to his flock that any further eulogium would but detract from the merits of a man whose days were occupied in unwearied exertions in behalf of religious and charitable institutions—whose benevolence was of the most active and expansive description, embracing good undertakings and good men in every department of Christian society. (1840-04-18, 3:4, D)

442. At the residence of her husband, Killymuddy, near this town, of inflammation, on Sunday last, aged 42 years, Mary Jane, wife of Robert Temple, Esq. She was a lady of the most amiable disposition and manners, and her loss is regretted by all who knew her. (1840-04-18, 3:4, D)

443. April 4, at Rostrevor, of consumption, Elizabeth, youngest daughter of the late William Magill, Esq., of Crieve, county Tyrone. (1840-04-18, 3:4, D)

444. At his residence, in the townland of Moy, near Castleblayney, on the 25th March, aged 73 years, Mr. Thomas M'Bride, universally respected during life and regretted at his death. (1840-04-18, 3:4, D)

445. On the 24th ult., at his residence, in Bellaghy, in his 76th year, Robert Steele, Esq., Second Lieutenant of the Bellaghy and Castledawson Yeomanry, and for many years Elder of the Presbyterian Church, Castledawson. (1840-04-18, 3:4, D)

446. April 14, in Eccles-street, Dublin, the lady of Isaac Butt, Esq., of a son. (1840-04-25, 3:3, B)

447. April 20, at St. Thomas's Church, by the Rev. Dr. Handcock, Surgeon Neville, to Jane Mayhey, daughter of the late Wakefield Hamilton, of Drogheda, Esq. (1840-04-25, 3:3, M)

448. April 21, at Rathfarnham Church, by the Rev. William Yeats, Rector of Tullyard, diocess of Dromore, Thomas H. Taylor, Esq., second son of the late Thomas Taylor, Esq., Dublin Castle, to Mary, third daughter of Capt. H. Terry, late Paymaster, 99th regiment. (1840-04-25, 3:3, M)

449. On the 14th instant, of fever, in Kilmacrenan, where he went on a visit to his brother, Doctor Molloy, Francis Lucas, the youngest son of the Rev. F.L. Molloy, of Fahan, aged 21 years. (1840-04-25, 3:3, D)

450. April 23, in the Cathedral, Londonderry, by the Rev. Charles Lyons Montgomery, John Barre Beresford, Esq., of Learmount, county of Londonderry, to Sophia, third daughter of the late Hugh Lyons Montgomery, Esq. of Laurenstown [Laurencetown], county of Down, and of Belhovel [Belhavel], county of Leitrim. (1840-05-02, 3:2, M)

451. In Cootehill, by the Rev. Mr. Adams, Dissenting Clergyman, Sergeant James Barry, late 58th regiment of infantry, pensioner, to Jane, relict of the late Mr. Hugh M'Farland, tailor. (1840-05-02, 3:2, M)

452. At Monkstown Church, Thomas Harpur, of Holywood, Down, Esq., to Mary Jane, daughter of the late Solomon Speer, of Granitefield, Dublin, Esq., barrister-at-law. (1840-05-09, 3:2, M)

453. At Drumcall, near Drum, county Monaghan, on the 5th inst., the Rev. Thomas Dawson, aged 84. His death will be long deplored by the poor, his friends and neighbors, on account of his many amiable qualities. He was frank, hospitable, and generous. (1840-05-09, 3:2, D)

454. On Thursday the 30th instant, aged 24 years, at his mother's residence, Thomas-street, Armagh, Jacob Haddock, printer, late of Dublin. Kind and humane, generous and charitable; he was beloved by all who knew him—in the prime of life, and in the full vigour of youth; he descended to the grave with a sure and certain hope of a glorious resurrection. (1840-05-09, 3:2, D)

455. May 11, in Templeport Church, by the Rev. George Beresford, Rector of Templeport, Robert Lanauze, Esq., of Dame-street, Dublin, to Nicolina, eldest daughter of the late John Bourke, Esq., of Bawnboy, county of Cavan. (1840-05-16, 3:2, M)

456. May 7, in Templenacarriga Church, by the Rev. Geo. E. Cotter, James Johnston, Esq., of Middleton, to Elizabeth Warren, youngest daughter of the late Samuel Swete, Esq., of Greenville. (1840-05-16, 3:2, M)

457. On Sunday, May 10, aged 50, Eliza, wife of Alexander Williams, hat manufacturer, Monaghan. She was in the full sense of the word a faithful wife, a good mother, and a steady warm friend; her patience under suffering, and the calmness with which she received the summons, were such as became a Christian; she finished her course, enjoying peace with God through the atonement. (1840-05-16, 3:2, D)

458. May 3, at Lausanne, aged 14 years, Isabella, eldest daughter of John Hamilton, Esq., of St. Ernans, county of Donegal. (1840-05-16, 3:2, D)

459. On the 14th instant, by the Rev. Alexander Henderson, John Kelso, Esq., M.D., of Lisburn, to Eliza, youngest daughter of the late Mr. George Gamble, same place. (1840-05-23, 3:3, M)

460. Samuel B. Dickson, Esq., of Finstown Cottage, Dublin, to Margery third daughter of the late Galbraith Hamilton, Esq., of Ballyfatten, Tyrone. (1840-05-23, 3:3, M)

461. Elizabeth, wife of the Rev. Stephen Radcliff, of Lisnadill Glebe, county Armagh. (1840-05-23, 3:3, D)

462. May 23, at Cavan, by the Rev. William Henry, Krause Duncan, third son of the late Alexander Robertson, M.D., Inspector-General of Military Hospitals, to Helen Frances, youngest daughter of the late Colonel Fraser, 18th Royal Irish, and of Chatsworth, in the island of Jamaica. (1840-05-30, 3:3, M)

463. May 20, in St. Mary's Church, by the Rev. Dr. Bardin, Rector of Derryloran, Neal O'Donel Browne, second son of the late Dodwell Browne, of Rahins [Raheens], county of Mayo, to Sarah, second daughter of Abel Labertouche, Esq., of Denneycarney [Donnycarney]. (1840-05-30, 3:3, M)

464. May 13, the Rev. Wm. Brown, of Duncrana [Buncrana], county of Donegal, to Matilda, second daughter of S. Haslett, Esq., of Foyleview, county of Derry. (1840-05-30, 3:3, M)

465. May 20, at Kilkeel, by the Rev. William Boyle, J.H. Rawson, of Clanbrassill-street Dundalk, Esq., to Mary, second daughter of Thomas Nicholson, of Seafield, county Down, Esq. (1840-05-30, 3:3, M)

466. On the 29th inst., by the Very Rev. Mr. Bell, Minister of Derryvalley, Mr. John Byers, of Corlea, county Monaghan, to Ann Jane, eldest daughter of Mr. Jones M'Call, of Madden, county of Armagh. (1840-05-30, 3:3, M)

467. On Thursday morning last, after an illness of a few hours, at his residence, Dublin-street, Monaghan, Mr. John Preston, an old and very respectable trader of this town. Mr. Preston had been suffering from gout for some time; but, on Wednesday, he was in good health, and on that evening he got a severe attack of gout in his stomach, which terminated his existence in a few hours. (1840-05-30, 3:3, D)

468. May 12, aged 29 years, Wm. J. M'Donagh, Esq., youngest son of the late Morgan M'Donagh, Esq., of Sligo. (1840-05-30, 3:3, D)

469. May 23, of consumption, at Cootehill, Mr. Richd. Giles, in the 21st year of his age, eldest son of the late Richard Giles, Esq., late of Cootehill. During his illness, he manifested the utmost patience and resignation to the Divine will, and died in the hope of a blissful immortality, through faith in the Redeemer of the world. (1840-05-30, 3:3, D)

470. May 23, at the Cottage, Athlone, Thomas Wyndham, eldest son of Wm. Cook, Esq., of Retreat, in the county of Westmeath. (1840-05-30, 3:3, D)

471. May 23, suddenly, Robert Johnston, third son of the late James Johnston, and brother of Joseph Johnston, Esq. of Knappa, in the county of Armagh. (1840-05-30, 3:3, D)

472. May 22, aged 12 years, Jane, only daughter of Dr. Lendrum of Fivemiletown, county of Tyrone. (1840-05-30, 3:3, D)

473. At Bath, the celebrated linguist, Mr. Thomas Manning, of Orange-grove, Dartford. (1840-05-30, 3:3, D)

474. In Dundalk, on Sunday last, the 24th instant, after a long and painful illness, which he bore with great patience, and Christian resignation, Captain Thomas Connick, merchant, aged 76 years. (1840-05-30, 3:3, D)

475. On the 5th inst., at the residence of his sister, Ballymena, after a protracted illness, in his 26th year, Robert Steele, officer of excise, Warrenpoint, son of the late Robt. Steele, Esq., Bellaghy. (1840-05-30, 3:3, D)

476. On the 16th inst. in Omagh, Michael Harkin, M.D., Member of the Royal College of Surgeons, London, &c., after a protracted illness, which he endured with the greatest resignation and patience. (1840-05-30, 3:3, D)

477. On the 18th instant, at Starling [Stirling], Janet, wife of Alexander Halliburton, Esq., late collector of excise in the county Derry. (1840-05-30, 3:3, D)

478. At Baltimore, U.S., William, second son of Alexander Davidson, Esq., of Laragh, county of Monaghan, to Sophia, youngest daughter of the late Stewart Brown, Esq. (1840-06-06, 3:3, M)

479. June 1, at Kingscourt, county Cavan, James Duffy, Esq. of Anglesea-street, Dublin, to Fanny, eldest daughter of James Lynch, Esq., of said place. (1840-06-06, 3:3, M)

480. May 31, by the Rev. John Porter, Captain James Reid, to Hessey, only daughter of Mr. John Garland, Belfast. (1840-06-06, 3:3, M)

481. June 3, in St. George's Church, by the Rev. Dr. Hare, S.F.T.C.D., uncle to the bride, William Roe, Esq., of Rockwell, county of Tipperary, to Elizabeth Hickman, second daughter of P. Clarke, Esq., of Mountjoy-square, Dublin. (1840-06-06, 3:3, M)

482. June 2, at her residence, Rockbrook House, county of Dublin, Mrs. Bridget Fry, aged 82 years, relict of Peter Fry, Esq. (1840-06-06, 3:3, D)

483. The Rev. Patrick Caraher, of Scariff, County Armagh. (1840-06-06, 3:3, D)

484. On Wednesday, the 3d inst., in St. Peter's Dublin, the Rev. Benjamin Maturin, fourth son of the Rev. Henry Marturin [sic], Rector of the parish of Fannet, county of Donegal, to Anne, daughter of the late John Johnston, Esq., of Ashlaw Lodge, in the county of Down. (1840-06-13, 3:5, M)

485. June 6, at Kingstown, in her 14th year, Augusta, second daughter of the late Honourable Richard Westenra, and grand-daughter of the Right Hon. Lord Rossmore. (1840-06-13, 3:5, D)

486. On the 10th instant, of typhus fever, in the 22d year of her age, at the residence of her brother-in-law, W.M. Brice, Esq., of Cavan, Mary Jane, youngest daughter of the late Mr. Alex. Johnston, of Monaghan—deeply and deservedly regretted by her numerous circle of friends and relatives. She died in the blessed hope of everlasting life, through the merits of Jesus Christ, her Redeemer. (1840-06-13, 3:5, D)

487. On Sunday morning, 7th instant, after a few hours' illness, Mary, the beloved infant and only daughter of T. M'Cullagh, Esq., Dunrimond House, county Monaghan. (1840-06-13, 3:5, D)

488. May 30, Thomas A. Sloane, youngest son of the late Charles Sloane, Esq., formerly of Lisabuck, county of Monaghan—a fine promising youth, who was unfortunately drowned in the Tolquay [Tolka] river, whilst bathing, aged 17 years. (1840-06-13, 3:5, D)

489. On the 31st May, after a very short illness, Mr. Richard Gregg, of Moneylegan, near Letterkenny, aged 60 years. (1840-06-13, 3:5, D)

490. At No. 11, New Row, Coleraine, on the 8th inst., Chas. Dalrymple Thornly, youngest son of Lieut. Thornley [sic], Sub-Inspector of Police. (1840-06-13, 3:5, D)

491. On the 11th inst., at Millmount, Monaghan, the residence of her father, Andrew Swanzy, Esq., the lady of Humphrys Jones, Esq., of Cameron-Lodge, county Dublin, of a daughter. (1840-06-20, 3:2, B)

492. On the 9th inst., by the Rev. Jas. Morgan, the Rev. Alexander Kerr, of Portadown, to Eleanor, eldest daughter of the late Robert Allen, Esq., of Belfast. (1840-06-20, 3:2, M)

493. On the 10th inst., by the Rev. Andrew Breakey, Andrew M'Donnell, Esq., of Ballywhite, near Portaferry, to Miss Carr, daughter of John Carr, Esq., Race-course, Killileagh. (1840-06-20, 3:2, M)

494. On the 15th inst., by the Rev. Dr. Hanna, Mr. David Rea, to Miss Sarah Sloan, both of Belfast. (1840-06-20, 3:2, M)

495. On the 11th inst., at Dublin, by the Rev. C. Wolsley, A. Macaulay Dobbs, Esq., second son of the late Rev. R. Stuart Dobbs, Bay Lodge, County Antrim, to Elizabeth Catherine, eldest daughter of the late George Kay, Esq., Vera Cottage, County Armagh. (1840-06-20, 3:2, M)

496. At Courtney Hill, Newry, on the 12th inst., in the 30th year of his age, Robert, youngest and last surviving son of the late Alexander Williamson, Esq., of Lambeg. (1840-06-20, 3:2, D)

497. On the 2d inst., in the 34th year of his age, Mr. James Greer, Esq., of Legmore, Derriaghy. (1840-06-20, 3:2, D)

498. On the 7th inst., at his residence, Laurel-Hill, Alexander Blackburn, Esq., aged 54 years. (1840-06-20, 3:2, D)

499. On the 6th inst., at his residence, Bunker's-hill, after a protracted illness, which he bore with Christian fortitude, John Madill, Esq., aged 59. (1840-06-20, 3:2, D)

500. On the 5th inst., at Silverbrook, county Tyrone, aged 39 years, Anna Charlotte, second daughter of John Carey, Esq. (1840-06-20, 3:2, D)

501. At Belmullet, by the Rev. Samuel Stock, Arthur Rose, Esq., to Mary Anne, second daughter of William Ivers, of Belmullet. (1840-06-27, 3:2, M)

502. On the 21st inst., aged 15 years, Andrew, only child of Mr. Samuel Thompson, of Kingorry, near this town. (1840-06-27, 3:2, D)

503. June 5, at her father's residence of rapid consumption, Anne Charlotte, youngest daughter of John Cary, Esq. of Silverbrook, county Tyrone. (1840-06-27, 3:2, D)

504. June 16, at the Glebe House, the Rev. Edward Chichester, Rector of Kilmore, in the Diocess of Armagh. (1840-06-27, 3:2, D)

505. June 18, at his residence, Retreat, county Cavan, the Rev. Benjamin Adams, in his 86th year. (1840-06-27, 3:2, D)

506. June 23, at Portoro House, Enniskillen, in the 80th year of her age, Lucinda, relict of Peter Graham, Esq., of Dublin. (1840-06-27, 3:2, D)

507. June 16, at Marseilles, Julia, wife of Alexander Hamilton, of Rutland-square, Q.C., and daughter of the late Michael Tisdall, of Charlesfort, county Meath, Esq. (1840-06-27, 3:2, D)

508. June 20, at Rathmines Road, in her 19th year, after a long and painful illness, Margaret, eldest daughter of the late William Kerr Nesbitt, Esq., of Heath Lodge, county Cavan. (1840-06-27, 3:2, D)

509. At Castleblayney, on the 1st inst., by the Rev. Thomas Boyd, Mr. John Hill, of Castleblayney, aged 98, to Miss Ann Jane Drane, aged 19, eldest daughter of Mr. William Drane, of Carrickaslane. (1840-07-04, 3:5, M)

510. July 1, in George's Church, by the Rev. John Gregg, John Brice Blake, Captain of the 47th Regiment, second son of the late Sir John Blake, Bart., of Menlo Castle, Galway, to Frances, eldest daughter of Jno. Drope M'Ilree, Esq., of Belturbet, county Cavan. (1840-07-04, 3:5, M)

511. July 2, in St. Werburgh's Church, by the Rev. Mr. White, Mr. John Connor, of Armagh, to Georgina, youngest daughter of Mr. Bartholomew, Dublin Castle. (1840-07-04, 3:5, M)

512. June 30, in Dublin, John Barlow, Esq., of Bushy Park, county of Roscommon, many years Magistrate for the county, sincerely and deservedly regretted by a numerous host of friends, to whom his excellent qualities of head and heart had endeared him. (1840-07-04, 3:5, D)

513. In Donaghadee, John Robert Irwin, Esq., of Cornagh House, county of Armagh, to Elizabeth Emily, daughter of Nicholas D. Crommelin, Esq., of Currowdon [Carrodore] Castle, county Down. (1840-07-18, 3:3, M)

514. At Aragonnel, on Saturday morning, the 4th inst., Mr. John Martin, in the 52d year of his age, many of which he was a ruling Elder (*continued...*)

514. continued... of the Presbyterian Congregation of Lisloony, in connexion with the late General Synod. He was distinguished for the strictest integrity, for cheerfulness and kindness of heart, and for sincerity in his friendship to all those who knew him. In him, the poor have lost a relieving friend. His death is greatly to be lamented by a large circle of friends and acquaintances. (1840-07-18, 3:3, D)

515. On the 22d instant, in Clogh church, by the Rev. Valentine Duke Christian, Alex. Johnston, Esq., of Cincinnati, Ohio, to Jane Anne, eldest daughter of Richd. Jackson, Esq., Hollywood, county Monaghan. (1840-07-25, 3:2, M)

516. July 16, at the College-road, Galway, Henry M'Dermott, Esq., son to the late Dr. M'Dermott, Hereditary Prince of Coolavin, and cousin-german of the O'Conor Don, M.P., to Mary, eldest daughter of the late Myles M'Sweeny, Esq., Drumquin, county Kerry, and niece to Daniel O'Connell, Esq., M.P. (1840-07-25, 3:2, M)

517. On the 21st ult., at the residence of her father, by the Rev. Mr. Adams, Mary Jane, youngest daughter of Joseph Rathburne, Esq., of Annisbrook, [Annsbrook] near Mullagh, county Meath, to Michael Eyre Murphy, son to Michael Murphy, Esq., of Newgrove Mill, near Cootehill, county Cavan. (1840-07-25, 3:2, M)

518. At Killyconigan, on Friday, the 10th instant, in the 73d year of her age, after a lingering and painful illness, which she bore with Christian meekness and resignation, Mary Elizabeth, relict of the late Doctor M'Adam of Monaghan, beloved and respected by all who knew her. She died in the sure and certain hope of everlasting life through Jesus Christ. (1840-07-25, 3:2, D)

519. July 17, at L. Blacker's Esq., near Donnybrook, aged 65 years, Elizabeth, wife of the Rev. Dr. Miller of Armagh. (1840-07-25, 3:2, D)

520. On Friday morning, at four o'clock, after a long illness, which she bore with that resignation that a fervent feeling of religion can only inspire, Jane, wife of Thomas Anketell, Esq., J.P., of Dungillick. She was a lady of the most benevolent disposition, and her loss is not only felt severely by her immediate family and friends, but by the poor and desolate of the neighbourhood, who deplore, in her decease, the loss of their best friend. (1840-07-25, 3:2, D)

521. On the 3d inst., the lady of S.R.B. Evatt, Esq., Mount Louise, of a son. (1840-08-08, 3:1, B)

522. August 8, at Dundalk, William James, the only son of Doctor Brunker, aged nine years and a half. (1840-08-15, 3:2, D)

523. August 5, at Catherine Grove, near Carlingford, of brain fever, Anne, the beloved wife of Richard Gernon, Esq.—She was only a few months married. (1840-08-15, 3:2, D)

524. August 10, at Kingstown, Christopher Reed, Esq., solicitor, who, for several years, had been sovereign of Hillsborough. (1840-08-15, 3:2, D)

525. At Mungret, near Limerick, Mr. Timothy Donovan, aged 102 years. (1840-08-15, 3:2, D)

526. On the 18th inst., Lieutenant-Colonel James Ross, at his residence, in Liscarney. His health had been greatly impaired by long and severe services in a most ungenial climate; and, humanly speaking, his life was latterly somewhat prolonged by the tender, unremitting attentions of his partner in life. As to his character—he was remarkable for candour, integrity and real Christian simplicity of soul. His loss is deeply felt. "Not lost," however, "but gone before." (1840-08-22, 2:5, D)

527. On Monday, August 24, in Monaghan Church, by the Rev. Henry Maffatt, William John, eldest son of Captain W. Allen, R.N., to Sophia, third daughter of the late Henry Wright, Esq., of the Diamond, Monaghan. (1840-08-29, 3:2, M)

528. In Meigh Church, county Armagh, Charles Leech of Newry, Esq., Barrister-at-Law, son of the late William Ansdell Leech, Esq., to Anna Maria, daughter of Hunt Walsh Chambre, Esq, of Hawthorn Hill, Armagh. (1840-08-29, 3:2, M)

529. At the house of her brother, John Walker Redmond, Esq., of Grange, Mr. William Sinclair, merchant, Newry, to Ellen, daughter of the late Abraham Walker, Esq., of Richhill. (1840-08-29, 3:2, M)

530. At Lifford, Mr. W. Clements, architect, to Miss Margaret Arnold, of Strabane. (1840-08-29, 3:2, M)

531. On Sunday, the 23d instant, at her father's residence, after a short illness, Anne Jane, eldest daughter of Mr. James Jebb, of Ashfield, formerly of Cootehill, having at the age of 14 been brought experimentally to know the joyful sound; from that period she walked in the light of God's countenance, looked with calmness on death and viewed the summons undismayed at the age of 19. A large circle of her friends and relatives deeply feel her loss, but the change to her is eternal gain. (1840-08-29, 3:2, D)

532. At New Orleans, on the 25th June last, Mr. Robert Breakey, a long resident of that city, and universally respected by his fellow citizens. He was a native of this county. (1840-08-29, 3:2, D)

533. At Dungannon, the Rev. Thomas Murray, many years curate of the parish of Ballygawley, county Tyrone. (1840-08-29, 3:2, D)

534. At Portaliffe, Cavan, Mary, daughter of the late Arthur Monypenny, Esq. (1840-08-29, 3:2, D)

535. At Farmhill, county Waterford, in her 80th year, Elizabeth, relict of George Grace, Esq., of Castle Brittas, Barrister-at-Law, formerly proprietor of the *Clonmel Herald*. (1840-08-29, 3:2, D)

536. At Bundoran, Mrs. Pressly, relict of the late Mr. Pressly, of Wattle bridge, county Cavan. (1840-08-29, 3:2, D)

537. August 29, at St. George's church, Charles Rochfort Mayne, Esq., youngest son of the late William Mayne, of Freamemount, county Monaghan, Esq., to Elizabeth, eldest daughter of the late Captain King, 20th regiment. (1840-09-05, 3:2, M)

538. August 27, at Aughnacloy, by the Rev. H.L. Baker, Henry James Macfarlane, Esq., of Huntstown House, county of Dublin, to Jane, third daughter of the late Hamilton Wallace, Esq., of Omagh. (1840-09-05, 3:2, M)

539. At Warrenpoint, on the 29th ult., aged 60 years, Alicia Eleanor, relict of the late George Bartley, Esq., of Monaghan. (1840-09-05, 3:2, D)

540. In Clones, on Tuesday night, the 25th ult., Mrs. Elizabeth Stewart, widow of the late Rev. James Stewart, Wesleyan Minister, aged 78 years. (1840-09-05, 3:2, D)

541. At Ballybay, in this county, after a short illness, which she bore with christian resignation and fortitude, Jane, the beloved daughter of Mr. Francis M'Sherry, aged 15 years. She was loved and respected by all who knew her, and is sincerely lamented by a numerous circle of friends and acquaintances. (1840-09-05, 3:2, D)

542. August 29, Anna, relict of Lieutenant-Colonel Kearney, of Armagh. (1840-09-05, 3:2, D)

543. On the 3d instant, at Castleblayney, the Lady of Hugh Swanzy, Esq., of a daughter. (1840-09-12, 3:5, B)

544. On the 30th ultimo, at Southampton, Viscountess Corry, of a daughter. (1840-09-12, 3:5, B)

545. On the 1st instant, at Balbriggan Church, by the Rev. Hugh Hamilton, Henry Ormsby, Esq., Barrister-at-Law, to Julia, youngest daughter of the late Henry Hamilton, Esq., of Tullylish House, County Down. (1840-09-12, 3:5, M)

546. On the 1st inst., at St. Pancras, by the Rev. Robt. Knox, Chancellor of Ardfert, the Rev. Thomas Knox, eldest son of the late Hon. and Venerable Charles Knox, Archdeacon of Armagh, to Eliza Winckworth, eldest daughter of the late Ellis Bent, Esq., Judge Advocate of New South Wales, and niece to the Hon. Chief Justice of British Guiana. (1840-09-12, 3:5, M)

547. At the same time and place [St. Pancras, London], by the Rev. R. Knox, Chas. George Knox, of Lincoln's Inn, Barrister-at-Law, third son of the late Hon. and Venerable the Archdeacon of Armagh, to Isabella Hannah, youngest daughter of the late Ellis Bent, Esq., Judge Advocate of New South Wales, and niece to the Honourable the Chief Justice of British Guiana. (1840-09-12, 3:5, M)

548. At Riversdale-House, Belturbet, on the 3d instant, by the Rev. J.S. Reid, D.D., Professor of Ecclesiastical history, Belfast College, S.D. Stuart, Esq., Carrickfergus, to Elizabeth Jane Hudson, eldest daughter of Robert M'Gowan, Esq., Customs, Killala. (1840-09-12, 3:5, M)

549. In Balrothyery [sic], Henry Courtenay, of Harrymount, county Down, Esq., nephew of the late Right Hon. John Courtenay, M.P., to Louisa, third daughter of the late Rev. Charles Seaver, of Treagh, county Armagh, and Minister of Saint Andrew's Parish, Dublin. (1840-09-12, 3:5, M)

550. On the 3d instant, at the house of his father, 15, Frederick-street Belfast, William M'Master, aged 32 years. (1840-09-12, 3:5, D)

551. On the 4th instant, at her house, in Ballymoney, Elizabeth, relict of the late Doctor Reynolds, aged 85 years. (1840-09-12, 3:5, D)

552. On the 27th ult. of fever, Mr. John Robinson, of Downpatrick, pawnbroker, in the 53d year of his age. (1840-09-12, 3:5, D)

553. On the 29th ult., at his house, Boat-street, Newry, Mr. Richard Whitehead, aged 69. (1840-09-12, 3:5, D)

554. On the 16th inst., at St. Martin's Church, York, by the Rev. Dorset Fellows, and afterwards according to the Rites of the Roman Catholic Church, J. M'Kenna, Esq., of this town, Solicitor, to Caroline, youngest daughter of the late James Currie, Esq., of Mersey View, Bootle, Lancashire. (1840-09-26, 3:3, M)

555. In the British Chapel, Copenhagen, John S. Brownrigg, Esq., 9th regiment, only son of John S. Brownrigg, Esq., to Katherine, second daughter of the Right Hon. Sir Henry W. Williams Wynn, G.C.H. (1840-09-26, 3:3, M)

556. On the 14th inst., at Mullyvilly Church, by the Rev. D. Babbington, Hamilton Blackham, of Portadown, Esq., to Jane, daughter of Henry Atkinson, of Ballyveagh House, county Armagh, Esq. (1840-09-26, 3:3, M)

557. At Ballyshannon, Mr. N. Guthridge, of that town, to Martha, fourth daughter of William Erskine, Esq. of Ballyshannon Cottage. (1840-09-26, 3:3, M)

558. On Tuesday, the 22d inst., at St. Thomas's Church, Dublin, by the Rev. John Fea, A.M., Henry R. Barker, of Harrymount, Newtownhamilton, Esq., to Caroline, second daughter of Hugh Moore, of Nootka Lodge, Carlingford, and Gloucester Terrace, Dublin, Esq. (1840-09-26, 3:3, M)

559. At St. James's Church, London, by the Lord Archbishop of Armagh, the Hon. Edward Kenyon, second son of Lord Kenyon, to Miss Susan Beresford, youngest daughter of the late Lord George Beresford. (1840-09-26, 3:3, M)

560. On the 9th instant, Vice-Admiral Lord Mark Robert Kerr, third son of William, fifth Marquis Lothian. His Lordship married Charlotte M'Donnell, daughter and co-heir of Randal, second Marquis of Antrim, and has left issue by her, Hugh Seymour, Earl of Antrim, and other children. (1840-09-26, 3:3, D)

561. At the very advanced age of 107 years, at her son's residence, Laurel Lodge, near Moy, Mrs. Casey, widow of Mr. Casey, of Grange, near Moy. (1840-09-26, 3:3, D)

562. March 16, at Canton, in China, in the 68th year of his age, John Jordan, Esq., formerly of Newry, in the county of Down, Ireland, and in early life a commissioned officer in his Britannic Majesty's service, who married a Chinese lady of exalted rank, and became possessed of a princely fortune, in consequence of which he became a resident gentleman in the Chinese territory. (1840-09-26, 3:3, D)

563. September 12, in Carrick-on-Shannon, of fever, in the sure and certain hope of a joyful resurrection, through faith in his Redeemer, on the anniversary of his 30th year, Robert Howard, Esq., son of the late Captain Howard, whom he survived three weeks. He has left a sorrowing widow and a large circle of friends to lament his melancholy and premature decease. (1840-09-26, 3:3, D)

564. September 6, at her residence in Beaumont-street, London, at the advanced age of 97, Mrs. Martha Blacker. This venerable and highly respectable lady was daughter of William Blacker, Esq., and sister of the late Rev. Dean Blacker, of Carrick, in the county Armagh. (1840-09-26, 3:3, D)

565. September 7, at the College, Armagh, aged 39 years, the Rev. Robert Miller, A.M., Rector of Newtownhamilton, in the diocese of Armagh. (1840-09-26, 3:3, D)

566. At his residence, Belfast, in the 46th year of his age, Wm. Hubbart, Excise Officer. (1840-09-26, 3:3, D)

567. On the 16th instant, at Caledon, in the county of Tyrone, Richard Robinson Lodge, Esq., Captain and Adjutant of the Royal Tyrone Regiment of Militia. (1840-09-26, 3:3, D)

568. Sept. 24, in St. Paul's church, by the Very Rev. the Dean of Emly, cousin of the bride, James Fawcett, Esq., of Strandhill, in the county of Leitrim, to Frances Elizabeth, second daughter of the Rev. W.J.H. Lefanu, Rector of St. Paul's, Dublin. (1840-10-03, 3:5, M)

569. September 17th, in Keady Church, by the Rev. Cosby Stopford Cosby Mangan, Samuel Alexander Kidd, Esq., of Dundrum, in the county Armagh, to Catherine, eldest daughter of Francis Stringer, Esq., of Tassagh House, in the same county. (1840-10-03, 3:5, M)

570. June 16, at Musserabad, from the bite of a snake, Lieut. Charles Atkinson, of the 10th Bengal Native Cavalry, third son of the late Lieutenant-Colonel Atkinson, of the King's County. (1840-10-03, 3:5, D)

571. Sept. 21, in Castlebar, Miss Cecilia Browne, of Woodstock, county of Mayo, aunt to Major Michael Browne, late of the South Mayo militia. (1840-10-03, 3:5, D)

572. At Dover, the Rev. Charles Palmer, Rahan, Kildare, Vicar of Carberry. (1840-10-03, 3:5, D)

573. At Ballybay, in this county, on the 26th ult., by the Rev. J.H. Morell, James, son of the late Mr. James Gray, to Sarah, second daughter of the late D. Williamson, Esq., of same place. (1840-10-10, 3:5, M)

574. October 3, Mr. Henry Hunter, of Castleblayney, to Catherine, second daughter of the Rev. William Curren, of Rushen, Isle of Man. (1840-10-10, 3:5, M)

575. In Dublin, James Grace, Esq., of Wexford, to Ellen, daughter of the late William Armstrong, of Farney Castle, Esq. (1840-10-10, 3:5, M)

576. In Great George's church, Charles Hill, Esq., barrister-at-law, son of Richard Hill, Esq., of Mountjoy-place, to Fanny, daughter of the late Charles M. Graham, Esq., Major of the 88th Regt. (1840-10-10, 3:5, M)

577. On the 3d instant, at Glennon, parish of Donagh, in this county, Anne, only daughter of Mr. James Aiken. During a severe and protracted illness, she bowed with meek submission to the will of her heavenly Father, and in patience possessed her soul. She knew in whom she believed, and was persuaded he was able to keep that which she had committed to Him; and, resting on the sure promises of the Gospel, she was enabled to regard the last enemy without fear, and to enter the dark valley, rejoicing in the hope of the glory of God. (1840-10-10, 3:5, D)

578. On the 1st instant, at Drummond, Armagh, aged 67, Mr. William Reilly. His illness was short but severe, and being prepared for death, his spirit passed away in peace. (1840-10-10, 3:5, D)

579. October 3, after a long and severe illness, which he bore with true christian fortitude, William Jackson, Esq., solicitor, son of Robert Jackson, Esq., Sackville-street. (1840-10-10, 3:5, D)

580. In St. Mary's Church, Newry, on Wednesday, the 14th inst., by the Rev. Dr. Campbell, John Busteed, Esq., of Tralee, to Isabella, second daughter of Donald Mackay, Esq., of Newry, H.P., 42d Regiment. (1840-10-17, 3:2, M)

581. On Monday, the 12th inst., after a painful illness, at the residence of his father, Robert Alexander Foster, Esq., aged 33 years, for a lengthened period one of the most useful and indefatigable office-bearers in the various charitable institutions of Newry. (1840-10-17, 3:2, D)

582. On the 12th inst., after 13 days' illness, of fever, in the 15th year of her age, Jane, the only daughter of Mr. John Guy, of Hill-street, Newry. (1840-10-17, 3:2, D)

583. On the 1st inst., of enlargement of the heart, at the early age of 16 years, John, eldest son of Mr. James M'Kenna, Mill-street, Newry. (1840-10-17, 3:2, D)

584. At Sydney, New South Wales, previous to the 20th of May last, Mr. Hugh W. Milford, formerly of Belfast. (1840-10-17, 3:2, D)

585. On the 6th inst., in the 25th year of her age, Julia, the beloved wife of Edward Boyle, Esq., of Newtonlimevady, and daughter of Major Stirling, of Walworth. (1840-10-17, 3:2, D)

586. On the 30th ult., at Dungannon, after a protracted illness, Samuel Davidson, Esq., Solicitor, aged 65. (1840-10-17, 3:2, D)

587. On the 6th inst., Frances Augusta, relict of Constantine Maguire, of Tempo, in the county Fermanagh, Esq. (1840-10-17, 3:2, D)

588. At his residence, in High-street, Newry, Mr. Thomas Carr, aged 78 years. (1840-10-17, 3:2, D)

589. On the 1st instant, at her residence, La Vallie, near Bray, Maria, eldest daughter of the late George Draper, Esq., of the Bank of Ireland, sincerely and deeply regretted by her numerous friends. "Blessed are the dead who die in the Lord." (1840-10-17, 3:2, D)

590. October 20, at Corville, county Cavan, the lady of Ralph Harman, Esq., of Middle Gardiner-street, Dublin, of a daughter. (1840-10-24, 3:2, B)

591. On the 21st instant, at the lady's residence, Diamond, Monaghan, by the Rev. Mr. Maguire, R.C.C., Mr. Peter M'Phillips, of this town, merchant, to Elizabeth, relict of the late Mr. James Curran, proprietor of the Westenra Arms Hotel. (1840-10-24, 3:2, M)

592. October 14, in Caledon church, by the Rev. Dr. Atkinson, Richard, fourth son of Lieutenant-Colonel Atkinson, of Cangort, King's county, to Mary Jane, second daughter of George Richard Golding, of Limepark, in the county of Tyrone, Esq. (1840-10-24, 3:2, M)

593. October 7, in St. Thomas's church, Dublin, by the Rev. Mr. Minchin, Denis B. Daly, Esq., of the island of Dominica, to Miss Augusta Da Butts, third daughter of the late Mark Anthony Mills, Esq., of Tempo [Timpaun?], in the county of Roscommon. (1840-10-24, 3:2, M)

594. On the 11th instant, at Cootehill, aged 64, Mrs. Jane M'Faddin, wife of Mr. Alexander M'Faddin, of that town. She was a loving wife, a fond and affectionate mother, and steadfast friend. During her illness, which was of long continuance, she bore her bodily pain with pious submission to the will of her Maker, and resigned her spirit into His hands who gave it, exclaiming—"I know that my Redeemer liveth, &c." (1840-10-24, 3:2, D)

595. Oct. 10, suddenly, at Blair Castle, N.B., Catherine, the beloved wife of William Nelson Clarke, Esq., and daughter of Sir Capel Molyneux, Bart., of Castledillon, in the county of Armagh. (1840-10-24, 3:2, D)

596. Oct. 14, Mrs. Graham, relict of the late Rev. James Graham, of Thornhill, county of Tyrone. (1840-10-24, 3:2, D)

597. October 16, at Clifton, Dorothea Helen, wife of William French, Esq., of Clonequin [Cloonyquin], county Roscommon. (1840-10-24, 3:2, D)

598. On the 17th inst., at her father's house, in the county of Antrim, Sarah Warren, the beloved wife of R. M'Naghten, Esq. of Coleraine. (1840-10-24, 3:2, D)

599. In Waterford, Mrs. Catherine Lacey, aged 112 years.—She retained her faculties unimpaired till within a few hours of her dissolution, and, except the natural debility attendant on her great age, enjoyed excellent health up to the same period. (1840-10-24, 3:2, D)

600. On the 22d instant, at Armagh, the lady of Geo. Armstrong, Esq., of a daughter. (1840-10-31, 3:3, B)

601. On the 27th instant, by the Rev. F.P. Le Maitre, Wesleyan Minister, D. M'Killop, Esq., South Great George's street, Dublin, to Isabella, second daughter of Andrew Kelly, Esq., of Newry. (1840-10-31, 3:3, M)

602. At Monkstown church, by the Rev. John Grant, Henry Savage, Esq., county Down, to Jane, youngest daughter of William Lawley, of Lee Gomery, Wellington, Salop, Esq. (1840-10-31, 3:3, M)

603. July 30, at Dublin, Ohio, United States of North America, by the Rev. Mr. Gilruth, William, son of John Graham, late of the county Cavan, Ireland, to Mary, daughter of Daniel Wright, Esq., of same place. (1840-10-31, 3:3, M)

604. At Buncrana, on the 21st inst., in the 73d year of her age, Miss Elizabeth Harvey, youngest daughter of the late James Harvey, Esq., of Derry. (1840-10-31, 3:3, D)

605. On the 21st instant, at Myrtle Grove, near Dungannon, Hannah, relict of the late John Gilmore, Esq., of Lisrone [Lisroan], county Tyrone. (1840-10-31, 3:3, D)

606. At Ballycolman, near Strabane, on Thursday se'nnight, in her 72d year, Mrs. Cowper, relict of the late James Cowper, Esq. (1840-10-31, 3:3, D)

607. Oct. 24, Fanny Edwina, second daughter of Edward Pratt, Esq., Paymaster of the 99th regiment, Royal Barracks, Dublin. (1840-10-31, 3:3, D)

608. In Tyholland Church in this county, Francis Lock, Esq., of Loughgall, to Mary, youngest daughter of Thomas Robinson, Esq., of Sallymount, near this town. (1840-11-07, 3:2, M)

609. On the 20th ult., by the Rev. Michael Keirns, C.C., at the house of her brother, Mr. Peter M'Kernan, of Drumgorin, county Monaghan, Mr. James Canavan, to Anne, youngest daughter of the late Mr. John M'Kernan, of same place. (1840-11-07, 3:2, M)

610. On the 27th October, by the Rev. William Smith, Mr. William Cargill, of Mullaban [Mullaghbane], county Monaghan, to Margaret, eldest daughter of Mr. John Reany, of Hillhall. (1840-11-07, 3:2, M)

611. On the 29th ult., by the Rev. James Davis, Banbridge, Mr. John Osborne, Bellubymore [sic], to Jean, second daughter of Mr. John Cully, of Ballydown, near Banbridge. (1840-11-07, 3:2, M)

612. November 3, at Castleblayney, by the Rev. Cuthbert Hackett, George Hodgens, of Lower Gardiner-street, Solicitor, to Anna Louisa Babington, daughter of Thomas King, Esq., of Castleblayney. (1840-11-07, 3:2, M)

613. On the 31st July, at Bhooj Cutch, of bilious remittent fever, the Rev. William Mitchell Burnell, Chaplain in the Honorable East India Company's Service, and eldest son of Maurice Burnell, Esq., of this town. (1840-11-07, 3:2, D)

614. On the 30th August, the Rev. Bernard M'Ardle, pastor of Belleville, New Jersey, America; a native of the county Monaghan, Ireland, aged 50 years. His loss will be long regretted by the congregation over which he had charge. (1840-11-07, 3:2, D)

615. At Enniskillen, on the 28th October in the prime of life, Mr. James Willis, proprietor of the White-Heart [sic] Inn of that town. (1840-11-07, 3:2, D)

616. On the 17th ult., at Kingscourt, county Cavan, of fever, Mr. Joseph Carolan, deservedly regretted by a numerous circle of friends. (1840-11-07, 3:2, D)

617. At the house of her brother, the Right Rev. Dr. Kernan, at Carrickmacross, on the 11th ult., Miss Kernan, at a very advanced age, respected and esteemed by all who had the happiness of her acquaintance. (1840-11-07, 3:2, D)

618. October 28, at her residence in Chiltenham [sic], Alicia Lady Steuart, relict of General Sir James Steuart, Bart., of Coltness, in the county of Lanark, N.B. Her Ladyship, who had nearly completed her 89th year (being born February, 1752), was daughter of Wm. Blacker, Esq., formerly of Carrick, in the county of Armagh. (1840-11-07, 3:2, D)

619. In this town, at the residence of her father, Alexander King, Esq., on Thursday night, the lady of John Irwin, Esq., sub-inspector of police, of a daughter. (1840-11-14, 3:4, B)

620. October 30, in Clones church by the Rev. Mr. Walsh, Mr. James Bowes, Bookbinder, of Enniskillen, and formerly of this town, to Eliza Clark, eldest daughter of the late Benjamin Clark, Esq., of Clones. (1840-11-14, 3:4, M)

621. November 2, at Cookstown, by the Rev. Dr. Bardin, Rector of the parish of Derryloran, William Bell, Esq., of Christianstown, county Louth, to Jane, second daughter of the Rev. C. Marshall, of Killeshill cottage, county Tyrone. (1840-11-14, 3:4, M)

622. In St. Andrew's Church, Dublin, by the Rev. James Nevin, Thomas T. Wyly, Esq., to Matilda, daughter of Edward Bell, Esq., of Newry. (1840-11-14, 3:4, M)

623. On Sunday, the 1st instant, at his residence in Glasslough-street, in his 64th year, Robert Mitchell, Esq., proctor of office of the diocese of Clogher, an old and very respectable inhabitant of this town. During his life, Mr. Mitchell was conspicuous for his mechanical genius, and even during his last years, he has invented some pieces of machinery well worth the observation of the curious. He is sincerely regretted by all who knew him. (1840-11-14, 3:4, D)

624. Nov. 6, at Belturbet, in his 45th year, of typhus fever, contracted in the discharge of his medical duties, James Morton Williams, M.D, L.R.C.S., Ireland. The community at large, and the poor in particular, will long have to deplore the loss of an individual whose skill and assiduity in the practice of his profession, and whose benevolence of heart, have justly endeared him to all classes of persons and rendered his loss irreparable. (1840-11-14, 3:4, D)

625. Nov. 13, at Dunkerrin Church, King's County, by the Very Rev. the Dean of Clonfert, James S. Heron, Killyleagh, Down, Esq. to Catherine, eldest daughter of the late Rev. Arthur Nelson, Redemon, county Down. (1840-11-21, 3:2, M)

626. November 4, by the Rev. Samuel Madden, Marcus Carew Russell, Esq., of Ballydavid, in the county of Tipperary, to Rebecca, relict of Alex. Boyle of Omagh, in the county of Tyrone, Esq. (1840-11-21, 3:2, M)

627. November 14, by special license, in Thomas's Church, and afterwards in the Roman Catholic chapel in Marlborough-street, Thomas Ferguson, Esq., the well-known proprietor of the race-horse *Harkaway*, to Fanny, eldest daughter of Thomas Timmon, Esq., of Navan, county Meath. (1840-11-21, 3:2, M)

628. Nov. 18, at St. Mary's Church, by the Rev. Thomas F. Miller, Assistant Curate of St. Andrew's,

Edwd. S. Smith, Esq., of 49, Lower Sackville-street, to Catherine Anne, daughter of the late John Smith, Esq., Monaghan. (1840-11-21, 3:2, M)

629. On Saturday morning, November 7th, at his residence in Caddah, of fever, Mr. Samuel Crawford, aged 53 years, deeply and deservedly regretted by his numerous friends and acquaintances. (1840-11-21, 3:2, D)

630. November 16, at 19, Lower Gloucester-street, Robert William Stephens, Esq., eldest son of the late Robert William Stephens, Esq., of Ballinacariggy, county of Cavan. (1840-11-21, 3:2, D)

631. Shot, while defending the important pass of Poolagee, on the 29th August last, Robert Moore, Esq., 1st Grenadiers, East India Service, third son of the late Christopher Moore, Esq., of Newry. (1840-11-21, 3:2, D)

632. On Thursday last, at the house of the lady's father, by the Rev. John Rankin, Seceding Minister, John Sloan, Esq., of this town, merchant, to Eliza, second daughter of Robert Hodge, Esq., of Monaghan. (1840-11-28, 3:2, M)

633. On the 18th instant, at Loughgilly Church, by the Rev. Doctor Steward, George Dickson, of Portadown, Esq., S.I., to Anna Eliza, second daughter of William Atkinson, Esq., of Glenanne. (1840-11-28, 3:2, M)

634. Nov. 19, in Anthony church, by the Rev. R. Dunning, John Carter Allen, eldest son of Admiral Allen, Torpoint, to Margaret, eldest daughter of the late George Scott, Esq., of Dublin. (1840-11-28, 3:2, M)

635. Nov. 19, at Beaumaris, by the Rev. Richard Howard, D.D., Christopher Rawson, Esq., of Liverpool, to Ellen Frances, youngest daughter of John Wright, Esq., one of her Majesty's Justices of the Peace for the county palatine of Lancaster. (1840-11-28, 3:2, M)

636. Nov. 19, at Omagh, James Hamilton, Esq., eldest son of Captain Hamilton, Fintona, to Anne Jane, only daughter of Francis Ramsay, Esq., Arvagh House, Clogher. (1840-11-28, 3:2, M)

637. On Tuesday, in Christ's church, Belfast, by the Rev. Thomas Drew, John Bates, of Belfast, Esq., solicitor, to Jane Anne, second daughter of J.G. Victorr [sic], Esq., Lieutenant Royal Navy. (1840-11-28, 3:2, M)

638. Nov. 23, aged 23 years, of a lingering illness, which she bore with Christian fortitude and resignation, Naomi, eldest daughter of James Dudgeon, Esq., of No. 38, Upper Fitzwilliam-street. (1840-11-28, 3:2, D)

639. On the 13th instant, at his residence in Keady, in his 39th year, Mr. Josiah Kidd, sincerely and deservedly regretted. (1840-11-28, 3:2, D)

640. Christopher Madden, Esq., Cahir, county Galway, aged 74 years. (1840-11-28, 3:2, D)

641. Nov. 19, at the residence of the Lady's father, by the Rev. Hamilton Dobbin, David, second son of Samuel Ruddell, of Fairview, Esq., to Jane, only daughter of Youngstan Brown, of Lurgan, Esq. (1840-12-05, 3:2, M)

642. On Tuesday last, in this town, of malignant fever, Wm. C. Michell, Esq., M.D., Superintendent of the Castleshane Dispensary. Although a stranger in the country, and a very short time a resident therein, his universal benevolence and uniform kindness of manners, had endeared him to a large circle of friends, who deplore his premature decease with unfeigned sorrow. (1840-12-05, 3:2, D)

643. Nov. 27, at his residence, Newry, in the 73d year of his age, William Hancock, Esq., merchant, generally and deservedly regretted. (1840-12-05, 3:2, D)

644. Nov. 4, at Naples, Mary Anne, wife of Colonel Benjamin Ansley, late of the 3d Regiment of Foot Guards, aged 61 years. (1840-12-05, 3:2, D)

645. Nov. 21, in Wilton-street, London, after a protracted illness, Everilda, the lamented wife of Lieut.-Col. Chesney, Royal Artillery. (1840-12-05, 3:2, D)

646. At Rome, on the 31st ult., aged 86 years, the Duchess di Torloni. (1840-12-05, 3:2, D)

647. November 20, at Omagh, county Tyrone, William Doherty, Esq., M.D., Moville, county Donegal, to Mary, fourth daughter of the late Thomas Harkin, Esq., of Omagh. (1840-12-12, 3:1, M)

648. In Kilronan Church, Meredith Thompson, Esq., of Knockadoo, county Sligo, to Kate, youngest daughter of the late Ffrench MacDermott Roe, Esq., of Alderford House, county Roscommon. (1840-12-12, 3:1, M)

649. Nov. 30, at Keady, county Armagh, Alex. Munkitterick, Ardee, Esq., M.D. (1840-12-12, 3:1, D)

650. November 30, of consumption, at the residence of her brother, Alexander Porter, Esq., of Lackagh, Jane, the beloved wife of Arthur G. Dunleavy, Esq., county of Donegal. (1840-12-12, 3:1, D)

651. On the 15th instant, at Drumsnat Glebe, the lady of the Rev. Allen Mitchell, of a daughter. (1840-12-19, 2:5, B)

652. December 8, at Fivemiletown Church, James Graham, Esq., of Aughnacloy, to Mary, only daughter of Robert Ley, Esq., of Grange, near Clogher. (1840-12-26, 2:4, M)

653. December 9, at St. Patrick's church, by the Rev. Alex. Nixon, Thomas Nixon, Esq., of Dunbar House, county of Fermanagh, to Juliana Mary Anne, relict of John Bovell, Esq. of Demerara, and eldest daughter of George Alcock, Esq., of Upper Pembroke-street. (1840-12-26, 2:4, M)

654. December 18, by the Rev. Edmond Hemphill, in St. George's church, Belfast, the Rev. Richard Hemphill, of Dublin, to Charlotte Jane, daughter of William Cranston, Esq., of Belfast. (1840-12-26, 2:4, M)

655. December 15, in Glengall-place, Belfast, Mrs. Mary Houghton, aged 66 years, relict of George Houghton, of Upper Pembroke-street, Esq. (1840-12-26, 2:4, D)

656. December 28, in Aughavea Church, by the Rev. John Whittaker, Thomas, son of Thomas Wilkins, Esq., of Becho, county of Fermanagh, to Miss Johnston, of Brookeborough, daughter of the late Surgeon Johnston, R.N. (1841-01-02, 3:1, M)

657. On Friday morning, aged 35, in this town, after a long and painful illness, Catherine, the beloved wife of Doctor William Murray. She was an affectionate wife, a cheerful member of society, and has left her disconsolate husband and six children to deplore her loss. (1841-01-02, 3:1, D)

658. On Wednesday, at Fairview, Cootehill, the residence of J. Jamieson, Esq., at the advanced age of 99 years, Jane, relict of the late Rev. Wm. Moore, of Kingscourt, county Cavan. During her long life she was distinguished for exemplary piety and goodness, and to the last hour, preserved the use of her faculties in an extraordinary degree. (1841-01-02, 3:1, D)

659. On Monday last, at Ashfield, near Clones, the residence of her son, J.G. Smith, Esq., at an advanced age, Sarah, relict of the late Wm. Smith, Esq. In every relation of life she was loved and respected, and though she left the world in fullness of years, her decease has been sincerely mourned by all who knew her. (1841-01-02, 3:1, D)

660. At Cootehill, Lieutenant Richard Dawson, of the Royal Navy, youngest son of the late Ralph Dawson, Esq., of Tanagh, in the county Monaghan. (1841-01-02, 3:1, D)

661. On the 3d instant, after a lingering illness, which she bore with exemplary patience, Bridget, the beloved wife of Mr. Michael M'Elroy, of Clones. She was highly gifted by God with every quality which renders woman amiable and valuable to society—a fond and faithful wife—an anxious, tender and vigilent [sic] parent—charitable to the distressed—kind and benevolent to all. She died deeply regretted by all who had the happiness of her society. (1841-01-09, 3:2, D)

662. On Thursday last, in the prime of life, at the residence of his father, Dublin-street, Monaghan, Dr. M'Kenzie King. (1841-01-16, 3:1, D)

663. At Portavo, on the 5th instant, the Lady of Matthew Anketell, Esq., of a son. (1841-01-16, 3:5, B)

664. On the 30th ult., at Middleton, the Lady of James Gregory, Esq., of a daughter. (1841-01-16, 3:5, B)

665. The Rev. Thomas Horner, Licentiate of the General Assembly of the Presbyterian Church in Ireland, to Maria, relict of the late Rev. Henry Kyd, and daughter to Robt. Bailie, Esq., of Belfast. (1841-01-23, 3:4, M)

666. At his residence, Newry, on Friday, 15th inst., of apoplexy, in his 82d year, Jonathan Seaver, Esq., of Heath-Hall, one of the oldest Magistrates of the co. Armagh. (1841-01-23, 3:4, D)

667. At Newbliss, on Saturday, the 23d inst., in the seventy-first year of her age, Ann, the beloved wife of Mr. Francis Thompson, whose mortal career closed in the delightful assurance of everlasting happiness and peace through the merits of Christ Jesus, her Redeemer. (1841-01-30, 3:3, D)

668. On the 22d instant, aged 80 years, after a lingering illness, which she bore with exemplary patience, Sarah, the beloved wife of Mr. Robt. Wright, of Feaugh, near Newbliss. She was a kind, fond, and faithful wife, an anxious, tender, and vigilent [sic] parent—charitable to the distressed, kind and benevolent to all. She died deeply regretted by a numerous circle of friends and acquaintances. (1841-01-30, 3:3, D)

669. On Wednesday, the 20th inst., Mr. James Kilpatrick, of Killilea, aged 62 years. He bore his last illness with patience, and while his body was subject to acute pain, his soul was stayed on Christ his Redeemer, whom he had served. To his very last moments, prayer was his constant delight, and his exhortations to his visitors were truly impressive and affecting. Kind and humane, generous and charitable—he was ever ready to assist the distressed, and relieve the afflicted as far as lay in his power. He yielded up his breath, in holy resignation, to the divine will, and without a single groan, his happy spirit took its flight from the body to mingle with those in a better and happier world. His departure is sincerely lamented by all who knew him, and he has left an affectionate wife and numerous family to deplore his loss. He has been a steady member of the Methodist Society for 41 years. (1841-01-30, 3:3, D)

670. Suddenly, of apoplexy, on the 28th ultimo, at his residence, Lisnadill, near Armagh, Doctor John O'Toole, in the 55th year of his age. (1841-02-06, 3:5, D)

671. On the 27th ultimo, of consumption, at the residence of his parents, Ballygowan, near Moira, in the 18th year of his age, Henry, youngest son of Mr. John Carville. (1841-02-06, 3:5, D)

672. On Sunday last, deeply regretted, Mr. Wm. Graham, Printer, in the 42d year of his age. Mr. Graham was for nearly ten years overseer in the office of this paper, where he was highly esteemed by all for his zeal, intelligence, and fidelity.—*Belfast Chronicle*. (1841-02-06, 3:5, D)

673. On Wednesday last, in the Church of Monaghan, by the Rev. V.D. Christian, Andrew Bell, Esq., of Carrowbarrow, to Kate, sixth daughter of the late Nathaniel Wright, Esq., of this town. (1841-02-13, 3:4, M)

674. On the 2d instant, at Cheltenham, by the Rev. Francis Close, Captain Bland, late of the Hon. East India Company's Army (Bengal Establishment), to Elizabeth, youngest daughter of the late Rev. William Pinching, Rector of Carrickmacross, county Monaghan. (1841-02-13, 3:4, M)

675. Feb. 4, at Feuter [sic] Lodge, in her 88th year, Margaret, relict of the late John Weldon Tarleton, Esq., of Killeigh, King's County. (1841-02-13, 3:4, D)

676. On Thursday, the 4th instant, at his house, Banvale, near Hilltown, in the 61st year of his age, universally regretted, Mr. Thomas O'Reilly. (1841-02-13, 3:4, D)

677. On the 3d instant, at the residence of his brother, Mr. John O'Neill, C.C., of the union of Dromore and Garvagh, in the 35th year of his age, and 8th of his ministry. He entered on the labours of his sacred calling in September. (1841-02-13, 3:4, D)

678. January 20, at the Grove, near Durham, aged 78, Elizabeth, relict of Stephen George Kemble, Esq. In early life, Mrs. Kemble, formerly Miss Satchell, was one of the first actresses of her day, in almost every range of character. (1841-02-13, 3:4, D)

679. On the 18th Instant, by the Rev. Samuel J. Moore, at the house of the lady's Aunt, Cleantough, the Rev. John H. Moore, Kells, county Antrim, to Margaret, eldest daughter of Mr. Henry Martin, Aughnacloy, County Monaghan. (1841-02-20, 2:5, M)

680. Feb. 18th, by the Rev. Y.B. Coulter, Mr. Wm. Smith, engineer, Carrickmacross, to Susanna, eldest daughter of Mr. Richard Mitchell of Castleblayney. (1841-02-20, 2:5, M)

681. On the 13th instant, at Donnybrook, near Nenagh, the seat of William Poe, Esq., Devaynes Smith, of Oakwood, in the King's County, Esq., aged 56 years. (1841-02-20, 2:5, D)

682. At the Clergy Sons' School, Lucan, of water on the brain, William Gore, youngest son of the late Rev. John Walsh, of Killflynn, county Limerick. (1841-02-20, 2:5, D)

683. At Releigh [Raleigh], near Macroom, Wm. Minhear, Esq., a magistrate of the county Cork. (1841-02-20, 2:5, D)

684. At Dromore, of fever, David Clotworthy, Esq., Surgeon. (1841-02-20, 2:5, D)

685. In Waterford, Mr. Thomas Raid. (1841-02-20, 2:5, D)

686. At Rathmines, Mr. Joseph Hoare Stedman, of Lower Gardiner-street. (1841-02-20, 2:5, D)

687. At Stondon-place, Essex, Ann, widow of the late Christian Paul Meyer, Esq. (1841-02-20, 2:5, D)

688. On the 3d instant, at the Glebe Cottage, Monaghan, the Lady of the Rev. W.L. Roper, of a son. (1841-03-06, 3:2, B)

689. On the 26th ult., in Ballinderry Church, by the Rev. Colin Ievers, the Rev. Edward Mockler, Curate of Killead, to Grace, second daughter of Mr. William Green, Ballinderry. (1841-03-06, 3:2, M)

690. In Newry, on Friday, the 26th ult., Isaac Glenny, Esq., J.P., in his 77th year. (1841-03-06, 3:2, D)

691. March 13, at Ballyleek, county Monaghan, the Lady of the Rev. John T. Whitestone of a son. (1841-03-20, 3:4, B)

692. On the 24th inst., in the 35th year of her age, Olivia, the beloved wife of John Shiell, Esq., of Castleblayney. In her, the poor have lost a friend indeed—the needy were never repulsed from her door. Her amiable disposition, and unaffected piety, endeared her to a very large circle of acquaintances. The esteem in which she was held was evidenced by the vast concourse of rich and poor that accompanied her remains to the grave. (1841-03-27, 3:3, D)

693. On Tuesday last, by the Rev. John Bleckley, Mr. Richard Bleckley, to Elizabeth, relict of the late Mr. James Swan, of Glasslough-street, and eldest daughter of Mr. Nathaniel Grecen, printer, Diamond, Monaghan. (1841-04-10, 3:2, M)

694. On Thursday evening, by the Rev. John Bleckley, Minister of the Presbyterian Congregation of Monaghan, Mr. John Carlisle, of this town, to Ann Jane, eldest daughter of Mr. George Cotterrell, of Glasslough-street. (1841-04-10, 3:2, M)

695. At Middletown, County Armagh, on the 18th ult., Mr. Richard Purdy, in his 50th year. (1841-04-10, 3:2, D)

696. Jan. 16, at Aurungabad, in the East Indies, George Lanauze, Esq., aged 35 years, Assistant Commissary-General in his Highness the Nizam's service, and third son of the late Andrew Lanauze, Esq, of the county Cavan. (1841-04-10, 3:2, D)

697. April 3, in Limerick, Joseph Gabbett Bouchier, Esq., of the Royal Tyrone Regiment. (1841-04-10, 3:2, D)

698. April 10, at Rockcorry, county of Monaghan, Mrs. Dorcas Bowes, at the advanced age of 80 years. (1841-04-17, 3:2, D)

699. April 6, in her house in Baggot-street, suddenly, in the 72d year of her age, Mrs. Montgomery Nixon, relict of the late Montgomery Nixon, Esq., M.D., of Lakeview, in the county of Fermanagh. (1841-04-17, 3:2, D)

700. April 18, by the Rev. David Stuart, Francis Nesbitt, youngest son of John M'Keon, Esq., of Drogheda, to Anne, eldest daughter of William Mills, Esq., of Slane, county of Meath. (1841-04-24, 3:3, M)

701. On the 1st instant, at the house of the bride's mother, Mr. George Whitten, of Lisnakea, County Armagh, to Jane, second daughter of the late Mr. Quintin Shannon, of Tullymore, near Poyntzpass, County Down. (1841-04-24, 3:3, M)

702. April 17, at Stradbally Church, county Waterford, by the Venerable the Archdeacon of Lismore, the Rev. William Campbell, of St. Matthew's Chapel of Ease, Belfast, son of John Campbell, Esq, county Down, to Elizabeth, daughter of the late George Roche, Esq., Youghal. (1841-04-24, 3:3, M)

703. April 17, at his residence, North Wales, John Latouche Powell, Esq. (1841-04-24, 3:3, D)

704. March 20, Elizabeth Madden, aged 24 years, and on the 17th instant, Lucretia Madden, aged 27 years, daughters of Major Madden, of the city of Kilkenny—in sure and certain hope of the resurrection to eternal life, through our Lord Jesus Christ. (1841-04-24, 3:3, D)

705. On the 10th instant, at his residence, Alistragh, in the county Armagh, Robert M'Bride, Esq. In the death of this Gentleman, society has lost an upright and useful member—the poor, a steady, and generous friend and benefactor—and his family, a tender, anxious and affectionate parent. He was in his 74th year. (1841-04-24, 3:3, D)

706. At his house, New Holland, near Keady, James M'Kean, Lieutenant Royal Navy, much and deservedly regretted. (1841-04-24, 3:3, D)

707. In Queen-street, Belfast, on the 18th instant, of typhus fever, John Caldwell, Esq. aged 22 years. (1841-04-24, 3:3, D)

708. On the 10th instant, Captain Henry, late County Inspector for Fermanagh. (1841-04-24, 3:3, D)

709. April 23, in St. Thomas's Church, Dublin, by the Rev. Edward Campbell, William Cummins, Esq., of Pettigo, in the county of Fermanagh, to Catherine, only daughter of the late Captain James Brier, Royal Tyrone Regiment. (1841-05-01, 3:4, M) *Note: This notice was largely illegible.*

710. In Clones, on the 23d ult., in the 53d year of his age, the Rev. Thomas Mogue, P.P. of Clones, and formerly of Rosslea. (1841-05-01, 3:4, D) *Note: This notice was scarcely legible.*

711. In Lough Oona, county of Monaghan, the residence of his grandson, A.A. Murray, Esq., the Rev. William Moffatt, aged 84, for many years the Rector of the parish of Curin, diocese of Clogher. (1841-05-01, 3:4, D) *Note: This notice was scarcely legible.*

712. On the 4th inst., at Clogher, county Tyrone, the Rev. John Hanna, of Clogher, to Matilda, youngest daughter of the late John M'Moran, Esq., M.D., of Monaghan. (1841-05-08, 3:2, M)

713. April 29, at Dunfermline, Adam Duncannon, Esq., Manager of the Ulster Banking Company, Enniskillen, to Jessie, only daughter of the late John Horn, Esq. (1841-05-08, 3:2, M)

714. April 28, in St. Thomas's Church, Dublin, by the Rev. Edward Campbell, William Crummer, of Pettigo, in the county of Fermanagh, Esq., to Catherine, only daughter of the late Captain James Brien, Royal Tyrone Regt. (1841-05-08, 3:2, M)

715. At St. Jude's Terrace, Liverpool, Harloe, eldest son of Thomas Trumble, Esq., Sligo Militia, Queenston, Canada, and formerly of Canebrook, county Sligo. (1841-05-08, 3:2, D)

716. May 5, at 10, Cambridge-terrace, Rathgar-road, Anne Carlton, the beloved wife of John Thomas Drought, of Whigsborough, in the King's county, Esq. (1841-05-08, 3:2, D)

717. At Carrickmacross, on the 8th instant, in the prime of life, of typhus fever, Evylyn John Evatt, Esq., M.D., Medical Attendant of the Carrickmacross Dispensary, brother to the late Rev. Charles Evatt, Rector of this town, and to Samuel Robert B. Evatt, Esq., of Mount Louise, county Monaghan. He was a gentleman of the mildest and most humane disposition, and was universally beloved in the neighbourhood in which he resided. (1841-05-15, 3:3, D)

718. On the 6th instant, Fanny, eldest daughter of the late Rev. James Morrell, of Fairview, near Ballybay. (1841-05-15, 3:3, D)

719. May 14, at Longfield Church, by the Rev. Archdeacon Hamilton, Thomas Simpson, Esq., of Ballyards, county Armagh, to Helena, youngest daughter of the late Robert Sproule, Esq., of Burrelsfolly [Burle's Folly], county Tyrone, and relict of Henry Maxwell, Esq., 98th Regiment. (1841-05-22, 3:2, M)

720. May 7, in Crosspatrick Church, county of Wicklow, by the Rev. P.J. Callanan, A.M., Carnew, John Connor, Esq., Bridgtown, Glasgow, to Robina, only daughter of the late Robert Caird, Esq., Portpatrick. (1841-05-22, 3:2, M)

721. May 13, by the Rev. Dr. Montgomery, Samuel Hunter, of Belfast, Esq., M.D., son of the late John Hunter, Aghadoey, Coleraine, Esq. (1841-05-22, 3:2, M) *Note: The bride's name was not stated.*

722. May 17, in Powerscourt Church, by the Rev. Arthur Wynne, Captain Croker, of the 17th Lancers, only son of John Croker, Esq., of Ballynaguard, county of Limerick, to Lady Georgiana Ellen Monck, fifth daughter of the Earl of Rathdowne. (1841-05-22, 3:2, M)

723. On the 23d ult., at Corvoy, Mr. John Crowe, aged 58 years. (1841-05-22, 3:2, D)

724. On Monday last, Mr. Rogers, of Tullyvogy, aged 92 years. (1841-05-22, 3:2, D)

725. May 15, in Drogheda, of consumption, in the 27th year of his age, Surgeon Thomas Sheppard Murphy, third son of the late George Murphy, Esq., M.D., Surgeon to the Louth Militia. (1841-05-22, 3:2, D)

726. May 3, at Dornock, Annan, N.B., William Little, Esq., aged 75, late proprietor of the salmon fisheries in the North of Ireland. (1841-05-22, 3:2, D)

727. May 12, in Paris, at the Church of Notre Dame, and afterwards at the British Embassy, the Baron de Bazancourt, grandson of the Countess Houdetot, to Annie, only daughter and heiress of the late David Nixon Donnelian, of Castlebellingham, county Louth, Esq., and Elizabeth, daughter of the late Honorable John Leeson, and grand-daughter of Brice, third Earl of Miltown. (1841-05-29, 3:1, M)

728. At the Glebe Cottage, on the 26th inst., of hooping-cough, Henry John, aged two and a-half years, the beloved child of the Rev. W.L. Roper, Rector of Monaghan. (1841-05-29, 3:1, D)

729. At his residence in Tydavnet, at an advanced age, much and deservedly respected, Mr. John M'Quaid, father of Mr. Peter M'Quaid, merchant, of this town. (1841-05-29, 3:1, D)

730. May 8, at Cootehill, in the 80th year of his age, Captain Samuel Beatny, formerly of the Royal Waggon Train. He spent upwards of 40 years in the service of his country, obtained a gold medal for his services in Egypt, and died a truly pious and resigned Christian lamented by his numerous friends. (1841-05-29, 3:1, D)

731. May 20, in his 81st year, the Rev. Alexander Leney, of Castledawson. (1841-05-29, 3:1, D)

732. May 25, Orr, second son of Wm. Gamble, Esq., of Solitude, County Down, to Sarah, daughter of the late Capt. Samuel Montgomery, Belfast. (1841-06-05, 3:3, M)

733. May 24, in Kilskeery, by the Rev. R.P. Cleary, A.M., Curate of Enniskillen, Thomas Wood, proprietor of the Leeds Woolen Mart, Enniskillen, Esq., to Anna Maria, eldest daughter of James Buchannan, Fintona, county of Tyrone, Esq. (1841-06-05, 3:3, M)

734. May 14, at the house of the lady's brother, at Omagh, by the Rev. John Arnold, Alexander M'Kee, Esq., of Florida Manor, county of Down, to Margaret, only daughter of the late John Mullin, Esq., of Omagh. (1841-06-05, 3:3, M)

735. June 2, by special licence, in Carrickmacross Church, George Bellamy, Esq., of Weldon, in Northamptonshire, to Barbara Frances, eldest daughter to John J. Cassidy, Esq., of Hunter-street, Brunswick-square, London. (1841-06-05, 3:3, M)

736. May 29, Denis O'Connor, Esq., eldest son of Matthew O'Connor, of Mount Druid, in the county of Roscommon, Esq., and great-grandson of Charles O'Connor, of Belanagare, to Margaret, eldest daughter of Nicholas Power, of Faithlegg, in the county of Waterford, Esq., and grand-daughter to the late Nicholas Mahon, of the Merchants'-Quay. (1841-06-05, 3:3, M)

737. June 1, at St. Peter's Church, by the Hon. and Rev. F. Howard, Charles William Hamilton, Esq, eldest son of Charles Hamilton, of Hamwood, in the county of Meath, Esq., to Letitia, daughter of the late William Henry Armstrong, of Mountheaton, in the King's County, Esq. (1841-06-05, 3:3, M)

738. At St. John's House, Cheltenham, in the 84th year of her age, Letitia, Dowager Lady Clonbrock. (1841-06-05, 3:3, D)

739. May 11, in London, James Montgomery, Esq., aged 73, late of the Hall, Donegal, brother of the late Sir Henry C. Montgomery, Bart., formerly M.P. for that county. (1841-06-05, 3:3, D)

740. May 22, at Portsmouth, Frederick Richard, youngest son of Captain Basil Hall, of the Royal Navy. (1841-06-05, 3:3, D)

741. At Boulogue [sic], John Aylmer, Esq, Admiral of the Red, in the 80th year of his age. (1841-06-05, 3:3, D)

742. May 26, in his 10th year, William Brownlow Barlow, third son of the Rev. William Barlow, Vicar of Carlingford. (1841-06-05, 3:3, D)

743. At Wiesbaden, in her 11th year, Henrietta Jane, only child of W. Lockwood, of Edenderry, King's County. (1841-06-05, 3:3, D)

744. June 8, in St. George's Church, by the Rev. A. Adams, of Ballymakenny Glebe in the county of Louth, Robert Adams, Esq., of Great Denmark-street, Dublin, to Mary, daughter of the late Alexander Nixon Montgomery, of Bessmount Park, county of Monaghan, Esq. (1841-06-12, 3:1, M)

745. June 4, at his residence in Henrietta-street, Bath, Geo. Cole, Esq., formerly Captain in the Cornwall Militia.—The deceased was uncle of Mrs. Cole, of Merrion-square, Dublin. (1841-06-12, 3:1, D)

746. On Thursday, of consumption, aged 17 years, John Anketell, second son of Mr. John Armstrong, Merchant, Diamond, Monaghan. He was a young gentleman of good promise, and interesting and amiable manners, and, during his protracted illness, displayed that patient resignation and holy faith in his Redeemer's promise, that pertaineth only to the regenerated, and which is now the chief consolation of his afflicted family. (1841-06-19, 3:1, D)

747. June 13, in Clones, at the house of his grandmother, Mrs. Armstrong, Thomas Armstrong Clarke, aged 11 years. During a lingering illness, he was divinely supported, and enabled confidently to rest on the atonement; his end was peace. (1841-06-19, 3:1, D)

748. June 11, at Strabane, Archibald Armstrong, Esq., Chief of Police, in that town. (1841-06-19, 3:1, D)

749. At St. Mark's Church, by the Rev. A. Franklin, D.D., Thomas Francis Gale, Esq., of Lower Mount-street, only son of the late Captain Anthony Gale, of Bellbrook, in the Queen's County, to Anna, only daughter of Adam Fuller, Esq., of Woodfield, in the King's County, and grand-daughter of Abraham Fuller, Esq., Deputy Lieutenant. (1841-06-26, 3:2, M)

750. June 16, at Newton Saville Church, by the Rev. Ewd. Burke, James Crooks Bell, of the city of Armagh, Esq., Barrister-at-Law, to Margaret, youngest daughter of Joseph Trimble, Esq., Clogher. (1841-06-26, 3:2, M)

751. June 19, in St. Thomas's Church, by the Rev. Henry Rochfort, Thomas F. Gerrard, of Kilsaren, county of Louth, Esq., to Amelia, only daughter of the late Captain Sweeny, 84th Regiment. (1841-06-26, 3:2, M)

752. At Belfast, the Rev. R. Quin to Edith, daughter of Major-General Sir Thomas Pearson, Commanding the Northern District of Ireland. (1841-06-26, 3:2, M)

753. Mr. Joseph Cassidy, Printer, to Miss Mary Ann Maher, of Dominick-street, Dublin. (1841-06-26, 3:2, M)

754. June 19, of hooping cough, at the Glebe Cottage, Monaghan, William Chamberlayne, infant son of the Rev. W.L. Roper. (1841-06-26, 3:2, D)

755. At Glasslough, on the 23d instant, in the 80th year of her age, Mrs. Jane Baxter, relict of the late Captain Robert Baxter. She was beloved through life, and her latter end was peace. (1841-06-26, 3:2, D)

756. June 21, Sarah Elizabeth, infant daughter of John Irvine, of Rockfield, county Fermanagh, Esq. (1841-06-26, 3:2, D)

757. On the 11th inst., of water on the chest, aged 50 years, Henry Grant, tanner, Lower Mill-street, Newry; and, on the 14th instant, of consumption, aged 46 years, Mrs. Grant. (1841-06-26, 3:2, D)

758. On the 5th instant, at the advanced age of 85, the Rev. William Harris, parish priest of Kileavan and Aughabog, and Roman Catholic Archdeacon of the Diocess of Clogher. (1841-06-26, 3:2, D)

759. By the Rev. A.C. Macartney, on Wednesday, the 30th June, the Very Rev. John Lee, D.D., LL.D., Principal of the University of Edinburgh, to Charlotte Ellen, third daughter of the late Joseph Wright, of Duncairne, Belfast, Esq. (1841-07-03, 3:3, M)

760. In this town on Friday morning, aged upwards of 80 years, Jane, relict of the late Mr. Alexander Barnes. (1841-07-03, 3:3, D)

761. June 26, at Ballyleck, county of Monaghan, of hooping cough, accompanied by influenza, John R. Russell, aged three months; and in the evening of the same day, James Roper, aged seventeen months, only children of the Rev. John T. Whitestone. (1841-07-03, 3:3, D)

762. July 5, in Christ's Church, Belfast, Richard Maffett, Esq., M.D., Glasslough, to Frances, third daughter of Thomas G. Ferguson, Esq. (1841-07-10, 3:3, M)

763. July 1, in the Parish Church of Cloone, by the Rev. Andrew Hogg, John Simpson Stuart, Esq., Sub Inspector, Constabulary, to Susan Lloyd, youngest daughter of George Beatty West, Esq., Drumdarkin House, county of Leitrim. (1841-07-10, 3:3, M)

764. July 5, at his residence Kingscourt, county of Cavan, after a few hours' illness, Phil. Ward, Esq., in the 76th year of his age. (1841-07-17, 3:3, D)

765. July 2, in the 17th year of his age, Andrew Y. Knight, third son of James J. Knight, of Green Cottage, county of Monaghan, and of Union Lodge, county of Dublin. (1841-07-17, 3:3, D)

766. June 30, of hooping cough, at Rathmines, deeply regretted by her family and friends, Sarah Eliza, second daughter of the late Rev. Richard Forster, and niece of Andrew Ker, Esq., Newbliss, county of Monaghan. (1841-07-17, 3:3, D)

767. At Magherafelt, on the 26th instant, the lady of John Dobbin, Esq., of a daughter. (1841-07-31, 3:3, B)

768. July 30, in St. Mary's Church, Newry, by the Rev. Dr. Campbell, John Colvan, Esq., M.D., Licentiate of the King's and Queen's College of Physicians, Ireland, and Physician to the Armagh Fever Hospital, &c., to Deborah, eldest daughter of the late John Coulter, Esq., of Carnmeen. (1841-08-07, 3:2, M)

769. July 27, in Forkhill Church, by the Rev. Dr. Campbell, Patrick Moore, Esq., S.T.C.D., to Ellen Mary, fourth daughter of the late Rev. Mr. Ashe, of Acton Glebe, county Armagh. (1841-08-07, 3:2, M)

770. August 2, at Booterstown Church, by the Rev. William Robert Nixon, Richard Field Mulvany, Esq., to Harriot, daughter of the late Neal M'Kenna, Esq., of the county Armagh. (1841-08-07, 3:2, M)

771. July 31, after a short illness, at the early age of nineteen years, William, eldest son of the Rev. James Lynar, Rector of the Parish of Kilderry, in the diocess of Ossory. (1841-08-07, 3:2, D)

772. August 3, at Carnagh House, in the county of Armagh, the residence of her son, John R. Irwin, Esq., Eliza, relict of William Irwin, Esq., late treasurer of the county Armagh. (1841-08-07, 3:2, D)

773. At his residence, Oakfield, county Fermanagh, on the 29th ultimo, in the 70th year of his age, John Pierce Hamilton, Esq., J.P., sincerely and deservedly regretted by his numerous circle of friends. He was an affectionate husband, a fond father and a steady friend. His true unaffected piety and faith in the merits of a crucified Saviour, give his relatives the consolation of believing him, "Not lost, but gone before." (1841-08-07, 3:2, D)

774. At the Parish Church, Stoke Fleming, Devonshire, on Monday, the 10th inst., Percy Hocken, Esq., of Dartmouth, to Mary Georgina Steuart Corry; and on Friday, the 15th inst., Henry Brooking, of the Island of Madeira, Esq., to Annette Caroline Steuart Corry, daughters of T.C. Steuart Corry, Esq., of the Manor House, Stoke Fleming, Devon, England, and late of Rockcorry Castle, in this county. (1841-08-21, 2:5, M)

775. At Monfieth, on the 10th instant, by the Rev. S. Miller, William Miller, Esq., Provincial Bank of Ireland, Monaghan, to Anne, third daughter of James Anderson, Esq., of Clocksbriggs, Scotland. (1841-08-21, 2:5, M)

776. At St. Luke's Church, Liverpool, on the 11th instant, by the Rev. Richard Graham, the Rev. James Graham, of Derry Cathedral, to Mrs. Gray, of Belfield-house. (1841-08-21, 2:5, M)

777. On the 2d instant, after a lingering illness, Mr. William Wilkin, of Ramakit, near Caledon, aged 54 years. (1841-08-21, 2:5, D)

778. On the 26th ult., the Rev. Robert Rusk, Presbyterian Minister of Ballyscullion, Grange, in the 42d year of his age. (1841-08-21, 2:5, D)

779. On the 11th inst., at his father's residence, in Sligo, after a protracted illness, John, second son of the Rev. John Nelson, Methodist Minister. (1841-08-21, 2:5, D)

780. August 13, aged 39 years, Isabella, the wife of the Rev. I. Steen, Head Master of the Mathematical Department in the Royal Belfast Academical Institution. (1841-08-21, 2:5, D)

781. August 16, James Walkinshaw Bell, Esq., Q.C., of Lower Gardiner-street, and one of the Benchers of the Queen's Inns. (1841-08-21, 2:5, D)

782. In Brownsville, Pennsylvenia [sic], on the 20th July, by the Rev. Wm. Johnston, Mr. George Taylor, Merchant, of Pittsburgh, to Miss Esther Graham, of Bridgeport Fayette, county Pa., formerly of Killycreen, near Monaghan, Ireland. (1841-08-28, 3:1, M)

783. On the 20th inst., at St. Mary's, Marylebone, Archibald Crawford, Esq., son of the late Arthur Crawford, Esq., of Belfast, to Elizabeth, only child of the late John Hennington Cosgrave, Esq., of Belfast. (1841-08-28, 3:1, M)

784. August 21, by the Rev. Mr. Gabbett, in the church of Templetenny, Wm. Burgess, Esq., M.D., of Clonmel, to Elizabeth Jane, eldest Daughter of Doctor Young, of Dublin, and niece to Thomas Carpenter, Esq., Ballunvillen, Michelstown. (1841-08-28, 3:1, M)

785. August 15, Robert, the beloved son of S.R.B. Evatt, Esq., J.P., of Mount Louise, in this county, aged one year and a fortnight. (1841-08-28, 3:1, D)

786. On the 16th instant, at Dabton, Dumfriesshire, aged 79 years, Henry M'Veigh, Esq., formerly a magistrate of the county Armagh. (1841-08-28, 3:1, D)

787. On the 20th instant, at his seat, Hooton, Cheshire, Sir Thomas Stanley Massey Stanley, Bart., aged 58. Sir Thos. was a gentleman beloved by his family and dependants for his domestic virtues, and highly respected in that part of the county in which he resided for his hospitality and attachment to old English sports, and for his benevolence to the poor and liberal contributions to local charities. (1841-08-28, 3:1, D)

788. On the 30th August, at the Cathedral, Cork, by the Lord Bishop of Cork, Cloyne, and Ross, the Rev. Richard Graves Meredith, eldest son of the late Doctor Meredith, F.T.C.D., to Maria, second daughter of Thomas Johnston, of Fort-Johnston, Esq., County Monaghan, and grand-daughter of the late Rev. Doctor Kingston, Vicar-General of Cloyne. (1841-09-04, 3:2, M)

789. On Thursday morning, at the house of the lady's father, by the Rev. Mr. Rankin, Presbyterian Minister, Doctor Thomas Reed, of this town, to Marianne, eldest daughter of Robert Hodge, Esq., of the Hill, Monaghan. (1841-10-02, 3:3, M)

790. On Wednesday, the 22d ult., in Coalisland Church, by the Rev. Isaac Ash, Mr. Thomas Timmerall, of Stone Bridge, near Richhill, to Isabella, fourth daughter of Mr. William Burns, Ballynakelly House, county Tyrone. (1841-10-02, 3:3, M)

791. Sept. 28, in St. George's Church, by the Rev. Henry Swanzy, A.M., Rector of Macroom, John Swanzy, Esq., of Hardwick-street, youngest son of Henry Swanzy, of Rockfield, in the County of Monaghan, Esq., to Fanny, second daughter of Francis Mills, Esq., of Mountjoy-square, Dublin. (1841-10-02, 3:3, M)

792. On Saturday, the 25th September, after a lingering illness, Sophia, wife of Mr. James A. Ross, of this town. (1841-10-02, 3:3, D)

793. Sept. 20, suddenly, of rupture of a blood vessel, at the residence of his son-in-law, Mr. Dobson, near Clones, where he had gone to spend the day, Mr. John Maxwell, of Green-mount, aged 61. (1841-10-02, 3:3, D)

794. September 30, at Ardbraccan Church, by the bride's uncle, the Venerable the Archdeacon of Clogher, the Rev. John West, D.D., Vicar of St. Anne's and Domestic Chaplain to his Grace the Archbishop of Dublin, to Bessie Margarette, eldest daughter of the Lord Bishop of Meath. (1841-10-09, 3:2, M)

795. September 30, in the prime of life, at his residence, Tubberpatrick, county Roscommon, Thomas Charles M'Dermott, Esq., Barrister-at-Law. The remains of this much regretted and highly talented gentleman were interred in the family vault at Kilronan. (1841-10-09, 3:2, D)

796. October 1, in St. George's Church, by the father of the bridegroom, John Edward Walsh, Esq, Barrister-at-Law, only son of the Rev. Robert Walsh, LL.D. and M.D., Vicar of Finglas, to Blair Belinda, only daughter of the late Gordon MacNeill, Esq., of Eccles-street, late of the 77th regiment. (1841-10-09, 3:2, M)

797. On Friday last, in Loughgall Church, Mr. Thos. M'Kell, of Moy, merchant, to Sarah, daughter of Mr. Robert Corrigan, of Moss Spring, near Charlemont. (1841-10-16, 3:2, M)

798. On the 4th instant, at St. Peter's Church, Dublin, Capt. Nugent, 36th Regiment, son of Andrew Nugent, Esq., of Portaferry, county Down, and nephew of the Viscount de Visci, to the Viscountess Bangor, widow of Viscount Bangor, of Castle Ward, county Down, and daughter of the late, and sister to the present, Lord Farnham. (1841-10-16, 3:2, M)

799. October 12, in St. Mary's Church, by the Rev. Mr. Mooney, Francis M'Grath, Esq., M.D., of Newtownbutler, county of Fermanagh, to Barbara Henrietta, second daughter of the late Robert Peare, Esq., of Newcastle, county Limerick. (1841-10-16, 3:2, M)

800. On the 10th instant, of fever, greatly lamented, Dickson, son of Mr. James Eakin, of Glennon, in the 16th year of his age. (1841-10-16, 3:2, D)

801. On the 2d instant, at Portstewart, in the 55th year of her age, whither she had gone for the benefit of her health, Elizabeth, relict of the late Robert Henry, Esq., M.D., Bray, county Tyrone, and daughter of the late Captain Thomas Cuppagh, Ballycastle. (1841-10-16, 3:2, D)

802. On the 2d instant, Margaret Campbell, of Glassmalough, near Dungannon, aged 87. (1841-10-16, 3:2, D)

803. On Thursday evening, after about twenty hours' illness, of Apoplexy, in his 67th year, at his residence, Fort-Johnston, Thomas Johnston, Esq., one of the oldest and most respectable magistrates of the County Monaghan. (1841-10-23, 3:1, D)

804. At Rosefield, on the 24th inst., of inflammation, after an illness of 26 hours' duration, in the 19th year of her age, Henrietta Louisa, youngest daughter of John Johnson, of Thornhill, Esq. Lovely alike in person and in mind, she evinced in death the character she had supported during her short life. Mild, amiable, and pious, in the most excruciating pain, she was sustained by a firm reliance on her blessed Saviour, and, with perfect resignation to his will, committed her pure and gentle spirit to him who gave it. This faint record of her virtues is given by one, who from her early childhood, had known, loved, and appreciated her worth.

"Weep not! She is not dead but sleepeth."

"Weep not" for her! Was ever mortal blest!
Free from all sin, from sorrow and from care;
'Tis she, who now with Jesus makes her rest—
With kindred spirits soars—their glories share.

"Weep not" for her! tho' many a passing year
You mourn that form, so lovely in your eyes;
Selfish it were to shed one sorrowing tear,
Or wish to bring her from her native skies.

"Weep not" for her! altho' a charm did seem
To dwell around her—in her very breath;
It seems to linger yet! I scarce can deem,
That brow has such repose—it can be Death!

"Weep not" for her! e'en tho' her soft, sweet smile,
Bright as a seraph's from the realms above,
Could from her dear ones, every care beguile,
And win them to her loveliness and love.

"Weep not" for her! tho' dreams of other days
Come like a whirlwind form the depths of thought;
Memory of her, who, like earth's hope decays,
The mild, the pious, loved, and unforgot!
(1841-10-30, 3:3, D)

805. On Wednesday last, at her residence, Glasslough-street, Anne, relict of the late Mr. Robert Murdock, of this town, in her 45th year. (1841-10-30, 3:3, D)

806. On Wednesday last, at his residence, Market-street, Mr. John Fitzhenry, aged 35, nephew of Mr. Samuel Richardson, of this town. (1841-10-30, 3:3, D)

807. Oct. 24th, at Newbliss, the lady of Richard Mayne, Esq., of a son. (1841-10-30, 3:3, B)

808. On the 3d instant, in the Church of Cashel, by the Rev. Thomas Newenham, the Rev. John Hare, Rector of Tully-Corbet, county of Monaghan, to Mary, eldest daughter of Mathew Pennefather, Esq., of Newpark, County of Tipperary. (1841-11-06, 3:2, M)

809. October 24, at Piercestown, by the Rev. Mr. Codd, Dr. Andrew Furlong, Kilmore, to Eliza, only daughter of Mr. James Clifford, Drinage Lodge, county Wexford, and sister to the late Captain William Clifford, 39th Regiment Bengal N.I. (1841-11-06, 3:2, M)

810. October 22, in Raphoe Cathedral, by the Rev. Thomas Irwin, Robert Montgomery, Esq., Civil

Engineer, Lifford, to Sarah, second daughter of Captain John Crawley, of the Constabulary. (1841-11-06, 3:2, M)

811. October 24, (his birth day), at Grangegorman-lane, aged 86 years, Lieutenant Francis Little, of the Royal Navy, second son of William Little, Esq., late Secretary to the Paving Board and brother of Dr. Little, of Sligo. (1841-11-06, 3:2, D)

812. On the 7th instant, at the residence of her father, by the Very Rev. Dean Bellew, Surgeon Rooney, Enniskillen, to Mary Anne, eldest daughter of James M'Kenna, Esq., Willville, Monaghan. (1841-11-20, 2:5, M)

813. November 18, in St. Andrew's Church, Dublin, by the Dean of Cashel, uncle to the bride, the Rev. William Watkins Deering, of Derrybrusk, in the county Fermanagh, to Elizabeth, second daughter of Charles James Adams, Esq., of Shinan House, in the county of Cavan. (1841-11-20, 2:5, M)

814. November 4, at Worleston Hall, Cheshire, Margaret Alsager Pollock, wife of Major R.C. Pollock, late 90th Light Infantry, and formerly of the 27th Enniskillen Regiment. (1841-11-20, 2:5, D)

815. Nov. 18, in George's Church, Dublin, by the Rev. Jas. Mathews, Rector of Bathcore [sic], Joseph Montgomery, Esq., eldest son of Richard Montgomery, Esq., of North Great George's-street, Dublin, and Cootehill, county Cavan, to Marianne, only daughter of H.B. Slator, Esq., of White Hill, Longford, and Belville, county of Meath. (1841-11-27, 3:2, M)

816. By the Rev. George Crolly, Mr. Robert Dillon, formerly of Drumespill, county Tyrone, and now of Belfast, to Anne, relict of the late Mr. Luke Wilson, of Belfast. (1841-11-27, 3:2, M)

817. On the 21st instant, at Belfast, Mr. James Garkin, York-street, painter, to Mrs. Logan, Melbourne-street, Belfast. (1841-11-27, 3:2, M)

818. On the 16th instant, William Park, jun. Esq., of Stewartstown, to Isabella, second daughter of Mr. Joseph Dudgeon, of Stewartstown. (1841-11-27, 3:2, M)

819. Sept. 4, at Charlestown, Mississippi, of fever, the Rev. Guy R. Pincking, youngest son of the late Rev. W. Pincking, Rector of Carrickmacross, county of Monaghan, aged 30 years, leaving a widow and two children. (1841-11-27, 3:2, D)

820. Nov. 16, at the house of his brother, Mr. West, 154, Capel-street, Dublin, Mr. John West, of Monaghan, in his 70th year. (1841-11-27, 3:2, D)

821. November 22, at his house, No. 18, Baggot-street, Dublin, Isaac D'Olier, Esq., LL.D., Treasurer to the Ecclesiastical Commissioners, aged 70 years, after a lengthened illness. (1841-11-27, 3:2, D)

822. November 29, in St. George's Church, by the Rev. Thos. Shaw, A.M., Hugh MacCaldin, to Eliza, eldest daughter of William Garner, Esq., of Belfast. (1841-12-04, 3:2, M)

823. Nov. 19, in Kilcronaghan Church, by the Rev. George Harris, John Burges Mee, Esq., of Music Hall, Tubbermore, to Jane, youngest daughter of Captain Godfrey, Leitrim House. (1841-12-04, 3:2, M)

824. November 14, at Brighton, Ellen, relict of Charles Albert Leslie, Esq., of Ballybay, in this county. (1841-12-04, 3:2, D)

825. November 20, in Ballyshannon, Mary Anne, third daughter of John Hardinge, Captain and Adjutant of the Donegal Militia. (1841-12-04, 3:2, D)

826. Nov. 24, at her house, Banbridge, county Down, in the 87th year of her age, Miss Euphemia Henry, only surviving sister of the late Mr. Robert Henry, of Dalkey Lodge, in the county of Dublin. (1841-12-04, 3:2, D)

827. Nov. 26, at Cheltenham, after an illness which commenced in Halifax, Nova Scotia, where he was employed on the staff of Major-General Sir Jeremiah Dickson, as Assistant Military Secretary, and in consequence of a recent cold contracted on his journey to this place, George Patrick O'Malley, Esq., late Captain in her Majesty's 88th Regiment. (1841-12-04, 3:2, D)

828. On the 29th of September, at St. Luke's Church, Antigua, by the Rev. Robert Holberton, A.M., David Brown, Esq., to Catherine Warwicha, eldest daughter of the Hon. Thomas Sanderson, Speaker of the Assembly, and Master in Chancery of said island, and grand-daughter of Robert Hyndman, Esq., (formerly of said island,) and now of 4, Belvidere-place, Dublin. (1841-12-11, 2:5, M)

829. Dec. 3, in St. Ann's Church, Belfast, by the Rev. A.C. Macartney, Vicar, and previously on the 23d of July, at Newtownbreda, John Gregg Murray, Esq., of Victoria-place, eldest son of the late James Murray, Esq., of Tully, county of Antrim, to Matilda, only daughter of William Edmonston, Esq., of Belvidere-place, Belfast. (1841-12-11, 2:5, M)

830. On the 4th instant, of consumption, at the residence of his father, in Cavan, Surgeon John H. Murray, late of London, in the 27th year of his age. He was an only son, and very much esteemed by all who knew him—yet his afflicted relatives had the consolation of witnessing his departure with a firm reliance on the merits of his crucified Saviour. (1841-12-11, 2:5, D)

831. November 18, at Cullenswood-avenue, near Dublin, aged 80 years, Miss Eleanor Devereux, sincerely and most deservedly regretted. (1841-12-11, 2:5, D)

832. December 5, at the residence of his son, Aughamore, county of Roscommon, in the 74th year of his age, John Lawder, Esq. (1841-12-11, 2:5, D)

833. At his residence in Tralee, in his 56th year, Charles Eager, Esq., proprietor of the *Kerry Evening Post.* He was generous, hospitable, an excellent friend, and liberal without ostentation in charity and benevolence. (1841-12-11, 2:5, D)

834. At Antigua, on the 19th of October, in the 54th year of her age, Mary Elizabeth, wife of the Hon. Thomas Sanderson, Speaker of the House of Assembly, Antigua, and eldest daughter of Robert Hyndman, Esq., (formerly of that island,) and now of 4, Belvidere-place, Dublin. (1841-12-11, 2:5, D)

835. At Ballymacrook, county Wexford, on Thursday sen., two sisters, Anastasia and Mary Furlong, the former 103, and the latter 105 years of age. They literally lived and died together, and their mortal remains now occupy the same resting-place. (1841-12-11, 2:5, D)

836. November 25, by the Rev. J. Sullivan, James Church, of Oatlands, Esq., in the county of Londonderry, to Barbara, only daughter of the late William Graham, Esq., of same county. (1841-12-18, 3:2, M)

837. December 9, at her house in Wellington-place, Belfast, Eleanor, wife of Hans S. Elsmere, Esq. Captain, Royal Navy. (1841-12-18, 3:2, D)

838. Dec. 5, at Larne, county Antrim, in the 67th year of his age, Henry William Baylee, Esq., formerly of Limerick, a gentleman whose name will be long remembered in that city, in connexion with the various charitable institutions, particularly on account of his fearless and indefatigable exertions to allay the ravages of typhus fever during the epidemic of 1817 and 1818. (1841-12-18, 3:2, D)

839. In Kilmore Church, on Wednesday, December 23, by Rev. Mr. Lloyd, Henry Hyde, Esq., Scotch-street, Armagh, to Mary, third daughter of the late John Atkinson, Esq., Fairview House, County Armagh. (1841-12-25, 2:5, M)

840. On Friday, the 17th instant, in Enniskillen Church, by the Rev. R.P. Cleary, Mr. William Alexander, printer, to Miss Elizabeth Miller, of that town. (1841-12-25, 2:5, M)

841. December 13, by the Rev. E.H. Allen, Presbyterian Minister of Athlone, the Rev. Wm. Crotty, Presbyterian Minister of Birr, to Kate, fifth daughter of the late Richd. Dempsey, Esq., of Mountmellick, and niece to the late Major-General Hays, of that town. (1841-12-25, 2:5, M)

842. December 21, in St. Anne's Church, Dublin, by the Rev. George Harris, of Kilcronaghan Glebe, county of Derry, Robert Holmes, eldest son of Randal Borough, Esq., of Cappa House, county of Clare, J.P., to Caroline, youngest daughter of the late Hugh Harris, Esq., of Ashfield, county of Armagh, and grand-daughter of the late John Porter, D.D., Lord Bishop of Clogher. (1841-12-25, 2:5, M)

843. December 15, by the Rev. William Castlemain, Samuel Jackson Cassidy, Esq., of Glenbrook, Magherafelt, to Miss Margaret Herron, daughter of the late Sir Robert Herron. (1841-12-25, 2:5, M)

844. December 14, Joseph M'Guire, Esq., of Heath Lodge, county of Cavan. (1841-12-25, 2:5, D)

845. December 18, at his residence, 7, Fitzwilliam-square, North, Hugh Faulkner, Esq., aged 64, sincerely and deservedly regretted. (1841-12-25, 2:5, D)

846. Dec. 20, at Stephen's-green, Dublin, Frances Haversham, wife of Dr. Ireland, after an illness of only thirty hours. (1841-12-25, 2:5, D)

847. On the 9th ult, by the Rev. J.P. Dickey, Mr. William Taylor, of Donoughmore, to Mary, only daughter, of the late John Harper, Esq., of Carnone. (1842-01-01, 1:3, M)

848. On Tuesday morning, at half-past six o'clock, at her residence, Hill, Monaghan, in her 23d year, after a short and painful illness, of effusion on the brain, Elizabeth, the beloved wife of Richard Mitchell, Esq., Solicitor, and eldest daughter of the late Henry Wright, Esq., of this town. In every relation of life, she was beloved and respected, and her melancholy death, which occurred in a few days after her accouchment, has cast a gloom over the thoughts of all who knew her. (1842-01-08, 2:5, D)

849. On Wednesday, at the residence of the lady's father, by the Rev. John Bleckley, Presbyterian Minister, Rev. John Lyons, to Jane, eldest daughter of David Horner, Esq., of this town. (1842-01-15, 3:3, M)

850. In the Church of Monaghan, on Saturday, the 15th inst., by the Rev. Henry Maffett, Thomas Spiller, Esq., of Londonderry, to Susanna, eldest daughter of Dr. James Geo. Lepper, of this town. (1842-01-22, 3:2, M)

851. January 13, by the Rev. Robert Johnston, in the Parish Church of Aughnamullen, Mr. Alexander Park, Woollen-draper, Castleblaney, to Mary Jane, third daughter of the late Isaiah Oliver, Esq., Derryrusk, county Monaghan. (1842-01-22, 3:2, M)

852. On the 12th inst. in Omagh, aged 63 years, John Buchanan, Esq. In his death, Omagh has lost one of its most respectable and valued inhabitants. He was mild, unassuming, kind, charitable, and humane—a true and steady friend—and, as a husband and a father, he was all that a fond wife and a loving family can deplore. (1842-01-22, 3:2, D)

853. On the 16th inst. aged 13 years, Eliza Anne Jackson, daughter to Mr. John Jackson, Newtownlimavady. She possessed great amiability of disposition, gentleness of manners, and filial affection. (1842-01-22, 3:2, D)

854. On the 7th inst., in the 48th year of her age, Margaret, daughter of the late Joseph Blake Esq., Marymount, near Dromore. (1842-01-22, 3:2, D)

855. Nov. 22d, at Naples, John Henry Vaughan, Esq. He was Judge Advocate to the Mauritius; his widow is daughter to Judge Blackburn, and niece to Lords Craven and Seaton, who, with one child, is left to deplore his loss. His sister, the wife of the Rev. George D'Arcy Irvine, was in daily expectation of his arrival in this country when the lamentable account of his death reached her. (1842-01-22, 3:2, D)

856. On the 10th instant, at Seaview, near Belfast, Mrs. Quinn, aged 68 years, relict of the late Henry Quinn, Esq., of Newry. (1842-01-22, 3:2, D)

857. On the 13th instant, at Kingstown, where she was removed for the benefit of her health, Miss Anne Atkinson, of the County Armagh. (1842-01-22, 3:2, D)

858. At Dublin, after a few days' illness, Richard Robinson Ellis, Esq. many years Proprietor of *The Warder* Newspaper. (1842-01-22, 3:2, D)

859. At Earlsgift, Tyrone, aged 17, Charles, second son of the Hon. and Rev. Charles Douglas. (1842-01-22, 3:2, D)

860. On the 4th inst., at Derrygonelly, Elizabeth Sarah, relict of the late Walter Bell, Esq., Dungannon, and youngest daughter of the late Rev. Thos. Vaughan Vesey, many years Rector of Drumglass, Co. of Tyrone, in the 85th year of her age. (1842-01-22, 3:2, D)

861. January 12, Captain John Alegeo, of Ravarra, near Saintfield, county Down, aged 38 years. (1842-01-22, 3:2, D)

862. On the 23d instant, in Cavan, after a protracted and painful illness, the lady of Lieutenant L. Canavan, Recruiting Officer. (1842-01-29, 3:2, D)

863. The 21st ult., at her residence, Redhill, of decline, aged twelve years, Elizabeth Howe, daughter of Mr. William Howe, postmaster. She was universally beloved by all her relations, friends, and acquaintances, who shall ever deeply regret the removal of her from among them. (1842-02-05, 3:1, D)

864. The 26th ult., at her residence in Clenfad, aged forty years, Arabella Lyttle, wife to Mr. Daniel Bell, of consumption, which she bore for the last four years with the greatest Christian fortitude, leaving behind her five children besides a numerous and respectable circle of friends to deeply deplore her loss. (1842-02-05, 3:1, D)

865. On the 28th ult., in Cavan, at the advanced age of 72 years, Mrs. Newman, relict of the late Mr. Robert Newman of that town, she was one of its oldest inhabitants. (1842-02-05, 3:1, D)

866. Feb. 9, 1842, at Liscarney, the lady of John Richardson, Esq., of a daughter. (1842-02-12, 3:1, B)

867. On the 12th inst., at the residence of the lady's brother, Newry, by the Rev. James Shields, James Lougheed, of Aughnacloy, county of Tyrone, Esq., to Elizabeth, eldest daughter of William Lockart, Esq., Tullyn, Newry. (1842-02-19, 3:3, M)

868. On the 15th inst., by the Rev. James Thompson, Drum, the Rev. Josias Mitchell, to Margaret Orr, first daughter of the Rev. Andrew Johnston, Newbliss. (1842-02-19, 3:3, M)

869. On the 6th inst., at his residence in this town, aged 75 years, Mr. James Doogan, an old and respectable inhabitant. (1842-02-19, 3:3, D)

870. On the 12th instant, at her residence, Tullyleer, within one mile of this town, Mary, relict of the late Mr. Robert Greacen, aged 70 years. She was one of the kindest mothers—charitable to the poor—kind and affectionate to all her friends and neighbours, and is generally lamented by all who knew her. (1842-02-19, 3:3, D)

871. At her residence in Rockcorry, on Monday, the 7th inst., after a few days' illness, Miss Mary Wilson. Her loss has left a great vacuum in a large circle of her friends and acquaintances, whose only consolation is, that she is not dead "but sleepeth," in sure and certain hope of a joyful resurrection. The large and respectable concourse which followed her remains to the place of interment told how she was esteemed and respected. (1842-02-19, 3:3, D)

872. On the 11th inst. at Crimlin, near Cavan, Mr. John T. Howse, late of Farnham, in the 58th year of his age. (1842-02-19, 3:3, D)

873. February 28th, 1842, at the house of Mr. S. Richardson, merchant, of consumption, in the 29th year of his age, Robert Hill Wilkinson, Esq., third son of Charles Wilkinson, Esq., of Tipperary. (1842-03-05, 2:5, D)

874. On the 9th instant, in St. George's Church, Dublin, by the Dean of Cashel, Chas. Coote, Esq. M.D., of 3, Upper Temple-street, second son of the late Major Coote, and grandson of the late Earl of Bellamont, to Mary, second daughter of Sir John Cooper, of 23, Lower Gardiner-street. (1842-03-12, 3:5, M)

875. On Friday, the 11th inst., in Castleblayney church, by the Rev. J.T. Whitestone, Samuel Clarke, of Rosslea, to Eliza, second daughter of Mr. Thomas M'Cann, of Castleblayney. (1842-03-12, 3:5, M)

876. February 19, in London, Louisa, daughter of the late Edward Young, Esq., of Knockbane Cottage, Tynan, county of Armagh, to Thomas Clarke, Esq., Upper Berkeley-street, Portman-square. (1842-03-12, 3:5, M)

877. On the 1st inst., by the Rev. Mr. Sweney, Presbyterian Minister of Croghan, John Browne, Esq., of Drumheriff, near Cootehill, second son of Archibald Browne, Esq., of Greenmount, to Margaret, fourth daughter of James Berry, Esq., of Croghan, near Killeshandra. (1842-03-12, 3:5, M)

878. On the 3d inst., in the Church of Tullycorbet, county Monaghan, by the Rev. John Hare, Henry Gilbert, Esq., of Corderrybane, to Miss Agnes Nesbit, of Drumlongfield, in this county. (1842-03-12, 3:5, M)

879. On the 24th ult., by the Rev. H. Cooke, D.D., L.L.D., Mr. James Nesbitt, North-street, Belfast, to Miss Shaw, Lagan Village. (1842-03-12, 3:5, M)

880. On the 27th ult., at Torquay, Devonshire, of consumption, Henry Jones O'Hara, only son of Henry O'Hara, of Portstewart, county of Londonderry, Esq. He had been pursuing studies at Oxford, and was a youth of strong intelligent mind, and considerable promise. His high honourable principles, amiable disposition and manners, endeared him to his disconsolate parents and all who knew him. (1842-03-12, 3:5, D)

881. On the 2d inst., at Rosebank, Sarah, wife of the Rev. Alexander Patterson, of Magherally, aged 71 years, and last surviving daughter of the late David Bleakley, Esq., of Greenvale, near Keady. (1842-03-12, 3:5, D)

882. On the 24th ult., at the advanced age of 89 years, James Hamilton, Esq., Corkey, near Ballymoney. (1842-03-12, 3:5, D)

883. On the 28th ult., at Donaghadee, in the 45th year of his age, William A. Getty, Esq., J.P., principal Coast Officer of Customs. (1842-03-12, 3:5, D)

884. On the 25th ult., at Downpatrick, in her 81st year, Mrs. Abigail Nevin, widow of the late William Nevin, Esq. (1842-03-12, 3:5, D)

885. On the 27th ult., at Leek, near Glasslough, Hannah, wife of William Cochran, Esq. (1842-03-12, 3:5, D)

886. On the 15th instant, by the Rev. Dr. Campbell, the Rev. John H. Morell, of Fairview, near Ballybay, to Mary, fourth daughter of the late John Russell, Esq., of Newry. (1842-03-26, 3:3, M)

887. March 15, at Mountjoy-square, Dublin, Henrietta, daughter of James Nixon, of Prospect, county Fermanagh, Esq. (1842-03-26, 3:3, D)

888. At Bath, John Alexander, Esq., aged 80 years, to Miss Bewley, of Quemerford-common, aged 18 years. The youthful bride is grandniece to the antiquated bridegroom. (1842-04-16, 3:3, M)

889. To the deep regret of his friends, killed in the pass of Khoord Cabul, Major Henry Walter Bellew, Assistant-Quarter-Master-General, Bengal Army, fourth and late second surviving son of the late Robert Bellew, Esq., of Ballendiness, Castle Martyr, county of Cork. (1842-04-16, 3:3, D)

890. On Thursday last, at Enniskillen, Mrs. Nixon, wife of George Alcock Nixon, Esq., of that town. (1842-04-16, 3:3, D)

891. On Saturday, the 2d inst., at his residence, Derrycourtney, near Caledon, Mr. Phillip Henderson, aged 80 years. (1842-04-16, 3:3, D)

892. On the 23d ult., aged 83, Sarah, widow of the late Mr. Thomas Bunting, of Portadown, architect. (1842-04-16, 3:3, D)

893. On the 26th Feb., at Genoa, Mrs. Sneyd, relict of the late Nathaniel Sneyd, Esq., many years M.P. for the County of Cavan. (1842-04-16, 3:3, D)

894. April 15, at St. George's Church, Dublin, — Atkinson, of No. 16, Upper Rutland-street, Esq., Barrister-at-Law, eldest son of Thomas J. Atkinson, of Cavan Garden, county Donegal, Esq., to Ellen, second daughter of Robert D. Mecredy, of Carnew House, county Down, and No. 2 Fitzgibbon-street, Dublin, Barrister-at-Law. (1842-04-23, 3:2, M)

895. April 19, in St. George's Church, John Kenneth Mackenzie, Esq., of the 60th Rifles, only son of the late Lieut. General John Mackenzie, of Belmaduthie, Rossshire, to Harriet Louisa, daughter of Edward Litton, Esq., q.c. and m.p. for Coleraine. (1842-04-23, 3:2, M)

896. April 22, at 20, Hanover-square, London, the Lady Cremorne, of a son and heir. (1842-04-30, 3:2, B)

897. On the 20th instant, in Lisburn Church, Francis Glenfield, jun., Esq., nephew of Francis Glenfield, Esq., Cromac, to Eleanor, daughter of Hugh Seeds, Esq., of Lisburn. (1842-04-30, 3:2, M)

898. On the 24th instant at Ballymacarrett, by the Rev. Mr. M'Ginity, Mr. John Faloon, of Belfast, to Miss Rose Ann M'Kenna, of Ballynafeigh. (1842-04-30, 3:2, M)

899. At her residence, Chichester-street, Belfast, on the 26th instant, Elizabeth, relict of the late Thomas M'Comb, Esq., merchant, deceased. (1842-04-30, 3:2, D)

900. In Margaret-street, Newry, in the 83d year of his age, Thomas Wilson, Esq., deeply and universally regretted. (1842-04-30, 3:2, D)

901. On the 6th instant, at Huntly, N.B., the Rev. James Walker, aged 84, for upwards of sixty years Incumbent of the Episcopal Church in that place. (1842-04-30, 3:2, D)

902. May 2, by the Rev. J. Collins, A. Durham, Esq., M.D., of the East India Company's Service, to Mary, eldest daughter of John Crozier, Esq., M.D., of Mullaghmore, near Caledon, county Tyrone. (1842-05-07, 3:5, M)

903. May 3, in St. George's Church, by the Rev. John Gregg, the Rev. William Morgan, Incumbent of St. James', Clithero, Lancashire, to Elizabeth, eldest daughter of Charles Cochrane, Esq., of Grove, county Donegal. (1842-05-07, 3:5, M)

904. May 1, in the 26th year of her age, at 9, Earl-street, Belfast, after a long period of suffering, Agnes, the beloved wife of Mr. Wm. Thetford, Officer of Customs, and second daughter of Mr. William Nocher, Arthur-street, Belfast. (1842-05-07, 3:5, D)

905. May 9, at Glynch Lodge, near Newbliss, the lady of the Rev. George H. Reade, of a son. (1842-05-14, 3:5, B)

906. May 4, in the Church of Trory, by the Rev. Thomas Ovenden, Rector of Magheracross, Mr. Abraham Dawson, Primitive Wesleyan Preacher, Ballyshannon, to Anne Jane, only daughter of Thomas Graham, Esq., Knockmanowl. (1842-05-14, 3:5, M)

907. On the 26th ultimo, John Johnston Brice, aged two years, youngest son of William M. Brice, Esq., of Cavan. (1842-05-14, 3:5, D)

908. In Castleblayney, on the 28th ult., at the advanced age of 76 years, Mr. James Rule, innkeeper, much and deservedly regretted by a large circle of friends and acquaintances. (1842-05-14, 3:5, D)

909. May 10, at her residence, Urney Park, near Strabane, much regretted, at an advanced age, Lady Galbraith, widow of the late Sir James Galbraith, Bart. (1842-05-14, 3:5, D)

910. May 9, at Dungannon, county of Tyrone, Miss Pettigrew, to the inconsolable affliction of her numerous friends and relatives, and to the severe loss of the poor of her neighbourhood, over whom she watched with parental care. (1842-05-14, 3:5, D)

911. May 8, in London, where he had arrived from China on sick leave, in his 18th year, Lieutenant Henry Southwell Coote, 37th Madras N.I., youngest surviving son of Chas. Coote Forest, Esq., deeply and deservedly lamented. (1842-05-14, 3:5, D)

912. On the 17th inst., by the Rev. V.D. Christian, in Clough Church, Samuel Clarke, Esq., of Cortrasna, to Miss Sally Anne, daughter of Benjamin Whitsitt, Esq., Rosslea. (1842-05-21, 3:1, M)

913. On the 3d inst., by the Rev. Mr. Boyde, Presbyterian Minister of Castleblayney, Mr. James Wilson, merchant, of Castleblayney, to Margaret, second daughter of Mr. Robert Harrison, of the Moy, county Monaghan. (1842-05-21, 3:1, M)

914. In George's Church, Dublin, and also by the Rev. Philip Farrelly, P.P., Moynalty, Joseph Francis Hopkins, of Possentown, in the county of Meath, Esq., to Eliza, daughter of the late Martin Tucker, of Petersville, in the same county, and relict of Hugh Parker, Esq. of Dundalk. (1842-05-21, 3:1, M)

915. On the 12th instant, by the Rev. E. Stewart, Clough, the Rev. Samuel Nicholson, Hillsborough, to Margaret, daughter of Mr. John Moore, of Knocksticken. (1842-05-21, 3:1, M)

916. On Sunday, the 15th inst., in Ballymacarrett, by the Rev. Francis M'Ginnety, C.C., at the house of the bride's father, Mr. Thomas Campbell, Belfast, to Miss Jane Gilmor, of Ballymacarrett. (1842-05-21, 3:1, M)

917. On Thursday evening last, of fever, at seven o'clock, at his house in Glasslough-street, Monaghan, Mr. George Moore, Coach Agent and Clerk of Petty Sessions. Mr. Moore was a man whose superior abilities and business habits rendered him an acquisition to the community in which he lived, and his death is sincerely deplored by all who knew him. He has left a wife and a young and helpless family to mourn his loss. (1842-05-21, 3:1, D)

918. On the 8th inst., aged 18, three days after his arrival in Europe, from China, at Chapel-street, South Audley-street, London, Lieutenant Henry S. Coote, of the Hon. E.I.C. Service, 37th Native Infantry, son of Charles Coote, Esq., of Bellamont Forest, county Cavan, and nephew of the late Lord Cremorne. (1842-05-21, 3:1, D)

919. May 13, after a few days' illness, Mr. John M'Dermott, aged 56 years, late of Dame-street, and formerly of Ormond-quay, one of the most respectable traders of this city for upwards of 30 years. His death has left a numerous and truly afflicted family wholly unprovided for. (1842-05-21, 3:1, D)

920. On the 12th inst., at her house, Armagh, Ellen, wife of J. Caulfield M'Kinstry, Esq., sub-sheriff of said county. (1842-05-21, 3:1, D)

921. May 12, at Drumrohill, Enniskillen, the residence of his father, George, eldest son of the Rev. Andrew Staples Clarke, aged 23 years. (1842-05-21, 3:1, D)

922. May 20, at the Rectory House, Castleblayney, the lady of the Rev. John T. Whitestone, of a son. (1842-05-28, 3:2, B)

923. May 23, at Cavan, the lady of the Rev. Decimus Wm. Preston, of a son. (1842-05-28, 3:2, B)

924. May 24, Mr. Edward T. Armstrong, of Ross, in the county of Fermanagh, to Anne Dawson, third daughter of the late Robert Henry, Esq., of Cookstown. (1842-05-28, 3:2, M)

925. On the 19th instant, in St. Peter's Church, Dublin, the Rev. William Filgate, of Magherally Glebe, county of Down, eldest son of Thomas William Filgate, of Arthurstown, county of Louth, Esq., to Louisa, third daughter of the late Rev. Henry Mahon. (1842-05-28, 3:2, M)

926. At his residence, Killenure, county Cavan, on the 18th instant, Lieutenant William Smyth, late of the Royal Dublin City Militia, aged 58 years. He was a sincere friend and an affectionate parent, universally beloved, and shall ever be deservedly and deeply regretted by all who had the pleasure and felicity of his acquaintance. (1842-05-28, 3:2, D)

927. On the 19th instant at Port Nelligan, Tynan, aged 74 years, after a long and lingering illness, Alexander Cross, Esq. (1842-05-28, 3:2, D)

928. On the 17th instant, at Ballystockard, near Comber, Hans Sinclair, Esq., in the 64th year of his age. (1842-05-28, 3:2, D)

929. On the 16th instant, at Ligoniel, aged 16 years, Sarah, sixth daughter of Mr. Thomas Darling, formerly of Belfast. (1842-05-28, 3:2, D)

930. On the 16th instant, Agnes, relict of the late Arthur Magennis, contiguous to Knockmore, near Lisburn, aged 101 years and ten months. She was a widow above half a century, and lived respected in her circle of relatives and acquaintances, and is much regretted by a numerous progeny. (1842-05-28, 3:2, D)

931. On the 15th inst., suddenly, at Stormont, Castleconnell, Lady De Burgho, relict of the late Sir John De Burgho, Bart., daughter of the late Colonel Waller, of Castle Waller, county Tipperary, and grand-daughter of the Marquis of Clanricarde. (1842-05-28, 3:2, D)

932. On Wednesday last, in the Church of this town, by the Rev. Henry Maffett, Joseph Wallace, Esq., of Ballaghnaid, county of Tyrone, to Jane, eldest daughter of Mr. William Alexander Barns. (1842-06-04, 3:2, M)

933. May 28, in Delgany Church, by the Rev. Francis Furlong, A.M., Edward Mayne Wadsworth, Esq., of Trinity College, Dublin, youngest son of Dawson Wadsworth, Esq., of this city, to Kate, second daughter of the late Robert Manning, Esq., of Mount Corballis, county of Wicklow. (1842-06-04, 3:2, M)

934. June 1, in St. Peter's Church, by the Rev. T.P. Brady, the Rev. D. Carlile Courtenay, Incumbent of Ballyeaston, county Antrim, to Dorothea, daughter of the late Francis T. Brady, Esq., of Willow Park, county of Dublin. (1842-06-04, 3:2, M)

935. May 23, at the residence of his son-in-law, Captain Robertson, of Tangier, Boyle, John Irwin, Esq., sen., of Camlin. (1842-06-04, 3:2, D)

936. May 21, at Portland-place, Glasgow, Catherine Anne, the wife of Robert Wilson, Esq., and second daughter of John Gibbs, Esq., of Upper Parnell-place, Dublin. (1842-06-04, 3:2, D)

937. At Marylebone Church, London, by the Rev. Henry Curtis Cherry, M.A., Rector of Burghfield, Berkshire, Edmond Percival, only son of the late Captain Morphy, of the Kilkenny Militia, to Susan, youngest daughter of John Gosling, Esq., Gloucester-place, Regent's-Park, London, and niece of the late John Cherry, Esq., Governor of Bombay. (1842-06-11, 2:6, M)

938. On the 3d instant, in the Cathedral, Lisburn, W.G. Robertson, Esq., of the Hon. E.I. Company's Service, son of the late Major Robertson, Perthshire, to Wilhelmina Wellington, third daughter of J.K. Clarke, Esq., Royal Artillery, Shamrockvale Lodge, Lisburn. (1842-06-11, 2:6, M)

939. On the 2d inst., at St. Bride's Church Liverpool, the Rev. Frederick W. Mant, second son of the Bishop of Down, Connor, and Dromore, to Isabella Connell, youngest daughter of J.T. Alston, Esq., of Abercrombie-square Liverpool. (1842-06-11, 2:6, M)

940. On the 31st ult., Dr. M'Dowell, of Maherafelt, to Miss Ann Crawford, of Winneyhaw, near Coleraine. (1842-06-11, 2:6, M)

941. In the city of Jackson, Mississippe [sic], Jane, wife of Major Wheelan, and eldest daughter of the late Doctor Sheil, of Ballyshannon. (1842-06-11, 2:6, D)

942. June 9, in Caledon Church, by the Rev. Wm. Maclean, Prebendary of Tyrone, the Rev. Stephen Radcliffe, of Lisnadill, to Mary Jane, only daughter of the late James Prentice, Esq. (1842-06-18, 3:1, M)

943. June 13, in Newtownards Church, by the Rev. Townley Blackwood, Mr. James Jamison, to Mary Patterson, only daughter of the late Samuel Patterson, Esq., Newtownards. (1842-06-18, 3:1, M)

944. May 28, by special license, by the Rev. Dr. Handcock, D.D., in St. Thomas's Church, William Andrew Dudgeon, Esq., Eden-quay, to the amiable and accomplished Miss Murphy, daughter of the late Arthur Knox Murphy, Esq. formerly of Lark-hill, county of Sligo. (1842-06-18, 3:1, M)

945. On the 7th instant, at his residence in Newry, Samuel Bell, Esq., aged 78 years. He was one of the oldest inhabitants, and esteemed and respected by all who knew him. (1842-06-18, 3:1, D)

946. At Montdruid, in the 88th year of his age, the Reverend Robert Trail, for 65 years Rector of the Parish of Ballintoy, Diocese of Connor. (1842-06-18, 3:1, D)

947. On the 25th ult., at Longdon in his 25th year, Billy Richardson. He was the tallest man in the neighbourhood, being as he lay in his shroud 6 [or 9?] feet 0[?] inches in height. (1842-06-18, 3:1, D) *Note: the numbers are blurred in the original.*

948. June 17, in Merrion-square, the lady of Loftus Tottenham, Esq., of daughter. (1842-06-25, 3:3, B)

949. June 21st, at Howth Church, by the Rev. Arthur Irwin, uncle to the bride, Maria, only daughter of the late Wm. MacLaughlin, Esq., R.N., of Ramilton, to Baptist J. Barton, Esq., Greenfort, county Donegal. (1842-06-25, 3:3, M)

950. In this town, on Sunday last, by the Rev. Mr. Maguire, C.C., Mr. P. Fallon, Master Tailor, to Miss Mary Keen. (1842-06-25, 3:3, M)

951. June 20, after a lingering illness, which she bore with patience and resignation, in her twenty-second year, at her residence, Mill-street, Jane, the beloved wife of A.W. Holmes, Esq., Editor and Proprietor of this paper, and second daughter of the late Henry Wright, Esq., of this town. (1842-06-25, 3:3, D)

952. On Friday morning, at Dromore, County Down, of disease of the liver, in the prime of life, after a few days' illness, Mr. John Clarke, of Monaghan, builder, sincerely and deservedly regretted by a wide spread connection, to whom he was endeared by a kind disposition, and a benevolent heart. The remains will be interred in Ballyalbany Church-yard, on Sunday evening, at 6 o'clock, and will leave Dromore, at 4 o'clock, A.M., passing through Aughnacloy at 1, P.M., and Emyvale at 3, P.M. (1842-06-25, 3:3, D)

953. June 28, at Newcastle, county of Down, the lady of P. Brenan, Esq., of a son. (1842-07-02, 3:3, B)

954. June 27, at Kilwood Vicarage, county of Down, the lady of the Rev. J. Perkins Garrett, of a son. (1842-07-02, 3:3, B)

955. On the 24th inst., by the Rev. John Rutherford, John Hutchinson, Esq., of Brague, to Martha, daughter of T. Hutchinson, Esq., of Banbridge. (1842-07-02, 3:3, M)

956. On the 20th instant, by the Rev. Edwd. Johnson, Wesleyan Minister, Dungannon, the Rev. William Hoey, Wesleyan Minister, of same place, to Miss Barnett, daughter of the late Moses Barnett, Esq., Stranford [sic], and niece to Mrs. Foster, Armagh. (1842-07-02, 3:3, M)

957. June 21, in Newmills Church, Drumglass, by the Rev. R. Darley, the Rev. W.J. Thornhill, of Arklow, to Mary Anne, only surviving child of the late Richard G.H. Young, Esq., of Cookstown, county of Tyrone. (1842-07-02, 3:3, M)

958. At Warrenpoint, on Friday last, aged 32 years, Mr. Thomas Knox, Armagh. For a long time he had been labouring under consumption, which he bore with exemplary patience; and while the dark shades of death were excluding from his mortal view terrestrial objects, supported by the immediate prospect of unfading unhappiness, his soul seemed more firmly stayed on his Redeemer, in whose merits alone he trusted; and while his beloved pastor was addressing the throne of grace on his behalf, his happy spirit took its flight to its merciful Creator.

He is gone to the grave, but we will not deplore him,
As Christ was his ransom, his guardian, his guide;
He gave him, he took him, and soon will restore him,
For death has no sting since the Saviour has died.

The immense concourse that attended his remains to their last resting place, showed that he was sincerely lamented and deservedly respected. (1842-07-02, 3:3, D)

959. On the 28th inst., of consumption, in the house of Mr. Samuel Bell, Mr. Joshua Fielding, aged 47 years, professor of music, and son-in-law to Dr. Fletcher, of Eden Cottage, near Carrickfergus. (1842-07-02, 3:3, D)

960. On the 25th instant, aged 39 years, Mr. John Shaw, Great Edward-street, Belfast. (1842-07-02, 3:3, D)

961. At Stonehouse, near Plymouth, on Monday last, Major-General Harry Perceval Lewis, R.M., in his 75th year.—He had served in many of the naval engagements during the last war in the royal marines, and was promoted to the Colonelcy on the 28th of Dec., 1830, and at the last brevet was made Major-General. (1842-07-02, 3:3, D)

962. June 29, at Brandrum House, Monaghan, the lady of Robert Thompson, Esq., of a son. (1842-07-09, 3:4, B)

963. July 2, in Booterstown Church, by the Rev. Robert Herbert Nixon, George, second son of the late Joseph Spearing, Esq., of Cork, to Mary, youngest daughter of the late Charles Warner, Esq., of Carlow. (1842-07-09, 3:4, M)

964. July 1, in Ballymascanlon Church, by the Rev. H.T. Hobson, Wm. Wellington Godfrey, Esq., of her Majesty's Customs, Newry, to Harriet, only daughter of Benjamin Thompson, Esq., of Ravensdale, county Louth. (1842-07-09, 3:4, M)

965. July 4, at his residence, Analore, near Clones, George Moore, Esq., aged 57 years. (1842-07-09, 3:4, D)

966. At Upper Gloucester-street, Dublin, Bridget, wife of R. Young Reynolds, of Fort Lodge, county of Cavan, Esq. (1842-07-09, 3:4, D)

967. July 1, at his seat, Kilmore, county of Clare, after an illness of some weeks' duration, Poole Hickman, Esq., Deputy-Lieutenant. (1842-07-09, 3:4, D)

968. On the 28th ult., in the Bow Island, near Pettigo, Mr. George Allington, sen., in his 100th year. (1842-07-09, 3:4, D)

969. On the 28th ult., at his residence, Sea View House, county Sligo, R.W. Hillas, Esq., Barrister at Law, aged 72 years. (1842-07-09, 3:4, D)

970. On Tuesday last, at the Church of Crossduff, by the Rev. Edward Mayne, Francis Dawson, Esq., of Forest-view, county Monaghan, to Louisa Maria Steuart Corry, daughter of Thomas Charles Steuart Corry, Esq., D.L., J.P., and formerly M.P. for Monaghan. After the ceremony, the happy couple left on a tour. (1842-07-16, 3:3, M)

971. On the 8th inst., by the Rev. Dr. Henry of Armagh, at the house of the lady's father in Portadown, the Rev. James M'Kee, Missionary to India, in connexion with the General Assembly, to Jane, second daughter of William Beattie, Esq., of Portadown. (1842-07-16, 3:3, M)

972. In the parish Church of Mevagh, by the Rev. George Prior, Curate, on the 28th ult., the Rev. James Crawford Rector of said parish, to Susan, eldest daughter of the late Rev. John Wilkinson, formerly Rector of that parish. (1842-07-16, 3:3, M)

973. On the 30th ult., by the Rev. James Collins, A.M., Dromore, Mr. Moses Patterson, of Tullyglush, to Martha, daughter of the late Mr. Mathew Scott, of Drummillar. (1842-07-16, 3:3, M)

974. On the 7th instant, in Killaghter [sic] Church, County Donegal, the Rev. John Harris Jameson, F.T.C.D., eldest son of Captain Jameson, of Clonkeen, county Monaghan, to Mary Anne, second daughter of Acheson O'Brien, Esq., D.L., J.P., of Drumsilla, county Leitrim. (1842-07-16, 3:3, M)

975. On the 6th instant, at Brighton, Captain George Johnston, of the Coldstream Guards, eldest son of William Ponsonby Johnston, Esq., of Walton House, Cumberland, to Fredrica, second daughter of Colonel Sir F. Hankey, G.C.M.G. (1842-07-16, 3:3, M)

976. July 13, in St. Mary's Church, Newry, by the Rev. Dr. Campbell, Vicar of Newry, John T. Godfrey, Esq., Solicitor, to Martha, youngest daughter of the late Isaac Glenny, Esq., J.P. and Seneschal of Newry. (1842-07-16, 3:3, M)

977. At Kingstown, Theobald Gore Kenney, Esq., of Rock-savage, county Monaghan, to Thecia, daughter of the late D.H. Callen, of Phillipstown, county Louth. (1842-07-16, 3:3, M)

978. On the 13th inst., at Barkley's Grove, Mr. John Dalzell, of the College, Belfast, aged 20 years. (1842-07-16, 3:3, D)

979. On Thursday, the 7th inst., at Kilelean [sic], Castlederg, Mr. John M'Farland, aged 106 years. (1842-07-16, 3:3, D)

980. On the 23d ult., in the 70th year of her age, after a short illness, Rebecca, wife of Mr. John Storey, of Innish near Dungannon. (1842-07-16, 3:3, D)

981. On the 8th instant, suddenly, at the residence of her nephew, Maurice Collis, Esq., Merrion-square, Catherine, daughter of the late John Day, Esq., of Cork. (1842-07-16, 3:3, D)

982. On the 10th instant, at Claremont, Rathmines, Emily, only daughter of the Rev. James Mathew, Rector of Rathcore. (1842-07-16, 3:3, D)

983. On the 10th instant, Mary, wife of Richard J. Mathews, Esq., of Newbridge, county Westmeath. (1842-07-16, 3:3, D)

984. On the 12th instant, by the Rev. George Crolly, C.C., Mr. Martin Leeson, of Belfast, to Mary Ann, eldest daughter of the late Mr. John Johnston. (1842-07-23, 3:3, M)

985. In Inniskeal Church, on the 30th of June, by the bride's brother, the Rev. Knox Barrett, Galbraith Hamilton, Esq., Eden, County Donegall, to Mary, daughter of the Rev. M. Barrett, Rector of said place. (1842-07-23, 3:3, M)

986. On Thursday, the 14th instant, by the Rev. Richard Dill, of Ballykelly, Mr. William Patchell, of Walworth, to Miss Isabella, daughter of Mr. D. M'Farland, of Drumacony. (1842-07-23, 3:3, M)

987. In Enniskillen, on the 17th inst., Mrs. Bridget Creden, relict of the late Mr. Wm. Creden, aged 85 years. (1842-07-23, 3:3, D)

988. July 13, in Dublin, after a protracted illness, in his 45th year, Mr. Richard Johnston, veterinary surgeon. (1842-07-23, 3:3, D)

989. Mrs. Reynolds, wife of Richard Young Reynolds, Esq. of Ford Lodge, county Cavan, and sister and co-heiress of the late George Nugent Reynolds, and Mrs. Richard Macnamara, of Loughscur, county Leitrim. (1842-07-23, 3:3, D)

990. July 13, of typhus fever, at the residence of Mr. John Hayes, Harrington-street Dublin, Mr. Geo. Robinson, Preacher, in the Primitive Wesleyan Methodist Connexion, in the 32d year of his age, and 12th of his itinerancy. (1842-07-23, 3:3, D)

991. On the 21st ult. in Cootehill Church, by the Rev. Mr. Brabazon, Andrew Higginbotham, Esq., of Brampton, Upper Canada, to Mary, third daughter of John Higginbotham, merchant, Cootehill. (1842-08-06, 3:3, M)

992. On the 26th ult. by the Rev. James Denham, Londonderry, Mr. Joseph Ferris, merchant, to Sarah, youngest daughter of Mr. David Denny, of Calkil [sic], near Omagh. (1842-08-06, 3:3, M)

993. On Wednesday, the 27th ult., at his residence New-Mills, near Newbliss, John Harpur, Esq., aged 27 years, a young gentleman of the most amiable disposition, and greatly beloved by those who knew him. (1842-08-06, 3:3, D)

994. On Thursday last, after a few days' illness, in the prime of life, John Anketell, Esq., aged 35. His remains will leave his residence, Mount-Anketell, for interment at Errigle, on Sunday morning, at nine o'clock. (1842-08-06, 3:3, D)

995. On the 25th ult. at Banbridge, John Loftie, Esq., formerly of Tandragee, in the county of Armagh, in his 67th year. (1842-08-06, 3:3, D)

996. On the 17th ult. at Clough, aged 82 years, Mr. John Moffett, merchant. (1842-08-06, 3:3, D)

997. On the 21st ult. in Newry, after a few days' illness, of inflammation in the bowels, Mr. John Kidd, aged 31 years. (1842-08-06, 3:3, D)

998. On the 24th ult., at his residence, Rockville, Ballyshannon, of inflammation of the lungs, Thos. Wm. Crawford, Esq., for many years Surgeon of the Donegal Militia. (1842-08-06, 3:3, D)

999. At Grinan Cottage, Newry, on Friday the 29th ult., in the 26th year of his age, Thomas Denvir, Esq., Member of the Royal College of Surgeons, late of H.M.S. *Impregnable*. (1842-08-06, 3:3, D)

1000. At Belvidere Cottage, Belfast, on the 28th July, Wm. Allen, Esq., aged 32, late of Demerara. (1842-08-06, 3:3, D)

1001. July 24, at Boyle, in the hope of a glorious resurrection, Mrs. Rossborough, relict of the late John Rossborough, Esq., of Cloncaulfield House, county of Longford, and Mullinagoan House, county of Fermanagh. (1842-08-06, 3:3, D)

1002. August 8, at St. Peter's Church, John Pennefather, Esq., second son of the Hon. Baron Pennefather, to Eliza, daughter of the late Hon. Edward de Moleyns, and grand-daughter of Thomas Lord Ventry. (1842-08-13, 3:3, M)

1003. On the 4th inst., in Armagh Church, by the Rev. James Disney, Mr. William Burns, of Killyman, to Miss Anna Clark, Corrandonabally. (1842-08-13, 3:3, M)

1004. On the 5th instant, in St. Anne's Church, by the Rev. Doctor Drew, Mr. Andrew T. Knight, of Downpatrick, to Mary, daughter of Thomas M'Kelvey, Esq., of Belfast. (1842-08-13, 3:3, M)

1005. On the 27th ult., by the Rev. Robert Morrison, Markethill, Mr. Alexander Jamison, Westland, near Armagh, to Miss Shields, daughter of Mr. Thomas Shields, Glasdrummon, near Markethill. (1842-08-13, 3:3, M)

1006. August 6, in Killarney, Thadee William Morphy, Esq., of Killarney, to Charlotte, third daughter of the late John Morphy, Esq., of Mount Prospect. (1842-08-13, 3:3, M)

1007. August 8, at Killyman, county of Westmeath, in the 80th year of his age, James Saunderson, Esq., Clover Hill, county of Cavan. (1842-08-13, 3:3, D)

1008. August 5, at his residence, near Kilkenny, John Banim, Esq., author of "Tales of the O'Hara Family," and other popular works of fiction. (1842-08-13, 3:3, D)

1009. June 2, of apoplexy, at Plasto Rico, Hugh Fitzsimons, Esq., formerly of Ballyhaise, county Cavan. (1842-08-13, 3:3, D)

1010. On the 4th inst., of apoplexy, Mr. Hugh Moffett, innkeeper, Rosstrevor, aged 54 years. (1842-08-13, 3:3, D)

1011. On the 1st inst., of fever, at Armagh, in the 22d year of his age, Mr. James Ellis, printer. (1842-08-13, 3:3, D)

1012. On the 3d inst., at Warrenpoint, aged 17 years, Frances, third daughter of James Benn, Esq., of Belfast. (1842-08-13, 3:3, D)

1013. On the 5th April last, on the highest hill to the right of Khyber Pass, Affghanistan, aged 23, Lieutenant James S. Cumming of the 9th Regiment, eldest son of the Rev. P.M. Cumming, Incumbent of Magheraclune, county of Monaghan. (1842-08-13, 3:3, D)

1014. On the 27th ult., at Strabane, in the 59th year of his age, Dr. Hunter, of Ramelton. (1842-08-13, 3:3, D)

1015. On Monday last, the 15th, inst., Mr. Patrick Brady, of Clones. We have rarely had a more painful duty than that of recording Mr. Brady's death. There are few whose loss will be equally deplored by those who knew him. He was kind, humane, generous, and charitable. To his good qualities, the people of Clones bore ample testimony, for, from the moment of his death, until the morning after his burial, not one shop in Clones was open; the whole town and neighbourhood, including all classes, and many of the neighboring towns attended the funeral, while the poor followed the corpse, with shouts and lamentations. (1842-08-20, 3:5, D)

1016. In Clones Church, on the 26th instant, by the Rev. Mr. Graden, Mr. Young Sloane, of Monaghan, to Matilda Jane, third daughter of the late James Fitzgerald, Esq., of Clonavilla, county Monaghan. (1842-08-27, 3:2, M)

1017. On the 13th inst., by the Rev. David Adams, Ahoghill, Mr. John Kernaghan, youngest son of Mr. John Kernaghan, of Drumrankin, to Jane, eldest daughter of Mr. John M'Kinney, of Ballybeg, county Antrim. (1842-08-27, 3:2, M)

1018. On Monday, the 22d instant, at the residence of his sister, English-street, Armagh, Doctor Vogan, aged 67 years. (1842-08-27, 3:2, D)

1019. At Ramelton, on the 20th instant, in the 63d year of her age, Miss Catherine Reid, only surviving sister of the late Rev. E. Reid, of that town, and of the Rev. Doctor Reid, of Glasgow College, much and deservedly regretted by a large circle of friends and acquaintances. (1842-08-27, 3:2, D)

1020. In Captain-street, Coleraine, on the 14th instant, aged 66 years, Paymaster Sergeant William Henderson, late of the 86th foot. He had served 18 years in India. (1842-08-27, 3:2, D)

1021. Suddenly, at Magherafelt, on the morning of the 20th inst., Mr. Benjamin Beatty, teacher. (1842-08-27, 3:2, D)

1022. July 15, at Tusket village, Yarmouth, Christiana, the beloved wife of Mr. Edward Kelly, formerly of Ballyshannon, and daughter of Captain John Jones, of the Donegal Militia, aged 35 years. (1842-08-27, 3:2, D)

1023. At Newmills, near Coleraine, on the 15th instant, after a long illness, Henry, youngest son of the late Mr. James Logan, of said place. (1842-08-27, 3:2, D)

1024. On the 17th instant, at the house of her son-in-law, Mr. John Kennedy, Belfast, Eliza, relict of the late Mr. James Donaldson, Ballymorran, county Armagh, aged 79 years. (1842-08-27, 3:2, D)

1025. On the 5th instant, at his house in Cavan, Capt. Edward Harrison, adjutant of the Cavan Militia. (1842-08-27, 3:2, D)

1026. On the 13th instant, in Tempo, aged 25, of a decline, Mr. D. Scoales, Manager of the Tempo Loan Fund. (1842-08-27, 3:2, D)

1027. At the residence of her son, Doctor Cuming, Castleblayney, Anne, relict of the late James Cuming, Esq., of Lixview, county Cavan, aged 82 years. (1842-09-17, 3:3, D)

1028. Sept. 16, in St. Mary's Church, Newry, by the Rev. Dr. Campbell, Mr. Robert Williams, of the city of Dublin, Merchant, to Margaret, eldest daughter of the late Mr. John Frazer, of Newry. (1842-09-24, 3:2, M)

1029. Sept. 15, at Carlow Church, by the Rev. Joseph Jameson, Robert Anderson, Esq., of Graigue, to Emily, second daughter of the late James Smyth, Esq., of Carlow. (1842-09-24, 3:2, M)

1030. Sept. 15, in St. Luke's Church, Cork, by the Rev. John D. Penrose, the Rev. James Crawford Gordon, of Delamont, county of Down, to Geraldine, daughter of James Penrose, Esq., of Wood-hill, county of Cork. (1842-09-24, 3:2, M)

1031. Sept. 16, in Dublin, after a lingering and painful illness, Jane, second daughter of Mr. John Drought, aged about five years and nine months, an engaging and very interesting child. (1842-09-24, 3:2, D)

1032. On Thursday morning, at his residence, in Clones, of Fever, Mr. Cornelius Cosgrove, deservedly regretted by all who knew him. (1842-09-24, 3:2, D)

1033. Sept. 16, at Drumcondra, Mary Magennis, relict of John Magennis, formerly of Arran-quay, in the city of Dublin—an eminent and highly respected solicitor. (1842-09-24, 3:2, D)

1034. On his voyage home from Calcutta, 20th April last, of apoplexy, on board the ship *Troubadoor*, which he commanded, aged 32 years, Captain William Smith, a native of Portaferry. (1842-09-24, 3:2, D)

1035. On the 12th inst., at his residence, Newry, James Warring, Esq. (1842-09-24, 3:2, D)

1036. On the 10th inst., at Blaris, Mrs. Sarah Toane, aged 45 years, relict of the late Thomas Toane, of Hillsborough. (1842-09-24, 3:2, D)

1037. Sept. 15, at Turlough, of dropsy, much and deservedly regretted, Wm. H. Woodhouse, Esq., late Lieutenant of the 37th party Revenue Police, and second son of Curran Woodhouse, Esq., of Portadown. (1842-09-24, 3:2, D)

1038. September 26, at the house of her aunt, Mrs. Cole, 31, Merrion-square, the lady of A.G. Lewis, Esq., of a son. (1842-10-01, 3:3, B)

1039. At Coothill [sic], on Saturday the 17th September, after a long and painful illness, which he bore with christian fortitude and resignation, Mr. John M'Cann, grocer, aged 57 years. (1842-10-01, 3:3, D)

1040. September 24, at Sydney-avenue, Blackrock, Eliza, the beloved wife of John Barton, Esq., of Rathkenny, county Tipperary, and Rossclare, county Fermanagh. (1842-10-01, 3:3, D)

1041. September 24, at Castledargon, county of Sligo, Mary Fortescue, eldest daughter of John Ormsby, Esq., aged twenty-three years. (1842-10-01, 3:3, D)

1042. September 27, Anna Maria, the infant daughter of John Swanzy Esq., aged seven weeks. (1842-10-01, 3:3, D)

1043. Oct. 6, in St. Peter's Church, by the Rev. S.W. Fox, the Rev. William Nesbitt, Incumbent of Hollymount Church, county of Down, to Dorathea, youngest daughter of the late Captain Digby, of Clonmethan, county of Dublin. (1842-10-08, 3:5, M)

1044. Oct. 4 in Ballymacarrett Church, by the Rev. Thomas Leonard, A.M., Wm. Breath Searight Esq., Maherafelt, to Mary, eldest daughter of Wm. Radcliff, Esq., Ballymacarrett. (1842-10-08, 3:5, M)

1045. On the 3d inst., of inflammation, Mr. William Hadzor, of Warrenpoint, greatly regretted by his friends and a large circle of acquaintances. (1842-10-08, 3:5, D)

1046. At Kilmainham Wood House, county of Meath, Miss Honoria Boyle, sister of the late James Boyle, Esq., of Tullivin, in the county of Cavan. (1842-10-08, 3:5, D)

1047. On Tuesday, the 4th instant, by the Rev. Mr. Stephens, R.C.C., Killybegs, Francis M'Hugh, Esq., Castlederg, county Tyrone, to Miss Mary M'Closky, eldest daughter of John M'Closky, Esq., Tyfannon House, county Donegal. (1842-10-15, 3:3, M)

1048. On the 27th ult., at Alderley, Gloucestershire, T.G. Willis, Esq., of Castlerea, county Roscommon, eldest son of W.R. Willis, Esq., of Willsgrove, in the same county, to Eleanor Theodosia, of Alderly and Cottles House, Wiltshire. The ceremony was performed by the Dean of Ossory, brother to the Earl of Mayo, and uncle of the bride. (1842-10-15, 3:3, M)

1049. At No. 2, Mount-street Crescent, Dublin, on Friday, the 7th instant, Miss Isabella Colthurst, youngest daughter of the late Rev. Charles Colthurst, brother of the late Sir Nicholas Colthurst, Bart., and grand-daughter to the Lady Charlotte Fitzmaurice. (1842-10-15, 3:3, D)

1050. On the 3d instant, at Warrenpoint, in the 57th year of his age, Mr. William Hadzor, one of the most respectable inhabitants of that town. (1842-10-15, 3:3, D)

1051. October 8, at Sandymount, Marion, daughter of Mr. William Kay, aged four years, from eating the berries of the phyracanthus. (1842-10-15, 3:3, D)

1052. October 10, at Little Bloomfield, county of Dublin, in the 52d year of her age, Margaret, the beloved wife of Nicholas Murray Mansfield, Esq., whose singleness of mind and benevolent disposition endeared her to all who had the happiness of knowing the goodness of her heart, and the amiable and cheerful simplicity with which she discharged the various duties of wife, mother and friend. (1842-10-15, 3:3, D)

1053. At his residence, Bloomfield-avenue, Mr. Robert Connolly, formerly preacher in the Primitive Wesleyan Methodist Society. (1842-10-15, 3:3, D)

1054. At Rathcoursey Cottage, Middleton, the Lady of the Rev. Richard G. Meredith of a daughter. (1842-10-22, 3:4, B)

1055. On the 13th instant, at Christ Church, Captain C.B. Carrothers, to Maria Anna, daughter of Captain Knox, Greenwood Park, county Mayo. (1842-10-22, 3:4, M)

1056. On the 11th instant, at Balteage Church, Robert C. M'Causland, Esq., of Broglascow, Newtownlimavady, to Matilda, relict of the late Robert Dallas, Esq., of Coleraine, and daughter of the late Henry Huey, Esq., of the same place. (1842-10-22, 3:4, M)

1057. On the 13th instant, Mr. James Given, of Drumquin, county Tyrone, to Miss Mary Graham, third daughter of Richard Graham, Esq., of Rahoney, county Tyrone. (1842-10-22, 3:4, M)

1058. On the 9th instant, at Causeway Hall, Bushmills, Mary, wife of Echlin Molyneux, Esq., Barrister-at-Law. (1842-10-22, 3:4, D)

1059. On the 3d instant, in London, after a long and protracted illness, Lady Charlotte Matilda Ward, daughter of the first Marquis of Londonderry, and relict of the late Michael Edward Ward, Esq., of Bangor Castle, county Down. (1842-10-22, 3:4, D)

1060. October 16, at Belfast, aged 25 years, Jane, wife of Jas. Ramsey Newsam, Esq. (1842-10-22, 3:4, D)

1061. October 18, after a long illness, at Arley Cottage, the seat of her son-in-law, the Hon. Somerset R. Maxwell, in the 64th year of her age, Jane, the beloved wife of the Hon. Baron Pennefather, and daughter of the late Judge Bennett. (1842-10-22, 3:4, D)

1062. October 9, of scarletina, Jane, eldest daughter of Marshall B. Thornton, Esq. of Belturbet. (1842-10-22, 3:4, D)

1063. On Friday last, at his residence, Berkeley-street, Claredon-square, London, George Whannell, Esq., who edited the *Fermanagh Report*er from 18–8 [*partially illegible*] and 1839. (1842-10-22, 3:4, D)

1064. On the 20th inst., at Warrenpoint Church, Mr. John M'Neill, Low Mills, Seagoe, to Eliza Ann, only daughter of Mr. Edward Plunkett, Woodbine Cottage, Warrenpoint. (1842-10-29, 3:4, M)

1065. On the 20th instant at Glenarm Church, by the Rev. William Crawford, Rector of the united parishes of Skerry and Rocavan, S. Wilson M'Neale, Esq. second son of John M'Neale, of Ballycastle, Esq. to Mary, only daughter of Thomas Davison, Esq. of Glenarm. (1842-10-29, 3:4, M)

1066. On the 20th instant, at Swords, by the Rev. Thomas King, the Rev. Thomas Moutray, son of John Corry Moutray, Esq., of Favour Royal, county Tyrone, to Eliza Catherine, youngest daughter of Andrew Crawford, Esq. of Auburn, county Dublin. (1842-10-29, 3:4, M)

1067. October 22, at his residence, Thomas Sadlier, Esq., for many years Clerk of the peace for the county Tipperary. (1842-10-29, 3:4, D)

1068. On the 15th inst., aged 80 years, Clara, relict of the late Alexander Mitchell, Esq., of Newgrove. (1842-10-29, 3:4, D)

1069. On Tuesday, the 2d instant, at the residence of the lady's aunt, Mrs. M'Phillips, Monaghan, by the Rev. Mr. M'Kenna, R.C.C., Mr. John Fay, Woollen Draper, to Miss Anne Malone, third daughter of Mr. Malone of Ennis, county Clare. (1842-11-05, 3:3, M)

1070. Of Scarlitena [sic], on the 31st of October, aged 20 years, Josephine, second daughter of Maurice Burnell, Esq., Hill, Monaghan. (1842-11-05, 3:3, D)

1071. On Wednesday night last, at 7 o'clock, aged 82 years, Mr. Ralph Campbell, of Market-street, an old and respected inhabitant of Monaghan. (1842-11-05, 3:3, D)

1072. Nov. 7, in Lucan Church, by his father, the Rev. T.R. Cradock, James Cradock, Esq., Sub-Inspector of Constabulary, to Matilda, daughter of Major John Wills, of Esker Lodge, county of Dublin. (1842-11-12, 2:5, M)

1073. Nov. 4, in the Cathedral of Derry, by the Rev. John Kincaid, Robert Martin, Esq., of William street, to Catherine, only surviving daughter of the late James Preston, Esq., of Derry. (1842-11-12, 2:5, M)

1074. October 31, at her residence in Boyle, Margaret, wife of James Read, Esq., Sub-Inspector of police. (1842-11-12, 2:5, D)

1075. November 7, after a short illness, the Rev. William Ball, Rector of Rossory, in the diocess of Clogher. Pious, benevolent, and friendly, Mr. Ball was beloved by all classes of persons who came within the sphere of his acquaintance; and by none more than the flock amongst which he laboured with zeal, assiduity, and Christian spirit, which must render his loss a serious bereavement to them, and a source of deep and lasting sorrow. He was a good man, a pious and cheerful Christian—a faithful and indefatigable minister of the Gospel. He has gone to his everlasting reward. (1842-11-12, 2:5, D)

1076. Oct. 31, in London, William Joseph Glenny, only son of Joseph Glenny, Esq., late of Newry, Solicitor, in the 35th year of his age. (1842-11-12, 2:5, D)

1077. Oct. 22, at Berne, in Switzerland, of typhus fever, to the deep regret of his family and friends, Edward Madden, Esq., late of the Royal Dragoons, and eldest son to the late Charles D. Madden, Esq., of Spring Grove, county Fermanagh. (1842-11-12, 2:5, D)

1078. In Glasslough Church, on the 18th inst., by the Rev. Mr. Malleverer, James Hill, Esq., S.I., Newry, to Alice, third daughter of the Rev. W.H. Pratt, Vicar of Donagh. (1842-11-19, 3:2, M)

1079. On Monday, the 14th instant, in Clough church, by the Rev. Valentine Duke Christian, Joseph Cooper Moorehead, Esq., of Golanduff, son to John Moorehead, Esq., of Ballintoppin, county Monaghan, to Margaret Jane, daughter to Benjamin Whitsit, Esq., Roslea, county Fermanagh. (1842-11-19, 3:2, M)

1080. Nov. 14, in Belfast, Charles G. Duffy, Esq., Dublin, to Emily, second daughter of Francis M'Laughlin, Esq., of Belfast. (1842-11-19, 3:2, M)

1081. Nov. 10, by the Rev. Mr. Maloney, in Seago church, William Rennix, Esq., of Camden street, Dublin, to Judith Johson, second daughter of Francis Johnson, Esq., of Knockmenagh, county of Armagh. (1842-11-19, 3:2, M)

1082. On the 1st inst., in Armagh, Mr. Robert Hamilton, to Miss Eliza Dunlap, both of that city. (1842-11-19, 3:2, M)

1083. On the 8th ult. by the Rev. Thomas Meharry, A.B., Secession Presbyterian Minister of Myroe, county Derry, John Moyle, Esq. of Stradeagh Mountain, to Elizabeth, third daughter of the late Joseph King, Esq., of Carrydoo Vale. (1842-11-19, 3:2, M)

1084. At Dungannon, aged 31 years, Catherine, the beloved wife of Mr. Francis Mackenzie. (1842-11-19, 3:2, D)

1085. On the 7th instant, in Strabane, after a lingering illness, in the 25th year of his age, Mr. Galbraith Frizzell, printer. (1842-11-19, 3:2, D)

1086. Nov. 14, at his residence, Strandtown, aged 77 years, Mr. William Ewing, for upwards of fifty years a merchant of Belfast. (1842-11-19, 3:2, D)

1087. November 18, in the Parish Church of Glasslough, by the Rev. James Mauleverer, A.M., Incumbent of Shantilly, county of Armagh, James Ponsonby Hill, Esq., Sub-Inspector, of Constabulary, son of Major Hill, of Bellaghy, county of Londonderry, to Alice, third daughter of the Rev. W.H. Pratt, A.M., Vicar of Donagh, and grand-daughter of the Very Rev. Wm. Pratt, Deane of Cloyne, and Vicar of Christ Church, Cork. (1842-11-26, 3:4, M)

1088. On the 16th instant, at Holy Trinity Church, Brompton, near London, Charles Rhind, Esq., Principal of the Ulster Institution for the Deaf and Dumb and the Blind, to Sophia Harriet, youngest daughter of William Oak, Esq., London. (1842-11-26, 3:4, M)

1089. On the 17th instant, in the Parish Church of Aughnacloy, Mr. James M'Mahon, Lisnadill, county Armagh, to Catherine, fifth daughter of the late John M'Williams, Carnteel, county Tyrone, Esq. (1842-11-26, 3:4, M)

1090. November 17, in Antrim, Mr. William John Scott, sincerely and deservedly regretted by a numerous circle of friends. (1842-11-26, 3:4, D)

1091. Nov. 12, at Tankardstown, in the 73d year of her age, Anne, relict of the late William Hawkins, Esq. (1842-11-26, 3:4, D)

1092. On the 12th instant, at Ballymoyer Glebe, Newtownhamilton, in the 86th year of his age, Richard Chaplin, Esq., formerly of Woodburn, Carrickfergus. (1842-11-26, 3:4, D)

1093. On the 12th inst., at Coleraine, Anne, wife of William Cavin, Esq., A.M. and M.D., and only daughter of the late Henry Newton, of Coleraine, Esq. (1842-11-26, 3:4, D)

1094. At sea, on the passage from Calcutta to Penang, to which place she was proceeding for the benefit of her health, Charlotte, wife of the Rev. John Vaughan, A.B., chaplain, Hon. East India Company's service, and third daughter of Lawford Transon, Esq., Newry, aged 19 years. (1842-11-26, 3:4, D)

1095. On the 18th inst., at his residence, Pump-street, Derry, in the 66th year of his age, James Gregg, Esq. For 37 years Mr. Gregg filled (as joint patentee with his brother, Mr. William Gregg) the office of Clerk of the Peace for the county of Derry. (1842-11-26, 3:4, D)

1096. At her residence, Fort-Singleton, county Monaghan, on Thursday last, aged 83 years, Annabella, relict of the late Thomas Singleton, Esq., of Fort-Singleton. The remains of this respected old lady will be interred in the family vault, in Errigle Churchyard, on Monday next, at eight o'clock, P.M. (1842-12-03, 3:1, D)

1097. At Castleblayney, on the 22d ult, in the 21st year of his age, Charles Moorhead, fifth son of Mr. John M'Kee, of said town. He bore a protracted and afflicting illness with Christian patience, fortitude and resignation; he was a member of the Wesleyan Methodist Society, and heartily devoted to its interests, being naturally of a reserved turn of mind; he professed less than he enjoyed, until within a few weeks of his departure, when he was enabled to hear a pleasing and satisfactory testimony of the willingness of God to save; he ended his course in peace, adopting language similar to the lines of the poet--

He hath loved me he cried—
He hath suffered and died,
To redeem such a rebel as me.
(1842-12-03, 3:1, D)

1098. December 1, in Clonallon Church, the Rev. Hunt Johnson, to Jane, youngest daughter of the late Savage Hall, of Narrow Water. (1842-12-10, 3:3, M)

1099. December 1, by the Rev. John Orr, of Portaferry, the Rev. Wm. M'Crea, of Ballindreat, county of Donegal, to Sarah Jane, eldest daughter of Robert Hunter, Esq., Collector of Customs, Strangford. (1842-12-10, 3:3, M)

1100. On the 1st inst., at the bride's residence, Portadown, by the Rev. J.S. Morrison, of Armagh, Mr. Robert Morrison, of Portadown, to Mary Jane, second daughter of Mr. Hector Saunderson. (1842-12-10, 3:3, M)

1101. Dec. 1, in St. Peter's Church, Dublin, by the Rev. Richard Ardill, Charles Williams, Esq., of Charlemont-street, Dublin, to Elizabeth Martha, daughter of the late Edward Tennant Esq., of Baggot-street Dublin. (1842-12-10, 3:3, M)

1102. December 2, at 9, Leinster Terrace, Rathmines, Eliza, the beloved wife of the Rev. J.T. Paul, and youngest daughter of the late Robert Holmes, Esq., Belfast. (1842-12-10, 3:3, D)

1103. Nov. 27, at Brookfield, Blackrock, Dorothea, fourth daughter of the late Mr. James Morrow, Dungannon, county of Tyrone. (1842-12-10, 3:3, D)

1104. At his residence in Blackwatertown, on the morning of the 24th, ult., Mr. James Hanna, who, from early life was a leading merchant there. (1842-12-10, 3:3, D)

1105. On the 27th ult., after a few days' illness, at the house of his uncle, Mr. Finley Anderson, of the port, county Donegal, Mr. William Anderson, a very promising youth aged 17 years, only son of Mr. Robert Anderson, Beleek, county Fermanagh. (1842-12-10, 3:3, D)

1106. On the 6th inst. by the Rev. Joseph M'Kee, Killead, Mr. William John White, Bridge-street, Ballymena, to Catherine, only daughter of Mr. Archibald Cooper, of Rosehill Nursery, near Antrim. (1842-12-17, 2:4, M)

1107. On the 5th inst. at Omagh, by the Rev. James Hill, John, second son of the late John Murphy, of Dominick-street, in the city of Dublin, solicitor, to Mary, eldest daughter of John M'Kenny, of Omagh, in the county of Tyrone. (1842-12-17, 2:4, M)

1108. On the 23d ult. by the Rev. J. Steele, Stranorlar, Mr. John Reid, of Carrickmagran, to Sarah, youngest daughter of Mrs. Shanklin, same place. (1842-12-17, 2:4, M)

1109. On the 11th October, in St. Mary's Church, Fort St. George, Madras, by the Rev. W. Mahon, A.M., Lieut. Loftus T. Cassidy, of her Majesty's 57th Regiment, son of the late Rev. M. Cassiday [sic], Rector of Newtownards, county of Down, to Jane, eldest daughter of Captain and Paymaster Barlow, of the same Regiment. (1842-12-17, 2:4, M)

1110. On the 7th inst. at Tullyvallen, by the Rev. Joseph Jenkins, Richard Henry, Esq., Surgeon, Newbliss, county Monaghan, to Anne Jane, only daughter of the late Alex. Donaldson, Esq., Tullyvallen, county Armagh. (1842-12-17, 2:4, M)

1111. On the 4th inst., at Lough Neigh Cottage, in the 34th year of his age, Edward Orbe, Esq., late of Clantilew. (1842-12-17, 2:4, D)

1112. On the 30th ult. Mr. John Burrows, tanner, of Dungannon, aged 43 years. (1842-12-17, 2:4, D)

1113. On the 23 ult., aged six years, William, only son of Mr. John Sloan, Armagh. (1842-12-17, 2:4, D)

1114. On the 1st inst., at Woodbine Cottage, Warrenpoint, Mr. Edward Plunkett, aged 57 years. (1842-12-17, 2:4, D)

1115. On the 1st inst. at Donaghmore, near Dungannon, Joseph Monro Hanson, eldest son of the Rev. James Hanson, in the 19th year of his age. (1842-12-17, 3:3, D)

1116. On the 15th instant, at the residence of the lady's uncle Samuel Cochrane, sen., of Christloughmore, Esq., by the Rev. Henry Wallace, the Rev. John Macky, Presbyterian Minister of Fahan, to Rebecca, third daughter of Mr. Joseph Cochrane, of Derry. (1842-12-24, 3:2, M)

1117. Dec. 31, at St. Peter's church, by the Rev. William Henn, Robert, youngest son of the late Richard Holmes, Esq., of Prospect, King's County, to Jane, daughter of William Henn, Esq., Master in Chancery. (1842-12-24, 3:2, M)

1118. Dec. 16, William Mahon, Esq., son of Bartholomew Mahon, Esq., of Russell-street, Dublin, and of Clonfree, Roscommon, to Jane, daughter of the late Wm. Davenish, Esq., of Mountpleasant, said county. (1842-12-24, 3:2, M)

1119. At Smithborough, of apoplexy, Mr. Francis Boylan, in the 72d year of his age, much and deservedly regretted by all who knew him. He was an old man, of whom few were ever found to say a "hard word," and against whom the tongue of calumny never pointed. (1842-12-24, 3:2, D)

1120. On the 9th inst. Richard, only son of Mr. John Ladly, of Downpatrick, solicitor. (1842-12-24, 3:2, D)

1121. On the 1st inst., at her residence, Forthill, aged 68 years, Mary, the beloved wife of Mr. Robert Malcolm, Ruling Elder for above 50 years in Connor Presbyterian Congregation. The numerous and highly respectable assemblage that accompanied her remains to the place of interment manifested the high esteem in which she was held by her numerous acquaintances. (1842-12-24, 3:2, D)

1122. On Saturday last, at Long-Stone, Lisburn, at the advanced age of 102 years, James Ferguson, a respectable inhabitant of that town. He perfectly recollected the circumstances of the French landing at Carrickfergus, having at that period volunteered his services in defence of his country. (1842-12-24, 3:2, D)

1123. On the 14th instant, rather suddenly, Mrs. Jas. Arthur, King's Arms Hotel, Dundalk. (1842-12-24, 3:2, D)

1124. Suddenly, on the morning of the 14th instant, at the hotel, Magherafelt, where deceased and his lady had been stopping for the last week, the Rev. Thomas Nevin Burgoyne, in the 39th year of his age. (1842-12-24, 3:2, D)

1125. On the 19th inst., aged three years, and six months, Elizabeth, eldest daughter of Mr. Richard Kerr, of Newbliss. (1842-12-31, 3:4, D)

1126. December 24th, to the inexpressible sorrow of his family and numerous friends, at his house in Paradise-row, Richardson Turckington, Esq., in the 65th year of his age, an old and respected Solicitor, of this city (Dublin)—he was a good husband, an affectionate father, and a truly sincere friend. (1842-12-31, 3:4, D)

1127. December 29, after a lingering illness, which she bore with saint-like patience, Anna Florence Eleanor, sixth daughter of the Honorable A.G. Stuart, Lisdhu, county of Tyrone. Though a very child in years, she was rich in faith, and departed this uncertain life in the sure and certain hope of a glorious resurrection, through the merits of her Blessed Saviour and Redeemer. (1842-12-31, 3:4, D)

1128. December 3, at Dunemanus, by the Hon. and Right Rev. the Bishop of Derry, Frederick Richard Surtees, Esq., second surviving son of the late William Villiers Surtees, Esq., of 40, Devonshire-place, and Rother-house, Rotherfield, Sussex, to Anne Jane, eldest daughter of the Honorable and Rev. Charles Douglas, of Earlsgift, county of Tyrone. (1843-01-14, 3:1, M)

1129. December 29, in Milltown Church, Wm. Cooke, Esq., of Levaghery House, Portadown, county Armagh, to Mary, only daughter of Wm. Fox, Esq., of Derrynain, Moy, county Tyrone. (1843-01-14, 3:1, M)

1130. On the 7th instant, at the house of the lady's father, by the Rev. P. Mooney, P.P., Lieutenant Macdonald, 54th Regiment, to Margaret Constantia, youngest daughter of William Carpenter, Esq., Dobbin-street, Armagh. (1843-01-14, 3:1, M)

1131. On the 29th ult., by the Rev. Mr. Shaw of Ballinahinch, Mr. Hugh Thompson, Comber, to Sarah, second daughter of Mr. John Jennings, Ballygawley. (1843-01-14, 3:1, M)

1132. On the 5th instant, at Moneymore, county Londonderry, by the Rev. A.K. Miller, William Saurin Cox, Esq., youngest son of the late Rev. Richard Cox, of Caherconlish, county Limerick, to Mary, only daughter of Rowley Miller, Esq., Moneymore. (1843-01-14, 3:1, M)

1133. January 6, in Kilkeel Church, by the Rev. John F. Close, Mr. William H. Thompson, of Castlewellen, county of Down, to Eliza Sophia Augusta, second daughter of Captain Hopkins, Wellington Lodge, Hillsborough, grand daughter of Captain Chesney, J.P., Packolet, and niece to Colonel Chesney, F.R.S. (1843-01-14, 3:1, M)

1134. In Trim Church, the Rev. A.P. Irwin, Temple Church, London, late of Roscommon, to Eleanor Gorgianna, daughter of David Thompson, Esq. (1843-01-14, 3:1, M)

1135. January 10, at St. Peter's Church, by the Rev. George Kemmis, Rector of Rosenalis, the Rev. William Henry M'Cusland, youngest son of the late Marcus Longford M'Cusland, Esq., Roe Park, county of Londonderry, to Martha, second daughter of the late Robert Fannin, Esq., of Leeson-street, in this city [Dublin]. (1843-01-14, 3:1, M)

1136. On the 6th instant, at Killygavna, in this county, of consumption, Alice, daughter of Mr. Robert Miller. She bore a long and afflicting illness, with that patience which religion only can impart, and died in the full hope of the blessed effects of the atonement. (1843-01-14, 3:1, D)

1137. At Clontibret, county Monaghan, on the 1st instant, of decline, in the twenty-fourth year of his age, Thomas, youngest son of Mr. Johnston of the above place, deservedly regretted. (1843-01-14, 3:1, D)

1138. On the last day of December, 1842, at Banagher Glebe, near Dungiven, aged 87, Mrs. Ross, relict of the late James Ross, Esq., formerly of Cumber-house, county Londonderry. (1843-01-14, 3:1, D)

1139. Sept. 26, of fever, after an illness of fifteen days, on board the *Princess Royal*, at Bonny River, Samuel Reid, third son of Robert Pooler, of Tyross, county Armagh, Esq., aged twenty-two years. (1843-01-14, 3:1, D)

1140. December 31, at Seven Churches' house, King's County, Henry Maxwell, second son of William Johnston, Esq. (1843-01-14, 3:1, D)

1141. January 5, at Newmarket-on-Fergus, aged 70 years, the Rev. Thomas M'Cullagh, vicar of Kilnasoolagh. (1843-01-14, 3:1, D)

1142. January 5, at Bath, universally loved and lamented, Harriet, the lady of the Rev. James Lowry, of Somerset, county Tyrone, Ireland, aged 71. (1843-01-14, 3:1, D)

1143. On the 11th inst., in St. Ann's Church, by the Rev. A.C. Macartney, Mr. J. Telford, to Sarah, only daughter of Mr. William Purdy, Denegal-street [sic], Belfast. (1843-01-21, 3:5, M)

1144. On the 12th inst., at Claremont, by the Rev. J. Monteith, Mr. Samuel Laughlin, of Derry, merchant, to Mary Jane, youngest daughter of the late James Walker, Esq., Holymount, Donemana. (1843-01-21, 3:5, M)

1145. Jan. 11, in St. Peter's Church, Benjamin Johnston, Esq., M.D., to Emma, daughter of the late Rev. Henry Maturin, Rector of Clandaradock, county Donegal. (1843-01-21, 3:5, M)

1146. Jan. 17, by the Rev. Fossy Tackaberry, Wesleyan Minister, the Rev. Gibson M'Millen, of Armagh, to Eliza, youngest daughter of the late Rev. John M'Arthur of Derry. (1843-01-21, 3:5, M)

1147. July 4, at Auckland, New Zeland [sic], Mr. A. Woodward, commander of the schooner *Velocipede*, to Miss Susanna Perry, of Warrenpoint. (1843-01-21, 3:5, M)

1148. Jan. 17, at 14, George's-hill, Miss Mary Jane Moran, niece of Messrs. A. and E. Crenan, of Dublin, to D.M. Hennessy, of Drogheda. (1843-01-21, 3:5, M)

1149. In Hardwicke-place, Dublin, on the night of the 13th instant, Sarah, the wife of Nicholas Ellis, of Lisnaroe, in the county of Monaghan, Esq. (1843-01-21, 3:5, D)

1150. January 15, at Hermitage, Crossdony, county Cavan, the residence of her grandchildren, Hannah, relict of the Rev. Thomas Lambert, of Callan, county Kilkenny, aged 89. (1843-01-21, 3:5, D)

1151. On the 13th inst., at the Rectory House, Ballymoney, county of Antrim, the Rev. William Greene, Rector of the Parish, in the 76th year of his age. (1843-01-21, 3:5, D)

1152. On the 11th inst., after a short illness, which she bore with resignation in the Divine will, in the 18th year of her age, Anna, second daughter of Mr. Arthur Gaffikin, Corn-market, Belfast. (1843-01-21, 3:5, D)

1153. On the morning of Friday, the 13th inst., in the 72d year of her age, Jane, relict of the late William Weir, Esq., Lenaderg Cottage, Banbridge. (1843-01-21, 3:5, D)

1154. On Thursday, the 26th ult., at the residence of the bride's father, by the Rev. J.H. Morell, Presbyterian Minister of Ballybay, Nathaniel Hilles, of Corrush, Esq., to Maryanne, eldest daughter of James Crawford, Esq., of Corrush, aforesaid, near Ballybay, in this county. (1843-02-04, 3:3, M)

1155. At her residence, Glenboy, county Tyrone, at the venerable age of 72 years, during which she earned and possessed the esteem of all who knew her, Mrs. Eleanor M'Knight, relict of the late Mr. Samuel M'Knight, and mother of Mr. James M'Knight, a respected merchant and inhabitant of this town. (1843-02-04, 3:3, D)

1156. On Wednesday last, in this town, in the 75th year of his age, Alexander Williams, in the full enjoyment of Gospel faith. (1843-02-04, 3:3, D)

1157. On Tuesday last, at Cornasoo, in the 88th year of his age, Mr. Robert Jameson. (1843-02-04, 3:3, D)

1158. Jan. 29, at Warrenpoint, after having given birth to a daughter, Georgiana, the beloved wife of Lawrence Tallon, Esq. (1843-02-04, 3:3, D)

1159. Jan. 11, at Exchange Buildings, Templehill, Troom, Mr. William Hendry, having nearly arrived at the patriarchal age of 100 years. He was a member of the Volunteers who assembled in Londonderry, in the year 1778, and originally belonged to the Parish of Cappagh, in the county of Tyrone. (1843-02-04, 3:3, D)

1160. February 14, at Mount-Temple Church, county Westmeath, by the Rev. S. Moffatt, Rector of St. Mary's, Athlone, Mr. William Haire, Hotel-keeper and Mail Coach Agent, to Bessie, daughter of Mr. Edward Lynch, both of Athlone. (1843-02-18, 3:5, M)

1161. February 2, at Rosevale, by the Rev. Hugh Bell, Hugh Montgomery, Esq., Ona Bridge, to Miss Jane Moneypenny, of Ballygawley. (1843-02-18, 3:5, M)

1162. February 8, at Ashton Church, Warwickshire, by the Rev. George O. Fenwick, Conolly Boyle, Esq., second son of Hugh Boyle, Esq., of Rush-hall, in the county of Londonderry, to Margaret, second daughter of Thomas Colman, Esq., of Green-house, Warwickshire. (1843-02-18, 3:5, M)

1163. November 15, at St. George's church, Kingston, Upper Canada, by the Venerable Archdeacon, John Gamble Horne, Esq., to Ellen, fourth and youngest daughter of the late Major-General Semour, Governor of St. Lucia, and Lieutenant-Colonel of the 15th Hussars. (1843-02-25, 3:6, M)

1164. February 17, at the bride's residence, by the Revd. Archdeacon Armstrong, James Patterson, Esq., Thornhill, near Beragh, to Miss Jane M'Farland, Woodbine Cottage, near Omagh. The parties are each upwards of 70 years of age. (1843-02-25, 3:6, M)

1165. In Derrynakish Church, on Wednesday the 22nd inst., Mr. Ambrose Hartley, of Old Castle, county Meath, to Jane, eldest daughter of Mr. Oliver Barret, of Clara, county Cavan. (1843-02-25, 3:6, M)

1166. On St. Valentine's day, at Manorhamilton, by the Rev. John Hamilton, Mr. Christopher Armstrong, merchant of that town, to Deborah, daughter of Mr. Allen Nixon, of Black Park, both of county Leitrim. (1843-02-25, 3:6, M)

1167. February 15, Arthur M'Guire Giles, Esq., to Maria M'Guire, daughter of the late Joseph M'Guire, Esq., of Heath Lodge, county Cavan. (1843-02-25, 3:6, M)

1168. Feb. 20, at 16, Lower Gardiner-street, Matilda Louisa, wife of Captain James Stacley Ireland, late Chief Magistrate of Police. (1843-02-25, 3:6, D)

1169. February 1, of influenza, to the heartfelt grief of those around her, by whom she was beloved and revered, Anna Maria, wife of Theobald Barnewall Donnelly, Esq., and daughter of the late Robert Fleetwood, Esq., of Parkstown, county Meath. (1843-02-25, 3:6, D)

1170. February 16, at his residence, Moyne Hall, County Cavan, Major Samuel Noble, late of the 2d Native cavalry, Bengal Establishment. (1843-02-25, 3:6, D)

1171. On Tuesday, Mr. Denis Maguire, of Enniskillen, Hardware merchant. (1843-02-25, 3:6, D)

1172. At Gledstown, Maguiresbridge, on the 2nd inst., Mrs. Dunne, relict of the late Mr. Richard Dunne, of Curraghpall [Curraghanall], parish of Aughavea, county Fermanagh. (1843-02-25, 3:6, D)

1173. Feb. 14, in Limerick, Holmes O'Brien, Esq., Solicitor, son of the late James O'Brien, Esq., of Quinborough, to the inconsolable grief of his family, and the sincere regret of all acquainted with his high character and engaging manners. (1843-02-25, 3:6, D)

1174. Feb. 16, at Hastings, of pulmonary consumption, in the 22nd year of his age, Charles Francis, son of James Lendrick, Esq., of Dublin, Barrister-at-Law. (1843-02-25, 3:6, D)

1175. Feb. 19, Edmund William Grimshaw, eldest son of Edmund Grimshow [sic], Esq., of Moosley, aged 35 years. (1843-02-25, 3:6, D)

1176. Feb 20 at Lurgan-lodge, county Sligo, the Lady of the Rev. Allen Lucas, Rector of Ballysumaghan, of a son. (1843-03-04, 3:4, B)

1177. On the 28th Feb, at Ballinode Church, by the Rev. J.R. Young, Mr. Robert Scott, of Carrihatty [Carrowhatta], to Mary, eldest daughter of Mr. Robert Wright, of Ballinode mills. (1843-03-04, 3:4, M)

1178. On the 9th instant, at St. Mary's Church, Dublin, by the Rev. Alexander Leeper, Henry Connell, Esq., of Mallow, county Cork, to Charlotte, relict of the late William M'Donnell, Esq., of Fairview and Mandaville-Hall, county Armagh, and of Blackwater-vale, Mullaghmore, Monaghan. (1843-03-11, 3:3, M)

1179. On Tuesday last, at his residence Rockfield, county Monaghan, aged 62, Henry Swanzy, Esq., Solicitor.—We do not speak in the common parlance of newspaper obituaries, when we say that his death is sincerely deplored by all who knew him. In the fullness of a ripe and respected old age, he has been called from a world in which he had not an enemy, and many a tear has been shed, and many a sigh heaved for his loss by those who, though unconnected with him by the ties of kindred, were firmly bound to the good old man in the strongest ties of friendship. Living he was loved, dead he is mourned. (1843-03-18, 3:3, D)

1180. On the 21st March, in Maguiresbridge church, by the Rev. Mr. Roe, Mr. George Henderson, of New York, America, to Mary Anne, second daughter of Mr. James Palmer, Maguiresbridge. (1843-03-25, 3:3, M)

1181. On the 17th instant, in St. George's church, Dublin, by the Rev. F. Brydge, Charles Columbine Jackson, Esq., of Ballintate, county Armagh, to Louisa, daughter of the late John Arthure, Esq., Barrister-at-Law, of Seafield, in the county of Dublin. (1843-03-25, 3:3, M)

1182. On the 12th instant, in the 25th year of her age, at the house of her father, John Byrne, Esq., Solicitor, Dundalk, of rapid decline, Elizabeth, relict of the late Henry Stewart Smith, Esq., formerly a Merchant in Newry, and lately resident in New York, from whence she had lately returned after burying her husband. (1843-03-25, 3:3, D)

1183. On the 11th instant, at Clogher, aged 12 years, Sarah Anne, only daughter of the late Mr. Thomas Steen. (1843-03-25, 3:3, D)

1184. On the 21st ult., at Ballycastle, by the Rev. Samuel Lyle, the Rev. Thomas Craig, of Chequer Hall, county of Antrim, to Jane, youngest daughter of James Kirkpatrick, Esq., Ballycastle. (1843-04-01, 3:3, M)

1185. On the 22d ult., in Tullylish church, by the Archdeacon of Connor, Leslie Edward Creery, of Dublin, Esq., to Eliza, second daughter of the late William M'Creight, Esq., of Gilford, in the county of Down. (1843-04-01, 3:3, M)

1186. On the 17th Dec. last, in the Cathedral of Bombay, by the Rev. Edward H. Essington, D.D., George Eccles Nixon, Esq., of her Majesty's 1st Royal Lancers, to Rebecca Henrietta, youngest daughter of the late Drelingcourt Younge, of Dublin, Esq. (1843-04-01, 3:3, M)

1187. March 22, on board the *Florence* Packet, on his passage home from Madeira, John Vignoles, eldest son of the Rev. Dr. Vignoles, Dean of the Chapel Royal, Dublin Castle, aged 31 years. (1843-04-01, 3:3, D)

1188. March 30, at Knockbride Rectory, in the 24th year of her age, eleven days after her confinement, Mary Anne Frances, the beloved and affectionate wife of the Rev. Guy Perceval L'Estrange, deeply lamented by the few who knew her. She met an early grave as it became the sincere Christian. (1843-04-01, 3:3, D)

1189. March 25, at Cavan, in his 30th year, George Gerard, eldest son of Samuel Moore, Esq., deeply regretted. (1843-04-01, 3:3, D)

1190. At Glasgow, on the 28th ult., the Lady of Doctor Robert Saunderson, of Newbridge, of a son. (1843-04-08, 2:4, B)

1191. April 9, at Anketell Grove, in this county, the Lady of Matthew Anketell, Esq., of a daughter. (1843-04-15, 3:4, B)

1192. On the 23d ult., by the Rev. T. Martin, Mr. W. Graham, Merchant, Bridgeport, United States, America, formerly of Killacreen, county Monaghan, to Mary Rebecca, daughter of Israel Millar, of same place. (1843-04-15, 3:4, M)

1193. April 5, in Keady Church, by the Rev. Cosby Stopford Mangan, Rector of Derrynoose, James Green, Esq., of Newholland, to Anna, eldest daughter of Dr. Magee, of Keady. (1843-04-15, 3:4, M)

1194. April 4, in Dunane Church, by the Rev. W.G. Macartney, Meredith, the eldest son of Hunt Walsh Chambre, Esq., of Hawthorn Hill, in the county of Armagh, to Mabella, the only daughter of the late Kennick Morres Jones, Esq., of Moneyglass House, county of Antrim. (1843-04-15, 3:4, M)

1195. April 5, at Seaville, county of Sligo, Mary, wife of Patrick I. Howly, Esq., in the 45th year of his age. (1843-04-15, 3:4, D)

1196. April 8, on Princes-quarry, Tralee, Denis Hill M'Gillicuddy, Esq., Lieutenant, R.N., and brother of M'Gillicuddy, of the Reeks. (1843-04-15, 3:4, D)

1197. March 27, at Bruges, after a short illness, Eliza, relict of the late Francis Whyte, Esq., of Red Hills, county of Cavan, most sincerely and deservedly lamented. (1843-04-15, 3:4, D)

1198. April 21, at Mount Louise, the lady of S.R.B. Evatt Esq., of a Daughter. (1843-04-22, 3:3, B)

1199. On the 18th instant, in Clough Church, by the Rev. V.D. Christian, Mr. William Burns, of Omagh, to Mary Anne, second daughter of the late Thomas Welsh, Esq., of Templetate, County of Monaghan. (1843-04-22, 3:3, M)

1200. April 19th, in Lucan Church, by the Rev. H.E. Prior, A.M., John Hannan, Esq., M.D., to Berri, relict of Evelyn Evatt, Esq., and daughter of the late Captain Bayley, formerly of the 5th Dragoon Guards. (1843-04-22, 3:3, M)

1201. Whitney Moutray, of Killibrick, county Tyrone, Esq., son of John Corry Moutray, of Favour Royal, Esq., to Annabella, daughter of Andrew Crawford, of Auburn, county Dublin, Esq. (1843-04-22, 3:3, M)

1202. On the 12th inst. in Glenavy Church, by the Rev. D. Bell, Mr. Arthur Gamble, of Drogheda, son of the late Robert Gamble, Esq. Belfast, to Isabella, daughter of the late Hugh M'Master Esq., Armagh. (1843-04-22, 3:3, M)

1203. On the 13th inst. by the Rev. William Glendy, Ballycarry, Mr. William Boyle Hill to Saragh Jane, youngest daughter of Mr. John Reid, both of Islandmagee. (1843-04-22, 3:3, M)

1204. On the 13th inst. at the house of the lady's brother, by the Rev. James Davis, Mr. James Thompson, merchant, to Miss Ann Mulligan, both of Banbridge. (1843-04-22, 3:3, M)

1205. On the 10th inst. in the 83d year, at her residence 35, Joy-street, Margaret, relict of the late Joseph Stephens, Esq. of Belfast, deeply regretted by a large circle of friends and sorrowing relatives. (1843-04-22, 3:3, D)

1206. On the 23d of April, at his residence, at Killymaddy, Dungannon, aged 88 years, Mr. James Brown, for upwards of 50 years a ruling elder in the congregation of Lower Clemannees. His remains were conveyed to the family burying-ground in Benburb, followed by a large concourse of people, who evinced the most sincere regret at the loss of a true friend, a devoted christian, and one who was pre-eminently remarkable for his virtues in all relations of public and private life. Mr. Brown was one of that almost extinct body of men, the Irish volunteers. (1843-05-06, 3:6, D)

1207. On the 6th instant, at the residence of his son, in Newbliss, Mr. Daniel Leary of Lisarley, aged 69 years. He was interred on Monday, and borne to the grave by the Members of the Masonic Institution, of which he was an eminent patron for the course of half a century. The numerous and very respectable concourse that followed his remains to the place of interment told how universally he was respected and beloved. (1843-05-13, 3:6, D)

1208. May 17, in Philipstown Church, by the Rev. William Little, Rector, Charlotte, second daughter of the late Mr. Joseph Jackson, of that town, to Mr. James Griffin, Primitive Wesleyan Preacher, Dublin. (1843-05-20, 3:6, M)

1209. May 16th, in George's Church, Dublin, by the Rev. Gibson Blake, Charles Henry Bingham, Esq., son of the late George Bingham, Colonel of the 35th regiment, to Jane, second daughter of James Stapleton, Esq., Riversdale-house, Drumcondra. (1843-05-20, 3:6, M)

1210. May 14, at Bangor, in the 18th year of his age, Robt. Johnston, of Ashley Lodge, Ballymacarrett. (1843-05-20, 3:6, D)

1211. May 15, at her brother's house, Grand Parade, Cork, Miss Martha Beauchamp, third daughter of the late John Beauchamp, Esq., of Graigue, in the county of Tipperary. (1843-05-20, 3:6, D)

1212. May 15, the infant son of T.O.K. White, Esq., of 19, Percy-place, Dublin. (1843-05-20, 3:6, D)

1213. May 15, at her daughter's residence, Merrion-avenue, Dublin, Ann, relict of the late Mr. Robert Jackson, of Edenderry, in her 74th year. (1843-05-20, 3:6, D)

1214. May 16, at Monkstown, after a protracted illness, in the 10th year of his age, James, eldest son of Surgeon Henry, 47, Summer-hill. (1843-05-20, 3:6, D)

1215. On the 23d instant, at Beech Hill, the residence of her nephew, Robert Murray, Esq., M.D., at the advanced age of 98, Miss Jane Allen, the last surviving sister of the late Rev. Andrew Allen, LL.D., formerly Archdeacon of Clogher. (1843-05-27, 3:3, D)

1216. On Friday, the 12th of May, inst., at his residence, after a few hours' illness, aged 71 years, in consequence of a fall from a car, Mr. James Clark, sen., an old and highly respectable inhabitant of Clones. (1843-05-27, 3:3, D)

1217. On the 12th March last, at Kyak Phoo Annacan, India, of fever, Ensign Thomas Robinson, of the 60th Regiment Native Bengal Infantry, Hon. E.I.C.S., aged 23 years, son of the late Thomas Robinson, Esq., Devinney, near Portadown. (1843-05-27, 3:3, D)

1218. At Slieveroe, county Monaghan, on Sunday, the 6th inst., Letitia, relict of the late Rev. James Rankin, who was for many years Minister of the Presbyterian Congregation of Ballyalbany, in same county. (1843-05-27, 3:3, D)

1219. On the 17th instant, in the prime of life, Mary, eldest daughter of John Bryan, Esq., solicitor, Dundalk. Her early removal will long be lamented by her bereaved parents, and those who enjoyed the pleasure of her society. (1843-05-27, 3:3, D)

1220. At Wilson's Hospital, Westmeath, the lady of the Rev. H. Taylor Ringwood, of a son. (1843-06-03, 3:4, B)

1221. At the Glebe House, Tuam, the lady of the Rev. John Galbraith, of a son. (1843-06-03, 3:4, B)

1222. At Fermoy, the lady of Edward Briscoe, Esq., late Captain, 60th Regiment, of a son. (1843-06-03, 3:4, B)

1223. At St. Peter's church, William Michael Reynolds, Delgany, in the county of Wicklow, Esq., to Frances Elizabeth, daughter of Edward Sherlock, of Dublin, Esq. (1843-06-03, 3:4, M)

1224. On Tuesday last, at Tyhollan church, by the Rev. Mr. Faulkener, Mr. John T. M'Auliffe, Printer, and Foreman in the *Northern Standard* Office, to Susan, eldest daughter of Mr. Richard Ellis, of this town. (1843-06-10, 3:3, M)

1225. On the 7th instant in Kinnawly Church, by the Rev. J.J. Fox, Mr. William Rawdon Holmes, of Emyvale, merchant, to Martha, second daughter of the late John Buchanan, Esq., of Drummany, Enniskillen. (1843-06-10, 3:3, M)

1226. March 24, killed in general action fought by the forces under Sir C. Napier, with the army of Meer Sheer Mahomed, near Hyderabad, John Crawford Smith, Lieutenant Bombay Horse Artillery, aged 21 years, third son of Robert Smith Esq., 10, Mountjoy-square, West. (1843-06-10, 3:3, D)

1227. June 5th, at the Murrough, Wicklow, in the prime of life, Robert Montgomery, Esq., third son of the late Alexander Nixon Montgomery, Esq., of Bessmount Park, County Monaghan. The remains of this lamented and deservedly regretted young gentleman will be interred this day (Saturday), in the family vault at Tyhollan Church, at 12 o'clock. The funeral will reach Castleshane at 10 o'clock, A.M., and proceed through that village to the burying-ground. (1843-06-10, 3:3, D)

1228. June 11, at Clontibret Glebe, county of Monaghan, the lady of Archdeacon Russell of a daughter. (1843-06-17, 3:6, B)

1229. June 14th, in Clones church, by the bride's brother, the Rev. John H. Jameson, A.M., William Middleton, Esq., M.D., of Fintona, to Fanny Anne youngest daughter of Captain Jameson, late of the 70th Regiment, Clonkeen, county Monaghan. (1843-06-17, 3:6, M)

1230. At Liscarney, on Monday, 26th June, the lady of John Richardson, Esq., of a son. (1843-07-01, 3:2, B)

1231. On Thursday, by the Rev. Mr. Deery, P.P., Mr. Thomas Slowey, of Monaghan, Builder, to Martha, youngest daughter of the late Mr. Maurice Herbert, of Clones. (1843-07-01, 3:2, M)

1232. June 28, at Leamington, Warwickshire, by the Rev. John Craig, A.M., Thomas Young Prior, Esq., Barrister-at-Law, of the Middle Temple, youngest son of the Rev. Thomas Prior, D.D., S.F., Vice-Provost of Trinity College, Dublin, to Jane Matilda, only surviving daughter of the late Rev. Robert Russell, D.D., of Ashbrook, in the county of Fermanagh. (1843-07-01, 3:2, M)

1233. June 28, in St. Paul's Church, by the Rev. Mr. Lefanu, Joseph Smith, Esq., late of the 48th regiment, to Jane Agnes, fourth daughter of George Fosberry, Esq., of Blennerville, county of Kerry. (1843-07-01, 3:2, M)

1234. June 15, at the Friends' Meeting-house, Moyallen, Joshua Robert Fennel, of Ronford, son of the late Robert Fennel of Garryone, county Tipperary, to Elizabeth Lacky Christie, second daughter of John Christie of Stramore, county Down. (1843-07-01, 3:2, M)

1235. On the 25th instant, at Clones, of scarletina, in her 30th year, Rebecca, the beloved wife of Mr. Joseph Porter.—During her life she was loved and respected by all who knew her, and her death is deeply deplored by her friends. (1843-07-01, 3:2, D)

1236. June 22, in Boyle, Lieut. J.W. Allingham, Barrack-master of the Boyle district, in his 44th year. His remains were interred with military honours by the 47th depot. (1843-07-01, 3:2, D)

1237. June 27, at his residence, at Foulksrath Castle, county Kilkenny, after a tedious illness, Stephen Wright, aged 77 years. (1843-07-01, 3:2, D)

1238. June 21, at Johnstown Glebe, William Roan Kennedy, Esq., M.D., fifth son of the Rev. P. Kennedy, Vicar of Loughmore, county Tipperary. (1843-07-01, 3:2, D)

1239. June 24th, at Banaghar, of malignant scarletina, after a few days' illness, Robert Owen Eurath, Esq., in the 24th year of his age, to the inexpressible grief of his afflicted relatives and sorrowing friends. (1843-07-01, 3:2, D)

1240. June 28, in Leeson-street, Dublin, after a protracted illness, which she endured with the meekness of a Christian, Sarah, the beloved wife of A.J. Watson, Esq. (1843-07-01, 3:2, D)

1241. June 26th at Monkstown, Major James Percival, of Barntown House, County of Wexford, aged 58. (1843-07-01, 3:2, D)

1242. July 1, by the Hon. and Rev. Arthur Perceval, Philip Perceval, Esq., of the Royal Horse Guards, eldest son of Colonel Perceval, of Temple House, county of Sligo, to Frederica Penelope, youngest daughter of Colonel Hugh Baillie, of Redcastle, Ross-shire, N.B. (1843-07-08, 3:3, M)

1243. July 3, at Greenwich, Alexander Holmes, of Calcutta, Esq., eldest son of the late Alexander Holmes, of Larne, county Antrim, to Jessica Maria, third surviving daughter of the late Richard Johnson, Esq., of Baker's Farm, Lybleheadingham [Sible Hedingham], Essex, and of Queen's County. (1843-07-08, 3:3, M)

1244. July 4, at St. Peter's Church, by the Rev. William Peacocke, Captain Gore, of the 72d Highlanders, son of Francis Gore, Esq., of Derrymere, county Clare, to Catherine, daughter of the late Hugh Faulkner, Esq., Fort Faulkner, county Carlow, and niece of Sir Thomas Butler, Bart. (1843-07-08, 3:3, M)

1245. On the 29th June, in the 20th year of her age, near Clones, Eliza, second daughter of the late Lieutenant Thomas Welsh, of the Leitrim Regiment of Militia.—Also, his relict, Olivia Welsh, at same place, on the 2d inst., in her 48th year. They both died with a blessed hope of a glorious immortality, which affords a strong consolation to her sorrowing friends and acquaintances. (1843-07-08, 3:3, D)

1246. July 5, at Tyholland Glebe, County Monaghan, Frederick Faulkiner, Esq., late of Congor-house, County Tipperary, aged 82 years. (1843-07-08, 3:3, D)

1247. On Tuesday, 27th ult., at Dungannon, in the prime of life, Mr. Andrew Vance, merchant. (1843-07-08, 3:3, D)

1248. June 30, at Port, in the county of Leitrim, the residence of her father, Captain Hamilton Peyten, Susanna, wife of Robert Peyten Graham, of Dublin, solicitor, aged 22 years. (1843-07-08, 3:3, D)

1249. June 26, at Franklin-place, Belfast, Louisa, the wife of the Rev. William Filgate, of Maherally Glebe, county Down. (1843-07-08, 3:3, D)

1250. At the residence of his son, Clapham, Surrey, on the 8th instant, after a severe illness, John Walker, Esq., in the 70th year of his age. He held an important situation in the India House for many years, and was for a period of more than forty years, connected with the old firm of Sir Francis Baring, Bart.; also, that of Mr. Alexander Baring, the present Lord Ashburton, to whom he was related. (1843-07-15, 3:5, D)

1251. On the 27th instant, in Monaghan Church, by the Rev. H. Maffatt, Mr. Thomas Scott, of Leagh, county Monaghan, to Margaret, eldest daughter of Robert Taylor, Esq., late of Bannaghban, county Monaghan. (1843-07-29, 3:5, M)

1252. July 23, in St. Pancras Church, London, by the Rev. Henry Melvill, M.A., the Rev. Redmond C. M'Causland, Rector of Desartoghill, in the county of Londonderry, to Martha, eldest daughter of Samuel Babington, of Rome Cottage, Monmouthshire. (1843-07-29, 3:5, M)

1253. July 24, in St. Nicholas's Church, Dundalk, by his father, the Rev. Henry Cotten, LL.D., Dean of Lismore, Henry Laurence Cotton [sic], Esq., grandson of the late Most Rev. Dr. Laurence, late Archbishop of Cashel, to Elizabeth Sarah, eldest daughter of Malby Crofton, Esq., and grand-daughter of Sir James Crofton, Bart., of Longford House, in the county of Sligo. (1843-07-29, 3:5, M)

1254. July 14, at Coromahen, county of Leitrim, Thomas N. Jones, Esq., aged 47 years. (1843-07-29, 3:5, D)

1255. July 23, John Henry Norton, Esq., Solicitor, of Dominick-street, Dublin. (1843-07-29, 3:5, D)

1256. July 23, at Crossmaglin, in the county of Armagh, Samuel Ball, Esq., Captain, H.P., Royal Marines, at the advanced age of 87 years. (1843-07-29, 3:5, D)

1257. July 25, at her residence, 129, Stephen's-green, Dublin, Elizabeth, relict of the late Rev. Henry Johnson, Rector of Magourney, county of Cork, deeply and universally lamented. (1843-07-29, 3:5, D)

1258. At Ramsgate, aged 71 years, George Bourne, Esq., Commander in the Royal Navy, brother of the late W.H. Bourne, Esq., of Terenure, county of Dublin. (1843-07-29, 3:5, D)

1259. On Tuesday the 1st of August by the Rev. James Bell, Tandragee, the Rev. Alexander G. Ross, Presbyterian minister of Markethill, and eldest son of James Alexander Ross, Esq., Monaghan, to Mariane, second daughter of Daniel C. M'Clure, Millmount, Markethill. (1843-08-05, 3:5, M)

1260. At Poplar Vale, Monaghan, on the morning of the 3d inst., Major Edward Richardson, D.L. and J.P., in his 75th year, deeply and deservedly regretted. (1843-08-05, 3:5, D)

1261. At the residence of his brother, Richard Mitchell, Esq., Hill, Monaghan, where he had been stopping for the benefit of his health, John Mitchell Esq., Provisional assignee of the Insolvent court, Dublin. (1843-08-05, 3:5, D)

1262. Aug. 16, at Dartrey, county of Monaghan, the Lady Cremorne, of a son. (1843-08-19, 3:5, B)

1263. August 14, at Askin Morrison's, Esq., Dublin, by the Rev. William B. Kirkpatrick, the Rev. Thomas Boyd, Presbyterian Minister of Castleblayney, to Jane Eliza, only daughter of James M'Birney, Esq., Millmount, county of Monaghan. (1843-08-19, 3:5, M)

1264. Aug. 17, in St. Anne's Church, Dublin, by the Rev. Thomas Gregg, Daniel Noble Wallace, Esq., M.D., of Boyle, to Mary Anne, only daughter of the late Mr. Alexander Kanning. (1843-08-19, 3:5, M)

1265. Aug. 12, in St. Martin's Church, Guernsey, the Rev. Charles Ross De Havilland, to Grace Anna Dorothea Verner, third daughter of the late David Verner, Esq., of Churchill, county of Armagh. (1843-08-19, 3:5, M)

1266. Aug. 15, in Nuncross Church, Wicklow, by the Rev. Alexander Royley [sic] Miller, A.M., Perpetual Curate of Baleek, county of Armagh, William Rowley Miller, Esq., Barrister-at-Law, to Elfrida, youngest daughter of the late Thomas Philips, Esq., of Edergale, in the county of Cavan. (1843-08-19, 3:5, M)

1267. Aug. 15, at Lisbellaw, by the Rev. Walter Going, Henry Thompson, Esq., to Lavinia Eleaner, eldest daughter of the Rev. J.G. Porter, Belle Isle, county of Fermanagh. (1843-08-19, 3:5, M)

1268. On the 22d instant, at Glasslough Church, by the Rev. William Henry Pratt, Vicar of Donagh, Charles Douglas, Esq., M.D., of King's-street, Glasgow, to Jemima, fifth daughter of the late William Campbell, Esq., of Portanaghy, county Monaghan, and niece of Robert Killen, Esq., of same place. (1843-08-26, 3:4, M)

1269. August 18, in St. Audoen's Church, Dublin, by the Rev. Thomas Scott, A.M., George Mahood, Esq., M.D., of Cootehill, County of Cavan, to Eleanor Anne, relict of Colonel Arthur Disney, E.I.C., late of Margaret-place, Dublin, and Ballysax, County of Kildare. (1843-08-26, 3:4, M)

1270. August 15, in Lurgan church, by the Rev. Mr. Oulton, Hugh Watson, Esq. of Lurgan, to Marianne, only daughter of William Armstrong, Esq., of same place. (1843-08-26, 3:4, M)

1271. August 15, in Cootehill Church, by the Rev. Philip Brabazon, William Mitchel, Esq., Surgeon, of Newbliss, county of Monaghan, son of Henry Mitchel, Esq., of Campstown, to Ann, second daughter of Mr. John Higinbotham, of Cootehill, merchant. (1843-08-26, 3:4, M)

1272. August 15, in Ballyclough Church, by the Rev. John Chester, Conway Blizard, jun., Esq., A.B., late of Grovefield, county of Down, to Dora, daughter of Thomas Haines, Esq., of Mallow. (1843-08-26, 3:4, M)

1273. August 17, at Rostrevor, Mrs. Fosbery, relict of the late George Fosbery, Esq., of Adare Farm, in the county Limerick, daughter of the late Thomas Rice, of Mount Trenchard, same county, and grandmother of Charles Powell Leslie, Esq., of Glasslough, M.P. for the county Monaghan. (1843-08-26, 3:4, D)

1274. August 22, at the Water, Blackrock, Dundalk, where he had been only a few days, Wm. Dermott, Esq., of Nappa, county Cavan, aged 60, whose loss will be long and deeply lamented by his sorrowing friends and relatives. (1843-08-26, 3:4, D)

1275. August 28, in the Church of St. Andrew, Westland Row, James, youngest son of William Flood, Esq., of Mountprospect, county of Kildare, to Honoria, eldest daughter of the late John Hogan, Esq., brewer, Dublin. (1843-09-02, 3:4, M)

1276. On Friday, the 18th inst., Alicia, relict of the late Mr. John Horan, of Cootehill. (1843-09-02, 3:4, D)

1277. Aug. 29, at Sea View, Clontarf, aged 13 years, Anne, only surviving daughter of Hugh Chambers Esq. (1843-09-02, 3:4, D)

1278. Aug. 26, at Rostrevor, of apoplexy, Charles Norman, Esq., of Glengollan-house, Fahan, county of Donegall. (1843-09-02, 3:4, D)

1279. Aug. 13, John Forster, Esq., at his residence, Summer-hill, in the 94th year of his age. (1843-09-02, 3:4, D)

1280. Aug. 29, at his residence, Richmond Hill, West, county of Dublin, Patrick Newman, Esq., sincerely and deservedly regretted. (1843-09-02, 3:4, D)

1281. On the 26th ult., at Derrygooney Lodge, County Monaghan, at the residence of her brother, Richard A. Minnit, Esq., Jane, the only surviving daughter of the late Captain Robert M. Minnit, aged 30 years. (1843-09-09, 3:5, D)

1282. On the 28th ult., of consumption, at the residence of her father, near Clones, in this county, Bessie, second daughter of James Knight, Esq., solicitor. (1843-09-09, 3:5, D)

1283. April 15, on her homeward passage from India, Elizabeth, wife of John Smith, Esq., M.D., Surgeon of the 64th N.I., Berampore, and second daughter of the late Captain John Joyce, 60th Rifles, and formerly Inspector of the Fermanagh Constabulary. (1843-09-09, 3:5, D)

1284. September 7, at Downpatrick, by the Rev. S.C. Nelson, James Murland, Esq., of Downpatrick, to Margaret, only daughter of the late William Beckett, Esq., of the same place. (1843-09-16, 3:4, M)

1285. September 11, by the Rev. James Steele, Stranorlar, James Holmes, Esq., Navney House, Stranorlar, Glencovet Cottage, county of Donegal, to Jane, fourth daughter of John Craig, Esq., Killygordon. (1843-09-16, 3:4, M)

1286. September 12, by the Rev. James Morgan, Mr. Joseph Lowry, to Ellen, eldest daughter of Martin Harper, Esq., merchant, Belfast. (1843-09-16, 3:4, M)

1287. September 12, in St. Mary's Bryanston-square, London, by the Rev. William Charleton, M.A., Charles Gubbins, of the Bengal Civil Service, second son of the late Major General Gubbins, to Maria Burnley, eldest daughter of Joseph Hume, Esq., M.P. (1843-09-16, 3:4, M)

1288. Sept. 13, Richard Falls, Esq., of Augnacloy, in the county of Tyrone, aged 61 years; he was much esteemed, and is sincerely regretted. (1843-09-16, 3:4, D)

1289. At Carrickmacross, on Wednesday last, of inflammation, Margaret, wife of Charles M'Mahon, Esq., Solicitor, of said town. (1843-09-16, 3:4, D)

1290. September 11, at Sans Souci, near Belfast, Dr. Purden, aged 73 years. (1843-09-16, 3:4, D)

1291. September 8, in Park-street, London, Blanche Eleanor, infant daughter of Lord and Lady Robert Grosvenor. (1843-09-16, 3:4, D)

1292. Sept. 10, at Cullinswood, Dr. James Fabie, late Master of the Royal School, Balanus. (1843-09-16, 3:4, D)

1293. Sept. 28, in Clontarf Church, by the Rev. Decimus Preston, the Rev. W.G. Ormsby, Curate of Clontarf, son of the late Rev. Owen Ormsby, of Kilmore, county of Roscommon, to Henrietta, daughter of Lieut. General Armstrong, of Woodville, Killester, county of Dublin. (1843-09-30, 3:4, M)

1294. Sept. 26, in Malahide Church, by the Rev. George Bennett, Edmond, son of George Bennett, Esq., Q.C., Merrion-square, Dublin, to Cecilia Mary, the eldest daughter of M.M. O'Grady, Esq., M.D., of La Mancha, county of Dublin. (1843-09-30, 3:4, M)

1295. Sept. 25, at Egremont, Cheshire, Edward Atkinson, Esq., of Carrickmacross, Monkstown, county of Dublin, Barrister-at-Law, to Jane, third daughter of the late B. Searight, Esq., of Liverpool. (1843-09-30, 3:4, M)

1296. On the 4th of October, in the parish church of Aughclooney, diocese of Derry, by the Rev. Mr. Roleston, John Hatchell, Esq., of Bessmount-park, High Sheriff of the county of Monaghan, to Elizabeth Anne, only daughter of the late Doctor Speer, of Glasslough. (1843-10-07, 3:3, M)

1297. On Tuesday, 3d October, at Finner Church, Bundoran, by the uncle of the bride, the Rev. John Auchinleck, Rector of Dunboyne, John Charles Doveton Coane, of Brookhill, county of Leitrim, Esq., to Anna Maria, second daughter of the late Richard Dane, Esq., of Killyhevlin, county Fermanagh, D.L., J.P. (1843-10-07, 3:3, M)

1298. October 3, in Finner Church, Bundoran, by the Rev. Alexander Eccles Auchinleck, of Templecarne, William, third son of Joseph Macartney, Esq., of Hollywood, county of Down, and grandson of the late Sir John Macartney, Bart., to Henrietta, third daughter of the late Richard Dane, Esq., of Killyhevlon, county of Fermanagh, D.L., J.P. (1843-10-07, 3:3, M)

1299. At Finner Church, on Thursday, the 28th September, by the Rev. Mr. Dunbar, Wm. Scott, Esq., of Omagh, to Jane, fourth daughter of Gerrard Lloyd, Esq., of Munville, county Fermanagh. (1843-10-07, 3:3, M)

1300. On the 28th ult., in the church of Mullaghdun, parish of Cleenish, by the Rev. Thomas Birney, rector of Templecarne, William Nixon, Esq., of Thorn Hill, county Cavan, to Rebecca, eldest daughter of Robert Macartney, Esq., of Moybane, county Fermanagh. (1843-10-07, 3:3, M)

1301. Sept. 29, in Mitchelstown Church, by the Rev. John Wade, A.M., George Wade, Esq., Sub-Inspector of Constabulary, second son of George Wade, Esq., County Inspector, Omagh, to Ellen, youngest daughter of the late Prince Crawford, Esq., of Dublin. (1843-10-07, 3:3, M)

1302. In Calry Church, Sligo, Robert Armstrong, Esq., son of Captain Armstrong, of Manorhamilton, to Maria, relict of the late Major Baines. (1843-10-07, 3:3, M)

1303. On the 28th ult. in the Parish Church of Belfast, by the Rev. Charles Oulton, Rector of Kilmore, county Down, Peter Smith, jun., of Glasgow, Esq., to Margaret Anderson, second daughter of John Cramsie, of Belfast, Esq. (1843-10-07, 3:3, M)

1304. On the 21st inst, at Coolock Church, by the Venerable Archdeacon Laugrishe, and afterwards at Charles Roper's, Esq., according to the rites of the Roman Catholic Church, Thos. Joseph Fitzgerald, Esq., of Ballinaparka, in the county Waterford, to Jane Ann, daughter of the late William Roper, Esq., and grand-daughter of the late Hon. and Rev. Richard Henry Roper, Rector of Clones, county Monaghan. (1843-10-07, 3:3, M)

1305. On the 28th ult. at Booterstown Church, by the Rev. R.H. Nixon, Fergus Massy, Esq., of Belfast, to Mary, eldest daughter of Ewd. Ferrar, Esq., of Sydney Avenue, county Dublin. (1843-10-07, 3:3, M)

1306. Oct. 1, at Cove, Mary, eldest daughter of the late Honorable Richard Westenra. (1843-10-07, 3:3, D)

1307. Sept. 25, at Market Hill, aged 83 years, Joshua Paul Barker, Esq., Captain and Adjutant of the Armagh Militia—for several years, an efficient and active Magistrate for the county Armagh. (1843-10-07, 3:3, D)

1308. Sept. 29, suddenly, James Hamilton, Esq., formerly of Mulnagore Lodge, in the county Tyrone, and many years a merchant in Dublin, deeply regretted by his family and friends. (1843-10-07, 3:3, D)

1309. Sept. 28, at Rathmines, Mrs. Avis Nuttal, relict of the late Captain Nuttal, whom she survived upwards of 70 years. She died at the advanced age of 101, having retained her mental faculties with perfect distinctness to the last. (1843-10-07, 3:3, D)

1310. On Friday, the 29th September, at his residence, Enniskillen, Mr. Denis Quinton, an old and respectable inhabitant. (1843-10-07, 3:3, D)

1311. On Monday morning, after a short illness, Mrs. M'Vey, of Enniskillen. (1843-10-07, 3:3, D)

1312. On Friday the 13th inst., in the Church of Monaghan, by the Rev. H. Maffatt, Mr. James Laing, Head Constable of Police, to Sarah Jane, second daughter of Mr. Richard Skelton, of Market-street, Monaghan. (1843-10-14, 3:2, M)

1313. October 8, in Newry, the Rev. W. Hamilton, aged 82 years. For fifty-five years, he was a zealous and faithful Minister of the Gospel in the Wesleyan Methodist connection. (1843-10-14, 3:2, D)

1314. October 9, at Sandymount, county of Dublin, Sidney, daughter of the Rev. John Harvey, late Rector of Boveragh [sic], county of Londonderry, universally beloved and respected. (1843-10-14, 3:2, D)

1315. On the 15th instant, at Castleblayney, the Lady of Hugh Swanzy, Esq., of a son. (1843-10-21, 3:2, B)

1316. The Lady of Wm. Walker, Esq., Architect, Monaghan, of a daughter, on the 17th instant. (1843-10-21, 3:2, B)

1317. At Drumbrain House, on the 19th instant, the Lady of Arthur Bernard Blazby, Esq., of a son. (1843-10-21, 3:2, B)

1318. October 24, in Cootehill Church, by the Rev. Joseph Welsh, Rector of Killaughter, in the county Donegal, his eldest son, the Rev. Charles Welsh, Curate of Clones, to Grace, youngest daughter of the late Major Coote, and sister of Thomas Coote, Esq., J.P. & D.L., Retreat, county Cavan. (1843-10-28, 3:3, M)

1319. On the 25th instant, at Clones Glebe, in her 69th year, Mary, wife of the Very Rev. Dean Roper, Rector of Clones. (1843-10-28, 3:3, D)

1320. October 27th, at Lisboy, Parish of Donagh, George Dunglass, aged 104. (1843-10-28, 3:3, D)

1321. Oct. 21, in St. George's Church, by the Right Hon. and Right Reverend the Lord Bishop of Meath, Walter Keating, Esq., of Sylvan Park, in the county of Meath, Barrister at Law, to Elizabeth, daughter of Richard Robinson Lodge, Esq., late of Caledon, in the county Tyrone, deceased. (1843-11-04, 3:6, M)

1322. Oct. 26, at Shipquay-street, Derry, by the Rev. William M'Clure, the Rev. Peter Dale, Minister of the united Parishes of Houston and Killalar, Renfrewshire, to Margaret, eldest daughter of the late Rev. George Hay, of Derry. (1843-11-04, 3:6, M)

1323. Nov. 2, at Knockbane, near Tynan, aged 91 years, Sarah, relict of Thomas Bond, of Bondville, county of Armagh, Esq. (1843-11-11, 3:6, D)

1324. Nov. 4, at Dawn View, near Coleraine, in the 86th year of her age, Elizabeth, relict of the Rev. John [Little? *illegible*] late of S–wegues [*illegible*], and Vicar of Drummaul, in the county of Antrim. (1843-11-11, 3:6, D)

1325. At the house of her sister, Mrs. Hairrington, How— [Howth?], at an advanced age, Anne, daughter of the late M— [*illegible*] Johnston, Esq., of Henry-street, Dublin. (1843-11-11, 3:6, D)

1326. October 29, in Dublin, Miss Montgomery, [*illegible*] daughter of the late John Montgomery, Esq., [*illegible*] Mills, county of Kildare. (1843-11-11, 3:6, D)

1327. November 7, at Ballykilty Church, by the Rev. John Olphert, John L. Robinson, Esq., of the

Diamond, Monaghan, to Hannah Little, of Newtown-limavady, eldest daughter of the late Patrick Little, of Dungiven, in the county of Londonderry, Esq. (1843-11-18, 3:5, M)

1328. On the 18th instant, at Lowtherstown, by the Rev. Edward Johnston, George Gilmore, Esq., Brackaville, county Tyrone, to Catherine, second daughter of the Rev. Wm. Douglas, Wesleyan Minister, Lowtherstown. (1843-11-18, 3:5, M)

1329. On the 11th instant, at Drumgroan, in this county, in the 86th year of his age, Thomas Humphrys, Ensign in the Volunteers and Lieutenant in the Ballyleck Yeomanry, universally lamented by his numerous relations and friends. (1843-11-18, 3:5, D)

1330. Nov. 11, at the Rectory, Castleblayney, the lady of the Rev. J.T. Whitestone, of a daughter. (1843-11-25, 3:4, B)

1331. At Cabra Lodge, the lady of the Rev. R.L. Tottenham, of a daughter. (1843-11-25, 3:4, B)

1332. Nov. 1, at the British Embassy, at Vienna, the Earl of Shelbourne, to the Honorable Emily Elphinstone de Flahault, eldest daughter of the Comte de Flahault, French Ambassador at Vienna, and Baroness Keith and Nairn. (1843-11-25, 3:4, M)

1333. Nov. 20, at Fitzwilliam Lodge, Blackrock, near Dublin, the Countess of Roscommon, after a short illness. (1843-11-25, 3:4, D)

1334. Nov. 19, at Bersted Lodge, Bognor, the Countess of Mayo. Her Ladyship's sufferings, for the last three weeks, have been severe, which she bore with the greatest fortitude and resignation. (1843-11-25, 3:4, D)

1335. November 28, at Retreat, county Cavan, the lady of Thomas Coote, Esq., J.P., and D.L., of a daughter. (1843-12-09, 3:4, B)

1336. November 20, Mrs. Joseph Lowry, of Ballieborough, of a son. (1843-12-09, 3:4, B)

1337. In Clogh Church, on the 7th inst., by the Rev. V.D. Christian, David Bruce, Esq., Officer of Excise, to Sarah, youngest daughter of the Rev. W. Gunn. (1843-12-09, 3:4, M)

1338. December 3, at his residence, Ardress, near Loughgall, county Armagh, George Ansor, Esq., aged 73 years. (1843-12-09, 3:4, D)

1339. December 3, in Devonshire-place, London, aged 84 years, General Edward Morrison, Colonel of the 13th Light Infantry. (1843-12-09, 3:4, D)

1340. On Monday morning, after a few minutes' illness, at his residence in Glasslough-street, John Johnston, Esq., Co. Inspector of Constabulary for Monaghan. The remains of this esteemed and respected gentleman were interred in Tyholland grave-yard on Thursday, and the long train of carriages and vehicles, filled with the gentry and inhabitants of the town and neighbourhood, proved the high position he held in the love of those who knew him.—Kind and courteous in his deportment, he performed his duties with benefit to the country and with credit to himself; and while he firmly carried into effect the necessities of the law, he smoothed, by his manner of doing so, its rigors. A large body of the Constabulary force in coloured clothes, marched beside the hearse to the cemetery; the coffin was borne to the tomb by the officers and head constables of the force under his command, who had long learned to look upon him as a father and a friend. (1843-12-16, 3:2, D)

1341. On Wednesday, in Glasslough Church, by the Rev. William H. Pratt, Vicar of Donagh, Mr. Robt. Crowne, of Minmurray, to Isabella, youngest daughter of Mr. Robert Wilson, of Dessart, county Monaghan. (1843-12-23, 3:5, M)

1342. In Tullycorbet Church, by the Rev. John Hare, Isaiah Gibson, Esq., Listrar, county Monaghan, to Anne, second daughter to the late W. Niblock, Esq., of Corlongford, county Monaghan. (1843-12-23, 3:5, M)

1343. On the 18th instant, by the Rev. Mr. Johnston, Mr. John Taylor, to Jane, eldest daughter of Mr. Robert Vance, of Belfast. (1843-12-23, 3:5, M)

1344. On the 15th instant, at Saintfield, by the Rev. James Wallace, Mr. Thomas Walker Davidson, of Lisroan, near Moy, to Miss Mary Rose Davidson, fourth daughter of the late Mr. William Davidson, of Mavesford, near Saintfield. (1843-12-23, 3:5, M)

1345. At Moneyrea, on the 16th instant, Mr. Wm. Patterson, in the 73d year of his age. (1843-12-23, 3:5, D)

1346. Suddenly, on the 5th instant of apoplexy, the Rev. H. Hutchinson, of Duneane. (1843-12-23, 3:5, D)

1347. On the 12th inst., Lieutenant-Colonel John Montagu, late of the Coldstream Regiment of Guards. (1843-12-23, 3:5, D)

1348. Dec. 27, in Booterstown Church, by the Rev. Samuel Magee, Andrew Taylor, Esq., to Annette Augusta, fourth daughter of the late Major James Flood, of Dundalk. (1843-12-30, 3:6, M)

1349. Dec. 26, Mr. James Meade, of 14, George's-hill, to Mary, daughter of the late Mr. James Kennedy, of Ormond-market, Dublin. (1843-12-30, 3:6, M)

1350. Dec. 22, by the Rev. J. Alfred Canning, Kilkeel, the Rev. Samuel J. Smith, Newcastle, to Miss Irvine, only daughter of William Irvine, Esq., Mourne, and sister to Hill Irvine, Esq., Newry. (1843-12-30, 3:6, M)

1351. Dec. 24, in Kilmore Church, by the Rev. Mr. M'Cullough, Mr. Robert Robinson, of Kilmore, to Ruth, second daughter of Mr. William Welsham, of Crossgar. (1843-12-30, 3:6, M)

1352. Dec. 20, at Janeville, county of Louth, having nearly completed his 87th year, Robert Younge, Esq., of L—burn [*partially illegible*], one of the Volunteers of 1778. (1843-12-30, 3:6, D)

1353. Dec. 23, Robert Horne, Esq., of Harleyford-place Kennington-common, many years of the Navy-office, in his 88th year. (1843-12-30, 3:6, D)

1354. Dec. 25, Joseph Singer, youngest son of the Reverend Robert Stavely. (1843-12-30, 3:6, D)

1355. On Monday last, at 3 o'clock, P.M., aged 72 years, Miss Elizabeth Ker, sister of Doctor A. Ker, proprietor of the town of Newbliss. A long life of usefulness made her beloved, and in the fulness of age and faith, she left this world for a better. (1844-01-06, 3:1, D)

1356. 12th January, in Drumcrin Church, by the Rev. John Thornhill, William Fitzgerald, Esq., of Clona-villa, County Monaghan, to Eliza, daughter of the late Robert Deverell, Esq., of M'Clone, in the Queen's County. (1844-01-13, 3:5, M)

1357. January 6, at Warrenpoint Church, by the Rev. J. Davis, Mr. David Mahood, of Warrenpoint, to Margaretta, daughter of the late Wolsey Atkinson, Esq., Edenvilla, near Portadown. (1844-01-13, 3:5, M)

1358. Jan. 4, in St. Mark's Church, Armagh, by the Rev. Silver Oliver, Rector of Loughgall, John Moore Tittle, Esq., of Farmhill, in the county of Londonderry, to Sophia, fourth daughter of the late William Hardy, Esq., of Loughgall House in the county of Armagh. (1844-01-13, 3:5, M)

1359. On the 10th instant, after a few days' illness, of inflammation, in his 26th year, Wm. Mitchell Dudgeon, Esq., of Rosefield, in this county, Stamp Distributor for Monaghan, and eldest son of the late lamented Captain Ralph Dudgeon, of Rosefield. (1844-01-13, 3:5, D)

1360. On the 11th instant, at her house in Clones, in her 76th year, Anne, relict of the late Dr. Armstrong, of that town. Her end was peace, as she was enabled to rest confidently on the atonement. (1844-01-13, 3:5, D)

1361. At his residence, Cloniffe [sic], on Sunday, the 7th instant, Thomas Wright, Esq., Barrister, in the 45th year of his age. (1844-01-13, 3:5, D)

1362. January 8, in the 82d year of his age, at his residence, Glencaira, near Castleblayney, in the county of Armagh, Arthur Irwin, Esq., formerly of Grenville-street, in the city of Dublin, Solcitor. (1844-01-13, 3:5, D)

1363. Jan. 8, in Molesworth-street, Jane, lady of Edward Mathews, Esq., and mother of Jeffery Brownrigg [Browning], Esq., Carass Park, Limerick, sincerely and deservedly regretted. (1844-01-13, 3:5, D)

1364. On Saturday, the 20th inst., in Warrington-place, Dublin, the Lady of Richard Mayne, Esq., Newbliss, county of Monaghan, of a daughter. (1844-01-27, 3:6, B)

1365. On Sunday morning last, of consumption, at his residence, Newgrove, in his 64th year, Mr. John Hamilton, a man beloved during his life for honest integrity, and lamented in death as a friend lost to all who knew him. He bore his illness with Christian fortitude, and died in the full hope of a glorious immortality. (1844-01-27, 3:6, D)

1366. On Monday, 22d January, in Saint David's Church, Exeter, by the Rev. R.C. Harrington, Rector, Henry Mayne, Esq., 49th Regiment, Portsmouth, to Rebecca Jane, Widow of Samson Yule, Esq. (1844-02-03, 3:6, M)

1367. On Sunday morning last, of consumption, at his residence, Newgrove, in his 56th year, Mr. John Hamilton, a man beloved during his life for honest integrity, and lamented in death as a friend lost to all who knew him. He bore his illness with Christian fortitude, and died in the full hope of a glorious immortality. (1844-02-03, 3:6, D)

1368. On Wednesday last, by the Rev. John Bleckley, at the residence of the bride's father, Mr. Robert Blackburne, of Legacurry, in this county, to Eliza, eldest daughter of Mr. Thomas Watson, of Drumlara, county Monaghan. (1844-02-10, 3:6, M)

1369. On the 31st January, in his 71st year, at Clones, Lieut. George Pratt, 27th Regt., where he had been a resident for upwards of thirty years. (1844-02-10, 3:6, D)

1370. David Hamil, Esq., of Rusky, in the county of Monaghan, to Elizabeth, second daughter of the Rev. D. White, Bailieborough. (1844-02-17, 3:4, M)

1371. On Wednesday last, after a short illness, in her 33d year, Maryanne, wife of Edward Fiddis, Esq., of Clenamully, in this county. This untimely and melancholy bereavement has cast a large family, and a numerous circle of friends and relations by whom the deceased lady was well and deservedly beloved, into the most poignant grief. (1844-02-17, 3:4, D)

1372. Feb. 20, in Swanlinbar Church, by the Rev. William Prior Moore, A.M., the brother-in-law of the bride, the Rev. Orange Sterling Kellett, fourth son of Robert Kellett, Esq., of Waterstown, county of Meath, to Mary Anne, third daughter of the Rev. William Grattan, of Swanlinbar, county of Cavan, and Bensfort, county of Meath. (1844-02-24, 2:4, M)

1373. At Kingrave [Kingarve], near Dungannon, James Hasty, aged 95. For the last 50 years he had been agricultural steward to Edward Evans, Esq. (1844-02-24, 2:4, D)

1374. Feb. 15, at an advanced age, Ignatius Kelly, Esq., one of the oldest Solicitors in Ireland. (1844-02-24, 2:4, D)

1375. Feb. 19, at Armagh, Leonard Dobbin, D.L., and J.P., and formerly representative in Parliament for the borough of Armagh. (1844-02-24, 2:4, D)

1376. February 23d, in Tullycorbet church, by the Rev. John Hare, Thomas, eldest son of James Irwin, Esq., of Grove Island Lodge, county Cavan, to Cherry, fourth daughter of Thomas B. Ferguson, Esq., 107, Canal-street, Newry. (1844-03-02, 3:5, M)

1377. February 5th, in Navan, Mr. Samuel Gass, Printer, fourth son of the late Mr. John Gass, of this town. (1844-03-02, 3:5, D)

1378. On the 2d inst., at Mountsedborough, county Fermanagh, in the 23d year of her age, Caroline, wife of Mr. William Mayne, deeply lamented by her husband and relations. (1844-03-09, 3:4, D)

1379. On the 26th ult., of croup, aged 4 years and 3 months, Frederick Moore Wilde, son to the Rev. Wm. White, Gransha. His sweet and gentle spirit resigned, without a murmur, this tenement of clay for a blessed immortality. (1844-03-09, 3:4, D)

1380. On the 8th instant, after a short but severe illness, James, younger surviving son of James Lyle, Esq., of Newry. (1844-03-16, 3:5, D)

1381. At Killyconigan Cottage, on the 28th of February, Catherine, the beloved wife of Mr. William Burns, formerly of Monaghan, in the 58th year of her age. (1844-03-16, 3:5, D)

1382. March 14, at Echlinville, county Down, the lady of the Rev. John R. Echlin, of twins—a son and a daughter. (1844-03-23, 3:4, B)

1383. March 20, at St. Peter's Church, by the Rev. Francis Saunderson, Gartside Tipping, Esq., eldest son of Thomas Tipping, Esq., of Davenport Hall, Cheshire, to Jane, eldest daughter of Robert Fowler, Esq., of Rathmolyn House, county Meath, and niece to the Earl of Erne. (1844-03-23, 3:4, M)

1384. On the 12th instant, in Drumcree Church, county Armagh, by the Rev. David Babington, William Cowan, Esq., of Whiteabbey, to Mary, only daughter of Robert Waddell, of Drumcree-cottage. (1844-03-23, 3:4, M)

1385. On the 5th instant, at St. George's Church, Dublin, by the Rev. John Reid, Rector of Ballee, diocese of Down, Philip E. Brabazon, Esq., Fellow of the College of Surgeons, Dublin, and Surgeon of the county Down Infirmary, eldest son of Charles Brabazon, Esq., of Neilstown, county of Dublin, to Letitia, elder daughter of the late Edward Hudson, Esq., of Loughbrickland, county Down, and Gardiner-place, Dublin. (1844-03-23, 3:4, M)

1386. At Rockcorry, on Saturday, the 9th instant, Alexander Wilson, jun., aged 24 years, during a lingering illness, which he bore with Christian fortitude, and in his last moments he was enabled to cast himself wholly and unreservedly on the atoning efficacy of a Saviour's blood and righteousness. (1844-03-23, 3:4, D)

1387. At Belturbet, on Sunday, the 10th instant, in his 104th year, Mr. John M'Vity. (1844-03-23, 3:4, D)

1388. March 6, of rapid decline, at Killarney, in the 28th year of his age, Patrick O'Connor, Esq., for some years past connected with the *Morning Advertiser*, as a parliamentary reporter. (1844-03-23, 3:4, D)

1389. On the 8th instant, Mrs. Elizabeth Johnston, widow of the late Mr. John Johnston, of Antrim-lane, Lisburn, aged 67 years. (1844-03-23, 3:4, D)

1390. On the 6th instant, aged five years, Abraham Hume Fisher, second son of Mr. James Fisher, of Ashvale, Maragall. (1844-03-23, 3:4, D)

1391. On the 7th instant, in London, George M'Murray, Esq. of Warringstown [sic], aged 50. (1844-03-23, 3:4, D)

1392. In Cootehill Church, on Wednesday, the 13th inst. by the Rev. P. Brabazon, Edward Harrison, Esq., of Kingston, Upper Canada, to Jane, eldest daughter of John Higginbotham, Esq., of Cootehill. (1844-03-30, 3:3, M)

1393. On the 3rd instant, near Glasslough, Eliza, the beloved wife of Mr. Joseph Murdock, in the 54th year of her age. She was much and deservedly esteemed for her unaffected sincerity, kindness of heart, and her truly charitable disposition; possessed of a cheerful temper, a good understanding, and a retentive memory, her society was agreeable and entertaining. Having lived the life of the righteous, her latter end was peace. (1844-04-13, 3:2, D)

1394. On Monday last, at Slieveroe, in her 75th year, Martha, relict of the late Hamilton Reed, Esq. (1844-04-13, 3:2, D)

1395. On the 30th ult., in Muff Church, by the Rev. George W. Steuart, George Woodhouse, Esq., of Londonderry, to Margaret, daughter of the late John Cochrane, Esq., of same City, Merchant. (1844-05-04, 3:3, M)

1396. On Thursday last, in the Church of Glasslough, by the Rev. William H. Pratt, Vicar of Donagh, Arthur W. Holmes, Esq., proprietor of the *Northern Standard*, to Jane, second daughter of James George Lepper, Esq., of the Diamond, Monaghan. (1844-05-04, 3:3, M)

1397. April 27th, at St. Peter's Church, Dublin, Henry M'Geough, Esq., youngest son of the late Joshua M'Geough, Esq., of Greenwood-Park, county of Down, to Sarah Patience, youngest daughter of the late William Mayne, Esq., of Fream-mount, in this county. (1844-05-04, 3:3, M)

1398. On the 26th ult., at Salford Barracks, Manchester, from the effects of a fall from a horse, in the 20th year of his age, Mr. Mark Anthony Montgomery, of the 67th Regiment, youngest son of the late Alexander Nixon Montgomery, Bessmont Park, Monaghan. His remains was [sic] interred in the family vault, Tyholland, on Friday, the 3d inst. (1844-05-04, 3:3, D)

1399. On 25th of April, Annabella, the beloved wife of Mr. Wm. Clarke, of Drummullen, near Newbliss. She died as she lived, full of the blessed hope of a glorious immortality. "Let me die the death of the righteous, and let my last end be like his!" (1844-05-04, 3:3, D)

1400. On Tuesday last, in the Church of this town, by the Rev. Henry Maffatt, William Johnston Rutledge, Esq., of Crevena, county Tyrone, to Sarah, only daughter of Joseph Robinson, Esq., of the Diamond, Monaghan. (1844-05-11, 3:4, M)

1401. On Friday, in Tullycorbet church, by the Rev. Henry Maffatt, William M'Keane, Esq., of Clones, to Mary Jane, only daughter of the late George Barkley, Esq., of Monaghan. (1844-05-11, 3:4, M)

1402. On the 16th inst., at her father's house, by the Rev. A.G. Ross, Alicia, eldest daughter of James Lyle, Merchant, Newry, to James Mollan Ross, second son of James A. Ross, of Monaghan. (1844-05-18, 3:4, M)

1403. May 22, at Tunniscollen, the residence of the lady's brother, Mr. Edward Sharpe, of Killyclare, to Isabella, eldest daughter of the late Mr. John Steenson. (1844-05-25, 3:4, M)

1404. On the 18th inst., at Plymouth, of rapid decline, in her twentieth year, Anne, the youngest and beloved daughter of James Bleazby, Esq., late of the South Jenose, Cork. (1844-05-25, 3:4, D)

1405. Lady John Beresford, of a son and heir. (1844-06-04, 3:4, B)

1406. 29th May at Bryandrum, Markethill, Mrs. Alex. G. Ross, of a son. (1844-06-04, 3:4, B)

1407. Of consumption, at her residence in Monaghan, on Thursday last, Margaret, the beloved wife of Mr. William Watson, aged 33 years. (1844-06-04, 3:4, D)

1408. On the 1st inst., at Mount Louise, the Lady of Robert B. Evatt, Esq., of a daughter. (1844-06-08, 3:4, B)

1409. May the 28th, in Shipquay-street, Derry, the lady of Baptist Johnston Barton, Esq., of Portserlon [sic], county of Donegal, of a daughter. (1844-06-08, 3:4, B)

1410. In Paris, by the Right Rev. the Bishop Luscombe, chaplain to the British Embassy at the Court of France, the Rev. Charles W. Leslie, Incumbent of St. Leonard's and St Mary Magdalen, Sussex, to Emily, widow of the late Arthur French, Esq., of Leslie-house, Ballybay. (1844-06-08, 3:4, M)

1411. May 31st, Castleblayney, by the Rev. Mr. M'Phillips, Mr. James Doogan, to Sally Jane Clyanse, second daughter of Joseph Clyanse, Bath-hill. (1844-06-08, 3:4, M)

1412. On the 31st of May, at her residence, York Terrace, Hyde-park, London, deeply and sincerely regretted by her family and a large circle of friends, Alicia Ann, relict of the late Andrew Seton Karr, Esq., at Kippilace, Roxburghshire, and youngest daughter of the late John Rawlinson, Esq., of Ancots Hall, Lancashire. (1844-06-08, 3:4, D)

1413. On the 2d. inst., at Newbliss, the lady of William Mitchell, Esq., of a son. (1844-06-15, 3:3, B)

1414. At 78, Charlotte-street, Glasgow, on the 1st instant, the Lady of Dr. Charles Douglas, of a son. (1844-06-15, 3:3, B)

1415. June 11, in Davenham church, by the Rev. Thomas France, A.M., Rector of Davenham, the Rev. Charles O'Neill Pratt, A.M., curate of Christ Church Macclesfield, to Elizabeth Roylance, second daughter of William Court, Esq., The Manor House, Cheshire. (1844-06-15, 3:3, M)

1416. On the 30th ult., by the Rev. Henry Cottingham, at Ballymacue Church, county Cavan, Mr. Thomas Howe, formerly of Enniskillen, now of Cavan, to Rebecca, eldest daughter of the late Mr. Charles Moore, of Lisdarren, county Cavan. (1844-06-15, 3:3, M)

1417. On the 30th ult., in St. Andrew's Church, Dublin, Frederick A. Malcomson, of Drumrora House, county Cavan, Esq., to Bessie, third daughter of the late Henry Deacon, of Carlow, Esq. (1844-06-15, 3:3, M)

1418. On the 3d inst., at Belturbet Church, by the Rev. H.M. Winder, Henry H. Dickson, Esq., of Armagh, to Letitia Eleanor, daughter of Robert M'Gowan, Esq., Collector of Customs, Youghal. (1844-06-15, 3:3, M)

1419. On the 30th ult., at Ballymacue Church, county Cavan, by the Rev. Henry Cottingham, Mr. John Moore, of Lisdarren, to Jane, only surviving daughter of the late Mr. Irwin Johnstone, of the town of Cavan. (1844-06-15, 3:3, M)

1420. Marriage in High Life.—On Monday the 10th of June, in Saint Peter's Church, Sir David Roche, Bart., of Carass, county Limerick, M.P., to Cecilia Caroline, youngest daughter of Henry Deane Grady, Esq., of Stilorgan [sic] Castle and Merrion-square,

East, Dublin, sister of the Viscountess Massarene, the Lady Edward Chichester, and the Right Hon. Lady Muskerry. (1844-06-15, 3:3, M)

1421. On the 2d inst., at Derygooney [sic] Lodge, in this County, the residence of her son, Richard Allen Minnitt, Esq., J.P., Mrs. Minnitt, relict of the late Captain Robert M. Minnitt, aged 72 years. (1844-06-15, 3:3, D)

1422. At Philadelphia, on the 40th [sic] April, Edward Holmes, a native of Strabane, Ireland. (1844-06-15, 3:3, D)

1423. On the 25th ult., at Magera [sic], aged 43 years, Mr. John Mulholland, proprietor of the Maghera hotel. (1844-06-15, 3:3, D)

1424. At his residence, Bishop-street, Derry, Mr. Samuel Walker, of that city, merchant, aged 70. (1844-06-15, 3:3, D)

1425. On Sunday last, June 9, at Annahilla, aged seven years and nine months, Edward, the only and beloved son of Michael Elliott, Esq.

In youth and beauty's freshest bloom,
Death came remorseless and sunk him to the tomb.
(1844-06-15, 3:3, D)

1426. On the 29th ult., at Fountain-street, Derry, Anne, wife of Mr. William L. Warnock, aged 38 [or 36?] years. (1844-06-15, 3:3, D)

1427. On the 5th inst., at the Commercial Hotel, Londonderry, Mr. James Caldwell, commercial traveller for the house of Messrs. Cash and Ledgard, Wood street, London. (1844-06-15, 3:3, D)

1428. On the 6th inst., Mr. John M'Colgan, of Evish, near Strabane. (1844-06-15, 3:3, D)

1429. On the 7th inst., at Lagg, Malin, aged 80 years, Mr. John Magennis. (1844-06-15, 3:3, D)

1430. On the 1st inst., at Greenwich, in her 14th year, Ellen, only daughter of Mr. Hugh Breen, of the Royal Observatory, late of Armagh. (1844-06-15, 3:3, D)

1431. June 8, at Bundoran, county Donegal, after a very short illness, which he bore with truly Christian resignation, aged 60, Charles Archdall, Esq., of Rivers-town, county Fermanagh, a Magistrate for the counties of Fermanagh, Tyrone, and Donegal. (1844-06-15, 3:3, D)

1432. In William-street, Kilkenny, after an illness of some duration, greatly regretted by her friends and acquaintances, Mrs. Baird, wife of Mr. Walter Baird, Esq., Accountant in the Kilkenny Branch of the Provincial Bank. (1844-06-15, 3:3, D)

1433. June 1, the Rev. James Hamilton, Rector of Ardingly, Sussex, and formerly Rector of Cootehill, County of Cavan. (1844-06-15, 3:3, D)

1434. June 18, by special license, in Sandford Church, by the Venerable the Archdeacon of Emly, the Hon. Judge Crampton, to Magaret [sic], eldest daughter of John Duffy, Esq., of Pembroke-road, Dublin. (1844-06-22, 3:4, M)

1435. June 13, in St. Peter's Church, Captain Grady, son of Henry D. Grady, Esq., Q.C., to Miss Harding, daughter of the late John Harding, Esq. (1844-06-22, 3:4, M)

1436. On the 7th instant, Mr. John Thompson, to Frances, eldest daughter of Mr. John Kitson, both of Armagh. (1844-06-22, 3:4, M)

1437. On the 12th instant, at Warrenpoint Church, William Thompson, Esq., of Salisbury-street, Liver-pool, and eldest son of the late David Thompson, Esq., county Meath, to Jane, second daughter of Leonard Watson, Esq., Warrenpoint. (1844-06-22, 3:4, M)

1438. In this town on the 14th instant, aged four years and six months, Louisa, only child of Mr. William Watson, Diamond. (1844-06-22, 3:4, D)

1439. At Clones, on Monday, the 15th inst., in the 46th year of his age, Mr. John M'Coy, merchant. He is greatly lamented by all who knew him, and has left a loving wife and family to deplore his loss. (1844-06-22, 3:4, D)

1440. On Wednesday evening, at Corbyfin, in this county, after a lingering illness, aged 75 years, Sarah, wife of Mr. Samuel Anderson, of same place. (1844-06-22, 3:4, D)

1441. June 20, at St. Clement's, Cornwall, by the Rev. G.W. Gibson, M.A., Edmond Henry Casey, of Newbook House, County Dublin, Esq., to Mary, second daughter of the late Philip Sandys Tom, of Rosedale, Cornwall, Esq. (1844-06-29, 3:3, M)

1442. June 25, at Rathfarnham Church, Henry G. Bourne, of Terenure, county Dublin, to Margaret, daughter of Captain R. Bourne, R.N., of Mountpellier-parade, Monkstown. (1844-06-29, 3:3, M)

1443. June 25, at his residence, 9, Peter-place, after a painfully lingering illness, Mr. William Maguire, deeply and deservedly regretted by his family and a circle of numerous friends. (1844-06-29, 3:3, D)

1444. June 20, at Earlsgift, county of Tyrone, Georgiana Frances, fifth daughter of the Hon. and Rev. Charles Douglas, aged 15. (1844-06-29, 3:3, D)

1445. June 18, at Aberystwith [sic], South Wales, aged 24, Arabella, eldest daughter of M'Gillycuddy of the Reeks. (1844-06-29, 3:3, D)

1446. June 2, at 22, Hardwicke-street, in this city, Anne, daughter of the late Townley Blackwood, Esq., of Cloneroy, county of Cavan. (1844-06-29, 3:3, D)

1447. June 18, at Warrenpoint, after a few hours' ill-ness, William Daniel, Esq., of Ballymackey, in the county of Monaghan, J.P. (1844-06-29, 3:3, D)

1448. June 2, in Blackwatertown, after a few days' illness, William Wilson, Esq., aged eighty-nine years, deeply regretted by his family and a circle of numerous friends. (1844-06-29, 3:3, D)

1449. Birth of an Heir to the Western Moiety of the Barony of Farney.—On the 15th of July, in Lordones-street, Belgrave-square, London, the wife of Evelyn Philip Shirley, Esq., M.P., for the county of Monaghan, eldest son of E.J. Shirley, Esq., M.P., was safely delivered of a son and heir. (1844-07-20, 3:4, B)

1450. On Monday, the 15th instant, of fever, in her 54th year, Matilda, wife of Mr. John Rowland, Governor of the county prison. (1844-07-20, 3:4, D)

1451. On Thursday morning, at the residence of her husband, deeply deplored by all who had the pleasure of her acquaintance, aged 24 years, Hannah, the beloved wife of John L. Robinson, Esq., of the Diamond, Monaghan. (1844-07-20, 3:4, D)

1452. July 25, in Bride's Church, Dublin, by the Rev. Mr. Davis, Richard Mitchell, Esq., of this town, Solicitor, to Susan, youngest daughter of Andrew Johnston, Esq., of Enniskillen. (1844-07-27, 3:4, M)

1453. April 1, in Australia, Robert Baker, Esq., of Drue-Wallakiama, youngest son of Henry Fry, Esq., of Fortescue Terrace, (late of Frybrook, county of Roscommon,) to Ellen Anne Jane, eldest daughter of Captain Collins, late of the 13th Dragoons. (1844-08-03, 3:4, M)

1454. July 18, at Bray Church, by the Rev. Mr. Dombrain, Major Hamilton Dundas, late of the 85th Light Infantry, to Mary Augusta, widow of Peter Holmes, of Nenagh, and Peterfield, Esq. (1844-08-03, 3:4, M)

1455. July 25, at Knoctopher Church, by the Venerable the Archdeacon of Glendalough, Peter Connellan, Esq., of Coolmore, county Kilkenny, to Anna Maria, second daughter of the Rev. Sir H. Richard Langrishe, Bart., of Knocktopher House, in said county. (1844-08-03, 3:4, M)

1456. May 19, at his house in Bath, at the advanced age of eighty-one, Major-General Edward Scott, K.C., of Scottstown, in the county of Monaghan. He was one of the oldest General officers in the army, had served with distinguished reputation in various parts of the world, but had for many years retired from the active duties of his profession. (1844-08-03, 3:4, D)

1457. July 27, in Newry, Edward Bell, Esq., of Hill-street, sincerely regretted. (1844-08-03, 3:4, D)

1458. July 26, at her residence, Drummilly, county Armagh, at the advanced age of 90, Sarah Arrabella, relict of Nicholas Archdall Cope, Esq., daughter of Archdeacon Meade, and niece of Bishop Cope. (1844-08-03, 3:4, D)

1459. July 25, at Belturbet, Cordelia, the beloved wife of John Gumley, Esq. (1844-08-03, 3:4, D)

1460. July 27, Emily Frances, daughter of Robert C. Christian, Esq., aged two years. (1844-08-03, 3:4, D)

1461. On Thursday, the 8th inst., in Monkstown church, Robert Holmes, Esq., Solicitor, to Rosalinda J. Johnston, of Carysfort Avenue, Blackrock, relict of the late Thomas Johnston, Esq., of Fortjohnston, county Monaghan. (1844-08-10, 3:5, M)

1462. At Galway, John Ribton Gore, Esq., son of the Hon. and Very Rev. the Dean of Killala, and grandson of the late Earl of Arran, to Frances Brabazon, daughter of J.D. Ellard, Esq., of Renmore, in the county of Galway, and R.M. at Tulla, in the county Clare. (1844-08-10, 3:5, M)

1463. At Trinity Church, Marylabone [sic], London, Henry Sudden, Esq., second surviving son of the Right Hon. the Lord Chancellor of Ireland, to Marianne, only surviving daughter of the late Colonel Cookson, of Durham. (1844-08-10, 3:5, M)

1464. At Lisaniske, in this county, on Saturday, the 3d of August, Caroline, the wife of Adam Gibson, Esq., in the 58th year of her age. (1844-08-10, 3:5, D)

1465. At Upper Rathmines, Mr. Joseph M'Dowell, in the 74th year of his age. (1844-08-10, 3:5, D)

1466. At Baden Baden, Fanny, the beloved wife of Captain W. O'Neill, and fifth daughter of the late Robert Lindsay, Esq., of Loughry, county Tyrone. (1844-08-10, 3:5, D)

1467. At Drumilly, county Antrim [sic], aged 90, Sarah Arrabelle, relict of Nicholas Archdall Cope, Esq., daughter of Archdeacon Meade, and niece of Bishop Cope. (1844-08-10, 3:5, D)

1468. After a few days' illness, at Lower Baggot-street, Lieutenant Colonel Skerrett, late of the 55th Regiment of Foot. (1844-08-10, 3:5, D)

1469. At her house, in Limerick, at an advanced age, Miss Maunsell, eldest daughter of the late Venerable Wm. Maunsell, Archdeacon of Kildare, and sister of Thomas P. Maunsell, Esq., M.P., for Northamptonshire, and sister of Captain Robert Maunsell, C.B., R.N., and of the Archdeacon of Limerick. (1844-08-10, 3:5, D)

1470. August 12, at Sharavogue, in the King's county, the lady of Lieutenant-Colonel the Hon. J.C. Westenra, M.P., of a son and heir, who only survived a short time. (1844-08-17, 3:4, B)

1471. August 5, by the Lord Bishop of Sodor and Man, Clarence Horatia Cary, Esq., of Doogery, county of Armagh, second surviving son of the late Colonel Cary, Royal Artillery, to Elinor, only child of the late Wm. Leece Drinkwater, Esq., of Leece Lodge, and niece of Sir George Drinkwater, of Kirby. (1844-08-17, 3:4, M)

1472. August 10, at Knock Abbey Castle, county Louth, William O'Reilly, Esq. Mr. O'Reilly was brother of the late Colonel O'Reilly, husband of the Dowager Duchess of Roxburgh, and of Mr. Dowel O'Reilly, the present Attorney-General of Jamaica. (1844-08-17, 3:4, D)

1473. Death of Lady Rossmore.—We regret to announce the death of Lady Rossmore, which melancholy event took place at her residence, the Dell, Windsor, on Tuesday, the 20th instant, at half-past nine o'clock, A.M. The intelligence reached Camla on Friday morning, when the deepest sympathy for his Lordship's bereavement was evinced by the inhabitants of Monaghan. (1844-08-24, 3:3, D)

1474. Aug. 15, at Bushmills, by the Rev. William Oliver, Mr. Samuel Boyd, merchant, to Hessie, youngest daughter of the late Mr. T. Gernon, of Bushmills. (1844-08-24, 3:3, M)

1475. Aug. 20, in the Friends' Meeting-house, in Eustace-street, William Uprichard, Esq., of Spring Vale, in the County of Down, to Hannah Maria, youngest daughter of Josiah Malone, Esq., of Cullenswood-avenue, in the county of Dublin. (1844-08-24, 3:3, M)

1476. Aug. 13, in Thomas's Church, by the Rev. Joshua Bernard, Mr. Hugh Brown, of Leinster-road, Rathmines, to Mary Anne, only daughter of Vere W. Riddle, Esq., of Fairview Avenue. (1844-08-24, 3:3, M)

1477. Aug. 19, in Listowel Church, by the Rev. Edward Maynard Denny, John E. Murray, Esq., of the English Bar, eldest son of Adam Murray, Esq., 47, Parliament-street, London, to Maria, third daughter of Richard Fitz Gerald, Esq., Listowel Castle. (1844-08-24, 3:3, M)

1478. In Glasslough, on Tuesday last, after a very short illness, Jane, second daughter of Mr. G. Smith, of that town. (1844-08-31, 3:3, D)

1479. In this town, on Sunday last, by the Rev. Mr. Maguire, R.C.C., Mr. Francis Brady, Head Constable of Police, to Eliza, second daughter of Mr. Mathew Vallely, of Market-street, Monaghan. (1844-09-07, 3:4, M)

1480. Sep. 3, in Castle Caulfield Church, by the Rev. Maxwell Carpendale, the Rev. John Thomas Paul, Curate of Castlecaulfield, to Henrietta, daughter of the Rev. T. Carpendale, Rector, of Donaghmore, county of Tyrone. (1844-09-07, 3:4, M)

1481. Sept. 4, Rathfarnham, by the Rev. Saunders Brereton, Henry Cornelius, Esq., of Gosbrook, in the Queen's County, eldest son of Henry Cornelius, Esq., of Castletown, in the Queen's County, to Elizabeth Mary White, daughter of the late Richard Giles, Esq., of Cootehill, in the County of Cavan, and co-heiress of the late Rev. Thomas Kemmis, of Straboe, in the Queen's County. (1844-09-07, 3:4, M)

1482. Sept. 3, Armagh, by the Rev. Dr. Henry, the Rev. Henry Sheil M'Kee, of Killucan, to Eliza, second daughter of H. Macmahon, Esq., late of Aughnacloy. (1844-09-07, 3:4, M)

1483. At Clones, much regretted, of rapid consumption, in the 22nd year of her age, Eleanor, eldest daughter of the late William Irons, Primitive Methodist Preacher. (1844-09-07, 3:4, D)

1484. Aug. 30, at her residence, Pump-Street, Derry, Mary Jane, relict of the late Lieutenant John Valentine, 99d regiment, aged 32. (1844-09-07, 3:4, D)

1485. September 7, in North Great George's-street, the Rev. William Blundell, D.D., for thirty-one years Prebendary of Ballintobber, and Rector of Kilkeevan, in the diocess of Elphin, and Vicar of Balscadden, in the arch-diocess of Dublin, aged 78 years, sincerely regretted by all who new him. (1844-09-14, 3:4, D)

1486. Sept. 13, by the Rev. Robert Anderson, Banbridge, Mr. William Noble, Swanview, to Elizabeth, third daughter of Mr. Richard Matchett, Sandymount College, both near Banbridge. (1844-09-21, 3:3, M)

1487. Sept. 16, at Argray, by the bride's brother, the Rev. Mr. M'Crea, David Graham, Esq., merchant, Londonderry, to Ellen, youngest daughter of the late Archibald M'Crea, Esq. (1844-09-21, 3:3, M)

1488. In Clones, on Tuesday, the 17th inst., Mr. William Elliott, aged 76. He has been a resident in that town for the last half century. (1844-09-21, 3:3, D)

1489. September 15, at the Brow of the Hill, Londonderry, of malignant scarletina, after little more than two days' illness, Henry Pakenham, eldest son of the Rev. Robert H. Burgh, aged eleven years. (1844-09-21, 3:3, D)

1490. September 15, at Elphin, Henry, second son of the late John Smith, Esq., aged 20. (1844-09-21, 3:3, D)

1491. September 11, at her mother's residence, Cabra Road, after a lengthened illness, Miss Eliza Mullen, youngest [daughter] of the late John Mullen, Esq., of Dublin. (1844-09-21, 3:3, D)

1492. At Liscarney, on the 25th inst., the lady of John Richardson, Esq., of a son. (1844-09-28, 3:6, B)

1493. On Wednesday 25th, in Monaghan church, by the Rev. Henry Maffatt, John Stevenson, Esq., of Roan-Mills, county Tyrone, to Sarah Jane, youngest daughter of Robert Hodge, Esq., of Killigoan Cottage, Monaghan. (1844-09-28, 3:6, M)

1494. At St. Mary's Church, Dublin, Bengamin Alcock Chamber, Esq., of Beacon's-town, county Meath, to Allicia Mona Rutledge, relict of David Rutledge, Esq. of John House, county of Mayo. (1844-09-28, 3:6, M)

1495. On the 30th instant, at Inish House, near Dungannon, Margaret, youngest daughter of the late James Brown, Esq., of Killymaddy Evans. She bowed with meek submission to the will of her heavenly Father, and patience possessed her soul; she knew in whom she believed and was persuaded he was able to keep that which she had committed to him, and, resting on the sure promises of the Gospel, she was enabled to regard the last enemy without fear and to enter the dark valley rejoicing in the hope of the glory of God. (1844-10-05, 3:6, D)

1496. On Tuesday last, after a short illness, Mr. Mathew Logan, of this town. (1844-10-05, 3:6, D)

1497. At Corra, in this County, Mr. Edward Mitchell. (1844-10-05, 3:6, D)

1498. Oct. 3, aged eighteen years, of tetanus, or lockjaw, caused by the puncture of a nail in the foot, Joseph, son of Mr. Samuel Jones, of Clogher, county of Tyrone. (1844-10-12, 3:1, D)

1499. On the 15th of October, in the Church of Moycosquin, by the bride's uncle, the Rev. John Richardson Young, Rector of Tydavnet, Thomas Scott, of Willsborough, Esq., High Sheriff, county of Londonderry, D.L., J.P., to Catherine Elizabeth, eldest daughter of the late Rev. Thomas Richardson, and sister to Henry Richardson, of Somerset, Esq., D.L., J.P., county Londonderry. (1844-10-19, 3:2, M)

1500. On Friday morning, at his residence, Election Hill, the Rev. Mr. M'Dermott, Parish Priest of the Parish of Errigle, in this County. Mr. M'Dermott held an influential position among his brother clergymen in this County, and will be much regretted by his numerous friends. (1844-10-19, 3:2, D)

1501. On the 22d inst., after a few hours' illness, at Banbridge, where he had gone on business connected with the Railway, Mr. Thomas Singleton Mellan [sic], youngest son of the late Mr. James Mollan of Monaghan, whose kindness of heart, and disposition endeared him to his sorrowing relatives. (1844-10-26, 2:4, D)

1502. On the 19th inst., at his father's residence, Cootehill, of violent scarletina, Master John Higinbotham, aged 14 years, universally lamented by all who knew him. From he was first seized by this insidious disease, he had strong forebodings that it might terminate in his dissolution. He had not only the privilege during his illness of the faithful and unremitting attention of his own minister, but also the ministers of other denominations who affectionately waited upon him, up to the very moment when his ransomed spirit fled to God. Happy, his parents can now look back on his memory, beatified as it was by all the traits which an early love of untainted moral excellence in its finest expressions could impart. In these, however, he had no confidence;—but when asked during his sickness, on appearing somewhat anxious, "did he want anything?" he replied, "nothing but Christ,"—as if he had said, having all his wants in Him sufficient.

Let others stretch their arms like seas,
And grasp in all the shore;
Grant me the smiles of Jesus's face,
And I desire no more.

"Blessed are the dead who thus lie in the Lord; they rest from their labours and their works do follow them." (1844-10-26, 2:4, D)

1503. At Glasslough, on Wednesday last, aged 48 years, of inflammation of the lungs, Doctor James George Lepper, sincerely regretted by all who knew him. (1844-11-09, 3:2, D)

1504. On Thursday the 7th instant, at the residence of the bride's father, by the Rev. Charles M'Alister, Sarah Ann, eldest daughter of Mr. Wm. Boyd, merchant, Armagh, to Mr. Robert Rainey, Maxwell Cottage, Co. Monaghan. (1844-11-16, 3:2, M)

1505. On Thursday, the 28th inst., at the house of the bride's brother, Thomas-street, Armagh, Miss Ann Hughes, to Mr. John Fanning of this town. (1844-11-30, 3:3, M)

1506. Nov. 25, at the house of her father, in Coalmarket, Kilkenny, Marcella, second daughter of James Morris, Esq., Manager of the Kilkenny Branch of the National Bank, to Alderman Hart, of High-street, same place. (1844-11-30, 3:3, M)

1507. On Saturday, Nov. 23, at Loftus, near Gisborough, Yorkshire, Lieutenant-General the Hon. Sir Robert Laurence Dundas, K.C.B., Colonel of the 59th Regiment. (1844-11-30, 3:3, D)

1508. November 28, at St. Peter's Church, in this city, by the Rev. Henry Stewart, Rector of Lucan, Joseph Weld, of Lodge, Esq., to Isabella, eldest surviving daughter of the late Captain James Woodwright, of Gola House, in the county of Monaghan, and of Fitzwilliam Square, in this city [Dublin]. (1844-11-30, 4:3, M)

1509. At Fethard Glebe, the residence of his father, George Henry Woodward, Esq., of the Middle Temple, Barrister-at-Law. In this much lamented gentleman, the English Bar has lost one of its ablest and most promising junior members. He had returned to Ireland for a change of air, after a long illness, and fell asleep in sure and certain hope of a joyful resurrection. (1844-11-30, 4:3, D)

1510. November 22, at Chillington, in her 81st year, the Right Hon. Lady Charlotte Giffard, relict of the late Thomas Giffard, Esq. (1844-11-30, 4:3, D)

1511. November 25, at Abbotstown, Louisa Jossevel, aged 41 years. (1844-11-30, 4:3, D)

1512. November 28, at 21, Fitzwilliam-place, Henry Shears, infant son of William Carey Dobbs, Esq. (1844-11-30, 4:3, D)

1513. On the 26th inst., at Rooskey, the Lady of David Hamill, Esq., of a son. (1844-12-07, 3:2, B)

1514. On the 4th inst., by the Rev. Wm. White, Margaret, second daughter of Mr. Thomas Graham, Smithboro', to Mr. Matthew Leming, Rockcorry. (1844-12-07, 3:2, M)

1515. By the Rev. John Elliott, on Thursday, the 12th inst., Rev. Robert Moorehead, Presbyterian Minister, of Garvaghy, county Down, to Eliza Ann, youngest daughter of Mr. Robert Lowry, Smithboro', county Monaghan. (1844-12-14, 2:4, M)

1516. Dec. 5, in St. Anne's Church, Belfast, by the Rev. Richard Oulton, Mr. James M'Henry, of Liverpool, second son of Dr. M'Henry, Consul for the United States, at Londonderry, to Lydia Hensworth, third daughter of Mr. James Gardner, Belfast. (1844-12-14, 2:4, M)

1517. Dec. 7, at Stephen's-green, Jane, relict of the late Garret Stack, Esq., 77th regiment. (1844-12-14, 2:4, D)

1518. Dec. 6, at Ballynanty, county of Limerick, the residence of her son-in-law, John Low, Esq., Sophia, relict of the late George Mahon, Esq., of Mount Pleasant, county of Mayo, aged sixty-five years. (1844-12-14, 2:4, D)

1519. Dec. 6, at Gortmerron House, Dungannon, in the most perfect resignation to the will of the Almighty, and in sure and certain hope of a resurrection to eternal life through the atoning blood of her Redeemer, Sarah Maria, the beloved wife of Edward Evans, Esq., in the seventy-third year of her age, deeply and sincerely regretted. (1844-12-14, 2:4, D)

1520. Dec. 10, in Lurgan church, by the Rev. Charles King Irwine, Rector of Magherafelt, A. Bredon, Esq., M.D., of Portadown, county Armagh, to Catherine, second daughter of Dr. Joseph Bredon, formerly of Fivemiletown, county Tyrone. (1844-12-21, 3:4, M)

1521. Dec. 13, at Drum, county Monaghan, Hugh Rutherford, Esq., aged twenty-two years. (1844-12-21, 3:4, D)

1522. At Gortmore-House, Dungannon, on Friday morning, the 6th instant, in the 73d year of her age, Sarah Maria, the beloved wife of Edward Evans, Esq. (1844-12-21, 3:4, D)

1523. On the 11th instant, at Drumgart, near Roslea, Mr. Wm. Gordon, aged 81, in the most perfect resignation to the will of his Heavenly Father, in sure and certain hope of a resurrection to life eternal. (1844-12-21, 3:4, D)

1524. On the 13th inst., aged 63 years, deservedly esteemed, and sincerely lamented by all who were acquainted with him, George Hearkness, of Tullyleer, a man of truth, a sincere christian, of general information, and of unbending integrity. (1844-12-21, 3:4, D)

1525. At Drumbrain-House, on the 22d instant, the Lady of Arthur Bernard Bleazby, Esq., of a daughter. (1844-12-28, 3:3, B)

1526. On the 10th instant, by the Rev. J. Radcliffe, Castledawson, Rev. Alexander Runde, to Matilda, eldest daughter of Robert Coffey, Esq., M.D., and Professor of Surgery in Belfast College. (1844-12-28, 3:3, M)

1527. On the 19th instant, in Trinity Church, by the Rev. Theophilus Campbell, Mr. Robert Owen, Custom-house officer, Belfast, to Mary, youngest daughter of Mr. John Coats, Finaghy. (1844-12-28, 3:3, M)

1528. On Sunday evening last, at the residence of her eldest son, the Rev. Henry Maffatt, Park-street, Monaghan, aged 62 years, Frances, relict of the late Mr. Thomas Hurst of this town. During a long and well spent life, this amiable lady gained for herself the sincere friendship of every class of society, and her death is deplored not only by an affectionate family but by an attached circle of friends. (1844-12-28, 3:3, D)

1529. On the 21st instant, at Crawfordsburn, Mable Fridiswid, wife of William Sharman Crawford, Esq. (1844-12-28, 3:3, D)

1530. On Tuesday, the 17th instant, at his residence, Seymour-street, Belfast, Mr. James Ferguson, aged 47 years. (1844-12-28, 3:3, D)

1531. On the 21st instant, aged 77, Mr. Arthur Quin, of High-street, Belfast. (1844-12-28, 3:3, D)

1532. On the 2d instant, Elizabeth, the beloved wife of Mr. Gawn Finlay, Elder of Clough Congregation. (1844-12-28, 3:3, D)

1533. On the 13th instant, Ruth, wife of Robert Stanley, merchant, and daughter of Robert Gaskin, of Bloomvale in the county of Down, Esq. (1844-12-28, 3:3, D)

1534. On the 11th instant, at Down, Ballymena, in the 86th year of her age, Elizabeth, relict of the late Mr. Edward Laird, of Ballywalter, near Doagh. (1844-12-28, 3:3, D)

1535. At his house in Drumasin, near Gilford, on the 17th instant, Mr. William Dunlop, an Elder of the Presbyterian Congregation of Tullylish. (1844-12-28, 3:3, D)

1536. On the 8th instant, at Ballymena, after a severe and protracted illness, Fanny, the beloved wife of Mr. John Mullen, aged 58. (1844-12-28, 3:3, D)

1537. On the 15th instant, at Bond's-hill, Derry, John M'Cammon Johnston, Esq., son of the Rev. James Johnston, of Coalisland. (1844-12-28, 3:3, D)

1538. January 2d, at his residence, Townview, Monaghan, aged 77, Samuel M'Dowell, Esq., M.D., Fellow of the Royal College of Physicians of Edinburgh, after years of suffering, which he bore with christian submission to the divine will. In the domestic circle, he was a kind husband, an affectionate parent, and a steady friend; and in his public capacity, as Surgeon to our County Hospital, (which he had held for upwards of 40 years) he ably discharged its arduous duties to the entire satisfaction of the governors. His bereaved family and friends sorrow not, however, as those without hope, as he died in the full assurance of a blessed immortality, through faith in his Redeemer. (1845-01-04, 3:2, D)

1539. On Friday, the 27th ult., at his residence, Cormeen, Mr. James Murphy, much and deservedly regretted. (1845-01-04, 3:2, D)

1540. January 1, the lady of Robert Tottenham, Esq., of a daughter. (1845-01-11, 3:1, B)

1541. January 1, in Londonderry, the lady of Edward James Hamilton, Esq., of Belfast, county of Donegal, of a son. (1845-01-11, 3:1, B)

1542. January 2, at Heavitree, Devon, by the Lord Henry Kerr, Charles Davers Osborn, Esq., second son of Sir John Osborn, Bart., of Chicksands Priory, Bedfordshire, to Louisa, eldest daughter of the Rev. Arthur Atherley, vicar of Heavitree. (1845-01-11, 3:1, M)

1543. January 7, in Monkstown Church, Daniel Campion, Esq., of Carlow, to Rachel, only daughter of the late Wm. Burke, Esq., M.D., of Sweetmount, Dundrum, and grand-daughter of the late Rev. John Burrows, Prospect House, Blackrock. (1845-01-11, 3:1, M)

1544. Jan. 7, in Mountmelick Church, by the Rev. Ralph Tagert, John H. Beare, Esq., of Dublin, to Kate, fourth daughter of William Brunskill, Esq., Irishtown House, Mountmelick. (1845-01-11, 3:1, M)

1545. Jan. 6, in Broadford Church, by his father, the Rev. Richard Studdert Welsh, of Newtown House, Maurice Studdert Welsh, Esq., to Mary Catherine, only daughter of the late James Going, of Violet Hill, county of Clare. (1845-01-11, 3:1, M)

1546. Jan. 6, in St. Thomas's Church, Dublin, Mr. Griffith Bertram Henry, of Lower Gloucester street, Dublin, to Mary Alicia Elizabeth, daughter of the late George Concanon, Esq., of Westland row, Dublin. (1845-01-11, 3:1, M)

1547. December 25, at 42 Dawson-street, Mrs. Steward, relict of John Steward, Esq., of Wilmont, county Antrim, and daughter of Thomas Smyth, Esq., Drumcree, county Westmeath. (1845-01-11, 3:1, D)

1548. December 27, at Aughafad, in the parish of Fintona, in the county of Tyrone, William Moore, Esq., aged 90 years. (1845-01-11, 3:1, D)

1549. January 1, suddenly, at his residence in Keady, Samuel Magee, Esq., M.D., aged 51. (1845-01-11, 3:1, D)

1550. Nov. 7 at Calcutta, Mary Charron, wife of William Toller, Esq., Commander of the *Wellesley*. (1845-01-11, 3:1, D)

1551. Jan. 4, at his residence, Auburn, county of Dublin, Andrew Crawford, Esq., most sincerely and deservedly lamented. (1845-01-11, 3:1, D)

1552. Jan. 8, at the residence of his brother-in-law, Dr. M'Leod, 62, Amiens-street, Dublin, John Brooke, Esq., deservedly and sincerely regretted by all who knew him. (1845-01-11, 3:1, D)

1553. Jan. 1, at Cheltenham, Sir Jacob Adolphus, M.D., Inspector-General of the Army Hospitals, a distinguished officer of the Medical department of the army, who had served in every quarter of the world. (1845-01-11, 3:1, D)

1554. Jan. 1, at Cheltenham, sincerely regretted by all her friends, Lady Burdett, relict of the late Sir William Burdett, Bart. (1845-01-11, 3:1, D)

1555. Jan. 16, in George's Church, Dublin, by the Rev. Edward Lloyd Elwood, Vicar of Kilmactranny, Isaac, eldest son of Thomas Willan, Esq., Carrick Hill, county of Dublin, to Susan, daughter of the late John Hone, Esq., of North Great George's-street. (1845-01-18, 3:3, M)

1556. Jan. 11, in St. George's Church, Dublin, by the Rev. Gibson Black, Frances Jane, only daughter of Joseph Mullan, Esq., North Brunswick-street, to Wm. Hugh, third son of the late John Taylor, Esq. (1845-01-18, 3:3, M)

1557. On Wednesday, the 8th instant, at Cumry, in this county, of consumption, in the 33d year of his age, Mr. James Irwin, sincerely and deservedly regretted by a large circle of friends and acquaintances. (1845-01-18, 3:3, D)

1558. On Saturday last, at Lifford, at an advanced age, Tasker Keys, Esq., father-in-law of Robert Keys, Esq., Fort Lodge. (1845-01-18, 3:3, D)

1559. On Tuesday, 14th instant, of consumption, in his 16th year, Robert, second son of Mrs. S. Ireland, 98, Ann-street, Belfast. (1845-01-18, 3:3, D)

1560. On the 14th instant, aged 34 years, Jane, eldest daughter of Mr. Robert Kennedy, brewer, formerly of Comber. (1845-01-18, 3:3, D)

1561. On the 2d inst., at Belvidere Terrace, Liscard, the Lady of James Donlevy, Esq., M.D., of a daughter. (1845-01-25, 3:1, B)

1562. January 21, in St. Michael's Church, by the Rev. W. Marrable, John Begley, Esq., of Three Castles, county of Wicklow, to Eliza Maria, second daughter of William Burgess, Esq., and niece of the late Richard Burgess, Esq., M.D., Clonmel. (1845-01-25, 3:1, M)

1563. January 21, in St. Mark's Church, by the Rev. John Gregg, Halwood Clarke, to Marcella, youngest daughter of the late Thomas Henry Egan, M.D., and grand-daughter of the late Dr. Egan, of Sackville-street. (1845-01-25, 3:1, M)

1564. January 18, at Fitzwilliam-square, in the 76th year of his age, the Rev. Thomas Blakeney, of Holly-well, county Roscommon. (1845-01-25, 3:1, D)

1565. December 12, at his residence, Barnfort Cottage, London, Upper Canada, Charles, youngest son of Major Madden, of the city of Kildare, aged 33 years. (1845-01-25, 3:1, D)

1566. On Monday, after a protracted illness, to the deep regret of a numerous circle of sincerely attached friends, and to the great loss of the numerous poor who were recipients of her liberal and extensive charities, Miss Waugh, of English-street, in Armagh. Miss W. had been ill for a series of years, but bore her illness with meek and truly christian resignation. She dispensed her bounty with a liberal hand, and none that appealed to her benevolence "went empty away." She was a faithful and bountiful dispenser of the wealth with which Providence had blessed her, for the benefit of the afflicted and destitute who came within the sphere of a mind, ever actively engaged, as we have been informed, in seeking out and relieving objects in distress. We regret that, in this hurried obituary, we cannot do more ample justice to the memory of one whose demise is generally regretted by all who had the pleasure of knowing her. (1845-01-25, 3:1, D)

1567. In Armagh on Tuesday, Margaret, eldest daughter of Doctor Gratton. She was an interesting child, and was removed from her now sorrowing parents and friends after a few days' illness. (1845-01-25, 3:1, D)

1568. In common with all who had the pleasure of knowing her, we this day regret having to record the death of Mrs. Gordon, wife of John Gordon, Esq., and daughter of J. Williams, Esq., of Newry. Mrs. G. died of fever, at Sheepbridge, on Wednesday last, very sincerely and deservedly regretted by a numerous circle of relatives and friends, and has left a sorrowing husband, and an interesting family of seven children, all young, to deplore the loss of an affectionate and indulgent parent. (1845-01-25, 3:1, D)

1569. Sudden Death.—With feelings of regret, we announce the sudden death of Mr. Daniel Bannon, owner of the *Shamrock* steamer, plying between Warrenpoint and Liverpool, who expired, while taking coffee at his lodgings in the above town, on Monday evening. Mr. B. was much and deservedly esteemed, and is generally and sincerely regretted. (1845-01-25, 3:1, D)

1570. On the 16th inst., at Prospect house, County Louth, the Lady of Maxwell William Boyle, Esq., of Tullyvin-House, county Cavan, of a son and Heir. (1845-02-01, 3:2, B)

1571. Jan. 27, at Fort William, county of Cavan, the lady of Thomas Coote, Esq., D.L., of a son. (1845-02-01, 3:2, B)

1572. In Clones church, on the 29th inst., by the Rev. George H. Reade, Rector of Curran, Captain John Johnston, late of the 70th Regt., to Isabella Eccles, daughter of Captain Jameson, Clonkeen, Clones. (1845-02-01, 3:2, M)

1573. January 16, at 114, Lauriston place, Edinburgh, Walter Thomas Miltown, Esq., of Singapore, to Jessie, only daughter of William Campbell, Esq., and widow of the late John Macan, Esq., of Lurgyvallen, county Armagh. (1845-02-01, 3:2, M)

1574. On the 16th December, in the Cathedral, Antigua, Joseph Glenny, Esq., eldest son of the late George Glenny, Esq., of Moorevale, County Armagh, to Anne Amelia, only daughter of the late Robert Martin, Esq., Antigua. (1845-02-01, 3:2, M)

1575. January 22, in Annaduff Church, county of Leitrim, Abraham C. Swayne, Esq., Surgeon, to Anne Alicia, daughter of the late Dr. Browne, Carrick-on-Shannon. (1845-02-01, 3:2, M)

1576. Jan. 22, at Lough Eske, Donegal, the residence of her nephew, Thomas Brooke, Esq., Mrs. Young, relict of the Rev. John Young, Killishil, county of Tyrone. (1845-02-01, 3:2, D)

1577. After a protracted illness, the wife of Dr. Joseph Murphy, of Clones. (1845-02-01, 3:2, D)

1578. Jan. 20, at Armagh, Miss Anne Rickard, second daughter of Mr. James Rickard, aged 19 years. (1845-02-01, 3:2, D)

1579. Jan. 16, at Augharney, near Dungannon, Mr. H. Irwin, in the 84th year of his age. (1845-02-01, 3:2, D)

1580. Last week, at his cottage near Killorglin, Eusebius M'Gillycuddy, Esq., eldest son of the late E.C. M'Gillycuddy, Esq., for many years Sub-Sheriff of the county Kerry. (1845-02-01, 3:2, D)

1581. January 24, after an illness of short duration, at the residence of her son, the Rev. Arthur Champagne, at Milltown, in the county Limerick, Mary, relict of the late Rev. Gustavus Wybrants, Vicar of Askeaton, in the diocess of Limerick, and of Castle Lyons, in the diocess of Cloyne. (1845-02-01, 3:2, D)

1582. Jan. 26, in Upper Dominick-street, Dublin, Louisa, widow of the late Leynard M'Nally, Esq., Barrister-at-Law, and last surviving daughter of the Rev. Robert Edgworth, of Lissard, in the county of Longford, Clerk, deceased. (1845-02-01, 3:2, D)

1583. Jan. 16, in the seventy-fourth year of her age, universally regretted, Mary, relict of H.B. Code, Esq., well known in the literary world for his talents and patriotic exertions. He was for years connected with the press of Dublin, and assisted to establish for the *Warder* newspaper the high character and position it now holds. (1845-02-01, 3:2, D)

1584. In Glasslough Church, on Thursday, the 6th inst., by the Rev. W.H. Pratt, Julius Brockman Travers, Esq., H.M. 25th Regiment, or King's own Borderers, second son of the late Captain Boyle Travers, of Cork, to Matilda, eldest daughter of Henry G. Johnston, Esq., of Fortjohnston, county of Monaghan. (1845-02-08, 3:3, M)

1585. February 3, at St. Peter's Church, by the Rev. Richard Booth Eyre, Robert Hedges, son of the late Rev. Dr. Eyre, of Hassop Park, Eyre Court, in the county of Galway, Esq., to Jane Elizabeth, youngest daughter of the late Robert Smith, Esq., of Fitzwilliam square, Dublin. (1845-02-08, 3:3, M)

1586. February 4, at St. Peter's Church, by the Rev. H.R. Hallahan, Thomas Hird Goodwin, Esq., of Marlborough street, to Maria, daughter of the late Robert Boroughs, Esq., Carlow. (1845-02-08, 3:3, M)

1587. February 1, at the residence of the bride's father, James Irwin, youngest son of Richard Irwin, of Rathmile House in the county of Roscommon, Esq., to Honores Olivia Letitia, third daughter; and on the same day, William Joseph, eldest son of the late Terence Henry, Esq., M.D., to Sahina Cecilia Evelina, fourth daughter of James Lynch, of Lancaster Park, in said county. (1845-02-08, 3:3, M)

1588. At his residence Tanagh, county Monagan, on the 3d inst., Captain Charles Dawson, D.L., J.P. The death of this respected gentleman, will place several noble and gentle families in Cavan, and Monaghan in mourning. (1845-02-08, 3:3, D)

1589. January 28, at Ringwald Rectory, in the 81st year of her age, Sarah, relict of John Monins, Esq., of the Archbishop's Palace. (1845-02-08, 3:3, D)

1590. February 2, at Mersham Hatch, of consumption, aged 20 years, Fanny Elizabeth, eldest daughter of Sir Edward and Lady Knatchbull. (1845-02-08, 3:3, D)

1591. On the 11th instant, by the Rev. W. M'Gowan, Greyabbey, Mr. Hugh M'Neill, Belfast, to Jane, second daughter of Mr. William M'Gowan, Crossnacreevy. (1845-02-15, 3:3, M)

1592. At Cullybackey, on the 11th inst., by the Rev. Hugh Hamilton, Mr. John Telford, of Galgorm Parks, to Elizabeth, daughter of the late Mr. Joseph Dixon, of Cullybackey. (1845-02-15, 3:3, M)

1593. On the 9th inst., by the Rev. Mr. Murphy, P.P., of Killeavy, Captain James O'Neill, to Biddy, daughter of Mr. Mathew M'Guigan, of Lower Watham [sic], near Newry. (1845-02-15, 3:3, M)

1594. Feb. 12, in George's Church, by the Rev. John Gregg, Edmund T. Cuppage, Esq., of Clare Grove, in the county of Dublin, to Susan, relict of the late Hans Johnson, Esq. (1845-02-15, 3:3, M)

1595. At Balnagarry, in this county, in the 28th year of his age, Thomas Cathcart, eldest son of the Rev. Thomas Cathcart. (1845-02-15, 3:3, D)

1596. Feb. 2, at Epworth Terrace, Upper Leeson-street, Dublin, aged eleven years, Harry, eldest son of John Sibthorpe, Esq. (1845-02-15, 3:3, D)

1597. Feb. 13, at Parker Hill, Rathmines, aged seventy-six, Mrs. Hannah Sibthorpe, relict of the late Henry Sibthorpe, Esq., of Cork Hill, Dublin. (1845-02-15, 3:3, D)

1598. Feb. 11, at Harrington-street, Dublin, Ruth, daughter of the late George Clibborn, Esq., of the Castle, Moate, county of Westmeath. (1845-02-15, 3:3, D)

1599. Feb. 9, at her house, Nelson-hill, Youghal, Alice, relict of the late Edward Greene, Esq., aged seventy-three years. (1845-02-15, 3:3, D)

1600. On the 12th inst., in the 11th year of her age, Margaret, daughter of Mr. James D. O'Connor, College-place, North, Belfast. (1845-02-15, 3:3, D)

1601. On Sunday, 2d instant, Mary, wife of Robert M'Entire, of Dublin, Esq. (1845-02-15, 3:3, D)

1602. On the 6th instant, after a protracted illness, in the 20th year of his age, James Orr M'Nally, of Ballyrobin. (1845-02-15, 3:3, D)

1603. On the 29th ult., at Illenan, near Baden, Margaret Gillespie Boyd, eldest daughter of the Rev. H.E. Boyde [sic], Prebendary of Dromore, County Down. (1845-02-15, 3:3, D)

1604. At 24, Great Charles-street, Dublin, on the 8th inst., Dorinda, wife of James Corry Lowery, Esq. (1845-02-15, 3:3, D)

1605. On Friday, the 7th inst., of apoplexy, in the 23d year of her age, Catherine, wife of Mr. Michael Crummy, innkeeper, Portadown. (1845-02-15, 3:3, D)

1606. At his residence, in Bridge-street, Banbridge, on the evening of Sunday last, the 9th inst., in the 63d year of his age, Mr. James Nelson, watchmaker. (1845-02-15, 3:3, D)

1607. Feb. 12, in Bryansford Church, county of Down, by the Rev. Christopher Usher, Captain De Courcy, Inspecting Commander of the Coast Guard, to Sibella, third daughter of Captain Morris, R.N., of the Barbican Cottage, same County. (1845-02-22, 3:2, M)

1608. Feb. 15, in St. Mark's Church, by the Rev. A. Franklin, John Harricks, Esq., Surgeon, Liverpool, to

Mary Anne, second daughter of the late Richard Harricks, Esq., of Westmorland-street. (1845-02-22, 3:2, M)

1609. On the 12th instant, by the Rev. W.J. Raphael, Ballyeaston, the Rev. D. Wilson, Presbyterian Minister of Limerick, to Jane, eldest daughter of Wm. M'Ferran, Esq., Cogry-house. (1845-02-22, 3:2, M)

1610. On the 6th inst., in Rossory Church, by the Rev. R.P. Cleary, Mr. Richard Lisburn, Editor of the *Armagh Guardian*, to Ellen, second daughter of Mr. Daniel Gibson, of Enniskillen. (1845-02-22, 3:2, M)

1611. On the 14th instant, in Rathfarnham Church, by the Rev. T.R. Cradock, A.M., Incumbent of St. Nicholas Within, Becher Hungerford, Esq., of Glen Camus, county of Cork, son of the late Captain Richard Hungerford, of the Island, to Anne Jane, eldest daughter of the late William Crossley, Esq., of H.M.'s 38th Regt. of Foot, subsequently Inspector of the Londonderry [Constabulary Force], and J.P. for the counties of Derry and Antrim. (1845-02-22, 3:2, M)

1612. On the 13th inst., at the Friends' Meeting-house, Cork, Jonathan Greenwood Pim, Esq., of Dublin, to Mary, youngest daughter of the late Reuben Harvey, Esq., of Cork. (1845-02-22, 3:2, M)

1613. On the 2d inst., in Cork, by the Rev. James O'Sullivan, Wm. Pearce, Esq., to Eliza, third daughter of Mr. John Hamilton, of Caroline-row, and grand-daughter of the late Alexander Richardson, Esq., of Summer-hill, Dublin, and Farlough, county Tyrone. (1845-02-22, 3:2, M)

1614. February 13, at the parish of Forkhill, by the Rev. Doctor Campbell, Henry Stanley, Esq., M.D., fourth son of John Stanley, Esq., of Armagh, to Frances Grace, only daughter of Captain Robinson, Sub-Inspector of Revenue Police. (1845-02-22, 3:2, M)

1615. February 13, at the Lisburn Cathedral, by the Rev. Dean Stannus, Edward Maxwell, Esq., of Leeds, to Mary, daughter of the late Dr. Nicholson, of Lisburn. (1845-02-22, 3:2, M)

1616. February 11, by the Rev. Hamilton Dobbin, the Rev. Thomas Millar, jun., to Isabella, youngest daughter of Mr. Gladwood, Lurgan. (1845-02-22, 3:2, M)

1617. February 13, in the parish church of Cappagh, by the Rev. H.H. Harte, Rector, Montgomery Armstrong, of the Island of Innishmore, Lough Erne, county Fermanagh, Esq., to Sarah, daughter of John Buchanan, Esq., Bunnynubber, near Omagh. (1845-02-22, 3:2, M)

1618. On Wednesday evening at Saloo-house, County Monaghan, after a short illness, Elizabeth, third daughter of the late Joseph Whitsitt, Esq. The deep sympathy evinced by all classes of society, for the loss of this amiable lady, is the best evidence of her worth. (1845-02-22, 3:2, D)

1619. At Coothill [sic], on Sunday morning, the 16th inst., under the happy influence of religion, (at the tender age of 11 years,) which she astonishingly evinced at her prayers to her God, under the endurance of nine days' suffering, Eliza Maria Coote, the dearly beloved, and only child of William Coote, Esq., M.D., Fellow of the Royal College of Surgeons, in Ireland. (1845-02-22, 3:2, D)

1620. October 6, at Chusan, China, Elizabeth, wife of Captain Charles Dunbar, of the 18th Royal Irish Regt. Two days before, Mrs. Dunbar gave birth to a still-born son. (1845-02-22, 3:2, D)

1621. On Saturday, the 15th instant, at Belfast, after a prolonged affliction, which she bore with christian fortitude, Mrs. Robert M'Neight, in the 39th year of her age. (1845-02-22, 3:2, D)

1622. Suddenly, on the 17th instant, in the 47th year of her age, Margaret, the beloved wife of Mr. Samuel Bell, No. 22, Robert-street, Belfast. (1845-02-22, 3:2, D)

1623. On the 14th inst., Ann, wife of Mr. Joseph M'Clure, Belfast, aged 64. (1845-02-22, 3:2, D)

1624. Feb. 13, Marianne Margaret, wife of Thomas Wm. Filgate, Esq., of Arthurstown, county of Louth. (1845-02-22, 3:2, D)

1625. July 7, at the residence of his father, of rapid decline, in the nineteenth year of his age, Alexander, eldest son of James Elliott, Esq., Annalee, county of Cavan. (1845-02-22, 3:2, D)

1626. On the 5th instant, in Tullylish Church, John Birch, of Birch-grove, eldest son of the late George Birch, J.P., Rector of Comber, County of Down, to Mary Jane, eldest daughter of the late Francis M'Connell, Esq., Farm-hill, Gilford. (1845-03-15, 3:2, M)

1627. March 6, in St. Peter's Church, Dublin, by the Rev. G.V. Sampson, Arthur Sampson, Esq., of Drummond, County Londonderry, to Louisa, youngest daughter of the late A. Rawlins, Esq., of Rutland-square. (1845-03-15, 3:2, M)

1628. On Sunday last, at his residence, in the Diamond, in his 76th year, David Horner, Esq. Mr. Horner, through his long and well spent life, earned, by every virtue which adorns the citizen and man, the highest respect and regard, not only of his friends and acquaintances, but also that of the community in which he so long dwelt. We do not generally deal in panegyrics on the dead, but we cannot refrain from giving to our readers the closing sentence of an eloquent address delivered by the Rev. John Bleckly, at the grave of the late lamented townsman, which was nearly as follows:—

"To call him a man of integrity is but to re-echo the public voice; to say that he was benevolent is to repeat the testimony of all the poor; to describe him as consistent in religious profession is to recall the long experience of the congregation of which he was a member; to represent him as charitable and forbearing is but to record the opinion of christians of every name. His liberality was the consequence of his own deep felt conviction, and very unlike that spurious kind which, having no creed of its own, is ready to adopt any form which fashion or interest may recommend. A Presbyterian from education and from prinicple, he was willing to believe that Christians of other names might be equally sincere; he granted to them that liberty of judging which he claimed for himself, and cultivated kindness and friendship with them all.

"It is right here to say that he ascribed much of his happiness and prosperity through life to the religious training of his early years, under the eye of a pious mother, and to the respect for the holy rest of the sabbath, to which he was accustomed in his father's home. Such were the principles with which he left this neighbourhood in his youth. We this day bring back his remains to consign them to the graves of his kindred. They need not refuse him a resting place among them. He maintained a character without reproach—and he has no blot upon his memory." (1845-03-15, 3:2, D)

1629. On the 7th instant, in Derry, at the residence of her son, the Rev. James Graham, Elizabeth, relict of the late Rev. John Graham, of Magilligan Glebe. (1845-03-15, 3:2, D)

1630. On the 9th instant, at No. 51, Stephen's-green East, Caroline, wife of James Hans Hamilton, Esq., M.P., of Abbotstown, County Dublin. (1845-03-15, 3:2, D)

1631. Tuesday morning, at the residence of the lady's father, Strand road, by the Rev. Dr. Brown, Moderator of the General Assembly, the Rev. M. Wilson, Presbyterian Minister, Ramelton, to Abigail, youngest daughter of the Rev. James Crawford, of Derry. (1845-03-29, 3:2, M)

1632. On Tuesday, the 25th instant, by the Rev. Samuel Carlisle, Mr. Robert Cooke, Merchant of Derry, to Mary, second daughter of Mr. Thomas Nevin, jun., Kilmaill, Coleraine. (1845-03-29, 3:2, M)

1633. On the 18th instant, at Auchtermuchty, Scotland, by the Rev. John A. Cooke, Free Church, Auchtergavin, James Gray, Esq., Auchtermuchty, to Maria Isabella, youngest daughter of the late Mr. J. Cooke, Strabane. (1845-03-29, 3:2, M)

1634. On the 20th inst., by the Rev. A. Buchanan, Mr. Ross Selfridge, of Ballykelly, to Miss Rebecca Tennent, of Koolkeeragh. (1845-03-29, 3:2, M)

1635. On Thursday, the 20th instant, by the Rev. Andrew M'Cullough, Presbyterian minister, Robert Wilkin, of Ramakit, Esq., to Elizabeth, youngest daughter of William Wilkin, Esq., late of Caledon, in the county of Tyrone. (1845-03-29, 3:2, M)

1636. On Saturday, the 22nd instant, in the Parish Church of Tynan, county Armagh, by the Rev. C.J. White, Robert Tod Huston, Esq., late Army Surgeon, to Mary, relict of James R. Allen, Esq., Surgeon, of Caledon, and daughter of the late Captain John Moore, of the Royal Tyrone Regiment. (1845-03-29, 3:2, M)

1637. On the 18th instant, by the Rev. J. Thomson, Raphoe, Mr. Nathaniel M'Night, of Glenmaquin, to Sarah, eldest daughter of Mr. Thomas Eaton, of Muntertinney. (1845-03-29, 3:2, M)

1638. On the 18th instant, at North Muirtown, Perth, by the Rev. John Y. Walker, the Rev. H. Perry, of Portglenone, to Anne, youngest daughter of the late James Wood, of Beglie, Esq. (1845-03-29, 3:2, M)

1639. On Tuesday, the 18th instant, in the Cathedral of Derry, by the Rev. John Kincaid, Mr. George King, to Mary, third daughter of Mr. James Thistle, both of Derry. (1845-03-29, 3:2, M)

1640. At Greenlees, on Wednesday, the 19th instant, at the advanced age of 103 years, Mrs. Henderson, relict of the late Mr. James Henderson of Laught. (1845-03-29, 3:2, D)

1641. On the 16th instant, at Dernaflaw, near Dungiven, aged 72 years, after a painful and lingering illness, which she bore with the patience and resignation of a Christian, Mary, the beloved wife of Mr. William M'Culley. (1845-03-29, 3:2, D)

1642. On the 16th instant, at Monglass, Mr. Thomas Forrest, aged 34 years. (1845-03-29, 3:2, D)

1643. On Tuesday, at Kilmacreden House, county Donegal, deservedly regretted by all who had the pleasure of his acquaintance, Thomas Nesbit Major, Esq. (1845-03-29, 3:2, D)

1644. March 27, at Killinchy, by the father of the bride, William Robert Ward, youngest son of the late Right Hon. Robert Ward, of Bangor Castle, county Down, to Arabella, second daughter of the Hon. and Rev. Henry Ward, Killinchy. (1845-04-05, 3:2, M)

1645. March 27, by the Rev. Wm. Sweeny, of Killisandra, William C. M'Bride, Esq., of Alestragh, county Armagh, to Mary Jane, second daughter of Charles Magee, Esq., of Tully, county of Cavan. (1845-04-05, 3:2, M)

1646. At Merrion-square, Martin Crean, of Obelisk Lodge, county Dublin, Esq., to Elizabeth Mary, youngest daughter of Charles Hurry, of Newcastle upon Tyne, Esq., and grand niece of D. O'Connell, Esq., M.P. (1845-04-05, 3:2, M)

1647. March 29, in St. Peter's Church, Cork, by the Rev. Robert Warren, Rector of Cannowee, William Morris, jun., Esq., of Castle Salem, to Catherine Beamish, eldest daughter of Richard Tonson Evanson, Esq., of Friendly Cove. (1845-04-05, 3:2, M)

1648. March 31, at Mountjoy-place, John J. Nugent, Esq., to Anna Mary, daughter of the late John Stapleton, Esq., of Cassino. (1845-04-05, 3:2, M)

1649. March 31, at Lincoln's-inn-fields, London, James Drake, Esq., of Rathmines, Dublin, to Jane, eldest daughter of Lieutenant J.A. Moore, Royal Marines Artillery (half-pay), of Guilford-street, Mecklenburgh-square, London. (1845-04-05, 3:2, M)

1650. March 27, at Belfast, by the Rev. J. Morgan, the Rev. Robert Irvine, of St. John's [sic], New Brunswick, to Elizabeth Mary, daughter of the late Robert Orr, Esq., Barrister. (1845-04-05, 3:2, M)

1651. On Friday, the 28th March, at the residence of Capt. Shanly, near Clones, in the 26th year of his age, George T.C.S. Corry, second son of the late Thomas C.S. Corry, of Rockcorry Castle, Esq. His remains were interred in the family vault at Killcrow, whither they were accompanied by a very large and respectable concourse of friends and acquaintances. (1845-04-05, 3:2, D)

1652. March 28, at his house in Portman-square, London, in the 59th year of his age, Colonel Turner Grant, late of the Grenadier Guards. (1845-04-05, 3:2, D)

1653. March 31, at Avon Lodge, Armagh, Major Thomas Shawe, aged 75 years, universally respected and regretted. (1845-04-05, 3:2, D)

1654. March 23, in Blackhall-street, of disease of the heart, Samuel Belton, Esq., aged 63 years. (1845-04-05, 3:2, D)

1655. March 31, in South Frederick-street, Thomas Herbert Orpen, M.D., in the 79th year of his age. (1845-04-05, 3:2, D)

1656. March 20, at Brook Hall, near Coleraine, Eliza, wife of James Boyce, Esq. (1845-04-05, 3:2, D)

1657. November 7, at Lewistown, Pennsylvania, James Wightman, Esq., formerly of Grove Green, near Lisburn. (1845-04-05, 3:2, D)

1658. March 26, at his residence in Glenarm, Thomas Davison, Esq. (1845-04-05, 3:2, D)

1659. March 20, at Belmont Terrace, Newry, Anastasia, wife of Captain Russell, Staff Officer, aged 24 years. (1845-04-05, 3:2, D)

1660. March 27, at her residence, Dalkey Lodge, near Dublin, after one week's illness, aged 77 years, Catherine, relict of Robert Henry, Esq., and daughter of the late Thomas Elder, Esq., of Dalkey Lodge, and formerly of Belfast. (1845-04-05, 3:2, D)

1661. March 18, James Prendeville, Esq., after a protracted illness of seven months. Mr. Prendeville was well known to the literary world, and has left a wife and three children totally unprovided for. (1845-04-05, 3:2, D)

1662. March 25, at Ilchester, in the county of Somerset, John Walker, Esq., M.A., only son of Dr. John Walker, Senior Fellow of Trinity College, Dublin, and founder of a sect that bears his name. (1845-04-05, 3:2, D)

1663. March 27, at 70, South Audley-street, Charlotte Granville, wife of G.T. Trench, Esq., Marino, Ireland. (1845-04-05, 3:2, D)

1664. On Thursday, the 3rd inst., at Newbliss, in the 47th year of his age, Mr. Daniel Leary, Merchant. The large and very respectable concourse that followed his remains to the place of interment, told how much he was respected and beloved. (1845-04-12, 2:4, D)

1665. April 12, in Donaghmore Presbyterian meeting-house by the Rev. Verner M. White, of Liverpool, Maxwell, youngest son of the late Thomas Simpson, Esq., Beech-hill, county of Armagh, to Mary, second daughter of the late Samuel Martin, Esq., Longhorse, county of Down. (1845-04-19, 3:6, M)

1666. April 15, in St. Thomas's Church, Thomas Smyth, Esq., Solicitor, to Alicia Rachael, eldest daughter of the late Jeremy Marsh, Esq., Captain, 90th Regiment. (1845-04-19, 3:6, M)

1667. At the residence of her brother-in-law, Merrion-avenue, Blackrock, Dublin, Rebecca, second daughter of Edmond Hanley, Esq., of Waterford, to Michael Joseph Power, Esq., Manager, National Bank of Ireland, Castlerea. (1845-04-19, 3:6, M)

1668. April 12, at Richmond Hill, Rathmines, Dublin, of pithises [sic], Bridget Bedelia, wife of Frederick Carter, Esq., Glenview, county of Waterford. "In death regretted as in life beloved." (1845-04-19, 3:6, D)

1669. On the 14th inst., Mr. Patrick Moore, of Little May-street, Belfast. (1845-04-19, 3:6, D)

1670. On the 7th inst., in the 25th year of his age, at the residence of his father, Mr. Hugh Rodgers, of Beragh, county Tyrone. (1845-04-19, 3:6, D)

1671. At Paris, Count Olivier de Boisguilbert, to Louisa, daughter of W. Bingham, Esq., of Philadelphia, niece of Lady Ashburton. (1845-04-26, 3:2, M)

1672. April 19, James Hamilton Stitt, grandson of the late Rev. William Stitt, of Dungannon, to Catherine, eldest daughter of the late John Porter, Belfast. (1845-04-26, 3:2, M)

1673. April 18, at Lurgan Church, Edward Leslie Falloon, Esq., Surgeon, of Liverpool, third son of the Rev. Marcus Falloon, Rector of Layde, Cushendall, to Eliza, third daughter of Joseph Breedon, Esq., Surgeon, R.N., of Sandstead Plain, East Canada. (1845-04-26, 3:2, M)

1674. April 20, after a long and painful illness, George Beresford Dawson, late of the Rifle Brigade, and second son of the Right Hon. George R. Dawson. (1845-04-26, 3:2, D)

1675. April 21, at Manor Highgate, county of Fermanagh, Kate Isabella, eldest daughter of Captain W.B. M'Clintock, R.N., aged one year and five months. (1845-04-26, 3:2, D)

1676. April 19, at Kincor [sic], the residence of his brother-in-law, after a long and protracted illness, which he bore with christian patience, John Parker, of Ballyboy, Esq., sincerely and deservedly regretted by a large circle of friends. (1845-04-26, 3:2, D)

1677. April 17, in Armagh, Dr. Bampfield, Surgeon in the 32d Regiment of Foot, aged 64 years, leaving a widow and four children, one of whom is in the 1st Royals. (1845-04-26, 3:2, D)

1678. At Dublin, Doctor Thomas O'Conner, of Cavan, to Rose, daughter of James O'Brien, Esq., of Cavan. (1845-05-03, 2:6, M)

1679. At an advanced age, Adam Gibson, Esq., of Lisaniske, in this county. (1845-05-03, 2:6, D)

1680. On Wednesday, the 30th April inst., the lady of Jas. M. Ross, Esq., Church-square, Monaghan, of a daughter. (1845-05-10, 3:3, B)

1681. On the 22d ult., in Connor Church, by the Rev. Mr. Hobson, Mr. Alexander Harman, Merchant, of Enniskillen, to Mary, youngest daughter of Henry Martin, Auchnacloy, county Tyrone. (1845-05-10, 3:3, M)

1682. In Dungannon, on Thursday, the 8th inst., Mrs. M'Gerr, wife of Mr. John M'Gerr, of that town, and daughter of Mr. Matthew Vallely, Monaghan. (1845-05-10, 3:3, D)

1683. April 26, at Portadown, of apoplexy, Robert Ball Calhoun, Esq., M.D. (1845-05-10, 3:3, D)

1684. On Sunday, the 27th April, in Eden, Enniskillen, Mr. Cockran, aged 60 years. (1845-05-10, 3:3, D)

1685. April 28th, Anne, eldest daughter of Mr. J. Bland, of Enniskillen, aged 3 years. (1845-05-10, 3:3, D)

1686. On the 26th ult., at Bell-Hill, after a short illness, John Armstrong, Esq., in the 76th year of his age. (1845-05-10, 3:3, D)

1687. At the residence of her son, Dr. Mervyn Crawford, Upper Berkeley-street, London, aged 78 years, Elizabeth, relict of Alexander Crawford, Esq., formerly of Miltown House, near Dublin, and of Millwood, county Fermanagh. (1845-05-10, 3:3, D)

1688. Deeply regretted, Jane Maria, the wife of Mr. Wm. Scott, draper, Omagh, in the county of Tyrone, fourth daughter of the late Jerald Lloyd, Esq., Munville, in the county of Fermanagh, in the 76th year of her age. (1845-05-10, 3:3, D)

1689. May 6th, at Shirley House, Hants, the lady of C.P. Leycester, Esq., of a daughter. (1845-05-17, 3:3, B)

1690. May the 14th, in Killevan Church, by the Rev. W.W. Deering, Thomas Lennard, son of the late William Mayne, Esq., of Freame Mount, county Monaghan, to Margaret Georgina, eldest daughter of the late Robert Thomas Mahony, Esq., Blessington-street, in the city of Dublin. (1845-05-17, 3:3, M)

1691. On the 1st inst., Mr. James M'Kee, of Castleblayney, to Ellen, fourth daughter of the late Thomas Walsh, Esq., of Templetate, county Monaghan. (1845-05-17, 3:3, M)

1692. At St. Anne's Church, the Rev. Robert Mann, of Saxmundham, to Harriet, the fifth daughter of the Right Hon. Sir Edward Sugden. (1845-05-17, 3:3, M)

1693. On the 13th instant, by the Rev. H. Dickson, Ballysillan, Mr. Thomas Horner, Ligoneil [sic], to Miss Jane M'Neece, Wolfhill. (1845-05-17, 3:3, M)

1694. On the 7th instant, by the Rev. H. Perry, in the third Presbyterian Church, Portglenone, Robert Hemphill, to Mary, eldest daughter of Samuel Young, both of Bracknamuckley. (1845-05-17, 3:3, M)

1695. May 3, at Cornmarket, aged 28 years, Mr. W.L. Fletcher, Printer. He was the author of many poems, amongst which was one published entitled, the "Frequented Village." (1845-05-17, 3:3, D)

1696. On the 12th instant, James, youngest son of the late James Ireland, Prince's-street. (1845-05-17, 3:3, D)

1697. On Thursday, 8th inst., at Larne, William Walsh M'Neill, Solicitor. (1845-05-17, 3:3, D)

1698. Very suddenly, on Tuesday the 6th instant, Mrs. Getty, wife of Mr. Moore Getty, Kirkmoil, near Ballymoney. (1845-05-17, 3:3, D)

1699. On the 2nd inst., at 50, Queen-street, Edinburgh, Mrs. Cunningham, wife of James Cunningham, Esq., Writer to *The Signet*, and sister of the Rev. D. Bagot, Newry. (1845-05-17, 3:3, D)

1700. On the 5th inst., at his residence, Ravensdale, Flurry-bridge, Richard Bennison, Esq. (1845-05-17, 3:3, D)

1701. At Banbridge, on the 6th inst., Miss Anabella M'William, sister to the late Mr. William M'William, of same place, aged 70. (1845-05-17, 3:3, D)

1702. On Sunday Evening, the 11th inst., James Foster, Esq., of Lisnabreen, county of Down, at the advanced age of 81 years. (1845-05-17, 3:3, D)

1703. May 8, John Martin, Esq., manager of the Dublin Banking Company, D'Olier Street. (1845-05-17, 3:3, D)

1704. In Benburb Church, on Tuesday, the 12th inst., by the Rev. Richard Wrightson, Mr. Andrew Wilson, of the Ordnance Survey department, to Miss Caldwell, of Armagh. (1845-05-24, 3:3, M)

1705. On Friday, the 9th inst., in Portadown Church, Thomas Sinnamon, jun., Esq., to Margaret Maria, eldest daughter of James Kinkead, Esq., of Tandragee, and sister to G. Kinkead, Esq., of Portadown. (1845-05-24, 3:3, M)

1706. On the 14th inst., in the Wesleyan Chapel, Sandys-street, by the Rev. Mr. Carey, Mr. Isaac Glenny, to Miss Anna Harcourt, third daughter of the late Mr. Richard Harcourt, both of Newry. (1845-05-24, 3:3, M)

1707. Yesterday, in Scotch-street, at the house of her son, Mr. Robert Barnes, Mrs. Barnes, relict of the late Wm. Barnes, Esq., of this City [Armagh], in the 71st year of her age, much and deservedly regretted. (1845-05-24, 3:3, D)

1708. At the residence of her uncle, in Dobbin-street, Armagh, aged 16 years, Isabella, daughter of the late Mr. James Star, of this City. (1845-05-24, 3:3, D)

1709. On the 10th inst., in the 88th year of her age, at the house of her son, Mr. Archibald Johnston, of Middletown, Mrs. Rachel Johnston, widow of the late Mr. M. Johnston, of Derryhaw, near Tynan. In all the relations of life, she was most exemplary, meek, and humble; she enjoyed comfort in death, and fell asleep in Jesus, in true and certain hope of a glorious resurrection. (1845-05-24, 3:3, D)

1710. On Wednesday, the 14th instant, at Summer Hill, the residence of her mother, Jane Anne, wife of Mr. Richard C. Vogan, of this City [Armagh], Merchant, in the 28th year of her age. (1845-05-24, 3:3, D)

1711. At Caledon, on Wednesday, the 14th inst., Anne, eldest daughter of Mr. John Taggart. (1845-05-24, 3:3, D)

1712. At his residence, Grann [sic], in the 84th year of his age, on Monday last, Adam Nixon, Esq., Clerk of the Peace for the county Fermanagh. (1845-05-24, 3:3, D)

1713. On the 9th inst., at Caledon, Mr. Marcus M'Clean. (1845-05-24, 3:3, D)

1714. On the 15th inst., at his residence, Annslough, near Middletown, of a tedious and painful illness, which he bore with the most christian patience and resignation, the Rev. Bernard Loughran, P.P., of Tynan. (1845-05-24, 3:3, D)

1715. May 13, at Castleblayney, in this county, James Molloy, Esq., of Dublin, Public Notary and Stockbroker. (1845-05-24, 3:3, D)

1716. On the 23d ult., at St. George's Church, Dublin, James Power, Esq., of Colehill-house, county of Longford, to Eliza, second daughter of the late Alexander Nixon Montgomery, Esq., of Bessmount-park, county of Monaghan. (1845-05-31, 3:3, M)

1717. On the 18th inst., in Caledon Church, Mr. Andrew Bampton, of Strabane, to Frances Elizabeth, fourth daughter of Henry Pilkington Ogle, Furz Park, County Meath. (1845-05-31, 3:3, M)

1718. On the 13th inst., at Moyleteragh Church, by the Rev. George Smith, Arthur, only son of Mr. Arthur Baxter, Coolnaman, to Mary, eldest daughter of Henry Hunter, Esq., of Castledawson. (1845-05-31, 3:3, M)

1719. On the 26th instant, in the Presbyterian Church, Linenhall-street, Belfast, Mr. James Madill, of Shankhill, to Catherine Neill, of Ballymacarrett. (1845-05-31, 3:3, M)

1720. On Friday, the 23d inst., by license, in the Presbyterian Church, Muckamore, by the Rev. J.M. Morrow, Mr. James Weir, millwright, Dunadry, to Margaret, daughter to Mr. H. Wilson, of Straidbally-morris. (1845-05-31, 3:3, M)

1721. May 26, in St. George's Church, Hanover-square, London, by the Bishop of Rochester, Lord Lovaine, eldest son of the Earl and Countess of Beverley, to Louisa, eldest daughter of Mr. Henry and Lady Harriett Drummond. (1845-05-31, 3:3, M)

1722. May 26, in Mountjoy-square, Prissilla, eldest daughter of the late Matthew O'Connor, of Mount Druid, county Roscommon, and niece to the late O'Conor Don, M.P., to John Chester, Esq., of Williamstown, county of Louth. (1845-05-31, 3:3, M)

1723. May 26, in Great George's Church, by the Rev. Wm. Burgh, Joseph Chambers, second son of Edward Elliot Chambers, Esq., late of Fitzwilliam-place, Dublin, to Harriet, youngest daughter of Nevill Barry, Esq., of Russell-street. (1845-05-31, 3:3, M)

1724. May 23, in St. Peter's Church, Henry, son of John Smith, Esq., of Somerton, county of Dublin, to Jane, youngest daughter of the late Robert Brattle, Esq., of Wateringbury, Kent. (1845-05-31, 3:3, M)

1725. May 22, at Cleland, Lanarkshire, by the Rev. Travis Sandys, A.M., Vicar of Beverley, and Domestic Chaplain to Lord Belhaven, John Dick Lauder, Esq., eldest son of Sir Thomas Dick Lauder, of Fountain Hall and Grange, Bart., to Ann, second daughter of North Dalrymple, Esq., of Fordel. (1845-05-31, 3:3, M)

1726. May 24, at Leamington, John Wilson, Esq., late Captain in the 37th Regiment, to Philippa, youngest daughter of the late P.L. Story, Esq., of Kemptown, Brighton. (1845-05-31, 3:3, M)

1727. May 26, Thomas Price, Esq., late of the 60th Royal Rifles, and youngest son of the late Sir Rose Price, Bart., of Trengwainton, Cornwall, to Anna, second daughter of the late Frederick Hayes Macnamara, Esq., formerly Lieutenant in the 52d Regiment of Foot. (1845-05-31, 3:3, M)

1728. At Newtownbutler, on the 23d instant, of consumption, Mr. Robert Allen, aged 25 years. From a boy, he was a member of the Primitive Wesleyan Methodist Society; when in affliction, he experienced the consolation and support of that religion he professed, and of which he was an ornament; he died universally regretted. (1845-05-31, 3:3, D)

1729. On the 22d instant, at her mother's house, at Kingstown, Margaret, relict of Philip Goraghty, late of Dungannon. (1845-05-31, 3:3, D)

1730. On the 12th instant, at Armagh, John Crosthwaite, only son of Joshua Thomas Noble, Esq., aged 19 years. (1845-05-31, 3:3, D)

1731. May 21, at Newcastle, after a few days' illness, deeply regretted by his brother officers, and all who knew him, Colonel Archibald Montgomery Maxwell, K.H., Lieut.-Colonel commanding the 36th Regiment. (1845-05-31, 3:3, D)

1732. May 25, in Ennis, of an affection of the heart, John, the second son of the Rev. L.W. King. (1845-05-31, 3:3, D)

1733. May 25, suddenly, at her residence, 18, Kildare-st., Elizabeth, relict of William Studdart, of Clonlohan House, in the King's County, Esq., and only sister of the late Rev. Launcelot Dowdall, D.D., of Dungannon. (1845-05-31, 3:3, D)

1734. May 24, at Belfast, Miss Donnelly, eldest daughter of Daniel Donnelly, Esq., of that town. (1845-05-31, 3:3, D)

1735. May 27, Mrs. Ellis, wife of Arthur Ellis, Esq., of Lower Gardiner-street. (1845-05-31, 3:3, D)

1736. March 16, at Hullyhall, near Darwar, Madras Presidency, Ensign John Edgar Leslie, of the 35th Native Infantry, eldest son of Major-General John Leslie, K.H., of her Majesty's service, commanding at Bellary. (1845-05-31, 3:3, D)

1737. June 3, at St. George's Church, by the Rev. Frederick Fitzpatrick, Rector of Sircock, county Cavan, and uncle to the bride, George Hicks, Esq., son of the late Charles Hicks, Esq., of Bath, to Eliza Mary, eldest daughter of the late Rev. John Salisbury Rainsford, formerly of St. Michan's in the city of Dublin. (1845-06-07, 3:3, M)

1738. May 28, in his 79th year, at his son's residence in Castleblayney, Geo. Richard Golding, Esq., of Limepark, county Tyrone. (1845-06-07, 3:3, D)

1739. On Saturday last, at Blackwatertown, Margaret, wife of John Crothers, Esq., aged 26 years. Seized by a fatal disease in the midst of youth and great usefulness, she was enabled to commit herself with complete resignation to the will of God, and has, through his Grace, exchanged the varied relationships of life, which she eminently adorned, for the rest of a glorious immortality. (1845-06-07, 3:3, D)

1740. In Belturbet Church, on the 11th inst., by the Rev. — Winder, Richard Clarke, Esq., of Bailieboro', to Ellen, only daughter of Mr. C. Reynolds. (1845-06-14, 2:6, M)

1741. On the 9th inst., at the Naval Hospital, Woolwich, William R. Surridge, Esq., Mate of H.M.S. *Hecate*. (1845-06-14, 2:6, D)

1742. At Lime Park, county Galway, the Lady of Charles Wallace, Esq., R.M., of a daughter. (1845-06-21, 3:1, B)

1743. June 11, at the Parsonage, Newbliss, the lady of the Rev. William Deering, of a daughter. (1845-06-21, 3:1, B)

1744. June 19, in St. George's Church, by the Rev. Henry Fry, cousin to the bridegroom, the Rev. Henry Fry, of Edenderry, in the King's county, eldest son of Henry Fry, Esq., of Frybrook, in the county of Roscommon, to Jane Thomasina, second daughter of Thomas Fenton, Esq., of Temple-street, in this city [Dublin]. (1845-06-21, 3:1, M)

1745. In Enniskillen, Mrs. Stewart, the beloved wife of Captain Stewart, and eldest daughter of the late Rev. Charles Lucas Bell. (1845-06-21, 3:1, D)

1746. At Stamford, Niagara, Maria, wife of Dr. Corry, of Rockcorry, county of Monaghan, and daughter of the late Major Baylis, formerly Deputy-Assistant-Adjutant-General in Dublin. (1845-06-21, 3:1, D)

1747. At Caen, where he had resided more than twenty years, J.S. Smith, Esq., brother of the late Admiral Sir Sidney Smith, and formerly Ambassador at Constantinople. He was well known as a learned antiquary, and for his general literary attainments. (1845-06-21, 3:1, D)

1748. At Gortmore, Omagh, the lady of R.D. Coulson, Esq., of a daughter. (1845-06-28, 3:4, B)

1749. June 25, in St. Mary's church, Newry, by the Rev. Dr. Campbell, Rector of Forkhill, George Casey, Esq., of Liverpool, to Mercy Boursequot, eldest daughter of George Glenny, Esq., late of Moorvale in the county Armagh. (1845-06-28, 3:4, M)

1750. June 18, in St. Peter's, Dublin, by the Rev. W.W. Deering, the Rev. Joseph North, only son of Roger North, of Kilduff House, in the King's county, Esq., to Emma, daughter of the late John Deering, Esq., Q.C., of Derrybrusk, county of Fermanagh. (1845-06-28, 3:4, M)

1751. On the 18th inst., at Derrycortrevy church, by the Rev. Mr. Major, Alfred Sotheren, of Bray, Esq., to Ellen, fourth daughter of the late John Gilmore, of Lisrone, county Tyrone, Esq. (1845-06-28, 3:4, M)

1752. Same day [18th inst.], in St. Patrick's Cathedral, Armagh, James Gardner, Esq., to Miss Anne Scott, niece of George Scott, Esq., of Vicar's Hill. (1845-06-28, 3:4, M)

1753. At Lisanisk, Carrickmacross, Charles C. Gibson, Esq., solicitor. (1845-06-28, 3:4, D)

1754. On the second inst., Mr. P. Kelly, Merchant, Monaghan, to Elizabeth, second daughter of Mr. Michael Campbell, Erskinore, County Tyrone. (1845-07-05, 3:6, M)

1755. On the 10th instant, in St. Catherine's Church, Dublin, by the Rev. Thomas Gregg, Mr. Wm. Williams, Hat manufacturer, Monaghan, to Alice, only daughter of Mr. James West, Pleasant-street, Dublin. (1845-07-12, 3:2, M)

1756. July 2, in St. George's Church, by the Rev. Richard Conolly, brother to the bridegroom, Francis Conolly, Esq., of Ballinamore, county Leitrim, to Elizabeth, second daughter of the late Thomas Fleming, Esq., of the Ordnance Department, Dublin. (1845-07-12, 3:2, M)

1757. June 27, in Cavan Church, by the Rev. Decimus William Preston, A.B., Wadham Wyndham Bond, Esq., Lieutenant, 4th King's Own Regiment, son of H. C. Bond, Esq., of Bondville, county of Armagh, to Catherine Charlotte, daughter of the late William Wilkins, Esq. (1845-07-12, 3:2, M)

1758. On Saturday last, at his residence, Clones, at an advanced age, and after a long illness, Mr. Hugh M'Mahon, proprietor of the Clones Hotel. Mr. M'Mahon was one of the most respected inhabitants of the town, and a general favorite with all classes in the community, as the concourse which followed his remains to its last home testified. (1845-07-12, 3:2, D)

1759. In Clones Church, by the Rev. Charles Welsh, Mr. Robert Irwin, Merchant, Clones, to Louise Maria, second daughter of the late John Clarke, Esq., Post-master, Clones. (1845-07-19, 3:2, M)

1760. At the Registrar's office, Monaghan, by John Goudy, Esq., on the 7th instant, Mr. Hugh Hamilton, to Miss Anne Presho, of Saloo. (1845-07-19, 3:2, M)

1761. July 9, in St. Mary's Church, Marylebone, London, by the Rev. Peter Hall, William Drummond Delap, Esq., of Monasterboice House, county of Louth, Ireland, to Mary, second daughter to the late Colonel Sankey of Fort Frederick, county of Cavan and Rutland-square, in this city. (1845-07-19, 3:2, M)

1762. At Castleblayney, on the 17th instant, at the home of the bride's father, by the Rev. Dr. M'Meel, P.P., Mr. James Quigly, Monaghan, to Maryanne, second daughter of Mr. James M'Mahon. (1845-07-26, 3:3, M)

1763. July 15, by the Rev. W. Bolton, at the residence of her Britannic Majesty's Envoy Extra-ordinary and Minister Plenipotentiary at Frankfort, Captain Adderly Beamish Bernard, of Kilcoman, in the county of Cork, to Anne Catherine, youngest daughter of Captain George Walker, Royal Navy, residing in Dusseldorf, Prussia, and late of Summer-seat, county of Wexford. (1845-07-26, 3:3, M)

1764. July 17, at Donoughmore Church, by the father of the bride, the Rev. Edward Hodgins, Curate of Carigrohan, to Margaret Anne, eldest daughter of the Rev. Joseph R. Cotter, Rector of Donoughmore, and senior Prebendary of Cloyne Cathedral. (1845-07-26, 3:3, M)

1765. At Armagh, John Hanna, of Terryskean, county Armagh, Esq., to the second daughter of the late William Wilson, Esq., of Blackwatertown, and niece of the late Sir Isaac Wilson, Knight, Surgeon in Ordinary to the late Duke of Sussex. (1845-07-26, 3:3, M)

1766. July 15, James Newell, Esq., Castle Hill, Rath-friland, to Fanny, daughter of Thomas Nicholson, Esq., Seafield, Kilkeel. (1845-07-26, 3:3, M)

1767. July 21, Michael Corcoran, of Gardiner-street, Esq., to Anna Maria, youngest daughter of the late Francis Magan, Esq., of Emo, county Westmeath. (1845-07-26, 3:3, M)

1768. On Thursday, in this town, after a protracted illness, which she bore with Christian resignation, Mary, second daughter of Mr. P. M'Phillips, proprietor of the Westenra Arms Hotel, Monaghan. (1845-07-26, 3:3, D)

1769. On the 19th instant, at his own residence, near Coothill, of Typhus Fever, the Rev. Philip Brabazon, who had been curate in the parish of Cootehill, for the last seven years. It is but justice to his memory to state, that during the above period of his ministry, he was a firm and zealous supporter of the principles of his own Church, a vigilant and laborious pastor of the poor, and ardent and indefatigable in the improvements of the young; who in hundreds attended his remains to their last resting place, and by their tears and cries, proved on the occasion, that "from the very mouth of babes and sucklings, the Lord can perfect praise,"—and that "blessed are the dead who die in the Lord! they rest from their labours, and their works do follow them." (1845-08-02, 3:6, D)

1770. July 28, at Dunamoine Glebe, county Monaghan, the lady of the Rev. Robert Loftus Tottenham, of a son. (1845-08-09, 3:3, B)

1771. August 4, at the Marriage Registry Office, 48, Dame-street, by the District Registrar, Christopher Thorpe, Esq., (of the Excise), to Jane, eldest daughter of the late Rev. Joseph Barnes, of Whigsborough, in the King's County. (1845-08-09, 3:3, M)

1772. In Clennanese Presbyterian Church, county Tyrone, Hamilton Boyd, Esq., of Lynchburgh, Virginia, North America, to Margaret, eldest daughter of the Rev. James Kinnier, of Lower Clennanease, near Dungannon. (1845-08-09, 3:3, M)

1773. July 31, in Derry, Arthur M'Corkhell, Esq., solicitor, to Jane, second daughter of David Gilmore, Esq., both of that city. (1845-08-09, 3:3, M)

1774. At Charlemont-place, Armagh, on Tuesday, 29th ult., Miss Jessie Paton, second daughter of James Paton, Esq., of Ayr, Scotland, aged 22. Her remains were taken to Ayr for interment. (1845-08-09, 3:3, D)

1775. On the 29th ult., at Brookeborough, aged 84 years, Doctor John West, the oldest medical practitioner in Fermanagh. (1845-08-09, 3:3, D)

1776. On Monday evening, 29th ult., at Willoughby-place, Enniskillen, at an advanced age, Mrs. Betty, relict of the late John Betty, Esq., Cappy. (1845-08-09, 3:3, D)

1777. At Castleblayney, on the 7th inst., by the Rev. Thomas Boyd, John M'Burney, Esq., M.D., to Abigail, youngest daughter of Mr. Henry Grier, of Hawk Cottage, Castleblayney. (1845-08-16, 3:5, M)

1778. August 17, in Lower Fitzwilliam-street, the lady of Richard Mayne, Esq., of Newbliss, of a son. (1845-08-23, 3:3, B)

1779. At Cloverhill, in this county, on Friday, the 15th last, Alexander Waddell, Esq., aged 78. Mr. Waddell, was one of the celebrated Volunteers of '82, and one of the three last survivors of this well known body in this county. There are two others yet in existence in the county Monaghan, and the three men enjoyed all the respect and esteem due to their early patriotism, their great age, and their respectability of character. (1845-08-23, 3:3, D)

1780. On the 22d instant, at Cartmel, Lancashire, the Lady of William Foster Elliott, Esq., of a daughter. (1845-08-30, 3:3, B)

1781. August 24, at his residence in Baggot-street, Dublin, after a long and protracted illness, C. Benson, Esq., Barrister. (1845-08-30, 3:3, D)

1782. September 2, at Cremoney [sic] Church, by the Rev. Dr. Drew, Henley R. Bass, Esq., of Glasgow, to Julia Vincent Duff, Mount Caulfield, county of Armagh. (1845-09-06, 3:4, M)

1783. September 2, in St. Catherine's Church, by the Rev. Thomas Gregg, Mr. Thomas Whitehead, of Pimlico, second son of Mr. George Whitehead, to Anna, only daughter of James M'Cartney, Esq., of Drogheda. (1845-09-06, 3:4, M)

1784. September 2, in Cliffe Castle, John, eldest son of the late C. Cahill, Esq., of Rathlesty, in the county of Tipperary, to Teresa Jane, youngest daughter of the late P. Russell, in the county of Limerick. (1845-09-06, 3:4, M)

1785. Sept. 4th, in Clontibret Church, by the Venerable the Archdeacon of Clogher, the Rev. John Evans Lewis, Rector of Moyntagh [sic], County Armagh, eldest son of the late William Lewis, Esq., of Sligo, to Margaret Jane, youngest daughter of the late Henry Swanzy, Esq., of Rockfield, county Monaghan. (1845-09-06, 3:4, M)

1786. June 3, in the island of Madeira, of fever, John G. Thomson, Esq., of Knockbryttas, county of Dublin, most deservedly and sincerely regretted. (1845-09-06, 3:4, D)

1787. September 2, at Ulster Terrace, Rathmines, aged sixty-seven, Isabella Maria, the beloved wife of B.T. Ottley, Esq. (1845-09-06, 3:4, D)

1788. August 31, at Annsbrook, Clontarf, George O'Brien, Esq., Solicitor of Hardwicke-street, aged sixty. (1845-09-06, 3:4, D)

1789. September 1, at Roundtown, Mr. William Smith, aged seventy-seven years. (1845-09-06, 3:4, D)

1790. August 31, at Clonegal, county of Carlow, W. Hope, Esq., Solicitor, aged sixty-one. (1845-09-06, 3:4, D)

1791. At Plumstead Church, Woolwich, William Morris Alcock, Esq., eldest son of Alexander M. Alcock, Esq., of Dunmore, in the county of Waterford, to Anna Maria, eldest daughter of the late Captain John Elgee, 67th Regiment. (1845-09-20, 3:4, M)

1792. September 11, in Magourney Church, county of Cork, by the Very Rev. the Dean of Cork, Hedges Eyre Chatterton, Esq., Barrister-at-Law, to Mary, daughter of the Rev. William Hallaran, A.M., Rector of Magourney. (1845-09-20, 3:4, M)

1793. In Clontarf Church, Neal Davis, Esq., of Upper Rutland-street, to Eleanor, second daughter of Thos. Palmer, Esq. (1845-09-20, 3:4, M)

1794. September 13, in St. Anne's Church, by the Rev. Charles Fleury, Chaplain to the Molyneux Asylum, Philip Phin, Esq., of Shelvenstown, in the county of Meath, to Alice, the daughter of James B. Archer, Esq., and grand daughter of the late Doctor Archer, of Dublin. (1845-09-20, 3:4, M)

1795. September 13, in St. Peter's Church, by the Rev. T. Dawson, Samuel Walker, Esq., 7, Rathmines Terrace, to Emily, second daughter of J. Place, Esq., of the county of Wexford. (1845-09-20, 3:4, M)

1796. September 11, in Aghada Church, by the Rev. R.B. Kirchoffer, R.T. Hill, Esq., only son of the Rev. J. Hill, Rector of Rostellan, to Maria Georgiana, third daughter of the Rev. W.R. Townsend, Rector of Aghada. (1845-09-20, 3:4, M)

1797. September 15, at Killarney, Bray, the Rev. Andrew Forster, deeply regretted. The remains of this lamented gentleman, who was brother to William Foster [sic], Esq., of Ballynure, J.P., D.L., were brought from Monaghan yesterday, for the purpose of interment in the family vault, at Ballinode. The funeral was attended by a large concourse of the gentry and clergy of the county. (1845-09-20, 3:4, D)

1798. September 15, at the Castle, Parsonstown, the infant daughter of the Countess of Ross, aged four days. (1845-09-20, 3:4, D)

1799. September 9, Julian Venables Verdon, eldest son of the proprietor of *The Sligo Champion*. (1845-09-20, 3:4, D)

1800. On the 24th instant, at Mount Louise, the Lady of S.R.B. Evatt, Esq., of [a] son. (1845-09-27, 3:2, B)

1801. September 18, at Cullies, near Cavan, the lady of the Rev. Dr. Carson, of a son. (1845-09-27, 3:2, B)

1802. On the 23d instant, in the Registrar's office, Monaghan, Mr. William Dodds, of Tattanclave, to Miss Agnes Graham, of Legacurry. (1845-09-27, 3:2, M)

1803. In Rossory Church, on Monday last, by the Rev. John Taylor, Doctor Adam Nixon, of Willoughby Place, to Matilda Susanna, only surviving daughter of Capt. John Stewart, of same place. (1845-09-27, 3:2, M)

1804. September 18, at Poyntzpass Church, by the father of the bride, Matthew Fleming Handy, Esq., third son of John Handy, of Barraghcore, in the county Kilkenny, Esq., to Isabella Sarah, second daughter of the Rev. Henry Gamble, of Drumnargoole, county Armagh. (1845-09-27, 3:2, M)

1805. September 23, in St. James's Church, by the Rev. R. Connolly, William, youngest son of the late Richard Conolly, Esq., of Rathmines, to Emily Jane, youngest daughter of Thomas Willans, Esq., of Susan Vale, county of Dublin. (1845-09-27, 3:2, M)

1806. September 16, in Aberdeen, by the Rev. E.S. Hutchinson, Vicar of East Stoke, J. Hadden, Esq., of Bramcote, to Annie Duncan, eldest daughter of the late Lieutenant-Colonel Macgregor, of the 33d Regiment, and niece of Sir James Macgregor, Bart. (1845-09-27, 3:2, M)

1807. September 21, at Carysfort Avenue, deeply and deservedly regretted by his family and numerous circle of friends, Joseph Montgomery, eldest son of Richard Mongomery [sic], Esq., North Great George's-street, Solicitor, and Cootehill, county Cavan. (1845-09-27, 3:2, D)

1808. September 22, sincerely regretted, Mr. James Le Bass of Castle-street, aged seventy-three. He was a sincere friend, a loving husband, an affectionate father, and in the true sense of the term, an honest man. (1845-09-27, 3:2, D)

1809. September 20, at Bath, aged 83, Mrs. Elizabeth Close, last surviving sister of the late Sir Barry Close, Baronet, and of the late Rev. Samuel Close, of Elmpark, county Armagh. (1845-09-27, 3:2, D)

1810. September 23, at Connaught Terrace, Rathmines, Emily, the beloved wife of Charles Gavan Duffy, Esq., proprietor of the *Nation* newspaper. (1845-09-27, 3:2, D)

1811. On Sunday, at Bundoran, where he had gone for the benefit of his health, Alexander Hassard, Esq., J.P., and formerly Captain in the Enniskillen Dragoons. He was a brave and distinguished officer, and an upright magistrate. (1845-09-27, 3:2, D)

1812. September 24, in Portaferry Church, by the Rev. W. Savage, Rector of Shinrone, uncle of the bride, Major Hall, youngest son of the late Savage Hall, Esq., of Narrow Water, to Anne, youngest daughter of Andrew Nugent, Esq., Portaferry. (1845-10-04, 2:5, M)

1813. September 25, H.E. Browne, Esq., to the Hon. Catherine Georgiana, daughter of the Right Hon. Lord Decies. (1845-10-04, 2:5, M)

1814. At Cheltenham, Aeneas R. M'Donnell, Esq., to Emma, daughter of Major-General George Briggs. (1845-10-04, 2:5, M)

1815. September 26, at Letchworth, Herts, by the Rev. S.H. Knapp, Captain Hall, to Georgiana Arabella Caldecott James, only daughter of the late Lord Bishop of Calcutta. (1845-10-04, 2:5, M)

1816. On Thursday last, at the residence of her grandson, J.G. Lepper, Esq., at the advanced age of 85 years, Susanna, relict of the late Doctor Thomas Cottenham, of Cootehill. During her long life, she earned the respect and esteem of all who knew her. (1845-10-04, 2:5, D)

1817. After a few days' illness, at the residence of her brother-in-law, Thomas Butler, Esq., Montpellier Crescent, Brighton, Anne, the beloved wife of Charles Butler, Esq., M.D., Abbey View, Monkstown, in the county of Dublin. (1845-10-04, 2:5, D)

1818. At Ryefield, county Roscommon, the residence of her son-in-law, Christopher K. Taaffe, Esq., aged seventy-four years, Catherine, relict of Michael Lynch, Esq., of Granagh, county Longford. (1845-10-04, 2:5, D)

1819. September 23, at Glinn House, Carlingford, Sarah Anne, relict of James Fforde, Esq., of Raughlan, county Armagh. (1845-10-04, 2:5, D)

1820. At sea, on the passage home from Bombay, Mrs. Moore, wife of Lieutenant Moore, of the 28th regiment. (1845-10-04, 2:5, D)

1821. September 27, Hanna Annette, the beloved and only daughter of Samuel Gerrard, Esq., Vernon Parade, Clontarf. (1845-10-04, 2:5, D)

1822. September 27, at the residence of his brother, Acheson Lyle, Esq., Chief Remembrancer, Hugh Lyle, Esq., of Carnagarve, in the county of Donegal, Deputy Lieutenant and Treasurer of the county of Londonderry. (1845-10-04, 2:5, D)

1823. September 28, at the house of her father, in Hyde Park Terrace, aged nineteen, Emily Octavia, daughter of the Hon. Charles Ewan Law, M.P., Recorder of Law. (1845-10-04, 2:5, D)

1824. At his residence, in Armagh, on Thursday morning, after a long illness, Mr. James Greacen, Printer, eldest son of Mr. Nathaniel Greacen, of Monaghan. (1845-10-11, 3:6, D)

1825. On Tuesday, the 14th instant, at Fort-johnston, the residence of her father, the lady of J.B. Travers, Esq., Paymaster of the 31st Regiment, of a son. (1845-10-18, 2:3, B)

1826. On the 14th inst., at Steynton Church, Pembrokeshire, by the Rev. Robert Synge, M.A., Rector of Walwyn's Castle, the Rev. Wm. W. Webb Bowen, Vicar of Camrose, to Olevia, only daughter of the late Captain Charles Duffin, of the Bengal Cavalry. (1845-10-25, 3:6, M)

1827. Suddenly, on Saturday last, Mr. W. Wilson, Clonickney [sic], county Monaghan. (1845-10-25, 3:6, D)

1828. October 23, at Glen Lodge, Sligo, Patrick, eldest son of George Harkan, Esq., Ross, county Roscommon, to Miss Gardiner, daughter of the late Charles Gardiner, Esq. (1845-11-01, 3:3, M)

1829. October 15, at Preston, Major Crofton, of the 6th Royal Regiment, grandson of the late Sir Morgan Crofton, Bart., of Mohill Court, county Leitrim, to Ann Agnes, only daughter of John Addison, Esq., of Preston. (1845-11-01, 3:3, M)

1830. August 12, at Cawnpore, Andrew Spottiswoode, Esq., Captain in the 9th Lancers, to Jane Emily, youngest daughter of Colonel Campbell, of the same regiment. (1845-11-01, 3:3, M)

1831. September 1, at Calcutta, Major Stuart Corbett, commanding the 25th Native Infantry, to Mary Augusta, youngest daughter of Henry Kellett, Esq., Barrister-at-Law, of Cork. (1845-11-01, 3:3, M)

1832. With sincere sorrow, we record the death of Jas. Smith, Esq., of Ashfield, near Clones—a gentleman beloved and esteemed by all who knew him. Mr. Smith had been in a bad state of health for some time past, but no immediate danger was apprehended. He was at the fair of Clones on Thursday, and intended to have gone to Dublin on Friday for medical advice, but, on his return from the fair, he got a sudden attack, and expired in a few hours. (1845-11-01, 3:3, D)

1833. October 26, in Portman-square, after a long and painful illness, the Lady Strafford, wife of General Lord Strafford, G.C.B. (1845-11-01, 3:3, D)

1834. October 15, drowned at Sunderland, whilst bathing, Archibald Baird, second son of Sir David Baird, Bart. Also, Robert Baird, his eldest son, through the heroic attempt he made to save his brother, not being able to swim himself, and when the attempt had failed by those who could swim. Thus, they perished together; the eldest brother displaying that gallantry and devotion which belongs to the family from whence he was sprung, and blighting the hopes of his relations and friends, who had looked forward to his nobly following the footsteps of the gallant Baird of Seringapatam and Corunna, of whom, as far as judgment could be formed of the early promise of no ordinary kind, he would have been a worthy successor. (1845-11-01, 3:3, D)

1835. October 3, in the neighbourhood of Gottenberg, in Sweden, in the 26th year of his age, Talbot Dillon Chester, Esq., late of the 1st Dragoon Guards, and son of Henry Chester, Esq., of Cartown House, D.L., county Louth. (1845-11-01, 3:3, D)

1836. October 23, at St. Stephen's-green, Francis Gore, of Derrymore, county of Clare, Esq., aged eighty-four. (1845-11-01, 3:3, D)

1837. October 24, at Woodbine Lodge, near Longford, Alexander Dudgeon, Esq., Lieutenant in the Monaghan Militia. (1845-11-01, 3:3, D)

1838. October 24, in Dublin, the Rev. Samuel Mathews, only son of the late Samuel Mathews, Esq., of Bonnetstown, county of Kilkenny. (1845-11-01, 3:3, D)

1839. October 17, in Skibbereen, Kate, the beloved wife of M. Doyle, Esq., Comptroller of Customs, and grand-niece to the late Sir John Doyle. (1845-11-01, 3:3, D)

1840. October 27, at his residence, Millsbrook, near Ballinamore, William Slack, Esq., aged sixty-five years. (1845-11-01, 3:3, D)

1841. On the 27th inst., in the parish church of Aughnacloy, by the Rev. A.M. Pollock, Manly Power Dudden, Esq., of Lara Vale, youngest son of the late Jacob Dudden, Esq., Captain, 32d regiment, to Susan, ninth daughter of the late Mr. John Beggs, merchant, Aughnacloy. (1845-11-15, 3:6, M)

1842. October 30, at the hotel of the British embassy, Paris, by the right rev. Bishop Luscombe, Captain George Agustus [sic] Henry, R.N., fourth son of Mr. and Lady Emily Henry, to Etheldreda Lucy Emily, only child of the late lieutenant-colonel Ferris, Treasurer of the Island of Mauritius. (1845-11-22, 3:4, M)

1843. November 14, at Oundie, in Northamptonshire, Harittea, relict of the late Rev. John Stack, rector of Dromaid, county of Sligo. (1845-11-22, 3:4, D)

1844. November 16, aged 28 years, at Backwell-house near Bristol, the residence of the Hon. Lady Le Poer Trench, William, son of the late hon. colonel Sir R. Le Poer Trench. (1845-11-22, 3:4, D)

1845. November 14, Miss Catherine Thomasine Herbert, Colton Hall, Staffordshire, youngest daughter of the late rev. Robert Herbert, and grand daughter of Thos. Herbert, Esq., of Muckruss Abbey, and the Hon. Frances, his wife, daughter of Nicholas Viscount Kenmare. (1845-11-22, 3:4, D)

1846. November 11, at an advanced age, at the residence of her son, H.C. Field, Esq., M.D., Blackrock, Rose, widow of the late William Hamilton Field, Esq. (1845-11-22, 3:4, D)

1847. On the 11th inst., at his residence in Corbrack, Ballibay, Mr. John Mitchell, aged 85 years. He officiated as a ruling elder in the Presbyterian church of Crieve for nearly half a century, and faithfully discharged the duties of his office—always manifesting the deepest interest in the prosperity of that church, even from its very commencement. His memory will long be revered by its members. In the various relations of life, his conduct was becoming his Christian profession. By his uniform strict integrity, and unassuming habitual piety, he has left an example to an extensive circle of relations and friends, who, while they sincerely regret his removal from them, rejoice in the hope which he cherished of a blessed immortality through a crucified Saviour. (1845-11-22, 3:4, D)

1848. In Monaghan Church, on Wednesday last, by the Rev. H. Maffet, Mr. Alexander Shekleton, to Margaret, youngest daughter of the late Mr. James Clarke, of Clones. (1845-12-06, 3:4, M)

1849. Married, on the 25th ult., in the Office of the District Register, Castleblayney, by the Rev. Thomas Cathcart, Mr. Robert Crane of Tullycahey, farmer, to Miss Agnes M'Kee of Tullynaglush, County Armagh. (1845-12-06, 3:4, M)

1850. Nov. 24, at Rosstrevor, by the Rev. P. M'Evoy, P.P., Thomas Whittington Egan, Esq., eldest son of the late Thomas Egan, Esq., Solicitor, Dublin, to Miss Kate, only daughter of the late Mark Devlin, Esq., Solicitor, Newry. (1845-12-06, 3:4, M)

1851. Nov. 27, at St. Ann's Church, by the Rev. William M'Ilwaine, Mr. Robert Atkinson, eldest son of Mr. John Atkinson, Portadown, to Susanna, daughter of the late James Bryson, Esq., Waring Street, Belfast. (1845-12-06, 3:4, M)

1852. Nov. 20, at Plumstead Church, Robert Ramsay Pringle, Esq., Deputy Ordnance Store-keeper and Barrack-master at Enniskillen, to Harriette, third daughter of Joseph Cheetham, Esq., Ordnance Store-keeper, Windsor. (1845-12-06, 3:4, M)

1853. Nov. 23, at the residence of her father, Jane, third daughter of Mark Berey, Esq., of Richmount, in the 21st year of her age. (1845-12-06, 3:4, D)

1854. At Agean, in France, the Honourable George Hely Hutchinson, nephew of the late, and brother of the present, Earl of Donoughmore. (1845-12-06, 3:4, D)

1855. November 37 [sic], at the residence of his brother, the Proprietor of the *Tipperary Vindicator*. (1845-12-06, 3:4, D)

1856. November 21, at her residence in Sligo, Mrs. Little, the wife of Thomas Little, M.D., LL.D., surgeon to the Sligo county infirmary. (1845-12-06, 3:4, D)

1857. November 20, at Merrion-square, south, Mary, widow of the late Robert Reeves, Esq., of the same place, in the 82nd year of her age. (1845-12-06, 3:4, D)

1858. On Wednesday morning last, in Ballyshannon Church, by the Rev. Mr. White, curate, Mr. Robert Kerr, Primitive Wesleyan Methodist Minister, to Miss Charlotte Patience Hardinge, youngest daughter of Captain Hardinge, Donegal Militia. (1845-12-13, 3:2, M)

1859. December 6, at her residence in Upper Dorset-st., in her 82d year, Mary, relict of H. Cross, Esq. late of Dublin, and formerly of Clones, county Monaghan. (1845-12-13, 3:2, D)

1860. December 7, in Summerstown, county of Meath, at an advanced age, Mrs. Ingham, relict of the Rev. C.D. Ingham. Her end was peace, having a sure hope in the merits of her Redeemer. (1845-12-13, 3:2, D)

1861. December 7, of water on the brain, Richard Joseph, youngest son of the late J. Montgomery, Eccles-street, aged thirteen months. (1845-12-13, 3:2, D)

1862. December 5, at his residence, Baggot-place, South Circular-road, after a protracted illness of an excruciating kind, which he bore with the most exemplary patience [and] Christian fortitude, Doctor John O'Brien, late Fellow of the King and Queen's College of Physicians. For upwards of thirty years, he was senior Physician to the Fever Hospital, Cork-st., Dublin. (1845-12-13, 3:2, D)

1863. Died of Fever, on Monday the 8th instant, at Ballybunnion, County Kerry, the Rev. Andrew Bell, Curate of same place. (1845-12-13, 3:2, D)

1864. On the 5th inst., at St. Martin's Church, Birmingham, by license, Mr. Robert M'Knight, sixth son of Mr. John M'Knight, of Culcavey, Hillsborough, to Miss Mary Ann, daughter of the late John Hilditch, Esq., Potteries, Staffordshire. (1845-12-20, 3:1, M)

1865. On the 8th inst., in St. Peter's Church, Drogheda, by the Rev. A. Wynne, Vicar, Lee W. Dickson, Esq., to Letitia, relict of the late Joseph Leland, Esq., Pembroke-road, Dublin, and daughter of Thos. Sheppard, Esq., Collector of Customs, Londonderry. (1845-12-20, 3:1, M)

1866. On the 3d inst., in the Presbyterian Church, Sandholes, by the Rev. Joseph Geddes, Mr. Isaac Harvey, merchant, Banbridge, to Miss Harriet Dickson, daughter to the late Robert Dickson, Esq., M.D., of Alder Lodge, Sandholes. (1845-12-20, 3:1, M)

1867. Dec. 16, in Bryansford Church, by the Rev. Christopher Ussher, Henry L. Lindsay, Esq., Melbourne Terrace, Armagh, to Helena, third daughter of the late Christopher Crawley, Esq., of Bryansford, in the county of Down. (1845-12-20, 3:1, M)

1868. On the 11th instant, in Belfast, James Alexander Henderson, Esq., eldest son of James Henderson, Esq., Newry, to Agnes, daughter of the late Alexander Mackay, jun., Esq., Mount-Collyer Park. (1845-12-20, 3:1, M)

1869. At his residence, Portanaghy, in this County, on Thursday night, after a few days' illness, Robert Killen, Esq., one of the largest capitalists in Ulster. (1845-12-20, 3:1, D)

1870. On the 8th Sept., aged 65 years, Mr. Joseph Russell, formerly of Rosepark, near Dundonald. (1845-12-20, 3:1, D)

1871. On the 30th Sept. last, Major-General Edward Henry Simpson, of the Benega [sic] Army, while in command of the Dinapore district. (1845-12-20, 3:1, D)

1872. On Monday morning last, in Enniskillen, at an advanced age, William Trotter, Esq., who [for] many years discharged the duties of coroner for this county. (1845-12-20, 3:1, D)

1873. December 7, at Thames Dion [*illegible*], Charles Sheffington Burgess [sic], aged 10 years, the beloved child of John Ynyr and Lady Caroline Burges. (1845-12-20, 3:1, D)

1874. Dec. 18, in St. Anne's Church, by the Rev. Ralph Sadlier, A.M., Henry Flavelle, jun., of D'Olier-street, to Margaret Jane, third daughter of the late William Page, Esq., of Leinster-street and Monkstown. (1845-12-27, 3:1, M)

1875. Dec. 6, at Corcloon Cottage, at the advanced age of ninety, universally beloved in every relation of life, Barbara, relict of the late John Ovens, of Raholton, county of Fermanagh, third daughter of the late James Montgomery, Esq., of Corry. (1845-12-27, 3:1, D)

1876. Dec. 15, at 23, Lower Camden-street, of water on the brain, Edwin George Roberts, the beloved son of Mr. William Roberts, Professor of Elocution. (1845-12-27, 3:1, D)

1877. Dec. 15, in Belvidere-place, aged four years, [the] son of Lieutenant-Colonel Charles Bowen. (1845-12-27, 3:1, D)

1878. Dec. 21, S. Nolan, Esq., of Haddington-terrace, Kingstown. (1845-12-27, 3:1, D)

1879. Dec. 15, in Waterford, aged seventy-five, the Rev. F. Newport, Vicar of Poulrone, diocese of Ossory. (1845-12-27, 3:1, D)

1880. Dec. 19, at the house of his son-in-law, T. Green, Esq., Wexford, W. Taylor, Esq., aged eighty, for years one of the proprietors of the late *Wexford Herald*. (1845-12-27, 3:1, D)

1881. Dec. 10, at Lakefield, aged seventy-eight, sincerely and deservedly regretted, D. Crofton, Esq., for many years a Magistrate and Deputy Lieutenant of the county of Leitrim. (1845-12-27, 3:1, D)

1882. In London, Lady Hariet Gallwey, relict of Lieutenant-General Sir W.P. Gallwey, Bart. (1845-12-27, 3:1, D)

1883. At Southfield, Frome, Somerset, Major George Warburton, aged sixty-four, late Inspector-General of the Constabulary Force in Ireland. He was the eldest male lineal descendant of the ancient Norman family of Warburton in Cheshire. (1845-12-27, 3:1, D)

1884. On Tuesday, the 30th ult., in Glasgow, the lady of Doctor Charles Douglas, of a daughter. (1846-01-03, 3:4, B)

1885. Dec. 31, in Carrickmacross Church, by the Rev. William Thompson, Mr. John C. Adams, of the City of Armagh, to Eliza, second daughter of Mr. George Rennick, of Carrickmacross. (1846-01-03, 3:4, M)

1886. Dec. 30, by the Rev. John Elliott, Smithborough, Mr. James Moorehead, Ballintoppin, to Eleanor Anne, eldest daughter of Mr. John M. Moorehead, Kilruskey. (1846-01-03, 3:4, M)

1887. 31st December, in Monaghan Church, by the Rev. H. Maffett, Mr. John Steward, to Margaret, third daughter of Mr. John Wright, of Drumloo House. (1846-01-03, 3:4, M)

1888. At her residence, Poplar-vale, in the immediate vicinity of Monaghan, at the advanced age of 87, Alice, relict of the late Major Edward Richardson. Beloved by a numerous circle of friends, and revered by the humbler classes, this estimable old lady passed a life of benevolence, and expired amid the deep and tearful regrets of poor and rich in this neighbourhood. (1846-01-03, 3:4, D)

1889. At his residence, Carrahor, in this County, at the advanced age of 78 years, Joseph Wright, Esq. (1846-01-03, 3:4, D)

1890. At Smithboro, in this County, Mr. Robert Lowry, merchant, much and deservedly regretted. (1846-01-03, 3:4, D)

1891. January 2, at Summerville, Nenagh, the lady of William Mitchell, Esq., and sister of the late Peter Holmes, Esq., of a daughter. (1846-01-10, 3:5, B)

1892. In the First Presbyterian Meeting House, Monaghan, by the Rev. John Bleckley, William Kinkead, Esq., of the Belfast Bank, Newry, to Margaretta, third daughter of the late David Horner, Esq., of Monaghan. (1846-01-10, 3:5, M)

1893. January 6, at Monkstown Church, by the Rev. Anthony Garstin, the Rev. Marlboro Sterling Berry, of Halfield, Herts, to Elizabeth, eldest daughter of Digby Marsh, of Aughalough, county Leitrim, and Brookfield, county Dublin, Esq. (1846-01-10, 3:5, M)

1894. December 20, at Marylebone Church, by the Rev. [Mr.] Hussey, Rector of Hayes, Kent, E.R. Wylde, Esq., of Cheltenham, to Flora Frances, eldest daughter of the late Colonel John Macdonald, of Summerlands, Exeter. (1846-01-10, 3:5, M)

1895. On the 2d of January, at his residence, William Adams, Esq., Acting Partner of the Ballyhaise Mills, County Cavan, deservedly regretted by all who knew him. (1846-01-10, 3:5, D)

1896. January 6, at Black Park, near Castledawson, county Derry, John Sheil, Esq., for many years Justice of Quorum for the counties of Antrim and Derry. (1846-01-10, 3:5, D)

1897. January 1, at the Rectory, Athlone, of severe hooping cough, Anna Maria, the beloved daughter of the Rev. J.R. Moffatt, in the seventh year of her age. (1846-01-10, 3:5, D)

1898. Jan. 13, in St. Peter's Church, by the Rev. Mr. Griffith, Samuel Rutherford Moorhead, Esq., of Clones, in the county of Monaghan, to Mary Elizabeth, only daughter of Henry Barton, Esq., of Clanbrassil-terrace, and grand-daughter of the late Thomas Hamilton Ennis, formerly of Dublin. (1846-01-17, 3:4, M)

1899. Jan. 14, at Tallaght Church, by the Rev. Wm. Robinson, William Irwin, Esq., Captain, 88th Regiment, to Elizabeth, only surviving daughter of the late Joshua Crump, Esq., of Carland, county Tyrone. (1846-01-17, 3:4, M)

1900. Jan. 13, in the Scotch Church, Adelaide Road, by the Rev. Mr. Hunter, Mr. A.S. Findlater, to Jane, eldest daughter of Mr. John Johnston, Dublin. (1846-01-17, 3:4, M)

1901. Jan. 13, in Cavan Church, by the Rev. W.M. Wilkins, C.B. Reynolds, Esq., to Rose Anne, youngest daughter of Mr. R. Davis, Bridge Street, Cavan. (1846-01-17, 3:4, M)

1902. On Sunday the 11th inst., in her 38th year, Isabella, the beloved wife of Mr. Joseph Holdcraft, of Derrylidigan, in this county. (1846-01-17, 3:4, D)

1903. On the 13th inst., at Lurgan, James Morisson, Esq., Manager of the Ulster Branch Bank. (1846-01-17, 3:4, D)

1904. On Monday, the 5th inst., Maria Jane, wife of Alexander Young, Esq., Castle-street, Ballymena. (1846-01-17, 3:4, D)

1905. On the 4th inst., Rebecca, wife of Mr. William Priestly, of Millview, Annahilt, County Down. (1846-01-17, 3:4, D)

1906. November 17, drowned, at Poona, deeply regretted by all who knew him, Arthur Webber Smith, Lieutenant of her Majesty's 22d Regiment, son of Major-General Webber Smith, aged 25, nobly sacrificing his own life to save that of one of his native servants. (1846-01-17, 3:4, D)

1907. January 7, in London, Charles Claude Hamilton, second son of the late John Hamilton O'Hara, Esq., of Crebilly, Ballymena, county of Antrim, leaving a wife and eight children. (1846-01-17, 3:4, D)

1908. January 6, at an advanced age, Jones Irwin, Esq., Captain in the Leitrim Militia. (1846-01-17, 3:4, D)

1909. January 7, at Outerarde, deeply and sincerely regretted by her family and friends, Margaret, the beloved wife of J.D. M'Illre, Esq., of Belturbet, county Cavan. (1846-01-17, 3:4, D)

1910. January 9, at Loughrea, in the 59th year of his age, Nicholas D'Arcy, Esq., for many years Sub-Inspector of the Constabulary Force. (1846-01-17, 3:4, D)

1911. January 7, at his residence, Lower Fitzwilliam street, after a painful and tedious illness, Robert S. Irvine, Esq., only surviving son of the late Doctor Irvine, of Johnstown, county Fermanagh, aged 73 years. (1846-01-17, 3:4, D)

1912. On the Twentieth of January, inst., at Cabra House, the residence of the bride's Father, by the Right Rev. Dr. Blake, Roman Catholic Bishop of Dromore, George H. Gartlan, Esq., of Carrickmacross, to Mary, eldest daughter of Alexander M'Mullan, Esq., J.P., county Down. (1846-01-24, 3:4, M)

1913. On the 19th instant, in Belturbet Church, by the Rev. Mr. Godby, Mr. R.A. Caddy, printer, to Elizabeth, only daughter of Sir Thomas Finlay, of Sugar-Loaf, in the county of Cavan. (1846-01-24, 3:4, M)

1914. On the 14th instant, at the Registry Office, Dungannon, by the Rev. Mr. Bates, the Rev. Mr. Aveo, Baptist Minister, to Miss Elizabeth Duncan, eldest Daughter of Mr. James Duncan, Perry Street, Dungannon. (1846-01-24, 3:4, M)

1915. On the morning of the 20th inst., in Carrickfergus, Mr. Thomas M'Caul, aged 25, late a Divinity Student of the Belfast College, and a resident master in Dr. Molony's school. (1846-01-24, 3:4, D)

1916. On the 11th inst., at Hillsborough, Thos. Nesbitt Moorhead, Esq., M.D., of fever, caught in the discharge of his professional duty. (1846-01-24, 3:4, D)

1917. On the 12th inst., aged 14 months, John Robert, youngest son of John Robert Irwin, Esq., of Carnagh-house, County Armagh. (1846-01-24, 3:4, D)

1918. On the 15th inst., at Portarlington, Frances, daughter of the late Rev. Richard Clarke, of Portarlington, and sister of Dr. Clarke, Blackwatertown. (1846-01-24, 3:4, D)

1919. At Rome, on the 13th ult., Mrs. Beresford, wife of the Venerable the Archdeacon of Lismore. (1846-01-24, 3:4, D)

1920. On the 13th inst., at his residence, Marorkin, County Armagh, Mr. Daniel Black, aged 90 years. (1846-01-24, 3:4, D)

1921. Jan. 16, at Shannon-bridge, W. Mitchell, Esq., for many years Supervisor of Assessed Taxes. (1846-01-24, 3:4, D)

1922. Jan. 19, at Belvidere-place, aged eleven and a half years, Thomas T. Mayne, eldest son of Francis G. Mayne, Esq., Friendship Park, Kingston, Jamaica. (1846-01-24, 3:4, D)

1923. On the 13th instant, at his father's residence, Altinamoichan, Newtownhamilton, after completing his undergraduate course in the University of Glasgow, Mr. John Jenkins, aged 21 years. (1846-01-24, 3:4, D)

1924. At Larne, on the 13th inst., Mr. W. M'Calmont, aged 73 years, a steady and highly respected member of the First Presbyterian Church, in connexion with the General Assembly. (1846-01-24, 3:4, D)

1925. On the 13th instant, Mr. Robert Edmonston, of Tullyrod, near Cloughmills, in the 86th year of his age. (1846-01-24, 3:4, D)

1926. On the 15th instant, at Larch Mount, Dungannon, Samuel King, Esq., of the firm of King and Newton, Coalisland Mills, and for many years a leading merchant in Dungannon, much and deservedly regretted. (1846-01-24, 3:4, D)

1927. On the 12th inst., at his residence, Wellington place, Dundalk, Thomas Coulter, Esq., aged 41. (1846-01-24, 3:4, D)

1928. November 26, at Meerut, East Indies, by the Rev. E.K. Maddock, George Frederick Long, Esq., Captain in her Majesty's 50th Regiment, (Queen's Own), to Charlotte Irvine, youngest daughter of the late Henry Loftus Tottenham, of Mac Murrough, county of Wexford, Esq. (1846-01-31, 3:5, M)

1929. January 28, in St. Thomas's Church, by the Rev. J.J. Molley, William Auchinleck, fourth son of the late Richard Dane, of Killyhevlin, in the county of Fermanagh, Esq., D.L. and J.P.., to Sarah, daughter of the late Benjamin Friel Foster, of Drumloo Cottage, in the county of Monaghan. (1846-01-31, 3:5, M)

1930. On Wednesday, the 28th inst., in the parish Church of Ballibay, by the Rev. Hercules Langrish, Mr. Robert Skelly, of Drogheda, Merchant, to Martha, daughter of Mr. Thomas M'Murry, of Ballibay. (1846-01-31, 3:5, M)

1931. In Warrenpoint Church, by the Rev. John Davis, Mr. Andrew M'Keown, of Warrenpoint, to Mary Anne, eldest daughter of Mr. Moses Searight, of same place. (1846-01-31, 3:5, M)

1932. Jan. 23, in Kilkeedy Church, by the Hon. and Right Rev. the Lord Bishop of Killaloe, William Peters Smith, Esq., eldest son of Robert Smith, Esq., of Mountjoy-square, Dublin, to Maria Frances, daughter of the Rev. Richard Dickson, Vermonty, county of Limerick. The bride was attended to the altar by the Honourables Sophia, Gertrude, and Kathleen O'Grady, daughters of Lord Viscount Guillamore, and by Miss Dickson. The newly married pair left for Castle Mahon, near Cork, the seat of Sir William Chatterton, Bart., uncle to the bride. (1846-01-31, 3:5, M)

1933. At a very advanced age, at his residence, near Coote-hill, Richard Murphy, Esq., for many years a magistrate of the county Cavan. (1846-01-31, 3:5, D)

1934. On Wednesday 28, at the house of his Son-in-law, Mill street, Monaghan, Mr. Francis Donnelly, aged 88 years. (1846-01-31, 3:5, D)

1935. January 28, by the Rev. James Bowes, at the Scotch Church, Cootehill, Joseph Armstrong, jun., Solicitor, second son of Joseph Armstrong, of Woodfort, in the county of Meath, to Kate, second daughter of Doctor Macfadden, of Cootehill, in the county of Cavan. (1846-02-07, 3:4, M)

1936. On Monday last, after a lingering illness, which she bore with christian resignation, aged 18 years, Helen, fourth daughter of the late Henry Wright, Esq., of this town. (1846-02-07, 3:4, D)

1937. On the 29th ult., in the 19th year of his age, Joseph, third son of Joseph Stevenson, Esq., of Roan-Mills, near Dungannon. His amiable disposition and uniformly gentle and kind demeanour, had secured to him the good-will of all with whom he had intercourse. His relatives mourn his early removal, but "not as those who have no hope." (1846-02-07, 3:4, D)

1938. On the 30th ult., at Tyrrels-Pass, in his 19th year, of billious [sic] fever, George, eldest son of Thomas Somers, Esq., of that place, and grandson of the late Dr. Armstrong of Clones. (1846-02-07, 3:4, D)

1939. At his residence, 100, James's-street, aged 33 years, P. Campbell, Esq., late Master of St. Patrick's (Swift's) Hospital. (1846-02-07, 3:4, D)

1940. January 22, in Ballina, Henry William Knox Gore, Esq., late Lieutenant of the 65th regiment, aged 33 years, third son of the late James Knox Gore, Esq., and Louise Knox Gore, of Broadlands Park, county Mayo. (1846-02-07, 3:4, D)

1941. At Barrackpoor, Bengal, Major Robert Verner, her Majesty's 61st regiment; his horse rearing up, fell back and killed him on the spot. (1846-02-07, 3:4, D)

1942. At Philipstown, Lady John Beresford, of a daughter. (1846-02-14, 3:2, B)

1943. On Friday, the 6th instant, at his residence in this town, Thomas Gillis, Esq., aged 40 years. (1846-02-14, 3:2, D)

1944. On the 29th ult., of rapid decline, at the residence of her father, in Cootehill, aged 25 years, Anne, second daughter of John Higginbotham, Esq., and wife of Dr. Mitchell, Newbliss, Co. Monaghan, she has left two infants and many sorrowing relatives and friends to deplore her early loss, but to her to die was a gain, as she departed this life in a sure and certain hope of a joyful resurrection. (1846-02-14, 3:2, D)

1945. At Channel Rock, by the Rev. Patrick Bannon, Mr. Laurence Brady, Innkeeper of Castleblayney, to Miss Mary Conlon, second daughter of Patrick Conlon, Swan Inn, County Louth. (1846-02-21, 3:3, M)

1946. On the 12th inst., in St. Peter's Church, Dublin, by the Rev. C.T. Black, William A. Williams, Esq., of Mount Carmel, County of Monaghan, to Frances Beasley, youngest daughter of the late R. Beasley, Esq., Lieut. in her Majesty's 9th Light Dragoons. (1846-02-21, 3:3, M)

1947. February 14, at 105, Lower Baggot-street, Miss Moore, sister of the poet, Thomas Moore, Esq., greatly beloved and respected by a numerous circle of friends. (1846-02-21, 3:3, D)

1948. February 13, at Carrig Glebe, in the county Cavan, in the 71st year of his age, the Rev. Thomas Skelton, Vicar of 39 years of the parish of Kildrumferton, in the diocese of Kilmore. (1846-02-21, 3:3, D)

1949. The Potato Disease.—Three deaths by fever occurred in Mallow last week, from eating bad food, particularly diseased potatoes. Fever is also greatly on the increase in the outskirts of the town from the same cause. (1846-02-21, 3:3, D)

1950. At Bellamont Forest, the seat of Richard Coote, Esq., February 21st, 1846, Mary Anne, widow of William Bennett, of Drumlavey, county of Cavan, Esq., at the advanced age of 72. Through a long period, under the trials and sufferings of a truly useful life, she was warmly benevolent, and a bright example of zeal, christian feeling, charity and love. Her Church has lost its dearest ornament, and her afflicted family a devoted parent, and a sincerely attached friend. She died as she lived, glorifying her Saviour. (1846-02-28, 3:5, D)

1951. March 5, in Tyholland Church, by the Rev. J.R. Tarleton, the Rev. Richard D. Falkiner, eldest son of John Falkiner, Esq., of Willsboro', county Tipperary, to Isabella, youngest daughter of the late Nathaniel Wright, Esq., of Monaghan. (1846-03-07, 3:3, M)

1952. March 2, in the Broomfield Presbyterian Church, by the Rev. S.B. Shaw, Andrew Hunter, Esq., Deputy-Agent to Viscount Templeton, county of Monaghan, to Sarah, daughter of the late Robert Lewers, merchant, Castleblayney. (1846-03-07, 3:3, M)

1953. Feb. 3, by the Rev. George Gould, Adam John Burr, Esq., of Nenagh, to Martha Jane Rosa, third daughter of Captain Matthew Foster, of Brunswick-square, London. (1846-03-07, 3:3, M)

1954. At his father's residence, Annyube, in this county, aged twenty-five years, of Consumption, Mr. James Lewers, a young gentleman of considerable literary attainments, and promising genius. His amiable disposition and retiring habits endeared him to all who knew him, and in every class of society in his neighbourhood, he has left friends who sincerely mourn his early departure. A frequent contributor to our columns when in health, we deeply feel his loss, and from an intimate knowledge of his integrity and sterling worth, we can say, that upon his tomb might with justice be graven the words of Davis—"He served his country, and loved his kind." (1846-03-07, 3:3, D)

1955. March 7, by special license, in 65, Stephen's-green, by the Rev. D. Flynn, Sir George De La Poer Beresford, Bart., to Elizabeth, second daughter of Davis Lucas, Esq., Clontibret, county Monaghan, and Glendalough, county of Galway. (1846-03-14, 3:6, M)

1956. In Clones, on Wednesday the 4th inst., at the residence of her Father, Mr. Henry Armstrong, in the 34th year of her age, after a short illness, Eliza, the beloved Wife of John Monahan, Esq., Sub-Inspector of Constabulary, Ardee. (1846-03-14, 3:6, D)

1957. March 12, at the residence of the bride's mother, Northumberland avenue, Kingstown, by the Very Rev. Doctor Yore, V.G., Charles David Ingham, Esq., Solicitor, second son of John Ingham, Esq., Solicitor, of John Ville, county Cavan, and grandson of the late Rev. David Charles Ingham, Rector of the united parishes of Kilmesson, Assay, and Balsoon, in the diocess of Meath, to Helen Anne, only surviving daughter of the late Patrick Hayne, Esq., of Dublin. (1846-03-21, 3:4, M)

1958. March 9, at his house, Corporation street, Belfast, Captain Robert Arnold, in the 34th year of his age, youngest son of the late Rev. John Arnold, Presbyterian Minister, Donaghadee. (1846-03-21, 3:4, D)

1959. On Thursday, at the Highland Cottage, Clones, from rapid decline, Maria, daughter of Captain John Ross, of the Monaghan Militia, aged 18 years. (1846-03-21, 3:4, D)

1960. On the 23rd inst., in Ballinode church, county of Monaghan, by the Rev. W.H. Pratt, the Rev. Edward O'Bryen Pratt, curate of Killymard, in the Diocese of Raphoe, to Geraldine Caulfield, relict of the late Thomas Caulfield Hanyngton, Esq., and youngest daughter of James Murray Gordon, Esq., of Balmaghie House, Kircudbrightshire, Captain in the Royal Navy, and grand daughter to the late Venerable John Caulfield, D.D., Archdeacon of Kilmore, Rector of Devenish, in the Diocese of Clogher, and of Derryloran, in the Diocese of Armagh. (1846-03-28, 3:4, M)

1961. In the Registrar's office, Monaghan, by the Registrar of the Monaghan District, Mr. Hugh M'Cleery, of Portinaghey, to Miss Mary Mitchell, of Derrygasson. (1846-03-28, 3:4, M)

1962. In the Registrar's office, Monaghan, by the Registrar of the Monaghan District, Mr. Alexander Burns, of Market-street, Monaghan, to Miss Jane Cavanagh, of Drumaclan. (1846-03-28, 3:4, M)

1963. At Gopaug [sic], 25 miles from Hyderabad, in Scinde, on the 2d of November 1845, when proceeding on medical certificate to Kurrachee, Ensign W.F. Fawcett, 4th Bengal Infantry, youngest son of the late Edward Fawcett, of Rowantree Hill, Esq., county Donegal, deeply and deservedly regretted by his brother officers. Struck down in the early dawn of life, it is no wonder that his loss should be mourned by his friends and relatives in this country, who have been plunged into the depth of anguish and sorrow by his unexpected death. He fell a victim to the effects of a tropical climate, whilst serving his country under Sir Charles Napier. (1846-03-28, 3:4, D)

1964. On the 20th instant, at Camptown Cottage, near Cootehill, aged one year and nine months, Henry, eldest child of Dr. W. Mitchell, of Newbliss. (1846-03-28, 3:4, D)

1965. On the 1st instant, the Lady of William Walker, Esq., Architect, 8, Apsley Place, Belfast, and Monaghan, of a son. (1846-04-04, 3:3, B)

1966. In this town, on the 28th ult., of dropsy and decline, which he bore with resignation to the Divine will, Mr. John Graham, aged 26 years. He left a wife and two young children to lament the loss of a kind husband and good father, and is deservedly regretted by all who knew him. (1846-04-04, 3:3, D)

1967. March 23, in Queen-street, Edinburgh, the Lady Grace Douglas, relict of George Douglas, Esq., of Cavers, and the only surviving sister of Francis, Earl of Moray, K.T. (1846-04-04, 3:3, D)

1968. March 28, suddenly, at his house in Brighton, Colonel Edward Wildman, late Lieutenant-Colonel of the Carbineers, and brother of Colonel Wildman, of Newstead Abbey. (1846-04-04, 3:3, D)

1969. At Island view, Enniskillen, on the 26th inst., Mr. Robert Frith, at the advanced age of 86 years. (1846-04-04, 3:3, D)

1970. On the 13th inst., at 10, Corn-market, Dublin, of inflammation of the lungs, Grace Bell, youngest daughter of Mr. Letford M'Cleland, Dungannon. (1846-04-04, 3:3, D)

1971. March 30, in Mountjoy Street, John H. Crawford, Esq., formerly of H.M. 34th Regiment. (1846-04-11, 3:4, D)

1972. Yesterday, at the residence of Mr. Samuel Richardson, her brother-in-law, Susanna Dugan, after a long and lingering illness, Aged 84. (1846-04-11, 3:4, D)

1973. At Lower Gardiner Street, Mrs. Elizabeth Donelan, much regretted. (1846-04-11, 3:4, D)

1974. April 6, at 61, Mary Street, Catherine, relict of the late James Charles, aged 70. (1846-04-11, 3:4, D)

1975. April 7, in the Cathedral of Londonderry, by the Rev. John Molesworth Staples, Pechell Irvine, Esq., of that city, to Margaret Jane, fourth daughter of the late T.W. Crawford, Esq., M.D., of Rockville, Ballyshannon. (1846-04-18, 3:4, M)

1976. April 7, in the Presbyterian Church, Dundalk, by the Rev. James Beatty, the Rev. E. Patteson, Free Church, Ellsridge-hill, Lanarkshire, to Ann, daughter of the late J. Dickie, county of Louth. (1846-04-18, 3:4, M)

1977. April 14, by the Rev. Michael Lennon, P.P., John Skipton Mulvany, Esq., to Eleanor, daughter of Joseph Burke, Esq., Culloville, county Armagh. (1846-04-18, 3:4, M)

1978. On the 11th instant, at his residence in Killaneel, near Monaghan, Mr. John Bryans, aged 64 years, universally regretted. During a lingering illness, he was remarkable for deep humility, patience, hope, and a thankful admiration of the plan of salvation which the gospel reveals. (1846-04-18, 3:4, D)

1979. Feb. 15 and 18, at Secunderabad, Madras Presidency, of cholera, Captain Osborne, 40th Native Infantry (second son of Sir Toler Osborne, Bart., and the Lady Hariette Osborne,) Anne, his wife, and their youngest child. They all three lie buried in one grave. (1846-04-18, 3:4, D)

1980. April 8, in Pembroke-street, Captain J.C. Fortescue, Deputy Quartermaster-General of the East India Company. (1846-04-18, 3:4, D)

1981. Feb. 13, at Masulipatam, Eleanor Jane, wife of Lieutenant F.H. Chitty, of the 40th M.N.I., beloved and deeply regretted by all who knew her. (1846-04-18, 3:4, D)

1982. April 10, at his residence in Dingle, the lady of the Rev. Charles Gayer. She has left a fond husband, and ten children, the eldest of whom is only fifteen, to bewail her loss. (1846-04-18, 3:4, D)

1983. April 11, at Fort Granite, county of Wicklow, the residence of his uncle, (T.S. Dennis, Esq.,) H. W. Harrisson, of Fort William, county of Westmeath, aged twenty-three. (1846-04-18, 3:4, D)

1984. April 12, at the Hanover Hotel, Hanover-square, the Right Hon. Lady Elizabeth Murray Macgregor, widow of the late Sir Evan John Murray Macgregor, Bart., and youngest daughter of the late John, Duke of Atholl. (1846-04-18, 3:4, D)

1985. April 13, at Fort William, county of Roscommon, Patrick Tighe, Esq., in the 86th year of his age. (1846-04-18, 3:4, D)

1986. February 9, at Ferozepore, of small pox, James Saurin Richards, Lieutenant in Her Majesty's 62d Regiment, aged 19 years, second son of the Rev. E. Richards, of Clonallan, county Down. (1846-04-18, 3:4, D)

1987. April 22, in St. George's Church, by the Rev. James Adams, Rector of Castlecorr, Captain John Adams, R.N., to Elizabeth, daughter of Henry Ellis, Esq., Eccles-street, Dublin. (1846-04-25, 3:3, M)

1988. On the 14th inst., in St. Anne's Church, by the Rev. Thomas Walker, Vicar, Newton, youngest son of Arthur Williams, of Richmond-house, county Dublin, Esq., to Mary, third daughter of William Orr, of Glenaline, county Antrim, Esq. (1846-04-25, 3:3, M)

1989. On the 14th inst., in St. Ann's Church by the Rev. James Collins, James Cromie, of Listallyna-curran, Esq., county Down, to Jane, second daughter of John Cain, of Drumboneth, of said county. (1846-04-25, 3:3, M)

1990. On the 15th instant, in St. Mark's Church, Armagh, by the Rev. Robert Haig, Robert Riddal, of Armagh, Esq., to Harriett, second daughter of Samuel Gardner, of Armagh, Esq. (1846-04-25, 3:3, M)

1991. On the 15th instant, in St. Mary's Church, Newry, by the Rev. Daniel Bagot, the Rev. James Hill, Head master, upper school, Royal Hospital Greenwich, to Anne, youngest daughter of Mr. John M'Cullough, Derry, and sister of Mr. William M'Cullough, Manager, Provincial Bank of Ireland, Newry. (1846-04-25, 3:3, M)

1992. At Newtownards, on the 17th inst., by the Rev. Townley Blackwood, Mr. William Kelly, Movilla, to Miss Eliza Bell, of same place. (1846-04-25, 3:3, M)

1993. On the 15th inst., in the Second Presbyterian Meeting-house, Portglenone, by the Rev. H. Perry, Mr. W. Adams, to Miss E. M'Goskey, both of Portglenone. (1846-04-25, 3:3, M)

1994. At St. James's Cathedral, Toronto, on the 14th ult., by the Rev. J. M'Cord, LL.D., William Ramsay, Esq., A.M., Barrister-at-Law, eldest son of Robert Ramsay, Esq., Sligo, Ireland, to Frances, eldest daughter of Capt. Hugh Eccles, late of 61st Foot. (1846-04-25, 3:3, M)

1995. At Toronto, on the 13th ult., by the Rev. A. Lillie, Hamilton Hunter, Esq., superintendent of education, of the Home District, to Sarah, fifth daughter of Francis Mulligan, Esq., late of Banbridge, Ireland. (1846-04-25, 3:3, M)

1996. April 16, by the Rev. George Tyndale, at Newtonlimavady, county Derry, Edward Senior, Esq., of Winterbourne, Gloucestershire, to Theodosia Sidney, second daughter of Marcus Macausland, Esq., of Fruit Hill. (1846-04-25, 3:3, M)

1997. April 14, in Wexford, James Cook, Esq., Sub-inspector of Constabulary, to Grace, only daughter of John Brown, Esq., late Collector of Excise, Wexford. (1846-04-25, 3:3, M)

1998. At Church-square, Monaghan, on the 22d instant, Alicia, the beloved wife of James Mollan Ross. (1846-04-25, 3:3, D)

1999. On Monday, the 13th April, at Rathmore, near Antrim, the beloved wife of Mr. Thomas Davison, aged 52 years. (1846-04-25, 3:3, D)

2000. On the 31st ult., Mr. James M'Gifford, of Carnagran, aged 77 years. The deceased was commonly known by the name of Laird M'Gifford. Though a man of kind and charitable disposition, he realised, by his industry, upon sixteen acres of land, the sum of £6,000, which he bequeathed to his relatives. (1846-04-25, 3:3, D)

2001. April 19, at his house, 26, Upper Brook-street, General Sir Moore Disney, K.C.B., in the 81st year of his age. (1846-04-25, 3:3, D)

2002. April 19, at Mountainstown, in the county of Meath, A.H.C. Pollock, Esq., aged 60 years. (1846-04-25, 3:3, D)

2003. March 9, at St. John's Church, Port Hope, Canada West, James J. Ward, Esq., second son of Thomas Ward, Esq., Port Hope, to Octavia Susan, youngest daughter of the late John Grierson, Esq., of Moville, county Donegal, and of Beaumont, county Meath. (1846-05-02, 3:4, M)

2004. April 28, in St. Peter's Church, Isaac Morgan, Esq., Professor of Music, to Maria Eleanor, daughter of the late James Reynolds, Esq., M.D., of Middleton [sic]. (1846-05-02, 3:4, M)

2005. On the 29th inst., Rev. Robert Lewers, for fifty-one years minister of second Clontibret Presbyterian congregation. During a period of 47 years, he discharged the duties of his office with a faithfulness, zeal, and success seldom equalled. He bore a lingering illness with christian resignation and departed in peace. Aged 72 years. (1846-05-02, 3:4, D)

2006. On Thursday the 30th ult., at his residence, Rooskey Lodge, near this town, Mr. William Quinn, after a lingering illness. (1846-05-02, 3:4, D)

2007. On Thursday last, in Market-street, in this town, Mr. Joseph Latimer, aged 69. (1846-05-02, 3:4, D)

2008. April 27, at Jennymount, near Belfast, aged 18, Eliza, daughter of the late Rev. James Blacker, Rector of Keady, and niece of Colonel Blacker of Carrick. (1846-05-02, 3:4, D)

2009. April 26, at Macloneigh Rectory, the Rev. Richard Jephson Rothe, rector of Kilmichael, county Cork, eldest son of the late George Rothe, Esq., of Salisbury and Mount Rothe, in the county of Kilkenny. (1846-05-02, 3:4, D)

2010. April 26, at 8, South Frederick-street, aged 93 years, Mrs. Jane Miller, relict of Major Arthur Miller, formerly of her Majesty's 6th regiment of foot. (1846-05-02, 3:4, D)

2011. April 27, in the tenth year of his age, William Henry, eldest son of Thomas Wensley Bond, of Fortescue terrace, Esq. (1846-05-02, 3:4, D)

2012. May 1, in St. Mary's Church, Newry, by the Rev. W.R. Williams, Andrew James Newton, Esq., of Cookstown, county of Tyrone, to Mary Jane, eldest daughter of the late James Searight, Esq. (1846-05-09, 3:4, M)

2013. April 28, by special license, in Taney church, by the Venerable the Archdeacon of Dublin, the Rev. Launcelot Dowdall, Vicar of Ballyhalbert, to Maria, fourth daughter of John Downing, Esq., of Rowesgift, and niece of G.A.D. Fullerton, Esq., of Ballintoy Castle, county of Antrim, and of Tockington, Gloucestershire. (1846-05-09, 3:4, M)

2014. April 30, in St. Pancras Church, by the Rev. C. Frederick Seymourr, Sir George Duckett, Bart., to Mrs. Saxe, of Gloucester Park Lodge, Regent's Park. (1846-05-09, 3:4, M)

2015. At Hamburgh, on the 22d ult., of intestinal inflammation, Francis, eldest son of the Right Hon. Edward Lucas, of Castleshane. (1846-05-09, 3:4, D)

2016. April 29, at his residence, Corballis, county of Meath, after a tedious illness, Christopher Prant, Esq., sincerely and deservedly regretted by his friends. (1846-05-09, 3:4, D)

2017. April 30, at Esher, Surrey, after a few days' illness, Miss F. Burdett, sister of the late Sir F. Burdett, Bart. (1846-05-09, 3:4, D)

2018. April 28, at Ore-place, near Hastings, Major General Sir H. Elphinstone, Bart., G.C.B., aged seventy-four. (1846-05-09, 3:4, D)

2019. May 7, at his residence in Cavan, on the third anniversary of his wife's death, and in the sixty-fourth year of his age, Francis Thompson, Esq., J.P., of Leggykelly and Killibandrich, in the county of Cavan, Captain in the Dublin Militia. In all the relations of life—as a landlord, magistrate, husband, father—he lived respected and esteemed, and died regretted. Of him, it may be truly said, he never made an enemy, and never lost a friend. His end was like his life, peaceful. (1846-05-16, 3:3, D)

2020. At the College, on the 7th inst., Wm. Meikleham, LL.D., Professor of Natural Philosophy in the University of Glasgow. (1846-05-16, 3:3, D)

2021. In Dublin, on 21st inst., William Trimble, Esq., editor and proprietor of the *Fermanagh Reporter*, to Anne, relict of John Farrell, Esq., of Westport, Merchant. (1846-05-23, 3:4, M)

2022. May 21, in Stillorgan Church, by the Rev. William Metge, Curate of Seapatrick, diocese of Dromore, and brother to the bride, William Hastings Minnitt, Esq., second son of the late Joshua Minnitt, Esq., of Annabeg, county of Tipperary, to Araminta Charlotte, daughter of the late Rev. James Metge, of Ballinasloe, county of Galway. (1846-05-23, 3:4, M)

2023. March 14, at Nassau, New Providence, Captain George Bartley, of Her Majesty's 2d West India Regiment, second son of the late Sir Robert Bartley, K.C.B., having survived his youngest brother, who was killed at Sobraon, but 32 days. (1846-05-23, 3:4, D)

2024. May 21, A.G. Hewitt, Esq., Richmount, Portadown, to Mary Ann, second daughter of the late Thomas Glasgow, of Lislea, near Keady, Esq. (1846-05-30, 3:4, M)

2025. May 19, in St. Mark's Church, Armagh, Mr. Wm. Glen, of Fivemile-town, to Anne, daughter of the late Oliver Vance, Esq., of Dungannon. (1846-05-30, 3:4, M)

2026. On Saturday last, of consumption, at the residence of her brother, Dromard, Clones, Miss Margaret Cochrane. (1846-05-30, 3:4, D)

2027. May 21st at Clones, of apoplexy, Mr. John George Fitzgerald, aged 38 years. (1846-05-30, 3:4, D)

2028. On the 17th instant, at Tullycreevy, A. Saunders, Esq., aged 77 years, formerly Captain in the 4th Foot. (1846-05-30, 3:4, D)

2029. June 2, at Carrick-on-Shannon Church, by the Rev. R.S. Clifford, A.M., Simon Bagge, of Ardmore House, in the county of Waterford, Esq., to Arabella, fourth daughter of Captain Cox, of Carrick-on-Shannon, in the county of Leitrim, J.P.(1846-06-06, 3:3, M)

2030. In Glasslough, at an advanced age, of apoplexy, Miss Rawdon, a respected inhabitant of that town. (1846-06-06, 3:3, D)

2031. May 31, at Stillorgan Castle, the Residence of his father, after a long protracted illness, Standish Deane Grady, Esq., eldest son of Henry Deane Grady, Esq., Q.C., of Merrion-square. Mr. Standish Grady was a gentleman of unobtrusive manner, great quietness of disposition, and amiability of temper. He was beloved and regarded by his family and friends; and was extremely popular in a circle of acquaintances widely extended. A better son, a more affectionate brother, or a truer hearted friend, never lived. (1846-06-06, 3:3, D)

2032. June 1, at Moyle Glebe, county Tyrone, after a protracted illness, Mary, eldest daughter of the Rev. R.H. Nash, EX. F.T.C.D. (1846-06-06, 3:3, D)

2033. May 31, at 101, Stephen's-green, in the 78th year of his age, Francis Prendergast, Esq., Registrar, of the Court of Chancery. (1846-06-06, 3:3, D)

2034. In Killievan Church, on the 1st of June, by the Rev. John Compton, William Mitchell, Esq., Surgeon, Newbliss, to Mary Jane, daughter of John Clark, Esq., merchant, of same place. (1846-06-13, 3:6, M)

2035. June 11, in St. Peter's Church, by the Venerable the Archdeacon of Dublin, the Rev. Lord Adam Loftus, Rector of Ballibay, county of Monaghan, third son of the Marquess of Ely, to Margaret, fourth daughter of the late Robert Fannin, Esq., of Leeson-street, Dublin. (1846-06-13, 3:6, M)

2036. On the 11th inst., at Cremorne Green, the residence of her husband, Ellen, wife of John Jackson, Esq., Secretary of the Grand Jury, county Monaghan—a lady as universally beloved as she was known, and sincerely lamented by a large circle of sincere friends. (1846-06-20, 3:4, D)

2037. At the residence of her son, on Monday the 15th inst., Seletia, relict of the late Mr. James Johnston of Derryhaw, at the advanced age of 78. In life she was cheerful, pious, and affectionate. Released from pain, she has entered upon an everlasting reward, and happy is she that believeth. Her remains were conveyed by a very extensive circle of friends and acquaintances, to the ancient family burying ground, Tynan, upon the 17th. (1846-06-20, 3:4, D)

2038. At Paris, on the 25th June, Maria Dorothea, wife of D. Barclay, Esq., M.P., and daughter of the late, and sister of the present, Sir Hedworth Williamson, Bart., and of the Countess of Zetland. (1846-07-04, 3:2, D)

2039. June 19, at Bath, at an advanced age, Hannah, relict of the late Simeon P. Boileau, Esq., Carnarvon, North Wales. (1846-07-04, 3:2, D)

2040. June 26, at Stephen's-green, Harriet, the beloved wife of Doctor Ireland. (1846-07-04, 3:2, D)

2041. On the 5th of July, at Niddrie House, N.B., the lady of Andrew Wauchope, Esq., Marischal, of a son. (1846-07-18, 3:3, B)

2042. At Clones, on Sunday the 21st June, the wife of Mr. Robert Irwin, of a son. (1846-07-18, 3:3, B)

2043. July 8, at Yoxall Church, Staffordshire, A.H.R. Mulholland, Esq., Master of the English School in the Belfast Academy, to Jane, youngest daughter of the late William Scott Smyth, Esq., of Headborough, county Waterford, and niece of the late Rev. Percy Scott Smyth, of Monatrea, Youghal. (1846-07-18, 3:3, M)

2044. On Sunday last, the 12th inst., at Mulladoo, Mr. John Cargill, in this county. (1846-07-18, 3:3, D)

2045. July 21, in St. Thomas's church, A.W. Gate, Esq., to Julia, relict of the late J.G. Bunton, Esq., Solicitor, Limerick. (1846-07-25, 3:3, M)

2046. On Tuesday last, after a few minutes' illness, Cole Fitzgerald, Esq., of Lisabuck, near Clones. (1846-07-25, 3:3, D)

2047. July 20, at Kingstown, Rear-Admiral Mangin, in the 65th year of his age. (1846-07-25, 3:3, D)

2048. July 21, at his residence, Wentworth-place, Peter Browne, Esq., universally esteemed and regretted. (1846-07-25, 3:3, D)

2049. On Wednesday the 22d inst., at No. 25, Hamilton-street, Francis Murray, Esq., in his 58th year. (1846-07-25, 3:3, D)

2050. On the 19th inst., at her residence, Rossborough-place, Rachael, wife of Mr. Bessborough, aged 60 years. (1846-07-25, 3:3, D)

2051. July 27, at Drumbraine House, the lady of A. Bernard Bleazby, Esq., of a son. (1846-08-01, 3:3, B)

2052. July 21, in Agherton Church, Portstewart, by the Rev. Stephen Gwynne, Rector, John Hilliard Lawlor, Esq., of the Provincial Bank of Ireland, Coleraine, fourth son of the late Jeremiah Lawlor, of Tralee, Esq., and grandson of the late Robert Hilliard, of Listrim House, county Kerry, Esq., to Catherine, eldest daughter of Colonel John Elliott Cairnes, K.H., late of the Scots Fusilier Guards. (1846-08-01, 3:3, M)

2053. July 23, at Templeport, by the Rev. Thomas La Nauze, Francis Pyner, Esq., Captain, 5th Fusiliers, to Mary Neilson, daughter of the late T. Grey, Esq., and relict of John Baker, Esq., of Ashgrove, county Cavan. (1846-08-01, 3:3, M)

2054. On the 22d inst., at North Shields, by the Rev. Samuel Dunn, Robert Lindsay, Esq., of Belfast, to Jane Elizabeth, eldest daughter of Cuthbert Hunter, Esq., Walker Cottage, Newcastle-on-Tyne. (1846-08-01, 3:3, M)

2055. On the 21st inst., at the Registrar's Office, District of Rush, by the Rev. Mr. King, the Rev. Alexander Bell, Independent Minister of Ballycraigy, near Belfast, to Miss Fisher, of Balbriggan. (1846-08-01, 3:3, M)

2056. On the 27th ult., at Redhills, county Cavan, in the 50th year of her age, Mrs. Ruth Topham, wife of Mr. John Topham, and sister to Mr. Thomas Howe, Monaghan. Greatly lamented by a numerous circle of friends. (1846-08-01, 3:3, D)

2057. On Sunday evening last, at Shrub-hill, James M. Sanders, Esq., M.D., aged 32 years.(1846-08-01,3:3,D)

2058. On the 29th inst., of consumption, aged 24 years, Eliza, fifth daughter of the late Mr. Jamer [sic] Gillis, formerly of Tullydraw House, Co. Tyrone. (1846-08-01, 3:3, D)

2059. On the 24th inst., in the 84th year of his age, Mr. John Munro, of Ballymacbrinnin, near Moira. (1846-08-01, 3:3, D)

2060. On the 20th inst., in the 88th year of her age, Margaret Gordon, relict of the late John Gordon, of Ballypallady. (1846-08-01, 3:3, D)

2061. On the 21st inst., at the residence of his uncle, R.H. Patton, Esq., Crohan-house, Ramelton, in the 22d year of his age, William Babington, youngest son of the late Thomas Keynes, Esq., R.N. (1846-08-01, 3:3, D)

2062. In London, Catherine Louisa D'Arcy Irvine, eldest daughter of Sir Georges Irvine, Bart., of Castle Irvine, county Fermanagh, and niece of John Caulfield Irvine, of Grove-hill, Esq. This lamented lady was sister to Viscountess Dungannon, and the Marchioness Incontri. (1846-08-08, 3:3, D)

2063. August 11, at Prince Edward Terrace, Black-rock, by special license, by the Rev. Gregory Lynch, William Roche, of Upper Pembroke-street, Esq., to Ellen Georgiana, youngest daughter of the late Geo. Anketel, Esq., of Dingle. (1846-08-15, 3:4, M)

2064. August 6, at Ballymoney Church, by the Rev. Jas. Dunseath, Rector of Layde, Francis Ogle, Esq., of Newry, to Sarah, youngest daughter of the late Richard Hutchinson, of Stranocum-house, Esq. (1846-08-15, 3:4, M)

2065. On the 11th instant, in the Presbyterian Meeting-house, Keady, by the Rev. Joseph Jenkins, Mr. Thos. Mason, of Rockmount, Keady, to Jane, eldest daughter of Mr. John Dobbin, of same place. (1846-08-22, 3:4, M)

2066. In the city of Toronto, on the 7th ult., at the residence of the bride's father, by the Rev. J. Harris, Richard Robinson, Esq., of Baltimore, United States, to Margaret, daughter of the Rev. Samuel Cuthbertson, formerly of Omagh. (1846-08-22, 3:4, M)

2067. In Ballygawly Meeting-house, on Tuesday, the 11th inst., by the Rev. Wm. Ferguson, Mr. Wm. Neely, of Ballygawly, to Miss Mary Anne Neely, daughter of Wm. Neely, Esq., Grange House, county of Monaghan. (1846-08-22, 3:4, M)

2068. In Mountfield Church, on the 13th instant, by the Rev. Wm. Samuel Cuthbert, John M'Cay, Esq., Kildrail House, to Margaret, eldest daughter of John Fullerton, Esq., Mayne House, County Tyrone. (1846-08-22, 3:4, M)

2069. On the 5th inst., at Acton Church, Poyntzpass, by the father of the bride, Henry Frederick, son of the late Captain Hole, R.M., of Newport, Devonshire, and grandson of the late Rev. Wm. Hole, Incumbent of Swimbridge, Devonshire, to Anne Hester, eldest daughter of the Rev. H. Gamble, of Drumnargoole-house, County of Armagh. (1846-08-22, 3:4, M)

2070. August 19, in St. Mark's Church, by the Rev. Charles H. Stewart, brother of the bridegroom, Robert P. Stewart, Esq., of Upper Baggot-street, to Mary Anne, youngest daughter of the late Peter Browne, Esq., of Wentworth-place. (1846-08-22, 3:4, M)

2071. In Enniskillen Church, on Thursday, the 13th instant, by the Rev. Newport B. White, James Jasper Macaldin, Esq., M.D., Coleraine, to Mary Jane, eldest daughter of Thomas Kernaghan, Esq., Enniskillen. (1846-08-22, 3:4, M)

2072. August 11, in the Parish Church, Belfast, by the Rev. Archibald Crayford, Mr. Norman Henry Smith, of Birmingham, to Jane, eldest daughter of the late Arthur Crawford Lodge, Esq., county of Antrim. (1846-08-22, 3:4, M)

2073. In Tanderagee, by the Rev. Henry Burdett, John Thomas Hinds, Esq., of Waterloo Lodge, Trim, to Emma, fifth daughter of the Very Rev. the Dean of Tuam. (1846-08-22, 3:4, M)

2074. On the 6th instant, at Parsonstown, of gastric fever, Maria, relict of the late Marcus Longford M'Causland, of Roe Park, county of Londonderry, deeply regretted by her family and friends. (1846-08-22, 3:4, D)

2075. On Thursday evening, of consumption, aged 26 years, Mr. George Buchanan, eldest son of James Buchanan, of Fintona, Esq. (1846-08-22, 3:4, D)

2076. Sept. 1, in Monkstown Church, by the Rev. Henry Stepney, James Collins, Esq., 58, Summer-hill, to Mary Napier, second daughter of the late Richard Phipps Irwin, Esq., Mountjoy-square, Dublin. (1846-09-05, 3:2, M)

2077. Sept. 22, at River View, Carrickmacross, the lady of Thomas R. Barry, Esq., of a son. (1846-09-26, 3:6, B)

2078. Sept. 28, at Harcourt-street, the lady of Thomas Coote, Esq., D.L., of a son. (1846-09-26, 3:6, B)

2079. On the 10th instant, in Loughgall Church, by the Rev. Francis John Crawford, Alexander John Pringle, only son of the late Michael Pringle, Esq., Sally Vale, to Miss Martha, second daughter of William Jackson, Esq., Ballymagerney. (1846-09-26, 3:6, M)

2080. On the 15th instant, in St. Mark's Church, Armagh, by the Rev. Robert Haig, Mr. John Smith, A.M., Principal of the Diocesan School, Abbey-street, to Miss Mary Power, of the Model School, Armagh. (1846-09-26, 3:6, M)

2081. September 14, in George's Church, Thomas Dawson, Esq., of Belvidere-place, eldest son of the late John Dawson of Annamartin, county Fermanagh, Esq., to Susan Frances, eldest daughter of Edward Moore, of Lower Gardiner-street. (1846-09-26, 3:6, M)

2082. On the 22d instant, aged six months, Joseph, youngest son of Mr. Robert Mitchell, of this town. (1846-09-26, 3:6, D)

2083. On the 16th instant, at Clark's Bridge, near Newtownhamilton, the beloved wife of the Rev. William M'Alister, Presbyterian Minister, sincerely and deservedly regretted. (1846-09-26, 3:6, D)

2084. On the 7th instant, at Dundalk, aged sixty years, Arabella, widow of the late John Martin, Esq., of that town. (1846-09-26, 3:6, D)

2085. September 17, at Drumbrain House, county of Monaghan, Anna Maria Alicia, aged one year and eight months, daughter of A.B. Bleazby, Esq. (1846-09-26, 3:6, D)

2086. On the 15th instant, Mrs. Lowry, relict of the late Rev. John Lowry, A.M., of Upper Clannaneese, after a tedious illness, which she borne with christian fortitude and patience, after expressing her trust in Christ, and anxiously hoping to meet her deceased husband, whom she survived only five months. (1846-09-26, 3:6, D)

2087. On the 13th instant, to the inexpressible grief of his beloved family, the Rev. James Thompson, aged 66, deservedly esteemed and regretted by all who enjoyed intercourse with him. For 45 years, he filled the situation of Pastor to the Second Presbyterian Congregation of Drum, county Monaghan, which he resigned only a few weeks since. (1846-10-17, 3:5, D)

2088. On the 14th inst., Mrs. Hamilton, wife of Dacre Hamilton, Esq., Newpark, county Monaghan. (1846-10-17, 3:5, D)

2089. On the 9th inst., at his father's house, 44, Tomb-street, of disease of the heart and dropsy, Captain W. M'Nally, aged 29 years. (1846-10-17, 3:5, D)

2090. On Wednesday evening, the 7th instant, at the Hibernian Hotel, of congestive apoplexy, James H. Harman, Esq., of the island of Antigua, in his 25th year. (1846-10-17, 3:5, D)

2091. On the 11th ult., at the residence of his mother, Kilmorey-street, Newry, in the 25th year of his age, Mr. William Gorden, Printer. (1846-10-17, 3:5, D)

2092. Oct. 21, in Agbawn Church, in the county of Fermanagh, by the Rev. Henry Lucas St. George, father of the bridegroom, Henry Lucas St. George, Esq., of Dromore Rectory, in the county of Tyrone, to Harriet Charlotte Rebecca Sterne, only child of William Sterne, Esq., of the city of Bristol, and Gola House, county of Fermanagh. (1846-10-24, 3:4, M)

2093. October 22, in Sandys Street Presbyterian Church, Newry, by the Rev. J.A. Canning, of Morne, Nathaniel Weir, Esq., of Newry, in the county of Down, to Anne, eldest daughter of M. Singleton, Esq., R.M., county of Armagh. (1846-10-31, 3:3, M)

2094. October 20th, in Newtownbutler church, by the Rev. H. Johnston, Mr. Mark Little, Cloughagaddy, to Isabella, eldest daughter of Mr. Edward Brown, county Fermanagh. (1846-10-31, 3:3, M)

2095. October 26, at St. Paul's Church, Knightsbridge, Sir John Edward Harington, Bart., of the Coldstream Guards, to Jane Agnes, youngest daughter of J.S. Brownrigg, Esq., M.P. for Boston. (1846-10-31, 3:3, M)

2096. October 24, at his seat, Up Park, Sussex, Sir Henry Fetherston-haugh, Bart., in his 92d year. (1846-10-31, 3:3, D)

2097. October 28, at his residence, Mountjoy-square, in his 94th year, and in full possession of his faculties, John Sweny, Esq., universally regretted. He was the eldest member of the Irish Bar living, being called in 1776. (1846-10-31, 3:3, D)

2098. On Thursday, the 5th inst., at Warrenpoint church, by the Rev. John Davis, John Fleming, Esq., of the Hill, Monaghan, to Mary, third daughter of Benjamin Atkinson, Esq., of Ballymoney, county Armagh. (1846-11-07, 3:4, M)

2099. On the 4th inst., in the Presbyterian Church, Lisburn, by the Rev. A. Henderson, Hugh Rea, Esq., Belfast, to Miss Kelsey, eldest daughter of William Kelsey, Esq., Plantation House, Lisburn. (1846-11-07, 3:4, M)

2100. On the 5th instant, in the Presbyterian Meeting house, Monaghan, by the Rev. John Bleckly, Mr. Joseph Petty, of Kingscourt, county Cavan, Woollen Draper, to Rebecca Jane, youngest daughter of Mr. James Williams, of Monaghan. (1846-11-07, 3:4, M)

2101. Nov. 6, in Monkstown Church, county of Dublin, by the Rev. John St. G. Williams, William Ashford, Esq., M.D., Dublin, to Mary, youngest daughter of Benjamin Oliver, H.M.S. *Prince of Wales*. (1846-11-14, 3:3, M)

2102. On Saturday last, at his residence, Hill Cottage, Monaghan, one of the oldest inhabitants of the town, Mr. John Rowland. His urbanity and impartiality in the fulfilment of his official duties earned for him the good opinion of all classes, and the humanity with which he discharged the duties of Governor of the County Prison, which office he held for we years, attested his kind and generous disposition. He died, much regretted, in the 78th year of his age, and the 53d of his public life. (1846-11-14, 3:3, D)

2103. At Caledon, on the 5th instant, William Pettigrew, Esq., aged 18 years, second son of the late George Pittigrew [sic], of Crilly, in the County Tyrone, Esq., and grand nephew of the late Sir James Pettigrew. (1846-11-14, 3:3, D)

2104. Nov. 10, at his residence, Harcourt-street, Dublin, Nathaniel Hone, Esq., in the 89th year of his age. (1846-11-14, 3:3, D)

2105. Nov. 6, Dacre, fourth son of the late William Hamilton, Esq., of Shankhill. His end was peace, being enabled to rest with confidence on the atonement of our beloved Lord. (1846-11-14, 3:3, D)

2106. Nov. 8, in Dundalk, John Coleman, Esq. (1846-11-14, 3:3, D)

2107. Nov. 8, at his residence, 29, Lower Leeson-street, Dublin, after a long and painful illness, Martin Keene, Esq., in the 66th year of his age, deeply and deservedly regretted. (1846-11-14, 3:3, D)

2108. At Monaghan, at the residence of his brother, the Rev. Henry Maffett, on the 15th instant, Richard Maffett, Esq., M.D., F.R.C.S.I., of Glasslough, in the 35th year of his age. As a Physician, he was highly esteemed, and as a friend, in all the relations of life, few were more generally beloved. The deep sympathy manifested by all classes in the community on this melancholy occasion, testify [sic] in the strongest manner the high estimation in which the character of Dr. Maffett was generally held by the public. (1846-11-21, 2:5, D)

2109. Nov. 12, at Waltham-terrace, Near Dublin, the Rev. H. Adair, third son of the late H. Adair, Esq., Mountjoy-square. (1846-11-21, 2:5, D)

2110. Nov. 14, aged fifty-three years, George Rankin, Esq., of Capel-street and of Enniskillen—an eminent Solicitor, deeply and deservedly regretted. (1846-11-21, 2:5, D)

2111. At Charlemont church, on the 16th inst., by the Rev. James Disney, Mr. Robert Cherry, of Derrycary, Verner's bridge, to Mary, daughter of the late Mr. John Madden, of Corr and Dunavally.(1846-11-28, 3:1, M)

2112. On the 17th inst., in Benburb church, by the Rev. Richard Wighton, curate of Clonfeacle, Miss Marrianne Neely, of Tullygoney, to Mr. James Hogan, of Benburb. (1846-11-28, 3:1, M)

2113. At Magherafelt, on the 18th inst., by the Rev. C.K. Irwin, Mr. Thomas York, to Miss Jane Williamson. (1846-11-28, 3:1, M)

2114. On the 13th inst., in the Ahorey Meeting-house, by the Rev. Thomas Kilpatrick, Mr. A. Wilson, of Ballynewry, to Miss Sarah Lewis, of Ahorey. (1846-11-28, 3:1, M)

2115. Nov. 25, in St. Thomas's Church, by the Rev. Henry Brownrigg, Rector of Arklow, and uncle to the bridegroom, Henry Brownrigg, Esq., only son of Thomas Brownrigg, Esq., of Greenfield, county of Dublin, to Mary Matilda, eldest daughter of the late Captain Alexander Hanna, 56th Regiment, and niece of Major-General Philip Hay. (1846-11-28, 3:1, M)

2116. It is our painful duty to announce the death of our dearly beloved friend, the Rev. Thomas Maunsell, of Castleroe Glebe, county of Kilkenny, on the 23d day of the present month, after a short illness, in the sixty-ninth year of his age, upwards of forty of which he discharged the duties of pastor of that parish. (1846-11-28, 3:1, D)

2117. Nov. 25, Fanny, the beloved and only child of Robert Maziere, Esq., of Eccles-street, aged one year and seven months. (1846-11-28, 3:1, D)

2118. December 3, at Dunany House, county Louth, the Rev. Thomas Coombe William [sic], of Fulmer, [*illegible*], to Elizabeth Blacker Nicholson, daughter of the [late?] John Nicholson, Esq., of Stramore House, county Down. (1846-12-12, 2:6, M) *Notes: (1) A fold in the right-hand margin rendered some of the article illegible. (2) From The Patrician, Vol. III, edited by John Burke, London: E. Churton, 1847, pg. 92:* WILLIAMS, the Rev. Thomas Coombe, S.C.L., of Catherine Hall, Cambridge, second son of Thos. Williams, Esq. of Cowley-grove, Middlesex, to Elizabeth Blacker Nicholson, youngest daughter of the late John Nicholson, Esq. of Stramore-house, county of Down, 3rd Dec.

2119. Dec. 4, at the Scots Church, Great James's-street, Derry, by the Rev. James Denham, brother to [the] bride, the Rev. Andrew Lowry, of Ballshannon, [to] Jane Eliza, daughter of the late Rev. Joseph Den[ham] of Killeshandra. (1846-12-12, 2:6, M) *Note: A fold in the right-hand margin rendered some of this and subsequent articles under this date illegible.*

2120. Dec. 3, at St. Mildred's Church, by the Rev. [*illegible*] Chorlesworth, Thomas Tribe, Esq., of Bombay, [son of] Lieutenant Tribe, of the Royal Navy, to H[*illegible*], daughter of W. Cuningham, Esq., late of Drom[*illegible*], county Antrim. (1846-12-12, 2:6, M)

2121. December 2, at Dundalk, in his 57th year, Ca[*illegible*] Robinson, brother of the Countess of Castlestuart. (1846-12-12, 2:6, D)

2122. December 3, at Cheltenham, in the 47th year of [his] age, Bessy, the beloved wife of the Rev. Geo. E[*illegible*], formerly of the city of Armagh, and daughter of [the] late William Murray, Esq., of Killymeal, in [the] county of Tyrone. (1846-12-12, 2:6, D)

2123. December 5, Mrs. Barclay, the beloved wife of [*illegible*] Barclay, Esq., of 13, Summer-hill, Dublin. (1846-12-12, 2:6, D)

2124. December 2, at her residence in George's-[street,] Dublin, (trusting with sincerity for her sal[vation] through the merits and suffering of Christ a[*illegible*,] Miss Ann Hall, sister of Lodge Hall, M.D., of D[*illegible*.] (1846-12-12, 2:6, D)

2125. December 6, R. Booker, Esq., of Dublin, Sol[icitor,] aged 73 years. (1846-12-12, 2:6, D)

2126. December 4, at Foster-street, aged 68, George Gerald, Esq., Solicitor. (1846-12-12, 2:6, D)

2127. January 5th, at St. George's Church, by the Rev. John Gregg, William Hubbert, eldest son of Major Wolsely, of Russell-place, to Elizabeth, daughter of the late John Dawson, Esq., of Annamartin, county Fermanagh. (1847-01-09, 3:3, M)

2128. In the city of Rochester, United States, on 28th Dec. 1845, aged 81 years, Mr. Philip Skelton, one of the first members of the "Monaghan Dismounted Cavalry," and Master of the Band, belonging to that Loyal Corps. Also, Martha, his wife, on the 11th June, 1846. (1847-01-09, 3:3, D)

2129. January 13th, at Stonebridge Presbyterian meeting house, by the Rev. William White, John Crumly, Esq., to Jane, eldest daughter of Mr. George Elliott, merchant, both of Clones. (1847-01-16, 3:5, M)

2130. On Wednesday, the 6th inst., in the First Presbyterian Church of this city [Armagh], by the Rev. Mr. Fleming, Mr. W.R. Ferris, of the firm of M'Culla and Ferris, Merchants, Armagh, to Maria, second daughter of Mr. Arthur Hughes of Scotch Street. (1847-01-16, 3:5, M)

2131. Of gastric fever, on Saturday last, aged 9 years, Nathaniel, fifth son of the late J.G. Lepper, Esq., of this town. (1847-01-16, 3:5, D)

2132. On the 5th instant, at Cootehill, Samuel Macfadin, aged 77 years. (1847-01-16, 3:5, D)

2133. On the 26th Dec., at Newry, Mr. Samuel Wallace, merchant, aged 52 years. (1847-01-16, 3:5, D)

2134. Of measles, aged eleven months, at Castleblayney, Maria, only child of Mr. William Twible, Master of the Castleblayney Union Workhouse. (1847-01-23, 3:3, D)

2135. On the 19th instant, at the residence of her husband, aged 74, Martha, wife of Robert Little, Esq., of this town. (1847-01-23, 3:3, D)

2136. At Gravesend, on Sunday, the 10th instant, in his 35th year, John Jones, Esq., Surgeon, son of J.E. Jones, Esq., of Monaghan. (1847-01-23, 3:3, D)

2137. On the 20th instant, at St. Kilda's [sic] Catholic Church, Hartlepool, Durham, by the Rev. William Knight, and subsequently on the same day, at the parish church, Stranton, Stockton-on-Tees, by the Rev. Rowland Webster, George Duggan, Esq., C.E., Birmingham, to Harriet Anne, second daughter of Thomas Casebourne, Esq., M.I.C.E., Resident Engineer at Hartlepool West Harbour and Docks. (1847-01-30, 3:3, M)

2138. January 5, in Hillsborough Church, by the Rev. Frederick William Mant, Rector of Armoy, county of Armagh, the Venerable Walter B. Mant, Archdeacon of Down, and rector of Hillsborough, eldest son of the Lord Bishop of Down and Connor and Dromore, to Emily Neville, youngest daughter of Marcus Corry, Esq., Homra House, in the Parish of Hillsborough. (1847-01-30, 3:3, M)

2139. At Newbliss, on the 27th inst., in her 40th year, Margaret, wife of Mr. G. Moffatt, Merchant, after a tedious illness, which she bore with fortitude and resignation, in the sure and certain hope of a joyful resurrection through the alone [sic] merits and mediation of Jesus Christ. (1847-01-30, 3:3, D)

2140. Jan. 16, at his residence, Mount Selim, Clones, the Rev. Adam Averell, in the ninety-third year of his age, and seventeenth [sic] of his ministry. This venerable servant of the Lord was ordained by the Bishop of Clonfert; but, like Mr. Wesley, he subsequently confined his labours to the promotion of religion amongst the Methodists; and for sixty years, his time, property, influence, and talent, were devoted to the advance of the cause of God through the instrumentality of that society. His strong attachment to the Established Church led him, at the time of the division of the Methodist body, to connect himself with those who adhered to the primitive principles; and so long as his health permitted, he presided at the Annual Conference of the Methodists, who continue in communion with the Church. His end was that of holy joy and triumph. (1847-01-30, 3:3, D)

2141. On the 16th of August last, by special license, at Perth Church, Jamestown, Van Dieman's Land, David Gibson, Esq., Glasslough, South Esk, to Caroline, third daughter of George R. Clark, Esq., Boyne Lodge, Drogheda, Ireland. (1847-02-06, 3:2, M)

2142. On the 27th Jan., at St Mary's Colton, by the Rev. J.O. Oldham, the Rev. Robert Haig, of Armagh, son of the late Robert Haig, Esq., of Dublin, to Matilda, daughter of James Oldham Oldham [sic], Esq., of Bellamour Hall, county Armagh, and late of the Bengal Civil Service. (1847-02-06, 3:2, M)

2143. On the 28th Jan., in Aughnacloy Church, by the Rev. Edward Henry Newenham, Mr. Thos. M'Mahon, Ballymacone, near Keady, county Armagh, to Isabella, youngest daughter of the late John M'Williams, of Carnteel House, county Tyrone, Esq. (1847-02-06, 3:2, M)

2144. Jan. 26, at his residence, Rosslea, of consumption, Mr. Hugh Timmons, in his 50th year, sincerely and deservedly regretted. (1847-02-06, 3:2, D)

2145. On Monday, 1st instant, at Derrybrusk Glebe, Rev. George Harris, aged 67. (1847-02-06, 3:2, D)

2146. Died on the 9th inst., at Ballybay, in the 30th year of his age, Mr. Samuel Foster; deeply and deservedly regretted. (1847-02-13, 3:1, D)

2147. Died on the 15th Feb., at Clones, of Consumption, in the 19th year of her age, Anna Maria Lions, Youngest daughter of the Late William Lions, Primitive Wesleyan Methodest [sic] Preacher. (1847-02-13, 3:1, D)

2148. On the 8th instant, at the residence of her mother, Whitehall, Blackrock, Susan, fifth daughter of the late Philip Hughes, Esq., of Newry, to Charles Gavan Duffy, Esq. (1847-02-20, 3:4, M)

2149. In Russell-street, Armagh, on the 11th inst., Mrs. Noble, aged 40 years, sincerely regretted by a large circle of friends. (1847-02-20, 3:4, D)

2150. On the 2d inst., at Killinure, county Cavan, the residence of Mrs. Bell, Mrs. Margaret Smyth, aged 83, upwards of sixty years housekeeper in the family of the late George Bell, Esq., Barrister at law. (1847-02-20, 3:4, D)

2151. On the 7th instant, at the house of his mother, 5, Chichester-street, Belfast, on his return from Africa, of a rapid consumption, Latimer Barklie, third son of the late James Barklie, linen merchant, Linenvale, County Armagh, aged 28. (1847-02-20, 3:4, D)

2152. On Saturday morning last, at the advanced age of 79 years, 52 of which he was Rector of the parish of Kilmore, in this county, the Rev. G.H. Schomberg, lineal descendant of the celebrated Duke Schomberg. (1847-02-27, 3:5, D)

2153. At Skegarvey, the residence of her son, Robert Harrison, Esq., on Monday last, aged 72, Jane, relict of the late Robert Harrison, Esq., of Skegarvey. (1847-02-27, 3:5, D)

2154. At Liscormack House, county Longford, the residence of William L. Crofton, Esq., Shuldham Johnston, Esq., aged 26 years, fifth son of Andrew Johnston, Esq., late of Ballymahon, county Longford, of consumption. (1847-02-27, 3:5, D)

2155. At Clones, on the 22d ult., by the Rev. Charles Welsh, Matilda, second daughter of Mr. David Thompson, of Gortnawinny Cottage, to Mr. Charles Graham, of Clones. (1847-03-06, 3:4, M)

2156. On Saturday, 20th instant, at Middleton [sic], County of Armagh, David Smyth, Esq., Surgeon and Medical attendant, of the charity estate of the late Bishop Sterne. His professional skill, and generous disposition—his unwearied diligence in the discharge of his duties, have excited the deepest regret in the breasts of all those who had the pleasure of his acquaintance, or had the advantage of his consummate skill. He lost his valuable life from a malignant fever, caught in the attendance of the numerous sick in his neighbourhood. (1847-03-06, 3:4, D)

2157. On Friday, at the residence of his son-in-law, James M'Knight, Esq., Diamond, Monaghan, in his 75th year, Thomas Wright, Esq., one of the oldest and most respectable inhabitants of the town. (1847-03-13, 3:5, D)

2158. On Saturday, 27th February, in the 20th year of her age, Elizabeth, daughter of Mr. John Kinnier, of Down, parish of Clontibret, after a painful and protracted illness of seven months, which she bore with exemplary patience and Christian fortitude. Few, indeed, called away at so early an age, have bequeathed to sorrowing friends such satisfactory evidence of that acceptance and meetness for glory, as the young person whose death is here recorded. (1847-03-13, 3:5, D)

2159. On Tuesday, at Woodbine Cottage, Tyhollan, the lady of the Rev. Richard D. Faulkner, of a daughter. (1847-03-27, 3:1, B)

2160. March 20, the Rev. Charles Sheridan Young, Curate of St. Paul's, Dublin, brother to Francis S. Young, 1st Sub-Inspector of Constabulary, and of Lissanymore, county of Cavan. (1847-03-27, 3:1, D)

2161. At Sea View Terrace, Donnybrook, of consumption, Henrietta Miller, youngest daughter of the late J.R. Miller, Esq., and grand daughter of the late Sir J. Bond, Bart. (1847-03-27, 3:1, D)

2162. On the 11th inst., in St. George's Church, Dublin, by the Rev. John Gregg, the Rev. Robert Warren Wolsley, youngest son of Major R.B. Wolsley, of Russell place, Dublin, to Georgina, seventh daughter of the late Jas. Nixon, Esq., Prospect, county Fermanagh. (1847-04-03, 3:5, M)

2163. March 23, St. Thomas's Church, by the Rev. W. Molloy, Alexander Henry, Esq., of Stickillen, county of Louth, to Jane, youngest daughter of John Sheckleton, Esq., of Drumnahall, county of Down. (1847-04-03, 3:5, M)

2164. Of Fever, on Friday the 19th March, Anne, wife of Mr. William Montgomery, master of the Clones workhouse, aged 46 years. She was appointed Matron of the establishment on its first opening, and always discharged the arduous duties of the situation to the entire satisfaction of the Board of Guardians, and the comfort of those placed under her care. Her character may be summed up in one word—a sincere Christian—and as such, her end was peace. The estimation in which she was held, was manifested by the unusually large and respectable attendance at her funeral. (1847-04-03, 3:5, D)

2165. On Thursday 18th inst., at Caledon, Michael Bragan—a miser, who through life had managed to scrape together a good deal of money. Previous to his death, he had a horse and cart brought to his house and was conveyed to a neighbouring grove to get his money—an hour before death, he took a hearty meal of bread and tea. (1847-04-03, 3:5, D)

2166. March 18, at Dartry, in the county of Armagh, the residence of William Olpherts, Esq., Sarah, relict of Dr. Macartney, Professor of Anatomy and Surgery, Trinity College, Dublin. (1847-04-03, 3:5, D)

2167. March 28, at Newry, W.H. Quinn, Esq., J.P., for the counties of Down and Armagh, aged thirty-eight. (1847-04-03, 3:5, D)

2168. In Anne's Church, Dublin, on the 5th inst., by the Rev. A.N. Bredin, Mr. George Drought, Printer, to Eliza, eldest daughter of Mr. Joseph Coutts, merchant-tailor, formerly of Edinburgh. (1847-04-10, 3:1, M)

2169. At St. Peter's Church, Dublin, by the Rev. Abraham Hamilton, Rector of Manorhamilton, John Elliott, Esq., Royal Marines, son of the late Captain Sir Wm. Elliott, R.N., to Georgina Francis, fourth daughter of the late Lieutenant-Colonel Cullen, of Skreeny, Co. Leitrim. (1847-04-17, 3:5, M)

2170. On the 2nd inst., at Blackwatertown, at an advanced age, Elizabeth, relict of the late John Crothers, Esq. (1847-04-17, 3:5, D)

2171. On the 25th ultimo, at the School for the sons of the Clergy, Lucan, of effusion on the brain, the dregs of scarlatina, Maxwell Close, youngest son of the Rev. Maxwell Carpendale, of Tamlaght, County Tyrone. (1847-04-17, 3:5, D)

2172. On Thursday night, at his residence, Cappog, in this neighbourhood, after a short illness, Mr. Thos. Mitchell, in his 56th year, much regretted by all who knew him. For many years, he discharged the duties of assistant to the secretary of the grand jury, and was most deservedly a favorite with the gentry of the county. (1847-04-24, 3:6, D)

2173. On Saturday, 17th inst., James Boyd, Esq., of Cootehill, eldest son of John Boyd, Esq., Clementstown, Co. Cavan, aged 45. Few have ever left this mortal scene, having with them the unseen tears and heartfelt prayers of their friends and acquaintances half so fully as the departed. In every station of life, his conduct was unimpeachable. In the sacred duties of [*illegible*] parent, friend, he was seldom if ever equalled; [*illegible*] the Psalmist says. 'Charity covereth, &c.' we [*illegible*] his noble conduct on that point is sufficient to [*illegible*] his spirit a Heavenly sleep in Jesus. (1847-04-24, 3:6, D) *Note: Blurring in the right-hand margin renders some of the words illegible.*

2174. On the 20th inst., in St. Mark's Church, Portadown, by the Rev. Arthur Malony, Rector of Derryloran, Cookstown, James, youngest son of the late James Searight, of Newry, Esq., to Elizabeth, youngest daughter of William Paul, of Portadown, Esq. (1847-05-01, 3:4, M)

2175. At Middletown, on Thursday the 22d inst., aged 48 years, Sarah Ann, beloved wife of Mathew Johnston, Esq., sincerely and deservedly regretted. (1847-05-01, 3:4, D)

2176. On the 20th inst., at the residence of his brother, Doctor Clarke, Blackwatertown, Edward Clarke, Esq., aged 23 years, youngest son of the late Rev. Richard Clarke, of Portarlington. (1847-05-01, 3:4, D)

2177. On Sunday last, of fever, Mr. Thomas Marrow, of Thomas street, Dublin, aged 40 years. (1847-05-01, 3:4, D)

2178. In Armagh, on Friday last, of fever, Anne, wife of Mr. William Hughes, aged 70 years. She was for upwards of 25 years matron of Armagh gaol. (1847-05-01, 3:4, D)

2179. At Moy, on the 22nd instant, of typhus fever, in the 61st year of his age, Mr. Owen Tomney, universally and deservedly regretted. (1847-05-01, 3:4, D)

2180. On the 17th of April, in the townland of Dernashallog, near Emyvale, Michael Traynor—commonly called "Michael Crutch,"—at the age of 117. One of his peculiarities was that of a stentorian voice, which he used with much power until a short time before his death; when in vigour, this organ was so loud, that persons now living, attest the fact, of his "call" having been distinctly heard at a distance of more than an Irish mile. In his younger days, to test his vocal power, he used to call his wife to return home when at Emyvale market, a distance of about one mile from his house.

In height, he never exceeded four feet ten, was always stooped in the back, and his head and chest very large, but remarkably small in the limbs, and which he trailed along in a manner denoting weakness.

His face was full of arch expression, increased by the undue size of his under lip, which hung over his chin, and from the corners of which, streams of saliva always meandered. His physiognomy was a perfect reflection of his mind, and in an instant, assumed various shades of feeling; he was, in fact, a perfect study for Lavater. A portrait of him was painted some years ago, by Mr. M'Manus, which reflects his very image. (*continued…*)

2180, continued: Michael Traynor, though generally good tempered, when excited, was ferocious, and thought little of leaving the mark of his "crutch" upon the pate of offenders. Not more than five or six years ago, he was summoned to Emyvale, for an assault, the nature of which, shook the gravity of the bench. His talent in discerning character was first rate; he had an intuitive knowledge of every man in his locality, and in this quality, might have aspired to the dignity of a rural Talleyrand, to whose physiognomy he bore a very near resemblance. His numerous witty and acute sayings, stamped at once his power of generalization.

Tranor's [sic] occupation, through life, was that of a herd, at Anketell Grove, in which capacity he was trustworthy, and a terror to all who interfered with his prerogative. He retired on a pension nearly forty years ago, and lived snugly, with his numerous friends around him. In the evenings, his house was the resort of neighbours, to whom, he often detailed the scenes of his youth—like Nestor, he had seen many generations of men.

He retained all his faculties, except partial loss of sight, and a slight loss of memory of very recent events, to the last, and up to the day of his death, smoked his pipe as usual. He had no organic disease, having been carried off by a sudden attack of dysentery. (1847-05-01, 3:4, D)

2181. April 29, at 4, Summer-hill, Kingstown, the lady of G. Morant, Esq., of a son. (1847-05-08, 3:4, B)

2182. May 1, at Black Castle, county Meath, the lady of Thomas Rothwell, Esq., of a son. (1847-05-08, 3:4, B)

2183. May 3, at Magheraclooney Church, in the county of Monaghan, by the Rev. J.H. Stubbs, Rector of Dromiskin, Samuel Usher Roberts, Esq., eldest son of Edward Roberts, of Weston, county Waterford, Esq., to Emily Isabella, daughter of Sir George Forster, of Coolderry, Bart. (1847-05-08, 3:4, M)

2184. On Monday was married, at All Souls Church, Langham place, by the Very Rev. the Dean of Chichester, the Marquis of Sligo, to the Hon. Ellen Sydney Smith, daughter of Viscount Strangford. (1847-05-08, 3:4, M)

2185. April 28, at Auldbar, the seat of P. Chalmers, Esq., Forfarshire, North Britain, by the Right Rev. Dr. Moir, Bishop of Brechin, Robert Spankle, Esq., of the Bengal Civil Service, to Mary Stewart Blakely, eldest daughter of the Very Rev. the Dean of Down. (1847-05-08, 3:4, M)

2186. May 1, at the Parish Church, Drumcondra, by the Rev. James Duncan Long, A.M., Richard Howard Gorges, youngest son of the late Rev. John Howard Gorges, in the County Mayo, to Harriet, eldest daughter of the Rev. Solomon Richards, of Solsborough, co. Wexford. (1847-05-08, 3:4, M)

2187. On the 1st instant, at Warrenpoint, Mr. J. Delamere, aged 64 years. (1847-05-08, 3:4, D)

2188. In London, on the 29th April, Henrietta Gartwood, second daughter of William Walker, Esq., Architect, Monaghan. (1847-05-15, 3:6, D)

2189. On Wednesday evening, of fever (after an illness of three days), Richard Jackson, Esq., seneschal of the manor court of Rosslea. (1847-05-15, 3:6, D)

2190. On the 9th instant, in the 43d year of her age, Elizabeth, wife of Mr. Robert Clark, of Fellows Hall, County Armagh, deeply and deservedly regretted by a large circle of friends and acquaintences [sic]. (1847-05-15, 3:6, D)

2191. May 10, at Florence Court, the Countess of Enniskillen, of a daughter. (1847-05-22, 3:3, B)

2192. On the 14th inst., Mrs. O'Neile, wife of Mr. D. O'Neile, Civil Engineer, Dobbin-street, Armagh, of a son. (1847-05-22, 3:3, B)

2193. May 20th, in Cootehill, the lady of Thomas Fitzgerald, Esq., of a son. (1847-05-22, 3:3, B)

2194. On the 11th inst., at Castleblayney, by the Rev. J.T. Whitestone, Mr. Joseph Crowe, Dundalk, to Jane Eliza, youngest daughter of William Molloy, Esq., Castleblayney. (1847-05-22, 3:3, M)

2195. On the 11th inst., at Newbliss, in the 65th year of her age, Elizabeth, relict of the late Alex. Donaldson, Esq., of Tullyvallen, co. Armagh. (1847-05-22, 3:3, D)

2196. At Enniskillen, on the 12th inst., of fever, Stewart Betty, Esq. (1847-05-22, 3:3, D)

2197. At Pettigo, of fever, the Rev. Simon Nelson, Presbyterian Minister. (1847-05-22, 3:3, D)

2198. At his residence, in Ballymena, on Monday, 17th inst., of typhus fever, the Rev. A. Patterson, in the 46th year of his age. (1847-05-22, 3:3, D)

2199. On the 13th inst., at his residence, Glenmore, near Lisburn, James N. Richardson, in the 67th year of his age. (1847-05-22, 3:3, D)

2200. On the 16th inst., Caroline, daughter of Mr. Richd. Brown, Belfast. (1847-05-22, 3:3, D)

2201. On the 11th inst., of typhus fever, Miss M'Moran, of Great Patrick-street, Belfast, aged 52 years. (1847-05-22, 3:3, D)

2202. On the 11th inst., in her 32d year, Jane, wife of Mr. A. Mearns, Belfast. (1847-05-22, 3:3, D)

2203. On the 11th inst., at her residence, Little May-street, Belfast, Hannah Osborne. (1847-05-22, 3:3, D)

2204. On the 13th inst., at his residence, 4, Johnston's Buildings, Shankhill Road, Belfast, Mr. Thomas Knight, boiler maker and engineer, aged 49 years. (1847-05-22, 3:3, D)

2205. On the 4th inst., Mr. Wm. Johnson, of Hillhall, in the 76th [70th?] year of his age. (1847-05-22, 3:3, D)

2206. On the 11th inst., at Clontibret, county Monaghan, at an advanced age, after a protracted illness, which he bore with christian resignation, M.J. Niblock, deeply regretted. (1847-05-22, 3:3, D)

2207. On the 9th inst., the Rev. Frederick M'Cullagh, curate of Magheracoolmoney, formerly of Kilmore, co. Down. (1847-05-22, 3:3, D)

2208. On the 13th inst., after a few days' illness, Theobald Kenny, Esq., of Thornfield House, third son of N.W. Kenny, Esq., of Rocksavage, co. Monaghan. (1847-05-22, 3:3, D)

2209. On the 1st inst., Letitia, second daughter of James Williams, Esq., of Newry. (1847-05-22, 3:3, D)

2210. On the 8th inst., at Corbally, co. Down, Agnes, wife of John Cowan, Esq. (1847-05-22, 3:3, D)

2211. Of inflammation, on Wednesday the 19th inst., at the house of his brother, in the town of Clones, Richard Thompson, in the 30th year of his age, much and deservedly regretted. (1847-05-22, 3:3, D)

2212. At Anketell Grove, on the 20th May, the lady of Matthew John Anketell, Esq., of a daughter. (1847-05-29, 3:4, B)

2213. On the 20th inst., in Belturbet Church, by the Very Rev. the Dean of Cashel, Theophilus Thompson, Esq., of Cavan, County of Cavan, to Isabella Olivia, second daughter of George Marshall Knipe, Esq., of Erne Hill, in the County of Cavan. (1847-05-29, 3:4, M)

2214. On the 3rd inst., the lady of Thomas L. Mayne, Esq., Governor of Monaghan Gaol, of a son. (1847-06-05, 3:5, B)

2215. On the 23d day of May last, at the residence of her father, in Monaghan, Maria M'Coy, in her 17th year, eldest daughter of Mr. P. M'Coy, of this town. (1847-06-05, 3:5, D)

2216. May 30, in Armagh, of bronchitis and dysentery, Mr. Joseph Soden, editor of the *Ulster Gazette*, aged 40. (1847-06-05, 3:5, D)

2217. May 7, in Sloane-street, after a lingering illness, the Hon. Lady King, relict of Lieut.-General the Hon. Sir Henry King, K.C.B., of Grove Lodge, Berkshire. (1847-06-05, 3:5, D)

2218. At No. 4, Charlemount-mall, after a protracted illness, in the twenty-second year of her age, Charlotte Vicars, the beloved wife of P. De Courcy Sheehy, Esq., and third daughter of James C. Egan, Esq., of Dublin. (1847-06-05, 3:5, D)

2219. At Stephen's-green, after a short illness, Mr. Alex. Patterson, aged forty-one. (1847-06-05, 3:5, D)

2220. June 1, at Mountjoy-square, East, Alice, only daughter of Charles S. Ottley, Esq. (1847-06-05, 3:5, D)

2221. February 13, at St. James's Church, Sydney, Australia, by the Rev. J.W. Bodenham, Mr. John Flavelle, youngest son of Mr. H. Flavelle, of D'Olier-street, Dublin, to Catherine, the third daughter; and at the same time and place, Mr. Samuel Brush, late of the county Down, to Gertrude Georgiana, the fourth daughter of the late Mr. Rossiter, of Wellbank, county Kildare. (1847-06-12, 3:3, M)

2222. June 3, at Aughanunshin Church, by the Rev. John Irwin, the Rev. C. Fausett, son of Robert Fausett, of Lisbofin, county of Fermanagh, Esq., to Anne Jane, eldest daughter of the late William Wray, of Oak Park, county Donegal, Esq. (1847-06-12, 3:3, M)

2223. On Tuesday last, Mr. William Scott, at the residence of his mother, Market St., Monaghan, Aged 16 years. (1847-06-12, 3:3, D)

2224. On the 1st instant, at Stonehouse, Plymouth, Samuel Bleazby, Esq., M.D., aged 26 years. (1847-06-12, 3:3, D)

2225. June 4, suddenly, Doctor Litton, Professor of Botany to the Royal Dublin Society. (1847-06-12, 3:3, D)

2226. Of fever, this week, at the county hospital, Monaghan, Mrs. Jane Campbell, head nurse of the institution. (1847-06-12, 3:3, D)

2227. On the 17th day of June, 1847, on Pound-hill, Clones, in the promise of life, and 32nd year of his age, Mr. James Gray, deservedly and universally regretted. Having been admitted a member of the Orange Society at an early age, he continued through life to act as a steady and consistent member of that society. His remains were attended to the grave by a large number of his sorrowing brethren. (1847-06-12, 3:3, D)

2228. On the 17th instant, in Castleblayney Church, by the Rev. J.T. Whitestone, B.V. Cumming, M.D., to Ann, second daughter of Edward Hunter, Merchant, both of Castleblayney. (1847-06-19, 3:3, M)

2229. June 16, in St. Thomas's church, Dublin, by the Rev. Josiah Lowe, A.B., Alexander Crothers, Esq., Blackwater-town, to Eliza, only daughter of the late Andrew Wilson, Esq., Solicitor, Lower Gardiner-st. (1847-06-19, 3:3, M)

2230. In Clones, of Fever, deservedly regretted, Mr. Thomas Hanna, merchant. His remains were interred in the grave yard of his native parish, Tydavnet, on Friday, amidst the sincere sorrowing of a large circle of friends. (1847-06-19, 3:3, D)

2231. June 14, at Rockdale House, county of Tyrone, James Lowry, Esq., aged sixty years. (1847-06-19, 3:3, D)

2232. June 15, at her residence, 20, Mountpleasant-square, in her seventy-sixth year, in perfect peace, trusting to the righteousness of Christ alone, Mrs. De Baviere, of paralysis, the attack of which she survived only eight hours. (1847-06-19, 3:3, D)

2233. Of fever, in the Trough Fever Hospital, on Saturday the 12th instant, while under the immediate care of her mother, matron of the institution, Mrs. M'Dowal, the beloved wife of Mr. Alexander M'Dowal, postmaster of Emyvale, aged 30 years. Her remains were carried to Tynan burial ground, followed by a large concourse of mourning friends, and sorrowing acquaintances. (1847-06-19, 3:3, D)

2234. June 11, at Newry, Susan, fifth daughter of Henry Waring, Esq., aged eight years.(1847-06-19,3:3,D)

2235. June 10, in Newry, Mr. Hans Baird, aged sixty-six. He was respected by a numerous and respectable circle. (1847-06-19, 3:3, D)

2236. On the 21st inst., at his residence near Clones, in the 36th year of his age, after a short illness, William Mayne Clarke, Esq., Inspector for the Ulster Canal Carrying Company, for the Western district—prompt, active, and talented while in life, his duties and cares have suddenly come to an end. (1847-06-26, 3:4, D)

2237. On the morning of Saturday, the 19th inst., at his residence, Clontibret, in this county, Alexander Reed, in his 65th year. (1847-06-26, 3:4, D)

2238. At an advanced age, at Phibsboro', Anne, relict of the late William Russell, Esq., formerly of Upper Baggot-street, and aunt of the Rev. Archdeacon Russell. (1847-06-26, 3:4, D)

2239. June 14, at Brislington, the Right Hon. Brinsley Butler, Earl of Lanesborough, aged sixty-three years. (1847-06-26, 3:4, D)

2240. June 18, of consumption, at Kildare-street, Hannah Maria, youngest daughter of the late Rev. L. Dowdall, D.D. (1847-06-26, 3:4, D)

2241. On the 18th inst., at his residence, Arthur-street, Belfast, John Pim Jackson, Architect, aged thirty-two years. (1847-06-26, 3:4, D)

2242. On the 20th inst., at her residence, 12, Chichester-street, Belfast, Jane, wife of Mr. Arthur Gaffikin. (1847-06-26, 3:4, D)

2243. On the 16th inst., William Thomas Ireland, son of the late James Ireland, Prince's-street, Belfast, aged 16 years. (1847-06-26, 3:4, D)

2244. On the 9th inst., at Belfast, of fever, in his 48th year, Mr. James Wallace. (1847-06-26, 3:4, D)

2245. On the 12th inst., at Belfast, of fever, in her 50th year, Mary, wife of Mr. James Wallace. (1847-06-26, 3:4, D)

2246. On the 15th inst., in her 87th year, Jane, relict of the late Adam Dickey, Esq., Hollybrook, Randalstown. (1847-06-26, 3:4, D)

2247. On the 13th inst., at Rockdale House, co. Tyrone, James Lowry, Esq., aged 60 years. (1847-06-26, 3:4, D)

2248. On the 13th inst., at Strabane, Mr. James M'Dougal, Clerk of the Strabane Union. (1847-06-26, 3:4, D)

2249. On the 11th inst., at Newry, Susan, fifth daughter of Henry Waring, Esq., aged 8 years. (1847-06-26, 3:4, D)

2250. On the 11th inst., of dysentery, at Derrigolin Glebe, Carrickmacross, James, child of Rev. Wm. Thompson, aged 6 years. (1847-06-26, 3:4, D)

2251. On the 12th, at Warrenpoint, after a short illness, Mr. Moses Searight, aged 48 years. (1847-06-26, 3:4, D)

2252. On Sunday the 27th instant, at Mount-Louise, the wife of S.R.B. Evatt, Esq., of a son. (1847-07-03, 3:5, B)

2253. On Tuesday the 29th instant, the Lady of Henry P. Lennon, Esq., of a son. (1847-07-03, 3:5, B)

2254. On the 1st instant, James A. Ross, Monaghan, to Anne, only daughter of the late Captain Alexander Waddel, of Lisnavane, one of the most distinguished officers in the Irish Volunteers. (1847-07-03, 3:5, M)

2255. At Newbliss, in the 80th year of her age, Mary, relict of the late Mr. James Bowes. (1847-07-03, 3:5, D)

2256. In Derry, on the 1st inst., Mr. Robert E. Hughes, of Armagh, second son of the late Mr. Arthur Hughes. (1847-07-10, 3:3, D)

2257. June 29, at her residence, Academy-street, Belfast, Anna, wife of Mr. William Thompson. (1847-07-10, 3:3, D)

2258. In Newry, on the morning of the 3d inst., of typhus fever, Mr. John Bennie, proprietor of the Eagle Iron Foundry. (1847-07-10, 3:3, D)

2259. In Newry, on the evening of the 3d inst., Mr. Adam Ledlie, merchant. (1847-07-10, 3:3, D)

2260. June 26, at Oatland Cottage, the residence of her uncle, T. Walkington, Esq., of rapid decline, aged 31 years, Eliza, wife of the Rev. Wm. Thomson, Derryolin Glebe. (1847-07-10, 3:3, D)

2261. June 27, at Greenwood-park, Eliza Sarah Livingston, aged 84 years, relict of the late Dr. Livingston, Newry. (1847-07-10, 3:3, D)

2262. July 9, at the Rectory, Castleblayney, the wife of the Rev. J.T. Whitestone, of a son. (1847-07-17, 3:3, B)

2263. On Thursday last, at his residence, Sallymount near Monaghan, at an advanced age, Thomas Robinson, Esq. Mr. Robinson had been for a long time ill, but made what was thought a rapid recovery during the last month, when a change for the worse took place and hurried him away amid the regrets of a large circle of friends. (1847-07-17, 3:3, D)

2264. July 9, at Dunmanway, of typhus fever, the Rev. Thomas Brodrick Tuckey, Curate of Fanlobbus, eldest son of the Rev. Thos. Tuckey, Rector of Drimoleague. (1847-07-17, 3:3, D)

2265. July 7, at Dunmanway, of typhus fever, Miss Ellen Jagoe, daughter of the late Abraham Jagoe, Esq., of Kilronan. (1847-07-17, 3:3, D)

2266. At Ballyfarnham, of typhus fever, caught in the discharge of his public medical duties, Dr. Hawkesworth. (1847-07-17, 3:3, D)

2267. July 5, James Verner, Esq., formerly Captain in the 19th dragoons. (1847-07-17, 3:3, D)

2268. At his residence, Drum, of fever, on Sunday last, Wm. Rutherford, Esq., J.P. (1847-07-17, 3:3, D)

2269. July 22, at 59, Lower Mount-street, Captain Charles Sharman, late of the Royal Irish Artillery, and formerly of Derrylusk in this County, aged eighty-four. "Blessed are the dead which die in the Lord, for they rest from their labours." (1847-07-31, 1:3, D)

2270. On the 30th June, in the Presbyterian Meeting-house, Castleblayney, by the Rev. Thomas Boyd, Mr. Samuel M'Birney, clerk to the Board of Guardians, Castleblayney, to Miss Donaldson, schoolmistress to the same union Workhouse. (1847-08-07, 3:3, M)

2271. August 3, in Monkstown Church, by the Rev. John Saint George Williams, James Shekleton, Esq., of Dundalk, eldest son of the late Alexander Shekleton, Esq., of same place, to Adeline Jane, youngest daughter of Zachariah D. Williams, Esq., Brighton Terrace, Monkstown. (1847-08-07, 3:3, M)

2272. On the 5th Inst., at Gallina, Monaghan, at the residence of his father, Alexander Fleming, Esq., Ex-Scholar of T.C.D., Barrister-at-law, aged 31 years, third son of Mr. Alexander Fleming. (1847-08-07, 3:3, D)

2273. May 29, at Ferozepore, Brevet Major John Loftus Tottenham, 3d Regiment Bengal Light Cavalry, Judge Advocate General at Lahore. (1847-08-07, 3:3, D)

2274. July 31, at Killiney, Mark Anthony Levinge, Esq., Captain in the Cavan Militia, aged 72 years. (1847-08-07, 3:3, D)

2275. July 31, at Wyatt Ville, Harriet Sophia, fourth daughter of James West, Esq., Upper Mount-street, Dublin. (1847-08-07, 3:3, D)

2276. June 24th, at Montreal, of typhus fever, contracted while ministering to the wants of the sick and destitute Irish emigrants, Lieutenant William Lloyd, R.N., of Montreal and Sherbrooke, Canada East, after twelve days' illness. (1847-08-07, 3:3, D)

2277. On the 9th instant, in St. Ann's Church, by the Rev. H.S. Hamilton, Edward Rodgers, Esq., Vicar-Choral, Cathedral, Armagh, to Charlotte, daughter of Wm. Campbell, Esq., late of her Majesty's 38th Regiment of Foot. (1847-08-21, 3:4, M)

2278. On the 12th inst., in Belfast, Wm. Allan, Esq., of Dundalk, to Anne, only daughter of the Rev. S. Brown, Castledawson. (1847-08-21, 3:4, M)

2279. On the 21st ultimo, in the First Presbyterian church, Newtownhamilton, Mr. John Thompson, of Tullenageer, to Miss Sarah Hanna, of Lissiness. (1847-08-21, 3:4, M)

2280. On the 10th instant, by the Rev. William White, Downpatrick, Mr. Robert Nesbit, of Belfast, Woollen-draper, to Sarah, second daughter of Mr. Wm. Rowan, Downpatrick. (1847-08-21, 3:4, M)

2281. August 1, of fever, at Broomfield, in the county of Monaghan, Jemima Matilda, the beloved wife of the Rev. Adderley Campbell. (1847-08-21, 3:4, D)

2282. On the 9th instant, after an illness of fourteen days, Roger Marlay, Esq., of Portadown. (1847-08-21, 3:4, D)

2283. August 16, in Moneyrea Meeting-house, by the Rev. Henry Montgomery, LL.D., the Rev. William Cochrane, of Aberdeen, to Jane, daughter of the Rev. Fletcher Blakely, A.M. (1847-08-28, 3:1, M)

2284. August 7, at Kinsale, Maria, the beloved wife of the Rev. Richard Graves Meredyth, and second daughter of the late Thomas Johnston, Esq., of Fort-johnston, county Monaghan. (1847-08-28, 3:1, D)

2285. August 23, Judith Anne Eliza, youngest daughter of Mr. Thomas Kelly, Market-street, Monaghan. Aged 17 years. (1847-08-28, 3:1, D)

2286. On the 2d inst., at Lara church, county Cavan, by the Rev. Mr. Erskine, James George Lepper, Esq., of Monaghan, to Eliza, only daughter of Robert Thompson, Esq., of Ravenwood. (1847-09-04, 3:2, M)

2287. August 25, at Walthamstow Church, the Rev. Thomas Hincks, M.A., Rector of Culfeightrim, Antrim, to Mary Annie, daughter of the late George Lewis, Esq., of Tottenham, Middlesex. (1847-09-04, 3:2, M)

2288. August 27, at Blackrock, Christiana, relict of R.T. Atkins, Esq. (1847-09-04, 3:2, D)

2289. August 29, Frederick, son of John Glenton, Esq., Charleville-mall. (1847-09-04, 3:2, D)

2290. August 30, of malignant typhus fever, caught in the discharge of his parochial duties, the Rev. John Stone, Curate of St. Michan's parish, aged 29. (1847-09-04, 3:2, D)

2291. On the 3rd instant, of typhus fever, in the 63d year of her age, Jane, the beloved wife of William M'Caldin, Tinary, Newbliss. By the removal of this excellent and pious woman, the poor have been deprived of a valuable friend, and to her family, the loss is incalculable. (1847-09-11, 2:6, D)

2292. At Belfast, on the 6th inst., of Diarrhoea, in the 52d year of her age, Jane, fourth daughter of the late William Anketell, Esq., of Dungillick, in the county of Monaghan, and sister of Thomas Anketell, Esq. (1847-09-18, 3:4, D)

2293. September 9, at Weybridge, Lady Follett, relict of Sir William Webb Follett, Attorney General. (1847-09-18, 3:4, D)

2294. September 2, at Manorcunningham, county Donegal, Miss Ellen Montgomery, aged eighty years. (1847-09-18, 3:4, D)

2295. September 11, in Newry, Margaret, relict of the late William Overend, of Portadown, Esq. (1847-09-18, 3:4, D)

2296. Sept. 13, in Kinsale Barracks, of dysentery, aged twenty-one years, John Jackson Hull, Esq., A.B., T.C.D., Ensign in her Majesty's 54th Regiment, youngest son of Perry Hall, Esq., of Tully House, Monaghan. (1847-09-18, 3:4, D)

2297. September 11, at Blackrocks, county of Louth, Sydney George Hamilton, youngest son of the Rev. Thomas Dawson Logan, of Ardee. (1847-09-18, 3:4, D)

2298. On the 18th August, of apoplexy, Patrick Fraine, Esq., of Carrickmacross, at the residence of Mrs. Campbell of Portenaghey, leaving a wife and son to deplore his loss. (1847-09-18, 3:4, D)

2299. At Antrim, on the 21st inst., Andrew A. Molyneux, surgeon. (1847-09-25, 3:2, D)

2300. On the 13th inst., in his 21st year, at the residence of John G. Copley, Esq., Richmond Hill, Manchester, William, youngest son of the late Samuel King, Esq., of Coalisland Mills, Dungannon. (1847-09-25, 3:2, D)

2301. Yesterday morning, at Anketell Grove, the lady of William R. Anketell, Esq., of a daughter. (1847-10-02, 3:2, B)

2302. September 23, in the parish church of Downpatrick, Robert Boyd, Esq., M.D., of Wells, Somersetshire, to Isabella, youngest daughter of the late Richard Keown, Esq., of Downpatrick, and grand-daughter of the late Henry Keown, Esq., J.P., of Tullymore, county Down. (1847-10-02, 3:2, M)

2303. September 28, at Celbridge church, by the Rev. Mr. Packenham, and afterwards by the Rev. Michael Dungan, P.P., of Blanchardstown, Mr. William Dirham, of Isher's [sic] Island, to Mary Christina, fourth daughter of the late Captain Browne, of St. Wolsten's, county Kildare. (1847-10-02, 3:2, M)

2304. September 16, at St. Dunstan's church, Cranbrook, the Rev. William Pennefather, son of the Hon. Richd. Pennefather, one of the Barons of the Court of Exchequer in Ireland, to Catherine, eldest daughter of the Hon. Rear-Admirable [sic!] and Mrs. King, of Angley-House, Cranbrook, and grand-daughter of Robert, second Earl of Kingstown [sic], and of the Most Rev. Euseby Cleaver, formerly Archbishop of Dublin. (1847-10-02, 3:2, M)

2305. In London, on Friday, the 24th Sept., at the advanced age of 83 years, the Rev. John Wright, for forty years rector of Killeevan parish, in the Diocess of Clogher. (1847-10-02, 3:2, D)

2306. September 21, at Stratford, county Wicklow, of malignant typhus fever, the Rev. John Marchbanks. Taken away in the prime of life, his memory will be long cherished, not only by his sorrowing friends and relatives, but by those among whom he so faithfully laboured, for he adorned the doctrine of God our Saviour in all things. (1847-10-02, 3:2, D)

2307. September 22, at Sydney-avenue, Black Rock, to the deep regret of their numerous friends, Catherine, eldest daughter, and on the 25th, Anne, second daughter of the late William Kelly, Esq., of Turrock, county Roscommon. (1847-10-02, 3:2, D)

2308. September 26, in Castlebar, of malignant typhus fever, Mr. Grier Hughes, deputy governor of Mayo prison. (1847-10-02, 3:2, D)

2309. On Wednesday, the third inst., the lady of Wm. A. Williams Kerr, of Mount-Carmel, of a son. (1847-10-09, 3:6, B)

2310. At Middletown, the Rev. James Mauleverer, curate of said place. (1847-10-09, 3:6, D)

2311. At Portadown, on the 2nd inst., Robert Waddell, Esq., formerly of Lisnavain, County Monaghan. (1847-10-09, 3:6, D)

2312. In Bailieboro church on Tuesday, the 12th inst., by the Rev. Charles C. Berresford, Rector of Bailieboro, James L. Bailey, Esq., Sub-Inspector of Constabulary, to Mary Ann, daughter to Rev. E. Mahaffy, Beckscourt, Bailieboro. (1847-10-16, 3:6, M)

2313. On Wednesday the 13th inst., at his residence, the hill, Monaghan, in his 76th year, Richard Mitchell, Esq., one of the oldest and most respectable inhabitants of this town, almost the only remaining burgess of the old borough corporation. (1847-10-16, 3:6, D)

2314. On the 20th inst., Mrs. Young, the lady of George W. Young, Esq., of Knockbawn, County Armagh, of a son. (1847-10-30, 3:3, B)

2315. In London, on the 21st instant, after a long illness, Bertha, the beloved wife of Michael M'Donald, Esq., and daughter of the late Richard Mitchell, Esq., of this Town. (1847-10-30, 3:3, D)

2316. Oct. 24, at his residence, in Carrick-on-Shannon, aged seventy-six years, John Irwin, Esq., universally respected in life, and regretted in death. His end was peace, for Christ was precious to his soul. (1847-10-30, 3:3, D)

2317. Oct. 24, at his father's residence, Sans Souci, Richard Andrew O'Reilly, Esq. (1847-10-30, 3:3, D)

2318. Oct. 21, in this city, G.A. Holmes, Esq., of Moorock, King's County, aged sixty years. (1847-10-30, 3:3, D)

2319. On the 27th of October, in Jubilee-place, London, aged 63, Mrs. Sarah Johnston, relict of the late Surgeon Johnston, of Castleblayney. Mrs. Johnston formerly filled the situation of Matron to our county gaol with zeal and efficiency, and had retired on a pension; she was a truly pious woman, and in all the relations of life, her conduct was most exemplary. (1847-11-06, 3:3, D)

2320. October 31, at the residence of her brother, the Rev. James Burrowes, Killanley Glebe, county Sligo, Hannah, widow of the Rev. Thomas B. Meares, aged 81. (1847-11-06, 3:3, D)

2321. On Wednesday, the 27th October, at Clones, of Fever, Mr. Frederick C. Gray, sincerely, and deservedly regretted, by all who had the pleasure of his acquaintance. (1847-11-06, 3:3, D)

2322. Nov. 16, at 31, Rutland-square, West, Dublin, the lady of Alexander Montgomery, Esq., of Kilmin, in the county of Meath, of a daughter. (1847-11-20, 3:1, B)

2323. On the 18th instant, at the Parish Church, Monaghan, by the Rev. W.L. Roper, Hugh Redpath, Esq., Morningside Bank, Edinburgh, to Elizabeth, youngest daughter of the late Alexander Russell, Esq., Kirkaldy. (1847-11-20, 3:1, M)

2324. On the 5th instant, in Clare Church, near Tandragee, by the Rev. James Wilson, Mr. John Stevenson, of Tandragee, to Harriet, second daughter of the late Rev. Thomas Walsh, Rector of Tartaraghan. (1847-11-20, 3:1, M)

2325. Nov. 15, at Virgemount, Wilhelmina Frances, relict of the late J.M. Cook, Esq., M.D. (1847-11-20, 3:1, D)

2326. On the 14th instant, at Carrickmacross, of fever, aged 35, Mr. Thomas Armstrong, bridewell keeper. (1847-11-20, 3:1, D)

2327. On the 11th instant, at his residence, Malone, Mr. Hugh Roney, aged 50 years. (1847-11-20, 3:1, D)

2328. On Sunday evening, the 14th inst., in the 21st year of her age, Sarah Hammersly, eldest daughter of Mr. James Johnston, Castledawson. (1847-11-20, 3:1, D)

2329. November 2, at his residence, Castlelawn, Douglas, Isle of Man, after a protracted illness, which he bore with Christian patience, William Percival, formerly a Captain in her Majesty's 9th Regiment of Foot. (1847-11-20, 3:1, D)

2330. November 18, in the Church of the Holy Trinity, Upper Chelsea, the Rev. Edward Mayne, of Lakeview, county of Monaghan, to Anna, relict of Henry Oswald Smith, Esq., of the 42d Native Infantry, Madras Army, and grand-daughter of the late Warden Flood, Esq., Judge of the High Court of Admiralty. (1847-11-27, 3:5, M)

2331. November 18, at Newcastle Church, Limerick, G. Bolster, Esq., Surgeon, eldest son of George Ievers Bolster, Esq., of Richmond Villa, county Limerick, to Frances, relict of Lieut. Robert Carte, Barrack-master of Newcastle. (1847-11-27, 3:5, M)

2332. November 18, at Eckington, William Lloyd Flood, Esq., of Farmley, county of Kilkenny, to Frances, only daughter of C.E. Hanford, Esq., of Woollas Hall, Worcestershire. (1847-11-27, 3:5, M)

2333. November 19, in the Parish Church of St. Andrew's, Holborn, Henry Augustus Dunn, second son of the late Arthur Dunn, Esq., Barrister, of the city of Dublin, to Caroline, youngest daughter of Mr. George Kirkman, of London. (1847-11-27, 3:5, M)

2334. November 10, in St. Peter's Church, by the Rev. R. Stack, Mr. A.B. M'Kee, to Charlotte, youngest daughter of Mr. R. Beere, of this city. (1847-11-27, 3:5, M)

2335. On the 16th instant, in the Meeting-house, Dunmurry, James S. Cosgrave, Esq., Surgeon, Malone, to Anne, fourth daughter of John O'Neill, Esq., merchant, Belfast. (1847-11-27, 3:5, M)

2336. November 21, at his residence, Dublin-street, in the 40th year of his age, Mr. John Macklen, Victualler, of this town. (1847-11-27, 3:5, D)

2337. November 18, at his house in Leeson-terrace, Dublin, Benjamin Adams, formerly Captain in the 17th Lancers, and lately Major in the 78th Highlanders, aged sixty-three. (1847-11-27, 3:5, D)

2338. On the 22d instant, at his residence, Chichester-st., Belfast, the Rev. John Davison, Senior Presbyterian Minister of Cookstown, county Tyrone, in the 79th year of his age, and 59th of his ministry. (1847-11-27, 3:5, D)

2339. On the 26th of November, at the residence of her son-in-law, Mr. Mathew Johnston, of Middletown, Martha Little, relict of the late Mr. Nicholas Little, of Kiltubride, aged 88 years. (1847-12-04, 3:1, D)

2340. December 1st, at Feagh, near Newbliss, Mr. John M'Cready, aged 70 years, thirty-two of which he had served, in the faithful discharge of his duties, as steward of Mr. Coote's family, of Brandrum House. (1847-12-04, 3:1, D)

2341. In Drumsnatt Church, County Monaghan, on the 9th Inst., by the Rev. W.H.E. Woodwright, Ralph Dudgeon, Esq., Lieutenant, 76th Regiment, son of the late Captain Dudgeon, of Rosefield, to Martha Caroline, second daughter of John Johnson, Esq., of Thornhill. (1847-12-11, 3:6, M)

2342. In Monaghan Church, on Wednesday the 8th, by the Rev. Henry Maffatt, Mr. James Warner, to Martha, eldest daughter of Mr. James M'Knight, both of this town. (1847-12-11, 3:6, M)

2343. At Ballingarry, county Cavan, by the bursting of a blood vessel, Mr. John M'Ardle. His death is greatly regretted by his friends and acquaintances. (1847-12-11, 3:6, D)

2344. On Saturday, the 11th instant, Jane, only daughter of Mr. James M'Murray, of Ballibay. (1847-12-18, 3:2, D)

2345. On the 22d inst., in the Presbyterian Church of Monaghan, by the Rev. J. Bleckley, John Highland, Esq., Newcastle, to Anne Jane, daughter of the late William Smith, Esq., of Orchard Vale, county Monaghan. (1847-12-25, 3:4, M)

2346. Dec. 18th, of malignant Typhus of 14 days' duration, Rosanna, the beloved sister of Dr. Duffy, Ballybay, aged 16. Of the forbearance [which] this amiable and bland young patient has shown during her deeply distressing illness, her friends, and many sympathizing visitors have had ample experience, but of the grief which must last as long as her memory, none but such as are acquainted with the vacuum she has left, can be sensible. To her, the poor of the neighbourhood own, and acknowledge, their lasting obligation. (1847-12-25, 3:4, D)

:: :: ::

3. News Accounts

2347. Death of Lord Castlemaine.—We have just heard a rumour, which we fear too true, that Lord Viscount Castlemaine breathed his last yesterday morning at Moydrum Castle, Athlone. Not having issue, his Lordship's title will devolve on some member of the Hancock Family, but we are not prepared to say which. His death, we have reason to believe, was unexpected.—*Packet.* (1839-01-12, 2:3)

2348. Death of the Earl of Carnwath.—We regret to announce the death of this gallant officer. The noble Lord was in his 71st year, having been born in 1768; he was restored to the forfeited honors of his ancestors by act of Parliament in 1826. He was twice married; in 1789, to Jane, daughter of Mr. Parker, who died soon after; and in 1784, to Adalucia, daughter of Lieutenant-Colonel Arthur Brown. By his first wife he had an only child, a daughter, who died at the early age of eleven; by his second wife he had not less than thirteen children, some of whom survive him. He is succeeded in the title and estates by his eldest son, Lord Dalzell, now Earl of Carnwath, who was born in September, 1797. The late Earl was a Major in the Army in 1798; Lieutenant and Captain, 1st Foot Guards in May, 1803; Lieutenant-Colonel in the army in September of that year; Colonel in the army in January, 1812; and Major-General, the 4th of June, 1814. He served as Deputy-Adjutant-General in Ireland, and was on the staff in Belfast. (1839-01-12, 2:3)

2349. Sudden Death from Apoplexy.—On the 10th instant, an inquest was holden in the townland of Cordoola, Parish of Tullycorbet, before Robert Murray, Esq. of Beechhill, Coroner for the county, on view of the body of Catharine Connolly, who was found in a ditch on said townland. Dr. Mitchell was examined before the jury, and found that apoplexy was the cause of death, when the jury returned a verdict as usual in such cases, of death by the visitation of God. (1839-01-12, 2:4)

2350. Funeral of Lord Norbury.—Durrow, Tuesday, Jan. 8.—Between one and two o'clock this day, the mortal remains of the late inestimable Earl of Norbury were conveyed to their last resting place, attended by a vast concourse of persons of all ranks, who seemed actuated by one common feeling of deep and sincere sorrow. The coffin was borne from the castle to the church by the gentry, including Captain Fox, Henry Magan, Esq., the parish priests of Tullamore, and Clara, the Rev. Messrs. Rafferty and Barry, Mr. Thompson, Mr. Oldham, and about 17 or 18 other Magistrates, who relieved each other at short intervals. The Earl of Charleville and Lord Oxmontown were pall-bearers, supported by the Rev. Mr. Shelton, Gresson, and Captain Tibeaudo. The chief mourners were, the late Lord Glandine, now Earl Norbury; his brother, the Hon. Otway Toler, and their brothers-in-law, Messrs. Vandeleur and Stewart. The service was performed by the Rev. Mr. Lever, Rector of Tullamore, who delivered a most affecting discourse. When the coffin was deposited in the vault the Rev. Mr. Rafferty addressed the people in the church-yard in terms most complimentary to the character of the deceased. The demeanor of the peasantry was most praiseworthy. They felt deeply, so seemed to feel sorrow, for the loss of one who was regarded as their best friend and benefactor. (1839-01-12, 3:5)

2351. Marriage in High Life.—At Marylebone church, Mr. H. Richardson, led to the altar Lady Emily Kerr, sixth daughter of Lord Mark Kerr. Lord Clinton, Sir William and Lady Gomm, Hon. Salina Kerr, Mr. Edward M'Donnell, and a select circle of friends were present at the solemnization. An elegant dejune was given by Lord M. Kerr to the wedding party, after which the happy couple started for Bick, Oxfordshire, to pass the honeymoon. (1839-01-12, 4:2)

2352. April 7, 1838. Mr. John Wynne to Lady Anne Butler, daughter of the late, and sister to the present Marquis of Ormonde. (1839-01-12, 4:3)

2353. April 20, 1838. The Earl of Clonmel to the Hon. Annette Burgh, eldest daughter of Viscount Downes. (1839-01-12, 4:3)

2354. April 25, 1838. Viscount Galway to Miss Milnes. (1839-01-12, 4:3)

2355. April 25, 1838. The Dowager Lady Huntingdon to Colonel Harris. (1839-01-12, 4:3)

2356. May 25, 1838. Lady Selina Hoste, daughter of the Dowager Marchioness of Hastings, to Mr. Charles Henry, nephew of the Duke of Leinster. (1839-01-12, 4:3)

2357. July 24, 1838. The Earl of Cavan to the Hon. Caroline Littleton, daughter of Lord Hatherton. (1839-01-12, 4:3)

2358. August 7, 1838. The Hon. Captain Hood, son and heir of Viscount Bridport, to Lady Mary Hill, daughter of the Marchioness of Downshire. (1839-01-12, 4:3)

2359. August 9, 1838. The Hon. Charles Ponsonby, M.P., eldest son of Lord De Manley, to the Hon. Miss Ponsonby, daughter of Lord Duncannon. (1839-01-12, 4:3)

2360. Sept. 10, 1838. Viscount Milton, eldest son of the Earl Fitzwilliam, to Lady Frances Douglas, daughter of the Earl of Morton. (1839-01-12, 4:3)

2361. October 2, 1838. Viscount Combermere to Miss Gibbings. (1839-01-12, 4:3)

2362. October 10, 1838. Mr. James M'Kenzie, to Lady Anne Wentworth Fitzwilliam, fourth daughter of the Earl Fitzwilliam. (1839-01-12, 4:3)

2363. October 16, 1838. The Hon. W. Stourton, second son of Lord Stourton, to Miss Catherine Scully. (1839-01-12, 4:3)

2364. Dec. 3, 1838. The Hon. Francis Clements, son of the Earl of Leitrim, to Miss Kings. (1839-01-12, 4:3)

2365. Dec. 8, 1838. Lord Teignmount [Teignmouth], M.P., to Miss Caroline Browne. (1839-01-12, 4:3)

2366. Dec. 15, 1838. Mr. Thomas Nugent Vaughan to Viscountess Forbes, relict of the late Viscount Forbes, and mother of the Earl of Granard. (1839-01-12, 4:3)

2367. Dec. 29, 1838. The Hon. Randal E. Plunkett, eldest son of Lord Dunsanny [sic], to Miss Elizabeth Evelyn. (1839-01-12, 4:3)

2368. January 13, 1838. Lord Farnborough, in his 78th year (title extinct.) (1839-01-12, 4:3)

2369. January 18, 1838. The Earl of Clonmel, in his 55th year. (1839-01-12, 4:3)

2370. April 5. 1838. The Dowager Viscountess Strangford, in her 82d year. (1839-01-12, 4:3)

2371. April 30, 1838. Lord Muncaster, aged 35. (1839-01-12, 4:3)

2372. May 22, 1838. The Marquis of Ormonde, in [his] 64th year. (1839-01-12, 4:3)

2373. August 25, 1838. Earl Annesley, in his 67th year. (1839-01-12, 4:3)

2374. September 18, 1838. Lord Carrington, at the advanced age of 86 years. (1839-01-12, 4:3)

2375. September 20, 1838. Lord Farnham (fifth Lord,) in his 71st year. (1839-01-12, 4:3)

2376. October 19, 1838. Lord Farnham (sixth Lord,) in his 65th year. (1839-01-12, 4:3)

2377. November 29, 1838. Hon. Mrs. Bowles, sister of Viscount Palmerston. (1839-01-12, 4:3)

2378. December 20, 1838. The Hon. William Waldegrave, brother of Lord Radstock, in his 43d year. (1839-01-12, 4:3)

2379. Tombstones.—We understand that in consequence of Sir Herbert Jenner's recent extraordinary decision in the case of *Breeks v. Woolfrey*, by which he has affirmed that praying for the dead is not inconsistent with the doctrines of the Church of England, many of the clergy have determined to exercise a rigid scrutiny into every inscription intended to be placed on a tombstone. In some instances, the excellent plan of giving public notice has been adopted, the clergyman announcing to his congregation that he will not allow any monument to be erected without his written authority, and requiring to see a copy of the inscription proposed to be engraved. Whether the decision of Sir H. Jenner be good or bad in law, we trust that the clergy will continue to inspect all inscriptions. They may thus prevent good taste and right feeling from being so constantly annoyed by the wretched and unbecoming trifling observable in too many of our churchyards.—*Berks Chronicle*. (1839-01-17, 1:2)

2380. The Last Adieu.

Cease fond friends,
He is my husband still! and I shall see him:
Heavens! what a change of features now!
And yet in death a calmness rests upon him,
That might shame a living mortal's look!
Hah! Edward, there is a fixity in those eyes
That was not wont to be, they used to roll in joy,
And, like the midnight dream of happiness,
Flashing in ideas quick across imagination,
Re-kindle soul and body in increasing
And untiring love.
Where are the accustomed smiles
To greet your weeping Amy's presence? they have fled,
And now are locked within the iron chambers
Of grim visaged death! and idol memory,
Must strain its nerve and utmost strength,
To raise a shadow of my former bliss.
Are thy cold hands,
Closed against my grasp! ope them,
If woman's strength in agony, can ought avail,
Ye stiffened fingers yield—I have thee now!
And ere they place thee in the solemn darkness,
Of thy cold, cold tomb, I'll bid a fond adieu,
Moistening thy pallid cheek with pure affection's stream
'Spite of the world's huge laugh of mockery.
Speak, love,
Although my fond words are choaked with sighs,
And buried in the bitterness of agonizing tears,
I'll answer thee; speak but chide me not!
The fervency of woman's love was ever with thee;
And now I swear my heart to oath irrevocable,
That as it lasted to the death, it shall not cease!
But dwell eternally with dust and ashes.
This pressure of thy changed and manly form
To my widowed heart, is mighty consolation:
Thy cheek is warm with the fever of my own,
And thine eyes for once deceive me—hah!
Those tears are mine—thy lips are glowing
Underneath my pressure, would that life's warmth,
By miracle profound, would break from lips to heart,
And starting from the icy coldness of your couch,
Calmly to ponder on my biding love!
When I should faint away.

G.L. (1839-01-17, 4:1)

2381. She Looks Upon the Ring.

She looks upon the ring,
In a dream of happiest days,
When the lips of one now dead and gone,
Were opened but to praise.
When life o'erflowed with promise
Of happy, happy years,
In one dead day that passed away
To torture and to tears.

She looks upon the ring,
In the bloom of purest youth,
And can recall, remembering all
His tenderness and truth.
The flowers he fondly gathered,
And in her bosom laid,
Have never lost their summer bloom—
Those flowers will never fade.

She looks upon the ring,
And the winter melts away—
The very air is golden—
It is the prime of May.
The fields through which they walked to church
She sees—the bloom, the sky—
And of the beauty of that day
The sense can never die.

She looks upon the ring,
And her cheek a moment glows—
Again seem blending in her hair
The lilly and the rose.
She sees a bridal party—
Of maiden white a gleam—
And the merry chime of village bells
Is mingling with her dream.

She looks upon the ring,
And her native home she sees,
As last she took a lingering look,
Beyond the village trees,
She hears her father's blessing—
She feels her mother's tears—
And in one moment knows again
The bliss and woes of years.

Richard Howitt.
(1839-01-17, 4:1)

2382. Approaching Marriage in High Life.—We understand that the beautiful and accomplished Miss Bateson, Bart., [sic] of Belvoir Park, will shortly be led to the hymeneal altar by J.W. Gladstone, Esq., son of John Gladstone, Esq., of Fasque Park, Scotland, and Carlton Terrace, London. Captain Smith, brother to the Princess of Capua, will shortly be married to the Hon. Miss Catherine Abbot, sister to Lord Tenterden. (1839-01-26, 3:2)

2383. Life.

Life! is the light shadow of a passing dream,
Reflected by the sickening mirrors of pallid woe—
And sorrowing ills; in its quick exit,
It fain would wipe our varying pangs away:
But, ah! it speeds to the world of spirits,
And a big reckoning must be made,
To Master-Spirits there.

Life! is like the early blossomed flower,
Perfected by a season's care of nature and of man:
Mark the expansion of the fragile thing!
To catch the sharp Zephyrs in their playful rounds:
But, lo! it shrivels o'er the courted treasure,
And fades and dies away.

Life! is like the silvered trail of horned snails,
Which to superficial glances seems most pretty:
Examine closely, and you'll quick discover,
That the spangled course is thin!
Unfit to hide the bitter blast!
Unfit to hide the drops of melting skies:
And here and there 'tis pierced with angled stones,
And sharpened thorns: while at the best,
'Tis but a path for enemies to crawl upon!

G.L. (1839-01-26, 4:1)

2384. Husband-Hunting.—Music is cultivated to fascinate the reluctant ear, painting to captivate the eye, and dancing to enrapture the touch. Botany has been studied as an excuse for solitary walks and maiden musing; geology, for a rocky nook, or a secluded pass; astronomy, that the silent hour of night, and the star of love may produce their wished for influence; poetry is to select tender and touching passages; and history is to quote examples of woman's undying affection. Attitudes are studied, sighs practised, fainting stimulated [sic], and a fountain of tears, ranged to pour out on all fitting occasions a shower of glittering pearls. (1839-01-26, 4:3)

2385. Death of Viscount Clements, M.P.—We regret to state that Lord Clements departed this life yesterday evening, at the seat of the Earl of Charlemont. The death of Lord Clements causes a vacancy in the representation of the county of Leitrim. (1839-02-02, 1:4)

2386. The Infidel's Death-Bed.

Loud the yells which echo there,
Dark that brow that once was fair,
And deep, wild, mad despair!
Breaks from his lips!

Mark the judgment of his sceptic mind,
Mark the mocking length of all his kind,
He goes in agonizing woe to find,
His portion with the damn'd!

Convulsion shakes him, list—his cries!
His joints grow stiff, and fixed his eyes,
He curses, quivers, madly dies!
Leaving earth's stage.

The judgment o'er, the loud "Depart,"
Breaks on his ears—strikes on his heart—
Shuddering he's borne to his curs'd part,
Within the flaming deep. (*continued...*)

2386, continued:

And Devil's gathering round in sinful ire,
Flap their broad wings on the liquid fire,
For agony creates a wild desire,
To pain the soul of others.

G.L. (1839-02-02, 4:1)

2387. The Best Mode of Dying.—The exchange papers are full of suicides. The easiest way to die is—to pay all your debts, and wait till your time comes. We've tried it. (1839-02-02, 4:4)

2388. The Right Hon. William Saurin.—Of the Right Hon. Wm. Saurin it is a matter of no small difficulty to speak in terms sufficiently panegyrical, for he was, in truth, a rare man—rare in talents, rare in dignity of mind, and rare in temper and disposition.

Mr. Saurin was of French extraction, and was one of four brothers, the present excellent Bishop of Dromore being the only survivor. On Mr. Saurin's being called to the bar, he speedily rose to eminence; but that which first paved the way to his high elevation in his profession, was the memorable contest for the representation of the county of Down, in the year 1792, which lasted nearly four months, and which laid the foundation of these subsequent acts of Parliament, limiting the duration of similar trials of strength, between the contending parties. By his signal display of forensick knowledge and tact, he was enabled, at the close of the most arduously contested election ever remembered in Ireland, to return to the Courts within ample purse, and the eyes of all his co-temporaries turned upon him.

"*At pulchrum est digito montrari, et dicier, hic est.*"

Soon afterwards, Mr. Saurin had the good fortune to be united to Lady Cox, the inestimable and sorrowing widow who now survives him. This lady is sister to the Marquis of Thomond, and at a very early age was married to Sir Richard Cox, Bart., of Dunmannaway, in the county of Cork, who, also, was under age, and was unfortunately drowned in his own lake, by falling out of his pleasure boat and being entangled in the weeds. By Sir Richard dying under age, and intestate, lady Cox, now lady Mary Saurin became entitled to her thirds; and thus an accession of income was made, in addition to the possession of a young, a beautiful, and accomplished woman. From this period Mr. Saurin steadily rose from step to step, until he was made, during (we believe) the Chancellorship of Lord Manners, Attorney-general of Ireland, an office which acquired both dignity and practical efficiency when held by this upright man and sound lawyer. But, however, creditable to the man was the performance of the high duties of this office, the circumstances under which he found it necessary to resign, and to refuse a peerage, will, in Ireland's history, reflect but little honor on his immediate successor, or indeed, on the party concerned in the affair.

From this period, Mr. Saurin withdrew from his practice, as a chancery barrister, and became, exclusively, a chamber lawyer, his opinion being sought by persons of all parties upon cases involving any intricacy of law, in all and every imaginable branch, in which he was ably assisted by his youngest son, whom he always associated with himself in forming his decisions.

But, alas! the great and good man is no more! He died in the plenitude of years, nearly 83, and in the full possession of all his fine faculties; but above all, in the entire trust and confidence of the atonement made by his blessed Redeemer. He was a man particularly Christian, and firm in the Orthodox faith of the Reformed Church, to which he was ardently attached, and of whose stability he was the uncompromising advocate.

Nor were Mr. Saurin's talents confined to his profession; for in the year of the rebellion, in 1798, he raised and commanded one of the finest corps of yeomanry ever brought upon parade, to which it was by no means confined, as events proved, the Lawyers' Infantry; and we remember to have seen him on the field, as a reviewing officer, put his own corps, and several others, through the most difficult manoeuvres, with a skill that drew forth both the admiration and applause of old and experienced military tacticians.

In stature, Mr. Saurin was about the middle size, with bushy eyebrows, and a French cast of countenance, but withal the most beautiful and benevolent look, so expressive of goodness and sweetness of disposition, as to attract the very heart of every one who looked in his face, and heard his language.

He is now gone to his high reward; and though we all are in no doubt that his lot is so glorious, still we may, with his many soaring friends, say—

"*Quis desiderio sit pudor, aut modus,*
Tam chari capitis!"

Memor.
(1839-02-16, 3:1)

2389. Death of the Right Hon. William Saurin.—Never, we may truly say, has it fallen to our lot to discharge a duty in every respect so painful as in announcing the demise of the illustrious and venerated William Saurin, which to the inexpressible grief of his family, and the irretrievable loss of his friends and his country, took place at 12 o'clock this day (Monday), at his residence in Stephen's-green. Mr. Saurin had been for some time in a declining state of health, but his demise was sudden and unexpected. He died without a pang, and resigned his gentle spirit into the hands of his Maker without a groan. Although in his 83d year, he retained to the last moment the full possession of his faculties, and maintained to the end that sweetness of temper and amiability of disposition which never forsook him during the stormy scenes in which he was for so many years a prominent actor.—*Evening Mail.* (1839-02-16, 4:1)

2390. Funeral of the Late Lord Clements.—The remains of this lamented young nobleman, whose death we announced on Saturday, were interred on Monday, in the family vault of St. Michan's Church.
The funeral was, as himself directed, private; but the deep and unfeigned grief with which the intelligence of his death has been received by all who knew him, of every rank and station, every religious and political opinion, bears testimony to the character of his life.
His services as a member of the legislature have been prematurely closed; but even in the short period of their exercise, sufficient was done to manifest his honest and liberal principles, his sound and unbiassed judgment, his talents and uncompromising independence, and his unpurchased devotion to his country. Nor was his private life less generally endeared. (1839-02-16, 4:5)

2391. Death.

The living beings of this world,
Around the precincts of the tomb,
Have dreadful visions o'er it hurled,
Of dark, and cold, and cheerless gloom!
Little the eye that's closed recks,
Of darkness, or of chill;
It is the living heart that breaks,
The dead, are calm and still.
The sleeping dust feels not "alone,"
Nor the senseless form "the grave;"
'Tis those who weep with anguish'd moan,
The one they'd die to save.

Yes! 'tis the living heart that breaks,
The dead no earth-born sorrow recks!
Death spareth neither age nor youth,
The floweret or the tree;
But, oh! he comes with startling truth,
And comes to set us free.
For what—what is it once to die?
Depending on a Saviour's love;
What, but in rest awhile to lie,
Then waken with his saints above;
Bend to the grave's restless power,
And lay the cumbered body down—
Give death and sin their passing hour,
And gain a living spirit's crown.

Em. Em. (1839-02-23, 4:1)

2392. The Wandering Piper.—The eccentric individual [Graham Stuart] known by this name died on Sunday night, at Mercer's hospital, in Dublin. It appears from his own account that he was induced many years since, for a bet of several thousand pounds, which were staked by a friend, to engage in his extraordinary mode of life. Had he relinquished the undertaking, the money would have been lost to his family. A similar result would have attended his supporting himself in any other way than by the precarious profits of his assumed profession during the stipulated period. Hence, although having expended large sums in charity, and on one occasion procured (it is asserted) a living in Scotland for a clergyman who had rendered him some assistance, here he died in indigence, as to his personal effects. By his death the bet is said to be cancelled; and it was his wish to die. He was admitted into Mercer's Hospital about three weeks since. By the kindness of the governors of that institution, he was allowed every reasonable indulgence adapted to his supposed better rank of life. Grateful to the medical officers of the hospital for the services rendered to him, he executed a testamentary document in its favor, probably, however, of but little value. As, however, he expressed great anxiety to communicate what he termed an important secret to a clergyman of the Church of England, and as he was visited by such, it is probable that something may be ascertained as to his rank and circumstances. The cause of his death was incurable disease of the lungs, aggravated by the effects of a severe injury of the hip, received many years since, and which latterly caused excruciating torments.—The injury was of a very unusual character, so much so, as to be without precedent, in the experience not only of the physicians and surgeons of Mercers Hospital, but also of the most eminent practitioners in Dublin, unconnected with that institution, who examined the body after death, and one of whom had attended the deceased as a private patient. (1839-03-02, 4:4)

2393. An inquest was held on Wednesday, on the body of a man named Peter Hughes, who dropped dead suddenly in the Church-square of this town. The cause of death as described by the medical attendant, was abscess on the liver, and we believe the jury returned a verdict accordingly. (1839-03-23, 3:4)

2394. Marriage of the Duchess of Kent and Lord Melbourne.—The preliminaries of the marriage of Lord Melbourne and the Duchess of Kent are, it is said, finally settled! The union is expected to take place in June. The Duchess of Kent will be 53 on the 17th of next August—Lord Melbourne 60 on the 15th instant.—*Globe*.

The *Globe* is too good authority for such an announcement as the above to leave any doubt of its truth. The report has been long prevalent; but the general impression was that her royal highness would scarcely descend so much below her present station, and at so mature an age, when girlish fantacies [sic] are supposed to have in a great measure lost their control. Assuming the account, however, to be fact, as we really must now assume it to be, all mystery vanishes as to the cause of the incapable Cabinet being so long forced upon the nation, and Lord Melbourne having obtained so free a run of the royal kitchen. We can hardly condemn the young Queen's conduct on the occasion. It was so very natural for her royal mother's inclination! We hope, however, that the noble viscount having once obtained the 30,000*l*. a-year and a Dukedom, we shall be spared any more sinister interference on his part with the interests of the state. His meddling would henceforth excite formidable jealousy. (1839-03-30, 4:2)

2395. Lieutenant General Sir H. Taylor, G.C.B.—There is every reason to believe that the report of the death of this gallant officer, the faithful and attached servant and friend of so many princes, is unfounded. Lord John Russell, it is said, the instant he heard the rumor, sent, with the most indecent haste, to the brethren of St. Katharine's for their charter, doubtless having an eye to the mastership himself. But it will be seen that even were there a vacancy, there is little chance of his lordship grabbing it. Respecting this point the *Morning Herald* remarked—

"The valuable place of Master of St. Katharine's Hospital, with the noble mansion attached to it in the Regent's Park, now vacant by the demise of Sir Herbert Taylor, is in the personal gift of her Majesty, unconnected with her ministers, though it is not improbable but one of them may have it."

It would be, doubtless, a very pretty sop for his fading lordship, but unfortunately the place is not in her Majesty's gift. By the will of the royal founder, the Mastership is in the patronage of the Queen Consort; should there be no such person, then of the Queen Dowager, and only in that of the sovereign when there are neither Queen Consort nor Queen Dowager. Her Majesty Adelaide, therefore, has the disposal of the patronage, and not Victoria; and we are quite sure that it will be properly bestowed.—*Age*. (1839-04-06, 1:3)

2396. Funeral of His Grace the Archbishop of Tuam.—Ballinasloe, Thursday Evening.—The mortal remains of the Archbishop of Tuam were this date deposited in the family vault at the ancient church-yard of Cruagh, near this town. At six o'clock this morning the funeral left Tuam, which is 25 miles from Ballinasloe, and was met on the road by large numbers of pedestrians, equestrians, as well as by persons in private carriages and hack coaches, and by the time it arrived here (one o'clock), the funeral procession had greatly increased, and the large numbers of all ranks and classes who thus came forward to testify their esteem for the dead, showed that his worth was estimated [sic] whilst living. The late Archbishop was a man, beyond all doubt, of the purest philanthropy and most universal benevolence, and that the poor of Tuam of all religious denominations, particularly the poor Catholics, as they were twenty to one in number, will long have cause to mourn his loss. His acts of charity and consideration for the poor could not be enumerated. Since the recent memorable storm he has had his men out directing and thatching the cabins of the poor throughout his own parish that were levelled by that awful visitation, the horrors of which will be long remembered. The hearse which contained the body, was followed by four coaches containing the principal mourners. In the first was the Rev. William Trench, son of the deceased, and some other near relatives. In the second carriage were Lord Clancarty, Admiral Trench and two of the archdeacon's sons. In the third were General Taylor, the brother-in-law of the deceased, and some members of his family. In the fourth were Hardiman Burke, late Mayor of Galway, and some of the clergymen of the diocese. In the next carriage followed his Grace's curates and domestic chaplain. The coffin, which was covered with a plain black velvet pall, was carried into the church-yard by ten clergymen of the diocese, supported on either side by the sons and near relatives of the deceased. The funeral service was read by the Rev. Mr. Purden, who also pronounced a beautiful and pathetic eulogy upon the virtues of the deceased. His Grace was in his 69th year; he had two sons and two daughters. One son was in the Army, and the other in the church. One of his daughters was married to the late Recorder of Galway; the other is unmarried, and is as remarkable as her father for unbounded acts of charity. (1839-04-06, 1:4)

2397. Marriage Law in different Countries.—A marriage countracted [sic] in a foreign country, by a fraudulent evasion of the laws of the state to which the parties belong might seem, on principle, to be void in the country of the domicil, though valid under the laws of the place where the marriage is contracted. Such are marriages contracted in a foreign state and, according to its laws, by persons who are minors, or otherwise incapable of contracting by the law of their own country. These cases seem to form exceptions to the general operation of the *lex loci contractus*, which no state is bound to admit where it injuriously affects its sovereign authority, or the rights and interests of its citizens. But according to the international marriage law of the British empire, a clandestine marriage in Scotland, or parties originally domiciled in England, who resort to Scotland for the purpose of evading the English Marriage Act, requiring the consent of parents or guardians, is considered valid in the English Ecclesiastical Courts. This jurisprudence is said to have been adopted upon the ground of its being a part of the general law and practice of Christendom, and that infinite confusion and mischief would ensue, with respect to legitimacy, succession, and other personal and proprietary rights, if the validity of the marriage contract was not to be determined by the law of the place where it was made. The same principle has been recognised between the different States of the American Union, upon similar grounds of public policy. On the other hand, the age of consent required by the French civil code is considered by the law of France as a personal quality of French subjects, following them wherever they remove, and consequently a marriage, by a Frenchman, within the required age, will not be regarded as valid by the French tribunal, though the parties may have been above the age required by the law of the place where it was contracted.—*Dr. Wheaton's Elements of International Law*.(1839-04-06, 4:5)

2398. The Late Archbishop of Tuam.—It is stated that in consequence of the late Dr. Trench having survived one day beyond the 24th March, his family will receive an addition to their property of from £20,000 to £30,000. His Grace's life was ensured for £50,000. (1839-04-13, 1:2)

2399. The marriage of Captain Smith, late of the 32d Regiment, brother of the Princess of Capua, with the Honourable Miss Abbot, sister to Lord Tenderden, will shortly be solemnized. (1839-04-13, 1:5)

2400. Death by Drowning—Kingstown, April 8.—One of the Port of Dublin pilots, Mich. Tallant, a fine seaman of eight-and-twenty, was drowned this morning, having missed his footing when in the act of leaping from his cutter on board of a schooner from a foreign port; and although he buffeted with the waves for a quarter of an hour, and every exertion was made by his comrades in the cutter, he sunk into the grave which annually swallows up so many of our brave, and too often undeplored, mariners. He has left a widow, but fortunately no children. The life of a pilot is but little known—it is one of extreme hardship and peril, and he is looked upon as nothing better than a "drunken swab" or a "sea hog." The first of these sobriquets is often attached to him by the generous libations liberally furnished to him when he has performed his duty well by the master of the ship he pilots; and as people often praise contraband goods more than those sold in the shops, so the pilot often thinks that the foreign wine and rum, offered to him so freely, is sweeter as it costs nothing, and would therefore be a sin to refuse it. This is the true origin of drunkenness among pilots, and it is certainly much to be deplored. (1839-04-13, 1:5)

2401. Inquest at Glasslough.—An inquest was holden in Glasslough, on a late hour on Tuesday, the 9th before Thomas Johnston and Thomas Anketell, Esqrs., on the body of Hugh Donlan, who had died the day previous. It appeared from the testimony of Dr. Richard Maffatt, that the deceased (Donlan) came to his death in consequence of several contusions of the body, caused by the passing of a cart wheel over his chest, which fractured some of the deceased's ribs and injured his lungs. The jury found a verdict to the same effect. The circumstances which were disclosed at the inquest appeared as follows:—On the evening of Monday, 8th, this unfortunate man had accompanied some persons as far as Glasslough, who were leaving the country, for America, when an attempt was made by a few individuals, to seize the goods for a trifling debt of about two pounds. The order for seizure having been demanded, and none having been produced, the party attempted to proceed, a scuffle ensued about the horse, which unfortunately terminated in the loss of life. (1839-04-13, 3:1)

2402. Earl of Caledon.—We lament that we have to record, this week, the death of the Right Hon. the Earl of Caledon, one of the most truly patriotic noblemen and best country gentlemen that the North of Ireland could boast of. His Lordship was in his 62d year, and until very lately had enjoyed most excellent health. To his spirited exertions this part of the country is mainly indebted for the construction of the Ulster Canal, of which he was the very life, and which is at this moment assisting to supply the town of Monaghan, and its neighbourhood, with flax-seed for the spring sowing, and which is extending its benefits far and wide. In his Lordship's own town of Caledon, the utility of this undertaking is most conspicuous, where his magnificent flour mill (the largest, we believe, in Ireland) is supplied with grain by its means, and the inhabitants with coals, and all the usual materials of mercantile profit. In the improvement of his tenantry there was no one his superior, witness the general appearance of his estate, where the numerous cottages, mostly built on the Swiss model, with two stories and precipitous roofs, fluted chimneys, and latticed windows, opening outwards, and with all the comfortable appliances so general in Germany, and so unusual in our land—all attest the purity of his taste, and his desire to raise their character. As a landlord, he was highly respected, and universally beloved; his tenantry, to a man, being thoroughly convinced that their interest and accommodation was no less an object of his constant solicitude, than the protection of his property. In performing the duty of a magistrate, he was upright, firm and impartial; and no one ever gave greater satisfaction than the Earl of Caledon, as Lord Lieutenant of the County of Tyrone, and as Colonel of that county regiment of militia. As a neighbour and friend, the affability and good nature, the sweetness of his temper, and the noble and general hospitalities of his table, endeared him to a large circle of acquaintances; and the cordial shake of the hand, now cold and in the grave, will be felt, in recollection, by all who have experienced the kindly pressure. Alas! the good man is no more!—and many and many a wet cheek will display the grip which he had on the hearts of all, who know his worth and prized his excellence.

Lord Caledon, graduated at Oxford, and in early life was Governor of the Cape of Good Hope; which office he administered to the advantage of the colony, and to the satisfaction of the government at home; nor should it be omitted that he was a staunch friend to the missionary interests in the south of Africa, exhibiting a rational zeal and a sound faith. He was, every way, a practical Christian.

On the resignation of his government of the Cape, Lord Caledon was united to the Lady Catherine York, second daughter to the late Earl of Hardwicke, by whom his Lordship had one child, the present Earl, now in his 27th year, and, until the demise (*continued...*)

2402, continued: ...of his father, M.P. for the county of Tyrone, and an officer in the Scotch Fusileer Guards. This amiable young nobleman had but ten days before Lord Caledon's death, returned from Canada, with despatches; and his inestimable father had just began to enjoy the society of his only child, under such endearing circumstances, when it pleased the Almighty to summon him to his high reward.

The Earl of Caledon was one of the Representative Peers for Ireland, and a Knight of the order of St. Patrick. His Lordship did not often speak in Parliament; but when he did he spoke well and to the purpose, and rarely, except upon some point involving the statistical interests of his country; his principles were Conservative, and he was always listened to with attention, because his judgment was sound, and his character upright and straight forward. He had a manly figure, and a good countenance, and benevolence shone in every feature. The charities of Lord and Lady Caledon were most munificent, and bounded only by sound discretion; and being very generally resident, they were perfectly and personally cognisant of most of the objects of their bounty; and though well founded hopes are entertained of the worth and goodness of his successor, still we may, and must indulge in the deepest sorrow for him whom we have lost. (1839-04-13, 3:2)

2403. Funeral of Lord Caledon.—On Monday, at seven o'clock, the procession of Lord Caledon's funeral commenced leaving Caledon Hall, in the following order:—

Curate. The Venerable Archdeacon Stopford. Curate;
8 Gents. with White Hatbands and Scarfs.
Two Physicians;
8 Gents with White Hatbands and Scarfs;
Hearse, drawn by four black horses;
Six Chief Mourners;
followed by near 400 of the Tenantry, with Hatbands, Scarfs, and Black Gloves;
with a concourse of spectators
from the neighbouring district
to the amount of at least 4,000;
after which followed
Fourteen Private Carriages.

The Clergy attended of all denominations. It having been understood the funeral was to be strictly private, a great number of the neighbouring gentry did not attend, or the concourse would have been still more numerous. As the corpse was being put into the church, one of his late Lordship's principal domestics, named Wm. Martin, dropped dead at the entrance of the church; excessive grief is supposed to have been the cause of his death, the poor fellow having been in his Lordship's service for many years.—*Newry Telegraph.* (1839-04-20, 3:2)

2404. The Keepsake.

That ringlet! how forcibly in memory's mirror bright,
Sad dreams, and visions of the past, it brings before my sight,
When life's young sky was cloudless, and it formed, though lonely now,
Part of the bright apparelling hung o'er an angel's brow.

That sunny lock, in memry's glass, reflects before my sight,
A fair form that's all array'd, like innocence, in white;
Her radient [sic] smile, and beaming eyes, and marble brow, are there,
Such as she was in life's young morn, so beautifully fair!

But she has gone! that much loved form, from earth has pass'd away,
All save that soft, smooth, burnished lock has moulder'd into clay,
Gone are those sunny tresses that oft lovingly were press'd,
Like a very shower of sunbeams, against my beating breast.

I gaze upon that ringlet, 'till it seems upbraidingly,
In mem'ry's ear, to whisper me, "Ah! weep no more for me;"
But oh! though many, many sad and weary years, have pass'd,
I never have forgotten her! my first love and my last—

Yes, though the bright but transient sun of her young life has set,
Her loveliness, her love, her truth, I never will forget!
Her memory still shall cheer me, till, life's sad journey o'er,
We meet beyond the grave, to be ne'er divided more.

Mask.

(1839-04-20, 4:1)

2405. The Hon. Somerset R. Maxwell, M.P. for the county of Cavan, brother of Lord Farnham, will shortly lead to the hymeneal altar, Dora, only surviving daughter of the Hon. Baron Pennefather. (1839-04-20, 4:3)

2406. Lieutenant Miller, 17th Royal Lancers, stationed at Colchester, will shortly lead to the hymeneal altar, Miss M'Mahon, eldest daughter of General Sir Thos. M'Mahon. Lieutenant Miller is possessed of extensive property, and will, on the decease of his grandfather, come into further large possessions in Scotland, and a title. Immediately on Sir Thos. M'Mahon's resigning the command at Portsmouth garrison, Lieutenant Miller will proceed to Ayrshire to select a house and grounds, shortly after which the nuptials will, we understand, take place. (1839-04-20, 4:3)

2407. We regret to say that Miss Blair died on Wednesday. (1839-04-20, 4:3)

2408. Suicide.—Lieutenant F.C. Fyers, H.M. 4th Light Dragoons, shot himself at Bommacore, in the East Indies, on the 14th of December last, while labouring under a depression of spirits. (1839-04-20, 4:4)

2409. We have been favoured, at our own request, with the following extract from a discourse preached in the Parish Church of Glasslough, on the 14th instant, being the first Sunday after the death of the lamented Earl of Caledon. The text was from the 7th chapter of Ecclesiastes, 4th verse:—

These reflections, I am sure you will all agree with me, are founded upon the sound general maxims of Christian duty; but, still, circumstances such as from time to time, occur near our doors, will bring more and more home to our hearts and understandings, the truth of the maxim, laid down by the wisest of men. Alas! it has pleased the Almighty to place the house of mourning close beside us; and though there may be a reasonable and scriptural ground for rejoicing, I mean in the hope and trust that our dear and inestimable neighbor is only gone from an earthly to a heavenly exaltation. Yet, we cannot but know that a widow's grief, and the sorrow of the fatherless, must, in the infirmities of human nature, bear hard for a season upon the individuals who, more than any others upon earth, must suffer by the sad deprivation! Nor is their loss confined to themselves: oh, no! the influence of the praise worthy conduct of the Earl of Caledon—the example set forth to all who viewed his useful life and habits—the proof of how well riches, power, rank and station could be dispensed, not for self aggrandizement, or to the bearing down with arrogant assumption those whose situation in society had been cast in an humbler scale,—the influence, I repeat, that this open picture must have had on all who contemplated it, will be felt, and with good effect too, for many a year to come; in fact as long as the memory of the good man will last with his personal survivors, and afterwards be handed down to posterity as a model of individual excellence, and a pattern of public benefactors. Nor was his duty as a country gentleman and landlord alone to be admired, I mean the exertions which he made to render all within the sphere of his influence industrious, orderly and happy; his domestic life was equally an object of praise and imitation, and in this I include his habitual demonstration of his respect for, and support of all the solemn observances of the Church of England. Never, while at home, did he omit his scrupulous attendance at the ordinance of the Lord's table; and the Sabbath day, was, as it ought to be, consecrated wholly to the cultivation of his immortal soul, and that of the family and domestics of his admirably regulated household, in all which he was well seconded by the inestimable partner of his happiness, now alas! the sorrowing survivor. It is true that we, immediately here, do not personally feel this great loss, but still in so close a vicinity, the example was precious, and its contemplation instructive. We are not, blessed be God, without our own objects of fine example and fostering kindness, and we well may hope for a long continuance of the same; nevertheless, the noble model of goodness, which so long held so distinguished a part in our locality, richly deserves any tribute we can offer of our veneration and respect, and a well grounded trust that there will be no diminution of the extent of the religious, the generous and humane duties—of those acts of mercy and goodness, which it has been our fortunate lot so long to witness, and admire! Truly did this good man "walk in the ordinances of the Lord, blameless." (1839-04-27, 3:2)

2410. On the Death of the Earl of Caledon.—"As the corpse was being put into the Church, one of his late Lordships principal domestics dropped dead at the entrance—excessive grief is supposed to have been the cause."—*Northern Standard.*

Slow tolls the solemn bell! and slow
Advance the mourning train—
Deep voices murmuring sadly flow,
And tears are checked in vain,
Sighs unrepressed heave faint and low,
From hearts which throb with pain,
As each vibration strikes the ear,
Or as the tearful eye observes the sable bier.

Deep tolls the bell!—that heavy bell!—
And often hath it tolled
The parted spirit's last farewell,
To earth so dim and cold,
And oft hath made the full heart swell
With feelings uncontrolled,
But never hath its accents sped
O'er mortal heart more good—o'er more illustrious dead!

Woe! to thee darkened Caledon
Cold sleeps thine honoured Lord
His final goal too soon is won,
Snapped quick life's silken cord
And his free heart and hand have done
Their blessings to award—
The shrine of pure philanthropy
Is "where the weary rest."—Woe Caledon to thee!

Weep! yea and tears become thee—weep!
Release each pent up sigh,
Stern is the heart which now could sleep
In stoic apathy—
Lo! one hath broken—anguish deep
Hath rent each earthly tie,
And now the thrilling notes are poured
O'er the cold corse of each—the servant and his Lord.

The Noble lieth proudly there,
Here sleeps the humbler heart—*(continued…)*

2410, continued:

Their spirits flee to mingle where
They never more shall part—
Oh! soul of love—thou couldst not bear
Thine idol should depart,
And boundedst from this "vale of tears"
To love again on high—above yon countless spheres.

Ashes to ashes! and be dust,
To kindred dust consigned,
The damp dark vault may hold in trust
The noble's clay confined;
The servant's meaner relics must
To dull earth be resigned,
But 'mid angelic hearts above
Alike their state and place—alike their joy and love.

J. B. P. (1839-04-27, 3:3)

2411. At a Meeting, held in Caledon, on the 15th day of April, 1839, the Archdeacon of Armagh in the Chair. —It was unanimously resolved, That the following circular be adopted, and distributed among the friends and admirers of the late lamented Earl of Caledon, and that a committee be appointed to receive subscriptions for the purpose of erecting a Testimonial in honour of his memory:—

"With feelings of deep sorrow, we have this day consigned to the tomb the mortal remains of the late lamented Earl of Caledon. A nobleman eminently distinguished by a rare combination of excellent qualities fitted to endear every private relation of life, to adorn every public station, and to confer lasting benefits upon the community of which he was a member.

"We presume not in this address to intrude into the sacred privacy of domestic affliction; neither is it our intention, as private friends, publicly to deplore the painful severance of those ties, which bound us in friendly union with so much excellence. But as members of the community, who enjoyed frequent opportunities of witnessing the judicious and well directed zeal, and of admiring the beneficial results of the untiring exertions of a true friend in his country, we feel justified in becoming the humble instruments of drawing forth a public expression of what we believe to be, the general sentiment of admiration of an exalted public character; and of holding up to general imitation, by a permanent memorial, an illustrious example of genuine patriotism.

"We propose, therefore, to perpetuate, by a public testimonial, the memory of a man whose ruling principle was zeal for the improvement of the social condition of all within the sphere of his influence,—a zeal tempered by prudence, and rendered effectual by sagacity to discern, and ability to open out, new sources of prosperity,—by munificence in forwarding the execution of beneficial plans,—and by perseverance in overcoming no common difficulty.

"This wise master-builder placed the superstructure of national prosperity upon the solid foundations of morality and religion. He established Schools for Education on Scriptural Principles, and was a liberal contributor to the erection of places of Public Worship. He endeavoured to show by the example of a happy tenantry that industry, morality and religion can exalt the humblest rank; whilst he proved by his own example, that Christian piety and unaffected humility are the brightest ornaments of an exalted station.

"As a Magistrate, by constant residence and regular personal attendance upon the administration of justice in his own particular district, he induced its inhabitants to regard the law as a guardian and protector and not as an enemy. As Lord Lieutenant of the County of Tyrone, he inculcated impartiality and forbearance. And by recommending the fittest persons for the Magisterial Office, and by conciliating the co-operation of an upright and independent Magistracy already established, their united efforts did not so much enforce the law, as by substituting in place of fear, the moral influence of conscientious obedience, render its enforcement unnecessary;—a model of industry, good order, and peace.

"If the dictates of sound policy and fervent gratitude prompt us to erect testimonials to Naval and Military heroes, who defeat the external enemies of our country, labouring to interrupt its peace, to destroy its prosperity and to overthrow our altars,—shall not like honor be paid to the patriot whose life was spent in converting subjects into friends, in increasing the prosperity of his country, in consolidating peace, and in building up our altars." (1839-05-04, 2:5)

2412. At an Adjourned Meeting, held at Dungannon, on Monday, the 22d of April, 1839, for the purpose of commemorating, by a Public Testimonial, the many virtues and estimable qualities of the lamented Late Earl of Caledon:—

Moved by the Hon. and Very Rev. Dean Maud, and seconded by Robert Montgomery Moore, Esq., that William Stuart Richardson, Esq., D.L., be requested to take the chair.

Moved by the Rev. R.N. Horner, and seconded by the Hon. A. Stuart, that the Address, read by the Archdeacon of Armagh, be adopted.

Moved by Edward Evans, Esq., seconded by George Buchanan, Esq., that the following be appointed a Sub-Committee, with power to add to their number, five to be a quorum—

Sir Hugh Stewart,
The Hon. A. Stewart,
R. Mongtomery Moore, Esq.
W. Stuart Richardson, Esq.
Archdeacon Stopford,
Rev. Francis Gervais,
Rev. Richard Stuart,
Rev. Thomas Stack,
Rev. R.N. Horner,
Rev. Thos. Carpendale,
Jas. Eyre Jackson, Esq., J.P.

Henry Pole, Esq., J.P.
Robert Hazzard, Esq.
Daniel Auchinleck, Esq.
Samuel Magill, Esq.
Charles Richardson, Esq.
Robert Evans, Esq.
Jno. Fallas, Esq.
Robert Foster, Esq.
George Buchanan, Esq.
James King, Esq.

Moved by the Rev. Richard Stuart, and seconded by Alex. Mackenzie, Esq., that a Subscription List be now opened for the purpose of erecting a Testimonial to the late Earl of Caledon.

Moved by the Rev. Francis Gervais, and seconded by James Eyre Jackson, Esq. that the Gentlemen present, and those named on the Committee, be requested to use their influence in obtaining Subscriptions in their respective neighbourhoods.

Moved by Robert M. Moore, Esq., and seconded by John Falls, Esq., that the Hon. A. Stewart be requested to act as Treasurer, and that Wm. Murdoch, of Annaroe, and Edward Golding, of Lime Park, Esqrs. be requested to act as Secretaries.

Moved by the Rev. Thomas Carpendale, and seconded by Danl. Auchinleck, Esq., that the following Bankers be appointed to receive subscriptions for the above purpose—

In England—Messrs. Coutts and Co., Strand, London.

In Ireland—The Belfast and Provincial Banks and their branches.

Moved by the Rev. Edward Stopford, and seconded by James Lindsay, Esq., that a General Meeting of the subscribers by held at Dungannon, on the 6th day of August, for the purpose of determining upon the species of Testimonial, and the place where it shall be erected.

Moved by Robert Foster, and seconded by James Scott, Esq., that the above Resolutions be Published in the *Dublin Evening Mail*, *Evening Post*, *Newry Telegraph*, *Ulster Times*, *Londonderry Sentinel* and *Northern Standard*.

Moved by Sir Hugh Stewart, and seconded by Major Humphreys, that Wm. Stuart Richardson, Esq., do now leave the Chair, and the Hon. and Very Rev. Dean Maude be called thereto, and that the marked thanks of this Meeting be given to Wm. Stuart Richardson, for his dignified and very proper conduct in the Chair. (1839-05-04, 3:3)

2413. Fatal Accident.—On Wednesday, Miss Byrne, a most interesting and intelligent young lady, daughter of John Byrne, Esq., of Rosmaskee, left her father's house about one o'clock, for the purpose, as was supposed, of taking a short walk, and at four o'clock, was found drowned in a rivulet at a short distance.—*Ballyshannon Herald.* (1839-05-04, 4:3)

2414. Death of Handcock Montgomery, Esq.—It is indeed a sad and grievous duty to add to the long, long bills of mortality a name so valued and so dear in every relation of life—in the domestic circle, the social board, and the hour of need—as that of the gentleman whose name appears above. But the ways of an all-wise though chastening Providence are inscrutable as they are beneficient, and our duty, as Christians, is a meek and holy submission to his will. Mr. Montgomery departed this life on Wednesday, the 10th instant, at his residence in Dublin, where he went a short time since to reside with his lady, to whom he has been united little more than twelve months. He was the fourth son of the late Major Alexander Montgomery of Bessmount Park, near this town, and his courteous and urbane manners secured to him the affections of every class of society. In this neighbourhood the most universal regret and the most sincere sorrow are felt for his untimely fate. The body, which is on its way from Dublin, will be interred in the family vault in the church of Tyholland, this evening. (1839-05-11, 3:1)

2415. Married, on Saturday last, at St. George's Church, Hanover-square, London, by the Bishop of Gloucester, John Royland Smith, Esq., Captain of the 6th Dragoon Guards, or Carabineers, son of the late Grice Blakeney Smyth, Esq., of Ballynatren [Ballynatray], county of Waterford, to the Hon. Catherine Alice Abbot, youngest daughter of the late, and sister of the present Lord Tenterden. (1839-05-18, 2:4)

2416. Mr. Law, brother of Lord Ellenborough, is about to be married to Miss Rochfort, daughter of Colonel Rochfort, a gentleman of large fortune in the county of Carlow. (1839-05-18, 2:4)

2417. Suicide.—A most determined act of self-destruction was perpetrated on Thursday last, within a mile of this town, Mr. Henry Addy, of Little Footstown, near Sydden, in the county of Meath. The deceased had gone on a visit the previous day to his brother-in-law, Mr. P. Heany, who resides at Oldbridge, where something occurred to irritate him, when he immediately went to that part of the river Boyne adjoining the Obelisk, and stripped off his coat and hat and plunged into the current. Two men who witnessed the catastrophe attempted to save him, but one of them was nearly drowned. The deceased was of a warm temperament, and there can be no doubt but he committed the act whilst in a state of insanity. Mr. Addy was about forty years old, and from his many social qualities, his premature and melancholy death is much deplored by a large circle of friends. He was respectably connected in the neighbourhood of Ardee. An inquest was held on the following day, and a verdict returned accordingly.—*Drogheda Journal.* (1839-05-25, 1:4)

2418. The Late Gideon Ouseley, Methodist Missionary.—We have been favored by the kindness of a friend with the following brief and affectionate memoir of the good and pious man whose name and calling we have prefixed.

This venerable and zealous minister of the gospel died in the city, after an illness of short duration, on Tuesday, the 14th instant, in the 78th year of his age. During 47 years, he was ceaselessly engaged in the arduous and important duties of his sacred mission. He was universally known, beloved, and respected by persons of every denomination. The announcement of his death will cause many hearts to mourn.

His first religious impressions were produced in the year 1791, by the careful perusal of the Holy Scriptures. He has often mentioned Young's works—the "Night Thoughts," especially his "Infidel Reclaimed," and "The Centaur not Fabulous," as singularly beneficial to him at that period.

Soon after he experienced the salutary influence of Christian truth, he became deeply impressed with the feeling that it was his duty to interest himself in the promotion of the spiritual good of others. Accordingly in the year 1792, he commenced his career as an out-door preacher. His first address was delivered at a church-yard, at a funeral, to a vast multitude assembled on the occasion. From thenceforward, in the fairs and markets, towns and villages, he continued to read the Holy Scriptures, and enforce divine truth with persuasive energy. He generally, when preaching in the open air, availed himself of his intimate knowledge of the Irish language to engage attention and instruct his hearers in Divine truth, through the medium of a well understood dialect. Numberless instances might be adduced, and persons who, through the blessing of God upon his persevering exertions, have been savingly converted from the soul-destroying Popish heresy, to truth as it is in Christ; and some of those persons are themselves at present engaged in the ministry of the Gospel in the Established and other Protestant Churches.

During the course of his long arduous career as a Christian missionary, he encountered, without dismay, difficulties of no ordinary description. To him might be applied, with truth, the apostle Paul's description of himself—"In labors abundant, in deaths oft, in journeyings often, in perils in the country; but none of these things moved him, neither counted he his life dear unto himself, so that he might finish his course with joy, and the ministry which he had received of the Lord Jesus, to testify the Gospel of the grace of God." Instances without number might be cited of his courage and fortitude, and of the meekness and patience with which he endured sufferings. On one occasion, some years since, while preaching in the town of Loughrea, in the County of Galway, he stood with his back to the wall which encloses the barrack; the mob, instigated, it is said by the priest, began pelting him with stones; but finding that this did not discompose him, they broke through the circle formed by the few friends who surrounded the chair on which he stood, and pulled him down. With difficulty he was got into the guard-room of the barrack, upon which the sergeant caused the gate to be closed. The mob, thus disappointed, became outrageous, cast stones over the wall, and threatened to pull down the barrack if the preacher was not given to them. The officer of the day was applied to, and he told Mr. Ouseley that he feared it would, under the circumstances, be contrary to his duty to permit him to remain. Mr. Ouseley, supposing that it would involve a breach of military discipline to shelter him, replied that he would go forth, assured that the God whom he served would save him from the power of his enemies. The officer, however, thought it better to consult the officer in command of the regiment, upon whose authority he ordered the men to arms, and then addressed the mob with effect, and caused them to disperse. On another occasion, while preaching in the streets of Monaghan, a Roman Catholic got so near Mr. Ouseley, as to spit full in his face; some of those present interfered, and were laying hold of the assailant, when Mr. Ouseley, who had by this time wiped his face, interposed and excused the man, and begged that he might be allowed to remain to hear what he had to say. On another occasion, while preaching in the street of Tuam, he had two of his teeth knocked out by a severe blow from a piece of hard turf thrown at him; he spit the teeth into his hand, and after a short pause, proceeded with his discourse without interruption, except occasionally to empty his mouth of the blood.

So fully was Mr. Ouseley's mind impressed with the solemn importance of the work in which he was engaged, and the vast value of the souls of men, that he could not be persuaded that all who wanted warning would be found to attend in any house to hear.

He therefore sought those who otherwise would not hear. Nor did he intermit this mode of preaching, when rebellion raged in the country. Regardless of danger, and uninfluenced by the temporizing prudence of cowardly professors, he affectionately and persuasively warned man to "flee from the wrath to come."

His zeal was not limited to Ireland; he frequently visited England and Scotland; and, perhaps, no preacher of the Gospel in modern times has been more abundantly successful; thousands were the crown of his rejoicing in the Lord; he travelled many thousand miles annually, and preached generally three sermons each day.

"*We fools counted his life madness.*"

He possessed a clear and comprehensive mind, stored with various learning, and improved by reading and close thinking; but all his acquirements were brought to bear upon the great concerns of eternity; his mode of address was simple, artless, and colloquial; he studied plainness of speech, and often observed, that as the larger number in every congregation could best understand truth when plainly expressed—if they understood what was said, those of a higher order of mind were sure to understand; he deprecated a gaudy and pompous style of uttering religious truth, because hearers, instead of judging themselves, were judging of the speaker; and, instead of admiring the Saviour, they admired the sermon, or were exposed to the temptation of doing so.

His spirit was truly Catholic; he was a stranger to sectarian asperity. To all, of every denomination, who love our Lord Jesus Christ, he was affectionately attached—not stumbling at non-essential peculiarities; and, although as a preacher and an author, he waged an interminable warfare against the soul-destroying dogmas of Popery, and against the compact confederacy of its priesthood, by which the spiritual interests and civil liberties of mankind are trenched upon—yet in his address to Roman Catholics, not one offensive word escaped his lips. He pitied them because he believed they were deceived—and he patiently instructed them without wounding their prejudices.

He was firm in his defence of truth—like a beaten anvil, he yielded not; yet he was gentle and easy to be entreated. In his journeyings, he was necessarily thrown into society of all grades; but whether with the rich or with the poor, his conduct and spirit were the same. He never forgot that he was a minister of God; and, as such, it was his joy and delight to speak to every man, in season and out of season, words by which they might be saved. Whether in the house or whether in the street—in his hours of retirement, and in his public ministrations—he was constantly actuated by the same spirit. When he spoke, his conversation was in heaven; and the hearts of his intense friends still burn within them on every recollection of the gracious words that proceeded from his mouth.

"*To means of grace the last respect he show'd,*
Nor sought new paths, as wiser than his God:
Their sacred strength preserved him from extremes,
Of empty outside, or enthusiast dreams."

To hoary age, he continued his active and laborious services, doing the work of an evangelist; within a few days of his confinement by the affliction which terminated his valuable life, he preached in the town of Mountmellick, three times on the same day; one service was in the open air. During the continuance of the affliction, although he suffered intense pain, not one murmur of impatience escaped his lips; on the contrary, he was enabled to praise God, and to rejoice in the hope of the glory of God. In a word, the grace of God, and the promises of Holy Scripture, which he delighted to recommend to others, in life and in death, were the support and rejoicing of his own heart.
(1839-06-01, 4:4)

2419. The Late Lord Langford.—On Friday last, the mortal remains of the late Right Honorable Hercules Langford Rowley, Baron Langford, of Summer-hill House, county of Meath, were deposited in the catacombs of the Harrow-road Cemetery. The funeral, in consonance with the wishes of the deceased, was strictly private. The only connections of the late nobleman present were Lord Langford, (a fine youth about 14 years of age,) his Lordship's brother, the Hon. Hercules Langford Boyle Rowley, their uncle, the Hon. Richard Rowley, and Charles Egan, Esq. The burial service was most impressively performed in the chapel of the cemetery by the Chaplain, the Rev. Joseph Trigger, M.A. By the demise of the late Baron, the following, amongst other noble families, will be placed in mourning—The Marquis Wellesley, the Duke of Wellington, the Visct. Burghersh, the Earl of Longford, and the Marquis of Headford.
(1839-06-15, 2:3)

2420. Estates of Lunatics.—The Lord Chancellor has stated that all applications for expending money on estates of lunatics must in future be made and approved of by the court of Chancery, before the expense is incurred, or it will not be allowed afterwards.
(1839-06-15, 3:3)

2421. The Corry Monument.—The foundation-stone of the public Monument to the memory of the late Trevor Corry, Esq., was laid on Monday, by the Rev. Dr. Campbell, Vicar of Newry, in the presence of a very large and respectable concourse of the inhabitants. (1839-06-22, 1:2)

2422. The Corry Monument.—(From the *Newry Telegraph.*)—On Monday the 17th inst., as announced in our last publication, the foundation-stone of the Corry Monument was laid by the Rev. Dr. Campbell, Vicar of Newry, who previously thereto addressed a large number of gentlemen, and many of the respectable inhabitants who had assembled to witness the interesting ceremony. The Rev. Doctor's address was as follows:—

Gentlemen,—We are assembled here for the purpose of laying the first stone of a monument to commemorate the private virtues and the public character of our late much-beloved and much-respected townsman, Trevor Corry, Esq. I have the honor of having been appointed by the Committee this day to perform the ceremony. In willingly and cheerfully undertaking the office, my only regret is, that it was not delegated to one better qualified to give expression, on this very interesting occasion to those feelings of sincere respect which they, and I trust we all entertain for the virtues and public character of our deceased friend. It is not my intention to dwell at any length in delineating either his private virtues or his public character. They are both well known to you all; and the honorable testimony to record them is sufficient proof that they are duly appreciated. (*continued...*)

2422, continued: ...Whether we regard him in the discharge of the various and interesting duties of private life, or in the performance of the more extended and not less arduous public duties as a magistrate, we find his character equally estimable and honorable. His firm and independent principles, his high and delicate sense of honor, his courtesy and urbanity of manner, and his private virtues in the discharge of the relative duties of life, endeared him to a widely-extended circle of friends. Well-versed in the office of the magistracy, he executed its duties for a space of 35 years, embracing some trying periods in the history of our country, with a devotion and assiduity, with a firmness of decision, and an uprightness and integrity of conduct, which justly merited the esteem of the community.

Famam extendere faetia
Hoc virtutis opus.

It is to commemorate and to perpetuate, by a permanent mark of our esteem, those virtues and that public character that we are now assembled. I shall not further trespass on your time, but proceed to lay the first stone of a Monument to his memory—first beseeching Almighty God to pour down the blessing upon us all, that in all our works, begun, continued, and ended in Him, we may glorify His holy name, through Jesus Christ our Lord.

Dr. Campbell then proceeded to lay the stone, in which a mortice had been cut for the purpose of receiving a phial that contained a scroll of parchment, on which had been engrossed the Address presented to Mr. Corry, 23d June, 1838, his Answer, and a Latin Inscription, as under:

Trevor Corry, Armigero,
Gratulatio.

Quingentorum Newriensis civium nominbus affixis xiii. Cal. Jul., millesimo octingentesimo trigesimo octavo, ad id selectis oblata fuit.

Hujusce exemplum infra positum necnon ejusdam praeclari viri responsum.

Hoc Momentum, quod eximias animi virtutes etiamque in rempublicam official, quibus pie functus est quinque et tringinta annos, commemorat, civium impensis gratorum extractum fuit.

Haud ali mercede affectus, praeter hanc virtutis honorumque comprobationis, obit Die Dominico xi Cal. August. Aetatis sexagesimo et tertio anno, 1838.

The ceremony gave general satisfaction; and we have no doubt that a monument will be erected worthy of the high deserts of the revered individual whose memory it is purposed to honor and perpetuate, and which will be creditable to the inhabitants, and ornamental to the Northern approach of Newry. (1839-06-22, 2:4)

2423. A horse, the property of Richard Robinson, Esq., of Parsonstown, drawing timber, ran furiously through that place, on Saturday, and killed Mary Dooley, aged 97. (1839-06-29, 1:4)

2424. The Highlander's Bride. (From the *Sunbeam.*)

It was evening,—and calmly the sun's setting ray
Beamed forth a farewell to the lingering day;
And a golden and rich flood of radiance threw
Over Glenallan's waters, translucent and blue.

On the banks of those waters, so tranquil and deep,
Where the whispers of evening seemed softly to sleep,
Sat a chieftain of Scotland, his hounds by his side,
And clasped in his arms his young beauteous bride.

Her hands o'er the strings of a mountain-harp strayed,
As, tuning its soft notes, a light air she played,
And her voice, like the breath of a spirit of song,
Thus warbled, as glanced her white fingers along:

"Oh, welcome, my own love,
Oh, welcome again;
Free and fleet as the falcon
That sweeps o'er the plain.
Long time have I waited
My true love to see,
For nought gives me pleasure
Like meeting with thee.

"Oh, welcome, my own love,
With bonnet and plume;
As the sunbeam dispelleth
The shadows and gloom,
So the shade o'er my spirit
Thou turnest to light.
And when darkness is around me,
Thou makest it bright.

"Then, welcome, my own love,
So faithful and true;
Oh, welcome again to thy
Deep waters blue:
The music and song,
With the harp's melody,
Shall ever be wakened,
My on [sic] love, for thee!"

Theodore.

(1839-06-29, 4:1)

2425. A boy died of hydrophobia at Cork, last week, from the bite of a dog. (1839-07-06, 1:1)

2426. Bequests. [At the General Synod of Ulster, Belfast, Tuesday, June 25.]—Dr. Cooke mentioned that a bequest, which undoubtedly had been left to the Synod of Ulster so long ago as 1726, and the will relating to which was in their hands at present, had been seized, and 700*l.* a-year had been quietly enjoyed by another body ever since. He had no doubt it could be recovered by ordinary process at the Quarter Sessions, and if his congregation, were young enough, he would try it in that way, but it must be a congregation of not more than four years.

After some conversation it was resolved to reserve the matter for interlocution and take the opinion of counsel. (1839-07-06, 1:4)

2427. Sudden Death of the Earl of Lucan.—The demise of the Earl of Lucan, which occurred at his residence, Serpentine-terrace, Knightsbridge, on Sunday last, was, we understand, awfully sudden. Soon after ten o'clock, having partaken of breakfast and made a hearty meal, he proceeded as was his custom, into his library, where he had not been many minutes before he was discovered in a dying state. Medical assistance was instantly sent for, but the noble Earl expired in about half an hour afterwards. His lordship's eldest son, Lord Bingham, was also immediately sent for.—*London Mercury Post.* (1839-07-06, 2:1)

2428. A wall fell lately, near Omagh, upon some workmen who were undermining it, and one man, named Clarke, was killed upon the spot. (1839-08-10, 1:1)

2429. The Lieutenant Governorship of the Isle of Wight is vacant by the death of that aged and respected veteran, Gen. Mervyn Archdall. (1839-08-10, 1:1)

2430. On the 2d instant, at Ardglass, a young man, named M'Cormick, was killed by a rock, weighing nearly three tons, falling and carrying him along with it into the sea. (1839-08-10, 2:2)

2431. A man named Barrington lately died, at Dundalk, from cholic, occasioned by drinking sea-water. He had been previously in a bad state of health. (1839-08-10, 2:2)

2432. On the 30th ult. Bryan Campbell fell from his horse at Ballinduff, near Dundalk, and fractured his skull, from the consequence of which he died next day. (1839-08-10, 2:2)

2433. J.B. OBrien, Esq., J.P., for Tipperary, was drowned in the river Suir, on Wednesday, by the upsetting of a boat. (1839-08-10, 2:2)

2434. On Monday last, the remains of the lamented and universally beloved, General Archdall, were interred at Templemaghery, in the family cemetery. The entire of the Nobility and Gentry of the country, the whole of the Archdall estate's tenantry, and a great portion of the respectable farmers of the county generally, were in attendance on the melancholy occasion. (1839-08-10, 2:2)

2435. Melancholy Accident.—Loss of Six Lives.—Kilkeel, 6th August.—An accident, attended with the most lamentable consequences, occurred here on the 1st inst. A number of boats went to sea for the purpose of fishing; during the day it commenced to blow a strong gale from the south; owing to the heavy sea they found it difficult to get ashore, and, melancholy to relate, one of them upset, and the crew, consisting of six men, met a watery grave. This awful calamity has spread a general gloom over the inhabitants of this part of the country. What renders it more distressing is, that the boatmen drowned left six widows and twenty-three orphans without any means of support. No trace of the bodies has yet been found. A meeting was held this day in the Court-house, Armor Boyle, Esq., Seneschal, in the Chair, for the purpose of raising a fund for their relief. The greatest liberality was shown by all present, and upwards of £20 was subscribed on the spot, and arrangements were made to collect further subscriptions, which are expected to amount to a considerable sum. The names of the men who perished are John Chambers, John Morgan, Hugh Cassidy, John Duff, William Curran, and Daniel Cunningham—all married. (1839-08-10, 2:3)

2436. Sudden Death.—An awfully sudden death occurred at Warrenpoint, on Friday evening, the 26th ult. Captain Neill, of the ship *Edward Reid* (which vessel had arrived the day previously from St. John's) was standing close to the shore, waiting for a boat to return to his vessel, when, suddenly, he tottered and fell, without having uttered a single word. A medical gentleman promptly hastened to the spot, and cut one or two veins; but in vain! life was extinct. The deceased had the appearance of enjoying good health. He had written that very day to Belfast, inviting his wife to join him at Warrenpoint.—*Newry Telegraph.*

(1839-08-10, 2:3)

2437. An inquest was held before Robert Murray, Esq., Coroner, on the 3d instant, on view of the body of a man named Patrick Tierney, who was found drowned in a hole, in the parish of Dona, near this town. (1839-08-10, 3:1)

2438. Melancholy Accident.—Ardglass, 2d August, 1839.—As one of the Cornish fishing boats was beating out of the harbour yesterday, a heavy sea running at the time, with the wind blowing in, it missed stays, and drifted on that part of the battery of the new pier, which had been carried away. Crowds of people immediately ran to the spot to render assistance; a line was got ashore from the boat, to where a number of people were collected on the very extremity of the ruins of the pier, by which means the boat was partly got off, when, sad to relate, a large stone, about three tons weight, which had been loosened by successive storms, gave way, and in its fall, carried a young man, named M'Cormack, along with it into the deep, in a moment, Mr. John Norris, Coast Guard, an inhabitant of the town, plunged in, and rescued the poor man from a water grave; but, alas! on being brought on shore, it was found, that in the fall, his arm was clean taken off by the shoulder, his ribs and legs broken, and his chest compressed. Dr. Harrison was in instant attendance, and had him conveyed to a proper place, where every attention was paid him; he survived, however, only a few hours. M'Cormack was a native of Ballynahinch, and a remarkably quiet, inoffensive man; and, in the season, followed the herring trade. He has left a wife and six small children to lament his fate.—*Down Recorder.* (1839-08-10, 3:2)

2439. On Wednesday last, in St. George's Church, Hanover-square by the Rev. Lord Wriotheseley Russell, Hamilton Gorges, Esq., to Miss Gertrude Bennett, niece to the Lord of Tankerville, and grand-niece to the Duke of Bedford. After the ceremony, the happy couple returned to Lord Tankerville's residence in Grosvenor-square, where a splendid dejeune was prepared. Amongst those present were the Marchioness of Abercorn, the Earl and Countess Jersey, and the Ladies Villiers, Lord, Lady, and Miss Wriothesley, Lord William Russell, Lord De Freyne, Mr. and Mrs. Russell, Mrs. Steuart, Mr. French, M.P, Miss Gore, &c. &c. After the dejeune, the bride and bridegroom proceeded to the Villa of the Duke of Bedford, at Camden Hill, where they are to pass the honey-moon. (1839-08-17, 1:2)

2440. The *Limerick Chronicle* says—On Monday the Duke de Roviego will lead to the hymeneal altar Miss Stamer, daughter and co-heiress of the late Colonel Stamer, Carnelly, county Clare. The Lady being a Protestant, and the Duke a Roman Catholic, the ceremony will in the first instances be performed by the Rev. Mr. Young, of Clare, and afterwards by the Rev. Mr. O'Gorman, P.P. The Duke is son of Savary, Duke Roviego, Chief of Police at Paris, under the Bonaparte dynasty, and successor to the celebrated Fouche in that department. (1839-08-17, 1:2)

2441. Fashions for August.—Bridal Dress.—White lace robe over white *pou de Soie*, the ground is richly flowered, and the border trimmed with two flounces placed near each other, the other one is looped at the side by a knot of white ribbon with long floating ends. The *corsage* is tight to the shape, pointed at bottom, cut en V at top, and edged with lace standing up. The sleeve tight and without ornament at the top, with the lower part very full, descending considerably below the elbow, and finished by a ruffle. The hair is dressed in a low knot behind, parted on the forehead, and arranged in a profusion of full but rather stiff curls at the sides. The bridal veil of *gaze zephir* is entwined round the knot of hair at the back of the head, and a sprig of orange blossom is attached at the side; a wreath of roses, disposed *en diademe*, completes the *coiffure*. (1839-08-17, 1:2)

2442. Mysterious Occurrence. (From the *Vindicator.*) —On Sunday 11th August, as some persons were making a grave, in Kilrush grave-yard, for the body of a man of the name of White, that was to be interred that evening, and after raising up the remains of the coffin, directly underneath the one they had just raised, which appeared to have been buried much deeper than was customary in years past. After digging about it, they discovered it to be a square box, which increased the surprise of those present; and on raising up one of its sides, it was found to be made of inch timber, unplaned, about 5 feet 5 inches in length, and three in breadth. On removing some of the earth, of which it was full, they discovered the remains of what must have been a very strong man, many of the bones, the shoulder blades, the arm and thigh bones, &c. being of great size. With these, were thrown out part of a hat, to the inside of which hair was sticking; also pieces of woollen cloth, &c. which left a strong impression that the man was murdered. It is also a curious fact, that the spot in which the box was found was very convenient to an old stile which formerly led into this burying-ground. (1839-08-24, 1:2)

2443. The bridal dress of the Duchess de Roviego was Limerick lace, which has, for some months, in the court and fashionable circles, eclipsed all others. (1839-08-24, 1:3)

2444. On Monday last a servant maid of Mr. M'Kay, of Bridge-street, Dundalk, was drawing two beautiful little twin sisters of her master's along the road, about half a mile from the town, when they were met by two carts, the foremost of which upset the little carriage, and before the girl could prevent it, the second cart passed over the body of one of the little innocents and killed it. (1839-08-24, 1:4)

2445. On Sunday, the 11th instant, as a young man named M'Mahon, from Inniskeen, in the county of Monaghan, was riding on the Blackrock strand, near Dundalk, his horse became restive, and threw the unfortunate rider, at the same time giving him a kick in the chest which killed him on the spot.—*Drogheda Argus*. (1839-08-24, 1:4)

2446. Kingscourt, August 16, 1839.—An accident of a very distressing nature, attended with the loss of life, occurred here a few days since, arising from the incautious use of fire-arms. The deceased, a young gentleman named Henry Bartrim, went to some of the adjoining covers, the property of Mr. Irwin, of the Plantation, for the purpose of shooting rabbits, and as he did not return for a considerable time, the family became alarmed, when intelligence was brought to them that he was found lying near the demesne of Cabra, which belongs to Colonel Pratt, in a state of insensibility, covered with blood. He was carried home, and notwithstanding all that medical skill could do, he expired. There was no inquest held, but for what reason the police and authorities of Kingscourt best know. It is said that the cause of his death arose from his placing the gun near his breast to conceal it, when it went off, and lodged the contents in different parts of the body, perforating the lungs and other vital parts.—*Drogheda Conservative*. (1839-08-31, 1:3)

2447. The Bridesmaid.

Bring roses—bring roses to deck the young bride;
Bring roses to crown her in flush of her pride:
Weave the gay crimson flower 'midst that raven dark hair;
Bind the pearls round that brown which so rivals them there.

Shade that beautiful neck with those ringlets so soft,
Which these hands have arranged with such pleasure so oft.
Now, reach me that veil to o'ershadow these charms;
And, ere thou'rt another's let me rest in those arms!

"Oh, sister! I dress'd thee: and, dearest! the heart
Which joys in thy joy is breaking to part
Mine own, only sister, companion, and friend.
Thou goest where thy footsteps no longer I'll tend;
Of thy voice I no longer shall hear the sweet tone,
And thy thoughts, heart, and feelings another shall own."

She ceased: and that bride, in her beauty and charms,
Looks lovelier still as she wept in her arms.

[From the *Book of the Dartrey Troubadors.*]
(1839-08-31, 4:1)

2448. The Widow.

She still exists: but life has lost its charm;
The vital spark of happiness is fled.
Oh, say not time shall yet, with wizard arm,
Unbind the chains which link her to the dead.

Mark you! the marble whiteness of that cheek;
The saddened lustre of that soft blue eye
Faint glimmering, like the pale illuming streak
Of sickly moonshine, through a clouded sky.

Oh! there's a summer of the heart, when all
The flowers of pleasure shed their passing bloom;
And there's a winter when the petals fall:
And sunny thoughts are lost, and all is gloom.

Hers was a love to vulgar minds unknown—
A love that falls not with the failing breath;
That deep pure feeling which survives alone
To shed its fragrance o'er the vase of death.

His was a kindred soul whose life was love—
A bright reflection of eternal light:
Awhile it sparkled and then soared above,
To share the glories hid from mortal sight.

No costly urn contains his sacred dust;
It lies embosomed in a fragrant sod
By angels guarded, till, with the just,
He wears the sun-clad image of his God.

And she, his widow'd bride, still lingers here
Like some fair flow'ret on a desert cast.
Nor aught on earth can charm her eye or ear;
Her dreams of earth-born happiness are past.

But there are visions left her brighter far
Than those the mem'ry of the past can bring,
Bliss which the hand of death no more can mar,
Draughts of unmixed delight from life's exhaustless spring.

[From the *Book of the Dartrey Troubadors.*]
(1839-08-31, 4:1)

2449. We regret to announce the demise of the Countess of Aboyne, which took place on Saturday. Her ladyship was the eldest daughter of the Marquis of Conyngham. (1839-09-07, 1:4)

2450. Last Saturday night, about half-past eight o'clock a sailor, named Neal M'Tormick, was drowned by falling into the water at Custom-house Quay. He belonged to the crew of the Schooner *Cumberland.—Vindicator*. (1839-09-14, 2:1)

2451. Lines, suggested on seeing the funeral of John Quin, of Newbliss.

Solemn and still they move along,
Silent sorrow has sealed each tongue;
Young shoulders bear the narrow bed
Which now contains the youthful dead.
The snow-white scarfs—the whispering breeze,
Gently rustling through the leaves,
Seems to waft, on every breath,
The awful, chilling, sound of death!
On they bear the widow's boy,
Once her fond hope—her greatest joy.

Alas! 'twas crush'd in midst of spring,
Like ev'ry other earthly thing.
One thought consoles his mourning friends,
As cries and sighs to Heav'n ascends,
Pains and toils to him are o'er,
He is not lost, but gone before,
Yes: he's gone—gone to a place of rest,

Within the mansions of the blest;
His weary nights are passed away,
He now enjoys eternal day.
With Zion's watchmen, from his youth,
He longed to preach eternal truth;
He now has join'd a nobler band,
Who night and day, in Heaven's land,
Enraptured, sing of wondrous love
Which brought God's equal from above
To seek and save a guilty race,
And by His all-constraining grace
Restore them to His Father's face.

September 21, 1839.
(1839-09-21, 4:1)

2452. Marriage in High Life.—Married, on Thursday, the 19th instant, at St. George's, Hanover-square, Robert Perceval Maxwell, Esq., of Finnebrogue, county Down, to Helena, only daughter of William Moore, Esq., of Moore-hill, and Sapperton, in the county of Waterford. The Hon. Edward Moore, Prebend of Windsor, officiated on the occasion; and amongst the company present were John Waring Maxwell, Esq., of Finnebrogue; William Moore, jun., Esq., of Moore-hill; the Countess of Kingston, the Hon. Lady and Miss King, Mr. and Lady Helena Cooke, Mr. and Lady Adelaide Webber, Rev. William and Miss Perceval, and several other friends.
(1839-09-21, 4:3)

2453. Cholera.—Patrick Kelly, blacksmith, of Downpatrick, has this morning, (Saturday,) after a few hours' illness, fallen a victim to asiatic cholera.—*Downshire Chronicle*. (1839-09-21, 4:5)

2454. The Emigrant Bride. by J.B.P.

Kind father, fare thee well! Another now
Must spring to linger gladly by thy side,
And other tones, to welcome thee, must flow,
And hail thy coming in the eventide;
Another hand must spread thy homely board—
Another heart thy comfort must devise—
To soothe, at eve, another's song be poured—
To glad thy breast must glisten other eyes.
Kind father, fare thee well.

My mother! oh, my mother! how from thee
Shall thy poor child, in such a moment, part;
Thou who hast watched each hour of grief or glee—
Whose voice breathed love—whose kindness won the heart—
Whose warm solicitude each care beguiled—
"With whom to dwell was ecstacy supreme"
Now, oh, my mourning mother! bless thy child,
Forgive these parting tears that sadly stream.
Loved mother, fare thee well!

And thou—gay partner of each happy time—
Sweet sister! sharer of my deepest love,
No more together shall our laughter chime—
No more o'er mountains shall we freely rove,
Our girlish joys and wanderings all are o'er,
We ne'er may call and twine the forest flowers,
Nor seek the pleasures which we sought before,
Nor feel the guilelessness of childhood's hours.
Sweet sister, fare thee well!

Have we not watched each starlet's twinkling beam,
Glowing resplendent from the mirror'd flood?
Have we not lingered by the brawling stream?
And gathered berries in the pathless wood.
The wild birds sung—responsive rose our voice.
No more our melody shall rise the same;
I now must roam with him—my heart's free choice,
And share his sorrows, pleasures, home, and name.
Sweet sister, fare thee well!

Mine is an altered lot; and I shall bend
Obsequious now to meet another's will.
Life shows a path of duty ne'er to end
Until my last cold dwelling-place I fill.
Oh! may a blessing hover o'er our way;
By consecrated love around us twined.
The husband fond—the hallowed home—be they
The gain I win for all I leave behind.
For ever fare ye well!

(1839-10-05, 4:1)

2455. Mortality in Demerara.—(Extract of a Letter from an Officer of the 76th Regt. dated Georgetown, Demerara, Aug. 12, 1839.)—As the Governor has kindly offered to send a letter by the *Mountaineer*, now sailing for England, I have only time to let you know that I am, thank God, still alive and well; but, I am sorry to say that the fever still continues unabated. Our band-master Mr. Heyder, died on the 3d instant; and poor Major Fitzgerald, (Brevet Major 76th,) who only came here from Berbice on the 27th July, to take command of the District, died on the 6th inst. of the same dreadful and treacherous disease. I have not now time to enlarge on the subject; but I may say of the poor Major that he was universally beloved by those who knew him. He had a noble disposition, even in his illness: he feared others might take the fever from him, and desired us not to go near him, which, of course we did not attend to. I was in his room one minute before he expired, but he was then senseless. I was speaking to him about two, p.m., and he said he did not know what was the matter with him; and he might seem to an experienced eye, not to be very ill, but he died at twenty-five minutes before nine at night. We have already lost eleven men this month, out of one hundred left here. I hope the draft may be sent out sooner this year than last year, on account of our unprecedented loss. Lieutenants Tydd, Whitter, Mr. Mrs. and Miss Preston are recovering. I am obliged to be off, as I am acting Captain, Subaltern, Commander of Royal Artillery, Fort Adjutant, and lots of other things. I hoped soon to be at home, but what is best for me I am sure will happen. Your affectionate Son, &c.—*Evening Packet*.
(1839-10-05, 4:5)

2456. The situation of Apothecary to the Adare Fever Dispensary, and Fever Hospital, is vacant by the premature death of Mr. Johnston—a young gentleman of great skill and assiduity in his profession, who fell a victim to the fever prevalent there, and which he caught in attendance on his patients. (1839-10-19, 2:1)

2457. Thirty Roman Catholic priests died this last month in various parts of Ireland. (1839-10-19, 2:4)

2458. Last Thursday, a child about two years old, living in Peter's Hill, was burned to death by its dress taking fire.—*Vindicator*. (1839-10-19, 4:4)

2459. Spinsters.—Formerly women were prohibited from marrying till they had spun a regular set of bed furniture, and till their marriages, were consequently called spinsters, which continues till this day in legal proceedings. (1839-10-26, 2:1)

2460. Death of Lord George Beresford.—We regret to learn that Lord George Beresford, who had been for some time previously on a visit with his distinguished relative, his Grace the Lord Primate, expired at the Palace, Armagh, on the morning of Saturday last. The Lord Primate, accompanied by his nephew, Lord John Beresford, has been passing the last week at Newcastle, in this county.—*Newry Telegraph*.
(1839-11-02, 4:2)

2461. The late Lord George Beresford bequeathed the whole of his property to his three daughters, the Hon. Misses Beresford, residing with their aunt, Lady Anne Beresford, sister of the Lord Primate, at Armagh. (1839-11-16, 1:3)

2462. Fire in Belfast.—Loss of Human Life.—Monday morning, about three o'clock, a small store in East-street, one of the by-streets diverging from Verner-street, in the direction of the river, was totally destroyed by fire, with almost all it contained which consisted of a large quantity of flax waste. The store was rented by Mr. Daniel M'Cartney, who had erected in it a stove, for the purpose of drying the waste, mostly purchased from the spinners in a moist state. Four young men, named Patrick King, John Roney, Martin M'Donnell, and Alexander M'Keown, had been, on Sunday night, in charge of the waste in progress of drying. The latter two were relieved by the others, about one o'clock on Monday morning; but, instead of returning home, lay down in the lower part of the store, and fell asleep near the stove. King and Roney took a candle up stairs, and, after turning the flax, had, it is conjectured, imprudently stuck the candle against the wall, and gone to sleep, like their companions. There is little doubt that Roney and King were intoxicated at the time. At three o'clock, M'Donnell and M'Keown were awakened by a suffocating smoke, and found the house in flames. They immediately made their escape by the door, and, calling out to apprize the other men of their danger, King leaped from a window, and received little injury. From the inflammable nature of the materials in reach of the fire, however, only a few minutes elapsed from it was discovered till the roof fell in, and buried poor Roney in the burning ruins. After the town fire-engine, which was soon on the spot, accompanied by a body of the constabulary and night-watch, under the orders of Mr. Armstrong, had secured the safety of the adjacent houses and hay-lofts, which were in great danger, search was made for the body of the ill-fated man, which, when found, was so horribly disfigured, as almost to defy recognition. This is the most lamentable accident that has occurred in Belfast for a long time; and ought to operate as a severe check to inebriety among workmen engaged in operations to similar risk to the above.—*Northern Whig*. (1839-11-23, 2:1)

2463. Since it first became our duty to record the decease of our fellow mortals, we have never conceived that duty more painful than while we note the death of Maria, the estimable wife of John Hatchell, Esq., of this town. In our last we stated, that she had, on the 8th instant, given birth to a daughter, and all was a scene of hope and joy, until the 9th day, when it pleased Almighty God to turn her home into a house of mourning. She became suddenly ill on the night of Friday, the 14th, and expired after 9 o'clock on Saturday morning. Mrs. Hatchell was daughter of the late Rev. Samuel Maffatt, and sister to the present Rev. Henry Maffatt, of Monaghan—a lady of the most amiable and Christian character—the darling centre of a devoted circle of friends, all of whom mourn her loss with scarcely less fervent sorrow than her fond husband. Her remains were deposited in the family vault, amid the deep and heartfelt regrets of a numerous train of friends, on Tuesday last. (1839-11-23, 3:1)

2464. Rejoicings at Mountfield, near Omagh.—Seldom has it been our lot to record a more marked testimony of the esteem in which a landlord is held than was manifested last week at Mountfield, on receipt of the joyous news that Lady M'Mahon had been safely delivered of a son and heir, to the extensive and highly improved estate of her husband, Sir Beresford B. M'Mahon, Bart. The tenantry vied with each other in their rejoicings—bonfires blazed in all directions, and loud and many were the prayers for the long life and happiness, not only of the young heir, but of the generous landlord and his amiable and kind-hearted lady, who, during their first and short visit to the estate, had endeared themselves, not only to their respectable and happy tenantry, but to all who enjoyed the pleasure of their acquaintance and hospitality. (1839-11-23, 3:1)

2465. Elegy.

Are there not bended heads,
And quivering lips, and many voices mourning,
And eyes o'er which the lid now drooping spreads,
To stay tears welling bitterly, and burning?
Lo! a dense train's advancing, sadly slow;
Emotion's sobbing floats upon the gale.
And hark! there soundeth shrill, o'er all their woe,
An infant's wail.

The branch is withered now,
And oh! how early is its freshness blighted;
The bud lives grafted on another bough,
But tears shall water—half-lit smiles shall light it.
How heavy this thy first sad loss—poor child!
Oh, who to thee may like a mother prove—
Who watch thee—guard thee—love thee, warm and wild
With mother's love!

Not thine the loss alone,
From kindred, and from strangers, sighs awaken.
The poor weep, hopeless—their best friend is gone,
And friendship mourns the treasure from her taken.
Oh, Death! why hath thy fleetest summons sped—
Why claim the wife—the mother, newly blest;
Oh, Grave! why call unto thy narrow bed
The kindest—best?
Hush! why should sorrow swell?
Hush! is a spirit's mortal care not ended?
Faith, o'er the righteous dead, breathes "It is well;"
Roses with gloomy cypress-wreathes are blended
"The Lord hath given;" then, oh! bless his name—

(*continued....*)

2465, continued:

"The Lord hath taken;" should praise be denied?
Lives she not now above you starry frame,
Beatified?
(1839-11-23, 4:1)

2466. We copy the following melancholy announcement from the *Newry Telegraph*, and regret that we omitted to do so in our last publication:—"We exceedingly regret to announce the death of the Rev. Charles James Maffatt, Perpetual Curate of St. Mary's, from that inveterate and malignant disease, the small pox, which melancholy event occurred at his late residence, Downshire Road, on the morning of Thursday, the 14th instant. During the long period that he resided here, his conduct, both as a minister of the Gospel, and a resident gentleman, was distinguished by the utmost zeal and assiduity in the discharge of the important duties pertaining to his station. In the promoting of the local charities, as well as in advancing the interests of true religion, his exertions were particularly conspicuous, and eminently successful. His premature death, is therefore deeply and sincerely lamented, not only by the congregation confided to his charge, but also to every one to whom the Rev. Gentleman was known. Mr. Maffett [sic] was also Chaplain to the Garrison of Newry and highly esteemed by the military quartered there. He was in his 37th year, extremely well looking, and has left a young widow, and two children to deplore his premature and unexpected call to his reward, proving, not only the uncertain tenure of this life, for the disease was most rapid in its progress, but also the necessity of the repetition of vaccinating after a certain period." (1839-11-30, 2:5)

2467. Lines on the Death of Mrs. Hatchell.

The fondly lov'd—the gentle one has faded;
And she that gladden'd many hearts hath pass'd
From earth away. Say, did not wealth, and youth,
And beauty, round thee linger? Could they not
Woo thee, with their brilliant charms, to waste
Thy love on earth? An, no! the God whose thou
hast been,
From infancy, hath call'd thee to far higher joys—
Pleasures imperishable. Yet was there nought
Could bind thee unto earth? Did thy pure soul,
Unfetter'd, break away from life without a sigh?
Alas! not so. How many chains of love, and hope,
And joy, had time around thee woven?
So soon to leave the long-expected one—the babe
To whom thy fond heart yearn'd with love
unspeakable.
Yet God had said, "I will protect the motherless."
And thou didst bow they soul in meek and firm
Reliance on his promise made. And she that bore
thee—
She that lov'd thee, with a mother's changeless
Fervent love: thy childhood's playmates too,
Must ye be parted; and him to whom thy plighted
faith
Was giv'n—round whom thy fondest hopes
Had twin'd themselves. Oh! it were vain
To speak now of thy anguish. Alas! 'tis always thus
Earth's fairest hopes—earth's brightest buds are
blasted!
And we must look from earth, and earthly things,
To those that are enduring.
Then mourn we not thy death as those that hope not.
The God that took thee to himself, and lov'd thee
Far above human love, hath sav'd thee from
Distress and pain which else thou might'st
Have suffer'd. And when life's weary cares—
Life's fleeting joys are over, may we
That lov'd and wept thee, meet where death
And sin shall have no more dominion.

Eliza.

Monaghan, 18th Nov., 1839.

(1839-11-30, 4:1)

2468. In such high estimation was the late Rev. Chas. James Moffatt [sic], Curate of St. Mary's, Newry, held, that at the time of his premature and lamented decease a considerable sum was actually in hands to build a church for the Rev. Gentleman, and also a residence close beside it—a strong proof of the value of his professional services. Mr. Moffatt had distinguished himself in College, and was A.M. of the University of Dublin. (1839-12-07, 2:4)

2469. Let us Think on Those that Sleep.

If we could see some warning hand,
Or hear some whisper calling
Each after each to join the band
Of death-struck mortals, falling,
In spite of human skill and care,
Into the gloomy sepulchre.

Amid the common words and smiles,
And friendly looks and greetings,
And all that every day beguiles
Our thoughts from other meetings
Than those which now, without misgiving,
The living hold with others living,

We sometimes—nay, we often—then,
Would think of those who often
Have met with us our grief, or pain,
Or cares of life to soften;
But now, from living converse gone,
Who sleeps beneath the surf or stone.

But, as if yesterday, their hand
With life's warm tide was flowing;
We grasp'd it, while th' expression bland
Was in their bright eyes glowing.
Death now has glas'd those eyes, and Death
Has stopp'd the warm blood and the breath.

Corruption triumphs now, in them,
O'er bodies which we pamper;

But ours, in turn, it soon will claim—
Ours soon the coffin hamper:
If the cold, rigid corpse could feel
The closeness of this bed of deal.

And is it, then, sure that we
Go where they're gone already?
As if, still beckoning, we could see
Their fingers, or a steady,
Calm, and unfaltering whisper said,
Close in our ear, "Come join the dead;"

'Tis very certain—those before,
Those following, placed between
The dead and living. Why, no more
Than if they ne'er had been,
Think we of friends of bygone hours,
Whose silent rest will soon be ours?

Carrigans. Kappa.
(1839-12-07, 4:1)

2470. Andrew Taylor, the steward of Lady Harriet Forde, was found dead in a pool of water, last Friday, near Hollymount. There were several wounds in his neck, apparently as if inflicted by some sharp instrument. It is thought that religious monomania had caused him to commit suicide. (1839-12-14, 2:4)

2471. On the 26th ult. Sergeant M'Auly, of Saintfield, was drowned near his own house. An inquest was held, and the jury returned a verdict died from excessive drinking of ardent spirits. (1839-12-14, 2:4)

2472. Last Monday, during the removal of the props from an arch in the mill of Mr. Daniel Collins, of Newry, the fabric fell, and three of the workmen were buried in the ruin. One of them was killed instantly, and the other two are not expected to survive. (1839-12-14, 2:4)

2473. Sudden Death.—On the morning of Friday, the 16th instant, a man of the name of Simpson, a native of Glasslough, who had been on a visit to his mother and sister, dropped down dead on the road, after having proceeded about a mile on his way home. He has left a wife and seven children to deplore their sudden bereavement. (1839-12-14, 3:1)

2474. Ode to a Departed Friend.

As oft, in melancholy thought, we tread
The lone and dreary mansions of the dead,
And shudder deeply at the mournful gloom
That ever hovers o'er the silent tomb;
Or gazing pensively, perchance, we roll
Our wand'ring vision on some recent scroll,
Which tells of one whose death doth almost seem
But as the fancy of a waking dream.
"Oft have we seen, in an untimely hour,
Some fair, unsullied, fondly-nurtured, flower
Droop to the earth its withered head, and lie
With stem recumbent—much too fair to die."
Of form more graceful, and of brow more fair;
Beloved more—if love there ever were—
Was she who slumbers 'neath that sculptured stone;
Nor unforgotten—nor, alas, alone!
Who lived, as 'twere, not only lived to bless
Her dear-bought offspring with a fond caress:
Smiled in his face who once had happily been
Her cherished partner in this earthly scene—
Gazed fondly once—and gazing, greatly sighed—
Breathed one, long, earnest, last farewell—and died.
Peace to thine ashes, Angelica, bright
As sheds the sun his noonday beam of light,
E'en brighter far thy pure example threw
A radiant halo round our enchanted view,
Bade our dull thoughts ascend to heavenly things
To Jesus, the Christ, the Lord, the King of Kings—
Taught us to gaze, with rapture, on the page
Which there pourtrayed the Eve of bygone age,
And see in thee, in every action tell
How true the semblance, ere, forsooth, she fell.
Once more, farewell, then, may thy spirit rest
'Loft in the regions of the ever blest—
Where nought save joy and innocence e'er reign,
And voices mingle in harmonious strain—
Where enter not a sorrow or a fear,
A pang of sadness, or a mournful tear.
Thou'st passed from earth, as if too pure to be
Tossed on the billows of life's troubled sea:
Nor needs thy urn an epitaph save this:—
She hath fled to mansions of eternal bliss.
(1839-12-14, 4:1)

2475. The Constabulary.—We regret having to announce the death of Lieutenant-Colonel Holmes, Deputy-Inspector-General of Constabulary, which took place on Thursday, at his residence in Rathmines. By a painful coincidence, it happened that his son, a fine boy, died of measles on the preceding day. (1839-12-28, 1:4)

2476. Death of John Deering, Esq.—We regret to announce the demise of this gentleman, which took place at his house in Mountjoy-square, Dublin, on Monday last. Mr. Deering was a bencher of the Queen's Inns, father of the North West Bar, (which he ornamented for nearly 43 years) and a magistrate and grand juror of the county of Fermanagh. His remains will arrive here on Saturday morning, and be interred at ten o'clock. —*Fermanagh Reporter*. (1839-12-28, 3:2)

2477. A young woman named Kennick drowned herself on Monday last, in the Derrymany river, between Greenhill and Brookborough, after having an altercation with her mother.—The mother's grief at discovering her daughter a ruined maid vented in reproaches which aroused the frail girl's remorse, and she went straight and drowned herself. (1839-12-28, 3:3)

2478. Advice to Young Ladies in selecting Husbands.—You are sitting some evening on a sofa, looking out on the clear moonlight, your adorer near by, also looking at the heaven in your lovely countenance. After a long breath, a tremulous motion of the heart, he murmurs forth his "love," "adoration," "declaration," "till death," "have pity," "say yes," &c. &c. You are to be quite cool and calm all the time, patting the carpet with your pretty little feet. You slowly turn round, and with one end of your soft melting eye upon him, proceed to the cross examination, thus:—first ask him, "do you take a newspaper?" If he replies "no," cut him at once as a savage and a barbarian—if he replies "yes," proceed to the next question. "What daily paper do [you] take?" If he replies the *Courier*, the *Express*, or any of the penny prints, then he won't do at all. A man who only takes such papers has no sentiment, no feeling, no light dawns on his soul—he can have no proper estimate of the qualities of an amiable, sensible and affectionate woman. Of course reject him. But if the unfortunate boy should say, "I take *Bennett's Herald*, that's my breakfast every morning," then the whole thing is done—pin him at once, and say

Gae ask my mammie—

have the wedding day appointed and you are a happy wife, with a devoted husband, as long as life doth run. "Pin at once"—forget not that.—*New York Weekly Herald.* (1839-12-28, 4:4)

2479. Approaching Marriages in High Life.—Baron Fortescue, Lord Lieutenant of Ireland, to the Lady Dover, sister of Viscount Morpeth.

Lord Grimston, eldest son of the Earl of Verulam, to the Lady Louisa Craven, sister of Lord Craven, who married the Lady Emily Grimston some three years ago.

The Lady Agusta Cadogan, eldest daughter of Earl Cadogan, is said to be affianced to a gentleman of large property; and connected with the Comptroller of her Majestys Household. (1840-01-04, 1:2)

2480. The lamented death of Philip Fogarty, Esq., Q.C., leaves a vacancy in the assistant-barristership of the county of Louth. Mr. O'Shaughnessy, it is thought, will preside at the January sessions in that county. (1840-01-04, 1:6)

2481. On the morning of the 28th ult. a poor man named Robert Mitchell, a resident of the Parish of Tydavnet, was killed by a fall from a tree, which he ascended for the purpose of lopping a branch therefrom.—He was alone at the time, but, was found shortly after his fall in an almost dying state. The spine of his back was severely injured, and, after lingering for a day or two in dreadful agony he expired. He was a thatcher, and bore an excellent character—had been in his place of worship on the preceding day, and the testimony borne to his humble worth and integrity by the minister of his Parish, who referred to the subject on the sequent Sunday, shews the value of the good esteem of our fellow-men, even in the lower walks of life. (1840-01-04, 3:1)

2482. The Mother's Lament.

My babe, my babe—my beautiful!
Art thou gone from thy sunny home?
From this joyous earth, in its summer time—
From the love that was all thy own.

Hast thou left the glad where thou didst list
To the wild-bird's song of glee,
Amid the flowers that the dew had kissed;
Thyself as wild and free?

Hast thou pass'd away from the cheerful hearth—
From the peace that around it dwelt—
From thy mother's tender kiss of love—
From the knee where thou has knelt?

Art thou gone, indeed? my child—my child!
Shall I see thy face no more?
Must I spend my life in mourning wild,
Since thy short life is o'er?

How willingly would I have died,
Hadst thou but liv'd to bless
All round thee with thy cherub smile—
Thy heartfelt loveliness.

But so it is: the wither'd leaf
Still lingers on the stem,
While the bud that blossom'd on the earth
Is taken up to heaven.

Be still, thou mourner; weep not thus
The dark'ning of thy sun,
But how thy soul before thy God,
And say, "Thy will be done."

Monaghan, 24th Dec. 1839.
(1840-01-04, 4:1)

2483. Matrimonial Hits and Misses, by J.B.P.

I want a wife!
Why, odds, my life?—
Good Sir, there's plenty;
Ye ne'er need fret—
I'll give you yet
Your choice of twenty;
All gentle dames, of all degrees—
All sizes, colors—what you please;
My namesakes first, Sir, all the P.s,
Who scarce are woo'd or won with ease;
Then comes the rest—there's Rachel Strong,
Miss Weeks, Miss Weekley, Bridget Long;
Or these may suit you to a tittle:—
Miss Short, Miss Low, and Sally Small;
Miss Shorter, then, or least of all
That little fairy thing, Miss Little.

There's more—still more,
Dear Sir; a score
We yet may grapple.
Next comes Vic. Church
Left in the lurch

By false Miss Chappel,
The Misses Britton, England, Scott,
Miss Welsh—shall Ireland be forgot?
Mis Cow-ley here, Miss Horse-ley there—
The Misses Love, Hope, Joy, and Cayre—
Eve Knight, Clare Day, Miss Frost, Miss Snow,
Miss Dove, Poll Pidgeon, fair Blanche Crowe,
Miss Sparrow, Julia Rooke,
Miss Henn, Miss Peacock, Anna Coote—
The Misses Hart, Hand, Head, and Foot,
Bell Butler and Grace Cooke.

There's some 'mid these
Antitheses
As good as any;
If they don't hit,
And no Miss fit,
Here still are many,
Miss Cole, Miss Peat, Miss Gass, Miss Sparke,
Miss Reed, Miss Rush, Field, Moore, and Parke,
And some almost of every hue—
Anne Black, Jane White, Miss Greene, Miss Blew,
Miss Dunne, Miss Scarlett, Gertrude Browne,
Miss Rose. Miss Gray is out of town
At Hughes, of Violet Hill.
Then next comes cutting Fanny Keene,
Miss Poynte, Miss Pierce—Miss Sharpe between
The Blunts, who're pretty still.

No choice?—I find
You're scarce inclined
For matrimony.
There's (ere we've done)
Miss Fryer, Miss Nunn,
And sweet Miss Honey,
Miss Mann, Miss Childe, who's quite annoy'd
To meet that tomboy chit, Miss Boyd;
The Misses Salmon, Pike, and Place,
Miss Heron, Haddock, Fry, and Dace;
The Misses Tree, Grove, Forrest, Woods,
The Rivers, Waters, Springs, and Floods,
And Hannah Brooke, the pretty quaker.
The Misses Bird and Fish are many;
There's Mary Goold and Susan Penny—
Ruth Cash—Hold there, Sir!—hold! Ill take her!
(1840-01-04, 4:1)

2484. Captain Paget, R.N., eldest son of the late Admiral the Hon. Sir Charles Paget, will in a few days be married to Miss Caroline M'Clintock, third daughter of Henry M'Clintock, Esq., Collector of Dundalk. Captain Paget is now at Dundalk, intending to remain there until the marriage ceremony is accomplished. (1840-01-11, 2:1)

2485. Melancholy Accident.—On the 7th instant, an inquest was held before J.M. Maghee, Esq., Coroner, in the townland of —, near Portadown, on view of the body of Thomas Lynas. It appeared the deceased had left home at an early hour on the morning of Monday the 6th instant, for the purpose of employing a horse and cart to draw home some turf. He got the horse and cart, and, on passing the house of John Dickson, near Blacker's Mill, he drew the cart over a draw-well, which had been partially covered with sticks; the sticks gave way, and the horse fell head foremost into the well; the deceased was drawn partially into the well, the wheel of the cart pressed him against its side, and in this position he remained until his cries alarmed Dickson, who immediately came to his relief. The weight of the horse, suspended from the cart, caused it to press so heavily against the unfortunate man, that great difficulty was experienced in extricating him; and not until the earth was cleared away from where he lay pressed were the people able to relieve him. He died immediately. The horse was also killed. A verdict of accidental death was recorded. The deceased was a young man, of good character; he had been but a twelvemonth married, and has left a widow and one child. (1840-01-11, 2:2)

2486. Child Burned to Death.—Last Monday a dreadful accident occured in Mary's Market, in this town. A woman named Steed, having occasion to go to a grocer's shop, left two children sleeping in the house. The eldest, a child, aged about two years, got out of the bed by some means, and having approached too closely to the fire, the flames unfortunately seized upon its clothes, when it was so severely burned that it died a few hours afterwards. We understand that two other children met a similar fate, on the same day in the above vicinity. Accidents of this kind are of frequent occurrence, and mothers cannot be too cautious about the safety of their children when they leave home.—*Vindicator*. (1840-01-11, 4:3)

2487. Inquest.—On Wednesday, the 25th ult., Mr. Wm. Ellis, Coroner, held an inquest on view of the body of William Campbell, an itinerant pedlar, beyond the prime of life, who died suddenly in a public house in Bishop street, the evening previous. From what we could learn respecting the deceased, it appears that he was for a number of years past addicted to indulge in the use of ardent spirits, but had from June last till within ten days of his death, totally abstained from intoxicating drink, when he again resumed drinking, but was not intoxicated at the time he died. Dr. Morton, who examined the body shortly after life became extinct, was examined on the inquest, and gave it as his opinion that his death was produced by apoplexy, arising from intemperance. Verdict—Died by the visitation of God.—*Londonderry Standard*. (1840-01-11, 4:4)

2488. A young girl of the name of Rennick, in the vicinity of Brookeborough, left her mother's house last week in a fit of anger, and has not yet been heard of. Apprehensions were entertained that she had drowned herself in a river contiguous to her dwelling, but of that there is no certainty, the body not yet being found.—*Erne Packet*. (1840-01-11, 4:4)

2489. The situation of Police Magistrate of Henry-street office, Dublin, is vacant by the death of James Blacker, Esq., one of the oldest divisional Magistrates in Dublin. (1840-01-18, 1:5)

2490. Melancholy Loss of Life.—Nine Persons Drowned in Lough Swilly.—On Thursday, the 9th inst., two boats from the west side of the lake proceeded to Doughbeg to fish for cod. On their return home, on the night of the same day, one of the boats struck on a rock in Pincher's Bay, when, melancholy to relate, all on board perished. Among the sufferers were a man named Callaghan and his two sons; two brothers named John and James Black, from Anney; and the rest of the crew were called Kerr or M'Elhare. The boat has been since picked up, with two of her boards stove in; but none of the bodies have yet been found. (1840-01-25, 2:3)

2491. Melancholy Accident.—On the night of the nativity, or early on the following morning of the 26th of December last, a man of the name of M'Cabe, who resided near Derranakesh church, parish of Drumgoon, and two young children, were killed by the falling in of his mud wall house. His wife fortunately escaped with some slight bruises and a discoloration of the eye. An inquest was held on the bodies, when the jury returned a verdict of "Died by the visitation of God." (1840-01-25, 3:2)

2492. On Monday night se'nnight, a young man of the name of Callan, who resided with his father, a comfortable farmer, near Derranakesh church, was found dead within a few perches of his home. He was seen quite well returning from the market of Bailieborough, where he had been on some business for his father, on that day. The verdict of the Coroners jury was, "Died by the visitation of God." (1840-01-25, 3:2)

2493. Sudden Death.—On Thursday morning last, as the *Shareholder* caravan from Newry to Dublin, was about to start, after changing horses at Caragher's public-house, Dundalk, Mr. James Richardson Martin, of Moy, merchant, while in the act of getting off the caravan, fell back upon the flags, with which the back part of his head came in contact, causing fracture of the skull, and consequent effusion of blood on the brain. He was immediately conveyed to the Louth hospital, and after lingering fifteen minutes, died in great pain. An inquest was held on the body, before John Byrne, Esq., coroner, and a respectable jury, when a verdict of accidental death was returned. It appears that upwards of £600 in debentures and bank notes have been found upon his person.—*Drogheda Constitution.* (1840-01-25, 4:5)

2494. Last Saturday, the wife of Patrick M'Carthy, a poor agricultural laborer, at Patrick's-well, near Limerick, gave birth to three full-grown infants—two boys and a girl. (1840-02-01, 1:4)

2495. Since the violent storm of Monday and Tuesday morning the weather is cold and boisterous, with occasional rain and hail showers, preceded or followed by squalls of wind. A great part of the country at both sides of the Shannon is flooded by the high tides, and within the circuit of three or four miles round this city, there are some hundred acres under water, the fields in all the agitation of a river. The inundation has been most injurious to the farmers, whose loss is considerable. On Monday night, a boat from Kildysart, laden with corn, was swamped in the storm and high tide, when four men named M'Mahon, Beaty, Behane, and Kinnane, were drowned; the boat was found on Wednesday, and the body of Behane in her.—*Limerick Chronicle.* (1840-02-01, 4:4)

2496. It is with the most painful feeling, we are obliged to record the death of the following lamented individual. The notification of his death is copied from the *Belfast Commercial Chronicle*, of February 5th:—On the 1st instant, at his residence, Donegall-Place, Belfast, John Wales, Esq., Surgeon. It is hard that one who so lately lived among us, admired, respected, and beloved, should be prematurely removed, without aiding to the record of such bereavement some faint expression of the grief with which this much-lamented person's death has filled the hearts of all who knew him. With every characteristic which distinguishes the high-minded and upright man, he was enthusiastically esteemed in the immediate circle of his acquaintance; while his humanity and skill in the practice of a profession which he adorned, and which, had he been spared he would have dignified, endeared him to the general community of this populous town. In the mourning breasts of those relatives, whose hopes and happiness have been thus crushed and blighted—and of those friends, over whose hearths his loss has thrown a gloom that will not soon be removed, is his best monument. His epitaph is breathed in the language of all—in the sorrowing regret of the affluent, the destitute, and the poor. (1840-02-08, 3:2)

2497. On the 6th instant, the village of Ballycarry was illuminated to celebrate the arrival of Mathew Anketell, Esq., of Anketell Grove, county of Monaghan, and his bride, Miss Ker, daughter of David Ker, Esq., Portavo, M.P. for Downpatrick, and granddaughter of the Marquis of Londonderry. (1840-02-15, 3:2)

2498. Marriage in High Life.—On Friday week, at Kensington Palace, by special license, Lord Dinorben, to Miss Gertrude Smyth, sister of her Royal Highness the Princess of Capua. His Royal Highness the Duke of Sussex gave the fair and accomplished bride away, and the Chaplain of Lord Dinorben officiated at the ceremony. The bride was attired in a rich white satin dress, trimmed and flounced with costly Brussels point lace, and wore a small bouquet of orange blossom in her hair, which was ornamented with brilliants.—The robe was confined at the waist by a superb band of diamonds at the first water. The ceremony took place precisely at a quarter past nine in the evening, his Royal Highness the Duke of Sussex having previously entertained his friend Lord Dinorben at dinner. Among the distinguished party present were—his Royal Highness the Duke of Sussex and Lady Cicilia Underwood, Prince and Princess of Capua, Duke of Devonshire, Duke and Duchess of Bedford, Lord Tenternen [sic], and the Hon. Miss Abbott, Capt. and the Hon. Mrs. Smyth, etc.

(1840-02-22, 1:4)

2499. F.A. Jackson, Esq., of Inone, county of Tipperary, will shortly lead to the hymeneal altar one of the lovely and accomplished daughters of the late Wm. Hutchinson, Esq., of Timony Park, same county.

(1840-02-22, 1:4)

2500. We regret to announce the demise of the Right Hon. Maria Countess of Leitrim, which took place at the Spa Hotel, Durham, on Wednesday last.

(1840-02-22, 1:4)

2501. Nine suicides occurred in New York the last week in January. An Irish gentleman, from Waterford or Tipperary, cut his throat at the tea-table. A German gentleman blew his brains out; and a lady, formerly in the service of George the Fourth, shot herself through the heart with a horse pistol. (1840-02-22, 2:1)

2502. The Caledon Testimonial—Laying of the Foundation Stone.—Monday, February 17, 1840—the day on which was embedded the first stone of a column intended to commemorate the name and perpetuate the remembrance of the virtues of the late Earl of Caledon—was to the people of the town of Caledon and the surrounding neighbourhood, a day of surpassing interest, and one, the incidents of which will not soon pass away from their memories. The morning was damp and lowering, but towards noon the weather became more settled and serene.

The site appropriately selected for the monument is on elevated ground, within the walls of the demesne, and immediately adjoining the lake. It is situated midway between the neat and rising town (itself a monument of the public spirit and taste of the deceased Earl) and Caledon House, and commands a view of the towns of Tynan and Killilea, as well as of a wide range of country on almost every side.

Long before the hour appointed for the ceremony, the grounds were occupied by a dense mass of the population. About one o'clock the carriages of his Grace the Lord Primate, of Mrs. Leslie, of Glasslough House, and of other distinguished individuals, drove inside the demesne, and drew up on the grand avenue, their occupants proceeding on foot to the site alluded to.

Amongst the crowded assemblage we observed the following individuals:—The Lord Primate, accompanied by the Rev. James Jones, his Grace's Chaplain; Mrs. Leslie, of Glasslough House, and her beautiful and interesting daughter; Archdeacon Stopford, Mrs. Stopford, and family; Acheson St. George, Esq., and family; Rev. William Mauleverer and family; Rev. Charles and Mrs. Alexander; William J. Alexander, Esq. and family; Rev. Mr. and Mrs. Nussey; Doctor and Miss Scott; H. Leslie Prentice, Esq., and family; William Irwin, Esq., Mount Irwin, and family; Captain Golding and family; Captain Lodge, and family; William Murdoch, Esq., and family; Mrs. Ellison and family; Rev. Mr. and Mrs. Kearney; Edmond Stronge, Esq., of Tynan Abbey; Robert Montgomery Moore, Esq., of Stormhill; Maxwell Cross, Esq., of Darton; Edward Golding, Esq.; Rev. Dr. Campbell, of Forkhill; Rev. Francis Gervais, of Cecil; Thomas A. Prentice, Esq.; Rev. Mr. Pratt; Rev. Alexander Miller; Rev. T.J. White; Rev. Henry Kennedy, of Blackwatertown; Charles Magee, Esq.; H. Harris, Esq.; W.T. Knox, Esq.; Michael Pringle, Esq.; Mr. and Miss Hogg; William Irwin, jun., Esq.; — St. George, Esq.; Wm. Forster, Esq., and Mrs. Forster, of Ballynure; Rev. Edw. and Mrs. Stopford, &c. &c.

The preparations having been completed, under the superintendence of the architect, Thomas J. Duff, Esq., and of the builder, Mr. Archer,

The Lord Primate accompanied by Mrs. Leslie, Archdeacon Stopford, Rev. W. Mauleverer, Rev. J. Jones, Rev. Dr. Campbell, and the gentlemen composing the Building Committee, descended into the cavity prepared for this ponderous stone.

The Rev. W. Mauleverer, holding in his hand a silver trowel and a mallet, and addressing his Grace, said:—My Lord, we are assembled here this day for the purpose of laying the first stone of a Testimonial to be erected to the memory of the late Earl of Caledon. It is, my Lord, an occasion deeply to be deplored; for he was a man universally esteemed and dearly beloved by every individual who had the slightest knowledge of him. Mr. M. here drew a brief outline of the late Earl's character. He first adverted to his humility, which ever added grace and lustre to his lordship's other virtues, and said that if ever the milk of human kindness overflowed in a human heart it was his. Of his lordship's integrity and public spirit it was, he said, superfluous to speak. The public voice proclaims the public loss. He was, in a word, a blessing to the country to which he belonged. The public praise followed him in life, and now consecrates his memory. His piety to God was most exemplary and conspicuous. Of his alms-giving how much might be said which he never suffered to be said of himself. Like holy Job, he might truly have said, "When the ear heard me then it blessed me, and when the eye saw me it gave witness to me, because I delivered the poor that cried, and the fatherless, and him that had none to help him; the blessing of him that was ready to perish came upon me, and I caused (*continued...*)

2502, continued: ...the widow's heart to sing for joy." My Lord (added Mr. M., in conclusion), as your Grace has come here for the purpose of laying the first stone of the Testimonial, I have been entrusted with this trowel to have it presented to your Grace, through Mrs. Leslie—a lady who has taken an active interest in forwarding this undertaking, and who has gone hand in hand with the late Lord Caledon in promoting the general interests of this neighborhood.

The Rev. Gentleman having handed the trowel and mallet to Mrs. Leslie, that lady gracefully presented them to the Primate.

His Grace then addressed the assemblage with deep feeling and energy. He said—

Gentlemen, I attend here at the request of the persons who were appointed to carry into the effect the plan which was agreed to for a monument to be erected to the late Earl of Caledon, and who have done me the honor to invite me to lay the first stone of that monument. I trust, therefore, that I shall be permitted to say a few words with reference to the occasion which has brought me hither. I mean not to deliver a labored panegyric upon the merits of my late noble and much-lamented friend. I feel that this is neither the time nor the place to lay before you a statement of his public services or private virtues—indeed any praise of him, upon the present occasion, appears to me to be superfluous, and, I fear, would appear to you to be cold, if not heartless—for no eulogium that could be pronounced to his character would confer so distinguished an honor upon it as the Testimonial which we are now about to erect in remembrance of him. No sooner was their purpose announced than subscriptions were sent in cheerfully and spontaneously: they were given, not from a consideration of the high station which Lord Caledon held in this country—not in consequence of personal favors which the subscribers had received at his hands—still less from a blind partiality to him—but from a well-founded judgment of his usefulness as a public man, and from an admiration of the worth and excellence he displayed in all the relations of social and domestic life. Allow me to remind you that the best proof which can be given of the sincerity of our attachment to the late Earl of Caledon will be to consider his life and conduct as an example which we ought to follow. Indeed, the contemplation of great and good men, with a view of imitating them, has ever been the delight of virtuous minds, and the higher the stamp of excellence which marks the man, the more advantageous will be the study of his character. I will only add, that it is the characteristic of a truly religious man, to enjoy with gratitude and moderation the blessings which Providence is pleased to bestow upon him, and to submit, with patience and resignation to the various ills and sorrows with which he may be afflicted. Among my acquaintances I know no one who manifested more thankfulness to God for the possession of those advantages which high rank and a large fortune enabled him to procure for himself, or for those who were dependent upon him, or who bore with more fortitude and submission the severe sufferings of an illness which though protracted, rendered his existence so precarious, that he could not count upon its continuance for a single hour. In both circumstances, religion was the source whence he derived strength, support, and comfort. Pious then as he was, and virtuous, and benevolent, and kind, let us humbly hope that he has exchanged that house which stands on yonder eminence for a house not made with hands, eternal in the heavens; and that, through the merits of his Redeemer, he now lives holy and happy in the presence of that Almighty God he feared—of that all-merciful Father whom he loved.

The illustrious Prelate delivered this short address in a manner at once dignified, powerful, impressive, and affecting. Once or twice towards the conclusion of it his Grace himself seemed to experience difficulty in restraining his feelings so as to find utterance for his words.—His Grace immediately proceeded with the ceremony. A bottle, hermetically sealed, containing an inscription, written on parchment—a copy of the *Newry Telegraph*, in which appeared an account of the opening of the Armagh Cathedral, and another of the *Dublin Evening Mail*, giving the particulars of the Queen's marriage—together with a number of gold, silver and copper coins of the present and late reigns—was deposited in the stone, which his Grace, assisted by the architect, deposited and covered in the usual manner.

The inscription on the parchment ran thus:—

Hocce Monumentum
in perpetuam verae
et sincerae admirationis memoriam
viri excellentissimi
Dupre, Comitis Caledoniensis Secundi,
Vox public dicat et dedicate
Obiit 6 Aprilis, 1839, Aetatis 62.
Reveradissimus Johannes Georgius Archiepiscopus Armachanus,
et totius Hiberniae Episcopus Primarius
primum lapidem, die decimo septimo
Februarii, Anno Dominii 1840,
posuit.
Thomas Johannes Duff, Architectus.

Building Committee:—
Sir J.M. Stronge, Bart.
John Ynyr Burgess, Esq.
Venerable Archdeacon Stopford.
Rev. William Mauleverer.
Henry Leslie Prentice, Esq.
Hugh Simpson, Esq.
James A. Jackson, Esq.
William John Alexander, Esq.
Joseph H. Scott, Esq.

Maxwell Cross, Esq.
Captain R.R. Lodge,
Rev. James Campbell, D.D.
Rev. Richard Allott,
Alexander Mackenzie, Esq.
John Falls, Esq.
Thomas Dobbin, Esq.
Rev. Francis Gervais.
Treasurer—Hon. A.G. Stuart.
Sub-Treasurer—Henry L. Prentice, Esq.
Secretaries—William Murdock, Esq.,
Edward Golding, Esq.

The trowel, of pure silver, and exquisite workmanship, bore the following inscription:—

Presented to
his Grace
John George, Lord Archbishop
of Armagh,
Primate and Metropolitan of all
Ireland,
on the occasion of his Grace's laying the
first stone of a Testimonial at
Caledon,
Erected by Public Subscription,
to the memory of
Dupre, second Earl of Caledon,
1840.

The ceremony having been brought to a conclusion, all the Gentry above-named, together with many others whose names we did not ascertain, proceeded by invitation to Caledon House, where a sumptuous repast had been prepared for them. We need only to add that the entertainment was, in every respect, such as might be expected at the table of a British Nobleman.

We cannot close our account of this interesting event, without expressing what appeared to be the general feeling of satisfaction at the very judicious and excellent manner in which, from first to last, the entire proceedings was conducted.

The Testimonial about to be erected in a column, of the Grecian Doric order, the proportions being taken from the Parthenon at Athens. It is to be fifty-seven feet in height, the shaft to contain a spiral stair which will lead to the Gallery over the abacus: above this will be raised a beautiful circular acroter, on which will be placed a colossal statue of the late lamented Nobleman, habited in proper costume. The whole height, including steps, stylobate, column, acroteria and statue, will be upwards of ninety-five feet.

*Another inscription, in English, was also deposited. It was as follows:

This Column
was erected to the memory of
the Right Hon. DUPRE, *2d* EARL OF CALEDON, *Kt. of St. Patrick, Colonel of the Royal Tyrone Militia, and Lord Lieutenant of this county.*
Dignified without pride; charitable without ostentation; prudent, courteous wise.
The Nobility and Gentry of this County, in admiration of his private virtues, and public worth as a Senator, Landlord, and Friend,
which would have exalted any rank, and dignified any station in life,
have raised this memorial of their esteem.
17th February, 1840.
(1840-02-22, 2:5)

2503. Death of Colonel Currey.—We regret to announce the demise of this gentleman, which took place on Monday morning, at Lismore Castle, county of Waterford. He was agent over the extensive estates of the Duke of Devonshire, in the counties of Waterford and Cork. Kind, affable, and obliging, he is most deservedly regretted by the tenantry of the estates over which he presided for more than twenty years. As a magistrate, grand juror, and country gentleman, none could surpass him for impartiality, justice, and uprightness of intention. (1840-02-22, 3:3)

2504. It has seldom fallen to our lot, as public journalists, to record the decease of an individual, whose removal from this world of trials, has filled the public mind with so much heartfelt sorrow as the death of Mrs. Lewis, the wife of our worthy and respected Provost, cousin-german to Lord Rossmore, and daughter to the late Richard Westenra, Esq., Rutland-square, Dublin—which event took place on Wednesday morning, at six o'clock—in the 49th year of her age. The high respect and universal esteem in which this amiable lady was held, in this town and neighborhood, are amply testified by the deep sorrow which has been manifested by all classes of society at her loss. To the poor she was ever a considerate indulgent and liberal benefactress, and in all the domestic relations of life she was beloved and honored. As a Christian, she was enabled, by Grace, to bear, with fortitude and resignation, a long and distressing illness. The love of God and the holy example of His blessed Son were the guide and rule of her life; and, therefore, for her we sorrow not, but for him on whom the principal weight of the sad bereavement falls most heavily—her afflicted husband—we feel the greatest sympathy; but he, like to her who is gone, is happily fortified by faith in Christ, and the God whom he has loved and honored through life, we feel conscious, will support him in his affliction. (1840-02-29, 3:2)

2505. Lamentable Accident. (From a Correspondent.)—On the night of Friday, the 21st instant, Mr. John Dermott, of Knappa, near Shercock, county Cavan, a highly respectable and wealthy gentleman farmer, left the market of Cootehill, on that evening in perfect health and proceeded towards his residence, which is distant from the latter town about five miles, and was met when about two miles from home by his servant boy with a horse for him, but as it was a cold frosty night, he declined riding, and sent them (*continued...*)

2505, continued: home before him, preferring to walk to keep himself warm; and when about five or six perches distant from Knappa bridge, on the Clones coach-road, where the river runs close to it, he unfortunately missed his way, the night being so extremely dark, and melancholy to relate, fell in the river and was drowned. Thereby proving most cogently the mutability of all human affairs, and that whilst in life we are in death. [sic] Mr. Dermott was generally beloved and esteemed by all who had the pleasure of his acquaintance and by none more than the writer of this article. His death has left a void in the circle of his friends and acquaintances on account of the urbanity of his manners and affability of his disposition that will not be easily filled up; as was evinced by the number and respectability of the persons who accompanied his remains to the place of interment. He was about 50 years of age and unmarried. (1840-02-29, 3:2)

2506. Death of Alderman D.F.G. Mahony. (*From the Limerick Chronicle.*)—Under the oppression of peculiarly distressing feelings we have to record the sudden and very alarming illness of Alderman Fitz-Gerald Mahony, who, on Thursday last, about mid-day was seized by an affection resembling paralysis, while in George's-street, and was immediately removed in his private cab to the family residence, Tontine buildings, where the faculty gave the most prompt and anxious attention to his case, and forthwith applied those restoratives which the best professional skill and experience could advise. The worthy Alderman derived a temporary relief, and slowly recovered from the first shock of the attack, which had been so violent and unexpected, but, alas, under a malady of so dangerous a complexion, little hope of improvement could be cherished, and on Friday morning their patient declined fast, and lingered until Saturday morning, at six o'clock, when the hand of death quietly released that spirit which animated his mortal frame. For fifty years he passed before his fellow-citizens of every rank and persuasion, as a man of business, a private gentleman, and a magistrate, conversant with all, respected and esteemed, without exception, by all. For a period of years, too, he took an active and valuable part, in connection with the *Limerick Chronicle*. In his domestic circle, the high and endearing relations of husband and parent were exhibited in the most amiable light—fond, indulgent, and affectionate to the wife and children of his bosom, the kind master, and liberal benefactor. A widow and ten children are left to deplore this calamitous bereavement, a visitation which no earthly influence can teach them to support, but the precept and example instilled by him who loved Christ for his own sake, and virtue for its intrinsic beauty and worth. (1840-02-29, 4:5)

2507. Last Sunday morning, a man named Hegarly, while in a state of intoxication, fell from the side of the road into a little stream, near Coleraine, and was unfortunately drowned. (1840-03-07, 4:4)

2508. (*Communicated.*) Armagh, April 1.—A melancholy accident happened here yesterday. A poor man named Pat M'Gaverney, of Charter School-lane, was employed by a man named Mac Kenna, to pull down some old houses in Barrack-hill.—Not having gone home, as usual, to his breakfast at nine o'clock, his wife wondering what had kept him, sent her daughter to inquire the reason of his stay. On arriving at the spot the old house was down, and she could obtain no information as to where he was gone. An alarm was immediately spread, and the poor man, after some delay, was dug out of the ruins, lifeless, and in a dreadful state. I think men, either as employers or servants, should pay more attention to the manner such operations are carried on, and not hurry themselves into eternity by undermining the walls, which if so done, must inevitably crush those engaged. I understand M'Gaverney was on his way to Scotland, and finding employment here he continued for months. He has left a wife and child to lament his loss. (1840-04-04, 3:2)

2509. Death of the Earl of Enniskillen.—A brave and noble spirit has departed from the world.—The Earl of Enniskillen is no more. After many months of suffering and decline, this distinguished Nobleman breathed his last, at his residence, Florence Court, in the county of Fermanagh on the morning of Tuesday. Frank, intrepid, and courteous in his manner, he was as much beloved by the friends, as dreaded by the enemies of his country. Just, considerate, and judicious as a landlord, he was the pride and the boast of his intelligent and independent tenantry; whilst the ardent affections of his family and the warm attachment of his friends—the solicitude with which they watched his declining health, and the sorrow with which his demise, though ripe and full of honors, has filled their hearts, are the honest evidence of that kindliness of disposition and universal benevolence of character which won him the respect, confidence, and affection of all who had the happiness of his acquaintance.

The noble lord is succeeded in his title and estate by his eldest son, Lord Cole, whose elevation to his present rank will create a vacancy in the representation of Fermanagh, of which he has been a member since the year 1831. (1840-04-04, 3:3)

2510. On Wednesday last a frightful occurrence took place near Dungarvan on the property of Lady Dover. Mr. Maher kindled a large lime-kiln until Wednesday when its operations became obstructed. One of the kiln-men went down to remedy the impediment, and remaining some time below, a second went down and after him a third, a fourth not seeing his comrades return, looked into the kiln, and saw them lying at the bottom of it; he immediately went down to see what was the matter, but a Protestant clergyman, the Rev. Mr. Brown, Rector of Dungarvan, who was present, apprehending the consequences, with a humanity that does him the greatest credit, went down himself, fastened a rope round the man's middle, and both were taken up. The man was perfectly insensible when taken up, and Mr. Brown himself fainted away on the bank, but both recovered in a short time. The other three unhappy men were taken up soon after, but life was extinct. (1840-04-04, 3:4)

2511. The report of the Earl Oneill's death is not true. Such an event would vacate the representation of Antrim, held by General O'Neill, his brother, and next heir; also the Colonelcy of the Antrim Militia. (1840-04-11, 1:2)

2512. Melancholy Suicide of Lieutenant-General Sir William Thornton.—We regret to announce the death of Lieutenant-General Sir William Thornton, K.C.B., Colonel of the 85th regiment of infantry, &c., who terminated his existence by self-destruction on Monday last. He retired to rest at his usual hour, and nothing was heard of him during the night, but about seven o'clock on Monday morning, a report of fire-arms being heard proceeding from his bedroom, on its being entered it was found that the gallant officer had destroyed himself. An inquest has been held on the body, and a verdict of "Temporary derangement" returned. Sir William Thornton succeeded the late Sir Herbert Taylor, Bart., as Colonel of the 85th foot. He also, in the lifetime of his late Royal Highness the Duke of York, filled the responsible office of Military Secretary to the Commander-in-Chief at the Horse Guards, and subsequently was, we believe, Governor of the island of Jersey. Sir William was in his 61st year, and unmarried. (1840-04-11, 1:3)

2513. The Late Elopement.—We hear—but find it difficult to credit the information—that Dr. Lardner has a daughter 15 or 16 years old, living under the same roof at Paris with himself and the unhappy companion of his flight!—He states, we are told, that he has been obliged to give up his Encylopaedia, which produced him near 2,000*l*. a year, but that he considers this a small sacrifice. It will be recollected that the elopement was in the first instance, intended to take place on a Tuesday, for which day apartments had been taken at the Adelaide Hotel, in London; but an accidental circumstance (that of an open fly having been provided, instead of a close one) caused its postponement till the following Friday. We understand that in the interval a lady called several times at the above hotel, to make inquires for Mr. and Mrs. Bennett, under which name Dr. Lardner and Mrs. Heaviside travelled.—*Brighton Gazette*.

At an early hour on Thursday, as Dr. Lardner was sitting at breakfast, at his lodgings, in the Rue Tronchet, Paris, he had the unwelcome visit of the husband of the lady whose affections he had seduced, and received summary chastisement at his hands.—The lady was, it is said, removed by her father, who accompanied her husband.—*Age*.

2513, continued: The following paragraph appears in Friday's *Galignani*:

—A correspondent informs us, that, at an early hour yesterday, a reverend gentleman, distinguished by his high scientific attainments, and whose recent flight from England occasioned a considerable sensation, was found at an hotel in this city, by the husband of the lady who accompanied the Doctor to the continent. The *rencontre* is described as having, in the extreme, been disagreeable to the latter, and was followed by the instant removal of the fair fugitive by her father.

Our correspondent in Paris sends the following version of this affair:—The occupants of the Hotel de Trouchet [sic], rue Trouchet, behind the Madelaine, in Paris, were disturbed from their slumbers on Wednesday night, or rather on Thursday morning, for it was between two and three o'clock, by screams of murder, and piercing shrieks. It appears that the hotel has amongst its lodgers Dr. Lardner and Mrs. Heaviside, whose flight from Britain and pursuit by her injured husband have been mentioned in the English newspapers. Mr. Heaviside and Col. Spicer (Mrs. Heaviside's father) who, with four servants, had arrived from England, had ascertained the address of the guilty pair, and having obtained an entrance, the lady was dragged out of her bed, notwithstanding her screams for assistance, and removed to the hotel de l'Europe, rue de Rivoli, and an hour afterwards was removed by her father from Paris, *en route* to England. Dionysius, it seems, was most severely punished by the invaders—he was beat most terribly and is covered with contusions and bruises. As my information emanates from a friend, through a gentleman living in the hotel, the facts may be relied on. I must add that rarely has a fracas given more satisfaction. (1840-04-18, 2:2)

2514. Horrible and Afflicting Tragedy.—From the *Limerick Reporter*.—This morning (Tuesday), one of the most shocking and awful cases of murder and suicide it has ever been the painful duty of a public journalist to record, occurred in Queen-street in this city. A gentleman, named Roche, a stranger in Limerick, and said to be from Cashel, the father of a grown and respectable family, cut his wife's throat with a razor, and almost severed the head from the body!! Mrs. R. had just risen from bed, and was in the act of lacing her stays, when, in a fit of insanity, the unfortunate husband seized a razor, and before assistance could be procured or alarm made, perpetrated the frightful deed. He then made an attempt to cut his own throat, but failed at first; in a second effort, however, the ill-fated maniac was successful. While he was in the very act of drawing the razor a second time across his throat, Miss Roche, his daughter, an interesting young lady, about eighteen years of age, rushed into the room but was too late. Our reporter had not seen the bodies, but the description given him was that they were lying on the floor in a pool of blood, presenting one of the most awful spectacles ever (*continued...*)

2514, continued: ...witnessed. These are the main facts of this awful tragedy.

An inquest having been held on the bodies before the Mayor, and a highly respectable jury, the following verdict was returned:

"That the deceased, Jane Roche, came by her death from the effects of injuries inflicted on her by her husband, Maurice Roche, by cutting her throat with a razor, he being at the time labouring under temporary insanity."—"That the deceased Maurice Roche came by his death from the effects of injuries inflicted on himself with a razor, he being at the time labouring under temporary insanity." (1840-04-18, 2:2)

2515. Noble Lindsay Wetherall, formerly 3d Light Dragoons, and who married Miss O'Brien, daughter of the sergeant-major, is committed to Cork gaol for bigamy. He is a native of Beaufort, Kerry, and respectably connected. (1840-04-18, 2:3)

2516. We are deeply concerned to announce the death of that most excellent nobleman and true philanthropist, the Right Hon. Lord Headly, at Aghadoe House, Killarney, almost adored, we may add, by his numerous tenantry and the poor of the neighbourhood, whose constant benefactor his Lordship was. Dying without issue, the title and estates descend to his nephew Mr. Winn. (1840-04-18, 2:3)

2517. Death of Thomas Drummond, Esq., Under-Secretary.—After four days of severe suffering, Mr. Drummond breathed his last, a few minutes after seven o'clock, on Wednesday, evening. Mr. Drummond had a dinner party on Friday evening, and rode into town, to Dublin Castle, on Saturday morning; and such was his devotion to public business that he spent nearly nine hours in his office on that day. On Sunday morning Sir H. Marsh, Bart., was suddenly called in when the most prompt means were taken to alleviate his complaint—inflammation of the peritoneum and kidneys. In the afternoon, the advice of Sir Philip Crampton, Bart., was availed of. On Monday, the violence of the symptoms increased; and on Tuesday, they had reached to such an alarming extent that the attending physicians pronounced the case to be hopeless. Since that time he has been occasionally in great suffering; but he died in perfect possession of his senses.—*Saunders's Newsletter*. (1840-04-18, 3:4)

2518. Death of Mr. Gregory.—The Right Hon. William Gregory, for many years Under-Secretary of State in Ireland, has paid the debt of nature. Full of years and of honors, his grey hairs have descended to the grave; and in the joyful expectation of the resurrection of the just, he rests from the labours of a well-spent life. (1840-04-18, 3:4)

2519. Melancholy Death of William M'Conkey, of Omagh, Esq., M.D.—We have this day the painful duty of announcing the premature death of this most estimable man. He left Omagh, during the evening of Monday last, to visit a patient in the neighbourhood, and did not leave, on his return, until about eleven o'clock. Early on Tuesday morning he was found lying on the road, a short distance from the house he had left, quite dead—his horse grazing near the body. At ten o'clock, when our information left, it had not been ascertained from what cause he had fallen from his horse—whether by accident or apoplexy. An inquest was about being held. The shops in the town were all closed, and every inhabitant seemed to sincerely regret the death of the humane, kind, and attentive Dr. M'Conkey, and to feel for the bereaved situation of a loving wife and interesting young family. The Doctor was the superintendent of the Omagh Fever Hospital, in which situation he had earned for himself the gratitude of hundreds of the poor of Omagh and surrounding country.—[*Derry Standard.*] (1840-04-25, 2:3)

2520. Death of Lord Guillamore.—We are concerned to announce the demise of the Right Hon. Standish O'Grady, Lord Viscount Guillamore, at the family residence, Rockbarton, in the county of Limerick, at eleven o'clock on Monday night last, when he departed this life, after an illness of long duration, and much suffering. His Lordship is succeeded in the title and estates by his eldest son, Colonel the Hon. Standish O'Grady, who represented this county, Limerick, for some years in parliament, and is married to a daughter of the Hon. Berkley Paget, niece of the Marquis of Anglesey. The late Peer was called to the Irish Bar in Easter Term, 1787, and was admitted a Bencher of the King's Inns in Michaelmas, 1798, an eventful period of his country's history, when he rose to distinction upon those high qualifications, natural and acquired, which he enjoyed in an eminent degree above most of his then distinguished forensic contemporaries. He was a man of superior mind, and mixed but little in the angry tumult of political agitation, but having filled the office of Attorney-General in 1803, was elevated to the dignity of Chief Baron of the Exchequer in 1805, where he presided for several years with consummate ability, and finally retired in January, 1831, the reward of his arduous labours in the public service being a Peerage and a pension for life of £3,500. His lordship married the sister of the late John Waller, of Castletown, Esq., formerly representative, in Parliament, for the county of Limerick, by whom he had a numerous issue.—*Limerick Chronicle*. (1840-04-25, 2:4)

2521. Chairmanship of Roscommon.—We regret to announce the death, from fever, of Thomas Forde, Esq., Chairman of Roscommon, which took place on Tuesday morning, at his residence in Mountjoy-square.—*Dublin Evening Packet*. (1840-04-25, 3:3)

2522. The remains of the late lamented Thomas Drummond, Esq., were removed [for] interment from the Under-Secretary's Lodge, Phoenix Park. 1840-04-25, 3:3)

2523. Lord Castlemaine died, of internal abscess, at Anne-street, Dublin, last Saturday morning. (1840-04-25, 3:3)

2524. A memorial is being got up by the principal members of the British Association for the advancement of Science to the council, praying them to remove Dr. Lardner from his office as one of their members, on account of his disgraceful conduct in the elopment from Brighton. (1840-04-25, 3:5)

2525. Stanzas, on the death of
the late Rev. Charles Evatt.

You who have slumber'd in soft pleasure's arms,
Who seek the halls, where wanton folly reigns,
Within whose home, woe spreads not her alarms,
Whose cheek the tear of sorrow, never stains:
Wake from your trance of dissipation now,
And mark how soon the living may lie low;
Reflect, though health may wear her rosy wreath,
The wily asp of death may lurk beneath.

We know not what the coming moment brings,
E'en as to him, (whose warning voice is still)—
The silent hours, may bear us on their wings,
The awful mandate of the sov'reign will;
He knew not, that his vesper blessing gave,
A last farewell, to those he strove to save—
Nor dream'd, while urging heavenward to stray,
That he, himself, should earliest lead the way.
Cold are the lips, that oft so fondly press'd,
A father's kiss, upon his children's brow,
And still the heart, within his yarning [sic] breast,
That felt for others, 'though so throbless now.
Beside his new made grave, the stranger stands,
And pays the tribute sigh, that worth demands.
His widow's tears, his orphan's cries are vain—
The good must die, and tyrant death must reign.
"Insatitate death," why like the lightning burn,
Peace from the hearth, where love so lately shone?
Why sever hearts, that wish'd to fill one urn,
Why leave the widow'd mother here alone?
Like the fierce simoom, on its winged way,
Thou blightest hope, and all her flow'rs decay;
Calm shall we sleep beneath thy cypress shade,
Ere skilful time can heal the wounds you've made.

"The young, the fair, the beautiful" have died;
Their Cemetery—earth—must close o'er all,
And conqueror and conquer'd, side by side,
Feed the same dust, and wait the judgment call.
Yet for the hope of resurrection given,
Let the sad mourner, raise her heart to heav'n,
She knows not, but the lov'd one that is gone,
May be the first to lead her to the throne.

April 15, 1840.
(1840-04-25, 4:1)

2526. Marriage with the Ring.—The practice of marrying with the ring for the female was adopted by the Romans; the bride was modestly veiled, and after receiving the nuptial benediction, was crowned with flowers. The ring, symbolic of eternity, having no termination, was given and received as a token of everlasting love. (1840-04-25, 4:5)

2527. Marriage in High Life.—On Thursday, at St. Mary's, Leamington Spa, Mr. William Charles Evans Freke, fourth son of the Hon. Percy Freke, and nephew of Lord Carbery, to Lady Sophia Wichcote, Widow of the late Sir Thomas Wichcote, Bart., and third sister of the Earl of Harborough. Her Ladyship is in her 45th year. (1840-05-02, 1:4)

2528. The Rev. Mr. Peacocke officiated at the funeral of Lord Castlemaine, who was interred on Monday, in Athlone Church. The Hon. Richard Handcock, eldest son of the late Peer, succeeds to the title and estate. (1840-05-02, 1:4)

2529. Inquests were held yesterday at Silverhill and Derrygore, in the neighbourhood of this town [Enniskillen], by Mr. Trotter, upon the bodies of two women who died suddenly. The one at Silverhill was a pauper, waiting at the gate of the Rev. Mr. Weir, and who had been in delicate health: she was waited upon by the charitably condescending lady of the rev. gentleman in person, who gave her some money, but observing her sickly state, she turned into the house for bread, and upon her return found life extinct. The other was a girl of the name of Kitty M'Kenna, servant of Miss Irwin of Derrygore, who came by her death in consequence of inflammation in the stomach and bowels, being induced by taking an emetic. She had been following her usual avocations the evening before.—*Fermanagh Reporter*. (1840-05-02, 2:2)

2530. We are sincerely grieved to record in this publication, the premature and melancholy decease of a young and talented townsman, Surgeon Hurst, who departed this life at an early hour on the morning of the 27th ult. In every circle of society he charmed around him the feelings and the affections of those he associated with, and it might be said, he claimed a home in the heart of every one who knew him intimately—talent of no ordinary description had marked his career in early life, and he had carried this touchstone of future success with unceasing industry through the years in which he sought after his medical honours, and to our knowledge, he has been, for the last few months, marked out by the gentry of the Monaghan poor law union, and by the approbation of a majority of the guardians, for filling the honorable situation of medical attendant to the poor-house of the district. He had concluded his studies, but desiring to do credit to their selection, was seeking with additional testimonials of professional respectability in Dublin, where, from assiduities of so unremitting and severe a description, he was seized with cough and other symptoms of pulmonary consumption, which, but too quickly, proved fatal. In (*continued...*)

2530, continued: ...his death, a widowed parent has been deprived (in God's inscrutable ways,) of a tender and affectionate son, and the other members of his attached family of a high-spirited and creditable relative—the society in which he moved of one of its brightest graces—the medical profession of an honorable and intellectual member—and the town and neighbourhood of Monaghan of one who would have gathered the laurels of professional success with the feelings of a gentleman. (1840-05-02, 3:2)

2531. Lines.—For the *Northern Standard.*

Another—yet another—
From the woodfires' cheerful light,
From the holy sunsets glancing,
Has departed from our sight;
And he pass'd amidst the breath
Of the spring time's gentle sigh,
When the winter winds had died,
And the summer yet was night,
And the zephyr made a sound
As he fled, that seem'd like weeping—
Murmurs thro' his casement low,
Like spring voices soft were creeping.

We have woo'd thee back to thy childhood's home,
That thou from its beauty no more might roam—
We have call'd thee afar from the city's din,
To rest thy mother's heart within,
And to dream of youth's bright home of bliss
In some fiery realm of happiness—
Where eyes must only glance to smile,
And heart must cherish heart the while,
Where time must linger in delight,
Unclouded by one shade of night,
And gentle as the twilight hour
It's [sic] close must be—in such a bower.
Would thy spirit rest from the world's strife,
'Till thy soul might wing its way to life;
Now the breeze is calling thee to thy home,
With a voice as soft as the ring-dove's tone—
And the Spring is spreading its beaming flowers,
To deck thy path to the fairy bowers;
Then list to their wooing—oh! linger awhile,
Till the earth in its beauty around thee may smile!
Why goest thou hence? is not thine the kiss
Of affection—pure—earth's dearest bliss.
And thy mother's bosom, that holy shrine,
Where earthly passion becomes divine,
Would pillow thee ever from sorrow's tears,
From life's rude blast and its wearying fears.
Oh! go not, for earth hath in store for thee,
Its brightest and fairest—return thee—oh! flee,
In thy youth's gay morn, and make thy home
On her beautiful bosom—amid thine own.

But it might not be the moaning
Of the dawn's sweet summer breath,
Could not bear back that young spirit
From the mighty grasp of death,
While above its gentle wailing
Were heard other holy tones,
That came like a gladsome singing,
From the far off spirit's homes.

We will bear thee afar on our glorious wings,
To the land where no earthly sorrow clings,
And its splendor will burst on thy dazzled sight,
Like the gleam of the summer morning's light,
And music shall breathe on thy soften'd sense,
Bearing thy pure soul in extacy hence.
We will waft thee to realms that the eagle's eye
Might not look on—where the bursting sigh—
Is unheard where the raging tempests case,
And the troubled bosom rests in peace.
Away with thy grief—tho' thy parting now
Cast a gloom and a shadow across thy brow;
Tho' thou leavest the lov'd on earth to dwell,
Yet dream not, thou sayest a last farewell,
And they, thy hearts cherish'd, the parted awhile,
Will welcome thee home with a joyful smile,
And never, thro' time, shall thy fond heart more,
Be torn from the happy ones gone before.
Then burst from the chains of the blighting earth,
That thy spirit may pass to its glorious birth.

And his bright soul burst in gladness,
From its fading form of clay
With the dying of that sweet song,
It past in peace way—
And the whispers of the wild wind,
Blent with the mourners' sigh,
Yet the earth smiles on in beauty,
Tho' its brightest flow'rets die.

28th April, 1840. Eliza.
(1840-05-02, 4:1)

2532. The Earl of Enniskillen.

The grey-haired patriot goes down to the tomb
Honor'd belov'd, and wept. The beauteous land,
Which hail'd him 'mong the first of freedom's band,
Faithful and dauntless in her day of gloom,
And spurning the foul chains of crimson'd Rome,
And raising up with spotless heart and hand
A prostrate cause, by perfidy struck down—
Ay! long and bitterly shall Ireland mourn
Him who has wended to that awful bourne
Whence traveller returns not! For the Crown
And Shrine he lived—for them he would have died
Joyously 'neath the banner of the brave,
Which scared the tyrant in his bigot pride,
When freedom cross'd the Boyne's exulting wave!
When Enniskillen charged, and Schomberg fell!
When flashed the gallant glaives of Freemen—when
Rome fled in curses to her gory den,
And sank, but not for aye, the savage yell
Of priestcraft's minions, reeking from the hell
Of vengeful superstition—say, who *then*
Could crouch and crawl to Popery? Display

The rankling chains of slavery? Untomb
The corse of tyranny—betray the blue
Banner of Runnymede—the Boyne—Torbay?
None! But the cravens of our latter day
Cherish the cause their ancestors had spurn'd!
Are freedom's tablets fragile as our clay?
Is Ridley's cause by Popery inurn'd?

Age.

(1840-05-02, 4:1)

2533. Sudden Death.—Yesterday an inquest was held at Bigfirs, near Clogher, by Dr. Blackwell, on the body of Mr. Thomas Kean, of Suffolk-street, Dublin, apothecary, who was found dead in his bed on Thursday morning; he was in a delicate state of health for some time previous. Verdict—"Died by the visitation of God."—*Drogheda Journal*. (1840-05-02, 4:1)

2534. Death by Drowning.—We have to record a melancholy accident which occurred on Wednesday last at Lisnalong, in the county Cavan. A Mr. James White of Cornary, county Cavan, went out in a boat to fish on Lisnalong lake, and whilst endeavoring to kill a large pike which he had hooked, the boat upset and, melancholy to relate, he was precipitated into the water where he sunk to rise no more. Some people who were working in a field adjoining saw the accident but could render him no assistance. His body was found shortly after and sent home to his residence. He was of a very ingenious turn of mind, being an excellent musician, a carpenter, mason, slator, plasterer, &c. He held an excellent farm of land in the townland of Knocknalosat, under Mr. Foulke Greville, and was on a visit with Mr. Brunker, of Lisnalong, at the time. He has left a widow and six children to deplore their loss. He was a quiet inoffensive man—much esteemed by all who knew him. (1840-05-09, 3:2)

2535. The Earl of Ranfurly, who had for many years resided in the Place Vendome, Paris, expired on the 26th ult., in the 86th year of his age. His Lordship married 2d of June, 1785, the Hon. Diana Jane Pery, eldest daughter and co-heir of Edmund Sexton Viscount Pery, and cousin of the Earl of Limerick, by whom he had issue, Thomas, the present Viscount Northland (now Earl of Ranfurly,) born 19th April, 1786, and married 28th February, 1815, Mary Juliana, eldest daughter of the late Hon. and Most Rev. Wm. Stuart, Lord Bishop of Armagh. There are several children by his marriage, the eldest of whom, the Hon. Thomas Knox (now Viscount Northland,) born 13th Nov., 1816, is M.P. for the borough of Dungannon. The late Earl of Ranfurly was brother to our esteemed Diocesan, the Lord Bishop of Limerick. A sum of £8,000 a-year reverts to the Crown by Lord Ranfurly's death.—*Limerick Chronicle*. (1840-05-09, 4:4)

2536. Marriages [England].—From the printed returns, it appears that in the year 1838 there were celebrated, of Broomstick marriages, 4,280—in the Orthodox from 107,201; making a total of 111,481; and showing pretty clearly what the feelings of the country really are upon that important subject, and what a great noise a very few people are capable of making. (1840-05-16, 1:5)

2537. Rejoicings at Anketell Grove.—On Monday last that part of the barony of Trough, surrounding Anketell-Grove, presented an appearance of joyous and unusual bustle—groups of farmers, in their holiday suits, and mounted on their best nags, were seen, from far and near, wending their merry way to a certain rendezvous where the tenants of William Anketell, Esq., were assembling to escort to the home of his ancient race, the heir of the Anketells, and his young bride, this being the first time that Major M. Anketell visited our county since his marriage. When all had collected, to the number of several hundreds, a procession of horse-men were formed, which proceeded, under the guidance of Thomas Anketell, Esq., of Dungillick, on the road by which the youthful pair were expected, and until they arrived at the point beyond Glasslough where the road branches off towards Tynan and Armagh. There they placed themselves in files, on either side of the way, in order to allow the carriage to pass in the midst, when the bridegroom was greeted with that deep and respectful deference which is more of the heart than the head. Mr. Anketell returned the salutes of his happy tenantry in a manner which shewed how deeply he appreciated the love of honest hearts, no matter how lowly, and the carriage passed on, accompanied by the *cortege*, in good order, until they approached the gate of the Grove demesne, over which a handsome arch was erected, bearing a banner and tablet, with the inscription of

"*Welcome to Trough.*"

Here were gathered all those who were not happy enough to possess horses to join the procession, and, on the approach of the cavalcade, one joyous cheer of welcome burst forth from at least five hundred lips, and was echoed again and again, until Mr. Anketell and his lady had reached the lodge, and entered its hospitable portals. In the evening refreshments were served out in abundance, and tar barrels and bonfires blazed in every direction in the neighbourhood. The town of Emyvale was illuminated—on every side was unbounded pleasure—and all went merry as a marriage bell.

The following day, Thomas Anketell, Esq., J.P., J.M. Johnston, Esq., J.P., and John Pringle, Esq., waited on Mr. Anketell, with a congratulatory address, signed by the tenantry on his father's estates, to which Mr. Anketell returned an answer, couched in those expressions of philanthropy and good-will which have always marked the conduct of his respected father and his family. The address and answer appear in another part of our sheet this day. (1840-05-16, 2:5)

2538. Lord Rossmore.—Several of our cotemporaries have been misinformed with respect to the death of Lord Rossmore. His Lordship is yet alive, but in a very weak and dangerous state. His medical attendant, J.S. M'Dowell, Esq., has, we believe, no hopes of his recovery. (1840-05-16, 2:5)

2539. At a Meeting of the Tenantry of the Anketell Grove Estates, held on Tuesday last, it was resolved unanimously to adopt and present to Major Mathew Anketell the following address, congratulating him on his recent marriage, and return to the home of his fathers.—It was also resolved that Thomas Anketell, Esq., J.W. Johnston, Esq. and John Pringle, Esq., be requested to present the congratulations of the meeting.

In accordance with the resolutions of the meeting the above named gentlemen waited on Mr. Anketell, and presented the address, which was received with much cordiality, and to which he returned the accompanying answer:

Address.

May 12th, 1840.

Dear Sir—In accordance with the unanimous wish of the Tenantry on the Grove, we feel sincere pleasure in presenting to you our congratulations on your recent marriage, and in having the opportunity of welcoming you and your amiable bride amongst us on so important and interesting an event, which we hail as the forerunner of increased happiness to yourself, and as calculated to cherish all the social virtues among those around you. We do not offer a tribute, merely of adulation, when we say that the amiability and kindness of disposition which you have ever shown in your intercourse with us, and your ready acquiescence in any measures suggested by your beloved father, for the advantage and improvement of his tenantry, demand the warm expression of our affection and esteem. We cannot, without doing violence to the feelings of our hearts, withhold this unostentatious manifestation of our feelings. We would hope, dear Sir, that you may be long spared amongst us to continue to imitate the virtues, and to reflect the qualities of your honoured and valued father; and, we would likewise pray, that he himself may live long to guide and encourage you by his bright example, to raise our neighborhood, as he has hitherto done, in civilisation and industry, and to preside over a happy and grateful tenantry. May you, and the bright ornament you have added to your house, long live in happiness and love—may the Grove never want an heir to inherit your united excellencies and respected name—and when the debt of nature is paid, may you together join the retinue of the Heavenly Bridegroom, and clad in the wedding garment, the righteousness of saints, sit down at the marriage supper of the Lamb to praise him throughout the endless ages of eternity. With every feeling of respect and attachment, we remain, dear Sir, very sincerely yours,

J.W. Johnston,	Thomas Anketell,
John Pringle,	John Anketell,
John Woods,	Robert Woods,
William Woods,	James Moore,
James Mullan,	John Boyd,
Robert Mitchell,	James Anketell.

Anketell Grove, 14th May, 1840.

My Dear Friends—The very flattering reception which awaited Mrs. Mathew Anketell and myself upon our arrival at Anketell Grove, in addition to the kind congratulations you have now presented to us, demonstrate beyond my most sanguine expectations, the warm interest you have evinced in our united happiness and prosperity.

To obtain the approbation and esteem of those with whom we are immediately connected, renders one of the highest favors which can be conferred upon an individual; and if, during my intercourse among you, I have contributed to cement our social circle, by inculcating, in private life, the doctrine of goodwill among persons of chequered religious and political opinions, be assured there is no circumstance which impresses me more agreeably than the attainment of so desirable an object. I am happy to feel that you are assured of my readiness to co-operate with my father in furtherance of improvements and projects, which he conceives will be most conducive to the welfare of his tenantry; and, let me add, that our mutual object will ever be, not solely the extension of possessions, so much as the securing the greatest prosperity upon a given surface.

In conclusion, allow me to offer, in the name of Mrs. Mathew Anketell and myself, our united thanks for the reception and congratulation with which we have been honored, as also for the solicitude you have so feelingly expressed in behalf of our temporal and eternal interests.

With best wishes for your happiness and prosperity, believe me, my dear friends, yours very truly,

Mathew Anketell.

(1840-05-16, 3:3)

2540. The following story is a new version of the tale—*She Stoops to Conquer*. The parties will be easily known:—At an early age, the daughter of a noble lord sold herself in marriage to a professional man, stricken in years, crippled, and so infirm, that at the time of his marriage he had to be assisted in and out of bed. At his death he honestly paid his youthful wife the value of her bargain; he left her 3,000*l*. a-year for life, provided she never married again! The young widow, liking the money better than the name, kept the former and changed the latter, and so managed matters as to get into the good graces of a personage of distinction. Marriage, for obvious reasons, was out of the question; if she married away went the 3,000*l*. per annum; if she did not, away went character. What was to be done? The broomstick settled the matter, and satisfied conscience.—The lady says she is married, and an honest woman, and she keeps 3,000*l.* a-year, left upon condition that she never married again! This is an honorable, just, and moral world we live in.—*Age.* (1840-05-16, 4:1)

2541. Dr. Unthank, was perhaps the oldest Physician in the south of Ireland. He expended large sums in the promotion of missionary settlements in North America, and the South Sea Islands. To the Illinois territory he transmitted £1000 some years ago, which the President of the United States publicly acknowledged. A considerable Government annuity has determined with his life. (1840-05-23, 1:4)

2542. Funeral of a Teetotaller.—On Monday last, a numerous body of Teetotallers of Charleville, wearing scarfs and hatbands, attended the remains of Mr. Francis Wyse, Petty Sessions Clerk of that town, to Effin church. A general feeling of regret pervaded all classes on account of this young man's death, for he fully exemplified the saying—an honest man is the noblest work of God. (1840-05-23, 1:5)

2543. The Hon. Henry R. Westenra, M.P., and the Hon. John C. Westenra, M.P., are at present at Cortolvin, attending the sick bed of their father, Lord Rossmore. His Lordship is still lingering in a hopeless state, each hour sapping the springs of a constitution that must in his youth have been of Herculean strength. (1840-05-23, 3:2)

2544. Melancholy Loss of Lives.—On Saturday, the 16th instant, three men, named Andrew M'Mullen, James M'Mullen, and John Leghey, were in a boat, sailing between Downhill and the Barmouth. It began to blow a hard gale, and the sea running high, the men saw that it was dangerous to remain any longer, and made for the shore: but before they got to the shore, a heavy sea came and swamped the boat. One of them seized the oar, and another got hold of the keel, from which, however, he was tossed by the advancing wave, and he then made for an oar which was at a distance, and caught it. Being encumbered with a heavy coat, he was unable to reach the shore, and perished. He has left a wife and two children. The third, Leghey, was not seen after the accident. It is supposed that he had been struck by the boat when it was swamped. The bodies of the two sufferers have not yet been found.—We must not forget to remark the most kind and humane conduct, on this occasion, of two of the Hon. the Clothworkers Company of London, who, together with C.J. Knox, Esq., happened to be present.—They used every effort in their power to restore M'Mullen to life, who came ashore, as, from so much suffering in the water, he was almost lifeless. He is now in the way of recovery. They gave to the wife of M'Mullen one sovereign, and half a sovereign to the person to whose house he was carried.—*Newry Telegraph.* (1840-05-23, 3:3)

2545. The late Mr. Drummond's Will.—It appears by the will of the late Mr. Secretary Drummond, that he died possessed of chattel property to the amount of 13,846*l.*, the stamp duty on which came to 155*l.* But it is said by recent purchases he left behind him real property to a vast amount.—*Warder.* (1840-05-23, 4:3)

2546. Will of the late Mr. Forde.—It appears by the will of the late Mr. Forde, Assistant-Barrister for the county of Roscommon, that he died worth the immense sum of 27,672*l.*, the stamp duty on which amounted to 260*l.* (1840-05-23, 4:3)

2547. On Saturday last, the coffin, containing the mortal remains of the late Earl of Ranfurly, arrived here from London, on board of the *Duke of Cambridge* Steamer. It was immediately placed in a hearse which was waiting on the quay, for removal to the family cemetery at Dungannon.—*Belfast Chronicle.* (1840-05-23, 4:5)

2548. Sudden Death of George Lee, Esq.—It is with feeling of regret that we have to announce the sudden demise of George Lee, Esq., solicitor, which event took place on Friday, the 22d, at Garnakeevan, the residence of Henry Smithwick, within four miles of Nenagh, from apoplexy, brought on by the bursting of a blood vessel, occasioned by a fall from a horse. Mr. Lee was in the 37th year of his age, and very generally esteemed. (1840-05-30, 1:3)

2549. Sudden Death of John Primrose, Esq.—We never witnessed a more awful illustration of the great Scripture truth, that in the midst of life we are in death, than the melancholy event which has torn from the bosom of an amiable and idolising family our respectable fellow-citizen whose name stands at the head of this obituary.

On Monday last, between two and three o'clock, Mr. Primrose had left his house in Denny-street, and had proceeded up Nelson-street, nearly opposite Mr. Cassidy's, upon some business connected with his duty as returning officer for this union, when he suddenly fell to the ground. Mr. Samuel Hilliard was immediately by his side, and promptly sent for Dr. Alton, who, in a few minutes, was in attendance. On his arrival, however, life was extinct, the temple artery, which was immediately opened, not affording the slightest drop of blood. The body was then removed into the house of Mrs. M. O'Connell, where it became the painful duty of the provost to hold an inquest. Dr. Alton was rather of opinion that death proceeded from the rupture of some vessel about the heart. The jury found a verdict in accordance with the circumstances of the case.—*Kerry Post.* (1840-05-30, 1:3)

2550. John Power, Esq., M.P., for the county of Waterford, was obliged to pay the Right Rev. Dr. Kinsella £100, to perform the marriage ceremony, as the Prelate demurred, for the bridegroom had not been at confession. (1840-05-30, 1:5)

2551. Dreadful Accident to Captain Otway.—A very serious accident happened on Friday evening, in Hyde Park, to Captain Otway, of the Royal Navy, eldest son of Admiral Sir Robert Otway, Bart. Captain Otway was riding a very spirited horse in the grass field on the left of Rotten-row, when the animal reared up, shyed at the hurdles, and at the same time, in consequence of the rider bearing the reins too tightly, both went over. Captain Otway fell on his back, and [the] horse upon him. By the concustion [sic] great internal injury arose, but no bones were broken. Captain Otway was immediately conveyed to the rooms of Colonel Cavendish, at the Knightsbridge barracks. Mr. Lane, the resident surgeon at St. George's Hospital, was the first medical attendant; but shortly after, Sir Astley Cooper and Sir Benjamin Brodie arrived.—Bleeding and fomentations were resorted to, the patient suffered the most acute agony. Lord Clarence Paget, who was riding with Captain Otway at the time of the melancholy occurrence, sat by the bed of the sufferer during the whole of Friday night. On Saturday evening Sir Robert Otway arrived from Sheerness, and the gallant Admiral has remained at the barracks ever since, except for a short period on Sunday, when he went to bring Lady Otway and her daughters to the melancholy scene. We lament to state that on Sunday evening there were but faint hopes of his surviving through the night. Captain Otway is about thirty years old, and a great favourite in the navy. The Queen has sent repeatedly to learn what hope the medical gentleman entertained. (1840-05-30, 2:2)

2552. Lord Rossmore.—Up to the hour of going to press we have learned that Lord Rossmore still lingers in a weak and hopeless state. It is impossible to say how long his lordship may linger—every hour diminishes his strength, and at present life is sustained merely by the effects of medical skill, acting on a strong and tenacious constitution. His sons are in constant and filial attendance on his sick couch—and it is impossible for them to calculate on an hour's absence, lest some unfavourable change might, in the interim, deprive them of a father. (1840-05-30, 3:1)

2553. Attempt at Self-Destruction.—A respectable looking young man, named John Mee, was charged by a police constable with attempting to drown himself in the Liffey.

The complainant stated that he heard a noise at the corner of Carlile-bridge the previous night; and on going to ascertain what was the matter, he saw the prisoner half over the wall, being held by a carman. He then took him away, but the prisoner made several efforts to throw himself over; witness then brought him to the station-house.

Inspector Mills said on going into the cell where the prisoner was confined he found him nearly choaked with one of his suspenders, which he had tied round his neck.

The prisoner said it was out of a family squabble he made the attempt, but promised to conduct himself quietly for the future.

The prisoner was then discharged. (1840-05-30, 4:5)

2554. Death of the Dowager Countess of Cork.—We regret to have to state that this venerable lady expired on Saturday morning at her house in New Burlington-street in her 95th year. Up to a short time ago, her ladyship was in excellent health, and even this year gave some parties. Her ladyship was taken unwell on Monday morning last, and gradually became worse. She was born the 21st of May, 1746, and thus had completed her 94th year a few days ago. (1840-06-06, 1:1)

2555. The Late Captain Otway.—Never were the better attributes of our nature more fully displayed than by the conduct of the officers of the 1st Life Guards during the late melancholy accident at the Hyde Park barracks. From the moment of the unfortunate gentleman being carried in, till his death took place, the whole establishment was devoted to the afflicted family. The splendid mess was broken up, and that house, which is usually the resort of gaiety and merriment, became suddenly one of silence and mourning. The very sentinels were seen to walk on their post on tiptoe for fear of disturbing the poor sufferer. Such was the conduct of this gallant regiment to their ill-fated brother in arms, and such should be the sympathy among the different branches of her Majesty's service. Let us hope that this bright example may long remain in the grateful memory of British sailors.—(*Morning Post.*) We have learned that the Queen, on hearing of the death of Captain Otway, immediately wrote in her hand a most kind and feeling note to Sir Robert and Lady Otway, expressing her own and Prince Albert's deep and sincere sympathy in their affliction. Such spontaneous acts of feeling speak for themselves, and must tend to rivet the affections, not only of those who are the immediate objects of such kindness, but of all who hear them.—*Globe.* (1840-06-06, 1:4)

2556. On Friday se'nnight, an unmarried female of the name of Rose Carroll, who resided with her brother, James Carroll, who rents a portion of the Glebe lands of the Rev. Archibald Douglas, Rector of Cootehill, in the townland of Killetee, got a hank of yarn, which she spun herself, put it across a beam, intended for a chimney-piece, in the kitchen, and making a noose at the other end, put her head through it, and then kicked away a low stool on which she was standing whilst adjusting it, but her weight having stretched the hank so far as to permit her feet to touch the ground, she might then have rescued herself from her irksome situation had she thought proper; but so determined was she to consummate the rash act that she actually contracted up her legs, until the work of death was complete; and when her brother, who is also unmarried, returned home to his dinner, from his agricultural pursuits, he found, on cutting her down, that life was extinct. No cause can be assigned for her perpetrating this heinous sin except that she was observed to have been very melancholy for some time previous. She was about forty years of age, of an irreproachable character. Dr. John M'Fadden, one of the Coroners for the county of Cavan, held an Inquest on her body on the evening of the same day, when the verdict of the Jury was—"That the deceased had hanged herself whilst labouring under a fit of insanity." (1840-06-06, 2:5)

2557. Melancholy Accident—On Friday morning last, as a poor woman of the name of Jane Clendinning, from Ashfield, was coming into the market of Cootehill, a horse, belonging to a man of the name of Corr, from the neighbourhood of Leesboro, county of Monaghan, which was in a cart, laden with cabbage plants, took fright in consequence of the wife of a dealing man having had some bickering with her husband, taking up a stone and throwing it at him, it ran across the footpath, adjoining the town, where poor Jane Clendinning was walking, knocked her down, and drew the cart across her. On returning, both horse and cart went again over her and killed her. (1840-06-06, 2:5)

2558. Lord Rossmore.—We have learned, since our last publication, that an improvement has taken place in his Lordship's health, and the favourable symptoms have been increasing up to the hour of going to press. His medical attendant, J.S. M'Dowell, Esq., M.D., entertains, we believe, much more sanguine hopes than hitherto. His sons still remain at Cortolvin Hills. (1840-06-06, 3:1)

2559. Captain Otway, R.N., who fell from his horse in Hyde-park, expired last night at ten o'clock. Admiral Otway remained in the barracks with his son. Sir Astley Cooper and Sir Benjamin Brodie continued in attendance. The case was hopeless; the injuries internal were of a most painful nature. (1840-06-06, 4:2)

2560. Mr. George Moore, of Moore-hall, county of Meath, dropped dead at Manchester-square on the 27th ult. (1840-06-06, 4:2)

2561. Feargus OConnor is treated like the vilest villain in York Castle, and the state of his health gives his friends just alarm. (1840-06-06, 4:2)

2562. The First Night in the Grave.

'Tis cold, 'tis passing cold, they say,
Here in this dark abode,
While clay is mingling with its clay,
And spirit gone to God.

Nay, winter's frost and summer's sun
Exert their powers in vain;
This cannot warm the icy limb—
That cannot give me pain.

My humble cottage, where I dwelt,
Could not this charm unfold;
In Summer's heat I gasp'd for breath,
In winter fled from cold.

But, though these chamber walls are damp—
Tho' winds around me moan,
And darkness reigns without restraint—
It is a peaceful home.

No melancholy thoughts depress—
No meteor hopes deceive—
No griefs this woe-worn heart distress
"The first night in the grave."

But oh! this only is the urn
Where dust awaits its change
Until the resurrection morn,
That morn so new—so strange.

The spirit is no slumberer here,
It rests above with God;
Nor eye hath seen, nor ear can hear
The joys of that abode.

But, oh! remember, to that place,
No thoughtless travellers stray;
'Tis there for sinners saved by grace,
And Christ alone the way.

(1840-06-13, 4:1)

2563. A Faithful Wife resembles the cable of an anchor, every single thread composing which a word might break—but when twisted by love into one solid rope of fidelity and esteem, the ship of matrimony may ride in safety amid the direst storm, if the anchor of faith to which that cable is attached, has only found a stratum on which to ground its certain hold. (1840-06-13, 4:4)

2564. The executors of John Harvey Ollney have appealed to the House of Lords against another decision of the Irish Chancellor, who valued two post obit bonds of the present Earl of Aldborough for £12,000, and £20,000, at the market price of £19,000. (1840-06-20, 1:4)

2565. Mr. Edward Palmer, one of the sons of the High Sheriff of the King's County, was shot dead, last Friday evening, by the accidental discharge of a gun which his brother, Mr. Henry Palmer, was in the act of giving to a servant boy to bring into the house. (1840-06-20, 2:4)

2566. Typhus fever prevails to a great extent at present in the county of Meath. (1840-06-20, 2:4)

2567. Lord Rossmore—Is still progressing towards convalescence, and is expected to be able to take an airing in a day or two. His recovery, if permanent, is little short of miraculous, and reflects the highest honor on the medical character of his attendant physician, J.S. M'Dowell, Esq. (1840-06-20, 3:1)

2568. The appalling rumour so current on Thursday, of four infant bodies being found in the great tank or reservoir of the water-works company, at Greenhill, and of which some factory girls were suspected of being the mothers, is totally destitute of truth, nothing having occurred to substantiate this wanton fabrication. (1840-06-20, 3:2)

2569. Elegiac Stanzas.

"Whom the Gods love die young."
Ours is the loss, not hers. Her spirit gains
A glorious paradise for hapless earth—
The widest freedom for life's galling chains
The fullness of ethereal joys for dearth.
Woe is the pilgrim's heritage while here,
Bliss is the franchised spirit's lot on high—
There partings pain not—sorrow wrings no tear,
Our God in mercy wipes each weeping eye.

The glory of each mundane crown is dim—
Each crown of ecstacy, of peace, of love—
Compared with those of that circle seraphim,
Whose raptures limitless as realms above.
Weak are the bonds that death may snap in twain,
And frail the fabric o'er which time may sway,
But there reunion ceases not again,
And there the spirit yields not to decay.

Why mourn then for the youthful who may flee
From human nothingness to all that's great,
Who cast the shackles of mortality,
And reach the glories of supernal state?
Theirs, an eternal holiday of love—
Theirs, an eternal and a holy place;
In uncreated radiancy they rove,
Which springs refulgent from Jehovah's face.

We wandered once beneath the evening star,
Our theme was heaven, and heaven's undying bliss;
"And wherefore—spake she—linger thus afar
From yon fair regions in a world like this."
Thrice sainted maid! thine aspirations high
Was heard and answered by thy spirit's king;
'Twas thine to say—"Grave, where's thy victory,
And death, oh, welcome death! where is thy sting."

Then mourn not for the sainted; yea, mourn not,
For human frailty, sorrow, trouble—care
Hath not had time to shadow o'er her lot,
That in its springtime and its bloom was fair.
'Twas well. She knew no agony of life,
And mercy called her ere life's winter came;
Now her pure soul with nameless rapture rife,
Shall dwell through all eternity the same.

P.

(1840-06-20, 4:1)

2570. Mr. Joseph Cardinal will this morning lead to the hymeneal altar the blooming widow of the late Mr. James Charles Doyle, the banns having been published in the Roman Catholic Cathedral on Sunday. Mrs. Doyle's maiden name is Blache; and although she is only in her twenty-seventh year, she has buried three husbands, the last having died on the 1st day of April last.—*Montreal Herald*, May 19. (1840-06-27, 1:4)

2571. Most Awful and Melancholy Occurrence.—On Sunday night a man named David Leo, residing on part of the estate of the Count de Salis, Loughgur, in a fit of delirium from fever, rose out of bed and turned his wife and family out of doors. He then bolted the door, and shortly after the house was enveloped in flames, which, together with the adjoining one (where the poor sufferers family took shelter) was burned to the ground. The unhappy maniac was literally burned to a cinder in his own cabin before assistance could be procured. The afflicted family calculate upon the landlord's kindness to them in their misery, should this meet his eye, and, we firmly believe, not without just hopes of success.—*Limerick Reporter*. (1840-07-11, 2:2)

2572. Death of the Chief Baron.—Accounts reached Dublin on Wednesday, announcing the death of Chief Baron Woulfe, which melancholy event took place, we learn, in England. (1840-07-11, 2:3)

2573. We were much gratified, and not a little surprised yesterday, to see Lord Rossmore driving through the town, accompanied by Captain A.G. Lewis. His Lordship seems to be acquiring a new constitution after the severe and dangerous ordeal he has for several months gone through. The recovery of his Lordship has given inexpressible pleasure to his numerous tenantry. (1840-07-11, 3:2)

2574. Death of James M'Moran, Esq.—We have just learned that this young gentleman died at Sheffield on the 15th inst., of rapid decline. He was son to the late John M'Moran, Esq., M.D., of this town. In politeness as a gentleman, integrity, as a merchant, and humble piety as a Christian, he had few equals. We understand that his remains will be deposited in the family vault at the Presbyterian Church here, but have not heard on what day the funeral may be expected. (1840-07-18, 3:3)

2575. The census of the population of Ireland is to be taken by the police force, and they are to commence that duty in May next year. Any person refusing to answer the required questions is made subject to a penalty of £5. (1840-07-25, 2:2)

2576. Within a few years not less than three Chief Barons of the Irish Exchequer have died, namely, Joy, Woulfe, and O'Grady, Lord Guillamore. (1840-07-25, 2:5)

2577. In relation to the melancholy catastrophe which occurred off the Cove of Cork, by which several lives were lost, in consequence of the upsetting of a sail boat, with a party of gentlemen, who were visiting the *President* steam-ship, we make the following extract of a letter from one of the party—Walter Johnston, Esq., eldest son of Henry George Johnston, Esq., of Cootehill, in this county:—

While engaged in a boating party off Cove, yesterday, I was nearly drowned by the upsetting of the boat, in which were fifteen persons, including myself. We were at Passage, looking at the *President* steamer, which is at present there; and were coming home, about a mile off Hawlbowline Point, and about three quarters of a mile off Cove, when the wind blew very strong off land, and struck the sail of the whale boat we were in, and which belongs to Dr. Cotter, who is at present from home, and capsized her. The persons in her were myself, Major Rogers, Mr. Roche, Lieut. Lawless, three sons of Mr. Welland's, the Rector of Cloyne, four boatmen, two policemen, to whom we gave a passage, Mr. Robert Murphy, inn-keeper of Cloyne, and a man named Guistine, making fifteen in all. Mr. Roche steered the boat, and Major Rogers managed the sail. When we fell into the water, the boat turned upside down; but, as we all clung to it, it turned over again, and we were precipitated into the water a second time. When I came up I saw the boat some yards off, and three of the oars beside me; the latter I instantly seized, and having secured them under my arms, made for the boat. By this time six persons were clinging to the vessel, and two more swimming for shore. Mr. Roche and Lieut. Lawless never came up after the boat went over;—the three Wellands—one of them about 18 years of age, another about 12, and the third 9 years old—were drowned. There was a boat about a hundred yards from us when the accident occurred, but—strange to say—would not come near us, nor render us any assistance. However, boats came speedily from the shore and picked us up. The Major was senseless when taken up, but is getting better.—There were five drowned and ten saved. (1840-07-25, 3:1)

2578. An inquest was held this week before Robert Murray, Esq., M.D., county coroner, on view of the body of a man named Carraher, residing in Cornasoo. The unfortunate man came by his death by a beam falling upon him while in bed, which crushed his skull and brain in a dreadful manner. Some foul suspicions were afloat previous to the inquest, as to a member of his own family being concerned in causing the fall of the beam, but for the sake of human nature, we are glad to say that he was acquitted by the jury, and a verdict of accidental death returned. (1840-07-25, 3:1)

2579. Death of the Rev. Robert Alexander.—At Portglenone House, in the county of Antrim, on the 25th July, the Rev. Robert Alexander, Rector of Aghoghill, and formerly Archdeacon of Down. Mr. Alexander was not less exemplary as an active and diligent Christian Minister, than estimable as a country gentleman and an upright magistrate—educated at Cambridge, in which University he distinguished himself. He was not less delightful as a companion in social life, than an ornament, as a scholar, in the sphere in which he quietly moved—cheerful without levity, and friendly without ostentation, (which, of all qualities, he abhorred;) he won the affections of his friends, the esteem of every one who knew him, and the respect of those who personally did not. Alas! it pleased the Almighty to summon him to his high reward in the 50th year of his age, leaving behind him a widow and nine children to lament the irreparable loss which they and many, many friends have experienced in his demise. Mr. Alexander was twice married; his first wife was Miss Catherine Staples, sister to the Marchioness of Ormonde, and daughter of the late Right Hon. John Staples, of Lissan, and the Hon. Harriet Molesworth. He was eldest son to the Lord Bishop of Meath, and a relative of the Earl of Caledon, and was second in remainder to the vast estates of his near kinsman, the Earl O'Neill. Mr. Alexander's second wife, (by whom he had no family) was a daughter of the late Colonel MacManus, of Mt. Divis, county of Antrim, Lieut.-Colonel of the Antrim Militia.

"*Quis desiderio sit pudor, aut modus*
Tam chari Capitis?
Multis ille bonis flebilis occidit;
Nulli flebilior quam."—*** [sic]

(1840-08-01, 2:3)

2580. Death of Lady Rossmore.—It is with painful feelings we record in our obituary this day, the sudden and unexpected decease of Lady Rossmore, whose departure, in good health, from Cortolvin, for England, in company with his Lordship, we announced a few days since. The sad event took place at Cheltenham, on Wednesday morning last, at six o'clock, after ten hours' illness. On the evening previous her Ladyship enjoyed her usual health, and had been taking exercise, but shortly after her return home, and while conversing with Dr. J.S. M'Dowell, the family physician, she was seized with apoplexy, and although she had the advantage of immediate medical relief, she never spoke a word from the period of the shock. Drs. Barron and Carron were also in attendance, but without avail—she lingered a few hours, and then the grave claimed its own. The intelligence of her decease caused a dreadful sensation in town yesterday, as she is deeply regretted by all who knew her, many of whom shared her bounty. Many families of the highest rank will be placed in mourning by her decease, as she was connected with a number of the most noble in the land. (1840-08-01, 2:3)

2581. Awfully sudden Death of the County Surveyor for Waterford.—Mr. Johnstone, county surveyor of Waterford, was sitting in the gallery of the crown court while the presentments were being passed, when he suddenly fell back, and was removed in a dying state to the apartment of the secretary of the grand jury. In two minutes, I was looking at his lifeless remains. The promptest medical assistance was resorted to, but without effect. The (*continued...*)

2581, continued: ...deceased was only thirty-two years of age, and up to the moment of the attack was in fine spirits;—but, within the last year he had been in a delicate state of health, owing to an affection of the heart of recent origin. Mr. Johnstone and his wife were stopping at the residence of Mr. Sampson Carter, his brother-in-law, county surveyor for Kilkenny, and the first announcement of her bereavement which the distracted widow received, was from a person who met her as she was driving to the court-house, happy in her ignorance. The event has caused a deep sensation here, and the most careless or indifferent cannot but feel sympathy for those who have been so suddenly deprived of a relative or friend. (1840-08-01, 4:4)

2582. Death of Major Rogers.—Death terminated this gentleman's sufferings about 11 o'clock on Wednesday. He had, up to Thursday last, proceeded rather favourably, and it was expected that he could have been in a few days moved to town. On Thursday, however, some person, a woman we believe, was allowed to see him, having said that she had obtained the permission of his friends. She inadvertently informed him of the fate of the young Wellands, who had been confided to his care upon the excursion that terminated so fatally, but a knowledge of which had been previously withheld from him. Since then inflammation set in, delirium followed, and he was continually exclaiming—There—there they are—Oh, God, will nobody save them?—poor Welland, poor Welland! —*Cork Constitution*. (1840-08-08, 5:5)

2583. Inquest at Cove.—On Tuesday, about one o'clock, the body of Lieutenant Lawless was found off Spike Island. It was brought to Cove and placed in the bridewell. The magistrates endeavoured to procure a coroner, but without success, and Dr. Millett, Captain Stubbs, and William Lambert, Esq., at seven o'clock in the evening, proceeded to hold the inquest.

Thomas Cashman sworn—I was in the boat the day deceased was drowned. Deceased was taken in at Passage from the *President* steamer. We left the steamer with fifteen persons on board. The boat was steered by Mr. Hugh Roche. All the party landed at Monkstown except Lieutenant Lawless. Lieutenant Lawless called Toomy, who had charge of the boat, and said here is 6d. to take some nourishment. Deceased told deponent to go likewise. He did, and took some bread. We remained at Monkstown about fifteen minutes, when all the same party went into the boat again, viz.: Mr. Hugh Roche, Lieut. Lawless, Major Rodgers, Masters William, Paul, and Thomas Welland, Mr. Custheen, Hubbard Murphy, hotel-keeper; John Higgins, John Cosgrave, a (dummy,) Mr. Walter Johnstone, Henry Roche, sergeant of police; and another policeman named Catchpole, Toomy, the boatman, and deponent. After pushing off, Mr. Roche desired Toomy to shake the reefs out, and hoist the sail, which was done. We sailed on towards Cove, the wind blowing north-west. We were going gaily. We passed a green boat with a man with his coat off at the helm. We were not five minutes past that boat when [the] sail was ordered to be lowered and shifted, I think by Mr. Roche.—It was hoisted again. They were then opposite Hawlbowline clock. A breeze came from the Cove side and the boat yielded to it. Witness said to Custheen that if Mr. Cotter was in the boat a reef would be taken in. Somebody said "ease the sheet," and Mr. Roche said, "hold, Major—don't give an inch." It was not one second or the clap of your hand after that when the boat was upset. The first thing I saw in the water was some one grasping at Tommy Welland, I think it was Mr. Roche. I saw the green boat we passed coming down, and Custheen made signals to her. She was from 100 to 200 yards off. I heard Custheen say, she is not coming to us. Witness does not recollect any thing after that. Witness could not swim. No person was tipsy in their boat.

By a Juror—The green boat was rowing, not sailing. The inquest was adjourned at a quarter to nine until next morning.

Before the Court rose a discussion took place between Doctors Cronin and Orpin as to which should be paid for examining the body.

Wednesday.—The body of Master Paul Welland, the second son, was found this morning, about five o'clock, near the Spit-buoy, by a fisherman on his return home. The face was dreadfully disfigured.

The jury having been sworn by the Magistrates,

Sergeant Roche, one of those saved, was sworn.—He corroborated Cashman's evidence as to what occurred up to their arrival at Monkstown. At Barry's public-house at Monkstown, Murphy, Cashman and witness took a glass of grog. Saw Mr. Roche and Major Rogers go up stairs. Saw two glasses of grog sent up stairs to them—I did not see them drink it—not one of the party was tipsy. Left Monkstown and proceeded towards Cove. Mr. Roche ordered the reef to be shaken out. When opposite Hawlbowline a whirlwind came. Mr. Rogers had the sheet in his hand (it was not belayed) and when the whirlwind came, Mr. Rogers pulled the sheet tight, and the boat upset. It upset to the Hawlbowline side. I went down and remained a long time under water. When I came up I was paddling, and Mr. Johnston caught hold of me, and said he could not swim. I told him to hold me but not to catch me too tight. Mr. Johnston then caught an oar and held himself up by it. I saw Toomy grasp the keel of the boat, and hold by it. I called to Toomy to hold firm and not be afraid. I was swimming away. A wave came over me and sunk me a little. I was afterwards taken up by a ring boat. From the time the boat was upset, I did not see either Mr. Roche, Mr. Lawless, or the three Wellands.

Several other witnesses were subsequently examined and their testimony was to the same effect. The jury returned the following verdict—"Came by their death by drowning."

The jury were then sworn in the case of Mr. Roche and returned a similar verdict. (1840-08-08, 5:5)

2584. At a few minutes to eleven o'clock last night (Aug. 14) Sir James Webster Wedderburn, Bart., dropped suddenly dead, when drinking with two females in Cooney's public-house, in Abbey-street, Dublin. The women who were in company with the unfortunate man were removed in custody to Frederick-lane station-house. Deceased appeared to be upwards of 50 years of age, of handsome countenance. The deceased had twenty thousand a-year in Scotland, was married to a sister of Lord Mountnorris, and was to be married on Monday to a Dublin Lady. (1840-08-22, 1:2)

2585. Sonnet, On the death of a Lady whose latter days were marked by much unmerited disgrace.

And art thou gone, thou persecuted one!
Thou victim of this cold world's cruel scorn?
Thou could'st not bear the scoffer's bitter tone,
And pierced thy tender breast the rankling thorn?
Far happier hadst thou been some peasant girl,
The peaceful intimate of some lowly cot—
Far, far removed from fashion's dazzling whirl,
Unenvied then had been thy humble lot.
But thou so favoured by high birth and fame,
Attracted envy's most malignant gaze;
Black malice tarnish'd thy time-honor'd name,
And crush'd thee in the spring-time of thy days!
Rest thee in peace, sweet maiden! till the day
When all shall burst this "tenement of clay."

M. A. M.

(1840-08-22, 2:2)

2586. Doctor Lardner will, we hear upon good authority, be removed from the council of the British Association for the advancement of science at the ensuing meeting at Glasgow. He has always been conspicuous for the prominent part he has taken at the head of the mechanical section, and has had charge of many money grants connected with steam improvement and mechanical discovery. (1840-08-22, 2:2)

2587. The Lord Bishop of Meath is dangerously ill; his Lordship is in his 80th year. The Bishop of Meath is a privy councillor ex-officio, and takes rank as the first suffragan Bishop. (1840-08-29, 3:3)

2588. Attempted Suicide.—At one o'clock on Wednesday last, a respectable woman, who resides near Bagenalstown, attempted to commit suicide under the following appalling circumstances. It appears that her husband was absent from an early hour in the morning, and in order to accomplish her destruction, she sent her servant maid to the post-office with a letter. When alone she bolted the windows, locked the front door, and went to her bed-room, took off her stays, and placed a basin very deliberately on the table to receive the blood, and then having seated herself opposite the looking-glass, she inflicted several wounds on her throat with a carving-knife.—Finding the knife did not effect her purpose, she got a razor, and threw it across her throat, and was found sitting in her chair, and life nearly extinct on the servant's return. The servant gave the alarm, and Drs. Roche and Johnson were promptly in attendance and bound up the wounds, which were five in number, and nearly two inches deep. Owing to the providential arrival of the physicians, hopes are entertained of the recovery of this wretched woman, who was, it is stated, in affluent circumstances, and whose diabolical attempt at self-destruction can only be accounted for by the fact, that she is said to express no small share of uneasiness about the loss of some property in the county Kildare. Her husband is a most respectable man, and is deeply concerned at the committal of this fearful act.—*Carlow Sentinel.* (1840-08-29, 4:3)

2589. The Lieutenancy of the county of Londonderry is vacant by the death of Lord Garvagh, a near relative of the late Right Hon. George Canning. His Lordship is succeeded in his title and estates by his only son, a minor. (1840-09-05, 1:4)

2590. James MCaw, baggage-porter of the Ulster Railroad company, was killed last week by the train from Lisburn to Belfast, from which he fell, and the carriages passing over him, he was crushed to death. (1840-09-05, 2:2)

2591. Lines on the Death of a Young Lady, who died at the age of fifteen, in Aug. 1840.

The fairest flower may soonest fade,
Its fragile stem in death decayed,
May droop no more to rise;
Yet thought the canker worm can part,
The petals of its fragrant heart—
Destruction it defies.

The summer's sunbeam strong and warm,
Will vivify its seed and form
And call to second birth,
Its dewy urn, a floral gem
Supported by a stronger stem
Will rise from mother earth.

The victim of an early tomb,
Thus youthful Jane hath met her doom
And closed her shortened day.
Consumption's fatal fingers stole
Her gifted and immortal soul
From its frail house of clay.

But yet, with energy divine,
The sun of righteousness will shine
And animate the dust;
Of all his faithful servants dead
For whom his precious blood was shed,
"The just for the unjust."

(*continued...*)

2591, continued:

Him you "did early" seek, lov'd girl,
He was as early found your joy,
Your grace and holy shield,
Your father in your ghostly strife,
Hath won for you eternal life,
On sin's dark battle field.

Ballybay, August, 1840.

1840-09-05, 4:1)

2592. Statistics of Marriages—Hints for the Ladies. (*from the Scotsman.*)—We published some years ago a table of the probabilities of marriage at the different periods of life, in the case of females, for which we have no doubt that the ladies of Britain feel grateful. It was founded, however, on limited data, which were derived entirely from records of marriages among the working classes. The table published in our leading article of Saturday supplies materials for more accurate conclusions, grounded on returns which comprehended all classes; and we think we shall confer a favour on our female readers by putting the results into a more distinct form than the table in its original shape did afford.

If we take 100 to represent the whole of a woman's chances of marriage between the ages of fifteen and seventy, the proportional chances in each period of five years will be as follows:—

Age.	Chances of Marriages.
15 and under 20 ...	... 14-1/2
20 and under 25 ...	... 52
25 and under 30 ...	... 18
30 and under 35 ...	... 6-1/2
35 and under 40 ...	... 3-3/4
40 and under 45 ...	... 2-3/4
45 and under 50 ...	... 1-1/2
50 and under 55 ...	... 3/4
55 and under 60 ...	... 1/4
60 and under 65} ...	one-
65 and under 70} ...	tenth.
	100

From the table it appears—

1. That one-seventh part of all the females who marry in England are married between the ages of 15 and 20, one-seventh part of a woman's chances of marriage lies between those years.

2. That fully one-half of all women who marry are married between 20 and 25, or one half of a woman's chances are comprised within these five years.

3. That between 15 and 24 precisely two-thirds of a woman's chances of marriage are exhausted, and only one-third remains for the rest of her life up to 70.

4. That at 30 no less than 85 chances out of the 100 are gone, and 15, or about one-seventh, only remains. She has strong reason for improving her time.

5. At 35, a fraction, a tenth, is all that remains to her—which is reduced to a twentieth at 40.

6. At 45, her chances of marriage have sunk to one-fortieth; and at 50, to one-hundredth. At 60 there is still a glimmering of hope, for it appears that among females about one marriage in 1,000 takes place at and beyond this age.

The number of women married between 15 and 20 is six times greater than the number of men.

The number of men and women married between 20 and 25 is very nearly equal, but the number of men married at all higher ages is greater than the number of women. (1840-09-12, 1:4)

2593. Deplorable Accident.—An inquest was held on the 4th instant, in the parish of Aughnamulla, before Robert Murray, Esq., M.D., Coroner for this county, upon view of the body of Mr. Patrick Mollen, who came by his death under the following melancholy circumstances:—The Rev. Francis Tierney, Roman Catholic curate of Aughnamulla, and deceased had been for some time previous exerting their skill in shooting at a target; deceased conceiving that the rev. gentleman had fired more shots than fell to his lot, endeavoured to wrest the loaded gun from him to have his turn, but melancholy to say—while some playful parrying was going on between them, the gun accidentally went off, and the contents lodged in Mollen's breast, and he instantly expired! Nothing could exceed the sorrow of Mr. Tierney, and he has been since labouring under severe illness. He and the deceased were intimate friends. The verdict was—"That the deceased came by his death from the effects of a gun shot wound, accidentally inflicted from a gun which the Rev. Francis Tierney had at the time under his arm." (1840-09-12, 3:1)

2594. An inquest was lately held at Downpatrick, on the disinterred body of the late Mr. Thomas Thompson, in consequence of various rumours respecting his death. The jury returned a verdict that the deceased had come by his death owing to his having taken some poisonous ingredient while labouring under temporary insanity. (1840-09-19, 2:5)

2595. It is said that the annual deaths from small-pox are not fewer than 12,000, out of perhaps 50,000 or 60,600 of the inhabitants of England and Wales afflicted by that disease. (1840-09-19, 2:5)

2596. Death of Captain Dumas.—On the 15th inst., in the 53d year of his age, at his residence in Cootehill, Captain Henry Dumas, late Sub-Inspector of the Constabulary for the county of Cavan, in which force he served for 18 years, and was lately obliged to retire from that situation in consequence of his arduous duties, which his great anxiety to improve the moral and social character of the community in that neighbourhood induced him to perform in a manner which was unfortunately injurious to his health and constitution, but to the perfect satisfaction of not only the authorities but the people at large. He was frank, generous, hospitable, and humane; as a proof of which, his demise is, in the neighbourhood, generally and deeply regretted. (1840-09-19, 3:3)

2597. Early Woo'd and Won, by Mrs. Abdy.

"Early woo'd and won,
Was never repented under the sun!"
German Proverb.

O! sigh not for the fair young bride,
Gone in her opening bloom,
Far from her kindred, loved and tried,
To glad another's home;
Already are the gay brief days
Of girlish triumph done,
And tranquil happiness repays
The early woo'd and won.

Fear shall invade her peace no more,
Nor sorrow wound the breast,
Her passing rivalries are o'er,
Her passing doubts at rest;
The glittering haunts of worldly state
Love whispers her to shun,
Since scenes of purer bliss await
The early woo'd and won.

Hers is a young and guileless heart,
Confiding, fond, and warm,
Unsullied by the world's vain mart,
Unscathed by passion's storm:
In "hope deferred" she hath not pined,
Till Hope's sweet course was run:
No chains of sad remembrance bind
The early woo'd and won.

Her smiles and songs have ceased to grace
The halls of festal mirth,
But woman's safest dwelling-place
Is by a true one's hearth;
Her hours of duty, joy, and love,
In brightness have begun;
Peace be her portion from above,
The early woo'd and won.

Metropolitan for Sept.
(1840-09-19, 4:1)

2598. The late Lord Mark Robert Kerr.—The deceased Lord who was uncle to the Marquis of Lothian and brother to Lord Robert Kerr, Adjutant-General of Scotland, was born the 12th November 1776, and was, consequently in his 64th year. In July 1779, his Lordship married Lady Charlotte Macdonnell, (Countess of Antrim), who died in October 1835, by whom his Lordship had issue the present Earl of Antrim and several children. The deceased Lord entered the navy at a very early age, and was Lieutenant of the *Sans Pereil* [sic] in Lord Bridport's action in 1795, assisted at the reduction of Minorca in 1798 when he commanded the *Cormorant* sloop, and captured in 1799 *El Vencejo*, of 26 guns. His Lordship served with distinction all the intermediate grades, and in reward for his gallant services, in Jan. 1837, he was made a Vice-Admiral of the White. (1840-09-19, 4:4)

2599. Melancholy Occurrence.—We learn from our Drumcondra correspondent, that an occurrence of a melancholy nature took place on Sunday evening last, at Cromartin, in the County Louth, by which two young women have lost their lives, and about thirty persons were maimed in a dangerous manner. It appears that on the evening of Sunday, a number of young persons of the village, amounting to seventy persons, male and female, congregated on the loft of a spacious house, which was in a ruinous state, and uninhabited, for the purpose of amusing themselves with dancing. In the midst of their mirth, the loft was observed to give way, together with one of the walls and every soul nearly buried in the ruins. As stated above, two persons died of the injuries they sustained and little hopes are entertained that some of the rest will recover.—*Drogheda Argus*. (1840-09-26, 2:1)

2600. Death by Drowning.—On Sunday evening, five young men went out boating on the river near Omagh, where, for some mismanagement of the canoe, at a very deep part of the river, she upset, and but for the intrepid exertions of Mr. John Buchanan, of Stragh-roy, and a servant-man, all must have perished. Four were rescued from a watery grave—but the fifth, a fine lad, named M'Crory, never came to the surface, and was consequently drowned.—*Derry Standard*. (1840-09-26, 2:1)

2601. Marriage of the Princess Amelia Bonaparte.—The *Presse* states that Count Demidoff has just married, at Florence, the Princess Amelia, daughter of Prince Jerome Bonaparte. One of the clauses of the marriage contract, it adds, is, that the Count will never bear arms against France. (1840-09-26, 3:3)

2602. The Young Widow.

Sorrow hath laid his hand on thee,
Lone mourner of the dead,
And blanch'd the glow upon thy cheek,
And bow'd thy stricken head;
There is a wildness in thy glance,
A look of mute despair,
That telleth, more than word or sigh,
What cause for grief lies there.

Widow! thine is no common woe,
That briefly doth subdue
The young soul's buoyant happiness,
With thoughts of sadd'ning hue;
No transient pains hath help to hail
The anguish they impart,
But one that gathers strength with thine,
The crushing of a heart.

Pale mourner! it is sad to think
That thou should'st bear alone
The burden of that stern regret
For him whose spirit's flown;

(*continued...*)

2602, continued:

But who could weep for him like thee,
Whose interchange of love
Was moulded, not for earthly bliss,
But holier joys above?

So young, too, and so beautiful,
Thus slow to pine away!
A star o'ershadowed by a cloud,
A lily in decay.
It seems as though some hand had loos'd
The bird, and set it free,
Well knowing to the same far home
The mate would, ere long, flee!

Bereav'd one! thou hast near'd that bourne
Where hope becomes divine;
Earth claims those sable weeds, but Heaven
That broken heart of thine,
Whose tender chords have given way,
Yet tremulous cling on,
To breathe its sorrow o'er the spot
From whence the loved hath gone!

Tait's Magazine.
(1840-09-26, 4:1)

2603. Marriage in High Life.—On Thursday were married, at Slindon House, Sussex, the seat of Anne Countess of Newburgh, Miss Rosamond Clifford, a near relative of Lord Clifford and of Sir Clifford Constable, Bart., of Burton-Constable, and niece of the late Cardinal Weld, of Lulworth Castle, to Theophilus W. Strachey, Esq., of the 29th regiment of Madras Native Infantry, nephew of Sir Henry Strachey, Bart., of Sutton Court, Somersetshire. Immediately after the ceremony, the happy couple proceeded to Bognor, from whence they will shortly depart on a tour of visits to the north, previous to their departure for India. The bride is distinguished, not only for her beauty, but for talents, which have already given celebrity to their possessor. (1840-10-03, 1:4)

2604. Death of Lord Kenmure.—John Gordon, Viscount Kenmure, and Lord of Lochinvar, in the Scotch peerage, died on the 21st inst, in the 91st year of his age. His Lordship's titles were restored in 1824, having been forfeited by his grandfather, the sixth Viscount. His Lordship married in 1781, Miss Morgan, who died in 1816, and by whom he had no issue. His Lordship is succeeded by his nephew, Lieutenant Adam Gordon, R.N., eldest son of his brother, Adam Gordon, who died in 1806. (1840-10-03, 1:4)

2605. The present year has witnessed the death of two of the oldest female members of the aristocracy—the venerable Countess of Cork, in her 93d year, and the equally venerable Countess of Dysart, in her 96th year. (1840-10-03, 1:4)

2606. By the death of Captain Henry Dumas, late Sub-Inspector of Police, and brother of the late Thomas Collins Dumas, Esq., of Killarney, a considerable property reverts to his nephew, Thomas Henry Brodrick, Esq., of Macroom. (1840-10-03, 3:5)

2607. It being the wish of many of the friends of the late Rev. Charles Evatt, to erect a plain, unostentatious Tablet to his memory, in the Church of Monaghan, which was built under his anxious superintendence, Notice is hereby given, That Donations, for carrying this purpose into effect, will be received by the Rev. W.L. Roper, the Rev. Henry Maffatt, Dr. J. Robinson, and Mr. R. Harrison, Churchwardens.

N.B.—The subscription list is now open to all classes and denominations. No individual donation to exceed £1, and the smallest sum will be accepted.

October 7, 1840.
(1840-10-10, 2:4)

2608. We are happy to learn that it is in contemplation to erect a testimonial in the body of our Church to the memory of the late Rev. Charles Evatt, Rector. This splendid building, the principal ornament of the town, was constructed under his superintendence—and the many excellent qualities that distinguished him through life as a Christian Pastor, an active, useful and intelligent citizen, his strong claims to the hearts of those who experienced his worth; and we feel certain that to his memory will be such as will convey to posterity the sentiments entertained towards the memory of the man. A subscription list is open for furtherance of the project.—(*Vide Advertisement.*) (1840-10-10, 3:4)

2609. Melancholy Occurrence.—Omagh, Oct. 7.
(*From our own Correspondent.*)

At about three o'clock, yesterday, Mr. James Love, sen. of Dry-bridge-street, in this town, a licensed vender of gun-powder, went from his shop to a store in the rere, in which the powder was kept, where he had been but a very short time when a terrific explosion took place. On some persons going to ascertain the cause of the explosion, it was perceived that it took place in the house where the powder was, the walls of which were scattered in every direction, and in the midst of the ruins were discovered the remains of the unhappy man, in a shockingly mangled state. The back part of his dwelling-house was forced in by the shock, and his family had rather a miraculous escape, as had Captain Wade, sub-inspector of police, whose office is contiguous to the powder-store, and which he had left only an instant before the awful event took place. The windows of his office were literally forced in, and his dwelling-house more or less injured. The deceased was 72 years of age. In August last, a son of his went to Australia, much against his father's wishes, since which deceased has laboured under a depression of spirits. An inquest was held on view of the body by Mr. Orr, coroner, and a verdict returned—"That deceased, James Love, while labouring under a fit of insanity, ignited a cask of gunpowder, which caused his death." (1840-10-10, 3:4)

2610. Gather Ripe Fruits, Oh Death!
(From Poems just published.)
By Thomas Ragg.

Gather ripe fruits, oh Death!
Strew not the pathway of the tomb with flowers.
Invade not childhood with thy withering breath,
Pass on, and touch not youth's bright sunny bowers.

There are enough for thee
Of hearths that long for they serene repose,
That fain among the lowly-laid would be,
Pierced deep with festering wounds that will not close.

Go to the desolate
Whom thou hast robbed of every star-bright thing,
On whom the smiles of hope no longer wait,
Whose loves have passed upon the morning's wing.

Go to the wearied frame
That seeks to slumber on the grave's cold breast,
That finds life's pleasures but an empty name,
And longs to flee away and be at rest.

Go to the saints of God
Whose souls are weary of the world and sin,
Who fain would tread the path their Saviour trod,
And greet the tomb that lets heaven's glories in.

Take these, take these to rest,
But smite not childhood in its mirthful play,
Snatch not the infant from his mother's breast,
Steal not the loved and loving ones away.

Gather ripe fruits, oh Death!
Strew not the pathway of the tomb with flowers,
Invade not childhood with thy withering breath,
Pass on, and touch not youth's bright fragrant bowers.
(1840-10-17, 4:1)

2611. Death of the Bishop of Meath.—Died, on the 21st instant, at his residence in Great George's-street, Dublin, in the eighty-first year of his age, the Right Honourable and Most Reverend Nathaniel Alaxander [sic], D.D., Lord Bishop of Meath. (1840-10-24, 1:5)

2612. Accounts reached Dublin on the 23d instant, leaving the Dean of St. Patrick's in a state of convalescence. He is a brother of George Dawson, Esq., late M.P., Derry, and a connexion of Sir R. Peel. (1840-10-31, 1:3)

2613. Doctor Beresford, Lord Bishop of Kilmore, is indisposed at Kilmore house, county Cavan. He is in his 76th year. (1840-10-31, 1:3)

2614. The Bank of Ireland have a vacancy for a manager at Kilkenny, by the death of Mr. Owen. (1840-10-31, 1:3)

2615. Sudden Death of Sir W. Brabazon, M.P.—With feelings of the most sincere sorrow we have, at the hour of going to press, heard that our excellent representative and friend, Sir William J. Brabazon, Bart., has closed his earthly career. The information which we have received is—that the hon. baronet had on this day (Saturday) returned from his customary ride, and that on some of his servants entering the parlour about four o'clock, they found their master lifeless in his chair. Medical aid was promptly summoned—Dr. Fitzpatrick was in instant attendance, but attention was vain—Sir William Brabazon had breathed his last.—*Mayo Mercury*. (1840-10-31, 1:4)

2616. Death of the Dean of St. Patrick's.—Died, on Saturday last, at Castlecomer, the Very Rev. Henry Dawson, M.A., Dean of St. Patrick's, and Rector of Castlecomer. It is almost unnecessary to say that this event has caused universal regret.

The Deanery of St. Patrick's and the living of Castlecomer are both rendered vacant by the demise of Dean Dawson. The election of the new Dean is vested in the Chapter, and of which the individual selected must be a member. (1840-10-31, 1:4)

2617. Suicide of a Chief Constable.—We learn with deep regret, that Chief Constable Cox, of Borris, county of Carlow, committed suicide on the 16th inst., while laboring under temporary insanity. The particulars are as follow:—It appears he retired to bed at a late hour, apparently in good health, although much depressed in spirits, and on next day he was found dead in his bed. An inquest was held on the body, when it was ascertained that he had taken a quantity of arsenic, a portion of which was found in a glass in his bed-room. It was supposed that temporary embarrassment led to the committal of this fearful act. The deceased had entered early in life into a dragoon regiment, and was at several engagements, particularly at Waterloo, where he was seriously wounded. He joined the Constabulary force several years ago, and was particularly distinguished for his fearless conduct and activity, as a public officer, during the disturbances in the Colliery. We regret to state that his two daughters are left in a state of utter destitution, and we sincerely hope the circumstance will not be overlooked by the government.—*Kilkenny Moderator*. (1840-10-31, 1:4)

2618. Death of Lieutenant-General Sir Joseph Straton.—By the death of this gallant Officer—one of the Spirits of Waterloo—which took place on Friday, in Park-street, Grosvenor-square, London, the Colonelcy of the 6th or Inniskilling Dragoons, which he held since April last, became vacant. Sir Joseph entered the service in December, 1794, in the 2d Dragoon Guards, in which corps he served two years and three months. He purchased a troop in March, 1797, in the 13th Light Dragoons, and the Majority of the same corps in August, 1801. He studied at the Royal Military College, High Wycombe, in 1804 and 5, from whence he obtained, on his examination, a diploma of the first qualification, and was appointed to the Staff of the Duke of Gloucester. He accompanied his Regiment to the Peninsula in February, (*continued...*)

2618, continued: ...1801, where he served, partly in command of the regiment and partly as second in command, for three years, and was in all the affairs and engagements in which it during that time bore part. In June, 1813, the Commander-in-Chief gave him, without purchase, in reward of his services, the Lieutenant-Colonelcy of the 6th Dragoons, of which he died Colonel. In April, 1815, he embarked with his regiment, and commanded it in the commencement of the battle of Waterloo, until the fall of the gallant Ponsonby, when the command of the brigade, consisting of the 1st, 2d, and 6th Dragoons, devolved upon him. This brigade, with the brigade of Life Guards, (Blues), and Kings Dragoon Guards, formed the two brigades of cavalry mentioned by the Duke of Wellington as having particularly distinguished themselves. Towards the close of the action Sir J. Straton was wounded, and his horse wounded twice. He received for his services the order of St. Vladimir of the 4th class from the Emperor Alexander of Russia, and was appointed a Companion of the Bath. In 1816 he took the name of Straton, his previous one being Muter. His last commission of Lieutenant-General, bears date June, 1838. (1840-10-31, 2:1)

2619. Death of N.A. Vigors, Esq., M.P.—We regret to announce the death of Mr. Vigors, M.P. for the county of Carlow, which took place at his residence in the Regent's Park, this morning, after a short illness—a vacancy is consequently created in the representation of the county. Mr. Vigors was elected for the county in February, 1837, in the room of the late Thomas Kavanah, Esq., opposed by H. Bunbury, Esq., who unsuccessfully petitioned against the return; was returned for Carlow in 1832, but was ousted in 1835; he was returned for the county in the same year with Mr. Alexander Raphael, High Sheriff of London, when both were unseated on petition.—*Sun* of Monday. (1840-10-31, 2:1)

2620. The Late Dean of St. Patrick's.—The Funeral.—It has been decided, on the suggestion of many anxious friends—and we think decided wisely—that the remains of this distinguished man and exemplary divine should not be interred in a remote and obscure village; but be deposited within the walls of that ancient cathedral, of which Dean Dawson was the ornament and head.—*Evening Mail.* (1840-10-31, 2:1)

2621. A false report of the death of Mr. Sergeant Jackson, M.P. for Bandon, was last Friday industriously circulated in Cork. (1840-10-31, 2:5)

2622. Dr. Lardner and Mrs. Heaviside were in New York a few days since, and are said to pass by the names of Mr. and Mrs. Bennett. They have not had an encouraging reception. (1840-11-07, 1:4)

2623. As the list of the subscribers to the tablet about to be erected in Monaghan Church, in memory of the Rev. Charles Evatt, late Rector, will be closed after this month for publication. We are requested to remind our readers who may be desirous to contribute to the fund for carrying the above object into effect, to forward their names and subscriptions to the Rector, Curate, or Churchwardens of the parish. (1840-11-21, 3:2)

2624. Captain Croker, 17th Lancers, is about shortly to lead to the hymeneal altar, Lady Georgiana Monck, the beautiful and accomplished daughter of the Earl of Rathdowne. (1840-11-28, 1:2)

2625. We sincerely regret to learn that a letter has been received from Canada, dated the 2d instant, announcing the death of Edward Ross, Esq., brother of D.R. Ross, Esq., of Rosstrevor, and secretary to Viscount Falkland.—*Newry Telegraph.* (1840-11-28, 1:4)

2626. Suddenly, of internal aneurism, at his house in Clones on Friday, the 20th inst., in his 73d year, Thomas Armstrong, Esq., for 45 years a highly respectable medical practitioner in that town. To his family, with whom he enjoyed a happiness rarely to be met in the domestic circle, he will be long an irreparable loss. As a warm supporter of, and liberal contributor to the charitable and religious institutions of the place, his death has left a blank that will not soon be filled up, and his removal will be long and deeply regretted by a numerous circle of friends and acquaintances. He possessed superior intellectual powers, which were highly cultivated and improved by various knowledge, derived from extensive reading. He was a man of sound unwavering religious principles, warmly attached to the Established Church, and during the greater part of his life, a zealous, consistent member of the Primitive Wesleyan Methodist Society. While in his life, he uniformly exhibited the steady demeanor of the Christian. [sic] He lived, humbly confiding in the merits of his Saviour, by whom, we believe, he is now exalted, to live with Himself for ever. (1840-11-28, 3:2)

2627. The remains of the lamented Henry Cole, Esq., Barrister-at-Law, were brought over from Leamington, where he died, on Saturday, the 14th instant, and deposited in the cemetery of Mount Jerome on Monday. Mr. Cole was in his 66th year. He was related to the Enniskillen and other families of distinction, and was for many years an efficient and active magistrate of the city of Dublin, and Seneschal of the Manor Court of Grange Gorman. (1840-11-28, 3:2)

2628. Death of Dr. Michell.—To the Editor of the *Northern Standard.*—Sir—Among the many respectable and sorrowing friends of the late Dr. Michell, I was solaced to witness you, almost a stranger amongst us, tendering to the merits and remains of respected worth, the last sad and solemn duty—I congratulate you, not only on your natural good feelings, but also on your sympathy with every person who has the happiness of his acquaintance—the individual who dedicates this ephemeral record to the virtues of departed worth, is amongst the many who have admired his manly bearing and deeply deplore his premature loss. In private, unaffected, bland and single-hearted; in public, unobtrusive and unpretending; yet, when occasions sudden and unexpected both in social and professional life, elicited his intellectual powers—he displayed a mind of no common order, and exhibited the varied stores of natural endowments, and acquired talent, which surprised his most enthusiastic admirers—a sympathising town by their universal testimony, have evinced their deep, unfeigned regret, while a private individual linked to him by all the sacred ties of private and professional regard, shares with him his portion of the tomb,

Quis desiderio sit pudor,
aut modus tam chari capitis.

(1840-12-05, 2:4)

2629. The Rev. Dr. Millar, of Armagh, whose recent decision on the law of marriage between members of the Church and Dissenters has attracted so much notice, has just published a reply to Dr. Pusey's letter to the Bishop of Oxford, which a correspondent eulogises thus—too brief, but well done. (1840-12-05, 2:4)

2630. Lamentable Accident.—A melancholy occurrence took place at Killaloo Glebe, the residence of the Rev. John Hayden, on Wednesday last, by which one of the sons of that estimable clergyman lost his life. Master George Hayden and two young friends were on a visit with him, retired after dinner to an apartment ordinarily used as a school-room. They had taken two guns with them for the purpose of cleaning them, intending to go on a shooting excursion the following morning. They had scarcely entered the apartment when a challenge passed in sport between Master Hayden and one of his young friends to fight a duel; one of the guns, however, unknown to any of the party happened to be loaded; and in going through the show of fighting the loaded gun went off, when young Master Hayden received its contents in the heart, and was killed on the spot. The event has plunged an amiable family into the deepest grief, in which there are many who sympathise with them. The deceased was a youth of the most ingenuous disposition, and of fine promise. The individual who was unwittingly the cause of this painful catastrophe, is, we understand, a relative of the family.—*Derry Standard.* (1840-12-05, 3:2)

2631. The Lament.—Addressed to the Ladies of the county Monaghan, by Six Young Gentlemen.

Say, ladies fair, is't not severe
That were pronounced to be
Old bachelors before we reach
The age of seventy-three?—
In vain we sigh, in vain we try
To please—hard destiny!
In vain were gay—the ladies say
Old bachelors you'll be.

We all can dance—we somehow chance
To be asked everywhere:
The ladies with us sometimes flirt,
But then—they all stop there.
They will not now let's breathe a vow:
Care not for poesy:—
In vain we try to find out why
Old bachelors we'd be.

We cannot tell why every belle
Combines to keep us so;—
Persons and manners passable,
We dress as others do;
We take great pains, yet without gains,
The right to let them see;
They all say Nay, too much you say,
Old bachelors you'll be.

Would that some fair her lot would share
With any of us six;
How we would laud her choice to heaven,
No matter where 'twould fix.
They'd then be taught that we would not
Submit to tyranny—
Then very soon they'd change their tune—
"Young bachelors" we'd be.

Signed, on behalf of the others,
X.Y.Z.

(1840-12-12, 4:1)

2632. The Reply of the Ladies of Monaghan to the "Lament" of the Six Disconsolate Young Gentlemen.

Dear gents. gallant, you're what we want,
We sigh for you, in truth;
There's few of you are "seventy-three"—
You've all enough of youth.
In vain we try, though something shy,
To coax you to agree;
With us; oh! dear, it would appear,
Old maidens we must be.

Oh! how we deck, make bare the neck,
Profuse our charms display,
To try and melt your frozen hearts,
But all are thrown away.
We blush, we sigh—a soft reply
We make to all, yet see,
Despire our arts to wound your hearts,
Old maidens we must be.

Dear sirs, your strain doth so complain,
And rolls the blame on us;
We must declare 'tis not our fault
To make you all rhyme thus.
So, now, dear Six, we'd have you fix
Your choice at once, and flee
To Hymen's bands, and join our hands,
Old maidens we won't be.

Do thus resolve our doubts to solve
About the marriage state,
Take us at once without a pause,

(*continued...*)

2632, continued:

Lest some should be too late.
Make no delay, we jointly pray,
The Priest, good soul, to see,
And we shall all come at your call,
The best of wives to be.

(Signed on behalf of our sex,)
Z.Y.X.
December 12, 1840.
(1840-12-19, 4:1)

2633. Census of Ireland.—The Lord Lieutenant has appointed William Tighe Hamilton, Esq., chief clerk in the office of the secretary of state; Henry John Brownrigg, Esq., inspector of constabulary; and Thomas Larcom, Esq., captain in the corps of Royal Engineers, to be the persons who shall superintend the carrying into effect the provisions of the statute for taking an account of the population of Ireland, the 3d and 4th Victoria, cap. 100. (1841-01-09, 1:2)

2634. They little know, who coldly talk of the poor man's bereavements, as a happy release from pain to the departed, and a merciful relief from suspense to the survivor—they little know what the agony of those bereavements is! A silent look of affection and regard, when all other eyes are turned coldly away—the consciousness that we possess the sympathy and affection of one being when all others have deserted us—is a hold, a stay, a comfort in the deepest affliction, which no wealth could purchase or power bestow.
(1841-01-09, 4:2)

2635. A man was frozen to death Thursday evening, the 7th instant, when proceeding in his cart along the Shankill-road. (1841-01-16, 4:5)

2636. Fatal Occurrence.—On Friday evening, the 15th inst. a melancholy accident occurred in the neighbourhood of Dungannon, by which the Rev. John Brydge, of Brydge Hall, a Presbyterian Clergyman, lost his life. The rev. gentleman, while on his way home from the sessions, had called at the house of a friend, where two of his daughters were spending the evening. After stopping there for a short time, he proceeded to get his horse and gig, his daughters walking forward before him. He overtook them on the road at a place where there was no fence, when, stopping to take one of them into the gig, the horse ran backwards, threw Mr. Brydge out, and both horse and gig unfortunately falling upon him, he was killed on the spot.—*Newry Telegraph*. (1841-01-23, 3:3)

2637. Two men died at Mitchell's confectionary-house, Grafton-street, Dublin, on the night of the 18th inst., from the fumes of charcoal in their bed-room stoves.
(1841-01-23, 3:3)

2638. The fee and inheritance of the Bawnboy estate, in the county of Cavan, as enjoyed by the late Nathaniel Sneyd, Esq., containing 1,100 acres, was sold on Friday in Master Goold's office, to Mr. Pearson, for 4,500*l*. (1841-01-23, 3:3)

2639. The situation of Governor of Mullingar gaol is vacant by the death of Mr. Fielding. (1841-01-23, 3:3)

2640. Suicide.—An inquest was held before Doctor Tyrrell, on Tuesday, the 5th instant, in the townland of Drumnagar, parish of Loughisland, county Down, on the body of a young woman, named Ellen Hall, who had committed suicide on the preceding Sunday, under the following circumstances:—The unfortunate young woman had resided in that neighbourhood for several years, in the capacity of a servant; she bore a good character, and was much liked by those who knew her. On Sunday, she requested two or three young girls to accompany her to the house of a friend. When they had proceeded about [a] quarter of a mile, she sat down convenient to a bog-hole, deliberately took off her shoes, cloak, and bonnet, gave her handkerchief to one of her young companions, and in a moment leaped into the hole, where she was drowned before timely assistance could be procured.—*Northern Whig*. (1841-01-23, 3:3)

2641. The Answer to the Reply of the Monaghan Ladies to the Six Young Gentlemen.

Ah! ladies, why to lure us try
And make us think that you
Would listen to our sighs or vows,
However deep or true.
'Tis cruel thus to sport with us,
And torture all our lives,
You think that we in jest must be—
Indeed we all want wives.

We try each way, we're sad we're gay,
Do all we can to please;
We sometime win a smile, but then
'Tis only given to tease.
You say that we are like the bee,
We rove from flower to flower,
In each we dip, its sweetness sip,
And leave it ere an hour.

Is't not a shame to throw the blame
On us who would not care
To wed to-day if we could find
Ladies our lots to share.
Would you were taught our inmost thought,
No flirts you'd find are we;
The fault's your own, and yours alone,
If e'er old maids you'll be.

We sure perceive that in your sleeve
You're laughing at the six,
Although you seem to think that we
At once our lots should fix;
The fair will not let's change our lot,
Altho' you all talk so;
We brave the task, the questions ask,
The answer's always NO.

X.Y.Z.
(1841-01-23, 4:1)

2642. Death of Sir John Godfrey, Bart.—Died, on Thursday, the 21st January, at Warwick house, Tunbridge Wells, in the 78th year of his age, Sir J. Godfrey, Bart., of Kilcoleman Abbey, in this county. Altho' this announcement can scarcely be called sudden, when the age of the venerable baronet is considered, yet there was nothing in the immediate illness to prepare his family, or numerous circle of friends and relatives, for the loss they have sustained; and a loss it will be acknowledged to be by every individual who had enjoyed the pleasure of his acquaintance. Indeed we have seldom or never been called upon to record the death of one whose course through a long life more fully entitled him to the praise of not having made an enemy, or left an ill-wisher behind him. Mild and benevolent in disposition, upright in principle, friendly and courteous in his manners, Sir John Godfrey deserved and won universal regard and respect. His tenantry and dependents looked up to him with that confidence and good-will which ever makes the relation of the landlord and tenant a benefit to both; and when a short time since he removed to England, both he and his estimable lady carried with them the regrets of all classes of society, but more especially of that circle, in which they had been the unceasing dispensers of advice, assistance and comfort. As the crowning characteristic of the venerable deceased, we would mention that real but unobtrusive piety—not a noisy, but living principle, which we have every reason to know shed a calm light over the evening of his days, and now affords his family and friends their best consolation in the reflection that he is not sleeping, but "awake in Him who is the resurrection and the life of man."

Sir John Godfrey succeeded his father in 1817; he married Eleanor, daughter of John Cromie, Esq., of Cromore, Londonderry, by whom he had a numerous family, and is succeeded in his title and estates by his eldest son, now Sir William Duncan Godfrey, Bart.—*Kerry Evening Post.* (1841-02-06, 3:3)

2643. Marriage of Mr. Charles Kean and Miss Ellen Tree.—It is stated in *Kidd's Dramatic Journal*, on the authority of a correspondent, that these performers have been privately married at Manchester. (1841-02-13, 1:4)

2644. The quiet and sober town of Lurgan, has experienced a good deal of excitement in consequence of the disappearance of Miss —, the beautiful daughter of a retired officer of the customs, with Mr. —, a young gentleman connected with a respectable banking office there. (1841-02-13, 1:5)

2645. Coroner's Inquest.—On the afternoon of Saturday last, the body of an elderly female, name and residence unknown, was discovered floating in the canal, a few perches below the Dublin Bridge. The body was dragged out and laid on the road, where it remained all the night and during the greater part of the day following. We know not what prompted to such unseemly exposure of the remains of a fellow-being, and therefore do we refrain from imputing blame to any party; but surely public decency—a regard to common humanity—should have suggested the depositing of the body within the walls of the bridewell or sessions house. At the inquest, the body was identified as that of a mendicant, named Sally Fegan, belonging to Killeavy, but who had no fixed place of residence. The verdict "Found Drowned," was then unanimously recorded. (1841-02-13, 2:4)

2646. The late Lord Henley was an Irish peer, and brother-in-law of Sir Robert Peel. A pension of £2,500, as ex-master in Chancery, reverts to the Crown. (1841-02-13, 3:1)

2647. Determined Suicide.—On Friday, the 5th inst., an inquest was held, in the townland of Drumlaughlin, near Rockcorry, on view of the body of a woman named Judith Duffy, who came by her death in the following manner, as appeared from the evidence adduced on the inquest:

Robert Elliott, in whose service deceased was, deposed, that he went to Tullyvin on Thursday, and on his return home found deceased attending to her business; observed nothing remarkable in her manner or appearance; deceased went to bed on that night rather earlier than usual—before supper; when supper was ready, witness's wife went down to the room in which deceased slept to call her to supper, but finding deceased and the children apparently asleep, she did not disturb them; after supper, witness and his wife went to bed, but in the course of the night witness was awoke by his wife, who told him she heard some noise in the house, and wanted him to rise and know the cause; witness replied that it might be the slapping of the window shutter, there being a pane of glass broken in the window; in a short time after, hearing the pigs grunting in the street, his wife said all was not right, and again told him to get up and look about the place; witness did so, and, on getting to the door of the room where deceased slept, and where the window was the shutter of which he thought was the cause of the noise, he found the door barred on the inside; he pushed it open, and went to the window-shutter which he found in the position he had left it the night before; on leaving the apartment he saw deceased standing (as witness thought) in one of the corners, and being somewhat surprised what she was doing there at that hour of the night, with her clothes on, he went over to where she was, and found deceased suspended by a hank of yarn from one of the joists; witness immediately called his wife, with whose assistance he cut deceased down; she was then in a lifeless state; witness then alarmed the neighbors and procured medical aid, but all to no effect, life was extinct. The jury, after viewing the body, and maturely considering the evidence, returned a (*continued...*)

2647, continued: ...verdict of "deceased came by her death by hanging herself while laboring under temporary insanity."

The deceased bore an excellent character, and was much esteemed by her master and mistress. What renders this melancholy case the more painful is the apparent self-determination of the unhappy woman to complete the work of self-destruction. The evening previous to the commission of the fatal deed, a neighbor remarked to deceased how cold she looked, to which she (deceased) made answer "she would be far colder that time to-morrow." "Why, where will you be?" Asked the woman. "O! I will be here," was the reply. On that evening, deceased left her master's house and remained out some time; on her return she appeared chilly-looking, and her feet wet; she slipped her shoes to one of the children, whispering her to put them aside. The next day her master, being made previously acquainted with this circumstance, took one of his neighbors with him, and, after examining all the water about the place, discovered a large flaxhole, the ice on the surface of which had been broken, it is thought by the deceased, in an attempt to destroy herself the previous evening. No cause has been assigned for the commission of the unhappy deed. (1841-02-13, 3:2)

2648. Melancholy Occurrence.—Seven Lives Lost.—On the night of Wednesday se'nnight a boat, with a crew of eight men, left the shore at Lacken to fish for herrings. Having been very successful, the unfortunate men were returning about eight o'clock, when, at the distance of a hundred yards from the shore, a wave broke over the boat, which instantly filled and sank. Of the eight men who were in it, only one escaped, having seized an oar, and being a good swimmer, on reaching the shore he gave the alarm, and Mr. Dalton, coast guard officer, manned his boat, and at great risk, from the darkness of the night and the height of the waves, proceeded to render assistance; but it was too late, the seven wretched men had sunk to rise no more. The names were—John Horan, Henry Dixon, Philip Nealan, James Early, Owen King, and Peter Lavin, all of whom left large families to deplore the sad event. On Saturday, Mr. Atkinson, coroner, held an inquest on the bodies of four of the deceased, which had been washed on shore; the other three had not been found. The expressions of grief uttered by one woman in particular were truly heart-rending—she had to lament the death of a husband, a father, and a brother.—*Mayo Constitution.* (1841-02-13, 4:3)

2649. Death of Judge Day.—We regret to announce the decease of the venerable Ex-Judge Day, which took place on the 8th inst., after a short illness, at his seat Loughlinstown House, in his 95th year. In 1819 the venerable judge resigned his station in the Court of Queen's Bench, which he had honorably filled during a period of twenty-one years.—*Post.* (1841-02-20, 2:2)

2650. Lines on the death of the late Sir W. Cusack Smith, Baron of the Court of Exchequer.

Nelson, triumphant in his glory, fell
The hero of the ocean. Thou hast stepp'd
To the Lethean slumbers of the grave
Like him—thy country's ornament and pride!
Like him, lamented by the good and just;
By virtue, wisdom, learning, hand-in-hand,
And by the weeping muses ever mourn'd!
Oh! ever, ever while recording fame
Shall breathe thy loved name, Baron Smith, a tear
Will fall upon thy urn—a tender tear
Of memory, fondly cherishing thy name!
A name that ever to the world proclaim'd
The gentleman and scholar!—that proclaim'd
(Fair truth assenting with a mournful smile)
A man of merit, modestly retired
Within himself, to shun the voice of praise—
To shun that praise which fame in whispers breathed
To many an ear, while pointing out a man
Presiding in the precincts of the Court,
Of intellectual endowments rare,
An ornament and honor to the bench
Judicial, by the learned bar allowed.

J.H.K. (1841-02-20, 4:1)

2651. Dreadful Fire near Letterkenny.—On the evening of Monday se'nnight, a fire, having most tragical consequences, broke out in the flax-mill of Mr. Samuel M'Clelland, at a short distance from Letterkenny, on the Kilmacrennan road. One of the men employed in the mill, named James Dogherty, had gone outside, after eight o'clock, to enter the lantern, which is apart from the interior of the mill, and having snuffed it with his fingers, part of the snuff, it is supposed, had fallen through a mouse-hole upon the floor of the mill, which instantly ignited. At first the flame was extinguished by Mr. M'Clelland throwing a leathern apron over it; but it instantly burst out with greater fury than before, and the persons employed in the mill—in all, the owner, four men, inclusive of Dogherty, and two girls, that person's daughters—found themselves in extreme danger. They rushed to the door; but, unfortunately, Dogherty had locked it; in trying to unlock it, the key dropped to the ground, it was recovered, and effectually used; but, in the interval, the seven persons were almost suffocated and scorched in the most shocking manner. On rushing out, some plunged themselves into the mill dam, and others into the stream, to extinguish the fire which was consuming them. Mr. M'Clelland, burnt as he was, managed to turn the water off the mill wheel, as the motion of the machinery driven by it assisted the fire in its progress; and neighbours having come to his aid, the conflagration was subdued, but not until nearly the whole roof and machinery had been consumed. Every possible attention was paid to the victims by the medical gentlemen of Letterkenny. The two girls, Doherty [sic], the one aged seventeen, the other fifteen, died—the first two days, and the other eight days after the accident, both having endured much suffering. The names of the men, besides Mr. M'C. who were in the mill, and who so narrowly escaped, but not without grievous torture, are John Doherty, James Bradley, Robert Chambers, and J. M'Kendrick. The verdict of the coroner's inquest held on view of the bodies of the two girls, was "accidental death." (1841-02-20, 4:5)

2652. Measles are exceedingly prevalent amongst the children of Cavan at present; even some adults are affected with the same disorder. There is hardly a family in which two or three children are not ailing—in some cases it has proved fatal. Two children of the same family died of the disease within one week of each other. (1841-02-27, 2:5)

2653. Frightful Accident at Newry.—Yesterday about the hour of eleven o'clock, this town was thrown into a state of alarm by a report that the Court-House had fallen and killed a number of persons; and the multitude pressing in that direction from every quarter, seemed to confirm the tidings.—The truth, however, soon appeared to be, that Miss Duff had been using the Grand Jury Room for the purpose of distribution, flowering work to a number of sewing girls, and making payment, &c., when the floor, owing to its rotten state, and the weight of these females, suddenly gave way, and all were precipitated into the area of the Courthouse.—Fortunately, there was only one old man (the keeper) underneath, and he happened not to be in the centre where the floor fell, and so escaped unhurt, by creeping out at the side. A great number of the females, however, were severely hurt, six or seven, we believe dangerously. We, ourselves, saw four or five, who seemed fatally injured. We have heard that one woman has died since her removal to the hospital, after giving birth to an abortive child. It is [a] matter of wonder that the use of this old building should be continued so long after sentence of condemnation had been pronounced upon it. Down with it, down with it in the name of humanity, before more lives are lost!—*Newry Examiner*. (1841-02-27, 3:2)

2654. ON DIT.—That the lady of a well-known joint of the tail—domiciled not one hundred miles from the kingdom of Kerry—has left her father's house, and taken with her a chosen servant to guide her footsteps, together with her four young children, to be the partners of her retirement. The cause of this step is said to be a gallant gay Lothario, who loved not wisely but too well, whose indiscretions became known to the servants, while the principally aggrieved person was attending his parliamentary duties. The affair will most probably be mooted pro and con by the gentleman of the long robe during the ensuing term. Some say the lady was met by a friend of the husband at Limerick, and that the children were taken from her. (1841-02-27, 4:1)

2655. Death of the Earl of Rosse.—We regret to announce the death of the Earl of Rosse, which took place on Wednesday evening, at his Lordship's residence in Brunswick-square.—*Brighton Herald* (Saturday.) The deceased was in his 83d year, having been born in May 21, 1758. He succeeded his uncle in 1807.—By his wife, Alice, daughter of J. Lloyd, Esq., he has left four children, the eldest of whom, Lord Oxmantown, who formerly represented the King's County in parliament, is in his 41st year, and married in 1836, Mary, eldest daughter of John Wilson Field, Esq., by whom he has several children. The late peer was one of the representatives of the Irish peerage sitting in the Imperial parliament: his death consequently creates a vacancy in the number of that body. (1841-03-06, 3:3)

2656. The noble house of Lansdowne has been again disappointed of an infant heir. The young Countess of Shelbourne has, however, pretty well recovered from the effects of her recent miscarriage. (1841-03-06, 4:5)

2657. The Marquis of Sligo on the birth-day of his son, Lord Altamont, entertained the King, Queen, and Court of Naples. (1841-03-06, 4:5)

2658. A dreadful accident occurred last Saturday in Great George's-street. An officer's servant was airing two horses, when one of them becoming restive, the man dismounted, in order to tighten the curbs. Upon remounting, both horses set off at full gallop, and coming in contact with a poor old man named Henry O'Neill, who was driving a coal-cart, ran him down. On being taken to the hospital, he only survived for about an hour. One of the horses knocked his head against a lamp-post, and instantly dropped dead. The servant man was thrown, and having hitched his foot in the stirrup, was dragged for some length along the road, but without receiving any serious injury. (1841-03-13, 2:4)

2659. In the case of *Heaviside v. Heaviside*, a divorce, on the plea of adultery, has been granted. (1841-03-13, 2:5)

2660. Lieutenant-Colonel G. Hillier, 62d Regiment, died of apoplexy at Calcutta, on the 15th of January. Major the Hon. G. Upton, formerly on the staff of Lord Clare, when Governor of Bombay, gets the late officer's rank in the Regiment; Captain Shortt, the Majority; and Lieutenant Jackson, the company. (1841-03-20, 1:5)

2661. The Commander-in-Chief of the Forces of Madras Presidency, Lieutenant-General Sir Samuel Ford Whittingham, died of apoplexy on the 19th of January, and the next senior officer is our gallant countrymen, Major-General Sir Hugh Gough, but pending his absence on the China expedition, Major-General Dick has taken charge of the Presidency. Lieutenant-General Whittingham was interred with full military honors, at Fort George. His son, Lieutenant Whittingham, R.E., was recently in this garrison upon the Ordinance Survey, and is now at Youghal. (1841-03-20, 1:5)

2662. A horse of Captain Crichton, Inniskilling Dragoons, took head in Belfast this week, and galloping through the town killed a man of the name of O'Neill; after which the infuriated animal dashed against a lamp post, and was killed on the spot. The soldier who rode the horse fell, and was dragged with his leg in the stirrup for some yards, and was severely hurt. (1841-03-20, 1:5)

2663. Awfully Sudden Death.—It is with feelings of sincere sorrow we have to record the death of William Erskine, Esq. Treasurer for the County Cavan, and Registrar to the Diocesan Court of Kilmore, both of which offices he has held for a long period. He was in his usual health on Saturday last—out through the town the whole of the day—took suddenly ill about six o'clock that evening when Dr. Halpin was called in, who prescribed some medicine, and did not consider his life in any danger, stating on leaving him at 10 o'clock that night, that he would probably be well enough in the morning. He became so much worse however in the course of a few hours, that the same medical gentleman was again called on, and before he arrived, although but the next door off, he had ceased to exist. He died at half past one o'clock, on the morning of Saturday, the 21st instant.

Mr. Erskine is deeply and deservedly regretted by the inhabitants of Cavan. He was a steady friend, and a useful member of Society—and of so munificient and charitable a disposition that the poor have sustained in him an irreparable loss. (1841-03-27, 3:3)

2664. Good Advice.—To Young Girls.—Never marry a boy whose mamma is afraid to have him go on the water, or whose papa cannot tell the difference between the toothache and the lockjaw.

To Young Men.—Have it fairly understood, before you wed, whether you intend to marry an individual or a whole family.

To Parents.—Do not let a silly ambition hazard the happiness of your children, nor your chagrin at the discovery of your own folly betray you into a violation of your obligations.

To Babies.—Remain with your mothers as long as you can, and do not get married before you are out of leading strings.

To Indiscreet Persons.—Never hire a printer to publish your folly in a book, for it is worse than being hung and paying the executioner forty shillings. (1841-04-03, 1:5)

2665. A lunatic in the Clonmel asylum, having obtained access to the medicine chest, last Saturday, regaled himself so freely of the contents, that he died in a few hours. (1841-04-10, 2:1)

2666. Melancholy Death from Suffocation.—On Thursday night last, a lovely girl, aged fifteen named Anne Jane West was suffocated in her bed in Omagh, under the following circumstances:—She believed her room was damp, and had induced one of the servant girls to sleep with her. They retired to bed about eleven o'clock, having left a dish of coals burning in the room, in which there was no fire-place. The girl awoke about seven next morning, and found the young lady's arm lying over her bosom, quite cold; she had just strength enough to rise and open the door, when it was found that Miss West was dead, having suffocated by the vapour from the coals. Had the girl not awoke when she did, she must also have perished, for though sensible she was speechless, and it was long before she recovered. The beautiful deceased was the only daughter of Mr. Robert West, of Fintona, who had removed to Omagh a few weeks before.—*Derry Standard*. (1841-04-10, 4:4)

2667. Mr. J. Gillespie, from Derry, has succeeded the late Captain Webb as Barrack-master at Waterford. Major Gossett, from Youghal, is appointed Barrack-master of Derry; and Lieutenant O'Donnell, from Newcastle, is appointed to Youghal. (1841-04-17, 1:1)

2668. Lord Belfast succeeds the late Lord O'Neill as Colonel of the Antrim Militia. (1841-04-17, 1:1)

2669. Death-Bed Scenes of Distinguished Men.—How deeply interesting it is to contemplate the death-bed scenes of those whose fame will be imperishable, so long as genius is admired, or science, art, and literature cultivated.

It is said that Haller, the great physiologist, died feeling his pulse. When he found that he was almost gone, he turned to his brother physician and said, "My friend, the artery ceases to beat," and died.

Petrarch was found dead in his library leaning on a book. Bede died in the act of dictating. Roscommon uttered at the moment he expired two lines of his own version of "Dies irae."

Rosseau, when dying, ordered his attendants to place him before his window, that he might once more behold his garden, and bid adieu to nature.

Addison's dying speech to his son in-law was characteristic of the *Spectator*. "Behold," said he to the dissolute young nobleman, "with what tranquillity a Christian can die!"

Alfieri, the day before he died, was persuaded to see a Priest, and when he came he said to him what [with] great affability, "Have the kindness to look in tomorrow; I trust death will wait four-and-twenty hours."

Tasso's dying request to Cardinal Cynthia was indicative of the gloom which haunted him through life; he had but one favor, he said, to request of him, which was that he would collect his books and commit them to the flames, especially his *Jerusalem Delivered.*

Clarendon's pen dropped from his fingers when he was seized with palsy, which terminated his life.

Chaucer died ballad-making. His last productions he entitled "A Ballad made by Geoffrey Chaucer on his death-bed, lying in great anguish."

Sir Godfrey Kneller's vanity was displayed in his last moments. Pope, who visited him two days before he died, says he never saw such a scene of vanity in his life; Kneller was sitting up in his bed contemplating the plans he was making for his own monument.

"I could wish this tragic scene was over," said the celebrated actor, Quinn; "but I hope to go through it with becoming dignity."

Bishop Newton died whilst in the act of setting his watch.

Bayle having prepared his proof-sheet for the printer, pointed to where it lay when in the act of dying.

The last words of Lord Chesterfield were, when the valet, opening the curtains of the bed, announced Mr. Drysdale, "Give Drysdale a chair." Warren observed that Chesterfield's good breeding only quitted him with his life.

Tell Collingwood to bring the fleet to an anchor, were Nelson's last words.

"I fear not death! Death is not terrible to me!" said Charles the First, when he ascended the scaffold.

Sir Thomas More, on observing the weakness of the scaffold on which he was about to die, said to the executioner, "I pray you see me up safe, and for my coming down let me shift for myself."

—The Physiology of Death by Mr. Winslow.
(1841-04-17, 1:5)

2670. The Approaching Census.—Active preparations are now being made for taking the decennial census, and instructions to this effect have already been sent to the registrars in the different parishes in the United Kingdom. Each parish will be divided into different districts, extending from fifty to eighty houses, and the inquiries will be made by intelligent persons residing in the neighbourhood, to be appointed by the local registrars. Each of the agents so appointed will have to deliver the notices at the houses, and on the 1st of July to fill up all the details respecting the age, sex, employment, &c. of the different occupants. On Monday, a circular was issued from the home office to the different district registrars, assigning as a rate of remuneration the sum of ten shillings for every ten houses above this number. The inspectors will be appointed from intelligent tradesmen and others in the different districts, by which means authentic details will be ensured. Inspectors have already been appointed for the purpose in most of the parishes in the eastern districts of the metropolis. (1841-04-17, 2:1)

2671. Approaching Marriage in High Life.—We understand the preliminaries are already arranged for the marriage of Sir William Heathcote, Bart., M.P. for North Hants, and Miss Shirley, daughter of Mr. Evelyn John Shirley, M.P. for South Warwickshire, of Lough Fra, county Monaghan. (1841-04-17, 3:2)

2672. The Bishop of London terms in one of his charges, the case of Churching a woman after accouchement, in a private residence unwarrantable and absurd. (1841-04-17, 3:2)

2673. Marriage in High Life.—On the 15th instant, at Leamington, by the Right Hon. and Rev. Lord Somerset, Charles Kemeys Tynte, Esq., late M.P. for West Somerset, only son of Colonel Kemeys Tynte, of Halswell Park, county Somerset, and Cafin Mably, Glamorganshire, &c., to Vincentia, daughter of the late Wallop Brabazon, of Rath House, county of Louth, Esq. After an elegant *dejeune* at Lady Teynham's (the bride's relative), the happy couple set off to pass the honeymoon at one of the family mansions in South Wales. (1841-04-24, 1:2)

2674. The Earl of Roden has taken his departure from London for his estate in Ireland. The noble Earl returns at the close of the ensuing week, to be present at the nuptials of his son, Viscount Jocelyn, with Lady Fanny Cowper, the daughter of the Viscountess Palmerston. (1841-04-24, 1:4)

2675. Marriage in High Life.—On Monday last, Captain Arthur G. Lewis, Provost of Monaghan, led to the Altar, Henrietta, relict of the late Hon. Richard Westenra, of Ballyleck, in this County, and third son of the Lord Rossmore. The Lady is only child of the late Henry Owen Scott, Esq., of Clanmacnelly in this county. The ceremony was performed by the Rev. Edward Jones Lewis, Rector of Loughran. On Tuesday evening, the town was illuminated in compliment to the Provost's nuptials. (1841-04-24, 2:5)

2676. Marriage in High Life.—In St. Andrew's Church, Dublin, on the 22d instant, by the Dean of Cashel, uncle to the bride, Thomas Coote, Esq., D.L., of Fortwilliam, in the county of Cavan, to Rebecca Horatia, eldest daughter of Charles James Adams, Esq., of Shinan House, in same county. (1841-04-24, 2:5)

2677. Marriage in High Life.—The marriage of Sir William Heathcote, Bart., M.P., and Miss Shirley, eldest daughter of Mr. E.J. Shirley, M.P., is to be solemnised early in the ensuing month. Sir Wm., who is in his 41st year, was married in 1825 to the Hon. Miss Caroline Perceval, daughter of the late and sister of the present Lord Arden, who died in March, 1835, leaving a family of four children. (1841-04-24, 2:5)

2678. Death of the Earl of Belmore.—With regret we announce the demise of this amiable and excellent nobleman, which took place, on Sunday last at Leamington. His loss will be sincerely deplored by his family, his connexions, and friends, and bitterly felt by his numerous tenantry, to whom he was an indulgent, kind, and benevolent landlord. His Lordship had been in a delicate state of health for some years, having suffered much from the climate while Governor of Jamaica. The death of Lord Belmore will cause a vacancy in the Irish representative peerage, being the third that has occurred within the brief space of a month.

(*continued...*)

2678, continued: ...The late Earl, Somerset Lowry Corry, Earl of Belmore, and Viscount and Baron Belmore of Castle-Coole, in the county Fermanagh, in the Peerage of Ireland; an Irish representative Peer, and Custos Rotulorum in the county of Tyrone. His Lordship was born on the 11th July, 1774, and succeeded to his titles on the 2d February, 1802, having been married on the 20th Oct. 1800, to the Lady Juliana Butler, second daughter of Henry Thomas, second Earl of Carrick. By her Ladyship, who was born on the 20th Sept. 1783, the deceased Earl has left two sons, Armar, Viscount Corry, (now Earl of Belmore), and the Right Hon. Henry Thomas Corry, M.P., the latter of whom was married on the 18th March, 1830, to the Lady Harriet Anne Ashley Cooper, second daughter to the Earl of Shaftesbury.

The present Earl of Belmore was born on the 23d Dec. 1801, and was married on the 27th May, 1834, to Emily Louise, youngest daughter of the late William Shepherd, Esq, and has issue—Somerset Richard, now Viscount Corry, born 9th April, 1835; the Hon. Armar, born 25th May, 1836; Lady Louisa Anne, born 17th November, 1837; and a son, born 17th June, 1839. (1841-04-24, 2:5)

2679. Monument to Mr. Erskine.—We are happy to find that a tablet, bearing a suitable inscription, is about to be erected in Cavan Church to the memory of the late William Erskine, Esq., to record the high sense in which the magistrates and gentry of the county held his character, both as a private gentleman and a public officer. It was moved by the Right Hon. Lord Farnham, seconded by Colonel Saunderson, and agreed to unanimously at a meeting, recently held in the Court-house, for the purpose of selecting a successor to the office of Treasurer for that county, vacant by Mr. Erskine's death—when Samuel Moore, Esq., jun., of Cullis was duly nominated to that situation. Subscriptions not to exceed one pound. There is already a large amount on hands, and the greatest willingness seems to pervade all classes to contribute towards that mournful duty. They are glad of this last opportunity of testifying their respect for the memory of a gentleman whose loss they so seriously deplore. (1841-04-24, 2:5)

2680. Ode to the Burial of Sir John Moore.—One of the most barefaced piracies that ever created a sensation in the literary world has been upon the *tapis* for some weeks past, originating in the claim of a Mr. Mackintosh to the authorship of the beautiful and admired poem, the name of which appears above.

Shortly after the poem appeared, it was attributed to the pens of both Byron and Campbell, but with the honesty of great minds, disclaimed by them. It was first printed in the *Newry Telegraph* of April 19, 1817, with the initials, C. W. attached—the initials of the Rev. C. Wolfe, who, we have the very best authority for saying, was the true and only author.

"The Ode was commenced in the year 1814," says the Rev. Samuel O'Sullivan, "in my presence—the first and last stanzas were composed, and in the course of a few days, during which it was upon the anvil, the Rev. Charles Wolfe read the production to me and claimed its authorship." Manuscript copies of the work were distributed amongst the college friends of Mr. Wolfe, amongst whom, as living witnesses, we quote the names of the present Bishop of Meath, Rev. Dr. O'Brien, the justly celebrated Anster, Mr. Geo. Downs, the Rev. Mortimer and Samuel O'Sullivan, all of whom can testify to the authorship; and to another of the little circle of friends, the Rev. John A. Russell, Clontibret, Archdeacon of Clogher, upon whom devolved the pleasing task of compiling the remains of this justly esteemed Divine. In this work, Mr. Russell not only gives the Ode as the composition of his friend, but in consequence of the previous disputes upon the subject, enters into an elaborate detail of proofs (*vide* pages 28, 29, and 32 of the Remains, Fifth Edition.) These proofs set the matter at rest for fifteen years until a Mr. Mackintosh, a Scotchman, having conquered the *mauvais honte* of his youth, endeavours, with matured muscle, to grasp the laurel wreath so deservedly earned by him who is gone. He states, that he composed the Ode in 1816, and that a Mr. Menzies was cognizant thereof, but unfortunately he is dead. He was about to submit it to Professor Christison, but his bashful temperament prevented him. How unfortunate again for the aspirant, as neither of these names can be appealed to! Again, he gave the Ode to a Captain Clapperton, a collector of lyrics, to publish, but he did not do so!! And, as a last resource, he wrote to the father of Menzies, requesting him to search amongst his son's papers for a manuscript copy, of which he says that person had many, but he got no answer to his letter!!! Was ever mortal so afflicted by coincidences.

In 1826, he learned that Archdeacon Russell arrogated the work to the Rev. Charles Wolfe, and published it to the world, in his compilation; yet he is silent until 1841, when in despite of all truth and seeming he comes forward and claims the offspring in its age which he deserted in its infancy. There is little of plausibility or seeming in this, but with our gifted friend, Mr. Russell, there is no doubt—he may see with Hamlet—"I know not seems, nay, it is." But in order to set the affair at rest in the minds of our readers, we publish the following correspondence:—

To the Rev. W. Muir.

"Rev. and Dear Sir.—The circumstances attending the writing of the lines on the burial of Sir John Moore, so far as I can recall them at the distance of time, are simple, and easily told. I had been long familiar with the details of the disastrous retreat to Corunna, and felt deeply interested in the fate of the gallant but ill-supported for John Moore.

"In the year 1816, while a student at the College of Edinburgh, I happened to lodge with Mrs. Henry, whose husband had been a sea-faring person, and, I remember well, lost his life at Corunna, while employed in the transport service, at the embarkation of the British troops. Mrs. Henry had a number of letters, which she sometimes took a melancholy pleasure in hearing me read to her, written by friends who had served under Sir John Moore, during the whole of the campaign. One of these, written by an eye-witness, depicted in forcible, though homely colours, the hurried interment of the devoted chief. It was on perusing this last, that I formed the idea of attempting a poetical description of that event. I had been accustomed from my childhood to feel singularly affected when witnessing the ceremony of a soldier's burial; and I have no doubt that an occasional sight of this kind from the window of my bed-room, which looked out upon the Greyfriar's church-yard, contributed in the present instance to draw my thoughts in that direction.

"About this time, a young man of the name of Menzies, who had formerly been a school-fellow, came to Edinburgh to attend the classes at the University, and, owing to the previous intimacy, was frequently in my company. Mrs. M. [sic] was an enthusiast in everything relating to the military profession, and would have esteemed it the summit of human ambition to be appointed to a commission in the British army. On seeing the ode, in the unfinished state it then lay among some other fugitive pieces, he professed himself highly pleased with it, but, at the same time, suggested some amendments which might be made on it, one or two of which I subsequently adopted. As Mr. M. took a copy of it oftener than once, I have always been of opinion that it was through his means it afterwards found its way into the public prints; although it would have been an easy matter for any person who had access to my lodgings to transcribe it without my knowledge. Whether this was the case or not, unfortunately I cannot positively say. I was soon afterwards separated from Mr. Menzies, who died about 1820.

"In the year 1817 I was a member of a small debating society, which met in Catherine-Street, when, on one occasion, I read the ode along with two or three other pieces, in place of the essay which it was customary for each of the members to read in rotation, before opening the debate; but, although I received some general prise [sic], I do not remember that the ode drew any particular notice.

"During my residence in Edinburgh, I had, in common with many other young men attending the University, experienced much kindness from the late Professor Christison. One evening, about this time, when going to call on him, I had put the ode in my pocket, with the intention of submitting it to his remarks, but during our interview, I had not the courage to present it. I have frequently regretted my diffidence on that occasion, as I have no doubt that Mr. Christison's exquisite taste would have at once appreciated those merits which the public were afterwards pleased to ascribe to it, and thus brought it into notice at a time when the author could not be disputed.

"In 1818, I left Edinburgh for my present situation.—It was a year or two afterwards when I first observed the Ode in print. It was in one of the Edinburgh periodicals, when a commendatory note subjoined, stated that it had recently appeared in one of the newspapers.

"About this time, the late Captain Clapperton, the African traveller, told me that a friend of his was getting up for publication a selection from the fleeting literature of the day, in which he wishes to insert *The Burial of Sir John Moore*, and, as he had been told that I was the author of that piece, wished to have my name adhibited to it, to which I consented. Captain C. shortly afterwards left this place, and I never learned whether the work was published or not.

"I never saw "Wolf's Remains" till you put the volume into my hands about two months ago.

"It was, I think, in 1826 that I learned that the author of the memoir of the Rev. C. Wolfe had claimed the ode for that gentleman. I felt somewhat indignant at this; and, with a view to place the matter in its proper light, wrote to the father of Mr. Menzies, who lived in a distant part of the country, requesting him to search among his son's papers for the manuscript of the lines, but to this letter no answer was returned.

"I then saw that I had allowed the proper time for asserting my claim to pass away; and, being apprehensive lest the public might be unwilling to believe that a piece, which had by this time made some little noise in the world, was the production of an obscure individual like myself, I judged it more prudent to forgo my claim, then to expose myself to any obloquy on its account.—I am, Rev. and dear Sir, yours very truly,

"A. Mackintosh.

"Temple, Jan., 1841."

To the Editor of the Edinburgh Advertiser.

Clontibret glebe, Castleblayney,
March 29, 1841.

Sir—An extract from your paper was forwarded to me yesterday by a friend, in which I read, with no small amazement, that the Rev. A. Mackintosh, (a native of Atholl, now master of the parish school of Temple,) has written what you call, *a very modest letter*, in which, he asserts his claims to the authorship of the celebrated Ode on the burial of Sir John Moore; and that his friend the Rev. W. Muir, (assistant minister at Temple), has furnished you with documents which seem to satisfy you that his claim is well-founded. Though I entertain no doubt, that so clumsy a fabrication can only bring disgrace on its author, I think it my duty to give you an opportunity of exposing the imposture which has (*continued...*)

2680, continued: been put upon you, and which your paper has been the means of circulating. You admit that the time which has elapsed since the Ode was written, has increased the difficulties of producing evidence of its authorship. The difficulties were of the new claimant's own creation. It appears from his own letter, that he had heard, (he thinks) in 1826, that the author of the Memoir of the Rev. C. Wolfe, had claimed the Ode for that gentleman. This was about a year after the publication of the work. He then vented his indignation in a private letter to the father of his friend Mr. Menzies. The natural course—the *only course* (if his pretensions were true), would have been to have vented it in a letter to the biographer, both by private communication and in the public prints. He says, "one evening, about the year 1817, he put the Ode in his pocket, to show it to Professor Christison; but he had *not the courage* to present it, and that he has since frequently regretted his diffidence."—Since that time, the gentleman certainly has wonderfully improved in *courage*, and seems now to have completely overcome his constitutional diffidence. It required more hardihood than usually accompanies the ingenuousness of youth, to have ventured on so barefaced a forgery, or to have hazarded an immediate and disgraceful detection. I have before me, at this moment, the Ode, and the Rev. C Wolfe's *own hand writing, which he wrote out in my own presence, soon after he had put the last finishing stroke to it*—he vowed it was his own, and I knew it to be so. I shall not occupy your columns farther, then by quoting a passage from a letter which I wrote to the Editor of *Blackwood's Magazine*, and which appears in the April number, 1826, page 489, and which enters into more special proof than I thought necessary to introduce into the memoir.—Mr. Wolfe wrote it out for me, soon after it was completed, expressly avowed himself to be the author. I can only testify, that he made the same declaration to many acquaintances in college, among whom, I have authority at this moment to name the now Bishop of Meath, the Rev. Charles Dickinson, (Chaplain of the Female Orphan House), one of his most intimate friends. I beg, leave, in conclusion, to refer to an extract of a letter from the Rev. Samuel O'Sullivan, in the last vol. (No. 10), of the *Annual Biography and Obituary* (pages 78 and 79), in which he states, that I had heard him more than once mention, that the poem was commenced "one evening in his *company*, by Mr. Wolfe—that the occasion which gave rise to it, was a paragraph which he had just read aloud to him, from the *Edinburgh Annual Register*, and that the first and last stanzas were actually composed in the course of the same evening, and were recited for him by the author, before he had committed them to paper. The other stanzas he completed within a very short time after." Mr. Mackintosh appeals to his friend Mr. Menzies, who *saw the same production* by him in its unfinished state, but Mr. Menzies (rather inconveniently) died about 1820. Happily I can appeal for corroboration of my statement, to *living* friends—the above named Rev. Samuel O'Sullivan, and his brother, the Rev. Mortimer O'Sullivan,—to George Downs, Esq., John Sydney Taylor, Esq., (a distinguished English barrister), to John Anster, Esq., and the present Bishop of Meath, and many others, I might name.

I feel more *regret* than *indignation*, that a gentleman educated for the ministry, and now a teacher of youth, should be capable of such a deliberate act of fraud, and that he should expose himself to public ridicule by his silly ambition to shine for a brief moment in borrowed plumes.

Moveat Cornicula risum
Furtivis nudata coloribus.—Hor.

J.A. Russell,
Archdeacon of Clogher.

P.S.—As I do not know Mr. Mackintosh's post town, may I beg of you to give him an opportunity of seeing the above letter, and to request, that he will furnish me with the date of his alleged composition as precisely as he can.

To the Editor of the *Edinburgh Advertiser*.

Sir—I shall answer the letter of the Rev. Mr. Russell with as much calmness as a man unjustly accused of "fraud" and "fabrication" can well command.

I had imagined it was merely the overweening partiality of friends that assigned the Ode to the Rev. Mr. Wolfe.—That I was mistaken in this, the respectable testimony referred to binds me to admit. But, while I revere as much as any man the maxim "De mortuis nil nisi bonum," a regard to truth, as well as to my own character and rights, compels me to declare that, when Mr. Wolfe avowed the lines to be his own, he stated what was not true, and that, having got a copy of my lines, by some means to me unknown, after having made a few alterations, he was induced, by vanity, or some other motive equally unjustifiable, to pass them off as his own.

Were I actuated by the "silly ambition" Mr. Russell imputes to me, I would certainly have long ago made public what I have often declared in private. I'm not so likely to be actuated by ambition now, after the lapse of so many years, and when I can derive no advantage from the assertion of my just rights.

Mr. Russell says, that when I heard he had claimed the Ode for Mr. Wolfe, "the only course (if my pretensions were true), would have been to have vented my indignation in a letter to the biographer, both by private communication and in the public prints," and not in a letter to the father of my friend. I readily confess that I should have made long ago the claims which I now assert. But Mr. Russell is the last person who should taunt me with having now "completely overcome my constitutional diffidence," for my diffidence has not been to his disadvantage.

After the statement I fearlessly gave to the public, it ill becomes Mr. Russell to call upon me to give the precise date of my "alleged compositions," who, in his attempt to appropriate the lines to Mr. Wolfe, after wading through a tedious course of circumstantial evidence, has avoided the giving of dates with a degree of caution which is sufficient to cast a doubt over the whole of his statements.

I have no time, and feel little inclination to protract a controversy of this kind. My claim to the lines is now before the public, who, I feel confident, will ultimately do me justice, however much I may be traduced at present by the interested, the prejudiced, or the malicious.

A. Mackintosh.

Temple, 13th April 1841.

(1841-04-24, 3:1)

2681. Fatal Accident.—Friday, the Rev. Robt. Quinn, Presbyterian clergyman of Fermoy, was knocked down and killed by a runaway horse in Patrick-street, Cork. The horse belonged to James Aspinott Tobin, Esq., of Ballincollig, who had just alighted, and given the horse in charge to a street-runner, a boy twelve years of age. The jury returned a verdict of accidental death, with a deodand of 20*l.* (1841-04-24, 4:3)

2682. Marriage in Scientific Life.—(From a New York paper.)—Dr. Lardner and Mrs. Heaviside, now in Philadelphia, will be married this week. By the last accounts, this lady has been divorced from Captain Heaviside; so there is nothing in the way of the two philosophers from becoming one. Will some one in Philadelphia give us a description of the wedding? (1841-04-24, 4:3)

2683. Wreck-a-shore.—The wreck of a foreign vessel drifted on Tuesday morning into shore at Maherrow, coast of Sligo, name *Urania*—a quantity of salted fish on board. The vessel contained five bodies in a state of decomposition. The name Stillot is written on a shirt belonging to one of the unfortunate sufferers. Some papers are on board written in the Norwegian language. The cargo consisted of fish, which seemed to have been saved without salt. She is supposed to have been a Norwegian. She is about 150 tons burthen, of a beautiful build, seemed quite new, and copper fastened. It is thought she was upset at sea. One of the sailors was found lying dead in his hammock. We regret to hear that the constabulary arrived at the wreck, the captain's box in the cabin was broken up, and whatever property was in it probably abstracted by some of the country people. An inquest was held on the bodies of the unfortunate men, by Mr. Burrowes. The eldest was about 30 years of age, and the youngest about 18. From their dress they appeared to be common sailors, neither the captain nor the mate were on board.—*Sligo Journal.* (1841-05-01, 1:3)

2684. The remains of the late Earl of Belmore arrived in this Town on Wednesday evening, on their way to the family burying ground near Caledon. The body was placed in the aisle of our church until next morning, at one o'clock, when it was conveyed to its last home. (1841-05-01, 2:5)

2685. The Earl of Limerick is the only one of the original representative peers for Ireland now alive. (1841-05-01, 3:3)

2686. Mrs. Osborne, the proprietrix of immense estates in the counties of Waterford and Tipperary, will shortly be married, at Rome, to a Neapolitan Count. (1841-05-01, 3:5)

2687. The Paintings of the Late Major Sirr.—The collection consists of about five hundred pictures, principally by the old masters. The exhibition also comprises a good array of fossils and minerals, some articles of *bijouterie*, a quantity of old china, a quaintly-carved cabinet, formerly the property of James II., a holster-pistol, which belonged to the same Monarch, an ancient Irish harp, several pike and spear heads, sundry skene-dhus, such as were used by the Kernes and Gallowglasses of yore, and various other curiosities too numerous to be specified by us.

The paintings are of various orders of merit: but taken as a whole, the collection is beyond all comparison, the richest that has been offered for sale in Dublin within our recollection.—*Packet.* (1841-05-01, 4:5)

2688. Saturday week was a woeful day from Galway to Connemara. Between Costello Bay and Thiddaw, twenty boats were wrecked, and eleven boats with sea weed were lost between the town and the salmon leap at Costello. The loss of life is not yet known but it must be very great. (1841-05-08, 2:1)

2689. The Census.—The Irish census will take place in July next. There are a number of extra hands employed in the Castle of Dublin preparing the books. (1841-05-08, 2:4)

2690. The O'Conor Don.—In consequence of the continued and increasing delicacy of Madame O'Conor's health, the O'Conor Don has been obliged to pair off for the remainder of the present session.—*Morning Register.* (1841-05-08, 4:5)

2691. Lord Headley is shortly to be married. (1841-05-15, 1:3)

2692. The situation of joint secretary to the National Education Board is vacant by the death of Hamilton Dowdall, Esq. The other secretary is Mr. Maurice Cross. (1841-05-15, 1:4)

2693. The Rectory of Derryloran, Tyrone, is vacant by the death of Rev. Dr. Bardin.—Patron, the Primate. (1841-05-15, 1:5)

2694. The parish of St. Mary's, diocese of Ossory, vacant by the demise of the Rev. Peter Roe, has been presented by the Lord Bishop of Ossory, to the Rev. Wilberforce Caulfield, and the Precentor's Vicarship in the Cathedral of St. Canice, Kilkenny, with the curacy of Moyne, vacant by the promotion of Mr. Caulfield, to the Rev. A.D. Perry, curate of St. Mary's, Ossory. (1841-05-15, 1:5)

2695. Census.—Head Constable Nolan commenced taking the census of the barony of Lurg on Saturday. The police on the other stations are also commencing. We hear only six days are allowed them, which, we fear is too short to do it correctly.—*Fermanagh Reporter*. (1841-05-15, 2:1)

2696. Ode on the Burial of Sir John Moore.—Literary Piracy is decidedly the worst species of robbery, because the thief is never driven to the commission of the base act by any necessity of nature—he avails himself of the want of a penal statute, and steals that which nought enriches him and makes the author poor indeed. It is therefore the duty of the periodical press to act as the defenders of this description of property, and to terrify, by its strongest censures, any attempt of the nature alluded to. Our readers are aware that a few weeks since a pedagogue in Scotland had the impudent audacity to claim as his own the much admired *Ode on the burial of Sir John Moore*, written by the Rev. Charles Wolfe, and published as his, in a compilation of his *Remains*, by our respected and clever countryman, the Venerable Archdeacon Russell. This Mr. Mackenzie, it now appears, by his own admission, longed and languished after notoriety—he should have it "honestly if he could, but if not, on any terms," and indeed he has now got a surfeit of it. The fellow imposed upon the Rev. Mr. Muir, the minister of his parish, by assertions and pretended proofs that he was the real author; nay, so far did his modest assurance carry him, that even after the subject became matter of public discussion, he presumed to rush into print himself, and unblushingly assert the lie he told in private to his friend, but conviction came in overwhelming force upon him, and the would-be poet has been obliged to acknowledge the imposture. The many witnesses still live who were aware of the true authorship to allow Mackintosh to persist in his tissue of falsehoods. Indeed, it was only necessary to examine Archdeacon Russell's work to convince the mind. We are happy to say that a new edition (the Eighth) of this valuable work is now in press, and will shortly appear with a lithographed copy of the ode in the original manuscript of Mr. Wolfe, as given by him, with an avowal of friendship, to his "dearest friend," Mr. Russell. The following letter from Mr. Muir, the first advocate of Mackintosh, appeared in the *Edinburgh Advertiser*, and does much credit to his candour in promptly avowing his error, but little to his discrimination in allowing himself to be the victim of Mackintosh's plausible duplicity.

To the Editor of the *Edinburgh Advertiser*.

Temple, 6th May.

Sir—It is with no little concern that I obtrude myself again on your notice and that of the public. A few weeks ago I came forward, with simplicity of design and desire, to vindicate the rights of an unfriended individual, who had given me the assurance, and presented me with strong presumptive evidence of his claim to a piece of literary property, of high value, about the authorship of which not a little discussion, at one time, was carried on.

Under impressions, strong and deep, of Mr. M'Intosh's claim to the authorship of the celebrated *Ode on Sir John Moore*, having his own repeated assertions to that effect, not being satisfied, besides with such evidence as had then come to my knowledge to prove the claim of Mr. Wolfe to it, and having also had presented to me several proofs by Mr. M'Intosh, which gave, in my view, the utmost credibility to his pretensions. I acknowledge I hastened, with the zeal of anxiety, to vindicate the property of one who had appeared to me to have been excluded from his due by the circumstances of his obscure lot, and the modesty and diffidence of his nature.

Feeling thus, I cannot say that there is ground for regret with me—that I betook myself to the supporting of the supposed right of one, whose place under me gave him a hold on my attention and care.

And surely, when I look back on the terms on which I advanced his pretensions, I have no cause to regret the mode in which I stated them; but I hasten now, with deep regret, on account of the unhappy position in which Mr. M'Intosh must now stand, as well as with equal regret at having been unintentionally the means of occasioning uneasiness to any friends to the memory of Mr. Wolfe, to convey to you, and through you to the public, that, first—upon new evidences, successively during these weeks past, brought forward to me, and these, at length, leading, alas! to the confession of the pretended author himself—the previous statement is without the shadow of a foundation.

Painful as this communication may be to the individual so deeply implicated in it, I have his authority, along with avowed sentiments of his contrition for what he has done, to make it, and in the explicit terms now used.

I am, Sir, your obedient servant,

William Muir,

Assistant-Minister, Temple.

This letter was read by Mr. Muir to Mr. M'Intosh in my presence, at Temple, on the evening of the 5th of May, 1841.

Thomas C. Latto.

(1841-05-15, 3:1)

2697. Suicide of Lord James Beresford.—A letter from Hastings, dated the 12th inst., advising the arrival of the *Tigris* there from India, states that Lord James Beresford, of the 10th Hussars, committed suicide on the 27th of April, on board that vessel, being on his passage to England.—*Times* of Friday. (This gallant young nobleman was brother to the Marquis of Waterford, and done duty in this garrison with the 90th Light Infantry, in which corps he was a Lieutenant previous to their embarking for Ceylon.)—*Packet*. (1841-05-22, 1:4)

2698. Suicide of Lord James Beresford.—Further Particulars.—Sunday morning the ship *Tigris*, Captain Symmons, arrived in the West Indian Import Dock from Columbo [sic], which place she left on the 20th December; Cape of Good Hope, February 28; and St. Helena, March 15. In consequence of a report which appeared in the *Times* on Friday morning that Lord James Beresford, of the 10th Hussars, had committed suicide on board that vessel, being on his passage to England, and which painful intelligence had not reached his lordship's noble relations, and being therefore generally discredited, our reporter proceeded to the West India Docks yesterday afternoon for the purpose of making inquiries on board the *Tigris* relative to the reported suicide of his lordship (brother to the Marquis of Waterford,) and he found that the report was unfortunately too true. It appears that Lord James Beresford, who was only in the 26th year of his age, embarked passenger on board the *Tigris* for England, and that it was remarked at the time, and at a subsequent period during the voyage, that his lordship appeared to be laboring under slight symptoms of insanity, and that his servant was in consequence ordered to pay more than usual care and attention to his lordship, which he did. On the night of Tuesday, the 27th April, his lordship was in his own cabin, and did not evince to the servant or to the passengers during the day anything particularly remarkable in his unusually somewhat eccentric manners. The servant, before going to lie down on his settee for the night, went to his lordship's cabin for the purpose of inquiring whether his lordship needed any further attendance that evening, and having repeatedly knocked at his state-room door without receiving any answer, the servant opened it, and discovered the cabin floor covered with blood, and on proceeding to the water closet adjoining the apartment he found his master (Lord James Beresford) reclining over the seat, with his head nearly severed from his body, and quite dead. The rash act was committed with a razor, and so determined had been his lordship to effect his dreadful purpose that only a small portion of skin at the back of his neck attached the head to the body. The alarm having been instantly given, the utmost consternation prevailed among the passengers (27 in number) and crew; but any attempt to restore life was beyond the power of human aid. After a consultation by the officers of the ship and passengers, the mangled corpse of Lord James Beresford was, with great solemnity, consigned to a grave in the abyss of the ocean. This lamentable event has created great grief and distress among the noble relatives of the deceased and the fashionable world generally.

The following is a copy of a letter from Captain Symmons, of the ship *Tigris*, to his Grace the Archbishop of Armagh:—

"Ship Tigris, May 14.

"My Lord Primate—According to your Grace's desire, I have the honour to forward the proceedings of the inquest held on board my ship, on the 28th of April last, upon the body of your Grace's nephew, the late Lord James Beresford. I beg leave to add, that during our long passage from Ceylon until the day previous to his death, his lordship enjoyed good health and very cheerful spirits; but early on the morning of the 27th he complained of an excruciating head-ache, and throughout the day it seemed to increase, until it deprived him of reason, and led to the sad catastrophe deplored by every individual on board, and by no one more sincerely than myself.

"It may, perhaps, be a melancholy consolation to your Grace and the other members of Lord James's family, to know that the act which thus terminated his life cannot be traced to any worldly cause whatever, but solely to a fever on the brain, and consequent temporary bereavement of reason, not to be accounted for; and that his lordship's kindness of heart and amiable disposition had won him the esteem of his fellow-passengers.

"I have the honour to be, your Grace's most obedient humble servant,

"John Symmons,
Commander of the ship Tigris.

"*To his Grace the Archbishop of Armagh.*"

(1841-05-22, 2:2)

2699. Marriage in High Life.—The nuptials of Sir William Heathcote, Bart., M.P., and Miss Selina Shirley, eldest daughter of Evelyn John Shirley, Esq., M.P., were solemnized on Monday. (1841-05-22, 3:2)

2700. Marriage in High Life.—His Excellency the Lord Lieutenant of Ireland is about to lead to the hymeneal altar the beautiful and accomplished Dowager Lady Somerville, widow of the late Sir Marcus Somerville, Bart. It is rumoured about the Vice-regal Court that the nuptials are fixed to take place next week. (1841-05-29, 3:1)

2701. Marriage in High Life.—Lord Cremorne will shortly lead to the hymeneal altar Augusta, youngest daughter of Mr. and Lady Mary Stanley. The bride elect is in her nineteenth year. (1841-05-29, 3:1)

2702. Ode to Sir John Moore.

To the Editor of the *Edinburgh Advertiser*.

May 11, 1841.

Sir—As I presume it is to you I am indebted for the *Edinburgh Advertiser* of the 7th inst., I beg to thank you for your kind consideration in forwarding it to me.

I am not disposed to deny you credit for honesty of purpose throughout the discussion in which you have lately engaged concerning the authorship of the poem on the *Burial of Sir John Moore*, &c. Now, that the claimant himself has publicly withdrawn his pretensions, and expressed his contrition for what he has done, I feel that it would be ungenerous on my part to embitter his feelings by any comment on his conduct.

You may relieve your own mind from the apprehension of having submitted the true author's friends to any painful process in the controversy, as none of them could have entertained a doubt of the result. We have only to complain that you should now think it necessary to account for your own over-estimate of an ill-formed claim, by charging them with culpable carelessness for their friend's honor and reputation. Happily, his honor and reputation rest on far higher ground than the loftiest literary distinction can attain. But, there seems no just cause of complaint that they have been negligent in vindicating his claim to celebrity as the author of a poem which has deservedly acquired universal popularity.

In the *Memoir*, which accompanied his *Remains*, I spoke of him as being the author from my own personal knowledge of the fact. I mentioned that the poem (with his initials) appeared in the *Newry Telegraph* long before any false claim was put forward. I quote the letter of an intimate friend, correcting some errors which had appeared in the printed copies. The omission of the date is all that is complained of. This, the author himself might not have been able to supply with precision; and, I am sure, there are many authors who may have read the poem, who would be at a loss to assign an exact date to some of their own compositions.

It is obvious, that had the date been given, it would not have been sufficient to deter a literary impostor from his purpose. On the contrary, it might have supplied a new facility, by tempting him to assume an earlier date, so that ultimately, the rival pretensions should be determined by other considerations. I did not, therefore, think it necessary to enter further into conflict with Mr. Mackintosh, but deemed it more proper to send the original manuscript to the publisher, Messrs. Hamilton and Adams, (whose property the work is) to have a fac-simile engraved for the 8th edition, which is shortly to appear, with a note, giving such further information as seemed requisite.

I beg to convey to Mr. Muir, through your columns, my full assurance that he was actuated by honorable motives in the zealous part which he took in behalf of his protege, and to give him due credit for his promptness in voluntarily avowing the error into which he was unfortunately drawn.

I have only to regret that he did not do me the honor of communicating with me on the subject before he ventured into print, as I think I should have satisfied him, that the numerous and ardent friends of the Rev. Charles Wolfe made no ungrounded claim for him, and that he himself was incapable of assuming an honor to which he had no title. Mr. Muir would have been thus saved no little mortification, and the public would not have heard anything of what the last literary compurgator of Mr. Mackintosh calls (more *appropriately* than *elegantly*), "the Corunna job, in which he saw him engaged."

I have the honor to be
Your obedient servant,
John A. Russell.
(1841-05-29, 3:2)

2703. Melancholy and Fatal Accident.—With feeling of the deepest regret we have to record the premature end of Charles Foster, Esq., fourth son of Baron Foster, which took place on Monday, under the following distressing circumstances:—On Saturday last he was to have accompanied the Baron and family from their residence, Rathescar, in the county Louth, to Dublin, but as he was to proceed on horseback, and the day being extremely wet, he deferred his journey to the following Monday. In the course of the morning of that day he and Mr. Arthur Foster, son of the Rev. Mr. Foster, vicar of Collon, and uncle to the deceased young gentleman, went out in a small boat on the lake of Collon, in the demesne of Lord Ferrard. They had been but a short time on the water when, owing, it is supposed, to some inadvertence in rowing, the boat upset, and both parties precipitated in twenty feet of water. A gamekeeper of Lord Ferrard's, with Mr. Delapp, son-in-law of that nobleman, happened to be on the bank of the lake at the time, and witnessed the melancholy accident. Mr. Delapp, an excellent swimmer, instantly plunged into the water, and quickly reached the fatal spot, where he caught a glimpse of Mr. Arthur Foster in the act of disappearing beneath the surface after a short but severe struggle for life. He succeeded in catching hold of him, and rescuing him, in a state of utmost exhaustion, and almost total insensibility, from his perilous situation, but his ill-fated companion had sunk to a watery tomb. Mr. Delapp dived repeatedly, to try at least to recover the body, but without success; and, although every possible exertion was made for the same purpose down to three o'clock in the afternoon, the remains were not found. At the above-mentioned hour, Mr. Delapp set off by post for Dublin, the bearer of the mournful tiding to the family in Merrion-square, who, it is unnecessary to add, have been thrown into a state of the most profound grief by this untimely bereavement. The deceased was in his nineteenth year, a fine-looking young man, and whose collegiate course here

was such as afforded proof of possession of talents of the first order, while his amiable disposition and the affability of his manners won for him a peculiar degree the attachment, not only of his more immediate connexions, but of all to whom he was known.
(1841-05-29, 4:5)

2704. Awful Suicide.—The spirit store at the Royal Canal Harbour not having opened at the usual hour on Monday morning last, the porter of the establishment knocked at the door, but was unable to obtain admittance; a ladder was then placed and an entrance effected through the bed-room window, when the proprietor, a person of the name of Barber, was found suspended from the roof, almost naked, and quite dead. The floor was covered with blood, and it is believed that the unfortunate man first attempted to cut his throat, but, not finding this succeed [sic] as quickly as he had expected, he got upon a table, and having made fast the rope, he accomplished his purpose by kicking away the table. No cause has as yet been ascertained which led to this fatal act.—*Mail.*
(1841-06-05, 1:3)

2705. On Thursday, Captain Edward Croker, late 17th Lancers, with his lovely bride, Lady Georgina Monck, daughter of the Earl of Rathdown [sic], arrived from Dublin at the beautiful mansion of Ballyneguard, county of Limerick, the hospitable seat of his father, John Croker, Esq., D.L. (1841-06-05, 1:5)

2706. Lord Ebrington's Marriage.—As it is not every day that a chief governor falls in love, it may be interesting to know the manner in which the arrows of Cupid pierces the heart of Lord Ebrington. He was partaking of the hospitalities of Mrs. Putland, at Bray, enjoying the delights of a *fete champetre*, some short time ago, when a thunder storm arose. The illustrious guest fled for shelter to a tree—an oak of the forest. It so happened that Lady Somersetville [sic] retreated to the same place of shelter. The storm continued for an hour—the fair lady became alarmed, he consoled her, and appeased her fears. An agreeable *tete-a-tete* ensued in spite of rain and thunder, and in that hour, tempestuous in weather but felicitous in love, the venerable and sedate Lord Ebrington became enamoured of the enchantress. It is also not a little singular that Sir W. Somerville offered the lady his hand before his father, Sir Marcus, proposed to make her the partner of his life; but she declined the honour, and took Sir Marcus for better for worse. Some years after the death of Marcus, the Hon. Hugh Fortescue, son of Lord Ebrington, sought the honour of relieving her ladyship from the weeds of widowhood, but she politely rejected his amatory offer. Lord Ebrington addressed her, and she has consented to be his wife. This rejection of two sons, and acceptance of two fathers, has given rise to much amusing chit-chat in the fashionable circles.
(1841-06-05, 2:2)

2707. The Marquess of Waterford is rather unwell, the melancholy death of his brother having greatly shocked his feelings. (1841-06-05, 3:1)

2708. The Rev. Dr. Magennis, of Maynooth College, succeeds the late Rev. Mr. Bogue, as P.P. of Rosslea, county Fermanagh. (1841-06-05, 3:1)

2709. We regret to announce the death of the Hon. Henry Dawson Damer, which took place in Hyde Park-terrace, May 27. Mr. Damer's death will be long and deservedly felt by his afflicted family and a numerous circle of friends, by whom he was much loved and respected. The Hon. gentleman was a captain in the navy, and next brother to the Earl of Portarlington, being also the next heir to the titles and estates, the Earl having no family. He was in his 56th year, married in 1813 Eliza, daughter of Captain E.J. Moriarty, R.N., by Lady Lucy Luttrell, sister of the late Earl of Carhampton. He has left several children, chiefly daughters; his eldest son, now heir presumptive to the honors and property of the family, is in his 19th year, having been born in September, 1822. The Hon. Colonel Damer, the member for Portarlington, is next brother of the deceased. (1841-06-05, 3:1)

2710. Death by Drowning.—On Tuesday last, a fine boy, of the name of Faucett, 11 years old, fell accidentally into a boghole, at Ballinacariga, and before he could procure assistance was drowned. (1841-06-12, 2:5)

2711. Death of the Dowager Lady Clonbrock.—Her ladyship died last week, at Cheltenham, after a short illness. The deceased, who was daughter and heiress of Mr. Clement Archer, married in 1776, Lord Clonbrock, grandfather of the present lord, by whom her ladyship had a family of three children, namely, the late Viscountess Ennismore, Luke, second Lord Clonbrock, and the Hon. Miss Letitia, who married the Hon. Sir Robert Le Poer Trench, K.C.B., and who still survives. Her ladyship was in her 84th year.
(1841-06-12, 2:5)

2712. The Census.—The impolicy of endeavouring to effect an inquisitorial or impertinent solution of the ages of the fair sex has been fully defeated by many of the beaux and belles of Parsonstown. The wishes of the latter have been responded to with a gallantry of the former, which would do credit to the era of chivalry. Numerous parties were given on the night of the 6th, where dancing was kept up until an advanced hour on the morning of the 7th. It might be said in sporting phraseology that the ladies on the night of the 6th slept no where!!—*Nenagh Guardian.*
(1841-06-12, 2:5)

2713. The country for miles around was illuminated on Sunday night by subshawns or fire brands, a demonstration ascribed to the universal fears prevalent in the minds of the lower orders upon the object of the census, which is to bear date from that night.—*Limerick Chronicle.* (1841-06-12, 2:5)

2714. Extraordinary Birth.—A poor woman, the wife of a labouring man named Dolan, living in the parish of Killaan, near Kilconnell, gave birth to five children on the morning of the 4th of June. The two first are boys, and are doing well, the other two girls and a boy were still born.—*Galway Advertiser*. (1841-06-19, 1:5)

2715. Marriage in High Life.—At St. George's Church, Hanover-square, London, on Monday, June 14, by special license, Henry Huchinson Hamilton O'Hara, Esq., of Cribilly House, county of Antrim, to Alicia Isabella, youngest daughter of the late General Sir Henry King, K.C.B., and niece to the Earl of Kingston and Viscount Lorton. There were present at the ceremony many of the relatives and friends of the young couple. Lady King, the Earl and Countess of Lichfield, Earl and Countess of Bandon, Earl and Countess of Mountcashel, and Lady Jane Knox, Hon. Harman King Harman and Lady, Mr. and Hon. Mrs. Lefroy, Sir Wm. and Lady Anson, Archdeacon St. Lawrence, Rev. Charles Leslie, Rev. R.J. MGhee, Colonel Perceval, M.P., and several persons of distinction. After the ceremony, which was performed by the Hon. and Rev. Edward Moore, cousin-german to the fair bride, the company adjourned from the Church to a splendid dejeuner at the house of Viscount Lorton, Eaton-square, whence the happy pair set off en route to Malvern. (1841-06-19, 2:5)

2716. We regret to announce the death of Madame O'Conor, the wife of the O'Conor Don, the lineal descendant of Roderick O'Conor, the last of the Kings of Ireland. This lamented lady was in her thirty-sixth year, and the mother of a large family. Her benevolence will long be remembered by the tenantry on her afflicted husbands estates.—*Globe*. (1841-06-19, 2:5)

2717. The late Marquis Camdon, who so nobly, but not wisely, surrendered nearly £400,000 to the Treasury, by giving up his pension as Teller of the Exchequer, has left his children so badly off that they are obliged to sell the family paintings. (1841-06-26, 1:4)

2718. Marriage in High Life.—The marriage of Lady Caroline Stanhope, sister of the Earl of Harrington, Duchess of Bedford, and Duchess of Leinster, and Mr. E.A. Sanford, M.P., was solemnised on Monday. A dejeuner was given by the Duke and Duchess of Bedford, in Belgrave-square, to a select circle of the members of the Bedford, Leinster, and Harrington families. Her Ladyship is in her fiftieth year. (1841-06-26, 2:5)

2719. Death of Alderman Darley.—With feelings of deep regret we annouce the death of this estimable man and excellent citizen, which event took place at his residence, Swanbrook, yesterday morning. Few men have passed through the vicissitudes of a long and varied public life with greater honour and credit than Frederick Darley; and not one of them has left behind him a higher character for sterling worth, strict impartiality, and undeviating probity. Bland in manner, social in habit, faithful in friendship, and uncompromising in spirit there were concentrated in his person all the qualifications and ingredients that render a public officer respected, and private friend beloved. It is but a few months since Alderman Darley ceased to discharge the duties of Chief Magistrate of Dublin—(he was one of the original divisional magistrates under the police act of 1808)—bearing with him in his retirement the affection and esteem of his associates and subordinates, and the approbation and regard of all who came within his sphere of action, either as a judicial functionary or a private gentleman. In his own family, and within the immediate circle of his intimate connexions, he was venerated with a love beyond the ordinary ardour of that sentiment; while his playful manners, amiable disposition, and gentleness of nature, endeared him to those who had the pleasure and the privilege of enjoying his friendship.

We are sure it will be a subject of gratification to his sorrowing relations, to find his conduct thus noticed, and his virtues thus recorded by a political opponent —the *Freeman's Journal*; and, we may add, that as a member of the press, it is to us a matter of pride to take such an extract as the following from a contemporary who can be generous as well as just:—

"We regret to announce the demise of Alderman F. Darley, which took place yesterday morning at his residence Swanbrook, Donnybrook Road. The deceased, in the course of a long life, upwards of 78 years, passed through the routine of civic offices in his native city. In 1798-99, he filled the office of high sheriff, and in the year 1800 was elected an alderman. In 1808, on the formation of the late police, he was appointed divisional magistrate of Marlborough-street. The following year he served the office of Lord Mayor, and in 1812 he succeeded Alderman Pemberton as chief magistrate of police. The Marquis Wellesley, in 1824, appointed him inspector-general of the county Dublin constabulary,which office was abolished in 1836, on placing that force under Colonel Kennedy. The deceased was superannuated in February last, when he retired on full salary (£6000 per annum), and was succeeded by our present truly estimable and most efficient chief magistrate, Alderman Fleming. The late Alderman Darley was the class-fellow of the late Lord Chancellor Plunket, and the school-fellow of the celebrated but unfortunate Theobald Wolfe Tone. By a rather curious coincidence it occurred that when, in the memorable year of 1799, the ill-fated Tone, condemned by military law, lay in the Provost prison, waiting the carrying into effect his sentence of execution by the common hangman—his earnest entreaty to die the death of a soldier being rejected—Sheriff Darley was entrusted with the writ of *habeas corpus* from the Court of Queen's Bench to have the convict brought before the civil tribunal. In all the relative duties of domestic life—as a husband, a father, and a friend—Alderman Darley was an ornament to the circle in which he moved. The deceased has left issue four sons, all members of the learned or distinguished professions. His amiable lady, who survives him, is sister of Arthur Guiness, Esq. Major-General Darley, we believe, is his only surviving brother."—*Evening Mail.* (1841-07-03, 2:2)

2720. An Epitaph—On the death of Rev. J.T. Whitestone's two infant children.

Two spotless souls have winged their way
To fairer worlds above,
Just in the morning of their day
When all their world was love.

They, like the fragrant flower, that blooms
In the meridian's beam—
Before the evening's threatening blast,
They bade adieu to pain.

While angels tune their golden harps,
Two harps for them are strung,
They, skilful, strike the tuneful strings
The angel choir among.

Let fruitless fears no more be seen,
For those we loved so dear,
With lustre far more bright they now
In spotless robes appear.

They've only crossed blest Jordan's stream,
A little while before;
Go on, ye parents, in the Lord,
You'll meet them on the shore.

(1841-07-03, 3:3)

2721. Scene in an Old Country Church-Yard.

Cold and cheerless was the night,
And the wind blew bitter and chill,
Sweeping the vail with echoing wail,
And the side of the bare brown hill.

And the wintry blast, with sudden gust,
Moaned round the ruined tower;
And the bell, as it swung in the tempest, rung,
At the fearful midnight hour.

And the pale moon, thro' the cloud outshone,
With dim and watery ray,
On the yew-tree tall, and the mouldering wall,
And the ruined belfry grey.

On the grass that waves above the graves,
It shone on the dead men's bones,
And it shone so bright on a lady white,
As she stood midst the church-yard stones.

That lady fair, why is she there
At midnight's fearful time,
When shapes of gloom, from the shadowy tomb,
Flit forth at the echoing chime?

Does she mourn o'er the grave of the true and brave,
In battles din laid low?
Is the faithful knight of that lady bright
Stretched stiff and stark below?

Does she sad watch keep by his grave so deep?
Does she mourn her young hope blighted?
Or does reason remain in her wandering brain?
Is the mind of the maiden benighted?

Is she not afraid in that place of dread,
In the haunted burying ground,
Where the white skulls grin, and the worms within
Creep loathsome and slimy around?

Where the spirit lost, and the sheeted ghost,
Glide along in their grave clothes white,
And the fiend so fell, with shriek and yell,
Leaps forth on the wandering wight.

From the cloud, the moon broke, and the lady spoke,
Does she call on her lover's shade?
Does she call from the gloom of the joyless tomb
The soul of the parted dead?

"I fear, alas, I will lose my place
If the chemise cannot be found,
This morning I left here to dry
On the hedge of the burying ground."

The pale moon shows her mistress's clothes,
As they fluttered all white in the storm,
And away to her bed trips the laundry maid,
With the chemise tucked under her arm.

H.L. (1841-07-03, 4:1)

2722. Reflections upon the Death of an Infant.—(Written impromptu on the blank pages of a Bible, in a very humble cabin in Co. Wicklow, near Glendelough, by a traveller, while looking on the face of a deceased child, which was placed in a cradle by his side, a few minutes after it expired. It was not four weeks old, and died in extreme agony, of convulsive disease. The scene took place, during a stormy night, in 1834.)

Sweet Babe, enjoy thy dreamless sleep,
Thy lot is now too bless'd to wish a change;
Thou did'st but venture on the stage,
And view our fallen world, and then withdrew.
How many pangs of sorrow hast thou shunned
By venturing no further?—Thou hast never sinned
By act transgressing God's holy law—
Thy breath was never corrupted by the fell contagion,
Which, like a leprous disease, degrades
The whole of Adam's race;
Thy tongue has never uttered accents
To offend the God of Love.
In this sin-parched wilderness,
Anguish and bitter tears awaited thee;
Satan his wiles had just prepared
To urge thee on to endless ruin—
Heaven is now thy home.

A few bitter pangs thou did'st endure;
A parent's heart was pained to see thee suffer,
But could neither shorten nor remove thy woes,
Though felt by her thy every pain. (*continued...*)

2722, continued:

Ah, heavy were thy sighs! long between
No breath could be discovered;
A mother's arm supported thee—
A mother's tearful eye beheld with
Pity's softest glance—
A mother's heart, oppressed with grief,
Wish'd thy sufferings o'er,
And long'd to see thy infant brow
Beaming with marks of early joy,
Covered with a pleasing smile,
But knew not which to choose,
Life or death—yet grace divine, within her heart,
Taught her to look to heaven,
And instantly she uttered, thy will be done,
My babe is thine, take it to thine arms,
If best it seem to thee, my Father, God.
Waked by thy mother's voice,
Ere yet the day had dawned,
Not in wailings loud, but in sweet resignation
Like the man of God.
While gazing on thy lifeless clay
She oft repeated, the Lord had given,
And the Lord hath taken away,
And blessed ever be the name of God.
Around I mingle with the little group,
The off-spring of thy parents,
And anxiously survey thy smiling dust;
And, though inwardly affection desires thy stay,
A mother's example draws from their youthful minds
A wish not to bring thee back to earth.
Silence is the scene to me, and fruitful in thought,
Though but an infant dies;
Directed by this holy book
To look beyond this mean abode,
On which the chilling winds are beating.
Rain in torrents, falling and finding access
To us who are left behind a little longer;
A few days or years, at most, and we too
Shall leave these tenements of clay,
And find (if found in Christ) with thee
A better home in that bright world above,
Where infants dwell,
And are with Jesus ever blessed.

Amicus Veritatis.

(1841-07-10, 4:1)

2723. To — on the Death of Her Cousin.

The Lord gave, and the Lord hath taken away, blessed be the name of the Lord. —Job I. 21.

Such were the words of holy Job,
And such should now be thine,
When e'er you think of her who's gone
To dwell with the Divine.

She's left a dark and wintry world
To enjoy a home of bliss;
Who would not gladly die to share
A joy so great as this?

From yonder sky she views thee here,
And couldst thou hear her voice,
It breathes reproof for every tear,
And tells thee to rejoice.

It tells that now she wears the crown
Her angel virtues won,
And calls upon her friends below
To do as she hath done;

And ne'er with impious sighs to mourn
That she hath gain'd the sky:
Cease then to weep—she is not dead—
The good can never die!

She lives not where death nor pain can come,
Nor grief distract the breast;
There hath she found that blissful home—
She sought and lovd the best.

No sad regrets, no struggling sighs,
Rose with her parting breath,
She rais'd her drooping eyes to Heav'n
And dying—conquer'd death.

The victory of the dying hour
Is all that death can boast—
A boundless—endless heav'n is gaind,
And earth is all that's lost.

Look up, dear girl—thy tears be dried,
Enjoy what Heav'n doth give,
And think—'twas when thy cousin died
That she began to live.

Be this our hope, be this our pray'r,
When life's short day is flown,
That we with her that home may share
Where God rewards his own.

Clones, 5th July, 1841. G.D.

(1841-07-17, 4:1)

2724. Death of James Rose, Esq.—Died, on Saturday, 17th inst., in the 46th year of his age, of paralysis, proceeding to inflammation of the lungs, James Rose, Esq., of Mullaghmore—a gentleman whose loss to the public, as well as to his friends, it will be found difficult to replace.

Born in another country, and bringing from thence political opinions opposed to those of most of the gentry of this neighbourhood, Mr. Rose was, nevertheless, but a short time settled in this county before he endeared himself to all with whom he came into contact, by his firm integrity—his active zeal for the public welfare—his disregard of self-interest—his mildness of manners, and generosity of disposition; with the guileless sympathy of childhood he combined acuteness of mind and extent of talent, fitted to deal successfully with the most difficult abstract questions, and to apply the results of his reasoning in the closet to the practical purposes of life. His numerous successful schemes of charity, and the unrivalled management of the considerable estate which he purchased here, are well known proofs of his acuteness in devising, and prudence in executing, plans of useful benevolence; but there are few who are fully acquainted with the range of his mental labours, and their effect upon the public interests. In this neighbourhood, it is owing to him that the land within five miles of the Ulster Canal is not under an annual tax for the construction and maintenance of that hitherto unprofitable speculation. The tenants of Church Lands in Ireland, by whom he was intrusted with the management of their interests, have acknowledged with gratitude his services towards obtaining for them fair and just terms in the recent acts of parliament: his suggestions upon the Irish Poor Laws have been received and acknowledged as most valuable and important, by those most competent to judge: upon the Corn Laws, it was he who collected and embodied in a masterly petition to both houses of parliament, two years since, the opinions of the best-informed persons in the county; and there is now no doubt, that if his plans for the extinction, or rather commutation, of tithes in Ireland, as developed in his able pamphlet, had been fully adopted, the clergy would have received their arrears in full, with exact proportionate justice to all, and without pressure upon the occupying tenant.

These, and other various subjects of equal importance, occupied what he called his leisure hours; while he was apparently devoted, without ceasing, to the more humble, but not less useful, details of public and private business in our county, in which his loss will not again be equally supplied.

He now lies buried in the silent grave, far from the land of his birth, and the friends of his early years; but there are those still left in the circle of his usefulness who will never lose the grateful recollection of his disinterested friendship, while the public will long lament an unwearied devotee to their interests—the poor, a never failing friend.

His remains were accompanied to the church-yard of Ballinode, on Tuesday last, by most of the gentry within reach, and notwithstanding incessant rain, by a vast crowd of his tenants and neighbours. An impressive address upon the occasion was delivered by his attached friend, Mr. Young, the Rector of the parish, which did his feelings much honour. We understand that his property is bequeathed to his niece, a minor, with legacies to several other relations in Scotland. (1841-07-24, 3:1)

2725. Lamentable Accident—Four Men Drowned.—I have just received intelligence of the most painful occurrence that took place in the channel between the Island of Rathlin and the main land, on Tuesday, the 6th inst. A fishing boat had put off from the above island to put shell-fish on board one of the Derry steamers; after having done so, the boat put into Port Morn one of the small watering places on the coast. When returning to Rathlin, the sea that had been very calm got quite tempestuous, the boat lived for some time, but was at last overpowered with the waves, and the four poor fellows who manned her met a watery grave; the boat and some of the tackle drifted ashore, but, by the latest accounts, none of the bodies have been recovered. One of the men has left a wife and seven children to bemoan his fate, and I have heard that the others have also left families unprovided for.—*Derry Sentinel*. (1841-07-24, 4:5)

2726. Rejoicings at Dartry [sic] House.—It having been ascertained that Lord Cremorne and his youthful and beautiful bride would arrive at his Lordship's romantic and picturesque residence (situate between Cootehill and Rockcorry, in this county) on Friday evening last, his grateful and attached tenantry made such hasty arrangements for their reception as the short notice which they received would permit; and, accordingly, preparations were made for illuminations, bon-fires, &c., to greet the useful and happy pair on their arrival. The tenantry and the people of the neighbourhood intended to meet him at Rockcorry, in procession, preceded by bands of music, torches, &c., take the horses from their carriage, and draw them home in triumph; but their kind intentions were frustrated by his Lordship arriving at a much earlier hour in the evening than they expected, he having heard of their intention, but being anxious to avoid any ostentatious display or parade, made arrangements to arrive at an earlier hour than he at first intended, to the no small disappointment of the people who were anxious to embrace this their first opportunity to testify their love and regard for their munificent landlord and benefactor. About half-past four o'clock, p.m., the very efficient and excellent amateur band of the Total Abstinence Society of Cootehill left that town accompanied by an immense concourse of people, followed by a great number of gigs, jaunting-cars, and other vehicles, who, on arriving at Dawson Grove, (the former name of Dartry demesne,) were much disappointed at learning that Lord and Lady Cremorne had previously arrived with his Lordship's brother, the Hon. Vesy Dawson, M.P., for Louth, who had been attending in Dundalk, at the assizes for that county, as a grand juror. The band, immediately after its arrival, struck up the popular air of *Haste to the Wedding*, and continued playing other exhilarating and enlivening airs during the remainder of the evening, to the great recreation and amusement of the people, large numbers of whom were momentarily arriving from Cootehill, Rockcorry, and the surrounding country, and continued to arrive until nine o'clock, and even up to a later hour.—Shortly after, the immense bon-fire which was directed at the terminus of the lawn, in front of the hall-door, was lighted, Lord and Lady Cremorne and Mr. Dawson made their appearance, (about half-past eight o'clock,) which was the signal for the most deafening and enthusiastic cheering, accompanied with the discharge of musketry, rockets, waving of torches, &c. Bon-fires and torches also (*continued...*)

2726, continued: ...now appeared to blaze on the adjacent hills for many miles around.

About half-past 9 o'clock the Ematris or Rockcorry Band, dressed in the uniform of a military band, was heard approaching in the distance, to join the gay and festive throng, playing *My Love she's but a lassie yet* and when it arrived there could not be less than 5 or 6000 persons assembled. His Lordship, with his very charming and interesting bride leaning on his arm, having proceeded to a convenient distance from the bonfire, very briefly addressed the assembled multitude, expressing how grateful he and his lady were, for the very friendly and enthusiastic reception they had experienced, he said that her Ladyship always esteemed and always admired the warm-hearted character of the Irish, and although born in England she made Ireland the land of adoption.—(cheers,)—and as a proof of her ladyship's partiality for the Irish, she selected himself, an Irishman for her partner for life, and added that he was certain when they knew her, they would like and esteem her as much as they did him.—(cheers, and cries, *we will, we will*). His lordship concluded, by saying, this reception was the more grateful as it was so unexpected. Her ladyship displayed the greatest affability, smiling most graciously all the time, and on retiring she most cordially shook hands with all the people indiscriminately, which condescension appeared to gratify them much as was evinced by the enthusiastic cheers which followed her departure. Refreshments were administered in a very profuse manner to all those who chose to partake of them. Dancing was kept up until a late hour, when the people retired to their respective homes in the most peaceable and orderly manner.

On Sunday last, Lord and Lady Cremorne attended Divine Service in Kilcrow Church, when her Ladyship put £10 into the poor box. (1841-07-31, 3:2)

2727. Sudden Death of Lord Dufferin.—A considerable sensation was created in Belfast on Wednesday, on the arrival of the *Reindeer* steamer, from Liverpool, on account of the sudden death, on board, of Lord Dufferin. His lordship complained of indisposition on leaving Liverpool on Tuesday night, and directed the steward of the steamer to bring him a dose of morphine, which he swallowed on going to bed. During the night he breathed heavily in his sleep; and at seven o'clock, on Wednesday morning, he was observed still asleep. At nine, a.m., he was found dead in his sleeping berth! His sister, the Hon. Mrs. Ward, was on board. An inquest was held on the body; but as the inquiry was not terminated on yesterday, we defer giving the particulars till our next publication. This is the third death of persons holding the title of Baron Dufferin and Clanboye, within less than five years; and there are now alive three baronesses of that name; two of them are generally residents in the North of Ireland; the third (now dowager and widow of the last deceased) is at present in Italy. The family is of Scottish origin; and derives its descent from J. Blackwood, Esq., a gentleman of respectable lineage in Fifeshire, who emigrated to Ireland towards the close of the 17th cenutry, and settled at Ballyleidy, in the county of Down, one of the handsomest residences in the Irish nobility. Robert Blackwood, Esq., was created a Baronet in 1763. He was succeeded in his title and property by Sir John Blackwood, Baronet, M.P. His successor was Sir James, who inherited the peerage, 18th, of February, 1808, at the decease of his mother, Dorcas created Baroness Dufferin and Claneboye, 30th July 1800. He died in August, 1836, without issue, and was succeeded by his brother Hans, at one time an extensive wine merchant in Dublin, who was twice married: by the first marriage, he had three sons—Robert (a captain of the army, killed at Waterloo,) Hans, (also in the army, who died in Naples,) and Price (whose premature death it is now our painful duty to record, and who acted as post-captain in the navy;) by the second marriage of Hans, second in the title, there were of issue the present Hon. William Steer Blackwood, in holy orders, now residing at Armoy, county of Antrim; and a number of daughters—one married into the Ward family. The late Lord Dufferin was born on the 6th of May, 1794; and on the 4th of July, 1825, he married Selina one of the beautiful and accomplished daughters of Thomas Sheridan, Esq. and consequently, grand-daughter of the celebrated Richard Brinsley Sheridan, and sister to the Hon. Mrs. Norton, and to Lady Seymour (the Queen of Beauty.) There is issue one son, Frederick, aged about fifteen years, heir to the title and large estates of Dufferin and Claneboye. This young nobleman is now at Eton, whilst, as before intimated, his noble mother is abroad, and ignorant of the calamity that has befallen her house. The nobleman now deceased was a Tory in politics, but a kind and considerate landlord.—*Northern Whig.* (1841-07-31, 4:4)

2728. Marriage a la Mode.—The noose matrimonial was never at so high a premium as it appears to be at present in, what is termed, high places, and it happened, singularly enough, that those who seek it are chiefly elderly victims. It was only at, what the Americans call the fall of last year, that the noble Secretary of State for Foreign Affairs (*pro tem.*) suffered himself to be bound in the silken chain of connubial felicity. A few months afterwards, the Lord Privy Seal, the Chancellor of the Exchequer, and the President of the Board of Trade followed the example of their colleague, and only a few days since the noble secretary for the Colonies accomplished his desire of returning to the *Home* Department. Another matrimonial conjunction is also about to be effected by the union of Lord Lieutenant of Ireland with a fair and accomplished lady. The planet Venus is certainly in the ascendant in the Whig Cabinet, and appears to occupy there the place of "Time the Consoler," in Voltaire's story of the "Chinese Widow." The next best thing to office is, no doubt, a comfortable domestic establishment; and it would really be worth the while of the few remaining benedicts of Downing-street to enter the market while there remains a quarter's salary in perspective. Perhaps Lords Melbourne, Morpeth, Macaulay, will take the subject into their serious consideration. The premier need not then be indebted for a dinner to the hospitalities of Buckingham House, and the Secretary would be enabled to pen those familiar epistles to his constituents from his wife's boudoir, which have heretofore been dated from Windsor Castle. (1841-07-31, 4:4)

2729. The Lady Frances Anne Emily Vane, eldest daughter of the Marchioness of Londonderry, to be united to the eldest son of Sir Charles Knightly, Bart. M.P. of Faulsley, Northamptonshire. (1841-08-07, 1:3)

2730. Melancholy Suicide.—We are under the painful necessity of recording one of those lamentable suicides, which, we regret to say, notwithstanding the progress of knowledge, the general spread of Christianity, and the wide circulation of the Holy Scriptures, are of too frequent occurrence, even in Ireland. The wife of a respectable tradesman, named James Graham, residing in Cavan, had been for some time since labouring under mental derangement, but not considered of so alarming a nature as to elicit particular watchfulness or apprehension, was found by her bereaved and afflicted husband at five o'clock on the morning of Monday last, the 2d instant, drowned in the river which flowed directly opposite the house in which she resided. The stream is not at present particularly deep, but the unfortunate and infuriated woman, in order to render her destruction certain, previous to throwing herself from the bank, suspended a large stone from her neck with a cord, which effectually kept her head under the water until life was extinct.

She must have been contemplating self-destruction for some time—as we understand, on Saturday last, she sent to an apothecary's shop for half an ounce of laudanum, which was prudently refused her messenger; and the cord she was known to have in her trunk for some time, but, of course, the design was not suspected.

She seemed rather better on Sunday, for she walked out with her husband on the evening of that day, when her general deportment was that of a sane person. Previous to her leaving the house on the morning of the fatal occurrence, she was observed to kiss her child in the most frantic and passionate manner, and soon after contrived to get out to the street unobserved. However, her husband, wondering at her delay, rose to look after her, when he discovered her as already described. A gold ring, which she wore since her marriage, Mr. Graham found in his [sic] pocket, after the body was taken out of the water. The deceased was a young woman, in the prime of life, and had no family except the child before alluded to. John M'Fadden, Esq., Coroner for the county, held an inquest on the body on Tuesday, the 3d instant, when the jury returned a verdict to the effect—"That she, in a fit of insanity, craftily terminated her own existence by drowning." (1841-08-07, 3:1)

2731. Coroner's Inquest—A Man Killed by a Bull.—John Macfaden, Esq., M.D., one of the Coroners for the county of Cavan, held an inquest at Loppa, near Stradone, on Tuesday, the 26th ult., on the body of James Hannigan, a small farmer, residing in that locality. It appeared in evidence that on Sunday last, whilst walking through his own land, he was attacked by a vicious bull, the property of his son-in-law, whose name is Brady, and tossed him into the air on his horns. He was rescued from the ferocious animal by some neighbouring men and dogs, who came to his assistance too late to save his life, as he died of his wounds and the injuries he had received on the following morning. He was a decent, quiet, inoffensive man, and a good neighbour. (1841-08-07, 3:1)

2732. At Mount Jerome, Harold's-cross, a monument is erected to commemorate the labours of the late Rev. Gideon Ouseley, with the following inscription:—"Gideon Ouseley departed this life, May 14, 1839, in the 78th year of his age. He was a zealous, laborious, and self-denying Minister of the Gospel of Our Lord Jesus Christ throughout the United Kingdom; and during nearly half a century, he was ceaselessly engaged in his Maker's work, in Ireland especially, in its towns and villages, fairs and markets, regardless of personal ease, fearless of danger, uninfluenced by the policy of those 'Who are prudent in their own sight,' he persuasively called on men to repent and believe the Gospel." (1841-08-21, 4:4)

2733. The pay-sergeant of the 60th Rifles, stationed at Beggar's-bush, Dublin, shot himself on Monday evening, in his quarters at the barrack. He locked himself up in a room, and blew his brains out with a loaded musket. His name was Cullen, and had fallen in love with a young lady in one of the squares, who returned his passion, but the officers interfered, and the man became desperate. The young lady is since in a state of distraction. (1841-08-28, 1:5)

2734. Appalling Suicide of a Head-Constable of Police.—One of the most frightful suicides which has occurred for years, took place at Cushendall police-barrack, on Wednesday, the 18th inst. About half-past six o'clock, p.m., and as the mail-car had started for Ballycastle, head-constable Wilder, of the above station, went into the gun-room and took his own double-barreled musket therefrom—such being the description of arms allowed to head-constables. He was distinctly heard by the rest of the constabulary (who were about the barrack door, enjoying themselves, it being a fine evening) running up stairs to his own room; he next appeared looking (*continued...*)

2734, continued: ...out of his room-window. After looking for a few minutes, he turned into the room, laid off his right-foot shoe, and the moment after, the loud, hollow report of the musket aroused the people outside of the barracks, and the heavy fall of the unfortunate head-constable was distinctly heard by many who were at a considerable distance. On entering the room, it was discovered that the lamentable occurrence was past remedy. Doctor M'Court was immediately in attendance, but the wound was mortal: the ball, entering at the base of the sternum, passed obliquely through the left lung, and, perforating the left scapula, spent its force against the wall and ceiling, and fell flattened at a distance. An inquest was held next day, before the Hon. Geo. Handcock and a jury of the inhabitants, when the usual verdict, "temporary insanity," was returned. A paper was found, written by deceased, a few minutes previous to the commission of the act, commencing with the horrid words, "when I shall have despatched myself, &c." In this document, he regulated his affairs with cool decision—requested the sad occurrence to be kept a secret from his mother, and to acquaint his sister in Longford with the full particulars of his unfortunate end. He assigned unpopularity, and his being a public servant, as the cause of his destroying himself. Such reasons were, however, only the false conclusions of a mind decidedly insane; head-constable Wilder, on the contrary, was universally respected for his moderate, inoffensive, and amiable manner. He was the son of a Protestant clergyman in the county of Cavan.—*Vindicator*. (1841-08-28, 2:1)

2735. Coroner's Inquest.—On the 17th instant, Doctor Macfaden, Coroner for the County Cavan, held an inquest in Knockbride Church-yard, near Shercock, on the body of a male child about two years of age, the son of William M'Minn, late of the townland of Knocknalosset, in the parish of Knockbride. The child died on Friday the 13th, and was buried on Sunday the 15th inst. The following are simply the facts of the case. Mr. M'Minn, the father of the child, died some short time previous to the birth of the child, previously making his will, in which he bequeathed a sum of £20 to his then expected issue, and in the event of its demise, he bequeathed said sum together with some other property to its mother. After the death of said Wm. M'Minn, a good deal of litigation ensued between the widow and the brothers and other relatives, of the deceased, about said property, and the widow got married to another man shortly previous to the death of the child. It was rumoured through the neighbourhood, that it came by his death by unfair means, in consequence of which, Doctor Macfaden deemed it his duty to have the body exhumed, which having been examined by Doctor James Sharpe, of Cootehill, the jury returned a verdict in consequence of his evidence,—"that the child died a natural death." (1841-08-28, 2:5)

2736. A new born infant was left this week in the confessional with the Rev. Mr. Tuohy at Birr. (1841-08-28, 2:5)

2737. Lord Morpeth, the Hon. H. Fortescue, and Mr. Geale, are the trustees in the marriage settlement of the Countess Fortescue; and the sum settled on her ladyship by his Excellency the Lord Lieutenant is 2,000*l*. per ann. (1841-08-28, 3:1)

2738. By the death of the Rev. James Edward Jackson, which took place in Paris a few days ago, the deanery of Armagh and a valuable living, in the gift of the Lord Primate, are vacant. The presentation to the deanery is, of course, in the gift of the government. (1841-08-28, 3:1)

2739. Awful and Sudden Death of the Rev. Mr. Keon, Parish Priest of Ballybay, County Monaghan.—This gentleman had been at Bundoran for the last fortnight. On Monday the 30th August, about three o'clock, he and the Rev. Mr. Maguire, Parish Priest of Maguiresbridge, and the Rev. Mr. O'Reilly, Parish Priest of Lowtherstown, went to bathe at the boat quay of Bundoran; they all leaped in, but immediately the Rev. Mr. Keon called for assistance: he was seized with a fit and must have immediately expired, but floated on his back in the sea, until taken up by a boat. Every remedy was used by the several medical gentlemen on the spot, but all was of no avail. Mr. Keon had been curate of Enniskillen parish for a number of years, but recently Parish Priest of Ballybay. His remains were interred at Boho on Wednesday. (1841-09-04, 2:4)

2740. Singular Case of Self Destruction Thro' Religious Fanaticism.—Tuesday last, the body of a woman was found in the lake, near Devonish [sic], towards the lands of Derryinch. An inquest was held yesterday before George Spear, Esq., J.P., in the absence of the coroner, and from anything that could be gleaned, she must evidently have destroyed herself under the influence of religious delusion. And it is further believed that it was in attempting to cross to the monastic ruins in Devonish—most probably under the belief that she was inspired, and could therefore walk on water. On examining the body, a leather belt was found round the waist, next the skin, on which there was a horn ring, and from which hung several lashes of whip-cord, knotted evidently for the purpose of inflicting bodily punishment on herself. From the neck were suspended two, what are called gospels, to which were attached two small brass medals, with the represenation of the crucifiction [sic], and other religious devices. In her breast was a spectacle-case containing a pair of spectacles, a slip of paper, with a couple of Latin lines nearly obliterated, but conveyng the idea that she had been at Lough Derg; from whence, as appears from the evidence of Mrs. Robinson, she said she had been turned off, we should suppose on the termination of the stations for the season, which we learn was about the 15th ult. The poor unfortunate woman was evidently the victim of a religious mania. She was rather well dressed, and was most probably herself the writer of the letter found by the policeman Stewart.—Mrs. Isabella Robinson deposed that deceased came to her house (near the lands where she was found) on Tuesday the 17th ult., and again on Wednesday morning. She gave her some refreshment. She said she had been in the island, (Lough Derg,) and had been put out of it. She said her husband's name was Reilly. She had written a kind of note hardly legible, directed to Father O'Connell, Dunard, county of Longford.

William Carleton deposed that while going up the lake fishing on Tuesday, he saw the body of a person floating and communicated it to his father, who came into town and informed the police.

Robert Stewart, acting constable, deposed that from the information of Carleton he went to Derryinch and took out the body to the shore. Found on her left arm a bundle containing a letter*, and a string of beads and a crucifix on her right. Found round her a strap and whip cord, and round her neck two small medals, one with a French inscription, and the other in the form of a heart, and bearing the picture of the crucifiction.

James Keirnan, Esq., M.D., carefully examined the body, and believed her to have come by her death by drowning. She did not appear to him to have any marks of violence on her body.

The jury therefore returned a verdict to the effect that deceased came by her death by drowning, while in a state of religious insanity.

*Dear Father O'Connell you know I was a liar I was at the island I seen heaven and hell I saw purgatory I showed example of charity I humbled pride I saw the light of Glory Round like the rainbow with two white like pigeons hell at the back of the altar dear father I have suffered near martyrdom I seen the glories of heaven and the torments of hell one on the one side and the other at the same I met.—The letter was directed thus—Father O'Connell parish Priest Dunard county of Longford.—*Enniskillen paper*. (1841-09-04, 4:1)

2741. The Rev. James Edward Jackson, D.D., Dean of Armagh, died at Paris, and the appointment is in the gift of the Crown—value £1,810 a-year, with 368 acres of land attached; also livings, Grange, English [sic], Lisdadell [sic], and Ballymoyer. (1841-09-04, 4:2)

NOTE: Three editions of The Armagh Guardian are missing between Sept. 4, 1841 - Oct. 2, 1841.

2742. The Earldom of Roscommon.—It is rumoured in Falmouth that a seaman called John Dillon, of the *Linnet* packet, is likely to obtain the title and estates of the earldom of Roscommon. His claim was urged some eighteen years ago, and he is now gone to London, having been summoned thither by a letter from the Court of Chancery.—*Plymouth Journal*. (1841-10-02, 1:3)

2743. It is generally believed the Rev. James Lombard, Rector of Carrigaline, will be promoted to the Deanery of Cork, vacant by the demise of Dean Burroughs. (1841-10-02, 2:5)

2744. By the death of the Rev. Chancellor of Dublin, the livings of Kilcullen and Glasneven [sic] are vacant; the Rectorial portion of this parish, valued at £420 a year, is in the gift of the Crown, and the vicarial portion, £462 a year, in the Archbishop. (1841-10-02, 2:5)

2745. Questions for a Wife.—Do you recollect what your feelings were immediately after you had spoken the first unkind word to your husband? Did you not feel both ashamed and grieved, and too proud to admit it? That pride, madam, was, is, and ever will be, your evil genius. It is the temper which labours incessantly to destroy your peace, which cheats you with a vile delusion that your husband deserved your anger when he really deserved your love. It is the cancer which feeds upon those glad and unspeakable emotions you felt on the first pressure of his hand and lip, and will not leave them till their ashes corrode your affections, blight your moral vision, and blunt your sense of right and wrong. Never forget that yours is a lofty calling—never forget the manner in which the duties of that calling can alone be properly fulfilled. If he is hasty, your example of patience will chide as well as teach him; your recriminations will drive him from you; your violence alienate his heart, and your neglect impel him to desperation. Your soothing will redeem him, your softness subdue him; and the merry twinkle of those eyes now filling beautifully with priceless tears will make him all your own.—*Chambers' London Journal*. (1841-10-09, 4:4)

2746. Melancholy and Fatal Accident.—Accident on the Ulster Railway.—The two o'clock train from Lisburn, on last Monday, was a quarter of an hour late in starting, owing to a fatal accident having happened to Hugh Kidd, Esq., of Newry. In getting out of the train at Dunmurry, this gentleman, it appears, intended paying a visit to some of his friends at Dunmurry, on his way to Newry. In getting out of the train at Dunmurry station, he from some inattention, did not get off at the proper time, and, in the effort to alight, came in contact with the wheels of the hindmost carriage just at the moment the coach was starting, by which one of his legs was shattered below the knee. One of the carriages was sent back for the unfortunate gentleman, to bring him to Lisburn, that medical assistance might be procured; but he had been taken into the house of Dr. Montgomery before it reached the fatal spot. Four medical gentlemen were immediately despatched to his assistance by the Company's officers at Lisburn; but the unfortunate sufferer expired a few minutes after their arrival.—*Vindicator*.

(From the *Newry Telegraph*.)—We have been pained to observe, in the Belfast Journals, an (*continued...*)

2746, continued: ... account of the death of Mr. Hugh Kidd, of this town, under very distressing circumstances. The deceased left Belfast, on Monday, by the Railway train, with the intentions of getting out at Dunmurry, a village about half-way between Belfast and Lisburn. When the train had stopped at the Dunmurry station, the usual time, it was again set in motion, and just then Mr. Kidd, who neglected to leave the carriage at the proper time, rashly leaped out, and coming in contact with (we presume) the steps of the vehicle, fell in such a position, across the rail, that the wheels of the hind-most carriages passed over one of his legs, and inflicted such injury as caused almost immediate death.

Mr. Kidd was a respected flour miller. He had resided in Newry for several years; and was generally esteemed by all who knew him. His numerous friends here, and in the County and City of Armagh, will long regret his awfully sudden removal.

(From the *Northern Whig*, Oct. 12)—Mr. Kidd had entered a carriage in the one o'clock up train, for the purpose of visiting the Reverend Doctor Montgomery, at Dunmurry, and, we believe, intended joining the first conveyance to Newry, at the Lisburn terminus, by one of the latter trains. The stoppage at Dunmurry is, usually, for a very short time; and the unfortunate gentleman, probably from his having been engaged in conversation with some person in the carriage, did not get out of it at the proper moment; but, after it was again in motion, he rashly leaped out of it, though, as we learn, every possible effort was made, by his fellow passengers, to prevent his doing so.—The consequence was, that the wheels of the hindmost carriage passed over one of his legs, crushing it in a frightful manner, and that he also received severe internal injuries, which resulted in his death, a short time after he had been removed to the house of his friend, the Reverend Doctor Montgomery.—It is right to add, that, immediately on the lamentable occurrence being made known, on the train reaching Lisburn, an engine and carriage were instantly despatched to Dunmurry, with a Surgeon, in order that every possible assistance might be rendered to the sufferer; but we are sorry to say, that this praiseworthy promptitude on the part of the Railway Company's officers, was unavailing. Dr. Montgomery had, also, procured the early attendance of Dr. H. Purdon, of Belfast. But Mr. Kidd had expired, ere that gentleman had time to reach the place. We understand, that an inquest will be held on the body, this day. (1841-10-16, 2:2)

2747. Fatal Occurrences.—(From a Correspondent.)—We regret to state that at the hour of seven o'clock on the morning of Saturday last, the 9th instant, Catherine Sheridan, a young girl of about 18 years of age, who lived in the capacity of a servant maid, with Mr. Jos. Trever, a respectable farmer, residing on the lands of Edermon, about a mile from Cavan, on the road leading from that town to Farnham, went out of her master's house in order to procure some water from an adjoining well, as she had been in the habit of doing, for culinary purposes; but not returning as quickly as was expected, another female member of the family went out to ascertain the cause of her delay, (the well not being more than two or three perches from the door). She could not see the girl in any direction; but observing the pitcher a short distance from the well's mouth, went over with the intention of fetching the water herself, but to her utter horror and amazement, on looking into the well which had not more than four feet of water in it, discovered the hapless girl with her head downwards and her feet projecting up, the well being of narrow dimensions. She was immediately pulled out, but, melancholy to relate, life had become extinct—the unfortunate creature was suffocated, although she had only been a few minutes absent. It appears she was subject to epileptic fits, and it is presumed one of those attacked her on this occasion, when she must have accidently rolled off the bank into the water, there being a considerable declivity from the place where the pitcher was found lying to the brink of the well. No indication of insanity or melancholy ever was discovered to exist with her, but on the contrary, she was an animated, amiable girl, and a good faithful servant, but for those fits already alluded to, which were not of frequent occurrence. John M'Fadden, Esq., M.D., the coroner, was in attendance at 12 o'clock next day, (Sunday) when he summoned a respectable jury, of which John Irwin Moore, Esq., of Waterloo-Cottage, was foreman, for the purpose of holding an inquest on the body. After short deliberation they returned a verdict of "Found drowned, occasioned by an epileptic fit." Her afflicted relatives conveyed her remains to the church-yard of Kilmore, some hours after the inquest where they are interred. (1841-10-16, 3:1)

2748. Extraordinary Sudden Death.—On Thursday, the 7th instant, a man named Thomas M'Avoy, of the townland of Crubany, about two miles from the town of Cavan, went out to a field adjoining his house, in order to dig some potatoes for present use, and desired his son, a lad of about 12 or 14 years of age to accompany him. The boy had some trifling delay to make, but proceeded to the field, about five minutes after to join his father, as desired, but when he reached, to his astonishment and sincere sorrow, he found him lying on a ridge a lifeless corps [sic]. He expired almost instantaneously in a fit of apoplexy. An inquest was held and a verdict returned accordingly. (1841-10-16, 3:1)

2749. Funeral of the Viscountess Lorton.—(From the *Boyle Gazette*.)—This last solemn duty to the lamented remains of this most inestimable lady, took place on Wednesday morning last. The procession left the house of Rockingham at a quarter before four o'clock. The stillness of the night, the profound silence of the procession, the deep and solemn gloom which pervaded every object around, the sincere and unuttered grief of those personal friends who accompanied the mournful procession,—produced such an indescribable impression, possessed such a reality of true sorrow and sympathy, with the mourning nobleman, as no words can possibly describe. It having been previously known to have been the earnest desire of the bereaved Viscount that the funeral should be in the strictest manner private, none presumed to intrude on the solemn procession; so that the universal respect for his Lordship's wishes was more delicately and gratefully paid than if thousands had accompanied the remains of his departed Lady to their resting place. The procession passed along through the demesne and thence by the mail coach road to this town, and reached the church-yard shortly after 5 o'clock.

The coffin was then borne by several gentlemen into the church, followed by Viscount Lorton, and his son the Hon. H.K. Harman, and accompanied by the Lord Bishop of Elphin, Right Hon. Dr. Lefroy, the Rev. Charles Leslie, the Rev. William Digby, the Rev. George Brittane, the Rev. Robert MGhee, M. Crofton, Esq., &c. &c. The funeral service was read in such a calm and solemn manner by the Rev. Mr. Maguire as exceedingly added to that impressive service; and this last office of duty and respect to the remains of this benevolent lady, whose virtues and excellent character shall long outlive her, were concluded as the dawn of morning began to appear.

We beg to subjoin from the *Dublin Evening Mail*, the following beautifully written account of the funeral of the departed Viscountess:—

On Wednesday morning, a little after five o'clock, the mortal remains of this inestimable Lady were laid in their last earthly abode, the vault of that noble family, in the Church of Boyle.

The mournful procession left the house of Rockingham at a quarter before four, and passed through the Boyle gate in solemn silence, towards its destination. Not a voice was heard; the measured tread of the horses, the slow rolling of the hearse and train of carriages that followed, were the only sounds that broke the stillness of the morning; and never did a mourning train follow the remains of one whose loss, in every relation of life that a Christian female could adorn, was more deeply and deservedly deplored.

About half-past four, the hearse reached the church of Boyle, which was lighted, and hung with black; and the solemn funeral service—so expressive of the vanity of all the glory of this life, and all the blessed hopes of that which is to come—never seemed more beautifully appropriate than when applied to one fallen from such an exalted station here, and laid in the tomb in such "sure and certain hope of the resurrection to eternal life through our Lord Jesus Christ."

The reverend gentleman who officiated, judiciously abstained from delivering any address on the occasion. It had been too much for his own feelings, and those not only of the mourners (her bereaved, afflicted Lord, and her son, the Hon. Harman King Harman), but for the feelings of all who were present. To speak of her loss were vain to those whose hearts were bowed down under the weight of sorrow, and commentary was unnecessary on the life of one whose life had been one speaking commentary on the truth and power of the Gospel.

It were intrusion into the sacred sanctuary of private grief to dwell on the blank left in her own family, and the mourning that pervades the afflicted house of Rockingham.—But Lady Lorton was in truth a public character.—Though one of the most humble, gentle, unobtrusive, retiring of human beings, her heart, her hand were open—her name and influence were known and felt wide as the range of pure religion and of Christian charity throughout the land.

What mission ever went through Ireland to advance the diffusion of the sacred volume—to send the Gospel to the benighted heathen—to proclaim the Blessed Messiah to the blinded Jew—to promote the hallowed cause of Scriptural education, which, while it found in the noble proprietor a patron, an open house, and a cordial welcome at Rockingham, did not find also a friend, a helper, a patroness, a liberal benefactress in Lady Lorton?

Who ever projected the erection of a building—the formation of a society—the founding of an institution—a plan for the promotion of any cause of true religion or benevolence in the land, for which the aid and influence of a Christian lady of exalted rank might be properly solicited, who did not, as it were instinctively, turn to the Viscountess Lorton, and whom did she ever send with a cold repulse, or an unkind response, away?

It might with confidence be stated that the history of Ireland does not present the name of a single female more prominent in promoting, to the utmost of her power, all that could redound to the glory of God and to the good of man, than that of the Viscountess Lorton.

Her charities to individuals—her consideration for the poor, the widow, the orphan, the stranger, were only bounded by her means of relieving their necessities. Her personal expenditure was restricted within the very moderate limits of the simplest, plainest gentlewoman. Her liberality was the noblest generosity of a munificent benefactress—yet withal unostentatious—silent—known in its extent but by herself and her God—

"True charity that came not in a shower,
Sudden and loud, oppressing what it feeds:
But, like the dew, with gradual, silent power,
Felt in the bloom it leaves along the meades."

She felt she was indeed a steward for her Heavenly Master, and she felt the power of the blessed principles of her Lord, "that it is more blessed to give than to receive."

Her numerous schools may be considered as models for the education of the poor. They have sent forth many, who have been trained in them, as valuable teachers into various parts of Ireland. (*continued...*)

2748,continued: ...Devotedly attached, on the soundest principles, to the Established Church, she was liberal in the truest sense, without compromise, and firm to her religion, without bigotry. She prized its sacred formularies, for the blessed principles of Christian truth enshrined within them; and for that truth's sake her heart expanded with the apostolic principle—"Grace be with all that love our Lord Jesus Christ in sincerity."

Quick and clear in her perceptions of all that militated against the purity of the Gospel—sensitively alive to every rise and progress of error—her library was ever well supplied with the best and ablest books to counteract it—few of her friends and visitors who have not profited by the wise selections of her judgment, and the liberal gifts of her affectionate and anxious generosity.

What liberal supplies of books has she not sent where she knew they were needed! What Bibles, Prayer-books, School-books, Tracts, has she not bestowed! Where has she travelled, at home or abroad, that she has not left behind for traces of her fidelity to the cause of her God, and of her ardent zeal for the temporal and eternal welfare of her fellow-creatures?

Yet these and all the varied excellencies, the graces and gifts of her character did not constitute one iota of the hope of her salvation. She wrought from love for Him who had saved her, but not to save herself. She "counted all things loss for the excellency of the knowledge of Christ Jesus her Lord." She was in her own eyes the very lowest of the earth, and all her hope was that of a helpless guilty sinner, washed in the precious blood, and clothed in the spotless righteousness of her Redeemer.

Panegyric cannot offend the ears of the dead; truth may profit those that are alive—and oh! that females in a lofty station could but know how hollow, how heartless, is the praise of the blush that glows upon the cheek—of the brilliancy or of the wit that sparkles in the eye—oh! that they could but know and feel how they grasp at shadows that are passing, and despise the solid joys that last for ever! If they would exchange error for truth—shadows for substance—vanity for peace, and vexation of spirit for happiness—if they would attain an eminence higher than rank or riches can confer, a hallowed reverence, which they never can command—if they would prefer that true heartfelt respect of all, to the hollow sycophantic flattery of a few—if they would be loved and honored when living, and have their memory embalmed in tears, and blessings when they are gone—if they would live and die like rational, accountable, redeemed, immortal beings—let them embrace the blessed faith, rest on the joyful hope, walk in the humble, holy love that formed the honoured character, and bequeath to her country and her sex the bright example of one whose name is epitaph enough—

FRANCES VISCOUNTESS LORTON.

(1841-10-23, 1:3)

2750. Death of the Bishop of Kilmore.—Died at the Palace, Kilmore, Cavan, on the morning of the 16th, the Right Rev. George De la Poer Beresford, D.D., Lord Bishop of Kilmore and Ardagh, in the 40th year of his episcopacy.

His loss is universally deplored by all who knew him, by none more than by those in the neighbourhood of Kilmore, by whom a long life of usefulness made him to be respected and beloved.

We understand he is to be buried in the episcopal vault in the churchyard of Kilmore on Wednesday next.—*Mail of Monday*. (1841-10-23, 1:5)

2751. Melancholy Accident.—Death of Mr. Joseph Nelson, of Charlemont.—A melancholy catastrophe occurred at Charlemont, county Armagh, on the evening of the 15th inst. Mr. Joseph Nelson, of that town, formerly a resident of Belfast accompanied by a young Gentleman, named M'Blain, of Dungannon, had been taking a pleasure sail in Mr. Nelson's canoe, on the Blackwater river, and were approaching Moy bridge. When nearing the Quay, at Mrs. Martin's, a little after 6 o'clock, p.m., the canoe, owing to some inexplicable cause, was capsized, and both Gentlemen were precipitated into the water; they struggled, for some time, with the current, and, instant alarm having been raised, a boat from the lighter *John William* put out, the man on board of which, William Erskin, caught hold of Mr. M'Blain, who was clinging to the bottom of the canoe and thus happily saved his life. Mr. Nelson had previously disappeared, and notwithstanding the utmost exertions of the multitudes who thronged the banks, his body was not discovered until an hour had elapsed. Doctor Martin, of Moy, who was on the spot from the first moment the alarm was given, assisted by Doctor King, left no remedy untried, which medical science could afford; but, alas, all in vain—the vital spark had fled! An Inquest was held on Sunday before Joshua M. Magee, Esq., and a highly respectable Jury, who returned a verdict of "Accidentally drowned." Mr. Nelson who has been thus suddenly cut off, in the spring of manhood, had secured the friendship and esteem of many, who deeply deplore his premature removal. His death affords another awful lesson of the uncertainty of human life. May it be felt and remembered, particularly by the youthful!
(1841-10-23, 2:3)

2752. Mr. P. Murphy, Assistant Barrister of Cavan, adjourned his Sessions Court, in order that the people might attend the funeral of the lamented Bishop of Kilmore. (1841-10-30, 2:1)

2753. In consequence of the continued indisposition of Mrs. Pennefather, the newly appointed Lord Chief Justice of the Queen's Bench, did not hold a levee on Monday last, the first day of the Michaelmas term.
(1841-11-06, 1:4)

2754. Sir Richard Cox's estate in the county Cork was sold by auction in that city on Wednesday, it fetched £40,000; the rental amounted to £1,500 a-year; the purchasers were Messrs. Hutchens, Doherty, Lucas, Gelgey, Wilplay, Reilly, Morragh, and Stephen Hayes. (1841-11-06, 1:4)

2755. On Wednesday night last, a farmer returning from Cahir races died from the inclemency of the weather. He was found dead on the road near the barracks, with the loss of his watch. (1841-11-06, 1:4)

2756. Lines suggested by the death of Miss Henrietta Johnson, Thornhill.

"Last noon beheld them full of lusty life—
Last eve in beauty's circle proudly gay."
Byron.

Awake! my lyre, thy saddest strains,
Let mournful numbers wildly flow;
Strew flowers upon her cold remains,
Nor stem the tide of bitter woe.

'Tis meet that we should weep, since one
So young, so lovely and adored,
Unto the silent tomb is gone,
By grieving friends to be deplored.

She based the gayest of the gay,
Mid splendid scenes of earth's delight,
As if it were on yesterday,
And lies a lifeless corse to-night!

Go mourn, ye youthful lovely dames,
With whom the graces love to dwell;
Extinguish all youth's joyous flames,
For brittle is life's tinsel shell.

Think not the charms of which ye boast
Can check the course of fell disease;
Ah! no, where beauty sparkles most
The hand of death may soonest seize.

Not all the blandishments of wealth—
Not all the glare of rich array,
Could purchase momentary health
When on her bed of death she lay.

She knew her soul was summon'd then
To join angelic hosts above,
And sing heaven's choicest—sweetest strain,
The anthems of redeeming love.

And when she knew her Master's will
She bid her weeping friends adieu—
Said to her beating heart, be still,
In Jesus I shall sleep; for who

Is like unto my God? Not all
The hopes and joys of this vain earth,
Which many do so much extol,
I feel their emptiness of worth.

She meekly closed her brilliant eyes,
So lately beaming with delight,
And flew to yonder lofty skies
To be a sinless saint of light.

Adieu! dear maid, we leave thy clay
To moulder with its kindred dust,
Until the awful Judgment Day
When Christ the silent tomb shall burst.

October 25th 1841.
Feventus.
(1841-11-06, 4:1)

2757. The Lord Bishop of Meath has appointed his chaplain, the Rev. Robert Mitchell Kennedy, to the Vicarage of Banagher, and the Rev. James Paul Homes, twenty-one years a Curate in the diocese of Meath, to the Vicarage of Gallen, both vacant by the death of the Rev. John Burdett. (1841-11-13, 1:3)

2758. The Rev. Mr. Chapman gets the living of Omagh, vacant by the death of the late Dean of Cork. This causes a vacancy in Mr. Chapman's present living.—*Fermanagh Reporter.* (1841-11-13, 1:3)

2759. Last Friday, at Annagor, near Drogheda, a man named Edward Reilly was gored to death by a bull. (1841-11-13, 3:5)

2760. Rejoicings at Hillsborough.—(*From a Correspondent of the Evening Mail.*)—"On Thursday morning, the 11th instant, the good news arrived here that her Majesty had, under the blessing of Divine Providence, safely presented her royal consort with a Prince, and her devoted people with an heir to the throne. Immediately the bells of our magnificent church, which had been for some time past kept in readiness, at a moment's warning to ring out the joyful intelligence, with more than usual fulness, and in tones that seemed to peal (not to repeal) the union of innumerable hearts in their sentiments of love and attachment to the Queen of this triple empire. This was continued with little intermission until a late hour at night, as well as on the following morning, when the town exhibited evident proofs of a determination further to testity the happiness and delight of every one on this auspicious occasion. Ever foremost in what is right and proper, the inhabitants of Hillsborough were all day busily preparing for a general illumination; and at half-past six o'clock in the evening, every window in the town appeared anxious to outshine its neighbour, and took pains, by its extra brilliancy, to show forth the brightness of honor which true loyalty ever cheerfully renders to whom it is due. It would be impossible to describe the variety of devices which were made use of, to exhibit the tastes of so many, each striving, with just emulation, to be seen 'in the very best light;' suffice it to say, that the meanest house was not without its appropriate motto—'God save the Queen.' The old castle—famous in history as having afforded a resting place to an illustrious ancestor of the royal infant just born to us—turned out its veteran warders, in their full uniform of the olden time, and, drawn up in the market square, fired many rounds of (*continued...*)

2760,continued:...musketry with admirable precision, each volley succeeded by a burst of cheering both loud and long. There were several six-pounders also actively at work; and, upon a cessation of their noisy joy, the Marquis of Downshire's celebrated band marched through every street playing the national anthem with remarkable harmony and effect. At each end of the town were immense bonfires; nor must I leave unmentioned, that, by the generous liberality of the soil, an abundant supply of excellent ale was distributed; and few there were, if any, who failed to drink, with all their hearts—'Long live the Queen and the Prince of Wales!'" (1841-11-20, 1:4)

2761. (From another Correspondent.)—Rejoicings at Edenderry.—On the happy tidings of the safe accouchement of our beloved Queen, and the birth of a young Prince, the bonfires were lighted, and the town resounded with shouts of long "live the Queen—long live the Prince." A grand salute was fired, and many a cheer was given to the health of the Prince in strong ale, which the noble proprietor of the town, the Marquis of Downshire, had ordered to be provided for the occasion. (1841-11-20, 1:4)

2762. Rejoicings in Kilcullen on the Occasion of the Birth of the Heir Apparent.—(From a Correspondent of the *Packet.*)—It would be impossible to give an accurate description of the joy and gladness, the enthusiasm which pervaded all classes in this town and neighbourhood since the above gratifying intelligence was communicated. Creed and party seemed to have merged into vying with each other in giving every proof which faithful subjects could possibly give of loyalty to the Throne and devotion to the Sovereign.—Amid other festivities, Mr. Carter, the proprietor of a considerable portion of this town, and to whose fostering care and practical patriotism it is principally indebted for its present prosperous and flourishing condition, gave a splendid entertainment, on Friday last, to his tenantry and labourers, with their wives and elder children. After feasting most sumptuously on beef and mutton, and all the other suitable accompaniments, dancing commenced, which was kept up till a late hour, during which the company was plentifully regaled with ale, negus, punch, and such as were teetotallers, coffee. The utmost gaiety and harmony prevailed, and on separating, all felt highly delighted with the kindness and hospitality of the host, which added considerably to the pleasures and enjoyments of the evening. (1841-11-20, 1:4)

2763. Meeting to Address the Queen.—A meeting was held in the new Court-house, Newry, on Monday, to vote an address of congratulation to her Majesty and Prince Albert, on the auspicious event of the birth of the Prince of Wales. A similar meeting was held in Belfast on the same day. (1841-11-20, 1:4)

2764. The Birth of a Prince.—On Saturday last, at twelve o'clock, the 29th regiment, under the command of Lieutenant-Colonel the Hon. A.C. Wrottesely, and the troop of the 4th Dragoon Guards, marched to M'Clean's Fields, and fired a *feu de joi* in celebration of the auspicious event of the birth of the Prince of Wales, after which the troops gave three hearty cheers. Sir Thomas Pearson, the general in command of the northern district, was present and received the salute.—*Belfast News-Letter*. (1841-11-20, 1:4)

2765. Military Rejoicings.—The Lieutenant-Governor, Sir Hercules Pakenham, by a garrison order, dated 11th inst., has directed that all soldiers, confined for military offences, should be released immediately, in consequence of the birth of a Prince of Wales. (1841-11-20, 1:4)

2766. Monaghan Illuminations, in Honor of the Birth of the Prince of Wales.—In consequence of an advice given in our last, and in accordance with the wish of a number of the inhabitants to display their joy at the birth of an heir to the Throne, a meeting was held on Saturday evening, when the propriety of a general illumination of the town was duly considered and resolved upon for Tuesday evening last; but the resolution not meeting the views and wishes of some persons who did not attend the meeting, another meeting was called upon Tuesday, at three o'clock, at which the non-contents found an overwhelming majority against them, so much so that they dared not put the question, of "illumination or no illumination," but sought, by various pretexts, an adjournment. After a long and stormy debate, the great majority of the inhabitants left the meeting, declaring their intention to illuminate whether the few persons who called the meeting, but who were, we must say, considerably the minority, chose to do so or not. We believe the last act of the minority was the getting up a requisition to the Provost, who was absent in England, to call a meeting to determine whether there should be, or should not be an illumination at some future day, but the attempt was a miserable failure. There was also a brilliant display of fire-works during the night, under the superintendence and management of Wm. Walker, Esq., Architect, which attracted general attention, and gave much satisfaction. We will offer no comment upon the reasons or motives which actuated the opponents, because out of Monaghan they would not be of any interest, and in it they are fully understood and duly appreciated. One thing we must say, that a factious and individual feeling should never be suffered to interfere with public actions, nor however humble or unworthy the individual who originates a good act, it should not be opposed on account of private pique or personal emnity. We like not to trust our pen farther with observations, but hesitate not to say, that with some of those who opposed an illumination upon this glorious occasion, the opposition was conceived in bad taste and carried on in worse temper. (1841-11-20, 2:4)

2767. Coroner's Inquests.—Determined Suicide by a Female.—On Monday the 8th inst., John M'Fadden, Esq., coroner for the county Cavan, held an inquest on view of the body of Anne Carolan, widow of Joseph Carolan,—the facts of the case, as they appeared in evidence are as follows:—The deceased had, for a few weeks previous to her death, been labouring under slight aberration of mind; on the night of the 7th, she went to bed as usual with her daughter and servant maid, and some time during the night got up and dressed herself unperceived, procured a hank of yarn, put the noose of one end round her neck and the other she attached to the crane of the kitchen fire-place, which was not more than four feet from the ground, and finding that that height would not suit her purpose, so determined was she to commit the rash act she had premeditated, that she very ingeniously twisted her body round and shortened the hank of yarn, but not finding that to answer she contracted her legs until she succeeded in her diabolical purpose. The servant girl gave the alarm to her neighbours, who found her in the situation described quite dead with the under part of her clothes and [a] portion of her body burned. The jury found that the deceased died from strangulation whilst labouring under temporary insanity. The coroner ordered the police to have the body interred after sunset, without benefit of clergy!! (1841-11-20, 2:4)

2768. Illuminations at Comber.—On Monday evening last, the 15th instant, the inhabitants of Comber and its vicinity displayed their joy at the birth of an heir to the British throne by a general illumination, bonfires, &c. The fineness of the evening and the frost which set in, made the streets so dry that every one was able to go out and witness the sight. The greatest quietness and harmony marked the conduct of the people, who returned to their homes about ten o'clock, highly delighted with the occurrences of the evening. (1841-11-27, 1:2)

2769. The Very Rev. the Dean of Down continues severely indisposed at his residence, Downpatrick. (1841-11-27, 2:2)

2770. Monument to the Memory of the Late Lord Bishop of Kilmore and Ardagh.—A public meeting was recently held in the Court-house of Cavan, for the purpose of considering the propriety of erecting a monument to the memory of the late Lord Bishop of Kilmore and Ardagh. Subscriptions not to exceed five pounds. A considerable amount has already been contributed for that purpose, and the greatest zeal is evinced by the neighbouring gentry to testify the high esteem in which they held the private virtues and public character of that worthy and lamented dignitary of the Church. (1841-11-27, 3:1)

2771. To the Prince of Wales.

Welcome, bright and lovely stranger!
Hails thee now exultant earth;
From each foe, false friend, and danger,
Angels shield thee from thy birth.

Born to bless great Albion's nation—
Scion of a princely tree—
Born to rule o'er wide creation,
Child of royal Victory.

The greatness of thy mother's spirit—
The graces of they father's heart—
May'st thou, all richly, boy, inherit,
And prove through life their counterpart.

And when has passed thine infant dreaming,
And when the palm of manhood's won,
When thy young light, now softly gleaming,
Breaks into its full noontide sun.

And when—but distant be the hour;
Long may it wind through bright delay;
May Heaven's all kind controlling power,
Proscrastinate the woeful day.

But when thy royal parent sleeping
Cold in death—as sleep she must—
Shall leave a sorrowing nation weeping,
O'er her consecrated dust.

To thee may wisdom then be given,
Rightly to sway thy sceptre o'er
(As representative of Heaven)
Thy kingdom wide from shore to shore.

May righteousness and peace be twining,
Bright o'er thy head their blossoms blest,
And 'neath the sacred shade reclining,
May all thy favoured subjects rest.

But should war rend the veil asunder,
And unprovoked the red spear fling,
May Heaven then point Britannia's thunder,
And each death-bolt with triumph wing.

Be then the royal bosom fired
With that same flame which, days of yore,
Saw thy great ancestors inspired,
When rolled the battle-field in gore.

And all creation shall exultant,
Of earth-born princes hail thee best,
When blazes forth that name triumphant—
VICTORIA—from thy burning crest.

And then they'll think on her that bore thee,
And tears commingle with their joy,
As bent in admiration o'er thee,
They bless the mother for the boy.

But when life's star shall wane above thee,
And of life's tree is snapped the stem,
May'st thou then, linked with these who love thee
Wear Heaven's deathless diadem,

Within redemption's sacred portal,
May'st thou, all blest, all glorious, be
Before the throne of God immortal,
That's gemmed for all eternity.

Welcome, thou bright, lovely stranger!
Hails thee now exultant earth!
From each foe, false friend, and danger,
Angels shield thee from thy birth.

Henry Ribion.
Dublin, Nov. 12th, 6, Victoria-terrace.
(1841-11-27, 4:1)

2772. Death of Lady Anne Beresford.—We regret to announce the death of Lady Anne Beresford, which took place, after a short illness, in Harcourt-street, on Saturday. Her Ladyship (who was in her 61st year) was sister to his Grace the Lord Primate, and aunt to the Marquis of Waterford. (1841-12-04, 1:5)

2773. The Lines on the Death of Sir John Moore.—A fragment of a letter addressed to Mr. Taylor, bearing the postmark of September 6, 1816, and written by the Rev. Chas. Wolfe, has been found, containing a complete copy of the lines on the death of Sir John Moore, and a sentence stating that his (Mr. Taylor's) praise of the stanzas first written had led him to complete the poem. This document will henceforth remove all doubt on the subject of the authorship of these beautiful lines. (1841-12-04, 1:5)

2774. Tablet to the Memory of Cairnes.—An elegant monument has just been erected in the Cathedral, to the memory of the gallant David Cairnes, one of the famous defenders of Derry in 1688. It has been erected at the expense of the Hon. the Irish Society, and bears the following inscription:—In the burial ground of this Cathedral are deposited the remains of David Cairnes, Esq., a pious Christian, an intelligent lawyer, and a heroic defender of his religion and his country, during the memorable struggle of 1688; after which he was returned for several years to parliament for the City of Londonderry. The original tribute to his memory having become mutilated and defaced, this tablet was erected by the Hon. the Irish Society, A.D., 1841. (1841-12-04, 2:1)

2775. Shipwreck and Loss of Ten Lives.—During the heavy gale of Wednesday morning, the 24th instant, about four o'clock, a.m., the schooner *James Cooke*, of Limerick, bound from Sligo to Glasgow with oats, &c., struck on the Glashedy rock, in the bay on the west side of Malin Head, and immediately went to pieces. The master and nine of the crew were unfortunately lost. One man, James Fitzgerald, was providentially saved, being cast upon the above mentioned rock, where he remained till Thursday, the weather being too rough on Wednesday to allow a boat to venture out to his rescue. At day-light on Thursday morning, the weather being more moderate, the Dunaff coast guard's galley and a number of county boats put off to the island, and the survivor was brought ashore in a very emaciated and exhausted state. The coast guard officers and constabulary are protecting the wreck, but nothing has come ashore except a part of the two lower masts, and some of the bulwarks, hatches, and broken spars.—*Derry Sentinel.* (1841-12-04, 4:4)

2776. Important Case Arising on the Marriage Law of Ireland.—The *Queen v. Samuel Smith.*—On Friday, the 26th ult., the twelve judges met in the Queen's Bench Chamber, to hear the arguments of counsel on a very interesting point arising out of the marriage law of Ireland.

It appears that the defendant was indicted for bigamy at last Armagh assizes, and was put on trial before Judge Crampton. It was proved that the prisoner was a member of the Established Church, and that in the year 1831, he intermarried with Margaret Smith, a Presbyterian. The parties were married by Mr. Bell, the Presbyterian minister of the congregation of Clare, in the county of Armagh, at his own house, at eleven o'clock at night, according to the forms of the Presbyterian Church. The prisoner lived with his wife for some years afterwards and then left her. In 1839 the prisoner married Jane Gordon, of Portadown, in the church of St. Ann's, in Dublin. The curate and clerk of that church attended and proved the marriage, and no objection was raised as to its validity; but Mr. Whiteside, for the prisoner, insisted that the prisoner was entitled to an acquittal on the ground that the first marriage was void, having been celebrated between a member of the Established Church and a Presbyterian, by a Presbyterian minister, and not by any priest in holy orders. Sir Thomas Staples, for the prosecution, insisted that at common law, the aid of a person in holy orders was not essential to the validity of a marriage in Ireland. The judge overruled Mr. Whiteside's objection, reserving the question for the opinion of the twelve judges, and the prisoner was found guilty and sentenced to be transported. The judges now met to hear the arguments on the point, when the Solicitor-General, Sir Thomas Staples, and Mr. Hanna, appeared for the crown, and Mr. Whiteside for the prisoner, and the discussion of the question continued the whole day. Mr. Whiteside, for the objection, in a speech of three hours, went through the statute laws of Ireland for regulation of marriages and relief of Dissenters, and quoted very largely from the statutes of the 12th George I., ch. 3; 9th George II.; 12th George II., ch. 13th; 17th and 18th Charles II., ch. 3d., 11th George II., ch. 10 and 21; and 22d George III., ch. 25; 32d George III., ch. 21, sec. 12 and 13; 57th George III., ch. 54; 58th George III., ch. 81, sec. 3; 3d and 4th William IV., ch. 102. He then went into a history of the common law as applicable to marriages, and read extracts and cases from Thelford on the *Law of Marriages*, Brown's *Ecclesiastical Law*, Sir William Scott, and several books on the law of Scotland; Jacob's note in 2d Roper, appendix 45; Lord Hale as to the necessity of the use of a ring in the ceremonies of marriage, and other English writers and books on the customs of the Saxons; several books on the Civil Law; the decrees of several of the Popes, and the proceedings of the Council of Trent, and the establishment of marriage as a religious ceremony all over Europe, and throughout the Christian world; and after reading a great portion of the judgement [sic] lately delivered by Doctor Millar, in the cause of *Lemon v.*

Lemon, concluded by submitting that, by the common law of Ireland, a priest or person in holy orders assisting was essential to the validity of a marriage in Ireland—that a Presbyterian minister was not a person known to the common law as being in holy orders—and as the statute law for relief of Dissenters to celebrate marriages amongst themselves, that is, between one Dissenter and another, the marriage of the prisoner, Samuel Smith, with said Margaret Smith, was void, and prisoner was entitled to his discharge. The solicitor-general in reply, insisted that the marriage of the prisoner with Margaret Smyth, was a good and valid marriage, and that the prisoner ought to be transported. There was no necessity whatever for the intervention of a priest or person in holy orders to make valid a marriage in Ireland. In support of this assertion he quoted Leathorp's case in Hansard's *Parliamentary Reports*, the *King v. Marshal*, Bunting's case, in *Moore's Reports*, and a variety of other authorities, all going to establish that, at common law, marriages in Ireland was [sic] a civil contract and not a religious ceremony; and that the law of Ireland does not now, nor ever did, require the intervention of any clergyman or person in holy orders to make a marriage valid, that the marriage before Mr. Bell, as a layman, or before any other person, was binding on the prisoner; and he prayed the judges by their judgment to confirm the conviction and so set at rest a question which, if decided in favor of the prisoner, would disturb and agitate society in the north of Ireland, and be productive of the greatest possible inconvenience and mischief.

At five o'clock, the judges adjourned the further hearing until the following day.

On Saturday, the 27th, the judges again met for hearing further argument of this case. Sir Thomas Staples, in support of the conviction, and Mr. Whiteside, in reply, occupied the entire day, and the judges adjourned again at five o,clock.

Counsel for the prosecution—The Solicitor-General, Sir Thomas Staples, and Mr. Hanna. Agent—The Crown Solicitor, North East District.

Counsel for the prisoner—Mr. Whiteside. Agent—Mr. J.O. Woodhouse. (1841-12-04, 4:5)

2777. Death of the Countess of Normanton.—We have the melancholy task of announcing the death, which took place on Thursday, the 2d of December, at the family seat, Somerly, Hants, of Diana, Countess of Normanton, after a protracted illness of four years. Her ladyship was the eldest daughter of George Augustus, Earl of Pembroke, and was married on the 17th of May, 1816, to Welbore Ellis, Earl of Normanton. Her ladyship leaves issue, James, Viscount Somerton; the Hon. Herbert, the Hon. Charles, and the lady Mary Agar. Lady Normanton united to a person of rare beauty and to accomplishments of the highest order a more than feminine understanding. Solid in judgment and quick in perception, she has left her family and friends the sad recollection of still more amiable qualities, which never can be forgotten.
(1841-12-11, 1:2)

2778. Mr. O'Connell's Marriage.—It is rumoured that the Right Hon. the Lord Mayor is about to re-enter the holy bonds of wedlock; and it even goes so far as to state the name and connexions of the lady (who is very young) who has overcome his Lordship's prejudices against an Union.—*Correspondent of London Standard.* —It is stated by a correspondent of the *Morning Herald* that the lady of his choice is a daughter of Sir James Murray—young handsome and accomplished.
(1841-12-11, 3:3)

2779. A melancholy accident occurred lately in Portadown. The children of a respectable family were breakfasting together in the nursery, and one of them a boy of nearly two years old, began to cry.—The nurse, instead of soothing him in the usual way, filled his mouth, while thus excited, with food, which, being principally fluid, went down the windpipe into the lungs. The irritation produced a convulsive suffocating cough. A little blood mixed with mucus, was vomited, and in less than a minute the child was dead.—*Newry Telegraph.* (1841-12-11, 4:3)

2780. Illness of Mr. Sharman Crawford, M.P.—We are deeply concerned to state that Mr. Crawford is at present suffering from an attack of typhus fever, at Crawfordsburn. We believe, however, that the symptoms of the disease have somewhat abated; and that there is ground to hope for the hon. gentleman's speedy recovery.—*Northern Whig.* (1841-12-11, 4:4)

2781. Marriage in a Wrong Name.—Dr. Lushington has lately decided that a marriage, in pursuance of banns, in which a wrong Christian name was given to the husband, with the knowledge of the wife, is void, and must be annulled. The fact of there being no children was alluded to, as if the court would have not so decreed had there been issue. (1841-12-18, 1:5)

2782. Fatal Case of Hydrophobia at Springfield.—It is our painful duty to record another case of hydrophobia—fatal, as we believe, almost every case proves. John M'Cartney, the cartman employed by Messrs. Stevenson, of Springfield, a respectable and trustworthy person, experienced, for the first time, some uncomfortable and unusual feelings, when passing the mill-dam, on his way from town, on Wednesday last; but it was not till he sat down to dinner that his wife and family perceived he was unwell. He spent a restless and excited night. On Thursday morning, medical advice was obtained, and the most active treatment pursued; but the spasms became more frequent and severe, and he expired at about three o'clock, being about forty-eight hours from the commencement of the symptoms. His mind remained clear, and it was not till Thursday that he suspected the (*continued...*)

2782, continued: ...nature of the disease. It is doubly painful to reflect that this poor man appears to have fallen a victim to his feelings of humanity to animals. About eight weeks ago, as he approached his own house, a number of savage boys were torturing and cruelly treating a poor little dog, whose leg was broken. He ran among them, to rescue the sufferer which, not being able to distinguish a friend from a foe, bit one of his thumbs slightly. It is said that he carried the animal into his own cottage, where it lay for an hour, and was afterwards led, by a person, quietly into town.—*Northern Whig.* (1841-12-18, 1:5)

2783. Death of Owen Wynne, Esq.—It is our painful duty to record the death of Owen Wynne, Esq., which took place at his residence, Hazlewood, county of Sligo, on Sunday, the 12th instant, in the 86th year of his age. He was one of the oldest and steadiest resident gentlemen of Ireland, and, we believe, the oldest Irish Member of the House of Commons, having represented the county of Sligo in the parliament of 1777, and sat in the Irish, and afterwards in the British Parliament, for many succeeding years. During a long life spent in the exercise of Christian and social virtues, and in the improvement of the neighbourhood in which he resided, he possessed the respect of all who knew him, and died endeared to his family and friends, by whom his loss will be long felt and deplored.—*Mail.* (1841-12-18, 2:3)

2784. We have good reason to believe that there is no truth in the newspaper statements respecting the supposed intended marriage of the Right Hon. Daniel O'Connell, M.P., and Lord Mayor, with the daughter of a fellow-citizen, whose name has found its way into some of the public journals.—*Packet.* (1841-12-18, 3:3)

2785. Mary Connelly, a married woman, and mother of four children, while in a state of starvation, attempted to drown herself at the Horseferry. The parish refused assistance, but offered to send her to Ireland, where the destitute woman said she would be now a stranger. (1841-12-25, 1:1)

2786. Death of Major Richardson.—We regret sincerely to announce the death of John Richardson, Esq., of Rossfad, in this neighbourhood, which took place on the morning of the 10th inst., in the 74th year of his age. He was brother in law of the late General, and of the present Colonel Archdall, of Castle Archdall, and uncle of our present county representative, Mervyn Archdall, Esq. He held the commission of Major in the Tyrone Militia, and was greatly esteemed by his brother officers, and by all the nobility and gentry of this and the surrounding counties. He is succeeded in his estates by his only son, Henry Richardson, Esq., who inherits all his father's virtues.—*Fermanagh Reporter.* (1841-12-25, 1:3)

2787. Death of the Dowager (Mary Anne) Countess of Belmore.—The above venerable lady died on Monday last, at Bath, in which city her ladyship had resided for many years, and was deservedly respected and esteemed for her manifold charities. The deceased countess, who was the eldest daughter of the late Sir James Caldwell, of Castle Caldwell, was third wife of Armer, first Earl of Belmore, grandfather of the present earl, to whom her ladyship was married in 1794. This countess had attained the great age of 86 years. (1841-12-25, 1:3)

2788. Her Majesty has been pleased to express her intention of becoming a sponsor to the infant son of Mr. and Mrs. James Marshall, daughter of Lord Monteagle, (late Maid of Honor to her Majesty.) (1841-12-25, 1:4)

2789. The Consistorial Court of Cloyne has given judgment in the case of *Wallis v. Horrigan, alias Moynihan,* for nullity of marriage, under 19th George 2d, cap. 13, and 33d George 3d, cap. 21, penal statutes against the union of Protestant and Roman Catholic by a Priest of the latter creed. Archdeacon Kyle announced the promovant, John Cooke Wallis, Esq., a Protestant, has established his suit, and that the marriage is null and void. (1841-12-25, 1:4)

2790. Dr. Lardner and Mrs. Heaviside.—Dr. Lardner is now creating a great sensation in all our fashionable and scientific circles. Some attack him on principles of morality, and others defend him on principles of astronomy. The issue can be easily divined—it will fill his lecture-room, and leave the moral questions as unsettled as the north eastern boundary. A few months after the arrival of the Dr. with Mrs. Heaviside in the country, they were married in Philadelphia, under a law of Pennsylvania. It seems also that all the property in the English copyrights has been swallowed up by the verdict given to Captain Heaviside. He has, therefore, been reduced to the necessity of working or starving—for it seems Mrs. Heaviside, now Mrs. Lardner, has no property, except a contingency on a death hereafter. Of course, Dr. Lardner prefers hard work at every risk. —*New York Herald.* (1841-12-25, 1:5)

2791. Melancholy Sudden Death.—A most interesting and intelligent girl, of about 14 years of age, the youngest daughter of Mr. John Davis, of Cavan, took suddenly ill on the night of Thursday, the 16th inst., of spasms in the stomach. She continued in the utmost agony during the night, no remedy affording her the slightest relief, until an early hour the following morning (Friday,) when death put an end to her sufferings. The fatal event has plunged the family into the utmost grief, as they were by no means prepared to meet with such a bereavement, yet they console themselves with the hope that their loss has been her infinite and eternal gain. (1841-12-25, 2:4)

2792. Extremely Sudden Death.—One of the most alarming sudden dissolutions, which it has been our duty to record for a long time, took place at Cavan, on Saturday last, the 18th instant, teaching us the solemn lesson, which, alas, too seldom reaches the heart to make any permanent impression there—that, "In the midst of life we are in death!" A poor widow, of the name of Campbell, an inmate of a charitable poor-house, on the Farnham-road, a few perches from the town of Cavan, erected by the Rev. Samuel Roberts, of Cootehill, when he was curate of the former place, was on her way thither, after purchasing some groceries in town, which she carried in her apron, suddenly fell on the road, and almost instantaneously expired. Medical aid, in the course of a few minutes, was in attendance, but, as the vital spark had already fled, of course could be of no avail. An inquest was held on the body, on Sunday, when a respectable jury was summoned, and a verdict of, "Died by the visitation of God, was accordingly returned." (1841-12-25, 2:5)

2793. Death of John Beatty West, Esq., M.P.—(From the *Dublin Evening Mail.*)—This is a sorrowful announcement. It will be afflicting intelligence to his friends—it will be heard with regret, even by his political opponents—enemies he had none.—The city—the county—the kingdom at large—will deplore the death of the Member for Dublin. The melancholy event took place this morning (Monday), at an early hour, at his villa at Mount Anville. Mr. West had been for some days labouring under the effects of a severe cold and influenza; but it was not until the afternoon of yesterday that any danger was apprehended. The aid of the most distinguished medical talents was prompt and unceasing—but in vain; fever and inflammation had set in, exhibiting the most alarming symptoms. At the hour of four o'clock this morning he expired, leaving an amiable and interesting family to bewail their domestic bereavement—to society to lament the loss of one of its most accomplished members—and to his country to follow to an early grave with sorrow a patriot as pure, ardent, and disinterested as she had ever given birth to.

The heart refuses at this period to enter on a biographical memoir of this distinguished gentleman. The hand is yet too unsteady to draw portrait of his character. Were it a time for admiration, we might dwell upon the sweetness and placidity of a temper seldom ruffled; upon affections pure, ardent, and permanent; upon manners simple, unaffected and graceful; upon the accomplishments and acquirements of the scholar; the learning, talents and conversational powers of the social companion—the sincerity of the friend, the fidelity of the husband; the blandness of parental love, the purity and wisdom of the politician—the zeal of the patriot—and the total integrity of the man—all of which, in a rare combination of the best qualities of head and heart, distinguished this amiable and lamented gentleman. Few were blessed with more friends—no man ever freer from enemies.

Upon the nature of our own private feelings, we dare not venture to dwell. Such sentiments are neither suited to our position nor fitting for the public eye. If sympathy for their loss can in any way alleviate the affliction of his surviving family, it is bestowed upon them to an extent such as it has never been our lot to witness. This death—alas, how sudden and unlooked for!—has cast a gloom over the whole city; and the merits and services of the public man—great and eminent as they confessedly were—are merged in the affectionate remembrances of the private friend. Even his political rivals and opponents loved him alive, and will honour his memory, now that he is no more.

We have the melancholy consolation of extracting the following notice from the *Morning Register*:—

"Death of J.B. West, Esq.

"We announce with unfeigned regret the death of J.B. West, Esq., one of the members for the city of Dublin.—The melancholy event took place at an early hour yesterday morning, at his villa, Mount Anville. Mr. West had been for some days laboring under the effects of a severe cold; but it was not until the afternoon of Sunday that the disease which carried him off began to manifest dangerous symptoms. On ordinary occasions it is an easy task to speak of the merits, and hold up the good example of departed worth to public approbation; but on an occasion like the present, when the writer feels that he has freqently done wrong to the man whose premature removal he deplores, it is a painful duty for the living to do justice to the character of the dead. Mr. West, however, requires no panegyric. His best and most endearing eulogy may be read in the heartfelt sorrow and unfeigned regret not only of those who agreed, but those who differed with him in sentiment and opinions. Perhaps no public man ever conciliated more of the good-will and respect of his political opponents than Mr. West. He has now ceased from his labours—he has gone down to the grave amidst the tears and regrets of a numerous circle of acquaintances and friends; but his name, and the remembrance of his many virtues and endearing qualities, will long live in the memory of those to whose interests he so generously devoted his time, talents and his purse.

"'Man goeth to this long home and the mourners about the streets,' was the saying of one who had reason to complain about the uncertainties and vicissitudes of this life; and never was the beautiful aphorism of the Scripture better or more forcibly exemplified than on yesterday, when it became known that the representative of Dublin had been removed from the cares and turmoils of this world, to 'that better place, where the wicked cease from troubling and the weary are at rest.'

"Newspaper eulogy is frequently little better than newspaper hyperbole; but we can safely praise the deceased without incurring the risk of having our sentiments misconstrued, or our motives misunderstood. Every one who knew Mr. Ward admired (*continued...*)

2793, continued: ...and respected him. They might dislike the politician, but there was no withstanding the urbanity of the man. They loved the straight-forward honesty of intention, which made him so esteemed in private, and respected in public—they felt a sort of veneration for the integrity of purpose which was one of his most striking characteristics; but they loved him, above all things, for that universal charity and kindliness of disposition which prompted him to make due allowance for all the failings and imperfections of his fellow-mortals. Mr. West, we need hardly say, was warmly attached to his peculiar religious and political opinions, but he never suffered his sentiments on either of those important subjects to interfere with the ordinary intercourse of society. He held and maintained the principles he deemed right, but he did so in such a manner, and in such a spirit, as to conciliate the good-will and respect of those who differed from him. The *Evening Mail* of last night has said, and said truly, that 'even his political rivals and opponents loved him alive, and will honor his memory now that he is no more.'" (1842-01-01, 1:3)

2794. The Church.—Owing to the much lamented demise, of the Rev. Chas. Smith, the late Vicar General of Elphin, the following promotions have now taken place in that Diocese:—The Rev. Henry Hunt, A.M., the Rector of Ahaskeragh, is appointed the Vicar-General, by the Lord Bishop of Kilmore, Elphin, and Ardagh; the Rev. Jos. Morton, appointed Surrogate of Elphin; the Rev. A.T. Gilmor, Surrogate at Sligo; and the Rev. Hugh Murray, Surrogate at Athlone. The Rev. John Maguire of Boyle, will be shortly collated to the Vicarages of Kilemanagh and Boyle. (1842-01-01, 1:4)

2795. Inquest.—An inquest was held by John M'Fadden, Esq., on the 24th ult., on the body of Maria Reilly, who fell dead whilst dancing at a teetotal ball near Kilnaleck, in the county of Cavan, on the evening of the 22d ult. It appeared that she had been in perfect health prior to her decease, and that her death was caused by the bursting of a bloodvessel.—*Impartial Reporter*. (1842-01-01, 3:1)

2796. Hydrophobia from the Bite of a Cat.—A lamentable instance of this disorder terminated in death on Saturday last, about three miles from Portadown, along the side of the river Bann. A person of the name of Patrick M'Connell, an old man, had been bitten by his own cat, which appeared in a rabid state in the month of September; but from the usual remedy being resorted to, and the wounds suddenly healing up, it was supposed no evil results could arise, and when three months had expired, all fears were at an end; but on Wednesday the 15th ultimo, he felt his limbs benumbed—he was stupid and rather dejected, with an incessant coldness, over the whole system. These symptoms were followed with great depression of spirit, which increased into horror of mind with the progress of the disorder; the mouth was parched, and the patient had a strong desire for drink, which, being offered, he involuntarily threw it from him, and a paroxyism [sic] followed. These continued at short intervals till Saturday evening when the patient became exhausted, the eyes fixed, and death ended his sufferings.—*Ulster Times*. (1842-01-01, 3:1)

2797. Effects of Intemperance.—An inquest was held on the 23d inst. on the body of a tinker named Thos. Campbell who was found in a ditch adjoining the road leading from Cavan to Ballyjamesduff. John M'Fadden, Esq., (the coroner) proceeded to the fatal spot attended by Lee M'Kinstry, Esq., the active and intelligent officer in charge of the district, and George Nixon Esq., the Surgeon to the Ballyjamesduff Dispensary. From the evidence, it appeared that the deceased had been drinking, and in endeavouring to make his way home had fallen into the ditch where he remained from Monday evening until Wednesday, prior to his being discovered. The jury found that the deceased had come by his death in consequence of his being under the influence of ardent spirits and being exposed to the effects of the cold. It is worthy of remark that Campbell was a Roman Catholic, and when brought to be interred in the Chapel-yard of Ballyjamesduff, the committee refused to admit his body inside the gate as the friends had neither money to pay the priest his due, nor for the ground the deceased would occupy. Application was made to the Rev. S.H. Lewis for ground in the Church-yard, who immediately consented, provided that the deceased should be buried according to the rites of the Protestant Church. His Friends agreed.—*Fermanagh Reporter*. (1842-01-01, 3:2)

2798. Death from Glanders.—John Hessian, a carrier between Dublin and Ballinrobe, died on Sunday morning, the 26th ult., of this dreadful disease, caught by infection from his own horse. The animal presented some signs of the disease, and about three weeks since the unfortunate owner supposed he might be able to save his beast by cutting out the swelled glands from under the animals jaw. It could not be ascertained that in this operation he suffered a cut. He came to Dublin with the same horse for a loading on the 16th ult. On the 18th he complained of being ill, and on the 22d he was received into the Hardwicke Hospital, under Doctor Corrigan, where he died on the morning of the 26th, with all the usual terribly repulsive symptoms of this formidable poison. Instances of this kind have, of late years, become not unfrequent both in this country and in France. Measures of inspection and prevention are already under consideration in France, and the growing frequency of the occurrence, with the certain termination of the disease in death, calls for something similar in this country. Not only is the disease certain death to the human being who first catches it, but it is equally fatal to those about the sick person should they happen to catch the infection; and some idea may be formed of the terrors inspired even in the medical profession by the disease, when it is known that bed and bedding are burnt which have come in contact with the glanders.—*Saunders's News Letter*. (1842-01-01, 4:4)

2799. A coroner's inquest was held in Derry on Sunday last, on the body of Nancy Green, a servant in the employment of Mr. John Colhoun, gas works. The deceased retired to bed on Saturday night in perfect health, and was found a corps [sic] in the morning. The verdict was—"Died by the visitation of God."
(1842-01-08, 1:4)

2800. His Excellency the Lord Lieutenant, accompanied by his amiable Lady, the Countess De Grey, paid a visit of condolence on Friday last, to Mrs. West, at her villa, Mount Annville, upon the occasion of her recent bereavement. There was a grace, as well as a graciousness, not only in the act itself, but in the manner in which the sad compliment was paid, and in the nature and tendency of the inquiries made in respect of Mrs. West and her afflicted family, which could only emanate from high and delicately-constituted minds.—*Mail*. (1842-01-08, 1:4)

2801. Judge Burton.—We are happy to learn, notwithstanding the recent deplorable event in his family, that Mr. Justice Burton enjoys good health, and that his lordship intends to preside in the Queen's Bench on the first day of next term.—*Evening Post*.
(1842-01-08, 4:4)

2802. The Police have yet received no remuneration for taking the census of the population last year.
(1842-01-15, 1:2)

2803. Most Important Decision of the Twelve Judges—Presbyterian Marriages.—The judges met on Monday in chamber, to consider a point of immense importance to the people of the north of Ireland, reserved by Judge Crampton from the last Armagh assizes.

The question simply was, whether a marriage between a Presbyterian and an Episcopalian Protestant, celebrated by a Presbyterian clergyman, be valid?

The meeting of the judges was private; but we have learned that their lordships have decided by a great majority, that such a marriage is not valid—is, in the eye of the law, NO MARRIAGE AT ALL!

It is impossible to over-estimate the importance of this decision. It will astound and afflict hundreds of the most respectable families in the north of Ireland, where such marriages have been of every-day occurrence, and have never heretofore had their validity brought into question.

There must be, of course, an instant appeal to Parliament on the subject. The decision is *retrospective* as well as *prospective* in its operation; and unless the Legislature pass an act to protect the multitude whom it will affect, its consequences must be really of a terrific character.

But we cannot doubt that the Legislature will interfere promptly and effectively, if the Presbyterians exert themselves for their own protection.

The judges were almost unanimous in this decision, there being ten for it, and only two dissentients—who are understood to have been Baron Foster and Mr. Justice Perrin.—*Register*. (1842-01-15, 3:2)

2804. Notice.—I hereby give Public Notice, that I will not be accountable for any Debt or Debts, contracted after this date by my Wife Honora Skeath, of Monaghan, and also Caution all persons against giving her Credit.

Dated this 14th day of January, 1841.

Richard Skeath.

(1842-01-15, 3:3)

2805. Awful Consequence of Intemperance.—On Friday night last a man named Halligan, a resident of this town, fell a victim to drunkenness. It appeared at the inquest that he had been in the habit of drinking a quart of whiskey each day for a week or a fortnight when the drunken fit set in—those periods of intoxication were far from being infrequent, and his death on Friday was the tragic close of one of those beastly fits of inebriety. Respecting the inquest in this case, a correspondent says, "I should like to know what necessity existed for a coroner's inquest? The man had been drinking for a week and fell by it; but the knowledge of that fact, which was notorious, would not serve the speculator's purpose! I thought the coroner had been paid a fixed annual salary for his services, which would save the functionary the trouble of reckoning his reward by the number of scalps. I know his satellite is paid after that fashion, a guinea, and sometimes two per skull, being demanded. If the services of those gentlemen were limited to mysterious causes of death, it would be a welcome boon to the feelings of humanity and a saving to the pockets of the Cess-payers of Fermanagh." Our respectable and respected coroner would, we doubt not, be happy at receiving a fixed salary from the public; but it is imperative on him, by the act, to take a surgeon to his aid on every inquest.—*Fermanagh Reporter*. (1842-01-22, 1:5)

2806. Law of Marriage.—We understand that the First Presbyterian Congregation of Armagh met, by appointment, on Thursday, in their church, to take into consideration the late decision of the Judges relative to the Presbyterian marriages, with the view of petitioning the Legislature on the subject.
(1842-01-22, 2:4)

2807. There are two livings in the gifts of Trinity College void by the elevation of Dr. O'Brien to the Deanery of Cork, and the death of the Rev. Mr. Maturin. The fellows have declined accepting them. One of the Parishes will, it is supposed, be conferred on the Rev. Mr. Porter, of St. Peter's Dublin.—*Limerick Chronicle*. (1842-01-22, 2:4)

2808. Presbyterian Meeting in Armagh.—The Marriage Question.—On Thursday, a meeting of the members of the First Presbyterian Congregation of Armagh took place in the Rev. Dr. Henry's Meeting-house, for the purpose of taking into consideration, and for adopting petitions in both Houses of Imperial Legislature, to avert, if possible, the danger which is already more than pending.

At a little after the appointed hour, the meeting was opened by an appropriate and earnest prayer for Divine direction as to the proceedings to be adopted on the important subject on which they were met to deliberate.After which,

Mr. Dobbin, J.P., moved, and Mr. Lee M'Kinstry, J.P., seconded the motion, that the Rev. Dr. Henry be requested to take the Chair.

Dr. Henry, on taking the Chair, proceeded to state the objects of the meeting in nearly the following terms:—Christian friends, we are assembled under circumstances painfully interesting to ourselves and others. Never in my memory have the Presbyterians of Ireland been more imperatively called on to exercise their civil privileges in defence of their social and religious liberties than at the present juncture—(Hear, hear.) From our settlement in this country as a branch of the Established Church in Scotland, down to the present time, our Ministers conceived they had the right of solemnizing marriages not only amongst the members of their own communion, but between their own hearers and the constituents of other denominations. Upon this understanding of the civil law we have ever, as a body, acted, and our uniform practice has been sustained by successive decisions from the learned Bench, as well as ratified by repeated acts of the Executive Government. It has frequently happened that miscreants in this province, reckless of the moral obligations which God and Nature imposes, have, through their law advisers, raised the point of the invalidity of Presbyterian marriages between an Episcopalian and one of our people, as a plea against the charge of bigamy, and as a shield against merited retribution, and it has till now as invariably happened that our judges and juries have ruled in favour of our practice. In consequence of this, many have suffered the penalty of transportation, and some are at this moment in banishment, making expiation of their bondage and punishment to the outraged laws of their country. It must be so, else they have been the victims of public cruelty and oppression. A case of this kind I have referred to occurred at Carrickfergus within these five years. Upon the testimony of one of our most respected Ministers,* that he had celebrated a marriage between an Episcopalian and a Presbyterian, the act was, without hesitation, ratified by the judge and jury, notwithstanding that the defence of invalidity was set up and ingeniously argued by counsel, and the bigamist in whose favour it was employed was forthwith transported. It is now twenty-four years since Captain Lethrope, an Episcopalian, was married by Dr. Black, of Derry, to a Miss Marshall, of his congregation. The parties removed to England, where Lethrope resided, and an attempt was afterwards made to deprive his daughter, the issue of this union, of her rightful property upon the plea of the illegality of the Presbyterian marriage performed between her parents. Lethrope himself was a party in this base attempt; and, not content with the iniquity of the disinheritance of his daughter, he added the crime of bigamy to his unnatural guilt. Doctor Black was summoned to England and proved the marriage. Not only was Lethrope defeated in his attempts, but he was transported for seven years, and Miss Lethrope put, by the Chancellor of England, on Dr. Black's testimony and marriage, in the undisturbed possession of all her rights. It has always been our united and individual practice, while manfully asserting our own privileges, to pay all due respect to law and constituted authority. Soon after my ordination, a clergyman of the Church of England, whom I most highly esteem, made a friendly verbal communication to me questioning my right to celebrate marriages in such cases. I had read and heard enough on the subject to satisfy myself, but to convince him, I applied to one of the safest men I knew, and had ample opportunities of being acquainted with the highest local authorities. A man who is an honour to his profession, Mr. Leonard Dobbin, jun.—himself a member of the Established Church—and without a moment's hesitation, he confirmed all my preconceived opinions. About seven years ago, I was summoned to give testimony in this city before our present Assistant Barrister regarding the degradation of one of our Ministers, who, after his deposition, had married an Episcopalian man to a Presbyterian woman. The husband had forsaken his wife, and she brought an action for maintenance. Even this marriage was held good, and I remember how the legal acuteness of the two attornies was unavailing, and how the man was thrown into the expense both of costs and yearly maintenance for his wife. It was then declared that a marriage contract entered into in this country before competent witnesses, if acted on afterwards in the public acknowledgment of man and wife by each other, was good and binding, though the parties might be of different persuasions, and the vow taken even before a layman. But to come to the case which now immediately concerns us—Smith, an Episcopalian, was married by one of my co-Presbyters, the Rev. John Bell, of Clare, to one of his hearers. After some years, he abandons his wife and two children; he removes to Dublin, and there marries and lives with another female. An action of bigamy is brought before Judge Crampton, at our last assizes. Mr. Bell proves the marriage; and though Mr. Whiteside, with his usual power, endeavours to invalidate it on account of the Presbyterianism of the Minister, it is sustained by judge and jury, and, in perfect conformity with previous analagous cases, Smith is sentenced to seven years transportation. But Mr. Whiteside, it appears, carries the question to the twelve judges, a majority of whom, for the first time, affirm the principles that the marriage of a regularly ordained Presbyterian Minister between his hearer and an Episcopalian is null and void. Thus, the man who was judicially doomed is now enjoying all the enlargement of freedom, and that without any change of circumstances or the light of any fresh evidence. I impeach neither the soundness of the judicial decision nor the integrity of her Majesty's Bench. No man entertains a higher opinion of the heads and hearts of the Irish Judges than I do myself, but I adduce these facts to vindicate myself and brethren against the charge of celebrating marriages either ignorantly or illegally. We rested implicitly on the deliverance of judges and the deliberate acts of Governments, and thought ourselves secure. Acting on this principle, nearly one third of my marriages have been of that kind which this decision dissolves, and some of my best friends and nearest relatives have been brought unwittingly by me into a state of public degradation. To argue the law of the case were futile. I take it up, and lay it before you as it stands. It is but justice to the Government to say, that to the last they were determined to transport Smith; and had not the deliverance of the judges necessarily altered that determination, no amount of interest could have prevailed on them to commute his sentence. I have testimony in my possession to this effect, and I conceive this an important and encouraging feature of the case that ought not to be lost sight of. And now, fellow-Christians, consider the awful and distressing circumstances in which we are placed. What is the fact? The marriages of many of you, of multitudes of your fellow-worshippers throughout Ireland, nay, over the face of the world, are dissolved. Your children and theirs, in such cases, are held up before Christendom as illegitimate, their right of inheritance broken, and the securities which you believe sacred and indissoluble, suddenly severed—(Hear, and applause.)—This is a blow that cuts us in the most vulnerable point.—Let a man's property be embezzled, and he may still, amidst the deepest poverty, find an asylum in the affections of his lawful wedded wife, and in the endearments of their legitimate offspring; but, whilst the foundation of his property is tottering, tell him, after years of mutual happiness, that the law disowns his wife, and writes bastardy upon his offspring, you strike him on the heart itself, you wound and blight him in his most hallowed sympathies. And shall we submit to this?—we, who are the very sinews of moral power of this flourishing Province—shall we tamely suffer our rights to be alienated, and our properties placed in jeopardy? The dead in many cases cannot be rescuscitated for another marriage ceremonial. We are most deeply grateful to the Attorney-General for giving us hope regarding the past. We thank him for his noble defence of our privileges, and for his intention of introducing a retrospective measure. We trust he will go farther, and apply the provisions of the Bill to *the future*. Now is the time to have it clearly understood, that less than this will not, cannot, satisfy us. We respect the rights of others; our own we are determined to support. Nothing short of unrestricted liberality to unite our hearers with those of other denominations can satisfy us. We confidently hope that none will be found so exclusive or tyrannical as to compel us to seek for those civil rights to which, by long usage at least, we are entitled, through the religious ceremonies of a Church with which, however respectable, we are not spiritually connected. Let us look for the cordial support of the Members of both Houses of Parliament in obtaining for us a prospective, as well as retrospective, measure of justice. Let that Member of the Legislature, be he Whig or Tory, who fails to stand by us in this struggle, be henceforth esteemed unworthy the support of any Presbyterian. (Applause.) Let all political differences be buried till we are again placed in the honourable position which we thought we held. Let us trust that through Ulster, all division will be forgotten; and with one heart, let us employ every legitimate means for securing, in all coming time, those immunities to which our numbers, wealth, and intelligence, as well as past practice, and the spirit of our glorious Constitution, entitle us. Let petitions from all quarters be poured in, breathing the language of loyal and obedient freemen. Others will assist us—multitudes of other denominations, men of feeling and honor, of justice and brotherly kindness. Many of the clergy and people of the Establishment sympathise with us. They will be anxious, moreover, to remove effectually what would bring us into direct and lamentable collision with them, and naturally produce jealousies and distrust where the most sacred feelings of husbands and fathers are concerned.—The dignitaries of the Church of England, especially those who may this year preside in Parliament, have now a fine opportunity of exercising their exalted powers in advancing our claims, in healing the wounds under which we are smarting, and of producing confidence and peace amidst the population of their respective jurisdictions. We trust that, when concessions have been made to many, privileges long enjoyed will not be wrested from our families. To force, and coerce, and drive us back from our position, in these days of religious freedom, is an experiment which, I pray God, may never be tried upon us. Notwithstanding this decision, and all the legal difficulties that may be raised, it will be ever felt by every right-minded and honourable man, that the wife of his bosom, united to him by the laws of God, through the act of a regularly ordained Minister of the Lord Jesus Christ, and in our case, by a Minister endowed and recognised by the State, is still united to him by moral and religious ties, sacred and dissoluble, which God has bound, and no man can break asunder, without incurring (*continued...*)

2808, continued: ...heinous guilt. And now, friends, before I call upon you to move and second the resolutions which are before me, I will give you an instance of the first fruits of this decision. I have here the documents detailing the facts of the case to which I allude.—A woman with four children applied on Tuesday last for admission into our workhouse, who had been [*illegible*]ed [deserted?] by her husband, after having been married to her for fourteen years, under the very pretence which this decision afforded him. He has abandoned her, and married a female in another quarter of this country, and her children, because of this, were publicly, on last Tuesday, on the books of the workhouse, designated as bastards. (Great sensation.) This is surely the time, when such occurrences as this are taking place amongst us, to be up and doing. The Rev. Doctor, after apologising for the absence of some of the leading members of the congregation, on account of sickness, and professional duties calling them elsewhere, concluded amid the warm applause of the meeting.

Mr. Dobbin, J.P., rose to move the first resolution.—The case to which he (the Chairman) had lately referred, came before him in his magisterial capacity. He had taken the informations of the woman against her husband, but, on account of the late decision, he was unable to act on them. By the late decision, the children of great numbers of them are rendered illegitimate, at least in the eye of the law; and if some healing measure is not adopted, the most disastrous consequences will ensue, causing utter confusion amongst the whole of the Presbyterian community. It was the more imperative on them to use every exertion for a satisfactory settlement of the matter, as a number of their young friends were, no doubt, looking forward to enter into the matrimonial state, who would be placed in a most unpleasant predicament, if things were allowed to remain as they were for any length of time. Mr. Dobbin then proceeded to read the resolution, which was seconded by Dr. Bryce, and carried unanimously.

Mr. John Kane moved the second resolution, which was seconded by Dr. Bell, who spoke as follows:—For many years, as you are all aware, it has been the practice in this country for Presbyterian Ministers to unite their hearers with members of the Established Church. This practice, though it may have been impugned elsewhere, was never until now formally condemned in the Courts of common law. On the contrary, it has been supported by legal decisions in criminal cases, and even in the Consistory Court of London, which is an Ecclesiastical Court, this practice may be said to have received the sanction of Lord Stowell, the presiding judge—for in the year 1811, in the case of *Dalrymple v. Dalrymple*, he is reported to have said, that, until the 26th of George II., the marriage law of Scotland and England was the same. Hence, presuming that the marriage law of Ireland was also similar to it, it has been inferred that in all the three countries, marriage was merely a civil contract, and that the performance of the ceremony between any parties, by any minister, could not render the union invalid unless it were forbidden by some special and prohibitory enactment.—Now, I do not mean to defend this expression of Lord Stowell's or the inference which has been drawn from it. I believe them both now to be indefensible, and I mention this merely to show that our ministers had some excuse for persevering in the practice of the above-mentioned, though we may regret that they had not the matter placed on a more certain foundation than this. It is true there exists no statute positively forbidding them to solemnise marriages of this kind, but I would draw your attention to two whose tenor seems to me to be very decisive on the subject—the 11th George II. chap. 10, and 21st George III. chap. 25. (Here the learned gentleman read the clauses of the Act referred to.) Now, does it not follow clearly from these, that before the first, Dissenting Clergymen could not marry even their own hearers, and that, before the second, they could only marry them after the minister and the parties had taken the oaths prescribed by the 6th George the First. Now, if these statutes were necessary to enable them to unite their own hearers and Roman Catholics, may we not fairly presume another statute would be necessary to enable them to marry Episcopalians. No such enabling statute is to be found—so that I think we must, in all candour, acquiesce in the opinion recently expressed by the Court of Queen's Bench. It may appear strange to some of you, upon this occasion, I should support the decision which has called us together to-day. But I do not think that such a course is at all appropriate. I believe in the propriety and stability of that decision; and if I have persuaded any of you to think with me, you will the more readily feel the necessity we are under of immediate and effectual relief. The learned gentleman concluded by seconding the resolution, which was passed unanimously.

The other resolutions were then separately proposed and carried, after which

Dr. Henry read a paragraph from the *Newry Telegraph*, which stated that means were being taken by the Law Officers of the Crown to have a bill prepared and brought in for the purpose of legalising all such marriages as the one which had been the source of so much unpleasantness to the Presbyterians of the North of Ireland. He said he had lately been one of a number who had drawn up the heads of a bill on the subject, and he would likely be one of those who would carry that bill to London on the ensuing meeting of Parliament. At the meeting at which the preparations of that bill was decided on, he was happy to say that there was but one opinion on the subject, and that was one of perfect unanimity.

The meeting then separated.—*Newry Telgraph.*

*The speaker alluded, it was understood, to the Minister of Lisburn Congregation.—*Reporter.*

(1842-01-29, 1:1)

2809. Mr. Fannin, of Leeson-street, Dublin, who died a few days since, has left fifty thousand pounds to each of his daughters. (1842-01-29, 1:3)

2810. It is said that Lord Morpeth is about to be married to a fair American, the daughter of a wealthy merchant of Boston, named Appleton. (1842-01-29, 1:3)

2811. The wife of a pensioner was burned to death at Lowtherstown, on Friday night last. (1842-01-29, 2:2)

2812. Presbyterian Marriages.—Last Sunday, after Divine Service in the Presbyterian Meeting-house of Donoughmore, county Down, a petition to both Houses of Parliament, in reference to the marriage question, was unanimously adopted by the congregation. (1842-01-29, 2:3)

2813. Sudden Death.—An inquest was held by John M'Faddin, Esq., M.D., coroner, in the gaol of Cavan, on Sunday last, the 23d instant, on view of the body of one of the female prisoners named Judy Dolan, who was found dead in her cell on the previous evening. It was at first supposed that the unfortunate creature had taken away her own life by some secret strategem; for, although ailing a little for some time, immediate death was not at all expected. She was committed to prison some months since, charged with having murdered her husband. Since her incarceration she was delivered of a child, who is still living, and not more than two months old at present—is still in the gaol; none of its hapless mother's friends have as yet applied for the infant in order to bring it up. The jury returned a verdict of "Died of water on the brain," which result, we are happy to say, removed the former unpleasant and harrowing suspicion. She was a tall, sturdy, middle-aged woman. (1842-01-29, 3:2)

2814. Presbyterian Marriages.—This subject, which has created a fearful excitement in Ulster, is now warmly taken up by the different Presbyteries in the Province, and petitions to the legislature are in course of signature in every district of the country. The tremendous effect which the decision of the Judges, in direct opposition to long established usages, would have upon the morality and the propriety of Ulster would be unlimited, if a salutary measure were not instantly adopted to prevent the evil. We know enough of human nature to be aware that in the many thousand marriages celebrated in the objectionable manner, hundreds, nay, thousands would gladly embrace an opportunity to dissolve bonds which incongruity of taste or dissimilarity of habits, altered circumstances, poverty or sickness have rendered irksome to both parties, and the doubtful position those persons would occupy, being actually "The Married Unmarried," would prevent them from ever entering into the holy covenant again, and although not in the sight of God, yet in the sight of man and man's law the stigma of bastardy would attach to their families; and when we consider the fearful quantity of litigation it would cause, when we know that property, instead of descending from father to son, would be claimed by distant relations, and a war for possession waged in every Court in the land, we confess we shrink from the contemplation with horror, and deem it to have been much better than our learned Bench had allowed the usage and precedent of centuries to be interpreted into law rather than to have dived into musty statutes, enacted for bigoted and perilous times, for the purpose of saving a malefactor from the well-deserved punishment of expatriation. The object of Government is to protect the weak against the oppression of the strong, and to secure the greatest good to the greatest number even to the inconvenience of the few. The obnoxious decision has had the contrary effect. It has entailed a multitude of evil upon the many and saved one man from the penalty of a crime, therefore it cannot be recognised as the law of a nation though it may be the law of a statute book long deemed obsolete; and there can be no greater evil to a country than the revival of an obsolete law, which has gradually fallen into disuse until none are acquainted with its existence except a few persons whose propensities lead them to pour over the mouldy records of antiquity. It is like setting a trap for posterity—it is strewing rushes over the mouth of the chasm, that the unwary may be led unwittingly to plunge into destruction. We sincerely admire the spirit with which the Presbyterians are acting—and it may be, perhaps, as well that this decision has been come to, because it lays the pit-fall bare to the eye and they must and will fill up the cavern which was only dangerous while concealed. This is a propitious moment to apply to our Conservative Government, pleased as they must be, and grateful for the unflinching support of the sturdy Northerns during the late arduous struggle for a Protestant Government. Sir Robt. Peel will remember that the men of Belfast first broke the chain that the Agitator was forging for Ulster, and that our Presbyterian brethren aided manfully in rending the last shred of his power at the Dublin Election. Loyal, firm, and uncompromising, they have formed a prominent portion of the Protestant force of Ireland, and Mr. Borland was not far astray when he said that it was the Presbyterians who held Ireland for the British Government. The line of demarkation between their Church and Popery is stronger marked than our own—and that between them and us a shadowy and ill defined difference—why then, we ask, should their ministers be deprived of the power with which they are worthy of being trusted, and which is given freely to our own institution, if their ministers submit to the restrictions and governances under which our Episcopal Clergy exercise the right. The Presbyterians have been in the habit of performing the marriage ceremony in private houses, which custom may be so abused, and marriage is so private, to suit circumstances, that it may be difficult to prove them afterwards and thus cause litigation in the descent of property, and (*continued...*)

2814, continued: ...evil report of those persons so married. We would, therefore, deem it right when the power (which we hope will be the case) is conferred upon Presbyterian ministers to unite their hearers to persons of any other denomination, that a restriction compelling them to perform the ceremony publicly in their chapels, will form part of the statute. They cannot object to that, as the Episcopalian Clergy are obliged to submit to it, and if they only seek an equality in power, they should also abide by the same limits. (1842-02-05, 2:3)

2815. Presbyterian Marriages.—Monaghan Presbytery. —On Tuesday last, there was a numerous and influential meeting of the Presbytery of Monaghan, at the Meeting-house in Dublin-street, for the purpose, amongst other matters, of discussing the necessity of petitioning the Legistlature to remedy the effects of the late important decision of the judges upon marriages by Presbyterian ministers.—Immediately adjacent to the reading-desk, we observed the Moderator of Monaghan Presbytery, the Rev. Mr. Smith, of Glasslough; Rev. Messrs. Bleckley, White, Rankin, M'Meehan, Borland, Elliott, Hendrum, Lyons, M'Cawley, and several others, with whose names we were not acquainted.

The Moderator opened the meeting by prayer, and called upon Mr. Bleckley to move the first resolution, to the effect that it was necessary to urge the Moderator of the Assembly to call an aggregate meeting in Belfast, to petition the Legislature against the Intrusion and Patronage Question in the Church of Scotland.

Mr. Bleckley proposed a resolution, that a requisition be forwarded to the Moderator of the General Assembly, requesting him to call a meeting of the Assembly for an early day, to take into consideration the present position of the Church of Scotland, and our duty in respect to it. [*Outline ensues of main points made in Mr. Bleckley's speech of nearly an hour and three quarters, including references to the Established Church, James I, Charles II, James II, Queen Anne, England, Parliament, Protestantism, Presbyterianism, Bolingbroke, Marnock, Edwards, the Presbyterian Church in Ireland, the Presbyterians in Ulster, churches in the south-eastern part of the Austrian dominions, the Puseyite College of Perth;Dr. Simeon, a Roman Catholic Bishop; and, Dr. Baines, of Bath.*]

Mr. Hendrum, of Middletown, seconded the resolution of proposed by Mr. Bleckley.

Mr. Borland proposed the second resolution upon the Marriage Question, and said—He rejoiced exceedingly at the resolution come to by the meeting respecting the Scotch Church; he approved also of the able and energetic address by which his Rev. brother, Mr. Bleckley, had preluded the resolution, and he hoped their Scotch brethren would not impute to a want of cordial sympathy, or to indifference, the postponement of their interference to the present moment. [*Further discussion of Irish support for the Scotch church.*] He would now call the attention of the meeting to a subject of paramount importance to the Presbyterian Church in Ireland. What he alluded to was the decision come to by the judges, respecting the marriages of Episcopalians and Presbyterians by Presbyterian clergymen. [*Further discussion, including references to: a brief outline of the history of Presbyterians in Ireland, and marriages celebrated by them.*] Twenty-five years had not elapsed since the legality of those marriages were first called in question—not in Ireland, but in England itself. The circumstances were these:—A Capt. Lethrope, an English Episcopalian, was stationed with his regiment in Derry; he was there married by Dr. Black, the Presbyterian Minister, to one of his hearers—a Miss Marshall. Subsequent to the marriage, they removed to England, and there Lethrope thought proper to abandon his wife and marry another woman. This man endeavoured, not only to destroy the wife of his bosom, but to defraud his only child of the property she was entitled to, and the plea he put in through his counsel was, that Miss Lethrope was illegitimate, as he (Lethrope) was an Episcopalian, and his marriage to Miss Marshall, by Dr. Black, was illegal; but, what was the decision of the highest law officers of the English crown?—Aye, the Chancellor of England pronounced the marriage a good marriage, and Lethrope was sentenced to seven years' transportation; and that Chancellor, if he still existed, could as easily wipe out the decision of those judges who decreed the contrary, as he (Mr. Borland) could lift or lay down the book before him. Again, it was not more than five years since the Rev. Mr. Henderson, at Carrickfergus, prosecuted a man for bigamy, whom he had united to a Presbyterian. In that case, Counsellor Scriven raised the objection, but the honest and upright Judge Moore overruled the objection, and refused to allow him to examine witnesses to sustain his objection. But it appeared that a new light had broken in on the Irish Bench, and they had discovered that, to use the language of Archdeacon Stopford—these marriages were pretended ceremonies, and that the Lord Chancellor and Judge Moore must have been doating when they decided on their validity.

(Here Mr. Boreland declared the circumstances attending the case of Smith, out of which the present question arose, but which has been several times laid before the public, and is unnecessary to repeat.) [*Mr. Borland outlined the difficulties ensuing from the present situation, concluding with:*] He would, therefore, move that the resolution he held in his hand be added to the previous one, requiring the Moderator of Synod to call a meeting for the joint purpose of petitioning in favour of the Church of Scotland, and for the necessary measures to rectify the evils arising from the late decision of the judges.

The Rev. Mr. Elliott, of Smithboro, seconded the resolution, which was passed unanimously, after which the Presbytery went into the routine business of the day. (1842-02-05, 2:3) *Note: This transcription is an extract of the original article, which runs to 2-1/4 columns.*

2816. Fatal and Melancholy Accident.—On the 26th ult., a fine, industrious young man named Edward Reilly, employed at the Ballyhaise mills, Cavan, proceeded to oil one of the wheels of that concern, and, in order to keep himself clean, put a sack or bag unfortunately about him, which accidentally caught on some part of the wheel and became entangled, so that the unfortunate young man could not succeed in his attempts to extricate himself from his perilous situation; the consequence was, that in spite of every effort made by those who witnessed the occurrence to stop the wheel, they could not possibly succeed in doing so, until, painful to relate, his arms and legs were broken, and otherwise so awfully bruised and lacerated that he died almost immediately. An inquest was duly held on view of the body, when a verdict of "Accidental death" was returned. Poor Reilly was the sole support of an aged mother and younger brother, who is an invalid. (1842-02-05, 3:1)

2817. To the Editor of the *Northern Standard*.—Sir—May I beg you will be good enough to contradict one or two erroneous statements which I unfortunately made in the short article I sent you about the inquest held in Cavan gaol, on view of the body of Judy Dolan. I wrote in such haste that I had not time to make inquiry from a proper source, as to the truth of every minutiae of the case. I gave the statements as I had heard them spoken of by several persons, whose words I did not then doubt in the slightest degree. It appears she was not found dead in her cell, but died in hospital, where she had been for ten days previous to her dissolution, the utmost care having been taken of her, and died, I might say, in the presence of Dr. Roe, the physician of the gaol, as he had been in attendance on her to the moment of her death, nor was there the slightest suspicion of her having committed suicide.—The other particulars are strictly correct. I would be sorry that an impression should be made on the public mind, to the effect, that the officers of the Cavan prison are not most attentive and correct in the discharge of their respective duties, and regret that the article in question had a tendency to lead the public to suppose the reverse.

I remain, dear Sir,
Yours faithfully,
A Cavan Correspondent.
Cavan, Feb. 1st, 1842.
(1842-02-05, 3:1)

2818. The Census—The Constabulary.—It is said that the accounts are now nearly made out, and that, in a short time, all who have any claim will be paid for their services. This will be good news for the Constabulary. (1842-02-05, 3:1)

2819. On Saturday week a poor woman named M'Donald was drowned while crossing a footstick on the lands of Clonmacfelemy, near Lisnaskea. (1842-02-05, 3:1)

2820. Mr. Maguire, an apothecary, died suddenly on Monday, in Maguiresbridge, in a fit of apoplexy. (1842-02-05, 3:1)

2821. An Epitaph.
Selected from Robinson of Cambridge.

Bold infidelity, turn pale and die,
Under this stone an infant's ashes lie,
Say, is it lost or saved?
If death's by sin, it sinned, for it lies here,
If heaven's by works, in heaven it can't appear;
Ah! reason, how depraved!
Revere the Bible's sacred page,
For there the knot's untied;
It died, for Adam sinned;
It lives, for Jesus died.

Amicus Veritatis.
Cootehill, Jan. 29th, 1842.
(1842-02-05, 3:2)

2822. Awful Loss of Life and Property.—We have just read a letter from Captain York, of the *Mayflower*, now at Ardbear Harbour, Clifden, in which he details his suffering upon Tuesday night last, hav-drawn [sic] his anchors, and lost his rudder and jib sail. He also communicates the melancholy intelligence of the loss of 35 fishing boats upon the same night with crews of from five to six persons in each boat, making a total loss of life of 170 to 180 unfortunate persons. This event took place to the north of Sline head.—*Galway Vindicator*. (1842-02-05, 4:3)

2823. Melancholy Shipwreck.—We regret to have this day again to record another shipwreck, but accompanied with more melancholy circumstances than the one mentioned in our last. At daybreak, on Wednesday morning, a schooner, the *Sarah*, of Waterford, Thomas Rossiter, master, sadly disabled, was seen to run ashore at Rastoonstown, a few yards west of Honor, where the sea continued to beat over her in mountains. The crew, five in number, were seen in the rigging, and although crowds, anxious to render every possible assistance, were within a few yards, all attempts proved fruitless. Benumbed with cold, and dreadfully beaten by the fury of the waves, the unfortunate men dropped one by one from the rigging, and melancholy to state, all perished save one seaman. The *Sarah* was laden with culm from Llanelly, and bound to Bannow. She has become a total wreck.—*Wexford Conservative*. (1842-02-05, 4:3)

2824. Another Melancholy Wreck.—On Wednesday morning a ship of about 600 tons, having lost her fore and mizen masts, struck on the Ring off the Saltees. When the wind veered to the N.W. she drove over the reef, and stranded on the Great Saltees Island. She is a Maltese, laden with wheat for Liverpool, and had seventeen hands on board, six of whom have perished. Fortunately there were some farm servants of Mr. Parie's on the island, who rendered (*continued...*)

2824, continued: ...every assistance to the crew as they reached the shore, else it is probable that none would have survived. Owing to the tremendous surf, no boats could put off from the main land until Thursday, when a portion of sails were brought on shore, and placed in charge of Captain Butler, R.N., of the coastguard. We find that the unfortunate vessel is the *Uronia* of and from Malta, Angela Marengo, master. The agent for the under-writers, Mr. Harper, has taken charge and acted with his well-known attention on these occasions.— *Wexford Conservative.* (1842-02-05, 4:3)

2825. Melancholy Occurrence.—This morning, at a quarter to one o'clock, as a private of the 12th Lancers, who had been in custody at the station-house of the C division of police for intoxication, was being led home by a sergeant and three of his comrades to the barracks, the unfortunate man, when close to the metal Bridge, made a race from his companions, and either flung himself or was precipitated over the Liffey wall. The policemen on duty ran for ropes and a boat, and every effort was made to save the wretched sufferer, but in vain. The body has not yet been found. —*Mail.* (1842-02-05, 4:4)

2826. The Marriage Question.—The Rev. Mr. Fleming, Minister of the Presbyterian Congregation of Cavan, has received the copy of a petition addressed to the House of Lords, and a like petition for the House of Commons, from Counsellor Gibson, of Belfast, who is at present in Dublin, with several clergymen from the North, devising measures to redress the grievances of the Presbyterians in the late decision of the twelve judges on the marriage question. (1842-02-12, 1:4)

2827. Presbyterian Marriages.—A very large and respectable meeting was held in the Second Presbyterian Church, Ballybay, on Wednesday, the 9th instant, at 12 o'clock, noon, to consider the late decision of the majority of the Irish Judges respecting Presbyterian Marriages. Samuel Cunningham, Esq., J.P., of Crieve, was called to the chair. After a few remarks from the Chairman, the Rev. M. M'Dowell moved, and Thomas M'Murry, Esq., seconded the first resolution, which was unanimously passed—"That we have heard with surprise and regret the late decision to which a majority of the Irish judges lately come [sic], declaring all marriages hitherto celebrated by Presbyterian clergymen, between Presbyterians and Episcopalians, null and void." The next resolution was moved and an excellent speech by the Rev. John H. Morell, and seconded by James M'Cullagh, Esq., and unanimously agreed to—"That the view now taken of the subject by the learned judges is directly opposed to the principles on which, in all time past, they have acted in administering the laws in the North of Ireland." The third resolution was moved by the Rev. David Bell, Derryvalley, and seconded by Mr. J.H. M'Ketterick, and passed unanimously—"That the natural consequence of the late decision is to induce unprincipled members of society to desert those whom they have solemnly vowed to protect and cherish, and to unsettle a large amount of property in this kingdom, hitherto held by an unquestioned title." The fourth resolution was moved by Mr. John Breakey, of Drumskelt, and seconded by Jas. M'Murry, Esq.,—"That we are impelled, by a sense of justice to ourselves, to come forward in defense of our dearest rights, and to petition the Legislature to pass an act, not only legalising all past marriages, solemnized under these circumstances, but prospectively securing to regularly ordained and recognised Ministers of the Presbyterian Church the right they enjoyed for time immemorial, of celebrating marriage between members of their own and all other denominations. The fifth resolution was moved by James Reid, M.D., Esq., and seconded by J. M'Cullagh, Esq.,—"That we earnestly call upon all our Presbyterian brethren to co-operate with us in vigorously urging upon the Parliament the duty and propriety of granting to the Presbyterians of Ireland an immediate and satisfactory settlement of this question. A copy of the petition was then read by the Rev. Mr. Bell; it was adopted and largely signed by the meeting. Thanks were voted to the chairman, and the assembly separated about 3 o'clock. (1842-02-12, 3:1)

2828. We copy the following from "The New Monthly Belle Assemblee," for January:—

The Soldier's Bride.
By Mrs. C.B. Wilson.

Nay, dearest! chase these tears away,
Though they enhance thy beauty;
The bugle sounds—I must obey
The stern commands of duty!

Unclasp these circling arms that hang
Their snowy links to bind me;
And let me think, without a pang,
On the Bride I leave behind me.

Again the echoing bugle calls!
One kiss, and then we sever;
And, oh! I believe, whate'er befalls,
My heart is thine for ever!

I swear it by this lingering tear,
Unchanging thou shalt find me,
As I believe the love sincere
Of the Bride I leave behind me!

And when this farewell hour is past,
And Hope comes gently stealing,
Like morn's faint tints, that radiance cast,
The day's return revealing;

Thou'lt own how vain it was to mourn
The lot that Fate assigned me;
And smiles will greet my glad return,
To the Bride I leave behind me.
(1842-02-12, 4:1)

2829. Downpatrick.—On Thursday, the members of the second Presbyterian Congregation in this town signed petitions to both houses of Parliament, praying that the Legislature would ratify the marriages hitherto celebrated between Presbyterians and Episcopalians by Presbyterian clergymen, and declare similar marriages to be valid in future, as they were always considered to be prior to the late decision of the twelve Judges. The first Congregation had also a meeting lately upon the same subject.—*Downpatrick Recorder.* (1842-02-12, 4:4)

2830. Law of Marriage.—Meeting of Presbyterians in Derry.—A large and influential meeting of the Presbyterian inhabitants of Derry was held in the first Presbyterian Church on Thursday evening, the 3d inst. for the purpose of taking into consideration what measures it would be most advisable for them to adopt in consequence of the recent alarming decision of the Court of Queen's Bench, regarding the marriage law of Ireland. Shortly after six o'clock, the following clergymen and gentlemen took their places on the platform:—John A. Smyth, Esq. Rev. H. Wallace, J.T. Mackay, Esq. John Mann, Esq. Rev. Wm. M'Clure, Rev. James Crawford, Wm. Leathem, Esq. John Bond, Esq. Rev. James Denham, Wm. Haslett, Esq. John Leathem, Esq. Patrick Gilmour, Esq. Doctor Hamilton, J.W. Johnstone, Esq. Rev. — Brown (Buncrana), James Thomas, Esq. S.L. Crawford, Esq. Rev. J. Canning, (Malin). M. Smyth was in the chair, and Mr. Crawford acted as secretary.—Several excellent speeches were delivered in the course of the evening, and a number of resolutions were agreed to, calculated to forward the object of the meeting. (1842-02-12, 4:4)

2831. The Presbytery of Ards, at their last meeting, on Jan. 25, resolved unanimously, the Moderator of the General Assembly shall be requested to call a meeting of that Court early in February, to deliberate on the subject of marriages celebrated by Presbyterian Ministers, and to consider the present situation of the Church of Scotland, as to the question of patronage. (1842-02-12, 4:4)

2832. Presbyterian Marriages.—On Wednesday last, the Presbytery of Magherafelt held a special meeting in Magherafelt in order to take into account what was its duty respecting the late decision.—After being met and constituted, various resolutions were proposed and passed unanimously—the general object and spirit of which were expressive of the astonishment which the late decision of the Judges excited, and of a determination to use all lawful means to influence the Government to pass a law which would, both for the past and future, save Presbyterians from such insecurity as that, because of a legal technicality, as expressed by Sir R. Peel, thousands of cases both of property and character could be disturbed. One peculiar feature of these resolutions was, that it was the duty of all Protestants, particularly those of the Episcopalian Church, to lend their aid in the present difficulty. After recommending all the congregations under their care to forward petitions on this subject without delay, it was determined that, except there could be a satisfactory adjustment of the matter as soon as could be reasonably expected, it would be advisable on the part of the Moderator to call a meeting of the Assembly. A petition to both Houses was then signed by the ministers and elders. (1842-02-19, 1:5)

2833. Newry Presbytery—Church of Scotland—Presbyterian Marriages.—On Tuesday last, the stated meeting of the Presbytery was held in the Presbyterian Church of the first Congregation, Sunday-street, Newry, Rev. William M'Gowan, Moderator—when they came to the unanimous resolution of respectfully requesting the Moderator to convene a meeting of the Assembly to take such steps as may seem necessary, in order to aid the Church of Scotland in the entire abolition of Patronage. It was unanimously resolved, to petition both Houses of Parliament, praying the Legislature not only to render valid all marriages between members of the Church of England and Presbyterians, celebrated by Presbyterian clergymen, but also to introduce into any bill that may be introduced a prospective clause, recognising the right of Presbyterian Ministers in Ireland to unite in marriage the people of their Church with the members of other communions. (1842-02-19, 1:5)

2834. Call of the General Assembly.—We are glad to announce to our readers that the Moderator is about to convene the Assembly for Wednesday, the 9th March, to meet in May-street Church of Scotland and [consider] the late decision of the Judges respecting Presbyterian marriages. (1842-02-19, 4:5)

2835. The Lord Bishop of Cork, Cloyne, and Ross, has presented the Rev. Wm. Fisher, A.B., curate of Kilmore, to the rectory of Kilmore, vacant by the death of the late Rev. Francis Langford. (1842-02-26, 1:2)

2836. The Rev. William Waller, of Castletown, has appointed himself to the rectory of Kilcornan, vacant by the death of the Rev. F. Langford. The vicarage of Chapel Russell, heretofore held by the Rev. Mr. Waller, reverts to the Bishop of Limerick. Its revenue is only £62 a-year, but Mr. Waller paid £75 to a curate for doing the duty. (1842-02-26, 1:2)

2837. Important Announcement.—Presbyterian Marriages.—With sincere pleasure we announce, on what, will be considered excellent authority, that the *prospective* measure so much desiderated by Irish Presbyterians, in reference to the Marriage question, will be granted by the Government. We hasten to place the documents from which we derive the pleasing intelligence in the hands of our readers:—

London, Feb. 11, 1842.

My Dear Sir—I have this moment received your letter of the 9th, and I lose no time in (*continued...*)

2837, continued: ...replying to it. On my arrival in London, I felt it my duty *immediately* to have a communication with Government on the late alarming decision of the Judges respecting marriages by Presbyterian ministers. I represented the strong feeling of alarm that prevailed in the North of Ireland; and I have the satisfaction to inform you and your congregation, that I received assurance that a law would be *immediately passed* to render all marriages legal and valid that have taken place; and also a law would be enacted to legalise future marriages. I have spoken to Dr. Cooke on the subject, who is in London; and he seemed satisfied that the matter would be all arranged to the satisfaction of the Presbyterian Church. I shall have much pleasure in presenting your petition when it arrives. You only do me common justice in saying—"that I have always been a steady and sincere friend of the Presbyterians"—and I beg to assure, that I shall, at all times be happy to sup- [sic] their just rights.—Believe me, my dear Sir, yours very truly.

Robert Bateston.

Rev. Wm. Browne, Upper Cumber.

The correspondence which follows is no less satisfactory than the above, as being in a great degree confirmatory of it:—

London, February 14, 1842.

Sir.—On my arrival at the House of Lords this day, I was favoured with your letter and accompanying petition. I have presented the latter, with others of a similar purport, and I can truly assure you that I have real pleasure in rendering any service to such respectable petitioners. I have the honour to be your faithful servant,

Starford.

Rev. Wm. Browne, Buncrannar [sic].

House of Commons, Feb. 15, 1842.

Dear Sir—I had the pleasure of presenting the petition from Buncrana, which you were so good as to entrust to me. I have great satisfaction in informing you that measures are in a state of forwardness to legalize the marriages that have been already solemnised, and to provide for future celebration.—Faithfully yours,

Edward Conolly.

Rev. Wm. Browne, Buncrannan [sic].

House of Commons, Feb 14, 1842.

Dear Sir—I am in receipt of your letter of the 9th inst., and the petition accompanying it. The latter I will take an early opportunity of presenting in the House of Commons. The circumstances which have occasioned your application to the legislature indicate a strange and anomalous state of the law, and have already engaged the attention of the Prime Minister who has announced his intention of forthwith introducing a bill, declaring the validity of all the marriages heretofore solemnised, which are called in question by the recent decision of the Judges. This announcement will go far to relieve the anxiety and dismay which must pervade so vast a number of my intelligent fellow-countrymen of the Presbyterian persuasion. As regards the future, the Prime Minister stated the subject was so very important that the Cabinet must take time to consider it, but that they should do so immediately, with a view to its adjustment, and bring forward a measure relating to it as early as possible, consistent with due and mature deliberation. This will, I confidently hope, prove satisfactory to you and to the Presbyterian Church, and eventually satisfy the just and reasonable expectations of your hearers. You may depend upon my rendering my humble aid in any way I can to procure an adjustment of this interesting and serious question.—I beg to remain, dear Sir, obediently yours,

John Young.

Rev. W. Sweeney, Killishandra.

(1842-02-26, 3:2)

2838. The General Assembly.—The meeting of the General Assembly, which is to take place on the 9th March, is looked forward to with the greatest interest by the Irish Presbyterians. Two subjects of vast importance are to come under consideration; the one, a question in which the Assembly and the congregations under its care have a deep personal interest—the late decision of the Judges on Presbyterian marriages; the other, a matter not less dear—the cause of their beloved mother Church of Scotland. The meeting, we have not the slightest doubt, will be an effective one. The sentiments and resolutions of the representatives of Ireland's 700,000 Presbyterians—the half of all the Protestants in the country—men not the least loyal, peaceable, industrious, and intelligent subjects of her Majesty's dominions—will have their due weight both in the Cabinet and in the two Houses of Parliament. They will rouse Ministerial apathy, banish Ministerial indifference, and awake Ministerial attention.

With respect to the first question, Presbyterian marriages—we observe that the Government are proceeding with sufficient promptitude, to bring forward the pitiful half-measure which they announced their intention to give for the present.—Lord Elliot, on Friday, in the House of Commons gave notice "that he would, on the 24th (Thursday next) move for leave to bring in a Bill to legalize marriages celebrated in Ireland, by Dissenting Ministers, between Dissenters and members of the Established Church." Taking this vaguely expressed notice, in connection with the previous explanations of the Duke of Wellington in the House of Lords, and Sir Robert Peel in the House of Commons, that a measure was in preparation for legalizing those marriages between Presbyterians and Episcopalians, which have been celebrated by Presbyterian ministers, and that further time would be taken to consider the whole question—we may conclude that a retrospective measure only is about to be brought forward. We are perfectly serious in expressing our deliberate opinion that it would be better for Presbyterians to remain as they are, even with the adverse decision of the Judges staring them in the face, than that a merely retrospective measure should pass.—Why do we advance this apparently strange opinion? For the following reasons. A new law on this subject, of the kind stated, would assume as its basis that the marriages in question are illegal, a position which even the decision of the Judges has not established. It is true that in the case of Smith, in a meeting of ten of the twelve Judges, owing to the neutrality of three, five were permitted, when the common law was never taken into account, and there was no counsel to plead the cause of the Presbyterians, to make a decision which liberated the prisoner. This decision, however, would not be more binding upon individual Judges no more than the decision respecting, the beneficial interest clause in the *Reform Act*. As in that case, two classes of electors are respectively admitted to the enjoyment of the elective franchise by Conservative and Liberal Assistant-Barristers; so, in the cases which involved the validity of the Presbyterian marriages, there would be two classes of Judges making opposite decisions. Baron Foster, or Judge Perrin, if a case of bigamy, similar to that of Smith, came before them, might transport the prisoner; and even some of the five, who have created so much uneasiness in the north by their decision, might, when they heard through the lawyer full evidence and argument on both sides, pursue the same course. Thus the law would remain in a state of uncertainty, one Judge taking one view of it, and another precisely the contrary—a state of things, however unpleasant, much to be preferred to the state after the passing of the contemplated bill, when it is certain the future marriages, of the kind under consideration, would be illegal. We may be wrong in this opinion, but whether we be right or wrong, the Presbyterian Ministers and people should make every possible exertion to prevail upon the Government to pass a complete bill, both ratifying past marriages, and declaring the future to be valid. The question is not so difficult or complicated as the question of the Corn Laws or Finance, which require time or consideration. It requires little time to settle the point—will we ratify by a declaratory enactment, the rights which Presbyterian Ministers have enjoyed for two hundred and thirty years in Ireland—rights which have never been successfully impugned till now? If it be right that past Presbyterian marriages should be ratified by law, it is equally right that the future should be celebrated not "in ignorance of law," as Sir R. Peel as rather carelessly stated, but in accordance with the law, as laid down by most eminent lawyers, and as acted on by Judges of the land; but if they had been celebrated in ignorance of the law, that would be a poor plea for their ratification in a country where it is assumed that every man is acquainted with the law. To ratify the past marriages, because they were celebrated in ignorance of the law, would be unconstitutional; there are higher grounds for their ratification, and these equally plead for the future as well as the past.

The several Presbyteries and congregations in connection with the assembly have done their duty in holding meetings and sending petitions to Parliament, and the Assembly will now complete the work at its ensuing meeting—so that, as far as Presbyterians are concerned, they shall have placed themselves in an attitude of firm but respectful determination to recover their rights—But why is it that Episcopalians are so apathetic upon a subject which equally concerns them? It is because the Government are spontaneously about to ratify past marriages? If, however, they would reflect for a little, they would see that it is a matter of no common interest that Presbyterian Ministers should retain the right of marrying the members of their own communion to Episcopalians. If, despite of the petty jealousies between sister Churches which are unhappily growing in these times, an Episcopalian and Presbyterian should become attached to each other, and desire their mutual affection to be cemented in marriage, would it not be a matter of no interest to the Epsicopalian, if a Presbyterian marriage were illegal, and the Presbyterian had religious scruples with respect to the propriety of being married by an Episcopalian clergyman? The thoughtless may ridicule the idea, but there are too many real cases in the world of heart-felt misery arising from matrimonial disappointments to check all levity upon such a serious subject.

We have not left ourselves space to say what we intended respecting the Church of Scotland. Her cause seems gloomy. Little, we fear, need now be expected from the Government. It is therefore of the more consequence to consider what is best to be done. Scotland is full of Church Defence Associations, so should the North of Ireland. At the very best, the Church of Scotland must have non-intrusion or nothing. The Evangelical Presbyterians of Scotland and the Orthodox Presbyterians of Ireland, united in close and cordial brotherhood, cannot be contemptible in the eyes of a British Minister, however strong he may be in the confidence of his supporters. If Presbyterians resolve to maintain the interests of religion in preference to those of mere secular politics—"to do all for the Church and some thing less for the State," they will force their righteous claims upon the attention of any Government. What is Whigism or Toryism, that either the one or the other should be supported to the neglect and ruin of higher and holier interests? But we must conclude. We hope the Assembly may be guided by wisdom from on high in its deliberations upon the important subjects which are to occupy its attention. —*Belfast News-Letter*. (1842-02-26, 4:1)

2839. Death of Major-General Coulson.—It is our painful duty to announce the unexpected death of this gentleman from an attack of apoplexy. He had been indisposed on Monday, and, on the afternoon of that day, had gone to Holywood in order to take a bath; but, before he left the bath-house, and when proceeding down stairs, he was taken alarmingly ill. All possible attention was paid to him. Medical aid from Belfast was promptly secured; he was bled, and other measures used to effect his recovery, but we regret to state, all proved of no avail. He was insensible from the time he experienced the attack till the period of his dissolution, and breathed his last at one o'clock on Tuesday morning. In his death, Belfast has sustained the loss of one of her most respected citizens. (1842-02-26, 4:5)

2840. Sudden Death.—An old man named M'Anally, a resident of the parish of Clontibrit [sic], had been transacting some business with H. Swanzy, Esq., in Castleblayney, on Tuesday last, when, finding himself becoming unwell, he left Mr. Swanzy's office and endeavoured to reach a house on the opposite side of the street—the moment he reached it, he fell down and instantly expired. (1842-03-05, 2:5)

2841. Awful case of Suicide.—On last Saturday, the steward of — Atkinson, Esq., of Cavan Garden, near Ballyshannon, in a fit of insanity perpetrated one of the most shocking acts of self-destruction perhaps ever heard of, by literally ripping open his belly, tearing out his bowels, cutting them in pieces and throwing them on the floor!! The day before he committed the horrible deed, he drank no less than a bottle of ardent spirits, from the deadly effects of which however, he was saved by medical aid. No cause can be assigned for his committing the frightful act save that it is reported by some of his neighbours that a person to whom he had lent some money fled to India, which preyed upon his spirits and led him to end his own existence. A little before he destroyed himself he went to his priest, made confession of his sins and received absolution. (1842-03-05, 2:5)

2842. General Assembly of Scotland.—A commission of this body was held on Wednesday last, at which, among other important matters, the case of the Irish Presbyterian Church, in reference to mixed marriages, was taken into consideration. An admirable speech was made on the subject by the eloquent and zealous Alexander Dunlop, who moved that petitions on behalf of their Irish brethren should be adopted.—*Derry Standard* of Wednesday. (1842-03-12, 1:3)

2843. Afflicting Case of Hydrophobia.—Yesterday, Mr. John Hindman, city coroner, held at the house, 83 Meclenborough-street, upon the body of a man named Michael Conran, aged 28, by trade a gardener. It appeared from the evidence, that about seven o'clock on the morning of the 6th of January last, the deceased was walking to the residence of Mr. Bushe of Clontarf, where he was used to work, when his attention was attracted upon the road by a very small dog of much beauty. He stooped down for the purpose of patting it, and having played with it for a minute or so, he spat inadvertedly [sic] upon it; the dog grew incensed, and springing towards the face of the deceased, who was still leaning over it, made a snap at him and bit him in the under lip. The deceased struck the dog down, who immediately ran away and he never after saw more of it. The wound on his lip healed up in four or five days, and he thought nothing of it until Friday morning last, when he was going to his work he complained of feeling very ill. He continued at his work that day, but returned very much worse about seven o'clock, when he complained of a great pain in his lip and general illness. He called for a drink of water, saying that he was thirsty, but when it was brought to him he shuddered at the sight and refused to drink, and said, that there was something the matter with his throat which prevented him from swallowing. All that night he raved in his sleep about the dog, imploring that it might be killed, and giving an accurate description of it. On Saturday, his malady increased fearfully. He shuddered at the sound of water, and, although he retained his consciousness and memory to the last, he occasionally leaped about so franticly that it was found necessary to call the police to hold him.—On Sunday Morning, he was conveyed to the Richmond Hospital, where he died about four o'clock. As the hour of dissolution approached, his sufferings appeared to undergo much mitigation, and he died composedly in the arms of his mother, being at the time in the full possession of his mental faculties. —Verdict, "died of hydrophobia." (1842-03-12, 4:4)

2844. On Tuesday last, the marriage of David S. Ker, Esq., M.P., was celebrated with much rejoicing in the village of Ballycarry. In the evening, Mr. Wright, the active and intelligent resident manager on the Red-Hall estate, regaled the labourers with abundance of bread and ale.—After dark, the village presented a very animated appearance—numbers of the neighbouring peasantry paraded the streets, and every house being brilliantly illuminated and tastefully decorated with evergreens; a number of houses in the neighbourhood were also elegantly lit up, among which we may mention Templecoran-house, the residence of the Rev. John Stewart, which, from its commanding situation, had a very imposing appearance, while the hills in the vicinity blazed with bon-fires until a late hour.—Every one seemed to vie with his neighbour in paying a tribute of respect and affection to their excellent and popular young landlord. (1842-03-12, 4:5)

2845. Suicide of the Earl of Munster.—The death of this nobleman by his own hand has been an engrossing object of conversation at the west end of the town this morning. The lamented action is stated to have occurred at a late hour last night, when his lordship's servant was alarmed by the report of a pistol. On going to the noble earl to ascertain the cause, he found his lordship wounded by the discharge of a pistol, and the earl desired the servant to fetch a doctor, as he was wounded. After the servant had so quitted him, the noble earl put a second pistol to his mouth, and thus destroyed himself.

The late nobleman was, besides being earl of Munster, Viscount Fitzclarence, and Baron of Tewkesbury, in the peerage of the United Kingdom; a Privy councillor, a Major-General in the Army, and Aide-de-camp to the Queen; Governor and Captain, also Constable and Lieutenant, at Windsor Castle; Colonel of the 1st Tower Hamlets Militia, and a Commissioner of the Royal Military College and Royal Military Asylum; Knight Grand Cross of the Order of Ferdinand of Wirtemburgh, Vice-President of the Royal Asiatic Society, and F.R.S. He was born Jan. 16, 1794, and was consequently in his 49th year.

He married, in October, 1819, Mary Wyndhom, daughter of the Earl of Egremont, and has left issue by her several children, the two eldest of whom are daughters. His eldest son, now Earl of Munster, &c., was born May 19, 1824, and is in his 18th year. The late peer was the eldest son of King William the fourth, by the celebrated actress Mrs. Jordan.

The Earl of Munster entered the army in Feb. 1807, and the date of his last commission, as Major-General, is Nov. 23, 1841. His lordship served in the Peninsula, and was severely wounded at Toulouse.

His Lordship was on half-pay of the 24th Dragoons. He served the campaign of 1808 in Spain, with Sir David Baird's army, as aide-de-camp to Adjutant-General Stewart, in 1813 as Deputy-Assistant Adjutant-General, and in 1814 with his regiment. He subsequently went to the East Indies, and acted as Aide-de-camp to the Governor-General, the Marquis of Hastings from 1815 to 1817, and returned to England overland in June, 1818, with despatches.

About six weeks since his lordship and family returned to town from Ostend, where they had been residing for some time, and since that period, it had been noticed that he was not in his usual spirits.—This fact was, however, attributed to the effects of several severe attacks of the gout from which he had suffered; and on Thursday last, on going to the House of Lords with some of the younger members of his family, his manner is said to have rather altered.—*Sun of Monday evening.*

The Inquest.—At seven o'clock on Monday evening, Mr. Higgs, coroner, and a jury of 12 gentlemen assembled at No. 13, Belgrave street, Belgrave-square, the residence of the deceased Earl, to determine the cause of his death. After several witnesses had been examined, the jury returned the following verdict—"That deceased died by his own hand whilst in a state of temporary mental derangement." (1842-03-26, 2:3)

2846. Major Eldred Pottinger, upon whom, on the death of Sir W.H. Macnaghten, the command at Cabool devolved, was also a native of the county Antrim; he was born in Lisburn. (1842-03-26, 2:4)

2847. Twelve soldiers' wives for every 100 men will be allowed to embark with each of the six Regiments for India. (1842-03-26, 3:1)

2848. Presbyterian Marriages.—We have received private information to the effect that the committee of the Lords, upon the state of the marriage law in Ireland, are prosecuting their inquiries with vigour; and that a disposition is manifested favourable to the rights of Presbyterians. All this we regard as evidence of the recent healthful agitation upon the subject; and it ought to encourage the Presbyterians to persevere. There ought to be no relaxation. Above all things, the cases reserved, by special verdicts, at the late Carrickfergus and Armagh assizes, should be pressed, with due diligence, inasmuch as the judgment of the House of Lords, in reference to them, is of the utmost importance to the Presbyterian body, let the committee of the Lords examine or recommend as they may.—*Northern Whig*. (1842-03-26, 3:1)

2849. At the Cork Assizes, a writ of inquiry was opened to assess damages in an action for trespass for seduction. The plaintiff is John Hawkes, of Kilena, Esq.; the defendant, his cousin-german, Samuel Devonshire Penrose, of Farren, Esq. The lady was Miss Nettles, of Nettleville. Damages were laid at 10,000*l*., and judgment was allowed to go by default. They were married in 1829, and in May, 1841, she eloped, taking the advantage of an invitation to visit a brother-in-law in the county Leitrim. Another brother-in-law, accompanied her to Dublin en route. She requested him to go to the theatre to amuse himself, which he did, and on his return to the hotel [he found that] she had fled with Penrose to England. Her eldest son is eleven years old, the youngest six years. The jury after three hours' deliberation, brought in a verdict of two thousand pounds damages, and sixpence costs. (1842-04-02, 2:2)

2850. Women at a Premium.—The Congress of Texas have passed a law, granting two thousand nine hundred and eighty-two acres of good land to every woman who will marry, during the present year, a citizen of that republic, who was such at the time of the declaration of independence. (1842-04-02, 2:2)

2851. A marriage is on the *tapis* between the Marquis of Waterford and the Hon. Miss Louisa Stuart, daughter of Lord and Lady Stuart de Rothsay, and sister of Viscountess Canning. We understand the marriage has only been brought about within the last six weeks. (1842-04-02, 3:1)

2852. Disaster at Sea.—The *Water Witch* cutter fell in with a barque, the *Queen*, of Hull, on the 21st inst., off the coast of Galway. She had been (*continued...*)

2852, continued: ...twenty-eight days water logged, and had lost all her sails and boats; and the bodies of five men were lying dead on the deck, who died with starvation and want of water. The master of the *Water Witch* supplied the two survivors with everything they required, but the master would not leave the vessel. The *Dolphin* revenue cutter was immediately sent out, and fortunately succeeded in falling in with her, and towed her up to the bay of Galway. (1842-04-02, 3:3)

2853. Sudden Death.—A boy, about sixteen years of age, named M'Kenna, dropped dead in our streets on Monday last. He was at once taken before a surgeon, but life was completely extinct. An inquest was held on the body, before Robert Murray, Esq., Coroner, and a verdict returned of died by visitation of God. (1842-04-09, 2:5)

2854. The Late Earl of Munster.—The funeral of the late Earl of Munster took place on Tuesday morning. The mortal remains of his Lordship were deposited in a vault in Hampton church, intended for the members of the Munster family. The funeral procession left Belgrave-street as early as eight o'clock. In consequence of the great number of applications on the part of the nobility to be allowed to have their carriages follow, as a mark of respect to the memory of the late Earl, it was determined by the relatives of the deceased to decline all such offers, and consequently the private carriages that followed in the rear were confined to those of the Queen Dowager and the other branches of the Royal Family. The mournful cavalcade passed through Belgrave-square, and thence by Knightsbridge to Fulham and by Wimbledon and Kingston to Hampton, which it reached by half-past eleven. The interment took place at twelve o'clock. Lord De Lisle and Major-General Wyndham are the executors of the late Earl. Lord De Lisle married a sister of the deceased, who died in 1837, and Major-General Wyndham is a brother of the Countess of Munster. The Colonelcy of the 1st Tower Hamlets Militia, by the death of his Lordship, is at the disposal of the Duke of Wellington. (1842-04-09, 4:4)

2855. We are much concerned to announce the death of Sir Hugh Dillan [sic] Massy, Bart., of Doonas, at his house in Fitzwilliam-square, Dublin, on Monday last, after an illness of some weeks. The name and celebrity of Sir Hugh Massy were associated with some of the most exciting events in the history of Ireland, immediately preceding the union. He was one of the most high-spirited and finished gentlemen of that memorable period—independent and patriotic in his principles—courteous in his manners—and devoted to his friends; Sir Hugh represented his native county. His only daughter is married to Captain Felix Smith, late of the Queen's Bays, but the deceased baronet having left no male issue, his titles and estates descend to his nephew, Captain Hugh Dillon Massy, of the Clare Militia, son of the late Rev. Charles Massy, Rector of Donagh.—*Limerick Chronicle.* (1842-04-09, 4:4)

2856. Death of Sir Ralph Gore, Bart.—This venerable and respected Baronet died at Brighton, on Friday last, after a short illness. The deceased Sir Ralph St. George Gore, of Manor Gore, county Donegal, was in his 83d year. He married lady Grace Maxwell, second daughter of Barry, first Earl of Farnham. The late Baronet was son of Mr. Richard Gore, brother of the fifth and sixth Baronets and succeeded to the family honours on the death of his uncle in 1102 [sic]. The ancestors of the late Baronet, since the reign of Elizabeth, held a high station in Ireland. The first Baronet was the commander of a cavalry corps in that country, when he was created by Elizabeth, and his fourth son was ancestor to the Gores of Lissadel. The fourth Baronet was distinguished for his military achievements, for which he was raised to the Peerage by the title of Earl of Ross, a title which expired with him, while the Baronetcy descended to his nephew, the subject of this notice. Mr. St. George Gore, eldest son of the deceased, succeeds to the title and estates. (1842-04-09, 4:4)

2857. Fatal and Melancholy Accident.—We regret to state that on Friday evening, the 8th inst., a most interesting female child, nearly seven years old, (Sarah Gorman,) daughter of Serjeant Gorman, of the Royal Artillery, at present on the recruiting service in Cavan, went out to the street in order to amuse herself with other children after her return from school. About half-past seven o'clock, her mamma became alarmed at her non-appearance, when a search was instituted, imagining she might, in all probability, be in some neighbouring house; but the search proving ineffectual up to 10 o'clock, Mr. Gorman considered it advisable to have the bell man sent round through the different streets, for the purpose of announcing that the child was missing, at the same time giving a description of her dress, &c. A great number of persons, prompted by feelings of commiseration for the bereaved and much afflicted parents, continued to search with the greatest assiduity and attention in every place where there was any probability of the unfortunate child being located. At length, as a last melancholy resource, a number of persons proceeded to search the river which flows in at the south end of the town, where they succeeded in finding the lifeless remains of the ill-fated little innocent, with barely as much water as covered her prostrate body, the river not being deep at that particular place.—It is a singular fact, that she was found almost in the very spot where Mrs. Graham drowned herself a few months since—(an account of which occurrence appeared in our columns at that period). It was absolutely heart-rending to witness the distraction of her truly afflicted parents on viewing the inanimate form of their beloved child. An inquest was held on the body, on Saturday, before Thos. Berry, Esq., the newly elected coroner for the County of Cavan, when a respectable and intelligent jury was sworn, of which Mr. Edward Kennedy, merchant, was foreman. Several of the children were examined, with whom the deceased was at play that evening, but nothing was elicited from them upon which the jury could place any reliance. After the most minute and careful investigation of verdict of "Lost, and found drowned," was returned. Her remains were conveyed to their last resting-place in Cavan burying-ground, on Sunday evening, accompanied by an immense concourse of the respectable inhabitants, who were anxious to testify their sympathy and respect for Serjeant Gorman, who has been for a considerable time a resident in Cavan, and is much esteemed by all who know him. (1842-04-16, 2:5)

2858. There is a letter in Dublin from Doctor Magrath's brother, which states that Doctor Magrath is not killed. Seeing the men of his own party (the 37th) all cut down, he joined about thirty of the 44th who stuck together, and they cut their way through the enemy, and escaped to a friendly fort.—*Mail.* (1842-04-16, 4:4)

2859. Coroner's Inquest—Mysterious Case of Suicide.—Yesterday John Elliott Hyndman, Esq., city coroner, held an inquest in the Chancery-lane station-house, on view of the body of a young woman, name unknown, who committed suicide by leaping into the river Liffey, on the morning of Sunday last. The circumstances were detailed in the evidence.

Joseph Kennedy, A 117.—I was on my bate yesterday morning on Wellington-quay, near half-past four o'clock, when I saw the deceased at the opposite side of the quay, at a good distance from me. When she came to the low part of the wall she looked wildly around her, sprang in an instant over the wall, and plunged into the river. When I saw her first she was coming from Essex-bridge to the Metal-bridge. There was no person on the quay at the same side of the river with deceased except myself. The tide was in at the time. I ran to the place whence she leaped, and sprung my rattle, when B 110 came up, whom I sent to try to get a boat. The boats were chained and locked, so we could not get one. She came to the surface of the water, and struggled for two or three minutes, then sank for ever. I think I saw the same young woman walking along the quay, when she appeared in a sorrowful and a very dejected mood. The body was found in an hour afterwards. When found she was lying on her face.

Verdict—"A woman unknown, in a state of temporary derangement, threw herself into the river Liffey, on Sunday morning, at half-past four o'clock, and was drowned."—*Freeman.* (1842-04-23, 1:3)

2860. Mixed Marriages.—The Rev. Dr. Miller, of Armagh, has arrived in Dublin, on his way to London, having been summoned by the select committee of the House of Lords on the question of mixed marriages in Ireland.

Our readers will recollect that Dr. Miller's able judgment on the Law of Marriages in Ireland, given in the Consistorial Court of Armagh, in the case of *Lemon v. Lemon*, (which was lately confirmed by the decision of the twelve Judges) has given rise to the present proceedings.

The Rev. Charles King Irwin, Rector of Keady, in the county of Armagh, has been likewise summoned. (1842-04-23, 3:2)

2861. Death of Connolly the Irish jockey.—Ever since his frightful fall at Oxford, in August, 1840, his existence was marked by sufferings of a most distressing nature; and, although he occasionally appeared to rally, yet it was only to experience relapses of increased severity. At length mentally and corporeally overthrown, he expired on Saturday, aged 35. At the age of 13, being in the service of Mr. Prendergast, and under the care of William Cleary, that gentleman's trainer, he made his debut as a jockey on the Curragh of Kildare, his first race being on Jemmy Gray, for a Handicap Peel course, on which occasion he weighed 3st. 9-1/2lb.! In 1821, he came over to England with Mr. Prendergast, and went with his stud to Newmarket, but soon after his arrival there Mr. Prendergast wrote to Mr. Cleary "to bring the horses up to London," which he did, and Connolly accompanied him. The horses were afterwards disposed of in various ways. The question being put as to what should be done with the "little jockey," it was proposed by Mr. Prendergast that he should be taken into the house, to fill a menial position then vacant. At this Cleary, to use his own expression, "burst into a blaze," and he repelled the offer with generous indignation. The next morning he returned to Newmarket, and on his arrival he made a present of Connolly (as he himself described the act) to Mr. H. Neale for two years and a half. In 1823, Neale put him on Lord Verulam's *Vaurien* for the Chelmsford Cup, which he had the good fortune to win, and from that time to his death Connolly found a liberal patron in his lordship. It will be recollected that Connolly was riding Lord Verulam's *Albert*, by *Waterloo* or *Moses*, out of *Varennes*, in a trial at Newmarket, when life became so suddenly extinct that, as Conolly [sic] said, "Albert was dead whilst yet he was in his stride." In the midway of his career, Conolly was put on the most celebrated horses, and such was his success, that he appeared to farm all the great stakes for the use and behoof of his employers. He won Derby, Oaks, and Leger; the first Eclipse foot at Ascott [sic], on *Priam*, and the Goodwood Cup two years following, on the same horse. In 1834 he was selected by Mr. Batson to ride *Plenipotentiary* for the Derby, which he won, *Shillelah* beimg second, *Glencoe* third. Six years ago he married Elizabeth, eldest daughter of Mr. Boyce, of Newmarket, who, with three children, the eldest four years old, the second two, and the youngest three weeks only, is left to mourn over his early grave. (1842-04-23, 4:3)

2862. Law Intelligence.—Court of Queen's Bench—April 23.—Presbyterian Marriage Case.—*The Queen v. Milles.*—This case, which has excited so much interest throughout the whole country, and particularly in the north of Ireland, came before the court in the shape of an argument upon a special verdict which was had at the last assizes of Carrickfergus.

Mr. Holmes, with whom was Mr. Nelson, Q.C., appeared on the part of the prosecution. He said he appeared as counsel for the Crown to pray the judgment of the court against the prisoner, who was tried at the last assizes of Carrickfergus, under an indictment for bigamy, upon which occasion a special verdict was found. He would state the facts with regard to the first marriage, as there was no question concerning the validity of the second marriage, and the whole case would be confined to the first, and the special verdict that was found in relation to it. The finding was to the effect that the prisoner, George Milles, did in the month of January, 1839, contract a marriage with one Hester Graham, then a spinster—that the marriage contract was entered into at Tullylish, in the county of Down, in the presence of the Rev. John Johnson, who was then and there a regular minister of the Christian community called Presbyterians, and that the said Rev. John Johnson then and there performed the religious ceremony of marriage between the parties according to the forms of the Presbyterian Church in Ireland. And that after the said contract and ceremony, the prisoner and the said Sarah Graham had cohabited together for two years, and that during that time he went by the name of Milles, and that the said George Milles was, at the time the said marriage was performed, a member of the Established Church of England and Ireland, and that the said Hester was not a member of the Established Church or a Roman Catholic. The jury also found that the prisoner had been married a second time, but about that there was no question, and the case set up for his defence was, that the first marriage was null and void according to law, that the prisoner was not therefore guilty of the crime imputed to him. The statute under which the trial took place was the 10th of Geo. IV., which provided that the accused party should be prosecuted in whatever county or city he might be arrested in.

Mr. Holmes then proceeded to address the court. He spoke for upwards of four hours, and quoted a variety of writers upon ecclesiastical law, as well as numerous decisions at common law, to show that marriage was a mere civil contract which did not absolutely require the presence of a clergyman to make it valid. He said—My lords, this is a case of mighty importance. The conviction or acquittal of the prisoner who is here charged with bigamy under the statute of James the First, is a matter of minor importance compared to the magnitude of the evil that would arise if hundreds—aye, thousands of the most respectable and virtuous families in Ireland were to have their peace invaded, their prospects blighted, their properties put in jeopardy, and their offspring deemed illegitimate by the decision which is called for here this day by the prisoner. [*Continuation of arguments for the prosecution, citing: Coke's Third Institute, Grotii de Jure Bell (in Latin), Story's Conflict of Laws, M'Kenzie's Institutes, Haltherden's digest of the laws of Scotland, Blackstone's treatise upon husband and wife, Kent's Commentaries, Dowe and Clark's parliamentary reports, Ferguson's Scotch Reports, Hale's History of the Common Law, Burne's Ecclesiastical Law, Haggard's Consistory Reports, the Coke-Littleton; a history by Father Paul, the Venetian; Sir William Scott; Lord Fitzmaurice, son of the Earl of Kerry; the Pope, Saint Peter, Roman Catholic priests, and Popery; Harry the Eighth; Lord Chatham; Dr. Cooke; a man named M'Adam, who kept a woman in his house as his mistress; mentions of the Council of Trent, and terms including Episcopalian, Protestant, Calvinistic, England, Scotland, clergyman, lawyer, America, Court of Delegates, Lord Chancellor, Jews, Society of Friends, the House of Lords, Armenian clergy, Puseyites. The article fills two columns, concluding with:*] The court then rose, and the case was adjourned to Friday. (1842-04-30, 2:3)

2863. Notice.—I Hereby give Notice, that from this date, I will not be accountable for any debt or debts contracted by my Wife, Norah Cunningham, and Caution any person from giving her Credit on my name.

Dated at Cordora, this 28th day of April, 1842.

Owen Cunningham.

(1842-04-30, 3:4)

2864. Death of Lady Charlotte Crofton.—Died, on Tuesday last, at Moat Park, the residence of her son, Lord Crofton, in the 65th year of her age, Lady Charlotte Crofton, relict of the late Hon. Sir Edward Crofton. Her Ladyship was born August 1777, and was daughter of John, Earl of Galloway.—*Roscommon Journal.* (1842-05-14, 2:2)

2865. Melancholy Accident.—A young woman, named Margaret Deane, lost her life on Sunday under very melancholy circumstances. She had gone up to the Cavehill in company with a young man, and having arrived at the top of M'Carts Fort, they were both standing close to the edge of the rock when she, under the impression that her companion was dangerously near the brink, stepped forward to pull him back, but in doing so by some means lost her footing, and was precipitated down the awful precipice, a depth of not less than 200 feet. The unfortunate girl was of course dashed to pieces on the spot, not a vestige of life being discoverable on her body being found. The poor girl lived, we understand, in Pinkerton's-row, and was a reeler in Messrs. Mulholland and Hind's mill.—*Belfast Chronicle.* (1842-05-21, 4:3)

2866. A melancholy accident occurred in this town last week, which terminated fatally. Miss M'Garraghan, of Castle-street, having incautiously held a candle over a chest from which she intended to take some clothes, her dress caught fire, and, before assistance could be rendered, she suffered injuries which occasioned her death on the following day.—*Sligo Champion.* (1842-05-21, 4:3)

2867. A young girl from the neighbourhood of Carrick-on-Shannon, whose name we could not ascertain, fell into the water at the quay on Friday evening, and, before assistance could be rendered, was drowned. The poor creature had come to Sligo for the purpose of embarking in one of our emigrant ships.—*Sligo Champion.* (1842-05-21, 4:3)

2868. Melancholy Death of Samuel Cleland, Esq., J.P., of Stormount House.—(*From the Belfast News-Letter.*)—It is our painful duty to have this day to record the death of this esteemed gentleman, which took place during the afternoon of Friday last, under the following melancholy circumstances:—Mr. Cleland has been, for some time past, making various alterations and improvements on the grounds immediately adjoining his own mansion, and on the day in question, he was superintending the labourers who were engaged in pulling down an old mud house. It appears that they were undermining the foundation of the wall, and, while so employed, the wall suddenly fell on the unfortunate gentleman and killed him on the spot. The workmen present immediately removed the rubbish, and underneath discovered the body, but life was completely extinct. His face was horribly cut and disfigured; one of his thigh bones having been broken, protruded through his pantaloons; and in fact, his whole body was bruised and smashed in a most shocking manner. He was speedily removed to the Hall, medical assistance instantly procured, but every means which skill could devise proved of no avail. Mr. Cleland's untimely death has cast a gloom over a vast number of the gentry of his own immediate country, and by many others who enjoyed the pleasure of his acquaintance. As a Magistrate, his loss will be felt—as a landlord, his sudden and unexpected removal will be regretted by his numerous tenantry, to whom he was always kind and indulgent, and as a loving husband and tender, affectionate father, his own domestic circle has sustained a heavy bereavement. Several of the labourers, we regret to state, were more or less injured by the falling of the house, one of them especially, at present lies in a very dangerous state.

Inquest on the Body.—On Saturday morning about half-past ten o'clock, an enquiry was held into all the circumstances connected with the sad event, before R.D. Coulson, Esq., J. Coates, Esq., J.P., and several other gentlemen, at Stormount House. The first witness examined was Samuel Shannon, who deposed that he was with Mr. Cleland on Friday last, undermining the wall of an old mud house; Mr. Cleland was standing within half a yard of the wall, when deponent saw the loose mould giving way, and called out to them all to run, as the wall was about to fall; deponent ran, but Mr. Cleland remained, and on deponent looking behind him, he saw the mud wall lying on top of Mr. Cleland and a workman named Melville; witness was of opinion that not more than three minutes had elapsed before Mr. Cleland was extricated from the rubbish, and when first discovered, betrayed no signs of life with the exception of a slight movement of his hand; witness stated, in conclusion, that in his opinion the accident was not caused through any carelessness on the part of any person engaged at the work. The medical gentleman, Francis Macminn, Esq., who first examined the body, stated that life was quite extinct at that time, and was of opinion that death was caused by excessive shock which the brain and nervous system received; he had received a severe compound fracture of the thigh bone, and death must have immediately ensued after the shock which the system had received. Samuel M'Ilveen, Esq., M.D., deposed that he also examined the body; and agreed with Dr. Macminn as to the causes to which he attributed Mr. Cleland's death. These being the only witnesses whose evidence was requisite, the Magistrates came to the unanimous decision that the melancholy accident was purely accidental, and that it was not through the carelessness of any person who had been present with him, and founded their verdict accordingly. On yesterday morning, the remains of this much lamented gentleman were removed for interment to the family burying-ground at Dundonald, and the attendance was very numerous—the procession of carriages extending for nearly a mile. (1842-05-28, 1:4)

2869. Coroner's Inquest—Important Case.—(*From the Londonderry Standard.*)—An inquest was held on the 19th instant, before Wm. Ellis, Esq., Coroner, on the body of James M'Connell, who died under peculiar circumstances on that day. The following evidence was taken:

Francis M'Aneany—Lives in the townland of Sheatrim, county Monaghan; knew the deceased James M'Connell, late of Tirleenan [sic], within two miles of Monaghan; about one month ago, deceased, in company with witness, Patrick Murphy, William Woods, and M'Briars, left Monaghan town, and proceeded to Glenties, county Donegal; about the 17th of May, a summons was served on witness, Murphy, and Woods, to give evidence before a Committee of the House of Commons in a certain petition pending between Lord Belfast and Mr. Emerson Tennent, in consequence of which they proceeded on their way from Glenties to this city, in order to go on board the steamer for Liverpool; they arrived here on the 18th, and stopped at the house of John Murray; on their from Glenties to Derry, the parties lunched together, deceased drank a tumbler of whiskey punch, and eat [sic] (*continued...*)

2869, continued: ...some bread and cheese, apparently in his usual good health; he drank only the one tumbler of punch in that house, but frequently desired to get drink on the way, in which he was prevented by the persons who were with him, as far as possible. They arrived at Murray's house in Derry between nine and ten at night, where witness went to bed sober, after taking two cups of tea; previous to going to his own bed, witness went into the room where deceased lay, and deceased then had in his hand a glass containing, as witness thought, spirituous liquor; next morning, witness got up and looked out of the window, when he saw deceased going down the street, apparently in his wonted health; witness then went down stairs, but on going to the street, he did not see deceased, nor did he seem him afterwards until a little after seven o'clock, when he saw him lying in the passage, apparently drunk; witness then spoke to deceased, asked him was he unwell, and whether a doctor should be sent for; deceased then said, "Oh, no, when I get a sleep, I'll be well enough;" witness then got him taken up stairs and laid on a sofa; witness again said he would go for a doctor, but deceased replied as before; about eight o'clock on that morning (19th), witness again visited him, and seeing him in a very dangerous state, went for Dr. White, but when witness returned as quickly as possible, and before the doctor arrived, James M'Connell was dead; deceased was between thirty and forty years of age, and was a married man.

To a Juror—Has known deceased for upwards of twelve years; never knew him to be subject to any disease; deceased was intoxicated before he left Glenties; is certain deceased drank upwards of half-a-pint of spirits on the road; they had a bottle of spirits on the car with them, of which William Woods and a person named Kane drank part; deceased, witness, and the other persons were all summoned to give evidence on the same side.

James Murray sworn—Lives in Belfast; is a Lithographic writer; knew the deceased for a short time; saw him first in Monaghan; witness was told that deceased had been at the late election in Belfast, and he and another gentleman went up to Monaghan to see deceased; deceased in company with witness and three or four others, left Monaghan about a month ago, and came to Glenties, where there was a poor-house in the course of erection; deceased was employed there for some time as a day-labourer, and was in the habit of receiving his money daily; he was much addicted to drink; witness left Glenties in company with deceased, and before leaving, gave him half-a-crown, which he believes was all spent by deceased in whiskey.

To a Juror—Was with deceased from Glenties to Monaghan.

To the Coroner—There was no force or coercion used to bring him from Monaghan to Glenties. He was at perfect liberty to return home if he wished.

To a Juror—Deceased had a black bottle full of whiskey with him on the car from Glenties, which was emptied, and again filled; there were two cars; deceased was not on the car with witness.

Catherine Donnelly, examined. —Is servant of Miss Hutchinson's of Ship-quay, publican; that morning (19th), three men came into the house and called for a naggin of spirits, which was drank; afterwards, one of them, whom witness believes was the deceased, called for a johnny and drank it.

Patrick Murphy, sworn.—Lives in Rakeeragh, about a mile and a half from the town of Monaghan, and came to Glenties, county Donegal, where they remained until yesterday (18th;) on that evening, arrived in Derry, and that day (19th), deceased, William King, and witness, went into a house at the Ship-quay, where they called for a naggin of whiskey, of which deceased drank about one glass, and afterwards he called for a johnny, which he also drank; on coming up the street, deceased became very unwell, and desired witness and King to stop till he should rest; he afterwards sat down, but again moved up the street; King assisted him, and when within a short distance of Murray's house, deceased becoming very feeble in his limbs, he fell, and King fell over him; witness ran into Murray's, and sent out a person to assist deceased; witness has not since seen him, but has heard that he died about eight o'clock same morning.

To a Juror.—Witness knew deceased upwards of twenty years; he was always a heavy drinking man, and frequently intoxicated.

Dr. White deposed to his making a post mortem examination of the body, assisted by Dr. Morton; is of opinion deceased came by his death in consequence of having drunk an excessive quantity of spirituous liquor.—Dr. Morton gave similar testimony.

The jury found accordingly.

(1842-05-28, 2:4)

2870. Calamitous Occurrence—A Magistrate of the County of Kilkenny Burned to Death.—The following particulars of the melancholy death of Gorges Hely, Esq., a brief account of which appeared in our last publication, are extracted from the *Kilkenny Moderator*:—

We have this day, with unfeigned regret, the painful duty of recording a most calamitous occurrence that took place on Sunday morning last, by which a respectable gentleman, Gorges Hely, Esq., of Violet-Hill, a magistrate of Johnstown district, in this county, has lost his life in a most appalling manner, and which affords another warning to the many already recorded of the awfully dangerous consequence of *reading in bed*!

It appears that the unfortunate gentleman, who was about 30 years of age, retired to bed at his usual hour, and commenced reading. It is supposed he fell asleep, when the curtains took fire, and the smoke was so great he was unable to render himself the slightest assistance, and he was suffocated. The bed was soon enveloped in flames, which reached his head, and which presented a shocking spectacle, being literally burned to a cinder.

The flames quickly burst through the bedroom window, which fortunately were seen, when the alarm was given, and the Johnstown police, with George Pinchin, Esq., Sub-Inspector, proceeded without a moment's delay to the spot, and notwithstanding the proverbial scarcity of water in that district, owing to the indefatigable and praiseworthy exertions of the sub-inspector and his party, the mansion and valuable library were preserved from destruction. This awful calamity has cast a gloom over the neighbourhood in which the deceased resided. (1842-06-04, 2:5)

2871. The Church.—His Excellency the Lord Lieutenant has been pleased to appoint the Rev. John Reed, Curate of Downpatrick, to the Rectory of Ballee, vacant by the death of the Rev. Wm. Bond. (1842-06-04, 2:5)

2872. Awful Occurrence—Cordial Drinking.—At a wedding which took place in the vicinity of Youghal some time since, a Teetotaler, got drunk with cordial; maddened by the damned drug, the wretched being imprecated that if the devil choked him he would drink enough, and, shocking to relate, he kept his fearful pledge—he drank until he dropt a hideous corpse. Shocked at this awful interruption to the bridal festivities, and wishing if possible to remove the responsibility of the madman's death from their own doors, some of the party removed the body to a neighbouring church-yard, where it was discovered on the following morning and an inquest held upon it. This calamitous and horrifying event has produced a deep sensation in the vicinity where it occurred.—*Waterford Chronicle*. (1842-06-11, 4:3)

2873. Melancholy Accident.—A fine young man named Lemon, aged about 20 years, was drowned, while bathing in Lough Ouna, on the morning of Sunday last. His brother, who was also bathing, made several ineffectual attempts to rescue him; and, had it not been for the prompt interference of a third person, who succeeded in rescuing him, he must inevitably have shared the same fate as his unfortunate relative. On the inquest, a verdict of "accidentally drowned" was returned. (1842-06-18, 2:4)

2874. Commission Court—Wednesday, June 15.—Bigamy.—A young man named Malachi Henry Moran, was charged with bigamy, in marrying Anne Maxwell, having previously intermarried with Catherine Sweeny.

It having been proved in evidence that the first marriage ceremony was performed by a Roman Catholic clergyman only, the prisoner being a Protestant, and Catherine Sweeny a Roman Catholic, the invalidity of the first marriage entitled the prisoner to be acquitted. (1842-06-18, 2:5)

2875. Death of the Earl of Erne.—His Lordship expired at his residence in the neighbourhood of London in the afternoon on Friday, and is succeeded in his title and estates by Colonel Crichton, of Crum Castle, in the county of Fermanagh, Lord Lieutenant of that county, and one of the best and most improving resident landlords in Ireland. The family is descended from a branch of the Crichtons, Viscounts Frendreught, in North Britain, which title ceased with Lewis, the fifth Viscount, about the year 1690. An ancestor of Lord Erne's commanded a Regiment of Foot at the battle of Aughrim in 1692. Another was celebrated for his gallant defence of the family seat of Crum Castle against a large body of King James's army. Having repulsed the assailants, young Crichton—for he was a very youth—made a sally at the instant that a corps of Enniskillenners were approaching to the relief of the Castle, which movement placed the besiegers between two fires, and caused dreadful slaughter. The enemy, attempting to accomplish his retreat across an arm of Lough Erne, near Crum Castle, that spot became the scene of such carnage that it has ever since borne the name of the bloody pass. (1842-06-18, 3:1)

2876. Marriage in High Life.—*On Dit*—E.P. Shirley, Esq., of Loughfea, M.P. for the county of Monaghan, is about to lead to the Hymeneal altar, Miss Lechmere, of Worcestershire, grand-daughter to Sir Andrew Lechmere—a lady of great beauty and accomplishments; and her mother was one of the Maids of Honor to the late Queen Charlotte; and is descended from the great Murray family, of Elibank, Scotland. The young lady is about 18 years of age. (1842-06-25, 3:1)

2877. Death of Lieutenant-General Sir Wm. Parker Carroll, C.B.—It is with feelings of deep regret that we have to announce the death of this distinguished officer, which took place at his seat, Tulla House, Nenagh, on the morning of Saturday last. He had been for some time labouring under water on the chest, which at length proved fatal.—*D.E. Packet*. (1842-07-09, 1:3)

2878. Death of the Right Hon. George Evans, late M.P. for the County of Dublin.—We regret to announce the demise of this gentleman, which took place on Saturday, between two and three p.m. At three o'clock a.m., Dr. O'Grady was called out of bed to hasten instantly to Portrane, near Swords, Mr. Evans' residence, as Mr. Evans had been suddenly seized with a fit of the gout.—*D.E. Packet*. (1842-07-09, 1:3)

2879. Death of Mr. Justice Foster.—(From the *Evening Packet*.)—It is with no ordinary degree of regret, that we have to announce the demise of the Hon. John Leslie Foster, which melancholy event took place after a very few hours' illness, in the town of Cavan, on Saturday night last. The deceased Judge had been on circuit, and had only arrived (*continued...*)

2879, continued: ...in Cavan on the evening of his demise, apparently in excellent health. The late lamented gentleman, who had been for many years third Baron of the Exchequer, succeeded to the vacancy in the Common Pleas, caused by the recent resignation of Mr. Justice Johnson. He was called to the Bar in Michaelmas Term, 1803, and was distinguished, while in Parliament, for his laborious exertions for the improvement of national education, on which subject he produced many valuable reports. As a scholar and a man of business he was universally admitted to hold a very high rank, and his death will be a source of deep sorrow to his numerous friends and acquaintances, by all of whom he was greatly and deservedly esteemed.

The following particulars of this sad event have been communicated to us by our Cavan correspondent:—

"A sad gloom was thrown over our village on yesterday morning, by a report that one of our judges was no more. 'Tis too true. Judge Foster arrived here at three o'clock from Longford, fiated the presentments, which occupied him until six. He dined with the high sheriff and grand jury, and left the party at a quarter before nine o'clock, apparently in good health —at a quarter past twelve he was no more. There were two eminent medical men with him for some time; but, although every means that their skill could devise was resorted to, they proved ineffectual. An express was sent off to Dublin at one o'clock on Sunday morning, and this morning Sir H. Marsh and Surgeon Cusack arrived, after remaining for two hours, returned for town. Sergeant Greene arrived at one o'clock and proceeded with the business of the Crown Court. It is thought that the judge burst a blood vessel." (1842-07-16, 1:3)

2880. Approaching Marriage in High Life—The marriage announced between Sir Henry Hervey Bruce, Bart., of Down Hill, Londonderry, and Miss Clayton, daughter of Sir Juckes and Lady Granville Clayton, will be solemnised in about a fortnight. (1842-07-16, 1:3)

2881. Marriage in High Life.—On Thursday last, at Hatfield-house, the princely seat of the most noble the Marquess of Salisbury, Mr. Alexander Beresford Hope, the grandson of the Viscountess Beresford, led to the altar of the Gothic Chapel, the Lady Mildred Cecil, the eldest daughter of the distinguished host. The ceremony was performed by the Lord Primate of Ireland, at the hour of one—the Marquess giving the lady away. The bride-maids were, Lady Blanche Cecil, Miss Harriet Beresford, Miss Beresford, Miss De Ros. (1842-07-16, 1:3)

2882. There are now two vacancies on the Staff of the Queen's Aides-de-Camp, by the death of Colonel Dennie, 13th, and the dismissal of Colonel Dundas, late 83d. (1842-07-16, 2:5)

2883. Death of the Bishop of Meath.—We are exceedingly pained in being called upon to announce the demise of this eminently-gifted and truly-amiable Prelate, which melancholy event took place on Monday night last, at the See-house, Ardbraccan, after a few days' illness. In noticing the elevation to the Episcopal Bench of the late Right Rev. and Right Honorable Dignitary, (for the Bishop of Meath is, *virtute officii*, a Privy Councillor,) we took occasion to express our opinion of his numerous virtues and varied acquirements as a clergyman and a scholar. That opinion, it is unnecessary to repeat now. It remains unchanged, and was the result of all we knew and heard of his transcendent character in all the relations of life.

Deeply do we regret the loss to the Church of so accomplished a Divine, and to his young and interesting family, of so excellent a father. As a pious ecclesiastic and a Christian gentleman, the Right Rev. Charles Dickenson, it may be said, with perfect truth, has left behind him no superior in any part of the United Kingdom. (1842-07-16, 3:3)

2884. Mr. George Robinson, Resident Preacher of the Wesleyan Methodist chapel, Bedford-row, who left this to attend the conference holding in Dublin, this week, has fallen a victim to fever, of which he died on Thursday after three days' illness, to the grief of his congregation in this City, who had cause to appreciate his ministerial labours, and esteem as a friend and director. He is to be succeeded here by Mr. John Stephenson, of the same connexion.—*Limerick Chronicle*. (1842-07-23, 1:3)

2885. The remains of the lamented Bishop of Meath were interred at Ardbraccan, on Friday morning, at eight o'clock—Archdeacon Russell and Dr. West, acting with his sons, as chief mourners. The funeral was attended by a vast body of the clergy of Meath, who testified their most sincere regret for the sudden loss they had sustained. (1842-07-23, 3:2)

2886. The Lonely Hearse.—*Written on seeing a Hearse containing a young Female, and almost wholly unattended, proceed through the streets of Paris on a cold rainy day. On the coffin lay a wreath of orange-flowers*.—By Lady Harriette D'Orsay.

Drearily the rain is falling
Upon thy maiden bier,
Though on thy wreath of orange-flowers
There is no mourner's tear;
Unheeded through the crowded streets
Thy lonely hearse moves on,
None miss thee from the busy earth,
None care that thou art gone.

And were there none to watch thee
Upon thy bed of pain;—
No friend to shed above thee,
Warm tears, albeit in vain?
Mournfully the spotless garland

Adorns thy coffin now;
As a bride before the altar,
It should have bound thy brow.

Whilst wandering on this dreary earth,
Dark and lonely was thy lot;
But now thou sleep'st a quiet sleep,
And thy sorrows are forgot.
Unheeded now, upon thy brow
Descend the snow and rain,
As would heaven's glorious sunshine
Fall on they grave in vain.

The cold world's harsh neglect and scorn,
The trampling of the proud,
These cannot reach thee where thou liest,
Wrapt in thy snowy shroud;
Though lonely is thy funeral,
There is a glorious throng
To welcome thee in Paradise
With the Redeemer's song.

There thou shalt see thy mother's face,
Who taught thy young lips truth,
And left thee in a dreary place,
In thy age of helpless youth;
But sadness now is pass'd away,
And thy pure soul shall raise
In sunny realms of endless day
Unceasing songs of praise.

(1842-07-23, 4:1)

2887. Melancholy and Fatal Accident.—On Monday, Sir N.W. Brady, city coroner, held an inquest at the house of Mr. Kellett, No. 25, Capel-street, on view of the body of a fine young man, named William John Morrison, aged about nineteen years, the son of Mr. Morrisson [sic], of Castle-street, who met his death in a very lamentable manner, by falling from the top window of the house, a height of at least fifty feet, on the previous night, about half past twelve o'clock. After the examination of some witnesses, the jury found a verdict, "That the deceased came by his death, in consequence of falling out of the window into the street, by which his skull was fractured, of which he instantly died." (1842-08-06, 2:3)

2888. Dreadful Steam-boat Explosion!—Loss of Fifty-eight Lives.—It becomes our painful duty to record one of the most distressing casualties which has occurred in this province since the introduction of steam on the St. Lawrence. The high-pressure steamer *Shamrock*, while between Lachine and Pointe Claire, on her way to Kingstown [sic], about ten o'clock on Saturday morning, burst her boiler, and, her bows being blown out by the explosion, she went down head foremost. There were on board of her at the time about 120 persons, of whom 48 were taken up unhurt by three barges in tow, and 18 were conveyed to the Montreal General hospital wounded—54 remain to be accounted for. Of the 18 conveyed to hospital, one has died under the amputation of both legs. The passengers were composed of English, Irish, and Scotch; of whom the English were supposed to have suffered the most from being in the fore part of the boat. The first engineer that was saved, declares he has no other consciousness of the transaction than that the explosion took place, and that he afterwards found himself on board one of the barges, the interval between those events being in his mind a perfect blank. Much money is said to have been lost, the emigrants being of a superior description. The captain was the last person who left the boat, and at the risk of his life swam out a considerable distance, and succeeded in saving one of the passengers from being drowned.—*Montreal Courier*. (1842-08-06, 2:4)

2889. Longevity.—Mr. Nagle, of Ballinamona Castle, county of Cork, writes as follows to the editor, in the last number of the *Southern Reporter*:—"I think you will not have any objection to insert in your next publication the death of a very old man, my pond-keeper, on part of the lands of Clogher, near Doneraile, named Louis Wholehan. He died yesterday at the age of one hundred and eighteen years and seven months; he was married to his first wife more than fifty years, and had no offspring. He married a second wife at the age of one hundred and nine years by whom he has a son, a fine boy and very like the father. From his great age I have given him his house and the parish pound many years rent free, which made him comfortable, and prolonged his life. He never lost a tooth, nor had he a gray hair in his head." (1842-08-06, 3:3)

2890. A lady paying a visit to her daughter, who was a young widow, asked her why she wore the widow's garb so long? "Dear mamma, don't you see?" replied the daughter; "this saves me the expense of advertising for a husband, as every one can see I am for sale by private contract." (1842-08-06, 4:4)

2891. Reasonable Enough.—An American editor says, "We don't mind recording the deaths of the people without being paid for our trouble, though that is not fair: but panegyricks on the dead must be paid for—we positively cannot send people to heaven for nothing." (1842-08-06, 4:4)

2892. Accident to Emigrants from Cork.—(*Halifax Register*, July 13.)—Great Disaster.—A St. John (N.B.) paper of the 4th gives an account of a most melancholy accident which occurred in the harbour of St. John on the 3d instant. We give the particulars. It appears that an emigrant ship called the *Silkworth*, filled with emigrants from Cork, had been lying at some distance from the wharfs, and a number of passengers being anxious to see their friends in the city, on the afternoon of Sunday, the 3d, took the long boat of the vessel to bring them on shore. After proceeding some distance (the weather being rather foggy at the time), they unexpectedly (*continued...*)

2892, continued: …met the ferry-boat which plies between St. John and Charleton. The poor people, fearing they would be run down, became extremely alarmed, and in their confusion upset the boat, which immediately sunk. The scene that followed is described as most painful and heart-rending; the air was filled with the shrieks and cries of men, women, and children—all struggling for life. Prompt assistance was rendered by the steamer and other boats from both sides of the river, and eight of the unfortunate beings were saved from a watery grave. The number of lives lost had not been ascertained, but it is supposed they would amount to eight or ten. This is an event pregnant with saddening reflection. The poor emigrant! he had triumphed over the dangers and perils of the sea, and when his heart beat high with hopes of happiness in the land that was before him, he was rudely dashed upon the changeless ocean of eternity! How many hopes are thus withered—how many homes made desolate—how many fond hearts blighted! (1842-08-13, 1:3)

2893. Marriages in High Life.—The marriage of Mr. Evelyn P. Shirley, M.P. for Monaghan, and Miss Lechmere, daughter of Mr. E.H. Lechmere, and grand-daughter of Sir Anthony Lechmere, Bart., was celebrated on Thursday last, at Hanley Church, Worcestershire.

August 11, in St. George's Church, by the Rev. William Mills, George Montgomery, Esq., fourth son of the late Alexander Nixon Montgomery, Esq., of Bessmount Park, Monaghan, to Elizabeth, third daughter of George Arbuthnot Holmes, Esq., of Moorock, King's county. (1842-08-13, 3:2)

2894. Death of Lord Rossmore.—This melancholy event took place on Wednesday evening, at half-past eight o'clock, at his residence, Cortolvin. His Lordship had been enjoying tolerably good health for some months past, so as to be able to drive about in his phaeton, and up to ten o'clock on Monday morning continued in his usual state, but immediately after breakfast he got an attack of apoplexy, which ended in paralysis, from which he never recovered. His family physician, Doctor Walsh, was in immediate attendance, and was shortly after aided by Doctors M'Dowell and Kidd, but without effect, as all feeling and consciousness was suspended; all their endeavours to restore animation were unavailing, and he remained insensible until the moment of dissolution. His Lordship, who was created a British Peer in 1838, was about seventy-eight years of age, and was much and deservedly loved and admired even by his political opponents, as an elegant and accomplished gentleman, a humane and benevolent landlord, and a frank and cordial friend. The last years of his life have been most earnestly devoted to the duties of Christianity, and he has left behind him many records of his thoughts upon religion, which show the softening and miraculous influence of the holy Gospel of God, in reforming the hearts of the gay and worldly. As far as the human mind can discern, he was long prepared to die, and was only waiting, with patience, the call of his Creator, to join her who had gone a short time before him.

His Lordship is succeeded in his titles and estates by our late representative, the Hon. Henry R. Westenra, who now goes into the House of Lords as a Peer of the realm.

The Hon. Colonel John Westenra was in attendance upon his parent until he expired.

The remains will be interred, on Tuesday next, in the family vault in Monaghan Church. (1842-08-13, 3:2)

2895. On Friday se'nnight, the 5th instant, Mr. Samuel Cornelius, Bridewell keeper and Clerk to the Cootehill Poor Law Guardians. Having finished writing a number of circular letters to the resident Guardians, apprising them of their next day of meeting (Friday, the 12th, yesterday), he sat down to look over a newspaper, when he was attacked with hemorrhage of the heart, and in less than half an hour was a breathless corpse. Medical aid was promptly procured for him, but without avail. He had been in a bad state of health for a considerable time past, but appeared to be recovering, and had ridden up to the mountains on the previous day; he was much esteemed by his acquaintances, and his death is very generally regretted. He was scarcely dead an hour when there were no less than five candidates for his situations, all eagerly canvassing for the appointments. (1842-08-13, 3:3)

2896. John Dallas Edge, Esq., Barrister-at-Law, and Seneschal of Castlecomer, arrived from Castlecomer, on Thursday, where he had been leaving his lady and two children on a visit with the family of his father. In the course of the same evening he was upset in a small row-boat on the mill-pond of the Mount Brown Distillery, and unfortunately drowned. (1842-08-20, 2:2)

2897. In Mary's Abbey Manor Court, Maria Roden-Berry, a handsome girl, was awarded 10*l.* damages against William Supple, clerk of the Four Courts Library, for breach of promise of marriage. (1842-08-20, 2:3)

2898. Funeral of the Late Lord Rossmore.—At an early hour on Tuesday, the day appointed for consigning the mortal remains of the late lamented Lord to his tomb, crowds of persons were seen approaching Rossmore Park from every direction; and as the appointed period approached, the extensive and beautiful grounds presented a picturesque and solemn appearance. Hundreds of horsemen were assembled in groups, all clad in the "panoply of woe"—their white scarfs and hat-bands, thousands of which were distributed, giving to them in the distance (as they lounged beside, or leant upon their long tailed and untrimmed nags, or seated themselves upon a rising knoll, or 'neath some spreading tree,) all the appearance of a huge eastern caravansary, resting in the great Oasis, after their weary pilgrimage across the burning sands of the desert; while the gloomy brow, and "dejected haviour of the visage," visible in each, strengthened the picture, leading the spectator to fancy that all were sadly brooding over the loss of some dear friend, of whom death had deprived them. About ten o'clock, a lengthened *cortege* formed by the carriages of the neighboring gentry, wound its way along the avenue, and was followed by a large number of cars and gigs containing the inhabitants of Monaghan and its vicinity who assembled to pay their last tribute of respect to their departed landlord; and when the procession moved through the demesne, we computed it to comprise at least five thousand souls.

At a few minutes after ten o'clock, Mr. John E. Jones, (to whom the important office of arranging the funeral in all its details, and who certainly deserves great credit for the ability and taste displayed by him,) had the body removed from the great Hall, where it had lain in state since the previous Thursday, and placed in the hearse, after which the order of procession was formed by Mr. Williams, the master of our work-house, and late sergeant-major in the fourth Dragoon Guards.

The coffin, which was of Irish oak, over a lead and cedar enclosure, covered with the finest black cloth, was richly emblazoned with the arms of the Westenra family in all its quarterings, and bearing all the paraphernalia of death in the gorgeous trappings in which custom, in this country, usually equips the departed great ones of the earth. The breastplate bore the following inscription:—

WARNER WILLIAM WESTENRA,
Lord Baron Rossmore,
Born
October, 1766,
Died
10th August, 1842.

Order of the Procession.

Four tenants a-breast, on horseback,
with scarfs and hat-bands.
Four hundred tenants on foot,
two and two,
with scarfs and hat-bands.

1st Carriage,
containing the Rev. W.L. Roper and Rev. H. Maffatt,
officiating clergymen.

FREEMASONS.
Members or Honorary Members of Lodge 790,
to act as bearers, viz.—

Colonel Cairnes, K.H.,	John Johnson, Esq.,
A. Dudgeon, Esq.,	William Temple, Esq., M.D.
Samuel Moorhead, Esq.,	Rev. Allen Mitchell,
Mr. Francis Fleming,	Francis Dawson, Esq.,
Mr. James M'Endoo,	Thomas Snowe, Esq.,
Henry G. Johnston, Esq.,	Thomas Phillips, Esq.,
Robert Bailey Evatt, Esq.,	Maurice Burnell, Esq.,
William Woodwright, Esq.,	Mr. John Rowland, Esq.,
Walter Stuart Corry, Esq.,	Mr. James Smith.

Six pensioners on the bounty of deceased, in mourning, as Mutes.	The HEARSE containing the Body.	Six old servants, in mourning, as Mutes.

Pall Bearers:

Colonel Cairnes, K.H.,	A.G. Lewis, Esq.,
Sir Nicholas Fitzsimon,	William Irwin, Esq.,
Maurice Lewis, Esq.,	Captain Seaver.

2d Carriage,
containing the Chief-Mourners,
the present Lord Rossmore and
Colonel J. Westenra, M.P.

3d Carriage,
belonging to the deceased, with closed blinds.

4th Carriage,
Colonel Henry Westenra, brother of the deceased.

5th Carriage,
Colonel Cairnes, as next of kin,
containing Captain Ross, Monaghan Militia, and
Captain Mosely, late 8th Hussars.

6th Carriage,
Doctors J.S. M'Dowell and Welsh,
family physicians.

7th Carriage,
John Lucas, Esq., of Raconnell.

8th Carriage,
Andrew Allen Murray, Esq., and Murray, Esq.

9th Carriage,
belonging to A.G. Lewis, Esq.,
containing Captain Seaver and Mr. Butler.

10th Carriage,
Rev. Mr. Tarleton.

11th Carriage,
Sir Nicholas Fitzsimon and Christopher Banim, Esq.

12th Carriage,
William Anketell, Esq., D.L., J.P.; Major M. Anketell,
and Thomas Anketell, Esq.

13th Carriage,
Right Hon. Lord Cremorne and Charles Boyle, Esq.

14th Carriage,
William Foster and Foster Cranston, Esqrs.

15th Carriage,
Rev. William Henry Pratt and E.P. Morphy, Esq.

16th Carriage,
William Mayne, sen. and jun., Esqrs.

(*continued...*)

2898, continued: 17th Carriage,
Rev. Gustavus Warner and John Johnson, Esq.

18th Carriage,
Right Hon. Lord Blayney's carriage,
containing Edward Golding, Esq., and
the Rev. John T. Whitestone.

19th Carriage,
William Irwin, sen. and jun., Esqrs.

20th Carriage,
James Hamilton, Esq., D.L., J.P.; George Foster, Esq.,
D.L., J.P.; Madden Hawkshaw, Esq.,
and Thomas Foster, Esq.

21st Carriage,
William Hamilton, Esq., and James S. Boyd, Esq.

22d Carriage,
Rev. Messrs. Schomberg and Hackett.

23d Carriage,
Henry George Johnston, Walter Johnston,
and John Jackson, Esqrs.

24th Carriage,
Rev. J.R. Young, and others.

25th Carriage,
Robert Thompson and Edward Fiddis, Esqrs.

26th Carriage,
Nicholas Ellis and Thomas Ellis, Esqrs.

27th Carriage,
A.K. Young, Esq., M.D., and William Brocas, Esq.

28th Carriage,
Robert Bailey Evatt, Esq., carriage empty, as Mr.
Evatt was in procession with the Freemasons.

29th Carriage,
Thomas Charles Stuart Corry's carriage.

30th Carriage,
Rev. Henry Tottenham, and Rev. Mr. Burnside.

31st Carriage,
John Hatchell, William Slate, and H. Mackie, Esqrs.

Eight gigs and cars,
containing tenants and friends,
in scarfs and hat-bands.

Six hundred tenants on horseback,
two and two,
in scarfs and hat-bands.

Tenants on foot.

In the above order, the procession occupied nearly two miles of the road leading into Monaghan. Upon reaching the Church gate, the footmen drew up in line on either side of the road; the body of Freemasons approached preceding the hearse, and as it was his Lordship's wish to be interred by the brotherhood of which he was a member, the gentlemen, whose names we give above, bore the coffin into the aisle of the Church. It was met at the Church gate by the Rev. Messrs. Roper and Moffatt, the latter gentlemen performing the burial service.—The funeral oration, a touching and eloquent appeal to the immense multitude who filled every corner of the Church, was preached by Mr. Roper, from the 20th chapter, of the first book of *Kings*.

On the arrival of the procession at the church, the powerful toned organ struck out the *Dead March*, in *Saul*, which was performed by Mr. N.W. Stack with great judgment. Notice is also due to the Funeral Hymn, *Vital spark of heavenly flame*, which was given with much pathos, proving that the exertions of our organist were of no trivial nature.

Upon the conclusion of Mr. Roper's address, the body was removed to the family vault in the churchyard, and consigned to the tomb by the brethren of the gentle craft, into the first degrees of which, he was initiated in Gibraltar many years ago, when serving there with his regiment; and he obtained the degree of Master Mason, in Lodge 6, Dublin, which ceremony was performed by brothers Thomas Snow, and Alexander Dudgeon P., Masters.

His Lordship was seventy-six years of age, having been born in the year 1766. He was created a British Peer in 1838, by the Whigs, of whom he was always a strong advocate, and has left issue, Henry Robert Westenra, the present Lord Rossmore, and Col. John Westenra, M.P. for the King's county, where he possessed considerable property. He was a patron of the fine arts, many specimens of which adorn the grand gallery of Rossmore Castle, and up to the hour of his death, he was engaged in having completed, by Mr. Brocas, the celebrated artist, the portrait gallery of his family. His lordship had, also, a passion for ancient architecture, of which his residence is a capital proof, and for works of *vertu*, many rare specimens of which are contained in his cabinets.

A short biographical notice of his family and descent from the Cairnes of Tyrone, and their intermarriage with the Blayney family, by which they became possessed of the Monaghan estates, will we think be appropriate at the present moment; and although we, as provincial journalists, residing upon his property, never received the slightest patronage from him, in justice to his many good qualities, we make the following extracts from Graham's *Ireland Preserved*, and Lodge's *Peerage*.

Sir Alexander Cairnes dying without male issue in October, 1832, was succeeded in the baronetcy by his brother Henry, who lived in the county Donegal, and died there. His tombstone yet remains, with a legible inscription on it, in the churchyard of Donnoughmore.

Though not recorded in the baronetcy, William Cairnes, his brother, succeeded Henry in the title, a full-length portrait of whom has been preserved in Rossmore Castle. On his death, the title became extinct; and his extensive estates devolved upon Sir Alexander Cairnes's daughter, Mary, already mentioned. She married Cadwallader, the seventh Lord Blaney, who died without issue by her, on the 19th of March, 1732; and she married secondly her cousin-german, the Right Hon. Colonel Murry, a Privy Counsellor of Ireland, and the successor of his father, as representative of the county of Monaghan in parliament.

He also left her a widow. He died on the 20th of February, 1752, on his way to Dublin, leaving issue by her four daughters, viz., Frances, who died 29th of February, 1752, had married Wm. Henry Fortescue, afterwards created Earl of Clermont, who had no issue by her. Elizabeth who died on 29 May, 1754, married the Rt. Hon. Lieutenant-General Cunningham, Commander-in-Chief of the forces in Ireland, member of parliament for Monaghan, and had no issue. Mary who died unmarried in 1774, and was a lady of great literary abilities, specimens of which she left after her, though never published, and yet extant among the Blenheim archives. Anne, married in 1761, to the Right Hon. Theophilus Jones, (by whom she had issue, but all died under age); and Harriet, who on 29th of November, 1761, married Henry Westenra, father of the present Lord Rossmore, who, in right of her, enjoys the large estates of this branch of the family of Cairnes.

The Westenras came to Ireland in consequence of the persecution of the Protestants in the Netherlands, by the Duke of Alva, in the reign of Charles V. of Spain. Afterwards, in process of time, they became possessed of considerable estates in the King's and Queen's County, as also in Meath, Dublin and Louth. Several of them were attainted by King James' parliaments, as appears by Archbishop King's *state of the Protestants of Ireland*; and there is a creditable tradition, that five of the distinguished name fought for King William at the battles of the Boyne and Aughrim, and Lord Rossmore, the present representative, was equally zealous in support of the crown and constitution during the disastrous period of 1798. His Lordship's *Survey of the River Shannon*, between Athlone and Portumna Bridge, was considered a most useful and important document of that day, having been the first that had been made. He was engaged in the defeating the Vinegar Hill army of rebels, and driving it back from its position there. With the king's army he cleared Ferns, and the Bishop's Palace there, of the rebels who had taken possession of both—over-awed Wexford—relieved General Loftus, who had been nearly surrounded near Ferns—interposed the division under his lordship's command between the Gorey army of rebels and the city of Dublin; thus intercepting the combined movements of the two great Wexford armies on the metropolis, which they had intended to make for the purpose of burning it, or becoming masters of it. He thus chained them both to their positions until Generals Lake and Needham came up with the king's army, which finished the rebellion.

Lord Rossmore afterwards drove Holt from Roundwood, on the eastern side of the Wicklow mountains, until the outlaw found it prudent to surrender. By these movements and successes he inspired the British troops with confidence, who had been dispirited and were falling back and giving up their posts after the defeat and death of Colonel Walpole and Major Lombard, of the North Cork militia. (See Gordon's *History of the Rebellion of 1798*.) By training the yeomanry brigade of Monaghan, of 3,000 men to chain, order and guerrilla service, Lord Rossmore contributed much to the safety of the country at this awful crisis; so that if his ancestors rendered service worthy of remembrance in 1688 and 1689, the same may be said of their Noble descendant in 1798 and 1799.

The family of Westenras, descended from that of Van Wassenear, of Wassenburgh, were of great antiquity in Holland, and bore the augmentation of the sea-horse, in reference to the valour of an ancestor, who, during the Duke of Alva's campaign, was actively employed against the enemy, and undertook to swim an arm of the sea, with important intelligence to his besieged countrymen.*

When civil and religious liberty were assailed by the Spaniards in the Netherlands, the families of the Westenras suffered severely from the support they gave to truth and freedom, by being compelled to migrate from a country in which their family had long flourished in the possession of wealth, and transferred themselves and their possessions to our island, at a time when the accession of intelligence and capital was of incalculable advantage to it, as it proved in the case of the Huguenots and other Protestant settlers in Ireland, from the days of Elizabeth to the present time.

The advantage of such families settling in our island is not the more evident in any circumstances connected with them than the hereditary disposition manifest by them with few exceptions, to maintain the true religion established among us; and it is due to them and to the Church to record them as they occur, to the encouragement of others to imitate their generosity, for "one good deed dying tongueless, slaughters a thousand waiting upon that."

The aunt of the present Lord Rossmore, (Elizabeth Murray, daughter of Lady Blaney, the grand-daughter and sole heiress of Sir Alexander Cairnes), bequeathed £1,200 for the building of the Church in Monaghan, which has been followed up by the Hon. Henry Westenra, with a splendid organ which cost £800, with a salary to the organist of £40 a year.

The late lamented lady, whose sudden death under peculiarly painful circumstances, deprived her lord of a source of comfort and happiness which may be more easily conceived than expressed, was Augusta, fourth daughter of Frances Lord Elcho, and sister of the Earl of Weyms (Weymms.) Her ladyship had made arrangements, which will no doubt, be followed up by an endowment for the building and support of ten alms-houses, for poor widows and orphans.

It is no adulation of the rich and the noble to record such deeds, and in days of trouble, rebuke, (*continued...*)

2898, continued: ...and blasphemy, when good Samaritans like these are seldom found it cannot be irrelevant to the present work to brighten its pages by such details.

Though last, not least, we may record another departed member of this honourable family, in justice to the late Major, the Hon. Richard Westenra, second son of Lord Rossmore. In his respective duties as a son, husband, brother, parent, and friend, his worth was only known to those who knew him, and could appreciate his value.—They were, indeed, pre-eminent, and the loss of such a parent to a young family, must have been as afflicting as irreparable. His departure, however to them untimely, may have been to himself a mercy. The ways of heaven are inscrutable, and "Blessed are the dead that die in the Lord," as we trust this noble and gallant gentleman did, after the example of more than one of his ancestors, whose eminent piety as well as indomitable courage, are on record in the pages of history. Possessed of a large portion of that uncommon attribute called common sense, he had, moreover, a very considerable portion of literary attainments, which, under control of native talent and cultivated taste, made him a delightful companion, particularly at the festive board, where the enjoyment, soaring above that of mere animal life, was the feast of reason and the flow of soul. It is scarcely necessary to add, that this gentleman's death left a blank in society not easily to be filled, and he departed this life universally regretted.

But the most distinguished of all the members of this family, was David Cairnes, of Knockmany, in the county of Tyrone, Esq., counsellor at law. He was born on the 15th of November, 1645, and was the first gentleman in Ulster, who went into Derry, on the arrival of Lord Antrim's regiment at the waterside of that city, and the 7th December, 1688.

*ARMS.—Quarterly: first and fourth per bend or. and ar. in chief a tree, and in base a sea-horse, reguardant, on Waves, all appar for Westenra. Second and third quarterly; first and fourth az. three bullets within a bordure ar. for Murray; second and third ar. three birds, martetts, close within a border, as for Cairnes; crest, a lion rampant.—*Burke's Peerage.*

Rossmore.—By deed dated 25th, and enrolled the 27th November, 1667, Colonel Grace sold to this Warner Westenra, of the city of Dublin, merchant, the town and lands of Clonleagh, Rahenhennagh and Lyagh, in the King's County.—*Note from the Westenra History—see Burke's Peerage.*

(From Lodge's *Peerage.*)

ROSSMORE, BARON. (WESTENRA.)

WARNER-WILLIAM WESTENRA, Baron Rossmore of Monaghan, county Monaghan, *in the Peerage of Ireland*; Lord Lieutenant and Custos-Rotulorum of the county of Monaghan, born 14th October, 1765, succeeded Robert Cunningham, the First Lord, 6th August, 1801, married 1st, 3d October, 1791, Marianne, 2nd daughter of Charles Walsh, Esq.; and her Ladyship dying 12th Aug., 1807, he married 2ndly, 3d June, 1819, Lady August Charteris, 4th daughter of Francis, late Lord Elcho.—*See* Wemyss. By the 1st marriage his Lordship had issue.

1 *Hon. Henry Robert, M.P., born 24th August, 1792, married 25th January, 1820, Anne Douglas Hamilton (daughter of Douglas, 8th Duke of Hamilton).

2 *Hon. Warner-William*, born 23d August, 1793, deceased.

3 *Hon. Charles*, born 14th November, 1794, deceased.

4 Hon. Richard, born 21st February, 1796, married 8th June, 1822, Henrietta, only child of Owen Scott, Esq., by whom he has issue,

1 Mary, 2 Augusta, 3 Henrietta.

5 Hon. Lieutenant-Colonel John-Craven, Scots Fusileer Guards, M.P., born 31st March, 1798, married 31st March, 1834, Eleanor-Mary, daughter of the late William Jolliffe, Esq., and widow of Sir Gilbert East, Bart.

6 *Hon. Charles*, Lieutenant 8th Hussars, born 23d Aug. 1800, deceased.

7 Hon. Marianne, born 16th August, 1801, married 17th July, 1824, Samuel-Gist Gist, Esq.

His Lordship's father, *Henry Westenra, Esq.*, was born 12th January, 1742, married 1st December, 1764, Harriet, 5th daughter of Colonel John Murray, and sister to Elizabeth, wife of Robert Cunninghame [sic], first Lord Rossmore; by this Lady, on whose sons and their issue male, the Barony is entailed, and who is now his widow, Mr. Westenra had issue.

1 WARNER-WILLIAM, PRESENT AND SECOND LORD.

2 *Mary-Frances*, born 16th January, 1769, deceased; having married 14th February, 1788, *Sir John-Craven Carden, Bart.*, widower, 1st, of the Hon. Mary Pomeroy—*See* Harberton; 2ndly, of Sarah, daughter of John Moore, Esq.; he married 4thly, Anne, Viscountess Dowager Monck—*See* Rathdown, and died 22d November, 1820.

3 Lieutenant-Colonel Henry, born 1st June, 1770, married 9th April, 1829, Anna, youngest daughter of the late Isaac Corry, Esq., who died 8th January, 1831.

4 Harriet-Hester, born 2d February, 1777, married 17th April, 1797, the Hon. Colonel Edward Wingfield. *See* Powerscourt.

Creation.—1796.

Genealogy and Arms.—See *Genealogical Volume*, and Plates of Arms, page 80.

Motto.—*Post praelia praemia*: Honours after battles.

Seat.—Rossmore-Park, county Monaghan.

(1842-08-20, 3:1)

2899. With deep regret we have to record the death of Doctor Maginn this day, at his residence, Walton-upon-Thames. Doctor Maginn was in his 49th year, and for the last year and upwards suffered from confirmed consumption. He has left a widow and three children, we fear without any provision but the claim of the lamented deceased upon the gratitude of the country, and more especially of the wealthy and high-minded Conservative party. That claim is, however, a strong one; for more than twenty years, Dr. Maginn laboured for the Conservative cause without relaxation, and to the support of that cause he brought more learning, more genius, and more zeal, than any other man connected with the public press during the same period.—*Standard*. (1842-08-27, 1:3)

2900. Suicide.—On Saturday morning a Dissenting minister from Bangor, who was stopping at a carman's inn in North street, took fourpence worth of laudanum, which caused his death. On the fact of his having taken poison being known, the usual remedies were applied by a medical gentleman in the neighbourhood, but the unfortunate man gradually sunk. About three o'clock, he was removed to the hospital, and every means were taken for his recovery, but in vain—he died a short time after having been brought to the hospital. We understand that the unfortunate man was lately irregular in his habits. He had a wife and family.—*Newry Telegraph*. (1842-08-27, 1:3)

2901. *On Dit.*—It is stated among the fashionable circles that the member for the borough of Dundalk is about to form a matrimonial alliance with the eldest daughter of an ex-M.P. and the head of one of the oldest and most respectable families in the county of Wexford. It is understood that the lady brings as dowry large landed possessions to the already independent fortune of the hon. member. (1842-08-27, 2:4)

2902. Melancholy Accident.—On Monday, a man named M'Laughlen, employed at the Lough Swilly embankment, unfortunately lost his life, in consequence of being buried by a fall of earth where he was employed in excavating.—He was dug out in a very short time after the accident, but life was extinct. (1842-08-27, 3:2)

2903. A Nuptial Piece.

Young Love your gentle hearts had twin'd
For many years together;
And now your hearts and hands are joind
For ever, and for ever;
The joyful Hymen sends a boon—
The sweetest, richest honeymoon.

The blushing rose of youth appears
Upon thy cheeks, sweet bride,
Wet with thy parents mingled tears
Of love, and joy and pride:
Pure as the silver light of day,
Sincerest love illumes thy way.

Away! ye cares of life, away!
Blest bridegroom ne'er repine:
Love, with thy spirits ever gay,
Gives thee a bride divine:
The fairy gifts of earth and sea
Are sacred, Love, when touch'd by thee.

The world below, the sky above,
With all their sun and shade,
Can boast no higher gem than Love—
O! happy youth and maid!
The richest pearls of sea and land
Are priceless made at Love's command.

Twenty summer suns have shone
Upon the gentle bride;
And now her maiden task is done,
So take her to thy side;
Now you are bound in holy ties—
Link'd in eternal sympathies.

Let the sweet kiss of sacred Love,
All tenderly be given;
And loving lips shall voiceless move
In fervent prayer to heaven;
Unutterable words shall bless—
Beseeching endless happiness.

When the brief human life is past,
And earth shall fade from mortal eyes,
In sweet companionship at last,
True lovers reach their native skies;
Crown'd with a rich unfading boon,
Love's waneless, blessed honeymoon!

(1842-08-27, 4:1)

2904. The Late Loss of Life in Lough Swilly.—Twelve of the bodies of the unfortunate men who were drowned in Lough Swilly, on the 8th inst., have been found within these few days. One, that of a man named Sweeny—a man of large stature, and powerful limbs—was found floating off Hawk's Nest, on the west side of the Isle of Inch. The other eleven were discovered between Buncrana and Linsford. One of the survivors tells an affecting story respecting five of these. He says that when the boat upset, he instantly sank to the bottom, but soon rose again to the surface, and, on looking around, and stretching himself, intending to swim towards the shore, his brother came up so close to him that his hand touched his outstretched arm. He (the survivor) then laid hold of the boat, and extended one of his legs in the hope that his brother would take advantage of the offered support, and be kept afloat till a boat should come to their assistance. At this moment, four others rose close to them, when the four and his brother caught each other in a deadly grasp, and sunk to rise no more, locked in one another's arms. Last week a hook from a drag line caught in the clothes of one of them, and the five bodies were hauled up in the same position in which they had disappeared, the struggles of death and the tossing of the waves not having separated them in their last embrace. (1842-09-03, 2:2)

2905. Evelyn P. Shirley, Esq., M.P. for Monaghan, and his lovely bride, were expected at Lough Fea on Friday (yesterday). We understand that this excellent gentleman's return to this county will be celebrated by a splendid *fete* at the princely mansion of his father, E.J. Shirley, Esq., M.P. for Warwickshire. It is rumoured that Mr. E.P. Shirley will become a resident at Lough Fea, a circumstance which must conduce materially to the happiness of his tenantry and of the neighbouring gentry. (1842-09-10, 2:4)

2906. The living of Desertoghill, vacant by the death of the Rev. William Smith, has been conferred, by the Lord Bishop of Derry, on the Rev. Redmond M'Causland, a Curate of long standing and high character in the diocese. (1842-09-10, 2:4)

2907. Death of Captain Cullen.—The deepest gloom has just been thrown over this town and neighborhood, by the death, this morning, of typhus fever, of one of its best and most valued members, Captain Cullen, after a few days' illness.—Had this lamented gentleman moved on a more busy and bustling stage than ours here—had he been a single, solitary being, still his demise could not possibly be looked upon with indifference; but the stroke of death makes a wide chasm in the village circle, and tells, with a scathing effect, when a beloved and devoted husband, a kind and affectionate father, a just and good man in all the relations of life, is summoned in the prime of his days too, to an untimely grave—one of whom it may be well said:—

"Heaven in his portrait show'd a workman's hand,
And drew it perfect, yet without a shade."

Carrick-on-Shannon, Sept. 7, 1842.
(1842-09-10, 2:5)

2908. Rejoicings in Farney.—To the Editor of the Northern Standard.

Carrickmacross, 14th September, 1842.

Sir—As your paper is the local instrument of our county, for the spread and diffusion of information connected with it, may I trespass so far to "play upon your organ" as to request the insertion of the following narrative of occurrences in this remote part of the county Monaghan, consequent on the arrival amongst us of E.P. Shirley, Esq., M.P., and his young and beautiful bride.

It was well known, for some time before, that the day fixed upon for their arrival at Lough Fea, the seat of E.J. Shirley, M.P., was Friday, the 9th instant, and in consequence, a guard of honor of upwards of 1,000 real "Stalwart" Farney yeomen, all tenants on the Shirley Estate, were prepared to go to the country verge, mounted, and dressed in their Baronial Costume (the far-famed Farney frieze), and there to give the happy couple a regular *caed milla failtha*, but from the fear of accident, and the inconvenience of bringing such a large concourse of people together, at a time of year when they had all their harvest business on their hands, it was kindly suggested that "the intention" would be taken for "the act," and out of pure respect to the parties with whom this suggestion originated, the idea of making this intended demonstration, was reluctantly given up. Mr. Mitchell, however, the active and zealous agent of the estate, took care that they should not "cross the border" without his knowledge, and he was accordingly in waiting at the county bridge—as the representative of the many—to escort the happy pair to Lough Fea, where every possible arrangement had been made to given them an "Irish" and, therefore, a hearty reception.

On the night of Friday, the 9th instant, when it became generally known that the youthful and happy couple had actually arrived at Lough Fea, the country around was brilliantly lighted up with bonfires. From the county bridge at Aghaclint, to the bridge of Ballitrain, a distance of eleven Irish miles, and from the boundary between the county of Cavan and the Shirley Estate, to the western part of the parish of Donaghmoyne, a distance of about six Irish miles, and comprehending an area of 30,000 acres of an undulating country, not a hill was observed without its light, the inhabitants of townlands vieing with each other in exhibiting in the celebration of the joyful event, their ardour! their warmth!! and their fire!!! Vollies were discharged and responded to from hill to hill, till the whole country were confirmed in the opinion that "the Boys" (very harmlessly, no doubt,) had "kept their powder dry."

During the following day (Saturday), arrangements were spiritedly in progress amongst the inhabitants of Carrickmacross, *the metropolis of Farney*, to give a *finish* and *eclat* to the popular effusion of good feeling, and nothing could be more admirable than the result. Order and peace were the rule of the night. Happiness, concord, and pleasure were exhibited in every countenance, and nothing could exceed the universal anxiety that prevailed, to do honor, and shew respect, to the heir apparent to the Shirley Estate, and his youthful bride. No expense was spared by the inhabitants in lighting up their dwellings—such seemed to be, and was really, the universal feeling of respect towards a worthy landlord and his worthy son. May Erin long be blessed with persons in their exalted walk in life, entertaining such humane views to practice, in such a praiseworthy manner. The excellent Amateur Temperance Band of our town, under the directions of Mr. Burke, their talented instructor, were in attendance, and proved by their performance the happy effects, and great moral improvement which have resulted from abstaining from the use of intoxicating liquors.—Ardent spirits they still have, and seem to know full well, as the present occasion testifies, how and when to use them. Fire-works were thrown up by Mr. White, of Dublin, and were conducted on such a brilliant scale as to call for the praise and the admiration of every one who witnessed them.

It is most gratifying to learn that the whole evening's entertainment passed off without any accident. Many of the neighbouring gentry brought their families to town, to witness the rejoicings of the night, and they certainly must have returned home well pleased.

During the evening, the Shirley family and their visitors walked through the town, and were most heartily and loudly cheered. This must have been a novel scene to them. The outbreak of Irish feeling is always genuine, and must, as a matter of course, have produced this effect, particularly on those who never witnessed it before. The band having played "God save the Queen" and the National air of "Patrick's day," retired, amidst the plaudits of the people. Thus ended the joyous proceedings of the night, all parties retiring in the best possible good humour, highly pleased with every thing they had seen and heard, and pouring blessings upon the young couple, whose union and presence had been the cause of this public manifestation of esteem and respect.

Entertainment to the Children attending the Shirley Estate Schools.—On Tuesday, the 13th instant, the children in attendance at the various schools of the Estate, supported by Mr. Shirley, were entertained in the new Baronial Hall, each of the schools headed in procession by their respective masters and mistresses, and walking, males and females distinct, two abreast. This was a truly interesting sight—six hundred and seven children sat down and partook of an abundant meal. The Rev. Mr. Morris, an English gentleman, now at Lough Fea, having first implored, in brief, but impressive terms, a blessing on the children present, and the food, so bountifully and humanely provided for them.

During the repast, the band played several of their best pieces, and the enjoyment was heightened by the presence and performance of our highly gifted countryman, Mr. Patrick Byrne, the celebrated Harper, who is, we are proud to say, a thoroughbred Farneyman. When the children had concluded their meal, three cheers were respectively proposed and given for Mrs. and Mr. Shirley, Mrs. and Mr. E.P. Shirley, Mr. Mitchell, &c., &c. After the entertainment within doors had been brought to a close, a new scene presented itself outside. The children having retired in the same order in which they had entered the Baronial Hall, were marched to the lawn, where there were in preparation several means of amusement. Gymnastic exercises were at once commenced, and when the members of the juveniles had enjoyed this sport to their hearts' content, the various schools having reformed, preparatory to returning, three cheers were given for the Shirley family, and the band striking up "God save the Queen," followed by "Patrick's day," the entire party moved homewards, highly pleased with the entertainments and amusements of the day. During the entire afternoon, the exertions and attentions of Mrs. E.J. Shirley, Mrs. E.P. Shirley and Miss Shirley were unceasing. Mrs. Shirley presented, with her own hands, the rewards to the female victors, all of whom bore their honors away.

Dinner to the Tradesmen, Labourers, &c.—This day (Wednesday) the 14th instant, having been fixed upon for giving a dinner to the tradesmen, labourers, &c., employed by Mr. Shirley at his building and in his farm and demesne, a strong muster of persons so employed, took place, and at three o'clock, 141 persons, all well and comfortably clad, sat down to a substantial dinner, with its appendages, to which they did most ample justice. During, and after dinner, ale, wine, &c., were supplied to those of the party who chose to use them, and for those who did not, cordials had been prepared.

During dinner, the band continued to play the most favorite tunes, and at proper intervals, that truly national instrument, the harp, was heard filling the Grand Baronial Hall—a room 79 feet long, by 34 feet broad—with its soft and swelling sounds, combining sweetness and mellowness of tone with grand and powerful effect. Indeed, Mr. Byrne is a "witch" in his way, he is really so enchanting.

After dinner, several toasts were given, and drank with the best possible feeling. The following were enthusiastically received and heartily responded to.

Mr. Mitchell proposed the health of E.J. Shirley, Esq., the Lord of the Soil, and expressed an ardent hope that he might be long spared in health and happiness, to practice those virtues of benevolence and charity, for which every one present knew he was remarkable. This toast was drunk and received (the company all standing) with loud and long continued cheering, which could hardly be suppressed. At length, silence being restored,

Mr. Mitchell proposed the health of E.P. Shirley, Esq., and his young and amiable bride, and expressed a hope that they would imitate the virtues of their predecessors of the noble houses of Shirley and Lechmere. Again, every person in the room raised his person, hand and voice, to show the respect with which this toast had been received and drank; and the succession of cheers, which lasted for many minutes, made the very "welkin ring."

Mr. Mitchell then said he had another toast to give, and, from the manner in which the previous toasts had been drank, he had no doubt it would meet with the reception it deserved; he therefore begged to propose the health of Mrs. Shirley and Miss Shirley, whose characters for humanity, benevolence, and every other virtue which could adorn ladies of their exalted rank and station in society, stood so pre-eminent.

E.J. Shirley, Esq., returned thanks for the manner in which the health of Mrs. and Miss Shirley and other members of his family had been received, and expressed a hope, that they would continue to merit such manifestations of public approval (*continued...*)

2908, continued: ...as he had, this day and previously, the satisfaction to witness.

Mr. Mitchell again rose and said—He had one general toast to give, about the reception of which he felt no misgivings; he therefore begged leave to propose The Ladies who had kindly honoured the company with their presence on this occasion—may they long live to witness and enjoy such scenes as the present.

On this toast being announced, the grand baronial hall rang from floor to roof, and from end to end, with one series of reiterated, loud and long continued cheers.

E.J. Shirley, Esq., then came forward and returned thanks on the part of the ladies, and begged to propose the health of a gentleman present, whom they all knew, and whose services both himself and those who heard him, had a just right to value. He, therefore, at once proceeded to propose the health of Alexander Mitchell, Esq., the active and worthy agent of the Shirley Estate.

Mr. Mitchell, when the cheering had in some degree subsided, returned thanks, and expressed the gratification he naturally felt at hearing from Mr. Shirley's own lips, that his exertions in every way, as his agent, had met with his approval, and he trusted that his future conduct, both towards the landlord and the tenantry, would be such as would be calculated to protect and guard the interests of the one, and to promote, in every practicable way, the interests of the other. Mr. Mitchell begged, in conclusion, to observe, that it would continue to be his most ardent wish, as well as his best reward, to have his conduct, as the agent of the estate, honoured by Mr. Shirley's approval.

Mr. Shirley again came forward, and said—He would, before they retired to enjoy the amusement of the lawn, propose the health of Mr. G. Sudden, Mr. W.G. Smith, and Mr. Brockie, all of whom, in their respective departments, had, at all times, given him and others with whom they had to do, such general satisfaction.

Three cheers were called for, and lustily given, when Mr. Sudden came forward, and briefly, but honestly, on the part of "himself and fellows," responded to this toast, and expressed his thanks for the compliment paid to himself and those with whom Mr. Shirley had been pleased to associate his name.

The health of Father Mattew and the Temperance Band, as also that of the servants at Lough Fea, whose attentions during the whole affair were unremitting, having been proposed by Mr. Mitchell, were received with nothing short of enthusiasm.

The greatest credit is due to Mr. Yarwood, the house steward, for the excellence of the culinary arrangements, and his evident anxiety to bear the family out in carrying their humane intentions into operation. At intervals, several Irish and Scotch songs were sung —each possessing its own national claim to attention. All were, however, very excellent, and the spirit and good humour in which they were given made them doubly acceptable.

The party now proceeded to the lawn, to enjoy the sports prepared for their evening's entertainment. Climbing soaped poles, running races in sacks, "blind man's buff," wheelbarrow races by persons blind-folded, &c., kept all parties actively employed. Dancing having commenced, and having been carried on for some time, the finale was given to the whole proceedings by a country dance, led off by E.J. Shirley, Esq., Mrs. E.P. Shirley, in which Miss Shirley, Mr. E.P. Shirley, Mr. Morris, Mr. Mitchell, &c., took a part.

The urbane and kind demeanor of the Shirley family and their visitors, is the general theme of conversation here. Such proceedings as were yesterday witnessed, at the two extreme points of our county, are admirably calculated to draw more closely together, in feeling and attachment, the various classes of which society is composed, for it surely cannot be imagined that the humble classes in the community will respect those above them less, because they love them more. Let the landlords of Ireland "do likewise," and they will soon find the same great moral and intellecutal change take place in the character of their tenantry, and the improvements of their estates, which has, by judicious management and kind and conciliating conduct, been effected in this once rude barony of Farney within the last twelve years. (1842-09-17, 2:6)

2909. Funeral of the Late Mr. Curry.—The funeral of the late lamented Master of Chancery, passed through this town on Wednesday last, attended by a numerous concourse of the gentry and inhabitants of Aughnacloy and its neighbourhood—Middletown and Armagh —many of whom came to Monaghan to meet the procession, and thus pay their last tribute of respect to one so much revered in life. The funeral arrived in Monaghan about 10 o'clock, when the train halted for breakfast, and about 11 o'clock again moved out of town, on its way to Aughnacloy, where the family burying place of the deceased is situated. The remains were conveyed in an elegantly equipped hearse, drawn by six long-tailed, black, full-bred horses, attended by two mourning coaches, each drawn by four horses of a similar description, containing the chief mourners—the Rev. Dr. Bruce, Halliday and Samuel Bruce, Esqrs.; Thomas and Alexander Dobbin, Esqrs.; Marcus and Robert Mazierre, Esqrs.; John Connor, Esq., and Alexander MCullagh, Esq. The procession consisted, on leaving Monaghan, of the hearse, mourning coaches, 16 carriages, and several gigs, cars, and horsemen. Amongst those present we observed the following gentlemen:—William Anketell, Esq., of Anketell Grove; James Montgomery, Esq., Thomas Montgomery, Esq., Lee M'Kinstrey, Esq., James and Henry Falls, Esqrs., Hugh Moore, Esq., John Falls, Esq., James Caulfield M'Kinstry, Esq., Joseph Mathews, Esq., Rev. Dr. Henry, Mr. Dixon, Rev. Dr. Bruce, Thomas Dobbin, Esq., John M'Kinstry, Esq., William Horner, Esq., Armstrong, Esq., John Simpson, Esq., of Clover Hill; Thomas Anketell, Esq., of Dungillick; Alexander Dobbin,

Esq., George Barnes, Esq., William Anketell, Esq., of the Cottage; J. Armstrong, Esq., and Mayne, Esq., besides many others whose names we did not learn. The procession was also accompanied out of town by many of our townsmen. We understand that when the hearse approached Aughnacloy it was met by a vast crowd of persons who assembled to do honor to the obsequies of their countryman.

We have received the following communication from a friend, and gladly give it insertion:—

Mr. Curry was a native of Aughnacloy—when young, his father sent him to the then celebrated school of Dr. Bruce, then the first in Belfast, where he distinguished himself, particularly in the classical department. In college, he bore away the gold medal from the present Attorney-General, and a number of such men. At the bar, he was distinguished by the soundness of his legal knowledge—the clearness of his views, as well as by his unbending integrity, and was much respected by judges, barristers, and juries. In private life he was most estimable, a warm friend, a safe adviser—and kind beyond conception—in the domestic circle, and in religion and politics, firm, but most tolerant to all, so that in fact, few men were so sincerely and universally beloved and respected.

In the year 1825, Mr. Curry was honored with a silk gown. In the year 1837, he was called on by the Whig constituency of Armagh, to stand in the room of his venerable uncle, Leonard Dobbin, Esq., then retiring under a weight of years, from the honorable position he had held as the first Member for Armagh under the *Reform Act*. Mr. Curry attended so arduously to his Parliamentary duties, that a few months after his return, his health became seriously impaired. On Election Committees his services were acknowledged by all parties to be most valuable. Whilst he stood high in the estimation of the Government, his political opponents, (private, he had none), all respected him. The Mastership of Chancery became vacant in the year 1839, and being offered to Mr. Curry, he thought it right to accept a situation, not only honorable, and profitable, but peculiarly adapted to his talents. Whilst discharging its duties most creditably to himself and beneficially to the public, God was pleased, after two or three days' illness, and by a dispensation most unexpected by his numerous and ardently attached relatives, to release him from the cares and sorrows of mortal life. There has seldom lived any man in Dublin, of whom so many northerns of different religions, and political creeds, could each in sincerity have said—"he is my friend." Though the funeral procession passed through Dublin at so early an hour as six o'clock on Tuesday morning, thirty private carriages were waiting to accompany it at Ball's Bridge. In his native town, a large assemblage paid the last sad tribute to departed worth; many whom he had materially served were amongst the number.

His wife, a daughter of the late Dr. Bruce, by whom he had no issue, died eighteen years before him. He lived and died a Presbyterian. (1842-09-24, 3:1)

2910. Marriage in High Life.—Married, on the 17th instant, in St. George's Church, Hanover-square, London, by the Rev. P. Scholefield, George D. Coleman, Esq., of the Honorable East India Company's Service, at Singapore, to Maria Frances, youngest daughter of the late George Vernon, Esq., of Clontarf Castle, near Dublin. (1842-09-24, 3:2)

2911. Death of the Master of the Rolls.—With deep sorrow and regret we have to announce the demise of Sir Michael O'Loghlen, Bart., Master of the Rolls, which deplorable event occurred at Brighton on Tuesday night.

The Right Hon. Baronet left Drumconora, county of Clare, some weeks for the benefit of change of air—he having suffered severely in health from his untiring and incessant application to the business of his court.

He did not close his court until he had disposed of every case on the list—in fact, he has fallen a martyr to the faithful and over-zealous discharge of his duties.

Sir Michael was one of the best judges that ever adorned the bench in this or any other country. All men of all parties, who had occasion to go to his court, were enthusiastic in praise of his pre-eminent abilities and zealous devotion to the interests of suitors. In every relation of life he was estimable; as a judge he was revered—as a citizen he was esteemed and admired—as a friend he was honoured and loved.

By his death the Irish bench has lost its brightest ornament. No man ever gave such universal satisfaction to all parties as he did. So great was public reliance and confidence in him, that the business of his court had increased more than two fold since his appointment. His loss can only be regarded as a public calamity.

We understand that Sir Michael O'Loughlen [sic] had been long labouring under the effects of internal disease, which, within the last few days, assumed so decided a character, as to justify the most gloomy anticipations. In obedience to a hasty summons from his father, Mr. Colman O'Loughlen arrived on Wednesday, when he learned that the melancholy event—now so universally deplored—had occurred a few hours before he reached the hotel.

Lady O'Loughlen passed through this city on Tuesday from Drumconora [sic], and arrived at Merrion-square on Wednesday. The late Sir Michael O'Loughlen, Bart., was fourth son of the late Colman O'Loughlen, of Port, county Clare, Esq., by his second wife, daughter of Doctor Finucane, of Ennis, born 1789, married 1817 to the daughter of Daniel Kelly, Esq., of Dublin, by whom he has left eight children, the eldest Coleman, born 1819, who succeeds to the Baronetcy. He was called to the bar in 1811.

When the distressing intelligence of the demise of the Right Hon. Sir Michael O'Loughlen reached Ennis, the inhabitants anxious to testify (*continued...*)

2911, continued: …their deep sorrow at the melancholy event to their excellent neighbour, closed their shops.—*Limerick Chronicle*. (1842-10-08, 1:5)

2912. Melancholy Accident.—On the 30th ult., an inquest was held before Geo. Walter Young, Esq., Coroner, and a respectable Jury, at Cullingtragh, in the County of Armagh, on view of the body of Mr. Andrew Black, son of the late Rev. Mr. Black. The first witness examined was William Bittles, who deposed, that on Thursday evening last, about 8 o'clock, he was returning from Newry on his way home in a cart, with deceased and Maria Bittles, his daughter. A short distance from Turley's public-house, in Tullyhappy, his daughter fell off the cart. The horse ran away; and, unfortunately, the reins broke, when the deceased fell out of the cart. After some time the deceased was found lying on the road quite dead, and a large quantity of blood beside him. The body was then removed to the house of the deceased. Some other witnesses deposed to the same facts. Surgeon Savage, who was examined, stated the deceased came by his death from the bursting of a blood vessel, occasioned by the fall. After a long and searching inquiry, the Jury returned a verdict of—"Accidental death." (1842-10-08, 2:2)

2913. The collection for the late Bishop of Meath's family progresses very slowly in the diocese. The Archbishop of Dublin has given the munificent donation of £1,000 to Mrs. Dickenson, to assist in paying that portion of the charge still due on Ardbraccan house, and also the profits of his late work on Christ's Kingdom. (1842-10-15, 2:3)

2914. The Late Sir Lowry Cole.—Few officers of the British army, or of that of any other nation, have served their country with more devoted zeal, energy, or ability, than General the Hon. Sir Galbraith Lowry Cole. His name is associated with many a deed of gallant daring in early life, and his after-career in Sicily, France, and the Peninsula, forms a bright page in our military annals. He wore a cross of four clasps, a distinction which is equivalent to eight medals, for his services at the battle of Maida, on the 4th of July, 1806, where he had charge of a brigade, and for his conspicuous bravery at Albuera, Salamanca, Vittoria, the Pyrenees, Neville, Othes, and Toulouse, on the 5th of May, 1811; 2d of July, 1812; 21st of June, 28th of July, and 10th of November, 1813; and 27th of February, and 10th of April, 1814; in each of which memorable actions he commanded a division. His other honorary decorations consisted of the Grand Cross of the Bath, which was conferred upon him immediately after the extension of that order in February, 1813 (he having been previously created a K.B.), and several foreign orders, although they are not enumerated in the Army List.

His commissions bear date as follow:—

Cornet, 12th Light Dragoons … March 31, 1787
Lieutenant, 5th Dragoon Guards … May, 31, 1791
Captain, 70th Regiment … Nov. 30, 1792
Major, 102d Regiment … Oct. 31, 1793
Lieutenant-Colonel, Wards Regiment … Nov. 26, 1794
Lieut.-Colonel of a newly raised corps … April 12, 1799
Lieutenant-Colonel, 27th Regiment … Aug. 4, 1804
Colonel by brevet … Jan. 1, 1805
Major-General … April 25, 1808
Lieutenant-General … June 4, 1813
General … July 22, 1839

In May, 1808, he was appointed to the staff in Sicily, whence he was removed, in August, 1809, to Spain and Portugal, where he continued to serve until the end of the war. In September, 1814, he was selected for the command of the Northern and Yorkshire districts; and in May, 1815, he proceeded to Flanders, but was not present in the action at Waterloo. In March, 1820, he went to Ireland, and commanded the forces there until April, 1823, when he was nominated Governor and Commander-in-Chief of the Mauritius, which responsible post he quitted in March, 1828, for the Governorship and command of the troops at the Cape of Good Hope. He was relieved from this, his last tour of active duty, by Sir Benjamin Durban, in October, 1833. He was appointed Colonel of the 103d Regiment on the 10th of January, 1812; of the 70th, on the 12th of January, 1814; of the 34th, on the 21st of May, 1816; and of the 27th, on the 16th of December, 1826. He received the public thanks of the House of Commons upon two occasions—namely, in February, 1812, and May, 1816. Sir Lowry Cole was in the 71st year of his age. The sinecure appointment of Governor of Gravesend and Tulbury Fort, which he had held since January, 1820, will now be abolished. (1842-10-15, 2:5)

2915. An Irishman, named John Henry M'Carthy, died on board the Michigan ship, when coming from New Orleans, and which arrived at Liverpool on Wednesday last.—When dying, Mr. M'Carthy gave the master of the vessel, Captain Hastings, a sum of £50 with some trunks to keep for his wife and child, who are both in some part of this country. It appears that M'Carthy was about two years in America, and was returning home to the land of his nativity when he unfortunately died. He was of a dark complexion, and about five feet ten inches in height. (1842-10-15, 2:5)

2916. The Late Sir Michael O'Loghlen.—The remains of the justly respected, and universally regretted Master of the Rolls, left Dublin at one o'clock, afternoon of Wednesday last, followed by very near 200 private equipages, of the highest public functionaries, and principal gentry of the Irish metropolis, of all creeds and politics, who collected to pay the last sad tribute of veneration for the virtues of their beloved countryman, whose decease, in the prime of life, and in the zenith of his fame, is not merely a loss irreparable to his own family, but a public calamity to Ireland. No judge within the last half century, has died so much esteemed and lamented. The funeral *cortege* rested at Monastereven on Wednesday night, and at Roscrea on Thursday night, entering this city at half past five last evening, the shops in the several towns in the line of route being closed, as a mark of respect when the melancholy cavalcade passed. A number of citizens left town to meet the procession, but as much uncertainy prevailed as to the time, many not expecting its arrival before night, the cavalcade was not near so great as otherwise it might have been. The procession consisted of a hearse drawn by six black horses, with ostrich sable plumes, followed by two mourning coaches containing the eldest son of the deceased, Sir Coleman O'Loghlen, the brothers of the deceased, Hugh O'Loghlen, and Bryan O'Loghlen, Esqrs. and his intimate friend, Michl. Finucane, Esq. as chief mourners. Then came the civic officers, two, and two, the Mayor and members of the Town Council, with crape bands on their right arms, a concourse of private citizens, carriages, and other vehicles. The mournful *cortege* entered by Clare-street, Assembly Mall, Bank-place, Rutland-street, Patrick-street, and turned into Denmark-street, where the remains were taken from the funeral car, and conveyed into St. Michael's Chapel, the Roman Catholic Clergy chaunting an appropriate hymn. The interior of the Chapel was lighted up, and the body, surmounted by a black velvet pall, with wax tapers at each side, lay upon a bier before the altar, during the night, attended by mutes, and, after office and high mass, at 7 o'clock this morning, for the dead, the funeral procession again moved on to Ruan, County Clare, its last resting place, attended by great crowds, of sorrowing spectators, who increased to a vast multitude on the road.

The funeral arrangements were respectably made out by Mr. Guerty, of Baggot-street, Dublin, and his representative on the route, was Mr. O'Donnell.

We should add, that in the evening and morning, a party of the City Police, under Sub-inspector Williams, attended, to preserve order about the Chapel, and were most useful in facilitating the funeral arrangements. (1842-10-15, 4:4)

2917. Fatal Occurrence.—Another of the many instances of loss of life, from the negligent and incautious use of fire arms, occurred in the neighbourhood of Moira on Monday last, a young man, named Bateman, a most respectable farmer, residing in that neighbourhood, on going out of his field, to superintend a number of workmen, whom he had engaged in making improvements, took out with him his fowling-piece. After looking about for a short time, without success, for a shot, he deposited the gun, for safety, in a thorn bush, convenient to the workmen. Wishing afterwards to return home he went to take up his gun, which he most imprudently took hold of by the muzzle, and in drawing it to him, the trigger was caught by a branch, by which it was discharged, and the contents, consisting of shot, were lodged in his chest.—He dropped down, and died in a few minutes. Deceased was married only a few months, and has left a young woman, with an aged mother and some sisters to lament his melancholy fate, an inquest was held on the body, when a verdict of "Accidentally Shot" was returned.—*Newry Telegraph.* (1842-10-22, 1:3)

2918. Inquest on the Body of a Man, name Unknown.—There was an inquest held in the townland of Maghanverry, near Markethill, on the 11th instant, by George Henry, Esq., coroner, on the body of a traveller, name unknown, who came by his death in consequence of having drunk a quantity of vitriol, which was given him, by mistake, for whiskey, in some public-house. He was a very stout athletic man, about forty-five years of age, and five feet eleven inches high, with dark hair, and a large nose, the lower end of which was flattened to the face. He had on a drab or greyish frock coat, with dark brown buttons, blue cloth waistcoat, with bright buttons, black silk neck-tie, check shirt, corduroy trousers, flannel drawers, grey socks, strong new shoes, and a wool hat, with maker's name inside, viz., Matthew Market, near Tullycorbit Church, county Monaghan. He had some money in his pocket, and clothes in a bag, which are now deposited in the police barrack, Markethill.—*Newry Telegraph.* (1842-10-22, 2:1)

2919. Dreadful Disaster at Sea.—(From the *Waterford Mirror.*)—Intelligence of the following disaster, there is some reason to fear, with the loss of the crew of the vessel run down, with the exception of one man, the writer of the subjoined statement, reached this city on Saturday. It appears that the brig *Dundonald*, of Troon, D. M'Nicol, master, which sailed from this port on Tuesday evening, for Troon, laden with ballast, was, shortly after her departure, in contact with the schooner *Kirby*, laden with slates from Dudden, a small seaport on the borders of Lancashire and Cumberland. The only particulars that we have yet learned are contained in the letter at foot, written by one of the crew of the *Kirby*, which letter he handed to the pilot authorities at Passage of Waterford, when he arrived in the *Maid of Mostyn*—it is to be remarked that the letter is not signed with the writer's name. The *Dundonald* took her departure from Hook Tower at eight o'clock on Tuesday evening, and her collision with the *Kirby* occurred about three hours after, and about sixteen miles from the Hook. We learn that the night was rather cloudy, but that the sea was smooth, with a light breeze. While we anxiously await some further intelligence, and in particular the version of the occurrence to be given by the *Dundonald*, we should think that it appears at least somewhat probable, from the following letter that the *Kirby* and the remainder of the crew went down:—

"This is to certify that the schooner *Kirby*, of Dudden, was bound on her passage from Dudden to Youghal, with a cargo of slates; and on Tuesday, the 11th of October, betwixt the hours of ten and twelve, p.m., the brig *Dundonald*, of Troon, and the said schooner got entangled with one another (*continued...*)

2919, continued: ...about a mile to the southward of the Connibegs light-ship, when the master of the schooner called out to the brig, 'You will run us down;' they said, 'Put your helm down,' and immediately the vessels struck, when our master called out, 'She is going down—save yourselves if you can.' With that I left the helm, and ran forward, and got hold of the brig's bobstay along with my shipmate, but I do not know whether he went overboard or not. There was none got aboard of the brig but myself. There was one of the brig's crew assisted me in getting over the bows. When I got on deck I heard my master say, 'Oh! dear captain, stand by us,' and he gave him no answer, but was giving orders to his men about his jib-boom, for it was carried away. I kept looking towards the schooner, and as near as I can calculate I saw her about twenty minutes, and the last words I heard my captain say were 'Oh, my dear wife.' I went to the captain of the brig, and said, 'you would better stand towards her,' and he said, 'what good can I do? let us get our own jib-boom in.' I wanted him to put me on board the Lightship, but he would not do it, and I remained on board of her till Thursday, the 13th, when I saw a schooner standing in for Tuskar Light. I asked the captain if he would allow his men to pull me abord of the schooner, and he said it was a day's work, she was so far off, and two of the men said they would go, and he said, 'Very well, call the hands up.' So we lowered the boat, and pulled toward the schooner, and made signal to her, and she hove to until we came up to her, which we found to be the *Maid of Mostyn*, Captain Edwards, bound to Ross, and I asked a passage from him, and he told me to come aboard. It was 3 p.m., then. She was about seven miles to the E.N.E. of Tuskar Light.

We have not learned the name of the writer of this statement. It appears that he was a north of England man, and has gone on to Youghal, in the expectation of finding the schooner was able to prosecute her voyage. We trust that the expectation will be realised. Her crew consisted of the master and three men, and it appears that the master's wife was also on board. (1842-10-22, 4:5)

2920. Hugh Gray, Esq., has been appointed a stipendiary magistrate, in the room of Mr. Esmonde, deceased.—*Evening Packet*. (1842-10-29, 1:3)

2921. Dr. Peter Kenny, of Charles-street, Seymour-street, late of Waterford, cut his throat on Tuesday night, and was a corpse in five minutes, having severed the carotid artery and jugular vein with a razor. (1842-10-29, 2:2)

2922. Fatal Accident.—Friday last, at Drumcroohan, near Derrygonnelly, a servant girl named Maguire came by her death from the kick of a horse. An inquest was held on Sunday by Mr. Trotter, coroner, and a verdict according to the above circumstances returned. (1842-10-29, 2:2)

2923. On the Death of J L, Aged Three Months.

As a flower weigh'd down by the midnight dew,
Breaks its frail stalk, and its rosy hue
Is lost 'mid the clods that it surround,
And sheds all its leaves on the moisten'd ground,

So lovely in form and in beauty he grew,
He smiled on all, and no evil knew;
His heart from every bond was free—
He seem'd a fair stem of a lovely tree.

But scarcely the fields their fruit had shed,
When tired of earth's joys, his way he sped
To a better place, where a joyful band
Hailed his approach to that happy land.

Then, farewell, sweet babe, no more I'll mourn,
Nor wish from that place my love to return;
Thou wert beauteous in death, and lovelier far
Than the bright twinkling light of an evening star.

No frown on thy brow foretold thy doom—
No pang thy companion to an early tomb;
With a pleasing smile thou did'st take thy flight,
And wing thy way to the regions of light.

Rescued from trials which we must bear—
Freed from all pain and anxious care—
No troubled sigh thy heart oppressed,
But now, with thy Saviour, art calmly at rest.

Yet I'll think of thee at night's still hour,
In the crowded hall or lonely bower,
Till I see thee in brilliant form arrayed,
When I shall have passed the grave's dark shade.

(1842-10-29, 4:1)

2924. Death of General Sir C.W. Doyle.—It is with deep and sincere regret that we announce the decease of a most worthy man and excellent officer Lieutenant-General Sir Charles Wm. Doyle, who died in Paris a few days ago—Sir Charles's services were of a varied and variable nature. In the Peninsula they were principally of a diplomatic kind, though connected with the military operations, the success of which may, in many important instances, be traced to his judicious and keen-sighted policy. It would be difficult to name an officer in the British army who was a more universal favourite than Sir Charles Doyle. An apt illustration of the correctness of this assertion is afforded by the consequences of the second battalion of the 87th Royal Irish Fusiliers, which at the time of his joining was in a very disorganised state. Such was his tact and management, and the influence which he possessed over the men, that by persuasion and a few friendly and well-timed admonitions, he succeeded in restoring the battalion without the infliction of a single lash, to a state of discipline and good order which has rarely been excelled.—He was a Grand Cross of the Royal Hanoverian Guelphic Order, a Companion of the Bath, a knight of the Legion of Honour, of Charles the Third of Sweden, and had the second class of the Crescent. He wore a medal for his services in Egypt, in addition to several decorations conferred upon him by the municipal authorities of Spain. Sir Charles's military career is honourably associated with the annals of the Netherlands and the conquest of our West Indian possessions.—*United Service Gazette*. (1842-11-05, 2:2)

2925. Marriage in High Life.—In Gelston Castle, Kirkcudbrightshire, Scotland, on the 25th of October, Charles Lionel Kirwan, Esq., of Gelston Castle above mentioned [*to Matilda Elizabeth, daughter of William Maitland of Auchlane and Gelston. Source: Burke, 1875.*] (1842-11-05, 2:2)

2926. Inquests.—An inquest was held at Cluntibunian, parish of Tedavnet, on the 28th ult., before Robert Murray, Esq., M.D., Coroner for the county Monaghan, on the body of Owen Coyle, aged about seven or eight years. It appeared, on evidence, that deceased was coming into Monaghan with a load of turf, when he was met by two boys, John Treanor and Michael Murrer, returning from Monaghan after disposing of their turf. One of them, Murrer, seized deceased by the shoulder with one hand, and with the other caught a rod which deceased had in his hand.—The deceased then fell into the ditch, and Murrer fell against him, but the witness, Treanor, who was along with Murrer at the time, did not think deceased was hurt by the fall.

Doctor Christian, who held a *post mortem* examination of the deceased, was of opinion that the cause of death was an abscess in the neighbourhood of the hip, which he conceived, in all probability, arose in consequence of the fall against the ditch. The jury found accordingly.

An inquest was held on the 3d instant, before Robert Murray, Esq., on view of the body of James Connor, a lad about sixteen or seventeen years of age, at Bradox, parish of Tullycorbet, county Monaghan. The finding of the jury was:—That deceased came by his death from a cart loaded with flax, being accidentally overturned upon him. The deceased was from Ballymoney, county Antrim, and had been with his master, James Johnson, a carman, in Ballybay market, from whence they were proceeding to Belfast, where the cart upset. He was under the load about half an hour before assistance could be procured to remove it. His master procured a coffin, and had the body conveyed to Ballymoney, where the mother of deceased, a poor widow, resides. (1842-11-05, 2:5)

2927. Illness of Lord Blayney.—We regret to announce the serious and dangerous illness of Lord Blayney, at his residence, Castleblayney. His Lordship is suffering from a severe attack of dysentery.—Our eminent and skilful county Surgeon, Doctor Andrew Knight Young, has been in constant attendance upon the suffering nobleman since Monday last, aided by Doctor Cuming, of Armagh; Sir Philip Crampton also met those gentlemen in consultation on Thursday and Friday. The last accounts received are:—That the dangerous symptoms have been held in check by the faculty, and that evidences of a favourable change are becoming apparent. The greatest anxiety prevails respecting the health of this humane and kindly nobleman, and we trust, from the favourable symptoms developing themselves, and the experience and skill of his medical attendants, that under Providence, he will be spared to his attached tenantry. We believe the title would become extinct in case of his Lordship's demise. Lady Blayney is at Castleblayney in attendance upon her son. (1842-11-05, 3:1)

2928. Rumoured Loss of Three Pilots.—On Tuesday evening last three pilots, Richard M'Greevey, and two men of the name of M'Keown, went down the lough on the look out for vessels. On Friday morning, the boat in which they went out was picked up near Bangor, with her stern out. It is supposed that either the boat has been run down by a steam boat, or has been capsized in a squall; the former supposition, it is to be hoped, will prove correct, as there will be then a greater probability of the men having been rescued from a watery grave.—*Ulster Times*. (1842-11-12, 1:3)

2929. Chairmanship of Kilmainham.—Mr. Max Blacker, whose state of health has for some time precluded him from discharging the duties of the office, has resigned the chairmanship of Kilmainham. Nothing definitive has been decided on as to the successor of the learned gentleman.—*Mail*. (1842-11-12, 1:5)

2930. Mrs. Colonel Copeland has applied to Queens-square office, for relief for herself and child, being left by her husband without provision, though she had her carriage and horses in Dublin not long ago. (1842-11-12, 2:1)

2931. Marriage in High Life.—The improving town of Tynan witnessed a very stirring and interesting scene on Wednesday, when the beautiful and accomplished Miss Stronge was led to the hymeneal altar by Capt. M'Clintock, R.N. The ceremony was performed by His Grace the Lord Primate. The gallant Captain was accompanied on the joyous occasion by his friend and companion in arms, Captain Tipping, R.N. The Diamond, though very spacious, was crowded with carriages. After the ceremony, the happy couple set off to Caledon Hall, the seat of the Right Hon. Earl of Caledon, where it is understood they intend to spend the honeymoon.—*Newry Telegraph*. (1842-11-12, 2:4)

2932. Inquest.—An inquest was held at Caddagh, parish of Tullycorbet, in this county, on Saturday last, the 5th inst., before Robert Murray, Esq., M.D., coroner, on the body of Susan Cassely, who poisoned herself by swallowing a penny worth of arsenic, which she purchased in Monaghan on the previous Monday, under the pretence of destroying rats. It appeared that the husband of the unfortunate wretch had gone to America some years since, (*continued...*)

2932, continued: ...and that he was about returning this season, and that she was in a state of pregnancy by another man, and fearing to meet her illtreated spouse, she put an end to her existence. She acknowledged the crime immediately after swallowing the fatal draught, and although every remedy was used to save her life they proved ineffectual. Doctor M'Lean, of Ballybay, applied the stomach-pump twice, and drenched the stomach, but to no purpose. She lingered from Tuesday until Saturday in the greatest agony—always expressing her determination to destroy herself even if that attempt failed—she said she wished to hide her shame in the grave, and was glad she took the poison, save that she did not expect to experience so much agony. The jury returned a suitable verdict. (1842-11-12, 2:4)

2933. Illness of Lord Blayney.—We have just heard from Castleblayney—Lord Blayney is in a very precarious state. He made a rally on Wednesday night, and favorable expectations were entertained. He had a bad and restless night on Thursday, and no appearance of improvement this morning; however, he is holding his ground, which is a great thing, and his medical attendants are yet sanguine.

The state of his Lordship's health has given rise to much Radical speculation in this county, which, it would be bad taste to animadvert on at present; but we have a rod in pickle for them, which we intend using unsparingly when his Lordship is restored to health, which we fervently hope will shortly be the case. In the event of his demise, the oldest title in Monaghan would be extinct, (the present is the twelfth Baron Blayney) and his extensive estates in Monaghan would become the property of Admiral Gordon, his brother-in-law, or his issue. Admiral Gordon is, we understand, a Liberal, and the chance of a transfer of the leading Conservative interest in the county into Liberal hands, has aroused the drooping spirits of the crest-fallen faction. Hence the rumours that have spread like wildfire through the country. Since the above, we have another account which states his Lordship is better. (1842-11-12, 2:4)

2934. Melancholy and Fatal Circumstance.—A very melancholy and fatal circumstance occurred in our jail last night. The facts are these:—This morning, at the usual hour, the turnkey of the felons' cell proceeded to that part of the prison, for the purpose of unlocking the cells. On reaching the centre cell, at the entrance to which an Arnold stove is placed, he was perfectly horror-struck to perceive three of the prisoners in a state of insensibility! Two of them were almost lifeless at the time they were discovered, and in a few minutes afterwards, life was completely extinct. Their names were Wm. Sullivan (under sentence of transportation for 7 years) and Edmund Burke, charged with the robbery of Mr. Holmes's fire-arms, in the Glen of Aherlow. The third man, named Callagher [sic], charged with a similar offence, still survives, and hopes are entertained of his recovery. It seems that this fatal occurrence was caused by an aperture in the flew [sic] of the stove, in which stone coal was burning, and the deaths were caused by suffocation. Since the foregoing was in type, the other unfortunate man, Gallagher, has died.—*Tipperary Constitution.* (1842-11-12, 4:1)

2935. Death of Lord Gort.—With feelings of intense sorrow, it is our painful duty to announce the death of one whose loss will create a greater blank in Irish political and social life, than almost any other name we could mention. Our justly esteemed and venerated friend, Lord Gort, expired yesterday evening, in Pembroke-place, in this city.

We cannot, at this moment, attempt to do justice to the various qualities which combined to render him the life and ornament of Irish society, still less to give that detailed notice of his public career which so remarkable a man deserves from the public journalist. For the present we can do no more than give a feeble expression to the universal sorrow which has spread throughout our city, for the loss of so rare an union of public and private worth.

His Lordship was Viscount Gort and Baron Kiltarton, in the Peerage of Ireland.

By his death a vacancy occurs in the Representative Peerage; and the office of constable to the Castle of Limerick reverts to the crown. He is succeeded in his title by his eldest son, the Honorable John Prendergast Vereker, (now Viscount Gort,) of Roxborough, in the county of Limerick.—*Evening Packet.* (1842-11-19, 1:2)

2936. Death of Colonel Cullen.—We very sincerely regret to announce the death of the above gentleman, which unexpected event took place on Wednesday last, at Screeny house, near Manorhamilton. He was an old and efficient Magistrate of the county of Leitrim, and few gentlemen were more generally beloved than the deceased. His amiable family are much to be pitied—two of his daughters had, only a few days previous to his death gone on a visit to their brother-in-law, the Rev. Edward Labatt, Rector of Killybegs, in this county, and will only reach Screeny in time to witness their beloved parent's funeral procession which takes place on Saturday next.—*Ballyshannon Herald.* (1842-11-19, 1:2)

2937. Several public schools in the vicinity of Dublin are closed in consequence of Scarletina and measles being prevalent with the scholars. (1842-11-19, 1:4)

2938. Death of the Bishop of Cashel.—(From the *Evening Packet.*)—We regret having to announce the demise of the Right Hon. and Right Rev. Stephen Creagh Sandes, LL.D., Bishop of the united diocess of Cashel, Emly, Waterford, and Lismore, which event took place at an early hour on Tuesday morning, at his Lordship's residence in Fitzwilliam-square, in this city. Doctor Sandes was for many years a Fellow of the Dublin University, where he was universally esteemed for the mildness of his manners, his profound learning, and numerous sterling but unobtrusive merits, as a gentleman and a divine.

In 1836, he was consecrated Bishop of Cashel and Emly, on the demise of the late Doctor Lawrence, and was in 1839 invested with episcopal jurisdiction over the other sees, immediately after the death of Dr. Burke, the preceding diocesan. Doctor Sandes's appointment was one of the very few which gave general satisfaction to all parties; for, although as an avowed Whig, and, to the last degree, a Liberal in all politics, he was yet, from his manifold good qualities and the unassuming simplicity of his character, a great favourite in every quarter where he was known. In short, to know Stephen Creagh Sandes, and not to love him, would be a very difficult thing indeed. The deceased prelate, who had long been in an extremely delicate state of health, only returned from England on Friday last, and since that period continued speechless.—His inability to articulate was caused by paralysis. He was, however, perfectly conscious of his approaching dissolution, and to the last recognized his friends. His death was in every sense that of a sincere believer in the merits of his Saviour's atonement. His remains are, we understand, to be deposited in the vaults of the University. (1842-11-19, 2:3)

2939. The preliminaries have been arranged for the marriage of Lady Fanny Emily Vane Stewart, eldest daughter of the Marquess and Marchioness of Londonderry, with the Marquess of Blandford, eldest son of the Duke of Marlborough, and the ceremony will take place in London at the close of the ensuing season, by which period the Marquess will have attained his majority. His lordship is now cruising with Captain Lynon, in the *Cirkassian* yacht, in the Mediterranean, whence he intended to make a tour in Syria and Egypt. (1842-11-19, 4:1)

2940. Rejoicings near Drumquin.—On the evening of Thursday, the 3d of November, the tenants of Sir James M. Stronge, Bart., in the neighbourhood of Drumquin, county of Tyrone, assembled to celebrate the nuptials of his daughter. Soon as the happy event was made known, the intelligence spread like wildfire through Sir James' numerous tenantry, and all being anxious to show their attachment to him, or to any member of his ancient and respectable family, they congregated on a hill in the neighbourhood, when, with bonfires, torches, firing of guns, and every demonstration of joy, they spent the evening in the greatest hilarity. The place chosen on this occasion was the stupendous hill of Mulnever, the grey top of which commands a prospect of some ten miles round over a rich and [*illegible; obscured by tax stamp*] country. The hill, as seen from a distance appeared [*illegible*] all in a blaze, its light illuminating the [*illegible*] and covered as it were with groups of happy [*illegible*] most interesting and amusing scene.—*Nenagh Guardian.* (1842-11-19, 4:1)

2941. Lord Blayney is, we are happy to say, rapidly recovering, and is now in a state of convalescence. (1842-11-26, 3:2)

2942. Shipwreck and Loss of Life.—We much regret to state that intelligence has been received of the wreck of the barque *Argyle*, of Waterford, R. Power, Master, for Quebec. She went ashore on the 15th ultimo, at Louisburg, Cape Breton, and the respectable and highly esteemed captain perished—there is too much reason to fear with all the crew, about sixteen in number. Seven of the bodies were recovered immediately afterwards. There were no passengers on board. The wreck was sold for £35. Stormy weather and shipwrecks had been unusually frequent throughout the American coast. (1842-11-26, 4:5)

2943. The Late Sir Michael O'Loughlen, Bart.—Meeting of Solicitors.—An adjourned meeting of attorneys and solicitors of Ireland was held on Saturday at the Solicitors' Rooms, Four Courts, for the purpose of carrying out the objects of their previous meeting, for collecting funds for the erection of a suitable memorial to the memory of the late lamented Master of the Rolls.

The committee reported that a sum of 507*l.* 10*s.* had been already subscribed by 264 out of 700 registered attorneys of Ireland.

A resolution was then carried to the effect, that the committee be empowered to nominate sub-committees for each county in Ireland, for the purpose of giving an opportunity to attorneys not resident in Dublin to send in their subscriptions, and that they report to a general meeting of the body, to be held on the day subsequent to the last day of next term.

On the motion of Mr. Richard Scott, it was resolved that the standing order, limiting the regular general meetings to two in each year, be rescinded, and that in future, a meeting be held on the first day after each term for the purpose of bringing members of the profession more intimately together.

The meeting then adjourned. (1842-12-03, 1:3)

2944. Inquest at Carlingford—Another Victim to Intemperance.—On Tuesday last, the 22d inst., an inquest was held at Carlingford, before J. Byrne, Esq., one of the coroners for the county of Louth, and a respectable jury of which Mr. C. Lane was foreman, upon the body of Thomas Murphy, tailor, of Carlingford, who came by his death under the following circumstances. It appears that deceased was drinking in a public-house kept by a man named Trainor, on Sunday night—that he left at a late hour, and, owing to the severity of the night, and the quantity of spirits which he had taken, was unable to procure lodging. The unfortunate man was found dead on the road side the following morning.—*Drogheda Journal.* (1842-12-03, 1:3)

2945. Death of Lieut.-Colonel Stephens.—(From the *Dublin Evening Post.*)—It is with the deepest grief we have to announce the death of our fellow-citizen, Lieutenant-Colonel Stephens, who was removed from the scene of his successes in the hour of victory, and when a glorious peace had terminated the protracted war in which this distinguished veteran had acquired new laurels, and added new lustre to a name associated with the most brilliant achievements in the Peninsula. From the commencement of the Chinese war, Colonel Stephens had been actively employed in every movement of the army. After the taking of Chusan, he had been appointed by the Commander-in-Chief, Sir Hugh Gough, to an important civil station in that island. Upon the resumption of active operations, he rejoined his regiment, the 49th, which he commanded in the attack upon Chin Keang Foo, on the 21st July; but the fatigue and sufferings of that day were too much for the brave veteran, and he did not long survive. In a postscript to the despatch of Sir Hugh Gough, we find the following:

"P.S., 29th July.—I am sorry to report that since the forgoing despatch was written, Lieutenant-Colonel Stephens, commanding the 49th Regiment, has died, in consequence, I fear, of the great fatigue and exposure to the sun which he underwent on the 21st inst."

It was thus that the distinguished soldier closed his brilliant career. In Murray's *Army List*, for 1842, we find the following record:—

"Lieutenant-Colonel Stephens accompanied the expedition to Walcheren, and was present at the siege of Flushing. Served in the Peninsula from March 1810 to the end of the war, including the battle of Busaco, siege of Almeida, battle of Fuentes d'Onor, storming the Forts at and battle of Salamanca (severely wounded through the thigh,) siege of Burgos, action at Cabecon, battle of Vittoria, blockade of Pampeluna, battles of the Pyrenees, Nivelle, Nive, Orthes, and Toulouse, besides many other minor actions and skirmishes." (1842-12-03, 1:4)

2946. Death of Charles Coote, Esq., of Bellamont Forest.—It is our melancholy duty to announce the demise of this lamented gentleman, which took place at his seat, Bellamont Forest, on Friday, the 25th of November. Mr. Coote had been for some time suffering from a severe attack of inflammation on the chest, which terminated fatally on the above day. The remains lay in Bellamont Forest House until Tuesday morning, when it was attended to the grave by a vast concourse of the deceased gentleman's numerous friends and tenantry. In consequence of the short distance from Bellamont House to the Church of Cootehill, and it being altogether occupied by footmen, a numerous train of carriages remained behind the procession. The remains were attended by the following gentlemen, as chief mourners:—R. Coote, Esq., Eyre Coote, Esq., Dawson Coote, Esq., (sons of the deceased), Thomas Coote, Esq., D.L., Dr. Coote, Col. Clements, M.P., and Vale, Esq. Among the crowd of Noblemen and gentlemen who joined the procession, we recognised the following:—Lord Cremorne, Sir Charles Ceote [sic], Charles J. Adams, Esq., Maxwell J. Boyle, Esq., Maxwell Boyle, jun., Esq., Charles Boyle, Esq., Dacre Hamilton, Esq., W. Mayne, Esq., Richard Mayne, Esq., Archdeacon Berresford [sic], Rev. Charles Walsh, Captain Stopford, Walter Corry, Esq., George Corry, Esq., Francis Dawson, Esq., Rev. Dr. Browne, Titular Bishop of Kilmore, —Donnelly, Esq., Dr. Walsh, William Rutherford, Esq., Joseph Montgomery, Esq., Charles M'Dermott, Esq., Rev. Mr. Harris, Rev. Mr. Deering, James Elliott, Esq., Samuel Rutherford, Rev. Mr. Wilson, Jameson, Esq., Rev. P. Reilly, R.C.C., Cootehill, Rev. Mr. Willey, Rev. Mr. Bones, &c. &c.

Mr. Coote will be long and sincerely regretted by all who knew him, for as an elegant and polished gentleman he had no superior. In his capacity as presiding Magistrate at Cootehill Petty Sessions, he earned the praise of every honest man, for the upright and correct manner he disposed of the business brought before him—the evil-doer always found him with a hand ready to chastise whilst the injured and oppressed found him always ready to hear their wrongs and redress their grievances.

Mr. Coote, in early life, was married to a Miss Heldon, of the county Louth, and afterwards to Louisa, youngest daughter of the late Richard Dawson, Esq., of Dawson Grove, county Monaghan, and sister to the late Lord Cremorne, and aunt to the present Lord.

Mr. Coote was for years a leader of *ton* in London, at that brilliant period when the princely splendour of George the Fourth made the British court the most magnificent in the world. He was almost the last survivor of the chosen companions of that Sovereign. Mr. Coote's estates devolve on his eldest son, Richard Coote, Esq. (1842-12-03, 2:5)

2947. Death by Drowning.—A melancholy accident occurred on Thursday last, at the Lagan water. As a young girl was crossing a foot-stick above Donaghcloney, she became giddy and called to a man who was standing convenient, to come to her assistance. The man ran forward to where the young girl was standing, and on reaching the spot, she fell, and in her fall caught hold of the unfortunate man and dragged him along with her into the water. A great number of persons collected about the place, but could render them no assistance, owing to the flood increasing. It was most heart-rending to behold the parents of the unfortunate individuals on the banks of the water deploring their loss. After the flood had subsided next day, an active search was made, and the body of the man was found a few perches [from] where the melancholy catastrophe occurred. The body of the young girl has not yet been found.—Correspondent of the *Belfast News-Letter*. (1842-12-03, 4:4)

2948. An action for breach of promise of marriage by an Irish member of Parliament, will be for trial next term in the London courts. (1842-12-10, 1:5)

2949. Lord Blayney is recovering, but still remains in a doubtful position. However, his health compared to last week, must be said to be better. There are evil symptoms still remaining, which require strict attention, and watchfulness upon the part of those around him. We heartily hope for his speedy recovery. (1842-12-10, 3:3)

2950. Sudden Death.—Last Friday evening as a respectable farmer, Mr. Robert Lendrum, was returning from road sessions at Omagh to his house, near Clogher, his horse stumbled by which he fell suddenly on his head, and was found dead early the next morning on the spot. (1842-12-17, 2:1)

2951. Before a man hangs himself for love, he should ascertain whether the lady of his dreams would like him any better with a rope round his neck. (1842-12-24, 1:2)

2952. Awful and Melancholy Death.—On Tuesday, the 13th inst., the inhabitants of Maghera were thrown into great consternation by the sudden death of D.G. M'Cullogh, Esq., M.D., late of the royal navy and 84th regiment. The circumstances attending his death were as follow:—On the above date, the late lamented gentleman and R. Barr, Esq., M.D., were visiting a patient, some short distance from town, and on their return, feeling thirsty they called at the Maghera Hotel, and got two bottles of soda water, when, awful to relate, whilst Surgeon Barr was in the act of uncorking one of the bottles, the cork flew, and struck Surgeon M'Cullogh somewhere about the jugular vein, and he fell almost instantaneously. Surgeon Barr, who was much agitated at the shock, was unable to render much relief. Surgeon Marcus Doorish was immediately called upon, who used every means possible to restore the unfortunate gentleman to life, but, alas! the vital spark had flown.—*Belfast Vindicator*. (1842-12-24, 2:3)

2953. On Saturday, Mr. Field, one of the collectors of police tax, died suddenly in the Lower Castle Yard, Dublin, as he was about proceeding to make his weekly return of the tax collected by him. (1842-12-24, 2:3)

2954. The Rev. Thomas Burgoyne, son of the late Sir John Burgoyne, of Strabane, died suddenly at the hotel, Magherafelt, on Tuesday night, where he had only just arrived with his lady. (1842-12-24, 2:5)

2955. Coroner's Inquest.—An inquest was held by Dr. M'Fadden, of Cootehill, one of the coroners for the County of Cavan, on Wednesday last, the 14th instant, at a place called Mullahard, near Shercock, in said County, on view of the body of a poor woman, a widow, of the name of Mary M'Kenna, who resided there. The following are the melancholy facts of the case, as they appeared from evidence. She, and her only son, a boy of about thirteen years of age, being alone in a house, out of which she had recently been ejected, for nonpayment of rent, but permitted to return and reside in it again, upon what is termed sufferance; they went to bed together on the night of Monday, the 12th inst., and, some time during the night, he heard a noise as if the couples of the house were breaking, and, immediately after, the roof (which was a thatched one) fell down in the bed on them, from which they could not extricate themselves. They kept up the conversation for about an hour, when death put an end to her sufferings, and the little boy lay by the side of his dead mother, in a pitiable state for five hours, when he was relieved by some of the neighbors who observed the roof of the house had fallen down, and came to his assistance, and rescued him from his perilous situation, by digging him out of the ruins, with only some slight bruises. (1842-12-24, 2:5)

2956. The King of Hanover has forwarded £200 towards the subscriptions for the relief of the widow and family of the late Dr. Maginn. (1842-12-31, 1:4)

2957. 1742 and 1842.

Man to the plough, Wife to the cow, Girl to the yarn, Boy of the barn, And your rents will be netted,	Man tally-ho, Miss piano, Wife silk and satin, Boy Greek and Latin, And you'll all be gazetted.

(1842-12-31, 1:5)

2958. Matrimonial and Clerical *on Dit*.—The morn was bright and balmy—the day clear and cheerful, when the congregation of the chapel of M—, of the county of Down, in twos and threes assembled from the neighboring country, on the Sabbath, to assist in the celebration of Mass. Mid-day came, and the expectant worshippers waited for the chief performer, the Rev. Mr. —. The service of the Mass has its meretricious attractions—the sumptuousness of the dress and ornaments—the inspiring incense—the solemn peal of the organ through the fretted vault; the reverence of the people for the earthly intercessor, and all the other charms attached to this superstition of the middle ages. But alas! the rev. gentleman forgot all these sacred things: a new worship, which if not so much esteemed, yet as pleasing, had ensnared his affections, and caused his feet to wander from the right way. A lady—start not, fair reader, it was one of Eve's lovely daughters, whose beauty like the radiance of the evening star, had allured the heart of our modern Abelard—

In those dark solitudes and awful cells,
Where heavenly pensive contemplate dwells,
Where ever-musing melancholy reigns,
What means this tumult in a vestal's veins?

(continued...)

2958, continued: ...His heart, for once true to nature, had felt the force of unconquerable love—the rights of a man prevailed above the dogmas of a cold and senseless vanity, which cheers neither in this world, nor in the world to come. Lo! he flies and prefers the balmy breath of the fair Eliza to the fragrant incense—the light of her blue eyes to the sacred flame from the altar—the soft music of her voice to the tinkling of bells, or the peal of the hymn of thanksgiving—the temple of hymen to the sanctuary—and the affection and love of a gentle being to the semi-idolatrous respect of a superstitious crowd of devotees who know not what they worship. Great was the consternation, and many the rumors in the chapel of M— that day. Some said that his reverence had turned Protestant, and was going to follow the example of Martin Luther, or the black-mouthed Calvin—others, that he had broken his leg, and had gone to the Dublin doctors, and was not able to return in time. The lady's parents are inconsolable, as she absconded on the same day that the priest did; the fair one's steps were traced to Belfast, where she sailed in a steamer either to Scotland or England. His reverence left at Warrenpoint for Liverpool, since which period (October) no accounts of the fugitives. Whether the good priest performed the sacred ceremony himself, (like father Tom of old,) or called in the assistance of the jolly Gretnagreen Blacksmith, we are not able to inform our readers.—*Drogheda Journal*. (1842-12-31, 2:1)

2959. Death of the Rev. Mr. Hone.—We extremely regret to state that this useful and beloved minister is now no more. At an early hour yesterday morning, a piece of meat stuck in his throat, and notwithstanding the prompt assistance afforded by Dr. Charles Ovenden, he never afterwards spoke.—The Rev. Gentleman was curate of Tempo, and rendered himself a most acceptable ambassador of his heavenly Master, by devoting his time and his talents to the building up those committed to his charge in the holy faith of the gospel. (1842-12-31, 2:1)

2960. Most Awful Catastrophe.—Thirty Lives Lost in a Roman Catholic Chapel.—We are indebted to the politeness of the editor of the *Galway Standard* for the following particulars of a melancholy catastrophe, resulting in the loss of no less than thirty lives, which occurred in the Roman Catholic chapel of Galway yesterday:—

"Galway, Dec. 25, 1842.—A melancholy accident occurred in this town this morning; and, as I do not publish before Friday, I beg leave to send you the intelligence exclusively. At early mass, in the parish chapel, there was an immense concourse of people—the gallery, as is usual on Christmas mornings, was crowded to excess—one of the rails of the staircase, by the pressure of the multitude, was broken, and some persons in the vicinity, having heard the crackling noise, gave the alarm, and cried out that the gallery was giving way; an indescribable but tramendous [sic] rush was made by the dense mass to escape.—The catastrophe was awful—thirty individuals, up to the time I am going to post, have been made the victims of the rashness of the assemblage. I enclose you the names of the killed, as supplied to me by Mr. Patrick Broughal, the apothecary of the town Dispensary, whose exertions to alleviate the sufferings of the wounded are most laudable. Doctors Calahan, Browne, Gray, Moran, and O'Grady were also at their posts, and exercising all their skill for the sufferers. The gallery did not give way.

"John Philips, James Walsh, Thomas Hardiman, Mary Laffey, John Downes, Thos. Cummins, Honor Laffey, John Summerville, John Burke, John Murray, Mark Laffey, Mary Synot, Honor Kelly, Michael Rooney, Mary Clougherty, Celia Commins, Pat. Cronnely, Pat. Forde, Luke Costello, Dooley, Connely, Mary Curley, P. Hemple, Biddy Reardon, Boulger, Henry—four names unknown."

(*From another correspondent.*)

"Galway, Christmas-Day.—I think it but right to tell you that a most tragical occurrence took place here, at six o'clock this morning, at the parish chapel, similar to what occurred in Dublin two years ago. Previous to the celebration of mass, the chapel was crowded to suffocation, and some person gave the alarm that the gallery was giving way; the consequence was, that a tremendous rush was made towards the stairs—numbers were thrown down the stairs and trampled to death by others getting into the street. At this moment (two o'clock), thirty-five persons are dead, and it is supposed that from ten to fifteen more are also numbered among the dead. There are a great many, besides, maimed; they are all of the lower class, such as poor tradesmen, labourers, and servants—no respectable person among them. There was no danger at all of the gallery giving way; it is very strongly built, and would bear four times the weight that was on it at the time. There must have been between four and five thousand people in it at the time. I never witnessed a more heartrending scene. I saw myself 25 dead bodies."

(*From another correspondent.*)

"Galway, Sunday Morning, 25th Dec.—I have just seen Dr. Gray, who informed me that he has ascertained twenty eight individuals to be dead, but he thinks there are a great many more, carried to different parts of the town by their relatives, that have not yet come under his observation. The town is in a frightfully agitated state. The sufferers are all of the working classes. I went through the chapel an hour ago; it is very strong, so that, if the foolish people had but thought for an instant, they might have been under no apprehension whatever of its giving way, and the lives of the poor creatures might have been spared. Two of our servants were in the chapel at the time, but escaped—they do not know how. This has been a scene very like that which took place at Kirkcaldy, and which I never can forget. (1842-12-31, 4:4)

2961. On Thursday, the 29th Dec. last, between the hours of two and three o'clock, was interred, in the Church-yard of Glasslough, the remains of Miss Rachael Fraser, aged 14 years, second daughter of John Fraser, Esq., Downpatrick. At an early hour on the morning of that day, but particularly from eleven to half-past one o'clock, numbers were seen, of the gentry, respectable farmers, and inhabitants of Glasslough and its vicinity, moving onward in the line of road leading through Caledon to Armagh, in order to meet the funeral. Precisely at two o'clock, the funeral procession entered the town, headed in front by two carriages, for the accommodation of Mr. Fraser, his friends and family, in the rere of which was the hearse, accompanied by a number of cars, &c., in regular succession, displaying emblems suited for the occasion, together with a large concourse of people. The corpse, being dislodged, under the superintendence of Mr. Wm. Johnston, Glasslough, was borne into the church, when the funeral service (a continuation of which was again resumed at the place of interment, so deservedly admired on such occasions), was read by the Rev. W.H. Pratt, after which, was again conveyed to the burying place, preceded by Mr. Fraser and his friends, and being covered in its clayey tenement, was consigned to moulder with its primeval dust. (1843-01-07, 3:2)

2962. Captain Rowan, barrack-master, from Nenagh, succeeds the late Captain Thompson, barrack-master at Belfast. (1843-01-07, 4:2)

2963. The Vicarage of Kilnasoolah, county Clare, value 100*l*. a year, is vacant by the death of the Rev. Thomas M'Culloch, and is in the gift of the Bishop of Killaloe. (1843-01-14, 1:3)

2964. Rev. Dr. Hinds, formerly Chaplain to the Archbishop of Dublin, has been preferred to the Prebend of Castleknock, of the yearly value of 570*l*. vacant by the death of the late Dr. O'Connor; the living of Donoughpatrick, diocese of Meath, held also by Dr. O'Connor, is not filled; but it is understood that the patron, Col. Everard, will nominate his brother, the Rev. George Everard, to it. (1843-01-14, 1:3)

2965. Catherine Keogh, who lived as servant with Miss Watson, of Monks-place, Phibsborough, Dublin, was engaged in washing clothes, when she complained of sudden weakness, and she had scarcely finished the sentence when she fell a lifeless corpse over the vessel at which she had been employed. (1843-01-14, 1:5)

2966. Birth of an Heir at Colebrooke.—Thursday last, the Hon. Lady Brooke gave birth to a son and heir. This joyous occasion was hailed by all the tenantry of Sir A.B. Brooke, Bart., M.P., and on Friday night every house and hill on his extensive estates were illuminated. Brookeborough was peculiarly festive, and was visited by the Maguiresbridge Amateur Band, who played suitable airs throughout the evening. (1843-01-14, 2:1)

2967. We are authorised to state, that a marriage is on the *tapis* between the Honorable and Reverend Lord John Beresford, brother to the Marquis of Waterford, and nephew to his Grace the Lord Primate of Ireland, and Miss Leslie, daughter of the late Charles Powell Leslie, Esq., of Glasslough, and sister to the present candidate for the County of Monaghan. (1843-01-14, 2:3)

2968. A fraternal address of condolence and congratulation, from the brotherhood of Masonic Lodge 181, to Eyre Coote, Esq., appears in our advertising columns, and we are happy to state that the feelings expressed by the brethren towards this respected gentleman are not confined to them alone, but find an echo in the breast of every one who knows Mr. Coote. This gentleman is second son to the late Charles Coote, Esq., of Bellamont Forest, the finest gentleman of his day, except his friend and companion, the Prince of Wales. The extensive estates of the late Mr. Coote descend to his son, Richard Coote, Esq., who now occupies the mansion of his father; and we are much pleased to find that his anxiety for his tenantry has induced him to commit the management of his property to his brother, Mr. Eyre Coote, a gentleman whose mild and benevolent disposition will be sure to benefit the people over whom he has been placed, and advantage his principal as much as he will serve the people. (1843-01-14, 2:5)

2969. Disinterment of the Corpse of a Convert from the Roman Catholic Religion.—The following particulars of perhaps the most barbarous and inhuman outrage which it has ever been our lot to record, have been furnished to us by a trustworthy correspondent:—Patrick Clarke, of Doon, in the parish of Bailieboro, and county of Meath, died of fever on Christmas-day, and, having been a convert from the Roman Catholic religion, the Protestant clergyman of the parish, accompanied by his curate, attended, in accordance with the wish of his father, Peter Clarke, at the grave-yard of Moybologue, to inter his remains. One of these gentlemen, the Rev. Mr. Petlland [sic], having been previously threatened with violence, while engaged in the interment of a daughter of Peter Clarke's, a party of police was in attendance on the occasion. This precaution had the effect of preventing actual violence; but every insult, short of that, was heaped upon the unfortunate parent of the deceased, as well as upon the senseless corpse. Upwards of one hundred boys and young men, apparently drilled for the occasion, interrupted the service by every species of annoyance, and by turning into ridicule every sentence uttered by the officiating clergyman. No person in the neighbourhood would lend the implements necessary for opening the grave, and it became necessary to send for them to a distance of two miles. But the climax of this brutal transaction had yet to be reached, and was consummated on new year's day by the disinterment of the (*continued...*)

2969, continued: ...body, which was exposed on the high road, with a notice, of which the following is a copy, attached to the coffin.

TAKE NOTICE

Bring this unsanctified beast home to Winning and let him plant him in evry where hell be convenient at his hand on the days of review where he'l have no more to do but call him in to the fridays feasts where this unhappy wrech bartered his eternal selvation for beacon and pelf and do not dare any More to inter his Infernal remains in the church of St. Patrick as he despised the church of the living god which is the pillar and ground of truth they moral faithful christians despises him and will not admit of his bones to Mouldner among the just if he'l be intered again he'l be taken up if they gard him for a year he'l be throwen out and you may as well bring for whin we'l lift him again, we will not lave him vissible aris ye dead and come to Judgment.

Into any commentary upon this horrible transaction it would be absurd to enter. The facts speak for themselves, and we presume they cannot be suffered to pass without suitable notice from the authorities of the country. That a fixed determination to exterminate the Protestant yeomanry of Ireland is entertained, cannot be doubted. How long will the richer members of the church be suffered to remain, if they do not make some prompt exertions to support their poorer brethren? What a mass of barbarity, ignorance and crime, have the priests of Ireland to answer for!
(1843-01-14, 3:1)

2970. Address to Eyre Coote, Esq.

At an Ordinary Meeting of the Masonic Lodge, No. 181, in their Lodge Room, Cootehill, on the 27th of December, 1842,—It was moved by Brother Richard Phillips, P.M., and seconded by Brother Ralph N. Higinbotham, that the following Address be presented to our Brother Eyre Coote, on his appointment to the Agency of the Bellamont Forest Estate:

Moved by Brother G. Leadbetter, and seconded by Brother Charles Cornelius,—that the following Brethren do present the Address, viz.:—Doctor James Sharpe, W.M., Richard Phillips, Esq., P.M., and R.N. Higinbotham.—Mr. Coote having appointed Monday, the 9th inst., for receiving the address, the Deputation proceeded to Bellamont Forest House, having presented the following Address, they received the accompanying gracious reply.

"Address of the
Cootehill Masonic Lodge, No. 81,
to Eyre Coote, Esq.—

"Sir and Brother,—Since it has pleased God to take unto Himself the soul of your late respected and much lamented Father; we the Master, Wardens, and Members of the Cootehill High Knights Templars Lodge, No. 181, do sincerely sympathise with you in the loss you have sustained, in being deprived of the care of so kind and affectionate a parent; while we have come to the loss of a Patron and able advocate, having been for more than thirty years a most zealous member of our Ancient and Honourable Institution.

"At present, we forbear to descant more largely on this our mutual bereavement, as we are not desirous of renewing your grief, by again bringing to your mind any of the many qualities which endeared him to all who knew him. However, we are rejoiced that we are not left as men without hope; as we are convinced, that in the person of the son, will be reflected all the accomplishments of the father, which fitted him for the society of those with whom even kings and princes deem it an honour to associate.

"Understanding, however, that you are appointed by your honoured brother, Agent over the extensive estates of Bellamont Forest, we beg leave to congratulate you on your appointment;—an appointment which reflects the greatest credit on your brother's sound judgment—as we are conscious that he could not confide the care of his splendid property to a Gentleman of more upright principles, stricter integrity, or more natural tender feelings for the sufferings of the poor; or one better qualified to give general satisfaction between landlord and tenant.

"We conclude this public token of our respect towards you, by praying that God may grant you long life and happiness; and that you may long continue over us in your present capacity. And we respectfully request you to do us the honour of appointing a day, at your earliest convenience, when you will dine with us in our Lodge-Room, where we will have an opportunity of shewing our respect for you as our Agent, and our esteem for you as a Brother Freemason.

"We beg leave to subscribe ourselves your, most fraternally, on behalf of selves and Brothers:

James Sharpe, W.M.	Richd. Phillips, P.M.
John Mayne, S.W.	James Beatty, S.W.

(Signed by Order),
Samuel Dundass, Secretary.
Lodge-Room, Cootehill, Jan. 9, 1843."

REPLY TO AN ADDRESS
presented by
The W. Master and Wardens of Lodge 181.

W. Master, Secretary, and junior Wardens and Brethren of Lodge 181, accept my most grateful thanks for the kind and delicate manner you have addressed me on the great loss I have so lately sustained; indeed, a father and a brother. May it please the Almighty Ruler of all, to grant your generous prayer, and make me capable to perform the duties placed upon me, with half that kind, generous, and fostering feeling.

My dear Brethren, I would add that your Agent did deserve all your praises—I will yet endeavour to deserve your love, as expressed, and hope yet to enjoy the love of all those placed under me. I will exert myself to bring the Tenant and Landlord together, in feelings of brotherly love; rather, I should say, he shall be a father to his people.

Pardon me, dear Brethren, if the season, as it is at present, and the impropriety of me being much out by night, should debar me accepting your fraternal invitation at this time; but it will afford me much pleasure to meet you in Lodge No. 181, at some other period.

I return you all my sincere thanks for the honour you have done by your address, and I'm proud of those feelings, so unanimously expressed by the Brethren of your lodge. May peace, love, and harmony abide amongst you; may all the social joys exist to cheer you on the way whither that Great Light leads: that your lives now may be pure and sober, and your end, honour and love.

I am, fraternally yours, Eyre Coote.
Bellamont Forest, Jan. 9, 1843.

After they received the Reply, the Deputation partook of a splendid *dejeune*, which was hospitably prepared for them, consisting of all the delicacies of the season and the choicest wines. (1843-01-14, 3:5)

2971. Melancholy and Fatal Accident.—Yesterday morning, as a young lad named Charles Moss, was proceeding to his work, and while passing through Francis-street, a dead wall, which for some time past has been in a dilapidated state, suddenly fell, and buried him under its ruins. A person named James Calwell, hearing the noise occasioned by the falling of the wall, ran to the spot, and while standing on the rubbish observed one of the legs of the unfortunate youth immediately under his feet. He instantly extricated him, and found his face dreadfully bruised, and one of his eyes entirely knocked out. Although mangled in such a dreadful manner, life was not entirely extinct, and he was speedily conveyed to the hospital, where every proper attention was paid by the medical gentleman in attendance, and every necessary means tried for the alleviation of the poor sufferer's pains, but all were of no avail, as death shortly afterwards terminated his existence.—*Belfast News-Letter*. (1843-01-14, 4:4)

2972. Death from Intemperance.—An old man, named Morrow, who had been drinking rather freely in Banbridge some night last week, on returning to his house on the road to Scarva from town, fell over a bridge near the residence of Mr. Brice Smith, and next morning was found dead. It is supposed that the drink incapacitated him from recovering himself after the fall, and that he foundered.—*Belfast News-Letter*. (1843-01-21, 1:4)

2973. By the death of the Rev. Doctor Lowry, a very extensive church living, in the county of Tyrone, is vested in the gift of the Fellows of Trinity College, Dublin. (1843-01-21, 2:3)

2974. Sudden Death of Colonel Clements, M.P.—It is with extreme regret that we have to announce the sudden death of Henry John Clements, J.P., and M.P., for the county Cavan, which melancholy event occurred at about six o'clock on the evening of Thursday, the 12th inst., at his seat, Ashfield Lodge, near Cootehill, of apoplexy, in the 62d year of his age. He had been out shooting in his Demesne on that day accompanied by his son Henry Theophilus Clements, Esq., (lately appointed Lieutenant-Colonel of the Leitrim Militia), and appeared to be in the enjoyment of his usual good health, and about two o'clock, without any apparent cause, he was attacked with a fit of apoplexy, and notwithstanding that Drs. Walsh and Horan, of Cootehill, were promptly in attendance and afforded him every medical aid possible, he died at the time mentioned, encircled by his amiable family, without being able to articulate a final farewell, which is another proof that—"In the midst of life, we are in death." Colonel Clements, who is nephew of the late Bishop of Kilmore, and cousin to the Primate and the Marquess of Waterford, and brother-in-law to Colonel Stuart, of Killymoon, county Tyrone, and a cousin of the Earl of Leitrim, was head Colonel of the Leitrim Militia, which regiment his father raised. He formerly represented the County Leitrim in the Imperial Parliament for several years, and succeeded Somerset Maxwell, Esq., brother of Lord Farnham, in the representation of the County of Cavan. For the representation of which, Richard Maxwell, another brother of the Noble Aaron, has addressed the constituency, on behalf of a fourth brother, a gallant Captain, now in the Island of Guernsey, who is expected in Cavan in a few days. Colonel Clements was a kind and indulgent landlord, and comparatively speaking, an impartial and honest Magistrate. He has left a disconsolate widow, one son (the said Lieutenant-Colonel H.L. Clements) and three daughters, to bewail their untimely and unexpected bereavement.

THE FUNERAL

Took place at about half-past eleven o'clock on Tuesday last, the 16th, and the remains of the honorable and gallant Colonel were attended from Ashfield Lodge, to the place of interment, underneath Ashfield Church, attended by a considerable number of the Nobility, Clergy, and Gentry, of the neighbourhood, and a large concourse of his surrounding tenantry, amongst whom we observed the Right Hon. Henry Lord Baron Farnham; Lieutenant H.T. Clements; the Rev. Marcus Beresford, who read the funeral service in a very impressive manner; the Rev. Archdeacon Douglas, Chaplain to his Excellency, Earl De Grey, Cootehill Glebe; the Rev. John Harris, Ashfield Glebe; Dr. Browne, R.C. Bishop, of the diocese of Kilmore; the Rev. M. McQuaid, P.P. Killsherdenny; The Rev. Messrs. Bones, Brabazon, Little, Willey, Thompson, Meares, Methodist Ministers; Drs. Horan and Walsh; Dr. Sharpe, Dr. Mahood, Cootehill; Maxwell James Boyle, Esq.; Maxwell Boyle, jun., Esq.; (*continued...*)

2974, continued: ...Charles Dawson and Chas. Boyle, Esqrs., Tanagh; Richard Mayne, Esq., Newbliss; Thos. Coote, Esq., D.L., Fort-William; Eyre Coote, Esq., Bellamont Forest; John Boyd, Esq., sen., Clementstown, agent of deceased and his two sons, &c. &c.

The funeral procession extended nearly from the Lodge to the Church. The remains of the deceased were encased in three coffins, viz.:—first, composed of deal; second, of lead, and the third of oak, covered with black cloth, with full mounting of the same sable color, surrounded with a black silk pall. The bier was born by twenty-four of the most respectable of the tenantry. There were twelve persons carrying white poles with black rosettes, who, with a strong party of the Constabulary, were appointed to preserve order. The following was the

ORDER OF THE PROCESSION.
The Servants of the deceased, in front,
two and two.

Pall Bearers.	The Coffin, and Bearers.	Pall Bearers.

Chief Mourners.
Nobility and Gentry, two and two.
The Tenantry and others, six deep.

The pall cloaks, scarfs, &c., were supplied by Mr. John Boyd, of Cootehill, and in a style that did much credit to the undertaker.

The Late Colonel Clements, M.P.—Colonel Henry John Clements, late member of parliament for the county of Cavan, and formerly M.P. for the county of Leitrim, was buried on the morning of the 17th, in the family vault at Ashfield Church, amid an immense assemblage of the gentry and yeomanry of the county, who testified their respect by the orderly and solemn manner in which they followed his remains to the grave. The pall was borne by Lord Farnham, the Hon. R. Maxwell, Messrs. Burrowes, Kilbee, Coote, Hamilton, Boyce, and Saunderson; and the last rites were performed by his friend and relative Archdeacon Beresford, assisted by the incumbent of Ashfield, the Rev. J. Harris. It has been the lot of few men to possess a more extensive and deserved popularity. Alternately the member for two counties, he was returned in neither by the overwhelming influence of great possessions, nor by lavish expenditure, but in both by the high respect in which his character was held, and by the personal attachment which the knowledge of his worth gathered around him. His strong attachment to the Protestant cause and party never led him to deviate from the strict line of the most impartial justice, or in any way to hurt the feelings of those from whom he differed. As a magistrate, his conduct was upright and unprejudiced—as a resident country gentleman he was alike the friend and protector of all classes; and, therefore, he earned alike the love of all. The Roman Catholic clergy and peasantry vied with the Protestant in testifying the esteem and regard in which they held him on the last solemn occasion on which they could be shown. (1843-01-21, 2:5)

2975. Another of the many instances of the uncertainty and brevity of human life, occurred in Aughnacloy, on the night of Saturday last, the 14th instant. A young man named John Collins, who had retired to rest in apparently perfect health, was, on the following Sunday morning, discovered to be a lifeless corpse. As was usual, being of a religious cast of mind, he devoted two or three hours previous to his going to bed, in attentively perusing the Sacred Volumes, and praying with the other inmates of the house in which he lodged.

How truly are the words of our beautiful service verified,—"In the midst of life we are in death." An inquest was holden on the body, on Tuesday. (1843-01-21, 2:6)

2976. Awful Loss of Life—Eighty Men Drowned. It has seldom fallen to our lot to record so melancholy a catastrophe as that which will be found detailed in the following statement, being an extract from a letter this morning received from a private correspondent at Dundrum in the county of Down. Eighty poor fishermen have fallen victims to the snow-storm of Friday, many of them leaving widows and helpless families to deplore their loss, and mourn over the untimely fate of brothers, fathers, husbands, and other relatives:—

"Dundrum, 15th Jan. 1843—Three o'Clock, p.m.—Friday morning was so very fine that almost all the boats from Newcastle to Annalong went out to their fishing in the bay, where they had quite an uncommon take of fish. About noon it came on to blow with snow. Up to this hour there are, I believe, seven boats from Newcastle and four from Annalong missing. They were skiffs manned with about six hands each. Some of them were seen to go down by the crew of the boats which got in. One made Killough, and sold five or six and twenty shillings worth of fish there; in fact, I believe they were all heavily loaded. One boat drifted in with two dead men in it. I think they reckon on the loss of forty-eight souls at Newcastle, and about thirty at Analong [sic], or eighty altogether; but I do not pretend to give you an official or authentic account of the numbers, only what appears to be the best and least exaggerated. You can easily picture the state of the unfortunate widows and children along the coast. It is the most afflicting event that has ever occurred in this quarter. (1843-01-21, 3:2)

2977. The Late Awful Calamity at Newcastle (Co. Down.)—A gentleman has furnished to us 1*l*., for the purpose of opening a subscription for the relief of the numerous families who have been left in misery and want, by the late melancholy catastrophe which occurred off the coast at Newcastle and Annalong. We sincerely trust, that all those who commiserate with the unhappy sufferers, will contribute as liberally as their means will admit of, for their alleviation, and evince that generosity which this most distressing occasion so earnestly demands towards our afflicted fellow-creatures. We will feel sincere gratification in receiving, and duly acknowledging, donations for the truly laudable object. (1843-01-21, 3:2)

2978. Melancholy Occurrence at Larne.—On Monday evening, 10th instant, a young woman, named Isabella Templeton, met with her death under the following circumstances:—She was left alone in the house and, by some means, her clothes caught fire. Notwithstanding the strenuous efforts of a neighbour to save her from the devouring element, the work of death was completed in a short time. She only survived about ten hours. She was about twenty years of age, of rather weak intellect, but of a peculiarly cheerful and amiable disposition. Her poor widow mother is in a very disconsolate state. (1843-01-21, 3:3)

2979. Lardner, the scientific scholar, is starving at Philadelphia, and Mrs. Heaviside, of Brighton, his *cher amie*, has eloped from him. (1843-01-21, 4:1)

2980. The Rev. Mr. M'Causland, who led Miss Fannin, of Dublin, to the hymeneal altar on Tuesday, with a fortune of £30,000, is private Chaplain to the Lord Bishop of Killaloe. (1843-01-21, 4:3)

2981. The Leitrim Militia.—It is rumored in well-informed circles that the Earl of Leitrim, as Lord Lieutenant of the county, intends performing the generous act of appointing the son of the late Colonel Clements to the Colonelcy of the Leitrim Militia, in the room of his deceased father. The son is at present the Lieutenant Colonel of the regiment, and was appointed by his father on the death of the late Colonel Cullen. (1843-01-21, 4:4)

2982. We regret to say that a letter was received this morning, conveying an account of the sudden and dangerous indisposition of Lord Ferrard. The Viscount Massareene, his Lordship's eldest son, instantly left town, accompanied by Sir Philip Crampton, the Surgeon-General, for Farnham, the seat of Lord Farnham, with whom Lord Ferrard was staying on a visit when he was attacked.—*Mail.* (1843-01-21, 4:6)

2983. The Late Storm—Shipwrecks.—In our last publication we alluded to the severe storm which visited us on Thursday night and Friday, but we were not then aware of the great mischief which had been done. *[Article includes description of property damage at the demesne of Pembroke, the seat of Thomas B. Boland, Esq., Passage West; also, to cottages on Tourin, and to the demesne of Marino, the seat of T.G. French, Esq.]* We regret that there has been a loss of life in some degree attributable to the effects of the storm. During the night of Thursday, the house of a farmer named Robert Hourahan, residing in the parish of Ahabollogue, about ten miles [west] of the city, was unroofed, and one end blown down. In consequence of the dilapidated state of the building, the family were compelled to seek shelter in the house of a neighbour, while three farm labourers went to sleep in the barn. Not having taken any rest on Thursday night, they lay down in the straw in the barn about nine o'clock on Friday evening, having taken a small bit of lighted candle in with them, which it is supposed they neglected to put out. However, about eleven o'clock, flames were perceived to issue from the house, and before any assistance could be rendered it was burned to the ground, and with it, the three unfortunate men. Saturday, their frames, for almost all the flesh was consumed, were dug from the ruins. —*Cork Constitution.* (1843-01-28, 1:3)

2984. Wexford, Jan. 13.—The *Santon*, Huxtable, from Calcutta to Liverpool, was driven ashore last night, in Ballyteague Bay, where she lies on her beam ends, with her deck to the sea—Captain and three men drowned. (1843-01-28, 1:3)

2985. The brig *Millman*, of Belfast, Blayne, from Monte Video and Falmouth to Antwerp, was off the North Foreland on the (4th instant, three days out from Falmouth), with bulwarks, stove, and one man washed overboard.—The fishing smack, *Fame*, of Ramsgate, put a man on board. (1843-01-28, 1:3)

2986. Captain Milligan, of the *Messenger*, arrived at Limerick port, picked up two fishing boats, on the 14th inst., between Dundrum and the Calf of Man, about 20 feet keel each. One called the *Isabella*, the other *Betty Jean*, of Newcastle. He makes no doubt, but the crews of both boats were drowned. (1843-01-28, 1:3)

2987. Melancholy Loss of Life in the Rosses, County of Donegal—Nineteen Persons Drowned.

Narin, 17th Jan., 1843.

On last Friday morning, as the boats belonging to the Rosses herring fishery were engaged in hauling their nets on the north side of the Isle of Arran, a violent gale of wind suddenly sprung up from the north, and in a very short space of time it increased to a perfect hurricane; every effort was made by the boatmen to reach the shore, but, alas! twelve poor fellows were doomed to a premature and watery grave, ten of whom formed the crew of one of Mr. F. Forster's large fishing yawls—the other two men were lost out of separate boats. A few days previous to this lamentable occurrence, as a boat was returning from Burton port to Arran she was capsized, and six persons out of nine were unfortunately drowned. One of the survivors died the following morning from the effects of the bruises which he received on the rocks while struggling to gain the shore.

The continued storm which we have had since the 4th, has paralysed the efforts of our hardy fishermen; and although there is every reason to believe that there is a large shoal of herrings off the island of Rananish, the tempestuous state of the weather has kept them from approaching the usual fishing ground. Twenty-seven train of nets, averaging (*continued...*)

2987, continued: ...7 each—in all about 190 nets, besides anchors, ropes, &c., have been lost by the Portnoo and Ballyhillagh fishermen on the morning of the 4th instant.

The losses sustained in the Rosses on the morning of the 4th and 13th inst., in nets, ropes, &c., will be severely felt by a vast number of fishermen.—*Ballyshannon Herald.* (1843-01-28, 1:4)

2988. On Friday night last, during the dreadful storm, a Galway wherry with fishing tackle for Killybegs, when entering that harbour, the night being dark, and they not being acquainted with the port, struck on the Rotten Island and went [to] pieces, throwing the crew (seven persons) on the mercy of the waves; three of the men sank to rise no more—the other four were driven on a rock, where they remained a few minutes, hoping they had escaped a watery grave, but they were washed off by another wave, and one of them, an old man, was drowned, the remaining three were once more left on the rock by the waves; and the sea falling, they were able to remain in their perilous situation until next morning, when some fishermen seeing them, went to their assistance, got them into their boat, and conveyed them to shore. Andrew Cassidy, Esq., of Bruckless, on hearing of the misfortune, brought a doctor to see them, and we are happy to learn they are doing well. One of them (the captain) is brother to the owner. The only article saved was about 200 sovereigns which the captain had sewed up in a purse and tied round his body, with which he intended to purchase salt and herring.—*Ballyshannon Herald.* (1843-01-28, 1:4)

2989. The Late Calamity at Newcastle, and Analong. —(*From the Mail.*)—It will be seen by the list of subscriptions which we publish this evening, that we were not mistaken in predicting that the grievous calamity under which so many of our fellow-creatures have perished, and so many others have been plunged into utter destitution, would be met by generous sympathy. We have been requested to state that the two committees formed at Newcastle and Morne for the relief of the sufferers in each of these localities, have united, and that all sums that may be collected are to go into a common fund. Steps have also been taken to bring the whole state of the case before the public, a preliminary meeting having been held in this city, at which a committee for receiving subscriptions was formed, consisting among others, of the Right Hon. the Lord Mayor, Admiral Oliver, Mr. Dombrain, Inspector-General of the Coast Guard, and Captain Neame, Deputy Inspector-General. The beautiful and Christian letter, addressed to the local committee, by the Earl of Roden, speaks for itself, although it can throw no additional lustre upon the character of its noble and excellent author. (1843-01-28, 2:2)

2990. It is stated that the Rev. Mr. St. George will succeed to the vicarage of Kilnasoolah, county of Clare, vacant by the Rev. Mr. Cullogh's death. 1843-01-28, 4:4)

2991. The Rectory of Ballymoney, Antrim, vacant by the death of the Rev. W. Greene, is worth £1,200 a-year, and is the gift of the Lord Bishop of Down and Connor. (1843-01-28, 4:4)

2992. A man of the name of Goulding returning from the market of Westport on Thursday, in a state of intoxication, fell into the river, near the church, and was drowned. He left a widow and six helpless children. (1843-02-04, 1:2)

2993. Accident.—As the wife of a man named M'Kelvey, resid[*illegible*] Aughnacloy, was in the act of skimming a large [*illegible*] in which the entrails of three or four pigs were [*illegible*] boiled, she unfortunately slipped and fell in. [*illegible*] persons who were convenient, hearing her scream[s] [*illegible*] [im]mediately endeavored to relieve the unfortunate w[oman] and succeeded in bringing her out in a very pre[carious] state. Since writing the above, death terminat[ed her] sufferings. (1843-02-04, 2:6) *Note: The inner margin is hidden within a fold of the paper, rendering many of the letters illegible.*

2994. Charitable Acknowledgment.—The Editor of the *Northern Standard*, acknowledges the receipt of 1*l.* [*numbers illegible*] from Mrs. Ker, of Mountain Lodge in this county, in aid of the fund collecting for the sufferers by the late storm off the coast of Annalong and Newcastle. (1843-02-04, 3:3)

2995. During the snow-storm last Friday, a young lad named Buchanan, perished at Rushy Hill, Collin Mountain. (1843-02-11, 3:2)

2996. Notice.—I Hereby give Public Notice, that I will not be accountable for any Debt or Debts, contracted after this date, by my Wife, Jane Mooney.

Dated, this 9th February, 1843.

William Mooney,

Garron, Parish of Clones East.

(1843-02-11, 3:4)

2997. Rumoured Loss of a Steamer.—It was reported yesterday in this town that the steamer *Rover*, of Londonderry, on her passage from that port to Glasgow on Friday night last, having experienced a severe gale of wind, was driven into the vicinity of Portrush harbour, where she became a total wreck, and all hands on board perished. Last night a gentleman, who had left Coleraine in the morning of yesterday, stated to us that the report was prevalent in that town; and a letter received in Belfast on Sunday from Coleraine mentioned the rumour. It was stated in the communication from Coleraine, that several of the dead bodies had washed ashore. We give the particulars of the report as they have reached us, hoping that the report itself may turn out to be unfounded, or at least greatly exaggerated.—*Ulster Times.* (1843-02-11, 4:1)

2998. Presbyterian Marriage Case.—House of Lords—Writ of Error—Feb. 13.—The judges were summoned to attend the hearing. The following judges attended:—Lord Chief Justice Tindal, Justices Patterson, Williams, Colbridge, Maule, Erskine and Cresswell; and Barons Parke, Anderson, and Rolfe. The lords present were, the Lord Chancellor, and Lord Brougham, Denman, Abinger, Cottenham, and Campbell.

This was one of two cases brought up to the House of Lords on error, from the Court of Queen's bench in Ireland, the alleged error being that the court below had held that a marriage not celebrated in any church of the establishment, but by a Presbyterian minister, under the circumstances stated in the case, was not such a valid marriage as to make a subsequent marriage in the church of England invalid, and to render the parties contracting the same liable to the penalties of bigamy. The facts of the case were thus set forth in the writ of error:—The defendant, George Millis, was indicted for bigamy under 10th Geo. IV., cap. 37, sec. 25 (Irish), at the spring assizes of the county of Antrim, held at Carrickfergus, for that county, on the 2d of March, 1842, before the Right Hon. Louis Perrin, one of the judges of her Majesty's Court of Queen's Bench in Ireland, then and there being one of the justices of oyer and terminer and general gaol delivery of her Majesty's gaol of Antrim, in the said county, in having, on the 1st day of September, 1828, at Banbridge, in the county of Down, in Ireland, married one Esther Graham, and afterwards, on the 24th day of September 1836, during the lifetime of the said Esther Graham, at Stoke Damerel, in the county of Devon, in England, feloniously intermarried with one Jane Kennedy; George Millis having pleaded not guilty to the indictment the jury returned a special verdict, finding the facts in reference to the offence wherewith the said George Millis was charged in the said indictment as follows:—

"We find that about thirteen years ago, to wit, in September, 1828, the prisoner George Millis, accompanied by Esther Graham, then spinster, and three other persons, went to the house of the Rev. John Johnstone, then and there being the placed and regular minister of the congregation of Protestant Dissenters, commonly called Presbyterians, at Tullylish, near to Banbridge aforesaid: and that the said prisoner and the said Esther Graham then and there entered into a contract of present marriage in presence of the said Rev. John Johnstone and the said other persons; and that the said Rev. John Johnstone then and there performed a religious ceremony of marriage between the said prisoner and Esther Graham according to the usual form of the Presbyterian church in Ireland; and that after the same contract and ceremony, the said prisoner and said Easther [sic] for two years cohabited and lived together as man and wife, the said Esther being after the said ceremony known by the name of Millis,

"And the jurors aforesaid, on their oath aforesaid, further say that the said George Millis was, at the time of the said contract and ceremony, a member of the Established Church of England and Ireland, and that the said Esther was not a Roman Catholic, but the jurors aforesaid do not find whether she the said Esther was a member of the said Established Church of a Protestant dissenter.

"And the jurors aforesaid, upon their oath aforesaid, further find that afterwards, upon the 24th day of September, 1836, while the aforesaid Esther was still living, the said George Millis was married to one Jane Kennedy, then Spinster, in the parish of Stoke, in the county of Devon, England, according to the forms of the said Established Church by the said officiating minister of the said parish, he being then and there a priest in holy orders. And the jurors aforesaid, upon their oath aforesaid, further find that the said George Millis afterwards on the 2d day of September, 1841, was apprehended, and in custody at Belfast, in the county of Antrim, on the charge of bigamy, because of his having so married the said Jane Kennedy as aforesaid.

"And the jurors aforesaid pray the advice of the court in the premises, and say that if the court shall be of opinion that the said contract and ceremony between the said George Mills [sic] and Esther Graham followed by such cohabitation as aforesaid, constituted a valid marriage in law, then the jurors aforesaid, upon their oath aforesaid, say and find that the said George Millis is guilty of the offence above laid to his charge, in manner and form as in the said indictment set forth; but if the court shall be of opinion that the same do not constitute a valid marriage in law, then the jurors aforesaid, on their oath aforesaid, do say and find that the said George Millis is not guilty of the said offence in manner and form as in the said indictment set forth."

The Attorney-General for Ireland having caused a writ of *certiorari* to be issued from the court of Queen's Bench in Ireland, directed to the justices of oyer and terminer and general gaol delivery of her Majesty's gaol of Antrim commanding the said indictment and special verdict thereon to be certified and returned into the court of Queen's Bench, the same was returned, and the law as applicable to the facts found in the same special verdict, was fully argued in the court of Queen's Bench in Ireland, in Easter and Trinity Terms last, by the Attorney-General for Ireland, and another on behalf of the Crown, and by counsel for the said George Millis; the counsel for the crown contending that, upon the facts so found, George Milis [sic] ought to be adjudged guilty of the said offence laid in the indictment, and the counsel for George Millis contending that he ought to be adjudged not guilty of the offence. The judges having heard the case so argued, and considered the same in Trinity Term, delivered judgement on the law as applicable to the facts so found in the said special verdict in favour of Millis, declaring him not guilty of (*continued...*)

2998, continued: ...the said offence.

Three of the judges only—viz., Justices Burton, Crampton, and Perrin heard this case argued (Chief Justice Pennefather, being absent from indisposition), and of the three judges who so heard this case argued, Justices Crampton and Perrin gave their decision in favour of the Crown, and Mr. Justice Burton in favour of the prisoner. In the case of *The Queen v. Carroll* (the other of the two cases now brought to the House of Lords), all the judges of the court were present and heard the arguments of counsel on both sides, and in this latter case, the learned judges were equally divided, Lord Chief Justice Pennefather and Mr. Justice Burton declaring their opinions to be in favour of the prisoner, and Justices Crampton and Perrin to be in favour of the Crown. But in both cases Mr. Justice Perrin, in order, as he said, that the cases might be carried to the House of Lords, and that the Attorney-general might be in a condition to bring a writ of error for that purpose, gave his formal judgement in favour of the prisoners, although still, as he expressed himself, retaining his opinion in favour of the crown; and accordingly, in both cases, judgement was entered up in the Queen's Bench in Ireland in favour of the prisoners.

The Attorney-General, the Solicitor-General in the Queen's Advocate, and Mr. Waddington appeared for the Crown; and Mr. Pemberton, Mr. Kindersley, and Sir John Bayley for the defendant in error.

The Attorney-General began his argument by contending that the same construction must be applied in civil as in criminal cases to an act to determine whether it was sufficient in itself to constitute marriage. There could be no doubt that enough had been done here to constitute a marriage valid by the laws of Ireland. The law regulating marriage in that country left it merely a civil contract, and did not require the presence or intervention of a clergyman in holy orders to give it validity. The law of Ireland resembled, in this respect, the law of most other countries in Europe, but particularly resembled the law of Scotland, where a contract *per verba de presenti* was a present marriage, and the contract *verba de futuro*, followed by cohabitation, sufficed to constitute a valid marriage. This had been the law of England up to the 26th Geo. II., c. 33., and the common law of Ireland had not been altered by that statute. It was clear, therefore, that the intervention of a clergyman in holy orders was not necessary to constitute a valid marriage in Ireland, the only real necessity being that there should be witnesses to attest the fact of the contract of marriage. But if the house should think that the intervention of some clergyman was absolutely necessary, then it was submitted that a person who was stated by the special verdict to have been present on this occasion was a person who fulfilled that condition, and by his presence gave validity to the ceremony. Mr. Johnstone was a regularly ordained member of the Presbyterian Church of Scotland, and held a cure in Ireland, where he was a member of the Synod, and enjoyed all the honours, rights, and advantages of a Presbyterian minister. He had performed the ceremony in the way in which it had always been performed by Presbyterian ministers since their settlement in Ireland in the reign of James I, and there could be no doubt that that ceremony, so performed, continues a valid marriage so as to render any second marriage between the same parties an act of bigamy. The learned counsel in a most able argument, cited all the English and foreign text writers, the cited cases, and the English and Irish statutes to support these positions. His argument on the statutes had not quite concluded when the house rose.

Adjourned till next day. (1843-02-18, 2:6)

2999. The wife of the caretaker of the Methodist Chapel, George's-street, Limerick, was suffocated on Sunday night, it is supposed from the effects of carbonic acid gas, and want of ventilation. (1843-02-18, 4:4)

3000. Marriage in High Life.—On Monday last, the 20th instant, the Hon. and Rev. Lord John Beresford, nephew to his Grace, the Lord Primate, was married, in Glasslough Church, to Miss Leslie, daughter to the late Colonel Leslie, and sister to Charles Powell Leslie, Esq., M.P. The ceremony was performed by his Grace the Lord Primate. The following distinguished persons were present on the happy occasion—the Marquis and Marchioness of Waterford; Lady Catherine and the Misses Beresford; Lady Louisa Fortescue; Earl of Caledon; Lord Bishop of Kilmore, &c., &c.; Rev. Charles Leslie; Hon. Mr. and Mrs. Kenyon; Lord Edwin Hill; Charles Powell Leslie, Esq., M.P.; John Leslie, Esq., and several friends of both families. The happy couple after partaking of a splendid *dejune*, set off for Ravensdale Park, the seat of Mr. and Lady Louisa Fortescue, where they purpose spending the honey moon. (1843-02-25, 3:3)

3001. Awfully Sudden Death.—Mr. John Stitt of Tynan, was found dead on the road early on Wednesday Evening, the 15th inst. He left Middleton [sic] at 7 o'clock, and shortly afterwards his horse was found without a rider, and melancholy to relate, Mr. Stitt was discovered lying on the road near Coolkill Nursery, entirely deprived of life. The Coroner, G.W. Younge Esq. and a respectable jury, of which David Leslie, of Leslie Hill Esq. was the foreman, returned after an adjourned and strict enquiry a verdict of "accidental death, caused by injuries on the brain." It is supposed that the horse had run away and thrown his rider, as he was seen galloping. Doctor Lochrane of Middletown, examined the body and stated it was his opinion, that death was caused by injuries similar to those received by the late Duke of Orleans. The neighbouring magistrates Sir James Stronge, Bart., D.L., Maxwell Cross, and Thomas J. Tenison, Esqrs., presided at the investigation, and took a deep interest in the proceedings; deceased for several years having with great ability filled the office of clerk to the Petit Sessions of Tynan and Middletown. (1843-02-25, 3:3)

3002. A respectable female named M'Donnell put an end to her existence a few days ago at Kilkenny, by throwing herself into the canal. (1843-02-25, 3:3)

3003. The Presbyterian Marriage Question.—The arguments in the case of Millis, which involves the legality of Presbyterian marriages in Ireland, were brought to a close on Friday in the House of Lords, after which their lordships put certain questions for the judges to consider, founded on the facts of the cases. Lord Brougham expressed a hope that the judges would give their opinions as soon as possible, considering the anxiety on the subject.

In the case of *Queen v. Carroll*, the Lord Chancellor inquired what the Attorney-General had to say to what appeared a defect in the special verdict, and which was fatal to the writ of error? In the special verdict, it was stated that the Presbyterian minister married James Carroll to Sarah Robinson according to the rules of the Presbyterian Church, without stating what those rules were. The Attorney-General was at a loss to account for the omission, and the Lord Chancellor said the judgment of the court below must be affirmed. (1843-02-25, 4:2)

3004. Loss of Life off the Coast of Donegal.—It [*illegible*] again our painful duty to ask for active sympa[thy] of the public on behalf of a number of sufferers fr[om] the calamitous storm of last month. The distres[s] of the unhappy families of the poor fishermen los[t in] Dundrum bay must be fresh in the recollection of [our] readers; but in the case of the sufferers on the co[ast] of Donegal, although not involving so large an amo[unt] of destitution, possesses another feature which gre[atly] enhances their claim upon public sympathy. [*Illegible*] reside in a district not possessing resident gentry—[*illegible*] consequently, are deprived of that solace in their [mis]fortunes, which so readily and so cordially sup[*illegible*] by the kind friends of the poor in the neighbourh[ood] of Annalong and Newcastle. (1843-02-25, 4:6). *Note: A fold in the margin rendered several words in this article illegible.*

3005. Hints to Ladies.—Men of sense—I speak not of boys from eighteen to twenty-five, during their age of detestability—men who are worth the trouble of falling in love with, and the fuss and inconvenience of being married to, and to whom one might after some inward conflicts, and a-course, perhaps of fasting and self-humiliation, submit to fulfil those ill-contrived vows of obedience which are exacted at the altar—such men want wives for companions, not dolls; and women who would suit such men are just as capable of loving fervently, deeply, as the Ringlet-tina, full of song and sentiment—who cannot walk—cannot rise in the morning—cannot tie her bonnet-strings—faints if she has to lace her boots—never in her life brushed out her beautiful hair—would not, for the world, prick her delicate finger with plain sewing, but who can work harder than a factory girl upon a lamb's-wool shepherdess, dance like a dervish at Almacks—ride like a foxhunter—and, whilst every breath of air gives her cold, in her father's gloomy country-house, and she cannot think how people can endure this climate, she can go out to dinner parties in February and March, with an inch of sleeve and half a quarter of bodice.—*Mrs. Thompson*. (1843-03-04, 4:1)

3006. Melancholy Occurrence.—In the beginning of last week, a most lamentable occurrence took place very near to St. Johnston. A young girl, who had previously borne a most reproachless character, and who resided with her parents and a grown-up brother, began to exhibit symptoms of her being in a situation which had not been suspected of by any of the family. The brother strongly upbraided her, and demanded to know the name of her betrayer, which she, from a romantic feeling of fidelity, refused to divulge. A man who lived near to them then entered the dwelling, and joined his upbraidings to those of the brother, upon which the distracted creature hurried out of the house into the piercingly cold air and the darkness of the night. A few hours afterwards she was discovered by a neighbour, lying in a state of insensibility at the side of a ditch, with a living infant in her arms. She was removed into that neighbour's house, and the usual restoratives were applied to her, but in a very short time she expired. The child, we believe, is still in life. —*Derry Journal*. (1843-03-04, 4:1)

3007. The Late J. Sydney Taylor.—The committee of noblemen and gentlemen who, with a sense of justice and propriety as honorable to their own feelings as it is to the memory of their departed friend, entered into a subscription for the above purpose, have within these few weeks completed the erection of a tomb in Kensal-green cemetery, as a memorial of the public and private virtues of this distinguished advocate and philanthropist:—The erection of this monument was confided to the management of W. Etty, Esq., R.A., and C. Moore, (sculptor), two members of the committee; and the manner in which these distinguished artists have fulfilled their sacred duty, shows that their appointment was most judicious. And we need hardly say that there is good taste, a propriety and solemnity of character, belonging to this tomb, which shows how intimately the gentlemen knew and estimated the leading features of his mind who now rests beneath its shadow. The form of this tomb is the simple block pedestal and plinth, planted on a massive slab, weighing nearly two tons and a half; the pedestal, which has an elevation of about seven feet, is surrounded by a cinerary urn, copied from one of the most elegant and suitable antique types in the British Museum, and especially selected for that purpose. The urn is above two feet high, so that the elevation of the work altogether is about ten feet. The material (*continued...*)

3007, continued: ...of which the whole is composed is the grey Aberdeen granite, every surface of which, except those of the basement slab, being polished as a mirror, an operation which renders granite impervious to atmospheric action, and is at the same time agreeable to the eye.

The work was accomplished at M'Donnell and Leslie's quarries, near Aberdeen, and sent up quite prepared for erection. The following inscription is carved on the east front of the pedestal:—

To
JOHN SYDNEY TAYLOR, A.M.
Trinity College, Dublin,
and Barrister-at-law of the Middle Temple,
who died Dec. 10, 1841, aged 45.
This Tomb was raised by the unanimous Vote of a
Public Meeting held in London, Feb. 19, 1843.
To mark his maintenance of the principles of
constitutional
Liberty, Christian Morality, and his successful
exertions in advocating the
Abolition of the Punishment of Death.

(1843-03-04, 4:3)

3008. Hydrophobia.—Melancholy Death.—In the month of November last, two men named Sweeny, living at Carnacon, five miles from this town, were bitten by a dog, one of them rather severely, the other slightly to the arm, through his coat. The dog was not supposed to be mad at the time, and consequently no means were adopted with a view to prevent any bad effects from the wounds. But on Monday se'nnight symptoms of hydrophobia were observed in Owen Sweeney [sic], the man who had been bitten slightly. On Thursday he was brought into this town to Doctor Acton, who gave his friends some medicine for him, but could, of course, do nothing towards a cure. After suffering the greatest agony the unfortunate man died on Saturday. His brother who was bitten at the same time, has been since affected with this dreadful malady, and his death was hourly expected.—*Mayo Constitution.*
(1843-03-04, 4:6)

3009. County of Down Assizes.—Crown Court.—Downpatrick, Monday, Feb.—Bigamy.—Fenton Tynan, a person of very plain appearance and about 35 years of age, was placed at the bar, charged with having, on 2d March, 1825, at Mountrath, in Queen's county, married one Mary Kelly, and that he, on the 11th of June, 1841, at Newry did marry Mary Campbell, his former wife being still alive against the peace and statute.

John Kelly, examined by Sir T. Staples.—Lives at Mountrath, in Queens County; knows Fenton Tynan (identifies the prisoner as the person); has known him for 25 years; he was born in Mountrath; was present, in 1835, when he was married to Mary Kelly, who is witness's step-sister; was one of the witnesses to the marriage; they were married by Father Conraghy, curate of the Roman Catholic Church; the prisoner was born and baptised a Roman Catholic; Mary Kelly was of the same religion; they lived together in Mountrath for nine months, until the first child was born; Tynan was brogue-maker by trade, saw Mary Kelly, his wife, in Dublin, on last Thursday; she was then alive; prisoner, some time ago, left Mountrath, looking for journeywork; he returned there a short time ago.

Prisoner—Where is the woman you are speaking about?—In Dublin. Why is she not here, where she should be?—Because she was not summoned. Will you swear what month or year it was we were married in?—I cannot swear it, but here is the Priest's certificate, taken from the registry book, of the day they were married.

Prisoner.—Pooh, sure pen and ink will refuse nothing.

Witness (to the Judge.)—The prisoner left his wife a year after the marriage.

Witness (to the prisoner).—If I would tell the whole of it on you, my boy, you would suffer for it.

Prisoner.—I would sooner take twenty-one years than be with your step-sister.

Mary Tate being examined by Mr. Hanna, deposed that she was present at the marriage between Mary Kelly and Fenton Tynan; they were married by Father Conraghy, according to the rules of the Roman Catholic Church; heard them called in Chapel twice before they were married; saw them live together after marriage.

Prisoner to witness.—Did you know Mary Kelly's father?—I did. What is his name?—Tom Kelly. Wasn't her father's name Delany?—The father I knew her live with, was Tom Kelly; perhaps she may have had a step-father, but I don't know. On your oath, was I drunk when the marriage took place?—No, you were not; it was at ten o'clock in the morning the marriage took place. Didn't you see me try to get out of the kitchen? No, I did not, but I saw you rustling at the door.

Prisoner.—I was taken by liquor completely, and I know nothing about it.

Alice Kelly, examined by Sir T. Staples.—Lives in Newry; was present in July, 1841, when the prisoner was married to her sister, Mary Campbell, in Newry Chapel; the Rev. Mr. Sharkey married them; her sister was a Roman Catholic, doesn't know what religion the prisoner is of; he lodged for six months in her house, and it was there he met her sister; did not hear them called before the marriage, as it is not the rule to call people before marriage in Newry; saw the prisoner put his hand to paper after the ceremony; can't say what day of the month it took place on, but it was June, 1841; saw them in the bed together, the night they were married. (Laughter.)

Prisoner—How long is it since that woman left me? —I cannot recollect, for you left her, and then she came to live with me. Ah, but how long is it since she left me?—I'll not answer any questions you put to me.

Chief Baron Brady—Answer him how long is it since your sister left him.

Witness—He left her, and she came and lived with me for a long time, until he came and brought her to Rathfriland, to make a holy show of her.

Priosner—I allow to this woman being married to me, and, if I get leave, I will keep her, and do for her.

Rev. Mr. Sharkey, P.P., examined by Mr. Hanna.—Is curate of the Newry Roman Catholic Chapel; saw the prisoner on 11th of June, 1841, in the chapel; he applied to witness to marry him, and on that day, he and a young woman, named Campbell, also applied for license; refused to marry them until he got some evidence that the prisoner was not a married man; in order to satisfy him of this, the prisoner produced a young girl whom he called his daughter; asked her if her father was married; she replied that her father had not been married since her mother died; he then performed the ceremony of marriage; the prisoner conformed to the rites of the Roman Catholic Church when he was married to Campbell; the woman to whom he married him is now in Court.

Chief Baron Brady briefly charged the Jury, who at once returned a verdict of Guilty.

Baron Brady then addressed him:—Fenton Tynan, you have now been found guilty of the crime of which you were given in charge to the jury, on evidence most clear and satisfactory; therefore, there can be no doubt of the justice of the verdict of the jury; and I can have no difficulty in passing on you the sentence of the Crown, which is, that you be transported for seven years. The prisoner left the dock without any remark. (1843-03-11, 1:2)

3010. Death of Arthur French, Esq.—It is with feelings of deep regret we have to announce the demise of Arthur French Esq., of Leslie-house, Ballybay. Mr. French, we understand, caught a slight cold, coming from Roscommon assizes, of which county he was Treasurer, and which ended fatally on Tuesday last. Mr. French was married to the daughter and heiress of the late Albert Leslie, Esq., of Ballybay, and was much esteemed and respected. His remains will, we understand, be conveyed to the family burying-place in French Park, County Roscommon. (1843-03-11, 3:3)

3011. The Magistracy.—The Lord Lieutenant has been pleased to approve of Wm. Talbot Crosbie, Esq., being appointed Deputy Lieutenant for the county Kerry, vice Arthur Blennerhasset, Esq., deceased. (1843-03-11, 4:3)

3012. Sudden Death of Alexander Mitchell, Esq.—It is with the most painful feelings we have to announce the sudden death of this esteemed and respected gentleman. The melancholy event took place on Monday last, in the Grand Jury Room of our Court-house, where he was engaged, as Secretary to the Grand Jury, in filling up the bonds of the High Constables, in order to have them executed. He was, a moment before, in the enjoyment of excellent health and spirits, and was chatting gaily to Henry George Johnston, Esq., one of the jury, when his head sank upon his breast, while the pen he held in his hand was tracing its characters on the paper before him. Mr. Sheils, of Castleblayney, was surprised that he ceased writing, and lifted his head, when he discovered that his eyes were fixed in death. —Doctor J. Christian was in immediate attendance, and opened the veins of his arms and temples, and although a little blood flowed, it was thick and congealing.—Doctors Young, Temple, and M'Dowell, also joined Dr. Christian, and all means were tried to restore animation, but in vain. It was supposed that some of the large vessels of the heart or brain suddenly burst, and caused instant death. Mr. Mitchell was agent to the extensive estates of E.J. Shirley, Esq., M.P., in this county; secretary of the Grand Jury, and a gentleman of considerable property himself. He held a conspicuous position in the direction of our county affairs; and, as a clever and intelligent gentleman, he had few equals. His sudden death has cause a blank in society that it will be difficult to fill up, and has plunged his numerous relations into deep affliction. (1843-03-18, 3:3)

3013. The Suicide.

I.

Oh! what a dark dread deed is Suicide!
To rush, uncalled, before the *Judgment Seat*!
To fling that Soul, for which the Saviour died,
As in defiance, at its Maker's feet.

II.

Man is with knowledge filled—proud self-depending;
He standeth like the century-nourished oak—
Though whirlwind sorrows come—erect, unbending!
Bows not, save unto Death's all-levelling stroke.

III.

Woman is simple, frail, and all-confiding;
Clinging, like ivy, to the forest king:
Her love, when fixed, though Heaven and earth be chiding,
Bows but to death—a lovely, priceless thing.

IV.

Earth hath nought like it, in its broad domain—
The Sun ne'er looked on aught so pure and holy—
In Heaven, alone, can we its like obtain;
Absorbing so, the soul's best feelings wholly.

V.

But generous-minded man doth oft abuse
That very life-pulse; for the grossest ends
Hell take advantage of it—none excuse
His victim; no—she'll find no pitying friends.

VI.

But, he is called a gallant mind—forsooth!
His sin glossed over; nay—'tis soon forgot;
While the fair flower, which, without fear or ruth,
He plucked; must bear a never-fading blot.

(*continued...*)

3013, continued: VII.

From every side the storm of slanders pelting—
Incessant falls its pitiless, keen shower;
Alone, she must endure that anguish, melting
Her heart away; she sees no shielding power,

VIII.

On which to cast herself—she sees Heaven frowning
The staff, on which she'd lean'd had pierced her hand
Despair at length comes, Hope's kind whispers drowning;
She thinks of, knows of, nothing, save *that* brand.

IX.

Frenzy comes on; she rushes recklessly
To self-destruction—peace is in the tomb
One long farewell she looks, and—suddenly
She's gone! with *that* which moved within her womb;

X.

Poor girl! by rope or water having sped
She's found; and then 'tis prosily decided,
What was her end—they can't prove where hath fled
Her spirit: yet, they judge, by custom guided.

XI.

Her burial is a dog's—unconsecrated—
While he, who caused that murder, passeth by,
With port erect—an upright man he's rated!
Her form seems swept from out his memory.

XII.

Should such things be? hath shame gone from the earth?
Oh! where is honour, truth, and pity gone?
That man will join society; his mirth
Unchequed; without a pang—hath conscience none?

XIII.

An honorable man! a villain rather!
A cool, unblushing, calculating one;
Hereafter—doth it not around him gather;
Chilling his heart? his crimes shall then be known.

J.S.
Castleblayney.
(1843-03-25, 4:1)

3014. The Married Man's Fare.

Happy and free are a married man's reveries,
Cheerily, merrily passes his life;
He knows not the bachelor's revelries, devilries,
Caress'd by and bless'd by his children and wife.
From lassitude free, too, still sweet home to flee to,
A pet on his knee, too, his kindness to share;
A fireside so cheery, the smiles of his deary,
Oh! this, boys, this, is a married man's fare.

Wife, kind as an angel, sees things never range ill,
Busy promoting his comfort around;
Dispelling dejection with smiles of affection,
Sympathising, advising when fortune has frown'd.
Old ones relating droll tales ever stating,
Little ones prattling, all strangers to care:
Some romping, some jumping, some punching, some munching;
Economy dealing the married man's fare.

Thus is each jolly day one lively holiday.
Not so the bachelor, lonely depress'd;
No gentle one near him, no one to endear him,
In sorrow to cheer him, no friend if no guest;
No children to climb up: 'twould fill all my rhyme up,
And take too much time up, to tell his dispair.
Cross housekeeper meeting him, cheating him, beating him,
Bills pouring, maids scouring, devouring his face.

He has no one to put on a sleeve or neck button;
Shirts mangled to rags, drawers stringles at knee;
The cook to his grief too, spoils pudding and beef too,
With overdone, underdone, undone is he;
No sons still a treasure, to business or leisure;
No daughter with pleasure new joys to prepare;
But old maids and cousins, kind souls! rush in dozens,
Relieving him soon of his bachelor's fare.

He calls children apes, Sir, (the fox and the grapes Sir),
And fain would he wed, when his looks are like snow;
But widows throw scorn out, and tell him he's worn out,
And maidens, deriding, cry "No, my, my love, no!"
Old age comes with sorrow, with wrinkle, with furrow,
No hope in to-morrow, none sympathy spares;
And, when unfit to rise up he looks to the skies up,
None close his old eyes up: he dies, and who cares?

(1843-03-25, 4:1)

3015. Sudden Death.—On Saturday last a melancholy instance of sudden death occurred in the neighbourhood of Bellaghy. Mr. Thomas Anderson, a highly respectable inhabitant of that town, had gone about two o'clock in the day to superintend some field labour, and during the temporary absence of the men at dinner, was seized with apoplexy, which terminated in his sudden death. He was a man of temperate habits, and, we regret to say, has left a widow and large family to lament his premature decease.—*Belfast News-Letter*. (1843-04-01, 2:4)

3016. Fight for a Bride.—On the 3rd inst., a scene occurred at Roster, in the parish of Lybester, which equals, if not surpasses, a late Glengarry salute to a wedding party. On that day, a bride and her party set out to meet her intended; they had to cross an unfrequented moor, and when about half-way, were attacked by a party armed with guns and other offensive weapons; the bride's party at first imagining it was a frolic, passed quietly on, but matters assuming a somewhat alarming appearance, the males of the bride's rejected, and as a "dernier resort," he adopted this mode of wooing. A scuffle ensued, and after a keen contest, the aggressors were defeated, and their guns broken. This action was fought on the identical spot that the Keiths and Gunns fought for Helen, the Beauty of Braemore, and in which the former were defeated.—*Glasgow Constitutional*. (1843-04-01, 4:4)

3017. Melancholy Suicide.—A woman named Mary Beattie, residing in Little York-street, committed suicide by hanging herself with her apron, which she suspended from the top of the door. The unfortunate woman had been observed for some time past to be labouring under some mental aberration, produced, it is said, by over anxiety, and singular notions on religious matters. The door of her house was observed to remain shut for a time long enough to excite a suspicion that all was not right, and the poor woman herself not making her appearance, the neighbours became alarmed, and, on proceeding to her house, rapped at the door in order to obtain admission. No person appearing, they forced the door open, and found the unfortunate woman as we have already described. Deceased was, by all accounts, a very respectable and industrious woman, and was known by the *soubriquet* of "Soft goods," a commodity in which she had dealt, for a great number of years, in this town.—*Belfast News-Letter*. (1843-04-15, 3:4)

3018. Testimonial to Sir G.L. Cole.—Six thousand pounds have been already subscribed toward erecting the testimonial to Sir G.L. Cole. We learn that many of the pensioners have subscribed or intended to subscribe "a day's pay," but that the army generally hesitate to contribute, because nothing has been done to perpetuate the memory of Lord Hill.—*Fermanagh Reporter*. (1843-04-29, 1:6)

3019. The Irish Census for 1841.—We understand that the census, which was simultaneously taken in every parish in Ireland, on a given day, in 1841, and which has occupied a considerable staff in its preparation for publication, will soon be printed and laid before parliament. A variety of curious and interesting details will be supplied for the first time. The exact amount of the population, rated according to sex and age—the diseases which are most prevalent and fatal—the number of insane persons under restraint, with other statistical details, will, it is said, be given with a surprising degree of accuracy. The following is a return of the population:

	Males	Females.
Leinster ...	963,747	1,009,984
Munster ...	1,186,190	1,209,971
Connaught ...	707,887	711,072
Ulster ...	1,161,846	1,224,579
	4,019,667	4,155,606
Total population ...		8,175,273
In 1821, the population was ...		6,801,827
In 1831, the population was ...		7,767,401
In 1841, the population was ...		8,175,273
Increase between 1821 & 1831		965,574
Increase between 1831 & 1841		407,872

From this it appears that the increase during the ten years up to 1841, was 557,702 less than it had been in the ten years preceding. This extremely reduced rate of increase is very remarkable and extraordinary.

The increase in England during the ten years 1831, to 1841, was 2,004,794, which was more than one-seventh upon the population of 1831.

The increase in Ireland, during the same ten years was 407,872, which was little more than one-twentieth of the population of 1831.

The increase in England has been in the ratio of nearly three to one, as compared with Ireland. This is the first time that Ireland has shown a less degree of increase than England. (1843-04-29, 4:6)

3020. Attempt at Suicide.—A respectable gentleman named Taylor, aged upwards of seventy years, who fills the situation of valuator to the South Dublin Union, was arrested on Thursday last upon a sheriff's writ. He was conducted, in custody of two bailiffs, to the Four Courts Marshalsea, Thomas-street, at three o'clock, and while the deputy governor, in whose charge he was given, was making out the requisite receipts for the sheriff's officers, Mr. Taylor, who was standing in the hatch, furtively took a pen-knife out of his pocket, and, drawing the blade, inflicted therewith a severe wound across his throat, in the direction of the left jaw. Dr. Benson, the physician of the prison, was immediately called in, and rendered prompt and effective assistance to the sufferer, who is now in a fair way of recovery. He appears, however, to be afflicted with great despondency, and threatens to repeat his dreadful attempt whenever a fitting opportunity may occur. (1843-05-06, 4:4)

3021. Inquests.—An inquest was held on the 17th instant, at Mullaghdermot, parish of Errigle, county of Monaghan, upon the body of a poor man named James Mullen, who came by his death in consequence of injuries inflicted upon him by his own bull, in the byre, where he had been attending it. He was discovered by his servant boy, who saw the bull standing at the door of the byre with his master's coat on his horns—and having beat him away, he found the poor man dreadfully mangled inside the door. Mullen lived for an hour after he was removed to his home.

An inquest was held at Annagola, parish of Kilmore, county of Monaghan, before Robert Murray, Esq., Coroner, upon view of the body of a male infant, which had been found in the Ulster Canal. The child appeared to be new born, and to have been thrown into the Canal immediately after its birth. The jury found upon the evidence of the medical gentleman examined, that it came by its death in consequence of the umbilical cord not having been tied. The body was much decomposed when it was found.

An inquest was held on Sunday 14th inst., at Ballinagarry, Parish of Kilmore, County of Monaghan, upon the body of David Gillespie.

Finding—That Deceased came to his death from natural causes. (1843-05-20, 3:3)

3022. Matrimony.—In the Consistory Court of Clogher. —*Cooper a. Cooper*.—The Plaintiff Catherine Cooper having filed a libel against her husband Robert Cooper, the Defendant, in a suit for divorce and alimony, by reason of cruelty. The defendant admitted the first article of the libel, alleging the solemnization of the marriage, but joined issue with Mrs. Cooper in the remainder, whereupon Mr. John Mitchell, Proctor, for the wife, moved the Court for allimony, pending the suit. In the mean time, however, the parties consented to a mutual agreement with leave of the Court.

Mr. John Mitchell—The plaintiff and her husband have come to a mutual arrangement, in which I fully concur; and as they are again united, and cohabiting together as man and wife, agreeably to their conjugal vow, the Court will be pleased to have the cause set down agreed.

The Court—I am happy to hear it—let the rule be entered accordingly. (1843-05-20, 3:3)

3023. The Blacksmith's Epitaph.—The following quaint epitaph, remarkable for its point and humor, graces a stone in one of the Parish churchyards at Ipswich, Suffolk:—

My hammer and anvil have declined;
My bellows, too, have lost their wind;
My fire's extinct, my forge decayed,
And in the dust my VICE is laid.

(1843-05-20, 3:4)

3024. Death of Major-General O'Malley.—Major-General O'Malley died at his residence in London, on Tuesday. This officer joined the army as a volunteer, in 1798, and served in Ireland during the rebellion of that year. He afterwards served with the 13th foot in the expeditions to Ferrol and Egypt. He was subsequently with the 101st Regiment upwards of seven years, in Ireland, Jersey, North America, and the West Indies. He was with the 2d battalion of the 44th foot at Waterloo, when he was twice wounded on the last day, and had two horses shot under him. In 1809, he obtained his Majority in the 30th foot; the date of his commission as Major-General was November 23, 1841.

The distinguished services of General O'Malley are well known, and were fully appreciated in the highest quarters, and those services were now likely to have received the reward which they so well merited, by the appointment of the lamented gentleman to one of the four regiments, the command of which is at present vacant. In all the social and domestic relations of life, the gallant General was eminently distinguished for those qualities of head and heart—sound and discreet judgment, honor, integrity, and most affectionate manners—which made him beloved and honored by those friends and relations whom his death has now plunged in the deepest affliction.

General O'Malley and the Brave 44th.—The 44th did gallant service at Quartre Bras and at Waterloo, though in point of numbers, the weakest regiment that came into the field. They numbered only 430 bayonets. In the year before, at Bergenop Zoom, they had suffered terribly—700 men went into action, 200 alone survived. Accordingly, at Quartre Bras, the men were for the most part recruits. When the French fire opened, many of them took to ducking from the shot. The officer then in command, Colonel O'Malley—a man of mould, and not of fiction—cried out, "Steady, men!—When you see me duck, you may duck; but the first man that ducks before I do, Ill cut him down!" "By Jupus," said an old grenadier, "that's pleasant!—if they will wait till the Colonel ducks, they'll wait till the cows come home."—*Fraser's Magazine*.

General O'Malley was a companion of the Bath. (1843-05-27, 1:4)

3025. Loss of the *Virginia* Packet-Ship.—Henry Gallwey, Esq., arrived in town this morning from his residence, near Clonakilty, and brings the intelligence that before he left home a country girl called at his house, and told him that she had been sent by her father to state that a large vessel had been driven into Derk [sic] Cove the night before, and had gone, or was fast going to pieces; that a boy had been seen coming from that direction with a piece of the stern of a small boat, on which the word *Queen* was painted; that some men were seen also coming from the same direction with a large piece of timber that had been washed ashore; and that numbers of the country people were seen hurrying off to the scene of the disaster. Mr. Gallwey immediately sent off messengers to ascertain the truth of the statement, and expects a letter per mail, at three o'clock, with full particulars. The following is an extract from a letter just received this moment, per mail, by Mr. Gallwey:—

The boys have this moment returned, and state that Morley, the coast-guard, told them that the vessel is the *Virginia*, packet-ship, supposed to have been washed ashore; and some bales have been seen floating round towards the island; but the report that the wreck was a steamer is totally unfounded.—*Cork Reporter of Saturday*.

We subsequently learned from Mr. Murray, the Ship Agent, that the *Virginia* Packet was to have sailed from Liverpool for Boston on the 9th instant, with passengers and goods, and for conveyance by which vessel Mr. Murray sent four persons to Liverpool who had been residents of this country. The following is a copy of a letter received yesterday:—

"To the Editor of the Cork Constitution.

"Milk Cove, Rosscarbery, May 21, 1843.

"Sir—Reluctantly I have to inform you of the loss of the *Virginia* Packet, parts of a portion of the deck, together with doors and wood work belonging thereto, having been picked up near this place, and brought in under my superintendence; and I have every reason to believe the crew all met a watery grave on the 19th inst. near this place.—I am, Sir, your obedient servant,

"W. Congdon, Lt. R.N."

The master of the *Highlander*, which arrived in Cove on Saturday, reported that about noon on the previous day, when it was blowing hard from the S.E., he observed a large three-masted vessel off the Old Head at Kinsale, on her broadside. She appeared to be lately out of port—she had painted ports and was copper bottomed—her anchors to the bowsmain mast and bowsprit broken, alongside could discover no name. —*Cork Constitution*. (1843-05-27, 4:4)

3026. Hydrophobia.—A woman named Ardill, wife of a respectable farmer living at Kilcarron, in the county of Tipperary, within a few miles of this town, was bitten by a dog about six weeks ago. On Monday morning last, symptoms of hydrafobia [sic] suddenly appeared, when a surgeon was sent for, and lost no time in going to her house, but, notwithstanding all his exertions, the symptoms continued to increase, and she lingered in great agony until Tuesday, when death terminated her sufferings. The dog, a small terrier, showed none of the usual symptoms of disease, and up to the time of this distressing occurrence, was allowed to go at large as usual. It has been since discovered that he has bitten several other dogs in the neighbourhood, and it is supposed, some sheep. Jonathan Walsh, Esq., J.P., Walsh-park, has lost twenty sheep from this cause.—*Leinster Express*. (1843-06-03, 3:4)

3027. The Christening of the Infant Heir of Colebrooke.—On Monday last this interesting event took place at the parish church of Colebrooke, in presence of a large congregation of the Colebrooke tenantry, and the following distinguished personages:—The Earl and Countess of Erne, the Earl of Belmore, Lord and Lady Cremorne, Captain Meade, and the Honorable Mr. Linsday, 43d L.I., and a large family circle.

From Lady Brooke's former connection with the Court, and the affection of her Majesty the Queen, graciously signified her wish to be sponsor, and by royal request the infant was named Victor Alexander. The font used on the occasion was presented by her Majesty. It was a large gold basin, richly chased; on a beautiful pedestal supported by three figures of the graces, and of elegant design and workmanship, bearing the following inscription "Presented to Victor Alexander Brooke, by Victoria Regina."

A large party of fashionables was entertained at dinner, and a splendid ball and supper was given in the servants' hall, which was kept up with music and dancing till a late hour.—*Enniskillen Chronicle*. (1843-06-24, 1:2)

3028. Mixed Marriages in Ireland.—In the House of Lords, on Monday morning, after the judges had given in their answers on the questions concerning the trial of persons supposed to be insane,

Lord Brougham wished to take that opportunity of asking the learned judges when it would be convenient for them to give their opinions respecting the law relating to mixed marriages in the north of Ireland (hear)? Now individuals did not know whether they were married or not. They did not know whether they were felons or not (laughter); therefore he trusted the law would be settled during the present session.

Lord Campbell trusted the Queen's judges would be able to give their opinions upon this important subject before going the circuits. It was a question of momentous importance to Ireland.

The Lord Chancellor said he had received a letter from the Lord Chief Justice of the Common Pleas on the subject, which he would read. His lordship then read the letter, which stated that the labours of the judges in circuit and their avocations in their own courts since, had been so incessant that they should not be able, with any satisfaction to themselves, to give an answer to the question relating to mixed marriages in Ireland before the long vacation, particularly as many of the books referred to on the subject were not to be found in the library of any of the courts.

Lord Brougham said he was glad the Chief Justice's letter had been read—it was deserving of the greatest attention; but he must think the judges, if possible, were bound to give their opinions, so that the subject might be concluded by parliament during the present session.

Lord Cottenham trusted another session would not be allowed to pass without the important question being settled.

The Lord Chancellor expressed a hope that the judges would be able to give their opinions on this great subject before going the circuit. He was certain they would do so, if possible, at the risk of personal inconvenience to themselves. It was most desirable, most important, that the law relating to mixed marriages in Ireland should be settled and defined with the least delay possible.

The subject then dropped, and the judges proceeded to deliver their opinions on cases relating to writs of error, of no public interest. (1843-06-24, 3:1)

3029. Awful Thunder Storm.—On Sunday, this town and neighbourhood were visited with a most awful thunder-storm, accompanied by vivid flashes of lightning, the rain pouring down in torrents. The heat during the early part of the day, and up to five o'clock (the hour at which the elements began to discharge the thunders of artillery upon the earth), was unsufferably warm. It is much to be feared that much loss to life and property has occurred. We have just heard that three boys, two of them brothers, named Gordon, of the ages of 17 and 19, and their cousin, a young lad named Grehan, was [sic] drowned while bathing, in a little lake at Errew, about two miles from town. It is supposed they were struck by one of the electric flashes.—*Castlebar Telegraph*. (1843-06-24, 3:2)

3030. Dreadful Accident.—On Saturday evening, a most afflicting accident occurred on board the canal boat coming to Limerick from Dublin. (*continued...*)

3029, continued: …When the boat was passing the lock near Clonara, the Rev. Mr. Cousins, a dissenting clergyman from England, who with his wife, were on their way to Killarney, looked out at one of the side windows of the boat to observe their position, when the boat received a sudden side move, as it generally does, by coming in contact with either side of the gateway, and the head of the unfortunate gentleman was caught between the boat and the wall of the dock, and he received such dreadful injury that he died at the hotel in Limerick a few hours after the occurrence. The accident, as may be supposed, threw a gloom over those present. Every attention possible was paid by the gentlemen present to his afflicted partner. The deceased was an aged man between 60 and 70 years. (1843-06-24, 3:3)

3031. Death by Drowning.—To the numerous deaths by drowning which we have recently had to notice, we regret to have to add that of Master Thomas Theodore Francis, only son of the Rev. Francis Craddock. The casualty occurred on Saturday, while bathing in the Lee at Carrigadrohid, and the sufferer, who was in his 15th year, was, we understand, a very fine lad, and during a short residence had won the esteem of all, for many miles around, with whom he had become acquainted. He could swim but little, and, getting out of his depth, the poor fellow probably became frightened, and unable to use that exertion for his safety of which in a calmer moment, he would probably be capable. The accident was witnessed by a young companion, who was aware of the depth and danger of the particular spot, but had not power to render him assistance. Heavy as is the affliction, his family are not without the only consolation that could mitigate its bitterness.—*Cork Constitution.* (1843-07-01, 2:1)

3032. Credulity of the Peasantry—A Priest's Miracle. —There was a boy drowned on Sunday, the 18th June, inst., when bathing in the river, near to Scarvey-bridge, in the vicinity of Cootehill, county of Cavan, in Bishop Brown's own parish. Divers were procured from great distances by the distressed parents to raise the body, but to no purpose. A priest of the adjoining parish, was sent for, when every effort had failed, and he, upon reading some prayers, caused the body to come to the top of the water, out of a depth of twenty-five feet, to the inexpressible joy of his parents, who never left the water edge for the space of five days.

The miracle, as it is called, is very generally believed by the poor ignorant Roman Catholics of this neighbourhood.—No wonder the priests have such power over their flocks when in the nineteenth century such cheats are practised by their reverences. The boy was drowned on the above day, the body not got out for five days, until the priest went there and read some prayers, for which, of course, he was well paid, as there were ten pounds offered for the body by the parents!—*Correspondent of the Packet.* (1843-07-01, 3:3)

3033. Dreadful Accident at Sea.—At half-past two o'clock, on Friday morning, the *Mersey* steamer, from Liverpool, ran down a Baldoyle fishing boat, which was at anchor a few miles off the Howth Light-house. Of the crew of seven men, six saved themselves by clinging to the rigging; the seventh was unfortunately drowned. (1843-07-01, 4:3)

3034. A Good Wife.—Oh, it is beautiful to live blameless under the poisoned glance of the world; poisoned, whether it please or blame; beautiful, not to be polluted by its observations, but more beautiful to be intimately known to one—to possess one—to possess one gentle and honest friend, and that one a wife! Beautiful to be able to read her pure soul in a mirror, and to be aware there of every blot on one's own soul, and to be able thus to purify it against the day of the great trial. (1843-07-08, 4:1)

3035. The Presbyterian Marriage Question.—House of Lords.—Friday, July 4.—*The Queen v. Millis—the Queen v. Carrroll.*—Writs of Error.—This being the day appointed for hearing the opinion of the judges upon the law of marriage with reference to the case of Dissenters in Ireland,

Lord Chief Justice Tindal, on behalf of his brother judges, read to the house the conclusions at which they had, in common with himself, unanimously arrived upon the questions upon which, in the judgment of the majority of them, those resolutions were based. The questions which had been put to himself and his brother judges upon the bench were to the following effect:—A, an Irish Protestant of the Established Church, entered into a contract of marriage, *per verba de presenti* with B, a Protestant Dissenter, in the house of a Presbyterian minister, and thereupon cohabited with her. A afterwards came to England, and married C according to the usual forms. Was A or was he not married to B, and did he or did he not, by his marriage with C, commit the crime of bigamy. In answer to this proposition, he would, in the first place, consider the effect of a contract *per verba de presenti* before the marriage act in 1827. The law as to the effect of contracts *per verba de presenti* was involved in much obscurity; and if Sargeant Maynard, Lord Holt, and others, had spoken on the subject with doubt and uncertainty, it surely became them, her Majesty's judges, to give to the questions before them all the care and consideration they possessed. It had only therefore, been after much doubt and fluctuation in the minds of some of his brethren, that he (the Chief Justice) was authorised to say, that by the law of England the contract of marriage between A and B did not constitute a marriage in fact. Until the time of the marriage act, a contract *de presenti* was indissoluble between the parties, but in itself it did not constitute a marriage the less made so by the intervention of a person in holy orders. It was essential to the constitution of a full and complete marriage, that besides the civil contract, there should be a religious ceremony.

That religious ceremony had varied in its form at different periods, according to the laws of the church, but its sufficiency had been left by the common law to be tested by the ecclesiastical courts, the law courts only requiring that the forms which had been sufficient at one time, should, if a priest in orders were present, be so again. In endeavouring to shew that these positions were correct, he would, in the first place, direct the attention of the house to the decisions on the subject in the courts of common law—secondly, to the various statutes passed by the legislature at different periods, throwing light on the subject; and, lastly, to the doctrines on the point recognised in the King's ecclesiastical courts.

[*Continued discussion, including mentions of: cases extending from Edward I. to Queen Anne; authorities such as 1 Rolls [Rolles] Abridg. 339 and 360, Perkins; legal cases such as Bunting v. Agnes, Weld v. Chamberlain, Hayden v. Gold, the Queen v. Fielding, Jessel and Camero, Dalrymple v. Dalrymple, the Cordery case; decisions made by Justice Gibbs, Sir W. Scott, Lord Edenborough, and Lord Kenyon; statutes such as 31 Henry VIII, 32 Henry VIII, 37 Henry VIII, 27 Elizabeth, 12 Charles II, 7 and 8 William III, 10 Anne c. 19, and 26 George II. Closing remarks delivered by Lords Brougham and Campbell, and the Lord Chancellor, included an acknowledgment of the great debt they owed to Chief Justice Tindal and her Majesty's other judges for the attention which they had bestowed on the subject, and included mentions of: her Majesty's courts at Westminster; England as the only country in Christian Europe which had adopted this peculiar law, and as a country in which the religion was originally Roman Catholic and in which appeals on spiritual subjects were originally carried to Rome; Sir William Scott upholding the law of Scotland.*]

The Lord Chancellor suggested to Lord Brougham, that he had better at present confine himself to the consideration of the course which ought to be adopted.

Lord Brougham said that that was his object—that his reason for making these remarks arose from this, that the news of the opinion pronounced by her Majesty's judges would go over to Ireland that night, and that he sought to give comfort to those who were alarmed, and warning to those who might feel inclined to marry again. It did not at all follow, because the judges had given such an opinion, that therefore their lordships should follow it; or even if they should do so, that a legislative act should not pass to provide for the emergency. He begged the attention of noble lords to the observation. He had known cases in which a plain and manifest error had crept into the law, as in the case of *Cabel v Palmer*, yet there the error being obvious, their lordships had refused, contrary to the opinion of the judges, to give effect to the conclusions necessarily deducible therefrom. He (Lord Brougham) ventured to submit that, considering the delicacy and importance of the present case to the interests of parents and children, and the widespread consequences depending thereon, the house would not confirm the decree of the court below. It was upon these grounds that, repeating his thanks to the judges for their careful and able consideration of the subject proposed to them, he thought that a still more serious consideration should be given to the remedial measures which ought to be adopted.

The Lord Chancellor, after expressing his concurrence in Lord Brougham's compliments and thanks to the judges, moved that the further consideration of the question be adjourned.

Lord Campbell, in seconding the motion, refrained from expressing any opinion on the subject at present. The opinion of her Majesty's justices was entitled to the most profound respect; but when the house did decide, it must do so upon its own judgment. He (Lord Campbell) would only add, that whatever desire he might have to come to the same decision as the judges, he would have great reluctance in coming to a conclusion which affected so many interests, would bastardise the children of Quakers and Jews, and all Dissenters in India and the colonies of the empire.

The motion of the Lord Chancellor was then put, and being carried, the further consideration of the question was adjourned *sine die*. (1843-07-15, 2:2) *Note: This transcript is an extract of the original article, which runs to 1-1/2 columns.*

3036. Death of Charles Kendal Bushe.—A great light has been extinguished—and the brilliant, the classical, the eloquent—he whose talents shed a lustre upon the senate and the bar—whose virtues reflected an honour upon the bench—whose wit illuminated everything it touched—whose vivacity gave life and cheerfulness and spirit to all within its sphere—is no more:—Bushe, the orator and statesman—Bushe, the advocate and the lawyer—Bushe, the scholar and the gentleman, has ceased to be!—The sad and afflicting event took place suddenly, on Monday afternoon, at Furry Park, the villa residence of his son, in the neighbourhood of Raheny. Under these circumstances, it is impossible for us to do more than announce the melancholy fact. The obituary of Charles Bushe should be recorded by the historian, not the journalist—for he was great amongst great men, and shone as a bright star in that galaxy of talent, when competitors for fame had to contend with such as Flood and Grattan—Ponsonby and Curran—Saurin and Plunket, and others of equal note, with whom it was never his fate to be discomfited. As a public or professional man, the late Chief Justice perhaps never had his equal for varied acquirements and literary knowledge and taste. In private life he was warm-hearted, kind, and affectionate; and by, and in his own family, and within his more immediate circle, he was rather adored than beloved.

He had come up from his seat, Kilmurry, county of Kilkenny, only a few days since, on a short visit to his son (Thomas Bushe, Esq.), and so recently (*continued…*)

3036, continued: ...as Friday, was in the enjoyment of as good health as he has had for some time, or since his retirement from the bench. A sudden effusion on the brain was the immediate cause of death of this truly great and good man.—*Mail* (1843-07-15, 4:3)

3037. Dr. Denis Phelan has been appointed a commissioner to inquire into the state of fever in Ireland. Is fever more prevalent in Ireland this year than usual? (1843-07-22, 3:1)

3038. Death of Doctor Radcliffe.—With feelings of deep regret, we announce the demise of the Right Hon. John Radcliffe, LL.D., Judge of the Prerogative Court, which event took place Tuesday evening, at his residence in Leeson street. (1843-07-22, 3:6)

3039. Presbyterian Marriages in Ireland.—A Bill intituled an *Act for Confirmation of certain Marriages in Ireland.* (Presented to the House of Lords by the Lord Chancellor, on Thursday.)

Whereas marriages have in divers instances been had and celebrated in Ireland, by Presbyterian and other Protestant dissenting ministers or teachers, or those who at the time of such marriages had been such, between persons being of the same or different religious persuasions, and it is expedient to confirm such marriages. Be it therefore enacted, by the Queen's most excellent Majesty, by and with the advice and consent of the lords spiritual and temporal, and commons, in this present parliament assembled, and by the authority of the same:—

I. That all marriages heretofore had and celebrated in Ireland by Presbyterian or other Protestant dissenting ministers or teachers, or those who at the time of such marriages had been such, shall be, and shall be adjudged and taken to have been or to be, of the same force and effect in law as if such marriages had been had and solemnised by clergymen of the said united church of England and Ireland, and of no other force nor effect whatsoever.

II. That this act may be amended, altered, or repealed by any act to be passed in this present session of parliament. (1843-07-29, 4:3)

3040. Stamp Duty—Irish Marriages.—According to a clause in a bill now before the House of Commons, the duty on marriage certificates in Ireland is repealed; and also the stamp duty upon leases for property of small value, under certain circumstances. (1843-08-05, 1:3)

3041. Explosion at Ballincollig Powder Mills.—(From the *Cork Examiner.*)—A fearful explosion of Gunpowder, in one of the granulating mills at Ballincollig, the property of Sir John Tobin and Sons, within four or five miles of this city, took place on Saturday. The shock, accompanied by a loud crash as of thunder, was felt in town, between the hours of one and two o'clock, and created considerable alarm. In the western part of the city it greatly shook the houses, and nearer to the scene of the casualty many residences sustained more or less damage. The explosion was soon followed by rumours to the effect that several lives had been lost—but on examination it was found that two persons only had been killed—viz., John Carrol and Jeremiah Long, labourers, young and unmarried, and both of them had gone into work but a few minutes before; and one of whom, it is said, was actually standing at the door at the time of the explosion. No possible light has been, or in all likelihood ever can be thrown on the origin of this affair; the mill in question, like the others in Ballincollig, was surrounded by water—its machinery, it is understood, was in good repair, and no danger whatever seemed to be apprehended by those in immediate charge of the concerns. Near this mill, separated from it only by a canal of ten feet broad, a plantation and a light paling, three troops of the 2d Dragoon Guards were drawn up in a line but a few minutes before the accident, under the inspection of General Sir Octavius Carey; but at the moment of the explosion, they were most fortunately at a distant part of the field, otherwise the consequences serious as they are, would certainly have been much more so. Slates, timber, lead and stones, were thrown to a great distance; not a stone of the mill was left standing; even its foundations were torn up and scattered; and the only part of its machinery standing is a large metal wheel used in the process of granulation.—The bodies of the unfortunate sufferers were cast a considerable distance, and in quite different directions. They were wholly denuded of clothes, and presented a shocking appearance—mutilated, and scarcely recognisable. Between the place in which the body of Long was found, and the mill, there is a wall some thirteen or fourteen feet high, over which he was cast with fearful violence. The body of Carroll [sic] was thrown far beyond the canal and plantation already spoken of, and into the field where the cavalry were exercising. Both the bodies, in addition to the mutilation they underwent, were as black as jet, and as we have observed, scarcely recognisable. In the barracks of Ballincollig, about half a mile distant, windows were shattered—houses in the village were shaken to their foundations, and in several of them articles were displaced—and the sensation caused in the minds of the inhabitants was as if an earthquake had taken place. The gunpowder which exploded amounted to 2,000lbs.!—one day's production in that particular mill!! quite a sufficiency to blow up an immense fortress—it was intended for immediate shipment.

On Sunday an inquest was held on the bodies of the deceased, John Carroll and Jeremiah Long, before H. Baldwin, Esq., when the jury were unanimous in returning the following verdict:—That the said Jeremiah Long and John Carroll, on the 29th day of July, in the year 1842 [sic], at Ballincollig powder mills, in the county of Cork, were killed by a quantity of gunpowder being accidentally and by misfortune exploded

in a granulating mill; and we are of opinion that all proper precautions were used by the proprietors of that establishment to prevent such occurrences.
(1843-08-05, 2:3)

3042. Sudden Death.—On Friday the 28th inst. as a poor man, a stranger, was crossing Barrack-street, Armagh, apparently in good health, he was seen to fall, and on being taken up, was quite dead. An inquest was held on the day following. (1843-08-05, 3:4)

3043. Life.

Life is a vapour that passeth away,
How rapid its progress, uncertain its stay!
From youth to old age, oh! how transient at best,
The life of a creature in mortality drest:
The view retrospective doth to mem'ry seem,
Like the fancied delight of a bright day dream.

Life's like a bubble on the broad ocean's breast,
Still constantly moving and never at rest;
In the sunshine 'tis seen all beautiful, bright—
Tho' round it the dark waters rage in their might;
But, ah! in a moment, as 'twere in the pride,
It is lost neath the foam-crested, swelling tide.

Life seems like a cloud, when it passeth away,
On the wings of the wind, in the bright noon day;
Tho' its motion appears at a distance, slow,
Yet it really with infinite speed doth go;
Whilst the place where 'tis born is unknown, unseen,
By the eye of a mortal, in earth, I ween.

Life resembles a vessel toss'd to and fro,
On the fathomless deep when the wild storms blow;
Tho' uncertain the hour of its sinking be,
It vanisheth soon 'neath the raging sea:
And no trace of it e'er appeareth more,
While its requiem issuing from shore to shore.

Thomas R.J. Polson.
July, 1843.
(1843-08-05, 4:1)

3044. We have just heard that an explosion took place at the Ballincollig Powder Mills, at one o'clock this day, (Monday), and have despatched a reporter to the spot to ascertain the particulars.—*Cork Reporter*.
(1843-08-05, 4:5)

3045. Consistorial Court.—The Archbishop of Dublin has appointed Dr. Joseph Radcliffe, son of the late excellent Judge of this Court, as successor of his father.
(1843-08-05, 4:6)

3046. Presbyterian Marriages.—Petition of the General Assembly.—The following is a copy of the petition presented to the House of Peers, from the General Assembly, in reference to the marriage case:—

"To the Right Honorable the Lords, Spiritual and Temporal, of the United Kingdom of Great Britain and Ireland, in Parliament assembled.

"The petition of the Ministers and Ruling Elders of the General Assembly of the Presbyterian Church in Ireland,

"Most Humbly Sheweth—That petitioners have been extremely disappointed in the opinion of the English Judges, on the subject of the validity of marriages, celebrated by Presbyterian Ministers in Ireland.

"Petitioners and their ancestors have believed, for upwards of two hundred years, that such marriages were valid in the eye of law, as they undoubtedly are in the eye of morality and religion. In this opinion they were supported by repeated decisions of Learned Judges, and the opinion of eminent civilians, not of the Presbyterians but of the Prelatic communion; and while they impeach not the learning or integrity of the Judges of England, they cannot conceal the astonishment which they feel at the opinion which they have on this day delivered.

"Petitioners have to lament, that in the lengthened and elaborate argument of the Crown Counsellors before your Lordships' House, the subject of Presbyterian holy orders was almost entirely omitted. Petitioners do not hold or approve of the lax and licentious doctrine, that marriages may be contracted privately, without the presence of a Minister of religion, or any religious ceremony; but they are prepared triumphantly to prove, by the testimony of all the Churches of the Reformation, not excepting the Church of England itself, that Presbyter and Bishop are two distinct names for the same sacred office, and, of course, that Presbyterian ordination confers the same holy orders as is conferred by Prelatic ordination.

"Petitioners, therefore, humbly, but earnestly, implore your Lordships not to decide this important question, until petitioners shall have had an opportunity, by two of their Ministers, or should that be inadmissible, by learned lawyers, of proving, at your Lordships' bar, that Presbyterian Ministers were introduced into Ireland by the Crown; that they have for upwards of two hundred years, been recognised as a Church, and endowed by the State; and that they are in holy orders for every purpose contemplated by the common law for the celebration of a valid marriage.

"Petitioners do further earnestly entreat your Lordships to order a return, if such can be obtained, of all the cases of bigamy tried in England and Ireland, for the last ten years, setting forth the religious denomination to which the bigamist belonged, and that of the Clergyman celebrating the second or criminal marriage, as petitioners are confident, that, in proportion to their numbers, there is not, among their people, a tithe of the general bigamy cases, and in very few instances, have bigamy cases been celebrated by their Ministers. And petitioners will ever pray

(Signed by order),

"Robert Stewart, D.D.,
Moderator of the General Assembly.

"John Boyd, Ruling Elder.
Belfast, July 12, 1843."

(1843-08-12, 2:4)

3047. Actions for crim. con. are rare in Bombay, and one which was tried lately in the Supreme Court has exhibited no small degree of curiosity. The parties concerned were both officers of her Majesty's 78th Highlanders; the plaintiff, Captain Cummin (now absent in Scinde); the defendant, Lieutenant Garrat. The husband recovered damages to the amount of £200. A duel had been previously fought. The lady is living under the protection of her seducer. (1843-08-12, 3:5)

3048. Death of General Sir A. Brooke.—We announce with feelings of sincere regret, the decease of Lieutenant General Sir Arthur Brooke, which occurred in London, on Wednesday last, the 26th of July. This excellent and much-lamented officer had been in the army nearly fifty-one years. He served from an early age in various parts of the globe. From May, 1794, to December, 1795, he was in Holland with his late Royal Highness the Duke of York, and in 1796, he was present at the reduction of the Island of St. Lucia. He afterwards faced the enemy in Egypt, Malta, the Mediterranean, and the Peninsula, and at the termination of the war there, proceeded to America, where he succeeded to the command of the army after the battle of Washington, where General Ross was killed.

He was greatly esteemed in private life for his many exemplary qualities, and respected and beloved by his brother officers of all ranks, for his integrity, bravery, and open-hearted generosity. His death has deprived society of an amiable man, and the British army of a gallant, and experienced, and a zealous officer.

Sir Arthur Brooke was a Knight Commander of the Bath, and had, we believe, several foreign orders, although they are not specified in the annual Army List. The Colonelcy of the 86th Regiment, in which he was appointed on the 24th of May, 1837, is, by his demise, placed at the disposal of his Grace, the Commander-in-Chief. (1843-08-12, 4:3)

3049. Melancholy Occurrence.—A fishing boat from Malin, having been out at Innistrahull Island on Friday night, was returning home on Saturday morning, when, a short distance from the island, she was struck by a sea, and upset, and, doleful to relate, five of the poor men who were in her met a watery grave. Four of the unfortunate sufferers have left widows and fifteen helpless children to deplore their loss; the other was a poor young man, the sole support of an aged father and mother, and four sisters.—*Londonderry Journal*. (1843-08-12, 4:5)

3050. The Earl of Seafield, an elderly Scotch Peer, with an income of 65,000*l.* a-year, is intent upon immediately forming an union with a very lovely young lady from the South of Ireland. (1843-08-19, 2:3)

3051. Galway Assizes.—Interesting Case—Breach of Promise of Marriage.—*Mahon v. Flanagan*. This case excited much interest in the County and town of Galway, in consequence of the respectability of the parties, and their connexion with some of the most influential families in the County. Immediately before the case was opened for the plaintiff, several ladies entered the Court, two of whom were accommodated with seats beside the Judge. They were, however, obliged to retreat in the course of the able speech of the Counsel for the plaintiff (Mr. Monaghan), in consequence of the delicacy of some of the topics to which he adverted. The facts of the case are these:—The defendant, Mr. Flanagan, residing at Woburn, in the neighbourhood of Eyrecourt, is a gentleman possessed of personal property to the amount of £8,000, together with landed property to the amount of £250 a-year. The young lady, a beautiful and interesting person, of eighteen years of age, lived some few miles from the residence of the gentleman, and having attracted his attention, he solicited a mutual friend (Mrs. Cowen) to introduce him. After an intimacy of a month or two, the gentleman became the accepted suitor of the lady. In the mean time, however, some qualms affected the conscience of the lover, and having a wish to break his engagement with the young lady, he had it circulated in the neighbourhood that a servant maid, who had been in the service of the family, was living in a state of conbuninage [*concubinage*] with him. This caused the negotiation to be broken off for a time, but again renewed, under the express condition, that the object of dispute should be removed. After appointing a day for marriage, and the eventful morning having at length arrived, the lady of the house was surprised by receiving a visit from the brother-in-law of the intended bridegroom, who announced the intention of the latter gentleman not to enter into a matrimonial engagement unless the servant were restored to her present lodging. This, of course, knocked up all further proceedings, and the gentleman having continued inexorable ever since the present action was brought. Mr. Monaghan opened the case for the plaintiff, in a very able speech.—The evidence adduced was of the most respectable and corroborative description, and was in vain endeavoured to be affected by an able speech of two hours' duration, delivered by Mr. Fitzgibbon, the Counsel for the defendant. After the evidence for the defence closed, Mr. Baldwin replied in a speech, which, at its conclusion, drew down the most enthusiastic cheers from the assembled multitude. The Learned Judge charged feelingly, and the Jury, after a quarter of an hour's consideration, returned a verdict of 2,500*l.* damages, and 6d costs. It is the intention of the Learned Counsel for the defendant to except to the charge of the Learned Judge, and apply for a new trial.
(1843-08-19, 3:5)

3052. Death of Mr. Pim.—With the deepest regret we have to announce the death of Mr. Richard Pim, superintendent of the mechanical department of the Dublin and Kingstown Railway. He had been labouring under severe illness for some months, but within the last few weeks improved so much in health as to be able to take carriage airings every day. On Saturday he drove out as usual, and seemed improved in strength and spirits, but it pleased an inscrutable Providence to release him at an early hour yesterday morning from his earthly sufferings. An effusion of blood on the brain was the immediate cause of his death. This young gentleman, from his scientific and practical skill, gave abundant promise of his attaining the highest eminence in his profession. He was in the thirtieth year of his age. His kindliness of heart and friendly disposition endeared him to a host of friends, while they secured for him the affection and respect of all who were placed under his superintending care and direction. A deep and general sympathy is felt for his sorrowing relatives.—*Saunders.* (1843-08-26, 1:2)

3053. Important—The Presbyterian Marriage Bill.—(*From the Belfast Chronicle.*)—We have reason to believe that this long disputed and important question will very soon be settled, in a manner which will give satisfaction throughout Ulster. A bill is immediately to be brought into Parliament, by the Lord Chancellor, of course having received his sanction, which, we feel satisfied, will remove all just grounds of complaint. We have not seen the bill, but we have authority to state the principal provisions contained in it. By it, the right of Presbyterian clergymen to marry members of their communion to Episcopalians, is completely recognised, and the most perfect equality established. There is, however, to be a publication of banns, as in the established church; the ceremony, also, is to be performed in the meeting-house, within canonical hours, and a marriage registry is to be kept. This is the gist of the bill, which is quite brief. Nothing can be more simple, and, in our opinion, more free from objection, or the likelihood of it; and we cannot entertain a doubt of its meeting the approbation of every reasonable man. The bill was introduced into the House of Lords on Wednesday evening, and was then to remain over for consideration during the recess; and we have excellent authority for stating that every expectation is entertained of its becoming the law of the land, unless some at present unanticipated obstacle be interposed. (1843-08-26, 1:2)

3054. Breach of Promise of Marriage.—It is currently reported, in Enniskillen, that a very aggravated case of the above description will engage the attention of the North-West Bar, at our next Assizes. The lady, who is young, amiable, and respectably connected, is a resident of our town, and the gallant gay Lothario (said to be wealthy) is on the wrong side of forty, and a merchant in the capital of Tyrone.—*Erne Packet.* (1843-09-02, 2:3)

3055. On Monday last, the 28th, two soldiers of the 14th depot, both of whom died the preceding day, were interred with military honors in St. Mark's Churchyard, Armagh; one of them would have been entitled to a claim for pension and discharge, had he survived two days. Their remains were deposited in the same grave. (1843-09-02, 3:1)

3056. County of Monaghan.—Auction.—Extensive Sale.—J.E. Jones, Begs to announce to the Public that he has received instructions from the Executor of the late Major Thomas Campbell Graham, to submit to Public Competition, at his late Residence, Scarva-House, (near Clones,)

On Monday, the 11th September next, and following days, at Eleven o'clock,

The whole of the choice and carefully selected Modern Furniture, all but a very short time in use, and in the best order; a neat Pedestal Sideboard; Ormoln Lamps; Pillar Dining Tables; Centre, Loo, Marble, and occasional Tables; Mahogany Balloonback, and Eighteen Parlour Chairs; Nelson Loungers; French Bracket Clock, with Glass Shade; Taberet Window Curtains and Draperies, with richly Carved Gilt and Burnished Cornices and Fittings; Brussels and Kidderminster Carpets and Hearth Rugs; Steel Fenders with Rests and Fire Irons; Mahogany, State, Fourpost, and Eliptic Bedsteads, with Chintz Hangings, Draperies, Fittings, and appropriate Bedding; Mahogany Wardrobe; Chests of Drawers; Wash and Dressing Tables; Slab Toilet Glasses; Towel-rails; Biddets [sic]; Commodes; Cane-seat Chairs; Carpets and Window Curtains; about sixty dozen of choice old Wines; Damask Table and House Linens, and a set of best Sheffield Ware (never in use); services of Dinner, Dessert, and Morning and Evening China and Glass; Kitchen and Dairy requisites; an open Carriage, with a Head Pole and Shafts, all in good order; a good Outside Jaunting Car; double and single Harness; Saddlery and Horse Clothing; a capital pair of Grey Carriage Horses, 15 hands high, 7 and 8 years old; a high-bred bright bay Mare, rising four years old, gentle, of good action, has been managed and intended for a Lady's use; two strong Cart or Farm Horses; In-calf Milch Cows and young stock of Cattle; Farming Carts; Farming Implements; growing crop of Oats, Potatoes, Turnips, and Mangle Wurzel. Terms.—CASH.

Approved Bills will be taken for 20 and upwards, including stamp and interest.

The purchasers to pay the Auction Duty.

Scarva-house, August, 1843.

(1843-09-02, 3:6)

3057. Loss of another Steamer.—The *Queen* steam-packet from Bristol to Dublin was totally lost off Milford Haven on Friday night, having struck on a rock during a dense fog. The cargo was all lost with the passengers' luggage, as in less than half an hour, she went to the bottom; the passengers and crew, with the exception of one old man, were saved. He was a pig-dealer, and is supposed to have been asleep in the hold when she went down. (1843-09-09, 4:5)

3058. Melancholy Death.—An account of a fatal and melancholy event has just reached us through our Clones correspondent, who states that on Tuesday last, the Rev. Mr. M'Kernan, Roman Catholic Curate of the Parish of Currin, in this county, was drowned in the Ulster canal. The rev. gentleman was riding along the bank when his horse stumbled and fell into the water, carrying his rider with him, and before assistance could be procured he had ceased to exist.

An inquest was held on the body before the Coroner of the county Fermanagh, and a verdict of "Accidental death" returned.

Our Correspondent, in detailing the above melancholy event, states an attending circumstance, which, for the sake of human nature, we do not wish to credit. He says that while the unfortunate gentleman was riding along the Canal bank, he was mistaken for a person of strong anti-repeal principles in the neighborhood, by a number of workmen who were reaping in an adjoining corn field—that those persons saw him fall into the canal, but would not render him any assistance, in consequence of their antipathy to the individual he was supposed to be. If this be true, it is a horrible state of society to contemplate.
(1843-09-16, 3:4)

3059. The Husband to His Absent Wife.

Dearest, come back, I cannot bear
These long, long days of pain;
Oh! come and soothe my grief and care,
Come, bless my sight again.

How the lone hours drag slowly on,
In creeping, drawling pace!
Oh! how I long to look upon
Thy dear, thy blessed face.

Come, dearest, come, and feast once more
My soul with rich delight;
Thou'rt cherished in my heart's deep core;
I live but in thy sight.

Come, love, and let me feel again
Thy warm heart beat gainst mine,
And let me tender kisses rain
On those sweet lips of thine.

Come, let me hear thy love-fraught sighs,
Not heaving oft in vain;
Come, let me see thy love-deep eyes,
My own dear wife, again.

Come, else my weary heart will fail,
My suppliant voice be dumb,
My love itself, unfed, grow pale;
Come home, then, dearest—come.

Oh, no, my love, I cannot bear
These long, long days of pain;
Then come and soothe my grief and care—
Come, bless my sight again.

(1843-09-16, 4:1)

3060. Inquest.—On Saturday the 9th inst., an inquest was held in this town (on view of the body of Mr. Peter Connally,) by John M'Faddin, Esq., Coroner of this county. It appeared in evidence that he had, on the 8th, been cutting wheat in the country, and in the evening he and his men indulged a little freely in partaking of the glass. On returning home, he mounted his mare perfectly well, but had not proceeded far when he became heavy, and leaned with his breast upon the saddle; his head having lowered to the beast's shoulder, breathing was consequently stopped. Verdict—"Died of suffocation, occasioned by the use of ardent spirits." The slightest caution would have saved his life; but no blame can be attributable to his servants, as both imagined he was all right, so long as they could keep him in his saddle.

On coming to his own house in Kingscourt, Surgeon Malcomson was immediately sent for, and as promptly attended, but the vital spark was totally extinct.

A general feeling of regret prevails through the entire neighbourhood for this death. Mr. Connolly [sic] was a kind-hearted, active, industrious, and rather intelligent man, and has left a wife and three young children to lament his loss. (1843-09-23, 3:3)

3061. It falls to our lot to announce the demise of the Vice Provost of Trinity College, Doctor Prior, which event took place at his residence, Mount Prospect, near Miltown, on Saturday last. His disease was paralysis. He was in his 79th year, and had been nearly fifty years a Fellow of Trinity College. The death of the Vice Provost leaves a vacancy among the senior fellows, to be filled by Doctor Lloyd, son of the late Provost; and his advancement creates a vacancy amongst the juniors for the next examination in June.
(1843-09-23, 3:4)

3062. How to Attain a Good Old Age.—All that genius, learning, study, wealth, and superstition could do have been brought in play for the attainment of this object, yet, how partial has been their success. Men have devoted their whole lives for but a partial insight into the supposed mysteries of this occult science. Thousands of pounds have been expended on quacks, and the remotest portions of the earth have been ransacked for medicines to aid man in his endeavours to reach that goal, which all mankind wish to attain. Notwithstanding all those endeavours, have we not seen men, aye, and women too, cut off in the prime of their youth, leaving friends, for whom they should live to love, bless, and make happy, to mourn over their early graves; yet, the panacea for all the woes entailed on suffering humanity was a secret—a secret, the very simplicity of which kept its wonderful efficacies unknown, and its powers untried. The possessor of this wonderful secret, fearful of being called a quack, or of too hastily imparting it until years of closest watching has put it out of the question. He now comes forward, and without fee or reward, most philanthropically bestows his secret, which, if dealt out with a niggard hand, would make Croesus a mere pauper compared to him, and the wealth of Ormus or of Ind but trifles in his treasury; and he hopes that the universal public will duly appreciate such liberality, and erect some splendid token of their unbounded gratitude to so great a benefactor of his race. Read, reader, and be instructed. Pay for your Newspaper in advance. We never knew a subscriber, who had paid for his paper in advance, die before his year was up; so make haste, and do not let one year overtake another. (1843-09-30, 3:4)

3063. The Dying Girl and her Father.—(From a newly published poem, "The hope that is in us.")

On a low couch, within a noiseless room,
Where the broad light was half subdued to gloom,
There lay a youthful sufferer, fair e'en now,
When the hard hand of death was on her brow.
Friends stood around; they knew her long and well;
They gazed, and bitterly their quick tears fell.
Sad, sad the scene, while all without was gay;
The small bird carolled to the sunny day,
Flowers breathed in perfume, and in cloudless glow
The blue heaven laughed to the green earth below;
But there, within the atmosphere of death—
The aching look, pale cheek, and labouring breath;
For she, who would have lived if love could save,
Would soon be lost to fondness in the grave!
But she, while sunk the iron hearts of men,
She only wept not, sighed not, shook not, then.
Strange! that in life unto her timid ear
The slightest sound came leaden with a fear;
Warm fancies fed her eager mind, which still
Saw in each sense some boding shade of ill;
While strong excitement in her vivid brain
Worked on each thought until it grew to pain;
But now, how great that change which meets their eyes.
Weak in herself, yet strong in Heaven, she lies;
No fear disturbs, no doubts, at life's still close,
Which hints of evil break her mind's repose:
Faith quiets nature's strife within the breast,
And warring passions settle into rest.
'Twas thus of old, when, rising dark and strong,
The tempest hurled the whitening wave along,
The Prince of Peace above the billows trod,
And the calm sea bowed down before its God.

But say, ye men of little faith, oh say,
When life has fled the unimpassioned clay,
How will ye dry the tears of those who stand
Around that couch of death—a sorrowing band?
Cease, till ye find some fitter creed to sneer
At that which whispers in each mourner's ear
She is not dead; she lives in freshened bliss,
Born into other worlds, though lost to this.
Live as she lived, and thou wilt welcome too
That death which gives both heaven and her to you.
And he who mourned her most above the rest,
Who knew her longest, and who loved her best
He, the sad father of her child, who stood
And gazed upon her face in tearless mood
That face o'er which used playfully to flit
Flashes of joy which love for him had lit
He looked upon her eye—'twas dull and cold,
Nor shone with answering glances as of old;
And that fond hand, which he was wont to clasp,
For the first time lay stiffly in his grasp.
Oh, had he deemed her all of life was o'er
That the cold mass lay there to raise no more
What would he then have felt! what thoughts of pain
Had scorched his very heart, and racked his brain,
As on his view the torturer memory brought.
Each small injustice, each scarce-acted thought
The wrongs of her he loved—each careless word,
Each hasty deed which jarred affection's chord:
These might have brought too soon that bitter day
Which death unpitying claimed his early prey.
And when, long hence, some pleasure for awhile
Won from his lips a melancholy smile
This, but for me, had been his mournful creed,
She might have shared, and I am lost indeed!
But now he knows, as but believers know,
That she is blest beyond all bliss below
Safe from all change, secure from all alarms,
And wrapt within the Everlasting Arms.

Such are the fruits religious faith can yield;
Death drops his dart, when hope uplifts her shield.
Take these away and the round world is then
But one vast tomb for all the race of man,
Which points to where, amid life's poor remains,
Decay has been, and death for ever reigns.
But give religion's pregnant hopes to man,
Existence then dilates its little span,
And longest years with which full time is rife
Are but the childhood of immortal life.
(1843-09-30, 4:1)

3064. Public Monuments to Eminent Men.—The following communication has been forwarded to Sir Robert Peel, conveying to C.L. Eastlake, Esq., the Secretary to the Commission on the Fine Arts, her Majesty's recommendation to the commissioners to enter fully on the subject of public monuments to scientific men, viz.:—

Whitehall, August 17, 1843—Dear Sir—A proposal was recently made to the House of Commons that the commissioners should be empowered by her Majesty to inquire into the best means of doing honor, by public monuments, in sculpture or painting, to be erected at the public charge, to the memory of men entitled to the gratitude of their country by eminent civil, literary, or scientific services. I was unwilling to devolve on the commissioners a general inquiry of this nature, not immediately connected (*continued...*)

3064, continued: ...with the original object for which the commission was appointed; but I willingly undertook to recommend to her Majesty to give to the commissioners full authority to consider whether there is a portion of this edifice intended for the accommodation of the houses in parliament, or of the building connected with that edifice, which could with advantage and propriety be allotted to the reception of monuments such as those to which I have before adverted, and to report their opinion to her Majesty; not only with regard to the particular site of such monuments, but in the event of an appropriate site in connection with the new houses of parliament being recommended by the commissioners, with regard to the principles, generally, which should govern the selection of the names to be honored by so distinguished a record of national gratitude, and the best mode of combining the public acknowledgment of eminent service with encouragement of the arts in this country. I am empowered by her Majesty to recommend the subject to the consideration of the commissioners, and to give them her Majesty's full authority for entering upon it.—I am, dear sir, your obedient servant, Robert Peel.—C.L. Eastlake, Esq. (1843-09-30, 4:1)

3065. The Population Returns.—The English and Scotch census for 1841 has been published in three folio volumes. The following details are interesting, as regards the extent of emigration from Ireland to Great Britain, and from Scotland to England:—

England.—The population of England (exclusive of Wales) by the census was 14,995,138. Among one thousand individuals of this population on an average there were—

Born in the county where they live, ... 807
Born in other counties, ... 159
Born in Scotland (59,907 males, 42,158 females), ... 6
Born in Ireland (148,151 males, 135,977 females), ... 19
Foreigners and British subjects born in foreign parts, 24,323 males, 14,305 females, ... 2
Not specified where born, 107,251 of both sexes, ... 7
Total, ... 1,000

It thus appears that the population of England in 1841 comprised 102,000 persons born in Scotland, and 284,000 born in Ireland. The returns for Wales show 1,173 persons born in Scotland, and 5,275 born in England.—Even if we add to these classes one-third of those who did not specify their native country, the number of immigrants from Scotland and Ireland is only 25 in 1,000, or 2-1/2 per cent., a smaller number than many supposed.

Scotland.—Population, 2,620,184. Among 1,000 individuals of this population there were—

Born in same county in which they live, ... 750
Born in other counties, ... 172
Born in England (18,562 males, 19,234 females), ... 14
Born in Ireland (66,502 males, 59,819 females), ... 48
Foreigners, and British subjects born in foreign parts, ... 1
Not specified, ... 6
Total, ... 1,000

It hence appears that there were in Scotland in 1841 37,000 natives of England, and no less than 126,300 natives of Ireland. The Irish immigrants form nearly 5 per cent. of the population of Scotland, while they form rather less than 2 per cent. of the population of England. (1843-09-30, 4:3)

3066. Emigration of Irish Harvest Labourers.—The following extract from the report of the census commissioners for Ireland contains some very curious and valuable facts:—

We have already stated that we have taken measures to obviate certain inconveniences, which we had reason to apprehend would arise from the lateness of the season at which the census was taken. Of these the principal arose from the fact, familiar to every one acquainted with Ireland, that in the month of June the agricultural population is in a state of considerable movement, the labourers resorting in search of work, to neighbouring counties, which require more labour than the resident population can supply, and many proceeding to England and Scotland for the purpose of reaping the harvest.—The numbers thus emigrating to Great Britain having been variously stated, we required from the police at every port an enumeration of all the deck passengers who embarked on board the various packets during the summer of 1841. For this purpose, a competent officer was stationed at each packet office, and each person as he receives his ticket for embarking was asked from what country he came. The results of this inquiry are exhibited in Table No. 3 of Home Emigration. The number who had gone before the 6th of June was 5,481, before the 1st of July, 13,997; and in the whole summer, 57,651. Of this number, Connaught furnished 25,118, and the single county of Mayo, 10,430. The great majority of these labourers embarked at Drogheda and Dublin, and disembarked at Liverpool. Ulster ranks next in point of numbers, having contributed 18,312, of whom the greatest portion from any one county came from Donegal. The next largest amount came from Londonderry, and the next from Tyrone.—These appear to have chiefly embarked from Londonderry and Belfast, and to have proceeded to Scotland.—Leinster has contributed 11,404, of whom 5,625 came from Dublin, and they appear to have gone to Liverpool. From Munster, the most populous province in Ireland, containing more than one-fourth of the whole population, i.e., 2,396,161, only 1,817 labourers proceeded to Great Britain. The following statements show the number which sailed from each port at which returns were compiled:—

	Male.	Female	Total.
Londonderry and Portrush, ……..	10545	772	11317
Belfast, ……….	6420	984	7477
Warrenpoint, …	1621	119	1740
Dundalk, ……..	1141	353	2184
Drogheda, ……	13321	466	13786
Dublin, ……..	15303	4388	19691
Wexford, …..	304	182	486
Waterford, …	47	2	49
Cork, ………	439	473	911
Total, ………	49911	7740	57651

We have no means of knowing how many of those people remained in England. On their return to Ireland they land in such haste, that all attempts to count them were abandoned. We had not the power to count them on embarkation at English ports, and the returns of the steam-packet companies are not complete. But if we are to assume 40,000 of these 57,651 to return, leaving the remainder as permanent residents or foreign emigrants, and each to bring back 5 with him, which we have been informed is frequently exceeded, we see at a glance the comparatively small cost to Great Britain at which this useful labour is annually purchased at a moment it is required, and the valuable equivalent in money brought back to Ireland. The singular thrift and foresight which has so faithfully been remarked as characterising these people is curiously illustrated by this table, in which it will be seen that no less than 12,256 Connaught labourers embarked at Drogheda, and only 8,308 at Dublin. This unusual circumstance is attributed to a small reduction in the fare from Drogheda, a few weeks before the season commenced, which reduction was industriously made known in all the towns through which the stream of labourers was likely to pass in its progress from the west. (1843-09-30, 4:3)

3067. Hugh Collum, Esq., was on Tuesday elected coroner for Fermanagh, in room of the late Lowther Brien, Esq. (1843-10-07, 1:2)

3068. Distressing Accident.—On Tuesday last, Mr. Griffith, superintendent of the fisheries of Lough Neagh and its tributary rivers, was in the act of stepping into a boat at Toome, to be rowed to Portglenone, and having a brace of double barrelled pistols, which had been lately sent him from London, he was asked to shoot a duck in a flock which were floating about. He did so, and, missing his aim, he was again asked to shoot one, and, in complying with the request, while raising his arm, the pistol went off, and melancholy to relate, the ball entered the body of Mr. William Pelan, son to Mr. Pelan, innkeeper, of Toome, who, with Doctor Godfrey, was standing on the slip at the time. Mr. Pelan exclaimed that he was shot, and at the same instant Mr. Griffith ran to his assistance. Mr. Pelan did not fall, but was assisted to a log of timber, on which he sat down. He was subsequently removed to his father's inn, not more than thirty yards distant; and expresses were sent off to Castledawson, Magherafelt, Randalstown, and Antrim, for medical aid. In a short time six medical gentlemen were in attendance; but the ball having entered between the seventh and eighth ribs, and perforated the abdomen, it was found impossible to extract it.—On Wednesday, Doctor Latham, of Antrim, arrived with a letter expressing deep sympathy with the sufferer, from that humane and praiseworthy nobleman, the Earl O'Neill, to Mr. Pelan; and Doctor Latham, having examined the wound and the patient, expressed hopes of his recovery. Dr. Godfrey was in constant attendance, as were also Dr. Neeson and others. Everything which surgical skill and attention could devise was done; and we are happy to say that, at six p.m., on Wednesday, the sufferer was considered by Dr. Godfrey to be in as good a state as could be expected. The young gentleman who met with this unfortunate accident is deservedly beloved by all who know him. It is but justice to Mr. Griffith to say that he is fully acquitted of any blame by the unfortunate sufferer and his relatives. He is known to be a most humane man in the discharge of his duties, and possessed of amiable qualities in private life. The accident, as may be readily conceived, has thrown him into the deepest distress.

In addition to the above, which we copy from a contemporary, we may mention that the young gentleman referred to, expired at five o'clock on the evening of Friday last, and the estimation in which he was held may be judged of from the fact, that his funeral was attended by an unusually large assemblage of persons of the highest respectability. Not less than 88 vehicles, of different descriptions, were to be found in the cortege, in addition to nearly 300 mounted horsemen. In fact, almost all the respectability of Ballymena, Castledawson, Magherafelt, and the adjoining vicinities, were in attendance, to testify their regard for the deceased, who was interred in the centre of the old church at Randalstown. On this occasion, an excellent address was delivered from *Deut.* chap. 32, v. 29, by the esteemed Protestant clergyman of that district, the Rev. S. Heatly. Amongst the auditors were Col. Kennedy, of Moneyglass, Major Hill, of Bellaghy, and other distinguished personages.—*Belfast News-Letter*. (1843-10-07, 1:3)

3069. Death of General Sir Thos. Browne, K.C.H.—We have to record the death of the above gallant officer, who expired on Wednesday, at Knockduffe House, near Kinsale, at the age of 72 years. He was son of Colonel Arthur Browne, Lieutenant-Governor of Kinsale and Charles Fort in Ireland, and married in 1803, Miss Wolseley, second daughter of Sir William Wolseley, Bart. The deceased entered the army in 1787, and in his early military career he ably distinguished himself during his services (*continued…*)

3069, continued: ...in the Mediterranean and Gibraltar. At the reduction of Corsica, in 1794, he rendered himself conspicuous amongst his companions in arms for his bravery, and he subsequently proceeded on active duty in the Windward, Leeward, and Carribee Islands. He was engaged in the reduction of Surinam, in South America, in 1799, and at the reduction of the Danish, Swedish, Dutch, and French West India Islands, in 1804. In 1812 he proceeded in command to the East Indies, where he remained until 1822. During his residence in India he rendered particular service in the Mahratta war, and was for six years in command of the Carnatic as Major-General of the Staff. In consideration of his distinguished services, he was in the receipt of the annual pension of 400*l*. He was for many years in the 69th regiment, from which he retired some time back. The commission of the gallant General was dated as follows:—Ensign, 24th of September, 1787; Lieutenant, 26th of September, 1719 [sic]; Captain, 3d of September, 1795; Major, 23d of August, 1799; Lieutenant-Colonel, 29th of March, 1801; Colonel, 25th of July, 1810; Major-General, 4th of June, 1813; Lieutenant-General, 27th of May, 1825; and General, 23d of November, 1841. (1843-10-07, 2:3)

3070. An event of uncommon interest was witnessed on Sunday last, the 24th ult., by the inhabitants of the surrounding neighbourhood of Loughgilly. Samuel Cohen de la Haye, an aged gentleman of the Jewish nation, who had been lately converted to the Christian faith, presented himself publicly at the baptismal font for Christian baptism. The Israelite convert to Christianity is, we are informed, nearly connected with the present excellent Bishop of Jerusalem, and has been, for a length of time, resident in the family of the Rev. William Foster, by whom he was baptised, in the presence of five hundred persons, and received at the same time the additional Christian name of Cornelius. Although the church was so overfilled that many could not obtain even a standing-place, yet a solemn stillness and silent emotion, indicative of the deep feeling which prevailed, marked the whole proceeding, and, we would hope, betokened a due appreciation of the Christian privileges.—*Newry Telegraph.* (1843-10-07, 2:3)

3071. Funeral of Miss Westenra.—Yesterday the remains of Miss Mary Westenra, eldest daughter of the late lamented Hon. Richard Westenra, son to the late, and brother to the present Lord Baron Rossmore, were interred in the family vault in Monaghan church-yard. This amiable young lady was in her 19th year, and had earned for herself the fondest affections of her family. The greatest sympathy was evinced by the inhabitants of this town, great numbers of whom went out to meet the funeral, and joined the procession. Several carriages belonging to the gentry of the county were present, and the tenantry of Lord Rossmore and the other members of the family, on horse-back, with scarfs and hatbands, had a most imposing effect. The body was conveyed into the aisle of the church at 12 o'clock, Colonel Henry Westenra, A.G. Lewis, Esq., Maurice P. Lewis, Esq., and Wm. Lucas, Esq., acting as chief mourners. The funeral service was read by the Rev. A. Alcock, and an eloquent and touching address delivered by the Rev. Henry Maffett, after which the remains were consigned to the family vault. (1843-10-14, 3:2)

3072. The Peasant's Funeral.

'Twas Nature's fairest flower that slumbered by their side,
'Twas one both young and innocent; in innocence she died;
And many a murmuring sob was heard, and many a broken sigh,
And sorrow fill'd the stoutest heart, and tears bedew'd each eye.

In a lovely little valley the village church was seen,
In the midst of shady willow trees and meadows bright and green;
The ivy twin'd around its walls and the wild rose tree grew there;
A sweet and pleasant resting-place for one so young and fair.

On the evning breeze there floated those sounds they knew so well,
The soft and sacred music of the faintly-tolling bell;
But such music was not welcome now, as on the Sabbath-day,
For it told them that her soul had fled its tenement of clay.

A robe of snowy whiteness next fluttered in the air,
And the white-hair'd village pastor came to read the funeral prayer,
While a deep and solemn silence reigned through all the country round,
As the coffin slowly disappear'd beneath the yawning ground.

Each peasant's face was overcast with sorrow deep and true,
And the earth was water'd with their tears as with the morning dew;
And the father clasp'd his trembling hands, and vacantly he smil'd
Upon the spot where rested now his young and only child.

There lies the little peasant girl, and high above her grave
Wild roses bloom, and hawthorn trees and honeysuckles wave;
But her soul has fled to glory, to the mansion of the blest,
Where the wicked cease from troubling, and the weary are at rest.

(1843-10-14, 4:1)

3073. Caution.—I Hereby give the Public Notice, that I will not be accountable for any debt or debts contracted after the date hereof by my wife, Margaret Kennedy, she having taken herself from under my protection. The Public are also cautioned not to give either my said wife or my son Robt. Kennedy, any credit to my account.

Monaghan, November 1, 1843.

Robert ✕ Kennedy.
Mark.

(1843-11-04, 3:6)

3074. The Irish Bride.

The gems glittered fair, in her soft golden hair,
And her plumes waved light and free;
And the sparkling hue of her eyes, as blue
As the ether that floats in the air;

Her blush was bright, as the roses of light
That bloom by the rivulet's side;
And faithful and free, as the bird o'er the sea,
Was the heart of this beautiful bride.

The zephyrs that glide, on the sweet silver tide,
And the lilies that modestly sigh,
So mild was her face with intelligent grace,
And bright was the beam of her eye.

When her pearls were set, she could not forget,
That an emerald stud should be there:
So, her plumes wav'd between her sweet favorite green,
And reclined on her forehead so fair.

And her sparkling ring, that mystical thing,
Attracted the dazzling light
Of the sun, as it rolled o'er its bosom of gold
And set, o'er her beauty bright.

And a far dearer prize, than the beam of her eyes,
Was the virtue her loveliness sought:
Retiring and kind, and chaste was her mind,
For grace was the flower of her thought.

Her tears were bright, and as ether light,
They glided as soon away;
Tho' her sighs were not deep, nature taught her to weep,
For she knew 'twas her bridal day.

Tho' her gems were bright, and her plumes wav'd light,
Unassuming she stept in the scene;
Thus flowers when they blow, the more lovely they grow.
And they cluster the leaves between.

(1843-11-04, 4:1)

3075. Sonnet,
On the Death of Lady Catherine Beresford,
by Thomas R.J. Polson.

Behold how night her gloomy mantle throws,
O'er Nature's fairest scenes: at evening's close,
Dark ebon shades involves us in a gloom,
As if this world were nothing but a tomb,
Wherein a numerous set of creatures slept,
In undisturb'd repose, whilst Hope still kept,
Like some bright star, the harbinger of day,
Shedding a placid, but inspiring ray;
Pointing, as 'twere, to some supreme delight,
Reserv'd for us, far from this vale of night.
E'en so it is with her; she only seems
As 'twere to sleep, whilst Hope, with vivid beams,
Invites from shades of night, her soul's away
To realms of bright, interminable day.

Armagh Model School, Oct., 1843.

(1843-11-11, 4:1)

3076. State Prosecutions.—Court of Queen's Bench.—[Thursday.]—Judge Burton sat at half-past ten o'clock, to hear motions of course.

Criminal Information.—The Queen at the prosecution of *Leech a. Hill.*—Mr. Fitzgibbon, Q.C., applied for liberty to file a criminal information in this case against the defendant.—His application was grounded upon the affidavit of the prosecutor, who was a barrister, and who deposed that a marriage, without the previous consent of the right honourable the lord chancellor, was solemnised between his brother-in-law, Mr. Meredyth Chambre and Miss Isabella Jones, who at the time of the marriage was a minor. The lord chancellor ordered the parties to attend before him, when the deponent was retained for Mr. Chambre as counsel and another counsel having stated that Mr. Chambre and his friends had managed to have said marriage take place, although the young lady's guardian expressed a wish to have it postponed, deponent replied that the marriage had been solemnised against the desire of Mr. Chambre, but with the free will and consent of the lady's guardian, and at her own house. He further deposed that such statement of his was according to his written instructions; and he believed it was perfectly true, after that statement was made. The deponent swears that he received a letter from the defendant, Mr. Hill, the young lady's uncle, alleging that the statement he made was untrue; that he (deponent) not only prepared, but saw Mr. Chambre, sen., sign an undertaking to execute a settlement a few days before the marriage, and saw the young gentleman and his sisters going to the wedding. The defendant also accused his (Mr. Fitzgibbon's) client of a desire to foment discord and litigation; but he, on the other hand, in the most unequivocal manner, said that his conduct was intended or calculated to create discord, and positively deposed that if his advice were taken, none of the litigation which took place would have taken place. He further states that the assertion made in the Court of Chancery, that Mr. Chambre, was not a consulting party to the wedding, was perfectly true, and was contained in his instructions as counsel for Mr. Chambre, jun. He (Mr. Fitzgibbon) had an affidavit that those instructions (*continued...*)

3076, continued: ...were given, and that they were perfectly true. Mr. Meredyth Chambre also stated that his father remonstrated with him against the marriage; and as to the statement of his sisters being at the wedding, it was deposed that they went there solely to please Mr. Chambre's mother, who was not opposed to the match.

Mr. Justice Burton inquired if the deponent stated on his oath, that Mr. Hill, the defendant, intended to provoke him to commit a breach of the peace?

Mr. Fitzgibbon replied that it was deposed that Mr. Hill's object to irritate and induce the prosecutor to call him out to fight a duel, which, however, he did not, very properly, do.

The Court granted the application. (1843-11-18, 2:1)

3077. Death of Miss Vereker.—Died, at an early hour on the morning of Tuesday, the 21st inst., at Finnoe, near Borrisokane, the residence of her brother-in-law, Thomas Waller, Esq., Harriet, daughter of the late John Vereker, of the city of Cork, Esq.—*Nenagh Guardian*. (1843-11-25, 2:2)

3078. Dreadful Suicide.—At an early hour on Monday morning, Surgeon James Dillon committed suicide by precipitating himself from the second floor window of his residence in Lower Dominick-street. He fell into the area, which presents a shocking appearance, the unfortunate gentleman's brains and blood being literally strewed all over the space. The deceased was a native of Ballymahon, in the county of Longford, and was very respectably attended.—*Evening Mail.* (1843-11-25, 4:4)

3079. We regret to announce the demise of Sir F.W. Macnaghten, which took place at Bushmills house on Tuesday. Sir Francis was in his eighty-second year, twenty-one of which he served in India. His health had been gradually declining since the intelligence reached this country of the death of his son at Cabool, whose melancholy end is fresh in the minds of us all. No hopes were entertained of the life of the venerable Baronet for the last ten days.—*Northern Whig.* (1843-12-02, 1:5)

3080. Death of the Countess of Rathdowne.—We regret to announce the death of the Countess of Rathdowne, which took place at Charleville, on Wednesday night. Her Ladyship, as a Christian, a wife, and a mother, discharged faithfully all the relative duties of life, and has left her family and extensive connections overwhelmed with grief at the loss they have sustained. (1843-12-02, 4:3)

3081. Caution to Persons Making Wills.—Since the passing of the new will act, in 1837, numerous wills have been set aside for want of due attention to the manner of attestations prescribed by that act.

Amongst the latest cases of hardship of this kind we may mention one that occurred in the Prerogative Court last week. The deceased signed his will in the presence of two witnesses, a man and his wife present at the same time, but the man having written the wife's name, the court held, that though the witnesses might have attested the signature of the deceased, they had not both subscribed the will, as the act required, and refused the probate of the will. (1843-12-02, 4:3)

3082. Funeral of the Late Countess of Mayo.—The mortal remains of the late amiable and venerated Countess of Mayo, were removed on Friday, from Bersted Lodge, Bognor, on their way to their last resting place in this country. They will be attended on their journey by her Ladyship's nephews, Mr. Bourke, and his two sons, Mr. Richard and Lieut. John Jocelynn Burke.

By order of his physicians, who apprehended the effect of the mournful occasion on his health, the venerable Earl is constrained to withhold his attendance.

Her Ladyship was first Lady of the Bedchamber to her Majesty the Queen Dowager, by whom she was highly valued and is deeply lamented. (1843-12-02, 4:5)

3083. Dreadful and Melancholy Accident.—On Thursday morning last, the two sons of Lord Oranmore, the Hons. Geoffery and Henry Browne, were shooting on the lands of Ballikinare, near Claremorris. The latter gentleman was getting over a fence, when on drawing the gun up after him, the trigger got entangled in the grass, in consequence of which the gun went off, the contents lodged in his side, and caused instantaneous death. The body was immediately conveyed to Castlemacgarret, the family residence, where an inquest was held. Doctor Frazer, a most eminent surgeon, lost no time in hastening to the tragic scene, but before he had arrived, the sufferer breathed his last.—*Freeman's Journal.* (1843-12-02, 4:6)

3084. Death of Abraham Colles, Esq., M.D.—It is with feelings of extreme regret that we have to announce the death of our highly esteemed fellow-citizen, and invaluable member of the medical profession, Abraham Colles, Esq., M.D. This sad event took place at his residence, in Stephen's-green, on Friday evening last. (1843-12-09, 1:4)

3085. Death of the Rev. Mr. Tyrrel, P.P.—The Rev. Mr. Tyrrel, Roman Catholic priest of Lusk, is no more. He died of inflammation, on Tuesday evening, in the 51st year of his age. He was one of those included in the indictment against Daniel O'Connell and others, for a conspiracy and other misdemeanors. His character is thus drawn in the *Freeman's Journal* of Tuesday:—

The rev. gentleman had been just three years the Catholic Rector of Lusk, but during that period his laborious and zealous discharge of his sacred duties—his sincere piety—his exemplary habits, and the kindliness and humanity of his demeanor—had won for him the affectionate reverence of all classes amongst his parishioners. Of his fifty-one years, nearly thirty years had been spent in the labours of his mission.

The rev. gentleman was, perhaps, of all his brethren in the ministry, the least likely to have placed himself in opposition to the laws of the land. Constitutionally he was rather timid—certainly retiring—and no man ever took a part in public life whose tastes and inclinations would lead him to avoid even an approach to notoriety, as did those of this excellent priest. His life was bound up in his sacred duties. He wished not for any celebrity beyond the precincts of his own parish. Having discharged his duties there conscientiously, he was satisfied with the approval of his own heart, and sought nothing from the *eclat* of his actions. But, deeply impressed with the miseries of his country—dwelling with a portion of her people of simple habits and of restricted wants, but against whom, nevertheless, those miseries are developed to an extraordinary degree, the Rev. Mr. Tyrrell felt, as the Catholic clergy in other portions of the kingdom feel, that he was bound by the obligations of his order, as well as by those of citizenship, to do whatever was in his power for the alleviation of the destitution of the people. Hence it was that the Rev. Mr. Tyrrell became a repealer.

Knowing nothing personally of the reverend gentleman, we are not disposed to question this sketch of his character. In his private, and even in his professional life, he may have been, and probably was, all that he is here pictured; but, the more amiable and retiring his disposition may have been, the more unfit was he for mixture with the desperate associates who dragged him reluctantly into their wild projects; and the more it is to be lamented that the intimidation and pressure of a formidable agitation should have constrained him to a course so ungenial to his nature and inconsistent with his habits.

We are loth to follow the *Freeman* into the insinuations connected with the cause of this gentleman's death, and we will not. But this we must observe, that if he has "fallen a victim," it is to arts and constraints imposed upon him, in common with many others as reluctant as himself, by the public disturber of his country's peace, and in a cause for which he has repeatedly said one human life—one drop of human blood—were too dear a purchase.

Need we pursue the reflection?

The following address has been issued from the Repeal Association; we will trust ourselves with a commentary upon its nature or tendency:—

"To the People of the Parish of Lusk and the Neighbouring Parishes.—A bitter affliction has fallen upon Ireland! One of her beloved and venerated priesthood—one eminent for his virtues even among them—the Rev. Peter James Tyrrell—has been snatched away by death from the midst of his flock, and lost to them and to the country which he so devotedly loved and served!

"Like the true pastor of the Gospel he has laid down his life for his flock! His zeal to warn and to save them from imminent peril, was the immediate cause of his contracting the mortal disease that had so suddenly terminated his career of usefulness and goodness.

"Humble, but most firm, is our hope—humble; but breathed from the innermost depths of our souls, is our prayer—that his may have been the reward of the 'good and faithful servant' of the Lord!

"The shortness of the notice will not allow—did other difficulties not exist in the critical circumstances of the time, and the ever-active malignity of our enemies; ever on the watch for opportunities to create disturbance—that no organized assemblage and procession worthy of the occasion should attend his honored remains to the grave.

"But you his parishioners and neighbours, and many of us from Dublin, who knew, revered, and loved him, will be there in peace—in silent mournfulness benefitting the occasion—allowing nothing to disturb or distract our minds from our grief and from our heart-breathed for his eternal repose; and when the last sad honours are paid, separating peaceably—quietly—silently—without giving our enemies a chance of creating disturbance—without offence to any one; and thus paying the best and fittest tribute to him we have loved and lost!

It will be the cure of the Repeal Association, without loss of time, to have upreared to his sacred memory a benefitting monument, which shall accord to our enfranchised posterity, his labours, his virtues; and his devotion to old Ireland!

Signed by order of the committee,

John O'Connell.

Corn-Exchange, Dec. 5, 1843.

(1843-12-09, 1:6)

3086. Funeral of the Late Thomas Waller, Esq.—On Friday, at half-past one o'clock in the afternoon, the funeral of Mr. Waller, the second victim of the barbarous onslaught at Finnoe, took place. The house and approach to it were crowded with the gentry of the neighbourhood anxious to testify their respect for the memory of the deceased and their deep horror at the murder. A deep silence reigned among them as they fell into procession, for the coffin was borne to the grave by persons of the higher class exclusively. It was preceded by a very large number of the clergy from the neighbouring district. It was most awful to witness the still blood-sprinkled state of the rooms and hall of the dwelling-house; especially the curtains of the latter, which was the chief scene of the deadly struggle, and which may have literally been said to be double dyed with crimson. The service was read by the parochial clergyman, the Rev. Mr. Goold, and the Rev. Mr. Cotter preached the funeral address. We understand that the butler walked out for a few moments on Friday, but was still very weak.—*Nenagh Guardian*. (1843-12-09, 2:4)

3087. Funeral of the late Doctor Colles.—The remains of the late Dr. Colles, attended by the Colleges of Physicians and of Surgeons in procession, by the Master of the Rolls, the Lord Chief Baron, and a crowd of distinguished and eminent men, whose carriages rendered the north side of Stephen's-green and Merrion-row impassable for an hour before the funeral, and followed by a large number of the poor to whom he was a benefactor, were conveyed on Thursday morning at an early hour to the cemetery of Mount Jerome. The chief mourners were five sons of the deceased; his brothers-in-law, the Rev. Thomas Ottiwell Moore, D.D., and Dr. Robert Harrison; and his sons-in-law, Major Harrison and James Arthur Wall, Esq., and his cousin, Edward Richards Purefoy Colles, Esq. We were particularly struck with the sight of a poor cripple, who with a distorted frame limped on crutches from the Incurable Hospital to Mount Jerome, to pay his last tribute to his benefactor, who had placed him in that hospital. The procession was the largest seen in Dublin since the funeral of the celebrated Dean Kirwan, in 1805. (1843-12-09, 2:4)

3088. Death of Sir Thomas Forster, Bart.—We have to announce the death of the Rev. Sir Thomas Forster, Bart., of Coolderry in this county, and Phillipstown, in the county Louth, which melancholy event took place at Coolderry, on Monday last. The deceased Baronet had reached the patriarchial age of 93 years, having been born on the 9th Sept., 1751. He married Dorcas, only daughter of the Venerable George Howse, D.D., Archdeacon of Down, and by her had issue one son, George, and two daughters, Letitia Anne, married in 1816, to Lieut.-Col. Shum, of the Royal Artillery, and Sophia Maria. The deceased Baronet was in holy orders, and was Rector of a parish in the county of Louth. He is succeeded in his title and estates by his only son George (now Sir George Forster, Bart.,) who married, in 1816, Anna Maria, eldest daughter of the late Matthew Fortescue, Esq., of Stephenstown House, in the county of Louth, and niece of Mr. and Lady Elizabeth M'Clintock, Drumcar. (1843-12-09, 3:4)

3089. Ballyhalbert—Horrible Death.—On Wednesday morning, the 20th ultimo, Samuel Doaldson, the individual who worked the water-mill in this village, lost his life in the following manner:—Deceased was in the act of adjusting some parts about the wheel, when missing his object, he was propelled forward, and his arm got entangled in the wheel, which turning round with its accustomed velocity, he was literally torn to pieces in its revolution. His remains, when collected, presented a most horrifying spectacle; while to his dependant family, who looked to him for support, and from whom he had a few minutes before parted at the breakfast board, the case was awful in the extreme.—*Banner of Ulster*. (1843-12-16, 2:3)

3090. Consistorial Court of Clogher.—*Hanah M'Kee and Jane Thompson, v. Joseph M'Kee and others.*—This cause was opened in court on the 19th of January last, by Samuel Hamilton, an executor, citing the legatees named in the will of Joseph M'Kee, sen., late of Knockreaghs [sic] Upper, in the county of Monaghan, to hear the said will proved in special form of law. In this stage of the proceedings, it was supposed that the will lodged in the Registry of the Court was not the real and true one, but a forgery. The proctor then used all possible means of detection, and found that the most artful devices had been resorted to that might render the fraud undiscoverable. It appeared that Samuel Hamilton was one of the executors named in the true will of the deceased—that deceased had entrusted it to him—that some days after, deceased wishing to add a codicil, sent for the will—put the codicil to it—gave it then to his wife, directing her to send it back to Hamilton—she put it into a chest which stood in a room where her son Joseph M'Kee, jun., went to lie. The chest was opened—the will was taken out of the envelope, and a clean sheet of paper left in its place. A will was afterwards forged, in which all the legatees named by the deceased were also inserted, but with only half the sums bequeathed to them by the deceased. So well was the forgery got up that the names of the two witnesses to the true will were also attached to it, as was likewise the very codicil put by the deceased to his last and true will. Here, indeed, were difficulties that many, if not all, would say were insurmountable; yet, the proctor managed so judiciously through the whole labyrinth, that he caused the executor to relinquish and resign, though it was a hard and difficult struggle.

Citations were then served on the other executor and legatees, to appear and prove the pretended will, which they declined to do. The Judge, on the 13th instant, declared and decreed that the will of Joseph M'Kee, senior, deceased, then in the Registry, was true and valid.

Robert Mitchell, Proctor for plaintiffs; William Jebb, Proctor for defendant. (1843-12-16, 3:1)

3091. To the Editor of the *Newry Telegraph*.

Carrickmacross, Dec. 4, 1842.

Sir,—A beautiful tablet has just been put up in the Church of Carrickmacross, by the Shirley family, to the memory of the late Alexander Mitchell, of Shirley-house, Carrickmacross, and of Drumreaske, near Monaghan, Esq., as a token of esteem and respect for departed worth.

The language and the terms of affection inscribed upon the tablet sufficiently show the high opinion the Shirley family have had reasons to entertain of the valuable services of their lost friend, Mr. Mitchell. In the management of the important trust committed into his hands, he brought to bear upon the duties he had to discharge a vigorous and comprehensive mind, a degree of foresight and decision, a promptitude and energy of action, and a determination of purpose, when necessary, but of forbearance and caution, when required, rarely to be met with in one individual.

Although at the time of Mr. Mitchell's undertaking the agency of the Shirley estate, he had many difficulties to meet and to overcome—yet, he approached them all with comparative ease, and overcame them with great success and advantage to the respective parties whose interests he had undertaken to protect and advance. Having been, from his early boyhood, accustomed to public business, and the discharge of public duties, as Secretary to the Grand Jury of the County of Monaghan, he had acquired an amount of experience, a degree of method and dispatch, which, in a public man, and to the public, were truly valuable.

In all the great interests of the County of Monaghan, his foresight, his intimate and accurate local knowledge, (and in danger, his gallant bearing,) were looked upon as likely to fix and seal the destinies of those opposed to him. Conservative and constitutional in principle, he was respected for his consistency, by the very party who feared his influence, and dreaded his mental vigor—yet his political bias never carried him too far.

In private life the late Mr. Mitchell was warm in his attachments, but very select in the immediate objects of them. Few who had the pleasure of enjoying his society, did not benefit by it. His maxims—his comprehensive sayings, and their immediate application to passing scenes and passing circumstances—gave a zest to his entertainments, which were always liberal, never extravagant. Many of his surviving friends will bear evidence of the truth of this picture. It is not, by any means, over-drawn.

To the persons in his immediate employ, his course was one of generous solicitude for their comfort and well-being; and it has been remarked that he never took any young man by the hand who did not succeed in life, if it were not his own fault. Correct and punctual himself, nothing but correctness and punctuality would please him. The virtues he possessed he wished others to practice.

As Agent of the Shirley estate, the late Mr. Mitchell, in conjunction with the respected Agent of the Bath Estate, James Evatt, Esq., effected many improvements in the town of Carrickmacross and its approaches. Under their auspices we have, and to their taste we owe it (aided liberally by their respective principals), a beautiful and well situated Fever Hospital, and a Court-house, both remarkable for suitableness of site, and elegance and permanency of structure.

The following is a copy of the inscription:—

"In the Burial-place of his Family, at Ballinode, in this County
are interred the Remains of
ALEXANDER MITCHELL, of Drumreaske, Esq.,
the valued Friend and Agent of
Evelyn John and Charles Shirley, Esquires,
Whose Estate, in this Barony, he managed,
With Unceasing Attention, and the Strictest Fidelity,
FOR THIRTEEN YEARS.
It pleased God to call him Suddenly from this World,
While in the Exercise of his duty as Secretary
To the Grand Jury of Monaghan,
On the 13th of March, 1843,
In the 46th year of his age.
Deeply do that Family
To whose interests he Entirely Devoted himself,
Lament his Irreparable Loss.
They have Erected this Tablet, in Grateful Remembrance
of their Warm-hearted and Grateful Friend."

Yours, &c.,
A Subscriber.
(1843-12-16, 3:2)

3092. Sacred to the Memory of Frances, Countess of Rathdowne.

"Was it by day she fell asleep, or night;
At morning's prime, ar at the twilight pale?"—
"O ask not when; for she is now at rest,
Beyond the reach of mutability."

"Where have they laid her?!"—"Oh! it matters not;
Even the adamantine rock would bloom
Around her; ay, the iron rock would spring
With tender woodbine, and sweet clematis."

"Where is her everlasting dwelling-place—
The sanctuary of her soul—her mansion blest?"—
"Be still—enough to know she is in heaven."

"Whither she has gone she has been before;
She is no stranger there—she is at home;
We wondered why she stayed so long below."

"When shall we see her again?"—"At the last day,
With all the ransomed people of the Lord;
Why seek ye still the living among the dead?"
(1843-12-23, 2:3)

3093. To the Editor of the Northern Standard.—Consistorial Court of Clogher.—*Hannah M'Kee and Jane Thompson v. Joseph M'Kee and others.*—Sir—Your paper of last Saturday contains what purports to be a report of the proceedings had in the above cause. As there are some allusions made to Joseph M'Kee, one of the defendants, which might tend to prejudice the minds of the public against him, I feel called upon, as his Proctor, to state that nothing whatever has appeared in evidence to warrant any person in even supposing he was accessory to forging the will of his late father, Joseph M'Kee. He was cited by the executor, with the other defendants, on the 13th of December, 1842, to see and hear a will of the deceased, which was on record in the registry of the court, proved in special form of law, and afterwards by the plaintiffs, to prove and approve same in special form of law, otherwise to shew cause why same should not be revoked, cassated and annulled, &c. Not having the means to prove the will, he was obliged, unwillingly, to renounce, as did also the other defendants; whereupon the will in the registry was set aside. Another part of the report (*continued...*)

3093, continued: ...is in the following words, alluding to the alleged forgery and suppression:—"Here, indeed, were difficulties that many, if not all, would say were insurmountable; yet the Proctor laboured so judiciously through the whole labyrinth as to induce the executor to renounce, though it was a hard struggle." Now, I am authorised by Mr. Hamilton, the executor, to state, that so far from its being a hard struggle that induced him to resign, he did so voluntarily, and altogether of his own accord. Hoping that these few observations may set the matter right, I remain, Sir, yours, &c.,

William Jebb.

Monaghan, 22d December, 1843.

(1843-12-23, 3:2)

3094. Omagh, 17th December, 1843.—The remains of the Rev. Mr. Jamieson, son of J.K. Jamieson, Esq., of Clonkeen House, county Monaghan, passed through town this morning on the way to Clones. He was an indefatigable labourer in the vineyard of his divine master, and is gone to rest in the sure and certain hope of a glorious resurrection. (1843-12-23, 3:3)

3095. Death of Lady Maria Somerville.—Intelligence was received in London of the death of the Lady Maria Somerville, wife of Sir William Somerville, Bart., daughter of the late Marquess and the Dowager Marchioness of Conyngham, and the sister of the present Marquess of Conyngham. Her Ladyship expired at Rome on the 3d of December. (1843-12-23, 3:3)

3096. Sudden Death.—On Tuesday last, after the Christmas examinations at the Carrickmacross school, a young lad, one of the pupils, was seized with apoplexy, brought on by the excitement consequent on the examinations, and died in a few hours.

A report has been in circulation that death was caused by an injury received from a school fellow, which, however, the evidence of Doctors M'Effer and M'Mahon, completely contradicted. (1843-12-23, 3:3)

3097. We have to record the death of the Rev. John Harris Jameson, son of J.K. Jameson, Esq., of Clonkeen, whose indefatigable zeal in his Ministerial duties exposed him to a malignant fever, of which he died after a short illness, leaving his bereaved family deeply afflicted, and his loss sincerely regretted by those amongst whom he laboured, as well as by the numerous circle of his acquaintances. (1843-12-23, 3:5)

3098. Glanders in Man and Horse.—Glanders and farcy are essentially contagious diseases, whether enveloped in man, or in the quadrumina. They are, moreover, decidedly infectious as well as contagious, in the latter class of animals—i.e., the contagious principle may be transmitted through the medium of the atmosphere, as well as by actual contact, from one animal to another. I have known several instances in which there was no possibility of contact with glanderous matter, and yet the disease was developed in healthy horses. A gentleman of fortune, in the west of Ireland, had had his stud infected with glanders. Every particle of wood-work in the stables, including stalls, rack, manger, &c., was taken down and replaced with new materials; the plastering on the walls was completely removed, and the pavement ripped up, and all was replaced with entirely new work, but the first horses that were again put into those stables became infected, and they were ultimately razed to the ground. It would even appear that the contagion remains for a long period, sometimes for years, in any stable or shed where glanders or farcy may happen to have been developed. (1843-12-30, 1:5)

3099. Marriage in High Life.—On Tuesday, the 19th of December, in Clifton Church, by the Hon. and Rev. Thomas Skeffington, David Ross of Blandesburg, Rostrevor, county of Down, to the Hon. Harriet Margaret Skiffington [sic], eldest daughter of the late Viscount Ferrard, and the Viscountess Massareene, and niece to the Dowager Lady Dufferin. The bride was attended to the altar by her two sisters, by her sister-in-law, the Hon. Mrs. Thomas Skeffington, and two of her brothers, the Hon. Chichester and Henry Skeffington; by Sir Augustus Foster, her Majesty's late Minister at the Court of Sardinia; and his son, Mr. Vere Foster; Mr. Corry and Mr. Robert Ross of Blandensburgh [sic], sons of the late gallant General of that name, who so distinguished himself in America, where he nobly fought and fell. (1843-12-30, 3:3)

3100. Concealment between Husband and Wife.—The first and most innocent step, says Mrs. Ellis, towards falsehood, is concealment. Before our common acquaintances there is wisdom in practising concealment to a considerable extent; but where the intimacy is so great, the identity so close, as between a husband and a wife, concealment becomes a sort of breach of faith; and with parties thus situated, the very act of concealment can only be kept up by a series of artful endeavours to ward off suspicion or observation of the thing concealed. Now, when a husband discovers, as in all probability he will, unless these endeavours are carried out to a very great extent—when he discovers that his wife had been concealing one thing from him, he very naturally supposes that she has concealed many more, and his suspicions will be awakened in proportion. It will then be in vain to assure him that your motive was good, that what you did was only to spare him pain, or afford him pleasure; he will feel that the very act is one which has set him apart in his own home as a stranger, rather than a guardian there—an enemy rather than a friend. Why then, should you begin with concealment? The answer, it is to be feared, is too familiar—My husband is so unreasonable. And here, then, we see again the great advantage of everything you think or do. After concealment has become habitual, there follows, in order to escape detection, a system of false pretences, assumed appearances, and secret schemes, as much at variance with the spirit of truth as the most direct falsehood, and unquestionably as debasing to the mind. But, as an almost inevitable consequence, next follows falsehood itself; for what woman would like her husband to know that she had, for days, months, or years, been practising upon his credulity. If he discovers what she has been concealing, he will also discover, that often, when the subject was alluded to, she artfully evaded his question, by introducing another; that sometimes she so managed her voice as to convey one idea while she expressed another, and that, at other times, she absolutely looked a lie. No; she cannot bear that he should look back and see all this, lest he should despise her; and, therefore, in some critical moment, when in that trying situation, in which she must either confess all, or deny, pronounces, at last, that fatal word which effectually breaks asunder the spiritual bond of married love. And now, it is scarcely possible to imagine a more melancholy situation than that of weak and helpless woman, separated by falsehood from all true fellowship, human or divine; for there is no fellowship in falsehood. The very soul of disunion might justly be said to be embodied in a lie. It is, in fact, the sudden breaking asunder of that great chain which binds together all spiritual influences; and she who is guilty of falsehood must necessarily be alone. (1843-12-30, 4:5)

3101. Suicidal Mania.—It may be laid down as an indisputable axiom, that in every case of this kind, bodily disease may, upon a careful examination, be detected. I never yet saw a case where the desire to commit suicide was present, in which there was not corporal indisposition. Instead of inculcating the notion that this morbid propensity is independent of material lesson, it should be our constant endeavour, and, in fact it is our duty, to establish the necessity of obtaining medical advice directly the idea of self-destruction takes possession of the mind. I have seen the most happy results ensue from adopting such a course. Patients have consulted me, complaining of being haunted by a desire to commit suicide, and I have invariably found them to labor under latent physical disease. To know ourselves is half our cure, is a wise maxim when applied to this subject. It ought to be our object to persuade those so unhappily afflicted, that the unnatural propensity is but the consequence of physical ailments, which are amenable to those medical principles which direct the medical practitioner in the treatment of diseases. We should diffuse through society the notion that it is a matter of essential importance that the patient, whose mind is haunted by the idea of suicide, should instantly subject himself to medical treatment. He should be informed that his feelings are but the effect of physical disorder, which is capable of being easily removed. In such cases the physician should be careful to ascertain whether there be congestion of the brain or abdominal viscera. The latter affection is often present in this class of patients.—*Forbes Winslow's Health of Body and Mind.* (1843-12-30, 4:5)

3102. Funeral of Arthur Hume, Esq.—The mortal remains of Arthur Hume, Esq., were yesterday removed from his late residence, Dawson-street, to their final resting-place, the family vault under St. Paul's church. The hearse, drawn by six mourning horses, was preceded by two mutes, and accompanied with eight pages with batons.

Immediately after the hearse followed the carriage of the deceased with the blinds closed, and the horses in mourning sheets.

Then followed three mourning coaches, containing the Rev. Mr. Hume, Mr. M'Cartney, Henry, [sic] and Captain Hume, nephews of the deceased; with the sons of the Rev. Mr. Hume, Mr. Dames, Major Brook Golding, &c., and nearest of kin. (1844-01-06, 1:4)

3103. The Will of Lord Rossmore.—The will and six codicils of Lord Rossmore have been proved in Doctors' Commons by the Hon. John Craven Westenra, the son of the deceased, and one of the executors named in the will, power of proving hereafter being reserved for the Hon. Henry Robert Westenra (another son of the deceased), and Arthur Gamble Lewis, Esq. The deceased gives his estates in King's County to his sons. To his wife he gives all diamonds, trinkets, jewels, &c. His furniture, glass, china, cabinets, plate (and also the plate purchased of the Cairness family), are to descend as heirlooms. In a codicil he enumerates the whole of the plate, which takes up seven closely-written pages.—His horses and dogs are to be sold by public auction, but his paintings of favourite dogs, horses, &c., and hunting pictures, he gives to his son, John, desiring that they should be carefully preserved. To three of his servants he gives legacies, of £10 each, to several others £5, and to an old and faithful servant £20 a-year for life.—In the last codicil he directs that his estates called "The Boy of Monieva" be sold by auction. One of the witnesses to the codicil is the governor of Monaghan gaol. The will has been proved here under £800, (within the province), a mere nominal sum to include property in England for that value only. The estates of the deceased in Monaghan county, King's County, &c., are immense, and, of course, when the will is proved in Ireland the amount will be proportionate.—*Britannia.* (1844-01-06, 1:5)

3104. General Assembly—Mixed Marriages.—We learn that the Presbytery of Ards, county of Down, has forwarded a unanimous resolution to the Moderator of the General Assembly of the Irish Presbyterian church, requiring him to call a *pro re nata* meeting of the body as early as possible, to consider the present position and legislative prospect of mixed marriages, celebrated by Presbyterian ministers.—*Northern Whig.* (1844-01-06, 2:5)

3105. An individual died here a short time since who obtained an unenviable celebrity more than twenty years ago. This was the Bishop of Clogher, who was indicted for a crime, committed in St. James's, London, in 1822, forfeited bail, and fled, was degraded from his ecclesiastical dignity, and has never been heard of till now. He kept house at No. 4, Salisbury-place, Edinburgh, under the assumed name of Thos. Wilson, to which he removed four years ago, having previously resided in Glasgow. His mode of living was extremely private, scarcely any visitors being known to enter his dwelling; but it was remarked that the post often brought him letters sealed with a coronet. His incognito was wonderfully preserved. It was only known to one or two individuals in the neighbourhood, who kept the secret till after his death. The application for interment was made in the name of Thomas Wilson. There was a plate upon the coffin which he had got prepared some years before, but without any name upon it. It bore a Latin inscription, the sense of which was as follows:—"Here lie the remains of a great sinner, saved by grace, whose hope rests in the atoning sacrifice of the Lord Jesus Christ." The preparation of this inscription years before shows that he was deeply penitent. He was very anxious to conceal his true name, having got it carefully obliterated from his books and articles of furniture. He gave instructions that his burial should be in the nearest churchyard, that it should be conducted in the most private and plain manner, and at six in the morning. His directions were complied with, except in the selection of the ground. His body was drawn to the new cemetery in a hearse with one horse, followed by five mourners in a one-horse coach, at seven in the morning. Such was the obscure and humble death of the Hon. and Rev. Percy Jocelyn, the son of a peer, who spent the early years of his life in the society of the great, and held one of the highest ecclesiastical dignities in the empire.—*Scotsman of Saturday*. (1844-01-06, 2:5)

3106. Inquest.—An inquest was holden at Cararghrin Chapel, on the 1st instant, before Robert Murray, Esq., M.D., Coroner, County Monaghan, on view of a female infant found exposed under suspicious circumstances, close to that building. One witness was examined who deposed to the discovery, &c., and Doctor Maffett, of Glasslough, after a *post mortem* examination of the child, gave evidence that the infant was "still born." A verdict was given according to the evidence. (1844-01-06, 3:1)

3107. We received the following communication on the 28th ult., but in consequence of its length, and the hour at which we received it, we were unavoidably compelled to postpone its insertion:—

To the Editor of the Northern Standard.—Consistorial Court of Clogher.—*Hannah M'Kee and Jane M'Kee v. Joseph M'Kee and others*.—Sir—Having, as an auditor, given in your paper of the 16th inst. a brief and, as I conceived, a true report of the case, as it terminated on the 13th, and finding, by last Saturday's paper, that Mr. Jebb accuses my statement as having been untrue and false, I beg you may have the kindness to permit me again to enter the auditoriam, that judgment may be had between the accuser and the accused. Mr. Jebb's first charge against what he says purports to be a report of the proceedings had in the above case is that, as there are some allusions made to Joseph M'Kee, one of the defendants, which might tend to prejudice the minds of the public against him, I feel called upon, as his proctor, to state, that nothing whatever has appeared in evidence to warrant any person in even supposing he was accessory to forging the will of his late father, Joseph M'Kee, senior; he was cited by the executor, with the other defendants, to see and hear a will of the deceased, which was on record, proved in common form of Law. Now, this shews, in the highest degree, the zeal and jealous care with which Mr. Jebb, as a conscientious proctor, watches over the interest of his client, and his determination to do the best he can for him, though that client was the — himself.

Nothing can be more innocent than that a person cited to hear a will (not the will) of his late parent read, and then proved in law; and this, in common with the other defendants (according to Mr. Jebb) was all the immaculate Joseph had to do. To detect falsehood and establish the truth, being Mr. Jebb's chief object, and, as the same desire actuates all honorable men, it now becomes necessary to divest some things here of their covering, to see how they look when undressed. As there are some allusions made to Joseph M'Kee, one of the defendants, which might tend to prejudice the minds of the public against him. It will be found that in the first notice of the case there was no allusion made to Joseph M'Kee having been the forger of the will then in the registry; it only stated that the true will was put into a chest which stood in a room where the said Joseph went to lie; that the chest was opened, the will taken out of the envelope, and a clean sheet of paper left in its place. That this is true, the widow of the deceased proves by declaring that she put the true will, as she got it from her late husband, into the chest, and locked it, and Mr. Samuel Hamilton, the executor, an upright man, declares that when he called the legatees to hear the will he had received from the widow read, and having opened it in their presence, found nothing within but the blank sheet. The first report stated that a will was forged. This Mr. Jebb acknowledges by saying when the defendants "were cited by the plaintiffs to prove and approve the same (meaning the will) in special form of law, otherwise to shew cause why the same should not be revoked, &c. Not having the means to prove the will, he was obliged, unwillingly, to renounce, as did also the other defendants." A higher authority (the court) proves the same truth, by its decree declaring the will of Joseph M'Kee, sen., void in law—that is, a forgery. Mr. Jebb again says, "I feel called upon, as his (Joseph M'Kee's) proctor, to state, that nothing whatever has appeared in evidence to warrant any person in even supposing he (Joseph M'Kee,) was accessory to forging the will of his late father, Joseph M'Kee, sen." Notwithstanding Mr. Jebb's aptitude and skill in dressing, this must be stripped, and it shall appear naked. In "evidence" of his client, Joseph M'Kee, jun., having been the actual fabricator of the forged will, may be adduced quotations from affidavits read in open court, Mr. Jebb himself being at the time present—

"Hannah M'Kee and Jane Thompson make oath on the Holy Evangelist, and say that they are the natural and lawful children, and two of the next of kin of Joseph M'Kee, sen., late of Knockreaghs [sic], in the county of Monaghan, and Diocese of Clogher, who did in his lifetime rightly and duly make and execute his last will and testament, of testamentary paper, in writing, and afterwards died without altering or revoking the same: that Deponents are informed, and believe that said will or testamentary paper is in the power or possession of Joseph M'Kee, jun., of Knockreaghs aforesaid, or in the power, possession, or knowledge of some persons or persons for him. And deponents further say that the alleged will now of record, in the Registry of the Consistorial Court of Clogher, bearing date the 17th day of September, 1842, and purporting to be the last will and testament of said Joseph M'Kee, sen., deceased, is not as deponents verily believe, the true, original, last will and testament of said deceased, but the same is a forged and fabricated document, introduced by said Joseph M'Kee, jun., for the purpose of defrauding these deponents and the other legatees of the bequests left them by their father, the said Joseph M'Kee, sen., deceased, in his said, true, original last will and testament suppressed by the said Joseph M'Kee, jun., aforesaid.

"Hannah M'Kee.

"Jane Thompson."

"Owen Mangan, of Castleblayney, in the county of Monaghan, and diocese of Clogher, writing clerk, maketh oath, and saith that on or about the 17th day of September, in the year of our Lord, one thousand eight hundred and forty-two, he (the deponent) reduced into writing the last will and testament of Joseph M'Kee, sen., late of Knockreaghs, in the county and diocese aforesaid, according to the instructions and intention of the said deceased: and saith that he afterwards became a subscribing witness to said last will and testament, and saw the same duly executed by the said Joseph M'Kee, sen., deceased; and deponent verily believes that said last will and testament is now in the possession or power of Joseph M'Kee, jun., of Knockreaghs, aforesaid, the natural and lawful son of said deceased, or in the power or possession of some person or persons for him. And saith that he has seen the pretended will now of record, in the Registry of the Consistorial Court, and that the same is not the original last will and testament of said deceased, nor is the same or any part therof in the handwriting of this deponent, and that the name Owen Finegan, signed to said pretended will, is not the handwriting of this deponent, but is a forgery, and deponent verily believes that the said will is a forged and fabricated document, introduced by said Joseph M'Kee, jun., for the purpose of defrauding the legatees named in said original last will and testament, suppressed by him aforesaid, Owen Finegan.

Sworn before me in the Court, the 22d day of March, 1843. R.L. Tottenham, Surrogate.

It may now be asked is there "nothing whatever" in evidence to warrant any person in even supposing he (Joseph M'Kee) was accessory to forging the will of his late father, Joseph M'Kee, sen. When Mr. Samuel Hamilton, the executor, received out of the memorable chest which stood in the innocent Joseph's room, the blank sheet only, where did Joseph the innocent get the forgery which he himself lodged in the Court? Mr. Jebb, in declaring the cause of his client Joseph M'Kee's unwilling renunciation was, "not having means to prove the will." It is difficult, indeed, to form an idea of the magnitude of the means necessary to prove forged lies to be authentic truths, or sufficient to rebut the recited affidavits and circumstances, and hence the cause of his "unwilling renunciation." Mr. Jebb next accuses the first report as not having said the truth, where it stated the difficulties were great, and the struggle hard, yet the labors of the Plaintiff's Proctor were so successful as to induce the executor to renounce. He, in endeavouring to refute the above, declares, "Now, I am authorised by Mr. Hamilton, the executor, to state, that so far from its being a hard struggle to resign, he did so voluntarily, and altogether of his own accord." That the difficulties must have been great in detecting a forgery so well devised and managed, as appeared in the first report, it is hoped will be admitted, and hence the struggle, necessarily hard; but during the progress of the cause in which Mr. Hamilton and the present defendants were plaintiffs, Mr. Jebb was not employed by Mr. Hamilton. It, then, may appear strange how Mr. Jebb came to know the cause of Mr. Samuel Hamilton's giving up the proceedings. Mr. Jebb concludes, "Hoping that his few observations may set the matter right." So do I; for it appears easy to set a matter right, when there has been nothing wrong.

Veri Amator.

(1844-01-06, 3:2)

3108. Death of the Dowager Marchioness of Clanricarde.—We have to announce the death of Urania Anne, Dowager Marchioness of Clanricarde, which took place at Sydney Lodge, on the 27th (*continued...*)

3108, continued: ... instant. Her ladyship, who was in her 77th year, was sister to the late, and only daughter to the 12th Marquess of Winchester, and was married on the 17th of March, 1785, to Henry, first Marquess of Clanricarde, of a second creation. She married, secondly, Colonel Peter Kingston, who was killed at the attack of Buenos Ayres, 22nd of May, 1897; and thirdly, 22d of May, 1813, Admiral Sir Joseph Sidney York, K.C.B., half-brother of Phillip, Earl of Hardwicke, and father of the present Earl, who was drowned on the 5th of May, 1831. (1844-01-06, 3:6)

3109. To the Editor of the Northern Standard.—Consistorial Court of Clogher.—*Hannah M'Kee and Jane M'Kee v. Joseph M'Kee and others.*—Sir—I find the few observations made by me, relative to the above cause, which you were kind enough to publish in your Journal of the 23d December last, has called forth from the pen of an anonymous writer a lengthened statement. I trust you will bear with me while I again vindicate the character of Joseph M'Kee, one of the defendants which that statement seeks to impeach.

"Veri Amator" begins by asserting that I accused his report of this case, published on the 16th December, as having been untrue and false; however, this may be the fact, I did not make use of any such expressions. What I stated then, I say still—that nothing whatever has appeared in evidence to warrant any person in ever supposing that Joseph M'Kee was accessory to forging the Will of his late father; and to contradict this statement, and saddle the forgery and fabrication on Joseph M'Kee seems to be the grand object of "Veri Amator," and to put it beyond the possibility of a doubt, he introduces copies of affidavits made, in open court, by Hannah M'Kee, Jane Thompson, and Owen Finigan [sic].

Now, it will be borne in mind that Hannah M'Kee and Jane Thompson are interested parties—this, it is hoped, will not be denied—they state in their joint affidavit, that they are legatees named in the Will and Testament of their late father, and I say they are also legatees named in the Will which has been set aside, but not to the same amount as in the Will said by them to be suppressed; and the sum and bonum of their evidence is to endeavour to entitle themselves, if possible, to a larger sum than what was bequeathed them in the Will which has been decreed void in law; for want of means, I again assert, of proving it by the witnesses, and not in common form, as "Veri Amator" would endeavour to lead the public to believe, was all the defendants were called upon to do.

"Veri Amator," in his first report of this case stated, that the Will in question was decreed true and valid, and in his last statement asserts that it was pronounced void in law—so much for his accuracy as an auditor.

I now come to the affidavit of Owen Finigan, and the purport of his evidence seems to be, "That on the 17th September, 1842, he wrote a Will for the late Joseph M'Kee, according to his instructions and intention, and became a subscribing witness thereto, and saw it duly executed, and that he has seen the pretended Will, now of record, in the Registry of the Court, and that same is not in his handwriting, nor is the name Owen Finigan subscribed thereto in his handwriting."

Now, I would be far from supposing for a moment that so clever a gentleman as Mr. Finigan could mistake his own handwriting, but I do confess it does seem a little strange that there are two other witnesses to the Will, and that neither of them is produced to corroborate the testimony of Mr. Owen Finigan, though they had as good a right to be produced as he had, and could have given very important evidence, as to whether their names subscribed to the Will were in their own handwriting, or a forgery. It may be asked why do I not allude that part of the affidavit which states, that a Will has been suppressed by Joseph M'Kee, and that a forged and fabricated document has been introduced by him, for the purpose of defrauding the legatees named in the Will, stated to be suppressed? I answer, it is only a matter of belief, for which there is no reason given, and I, therefore, pass it over without any comment, more than this, that if Joseph M'Kee did fabricate a Will, he might, instead of fifty pounds to each of the plaintiffs, have inserted some nominal sum as a devise to them.—I ask "Veri Amator" what authority he has for the statements he has made of the true Will having been put into a chest which stood in a room where Joseph M'Kee went to lie, and of its having been taken out of the envelope, and a clean sheet of paper left in its place? I trust he will not say this has been given in evidence; but sure it has been declared by the widow, and that is just as good, but I don't say so; and, what is more, I don't believe the widow ever said any such thing, or if she had such a belief, I don't think she would have came forward as she did (though too late) to exhibit an allegation, propounding the very Will which has been set aside. I think it right to mention that the affidavits which "Veri Amator" seems to lay so much stress upon, were not acted upon in any way by the Court, in pronouncing the Will on record, in the Registry, void in law; and if it be considered a crime not to prove a Will by witnesses when called upon, whether having the means or no, the other defendants have a right to their portion of the blame as well as Joseph M'Kee, as they were called upon in common with him.

I will now account for my having come to know the cause of Mr. Hamilton, which "Veri Amator" seems to think so strange. It is true I was not employed during the progress of the cause originally instituted; but I now tell "Veri Amator" that I was subsequently employed by Mr. Hamilton, and it was then that I learned the fact, that he did renounce voluntary and altogether, of his own accord, so that the struggle could not be very hard, nor were the difficulties great in detecting the alleged forgery, as a simple citation to prove it, in special form of law, brought the question at once to an issue.

I will not say one word about "Veri Amator's" accusing me of being able and skillful in dressing, but will leave the public to judge between us; but would wish if he again enters the auditoriam, he will give his real name, a conviction that Joseph M'Kee has been unjustly accused, and a desire to remove any unfavourable impression that may have been made concerning him, is the only apology I can make for thus trespassing on the columns of your valuable Journal.

I remain yours, &c.,

William Jebb.

Hill, Monaghan, 11th Jan. 1844.

(1844-01-13, 3:4)

3110. Epitaph.

There lies in the dust a musician of fame,
The tones of whose fiddle enchanted;
It is said, while he liv'd, he was one and the same,
And the spot where he now rests is haunted.

Armagh. P.

(1844-01-20, 4:1)

3111. Alleged Case of Crim Con—A case of crim con., which has caused no small sensation in the county of Tyrone, is, we understand, to undergo investigation at the ensuing Omagh assizes. The persons alleged to be guilty are both married; and the plaintiff has laid his damages at five thousand pounds.—*Londonderry Journal*. (1844-01-20, 4:1)

3112. The will and codicil of the Marquis Wellesley have just been proved by Mr. John Thornton Down, the sole executor, who has a legacy of one thousand pounds. He bequeaths to Mr. Alfred Montgomery his private secretary, one thousand pounds, in regard of his affectionate, dutiful, and zealous services, and the residue of his property to his wife, Mary Anne, Marchioness of Wellesley. By the codicil he gives to his Secretary (Mr. Montgomery), in addition to the legacy in his will, all his manuscripts; and gives the following directions which are *verbatim*:—"And I desire him to publish such of my papers as shall tend to illustrate my two administrations in Ireland, and to protect my honor against the slander of Melbourne and his pillar of state O'Connell. To Lord Brougham he leaves "Homer," in four volumes, and earnestly desires him to assist in publishing his MSS., saying "I leave my memory in his charge confiding in his justice and honor." To Earl Grey "my George, carved on an amethyst, and worn by George II." To his valet he leaves his apparel, robes, stars, &c., "for his kindness during my illness." The property is sworn under £6,000.—*Britannia*. (1844-01-20, 4:4)

3113. Vice Chancellor's Court.—London, Monday.—*Lord John Beresford v. The Archbishop of Armagh and others*.—The further arguments of counsel in this [case] which was several days before the court, were [res]umed this morning on the point raised by the pla[intiff] on further directions—namely, the right of the [pers]onal representatives of the late Lord Waterfo[rd to] have his personal estate now recoupled by the [pre]sent Marquis of Waterford out of the rents and [pro]fits of the Londonderry estate to the extent of [the] principal sums, with interest at 6 per cent., advan[ced] by the late Lord Waterford in his lifetime out of [his] own proper monies to pay off certain incumbr[ances] and debts upon the family estates. The claim made by the plaintiffs who represent all the you[ng] children of the late Lord Waterford, amounts, in[clu]ding principal and interest since 1826, the pe[riod] since that nobleman's death, to no less a sum [of] 90,000*l*.

The Vice-Chancellor proceeded to give judg[ment] upon this important question. His honour [said] that, as he determined the case, it really cam[e to] this, whether on the will of George Marquis of [Wa]terford, and the deed of 1822, taken together, it [is or was] to be considered that the late Marquis Henry [was?] originally placed under an obligation, or that he [had?] put himself under an obligation to apply what [his] Honour might call the surplus rents, and was, [?] as should remain after the current charges, w[hat] must have been paid with interest and so [?] whether the surplus rents, were to be applied [to] the liquidation of what he would call the ca[?] sums? That was the point. Now, it really appe[ared] to his honour that no such construction would be [fol]lowed in this court on the will of Marquis Geo[rge] and the utmost effect which could be given to [the *or* those *or* these] words with regard to rents and profits was that they would be applicable to keep down [the] principal if necessary, and in short, it left [every?]thing precisely as it would have been. There w[ould] merely have been a charge of debts and legacies [?] the simplest form on the Londonderry estates; [?] then with respect to the deed of 1822, it re[?] appeared to his Honour that if there had been a [writ?] filed for the purpose of carrying into execution [?] trusts of a deed, and it had been insisted on by t[hose?] who filed the bill that the construction to be g[iven] to it was such as was now contended for, the c[ause?] in considering the question, must take the whole [of] the instrument together, and taking the whole of it together no such construction could in his Hon[our's] opinion be made out of it; and although his Hon[our] admitted that there were very foolish and blunder[ing] words in the deed (it was drawn in Ireland), in t[he] part of that thing which was the witnessing part [of] it, just after the *habendum*, yet it appeared to [be] such a construction as that contended for by [the] present Marquis's counsel was utterly inconsis[tent] with (*continued...*)

3113, continued: ...the plain intention appearing on the rec[?] and his Honour also thought it utterly inconsis[tent] with those latter words at the end of the deed; an[d] therefore it appeared to his Honour that it would [be a] great surprise and a lamentable calamity of this n[oble] family if any other mode of dealing were allo[wed.] His honour should therefore declare that the ex[ecu]tors of the late Marquis Henry were entitled to [have?] a lien upon the rents and profits of the Londond[erry] estates to the extent of the principal of the inc[um]brances and debts paid off the family estates by [the] late Marquis Henry in his lifetime.

The result of this decision is to add a sum [of] 90,000*l.* to the personal estate of the late Mar[quis] which is divisable for the benefit of his you[ng] children. (1844-01-27, 2:6) [*Note: A fold in the margin renders many of the words illegible. Possible interpretations appear within square brackets.*]

3114. Death of Thos. Chas. Steuart Corry, Esq.—It is our duty to record the death of Thomas Charles Steuart Corry, Esq., who, for many years, represented this county in the Imperial Parliament. The melancholy event took place at Stoke Manor-house, Devonshire, on the 17th inst., after a protracted but not severe illness. Mr. Corry, on attaining his majority, was possessed of one of the largest estates in this county, together with an enormous sum of money accruing during a long minority. Handsome in person, and brilliant in manners and accomplishments, he shone for some years [as] the ornament of his native county, the observed of all observers. A staunch Conservative in politics, he was one of the most active leaders of the high Tory party in Ulster, and distinguished himself in Parliament by talents of no ordinary kind. During late years he retired from public life, and resided at Rockcorry Castle, and Loughbawn House, in this county, and Stoke Manor, in Devonshire, where he turned his mind from this world, and devoted himself to religion. He bore his illness with resignation and fortitude, and committed his spirit to his Maker with a lively faith in the atonement. (1844-01-27, 3:2)

3115. An inquest was held on Sunday last, before Robt. Murray, Esq., M.D., Coroner, on view of the body of a man named Forsyth, who fell into the Ulster Canal, at Cortolvin Bridge, near this town, on Saturday night, and was drowned. (1844-01-27, 3:2)

3116. Extraordinary Abduction.—Three men and two women were committed to our gaol on Friday, charged with having broken into the house of Michael Connery, near the Silvermines, assaulted the habitation and the inmates and forcibly took from out of it Timothy Ginane, whom they brought to the house of Father M'Grath, for the purpose of forcing him to marry Judy Ryan, who was there waiting for the man of her heart to be married to him; and Sally Ryan was also in waiting to act as bridesmaid to Judy. The names of the men engaged in this singular abduction are William Cagles, Michael Kennedy, and Denis Ryan.—*Nenagh Guardian.* (1844-02-03, 2:1)

3117. Colonel C.M. Vandeleur, D.L., Kilrush, acquires an accession of 2,000*l.* a year landed property, by the death of Tenkins Brew, Stipendiary Magistrate. (1844-02-03, 2:6)

3118. Nathaniel Gore, Esq., Inspector of Stamps, is at present in charge of Monaghan District, until such time as a successor to the late Wm. M. Dudgeon, Esq., is appointed. (1844-02-03, 3:4)

3119. Death from Hydraphobia.—A most distressing calamity has recently befalled [sic] the family of an officer of the Royal Engineers, who was stationed in Limerick garrison a few months ago. A lovely infant, three years of age, was bit by a little pet dog with whom she often exchanged caresses. The innocent child suspected nothing, and did not think of repulsing him, but it soon appeared that the dog had slightly cut, or rather, scratched her lip. The family did not regard the hurt with any apprehension, for it was scarce perceptible, and soon left no visible trace. However, in six months after, the usual symptoms of Hydrophobia set in, and in a few days the little innocent sufferer died a victim to the fatal malady.—*Limerick Paper.* (1844-02-03, 4:6)

3120. Melancholy Death by Burning.—An inquest was held on Saturday last, by G.W. Young, Esq., coroner for the county of Armagh, and Thomas J. Tenison, Esq., of Portneligan, J.P., on the body of John Ryan, an aged pauper, who lived in a small hut, in the townland of Derryhaw, Parish of Tynan, and was supported by the charity of his neighbours. The jury, being impanelled, proceeded to view the body which presented a most frightful and harrowing appearance; the lower extremities were literally burned to a cinder. The foreman, Mr. Gamble, of Beltagh Mills, the Poor-law Guardian for that electoral division, informed the jury that he had repeatedly requested the deceased to go into the Armagh Poor House, but without success. On the evidence of William Henderson, of Derryha [sic], farmer, the person who pulled the deceased out of the flames, and Dr. Lochrane, of Middletown, the jury returned a verdict of accidental death caused by suffocation and burning. (1844-02-10, 3:5)

3121. Rejoicings at Fivemiletown.—On Monday the 29th ult., H.R.S. Montgomery, Esq., with his lovely bride, daughter of the illustrious de Felleuberg [sic], of Hofyl, in Switzerland, arrived at his mansion at Blessingburn. Probably on no similar occasion were more judicious arrangements ever made than on the present by the excellent agent, Mr. Patterson. A most respectable array of horsemen, the tenants of the Tyrone estate, went as far as Clogher to meet their justly-beloved landlord, who on that morning started from Gosford Castle, the seat of his noble relative, the Earl of Gosford, so as to arrive punctually at the appointed hour, 2 o'clock.—The footmen met the procession about half a mile from Fivemiletown, took the horses from the carriage, drew it through the town and back again to the mansion House, preceded by a most respectable body of musicians. Every eye was directed to the stranger bride, and never did any female better stand the scrutiny. Here there is both room and temptation greatly to enlarge, but we will confine ourselves to saying what we believe will be more agreeable to the Lady and her most excellent husband. Her countenance is benevolence itself. No people in the world are more sensible of kindness than the Irish, and Mrs. Montgomery took a most effectual way of getting into the good graces of the surrounding multitude by condescendingly shaking hands with every one within her reach. This act appeared as natural to her as it would be to the warm-hearted person present. Illuminations on an extensive scale took place at night together with burning tar barrels, &c. Some very well executed and appropriate transparencies adorned the windows, the tendency of which was to welcome the bride, and eulogise her venerable father and her native land. On the arrival of the cortege at Blessingburn, the multitude was addressed by Mr. Montgomery in a speech neat and well suited to the occasion and auditory, which he concluded by directing them to return to this town and partake of the festivities there; to make themselves as happy as possible; to strike as much fire as they please, but don't, said he laughing good humouredly, set fire to my lough.—This elicited a burst of applause, and a call for three cheers for Mr. and Mrs. Montgomery, three cheers more for the Rev. Doctor Otto Schmidt, who visited this country in the winter of 1842, in company with Mr. Montgomery when the latter gentleman came to take possession of his estates, and three cheers more (as the proposer justly remarked by way of preface,) though last not least deserving, for our friend Mr. Patterson, the agent of the estate.

A copious supply of ale was distributed to the tenantry at the several public houses, and an open house was appointed to which all strangers were directed, also a temperance free hotel for all members of that society.

We are happy to add that not the slightest accident occurred from first to last. After the crowd had dispersed, the whole body of police partook of an excellent supper in the session-house, provided by order of Mr. Montgomery. (1844-02-10, 3:5)

3122. Accident.—On Tuesday, a house fell upon two children named Maguire, at Tonymore, near Belturbet, and killed them. Mr. Hugh Collum held an inquest on yesterday, and a verdict of accidental death [was] returned. (1844-02-10, 4:6)

3123. Death of Major Eldred Pottinger, C.B.—It is with deep regret we have to announce the death of our distinguished fellow-townsman, Major Pottinger, C.B. The lamented event occurred at Hong-Kong, on the 15th November last. He fell a victim to the fever which has been so fatal in our new colony, his constitution being sadly broken by his wounds, and particularly by his unparalleled sufferings, during his retreat to Cabool. The short and brilliant career of this young officer is a matter of history;—his name will be handed down to posterity as one who served his country nobly, under circumstances of appalling danger. We are in possession of circumstances of his private life, which shew him to have had the warmest and most affectionate heart; and sincerely do we sympathise with his afflicted family. It is a consolation, that it pleased God that he and his fellow-prisoners should have been released from their captivity, to allow an inquiry into the history of our Cabool disaster; for, although no person who knew Major Pottinger could, for a moment suppose, that any personal consideration weighed with him who had won his laurels at Herat; still, there would have been something unexplained, relative to the Cabool affair. His friends can now point, with pride, to the recorded opinion of the Court of Inquiry, confirmed by the Commander-in-Chief, and Governor-General, and warmly responded to by a grateful country. The Court declared they could not separate without an expression of their opinion of Major Pottinger's conduct, that, in circumstances of unforeseen and almost unparalleled difficulty and danger, he had shewn a degree of energy and manly firmness which stamped his character as one worthy of high admiration. History affords scarcely a parallel to the conduct of Major Pottinger, and his devoted band of eight hundred men, just prior to the Cabool outbreak, who held their post for a fortnight, against as many thousands, until every officer was killed but two, and the regiment reduced to one hundred and fifty. Major Pottinger, having been badly wounded, had himself lifted from his bed, and carried on a door to the scene of slaughter, to encourage his men. Finding it impossible longer to hold out, this little party, carrying their two surviving officers, both badly wounded, called out, to cut their way to Cabool. Out of the eight hundred men, four men only survived, to tell the tale of blood! Major Pottinger had been expected to arrive in England with the last mail; but, alas! while his friends were anxiously looking forward once more to welcome him to his native land, it had pleased God to remove him; and the mail with which he was expected brought the account of his death. Major E. Pottinger was eldest son of the present Thomas Pottinger, Esq., formerly of Silverstream; and nephew of Sir Henry Pottinger, now at Hong-Kong. He was only in the 35th year of his age.—*Northern Whig.* (1844-02-17, 3:4)

3124. A special meeting of the Irish General Assembly has been convened for Wednesday next, to consider the present state of the Marriage Question, and the duties of Presbyterians with reference to it. The meeting is to be held in Dr. Cooke's Church, May-street.—*Northern Whig.* (1844-02-17, 3:4)

3125. Death of Robert Bateson, Esq., M.P.—We are sorry to announce the death of Robert Bateson, Esq., M.P. for Derry, eldest son of Sir Robert Bateson, Bart., of Belvoir Park. This melancholy event took place at Jerusalem, from an attack of fever, caught during Mr. Bateson's journey across the Desert, after having visited Palmyra, Balbeck, and other interesting portions of Asia Minor. He was on his return to Europe, by way of the Holy Land. Mr. Bateson possessed a most amiable disposition; and bore an unimpeachable character. He was universally beloved and respected; and his loss will heavily fall on the hearts of his family and friends. By this event, a vacancy occurs in the representation of the County Derry. (1844-02-17, 4:3)

3126. By the death of the late Rev. Francis Lascelles, the living of St. Andrew's (Kircubbin), county of Down, is vacant. It is a union of three parishes which will now, probably be disunited. It is in the patronage of his Grace the Lord Primate. (1844-02-17, 4:3)

3127. Death of John Falls, Esq.—It was our painful duty, in our paper of last Saturday, to announce the death of John Falls, Esq., of Dungannon, a gentleman of the most upright principles, and amiable disposition. His premature decease arose from gangrene in the toe. He was much esteemed by all classes; and his loss will be generally felt in and around Dungannon. (1844-02-17, 4:5)

3128. Death from Cold.—On Thursday last, a poor boy was found dead, near Ballybay, having perished from the severity of the weather. (1844-02-17, 4:5)

3129. Appeals and Writs of Error.—House of Lords—Friday, Feb. 23.—Presbyterian Marriages—Ireland.—*The Queen v. George Mills.*—This was one of two cases brought up to the House of Lords, on error from the Court of Queen's Bench in Ireland, the alleged error being that the court below upheld that a marriage not celebrated in any church of the establishment, but by a Presbyterian minister, under the circumstances stated in the case, was not such a valid marriage as to make a subsequent marriage in the church of England invalid, and to render the parties contracting the same liable to the penalties of bigamy.

The Lord Chancellor said that, as this was a question of the greatest possible interest and importance, he had reduced his opinion to writing, and, with the permission of their lordships, he would now read it. The noble and learned lord went through all the authorities of text writers, and of decisions on contested cases in the ecclesiastical courts and at common law, and declared that these authorities had established in his mind these propositions—that, though a contract *per verba de praesenti* was a perfect marriage in other countries, it had never been so in this, without the presence of a person in holy orders; that it had indeed, been called *cerum matrmonium*, but it was only so for certain purposes; that it did not absolutely prevent another and succeeding marriage being validly celebrated *in facie ecclesiae*, the land of the father, and that their mother was not entitled to dower out of the father's [land?]. As the marriage *per verba de praesenti* wanted these incidents of a perfect marriage, it wanted in his opinion, that which showed it to be a perfect marriage. He was therefore of opinion that the marriage which had taken place in this case was one which could not be supported, and that the judgment of the court below ought to be for the defendants on the first point. He was of same opinion with respect to the second point, because if the presence of a person in holy orders was necessary to make a valid marriage, it was clear that that person must, either in England or Ireland, be a person in holy orders, according to the establishment of this country. A Presbyterian minister was not a person who fulfilled that condition in Ireland, and therefore a marriage by him there was invalid. On both these points he was of opinion that the judgment ought to be for the defendants.

Lord Cottenham expressed his concurrence with the Lord Chancellor on both these points, after he had most elaborately gone through the authorities which he had quoted as well as the arguments at the bar.

Lord Brougham, after paying a high compliment to the learned and able opinions just delivered by his two noble and learned friends, said that at present they had not in the least degree shaken his original opinion. But a further consideration of them was required to enable him to determine this point, and he therefore moved that the opinions just delivered, and that the further consideration of this case, be postponed. As this matter now stood, it was impossible to give judgment, for there were three law lords on each side of the question.

Lord Campbell seconded the motion of his noble and learned friend. Though not at present shaken in his previous opinion on the subject, he was most desirous of being able to consider in the most serious and deliberate manner the very learned and admirable arguments which had been delivered.

The motion was agreed to. (1844-03-02, 1:1)

3130. Dreadful Storm and Loss of Life.—We (*Cork Examiner*) have received the following letter from a respected correspondent:—

Cappoquin, March 2, 1844.—On yesterday, this part of the country was visited with the most terrible hail shower I ever witnessed. I have taken up some of the hailstones, and I assure you they were larger than the largest marbles I ever played with. We had also the most terrible thunder and lightning, and melancholy to relate, a woman and her son were killed—the boy, fourteen years old, was sitting by the fire, and the woman was in the garden. There were also two children severely injured. This occurred in the parish of Slievegore, between Cappoquin and Clonmel. (1844-03-09, 2:3)

3131. Breach of Promise.—Proceedings at law have been instituted by the son of a respectable shopkeeper in Listowel, who held a situation in a woolen draper's establishment in Manchester, against the daughter of a wealthy farmer, residing in the vicinity of that town. The fair defendant, forgetful of her former swain, lately got married to a rich shopkeeper in Limerick, older it is said by almost 30 years than the former partner of her choice. Two writs have been already served on the venerable bridegroom and his fair bride, and damages laid at six hundred pounds. The case is to be tried at Limerick, but not at the next assizes, as the declarations were not filed last term, and no notice of trial served.—*Kerry Examiner*. (1844-03-09, 4:6)

3132. Death of the Rev. John Graham, A.M.—At Magilligan glebe, in the county of Londonderry, on the 6th instant, in the 70th year of his age, the Rev. John Graham, M.A., Rector of Tamlaghtard, leaving a large family to deplore the loss of the most affectionate of husbands and parents. (1844-03-16, 3:3)

3133. Melancholy and Fatal Accident on the Belfast Lough—Eight Lives Lost.—One of the most melancholy and calamitous occurrences which we have ever been called upon to record, took place in the bay of our own town on the morning of Saturday last, whereby eight persons belonging to the guardship at Garmoyle, were almost in an instant hurried into eternity. It appears, that about half-past nine o'clock, a foreign brig, named the *Sylph*, had entered the harbour, and was passing up the river, and, as our readers are aware, it being the duty of the officers in the guardship to board all such vessels to ascertain if everything is right as regards their cargoes, Lieutenant Victor and a crew of seven men, proceeded in a six oared gig for this purpose; the wind at this time was blowing very fresh from the East, causing a great swell on the water, and when they came alongside, one of the brig's crew threw out a rope to the party in the boat. The rope was caught by a man named Cowan, but, owing to the storm and the agitated state of the water, the bows of the boat went down, right under the brig's counter, and it immediately filled and sunk. The brig was sailing at the rate of 7 or 8 knots an hour, but it does not appear that her crew made the least exertion to rescue the unfortunate men, who in the discharge of their duty, met an untimely end. They were observed for more than ten minutes struggling with the waves—one of them in particular swam for a short time—but before any assistance could reach them they had ceased to exist, and when shortly afterwards a boat reached the spot, no trace of either men or boat could be seen. We are informed that this lamentable occurrence took place within two hundred yards of the guardship, and in sight of Lieutenant Victor's lady, who was standing on deck all the time. What her feelings must have been at this fearful moment—witnessing her husband's peril, and, although the distance was but short, unable to render the least possible assistance—can be better imagined than described. Mr. Victor had been labouring under an attack of erysipelas for some time past, and as he had not altogether recovered, and being anxious to return to his duty, Mrs. Victor, with that tender concern for her husband's health which ever characterises the affectionate wife, accompanied him to the guardship, and remained with him several days previous to the morning of this fatal occurrence. We may mention a fact in reference to Mr. Victor, which, to those who are ever ready to sympathise with the afflicted, and whose first anxious enquiry, when similar accidents take place, is as to the manner of living of those whom death has snatched away in a moment, it cannot but be gratifying, as a pleasing instance of Christian conduct and assurance that though death was sudden, yet that he himself was not unprepared for it. We have been told that not more than a few minutes before the boat was launched to board the brig, Mr. Victor had just risen from his knees, where for a considerable time he had been occupied in the solemn exercises of religion and communion with his God. He was a man respected and esteemed, and had been, for a period of 36 years, employed in the Custom-House of this port. He has left a large family to deplore his loss, but we trust that a handsome provision will be made for their relief, and also for the wives and children of the men who perished with him. The names of the men who accompanied Mr. Victor in the gig are—Alexander Culviner, Owen Murphy, John Caughey, Patrick M'Gowhan, Henry Smith, James Boyce, and John Cowan. The only individual saved out of the entire crew of the guardship, was Arthur M'Kee, who remained on board with Mrs. Victor, and saw the boat upset. About an hour and a half after the accident, one of the bodies (that of Culviner) was picked up by John Stafford, master of the schooner Margaret. None of the others have yet been found.

An investigation into all the circumstances of this deplorable occurrence was held yesterday before the Magistrates at the Police-office. Several witnesses were examined as to the facts already mentioned. It was stated by one of the crew of the *Sylph*, that it was entirely out of their power to render the boat's crew any assistance, as all their boats and spars were lashed, and that before it would be possible to get a boat launched, they would be several miles (*continued...*)

3133, continued: ...distant from them, however, they used no effort to recover any of the men, as the captain said there was no use in attempting it.

At the conclusion of the enquiry, Mr. Verner stated, that he was of opinion that there was some blame attributable to the Captain of the *Sylph*—not that he thought any of the men could have been saved, but he (the Captain) might have, at all events, made an effort. (1844-03-23, 1:3)

3134. Memorials of the Late Rev. John Graham.—We feel it a duty we owe to all who have known, admired and loved the aged pastor of Magilligana-mong whom we include not a few of our readers, for whose instruction Mr. Graham devoted many a column in the *Londonderry Standard*—to put together a few notices of the most remarkable periods of his life, and traits of his character. We are aware how imperfect must be the result of our present task, on various accounts, but Mr. Graham's friends will have no reason to complain of any want of desire in us to do all justice to the memory of one, who on all occasions of intercourse with us, entitled himself to our regard and admiration.

Mr. Graham was born at Balfour-house, county Longford, on the 21st of April, 1774, and was the eldest son of James Graham, Esq., of Clones, in the county of Monaghan, and Anne, daughter of Andrew Hart, Esq., of Newtown, county Longford. Both his paternal and maternal ancestors were among the defenders of Enniskillen and Derry, holding commissions in the army. At the early age of 17—that is to say, in 1791, he served as Sub-Sheriff of Longford with much credit. In 1794, he entered Trinity College, Dublin, having obtained the distinguished honor of first place. Throughout the whole of the Irish rebellion, he served in the College corps, the most remarkable for its discipline, zeal, and the terror which it struck into the hearts of the rebels, of any of the bodies of the same nature then organised. In 1799, he was ordained to the curacy of Kilrush, in the county Clare, and was afterwards Curate in the parishes of Maghera and Lifford, in this diocese. He was 25 years a curate before he was presented with the small and remote benefice of Magilligan—a poor reward for the rich fruits of an inexhaustible genius, and for so many years of Christian labor. He remained the incumbent of this parish until the day of his death, contented with the humble income which he reaped from it, but more than satisfied with the romantic beauty of the situation, and the sphere of usefulness in which he moved.

Mr. Graham was always an industrious gatherer of statistical and historical knowledge, with which he stored his mind for the recreation of those hours which were not devoted to the imperative duties of his profession. With these acquirements, he also delighted and improved the public, both in works published by himself and in the prints of the day. He also aspired to the character of a lyrical poet, though nearly all of his rhythmetical compositions are filled with local allusions and references to the polemics of the period, that they cannot pretend to a higher fame than they at once received—that of a ready reception among all classes of Protestants, as echoing every Constitutional sentiment to which their hearts gave admittance. He wrote a very celebrated history of the siege of Derry, and also, the *Annals and History of Ireland from 1535 to 1692.* He published in Shaw Mason's survey of Ireland, statistical accounts of the parish of Maghera, Shruel, and Kilrush. He also published a curious poem entitled, *God's revenge against rebellion*, and, *Ireland preserved*, a new edition of an old and rare dramatic work.

As a member of the Orange Society, up to the formal dissolution of that body, he was distinguished for his uncompromising principles, and for the wholesome spirit of religious confidence which he infused into his councils. After it became an open association, he was unceasing in the use of his influence with the Orangemen, to preserve them from infringing in the least the new laws, and his word was a law in itself with them.

It is not easy to describe the nature of Mr. Graham's oratory. His enunciation was rapid and voluble as thought itself, and his voice and gestures were impassioned to an extent hardly to be credited by those who never had the pleasure of hearing him.—Few persons ever possessed the fluency enjoyed by him—no reporter could follow him for more than a few mintues together. His wit was boundless, and his features sparkled with the various modes of feeling to which his lips gave utterance—it was the same whether he spoke from the pulpit or the platform, or from the tables of the Conservative festivals. Many of his speeches at the Anniversaries of the Relief of Derry will be long preserved amongst us as faithful memorials of a mind of no common grasp.

As a domestic man, Mr. Graham was all that he could and ought to be—doatingly [sic] fond of his wife and children, while he edified them by the example of a house-loving, temperate, sin-hating, and vice reproving man. He was hospitable even beyond his means—open as day to melting charity, many a poor orphan, and destitute widow, benefitted both by his own little dole and by the urgent and ceaseless appeals made by him on their behalf to his wealthier friends. Possessed of many good and kind friends himself, among the noble and the great, he could feel for those who stood in hope of his exertions for their welfare, and trusted almost wholly to them. In his disposition he was simple and unworldly to a fault. Without any guile in himself, he could see none in any of those who moved beside him.—Though in public he protested loudly against all bad principles in politics and religion—in private he had a niche in his bosom for many of those whom he believed to be the victims of those vicious principles.—In fine, what was written of Gay, by Pope, might be fitly inscribed on the tomb of Mr. Graham:—

Of manners gentle—of affections mild—
In wit a man—simplicity a child.

His funeral was attended, notwithstanding the severity of the day, by a very large concourse of his parishioners, of all denominations, to as many of whom as could find room in the closely crowded Church; a very solemn and affecting sermon was preached, after the Church service, by the Rev. Wm. Hughes, rector of Aghanloo. (1844-03-23, 2:5)

3135. Presbyterian Marriage Question.—In accordance with a resolution passed at the recent special meeting of the General Assembly at Belfast, the first of the public meetings, to take into consideration the present state of the marriage question, and to forward petitions to Parliament on the subject, was held in Derry on Monday evening, in the church of the first Presbyterian congregation, at seven o'clock, at which hour an immense audience had assembled to testify their interest in the proceedings. The chair was taken by William Haslett, Esq., Mayor of Derry, and a series of resolutions, in accordance with the object of the meeting, were proposed and carried with enthusiasm. Petitions to the Houses of Lords and Commons were unanimously adopted.

A meeting for a similar purpose was held in the Presbyterian Church, Belfast, on Tuesday, when it was also agreed to petition Parliament on the subject. (1844-03-23, 2:6)

3136. Melancholy and Fatal Accident.—On Thursday morning, a fine boy, about 16 years of age, named Charles Hanna, apprentice to Mr. Francis Fleming of this town, shot himself through the abdomen. He had taken out his master's gun, without permission, to shoot sparrows in the garden, and having to pass over a hedge he laid the gun against it till he got over himself, and then turned around to pull it after him; some of the brambles caught in the trigger, and as the muzzle was within an inch of his body, he received the whole charge immediately under the ribs on the right side. Medical assistance was instantly procured by his master, who was sincerely afflicted, but in spite of all endeavours to save his life, he died on Thursday evening. He was an exceedingly fine, lively boy, and very much liked. (1844-03-23, 3:2)

3137. Notice.—The Adminstrator of the late John C. Hannigan, of Market-street, Monaghan, hereby gives Notice to all Persons to whom the deceased was indebted, that he will meet them at Mr. Patrick Sullivan's, Market-street, Monaghan, on Friday, the 12th of April next, for the purpose of finally arranging the affairs of the deceased; and all persons who are indebted to the deceased are requested to settle their respective accounts on or before the above date.

Thomas Hannigan.
(1844-03-23, 3:5)

3138. Notice.—The Creditors of Mr. James Reid, formerly of Slievroe, are requested to forward the particulars of their several claims against him, and the actual amount now due on foot of said demands, to me, on or before the 15th of April next.

Monaghan, 19th March, 1844.
Edmond P. Morphy.
(1844-03-23, 3:5)

3139. The Wife to Her Dying Husband.

I have loved thee in thy beauty,
Thy glory and thy power—
And shall I now desert thee,
In thy sorrow-stricken hour?
There is no hand save mine, to wipe
The death damps from thy brow;
Oh false as thou hast been to me,
I will not leave thee now.

Thy friends and boon companions—
The gallant and the gay—
The lovely and beloved ones,
Look round thee—where are they?
No trusted friend is near thee now;
No gentle love appears,
To hang o'er thy death swimming eyes,
And bathe them with her tears.

And I alone return at last,
My right in thee to claim;
I, with my sad and broken heart,
My blighted hopes and name.—
I, with my love, which, strong as death—
Alike in good and ill—
Hath clung to thee, in scorn and shame,
Unchanged, unchanging still.

But I come not to reproach thee—
(Ah, would I come to save!)
I can but smooth the rugged path
That leads thee to thy grave.
But sit for ever at thy feet,
Weeping in hopeless woe,
Ah! best beloved! would for thee
Mine own heart's blood might flow.

I have loved thee in thy beauty,
Thy glory and thy power,
I will not now desert thee,
In thy sorrow-stricken hour.
There is no hand save mine, to wipe
The death damps from thy brow;
Oh! dearest to my heart and soul!
I will not leave thee now.

(1844-03-23, 4:1)

3140. Violent Storm—Shipwrecks and Loss of Life. —One of the most violent storms experienced for many years blew from the eastward on Friday and Saturday morning. The injuries sustained by vessels and the damage done to property has been very considerable. On Saturday the sea was (*continued...*)

3140, continued: ...so convulsed and the weather so tempestuous, that the railway trains could only run upon the trains furthest from the shore, as the waves, for a great portion of the line, made a clear breach over the wall, in some places washing the ballasting away. The down train at a quarter before 8 o'clock, consisting of the Kingstown engine and 8 carriages, got off the line, the rails having been disturbed by the terrific force of the sea. In less than three hours, all was again set right without any injury either to engine or carriages.

On Friday the sea was comparatively placid, though the skies looked rather sulkily, and the keen eye of a seaman might be able to recognise in the breeze the indications of a gathering tempest. Between two and three o'clock, a.m., it came on to blow, and from that time until the evening, continued with unabated violence, the waves overcoming every impediment in their way, and dashing even against the windows of Victoria-terrace. Those who witnessed the scene describe it as most appalling and at the same time the the [most] magnificent that they ever beheld.

It is with great pain we have to report the disasters which have occurred in Kingstown Harbour from the violence of the tempest of Saturday. The gale blew from E.S.E., commencing about four, a.m., and did not terminate until Sunday morning; a more angry and awful sea has not been witnessed for many years in the Bay of Dublin, and to a certain extent it raged within the harbor, by which many vessels have been wrecked; but fortunately no lives [were] lost, although some of the crews had to clamber along a hawser to gain the shore and others were brought, through a heavy sea, by our hardy boatmen. Three brigs and two schooners drove on the rocks near Mr. Fagan's ship yard, and have become perfect wrecks; several others run into the old harbor, which is anything but a safe retreat. They had either burst their chain cables or slipped them when fouled by vessels that had broken adrift. Those unfortunate vessels have likewise suffered terribly.—Melancholy to state, the schooner *Seymour*, of Bray, coal laden, from Whitehaven, was overwhelmed by a sea when crossing the Burford Bank, and all hands perished. This sad sight was seen by the crew of the brig *Endeavor*, of Whitehaven, who also struck on the bank and expected to have been swallowed up in a similar manner. All the vessels that anchored within that part of the harbour, which is sheltered by the East Pier, held fast.

The steamer *Queen Victoria*, and *H.M.S. Urgent*, that should have sailed on Saturday evening, did not start until Sunday morning. The *Holyhead* steamer started in the morning through a frightful sea and hurricane. The names of the vessels wrecked are as follow:

Brig *Hemer*, of Maryport—total wreck.

Brig *Mary*, of Whitehaven—sunk.

Schooner *Betties*, of Liverpool—sunk.

Schooner *Tom*, of Whitehaven—sunk.

Thomas *Agnes*, of Preston—sunk.

Schooner *Belleview*, of Gravestones—perfect wreck.

Jane and Francis, of Wexford—much injured.

Brig *Pandora*, of Whitehaven; sloop *Colonel Smith*, of Carnarvon; sloop *Catherine*, of Newry; *Maria*, of Whitehaven—all more or less damaged.

The Kish Light Ship either parted or slipped and run for Dublin on Sunday morning, on the gale having ceased, which is very extraordinary. No calamity is likely to arise from this circumstance, as care has been taken to warn the Liverpool and Holyhead packets. It has also been communicated, no doubt, long since, by means of telegraphs all round the coast. Several of the small vessels enumerated were wrecked in view of two packets which were anchored in the harbor, and dared not attempt to offer them the least assistance, as such a step might have proved destructive to themselves. As far as can be ascertained, no life has been lost in the harbor, nor was it necessary to use the life boat, but every exertion which could be made to rescue the vessels and save the men was made by the sailors and pilots, under the control of Captain Hutchinson, Harbor Master.

A quantity of the substantial paling erected in the Phoenix-park to protect the young plantations, was prostrated by the violence of the gale, but effectual means were taken to keep the deer from injuring the trees. (1844-03-23, 4:5)

3141. Titles.—Title and ancestry render a good man more illustrious, but an ill one more contemptible. Vice is infamous, though in a prince; and virtue honourable, though in a peasant.—*Addison.* (1844-03-30, 2:4)

3142. Presbyterian Marriages.—A highly important and respectable meeting took place on Tuesday last, in the Presbyterian Chapel of this town, to petition Government to take into consideration the present state of the marriage law. The Chair was filled by A.G. Lewis, Esq., a Church of England Protestant, and several of that communion were present. The meeting was addressed by Mr. Lewis, and the Rev. Messrs. Bleckley, Borland and White. [Ow]ing to circumstances, we cannot publish the speeches this week, but in our next we intend giving a full report. (1844-03-30, 3:1)

3143. Dangers of Quackery.—A countryman, in the neighbourhood of Monaghan, lately received the following recipe for the cure of a disease from which he was suffering:—Three pennyworth of muriatic assit, take one half glass three times dayly.

When such things be, we only wonder that there is not more work for the Coroner. (1844-03-30, 3:2) *Note: Muriatic acid is a poisonous and corrosive substance.*

3144. Most Melancholy Accident.—On Wednesday morning last, an accident of a most distressing nature occurred in this neighbourhood which will throw many families of high respectability into deep affliction.

Mrs. Tuthill, (sister of the hon. Judge Jackson, and the wife of John Tuthill, Esq., of Rapla,) within a couple of miles of Nenagh, being in the upper part of the house, and on pushing out the Parisian blinds, did so, without perceiving the danger of the act, by which she lost her balance, and was precipitated from a fearful height into the area beneath. Death was instantaneous, and deprived a large family of a kind and affectionate parent—her bereaved husband of an old and beloved companion—and the poor of a benevolent and charitable friend. Mrs. Tuthill, we learn, was about 40 years of age—and this lamentable occurrence has thrown a gloom of sorrow and regret around the circle of acquaintances in which she moved, and by whom she was so highly esteemed.—*Nenagh Guardian.* (1844-03-30, 4:1)

3145. Approaching Marriage in High Life.—We understand that among the early alliances in high life will be the marriage of Miss Harriet Beresford, second daughter of the late Lord George Beresford, and niece of the Archbishop of Armagh, and Mr. G. Dunbar, late M.P. for Belfast. The Lord Primate and family are shortly expected from the palace, Armagh, and the ceremony is expected to be solemnized the week after the Easter recess. (1844-04-06, 1:3)

3146. Presbyterian Marriage Question.—According to the promise given in our last, we this week publish at length the speeches delivered at the meeting held in the Meeting-house of this town, for the purpose of petitioning Parliament to satisfactorily arrange this important question,

A.G. Lewis, Esq., in the Chair.

The Chairman rose and said—The kind feeling which has prompted you to pay me the high honour of placing me in this Chair, will, I have no doubt, bear with me for a few minutes, whilst touching upon one or two topics which may not be altogether irrelevant to the subject which has called us together; and first, with reference to the conduct and feeling of the distinguished head of the Established Church in Ireland; it is my earnest desire to speak with all the respect becoming his exalted situation, and without claiming for him the idea of infallibility, to say that if he has supplied the funds (as is stated) for carrying on the litigation which has enabled a culprit to escape the penalty of his offence, and thus brought about the present dilemma, in which the Presbyterian body has been so unexpectedly involved—that his conduct has proceeded from error in judgment. He is but a man, "of the like passions with ourselves;" and I would add, what as Presbyterians you must all admit, unless you have been inoculated with the insidious system, so softly terms Puseyism—that the Primate is not "the Church"—a designation which I understand is applicable to the worshipping people of Christ, whether Episcopalian, Presbyterian, or Moravian. I am thankful to say that I entertain this view in common with some of the most eminent Ministers of the Established Church, both in England and Ireland, who are in the habit of terming the Presbyterian as "our dear twin sister of the Reformation." I might mention names not unknown to this meeting, who entertain this view, but I shall content myself by referring to one whose numerous and valuable works we must be all more or less acquainted with, viz.:—the Rev. Edward Bickerstath; no doubt there is a difference between these sister churches, but it is only one of discipline, not of doctrine; for in the essentials of salvation there is none. Another erroneous impression I am induced to think prevails, as to the conduct of the Government: I beg to state distinctly that I am not their apologist: on the contrary, I consider they have acted a vacillating part, not on this occasion alone, but on others, which I attribute to a desire of pleasing the High Church, or Puseyite party, who are, I am aware, a powerful party in England; but, however, I am fully satisfied the Government stand exonerated from blame in the transaction, except so far as that they did not manfully come forward with a full and fair measure of redress, for a grievance affecting probably half of the Protestantism of Ireland—a grievance which would affix the brand of inferiority even by their mode of redress, upon the Church of Scotland, for I cannot understand why the Episcopalian Minister should have the power of uniting a member of the Presbyterian Church to one of his hearers, and the same right should not be equally exercised by the Presbyterian Ministers.—Away with such distinctions; I would say to each, "Ye are brothers, mutually interested in each others welfare—mutually necessary to the support of each other: that it is only thus each can stand, and that should one fall, the doom of the other is decreed." In urging this peaceful course, I am very far from recommending the Presbyterian body to do what I would not do, if similarly situated—that is to remain quiescent; on the contrary, I am only anxious that their endeavours should be made in a temperate manner, whereby I am well convinced they will carry with them the sympathies and best wishes of every well-meaning man of every party.

Mr. Bleckley addressed the meeting in a speech of which we are able to give but an imperfect outline. He characterised the proceedings in the Marriage Question as part of a systematic attack upon the privileges of Presbyterians, in common with other dissenting bodies, carried on of late years in different parts of the British empire—the attempt to prevent Presbyterian Ministers from celebrating marriages in Australia—the effort to exclude them from their just share of the clergy reserves in Canada—the inroads made upon the rights of the Church of Scotland—the Factory Bill in England and the Marriage Question in Ireland were all the works of a bigoted faction, which seemed to be neither tired with its labours, nor (*continued...*)

3146, continued: ...discouraged by its defeats. He defended the practice of Presbyterian ministers celebrating marriages, as cautious and guarded, because their duty to God required them to be so. He read the regulations of Assembly on that subject as being sufficiently strict. He showed that no evils had resulted from the liberty hitherto enjoyed by the Presbyterians in this kingdom, and stated the fact, that in this county, containing from 20 to 30,000 Presbyterians, there was not one arraigned at the last assizes. He then took up the decision given in the case of the *Queen v. Millis*, showed that the law on which that decision was founded was equally at variance with the laws of God and the laws of equity. That a vow was by that decision only binding because a mass-priest was a witness, and that a villain was allowed to profit by his own delinquency, which is contrary to the first principles of equity. He showed that "Holy Orders" meant "Mass Priests," that these only were allowed to celebrate marriage as a matter more sacred than any other rite of religion; for the twelve Judges lately decided in the case of the Canada reserves, "that there are other Protestant Clergy in this realm besides the Clergy of the Church of England." They are Clergy but not in Holy Orders. These Holy Orders belongs exclusively to the Churches of England and Rome. He expressed his expectation that no body of Christians could grudge the Presbyterians the full exercise of the liberty they possessed; that he could not believe that the members of the Established Church, generally, sympathised with the Puseyite faction. He knew that Puseyism was getting into this country by retail, but he did not expect, at this time, that the people generally, and Protestants in particular, would join in advocating the claims of the Presbyterians. If it were otherwise—if professions of liberality were hollow—it would be well to know it. The Presbyterians may be obliged to occupy new ground, and wage a determined warfare, not with men, but with the figments of superstition, which are the ground-work of all the annoyance to which of late they had been subject. He concluded by observing that there was no reason for despondency, but much for steady, united, persevering exertion, to let it be seen that while they sought no more than others enjoyed, they would be satisfied with no less. He then moved a series of resolutions expressing the alarm with which the Presbyterians contemplated the aggressions made upon their just privileges—their determination to use every lawful means to defend themselves, and to defeat the machinations of their adversaries—and, finally, that petitions be forthwith prepared to receive the signatures of all in the town and neighbourhood who were friendly to their claims; that the one to the Lords be intrusted to their tried friend, Lord Rossmore, and that to the Commons to C.P. Leslie, Esq., M.P.

The Rev. Mr. White, Wesleyan Minister, seconded the resolutions. He bore witness to the caution observed by Presbyterian Ministers in celebrating marriages. He believed some of the second marriages of bigamists had been celebrated by a Presbyterian. He expressed the sympathy of the denomination to which he belonged, with the Presbyterians in their present trials. He exhorted them to trust in God, and take courage; and closed a very excellent speech by again assuring them that the Wesleyans, at least, would stand by them in the hour of their need.

The Rev. Mr. Boreland [sic] rose and said—Sir, it is with considerable reluctance I rise to address you. I feel my inadequacy to do justice to the great cause which has brought us together. I have been so much occupied with my parochial duties for the last ten days, that I have not had a single moment to arrange my thoughts. Another reason why I feel unwilling to address you is, that I have already, in this very place, stated at length, my views on this perplexing question. And, sir, I recollect well, that on that occasion, after I had concluded, a friend of mine whom I don't see here, said to me in an under tone, "You borrowed all that speech from Dr. Henry" (a laugh.) Now, sir, although I do not expect to be *complimented in this way* to-night, yet I fear very much that I may afford an opportunity to some one, to repeat in my hearing, in a tone, louder than a whisper, the Scottish proverb—"Cauld kale het again."—I must state also, that my unwillingness to appear on this platform has not been lessened by what has taken place since we met. I admire very much the sentiments you gave utterance to in taking that chair;—especially did I admire the counsel you gave. "Combine *moderation* with *firmness*, in the expression of your opinions," is wholesome counsel, nor has it been lost upon us. The speakers who have preceded me have exemplified it—they have exhibited, in a remarkable degree, the *suaviter in modo* with the *fortiter in re*. I fear, however, I will not be able to follow in their footsteps; my temperament is not the coolest in the world—(a laugh)—and it is my infirmity that I cannot but speak warmly when I feel warmly. And surely, sir, of all questions, the one we've met to consider is the most calculated to excite every true-hearted Presbyterian (hear, hear.) Not only have our marriages been characterised "pretended ceremonies"—not only have the husbands and wives belonging to our communion, been represented as living in concubinage—not only have their children been stigmatized as bastards, but our authority to preach the Gospel, and even our right to call ourselves a Christian Church, have been broadly and openly impugned. Sir, when thus assailed, it is difficult, very difficult indeed, to avoid hard speeches. The very worm, when trodden on, will turn on its oppressor, and it is [in] no way strange that, placed, as we have been, in the pillory for the last three years, and exposed to the sneers of the inter-meddling curates and lordly prelates, we should not be always able to repress our indignation, and employ phraseology fitted to sooth (cheers.) Mr. Bleckley has, in the course of his very excellent address, reviewed at length, the various attempts made of late years, to strip Presbyterians of their rights and privileges: he has shewn that in New South Wales, in Canada, in Scotland, in this kingdom, in fact in every part of the wide domain of Britain, the most strenuous efforts have been made to overthrow our beloved Sion. The cry of our enemies has been "raze it, raze it, even to the foundations thereof." I will not try to deepen this impression which his observations have made; nor will I add ought to what he has said on those most mysterious of doctrines—"Apostolical Succession" and "Holy Orders;" and, sir, to be candid, I must say that the reason why I avoid touching on those topics is, I really don't know what is meant by "Apostolic Succession" and "Holy Orders" (a laugh.) Hitherto I have placed them in the same category with "Holy water," and I think it best to leave them there—(renewed laughter)—should any of you, however, have a taste for such studies, I would strongly recommend to your consideration—"Powell on apostolical succession" (hear, hear.) No doubt, it is stated in one of the resolutions now before this assembly, that God has overruled all the machinations of our enemies for good to our Sion. I most fully agree with this sentiment, although the originators of the crusade against the validity of our marriages, thought not so; nor was it in their hearts so to do. Yet have they been the instruments—the unconscious ones I admit, under providence, of doing us good;—so fully convinced am I of this, that as I journeyed here to-day, I had almost resolved to go down to Armagh, on Thursday next, and at the great meeting to be held there on that day, move a vote of thanks to his Grace the Lord Primate, Dr. Miller, and *hoc genus omne*, for having conferred so many benefits upon us (laughter.) Allow me, sir, to state briefly a few of the kindnesses they have conferred on us (continued laughter.) 1st, They have made us known. A few years ago, in this very kingdom, in which our Church has existed for more than two centuries; the greatest ignorance prevailed, relative to our principles, our numbers, and our history; and with regard to England, the people of that kingdom knew nothing of us. But, thanks to our enemies, we are no longer an "obscure sect;"—they have brought us into notoriety. It is known now, and it will be better known—on this controversy terminating—that Ulster Presbyterians constitute half of the Protestants of Ireland and the bond of union between this country and Britain (cheers.) 2nd, They have borne testimony to our genuine Protestantism. We are not "Mass Priests," nor have we our orders from Rome (cheers.) Many thanks to you, my Lord Lyndhurst, for these statements; they will prove hereafter "a heavy blow and sad discouragement" to the agents of the Church Education Society; but what of that;—3rd, they have attested the efficacy of our teaching. Not one of the bigamists belong to the Presbyterian Church. Our people have been taught to consider the marriage covenant a solemn oath, and they have not been taught in vain. All the bigamists belong to the only true and apostolic Church. Make a present of the whole batch to the Lord Primate; he may, if to so please him, make "a kirk and a mill of them" (laughter.) 4th, they have fully vindicated the conduct of Presbyterian ministers, in the celebration of marriages. In the bigamy cases now *sub judice*, in no instance was the second marriage performed by a Presbyterian clergyman (hear, hear.) On the contrary, in every one of those cases, the honor of presiding at the second marriage was reserved for one of the clergy of the establishment. Now, sir, this circumstance should teach our opponents the propriety of talking less about the "irregular and clandestine marriages of dissenters." "Those who live in glass houses should not throw stones first," is an adage I would advise them not to lose sight of. While on this subject, I may be allowed to say, that I have heard a great effort has been made before the "Marriage Committee" of the House of Lords to blacken the characters of Presbyterian ministers (hear, hear.)—Witnesses have been taken before it to retail all the evil deeds of drunken and degraded ministers; and what is still worse, letters the most calumnious have been tabled before that Committee. I am told that one of these letters, written by a dignitary in the Established Church, is to this effect—"Presbyterian ministers' houses in and around Derry are so many Gretna Greens" (cries of shame, shame.) Think of that! William M'Clures house a Gretna Green! James Denham's house a Gretna Green! Henry Wallace's house a Gretna Green! Vile calumny! Futile attempt to blast the reputation of men who will be loved and revered as long as genius, learning and piety are held in admiration, and the head and front of whose offending is, that they had something to do with "the plea of the Presbytery" (hear, hear.) Sir, I will not be tempted to retaliate on the ministers of the establishment; the puddle is too filthy to be stirred. I know—every minister in this house knows—that the reply of all parties, when we refuse to marry, is "Well, we don't care; we'll go to church" (hear, hear.) 5thly, I say again, Sir, these proceedings have promoted very much what is dear to us all—the union of Evangelical Protestants. This meeting is a proof of this (hear, hear.) Here are Evangelical, Episcopalians, Presbyterians, Methodists, and Independants, all mingled together; "how good and how pleasant it is for brethren to dwell together in unity." Sir, I have detained you too long (no, no,) and I must have done. Let me, then, sir, say to the Presbyterians now before me—hold fast your principles—barter not the truth of God for worldly mammon—listen not [to] those (*continued...*)

3146, continued: ...who would tempt you by worldly inducements to forsake the good old ways. Believe me, you have no reason to be ashamed of your principles; they have been tested for ages, and the more they are tried, the purer they appear. Extend your principles; and strive, especially, to extend them by the holiness of your lives. "Let your light so shine before men that they may see your good works, and glorify your father which is in Heaven." Cherish a Catholic spirit; look upon all who love the Lord Christ Jesus as brethren; unite with them in every good work; and let it be the anxious prayer of your hearts that all God's people may be "of one heart, and of one soul," and that they may all "strive together for the faith of the Gospel." Be not cast down on account of the enemies of our Sion—she cannot be overthrown—she is built upon the rock of ages, and the gates of hell cannot prevail against her. God has already made (as I have attempted to shew you) her very enemies to do her good, and he will yet do more for her.

God in the midst of her doth dwell;
Nothing shall her remove;
The Lord to her an helper well,
And that right early prove.

(1844-04-06, 2:6)

3147. Presbyterian Marriage Question.—Public Meeting in Armagh.—This meeting, held on Thursday, was large and highly respectable. On the platform were—The Earl of Gosford, lieutenant of the county; Lord Acheson, M.P., A. Shafto Adair, Esq., J.P., Rev. Dr. Henry, the Rev. Messrs. Bell, M'Alister, &c. &c. The *Banner of Ulster* gives the following report of the proceedings.—On the motion of the Rev. Dr. Henry, the Earl of Gosford was called on to preside.

His Lordship, in his opening address, said he had ever held high in his esteem the Presbyterians of Ireland; for, in all his intercourse with them, he had always found them a quiet and intelligent people. He had fondly trusted that meetings on such a subject as the present would not have been necessary; but he hoped that the unhappy differences that had arisen would be amicably settled. Presbyterians had a duty to perform, but he hoped they would go forward in that Christian spirit, but with all the determination that had ever been so characteristic of their forefathers. When he thought of the numbers who were interested in the present dispute—when he remembered that their Presbyterian forefathers had ever been the bold and unflinching advocates of civil and religious liberty—he (Lord Gosford), as a friend also to liberty, would not withhold his aid, humble though it might be (applause.) He called on all present, and indeed on Presbyterians in general, to be firm and united. Their enemies, he said were strong and powerful, and it was only by putting themselves in a posture of sure defence that they could hope to be successful in the present movement. His lordship was repeatedly cheered in the course of his short but excellent address.

The Rev. Mr. Bell, in a speech of considerable length, gave a detailed account of the rise and progress of the present troubles, which he traced to the neighborhood in which the meetings were at that time congregated.

The Rev. Mr. M'Alister spoke next in vindication of Presbyterian ordination, and quoted a number of authorities, both from ancient and modern authors in favour of that system.

The Rev. Mr. Jenkins followed, and, in an able address, adduced a number of additional arguments in favour of the system of Presbyterian church government.

The Rev. Mr. Elliot spoke next, and in the course of his address, quoted largely from the Puseyite publications, in order to trace the spirit that had actuated the present disgraceful proceedings against Presbyterian rights and privileges.

Lord Acheson next addressed the meeting, and said he entirely concurred in its object, and he felt called on to say so, both as a member of the community at large, and as a representative in Parliament of the county of Armagh; and whether in or out of parliament he would never shrink from making a manly and open avowal of his sentiments (cheers.) He was happy that the meeting had afforded them an opportunity of stating his opinions, and he felt it a privilege, also, to hear statements of their grievances, for by such we would be the better enabled to steer his course. With respect to those who were the first promoters of the quarrel, he would not pass any opinion; but he thought that any government would not be consulting their own security or comfort who would not take the earliest opportunity of settling their grievances. He concluded by saying that Presbyterians had enemies both in this country and in England, and that they need not expect any sympathy from them, and therefore they must use the means themselves, and all the assistance that lay in his power he would cheerfully give to carry them out of their present difficulties.

Dr. Henry then addressed the meeting in an eloquent speech, and he was followed by a number of other gentlemen.

Resolutions, embodying the sentiments of the meeting, were unanimously carried, as was also a petition to the legislature for a redress of their grievances.

(1844-04-06, 3:2)

3148. Presbyterian Marriages (Ireland.)—House of Lords—March 29.—*Queen v. Millis.*—Upon the Lord Chancellor entering the house, at half-past four o'clock, a long conversation ensued between his lordship and Lords Brougham, Cottenham, and Campbell.

The Lord Chancellor eventually took his seat on the woolsack, and the above case was then called on.

Lord Brougham thereupon moved that judgment be entered for the plaintiff in error. (Had this proposition been adopted, the first marriage—namely, that which had been performed according to the Presbyterian form *per verba de praesenti*, would have been held to have been a valid marriage.)

The Lord Chancellor having put the question, declared the division to have been in favour of the "Contents."

Lord Cottenham then moved that the house do divide.

Strangers were ordered to withdraw, and the house divided, when there appeared—

Contents ... 2

Non-Contents ... 2

The result of this division, therefore, will be, that the judgment of the court below, declaring the first marriage to be invalid, will stand undisturbed, each party of the law lords present being equal in number. (1844-04-06, 4:5)

3149. Awfully Sudden Death.—On Monday, the 8th instant, an inquest was held at the County Court-House in this town, on the body of Evan Bevans, coachman, to Major M'Cann, of Greenmount. It appeared in evidence that deceased came to Dundalk on that morning with a pair of his master's horses, to take home a carriage which had been undergoing repairs at Messrs. Sheckleton's. On alighting from the horse, he stated to Mr. Arthur's hostler that he felt extremely ill. The hostler, very properly, took him over to the shop of Dr. Scott, when some restoratives were administered, but without effect, as he died immediately after. The jury returned a verdict in accordance with the above facts. Major M'Cann gave the poor fellow a good character, and felt sincerely pained at the unfortunate occurrence. He was engaged to be married next Saturday, but alas! for the vanity of human hopes—his wedding garment is a shroud, and his bridal bed the cold damp grave. (1844-04-13, 1:5)

3150. Melancholy Death of Captain Vigors.—This lamented Captain Vigors was considerably in advance of the rest when he came boldly at the fence, consisting of a single ditch with a large dyke, his horse making a stumble at the ditch, threw him headlong on the opposite bank, upon reach which the horse immediately fell with his whole weight upon the rider, and rolled from him into the dyke. Surgeons Addison and Heighinton, who were standing within a few paces of the spot, ran to his assistance, and succeeded in dragging the body from beneath the horse; for some short time he was perfectly lifeless, but when he showed signs of life, every means were used to restore animation. He was, as soon as it could with safety be done, removed on a door to a neighboring cottage; at this time many other medical men arrived, and the unfortunate gentleman was intrusted to the care of Surgeon Russell, of the 36th regiment, but all endeavours were unavailing—he expired about an hour after his removal, notwithstanding the unremitting attention paid him by the medical men present. (1844-04-13, 3:1)

3151. Death of E. Williams, The Comedian.—Edward Williams, formerly of the Theatre Royal, Dublin, calmly died at his house at Clonliff, on Monday, the 8th of April, at the advanced age of eighty-one years. He was a favourite with the Dublin audience for nearly forty years; his amiable and convivial qualities endeared him to, and secured him troops of friends to the last. Mr. Williams was formerly proprietor of the Brighton Theatre, and came to Dublin soon after Frederick E. Jones succeeded Daly as patentee of the old Crow-street Theatre. The part of Michael in the *Adopted Child* at once stamped him as an actor of superior talent, and in similar characters no actor ever gave a more agreeable representation of the bravery and humanity of a British tar. It was not in these alone, but in many other parts in comedy that he excelled. Who that has seen him in Old Dornton, Peachum, Job Thornberry, Farmer Ashfield, Jobson, Vigil, (with the veteran Fullam,) Dogberry, and, last not least, the Grave Digger in Hamlet, will forget him on the stage as an actor, or off it as a man! Alas! poor Williams! I knew him well—a fellow of infinite mirth and excellent fancy, with flashes of merriment that were wont to set the table in a roar.

Mr. Williams retired from the stage a good many years ago in comfortable circumstances, and died with his dearest friends around him. (1844-04-13, 3:4)

3152. The Irish Marriage Question.—Lord Campbell's Protest.—House of Lords—Friday, March 30.—*The Queen v. Millis*—Writ of Error.—The order of the day being read for the further consideration of this cause, the house proceeded to take the same into consideration: and it being moved to reverse the judgment complained of, the same was objected to; and the question was put, whether the judgment complained of should be reversed? Lord Cottenham and Lord Campbell were appointed to tell the number of votes; and upon report thereof to the house, it appeared that the votes were equal, viz., two for reversing, and two for affirming. Whereupon, according to the ancient rule in the law, *semper presumtur pro negante*, it was determined in the negative: therefore the judgment of the court below was affirmed, and the record remitted.

Dissentient,

1. Because it appears by the special verdict that George Millis, before his second marriage (the regularity of which is not questioned,) had been married to Esther Graham by a Presbyterian minister, who they believed had the authority lawfully to marry them, and that having intended to enter, and believing that they had entered, into present marriage, without contemplating any further ceremony to complete their marriage, they cohabited together as husband and wife, and, there being no statute to affect the validity of such a marriage in Ireland, it is valid by the common law of England, which is admitted to be the law of Ireland upon this subject. *(continued...)*

3151, continued: ...[*Extract*: Dissentient argument continues, filling one column, and includes mentions of: the only objection made to the validity of this marriage was that it was not solemnised by a priest episcopally ordained; until the Reformation, the validity of marriage was a matter of ecclesiastical recognizance in England and the rest of Europe; canon law regulating marriage in Europe; prior to the Council of Trent, a priest was not necessary to a valid marriage; the presumption being in favour of the validity of this marriage, the onus lies upon those who question it to prove its validity; the marriage between George Millis and Esther Graham cannot properly be considered as a mere pre-contract; where a man and woman entered into marriage, and lived together as husband and wife, without the intervention of a priest, the church in England always considered the relation between them *verum matrimonium*, insomuch that they could not be proceeded against for fornication, that they could only be compelled to celebrate the existing marriage in the face of the church; only two cases leading to a contrary conclusion have occurred, in the reign of Edward I, but cannot be relied upon because we have no satisfactory statement; Lord Hardwicke's act (1817); no certain rule is laid down for the guidance of the public with respect to the class of clergymen, including Roman Catholic priests who have been admitted into the church of England, who are duly qualified to solemnise marriage between English subjects in countries where the English statutes respecting marriages do not prevail; in this case, the marriage solemnised by a Presbyterian minister whom the parties believed to be sufficiently authorised to solemnise it, is a nullity; the marriages of Quakers and Jews have ever been considered to be, and are valid, without the intervention of a priest in orders; in countries where the attendance of such a priest cannot be obtained, a valid and regular marriage may be entered into by the consent of the parties before witnesses; the legislature, in passing acts of parliament in Ireland and India, the prior validity of which depended upon the same principles as the validity of the marriage in question, has declared them to be valid, thereby admitting their prior validity; by the common law of England, the consent of the parties without the intervention of a priest was sufficient to constitute a valid though not a regular marriage—*Dalrymple v. Dalrymple* promulgated by Lord Stowell, and law laid down upon the subject also by Lord Ellenborough, Lord Tenderden, Lord Chief Justice Gibbs, Sir J. Nicholl, Sir H. Jenner, and Lord Eldon; there have been many convictions for bigamy in Ireland where the first marriage was solemnised by a Presbyterian minister, although both parties were not dissenters, and the persons so convicted have been sentenced to transportation; *article concludes with*:]

19. Because the noble and learned lords by whose opinion this judgment is affirmed admit that they are obliged to overrule authorities to which the greatest respect is due; all the recent authorities are uniformly in favour of the validity of the marriage in dispute; upon all questions it is desirable, that when the law has once been considered settled by judicial decision, it should not be again disturbed; and this is particularly the case with respect to the law of marriage, for the sake of honourable women and innocent children.

CAMPBELL.
(1844-04-13, 4:2)

3153. The Rev. Mr. Burke, formerly P.P. of Liscannor, recently curate of Lisdoonvarna, was married last week to the widow Kennedy, of the latter place, at Kilfenora church, by the Rev. Mr. Ryan, curate to Dean Stacpoole. (1844-04-20, 1:1)

3154. Marriage in High Life.—On Saturday last the marriage ceremony was celebrated in the Cathedral Church of Armagh, by the Lord Primate, assisted by the Precentor and Chancellor, between George Dunbar, Esq., late M.P. for Belfast, and the Hon. Harriet Beresford, second daughter of the late Lieut.-General Lord George Beresford, niece to the Primate, and cousin to the Marquis of Waterford. A numerous party were entertained at breakfast in the Palace; and we observed the following ladies and gentlemen with the bridal party at the Church:—Miss Beresford, the bride's sister; Miss Pilkington and the Misses Jone, as bridesmaids; the Rev. R. Abbott; the Rev. Dr. Blacker and Mrs. Blacker; W. Blacker, Esq.; the Rev. Dr. R. Robinson, Mrs. and Miss Robinson; Rev. Dr. Elrington and Miss Elrington; the Rev. James Flavell; the Rev. R. Quinn and Mrs. Quinn; the Rev. A. Irwin and Mrs. Irwin; the Rev. E. Disney; Dr. and Mrs. Kidd; Dr. and Mrs. Robinson; the Misses Patons [sic]. The interior of the Cathedral was crowded to excess, with persons anxious to witness the interesting ceremony; and on the arrival of the bridal party they were received with long and hearty cheers by the crowd without. The ceremony was performed immediately after Divine Service. We are no connoiseurs in the ladies' fashions, but we may say that the dresses of the bride and bridesmaids were exceedingly rich and beautiful; the bride wore a robe of blond tissue, and a magnificent necklace of pearl, clasped with very valuable brilliants. On the party leaving the Church, they were again received with renewed cheers, plainly indicating the estimation in which the family of his Grace is held by the inhabitants of Armagh. A sumptuous *dejeuner* was prepared for the guests on their return to the Palace, shortly after which the noble and happy couple started, we believe, for the residence of the Rev. Mr. Jones. (1844-04-20, 2:6)

3155. Auction.—J.E. Jones Begs to announce to the Public, that he has received Instructions from the Relatives of the late Mrs. Armstrong, to submit to Public Competition—At her late Residence in the Diamond of Clones, On Monday, the 22nd of April, instant, and following days at eleven o'clock,

All Her Household Furniture, which are chiefly of the best description, and in good order. A very excellent fine toned Piano Forte (by Willis of London;) a superior Mangle with Mahogany Beds; an excellent Dublin made Outside Jaunting Car; a set of Harness, nearly new; a capital good light Gig; a Farm Cart and Harness; some Farming Implements, Beam, Scales and Weights; a quantity of well saved Hay, &c., &c.

The Furniture comprises, in the Parlor,—A Mahogany Cellaret Sideboard; Mahogany Dinner Tables and Loo Table; 12 Mahogany Grecian Chairs, with moveable seats, in Satin Hair-cloth; a very handsome Mahogany Secretary and Book-case; a crimson Moreen Window Curtain and Fittings; a neat Mahogany Book-shelf; a large folding door Screen and Chair back Screens; a Plate-warmer; a Kidderminster Carpet, Crum Cloth and Hearth Rug; Brass Fender, Fire Irons, Turf-box and Bell Pulls.

In the Hall and Staircase,—A Mahogany Hall Table and Rack; a Hall Lamp, Umbrella Stand, an excellent Eight-day Clock; Venetian Stair Carpeting, Covers and Brass Rods.

In the Drawing-Room,—A fine toned Piano Forte and Music Chair and Music Stool; a Chintz Window Curtain and Fittings; a Grecian Sofa; 12 Mahogany Grecian Chairs, with moveable seats, in Damask Moreen; a large Indulging Chair; a Mahogany Sofa Table; a set of Dunstables; a Card Table; Spider and Ladies Work Tables; a Brussels Carpet; Green Baize Cover and Hearth Rug; a Brass Fender, Fire Irons, Turf-box and Bell Pulls.

In the Bed-rooms,—Mahogany Four Post Eliptic [sic] and Waggon Roofed Bedsteads, with chintz and other Hangings; Pallyasses; Pure Curled Hair Mattresses; choice Feather Beds and Bedding; Children's Mahogany and other Bedsteads; Bedsteps; two excellent Mahogany and other Dressing Tables and Toilet Glasses; Basin Stands and Toilet Delph, Cloths Airers, Commodes and Bidets; Mahogany Cane Seat and other Chairs; Mahogany Cane Seat and other Chairs; House Presses, Window Curtains, Carpets and Hearth Rugs, Fenders, Fire Irons and Turf boxes.

In the Pantry,—A Dinner Service of Blue Ware; a full Service of Breakfast China and an Evening set of do.; Tea and Coffee Urns; Table, Kettle and Stand; a variety of rich Cat and Plain Class [sic]; Plated Ware; Japanned Trays; Dairy and Kitchen Requisites; Dish Covers and Jack; a Stone Trough and Water Pipe, &c., &c.

Terms—Cash, and the purchasers to pay the Auction duties. Clones, April 3rd, 1844.
(1844-04-20, 3:5)

3156. The Quarters of Life.—The seven ages of man have become proverbial; but in respect of the condition of our minds, there are granted to the best of us but four periods of life. The first fifteen years are childhood. We know nothing—we hope. The next fifteen are passion and romance—we dream. During the third period of fifteen years, from thirty to forty-five, we are what nature intended us to be. Character has formed; we pursue a course of life; we reason; we meditate. This is the period in which we may be said with most propriety to live. The fourth period is that of commencing decay. We may grow wiser, but it is the wisdom that speaks in a shake of the head. Pain and penitence begin—we sorrow. Nevertheless, if the third period has been passed in providing against the fourth, nature is changed, our declining years are lighted with happiness and love, and, as they approach their destined end, instead of the gloom naturally accompanying decay, they are tinged with a ray from before them, the shadows are cast behind us on our path, feelings spring up, unfelt even in magic periods first traversed by us—we rejoice.—*Dublin Magazine*.
(1844-04-20, 4:4)

3157. Melancholy and Sudden Death.—Coroner's Inquest.—Doctor Kirwan, one of the city coroners, held an inquest on Friday, at two o'clock, at No. 11, Peter's-row, upon the body of Barry Maxwell Fitzgerald, Esq. who was found dead in his bed between twelve and one o'clock yesterday morning. The house in question is one of ill-fame, and the particulars of the melancholy occurrence will fully appear in the following evidence:—

James Frederick Hojel examined—I live at No. 10, Beresford-place; I was not acquainted with the deceased, but I saw him first, to know his name, more than a year ago. On Tuesday night I was at the Abbey-street Theatre, in company with Mr. Morgan. He told me that he was informed by a woman named Mary Clarke (with whom the deceased was living) that he was very unwell, and had been so for some time, and that she had applied to a person named Mapleson (a cupper) to come and see deceased as he was on intimate terms with him; she said he refused to do so, and she then requested Morgan to go and see Fitzgerald; Morgan asked me if I would go, and see him, and I did so; we found him in bed apparently delirious, but he was perfectly sober; he was wandering very much; in the course of the evening he said that on Thursday night previous the female (Clarke) wanted to go to the theatre, and that he endeavoured to prevent her when she gave him a kick on the right side (pointing to the spot) of the lower part of the abdomen; he complained of the great pain at intervals; we came at half-past ten, and remained until one or half-past it; we left him with the woman Clarke and another woman, both of whom seemed anxious about him; Clarke seemed greatly agitated at the state he was in, not however from fear, but from anxiety about him; Morgan then went to Mr. M'Carthy's in Aungier-street, and a young gentleman came over who I believe to be Dr. M'Carthy's son; he examined the deceased; I waited down stairs until he came, and then went to the room above, where we found deceased sitting by the fire with his top coat on; in answer to a (*continued...*)

3157, continued: ...question, he said he felt better when sitting up than lying down; he did not then or afterwards make any charge against the female Clarke. Mr. M'Carthy examined him, desired that he should be stuped, and order him a draught and a blister; Morgan and I stuped him for about half an hour, gave him the draught and applied the blister, and having made him as comfortable as possible, went away.

Doctor Edward Leeson examined—I examined the deceased, but could not discover any marks of external violence; there is, however, a mark on the right side as if from a blister; I opened the cavity of the abdomen, and found the liver tuberculated, which arises from too much drink; the stomach was highly inflamed, as were the rest of the intestines. These appearances were not sufficient to account for death; I then opened the chest; I found inflammation of the investing membrane of the lungs, and of the lung itself, together with infusion into the cavity of that side; there was also inflammation of the paricardium, and a commencement of inflammation of the heart; he died of inflammation of the substance of the lung; there was no internal mark of violence by a kick in the side.

Mr. Morgan corroborated Mr. Hojel's testimony in every particular, and further stated that he knew the deceased for four or five years, and knew that his habits were very dissipated; he served his time to an attorney, but was not admitted, and latterly he did business for Mr. John Bates, the solicitor, of Belfast; witness saw the deceased for the last time yesterday, and knew then that he was dying.

Mary Clarke, examined—I reside at No. 11, Peter's-row, in this house; I am an unfortunate girl, and I knew the deceased for about seven months; he has been living with me for the last three months, with the exception of one or two days, and was confined to bed for the last week; he complained one time of cold and another of heat; he asked me to get him a draught to put him into a heat; I said I would and I sent to Mr. M'Carthy for it by the servant, but the gentleman in the shop would not give it without seeing the deceased; he then came over, but Mr. Fitzgerald would not let him into the room, as he was ashamed of being seen in such a place; however, I brought out word what was the matter with him, and got the draught and a pill which he took; I bathed his feet, and continued to take care of him until he died about twelve o'clock last night; I never gave him a kick, so I think he must have been delirious when he said so; I met Mr. Mapleson, the cupper, at William's public-house, in Abbey-street, on Tuesday night; I asked him to come and see him but he refused, and I then asked Mr. Morgan (whom I saw him once walking with) to come and see him, which he did; I never knew him to have a quarrel with any one, or knew any one to kick him; Dr. M'Carthy's young man said he was too bad to be removed, and that he was dying.

The jury at once found a verdict, that the deceased Barry Maxwell Fitzgerald, died at No. 11, Peter's-row, between twelve and one o'clock on Thursday morning, of inflammation of the lungs.

A pocket-book was found on the person of the deceased, containing several letters from Mr. John Bates, of Belfast, discontinuing his services as conducting clerk, upon account of his being latterly inattentive to his business; and also a great number of duplicates, dated in March last, (some of them for very trivial articles, such as razors, &c.,) which showed that he must have been rather in straightened circumstances for some time back.—*Dublin Paper*. (1844-04-27, 1:2)

3158. On Sunday week, Mary Ridgeway, an unmarried lady, of considerable fortune and the highest respectability, a member of the body of White Quakers, died at their meeting house in Mountmellick. For some time past she had been suffering under a painful disease, but such are the extraordinary opinions of these people, that during her illness neither a physician nor her brothers would be permitted to see her.—An investigation into the circumstances of her illness and death was held by the magistrates and police, to satisfy public feeling. Her remains were interred on Tuesday morning in the new burial-ground of the White Quakers, attended by twelve of Joshua Jacob's followers, and a large crowd of spectators. Head-Constable Malony and the police were active in preserving order and decorum. No less than five of the White Quakeresses preached on the occasion, and lastly Samuel Jacob, brother of the notorious Jos., enlightened his audience with a short discourse in his own felicitous style. The number of this extravagant sect is daily diminishing. Last week a person of the name of Roberts, one of their corner stones, quitted them in disgust, regretting that he was ever so infatuated as to be in the leading-strings of Jos. A few more months, it is believed will still further lessen their ranks, and Jos. will find that his occupation is gone.—*Leinster Express*. (1844-04-27, 4:3)

3159. A deputation respecting the Presbyterian Church, consisting of Dr. Stewart, Dr. Brown, Dr. Henry, Dr. Boyd, Dr. Huxton, Rev. Mr. Dobbs, Rev. Mr. Gray, and the Rev. Mr. Alexander, had an interview with Sir Robert Peel, on Monday, at his official residence in Downing-street. (1844-05-04, 2:3)

3160. Distressing Accident on Lough Neagh.—We have to announce a very afflicting calamity that occurred on Lough Neagh, on Friday, by which Mr. Alexander Charters, son of our esteemed townsman, Mr. John Charters, Mr. Henry Nelson, son of Mr. James Nelson, Ballinderry, and Mr. Allen Bell, Glenavy water-foot, have been consigned to an early grave. They had that day gone on the lake, on a pleasure excursion, and between three and four o'clock in the afternoon, when rounding Ram's Island, the boat in which they were capsized in a sudden squall, and sunk, when the three young men perished. Several persons on the shore witnessed the occurrence; but, at the distance, and the wind blowing an unusually stiff gale from the north, no assistance could be afforded. All the bodies have been recovered. (1844-05-04, 2:5)

3161. Captain Scott, of the 5th Fusiliers, was killed by a fall from his horse, on Tuesday, while with his regiment in the Phoenix Park on duty. He was a native of Bath. (1844-05-04, 3:3)

3162. Births Extraordinary.—The wife of John Tynan (a game-keeper of the Marquis of Ormonde) living at the park of Dunmore, was delivered of four children, on the 30th ultimo! Two of them (boys) with the mother are doing well; the other two were still-born. Tynan was married on the 22d of August last.—*Kilkenny Moderator*. (1844-05-11, 2:4)

3163. Death of Lieut. Scott, 5th Fusiliers.—Coroner's Inquest.—On Thursday, Dr. Kirwan and Mr. Hyndman, the city coroners, held an inquest on the body of First Lieutenant Henry Lockman Gordon Scott, of the 5th Fusiliers, who, on last Tuesday evening was thrown from his horse while riding in the Phoenix Park, and sustained, as has appeared from the event, fatal injuries. Immediately after the accident occurred, he was conveyed to the house 20, Parkgate-street, from whence it was found impossible to remove him without hastening his death, which took place at 12 o'clock on Thursday. The inquest was held at the house above mentioned.

William Smith deposed that he was a groom in the service of the deceased. His master was a lieutenant in the 5th Fusiliers, and resided in Ship-street Barracks. On Tuesday evening, about five o'clock, he went to ride in the Park, and witness did not see him after until he saw him in that room in a state of insensibility.

Robert Keane stated that he was in the Park on Tuesday evening, and saw the deceased there riding in the Fifteen Acres. Saw his horse run away with him and throw him up against a tree. Witness, assisted by a friend, lifted up the deceased who was quite insensible at the time. He bled from the left ear. Left the deceased in care of his friend and went without delay for the police.

Dr. William Baird, Surgeon of the 34th Regiment, deposed that a little before six o'clock on Tuesday evening, a gentleman galloped into the Royal Barracks and inquired for a medical man to see an officer who had been badly hurt in the Park. He immediately went on a car after the gentleman into the Park, and found the deceased lying under a tree near the Fifteen Acres. He was quite insensible. Witness examined him, and found a severe wound on the left side of the head, above the temple, extending about an inch and a half on either side of it, but did not detect any fracture of depression of the bone. The deceased's left ear was bleeding. It was filled with blood, but the flow was trifling. Witness and the other gentlemen who were on the spot searched for an hour for a stretcher to bring the deceased into town. Before they removed him, he was examined by Dr. Henderson, another medical man. They then had him conveyed to that house, and witness remained with him until half past eight o'clock. Witness examined the tree under which the deceased lay. Found a piece of it upon the ground, but did not observe any blood on it. Witness shaved the deceased's head, and found no fracture of the skull. His impression then was, that there were symptoms of concussion and compression of the brain. At ten o'clock that night, he visited the deceased with Dr. Cusack. Saw him at eight o'clock the next morning. He remained insensible, and did not speak. Witness was of opinion that his death was caused by concussion and impression [sic] of the brain.

Surgeon Henderson, of the 5th Fusiliers, deposed that the servant of the deceased, accompanied by a policeman, came to him on Tuesday evening, and brought him to see the deceased. He corroborated Dr. Baird's evidence, and stated that he was not absent from the deceased from ten o'clock the previous night. His opinion concluded [sic] with Dr. Baird's, as to the death of the deceased having been caused by concussion and also compression of the brain.

Surgeon Mackay, who was also in attendance upon the deceased, expressed a like opinion as to the cause of his death. He was with him until half-past twelve that morning, when he breathed his last.

The jury returned the following verdict:—That the deceased, Henry Lockman Gordon Scott, died from compression and concussion of the brain, in consequence of injuries which he received from having accidentally come into contact with a tree, his horse having run away with him while he was riding in the Phoenix Park on Tuesday evening last. (1844-05-11, 4:4)

3164. Inquest.—An inquest was holden on the 11th inst., in the County Infirmary, by Robert Murray, Esq., M.D., on the body of Francis Murphy, who came by his death in the following manner:—He, along with some other men were engaged in felling a tree at Raconnell; one of the men was up in the tree cutting a branch, which, when nearly cut, he called to Murphy to get out of the way lest it should fall on him; on being so cautioned Murphy unfortunately stepped in towards the tree, and the falling branch struck him on the back of the head, and caused his death. The jury returned a verdict accordingly. (1844-05-18, 3:3)

3165. Extraordinary Longevity.—Died, on Monday, the 17th instant, at Crosmolina [sic], near Broadhaven, in Erris, Grace Devit, at the extraordinary age of 122 years. She was born in the year 1722, and had an accurate recollection of all the public occurrences of note in her native district for a full century preceding the last ten years. But of the events of that latter period she knew nothing, and even (*continued...*)

3165, continued: ...matters that regarded herself no trace in her memory. Her mental faculties seemed unimpaired when she conversed of things long gone by, but she spoke like a child on the affairs of later years. Grace Devit, notwithstanding her long life, never travelled out of Erris, and never saw a tree or crossed a bridge in the whole course of her protracted existence. She had several children, but one alone survives; and although he has reached his 80th year, she never called him any other name but, my poor boy Peter. Peter is still a bachelor, and if asked at any time for the last forty years to take a wife, his reply invariably was that he could not think of doing so while his mother lived.—*Mayo Constitution.* (1844-05-18, 3:4)

3166. A little girl about thirteen years of age, named Bridget Mack, whose mind seems distracted, was very humanely taken up at Killyleagh by the Police Serjeant, and placed in the Poor-house. She stated that her father and mother are both dead, and that she has a brother, a cork-cutter, in London, who sent money to a Mrs. Little, in Ormond-market, Dublin, to take her over, and which has been kept from her. She has come round the coast all the way from Dublin, looking anxiously for a vessel bound to London, appears to be in a deplorable state, and in great dread of Mrs. Little. Perhaps this may meet the eye of some person who knows the real state of her case. (1844-05-25, 4:6)

3167. On the Death of
Miss Elizabeth Courtney, Clones.

And art thou, youthful maiden, gone,
And has thy gentle spirit flown
So soon to Him who gave;
And must that form so mild, and fair,
Ere it has felt one pang of care,
Be shrouded in the grave?

Oh, must thy smiles and cheerful voice
No more thy parent's heart's rejoice;
And must thy sisters dear,
Who loved, and were beloved by thee,
No more enjoy thy company,
Nor ever meet thee here?

What mournful peels now strike my ear,
Alas! it is the bell I hear
That calls her to be laid
Beneath the very spot of earth
Where often she, in harmless mirth,
With her companions played.

Ah, Death, why aim'st thou not thy darts
At those whose care-worn, broken hearts,
By misery are oppressed,
Who, tired of every thing below,
Might gladly quit this vale of woe
To find a place of rest.

But why thus wholly void of rath [sic]
Cut off a child in bloom of youth,
At life's most joyous stage;
In whose mature enlightened mind
An infant's innocence combined
With all the sense of age?

Nor you, her friends, I'd ask to keep
From tears, while even I could weep,
Yet mourn her not as those,
Who have no hope; for she, ere this,
Is in the realms of endless bliss,
Where living water flows.

Then why should weak short-sighted man,
The ways of God pretend to scan;
Perhaps from grief and pain,
And dire afflictions yet to come,
Her God in mercy call her home,
Shall we his will arraign?

What though her flesh returns to clay,
Methinks I hear the saviour say
To every friend that weeps
Weep not, when Time's short space is o'er
I'll her to better life restore,
She is not dead but sleeps.

W.P.
21st May, 1844.
(1844-06-04, 4:1)

3168. Marriage.—Of all actions of a man's life, his marriage does least concern other people, yet of all the actions of life, it is most meddled with by other people. (1844-06-04, 4:2)

3169. Child Burned to Death.—On Sunday last a fine little boy, named John Love, aged eight years, was burnt to death in Fanet, in consequence of his clothes having taken fire, while he incautiously meddled with the fire during the absence of his friends at Church. Though so young, he displayed extraordinary self-possession on the occasion. He first ran to a neighbouring house, and finding it locked up, he then rolled himself on the ground, in the endeavour to extinguish the flames. This proving ineffectual, he finally ran to a well, where he succeeded in quenching the flames with which he was literally surrounded, but not until he had been so severely burnt, that, on Monday evening, death put an end to his sufferings. It is a remarkable coincidence that on the previous Sunday, the Clergyman had addressed the children of the Sunday-school (of which this child was one) on the sinfulness of absenting themselves from divine service and had also, in the course of his sermon, strongly enforced upon parents the duty of bringing their children, morning and evening, to the house of God on the Sabbath-day. Had this admonition been duly attended to, the above painful occurrence should not have to be recorded.—*Derry Sentinel.* (1844-06-04, 4:4)

3170. On Thursday last, the 6th instant, a woman of about forty years of age, of the name of Eliza Roggers, was found drowned in the Blackwater river, at

Faulkland bridge, within three miles of this town. An inquest was, on yesterday (Friday) holden, in view of the body, before R. Murray, Esq., M.D., coroner, when it appeared in evidence, she had long been subject to violent fits of apoplexy; and that upon the day in question, she was seen about a half an hour before the fatal occurrence, sitting upon a bough of a tree, within a few yards of her own dwelling. Some short time after her brother happened to be passing by the spot, when his attention was attracted by her lifeless body, with her head only immersed in water; which indicated that, she had fallen in, insensibly, as the slightest effort of her own, would inevitably have saved her. The finding was accidentally drowned. (1844-06-08, 2:6)

3171. Melancholy and Fatal Accident.—On the morning of Sunday last, the 2d inst., a boy of the name of Hamilton, lost his life almost instantaneously, by falling off the water-wheel of one of Mr. Whitsitt's mills, near Saloo. The ill-fated lad, who was only sixteen years of age, and the son—we understand, the only son of a wretchedly poor widow, was, with others of his playfellows, amusing himself by walking incautiously on the upper part of the wheel, when he stumbled, and was precipitated against some of the projecting stones of the mill-dam, and was in a moment taken up a lifeless corpse. An inquest was holden on Monday, in view of the body, before Robert Murray, Esq., M.D., coroner, when a verdict of "Accidental Death" was immediately returned. (1844-06-08, 2:6)

3172. Fatal Accident on the Dublin and Drogheda Railway.—On Thursday week, Mr. John Galbraith, a contractor in the formation of the above railway, met his death in the following manner:—On the arrival of the train from Raheny, the passengers left the carriages to partake of the entertainment provided; when about to leave, deceased changed into a first class carriage, and on its having started, going at the rate of fifty miles [sic], he attempted to close the door with his foot, when it was caught between the stage and the door, and, shocking to relate, he was drawn out and almost dragged to pieces. He was conveyed to one of the Dublin Hospitals, and after a few hours' suffering, ceased to exist.—*Dublin Paper*.—The train which arrived at Drogheda about 3 o'clock met with a misadventure. The engine overran the terminus, and knocked down the flag staff and wooden paling, but no other injury was done.—The number of tickets sold on Saturday reached twelve hundred. (1844-06-08, 3:3)

3173. Alarming Boat Accident.—On Monday evening while the fly-boat from Longford was on its passage to Dublin, on the Royal Canal, on its arrival at Ballinacarriga, about nine miles below Mullingar, a very alarming accident occurred under the following circumstances:—The boat contained a large number of persons who were about emigrating to America, and at the above station, as the vessel was descending the chamber of the lock, upwards of one hundred persons, friends of the emigrants, rushed on board with the intention of bidding them farewell.—The rush was so sudden that the boat struck on the sill of the lock, and was partially sunk, when the water rushed into the after cabin, where a child, aged about four years, the daughter of one of the passengers, was unfortunately smothered. A great deal of confusion prevailed on the occasion, but after some time, with the exception of the melancholy accident to the ill-fated child, all was got to rights, and the boat was enabled to proceed on her passage. There is a police station at Ballinacarriga, and the men stationed there are always in attendance to prevent accidents from such pressures by taking leave of their friends, but in consequence of their being absent at a neighbouring fair, the present fatality could not be guarded against. The boat arrived at one o'clock, on Tuesday, at the Broad-Stone, instead of at nine in the morning, the hour at which it was due. No blame whatever is attached to the company. (1844-06-15, 1:5)

3174. Spinsters.—Formerly, women were prohibited from marrying until they had spun a set of bed furniture; and, till their wedding, were consequently called spinsters, which they continue to this day, in all legal proceedings. (1844-06-15, 4:1)

3175. On yesterday (Friday), a man of the name of Donnelly, fell against the paving, from a height of about twenty feet, while thatching a house in Glasslough-street, in this town. The unfortunate man was standing on one of the transverse bars (near the top) of a ladder, which extended from the street up along the side of the house, when the wheel of a carriage, which was passing at the time, came in collision with the ladder near its base, upon which it instantly fell prostrate on the road, and though he clung to it till he came to the ground, there are only faint hopes entertained of his recovery. (1844-06-22, 3:1)

3176. Death of the Hon. Arthur Cole.—When we recently noticed the retirement of the Hon. Arthur Cole from parliamentary life, we little contemplated the painful task which is now before us of recording his death. Aware that his health had suffered serious impairment, we indulged the hope that relaxation from the cares that had worn him out, and the soothing restoration of domestic quiet in the bosom of an affectionate family, would have repaired his declining energies and prolonged his days. But, alas! disease had taken too deep a root, and death was not to be averted either by prayers of attached friends or the adoption of the hopefulest remedies.—He closed his eyes to this world, in the firm expectation of a happy resurrection in the next, on the morning of Saturday, the 10th instant, at his residence in Manchester-square, in the 64th year of his age. (*continued...*)

3176, continued: ...The death of this excellent gentleman will be a serious loss to the society in which he moved, to the friends who could estimate his qualities, to the family by whom he was beloved for his virtues no less than his kindred. Between him and his amiable and accomplished sister, the Countess de Grey, the most ardent affection subsisted. Deeply do we sympathise with a sorrow which, in this world, can know no consolation but the assurance that the object of her sisterly affections has passed from life unto death, and again from death into life, through the gates of mercy opened by the hands of a gracious Redeemer, and now enjoys the blessedness reserved for those who love and fear God as revealed in his Holy Gospel. (1844-06-22, 3:4)

3177. "What harm is there in a pipe?" says young Puffwell. "None that I know of," replied his companion, "except that smoking induces drinking; drinking induces intoxication; intoxication induces bile; bile induces jaundice; jaundice induces dropsy; dropsy terminates in death. Put that in your pipe and smoke it." (1844-06-22, 4:4)

3178. An American paper says, in an obituary notice, that the deceased had been for several years director of a bank, notwithstanding which he died a Christian, and universally respected. (1844-06-22, 4:4)

3179. The Loss of the *Manchester* Steamer.—The following letter was received this morning by the Secretary at Lloyd's, from the agent at Hull, dated June 21, half-past three, p.m.

"The *Leeds* steamer, from Hamburgh, has just arrived, bringing accounts, dated 18th instant, from Mr. Dutton, of Cuxhaven, stating that the *Manchester* steamer, Captain Dubley, which sailed hence 14th inst., appears to have been totally wrecked at the entrance of the Elbe, during a heavy gale, on the 16th and 17th inst., from the northward. The boats, broken, and also considerable quantities of broken bales of cotton twist and other goods and wreck, have been washed ashore at Cuxhaven. As there is no account of the crew and passengers, it is feared that the whole have perished. The ship had a very valuable cargo on board.

(Signed)

"Edward Moon."

P.S. Twenty minutes past four p.m.—Captain Mowle has no doubt that the whole of the crew and passengers are drowned.

We see by a second edition of the *Hull Advertiser* the following amongst the names of those unfortunate persons lost on board the *Manchester*, Hamburgh steamer:—"Mrs. Smith, a lady, 46 years of age; her daughter, Miss Emily Smith, 21 years of age; and Mr. St. George Smith, her son, 27 years of age. This family came from Drogheda, in Ireland, and were going to Graffenburgh, in Silesia, for the benefit of their health." (1844-06-29, 2:3)

3180. Coroners of Ireland.—A meeting of the coroners of Ireland took place on Wednesday at Bradley's Hotel, for the purpose of taking into consideration the provisions of a bill now before Parliament for the regulation of that office, and which we understand will materially affect the rights of that body. A parliamentary agent was appointed to superintend the bill throughout Parliament, and arrangements made to have as far as possible the objectionable clauses removed.—*Pilot*. (1844-06-29, 2:3)

3181. Melancholy Accident, and Loss of Life.—On the 21st instant, at Riverstown, near Carlingford, as a young man, named Douloughan, a miller, in the employment of Messrs. John and Laurence Feeban [sic], of Castlecarragh, was cleaning the dust off the wheel of the mill, inside the house, a heavy rain fell, which (from the channel conveying water to the mill) filled one of the buckets of the wheel outside, and turned it; of course, the effect was produced on the wheel inside, and Douloughan was caught by the arm. He called for assistance, and a person standing by, who saw his immediate danger, to save his life, succeeded in throwing him over the wheel, and fell under it. His sister, a fine young woman, instantly sprung to his assistance, with all those natural and excited feelings more easily imagined than described in witnessing such a scene, but sad to relate, she also was caught by the arm, and in an instant, the brave, the tender and affectionate sister became a mangled corpse. Before she was extricated, life was quite extinct. The brother was taken up seriously bruised, and frightfully mutilated—the flesh literally stripped to the bones from his leg and arm. He continues to linger in a precarious state. A man named M'Cann, while in the attempt to save them, had his finger caught, and was about being dragged in also, but with great presence of mind and exertion, he permitted the finger to be wrung off him. So fatally and sure was the powerful machine continuing to perform its destructive ravages on everything near it, that two others narrowly escaped. It was providential, when it is considered that the movement of the machine was unexpected, several persons being employed about the part where the greatest danger might be apprehended, and no time to escape. On the day after the occurrence, an inquest was held on the body of the young woman, before one of the coroners of the county of Louth, and John R. Croghan, Esq., S.I., when Surgeon Strong, of Carlingford, who made an examination of the body, and other witnesses, were examined. The jury returned a verdict according to the facts as above given.—*Newry Telegraph*. (1844-06-29, 2:5)

3182. Laying the Foundation Stone of Major-General Gillespie's Monument at Comber.—Monday last being the day appointed for laying the foundation-stone of a monument to the memory of the late Major-General Sir R. Rollo Gillespie, that interesting ceremony was performed by Colonel Cairnes, K.H., (who was deputed by the Marquis of Londonderry,) with all masonic honors, and in presence of several thousand spectators. The day was appropriately selected, being the anniversary of St. John's; and as the gallant individual, to whose memory this tribute of respect was shown, was of high order amongst the fraternity of Masons. By the permission of the Grand Lodge of Ireland, the brethren of the mystic tie for many miles round, were allowed the privilege of being present.—Notwithstanding the unfavourable state of the weather, the rain having fallen in torrents from about nine o'clock in the morning till three in the afternoon, the town of Comber was thronged by persons anxious to witness the ceremony. About the hour of two o'clock, the respective lodges of the district began to arrive in succession, and entered the town with much order and regularity, accompanied by bands of music playing appropriate airs. At half-past three o'clock, the rain ceased, and immediately afterwards the procession, headed by Colonel Cairnes, marched to the site of the intended erection, which is almost in the centre of the square. A platform was erected for the occasion, on which we observed Percy Boyd, Esq., John Andrews, Esq., J.P., John Miller, Esq., J.P., Major Haughton, Capt. Powell, Guy Stone, Esq., Reverend R. Jex Blake, W.T. Higgins, Esq., &c. Immediately below the platform was an open space, in the centre of which was placed the stone, and around it were the flags of the different masonic lodges. The scene at this moment exhibited a most interesting appearance. The masters of the various lodges were attired in their different robes of office, and at the word of command, formed a circle round the foundation-bed. Colonel Cairnes opened the proceedings, by reading a letter from the Marquis of Londonderry, apologizing for not being able to attend in person at the ceremony, and deputing the gallant Colonel to act in his absence. The Colonel then proceeded to allude to the object for which they had assembled, and expressed the satisfaction he felt at being entrusted by the noble Marquis with such an honorable duty, as that which he was about to discharge. He called attention to the character and exploits of General Gillespie, whose zeal for his country's glory had caused him to rank amongst the many brave officers whom Ireland had the honour of calling her sons. He (Colonel Cairnes) rejoiced to see so many persons assembled in the town which was the birthplace of Gillespie—a general who fought and bled for his country—for the purpose of doing honour to his memory, and that he had the pleasure of seeing around him a number of that illustrious man's friends, some of whom had also fought for their country, and other gentlemen, including Mr. Andrews, the noble Marquis of Londonderry's agent, and Rev. Mr. Blake, who had taken such an active part in furthering the good work, which they were about to commence. The gallant Colonel then called upon Percy Boyd, Esq., the Secretary to the subscribers, who addressed the meeting in an eloquent and spirited speech, enumerating the several acts of bravery for which Major-General Gillespie has been famed, and setting forth the claims which he had upon the affections of his countrymen, especially those of his native country. Major Houghton next addressed the meeting. He said he had come there that day to do honour to the memory of a gallant man, a relative of his own, but in doing so, he had no doubt that he would have heard the handsome eulogium which his kind friend Colonel Cairnes had been pleased to pass upon his services to his Sovereign and his country; but in doing which he (Col. Cairnes) had refrained from mentioning the weighty claims which he himself had upon the regard of his native land. Colonel Cairnes had been fighting the battles of his country during the best part of his life under the burning sun of India, and under the command of that distinguished General to whose memory they were about to erect a monument.—The person selected to lay the first stone was the companion of Sir Robert Rollo Gillespie, the companion of his early years, and a more appropriate person, or a more worthy man, could not have been chosen. Rev. Mr. Blake and John Andrews, Esq., next addressed a few remarks to the assembly, expressing the pleasure they felt at the commencement of a work in which they had all taken such an interest. Colonel Cairnes then proceeded to lay the stone. He first deposited it in a sealed bottle, containing copies of the Belfast newspapers, several coins of the realm, an almanac for the present year, the names of the subscribers, alphabetically arranged, and written on parchment, the names of the contractor and architect, and a document narrating the circumstances which led to the erection of the monument, and also signifying the respect which was entertained for the memory of the officer to whom it was erected. The stone was then lowered, previous to which the gallant Colonel, with a silver trowel, went through the usual ceremony of spreading a little cement and striking the stone three times with a mallet. This having been concluded, Mr. Higginson addressed a few words to the brethren, calling upon them to return home with good order, and to add to their many qualities that of sobriety. The bands present then played the national anthem, and after giving three cheers for the Queen, the meeting separated. We have not heard of the slightest disturbance having taken place during the day.—*Belfast News-Letter*. (1844-06-29, 2:6)

3183. Funeral of the Late Hon. Arthur Cole.—Monday morning last, the remains of the lamented Hon. Arthur Cole were interred in the family vault in Enniskillen Church. The very large and highly respectable body of persons which formed the procession, and the expression of sorrow in every countenance, in paying this last sad tribute of respect to departed (*continued...*)

3183, continued: ...worth, were manifestations such as were justly due to the deceased gentleman in every relation of life, both public and private. From an early hour in the morning, carriages and cars, together with horsemen and footmen, were in constant movement towards Callow-hill, in which Church the remains had lain for the previous night, having reached there on Sunday evening. The funeral left the Church at seven o'clock, a.m., and from there until it reached Enniskillen, the procession was gradually increasing. While passing through the Ballinaleck district, the Church bell of the parish tolled its notes of sorrow, and when within about two miles of this town, our Church bell commenced. The funeral reached the town at eleven o'clock.

On arriving at the Church gate, the body was removed from the Hearse, and borne by twelve respectable men from Florencecourt, into the Church, where the service was read with great solemnity by the Hon. and Rev. Mr. Maude, and the Rev. Mr. Cleary.—The Church was crowded almost to suffocation.—After the service was concluded, the body was borne to the vault in the rear of the Church, and placed with the remains of the deceased's ancestors and other relatives.—*Erne Packet.* (1844-06-29, 3:3)

3184. The preliminaries for a marriage have been arranged between a youthful Earl possessing extensive estates in Leicestershire and Staffordshire, and the lovely and accomplished grand-daughter of a noble Marquis in the north of Ireland. (1844-06-29, 3:3)

3185. The Presbyterian Marriage Bill.—This bill has not yet been printed; but we understand that it only provides for the celebration of marriages by Presbyterian ministers between their own members and those of the Established Church—excluding altogether the Methodists, Independents, Baptists, and other dissenters; the law with regard to Jews, Roman Catholics, &c., remaining as it is at present. The Rev. Thomas Waugh has left town for London for the purpose of appealing against the measure as regards the Wesleyan Methodist body.—*Statesman.* (1844-06-29, 3:4)

3186. Death of Colonel Madden.—With sincere sorrow, we announce the death of this venerated country gentleman. The melancholy event took place on Tuesday last, at Sandy Cove, Kingstown, where he usually spent the bathing season. For many years, he acted as a leading Grand Juror for this county. In every work of benevolence, he was foremost; in fact, he was a perfect specimen of the fine old Irish gentleman. He has left none behind him of more real worth, and his loss will not only be severely felt, and deeply deplored by those of his own rank, but the poor and the oppressed will have to mourn a steady friend and protector. Peace to his ashes. We will see few men of more real instrinsic worth. (1844-07-13, 3:3)

3187. Marriage in High Life.—On Tuesday, the marriage of Lord Charles Wellesley, youngest son of the Duke of Wellington, and Miss Augusta Sophia Anne, only child of the Right Hon. Henry Manvers, Pierrpoint [sic] and the late Lady Sophia Pierrpoint, was solemnised in St. George's Church, Hanover-square, London. (1844-07-13, 3:3)

3188. Prerogative Court, Dublin—July 6.—(Before the Right Hon. Judge Keatinge.)—*Enward* [sic] *Lennon Nugent a. the Right Rev. Dr. Wm. Higgins, Roman Catholic Archbishop of Ardagh.*—This cause, which has been before the Court for a considerable period, came on for judgment on Saturday, when the question to be adjudicated upon was, whether the will of the promovent's uncle, which was made *in extremis*, should be deemed good?

Sir H. Meredyth, Bart., and Sir T. Staples, Bart., with Messrs. J. and R. Staples Swift, appeared as advocates and proctors for the promovent; and Dr. Radcliffe and Dr. Wily, with Mr. Robert Orme, attended for the impugnant.

His Lordship, in pronouncing judgment upon the case, said that the suit was instituted to establish the will of Thomas Lennon Nugent, who died upon the 25th of January, 1843, and the parties appearing before the Court were the deceased's nephew, Mr. Edmund Lennon Nugent, the promovent, who alleged instances, and the Right Rev. Doctor William Higgins, the impugnant, who came forward in the capacity of residuary legatee to the will, to which an executor had been appointed, who renounced. The executor was a gentleman whose name had been very much mentioned in the case. The Rev. Edward M'Gaver, a parish priest, residing in the county of Longford, at whose instigation it appeared that the will had been made [sic]. The deceased was a very aged man, having passed his eighty-third year; and the alleged will, which was drawn out by the executor, and signed by himself as a witness, and by two other persons, whose wives were left legacies, appointed the right reverend impugnant as a residuary legatee to the remainder of the property, which was considerable, for the purpose of completing the Roman Catholic cathedral of Ballymahon, in the county of Longford, which bequest the promovent endeavored to show had been made within two hours of the deceased's dissolution, (which was not denied,) when he was in a state of mental incapacity, so as to render him wholly incompetent to know what he was doing. The learned judge having minutely gone through the evidence of the witnesses examined upon both sides, decided that the writ should be established, as there was no ground for imputing fraud to the Rev. Mr. M'Gaver. However, he gave the promovent his costs out of the estate, inasmuch as he considered the case to have been one of great suspicion, and deserving of investigation. (1844-07-13, 4:5)

3189. Death of the Rev. Andrew M'Caldin, Presbyterian Minister.—This melancholy event took place on Wednesday evening, the 10th instant, at his residence, Hanover-place. He had been, for twelve months past, afflicted with an affection of the heart, but was only confined to his room for the last few days. He was 64 years of age, and 42 years a minister of the Gospel, thirty-four of which were spent here [Coleraine], in ministering to the congregation of the first Presbyterian Church. He was a minister much beloved by his own people, and respected by those of other denominations; and as a preacher, his discourses were characterised by much fervency and feeling. He departed this life rejoicing in the consolations of that Gospel which he had so often tenderly administered to others, and knows we are persuaded now that to depart and be with Christ is far better. "Mark the perfect, and behold the upright, for the end of that man is peace."—*Coleraine Chronicle*. (1844-07-20, 3:4)

3190. The Loss of the *Manchester*.—Eleven Bodies Recovered.—By the late arrivals from Hamburgh, we learn that the relatives of the unhappy persons who perished with the *Manchester* steamer at the mouth of the Elbe have at last the melancholy satisfaction of knowing that the remains of those so dear to them have been cast from the deep, no fewer than 11 bodies of the sufferers having been picked up, comprising the whole of the passengers, Captain Dudley and a part of his crew. The *Neptune*, General Steam Navigation Company's steamer, from Hamburgh, brings the exact particulars concerning their recovery, as received by the managers of the Hanseatic Steam Company, at Hamburgh. It appears that Captain Dudley was picked up off Busom; also Mrs. St. George Smith, and her son, Mr. George Smith, two of the seamen, and the body of a gentleman unknown, with a large sum of money amounting to 3,900 marks, being adjusted round his neck. The gentleman was attired in a black dress coat, with black silk lining, black velvet waistcoat, greyish brown striped buckskin trousers, flannel waistcoat, and white cotton drawers. A gold watch was found in one of his pockets, the words "Peak of Teneriffe" engraved on the back; "Mr. Potrey, No. 8630" gold face, with four holes jeweled, statuture about five feet six inches, with very small feet. Near Cuxhaven were cast on shore the bodies of Miss Emily Smith, daughter of Mrs. St. George Smith; Mr. Rothery, of Leeds; Mrs. Webb, the stewardess, without covering, and right leg broken just above the knee, and two seamen, one apparently the first or second mate. A friend of Edgington, a magistrate of Hull, who was deputed to remain at Cuxhaven to identify the bodies of Mrs. Smith, and her son and daughter, has taken charge of the bodies, and it is understood will convey them by the earliest steamer to Hull for interment. That of the unfortunate commander, and the other persons, have been buried in the churchyard of Wasselbusom, but the authorities have signified their intention of allowing them to be disinterred should any of their relatives wish it. The face of Mrs. Webb was much disfigured by friction on the sands, and by fish. The wreck on the north end of the Riepen Sand has been completely broken up, and what has been saved of ship and the cargo has been sold by auction for 1,200*l*. for the benefit of the salvors.

The bodies of Mrs. St. George Smith, Mr. St. George Smith, jun., and Miss Emily Smith, were brought to Drogheda by the *Green Isle* steamer on the 17th instant, and interred on the 18th in St. Peter's church-yard. All the gentry of Drogheda, and its vicinity attended, and testified the deepest sorrow for the melancholy fate of individuals so universally respected and beloved. (1844-07-27, 4:2)

3191. Leap Year and the Ladies.—The report of the registrar-general bears witness, clear and undeniable, that the ladies avail themselves of the privilege which belongs to them in leap year. In all and every of the eight several divisions into which England and Wales are divided for registration purposes, there were more marriages in 1840 than in either 1839 or 1841! In the northern district, 1,444 of every 100,000 ladies living in 1839 entered into the holy state of matrimony; and in 1841, the proportion was 1,415; while in 1840 (leap year), 1,526 of every 100,000 ladies succeeded in leading as many men into the married state; the fair sex, of course, will be no less busy in the present year. (1844-07-27, 4:6)

3192. Elopement to Gretna Green.—On Thursday last, Lieutenant Leeson, nephew of Lord Milltown, and youngest son of the late Hon. Mr. Leeson, of the Thorn near Penrith, Cumberland, who is on leave of absence from his regiment, which is in the East Indies, eloped to Gretna-green, with Miss Laura Bristow, a daughter of John Charles Bristow, Esq., of Ensmere-hill, with great skill. Wednesday last was the day in which he intended to so have stormed the works, but the garrison having, doubtless, been apprised of his intentions, manned the walls so well all that day and night, that the besieger thought it right not to commence operations at that time. Next morning, however, the besieged, thinking all safe, made a sortie, and set up sail up the lake of Ullswater to Patterdale, taking the young lady with them. The besieger was not aware of this, and the besieged had nearly made a safe retreat into the garrison again; but one of the gallant officer's sharpshooters lay concealed among the brushwoods, who seized the fair prize, and away she was taken to her betrothed, who was waiting at a short distance with a coach and four, and off the young officer went with his booty. Pursuit was in vain; the fugitives soon passed over the six-and-twenty miles to Gretna-green, were married, and it is said, they contemplate a speedy embarkation for India; but it is expected that a reconciliation with her family will first take place, for that which is passed cannot be reversed. (1844-07-27, 4:6)

3193. Fatal Accident.—A few days ago as George Percy, Esq., of Garradice, county of Leitrim, was amusing himself by shooting rabbits, the gun, owing to some mismanagement, or a faulty lock, went off, lodging its contents under the unfortunate gentleman's arm, and inflicting a wound so dangerous in its nature that every means which medical skill could devise proved ineffectual, and he expired on Tuesday. The premature death of this gentleman, under circumstances so painful, has thrown the deepest gloom over a large circle of their friends, but to none will the affliction be so heavy and insupportable as to this young and interesting widow, to whom he had not long been united.—*Boyle Gazette*. (1844-08-03, 2:3)

3194. Hydrophobia—Another Victim.—(*From the Cork Examiner*.)—Painful indeed is our duty, to announce the death of Mrs. Delacour, the second victim to this malady in one family, within the short space of five months. The sad death of the young and graceful girl, the first victim, excited general horror and consternation; but who can describe the feeling with which the announcement of the second death will be received by the public. For more than five months, the terrible poison lurked in the veins of this amiable lady, until it at last manifested its presence in that horrible agony which heralds the dissolution of the sufferer. The following is from a respected correspondent:—

"Since writing the above, an account of Mrs. Delacour's death has reached town. She fell a victim to that dreadful malady against whose ravages science has as yet discovered no antidote—hydrophobia. It appears that the little dog which caused Miss Delacour's death, about five months since, licked Mrs. Delacour's face at that time, and she since had a horror of the fatal disease. R.B.B." (1844-08-03, 2:4)

3195. On Monday past, the 29th ult., a male child of three years old, of the name of Carr, was found drowned in a dyke of water near Emyvale police station. When found, there was no part of the body immersed but the head and hands, which were entangled in some fibrous weeds that covered the bottom. (1844-08-03, 3:1)

3196. Death of Major-General Edward Scott.—We have to announce the death of the above gallant officer, who died on Friday last, at his residence at Bath, at the advanced age of 82 years. The deceased had served with distinction in the 94th Foot, at St. Domingo, in 1794 and '95; and was on his return to this country sent with his corps to Ireland, for the suppression of the Irish rebellion in '98. He accompanied the expedition to the Ferrol and Cadiz, under Sir James Pulteney; and afterwards repaired to Egypt for the campaign of 1801, and was present at nearly all the engagements in that year, including the actions of the 8th, 13th, and 12th of March, in which last he was severely contused on the breast by a musket ball. For his services in Egypt, he was rewarded with a medal, and he had the Order of the Crescent conferred upon him by the Turkish government. His commissions were dated as follows:—Ensign, June 29, 1780; Lieutenant, August 4, 1781; Captain, June 30, 1795; Major, September 1, and Major-General, June 4, 1843. (1844-08-03, 3:1)

3197. Dr. Cooke, the Primate, and the *Marriage Bill*.—The following letter has excited no small curiosity n the province. We are bound to believe Dr. Cooke when he asserts that the Primate, throughout the whole of the negociations regarding the *Marriage Bill*, was friendly to Presbyterians; because it may be said of him as Cardinal Colonna said to Petrarch—"As for you your word is sufficient." We can only say that Dr. Cooke would have protected his Grace, the Lord Primate, from much misrepresentation an annoyance, had he earlier corrected the error into which the Presbyterian public have fallen, by giving the sanction of his name to the disclaimer, which for so long a time had no better authority than the anonymous *ipse dixit* of a Newry editor, unfriendly to the late agitation which took place on the Marriage Question:—

To the Editor of the *Newry Telegraph*.—Dear Sir—I feel much obliged by the copy of the *Telegraph* of the 16th inst., for which, I suppose, I am indebted to your kindness. And although, in one point of view, I feel much annoyed by its reference to myself in connexion with your report reflecting on the Lord Primate, yet, in another point of view, I feel satisfied, as it affords me a legitimate opportunity of expressing in *public* what you know I have always expressed in *private*—my firm conviction that, through all the Parliamentary management of the Marriage Bill, his Grace was *one of the best friends of the Presbyterians*. This opinion, founded not upon conjecture, but solid facts, I long ago authorised you to state, without making my name public, but with full power to use it in private, should your statement be called in question. The bill has now, for some time, passed the House of Lords, and I am happy to reiterate, in the most public manner, my unchanged opinion, not only of the good wishes, but also of the kind and efficient services of his Grace in the settlement of this question in a manner, as I humbly conceive, highly advantageous and honourable to the Presbyterian community.

Dr. Stewart being now in London, I have no opportunity of learning from himself what he did report to the Assembly at Derry. But knowing, as I do, the unavoidable imperfections, and, upon new topics, the errors of the best newspaper reporting, I can have no doubt that the report of his statement is incorrect. In fact, as reported, Dr. Stewart well knew I never could have said that Presbyterians would resist to the utmost of their power the giving of a notice of a proposed mixed marriage to the rector or other incumbent of the Established Church—for he knew that the whole deputation had already, in the most formal manner—in their own draft of a Marriage Bill—proposed to give such notice. And he knew that, in the absence of a deputation, I was limited to adhere to all that they had proposed.

It certainly was stated to me, as I stated to Dr. Stewart, that the object of the Lord Primate in bringing the bill again before the Select Committee was supposed to be the introduction, not of a notice clause of his own, but of the clause which the Presbyterian deputation had proposed, and the House of Lords had omitted. But such notice I never proposed; and, by the terms imposed upon me by the deputation on their return to Ireland, I dared not have proposed to resist, because it had already received their sanction. What I respectfully entreated my informant to guard against, and stated we should resist, was a notice conferring a *veto* upon mere will, or upon any except legal grounds—such as want of consent of father or guardian, in case of minors, forbidden degree of consanguinity, or previous contract of marriage. Neither did it ever enter into my mind that either the Lord Primate contemplated such a *veto*, though the report of Dr. Stewart's speech appears to attribute the intention to his Grace; my fears arose from a different quarter; and, whether well or ill founded, now, matters little, as I presume the whole question is by this time at rest. In point of fact, if my information was correct—and I have little reason to doubt it—the difficulties in the way of a Presbyterian Marriage Bill arose not from the quarter whence opposition was most dreaded, but whence patronage and assistance were most confidently anticipated. But be this as it may, I again repeat what I have uniformly stated, whether in England or in Ireland, and whether in public or in private, that, whatever appearance might indicate, or conjecture suppose, his Grace, the Lord Primate was, in my opinion, uniformly anxious for a settlement of the question consonant to the feelings and honourable to the position of Presbyterians, with restrictions merely preservative of the public decencies and proprieties of marriage.

Believe me, dear Sir,
Yours truly,
H. Cooke.
Belfast, 18th July, 1844.
(1844-08-03, 3:2)

3198. Marriages in High Life.—July 23, in the Cathedral of Clogher, by the Hon. and Very Rev. Dean Maude, Robert George Archibald Hamilton Gun Cunninghame, Esq., of Mount-Kennedy, county of Wicklow, to Isabella, only daughter of the Lord Bishop of Clogher and Lady Robert Tottenham.

(From our Correspondent.)

Clogher, July 25.

The 23d of July will long be remembered with pleasure by the inhabitants of Clogher and its vicinity, being the day on which the nuptials of Robert G.A.H. Gun Cunninghame, Esq., and the lovely and accomplished daughter of our respected Prelate were solemnised.

The fair bride was conducted from the Palace to the Cathedral by her noble father, (who gave her away,) accompanied by the Marquess and Marchioness of Ely and Lady Anna Loftus, (one of the fair bridesmaids,) the Hon. Mrs. Maude, the Hon. and Rev. J.C. Maude, Captain the Hon. Francis Maude, R.N., the Misses Maude, the Messrs. and Misses Tottenham and the leading gentry of the neighbourhood.

The procession (enlived by the tasteful dresses of the numerous bridesmaids) as it passed along under an archway formed of festoons of flowers, with the merry faces of dense masses of the country people in the distance, in their holiday attire, formed a most picturesque *coup d'oeil.*

After the ceremony (which was performed by the Hon. and Very Rev. Dean Maude) the whole party partook of a sumptuous *dejeuner* at the Palace.

In the afternoon, the Bishop's numerous laborers and their families, together with the poor of Clogher and surrounding district were, with his lordship's usual liberality, plentifully regaled with roast beef, &c., &c., nor were the inmates of the poorhouse forgotten on the festive occasion.

"Soon as the evening shades prevailed," tar barrels blazed in all directions, and the town of Clogher was brilliantly and tastefully illuminated, whilst the bells of the Cathedral rung out a merry peal, and several amateur bands supplied music—that "food of love," and contributed, by enlivening airs, to the general harmony.

The utmost order and decorum were observed by the thousands who thronged to the festive scene; and it was gratifying to observe persons of all classes and religious persuasions vieing with each other in tokens of respectful attachment to our justly-esteemed Prelate, and his family. (1844-08-03, 3:2)

3199. Marriages in High Life. ... On the 22nd inst., by special license, at Charleville, the seat of the Earl of Rathdowne, by the Very Rev. the Dean of the Chapel Royal, Dublin, Charles Stanley, eldest son of the Hon. C.J.K. Monck, to the Lady Elizabeth Louise Mary, third daughter of the Earl of Rathdowne.
(1844-08-03, 3:2)

3200. Provide for Old Age.—It is not well that a man should always labour. His temporal as well as spiritual interest demand a cessation in the decline of life. Some years of quiet and reflection are necessary after a life of industry and activity. There is more to concern him in life than incessant occupation, and its product—wealth. He who has been a slave all his days to one monotonous mechanical pursuit can hardly be fit for another world. The release from toil in old age, most men have the prospective pleasure of; and in reality, it is as pleasing as it is useful and salutary to the mind. Such advantages, however, can only be gained by prudence and economy in youth; we must save, like the ant, before we can hope to have any rest in the winter of our days.—*Book of Symbols.*
(1844-08-03, 4:1)

3201. Consolatory.—An English gentleman travelling through the county of Kilkenny, came to a ford, and hired a boat to take him across. The water being rather more agitated than was agreeable to him, he asked the boatman if any person was ever lost in the passage. "Never," replied the boatman, "my brother was drowned here last week, but we found him next day." (1844-08-03, 4:3)

3202. Death from Lockjaw.—We regret to have to mention the death of a fine and promising member of the medical profession, a son of the Rev. W. Townsend, of Aghada. This young gentleman, who had been for some time at Hobartstown, where he was on the staff of the governor, was returning from, we believe, a visit to a patient, when he was thrown from his horse. Beyond a few bruises and a slight abrasion of the skin a little above one of the knees, no injury was apparent, nor any inconvenience felt. In a few days, part of the knee which had been bared resumed its accustomed appearance, and the accident was forgotten. Three weeks, however, after the fall, Doctor Townsend was seized with lockjaw, and in about an hour, he was dead. The deceased was nephew to Doctor Edward Townsend of Cork, to whom he served his apprenticeship. (1844-08-03, 4:6)

3203. Awful Accident.—It is our painful duty to record one of the most awfully fatal accidents which has occurred within our recollection in the neighbourhood of Sligo. On Thursday night last, Gregory Cuffe Martin, Esq., accompanied his lady, left town in his car, at about nine o'clock, for the purpose of going to a bathing lodge, on Dorren's Island. The parties were last seen getting out upon the Cummin strand, at Scardon mills. In the morning the car was found (the horse drowned,) close to the seal-bank. But neither Mr. Martin nor his lady could be discovered; their melancholy fate, however, cannot now be questioned; the unfortunate gentleman must either have mistaken his course and have gone to the deep water, or (which is more probable) the horse must have lost his footing while crossing one of the small channels, and the current swept the victims into the deep, where they perished. It is impossible to describe the sensation which this terrible calamity, created in Sligo the moment it became known. Horror was depicted in every countenance, and hundreds of persons left town to search for the bodies, but up to this time they have not been recovered. Mr. Cuff [sic] Martin was second son—(and owing to a late afflicting accident which happened to the eldest son)—probable heir of Abraham Martin, Esq., now unquestionably the most bereaved man in Sligo. The commiseration which is felt for this gentleman is universal; and if it were any alleviation to his sorrows, we can safely say they are mourned by all. Saturday, Twelve o'Clock.—Boats were out all night in search of the remains of Mr. and Mrs. Martin, but we regret to say not a trace of them could be found. We are now inclined to think that they were forced by the current (which runs with such tremendous force between the two islands) out to the ocean, in which case there is scarcely a hope of their ever being recovered. The sufferers have left five infant children.—*Sligo Champion.* (1844-08-10, 2:4)

3204. Suicide.—On Friday, a man named John Mullan, who resided in Kennedy's-row off Smithfield, put an end to his life by hanging himself in his own house, about two o'clock. He was discovered by his son, a little boy, shortly after he had committed the act, who alarmed the neighbors, and they immediately cut him down, but life was extinct. He had been, we understand, a teetotaller, but had broken the pledge and was for some time back greatly given to drink, and it is supposed that this caused him to commit the fatal act. He kept a stall for the sale of small wares in Smithfield. He has left a wife and family to mourn his untimely end.—On the following day, an inquiry into all the circumstances of the case was held by the magistrates, at the Police-office. The first person examined was Ann Ferguson, a woman who resides next door to the house of the deceased. She stated that on the day of this melancholy occurrence, she saw deceased alive in Smithfield, and a few hours afterwards, saw him hanging by the neck from a beam in the attic story of his own house; observed a stool convenient to his feet; deceased drank a little that day, and was in general much addicted to whiskey; he had taken laudanum on a former occasion; witness lived next door to deceased, and was attracted to the room by the cries of his child; when the door was opened, deceased was quite dead. Constable M'Kendry deposed that he proceeded to the residence of deceased, and saw him in the position described by last witness.—Dr. Harkins was called in and attempted to bleed him, but without success. The wife of deceased stated to the bench that she had not seen her husband from nine o'clock in the morning till she saw him with the rope round his neck, hanging from the beam, and that he was a drunkard. A son of the unfortunate deceased was also examined. He saw his father about two hours and a half before he hanged himself; deceased told him to go out till he would get half an hour's sleep; witness went out, and deceased barred the door after him; returned and could not get the door opened; procured a fork and opened it, and when he went in, his father was hanging from the beam, quite dead.—*Belfast News-Letter.* (1844-08-17, 2:3)

3205. Marriage in High Life.—The nuptials of Lord Viscount Loftus, with Miss Hope Vere, will be solemnised with unusual splendour the ensuing month. The noble Viscount is eldest son of the Most Noble the Marquis of Ely, and heir to immense property in the county of Fermanagh and Wexford at the death of his noble father, which we trust may still be long protracted. (1844-08-17, 3:4)

3206. County of Monaghan.—House and Lands to Let.—To be Let,—For Seven Years from the first of November next,—The Dwelling House and Lands of

Ballymackney,

The Residence of the Late William Daniel, Esq., J.P.

Ballymackney is situate on the verge of the Counties of Monaghan and Louth, Two Miles from Carrick-macross, Eight from Dundalk, Seven from Ardee, and within 2-1/2 hours' drive of the Railway at Drogheda.

The House is modern, and in perfect repair, with ample accommodation for a large family, and having attached a handsome Lawn, Garden, and Orchard, with extensive Out-offices, consisting of Stables, coach-houses, Cattle-sheds for 80 head of Cattle, large Barn and Threshing-Mill, and every other requisite for a gentleman's country establishment.

The Farm comprises upwards of 70 Irish Acres of Prime Land, well fenced, planted, and watered, and in the highest condition, having been for the last several years cultivated on the most improved system of agriculture, with a plentiful supply of Meadow and Turbary of excellent quality and ease of access.

The Garden is large, in good order, and well stocked with all kinds of Fruit and Vegetables; and, in short, no pains or expense have been spared for many years, in making Ballymackney a desirable residence for a respectable family.

The Louth Fox Hounds and two packs of Harriers hunt regularly in the neighbourhood, and good Shooting and Fishing can be had on the Lands and in the adjoining River and Lakes.

Application may be made to Mr. Robert Geoghegan, Bank of Ireland, Dublin; Charles C. Gibson, Esq., 122 Lower Gardiner-street; and to Mr. John Thomas Holland, Carrickmacross, who will show the premises.

22d July, 1844.

(1844-08-17, 3:5)

3207. Fatal Occurrence.—On Thursday week, Mr. Patrick M'Kenna, of Maghera, grocer (father of Mr. John M'Kenna, fruiterer, Academy Street, Belfast), was returning from Magherafelt, where he had been for a load of timber, in company with his son. A cow which they were conveying home straying off the road, the son leaped off the cart, to bring her back. The old man observed that the horse began to be restive, and got off the cart. The horse started off, when Mr. M'Kenna was knocked down, and the wheel passed over him; he was killed on the spot. The son also suffered materially in endeavouring to extricate his father.—*Belfast News-Letter*. (1844-08-17, 3:5)

3208. Marriage in High Life.—The marriage of Captain R. Bernal, M.P. for Wycombe, and Miss Catherine Isabella Osborne, sole heiress of the late Sir Thomas Osborne, and daughter of Lady Osborne, was solem-nized on Tuesday at St. George's Church, Hanover-square, London. (1844-08-31, 1:4)

3209. Tragical Occurrence at Gughard.—(*From a Correspondent.*)—Situated about eight miles to the south-west of Tarbert, in the parish of Liselton, in this county, is a conical hill on a denomination of College property, called Gughard. The hill is about 200 yards from the base to the summit, which is surmounted by an ancient fort. On a lower position, at a distance of about a quarter of a mile towards the west, is another fort.—On Thursday last, as some men were raising stones at the foot of the hill in a line between the two forts, they came to a vertical aperture of about two feet square, like the entrance of a vault, and about six feet below the surface of the ground. On that day and Friday, some boys entered the opening, and having advanced for four or five feet, they returned in safety. On Saturday, a young lad named Bunnian, and a boy named Kennedy entered; they not returning as soon as was expected, the people outside became alarmed, and at length the tidings reached Kennedy's father, who was working at a lime-kiln at some short distance. The father hastened to the spot, and at once entered; but, not returning, three young men, named Hennessy, Coghlan and Sullivan, followed to seek for their friends. The day passed over, and night came on, and still none of the six persons appeared.

Yesterday (Sunday), thousands assembled at the fatal spot—several ineffectual attempts were made by the Roman Catholic curate and others to extricate the bodies, and at length about six o'clock, p.m., a power-ful young man named Bunnian, a distant relative of the first named person, headed a party of six, who entered. They proceeded through the narrow passage before described, and at a distance of a few feet were able to stand nearly erect; they thus advanced through four cellars, each about six feet long, connected in a circuitous direction by narrow apertures, the walls of the cellar being formed of grit-stone, overlapping each other. Having passed through these, the party reached a straight hall, about twelve feet long, at the end of which the leader (Bunnion [sic]) struck upon one of the bodies they were seeking. He proceeded to drag out the body, and the rest of the party were returning before him—but immediately after they heard the body drop from his hand, and himself fall on it, gasping in a state of suffocation. At this time, Lyons, one of the party, dropped, and Casey, another of them, succeeded in bringing him out alive. A second of the party was overpowered, and he was, likewise, saved by another. Poor Bunnian was lost.

Thus Sunday passed over—but to-day (Monday), the people dug down, over the place where the party who escaped lead them to suppose the bodies were, about thirty feet from the original entrance. They thus found the body of old Kennedy, with his arms clasping the body of his son, and near them the body of Bunnian, who entered with the latter.

The fresh air being admitted through the cellars, others entered and released the bodies (*continued...*)

3209, continued: ...of the other Bunnion, and Coghlan, Sullivan, and Hennessy. It was heartrending to see the widow Kennedy throw herself, in a state of distraction, on the coffins that contained the bodies of her husband and son, as they lay on the road in front of her cabin—they were her only support.

Coghlan and Sullivan were step-brothers, and their common mother is in her second widowhood, having survived both her husbands. The elder Bunnion also left a widowed mother to deplore his untimely end—she lost three daughters last year on their passage to America. Casey and the rest of the party who entered with him deserve to be rewarded for their exertions.

The property on which the disaster occurred is held under the College, by the representatives of the late Mr. Maxwell Blacker, Q.C.

A letter in the *Limerick Reporter* gives the following account of this sad affair:—"On Saturday last, as a man named Scanlan was raising earth on his land, at Gughard, about three miles from Ballybunion, County Kerry, he discovered the entrance to a subterraneous passage, which he entered, accompanied by two other persons, but a considerable time having elapsed without their reappearance, they were followed by six others, who went in for the purpose of bringing them out. Those, also, not appearing, the apprehensions of their friends, who were outside, became excited, and intimation of the circumstance having been conveyed to the Rev. Mr. Enright, C.C., he immediately repaired to the spot and entered the cavity with a view of rescuing those who preceded, but he had not gone far from the entrance, when he fell senseless under the noxious influence of the atmosphere, and was with difficulty brought to the surface. The alarm of the bystanders now became excessive, and further efforts having been made, three of those who had gone in were brought out apparently lifeless, but have since recovered. The scene at this time was heartrending, from the cries of the relatives of those who remained within, and this was further increased by the non-appearance of a man who ventured in in search of his son, against the entreaties of his friends. The Gunsboro' police were in attendance during the night, and succeeded in bringing out the bodies of four, amongst whom was the body of the man who went in search of his son, with the body of the latter clasped in his arms, having apparently perished in attempting to bring him out. Crowds of the country people having collected on yesterday, renewed exertions were made to discover the bodies of two persons still missing, and about five o'clock, three men having descended for the purpose, two returned in a state of exhaustion, leaving the third, who was unable to come with them, to share the fate of the others. A number of men are engaged in excavating the ground about twenty feet from the surface, hoping to reach the extremity of the cavern. This appears to be a work of great difficulty, as the opening is at the foot of a high bank on the side of a hill, and the passage leads downwards. Although the entrance is not more than two feet in diameter, the interior is lofty, and arched with masonry.—*Limerick Reporter*. (1844-08-31, 2:3)

3210. County Monaghan.—Important Sale of Stock, at Hilton, near Clones.—J.E. Jones Begs to announce to the Public, that he has received Instructions to submit to Public Competition at Hilton, late the residence of Colonel Madden, Deceased,—On Friday and Saturday, the 30th and 31st Days of August, at Eleven o'Clock,

The Valuable stock of Thorough-bred Durhams; Thorough-bred Colts and Fillies, by Bay Higham; Brood Mares; a Thorough-bred Entire Horse; Farm Horses; Brood Ewes and Lambs of the purest Leicester Breed; Fat Sheep and Pigs;—Farming Implements, &c., &c.

A thorough bred Bull of the purest Durham Blood rising 3 years.

4 thorough-bred Milch Cows, in calf to the aforesaid Bull;

4 thorough-bred Two-year-old Heifers;

8 do. Five-quarter-old do.

9 do. Weanling do.

11 Fat Heifers.

Horses—2 Two-year-old Colts, and 2 Two-year-old Fillies;

3 Yearling Fillies;

3 Brood Mares, high-bred (one thorough-bred) with Two Foals at foot.

Sheep—21 Brood Ewes and 19 Lambs;

13 Yearling Ewes;

23 Fat Sheep and a Three-year-old Ram.

Farming Implements; a Metal Roller and Frame; Threshing Machine, a Circular Saw and Frame; about 50 Dozen Sawn Ash Spade Shafts, &c., &c.

About 100 Meadow Cocks of Well-Saved Hay.

Terms, Cash—The Purchasers to pay the Auction Duties on such Stock as are subject to same.

Hilton, August 19, 1844.

(1844-08-31, 3:5)

3211. Melancholy Death of Captain Eliot.—We take the following particulars of this deplorable event from the *Athlone Sentinel*, omitting the copy of the verdict, as found by the jury, which, from its absurdity, ignorance of the simplest rules of grammar and ludicrous affectation of legal technicality, is calculated to throw a tinge of ridicule on even this lamentable affair:—

On Wednesday last, our town was thrown into a state of no inconsiderable excitement, in consequence of a report being rather prevalent that Captain Granville Heywood Eliot, of the 4th Dragoon Guards, and a small boy, his servant, of about twelve years of age, of the name of Curly, were drowned at the long island. Accordingly, one of the gun boats was immediately manned and repaired to the spot, accompanied by a number of small boats. After dragging the river for some time, the rumor turned out to be a sad reality. The first thing they succeeded in finding was the boat, which confirmed their worst fears and apprehensions. But they were not allowed long enough to remain in suspence [sic]; for within a few yards of where the boat was raised, both bodies were found, almost side by side, grasped in the strong arms of death. The bodies were lifted out of the water, put into the gun boat, and brought into town; but when they arrived at the canal, the sight was certainly such as to unman the stoutest heart. There could not have been less than 3,000 persons assembled on the banks of the canal, and their grief burst forth in loud exclamations. When the boats arrived at the canal harbor, the bodies were taken out and carried on a bier to the barracks, where the inquest was held by Mr. E. Lynch, coroner. The first witness examined was Keeran Mealy, who proved to having found two hats and a basket, which first gave rise to suspicion. Michael Dowling proved that when coming from Shannon Bridge, he met Healy [sic], who informed him that he found the hats and the baskets, and that he was present at the time the bodies were taken out of the water. Major Hodge stated that, when he was informed that two hats had been found convenient to the long island, and believing them to belong to the late Captain G.H. Eliot, and his boy, Pat Curly, he immediately repaired in a boat to the spot, and was present when the bodies were taken out of the water. This closed the evidence, and the jury, after a short deliberation, returned a verdict of accidental death.

The sequel of the melancholy catastrophe remains yet to be told. The father of the boy, on hearing the news of his death, became a prey to grief, whose ravages proved too much for the constitution of the poor old man, and he, on the morning of the next day, followed his son to that undiscovered country from whose bourne no traveller returns. He died breathing the name of his child, and his last convulsive effort was over his lifeless corpse!

We understood that the remains of Captain Eliot will be consigned to the tomb on Monday with all the military honors. He was a good and charitable man, and the voice of poverty always found in him a responsive echo. Captain Eliot was in the 29th year of his age, and was a rather well-looking man of about six feet high, of athletic frame, with considerable roundness, but not superfluous flesh. (1844-08-31, 4:4)

3212. Ante-Nuptial Experience.—A young lady offers the following serviceable and original rules for guidance of spinsters:—Before marriage it is necessary that a young woman should see her intended husband in four situations, viz.—1st, tipsy; 2dly, playing at cards and losing; 3dly, waiting for his dinner; and lastly, in a ball room. (1844-09-07, 3:2)

3213. On Thursday last, the children connected with the schools established and supported by the generous liberality of Charles P. Leslie, Esq., M.P., over his extensive property, were entertained at a sumptuous dinner in honour of his birth day by Mrs. Leslie. The tables were arranged in the Lawn, in the immediate vicinity of Glasslough-House; every accommodation was provided for the comfort of the youthful party, amounting to upwards of 620 in number. Mrs. Leslie, Miss Leslie, Lord and Lady John Beresford, Thomas Leslie, Esq., and the other members of the Glasslough family were most assiduous in their attentions to the children. The substantial fare consisted of Roast Beef and Plumb Pudding, &c.; it is pleasing to state that the children conducted themselves in the most orderly manner; and felt deeply gratified for the unremitting kindness of their beneficent hostess, and the other members of her family, on this joyful occasion. (1844-09-14, 2:1)

3214. Triennial Visitation of his Grace the Lord Primate.—On Tuesday last, his grace held a visitation of the Diocese of Clogher, in the church of this town. The attendance of clergy was numerous. Divine service was performed by the Rev. Wm. L. Roper, and the Rev. Henry Maffatt, after which his Grace delivered his charge, an abridgement of which we give as follows, copied from a report taken of the same charge at Armagh, and published in the *Newry Telegraph.*

His Grace commenced by explaining the change in the existing law which will be produced by the *Marriage Act* of the last sessions of Parliament, so far as the clergy will be affected thereby. A Surrogate is to receive seven days' notice from parties intending to be married, previous to his granting a license, a copy of which notice he is to enter in a book to be open for inspection; and he is also to forward a copy of the notice to the incumbent of the parish where the parties reside—or, if they reside in different parishes, to the incumbent of each. If the marriage shall not take place within three months after the notice has been given, the license that has been granted will be void. In addition to the three modes which heretofore existed of authorising marriages—namely, banns, special licenses, and licenses by a Surrogate—the recent statute has added a fourth—viz., a certificate from the registrar of the district. The lord lieutenant is empowered to appoint a registrar-general, under whom registrars are to be stationed in districts of convenient extent throughout the whole country. To these registrars, any parties intending to be married may give notice; and at the end of twenty-one days, if no objection to it be entered on the books of the registrar, he is to issue a certificate authorising the celebration of the marriage. If such a certificate be addressed to any clergyman, he is to receive it and act on it, as standing instead of the publication of banns, provided that his church is situated within the distance of the registrar who issued it. **.../**

3214, continued: ...His Grace then briefly adverted to the change of the law as regards Dissenters, and the power given them of celebrating marriages in certified places of worship, in the presence of a registrar, between eight and two o'clock; and the powers conferred on Presbyterian ministers of solemnising mixed marriages, where one of the parties is certified to have been a Presbyterian for a month previously; and he concluded this portion of his charge by expressing his confident hope that the act will put an effectual stop to the trade carried on in clandestine marriages, which has been such a fruitful source of unhappiness in many parts of the country. "The effecting of this desirable object," observed his grace, "was the principal design I had in view of the part which I took relating to the passing of this law." [*The Primate's charge continues, addressing such subjects as the dangers to which the Church is exposed at the present time, the attempts of the commissioners of national education to remove objections to their plan, and the Additional Curates' Fund Society.*] (1844-09-14, 3:2)

3215. To be Let,—In the County Monaghan.

Equity Exchequer.

William Rutherford, Esq. Plaintiff, Mrs. Grace Cottnam, widow, and others, Defendants.

Pursuant to the Order made in this cause bearing date the 14th day of June, 1844, I will, on Tuesday, the 1st Day of October next, at the Hour of One o'clock, in the Afternoon, at my Chambers, on the Inn's Quay, Dublin, Set up, and Let, to the highest and fairest Bidder, for Seven Years, pending this Cause, from the 1st of Nov. next, All That and Those, the Mansion-house and Demesne Lands of Minore, situate in the County of Monaghan, in the pleadings in this Cause, and in said Order mentioned, dated this 24th day of August, 1844.

For the Chief Remembrancer,

Wm. Hamilton, S.R.

The Demesne Lands are in Three Divisions, and will be let either separately or together; No. 1, with the House, containing 73A. OR. 18P., Statute Measure, with 1A. 1R. 28P. of Bog. No. 2 contains 59A. 3R. 4P., Statute Measure. No. 3 on the south side of the Road, from Drum to Cootehill, contains 64A. 2R. 2P., Statute Measure.

The Mansion is a most convenient and modern Edifice, built by the late Captain Cottnam, suited for a family of large or moderate means, commanding a fine view of Wood and Water, which requires to be seen to be justly appreciated. The Demesne is tastefully planted, situate 1/4 of a mile from Drum, 2-1/2 from Cootehill, 2 from Newbliss, and five from Clones. The Coach from Clones to Dublin passes daily within one Mile of the Gate.

For Further Particulars, apply to Samuel R. Moorehead, Esq., the Receiver, Lake-Lodge, Newbliss, or to Mr. Alexander Dudgeon, Attorney for the Plaintiff, and Receiver, 98, Talbot-street, Dublin, or Sterling-Lodge, Clones. (1844-09-14, 3:5)

3216. Frightful Case of Hydraphobia.—The *Castlebar Telegraph* contains the following melancholy statement:—About three months ago, a boy named Michael Colerare, aged twelve years, and son to a tenant of George Moore, Esq., Moore Hall, went out to herd some sheep that were grazing in his father's field at Millerhill, near the Abbey of Ballintubber. On getting into the field, the boy perceived a large dog attacking the sheep; he went to drive it off, but the dog, which was raging mad, flew at, and bit him in the hand. The boy instantly ran home and told his mother of the occurrence. She being under the impression that sea bathing would prevent any evil consequences, brought him without delay to the salt water, and besides making him bathe, caused him to drink of it plentifully. At length, the wound on his hand being healed, the boy and his mother returned home. There was no symptom of any bad effects from the bite, until last Sunday week, when the boy, while attending mass at the Abbey of Ballintubber, suddenly felt a thrilling sensation running from his hand to his shoulder, as if he had struck his elbow against the wall. The painful thrill continued to extend until it had soon spread itself over his entire frame. Then the boy became conscious himself that he was infected with hydraphobia; yet he was [at] intervals collected in his intellect, during which time he received from the Rev. Edward O'Malley the sacrament of confession. He told the clergyman that he could not endure the appearance of any liquid, he continued sensible for a long time, and told his mother he was aware he would soon die; that he would get violent, and to tie him, lest he should do any injury, but not to bleed him to death, as had been done in the village about twelve months previously to another person affected with hydraphobia. At length, the madness had reached its crisis, black froth and curdled blood foamed from his mouth, and he died in an awful paroxysm of violence and excitement. (1844-09-21, 2:3)

3217. On the Death of the Baroness Rossmore.

Angel of life! whose beatific wing
Shall ne'er be folded long as humankind
To this dark vale of sorrow is confined,
Still hovering o'er the homes of suffering!

Yonder, thy cloud-dispelling pinions fling,
Seek those mysterious solitudes assigned
Unto the mourner's melancholy mind,
And say that to the just, Death peace doth bring.

In sign, whereof, this votal wreath present,
Twined for the wan brow of the noble dead,
Of dewy cypress with green olive blent.

This token take, that they who now do shed
Tears, bitter tears, no longer may lament
To yield their lost a prize to Him who bled.

(1844-09-21, 3:2)

3218. Notice.—All Persons indebted to the late Wm. Thompson, deceased, are requested to settle with his Executors, Messrs. Samuel Armstrong and James Taylor, forthwith, otherwise they will be obliged to take legal proceedings.

John Mitchell, Proctor for the Executors.

18th Sept., 1844.

(1844-09-21, 3:4)

3219. Notice.—Notice is hereby given that Letters of Administration, with Will annexed, of Robert Hill, late of Errerow, in this County, Gentleman, deceased, have been granted to his Widow, Mrs. Jane Hill, from her Majesty's Court of Prerogative. All persons indebted to his Estate are requested to make immediate payments; and those having claims against said Estate, to present them properly authenticated.

Monaghan, 16th September, 1844.

John Mitchell, Proctor for the Administratrix.

(1844-09-21, 3:4)

3220. Rumoured Death of the Marquis of Donegall.—A report was very generally circulated in town yesterday forenoon, that the Marquis of Donegall, whose health for some time past has been such as to preclude all hopes of its re-establishment, had died in the course of the morning at Ormeau. It soon became known that the rumour was unfounded, and that his lordship, though still alarmingly ill, was not worse than for some days past. It is, however, to be feared that an event which would be a subject of universal regret, not in Belfast alone, but throughout the entire of the north of the Ireland, is not far distant.—*Banner of Ulster*. (1844-09-28, 2:2)

3221. Motive to Matrimony.—A young lady, who was lately led to the altar from a boarding-school, confessed that she had become a wife in order that she might be at liberty to lie in bed as long as she pleased in the morning, and have buttered toast for breakfast and sugar in her tea! (1844-09-28, 2:2)

3222. On Saturday last, the 21st inst., an old woman of the name of Jane Mills, (who was under treatment as a lunatic for some time previously,) hanged herself with a handkerchief, from the uppermost tranverse bar of a gate in the interior of the prison of this town. An inquest was holden before R. Murray, Esq., M.D., coroner, in view of the body, when the following verdict was returned, "hanged herself while labouring under mental derangement." (1844-09-28, 3:1)

3223. Suicide.—A man named Morris, who was a servant in the employ of an English clergyman, residing in Hume-street, put an end to his life on Tuesday last, in Quinne's-lane, off Pembroke-street, by taking a dose of oxalic acid. It appeared at the inquest that the deceased was about 50 years of age, and had lived with the gentleman to whom we have referred in the capacity of a coachman. The family returned to England some time ago, and owing to some misconduct on the part of the deceased, his master took another servant out to the carriage. The deceased was so annoyed at this circumstance, that he went into a public-house, kept by a person named Cullen, took the poison in a glass of punch, and died in two hours afterwards. The deceased fought at the battle of Waterloo, and was a man of general good character. A verdict was returned in accordance with these facts. (1844-09-28, 3:1)

3224. County Tyrone.—Auction at Killishiel Glebe House.

J.E. Jones—Begs to announce to the Public, that he has been favoured with Instructions to submit to Public Competition, at Killishiel Glebe House,—Late the Residence of the Rev. J. Young, Deceased,—On Monday, 14th October next, and following Days, at Eleven o'Clock, all his

Household Furniture,—Which are of the Best Description, in Good Order, and High Preservation.

Beautiful Specimens of Colored Prints, Drawings, and Original Oil Paintings, by Copley, Laport, Moncheran and Both, in Massive Rich Carved, Gilt and Burnished Frames. A Large Sized Brilliant Chimney-Glass, in Gilt and Burnished Frame; a Convex Mirror for Four Lights; Chandeliers; Sets of Dinner, Dessert, Morning and Evening Rich Colored Stone China; Plain and Rich Cut Glass; Brass-framed Hexagon Hall Lantern; a Patent Mangle and Shower Bath.

A Green-House Complete,—with a Splendid Variety of Plants and Exotics in Pots; Dahlias in Wood and Iron Frames; a Sundial on Stone Pillar.

The Furniture Comprising

In the Drawing-room.—A Grecian Sofa and Cover; Eight Chairs, and Four Arm-Chairs to Match; Two Indulging Chairs; Two Blue Satin Moreen Window Curtains and fittings; A Mahogany Loo-Table on Pillar; a Sofa-Table; a Brussels Carpet and Hearthrug; A Brilliant Chimney-Glass; a Convex Mirror; a Pier Cabinet; a Chandelier; a set of Chimney Ornaments; a Brass Fender and Fire-Irons.

In the Dining Parlor.—A Mahogany Celaret Sideboard; a set of Trafalgar extending Dining Tables; Twelve Mahogany Chairs, in Satin Hair Cloth; two Arm Chairs to match, a Guardi-vin Complete; Two Dumbwaiters; a Tray Stand; Two Scarlet Moreen Window Curtains, and Fittings; a Chandelier; Carpet and Hearthrug; Oil Cloth; Brass Fender and Fire Irons.

Breakfast Parlor or Study.—Two Mahogany Occasional Tables; Six Mahogany Chairs; a Mahogany Washtable; a Tea store; Two Scarlet Moreen Window Curtains; a Brussels Carpet and Hearthrug; Three Large Glazed Library Book-cases; Brass Fender and Fire-Irons.

A Hall Oilcloth; a Large Mahogany Table; Six painted Hall Chairs; an Eight Day Clock.

Stair-Carpeting and Brass Rods.

In the Bedrooms.—Superior Fourpost Bedsteads, with strong Reeded Pillars and Deep Footboards, with Satin Moreen hangings and Fittings; (*continued...*)

3224, continued:...Eliptic and Waggon Roofed do., with Chintz hangings, Prime Featherbeds and bedding; Pure Curled hair Mattresses and Palyasses; Mahogany Dressing tables and Toilet glasses; Wash tables and Toilet delph; Commodes and Biddets, Mahogany Wardrobes; a Mahogany Sloping desk and Glazed Bookcase; a Mahogany Secretary; Bedroom Chairs, Window Curtains, Carpets, hearth-rug, Fire-irons and Fenders.—Servants' Bedsteads and Hangings; Feather-Beds and bedding; a Linen Screw Press; House-Presses; Pantry, Dairy, and Kitchen Requisites; a Large Patent Kitchen Range.

In Calf Durham Milch Cows and 2-year-Olds; Yearlings and Wainling Heifers; a Brown Carriage Horse; Two Farm-Horses; a Gig with Patent Axles; an Outside Jaunting Car and Harness; Three Large Pikes of Hay; 15 Stacks of Oats; 4 Large Stacks of Turf; 5 Acres of Potatoes and 2 Acres of Turnips; Farming Implements; an Iron Plough, Harrow, Dril-plough, and Dril-harrow, and Turnip-barrow; Stone and Wood Rollers; about Nine Tons Oral or best Wiggin Coals.

Ladders, Barrows, Garden Tools, &c., &c.

Terms Cash—and the Purchasers to Pay the Auction Duties.

Killieshiel Glebe House,
September 28th, 1844.
(1844-09-28, 3:2)

3225. Equity Exchequer.—Wm. Rutherford, Esq., Plaintiff,—Mrs. Grace Cottnam, Widow, and others, Defendants.—Pursuant to the Decree made in this cause, bearing date the 19th day of June, I hereby require all Creditors and Legatees of Thomas Cottnam, deceased, in the pleadings named, and all persons having charges or incumbrances affecting the real and Freehold Estate of the said Thomas Cottnam, to come before me at my Chambers on the Inn's-quay, Dublin, on or before the 21st day of October next, and prove their respective demands; otherwise, they will be precluded the benefit of said Decree.

Dated 24th day of August, 1844.
For the Chief Remembrancer,
W. Hamilton, S.R.
Alexander Dudgeon, Plaintiff's Attorney,
98, Talbot-street.
(1844-09-28, 3:2)

3226. Mr. Ambrose (health guard officer on board of the *Norfolk*, from Renkin) was found dead in his berth on board the vessel on Monday morning. He retired to rest at half-past ten the night before in perfect health. —*Cork Constitution*. (1844-10-05, 1:6)

3227. A man named Murphy, on Monday, was killed by a stallion, near Kill, county Waterford. The man was turning off the high road into the field, to make a short cut, though advised to turn back, or else he might be killed by a wild horse he should have to pass. Fatally for himself, he trod the forbidden ground. In four hours after, his body was found torn to pieces. The horse's hoofs and mouth were incrusted with the blood of his victim. (1844-10-05, 1:6)

3228. Melancholy and Fatal Accident.—On Wednesday last, a respectable old woman, of the name of Eliza Soraghan, (who had been confined to bed for twelve months previous,) had her brains dashed out, by falling on the paving, from a garret window, three stories high, in her son's house, in Park-street in this town. The unfortunate woman, it appears, was laboring under mental derangement when she met with the sad and fatal accident. (1844-10-05, 2:5)

3229. Funeral of Lady Heytesbury.—Nothing has been as yet definitively ascertained, nor we believe, decided upon with respect to the funeral arrangements of this lamented lady. Immediately after her Ladyship's demise on Sunday last, a special messenger was despatched with the melancholy intelligence to England, until whose return no measures, preparatory to the conveyance of the remains from this country to the family burying-place, will be adopted. We may mention, however, on authority that the funeral, which is expected to take place towards the end of the week, will be strictly private. To Mr. Williams, of Stafford-street, has been entrusted the duties of undertaker on the occasion.—*Freeman's Journal*.

The time for the performance of the last sad obsequies of the lamented deceased is not yet definitely fixed, but the funeral will take place on either Saturday or Monday morning. It will be strictly private, and her Ladyship's remains will be conveyed to the family vault at Heytesbury, there to be interred. An Admiralty steamer has arrived in Kingstown Harbour to convey the body to Bristol. His Excellency the Lord Lieutenant, his brother, and son, will proceed by the same conveyance.—*Saunders*. (1844-10-12, 2:4)

3230. Death of Admiral Sir J. Poo Beresford, Bart., K.C.B., and G.C.H.—This distinguished flag officer expired on Wednesday evening last, at the Hall, Bedale, Yorkshire, after a protracted illness.

The deceased Admiral Sir J. Poo Beresford, Bart., was born in 1769, and was the illegitimate son of George, first Marquess of Waterford, and brother of Viscount Beresford. He married three times—first to Mary, daughter of Captain A.J. Pye Molloy, R.N., who died July, 1813, by whom he had issue an only son, Captain George Beresford, Bart.; secondly, the 17th of August, he married Miss Henrietta Peirse, of Bedale, Yorkshire, and by that lady, who died in 1825, he had issue two sons and four daughters. Sir John married, thirdly, 26th of May, 1836, Amelia, daughter of the late Mr. James Baillie, uncle of Colonel Hugh Bailie, M.P., and widow of Mr. Samuel Peach.

Sir John at an early age entered the navy, as the date of his entry is in the year 1782.

1796, then Captain Beresford, while commanding the *Lynx* sloop, he captured *La Cocarde*, of 14 guns; and, when captain of the *Raison*, fought a gallant action with the French frigate *Vengeance*. He assisted at the capture of the Islands of Bartholomew, St. Martin,

&c. in 1801. He commanded the *Theseus* at the attack on the enemy's fleet at Aix roads. In 1813 and the earlier part of 1814, he was actively employed on the American station, then in comand of the *Poietiers*, and by the indefatigable zeal he displayed in that particular service, he rendered considerable protection to our commercial enterprises in that part of the world.

His naval commissions were dated as follows:—Lieutenant, November 4, 1790; Commander, July 6, 1794; Captain, July 25, 1795; Rear-Admiral, June 4, 1804; Vice-Admiral, June 28, 1838.

In August, 1819, he was nominated a Knight Commander of the Most Honorable Order of the Bath; and subsequently, in May, 1836, was nominated by the late King of Knight Grand Cross of the Royal Hanoverian Guelphic Order.

By the demise of this estimable and much-regretted Baronet, the families of the Archbishop of Armagh, Viscount and Viscountess Beresford, the Marquess and Marchioness of Waterford, Viscount and Lady Sarah Ingestre, the Hon. Mr. and Mrs. Kenyon, Mr. and Mrs. Dunbar, Lord Decies, Lord and Lady John Beresford, &c., are placed in mourning. (1844-10-12, 2:4)

3231. Death of the Marquess of Donegall.—It is this day our melancholy duty to announce the demise of the most noble the Marquess of Donegall. His lordship has been for some time in a declining state of health, and his medical attendants having recommended sea air, he resided during the summer in the beautiful cottage near Cultra, lately occupied by the Dowager Countess of Dufferin. During the last few weeks he was sinking fast, and on the 21st ult. he was removed to Ormeau, where he expired on Saturday morning last at three o'clock.

His lordship, George Augustus Chichester, Marquess of Donegall, (Viscount Fisherwick, in England,) Lieutenant of the county of Donegall, Knight of St. Patrick, &c., was born in 1769, and was consequently in the seventy-sixth year of his age. He is succeeded in his title and estates by his eldest son, the Earl of Belfast, Lieutenant of the county of Antrim.

The mortal remains of the late Marquess, will, we understand, be removed for interment in the family vault at Carrickfergus church, on Monday the 14th inst.—*Belfast Chronicle*. (1844-10-12, 2:4)

3232. Effects of the Storm of Wednesday Night.—A violent storm from the S.S.E. has prevailed during the last two days, and last night it blew with terrible severity, almost equalling the memorable gale of January, 1839. An immensity of damage to property has been caused in this city and its vicinity, and, we regret to add, the loss of life has also been great. The tide in the river Liffey has not risen to a similar height for the last twenty years, the flood being several inches deep on the roads and pathways of the quays, and the adjoining streets.

The damage done to the shipping in the river has been unusually extensive. In Halpin's Pool, a place of shelter for vessels, situate at the extreme end of the North wall, several ships were injured, and one, the *Thistle*, of Wick, with a full cargo of oats, was completely sunk, having first been dashed with much violence against the jetty as to do considerable damage to that massive work. The following vessels were driven ashore:—*The Good Hope of Wales*; the *Falcon* of Dublin; the *Volunteer* of Dublin; all of which were materially injured. The *Shannon* steamer, lying at anchor in the pool, was driven from her moorings bow foremost against the patent slip, when her larboard paddle-box and wheel were carried away.

The island of Clontarf, well known as a bathing place, was completely covered, and an unfortunate man named Cromwell, with his son, who resided in a small house on the island, were swept away by the resistless flood.—Not a vestige of the building now remains; and such was the fury of the waves that the bed of the unfortunate couple was washed up on the Clontarf high road. (1844-10-12, 3:1)

3233. Hydrophobia.—An awful case of hyrdrophobia occurred at Marshalstown last week. There had been a pig, belonging to a Mrs. Coffey, bitten by a rabid dog; the pig was killed, and a cat in the house ate part of the entrails; the cat a short time after bit Mrs. Cyffey [sic] and her daughter—the melancholy result was the death of both last week from the dire malady.—*Cork Constitution*. (1844-10-19, 1:6)

3234. Poetry.—The very beautiful lines we this day present to our readers are extracted from a volume of early poems by our celebrated countryman, Doctor Anster. There is in them more than the promise of that genius which has since made the name of their author renowned among the poets of Europe. We spare the reader the unnecessary formality of further introduction:—

Elegy.

Oh, breathe not—breathe not—sure, 'twas something holy.
Earth had no sounds like these. Again it passes
With a wild low voice, that slowly rolls away,
Leaving a silence not unmusical!
And now again the wind-harp's frame hath felt
The spirit like the organ's richest peal
Rolls the long murmur; and again it comes,
That wild, low, wailing voice.
These sounds to me
Bear record of strange feelings. It was evening,
And this same instrument lay on my window,
That the sighing breezes there might visit it.
I then did love to leave my lonely heart,
Like this soft harp, the plaything of each impulse,
The sport of every breath. I sate alone,
Listening for many minutes. The sounds ceased,
Or, though unnoted by the idle ear, (*continued...*)

3234, continued:

Were mingling with my thoughts. I thought of one,
And she was of the dead: she stood before me,
With sweet sad smile, like the wan moon at midnight,
Smiling in silence on a world at rest.
I rushed away; I mingled with the mirth
Of the noisy many. It is strange that night,
With a light heart, with light and lively words,
I sported hours away; and yet there came
At time wild feelings—words will not express them;
But it seemed that a chill eye gazed upon my heart;
That a wan cheek, with sad smile, upbraided me.
I felt that mirth was but a mockery;
Yet I was mirthful.

I lay down to sleep:
I did not sleep—I could not choose but listen;
For o'er the wind-harp's strings the spirit came
With that same sweet low voice. Yes thou mayest smile;
But I must think, my friend, as then I thought,
That the voice was hers whose early death I mourned;
Which like a spell possessed the soul.
I lay
Wakeful, the prey of many feverish feelings,
My thoughts were of the dead! At length I slept—
If it indeed were sleep. She stood before me
In beauty the wan smile had passed away—
The eye was bright—I could not bear its brightness.

Till not I knew not death was terrible,
For seldom did I dwell upon the thought;
And if in some wild moment, fancy shaped
A world of the departed, 'twas a scene
Most calm and cloudless; as if clouds at times
Stained the blue quiet of the still soft sky,
They did not dim its charm, but suited well
The stillness of the scene, like thoughts that move
Silently o'er the soul, or linger there,
Shedding a tender twilight pensiveness!

This is an idle song! I cannot tell
What charms were hers who died. I cannot tell
What grief is theirs whose spirits weep for her!
Oh, many were the mockeries of prayer,
And many were the agonies of hope,
And many a heart, that loved the weak delusion,
Looked forward for the rosy smiles of health;
And many a rosy smile passed o'er that cheek,
Which will not smile again; and the soft tinge
That often flushed across that fading face,
And made the stranger sigh, with friends would wake
A momentary hope—even the calm tone
With which she spoke of those whom most she mourned
To leave, and when thought clear calm tears the eye
Shone with unwonted light, oh, was there not
In its rich sparkle something that forbade
The fear of death?—and when in life's last days
The same gay spirit that in happier hours
Had charactered her countenance, still gleamed
On the sunk features—when such playful words
As once could scatter gladness on all hearts
Still trembled from the lip, and o'er the souls
Of those who listened shed a deeper gloom
In hours of such most mournful gaiety,
Oh, was there not, even then, a lingering hope,
That flitted fearfully, like parent birds
Fast fluttering o'er their desolate nest?
Mourn not for her who died! She lived as saints
Might pray to live; she died as Christians die.
There was no earthward struggle to the heart,
No shuddering terror, no reluctant sigh.
They who beheld her dying fear not death!
Silently—silently the spoiler came,
As sleep steals o'er the senses unperceived,
And the last thoughts, that soothed the waking soul,
Mingle with our sweet dreams. Mourn not for her!

Oh, who art thou, that with weak words of comfort
Wouldst bid the mourner not to weep?—wouldst win
The cheek of sorrow to a languid smile?
Thou dost not know with what a pious love
Grief dwells upon the dead!—thou does not know
With what a holy zeal grief treasures up
All that recalls the past! when the dim eye
Rolls objectless around—thou does not know
What forms are floating o'er the mourner's soul!
Thou does not know with what a soothing art
Grief that rejects man's idle consolations,
Makes to itself companionable friends
Of all that charmed the dead: her robin still
Seeks at the wonted pane his morning crumbs,
And surely not less dear for the low sigh
His visit wakes!—and the tame bird, who loved
To follow with gay wing her every step,
Who oft in playful fits of mimicry,

Echoed her song, is dearer for her sake!
The wind, that from the hawthorn's dewy blossoms
Brings fragrance, breathes of her!—the moral lay
That last she loved to hear, with deeper charm
Speaks to her spirit now—even these low notes
Breathed o'er her grave will sink into the soul,
A pensive song, that memory will love
In pensive moments.

Mourners is there not
An angel that illumes the house of mourning?
The spirit of the dead—a holy image,
Shrined in the soul—for ever beautiful,
Undimmed with earth—its tears—its weaknesses
And changeless as within the exile's heart
The picture of his country—there no clouds.
Darken the hills—no tempest sweeps the vale
And the loved forms he never more must meet
Are with him in the vision, fair as when,
Long years ago, they clasped his hands at parting.
(1844-10-26, 4:1)

3235. Melancholy Accident—Death of John Walsh, Esq.—It is with feelings of the most unfeigned sorrow that we have this day to record the death of John Walsh, Esq., barrister-at-law. This melancholy event, which has plunged in the deepest affliction the numerous circle of friends to whom the lamented gentleman was endeared by his amiable qualities, occurred on Saturday last under circumstances of a character peculiarly painful and distressing. Having been engaged during the early portion of the day in the discharge of his professional avocations at the Insolvent Court, Strand-street, he quitted the court about twelve o'clock, accompanied by his favourite dogs, two fine animals of the Newfoundland breed, for the purpose of taking a walk in the country—a recreation to which he was greatly attached. He proceeded as was his usual practice, in the direction of the Royal Canal, and at half-past one or twenty minutes to two o'clock, was observed by Police-constable Rendle, 83 D, who was on duty to the immediate vicinity of the Tolka-bridge, which lies, as our readers will remember, in a valley to the right of the canal outside the city, and is distant about an English mile from the village of Phibsborough. The constable was standing on some high pasture lands which overhang the bridge, and from that position saw a gentleman, who was accompanied by two dogs, cross the bridge. This gentleman who from appearance he immediately supposed it to be Mr. Walsh—though the distance between them was too great to admit of identifications by features—turned into the valley on the right which lies in the direction of Finglas, and was walking leisurely with his dogs by the side of the river Tolka, when he was lost to the constable's view. The constable had not proceeded many yards upon his beat when his attention was challenged by a scream, and turning his eyes in the direction of the river, he saw a man's head above the surface of the water—his hands were lifted to his eyes—his hat was floating on the stream, and the dogs were howling on the shore. The constable ran down the valley with all possible expedition, but before he had reached the spot, the unfortunate gentleman had sunk, never again to rise a living man. The place into which he fell is a quarry-hole, or, more properly speaking, an enormous pit of from 60 to 80 feet in depth, which lies in the bed of the river elsewhere shallow and insignificant, and the exact situation of the spot will be understood by those who are conversant with the locality, when it is stated that it lies immediately opposite to the residence of Captain Mackenzie (or Marenzie,) in the valley leading to Finglas wood. The general impression, and that which would appear to be the most favored by probability, is that one of the dogs was swimming in the quarry-hole, and that Mr. Walsh, in stooping over the bank for the purpose of lifting him out of the water, lost his footing, and was precipitated into the pit. The bank is exceedingly steep and slippery, sinking abruptly within half-a-yard of the shore to the enormous depth already stated, but had the lamented gentleman been able to swim, he might possibly have saved himself, as a few strokes would have brought him to the other side, where the bank being level, a landing could be easily effected. The constable who, arriving on the spot, found Mr. Walsh's umbrella lying on the bank, lost no time in giving the alarm. A large group of villagers and several of the police force crowded to the scene of the tragic event, and boats were procured with as much expedition as possible, under the circumstances, for the purpose of having the river dragged; but more than two hours and a half elapsed before the body was discovered. When at length it was drawn up, and that the worst apprehensions as to the identity of the deceased were confirmed, it is impossible to conceive anything more heart-rending than the anguish endured by his friends and relatives who had assembled on the shore to witness the mournful sight. He was attired in a black frock, light tweed trousers, velvet waiscoat, and white neckcloth. A considerable sum of money was discovered in his pockets, and his watch, which was held by a gold guard, was found safe in his waiscoat fob. It had stopped at ten minutes to two o'clock. The body was conveyed to the cottage of a peasant resident in the neighbourhood.

Mr. Walsh was a zealous and eloquent advocate, and enjoyed an excellent reputation as a criminal lawyer. His practice was becoming every day more extensive, and his professional emoluments, particularly during the last three years of his life, must have been very great. He descends to his premature grave honored and lamented by all who had the pleasure of his acquaintance.—He was formerly a very leading member of the Trades Union, and subsequently edited a weekly paper called the *People*; during that period, he suffered six months imprisonment for a political offence; latterly he took no part in politics, and when going to the fatal place from whence he never returned alive, he gave one shilling and six pence in charity to a little girl who was working in an adjoining field; after the body was taken up, the object of his benevolence wept bitterly over the remains of her benefactor. It appears he had a great dread of water, and was most sensibly affected by the late calamity at the island on the north wall.

The Inquest.—Shortly after five o'clock, when the body was recovered, Dr. M'Carthy, senior coroner of the county, arrived and, having selected the following respectable jury, proceeded to hold the inquest:—John A. Curran, Esq., foreman; Thomas Carr, Charles Arabin, Bartholomew Scully, Daniel Nolen, John Fergusson, Bartholomew Josephs, James M'Cabe, George Carolin, Michael Kearney, James Markey, Peter M'Kenna, John Dillon, Alexander Dunne, Laurence Fottrell, and Peter Hickey, Esqrs.

The jury having viewed the body, retired to the "Brian Boroihme" public-house, near the (*continued...*)

3235, continued: ...turnpike at Glasnevin, when the following evidence was given:—On this day, I saw a man in a quarry hole near Finglass. At first, I heard dogs barking shortly after two o'clock in the afternoon. The man seemed standing up in the water with his hands towards his forehead, and his head partly over the water. Heard his shout once or twice. He remained in that position for three minutes. I called men from an adjoining field to come, saying I thought there was some person drowning. I went to the quarry as quick as possible. The body had disappeared before I got to the other side. The quarry is some perches in breadth. There was a hat floating on the water, and an umbrella on the weeds of the adjoining bank near where the body was found. The umbrella was lying up against the bank. One of the men who was called came up in a moment. Saw children near the place, about 40 or 50 perches from the quarry. The eldest of the children was about 13 years of age. Did not see any person pass from the quarry.—The inquest was then adjourned. When the jury had been discharged for the night, the remains were placed in a shell, and conveyed to Dominick-street, where a great number of professional and other respectable persons had assembled to condole with the family of the deceased on their irreparable loss.

The adjourned inquest on the body of the late Mr. Walsh was held yesterday evening, about seven o'clock, at the Brian Boroihme Tavern, Glasnevin, before Doctor M'Carthy, the senior coroner of the county.

The same jury as on the previous occasion having been sworn,

The police constable who was examined on the previous occasion having no further evidence to give,

Mr. Curran begged to ask the constable some questions as an impression had gone abroad that the police man had not done all he might have done to save Mr. Walsh under the circumstances.

Police Constable Joseph Rudden 83 D deposed.—I was at the Dublin side of the pond when I saw the person in the water. He was at the opposite side. To the best of my opinion, there was a distance of fifty perches between us. The men whom I saw digging potatoes were in a field beyond me. I went down by the bridge. I had then to turn back and go an opposite direction from where I then stood. It was about twenty perches from the bridge. It took me about three or four minutes to go to the side of the pond.

By another Juror.—When I first saw Mr. Walsh, he appeared about six or seven yards from the bank.

Matthew Donnellan sworn and examined.—I was called by policeman 83 D on Saturday last to assist in taking a body out of the water. I went as fast as I could, but the policeman was before me. I saw deceased a short time before this. He was standing at a gate near where I was at work, and had two dogs with him. There was no noise except the noise of the dogs barking.

Peter Donnelly being sworn, deposed to the same effect as the previous witness, and testified that no one could have acted better than the policeman did.

Mr. Curran said he had seen the policeman after the circumstance had taken place, and no one could have acted with greater feeling.

The jury returned a verdict, "that the deceased had died by accidental drowning." (1844-10-26, 4:4)

3236. Body Found.—The body of the boy, Hugh Dykes, who lost his life at the North Wall, on the night of the storm, was picked up on Sunday by the police near where the bodies of poor Cromwell and his son were found. (1844-11-02, 1:2)

3237. The Tracey Peerage.—On Monday last, an inquiry was held at Castlebrack church yard, before Captain Tibeaudo, George Newcombe, J.W. Tarleton, and Samuel Sheane, Esqrs., magistrates, relative to the genuineness of the tombstone, by which James Tracey, Esq., proves his title to his long disputed peerage; and which the House of Lords decided in his favour, subject to their proving of this stone. A great number of respectable people attended to give evidence, as well as to hear such a novel inquiry. Mr. John Rafter, a stone-cutter and builder, proved that the four pieces of stone produced must have originally been in one—they all corresponding with the grain, breaks, and letters, when laid together closely to form one stone—and it was his opinion that the said stone was the original one belonging to the family, placed there as a tombstone; in which other witnesses also concurred, and signed declarations to that effect.—*Leinster Express*. (1844-11-09, 1:3)

3238. On Wednesday, a fatal occurrence took place at Hillsborough. Two boys, named Kelly and Collins, aged respectively ten and eight years, were sent by a spirit dealer to the excise officer on duty at the distillery for permits; and while there they, without having been perceived, drank a quantity of impure spirits, called feints. Shortly after they were both taken ill, and the younger of the two died the same evening. An inquest was held by B. Ward, Esq., coroner, and the following verdict was returned, viz.: "That the deceased came to his death by drinking a large quantity of spirits at the Hillsborough distillery. That neither the proprietors nor any person in their employment were blameable, the spirits having been at the time in charge of the excise officer." The jury, at the same time, unanimously expressed their opinion that no blame could possible be attributed to the officer.—*Whig*. (1844-11-09, 1:4)

3239. Two statues have been erected in Enniskillen church at either side of the communion table, to the memory of John Willoughby Cole, late Earl of Enniskillen, and his brother, General Sir Galbraith Willoughby Cole, Colonel of the 27th Regiment. (1844-11-09, 1:4)

3240. Auction.—J.E. Jones Respectfully Begs to Announce to the Public that he has received Instructions to submit to Public Competition,—On Tuesday, 12th November, and following Days, at Eleven o'clock, —At Castleblayney Hotel, late the residence of Mr. James Rule, deceased—all his

Household Furniture,—House Linens; Plate; Plated-ware; China; Delph and Glass; an Eight-day Clock; Hall, Yard and Portico Lamps; Mangle, and every Requisite necessary for such an Establishment.

Three Post Chaises and 4 Post Cars; Single and Double sets of Harness; with Leading Harness and Postillion Saddles; 13 Post Horses and a Cart Horse, all in Good Working Order; 14 Fat Cows; 4 in-calf Milch Cows; 3 Yearling and 3 Wainling Bullocks and Heifers; 4 Ewes; 4 Wedders and 9 Pigs.

Eight large Pikes of Prime Hay, 14 Large Stacks of Excellent Oats; about 2 Acres of Potatoes; a large Stack of Turf, and a Large Houseful of the best do., 3 Farm Carts and Harness; an Iron Plough; Single and Double Harrows and a Winnowing Machine; Winnow Cloth and Sacks; a Water Cart and Vessel, with several Washstands; Several sets of Old Chaise, Jaunting Car Wheels, Springs and Harness; a Large Oatbin; a very Good Long Ladder, and several other do., Box and Turf Barrows, &c.

Also That Farm of Land, (in the most improved condition) in—Drumcrew and Conaberry—adjoining the Town, containing 30A. 3R. 25P. Irish Plantation Measure, held by Lease, (for two good lives in being) under the Hon. Lord Blayney, at the Yearly Rent of 52*l*. 6s. 6d., including Tithe Composition.

The Cattle, Crop, and Farming Implements, at Twelve o'clock on Thursday, the 14th inst., and the interest in the Lease of Drumcrew, and Conaberry, on Friday the 15th, at One o'clock.

Terms Cash—and the Purchasers to pay the Auction duties on such articles as are subject to same. Castleblayney, Nov. 2, 1844. (1844-11-09, 3:2)

3241. Eptihalamium,
On the Marriage of Lord Viscount Loftus
with Miss Hope Vere.
By Thomas R.J. Polson.

Happy spirits, light and gay,
Trip it round the world away,
Full of mirth and full of play;
This is Loftus' bridaly day!
On the golden solar ray,
On the ocean's silvr'y spray;
Happy spirits, light and gay,
Trip it round the world away.
Guardian spirits hid from sight,
Full of beauty, full of light,
Chase the shadows of the night,
Make it beautiful and bright,
Lull them, wrapp'd in sweet delight,
To sweet dreams of fancy's height;
And may virtue, spotless queen
Of purity, adorn the scene;
Sitting with angelic mien,
Soul-enchanting, look serene;
May the graces smiling there,
Greet the happy bridal pair!
What is life without a ray
Of fond hope to cheer one's way?
But as wild as 'twere o'ergrown
But as wild plants at random sown,
By the winds—borne from afar,
Wafted on Borea's car;
Where there's not a flow'r to please,
To throw its fragrance on the breeze;
Where there's nought to give a zest
To relieve the anxious breast.
Welcome hope, then, to attend,
And be life's familiar friend.
Happy spirits, light and gay,
Round the world now haste away;
Guardian angels full of light,
Round the earth now take a flight;
Trip it lightly, trip it gay,
This is Loftus' bridal day:
Hope will be his constant friend,
Hope will all his ways attend.

Oct. 20, 1844.
(1844-11-09, 4:1)

3242. Results of Tight Lacing.—We regret to learn that a painful and unexpected affliction has fallen upon the family of a respectable citizen. The particulars, as we have heard them, are as follow:—In the early part of the week, his daughters were taking a walk on the Upper Road, when one of the young ladies suddenly complained of illness, and on being assisted into an adjoining house, symptoms of rupture of a blood vessel became apparent. She was immediately conveyed to her father's residence, when medical aid and skill was at once brought into effect, but we are concerned to hear that the young lady still continues seriously and dangerously indisposed.—*Cork Reporter*. (1844-11-09, 4:4)

3243. The Late Storm.—On Saturday morning, during the tremendous gale which continued with unabated violence from the previous evening, a steamer was totally lost off Lambay, and all hands, we regret to say, perished.

Dalkey.—The storm was experienced here with much severity, and caused great and wide-spread injury to the roofs, windows, and chimneys of houses contiguous to the shore. The large protecting wall in front of Loretto House Convent was wholly washed away, and a metal railing, which ran for several hundred feet into the sea in a continuous line from the wall, was, notwithstanding that it was firmly fastened in the works, shattered in pieces. The windows of Mr. Richardson's house were nearly all smashed. **.../**

3243, continued: ...Killiney.—At this place, too, the storm raged with considerable power, and committed ravages similar to those described as having occurred at Dalkey. On Saturday, some firkins of butter and a dead pig were found on the strand, and on Sunday, we were shown a piece of plank driven in by the sea in the course of that morning. It bore the letters M A R, and evidently belonged to some ill fated vessel. Immediately following the R, there appeared either the lower part of an E or an L, but here all clue to further surmise was lost. (1844-11-09, 4:5)

3244. Remedy for Sea Sickness.—The following is a very simple remedy, if not always a preventative; it has been tried with the most surprising effect, and can be used without inconvenience or danger. The creosote, which is advertised as a remedy for toothache, may be now regarded as infallible; for it does not always prevent sea-sickness, it never fails to prevent the suffering which that malady usually occasions, and the straining of the nerves and muscles, which is sometimes productive of very serious consequences. In nine cases out of ten, and unless the sea be very rough, the sickness will be prevented; but if it does take place, there will be a relief of the stomach without straining; and the traveller, instead of lying prostrate during the whole of the voyage in a state of suffering which is indescribable, will be able, after the stomach is emptied, to keep his legs and even enjoy the motion of the sea. The creosote may be had of any respectable druggist, and is to be thus taken:—About half an hour before the passenger embarks, he is to take three drops in a small quantity of water. When on board, if he feels a little nausea, or if sickness comes on after the stomach has been relieved. The creosote is at the same time tonic and sedative; and independently of its value as a remedy at sea, assists the digestion by tranquillising the nerves of the stomach.—*Belfast Chronicle.* (1844-11-23, 2:2)

Note: Creosote is a toxic substance. This transcription is provided only for historical interest.

3245. To be Sold by Auction,—The Lands of Leitrim, in the parish of Tyhollan—in the Barony and County of Monaghan.

The above Lands are situate within three miles of the Town of Monaghan, and are of the best quality. They will be Sold by Public Auction, at the Commercial Buildings, Dublin, on Monday, the 13th of January, 1845, unless previously disposed of by private sale.—These Lands contain about 140A. 2R. 84P., late Irish Measure. They are held (with other Lands) under a Lease, bearing the date the 25th of May, 1710, for the term of 999 years, computed from the 1st day of May, 1688, at the Yearly Rent (in the Whole) of £20 late Irish Currency.

The Lands to be Sold yield a gross yearly rent of £206 12s. 1-3/4d., subject to £13 16s. 11d. yearly, a proportion of the above head-rent, and £1 8s. 6d. yearly, a proportion of Quit rent, and to the Tithe rent charge for the Lands held at will.

These Lands were purchased in the year 1837, by the late Thomas Johnston, Esq., at Sale under a Decree of the Court of Exchequer. The title was then fully cleared up to that time; and the Lands are now to be Sold by desire of the Administrator and other next of kin of the late Mr. Johnston, previous to a distribution of the Assets.

Proposals will be received by Henry George Johnston, Esq., of Fortjohnston, Glasslough, Administrator of Thomas Johnston, Esq., deceased, and by Thomas Reilly, Esq., Solicitor, 49, Lower Dominick-street, Dublin.

The Ulster Railway has been measured through the above Lands.

November 18, 1844.

(1844-11-23, 3:3)

3246. In Chancery.—Matthew Brinkley, Esq., and the Rev. Richard Hastings Graves, Executors of The Right Rev. John Brinkley, late Lord Bishop of Cloyne deceased, and Robert James Graves, Esq., M.D., Plaintiffs. The Rev. John Wright, Clerk, and others, Defendants.—Pursuant to the Decree in this Cause, bearing Date 6th day of July, 1844, I require all persons having Debts, Charges, or Incumbrances, affecting the Lands and Premises of Lisabrick, in the County of Monaghan, in the pleadings in this Cause mentioned, to come in before me, at my Chambers, on the Inns Quay, City of Dublin, on or before the 16th day of December, next, and proceed to prove the same; otherwise, they will be precluded the benefit of said Decree.

Dated, this 11th day of November, 1844.

J.S. Townsend.

Litton and Weld, Solicitors, for Plaintiffs,
No. 26, Leeson Street, Dublin.

(1844-11-23, 3:3)

3247. To be Sold by Auction,—on Thursday, 28th inst., and Following Days, for ready money,—At Election Hill, Near Emyvale,—The Household Goods, Stock, and Farming Utensils, Gig, Phaeton, and Harness, &c.

The Property of the Late Rev. Charles M'Dermott. Sale to commence on the first day at 12 o'clock, and on the following days at Eleven. (1844-11-23, 3:3)

3248. The Wife's Address to Her Husband.

You promis'd a long time ago, dear,
To leave off your treating me so;
But this eye, and this cheek plainly show, dear,
The result of last evening's blow;
'Tis strange that a man in his senses,
Should evince such a fondness for strife,
Since nought on his part recompences,
For sorrow once caused to his wife.

Your present irascible temper,
Your fickle and changeable mind;

Shows plainly some fatal distemper
Must prey on your senses I find;
'Tis only a fortnight since nearly,
That you promis'd you never would curse,
That you said you would change and love dearly,
But, alas! you have changed for the worse.

Now is it not very provoking,
To see you get on in this way;
To look at your snuffing and smoking,
And drinking, perhaps half the day;
What time you waste over those glasses,
Of whiskey and punch, that you drink;
All that ever I knew it surpasses;—
What prompts you, I really can't think?

And if that you see me but laughing,
You swear I have nothing to do;
While days you've been known to be quaffing,
And whole nights oft added thereto:
I think you have no cause to rail now,
But weigh matters o'er in your mind;
And your common sense cannot fail now,
To tell you, you're very unkind.

T.R. J.P.
October, 1844.
(1844-11-23, 4:1)

3249. Curious Epitaph.—On a Tombstone in Alstone churchyard, to the memory of a cobbler of the name of Jefferson:—

My cutting board's to pieces split,
My size-stick will no measures meet,
My rotten last's turned into holes,
My blunted knife cuts no more soles,
My hammer heads flown from the haft,
No more Saint Mondays with the craft,
My nippers, pinchers, stirrup, rag,
And all my kit have got the bag;
My lapstones broke, my colours o'er,
My gum-glass froze, my paste no more,
My heels sewed on, my pegs are driven,
I hope I'm on the road to Heaven.

(1844-11-23, 4:1)

3250. Melancholy Shipwreck.—Monday morning, intelligence was received of the shipwreck of the smack *Jane and Leany*, captain J. Quayle, belonging to Port St. Mary, Isle of Man, with the loss of the master and three female passengers. She had sailed on Sunday week from Ardglass, Ireland, for Port St. Mary, in ballast, having on board, besides the captain and crew, eleven passengers, seven men, and four women, most of them going out to service in Douglas. The *Jane and Leany* had got within a mile and a half of the Isle of Man, when, on Monday night, shortly before 12 o'clock, she was overtaken by a severe storm of wind and rain. The fury of the gale split her sails into pieces, and she was driven at the mercy of the waves for nearly 24 hours, when she went ashore at high-water mark at Bishampwith-Norbreck, near Poulton-le-Fylde, about ten yards from the shore. Some of the passengers leaped into the water, and escaped to the shore; the others, in the roll of the vessel, were washed overboard, and amongst the number four ill-fated individuals, Captain Quayle and three of the female passengers, were unfortunately drowned. Another woman had a narrow escape; the swell was carrying her away when her husband seized hold of her and saved her from a watery grave. All the bodies were subsequently found—two on the beach of Norbeck [sic], and the other two at Rossall. They were interred at Bispham on Wednesday last.
(1844-11-30, 4:2)

3251. Will of Sir J.P. Beresford, K.C.B.—The will and codicil of the late Admiral Sir John Poo Beresford, K.C.B., have just been proved in Doctors' Commons by his son Henry William De la Poer, Viscount Beresford, the other executor having declined to act. The personal property has been sworn under 4,000*l*. By the will, the deceased gives his mansion in Harley-street, to his three daughters for a residence, but directs that if they should decline accepting it for that purpose, it be sold by auction, and the proceeds divided between them on their attaining the age of twenty-one. He observes that his sons being provided for, he shall only bequeath them the family portraits with the exception of the eldest, who is left some valuable jewellery, which is to descend as "heirlooms." The daughters have also a great many articles of plate and jewellery. The codicil revokes the bequest to his daughters of the house in Harley-street, and bequeaths it to his eldest son, the executor.—*Britannia*.
(1844-11-30, 4:3)

3252. Lines.—Selected from
"Poetical Remains of a Clergyman's Wife."

"There was silence in heaven."—*Rev. viii. 1.*

Can angel-spirits need repose
In the full sunlight of the sky!
And can the veil of slumber close
A cherub's bright and beaming eye!

Have seraphim a weary brow
A fainting heart, an aching breast?
No, far too high their pulses glow—
To languish with inglorious rest.

How could they sleep amid the bliss,
The banquet of delight above?
How bear for one short hour to miss
The presence of the Lord they love?

Oh! not the death-like calm of sleep
Could still the everlasting song,
No fairy dream, no vision deep,
Absorb the blest and holy throng.

Yet not the lightest sound was heard
From angel harp or angel hand;
And not one plumed pinion stirred
Among the rapt, adoring band:— (*continued...*)

3252, continued:

For there was silence in the sky,
A joy that angels could not tell,
As, from its veiled fount on high,
The peace of God upon them fell.

Oh! what is silence here below?
The quiet of conceal'd despair—
The pause of pain—the trance of woe—
It is the rest of rapture there!

And to the way-worn pilgrim here,
More needful seems the perfect peace
Than the full chaunt of joy to hear
Roll on, and never, never cease.

From earthly agonies set free,
Tir'd with the path too slowly trod,
May such a silence welcome me
Into the temple of my God.
(1844-12-07, 2:3)

3253. County Monaghan.—Sale of Lands,—with valuable Linen Cloth and Corn Mills thereon.

To be Sold by Public Auction,—At the Head Inn, in the Town of Monaghan,—On Friday, the 3rd day of January, 1845,—At the Hour of one o'Clock in the Afternoon,

All That and Those, the Towns and Lands of Laragh, and Cornecarrow, (formerly the Property of William Oliver, lately deceased), with the Several Valuable Buildings thereon; consisting of Dwelling Houses, Offices, and Extensive Mills, some of which are quite new, with Machinery of the most improved kind, and inexhaustible supply of Water, of great power, and sufficient Bog for fuel.

These Lands contain in the whole 300 Acres, late Irish Plantation Measure or thereabouts, and are held as to part thereof, for a Term determinable upon the death of an old Life, now living in America, and supposed to be about 76 years of age; and as to the remaining parts therof, under covenants, for Lives renewable for ever. The Head Rent to which the whole is subject, is only 9s. 2d. an Acre. The Renewable Fines are 9*l*. 4s. 7d. on the fall of each Life.

The greater part of these Lands is let to tenants at considerable annual profit.

About Sixty Acres of said Lands, together with Dwelling-House, Offices, Five Mills, and sufficient Turbary for Firing, are held for lives renewable for ever, at a nominal Head Rent of about Two Pounds per Annum, and of which the Purchaser can have immediate possession.

The Premises are situated within 5 Miles of Carrickmacross, 5 of Ballybay, 5 of Castleblayney, and 12 of Dundalk.

Further Information, if required, will be supplied on application to David Leslie, Esq., Leslie-Hill, Armagh, or to James Meares, Esq., 35 Upper Dorset-street, Dublin, or to

J.E. Jones, Auctioneer, Monaghan.

December 6th, 1844. (1844-12-14, 3:1)

3254. *Limerick Chronicle* Office.—Dec. 28.—The remains of the late Lord Limerick passed our office to the cathedral, amidst the groaning and shouting of a fierce rabble, who abused the most respectable persons in the procession, especially Lord Monteagle, son-in-law of the deceased, and Sir A. de Vere, nephew, both of whom were pelted with stones, and compelled to alight from their carriage and take refuge in a house opposite the cathedral. The conduct of the mob was most disgraceful—the magistrates called out the dragoons and infantry, whose appearance restored order, after much confusion. (1844-12-28, 2:5)

3255. Frightful Accident.—On Friday last, as Mr. Joseph Watkin, only son of Wm. Watkin, Esq., solicitor, was returning to Enniskillen in a boat from the island of Devenish, where he had been shooting, he stretched out his hand and seized the gun by the muzzle, for the purpose of placing it more out of the way, when the gun discharged itself. The shot entered at the wrist, and passing along the arm to the elbow, frightfully disfigured the arm; but, we believe, he is not seriously injured. A person sitting in the boat behind Mr. Watkin narrowly escaped. (1844-12-28, 3:1)

3256. Approaching Marriage in High Life.—Mohum Fat, the celebrated Orientalist, at present in Dublin, will shortly lead to the hymeneal altar a beautiful young lady, a native of the Irish metropolis, and her entire family intend to accompany the happy couple to Persia! Mohum gave £10,300 towards the ransom of Lady Sale and Lady M'Naughtan.—*Limerick Chronicle*. (1845-01-04, 3:4)

3257. Last week, John Sheridan, a native of Glen, County Cavan, was found drowned in a gravel pit adjoining his residence.—An inquest was held on the body, and a verdict of "accidental death" returned.—*Fermanagh Reporter*. (1845-01-11, 2:3)

3258. Birth Extraordinary.—Dec. 20, Mrs. Mary Dunne, of Castledermot, was safely delivered by Dr. Carter of three male infants, who with the mother are doing well. (1845-01-11, 3:1)

3259. Alleged Breach of Promise.—We have heard from a quarter that may be called good authority that the friends of a lady—a native of the city of the violated treaty—purpose seeking redress by an action at law against a gentleman well known in Dublin, who is attached to a public office of importance, for an alleged breach of promise of marriage. It is understood that all negociation for an amicable arrangement has failed, and that a declaration, if not already filed, will be prepared in a few days, and it is probable the case will be tried at the ensuing term.—*Freeman*. (1845-01-11, 3:1)

3260. Melancholy Accident and Loss of Life.—A most appalling accident, attended with the loss of four children, took place on Saturday evening, about four o'clock, at the little hamlet of Knockmaroon, which lies contiguous to the southern and western wall of the Phoenix Park, and the low road to the Strawberry Beds and Lucan, &c. The commissioners of woods and forests, in their late extensive and valuable improvements in the Phoenix-park, constructed a new road at the back of the Royal Hibernian Military School through what is familiarly known as the Furry Glen, about midway from the summit level of the ground to that of the valley alongside the river Liffey. The place was so romantically beautiful in its aspect that it was resolved to add to its appearance by forming the upper part of the glen into an artificial lake, nature having provided for a supply of water by a rivulet which ran along, emptying itself into the Liffey, and formed the boundary between the parishes of Chapelizod and Castlenock [sic]. The usual precautions to permitting the overflow of the lake to pass away [were] provided for by means of a sewer. The boundary wall of the Park was at the bottom of the glen, and about 100 yards from it were the houses, the inmates of which fell victims. It would appear that the masonry work of the sewer gave way, and the great body of water rapidly filled the lower glen, as it is stated, to the height of seven or eight feet, the opening in the wall being quite insufficient to let off the rush of water; its weight soon bore down about twenty or thirty feet of the wall, and the all overwhelming flood swept into the houses, and in a few minutes, before any human help could be afforded, four children and a cow, the chief support of one poor family, were drowned. In the strawberry garden at the back of one house stood a rick of hay, and this was carried off into the culvert which crossed the Knockmaroon road, and served as the passage for the rivulet into the Liffey. The obstruction was so great that the water burst its way up into the road, breaking the arch of the culvert. Every one in the hamlet were ready to give assistance, and a number of policemen were soon on the spot; but relief was impracticable, the depth and violence of the rushing water was so great. An officer, whom we understand to be Mr. De Lancy, of the 1st royal dragoons, was riding fortunately along the road, and with intrepid humanity, which does honor to him, rode into the water, and succeeded in rescuing an aged woman and three children from destruction. Three others of the houses were not approachable. The name of the sufferers are—Roger Fox, by trade a weaver, but who is a fireman now on board one of the London and Dublin steamers, and at present on duty, lost three children, the eldest eleven years, the youngest an infant, the third about four years old. One of the children, aged nine, providentially saved herself by climbing on top of her father's loom, and was found in that position half dead, clinging with [a] death like grasp to it. The eldest girl, it is supposed, lost her life in her anxiety for the infant and her youngest sister. The poor mother was at market, providing some necessaries for the week's support, and returned but to witness their dead bodies, and that of the cow, their chief means of support. Coyle had one child drowned. A man named Mullen, by trade a smith, living on the bank of the Liffey, the opposite side of the road, had his house and furniture all wrecked and destroyed. A respectable tradesman named Butler had his furniture destroyed. It was to the courage, decision, and humanity of Mr. De Lancy, that this man owes the preservation of his mother and children's lives. The furniture, bed-cloths, store of potatoes, firing &c., were all destroyed upon these poor people, and a scene of more unqualified misery than these wretched dwellings presented could not be imagined. Some prompt measure of relief should be devised for these suffering families; but it is imperatively incumbent upon the commissioners of woods and forests to compensate them for the injury thus unwittingly inflicted upon them.

An inquest was held on the bodies yesterday, when the jury found that the deceased children came by their deaths on Saturday, the 4th inst., by reason of an embankment at the pond on the Furry-hill, in the Phoenix Park, giving way, when the water rushed into the rooms and drowned them; and the jurors further said, that the embankment built, or caused to be built, by the commissioners of woods and forests, was built in an insecure and insufficient manner, and wholly incapable of supporting the body of water therein confined, and that such insecurity and insufficiency were the cause of the accident; and the jurors begged to call the attention of the commissioners of woods and forests to the great injury and loss of property sustained by several poor persons, through the negligence of their servants. (1845-01-11, 4:3)

3261. A Church-Yard Scene.

Long, long, she gazed upon the ground,
On one small spot alas!
Which seem'd to swell to meet the hand
She laid upon the grass;
Her hand she laid upon the grass—
Retired, yet lingering stayed,
And aye upon the silent grass
Her long thin hand she laid.

That hand had often smoothd the couch
Of him who slept beneath,
And the love by which 'twas guided seem'd
A love that knew not death.
And so she knelt as if to feel
If earth were warm or soft
As the pillow—vacant now—on which
His head had lain so oft.

Ah me! what depth of love was hers,
Who thus her home forsook,
And all the living world beside,
Upon his grave to look!
I could not see the tears she shed, *(continued...)*

3261, continued:

They flowed not to be seen—
But well I knew the grass was wet
O'er which her eyes had been.

And still the grass she gently touched—
And bended meekly o'er,
As if to give her hand to him
Who took it once before;
That so she might bring back the time,
The morning time of life,
When by his side—a girl in years—
She felt in heart a wife.

Or haply 'twas in memory
Of some old early vow,
To love him even after death,
That she sought his grave place now—
Or, for some word unkindly said,
Though not unkindly meant,
Perchance upon his grave to shed
Atoning tears she went.

And oft upon that grave she look'd,
And of [oft?] she look'd above,
As if between that spot and heaven
She shared her whole heart's love!
(1845-01-18, 1:6)

3262. Sale of Arsenic.—Suicides and murders are so frequently caused by arsenic, which is generally dispensed for the alleged purpose of destroying rats, that we think there ought to be some legislative enactment to prevent the sale of poison for such uses. No inconvenience would be caused to the public by such a law, as rats are easily extirpated by throwing unsacked lime into the holes of the vermin.
(1845-01-25, 3:3)

3263. On the night of the 10th inst., a man named Mullan was found dead at the Lockpit of the Ulster Canal, near Moy. An inquest was held on the body by George Henry, Esq., of Tassagh, and a verdict returned that the poor man had foundered, owing to the inclemency of the weather, having wandered out of the direct way to his own house, which was in the neighbourhood.—*Ulster Gazette*. (1845-01-25, 4:6)

3264. Fatal Accident.—On Saturday last, a man named Hughes, while engaged in the act of emptying some shelling into the hopper of Mr. M'Kinstry's corn mill near this city, was caught in the works and so mutilated that he expired in a few hours after.—*Ulster Gazette*. (1845-01-25, 4:6)

3265. Shipwreck.—The brig *Robert Burns*, of Liverpool, 296 tons register, from St. Petersburgh to Liverpool, with a cargo of deals, sailed from Rathmullan, in Lough Swilly, at an early hour on Thursday morning last, in, as her crew supposed, a seaworthy state. Shortly after sailing, she encountered very strong gales from the south-west; and the ship laboring heavily, at two, p.m., every effort was made to reach Lochindall, the nearest port, in order to save their lives and the ship, but all the attempts of the crew proved fruitless, and at four o'clock, p.m., the vessel was struck with a tremendous sea, and immediately went on her beam ends, the captain at this time being washed overboard. The crew lashed themselves to the main chains, and remained in this perilous condition on the wreck, nearly dead from cold and exhaustion, till they were picked up by the crew of the *Perseverance*, of Dumfries, John M'Ghee, master and owner, when they were taken on board his vessel, and landed safely by him in this city yesterday. Great praise is due to Captain M'Ghee for his exertions at the risk of his own life and that of his crew, in rescuing ten fellow-creatures from a watery grave. The crew of the Robert Burns consisted of the following persons, all of whom have been saved:—William Hawthorns, mate, and his wife; Thomas Welling, Francis Morris, R. Hawthorn, John Stewart, Richard M'Ilree, J. Denny, John Quigley, and S. Farrell. The captain was the only person belonging to the vessel who perished.—*Derry Sentinel*. (1845-02-01, 1:5)

3266. Melancholy and Fatal Catastrophe.—(From the *Limerick Reporter*.)—On Sunday night, about eight o'clock, this city was thrown into a state of consternation by a most appalling and fatal accident. It appears that a woman named Mary Shaughnessy, wife of James Shaughnessy, resident in Sheep-street, off Athlunkard-street, had died in the morning, and her husband, conceiving that he had not sufficient room to wake the corpse in his own house, applied to a man named George Mason, who lived opposite, for the use of the upper part of the house for the purpose. Mason knowing the rottenness of the timbers, and fearing the consequences, strongly objected, and went to the landlord, we understand, to induce him to interfere in the matter. Even the mother of deceased (who lies at the hospital, badly wounded), offered her house, which had no lofts, and where no accident could have occurred. But all was of no avail, Shaughnessy persisted in having the wake at Mason's—and we now proceed to relate the frightful consequences. The house consists of three stories, and the upper, or attic, one being unoccupied, the wake was held there. A large number of women and two men were collected in the evening, when, about eight o'clock, the floor gave way in the centre, and the entire were precipitated to the floor beneath, which also gave way, and all came to the under floor or kitchen with a tremendous crash and a wild shriek, which was heard at the distance of several streets. People ran in every direction, many not knowing the locality of the tragedy, and others not even knowing what calamity had led to the concourse. At length, the shrieks of the relatives and of the wounded, which, together with the darkness of the dreary night, added horror to the fearful reality, attracted the multitude to the spot, when every assistance was given to extricate the dead and dying, the wounded and those who escaped unhurt, or with slight bruises, from the mass of ruins in which they were involved. It was ascertained that ten were killed in all—namely, Mary, wife of Cornelius Murphy, a bailiff; Catherine, wife of Michael Haneen, labourer, Garryowen; Catherine Madden (unmarried), Garryowen; Mary Molony (unmarried), Mary-street; Jane Boland (unmarried), of the Abbey; Bridget Rourke (widow), and her daughter Margaret (unmarried), Garryowen; James Enright, a youth, son of James Enright, and James Lynch, Garryowen, labourer. Three of the unfortunate women were far advanced in pregnancy. There were only two men present, and one of them escaped, while the other was killed in the effort to save his wife, who is pregnant, and severely, and, we fear, dangerously bruised. It was fortunate the calamity did not occur at a later hour, when a number of men would have collected and have been on the second floor, where they must have perished. On the kitchen floor was Mason, with a child in his arms, seven years of age, an interesting little creature, and by moving into the chimney, when he heard the crash, escaped being killed himself, but with a severe bruise in the loins. We saw it yesterday at the hospital, and it is doing well. Strange to say, there was a third party on the under floor, namely, Manahan, a cooper, who escaped completely unhurt, having got into some recess from which he shouted loudly, and was, of course, immediately extricated. The suspense of the unfortunate relatives, as each waited to see whether his or her relative was living or dead, and the burst of lamentation that fell upon the ear as each successive corpse was dragged from the rubbish, was terrible in the extreme. The Mayor, the police, and a large detachment of the 15th Regiment, from the Castle Barracks, were in attendance, and rendered every assistance. It required the exertions of the soldiery, even with fixed bayonets, to keep off the crowd, and to preserve order. The dead and the wounded were conveyed to Barrington's Hospital, where medical assistance was rendered by the Mayor, by Surgeon Kane, Sir Richard Franklin, Surgeon Thwaites, Dr. Brodie, and Mr. Allen, the Apothecary. Both the dead and the wounded are all of the humbler classes. Of the latter, we have ascertained the following names:—George Mason, Alice Grady, Margaret Grady, Margaret Halman, Margaret Jordan, Catharine Jordan, Ellen Fitzgerald, Bridget Kennedy, Mary Barlow, Margaret Lee, Henry Enright, and Rachel Lynch. There is a number of others bruised and wounded, for whom there was not accommodation, or whom their friends preferred having under their own care, and whose names therefore we have not learned. Were it not for the poor man, a tailor, who got under the ruins, several more would have been killed, whom he dragged out at the risk of his life. Yesterday, the dead bodies with the corpse that had been waiting, lay in one of the rooms of the hospital, side by side upon the floor, and presented a horrible spectacle. The swollen features and livid appearance of the face indicated that the majority were suffocated rather than killed by wounds, those who fell in the centre having been smothered by the others falling over them in consequence of the slanting of the broken boards in that direction. At four o'clock yesterday, an inquest was held on the bodies by George Bennett, Esq., when a verdict was returned in accordance with the foregoing facts. (1845-02-01, 2:2)

3267. Accouchement of Lady Cremorne.—It affords us much pleasure to state, that this estimable lady gave birth to a son, on Thursday the 30th ult. The health of her Ladyship and baby, is in as favorable a state as her medical attendant can desire. (1845-02-01, 3:1)

3268. The Cry of the Human.—By Miss Barrett.

"There is no god," the foolish saith—
But none, "There is no sorrow;"
And nature, oft the cry of faith,
In bitter need will borrow;
Eyes which the preacher could not school,
By wayside graves are raised;
And lips say, God be pitiful,
Who ne'er said God be praised.
Be pitiful, O God.

The tempest stretches from the steep
The shadow of its coming—
The beasts grow tame, and near us creep,
As help were in the human—
Yet, while the cloud-wheels roll and grind,
We spirits tremble under—
The hills have echoes; but we find
No answer for the thunder.
Be pitiful, O God.

The battle hurtles on the plains—
Earth feels new scythes upon her:
We reap our brothers for the wains,
And call the harvest—honor—
Draw face to face, front line to line,
One lineage all inherit,
Then kill, curse on, by that same sign,
Clay, clay—and spirit spirt.
Be pitiful, O God.

The plague runs festering through the town—
And never a bell is tolling:
And corpses jostled 'neath the moon,
Nod to the dead-carts rolling.
The young child calleth for the cap—
The strong man brings it weeping;
The mother from her babe looks up,
And shrieks away its sleeping.
Be pitiful, O God.

The plague of gold strikes far and near—

(*continued…*)

3268, continued:

And deep and strong it enters:
This purple chimar which we wear,
Makes madder than the centaur's.
Our thoughts grow blank, our words grow strange
We cheer the pale gold-diggers—
Each soul is worth so much on Change,
And marked, like sheep, with figures.
Be pitiful, O God.

The curse of gold upon the land,
The lack of bread enforces—
The rail-cars snort from strand to strand,
Like more of Death's white horses.
The rich preach "rights" and future days,
And hear no Angel scoffing:
The poor die mute—with starving gaze
On corn-ships in the offing.
Be pitiful, O God.

(1845-02-01, 4:1)

3269. Catching a Husband.—(From "Strathern"—A New Novel, by the Countess of Blessinton.

"Yes, this is better, infinitely better. By Jove! you improve amazingly."

"Thanks to your instruction," observed Lady Olivia, with a glance full of gratitude. "Oh! how I should like to have fine horses, exclaimed she, with assumed enthusiasm, and go into the stable, and see the dear animals feed."

"Would you indeed," asked Lord Fitzwarren, his face brightening up.

"Above all things in the world," resumed the lady; "excepting going out hunting. That has ever been my utmost ambition, *meas helas*, I have no chance of such happiness, and she sighed deeply."

"Who knows? Don't despair," said Lord Fitzwarren.

"You must not give me false hopes, for mamma would never let me go out hunting, even if I had a horse," observed Lady Olivia. "Would you mamma?" turning to Lady Wellerby, who affected to be busily engaged reading her English letters at the other end of the room, but who was a pleased and attentive spectator of the scene in which her artful and well-schooled daughter was so cleverly acting her part.

"Did you speak to me, Olivia?" asked the lady-mother slowly raising her eyes from the letter she was affecting to peruse.

"Yes, mamma; I asked you if you would permit me to go out hunting."

"Go out hunting, child. An unmarried woman go out hunting? I never heard such a thing;" and Lady Wellerby elevated her eyebrows, and opened her small eyes to their utmost extent, with a look of well acted astonishment.

"You see I was right," said Lady Olivia, and she sighed profoundly. "No; such happiness is not reserved for me. I shall never be able to go out hunting, and she shook her head slowly, and looked with a melancholy expression at Lord Fitzwarren.

"Not until you are married," replied he.

"So few men are really good riders, and only such could teach their wives to ride, that I have little chance of being so fortunate as to be selected by one," and Lady Olivia sighed more deeply than ever.

"Don't despair. What wager will you bet me that before six months you are not married to a regular fox-hunter?"

"You are jesting, Lord Fitzwarren; I see you are," and the lady pouted and looked more sad than before.

"By Jove, I am not. Never more serious in my life. I'll bet you five guineas to two; I'd make it fifty, only that I know young ladies seldom have much pocket money, and I don't want to win all yours.

"I would take your wager," said Olivia, in a low voice, "only that mamma would be angry, as she never allows us to make bets."

"She need know nothing about the matter," whispered Lord Fitzwarren, "so take my wager."

"Done," said Lady Olivia, and she nodded her head knowingly, and held out her hand to him saying, "I shall be sure to win your five guineas; for, fond as I am of horses, and must as I should like to go out hunting, I dont know a single fox-hunter that I would marry."

Lady Wellerby, on whom not a word of this discourse had been lost, and who augured the happiest result from it, was so alarmed by this unexpected speech of her daughter, that she positively started, and turned up her eyes towards the ceiling as if appealing to heaven against the stupidity of that young lady. But Lady Olivia, who observed the movement, smiled inwardly at her own superior tact, while waiting to see what effect the *naivete* of her declaration would have on him to whom it was addressed.

Lord Fitzwarren looked perfectly astounded and crest-fallen as he gazed inquiringly on the unconscious countenance assumed by Lady Olivia, and after a pause of a few minutes, exclaimed,

"And so you don't know a single fox-hunter whom you would marry?"

"No," replied the lady.

"Then, I suppose you won't marry me, eh?"

"But you are not a fox-hunter," said the lady, looking most innocently, "are you?"

"Why, what the devil else have you taken me for?"

"You never told me you were, and I—I—" and she cast down her eyes, and raised her handkerchief to her face, in affected confusion, to conceal, not her blushes, but the want of them.

"Well, I did not take you to be such a simpleton," said Lord Fitzwarren, his countenance brightening up, "But now you know that I am a fox-hunter—ay, and a most determined one, too—what do you say to your wager at present, eh? Come, confess that you haven't much chance of winning."

Lady Olivia still kept her handkerchief to her face, and seemed speechless from emotion.

"What will you give to get off, eh? But hang me if I can account for you not knowing that which every one of my acquaintances is aware of, namely, that Melton has not a more thorough-going Nimrod than myself. Well, is there now a fox-hunter of your acquaintance that you would marry? Don't keep hiding your face, but say, will you have me or not?"

Lady Olivia extended her hand to him, and whispered, "Oh! I am so happy; but do ask mamma, for I am so overpowered." (1845-02-01, 4:4)

3270. Fatal and Most Melancholy Fire.—At an early hour yesterday morning, a dwelling-house, near the fair green of Donnybrook and near Dodder-row, the residence of Captain Austin, was found to be consumed by fire, the interior being completely burned, and the walls only standing. The family consisted of the Captain, a very fine, athletic man, his wife, two children, and a female servant. The servant, on leaving home on Sunday evening, left the family in good health, and on her return yesterday morning, found the house a wreck, and no trace of its inmates. At an advanced hour of the afternoon of yesterday, a portion of the remains of the Captain, an arm and a portion of the trunk of his wife were dug from the ruins, with some small bones, supposed to be those of their children.

It is pretty clear that the whole family has been sacrificed to the devouring element, and that the fire must have been accidental, having spread its ravages while the inmates were locked in sleep.

It is a most piteous and afflicting tale. A coroner's jury has been summoned for this evening; but there does not seem to be the smallest chance of eliciting any information as to the cause of the frightful catastrophe. (1845-02-08, 1:6)

3271. Awful Visitation.—We regret to announce the awfully sudden death of Mrs. Dawson Hutchinson Vaughan, of Golden-Grove, King's County, which took place on Friday, at her residence. Seldom has a melancholy event of the kind caused more sincere sorrow, not only to her immediate relatives and friends, but to the poor, to whose wants and necessities she was at all times a ministering angel. On the day in question, whilst in the act of handing wine to a visitor, four or five of whom were present at the time, she fell back and instantly expired! She had been but eighteen months married, and has left an infant son and an afflicted husband to mourn their bereavement. Mrs. Vaughan was niece to the Earl of Rosse, and related to some of the most distinguished families in the King's County. She was young and beautiful, but better than all, good and charitable, and the memory of her virtues will long be cherished in grateful recollections of all who enjoyed the privilege of her acquaintance. She was the last of the Vaughan family, of Golden-Grove. (1845-02-08, 2:2)

3272. The Church.—By the death of the Rev. Henry Martin, surrogate of the diocese of Clonfert, the rectory of Aughrim is vacant, and at the disposal of the Hon. and Right Rev. Dr. Tonson, Bishop of the United parishes of Killaloe, Kilfenora, Clonfert, and Kilmacduagh, whose disposal of the patronage vested in him, from time to time, has reflected the highest credit on the Established Church, of which he is a distinguished ornament. This is the third living at the disposal of the Bishop, in the diocese of Clonfert, within a little [more than?] a week. (1845-02-08, 3:2)

3273. Death of the Marquess of Sligo.—We regret to announce that the rumors of the death of this nobleman, which have been circulated in this city, have proved correct.

The noble Marquess expired at Tunbridge Wells, on Sunday, the 26th ult., at one o'clock at noon [sic], after a protracted illness. The Marquess, with the Marchioness and family, had been residing at Tunbridge Wells since August last, with the almost hopeless view of benefiting his health. About three years [since,] his lordship was seized with a paralytic attack, by which he partially lost the use of his limbs and sadly impaired his intellects.

The Earl of Altamont (now Marquess of Sligo) is absent on a tour in Spain and Portugal, in company with his sisters, Ladies Elizabeth and Harriet Browne.

The Marchioness and Lady Emily Browne and the youthful members of the family were with the noble Marquess at his dissolution. Lord James Browne is abroad with his regiment, the 9th Lancers.

The Marquess's eldest son, George John, Earl of Altamont, born January 31, 1820, succeeds to the family titles and estates.

The late Marquess was Colonel of the South Mayo Militia, Senior Warden of the Irish Grand Lodge of Freemasons, a Trustee of the Irish Linen Manufacture, and a Knight of the Most Illustrious Order of St. Patrick.

The families of the Marquess and Marchioness of Clanricarde, Earl Howe, the Hon. Lady Bromley, the Hon. R. Curzon, the Earl of Howth, Mr. Charles and Lady Louisa Knox, the Earl of Desart, Mr. J. Browne, &c., are placed in mourning by the lamented death of his lordship.

The Marquess and family have descended from Captain Browne, an English settler, who fixed his residence at Neale, in the county of Mayo, in 1565. His son, Josias Browne, was father of Sir John Browne, created a Baronet of Nova Scotia, in 1636. His eldest son, Sir George, was an ancestor of Lord Kilmain. Colonel John Browne, a younger son, was a brave officer in King James's army, and was twice taken prisoner—at Galway, in 1691, and at Limerick. He died in 1705. Peter, his eldest son, was father of Mr. John Browne, who represented Castlebar from 1749 to 1760, in which year he was (*continued...*)

3273, continued: ...created Lord Monteagle, and in 1768 Viscount Westport; and subsequently, in 1771, Earl of Altamont, a title he only enjoyed five years, as he died in 1776. He was succeeded by Peter, his son, who died in 1780, leaving John Denis, the third Earl, (father of the deceased Marquess,) who was created Marquess of Sligo in Dec., 1800, and and an English Baron, by the style of Baron Monteagle in February, 1806.

The funeral is appointed to take place to-day, when the remains of the Marquess are to be conveyed by a special train from Tonbridge, and ultimately be removed for interment in a family vault in the cemetery at Kensell-green [sic]. The obsequies will be conducted as privately as possible, it having been the wish of the deceased nobleman that his remains should be interred without the least ostentation.—*Herald of Monday*. (1845-02-08, 4:5)

3274. Woman Found Dead.—An inquest was held by Joseph Orr, Esq., coroner, on the 4th instant, on the body of Bridget Green, who was found dead in a trench between potato ridges, in a field near Lowtherstown. It is supposed she had lain where she was found since the 25th ult., as she was not discovered until the thaw had cleared away the snow by which she was covered. Verdict—"Died from the inclemency of the weather."—*Tyrone Constitution*. (1845-02-15, 3:2)

3275. The Dying Child.—By Charles Piesse, Esq.

Oh mother? what sweet sounds I hear
So softly breaking on mine ear;
Whence this sweet music in the dark?
There? now again? Hear you it? Hark!

I hear no music, my sweet child,
Sleep! sleep again, thou dreamer wild;
No music sweet, or sound I hear,
Rest, my sick child! rest there, my *dear*!

Ah mother! No! I heard its sound,
Sickness and pain no more shall wound;
Good angels call me. See—that light—
My mother dear—good night—good night—

(1845-02-15, 4:1)

3276. The Twins.

Two sweet children, girl and boy,
Shared each other's tears and joy;
They were ever side by side
Like the Graces beautified.
Form without, thought within,
Linked them by the name of twin.
They had lost a mother's kiss,
Which is musical with bliss;
For the lips that smiled and burned
With the children's kiss returned,
Lost to all they took and gave,
Lay and rotted in the grave.
Oh, there are some mothers living
Busy as the angels giving
Showers of joy where'er they thread;
And there are some mothers dead
Who deserved to live for ever.
Death may blush at times to shiver
Mirrors that reflect, indeed,
Love which is a mother's creed!
Oft throughout the summer weather
Would the children range together,
When the sun in kingly power
Made a mint of leaf and flower.
There his yellow coin to cast,
Coin that long hath current passed—
Poets now, like bards of old,
Deem it earth's most genuine gold.
They had rambled far one day,
In their hasty footed way,
And the hours were robed in shade
'Ere they saw their toilet made.
Childhood never was Time's slave,
So upon their mother's grave
Both the pilgrims sat and wept,
And, outworn with weeping, slept.
With a stern eye, flashing fire,
Came the children's tyrant sire;
All unmoved by that dear pair,
While the eve-breath shook their hair,
There the father swore an oath,
And he struck the sleepers both.
"Mother!" shrieked the boy in pain—
But she answered not again;
"Mother, mother," shrieked the other,
But the echo babbled "mother."
More than Cain that man is cursed
Who believes the nurse and nursed
Can wipe out love's every feature:
Child and mother have one nature.
One warm pulse and heart between them,
So that death can never wean them.
Who would not give lands and gold,
Though their value was untold,
Could he keep alive the breast
That hath warmed his infant rest?
'Tis a cause for watery eyes
When a doating mother dies.

E.F. Babbington.
Bridgewater.

(1845-02-22, 2:4)

3277. County of Monaghan Assizes.—(From our own Reporter.)—Monaghan, Monday, Feb. 21.—Crown Court—Feb. 25, 1845.—John Feehan, for the abduction of Jane M'Kee, against the consent of her parents, she being under the age of 16 years, and also for riot and assault.

Sir Thomas Staples briefly stated the case to the jury, and cited the act which made a misdemeanour of the abduction of a girl under the age of 16 years, though she herself consented, if the parents were non-content.

John M'Kee examined—is a Covenanter or a member of the reformed Church of Scotland; his daughter, Jane M'Kee, is of the same faith; she is his only child; she was 15 years old on the 22nd of this month; witness lives in the Parish of Mucknoe; near Castleblayney; holds a farm of about 10 acres, at £2 8s. 6d.; his daughter was at home on the night of the 10th of April last; about 9 o'clock, in the evening; her mother told her to drive some pigs from before the front door; she went to do so and remained out for some time; her mother went out to see what detained her; heard his wife call her and immediately after, heard her cry out, "Oh mamma, mamma, send daddy here fast, fast;"—witness ran out and saw a large crowd outside; they ran away like a hunt, and it was too dark for him to ascertain who any of them were; witness ran after them, and when he came up with them, some of them cried out "kill the damned rascal, he ought to be killed long ago;" some of them cut him severely on the head; he did not see his daughter any more; witness and his wife went to the prisoner's mother's house, to see the girl on the following Monday; his wife saw her but he did not; the prisoner said then that he was the person to blame, and that he had the girl and would not give her up; knew the prisoner before the 19th of April; he was a friend of witness's servant girl; that girl lived with him for five years previously; he never slept in prisoner's house, or eat or drank at his expense there; the prisoner never spoke to him about his daughter; the prisoner would not allow the girl to go home; they took her to a great many places, and he sought her sorrowing far and near, at great expense, for he would sooner they had parted his soul and body the night they took her away.

Cross-examined by a juror; did not see her among the crowd.

Cross-examined by Mr. O'Hagan—The party did not knock at the door; can't say how many persons were in the crowd; did not see the prisoner in the crowd; knew the prisoner before, but not intimately; he did not go to the house as his friend, but as the friend of the servant girl; has heard that the prisoner has about 7 acres of land, or rather his mother has it; knows Owen M'Mahon; was on good terms with him as a neighbour before this affair; M'Mahon came to his house with the prisoner, but it was as the friend of his servant; never heard of a courtship going on between the prisoner and his daughter; never observed any freedom between them when the prisoner was in his house; the first time the prisoner came there, was to dig some potatoes for Bridget M'Mahon; was with him on that occasion; the prisoner bought a horse from witness; they have bought and sold pigs in different fairs together.

Mary M'Kee examined—Is wife to the last witness, and mother to Sarah Jane M'Kee; Sarah was 15 years of age last Saturday; I remember her leaving my house on the 19th of April last; she went out, and, as I thought she was stopping too long, I went after her and heard her say, "No, no;" I then said "Sarah Jane dear, where are you?" she then shouted, "Ma dear, send my da here fast, fast!" her father then came out, and some of the party said "Now's the time, boys, make away with her;" her father then followed shouting "Murder;" I went into the house, as I could not bear to see anything. (The witness then described different attempts made by her and her husband to get seeing her daughter.) On the 22d April, she saw her in John M'Shane's, who is uncle of the prisoner; her daughter was brought there by the prisoner himself; when she saw her, she asked her daughter to come and speak to her, but the prisoner said there should be no *cologuing* there; that was the very expression he used; he then took her away, and put her into a room; I cried and lamented both, for I couldn't help it; they brought her out again, and I asked her would she come home? she looked over to the prisoner as if to know his mind, and said, "I will go very quietly if John comes with me;" they wouldn't let her speak any more to me, and with pure vexation, I almost tore my clothes off; I did not see her for seven months after; she is at present in this town; in Castleblayney fair, about six weeks before this, my daughter, who was with me, was taken away from my presence for about an hour under some excuse.

Cross-examined by Mr. O'Hagan—The first time I saw the prisoner was once buying a pony from my husband; he was not frequently at our house; he was only a friend of the girl's; I never saw the prisoner speaking anything past the common to my daughter; I never thought of anybody speaking to her in loving terms; she did not speak privately to him; I never saw Hugh M'Mahon in our house before this; I never spoke to Owen M'Mahon of marriage; I wouldn't even her to any man, she was so young; I had only the one child, and my heart is in her; I had heard of the marriage before she was taken away; I heard it occurred at the fair; I saw Owen M'Mahon on the Saturday after the marriage, he called me into the room and said—"Oh, Mary, that's a cruel thing that's happened to Sarah Jane, for Eleanor Feehan tells me she was married to John Feehan, at the fair, on the Wednesday before." I exclaimed—"It could not be the case, for she was not long from my presence;" my husband said he would get advice in Dublin; after we heard of the marriage, we sent our daughter to her grandmother's; I never had any conversation with Owen M'Mahon or Eleanor Feehan before the marriage, about the girl; I never said to Owen M'Mahon that though my daughter was a Covenanter, and John Feehan a Roman Catholic, that I would prefer him before any person for a husband to my daughter.

Sarah Jane M'Kee, a smart looking country girl, was then examined by Mr. Hanna—I recollect being at home, in my father's house, on the 19th of April; it was a Friday evening; I went out of the door, (*continued...*)

3277, continued.: ...and went up to the end of the garden; I met John Feehan and another person there; when I was standing with them, my mother came to the door and asked me where I was? I said I was there; there were some other persons with Feehan, but they were at a distance; he brought me to Con. O'Neill's house, and remained with me that night; he brought me to different places for the next seven months, and came with me.

Cross-examined by Mr. O'Hagan—It was a good while before this that I knew John Feehan; I was married to him about six weeks before this; I had sent for him to take me away on this night; he was up at the end of the garden; none of the people were there; I do not recollect calling to my father that night, I did not call out anything, such as "Dadda, dadda, come here fast!" on my oath, I did not call upon either father or mother; Mr. M'Phillips married us; it was in the town of Castleblayney we were married; there was a license got for the marriage; Owen M'Mahon, Bridget Feehan, Felix Feehan, and John Feehan were present at it; I went away with my own will and accord on this night; I have lived with him ever since as his wife.

Mr. O'Hagan said that there were two questions to be discussed upon the evidence in this case, and the statute on which the indictment had been founded. One was a question of fact for the jury, and the other a question of law for the court. He submitted that the prosecution must fail, as it had appeared that a marriage had been celebrated between the prisoner and the daughter of the prosecutor, before the alleged abduction took place, as the act on which the indictment was founded referred to unmarried females. That marriage was performed by a Catholic clergyman, and it would be contended for the crown, that, under the 19th Geo. II., c. 13, the marriage was null and void. He submitted that the case before the court was not affected by that statute. Its terms were—"That a marriage between a Papist and a Protestant, or between two Protestants, if celebrated by a Popish Priest, shall be absolutely null and void to all intents and purposes, without any process, judgment, or sentence of law whatsoever." Now, the persons who had been married by the Rev. Mr. M'Philips [sic] were a Catholic and a Covenanter, and upon the true interpretation of the statute, and upon a comparison of its purposes with those of the numerous penal acts passed about the same period, he (Mr. O'Hagan) conceived that the word Protestant must be held to have been void in reference to members of the church by law established, and not Dissenters from that church. It would be found, that the distinction had been clearly taken throughout the old penal statutes, and generally through the Irish statutes, bearing upon the law of marriage, between Protestants of the Established Church and Presbyterians, and other dissenters. Mr. O'Hagan referred to several acts, and insisted that, as the marriage of a Roman Catholic Priest was unquestionably effectual in law, unless nullified by express enactment, and as the statute relied on in this case did not affect any persons dissenting from the establishment, the prisoner was legally, as well as religiously, the husband of the woman, with whose abduction he was charged, and that, therefore, he was entitled to an acquittal.

Judge Torrens said that he had never known the question raised before. He had always understood that the word "Protestant" included Protestant dissenters as well as Protestants of the Established Church; and at the time the act was passed, the Presbyterians were an influential and recognised body in this country.

Mr. O'Hagan observed, that the legislature at that time made, he conceived, a clear distinction in dealing with Presbyterians and the members of the Established Church; and his Lordship would find, by referring to Dr. Reid's history of the Presbyterian church, that in Ulster, the treatment of the two bodies had been essentially different, and not such as would have been exhibited to those who were considered to belong to the same religious community. He said that he had himself raised this question at the last Spring assizes, before Judge Perrin, in Downpatrick, in a civil case, in which Mr. Tomb and Mr. Nelson were on the other side; and that Judge Perrin had reserved the matter for consideration, and had not, he believed, yet pronounced any judgment upon it.

After a good deal of discussion, his Lordship took a note of the point for consideration before the judges, should there be a conviction.

Mr. O'Hagan, for the defence, contended that, if the marriage celebrated by the Priest was a good one, the indictment could not be sustained, and at some length argued that the marriage was not null and void, for though there was a statute prohibiting a marriage between Protestants of the Establishment and Roman Catholics, when celebrated by a Popish Priest, it did not apply to protesting Dissenters.

Judge Torrens thought that the construction of the statute included all the Protestant community.

Mr. O'Hagan thought he would be able to show his Lordship from the statute that, at the time of passing the Act he had referred to, it was only meant for Protestants of the Established Church.

The question was reserved for the consideration of the Judges.

Mr. O'Hagan then, at some length, and with considerable ability, addressed the Jury for the prisoners, after which he called the following witnesses:—

Owen M'Mahon, examined by Mr. O'Hagan—Knows the prisoner and family; knows also the prosecutor and his family; recollects going to M'Kee's house, with the prisoner, in the year 1843, when they were treated very respectfully; saw the young woman in company with the prisoner, and there was no objection made; recollects having a conversation with the mother of Jane M'Kee about a marriage; she said she (Sarah Jane) was delicate in health; she and prisoner were of different religions, and Mrs. M'Kee said that she would like to be a Roman Catholic; she said she did not object to the prisoner for being a Roman Catholic; knew of the prisoner being in town; met John M'Kee in fairs and markets; witness was present at the marriage in Castleblayney; met the Parish Priest and his two curates coming into town, and one of the curates went into the house of a man of the name of M'Donald, and celebrated the marriage there; prisoner's mother has ten or twelve acres of land.

Cross-examined by Sir T. Staples—Minds going with the prisoner to M'Kee's house, on the 1st of June; Jane M'Kee was big enough to be 18 years old; saw Mrs. M'Kee in Castleblayney on the day of the marriage; did not tell her of the marriage; Sarah Jane M'Kee went home the same day with her mother, and lived with her father for six weeks; witness was called to a room to be asked, was it true that the marriage had taken place? the father said he never would consent to the marriage.

Hugh M'Mahon, examined by Mr. O'Hagan—saw the prisoner and M'Kee together, and heard M'Kee say that when the two harvests were settled, the prisoner should spend three or four days with him; saw the prisoner and Jane M'Kee frequently together; was with the prisoner's mother in the town of Castleblayney; saw Mrs. M'Kee treat the prisoner's mother, and heard her say she would be quite happy if the prisoner was with her daughter; she said she would make her daughter worth £200; thinks Mrs. Feehan would not be satisfied with the marriage, as she was a widow; witness lives within about half-a-mile of prisoner's mother's; heard of Jane M'Kee being taken away to Scotland, and to different other places.

Eleanor M'Shane, otherwise Feehan, the mother of the prisoner, heard of her son going to M'Kee's house; met Mrs. M'Kee in the street of Castleblayney, who asked her if her son was out, or if she saw her daughter, and said she would not be uneasy if she knew that her son was with her; she spoke of marriage, and the witness said "she would not be at it."

Cross-examined by Sir T. Staples—Witness heard of the marriage the day before it took place, but did not tell Mrs. M'Kee about it; holds about nine acres of land; pays £5 4s. a-year; has six sons; the prisoner is the eldest; prisoner did not take his wife home with him the night of the marriage.

The Jury were then charged by the Judge, and after some consideration, they returned a verdict of Guilty, with a recommendation to mercy.

The prisoner was sentenced to one year's imprisonment, six months at hard labour, and fined £25, and to find sureties to keep the peace.

Judge Torrens and Judge Crampton, both ruled that Mr. O'Hagan's motion was null and void, and declared the marriage to be perfectly illegal. The girl presented a petition in favour of the prisoner, and begged to be allowed to go into prison with the prisoner: refused.
(1845-03-01, 2:1)

3278. Marriages in Ireland.—Notice furnished by the Registrar-General, under the provisions of the *Act for Marriages in Ireland* and for registering such marriages.—Acts required to be done by persons who may be desirous of solemnizing Marriages after 31st day of March, 1845, under the provisions of the *Act of the 7th and 8th of Victoria, cap. 81.*

1. Marriages according to the rites and ceremonies of the United Church of England and Ireland, may be celebrated after publication of Banns, or by Licence, or by Special Licence as heretofore, or they may be celebrated upon the production of the Registrar's Certificate, granted under the provisions of the recent Act, in lieu of Banns.

When it is intended that a Marriage shall be solemnised by licence (other than a special licence,) a notice must be given by one of the parties who shall have resided for not less than seven days in the parish named in such notice, to the Surrogate, or other person having authority to grant the licence; which notice should be signed by the person giving it, and should be in the form prescribed in the schedule A, annexed in the act, or to the like effect.

The licence cannot be obtained until after seven days from the giving of such notice.

When it is intended that a Marriage shall be celebrated upon the Registrar's Certificate, and both parties have resided in the same District for not less than seven days, one of the parties shall give the Registrar of such District a Notice, pursuant to the form directed by Schedule A, annexed to the Act, and containing the following particulars:—

The Name and Surname of each of the parties.

Whether Bachelor, or Widower, Spinster or Widow.

Their respective Rank or Condition.

Whether Minors or of full Age.

Their respective Dwelling-places.

Whether they have resided within the District more than one calendar month, or, if not, how long.

In what Church or Building the Marriage is to be solemnised.

The District and County in which the other party resides, when they dwell in different Districts.

In case the Parties shall reside in different Districts, notice must be given to the Registrar of each District, by one of the Parties who shall have dwelt not less than seven days in each District respectively.

A Copy of such Notice will be entered by the Registrar of the District in a book called *The Marriage Notice Book*, which will be open at all reasonable times, without fee, to all persons desirous of inspecting the same.

All Notices of intended Marriage received by the Registrar of the District, are to be transmitted by him to the Clerk of the Guardians of the Poor, and such Clerk shall read the same at the three weekly meetings of the Guardians, or, if such (*continued...*)

3278, continued: ...meetings are not held weekly, at any meeting of the Guardians within twenty-one days from the day of the notice being entered in the *Marriage Notice Book.* And after the expiration of seven days if the Marriage is to be solemnised by Licence, or of twenty-one days if the Marriage is to be solemnised without Licence, after the entry of the notice, even though no such meeting of the Board of Guardians shall have been held, and if no impediment has been shown, the Registrar of the district may be required to issue a certificate.

2. Marriages between parties both of whom are Presbyterians, or of whom one only is a Presbyterian, may be solemnised according to the forms used by Presbyterians, by the Licence of a Presbyterian Minister authorised to grant Licences, in Meeting-houses, duly certified between the hours of Eight in the morning and Two in the afternoon, with open doors and in the presence of two or more creditable witnesses; provided there be no lawful impediment to the Marriage of such parties.

After the 31st day of March, 1845, in every case of a Marriage by a Presbyterian Minister between two Presbyterians, otherwise than by Licence, Banns of Matrimony shall be published by or in the presence of a Presbyterian Minister in the Presbyterian meeting-house, duly certified, frequented by the congregation of which the parties to be married shall be members, upon three Sundays preceding the solemnisation of the Marriage, during the time of divine service, and not elsewhere; and whenever it shall happen that the parties to be Married by a Presbyterian Minister shall be members of different congregations, the Banns shall in like manner be published in the certified Presbyterian meeting-house frequented by the congregation of which each of the parties to be Married shall be a member; and any such Marriage by a Presbyterian Minister shall be solemnised in one of the certified Presbyterian meeting-houses, where such Banns shall have been published, and in no other place whatsoever; and before such Marriage shall be solemnised, the certificate of the Presbyterian Minister by whom or in whose presence the Banns shall have been published in the other certified Meeting-house, shall be delivered to the Presbyterian Minister solemnising such Marriage.

The person to be married shall, six days at the least before the time required for the first publication of such Banns, deliver or cause to be delivered to such Presbyterian Minister a notice in writing of their true christian and surnames, and of the congregation or congregations of which they shall respectively be members, and of the house or houses of their respective abodes, and of the time during which they have dwelt, inhabited, or lodged in such house or houses respectively.

One of the parties intending Marriage shall appear personally before the Presbyterian Minister authorised to grant Licences, and shall make and subscribe an Oath, or a solemn Affirmation, or Declaration, instead of taking an Oath (which Oath, Affirmation, or Declaration, such Minister is authorised to administer,) that he or she believeth that there is not an impediment of Kindred or Alliance, or other lawful Hindrance to the said Marriage, and that one of the said parties hath for the space of fifteen days immediately before the day of the grant of such Licence had his or her usual place of abode in the Presbytery within which the Marriage is to be solemnised, and that they are both of the full age of twenty: one years: or, when either of the parties shall be under the age of twenty:one years, that the consent of the person or persons whose consent to such Marriage is required by law has been obtained thereto, or that there is no person having authority to give such consent, or that such party is a widower or widow, as the case may be.

And the party so appearing personally, shall seven days before the Licence shall be delivered to him, produce a certificate according to the form prescribed in the Act, or to the like effect, from the Minister of the congregation of which he or she shall be a member and has been a member for at least one calendar month preceding; a true copy of which certificate shall be entered in a book to be called *The Marriage Notice Book*, which book shall be opened at all reasonable times, without fee, to all persons desirous of inspecting the same; and for entering every such notice, the Ministers shall be entitled to a fee of one shilling.

Any person may enter a caveat with the Minister authorised to grant Licences, against the grant of a Licence for the Marriage of any person named therein, and if any caveat be entered with such Minister, such caveat being duly signed by or on behalf of the person who enters the same, together with his or her place of residence, and the ground of objection on which his or her caveat is founded, no Licence shall issue or be granted until the Minister shall have examined into the matter of the caveat, and is satisfied that it ought not to obstruct the grant of the Licence for the said Marriage, or until the caveat be withdrawn by the party who entered the same; and in cases of doubt, it shall be lawful for such Minister to refer the matter of any such caveat to the Presbytery by which he shall have been appointed, which shall decide upon the same.

3. Persons (except Quakers and Jews) desirous of solemnising Marriage not according to the rites and ceremonies of the United Church of England and Ireland, may be Married according to the other rites and ceremonies, on production of a certificate, (obtained as above mentioned,) in a registered place of worship (stated in the notice of such Marriage), provided that every such Marriage shall be solemnised with open doors, between the hours of Eight in the morning and Two in the afternoon, in the presence of the Registrar of the District in which such registered building is situate, and of two or more credible witnesses; pro-

vided also that in some part of the Ceremony, and in the presence of such Registrar and witnesses, each of the Parties shall declare the following:

"I do solemnly declare that I know not of any lawful impediment why I, A.B., may not be joined in matrimony to C.D." And each of the parties shall say to the other, "I call upon these persons here present to witness that I, A.B., do take thee, C.D., to be my lawful wedded (wife or husband)." Provided also that there be no lawful impediment to the marriage of such parties.

After *seven* days from the entry of the notice, if the marriage is intended to be had by *Licence*, and after *twenty-one* days, if *without* Licence, the Registrar of the district may be required to grant his Certificate for marriage, but only for marriage in buildings registered *within his District* or in his office; but before any such Licence can be granted by him, one of the parties intending marriage must appear personally before him, and in case he shall not be the Registrar of the district to whom the notice of such intended marriage was given, shall deliver to him the certificate of the Registrar of the district to whom such notice shall have been given; and such party shall make oath, or shall make his or her solemn affirmation or declaration, instead of taking an oath, that he or she believeth that there is not any impediment of kindred or alliance, or other lawful hindrance to the said marriage, and that one of the said parties hath for the space of fifteen days immediately before the day of the grant of such Licence had his or her usual place of abode within the district within which such marriage is to be solemnised; and where either of the parties shall be under the age of twenty-one years, that the consent of the person or persons whose consent to such marriage is required by law, has been obtained thereto, or that there is no person having authority to give such consent, or that such party is a widow or widower, as the case may be.

4. Persons objecting to be married either according to the rites and ceremonies of the united church of England and Ireland, or according to the forms prescribed for marriages by Presbyterian Ministers, or in any such registered building, may, after notice and certificate as aforesaid, solemnize marriage on any day except Sunday, at the office of the Registrar of the district, with open doors, between the hours of eight in the morning and two in the afternoon, in the presence of the Registrar of the district, and in the presence of two witnesses, making the declaration and using the form of words required in the case of marriage in a registered building.

Quakers may contract and solemnize marriage according to the usages of their Society, provided both parties are of that society, and that notice shall have been given to the Registrar of the district and a certificate of such Registrar shall have been issued as before-mentioned.

Jews may likewise contract and solemnise marriage according to the usages of the Jewish religion, under similar provisions and restrictions, as stated in respect of Quakers.

Every marriage of which notice has been entered as aforesaid must be solemnised within three calendar months after such entry, or the notice must be renewed.

Every marriage solemnised after the 31st of March, 1845, under the provisions of this act for marriages in Ireland, in any other manner than as therein directed, will be null and void. But there is no alteration in regard to marriages by Roman Catholic Priests; such marriages may continue to be celebrated in the same manner and subject to the same limitations and restrictions as heretofore.

Be it also particularly observed that if any valid marriage shall be had under the provisions of the *Act for marriages in Ireland* by means of any wilfully false notice, certificate, or declaration is therein required, Her Majesty's Attorney-General or Solicitor-General may sue in the Court of Chancery or Court of Exchequer in Ireland, for a forfeiture of all estate and interest in any property accruing to the offending party by such marriage; and the proceedings thereupon and consequences thereof shall be the same as are provided in the like case with regard to marriages solemnized in England by Licence before the passing of this Act, according to the rites of the Church of England.

N.B.—Copies of the several forms and notices referred to in the foregoing, can be had on application at the office of the respective district registrars.

The districts to be established under the provisions of the Act, will be co-extensive with the Poor Law Unions, at the centre of which [the] Registrar must hold his Office.

William Donnelly, Registrar-General.

(1845-03-15, 1:1)

3279. The Lord Lieutenant has been pleased to appoint John Goudy, Esq., of Coolmaine, Registrar of Marriages, for this District, under the New Presbyterian Marriages bill. This appointment will give general satisfaction. (1845-03-15, 3:1)

3280. In Chancery.—Jane Harpur, Administratrix, of Henry Kidd, deceased, Plaintiff;—Henry Boyd, Defendant.—Pursuant to the Decree in this cause, bearing date the 20th day of January, 1845, I require all persons having charges or incumbrances affecting the lands of Bridgefarm, in the pleadings in this cause mentioned, to come in before me at my Office, Inns Quay, City of Dublin, and proceed to prove the same on or before the 1st day of May next, otherwise they will be precluded the benefit of said Decree.

Dated this 15th day of March, 1845.

R. Litton.

John Bates, Plaintiff's Solicitor,
38, Lower Ormond Quay.

(1845-03-22, 3:6)

3281. To the Memory of Mrs. James Gray.
By Francis Browne.

The spring hath woke her woodland choirs,
Of bird and stream and breeze,
And touched the sweet but viewless lyres,
That sound from quivering reeds and moss-grown trees;
Deep in the old untrodden woods,
When early sunbeams greet
Their green forsaken solitudes,
Waking the first young leaves and violets sweet.

But who shall wake for yearning love,
The voice whose echoes rise
From memory's haunted depths, above
All other pleasant sounds of earth and skies:
And who shall wake for us the chord,
That caught from classic strings,
The old world's dreamy music poured
In laurel groves, beside the Grecian springs?

How hath the hush of silence come
Upon the lip of song!
Why is there sorrow in the home
Where household love and gladness dwelt so long?
We for the grave that closed so soon
On life's unshadowed light,
The glory of a summer's noon
That saw no sunset fading into night!

Thou art not of the common Dead,
Lost sleeper! and we mourn
Thee not as they. No dews are shed
From the dark fount of Lethe on thine urn;
But, far along the wastes of time,
Each loving heart and ear
Will catch the song, as from the clime,
Where sounds the harp, hushed, but unbroken, here.

Stranorlar, February, 1845.
University Magazine.
(1845-03-22, 4:1)

3282. Awful Depravity.—On Friday, the 21st ult., an inquest was held before Franklin Baldwin, Esq., coroner of the county, on the body of a woman, under peculiarly revolting circumstances.

It appeared from the deposition of Thomas Kelly, one of the watchmen of the town of Bandon, that whilst he was going his rounds, and calling the hour of two o'clock, on Thursday morning, 20th instant, in the Shannon and Boyle-street beat, his attention was arrested by a person running after him, who requested him to go back with him to his lodgings in Shannon-street, as his kitchen or room was on fire. The watchman asked the man how it happened? To which he replied, "the old boy has set fire to my kitchen and room, dragged my wife off the table, threw it about the table, and would have dragged her up the chimney but for me, for I blessed myself, and rushed out of the door in a blaze of fire." On entering the kitchen, into which he was led by the man, the watchman found the dead body of a woman lying on the floor, with her face in a horrid ghastly manner towards the door, and within a quarter of a yard of a large blazing fire, and perceived a strong smell of something burned. The watchman did not make any particular examination of the body at the time, and saw no person in or about the room or house but the man who called him; he, however, saw four candles lighting, and part of a white cloth under the candlesticks, on a table, that had been burned, and he said, from the manner of the man both in speaking and walking, he must have had plenty of whiskey in him. At four o'clock, he returned, accompanied by two other watchmen (Lannan and Gallagher), and found the man sitting at the fire, and the dead body removed from the place where he first saw it, and found the left hand and arm much burnt—the upper part of the right side of the chest and the breast were also extensively burned; there was also a large hole burned in a shawl that was covering the body; the clothes on the body were also much burned. The watchman again asked the man the cause of all these appearances, and he replied she drank so much whiskey, she fell off the table in a fit and was burned; the watchman and one of his comrades then took the man in charge, and sent the other watchman to give information to the police.

From the deposition of Mary Kelly, it appeared that she knew the man now in custody, and the deceased woman for the last seven years; that his name was William Kelly, and that on Wednesday, the 10th instant, he came to her house and asked her to come down to his lodgings in Shannon-street and wash Kate (the deceased), who was dead, which she did and found no marks of violence whatsoever on the body; she and the prisoner laid out the body on a table near the fireplace.

On being asked by the coroner what he had to say for himself, the prisoner said that his name was William Kelly; that he was a pensioner, and received a pension of one shilling and fourpence per day; that he was discharged from the 59th Regiment, in August, fourteen years ago; that the deceased woman was his sister; that she was a married woman; that her husband was alive; that she had several children by her husband; that she was separated from her husband for the last seven years; that for that period, she lived with him (the prisoner) as his wife; knows that it was because of the life that he and the deceased led, that her husband would not live with her. Deceased was over 60 years of age.

The above statement of revolting depravity produced the most marked sensation of disgust and abhorrence in all present, and the Coroner expressed, in the warmest terms, his regret that he had not it in his power to inflict upon the prisoner such punishment as his almost unheard of depravity deserved.

From the conduct of the prisoner before and since the death of his wretched sister, he was evidently a determined drunkard. He attributed all the wretched scene the watchmen had witnessed to his drunken habits.

From the post mortem examination of the body, made by Wood, it appeared that the deceased had died from several visceral diseases, particularly of the lungs, which presented extensive marks of the last stage of consumption.

The jury, after a careful and lengthened examination, brought in a verdict, "Died by the visitation of God."—*Cork Constitution*. (1845-03-29, 2:4)

3283. Fatal Accident.—One of those harrowing occurrences which have latterly become so frequent through the ignorance of the public respecting the chemical properties of coal fume, where sufficient ventilation does not exist, took place on Friday night, in the house of Samuel Hemming, Esq., of Campsie, near this city. —A young couple only eleven months married, named Ellis, the domestic servants of Mr. Hemming, had retired to bed at their usual hour, but were not found stirring along with the other servants in the morning. Their room having been entered, they were found dead in their bed, locked in each other's arms, just as they may be supposed to have fallen asleep the night before. The cause of their death was at once evident. The room having been fresh plastered, a fire was put in the fireplace in order to protect the occupants from the effects of the damp, but either the high wind or the bad construction of the chimney prevented the flue from drawing properly, and the smoke was driven back into the room, whence there was no escape for it, the door and window being closed airtight. The man was yet warm when thus discovered, but the body of the poor young wife was quite cold and stiff. We have heard that they were warned against making use of the room by the other servants, but unhappily they were unheeded. An inquest was immediately held on the corpses, and a verdict in accordance with the facts was given. This is the second accident of the same kind which we have had to record within the last few weeks—four lives being thus sacrificed by the incaution of the sufferers. It is to be hoped that in these districts, at least, no one who has heard of these occurrences will be so foolish as to commit himself to a sleep from which he may never awaken, in an apartment with fire, whether in a grate, or stove of chafing dish, when there is not sufficient circulation of fresh air to carry off the pernicious fumes of the carbon. (1845-04-05, 2:1)

3284. The Irish Marriages Act.—On Thursday, the act of last session came into operation.—The *Newry Telegraph* says:—"It is a singular circumstance that, under the provisions of the act, no marriages can be legally celebrated in Ireland, by the clergy of any Protestant denomination, or by the registrars, during the ensuing eight days! The act requires that seven days' notice must be given before license can be issued, and a notice could not be served under the act before the 1st of April; it consequently happens that until this day (Wednesday) week, there can be no marriage lawfully performed in Ireland, save by Roman Catholic clergymen, an unprecendented anomaly." (1845-04-05, 2:3)

3285. A Breach of Promise of Marriage.—A verdict of two hundred and fifty pounds damages and costs was obtained on Wednesday, at the Cork assizes, after a two days' trial, by the Rev. Mr. Forrest, of same county, against Captain Donagh O'Brien, of the 72d Foot, for having broken his promise of marriage with plaintiff's daughter. The young lady is eighteen, and the gallant captain about forty. (1845-04-05, 4:5)

3286. Let the Dead Slumber Softly.

Let the dead slumber softly, recall not a name
That breathes to the living an echo of shame;
If souls must account for the ills they have done,
'Tis sinful to murmur the race they have run!
But, oh! if their deeds were the sunshine of life—
If they lived apart from seduction and strife—
If they charm'd the rude world, and sooth'd down its pain—
Oh, name them for ever again and again!

I love those who lend to their country a charm,
Who can sooth every sorrow and ward every harm,
Who can guide through each fierce rolling tempest that blows
The weak bark of life that is loaded with woes—
Then tell me of those who are offsprings of Fame,
Who have left in our breasts their endearment and name;
These charm'd the cold world and smooth'd down its pain,
Oh, name them for ever, again and again!

Oh, speak not of tyrants who ruled with the rod;
Of oppression, that crush'd every flower where it trod;
Of minions, who bent low the knee to the same,
And made them more bold in their actions of shame—
Such men are a curse to the earth we enjoy,
Inventors of discord and friends of alloy;
So tell me of those who have charm'd all our pain—
Oh, name them for ever, again and again!

(1845-04-12, 2:3)

3287. The following Presbyterian Meeting Houses being in the District of Castleblayney, and Presbytery of Ballybay, have been registered according to the provisions of the late Marriage Act.

Townland in which situated.	Parish.	County.
Derrykin,	Mucknoe,	Monaghan.
Broomfield,	Donomoyne,	do.
Derrynaloobina,	Ballybay,	do.
Derryvalley,	do.	do.
Alnameckan,	Newtownhamilton	Armagh.

William Rule,
District Registrar.
(1845-04-12, 2:4)

3288. Notice.—The Stone-bridge Presbyterian Meeting House, in the Presbytery and County of Monaghan, of which the Rev. William White is Minister, has been duly Registered for Solemnizing Marriages therein, agreeable to the *Act of 7 & 8 Vic., cap. 81.*

April 17th, 1845.

(1845-04-19, 3:2)

3289. Inquest on the Body of the Late Marquess of Downshire.—An inquest on the body of the lamented Marquess of Downshire, whose sudden death we recorded in our last publication, was held at six o'clock on Tuesday evening, in the court-house at Blessington, before Abraham Tate, Esq., of Rathdrum, coroner of the county Wicklow. A respectable jury of the tenants of his lordship was empannelled, and evidence was given corroboratory of the melancholy occurrence, as before stated by us.

Dr. Kellet, of Naas, was examined, and gave it as his opinion that he died of an effusion of blood on the brain.

Surgeon Cusack, of Dublin, who saw the remains of the deceased nobleman on Saturday night, was of a similar opinion.

The remains were conveyed on Monday evening, in a private manner, from Kippure Lodge to the house of Mr. Owen, at Blessington, to await the inquest.

The jury found the verdict that his lordship "died by the visitation of God."

The present Marquess of Downshire arrived at the Gresham Hotel on Tuesday evening, from London, and immediately proceeded to Blessington, to make the necessary preparations for the interment of his noble and much lamented father.—*Packet.*

(1845-04-19, 3:5)

3290. Sudden Death of the Marquis of Downshire.—We lament to record the very sudden and unexpected death of this estimable nobleman and venerated landlord.—His lordship was on Saturday engaged in paying his annual visit to the Blessington estates, in company with his agent, Mr. Owen. After riding to Sallygap, on his return he called at the residence of Mr. J.T. Armstrong, of Keppure Park, near Kilbride, where he lunched, and after riding about a quarter of a mile, he requested of Mr. Owen to ride on and acquaint some of his tenantry that he wished to see them, and inquire, as was his wont, how they were succeeding in their pursuits. Mr. Owen had scarcely left him when he happened to turn round, and found the noble marquis on the ground, the mare on which he rode walking over him. He hastened to his assistance, and on taking him in his arms, inquired if he was hurt, the only reply he received was a slight groan, when his lordship instantly expired.—The body was removed at once to Mr. Armstrong's on a temporary litter, where it lies to await a coroners inquest.

The lamented marquis was born on the 8th of October, 1788; he succeeded to the title in 1801; married, in 1811, Lady Maria Windsor, (born 30th of May, 1770,) eldest daughter of Other Hickman, fifth Earl of Plymouth.

His lordship's titles were Marquess of Downshire, Earl of Hillsborough, Viscount Hillsborough and Kilwarlin, and Baron Hill of Kilwarlin, county of Down, (Earl of Hillsborough, Viscount Fairford, Gloucestershire, and Lord Harwich, Baron of Harwich, Essex, in Great Britain,) Knight of Saint Patrick, Hereditary Constable of Hillsborough Fort, Lieutenant of the county of Down, [and] Colonel of the South Down Militia.—He is succeeded in his title by his son, Arthur Wills Blundell Sandys Trumbull Windsor, Earl of Hillsborough, M.P., born 6th of August, 1812, who married, 23rd of August, 1837, the Hon. Caroline Frances Stapleton Cotton, born 1815, eldest daughter of Stapleton Viscount Combermere. His other children are Lady Charlotte Chetwynd, Lady Mary Hood and Lord Arthur Edwin Hill.

Lord Arthur proceeded to England on Sunday morning, to convey the doleful intelligence to the Marchioness of Downshire, now at the Clarendon Hotel, Leamington Spa, on a visit to her daughter, Lady Charlotte Chetwynd, who is prolonging her stay at the Spa until after her confinement, which is shortly expected. It was the intention of the lamented nobleman to have joined the noble marchioness to Leamington in the latter end of this week. His departure was delayed until after the Royal Dublin Society, of which institution the noble marquess was a vice-president, and a strenuous friend and supporter.

(1845-04-19, 4:3)

3291. Diocess of Derry—Deplorable Event.—We feel exceeding pain in communicating to the public the sudden death of the venerated Bishop of Derry, the Right Rev. Dr. M'Loughlin, under circumstances exceedingly deplorable.—Accounts conveying this intelligence were received in town this morning, and have caused among all those who have known the personal and ecclesiastical worth of the deceased prelate, the most unmitigated pain. We shall not, for the present, enter more into the circumstances of this distressing event than thus briefly to record it. No doubt, a day or two will tend fully to explain what, being now known imperfectly, might unconsciously be aggravated.—*Evening Freeman of Monday.* (1845-04-26, 2:3)

3292. Representation of Down.—We have authority for stating that immediately after the sad obsequies of the late Marquis of Downshire shall have been performed, Lord Edwin Hill, the brother of the present Marquis, will offer himself to the electors as a candidate for the representation of the county. In any event, a member of the Hill family—adopting the same course, and advocating the same principles as those pursued and acted upon by Lord Hillsborough, the late member—would be sure of his return, but, under existing circumstances, we take for granted that there will be no contest.—*Mail.* (1845-04-26, 2:4)

3293. Death of a Waterloo Hero.—Sergeant James Graham, late of the Coldstream Guards, (light company,) departed this life on Thursday, at the Royal Hospital for ancient and maimed officers and soldiers, at Kilmainham. Graham was a native of Monaghan, and a most distinguished soldier. His gallant dexterity during the defence of the farm of Hugomont, during the battle of Waterloo by his intrepid corps, secured for him the admiration of the officers and men of that distinguished regiment. He was one of the party of the guards, headed by Lord Fitzclarence, which attacked the Cato-street gang. On that memorable occasion, Graham was one of the instruments by which, under Divine Providence, the life of the noble lord was saved. Graham and a brother soldier pulled the noble Lord down the ladder, at the instant that the fellows in the loft had their arms levelled to shoot him. Lord Fitzclarence met Graham some time back in Dublin, greeted him most cordially, and begged his acceptance of a pension which he has ever since enjoyed. He also fought gallantly in Spain, and returned from that country very little the worse of the wear.

The Rev. Mr. Norcross, rector of Framlingham, in Suffolk, having in 1815 requested that the Duke of Wellington should name a deserving soldier for a pension of £10 a year for life, which his reverence was desirous of conferring, his Grace directed that such a person should be named from the second brigade of the Guards by Major-Gen. Sir J. Byng, and the lot fell upon Graham as the most distinguished man in the action of the 18th of June in that year. This mark of distinction was communicated to the Sergeant by Colonels Woodford and Macdonald, in compliance with a brigade order, dated at Paris, August 9, 1815. The Sergeant was about 60 years of age when he resigned his spirit. Mr. Brocas, one of the eminent artists of that name, prevailed on Graham some time ago to sit for his portrait, which is a very fine picture. Captain Siborne has rendered the name of Graham immortal in that gallant officer's far-famed history of Waterloo. (1845-04-26, 3:1)

3294. The Right Hon. George and Mrs. Dawson have sustained a heavy affliction by the demise of Mr. George Beresford Dawson, late of the Rifle Brigade, their second son, who died on Monday morning. He was in the prime of life, not having attained his 23d year. The deceased gentleman had been gradually declining in health for some months. (1845-04-26, 3:2)

3295. Death caused by Glanders.—On Monday, a man named David Smith, of Creggan, died of glanders in the fever hospital attached to the county infirmary. He was infected by a horse of his own, which was labouring under that complaint for some time past. The diseased horse, we were informed, was not destroyed until late on Monday evening, and a sister of the deceased man continued to attend it, although she had been warned of the danger of doing so. It cannot be too generally known that glanders is communicated from the horse to man, and that in the latter, it is invariably fatal. Among the carmen employed in the city, we have been informed several other horses affected with the same disease are to be found, and it cannot be impressed too strongly on those whose duty it is to rid the city of such loathsome animals, that the promptest measures are required for the public safety.—*Derry Standard.* (1845-04-26, 3:2)

3296. Notice—Is hereby given that a separate building, named the First Presbyterian Meeting-House of Clontibret, situated in the townland of Legnacrave, in the parish of Monaghan, in the county of Monaghan, and in the district of Monaghan, being a building certified according to law, as a place of religious worship, was, on the fourteenth day of April, 1845, duly registered for solemnising Marriages therein, pursuant to the *Act of 7 and 8 Vic., cap. 81.*

Witness my hand this 16th day of April, 1845.
John Goudy, Registrar of Marriages
for the district of Monaghan. (1845-04-26, 3:3)

3297. Notice is hereby given that a separate building named the second Presbyterian Meeting-House of Clontibret, situated in the townland of Braddox, in the parish of Tullycorbet, in the county of Monaghan, and in the district of Monaghan, being a Building certified according to Law, as a place of religious worship, was, on the fourteenth day of April, 1845, duly Registered for Solemnising Marriages therein, pursuant to the *Act of 7 and 8 Vic., cap. 81.*

Witness my hand this 16th day of April, 1845.
John Goudy, Registrar of Marriages
for the district of Monaghan. (1845-04-26, 3:3)

3298. Notice is hereby given, that a separate building named the Glennan Meeting-house situated in the Townland of Glennan, in the parish of Donagh, in the county of Monaghan, and in the district of Monaghan, being a building certified according to Law, as a place of religious worship, was, on the fourteenth day of April, 1845, duly registered for solemnising Marriages therein, pursuant to the *Act of 7 and 8 Vic., cap. 81.*

Witness my hand this 16th day of April, 1845.
John Goudy, Registrar of Marriages
for the district of Monaghan. (1845-04-26, 3:3)

3299. Notice is hereby given, that a separate building named the First Monaghan Meeting-house situate in Meeting-house-square, in the town of Monaghan, in the Parish of Monaghan, in the County of Monaghan, and in the District of Monaghan, being a building certified according to Law as a place of religious worship, was, on the fourteenth day of April, 1845, duly registered for solemnising Marriages therein, pursuant to the *Act of 7 and 8 Vic., cap. 81.*

Witness my hand this 16th day of April, 1845.
John Goudy, Registrar of Marriages
for the district of Monaghan. (1845-04-26, 3:3)

3300. Notice is hereby given, that a separate building named the second Monaghan Meeting-house, situated in the townland of Mullaghmore, in the parish of Tydavenet, in the county of Monaghan, and in the district of Monaghan, being a building, certified according to law, as a place of religious worship, was on the fourteenth day of April, 1845, duly registered for solemnising Marriages therein, pursuant to the *Act of 7 and 8 Vic., cap. 81.*

Witness my hand this 16th day of April, 1845.
John Goudy, Registrar of Marriages
for the district of Monaghan. (1845-04-26, 3:3)

3301. Notice is hereby given, that a separate building named the Cahans Presbyterian Meeting-house, situated in the townland of Lisnavane, in the parish of Tullycorbet, in the county of Monaghan, and in the district of Monaghan, being a building certified according to law, as a place of religious worship, was on the fourteenth day of April, 1845, duly registered for solemnising Marriages therein, pursuant to the *Act of 7 and 8 Vic., cap. 81.*

Witness my hand this 16th day of April, 1845.
John Goudy, Registrar of Marriages
for the district of Monaghan. (1845-04-26, 3:3)

3302. Notice is hereby given, that a separate building named the Emyvale Meeting-house, situated in the townland of Carrigans, in the parish of Donagh, in the county of Monaghan, and in the district of Monaghan, being a building certified according to Law, as a place of religious worship, was on the fourteenth day of April, 1845, duly registered for solemnizing Marriages therein, pursuant to the *Act of 7 and 8 Vic., cap. 81.*

Witness my hand this 16th day of April, 1845.
John Goudy, Registrar of Marriages
for the district of Monaghan. (1845-04-26, 3:3)

3303. Notice is hereby given, that a separate building, named the Smithborow Meeting-house, situated in the town of Smithborow, in the parish of Clones, in the county of Monaghan, and in the district of Monaghan, being a building certified according to law, as a place of religious worship, was, on the fourteenth day of April, 1845, duly registered for solemnising Marriages therein, pursuant to the *Act of 7 and 8 Vic., cap. 81.*

Witness my hand this 16th day of April, 1845.
John Goudy, Registrar of Marriages
for the district of Monaghan. (1845-04-26, 3:3)

3304. Notice is hereby given, that a separate building, named the Scottstown Presbyterian Meeting-house, situated in the village of Scottstown, in the parish of Tydavnet, in the county of Monaghan and in the district of Monaghan, being a building certified according to law, as a place of religious worship, was on the fourteenth day of April, 1845, duly registered for solemnising Marriages therein, pursuant to the *Act of 7 and 8 Vic., cap. 81.*

Witness my hand this 16th day of April, 1845.
John Goudy, Registrar of Marriages
for the district of Monaghan. (1845-04-26, 3:3)

3305. Notice—Is hereby given that a separate building, named the first Presbyterian Church, of Castleblayney, situated in the townland of Derrykip, in the parish of Muckno, in the county of Monaghan, in the district of Castleblayney, being a building certified according to Law, as a place of religious worship, was on the eighth day of April 1845, duly registered for solemnizing Marriages therein, pursuant to the *Act of 7 and 8 Vic., cap. 81.*

Witness, my Hand this 24th day of April, 1845.
William Rule, Registrar of Marriages
for the district of Castleblayney. (1845-04-26, 3:5)

3306. Notice is hereby given that a separate building, named the Presbyterian Church of Bloomfield, situated in the townland of Broomfield, in the parish of Donnomoyne, in the county of Monaghan, in the district of Castleblayney, being a building certified according to Law, as a place of religious worship, was on the eighth day of April 1845, duly registered for solemnizing Marriages therein, pursuant to the *Act of 7 and 8 Vic., cap. 81.*

Witness, my Hand this 24th day of April, 1845.
William Rule, Registrar of Marriages
for the district of Castleblayney. (1845-04-26, 3:5)

3307. Notice is hereby given that a separate building, named the first Presbyterian Church of Newtownhamilton, situated in the townland of Newtownhamilton, in the Parish of Newtownhamilton, in the county of Armagh, in the district of Castleblayney, being a building certified according to Law, as a place of religious worship, was on the 9th day of April 1845, duly registered for solemnizing Marriages therein, pursuant to the *Act of 7 and 8 Vic., cap. 81.*

Witness, my Hand this 24th day of April, 1845.
William Rule, Registrar of Marriages
for the district of Castleblayney. (1845-04-26, 3:5)

3308. Notice is hereby given that a separate building, named the Presbyterian Meeting-house of second Ballybay, situated in the townland of Dernaloobina, in the parish of Ballybay, in the county of Monaghan, in the district of Castleblayney, being a building certified according to Law, as a place of religious worship, was on the ninth day of April 1845, duly registered for solemnizing Marriages therein, pursuant to the *Act of 7 and 8 Vic., cap. 81.*

Witness, my Hand this 24th day of April, 1845.
William Rule, Registrar of Marriages
for the district of Castleblayney. (1845-04-26, 3:5)

3309. Notice is hereby given that a separate building named the Presbyterian Meeting-house of Derryvalley, situated in the townland of Derryvalley, in the parish of Ballybay, in the county of Monaghan, in the district of Castleblayney, being a building certified according to law, as a place of religious worship, was on the ninth day of April 1845, duly registered for solemnizing Marriages therein, pursuant to the *Act of 7 and 8 Vic., cap. 81.*

Witness, my Hand this 24th day of April, 1845.
William Rule, Registrar of Marriages
for the district of Castleblayney. (1845-04-26, 3:5)

3310. Notice is hereby given that a separate building named the Presbyterian Church of second Castle-blayney, situated in the townland of Annyart, in the parish of Muckno, in the county of Monaghan, in the district of Castleblayney, being a building certified according to Law, as a place of religious worship, was on the twenty-second day of April 1845, duly registered for solemnizing Marriages therein, pursuant to the *Act of 7 and 8 Vic., cap. 81.*

Witness, my Hand this 24th day of April, 1845.
William Rule, Registrar of Marriages
for the district of Castleblayney. (1845-04-26, 3:5)

3311. Frightful Suicide.–An unfortunate wretch of the most abandoned character, named Alice M'Mahon, committed suicide on Saturday morning last, about the hour of 5 o'clock, a.m., in the Carrickmacross Bridewell, to which she had been committed for stealing a quantity of shop goods from a person named Doyle, a Taylor. She affected her dreadful purpose, by tying a handkerchief to her apron, then connecting both with one of the iron bars of her cell window, thus constituting a hank, into which she deliberately put her head, and sliding her feet into two of the small squares or iron holes forming the bottom of her bed (having first deliberately removed the mattress) she dropped in such a manner as to prevent the possiblity of extricating herself, and in the fall broke the vertebrae of the neck, which came in contact with the sharp edge of the window-stone, and deprived her of existence at once. On the previous day, she attempted self-destruction, by throwing herself down the stone stairs of the Bridewell, by which she got a frightful fracture on the right eye, extending across the temple. Mr. Armstrong, governor of the Bridewell, paid her the most humane and unceasing attention since she received the wound, visiting her cell almost hourly, and had been there asking how she felt, at four o'clock on Saturday morning. At five o'clock, again when he went to make a similar enquiry, when he discovered her as above described, and sent for Doctor M'Effer, who immediately attended, but found that life was extinct. It is probable the annals of human depravity can bear no parallel with the abandoned life led by this victim of juvenile prostitution. Not yet 10 years of age, she has been summarily committed by the Carrickmacross Bench, at Petty Sessions, seven times! Informations were returned and convictions obtained before the sitting Barrister of the County, against her, on six different occasions, for each of which she expiated her varied offences by imprisonment of two to six months, with hard labour! and twice has been presented for as a vagrant, by the Grand Jury, and escaped transportation through the mercy of the Judges, from a consideration of her extreme youth, and the solemn promises so frequently made to change her abandoned and reck-less career. On a previous occasion, the same individual attempted suicide, while a prisoner in the gaol of Monaghan.—*Armagh Gazette*. (1845-04-26, 4:3)

3312. Distressing Accident.–On Saturday last, a young lad of ten years of age, named Thomas Murphy, went, in the absence of his parents, to amuse himself by cutting sods of turf with a spade on the brink of a bog dike, near his father's residence, at Kilmore, near this town, when unfortunately the spade slipped, and the ill-fated lad was precipitated into the water, where his remains were found next morning, after his bereaved parents—who had no son but him—had searched the whole neighbourhood for him. The cause and circum-stances of death being obvious, the Coroner deemed it inexpedient to hold an inquest on the body.
(1845-05-03, 2:4)

3313. Death of Henry Faulkner, Esq.—It has become our melancholy duty to record the death of Henry Faulkner, Esq., of Castletown, in the county of Carlow, Deputy Lieutenant, which sad event took place on Saturday last, at No. 3, Percy-place, in the 73d year of his age.—For several years an active magistrate of the same county, his many public virtues gained for him the respect and esteem of all who were acquainted with him; while his character as a private individual bespoke the unostentatious Christian and the sterling friend. As a relative he was inestimable, being as a brother and an uncle the most fond, kind, and endearing. He died as he had lived, in displaying a meek submission to his Creator's will; and with a confiding trust in his Redeemer's love, he fell asleep in Jesus. (1845-05-10, 1:6)

3314. Mr. Grey Porter, the Federalist, is grandson of Dr. Porter, Bishop of Clogher, who died worth £300,000. (1845-05-10, 2:6)

3315. Death of Mr. Gilbert, Assistant Poor Law Commissioner.—We exceedingly regret to learn that Mr. Gilbert, the assistant poor law commissioner for this district, died yesterday, at his residence, Ross-trevor, of fever, after ten days' illness. His decease was most unexpected. Dr. Cuming, of Armagh, who had been summoned specially to visit him, arrived but a short time previously. Mr. Gilbert was greatly esteemed by those who knew him. (1845-05-10, 3:2)

3316. Notice is hereby given that a separate building, named Shancoagh Presbyterian Meeting House, situate in the parish of Magheross, in the County of Monaghan, being a building certified according to law, as a place of religious worship, was on the 22d day of April last, duly registered for solemnizing Marriages therein, pursuant to the *act of 7 and 8 Vic., cap. 81.*

Witness my Hand, this 7th day of May, 1845.
William Smith, Registrar of Marriages
for the district of Carrickmacross.
(1845-05-10, 3:4)

3317. Strange if True.–In the notice to correspondents published in the London *Medical Times* of the 26th ult., the following strange statement appears:—Dr. Davis, of Manorhamilton, sends us an (*continued...*)

3317, continued: ...authenticated statement, that in the neighbourhood of Londonderry, several ladies had gone to bed quite well, and in the morning, have been found in a complete state of insanity. More than six cases have occurred in a rural district within a circle of twenty miles. The mania is uncontrollably violent, and characterised by an extreme anxiety for the nudity of nature. Our correspondent speaks of the visitation as an epidemic like some of those that are recorded as taking place in the sixteenth and seventeenth century in Germany and France.

We have not heard of this singular malady, and therefore do not believe in its existence. If it should prove to be a slanderous imputation against our fair friends, we would recommend that the author of it should be tried by a jury of matrons, and, on conviction, be sentenced to wear, for the residue of his natural life, those garments of which he alleges the ladies of our neighbourhood are so desirous to divest themselves.—*Derry Sentinel*. (1845-05-10, 4:3)

3318. Coroner's Inquest.—Determined Suicide.—John Macfaden, Esq., M.D., one of the coroners for the county of Cavan, held an inquest at Lurgan, parish of Munster-connaught, near Oldcastle, in that county, on the 26th ult., on view of the body of a man of the name of Pat Tuite, a small farmer, who resided there, who cut his throat with a reaping hook. The coroner having impanelled a respectable and intelligent jury, the following are briefly the facts of the case, as elicited in evidence:—The deceased was charged with having, about nine years ago in that neighbourhood, killed a man with a loy (a kind of spade), for which he was brought to trial at the next Cavan Assizes, when the jury before whom he was arraigned returned a verdict that he (the deceased) stood mute by the visitation of God, and was at the time of the commission of unsound mind, and in consequence of which, he was sent to the Armagh Lunatic Asylum, by order of the then Lord Lieutenant, where he was kept for two or three years, and then sent home to his wife and family, having been considered sufficiently recovered from his melancholy malady to be discharged from that institution; and on the day previous, Thursday sennight (24th ult.), the deceased, who appeared to be in the enjoyment of his usual health, occupied himself in cleaning corn in his barn, and was discovered by his eldest daughter, a grown up young woman, on his knees with his throat cut, in a few minutes after his having committed the rash act, and the fatal reaping hook lying by his side, in the midst of the blood which flowed from the ghastly wound which he had inflicted on himself. He walked from thence to the dwelling house with her, where he was attended by a medical gentleman and a clergyman, who rendered him all the assistance in their power, but without avail—he never uttered a sentence from the time he was discovered by his daughter until he died. He was about sixty years of age. The jury returned a verdict in accordance with the foregoing facts.—*Drogheda Conservative*. (1845-05-17, 1:5)

3319. Death of Lord Carberry.—With extreme regret, we copy from the *Cork Constitution* of Tuesday, the following melancholy announcement:—

"Death of Lord Carberry.

"His Lordship died on Monday morning at ten minutes after nine o'clock, and his death will excite regret for the loss of a good landlord, a sincere friend, an independent, honorable, and high minded man. His Lordship was born in 1765, married in 1783 the third daughter of the Earl of Arran, succeeded his father in the Baronetcy in 1777, and his cousin in the Peerage in 1807, and was 80 years of age at the time of his decease." (1845-05-17, 2:4)

3320. On Sunday morning, a boat containing four men and one woman was [sic] proceeding from Cahirciveen, to Dingle, when on passing Cromwell's Fort, off the island of Valentia, the boat was upset in a sudden squall of wind, and all on board perished. (1845-05-24, 1:6)

3321. On Thursday, James M'Carthy, Esq., senior coroner of the County of Dublin, held an inquest at Kingstown, on view of the body of E.G. Simonds, a rich Jewish merchant, who died on board the packet from Liverpool to Dublin, on Wednesday night. It appeared that deceased came from Hamburgh *via* London, and had a large and very valuable stock of goods in his possession. He complained of a pain in his heart, and it was stated in evidence that he had been under treatment in London for the complaint.—Nothing particular occurred during the night, and in the morning, he was found dead in his bed in the packet. Some witnesses were examined and proved the above facts. The jury found a verdict that deceased died by the visitation of God. (1845-05-24, 1:6)

3322. Inquest.—On Thursday sennight, Mr. Atkinson, coroner, held an inquest at Ballycastle, on the body of Mrs. Eliza Harding, wife of Lieutenant George Harding, of the Coast Guards, stationed at Belarrig. The lady's death was very sudden, and many unpleasant reports injurious to the character of her husband were in circulation, owing to a servant maid who left her service a short time previous to her death. Many witnesses were examined, all of whom bore testimony to Lieutenant Harding being a kind and affectionate husband. Dr. Layng, of Ballycastle, who was in the habit of attending the deceased for some years, gave evidence as to her manner of living, and had seen her in fits, which appeared to him to be delirium tremens. Dr. Neilson made a post mortem examination, after which he gave the following evidence:—That on the left breast, there was the mark of a slight contusion, but it was not of consequence, as producing any material injury. The lungs were small, but in other respects, appeared healthy. The left extremity of the stomach was very much inflamed, and the greater portion of the small intestines were also in an inflamed state; the liver was gorged with

blood. He was of opinion that the state of the liver and also the inflamed state of the stomach and intestines could be satisfactorily accounted for from the intemperate habits of the deceased; and although there was no proof of excess of drinking ardent spirits for some days prior to death, he was [of] opinion, that a chronic state of inflammation of the stomach and intestines had existed for some time; he was, however, of opinion that the immediate cause of death was epilepsy. The jury returned as their verdict that the deceased, Eliza Harding, came by her death by the visitation of God.—*Athlone Constitution.*
(1845-05-24, 2:4)

3323. Notice—Is hereby given, that a separate building, named the Crieve Presbyterian Church, situated in the townland of Crieve, in the parish of Aghnamullen, in the county of Monaghan, in the district of Castleblayney, being a building certified according to Law, as a place of religious worship, was on the 23rd day of April, 1845, duly registered for solemnizing Marriages therein, pursuant to the *act of 7 and 8 Vic., chap. 81.*

Witness my Hand, this 21st day of May, 1845.
William Rule, Registrar of Marriages
for the district of Castleblayney.
(1845-05-24, 3:4)

3324. Notice is hereby given, that a separate building, named the Creggan Presbyterian Church, situated in the townland of Freeduff, in the parish of Creggan, in the county of Armagh, in the district of Castleblayney, being a building certified according to Law, as a place of religious worship, was on the 15th day of May, 1845, duly registered for solemnizing Marriages therein, pursuant to the *act of 7 and 8 Vic., cap. 81.*

Witness my Hand, this 21st day of May, 1845.
William Rule, Registrar of Marriages
for the district of Castleblayney.
(1845-05-24, 3:4)

3325. There are two vacancies in the Governors of Carlow Asylum by the death of Mr. Falkner and the removal to England of Mr. Evans. (1845-05-24, 4:5)

3326. On Monday, the marriage ceremony was performed in Nenagh gaol, between a male prisoner, against whom a charge of a serious assault was sworn, and the female whose informations were taken against him. After the ceremony, the pair were ushered outside of the prison. (1845-05-24, 4:5)

3327. Doctors Differ.—It will be in the recollection of our readers that a Roman Catholic Clergyman named M'Phillips, was tried at our last Quarter Sessions, for rescuing himself from a Bailiff who arrested him under a decree for debt. The arrest took place at a funeral where Mr. M'Phillips was officiating; and James Major, Esq., our Assistant Barrister dismissed the case, as he deemed a priest performing the offices of religion was not liable to arrest, under the *10th Geo. 4, sec. 27, cap. 34.* Mr. M'Phillips since summoned the bailiff before the Magistrates at Newbliss for making a false arrest. The Magistrates—R. Mayne, J. Moorehead, and C. Wallace, Esqrs., refused to decide the case without reference to the Law Officers of the Crown. A case was therefore laid before the Law advisers, and they have decided that the arrest was legal, and that a priest officiating under the circumstances did not receive the protection of the statute. (1845-05-31, 3:1)

3328. The Queen's Birth Day.—There was a grand review of the troops in garrison in Phoenix-park on Tuesday, commencing a quarter before twelve o'clock. In addition to the Grand military spectacle, the Locals and the boys of the Royal Hibernian School were ordered to parade on this occasion of the celebration of her Majesty's birthday. (1845-05-31, 4:4)

3329. Equity Exchequer.—Robert Killen, Plaintiff. Esther Connolly, Admnx. of Charles Connolly, Deceased, and John Corley, Defendants.

Pursuant to the Decree made in this Cause, bearing date the 7th day of February, 1845, I hereby require all persons having Charges and Incumbrances affecting the lands of Listillen, in the county of Monaghan, being the Mortgaged lands and premises, in the pleadings in this Cause mentioned; and, also, all Creditors of Charles Connolly, late of Listillen, aforesaid, deceased, in the Decree named, to come in before me, at my Chambers, on the Inns Quay, Dublin, on or before the 3rd day of November next, and prove their respective demands; otherwise they will be precluded the benefit of said Decree.

Dated this 4th day of June, 1845.
Entd. J.S. Acheson Lyle, C.R.
Thomas Edmund Wright,
Plaintiff's Attorney.
(1845-06-07, 3:3)

3330. Mad dogs, it is reported, are now doing harm in this county. We know not, but perhaps the police should be actively alive to the matter, and use suitable precaution.—*Fermanagh Reporter.* (1845-06-07, 3:3)

3331. Fever is very prevalent in the rural districts about Enniskillen. Some poor families in Enniskillen have been attacked. (1845-06-07, 3:3)

3332. The situation of resident apothecary to the Cork fever hospital is vacant, by the demise of Mr. Downing, who fell a victim to the contagion.
(1845-06-14, 4:5)

3333. Sudden Death of Arthur B. Cooper, Jun., Esq. —It with the most poignant regret we have to record the death of Arthur B. Cooper, jun., Esq., Cooper's Hill. In the fulness of youthful health, this amiable and highly esteemed young gentleman (*continued...*)

3333, continued: ...suddenly died on Thursday morning, at Fortland, the residence of Robert Jones, Esq., where he and his lady were on a visit. He rose early in the morning, and having looked out his bed-room window, remarked on the fineness of the day, and again retired to bed. He was only a few minutes in bed when he was heard to breathe oppressively, and alarm being excited, Dr. Homan, who happened to be at Fortland, was called on, but though only a few minutes had passed, he was dead. The intelligence of his death produced the strongest feeling of sorrow in Sligo, for wherever he was known, he was esteemed and respected, being of the most kind, generous, and charitable disposition. He filled the office of treasurer for the county, since the death of the late Mr. Dodwell.—*Sligo Journal.* (1845-06-21, 1:6)

3334. Melancholy Accident—Death by Drowning. A young man named Samuel Tood, a native of Belfast, who was in the employment of Mr. M'Coy, plumber, of this town, after finishing his day's work at the residence of C.P. Leslie, Esq., M.P., Glasslough, went to bathe in the adjoining lake; he plunged in, and sank to rise no more with life. He was taken out the next morning, and from the contorted state of some of his limbs, it is probable that he was seized with cramps, which, though a good swimmer, prevented him from making any effort to save himself. (1845-06-21, 2:5)

3335. James M'Donnell, Esq., M.D.—The late Doctor M'Donnell, of Belfast, whose death took place in the month of April, was a gentleman of the very first eminence in his profession, and had occupied the foremost rank not only in that great provincial town, but throughout a wide and important district, in the north of Ireland, for half a century.

Although not a native of this town, he was nevertheless one of its oldest inhabitants, having been sent there along with his two brothers, at a very early age, to be educated in the school of Mr. Garnet, at that time, and for some years subsequently, the most eminent teacher in the province of Ulster. The charge of his school-boy days was committed to his mother, a lady of strong intellectual powers, who, induced by maternal solicitude, accompanied her sons, on their first removal from home, and resided in Belfast until the death of her husband, when it became her permanent and final abode; and to the gentle, but powerful influence, of this maternal culture, the high development of mind and disposition, displayed so conspicuously in after life, may, in a great degree, be attributed.

That Doctor M'Donnell's progress in learning must have been more rapid than usual in those days, will appear from his having the degree of M.D., in the University of Edinburgh, at the age of twenty-two, and that he commenced his distinguished and successful career as a practising physician in the year 1784-5. The late Doctor Haliday of Belfast, a gentleman of independent fortune, whose name was in those days, (and still handed down in Hardy's *life of Lord Charlemont*), conspicuous as associated with that venerated nobleman, was also in the first and highest range of practice in Belfast, and to his friendship, and patronage, the young physician was in no trifling degree indebted for his success and distinction. Attached to the principles of civil and religious liberty, which that party, as Whigs of 1688, decidedly professed, Doctor M'Donnell, was from the commencement of his professional career to the close of his long and useful life, their consistent advocate.

His nature, however, was cast in a mould too gentle, to qualify him for the fierce encounter of party strife, in which the maintenance of his principles failed not to involve many, whose temper was not so mild, and whose judgement was not so penetrating. And though his reliance upon their ultimate success, which he lived to witness, was never a subject of doubt to the doctor, his calm spirit shrunk from the fearful extremes, which he saw those of a bolder temperament exhibit, to their own injury, and to the retarding of the prosperity of their country.

We would therefore desire most to contemplate the character of Doctor M'Donnell in that point of view, in which its features shine forth with peculiar lustre, indicating the enlighted christian, and warm hearted philanthropist, whose benevolence will long shed a sacred halo round his honoured memory. To the gratification of that benevolence, his profession afforded the most frequent and ample opportunities; at the same time that it made upon his sympathy and charity the most numerous demands; the former were never neglected; the latter never refused, though his aversion to ostentation, led him to conceal from all the world the extent of his generosity, which was rarely discovered, except by accident.

Amongst the many institutions in Belfast, for the relief of the poor, there is not one of which Dr. M'Donnell was not the liberal supporter; of not a few, he was, if not the founder, at least among the first promoters. The fever hospital and dispensary were long the scenes of his most active labours; and the system of district visitation, by which medical attendance is gratuitously provided at their own dwelling, for the poor, was chiefly organised at his suggestion, if not entirely so. The prosperity of the Belfast Academical Institution, and the establishment of the medical school connected with it, were also long the object of his watchful attention; and his exertions and influence contributed not a little to the obtaining of the grant of the endowment, however inadequate, which it receives from the state. The high estimation in which he was held by many noblemen and personages of rank, always giving him considerable weight, which was frequently exerted, and successfully too, in the advancement of young persons of humble rank, but of high qualifications, who, without the friendship and introduction of the Doctor, might have continued in obscurity.

Amidst the ceaseless anxieties attending his profession, Dr. M'Donnell still found intervals of leisure for the cultivation of philosophical and scientific pursuits, the latter generally connected with his own particular department of study. His name was, therefore, well known, and highly estimated amongst the various literary circles throughout the empire, and not unknown in the academies of science abroad; and whilst an introduction to his acquaintance was eagerly sought by strangers visiting Belfast, as a privilege and a valuable distinction, an introduction from him was prized as a passport, which would elsewhere realize for its bearer the most favourable consideration.

Descended from the ancient lineage of the M'Donnells of the Glens, as one of that enobled clan of which the Antrim family is the head, the Doctor felt the most devoted attachment to his native land, and his strong nationality led him, as a matter of course, to take the deepest interest in its early history and antiquities at a time when these subjects were rarely studied, as they have been since; whilst of late years, its industrial resources, the improvement of the moral and physical condition of his countrymen, with the details of hospital statistics, in which he took an unabated interest, were the subjects which engrossed the largest part of his leisure, when free from bodily suffering. Endowed by nature with a most retentive memory, his mind was stored with a mass of information which from its great variety, and extraordinary extent and accuracy, always excited the admiration of those in whose society he was accustomed to lay aside his natural diffidence, and display its solid treasures. Although the debility of advanced life had, for the last few years, confined him closely to his house, his mental activity long survived his corporeal powers, and it is within this very year, amid the circle of a few friends, all his juniors, whom he favoured with his friendship and invited to his family circle, that he was wont to pour forth, in the short interval of ease, which evening generally brought, a copiousness of observation connected with his favourite pursuits, blended with apt illustrations, amusing anecdotes, and the warmth of enthusiasm of his youthful days, which will not soon be forgotten by those who enjoyed this privilege, for such it was considered. But there are others with whom his memory will long be held in warm affection; we speak not of his family, to all members of which he was endeared by the strong ties of love and veneration, but of the poor and destitute who were accustomed to crowd around his door, or to fill his hall, so as actually to block up the passage, unchecked by any person; for to do so would be highly displeasing to him—to these admittance was never denied, until nature had denied to himself the strength to receive them.

Doctor M'Donnell, at the period of his death, which took place on the 8th of April, 1845, was in his eighty-second year. He must, in his youth, have been a very handsome man; his smile was the sweetest imaginable, and natural withal. He was in person rather tall, perhaps five feet ten inches at least. He was negligent of his dress, delicately cleanly, and generally wore top boots, though he never rode, but always went in a gig, driven by his well-known servant, Mick, a great curiosity in his way, with his hammer for breaking off specimens of minerals, &c., which they carried back in quantities. His library was extensive and valuable, and his dinner room was crowded with books, minerals, pamphlets, and innumerable tracts, and other papers; and although these seemed to be in a mass of inextricable confusion, he could lay his hand on any paper required, in a moment, and in his last illness, could direct a person to do the same. His intellects were clear to the final hour, and he died in faith and trust in the atonement made for him by his blessed Redeemer: receiving at his own request the Sacrament of the Lord's Supper from the hands of the minister of his parish, and professing his warm attachment to the doctrines of the Church of England. Alexander M'Donnell, Esq., resident Commissioner of the Board of Education, is the eldest son of the great and good man whose memoir I have attempted to shape, partly from a Provincial paper, and partly from an intimacy I had the happiness to enjoy from him for nearly forty years.

Quis desiderio, sit pudor, aut modus
Tam chari capitis?

Robert Short.
(1845-06-21, 2:6)

3336. Drowning.—The only son and principal support of a widowed mother named M'Keany was drowned on Sunday, 15th inst., at the Broad Meadow, adjoining Enniskillen. He was a shoemaker, and had gone in to wash himself. After 9 hours searching, his body was found, when Mr. Wm. Trotter, coroner, held an inquest, and a verdict of accidental drowning, was returned. (1845-06-21, 3:1)

3337. Cure for Hydrophobia.—A correspondent writes to the *Times* as follows:—"Observing in your journal of late several instances of this dreadful disease, allow me to call the attention of the faculty, and your readers generally, to the fact that French vinegar given in large doses (half a pint or more at a time) has proved of the greatest service. I do not mean to maintain that it will prove an infallible remedy, but that it has afforded relief, and in one case of dreadful suffering a permanent cure, I was assured by a gentleman some time since, who knew of it been [sic] practised to some extent in the French hospitals. Should this hint prove of avail, or lead to the means of drawing attention to it, I am sure you will give publicity to it." (1845-06-21, 3:1)

3338. Accident.—Daniel Peterson, in the employment of Wm. A. Dane, Esq., solicitor, rode to Maguiresbridge on Saturday morning on business, and letting the reins slack, he was pitched upon his head by the horse starting at a bird, and is not expected to recover. (1845-06-21, 3:3)

3339. The office of Secretary to the Louth Grand Jury is vacant by the death of A. Shekleton, Esq., of Dundalk. (1845-06-28, 1:2)

3340. We have heard, with great regret, that the child of Mr. Booth Bell, who had his arm fractured by a fall from the gig when his father was shot, has since died. (1845-06-28, 2:6)

3341. Death of Chas. Gibson, Esq.—We regret to announce the decease, of this estimable and worthy man. A short time since, we congratulated the tenants of Mr. Shirly [sic], upon having him placed over them as an agent.

"Man proposeth but God disposeth."

We trust he now enjoys the blessings earned by an honorable and well spent life. Public feeling and sympathy may console the living, and if ever it had that effect, the relatives of our friend have great consolation in knowing, that he died without an enemy, and loaded with blessings. (1845-06-28, 3:1)

3342. Melancholy Accident.—On Tuesday last, a groom of C.P. Leslie, M.P., while attending a Clydesdale Horse belonging to that gentleman, in Armagh, was killed by a kick from a mare, belonging to Mr. Thornton. The animal struck him in the chest on the left side, and the unfortunate man expired in a few moments. (1845-06-28, 3:2)

3343. The Orphan's Cry.—By Thomas Mills.

Tune—"Weep not for me."
Pity a poor helpless stranger,
Oh! think on me;
'Midst a world of want and danger,
Oh! think on me.
To the door of mercy flying,
Hear the helpless stranger crying
Save—oh, save an orphan dying,
Oh! think on me.

Once I had a tender mother
To think on me;
Then my heart ne'er sought another
To think on me;
But, by time and sickness shaken,
She at last from earth was taken,
Now, by all the world forsaken,
Oh! think on me.

Now life's road seems long and weary,
Oh! think on me;
Darker grows my path and dreary,
Oh! think on me.
Hope no more her bright lamp lighting,
Fate its dying embers lighting,
Nought on earth my soul delighting,
Oh! think on me. (1845-07-05, 1:3)

3344. Awful Visitation in Clare.—One of the dreadful and extensive calamities with which it has pleased Providence to inflict any portion of this county for many years, occurred to the tract of country lying between Broadford and Glenomera, a distance of nearly five miles, on Friday last. The morning was particularly calm and serene, but about two o'clock, rain fell with such violence, and came in such impetuous torrents from the mountain tops as completely to inundate the lower parts of the country. Such was the awful violence of the deluge (it could be called by no other name) that it swept before it three bridges, two of whose names we could for the present only learn—viz., Kilbawn and Ballymacdonnell. Flocks, herds, houses, and tillage, including immense quantities of wheat and potatoes, were alike victims to its ungovernable fury. It swept by the old chapel of Kilbawn and laid part of it prostrate. Amid the general ruin, we have yet heard of only one loss of life, that of Mary Kinneen, a girl of about fourteen years of age, whose body, all bruised and disfigured, with every limb broken, was found at a distance of about half a mile from the place where her residence stood but a few hours previously. An inquest was held on her remains by James Martin, Esq., coroner. Over seven hundred acres of meadowing have been completely ruined, the mountainous waters leaving mud scattered upon it so as to render it perfectly useless for the present season. Of the amount of the damages sustained, it would be difficult for the present to form a conjecture; but we fear that years must elapse before the inhabitants of the neighborhood can recover from the effects of this awful calamity. We have heard of similar devastations in some of the adjoining parishes, but nothing so authentic as to warrant a public notice. Would it not be well to open a subscription for the unhappy sufferers. Such a piece of active benevolence would be worth all the mock liberality and pulling patriotism that have so long traded on Irish credulity. Our columns may be commanded to forward such a laudable undertaking as this would prove.—*Clare Journal*. (1845-07-05, 2:6)

3345. Notice—Is hereby given, that a separate building, named the 2nd Newtownhamilton Meeting-house, situated in the town of Newtownhamilton, in Castleblayney-street, in the parish of Newtownhamilton, in the county of Armagh, in the district of Castleblayney, being a building certified according to law, as a place of Religious Worship, was on the 24th day of June, 1845, duly registered for solemnizing Marriages therein, pursuant to the *act of 7 and 8 Vic., cap. 81.*

Witness my hand, this 3rd day of July, 1845.
William Rule, Registrar of Marriages
for the district of Castleblayney.
(1845-07-05, 3:2)

3346. Birth-Day Recollections.
By Robert Gilfillan.

Oh! for the songs of other years,
When life and joy were young;
When nought but gladsome tales were told,
Or mirthful strains were sung!
When birth day healths, with welcomes high,
Were given with cheerful brow;
Our cups, alas! in silence pass—
We've nought but memories now.

And round our little social board
Was seen that watchful eye—
One who, though knit to us on earth,
Yet raised our hopes on high.
She who in childhood's helpless days
Around our couch did bow—
A mother's name—no more gives fame—
We've nought but memories now.

Oft in the stormy sea of life,
Our bark, by tempest driven,
Full dashing on the shoals of fate,
With cords and canvass riven,
A mother's love, a mother's look,
Like angel at the prow,
Would cheer us to the haven of health—
We've nought but memories now.

Youth's days are fled, and in their stead
Come sorrow, grief, and tears;
And for the sunny morns of song,
We number heavy years.
Fond friends are gone, and we alone
Must 'neath affliction bow—
Time was when we gave happy healths—
We've nought but memories now.

University Magazine for July.
(1845-07-05, 4:5)

3347. The Poet's Bride.

O wouldst thou be a poet's bride,
Think not his eyes are always bright;
Think not that joys all rapturous tide
For ever laves [sic] his soul with light;
The sweetest strains to music given
In lowest breathings oft are played,
The bird that nearest soars to heaven
Reposes in the silent shade.

So he who sometimes blithely soars
Far in the bright and sunny clime,
Whose harp its sweeping numbers pours,
And present brings the bygone time;
Whose mounting spirit loves to roam
In thought-built worlds where none may rest,
Wearied with soaring seeks a home
Upon affection's peaceful breast.

A poet is a human shrine,
Lit up at times by heavenly fire.
And, wouldst thou call the poet thine,
In silence oft may hang his lyre;
His wounded spirit oft may need
Love's hand to staunch the bleeding tide;
Say, wilt thou make that tide recede?
And may'st thou be a poet's bride.
(1845-07-12, 4:1)

3348. Coroner's Inquest.—On Monday last, an inquest was held, by George Henry, Esq., coroner, upon the body of William Dunn, Esq., a blacksmith, employed by Mr. James Scott, of Ballymacally Cottage. It appeared in evidence, that the deceased, on the day previous, had taken his dinner in the house of his employer, in good health—had gone out afterwards, during which time he had partaken freely of whiskey, but returned about six o'clock in the evening, apparently sober, and sat quietly down upon a chair, where he remained for some time, when he suddenly fell from thence upon the floor. He was immediately removed to bed, medical advice sent for, and every attention paid which his situation required, but without effect, for he expired about two o'clock on Monday morning. A verdict was returned of "Died by apoplexy, caused by drinking whiskey." (1845-07-19, 1:4)

3349. It affords us sincere pleasure to state that Robert Smith, Esq., Clerk of the Peace of this county, who was attacked with a severe fit of gout, is recovering. This announcement will be hailed with satisfaction by the numerous friends of this most estimable gentleman. (1845-07-19, 3:2)

3350. Poor Ben's Grave.

Yon broken oar on barren shore
Points out the sailor's pillow,
Where keel led by deeps in death he sleeps
Beside the rolling billow.

He rests alone, no pompous stone
His deeds or nation numbers;
His arm seem'd spread beneath his head
To take his cottage slumbers.

The hand that press'd his manly breast
Where Death's last pangs did hover,
Show'd what deep care had struggled there
Of parting grief now over.

Yet never more the sigh'd-for shore,
Nor cottage home shall greet him;
Nor wife nor child, in rapture wild,
With fond caresses meet him.

High o'er the sands a mourner stands,
Whose eye the tear is dimming;
Who views a shroud in every cloud
O'er misty ocean skimming.

How oft his shade, the anxious maid,
Sees through the lattice gazing,
In taper meets the winding sheets,
Learns death from faggot blazing.

Many a son his race shall run, (*continued...*)

3350, continued:

And dizzy speck shall vanish,
O'er sea's white foam, and tall ship roam
Ere Hope her spell shall banish.

His sleep is sound, where wreck'd were drown'd
Time flies as hope fades paler:
Gulls shriek their dirge, 'mid storm and surge
O'er Ben the shipwreck'd Sailor.

(1845-07-19, 4:1)

3351. Sudden Death.—An itinerant dealer in old rags and iron, named Murphy, was found dead in his bed on Thursday morning. Deceased was about forty years of age, and resided in Alexander-street. He was a confirmed drunkhard [sic], and it is believed that the unhappy man was suffocated through the effects of his own intemperance. Murphy has left behind him a wife and five children. (1845-07-26, 1:3)

3352. From the 1st of January next, all marriages at Gretna Green are declared illegal. (1845-07-26, 3:1)

3353. Death by Drowning.—On Friday last, a middle-aged woman, named Ann Aull, was found immersed in a pool of water, near where she lived at Aughnaseda, near this town, and on being taken out, life was found to be so nearly extinct that, she expired some minutes afterwards. That the unfortunate woman committed suicide, is apparent, from the fact, that on the previous day, she was prevented from committing self-destruction, in the same pool, by a person who came to the spot when she was throwing herself in, and that for some years past, she was subject to periodical paroxyms of insanity. (1845-07-26, 3:2)

3354. Chancery.—The Rev. Robert Hogg, Clerk, Plaintiff.—Charlotte Mitchell, Henry Mitchell the Elder, Henry Mitchell the Younger, and others, Defendants.

Pursuant to the Cause bearing Date the 21st day of June, 1845, I hereby require all Creditors and Legatees of Alexander Mitchell, Esq., late of Shirley House, Carrickmacross, in the county of Monaghan, Esq., Deceased, The Testator in the pleadings in this Cause named, and all persons having Charges and Incumbrances affecting the lands of Annaghcore, Killaneel, Garron, Lecklevery, situate in the county of Monaghan, aforesaid, or the several Messuages or Tenements, in the town of Monaghan, in the pleadings mentioned, to come in before me, at my Chambers on the Inns Quay, Dublin, on or before the 1st day of October, next, and proceed to prove their Debts and Charges, and claim their Legacies; otherwise, they will be precluded the benefit of said Decree.

Dated, this 19th day of July, 1845.

Thomas Goold.

Robert Murdoch, Plaintiff's Solicitor,
Chambers, 31, College-green.

(1845-07-26, 3:4)

3355. Approaching Marriage in High Life.—It is said that a matrimonial alliance is settled between Lady Jane Grimston, youngest and only unmarried daughter of the Earl and Countess of Verulam, and the Earl of Caledon. (1845-07-26, 4:5)

3356. Inquest.—On Monday last, 28th inst., an inquest was holden before Lord Cremorne, and Charles Boyle, Esq., at Rockcorry, on the body of an infant child, found dead in a pool of water near that town, by a man named Patrick Campbell. That it was destroyed by its natural parent seems probable, from its being carefully sewed up in a bag. It was floating when found; and the following verdict will best indicate how long it had been drowned:—"We find that this child, which it appears from the evidence of the Doctor, must have been in the water some weeks, and consequently became so decomposed as to prevent him giving us any professional proof or information as to its death. We find ourselves, under the circumstances, unable to say, whether the child was born alive, and if so, whether drowned or suffocated."
(1845-08-02, 3:3)

3357. Notice.—Notice is hereby given that a separate Building, named the Presbyterian Meeting-house of Clarkesbridge, situated in the townland of Curtamlet, in the parish of Newtownhamilton, in the County of Armagh, in the District of Castleblayney, being a building certified according to law, as a place of Religious Worship, was, on the 23rd day of July, 1845, duly registered for Solemnizing Marriages therein, pursuant to the *act of 7th and 8th Vic., Chapter 81.*

Witness my hand this 30th day of July, 1845.

William Rule, Registrar of Marriages
for the district of Castleblayney.

(1845-08-02, 3:4)

3358. The Grave.

The Grave it is deep and soundless,
And canopied over with clouds;
And trackless and dim and boundless
Is the Unknown Land that it shrouds,

In vain may the nightingales warble
Their songs—the roses of Love
And Friendship grow white on the marble
The Living have reared above.

The virgin, bereft at her bridal
Of him she has loved, may weep;
The wail of the orphan is idle;
It breaks not the buried one's sleep.

Yet every where else shall mortals
For peace unavailingly roam;
Except through the shadowy portals
Goeth none to his genuine home.

And the heart that tempest and sorrow
Have beaten against it for years,
Must look for a sunnier morrow
Beyond this temple of tears.

—*German Anthology by Maugan.*

(1845-08-02, 4:1)

3359. New Marriage Act.—A circumstance of a rather singular and unpleasant nature, and which shows the strictness of the new law, took place a short time since at Charlemont. A couple in the act of weaving the silken chord, and when the ceremony was half gone through, was stopped suddenly by the officiating minister receiving a notice to the effect that the bridegroom was a minor. Disappointed, the bridal party left the altar, and the expiration of three weeks again returned, fully qualified, when the remaining part of the interesting scene was effected. (1845-08-02, 4:5)

3360. Fact for Smokers.—German physiologists affirm, that of twenty deaths of men between 18 and 25, ten originate in the waste of the constitution by smoking. (1845-08-09, 4:6)

3361. Edward Scully, sub-constable, city police, died rather suddenly, at Corbally station, about seven o'clock on Thursday evening. (1845-08-23, 3:6)

3362. The nuptials of the Earl of Caledon took place on Thursday; and his Lordship and Lady are expected at Caledon-hill on Monday.—*Armagh Guardian.* (1845-09-06, 4:6)

3363. Inquest.—On Thursday, the 4th inst., an inquest was holden before Robert Murray, Esq., county coroner, on the body of Catherine Larkin, of Coolartner, who had cut her throat with a razor. Dr. Christian, of this town, deposed that the deceased had called on him to remove a lump, which she stated was in her throat; there being no lump, he considered her to be insane, and advised her friends to confine her. A verdict of insanity was consequently returned. (1845-09-13, 3:1)

3364. Suicide.—Yesterday, an inquest was held at 41 Francis-street, by John E. Hyndman, Esq., one of the city coroners, on view of the body of a servant girl named Mary Waters, who cut her throat about nine o'clock on that morning, (Thursday.) It appeared that deceased lived as servant in the above house, and that for some time past, she was in a very desponding state of mind, but no person could discover the cause. On yesterday morning about nine o'clock, she prepared breakfast for the young men of the house, and in some time after she was found dead in her own room, with her throat dreadfully cut in three places, which wounds were inflicted by herself. There was a verdict of "died by her own hand," the wounds being inflicted by herself, while labouring under temporary insanity. (1845-09-13, 3:1)

3365. Death of Thomas Osborne Davis, Esq., M.R.I.A., Editor of *The Nation.*—It has never been our habit to limit our sympathies for the sufferings of men of genius by the narrow boundaries of party feuds, and it is, therefore, with deep and sincere regret that we now announce the death, after a painful illness, of Mr. Thomas Davis, one of the Editors of the *Nation.*

Though employed in a cause which our judgment forbids us to sanction, Mr. Davis's talents were of a quality which necessarily enforced the admiration of all parties. Great vigour of intellect, great clearness of thought and purity of language, intense sincerity, and unflinching boldness, characterised his political writings; and if there was something to be forgiven in their tendency, still the learning, the science, the accomplishment—nay, the very enthusiasm of the gifted individual, disarmed the severity of censure, and disposed the mind to wish that talents so admirable were arrayed in a better cause, and to hope that time and experience might rectify his views.

In subjoining to this brief and hurried notice, the obituary record of a journal in whose eyes Mr. Davis's political principles were no abatement of his merits, we have only to add, that many gentlemen of first eminence, and of very different party persuasions, have expressed their intentions of paying (without reference to any political considerations whatsoever) the last tribute of respect to the memory of a man of genius, by attending his funeral, which is to take place at eight o'clock, to-morrow evening. Death levels all distinctions—why should not the grave suspend, at least, our political animosities.—*Mail of Wednesday.* (1845-09-20, 3:4)

3366. Death of Mr. Davis.—By the early death of this estimable gentleman, the press of Ireland has lost its brightest ornament—the country an honest, zealous, and enlightened patriot, and literature, a pillar of strength, decorated by the learning of the sage and the genius of the Poet. As a political writer, he was distinguished by a beautiful style, seldom brought into that field of rude struggle and keen encounter. There were evident in his productions an earnestness and honesty of purpose, fearfully dangerous to his opponents. Although holding opinions most diverse, and deeply impressed with the error of his views, we always admired his writings and gave him credit for having the most complete conviction that he was working out the regeneration of his country! His patriotism was true love of fatherland, unsullied by the slightest tint of sectarian bigotry, he sought out what he believed would be for the good of all, and if he was mistaken, it was the error of the head, not of his heart—a heart which overflowed with the purest philanthropy, the most delicate sensibility, and the kindest sympathies. Indeed, the concluding stanza of his beautiful imagery of a patriot's grave is a simple but exquisite epitome of his sentiments.

"Be my epitaph writ on my country's mind,
He served his country and loved his kind."

And if ever the fancy's sketch of a poet's vision were realised by man, it was in his case.—His remains were followed to the tomb by myriads of his countrymen of every denomination. The statesman and the philosopher—the dignitaries of his native land—the great, the good, of all parties, united in doing honor to the departed genius of the gentleman and the scholar; and as long as Ireland boasts of literature, the name of Thomas Davis will be writ indelibly on the mind of Ireland. (1845-09-27, 3:2)

3367. Death of Mrs. C.G. Duffy.—With the deepest feelings of regret, we copy the following record of a melancholy event, from the *Freeman's Journal* of Tuesday—and if the fullest sympathies of the friends of his childhood, and the admirers of his maturity can, in aught, alleviate the domestic sorrows of the afflicted and bereaved husband, we tender them, with our own, to our esteemed friend, and we trust that HE who supports good men in their troubles, may give him strength to bear up against the many sorrows of a most fatal period—fatal indeed to him, who in one short week is deprived of the blessings of love and friendship:—

At Connaught Terrace, Rathmines, on Tuesday morning, Emily, the beloved wife of Charles Gavan Duffy, Esq., proprietor of the *Nation* newspaper. Consumption had early developed its traces in the constitution of this lady, and to that insidious and immedicable malady her life has been yielded at the early age of 25 years. Though years had scarcely brought her beyond the opening of the life of womanhood, she had lived long enough to win the kindliest regard from all those who came within the sphere of woman's sweetest influence—her home.

For a considerable time, the ravages of the malady which consumed her mortal part had progressed beyond the power of medical skill even to retard, and her sorrowing husband, while he sat by the death-couch of the young partner of his life, and watched the ebbing of the vital tide, was hourly tortured by the anticipation of that consummation of which no anticipation could yet alleviate the crushing weight. The measure of Mr. Duffy's grief must, indeed, be great, losing within one short week his brilliant friend and his fondly cherished wife! How desolate is his home!

Mrs. Duffy, who was a native of Belfast, was of Connaught extraction, her maternal grandfather being the M'Dermott, of Coolavin. (1845-09-27, 3:2)

3368. Fatal Accident on Lough Swilly.—On Saturday last, the 20th instant, about eleven o'clock, a.m., as the *Zulieka* pleasure boat, the property of Major Snow, R.M., was sailing on her way from Rathmullan to Buncrana, she capsized off Killygarvan Point, and went down immediately. The crew were all drowned, consisting of James and Robert Aikin, H. Caulfield of Rathmullan, and W. Russell, of the parish of Aughenish, who was getting a passage across. It was blowing pretty fresh at the time, with a heavy sea, when she was struck by a squall which caused her to lay over and ship water. She was immediately run up in the wind, when the water she had shipped dropped to the stern, and she went down stern foremost with all on board. It is supposed the crew were entangled in the rigging, as they never rose to the surface.
(1845-09-27, 3:4)

3369. An inquest was held at the Ferry Boat, Mexbrough, on view of the body of Henry Graham, an Irish labourer from Armagh. It appeared in evidence that the deceased, along with four other Irishmen, had been shearing for several days for Mr. Dickenson, of Mexbrough, and on the previous day (Sunday) were proceeding in the afternoon to Laughton-en-le-Morthen to harvest for Mr. Pigott; four of the men crossed the river Dun by the Ferry-boat, and paid the usual charge of one penny, but it appears that Graham (who was of so close and saving a disposition) rather than pay the penny, went some distance below the ferry and was attempting to cross the river Dun on some stones, when he slipped off and fell into deep water, and was unfortunately drowned in the presence of his companions, the ferry-man and others, without their being able to render him any assistance. The deceased had lived for three weeks on 6s. 8d., but £3 9s. 6d. in money [was] in his pockets, and had left £10 in the hands of a person at Marsden, near Huddersfield, for whom he had been working. A verdict of "accidentally drowned" was recorded.
(1845-09-27, 4:2)

3370. Serious Accident.—On Saturday evening last about four o'clock, as Mr. George W. Biggs, of Bell-view near Borrisokane, was in the act of gathering nuts from off a large tree, a branch gave way, when he fell a distance of ten feet across a stone wall. Mr. Biggs, who is only eighteen years of age, was shortly afterwards discovered by his brother-in-law, Mr. Egan, in an insensible state. He is under the medical treatment of Dr. Hobbs, of Borrisokane, but is in rather a precarious state at present.—*Nenagh Guardian.*
(1845-10-04, 2:1)

3371. Death of the Most Noble the Marquis of Ely.—It is our painful duty to announce the demise of this distinguished Nobleman, which took place on the evening of Friday, after a very short illness. His lordship had but lately returned to Ely Lodge, and appeared to be in the enjoyment of more than his usual health and spirits. On Thursday, he experienced an attack of English cholera, and notwithstanding the prompt attendance of the most eminent medical men in the neighbourhood, expired, to the inexpressible grief of his family and friends, in the course of the following day.

By the death of the Marquis of Ely, the Protestants of Ireland have lost one of their most distinguished and consistent members, the district in which he resided a kind and considerate landlord and country gentleman, and the county at large a magistrate upon whom dependence could be placed at the present eventful crisis.

The deceased Nobleman enjoyed the title of Marquis and Earl of Ely, Viscount and Baron Loftus, of Loftus Hall, in the county of Wexford in the Peerage of Ireland; and of Baron Loftus, of Long Loftus, in the county of York, in the peerage of the United Kingdom: he was also a Baronet. He was born on the 15th of January, 1770, and was consequently in his 76th year: married on the 2d of May, 1810, to Anna Maria, eldest daughter of Sir Henry Watkin Dashwood, Bar. His Lordship was a Knight of St. Patrick, a Privy Councillor in Ireland, Custos Rotulorum of the county of Wexford, and Colonel of the Wexford Militia.

His Lordship is succeeded in his title and estate by his eldest son, Lord Viscount Loftus, born the 9th of January, 1814. (1845-10-04, 2:4)

3372. The Late Marquess of Downshire.—Letters of administration of the personal estate of the late Most Hon. Arthur Sandys Trumbull, Marquess of Downshire, deceased, have been granted by the Prerogative Court of Ireland, to the Most Hon. Arthur Sandys Trumbull Windsor, the present Marquess. The property (exclusive of real freehold) was sworn to be under the value of 200,000*l*. on which the enormous stamp duty of 4,050*l*. was paid, being the largest amount ever paid in Ireland on any single case, and besides which there are further duties payable to the Crown on all the residue of the estate after payment of debts and charges. The deceased died intestate. Had he made a will, a saving to his estate of 1,350*l*. would have been effected, as, in that case, the stamp duty would have been only 2,700*l*.—*Leinster Express*. (1845-10-04, 2:4)

3373. Approaching Marriage in High Life.—We are enabled to announce that the matrimonial alliance some time since alluded to as in contemplation between the Right Hon. the Earl Howe and Miss Gore, Maid of Honour to her Majesty the Queen Dowager, is now definitively arranged. We believe we are correct in stating that the 16th of the ensuing month is fixed for celebration of the ceremony, which, in accordance with her Majesty the Queen Dowager's expressed desire, will be solemnised at Witley Court.—*Morning Post*. (1845-10-04, 2:4)

3374. The Wife's Last Vigil.

"Thou has watched beside the bed of death,
Oh, fearless human Love!
The lip received the last faint breath,
Ere the spirit fled above.
The prayer was heard by the parting bier,
In a low and farewell tone."

How fades the day within this darkened room,
The evening shadow casts a deeper gloom—
How have I wearied for the setting sun,
That I might use the boon which I have won
By prayers and burning tears! once more Mine Own,
With thee to hold one midnight watch alone?
My heart hath panted for this hour—my soul
Hath felt as if it stretched towards a gaol
Of Hope through all the day—of wild relief
From the oppression of a stormy grief.
Why linger thus my friends? Oh! could you know
With what a gush of tenderness I go
To this last vigil, you would not unite
Your voice in so mournful a "good night!"
Mixed with such tearful blessings: know ye not
This is the last sad pleasure that my lot
In life henceforth affords?
The lamp is lit,
The door hath closed, the lingering steps are gone;
And now beside the silent couch I sit
With thee, with thee, beloved One, alone,
Feeling once more that thou are only mine,
That not even Death our being could untwine.

I lift with gentle hand the shadowy veil;
How like thyself thou art, and yet how pale!
The same dark hair above the lofty brow,
In its still beauty white and pure as snow,
Though mights't be sleeping that untroubled sleep
I often watched when resting by thy side,
But on thy face there is a calm more deep,
And on thy lips a rest more purified;
I touch thy hand—ah, now I feel the change,
For when was touch of thine so cold and strange?
And no uplifting of those shadowed eyes
That ever opening looked for love in mine;
No answer to those holy sympathies,
Whose magic trembled from my heart to thine.
My love, my love, it cannot be thy clay
That makes me shudder thus and turn away,
Away from thee—forgive—forgive! the thought
Was from a momentary terror wrought.
Wretch that I was to dread thee!—Lo, I rest
My head once more upon thy marble breast
As if it were a refuge still. O love!
That word of mine could one dear answer more
From these cold lips! Surely thou still must share
Some comfort from my watching and my care;
Surely we shall not part. Oh, joy for us
If we might ever be together thus—
That I could bear thee even as thou art
To some lone cavern, where my aching heart
Might have thee to itself, and none intrude
For ever on that sunless solitude,
Nay, is not our own chamber a defence?
Who hath a right from me to take thee hence.
From me, thy wedded wife?
Vain thoughts, vain words
Thrilled from the heart when its strained chords
Are swept by gusts of agony. I know,
And, spite of all these words and feelings wild,
That I shall sit submissive as a child
Till all is done—and thou art borne away
Where I shall never see thee more—Oh, day
Be long in breaking! Linger gentle night
My lamp of mournful joy will fade when light
Bursts on the world—this tune is all I have
Some further memories of the loved to save
As treasures for the future—and too soon
I see the low beams of the setting Moon.

—*University Magazine*.
(1845-10-04, 4:1)

3375. A Capital Farm of Land—In Raffeenan.—To be sold by public Auction,—By order of the Executors of the Late Mr. John Wright, of Raffeenan, Deceased, On Thursday, the 16th October instant, On the Premises, at Eleven o'Clock,

All the Deceased's Right, Title and Interest in and to that Capital Farm of Land in Raffeenan, containing 19A. 3R. 20P. late Irish Measure, together with the Dwelling-House, and Offices thereon, held by a Lease for two good Lives, in being, at the Yearly Rent of 24s. 3d. an acre, including rent-charge. And by a clause in his will, a residence for his mother therein as now in her possession (namely Esther Wright, aged about 80 years) as also the grazing of a Cow and Foddering and Wintering yearly for her, and Six pounds sterling annually, payable half-yearly to her, on every 1st day of May and every 1st day of November, in every year, during her natural life.

The Purchaser, on being declared the buyer, will be required to deposit in the hands of Mr. Robert Wright (one of the Executors,) one-half of the purchase Money, and the remainder on a day to be agreed upon at the Sale, on perfecting the deed of assignment and getting possession.

At same time, all the deceased's Household Furniture, Cattle, Farming Implements, &c. Comprising Mahogany and Oak Tables; Chairs; Mahogany Desk and Bookcase, a Mahogany Chest of Drawers, a Writing Desk; a Guardevine, a Glazed Beaufet; Bedsteads and Hangings; Cradle and Press Beds; Feather Beds and Bedding; a Toilet Table and Toilet Glass; Basin-stand; Presses; China, Delf and Glass, Dairy and Kitchen Furniture; a Meal Ark, &c., &c. A Good Farm Horse; a Milch Cow; an Iron Plough; Harrows, and Tackle; a Cart and Harness; a Hand Cart; a Water Barrow and Vessel; Box and Slane Barrows, Ladders, &c., &c.

Terms—Cash.

October 1st, 1845.

J.E. Jones, Auctioneer.

(1845-10-11, 3:2)

3376. *Errata.*—In our last Number, a mistake occurred in noticing the death of Mr. James Wilson, of Clonlick—who died suddenly on Saturday 18th ult.—we said Mr. William Wilson, of Clonlickney; this gentleman, we are happy to say, is in the enjoyment of excellent health. (1845-11-01, 3:1)

3377. Death of Major-General Bredin.—We regret to record the death of Major-General Andrew Bredin, of the Royal Artillery, which event took place on Wednesday last, at his residence on Fox Hill, Plumstead Commons.—The deceased officer, who was in the 74th year of his age, received his commission as Lieutenant on the 9th of September, 1794; Captain, 6th July, 1798; Brevet-Major, 25th July, 1810; Regimental Major, 12th June, 1813 [1818?]; Brevet-Lieutenant-Colonel, 12th August, 1819; Regimental-Lieutenant-Colonel, 17th October, 1823 [1828?]; Regimental-Colonel, 28th July, 1834; and Major-General, 23rd November, 1841. Previous to joining the Royal Regiment of Artillery, he belonged to the Royal Irish Artillery, and joined the service from that brigade. He was at the capture of Grenada, St. Vincent, and St. Lucia, under Sir Ralph Abercrombie, and also served in the Peninsula. He retired from the corps on attaining the rank of Major-General. His body was interred with military honors. (1845-11-08, 4:5)

3378. Court of Queen's Bench.—Thursday, Nov. 6.—Lessee James C. Bell, Esq., and others, plaintiffs; Henry King, Esq., defendant.

This case, which excited so much interest in the county of Tyrone, and was fully reported in the *Telegraph* of the 13th of March last, was this day finally disposed of, on a motion made by plaintiff, to show cause against the conditional order obtained by defendant to set aside the verdict. James Sheil, Esq., in a forcible and eloquent appeal, addressed the court at considerable length in support of the verdict. James Major, Esq., Q.C., with his usual ability, detailed all the circumstances of the defendant's case in support of the conditional order, and forcibly dwelt on the fact of the codicil having been drawn up by the plaintiff, a barrister, six days before the death of the testator, James King, Esq., in April, 1844, revoking the bequest made to Dr. King, his brother, in the will of 1842, and bequeathing his estate to Mr. Bell in trust for his own child, an infant aged two years, and no relation to the testator. John Brooke, Esq., Q.C., was also heard on the part of the defendant, and Oliver Sproule, Esq., on the part of plaintiff. The court was pleased to order that the verdict had for plaintiff at Omagh, for all testator's lands in Farlough, be changed to a verdict for 16A. 3R. 1P., being the two farms held by deceased under Mr. Pike, at £2 5s. per English acre, the defendant retaining possession of the freehold estates in Farlough, including the mills, quarries, &c., each party paying their own costs of the motion. (1845-11-15, 2:1)

3379. Death of Mr. John Irvine, M.P.—This highly-respected gentleman died on Monday morning, at his residence in Richmond Terrace, at the age of seventy-eight.—His death caused a vacancy in the representation of the county of Antrim.—*Sun.* (1845-11-15, 3:4)

3380. Notice—Is hereby given that a separate Building named the Newbliss Presbyterian Meeting House, situated in the Townland of Drumahannon, in the Parish of Aghabog, in the County of Monaghan, in the District of Clones, being a Building certified according to Law, as a place of Religious Worship, was, on the Eighth day of November, 1845, duly registered for Solemnizing Marriages therein, pursuant to the *Act of 7 and 8 Vic., Cap. 81.*

Witness my hand this 18th day of Nov., 1845.

Richard Reed, Registrar of Marriages
for the District of Clones.

(1845-11-22, 3:6)

3381. Deplorable Accident—Sixteen Lives Lost.—At a late hour last night, accounts reached town of the occurrence of a calamity of the most deplorable nature, of which, in the course of the evening, the Royal Canal was the theatre by which the lives of many of our fellow creatures were sacrificed. It is certain that sixteen are already dead! Of course, the particulars of this shocking affair are not yet fully known, but the following facts may be relied upon, having been communicated to us by an individual who arrived in town in the course of the night from the scene of the tragedy.

The nightboat to Longford started on yesterday at the usual hour, two o'clock in the afternoon. There were eight passengers in the fore or principal cabin, and considerably upwards of twenty in the after-cabin. Upon reaching the neighbourhood of Clonsilla, the steersman went below to dine, and unhappily committed the rudder, as we have been informed, to a boy employed on board the boat. This boy, either knowing nothing of the proper mode of steering, or not attending to the serious duty unfortunately and rashly committed to him, permitted the boat to run upon the banks of the canal, which caused her immediately to capsize, and speedily to fill with water. The fore-cabin passengers were saved, as that portion of the boat lay almost out of the water, which is, of course, shallow at the bank; the unhappy after-passengers, plunged into the deepest portion of the canal, could not extrictate themselves, and as no assistance was at hand, many of them have perished in the waters. At the time our correspondent left Clonsilla, sixteen of the drowned already crowded the banks, and the drags were plying busily in search of more.—This is a horrible calamity. It must be rigorously inquired into, and this frightful sacrifice of human life be excused by evidence or punished by law.—*Freeman.*

Another Account.—We regret to state that the night boat, which left Dublin at two o'clock yesterday afternoon, upon her arrival at a point near to Clonsilla, struck upon a projecting rock in the canal bank, and went down, in consequence of which seventeen persons lost their lives.

We understand that the Board of Directors are insituting a rigid inquiry, with a view of eliciting the fullest information as to the cause of the melancholy accident, and we have been requested to state, that since the management of the canal became vested in the directors of the Midland Great Western Railway Company, no change has taken place in the officers or servants of the company, or in the system of management. (1845-11-29, 2:2)

3382. The Late Accident on the Royal Canal.—In the case of the accident on the canal, James Dunne, the steerer, who gave the helm to Teeling, was, by the direction of the Attorney-General, held to bail on Monday, in 40*l.* himself, and two sureties in 20*l.* each, before Henry Davis, Esq., coroner, to stand his trial at the commission, with Teeling for manslaughter. (1845-12-06, 2:1)

3383. A young woman named Carr, who was lately a domestic servant in Lord Strangford's family, has become possessed of a fortune, estimated at ten thousand pounds; the luck really happening through the novelist's hackneyed incident, the death of an uncle in India. (1845-12-06, 2:5)

3384. Sudden Death.—We sincerely regret to announce the death of Doctor Shaw, of Rosslea [sic], who was found dead in his bed on Thursday morning. He went to bed in his usual good health, and on his servant going into his bedroom in the morning, he was a corpse. It is supposed apoplexy was the cause of his untimely end. He was highly respected and esteemed in his neighbourhood, and his death is deeply deplored by a numerous circle of friends. (1845-12-06, 3:4)

3385. Sudden Deaths.—Our Philipstown correspondent reports the sudden death, on Sunday last, of Thomas Whitfield, Esq., inspector of weights and measures—a man highly esteemed for his upright and humane disposition. He was in the act of changing a flannel vest, when a sudden rush of blood to the chest deprived him of life ere a medical attendant had arrived.

John Jones, a farmer, aged 80 years, residing about two miles from Philipstown, was found dead in a bed on Sunday morning.

The coroner, James Dillon, Esq., held inquests on the bodies, and the jurors found verdicts of "died by the visitation of God."

The same coroner held inquests, same day, on the body of a woman named Bridget Gavan, found drowned in a ditch near the Canal, and the body of a child supposed to have been murdered, but which died of the small pock for want of care, the mother being a wandering pauper. (1845-12-13, 1:2)

3386. Death of the R.C. Bishop of Ossory.—Just as we were about to go to press, we learned that the Right Rev. Doctor Kinsella, R.C. Bishop of this Diocese, had died a few moments previously, from the effects of a fit of apoplexy with which he had been seized on Thursday last.—*Kilkenny Moderator*. (1845-12-20, 1:3)

3387. Death of the Earl of Belmore.—With the deepest regret, we have to announce the death of the Earl of Belmore, which melancholy event occurred at Castle Coole, at half-past three o'clock on Wednesday morning. In our last publication, we informed our readers of the sudden illness of the noble Lord, and of the anxiety entertained by his family and medical attendants as to his recovery, the attack being gout erratic in a debilitated constitution; since then, his Lordship appeared to improve daily, and on Tuesday morning, the disease having seized upon the feet, the most (*continued...*)

3887, continued: ... favourable result was anticipated, but at the hour we have already stated, a transition to a vital organ took place, so suddenly, that life was extinct before Dr. Ovenden, who was in the room, could reach his Lordship's bedside. Armar Lowry Corry, Earl of Belmore, Viscount and Baron Belmore of Castlecoole, Co. Fermanagh, born on the 23d of December 1801, succeeded his noble father April 18, 1841. On the 27th of May 1834, he married Emily Louisa, youngest daughter of the late William Shepherd, Esq., of Bradbourne, Kent, by whom he has left eighteen children; the oldest, Somerset Richard, Viscount Corry, was born on the 9th of April, 1835.—*Fermanagh Reporter*. (1845-12-20, 2:4)

3388. Accidental Death by Drowning.—On Wednesday night last, a lock-keeper on the Ulster Canal, named Sharp, while engaged in opening one of the sluices of the lock, missed his hold of the bar, and was precipitated into the lock, which was nearly filled with water. No assistance being near, the unfortunate man was drowned. (1845-12-20, 2:4)

3389. Mysterious Case.—On Saturday last, the gardener of Dr. Cathcart, who resides at 21, Eccles-street, was digging in the garden, when he discovered the remains of a human body about two feet under the surface. The skeleton, although evidently many years in its present position, was in fair preservation. Dr. Kirwin, city coroner, was apprised of the circumstance, and attended yesterday in order to institute an inquiry on the subject, should such be necessary. On examination, Dr. Kirwan found that the body was that of a person somewhere about seventeen years of age, but whether male or female, he could not discover. He was enabled to arrive at the above conclusion from the formation of the skull. It was supposed that the remains had lain in the earth for nearly half a century, and that the body was used for dissection by some medical man who probably resided in the house, and that after dissection, the remains were interred there. Dr. Kirwan did not consider it necessary to hold an inquest, as in fact nothing save as to the discovery of the body could be given in evidence. The circumstance caused considerable sensation in the neighbourhood. The coroner gave directions for the reinterment of the body. (1845-12-20, 3:1)

3390. Death of the Rev. Samuel Dill, of Donoughmore.—It is our melancholy duty this day to announce the death of the Rev. Samuel Dill, of Donoughmore, in the county of Donegall. Mr. Dill was for about half a century in the ministry of the Presbyterian Church, and during this long period, he sustained in a most exemplary manner the respectability of the pastoral character. (1845-12-20, 3:3)

3391. The marriage of the Hon. Captain Daly and the Hon. Miss A'Court is to take place on Saturday next, the 27th instant. (1845-12-27, 1:1)

3392. Remarkable Birth.—Mrs. Shee, the wife of a respectable victualler of Enniscorthy, in the 66th year of her age, gave birth to a male child on the 27th or 28th of last month to the surprise of the inhabitants of that locality. Her eldest child is upwards of forty seven years of age. (1845-12-27, 2:2)

3393. To the Ladies.

For sixty-three years having led
A solitary life,
I lately took into my head
To look out for a wife.

I'm now resolved to change my state
For fortune I don't care;
But as I have a large estate,
I'm anxious for an heir.

The lady must be young and fair
Not older than eighteen;
She must have a *distingue* air
I hate a milk-maid's mien!

She must be over middle height,
Yet by no means too tall;
Her figure must be round, but slight;
Her feet and ankles small.

She must have eyes of clear bright blue,
And curls of silken hair;
She must have skin of snowy hue
No costly clothes must wear.

Her birth must be respectable
My rank in life is so;
She must be educated well,
The rule of three must know.

I would not wish her musical,
An uproar I can't bear.
No lady qualified to squall,
My home shall ever share.

I have a country residence,
A house in town beside;
For which I've gone to great expense,
And fitted for a bride.

Her father never must ask me
To join in a bank bill,
I hate to stand security
I never did nor will.

She must be gentle, fond and kind
A tender-hearted nurse;
For as I older grew, I find
My health is growing worse.

If I could meet with such a wife,
From all encumbrance clear,
I'd settle on her, for her life,
One Hundred Pounds a Year!!

(1845-12-27, 4:1)

3394. A House and Three Persons Burned to Death. —On Friday night last, Maurice Conroy, a small farmer, residing within two miles of Mountmellick, on the verge of the King's County, went, accompanied by his son, to look for a horse to bring oats to their market, leaving his wife and three daughters behind in the house. On his return, he found the house in one sheet of flames, past all remedy. The three daughters, of the respective ages of twenty, sixteen, and thirteen, horrible to relate, were burnt to a cinder, with all the poor man's Property. The wife miraculously escaped, having left the house on some business immediately before the fire commenced. The lamentable occurrence is considered an accident. (1846-01-03, 2:4)

3395. Fatal Accident—Upsetting of the Derry Mail. Yesterday morning, when the down Derry Mail, had proceeded about two miles from Castleblayney, by some mismanagement, the wheels got into the water-table, which was very deep, and the coach immediately upset. The guard, and an outside passenger, were flung over the ditch, into the adjoining field, and providentially escaped unhurt—not so, unfortunately, with the driver, (P. Shanly), who was flung against the ditch, and instantly killed. On examining the body, no wounds appeared except a slight scratch above the right eye; and as he was not entangled with any part of the coach or horses, it is supposed that his death was caused by dislocation of the spine. There were two inside passengers, who, we are happy to say, received no injury. (1846-01-03, 3:2)

3396. Fire and Melancholy Loss of Life.—On Saturday morning last, between the hours of five and six o'clock, the dwelling house of a small farmer near Quarrymount, between Mountmellick and Tullamoore, was discovered to be on fire, by a young man, who instantly gave the alarm, and on effecting an entrance, an appalling spectacle presented itself. The house consisted of but two apartments, in one of which three fine young women were burnt to death—the head being separated from the body of one. In the other apartment, the parents were asleep, and would doubtless have also perished but for the exertions of the person above referred to. Subsequently, an inquest was held on the bodies by Thomas Budds, Esq., Coroner, and a verdict in accordance [with the facts] was recorded.—*King's County Chronicle.* (1846-01-03, 3:3)

3397. Melancholy Death by Drowning.—The sad intelligence reached this [town] yesterday morning that Charles Montgomery, Esq., (youngest brother of A.H. Montgomery, Esq., of Tyrella, treasurer of this county), and his companion, one of the Mr. Reilly's, of Scarva, have been drowned in the Bristol Channel. They had been missing for several days, and the pleasure-boat in which they were sailing has not yet been found. A writing desk, belonging to Mr. Montgomery, was at Ardglass, with the same boat in which he has now unfortunately perished.—*Down Recorder of Saturday.* (1846-01-03, 3:4)

3398. Suicide of Mr. Nott, Dame-street.—Mr. Nott, of the firm of Nott, and Son, tea merchants and brokers, residing in Dame-street, committed suicide on Friday evening at the house of his brother-in-law, Mr. John Jones, of Burton Hall, near Whitechurch, Rathfarnham. When the melancholy intelligence reached town on Saturday morning, considerable excitement prevailed in the mercantile circles, as the unfortunate gentleman was well known and very generally esteemed amongst his brother merchants in this city. The rumours as to the cause and the means of death resorted to by the unfortunate deceased were various and contradictory, and it was even confidently asserted by many that the report was totally void of truth. We are sorry, however, to say that the fact was otherwise, and that the report of his death was unhappily too true. The following are, as far as could be collected, the facts of this lamentable case. The deceased gentleman went out to Curton [sic] Hall, the country seat of his brother-in-law, Mr. Jones, on Friday, and in the course of the evening, his body was discovered suspended by a cord and handkerchief from a stair case which led into the water closet. The body was at once cut down, and medical aid procured, but all to no purpose, as the vital spark had been extinguished for some time. Deceased was in his 58th year, and lived on terms of the greatest affection with his family and relations. Mr. Nott had been labouring under disease of the head for some time, and was heard a week since to say "that it would be no wonder if a person suffering as he was would commit suicide." There was an inquest held on Saturday evening on the remains, when a verdict to the effect that he committed suicide while labouring under temporary insanity was returned.—*Freeman's Journal.* (1846-01-10, 1:6)

3399. Illegal Marriages.—The Inspector General of Constabulary has issued a circular to the various stations of the force, stating that information having been received that marriages are not unfrequently solemnized by degraded clergymen, or other unauthorised persons, contrary to the *7th & 8th Victoria, chap. 81*; and the celebration of all such marriages being a felony, the attention of the constabulary should be particularly directed, in order [that] offenders may be apprehended and proceeded against as the law directs. (1846-01-10, 1:6)

3400. Deaths by Shipwreck.—On the 31st of December, Mr. Atkinson held inquests on the bodies of five men and a boy in Erris. It appeared that their bodies were washed in on the shores of Cross Drum and Plot Barrett, on the night of Sunday and Monday, the 28th and 29th.—Some of the bodies were greatly mutilated, as if knocked against rocks, and one had the face eaten away, supposed by a dog. Much to the discredit of some of the country people, the bodies had been stripped of their clothes. It is supposed that these persons belonged to a ship called the (*continued...*)

3400, continued: ...*Kate Nickleby*, of Glasgow, the wreck of which came in along these shores at the same place and time. It is thought she was outward bound for a cargo, as a great number of empty puncheons came ashore. The wreck, as fast as it came in, was carried away by the country people. It is supposed that the captain's wife was on board, as a band-box and bonnet, a lady's work-box and boots and shoes came ashore. There were thirteen hands on board, as appeared in a book which some of the people picked up and took away. It was believed that she must have struck on Saturday night, on either the island of Ennisglory or Enniskea. It was stated that some of the country people cut the finger off one of the men to get a ring off it.—*Mayo Constitution*. (1846-01-10, 2:3)

3401. We learn with much regret that Mr. Sheil, M.P., has lost his only son, who died at Madeira, on the 9th November last. (1846-01-17, 1:1)

3402. Lord Rossmore, who went to Ireland on account of the sudden illness of his brother, the Hon. Colonel Westenra, M.P., returned to Brighton on Thursday last.—*Packet*. (1846-01-17, 1:1)

3403. The Earl of Portarlington's sisters, the Misses Dawson Damer, will shortly receive the rank and precedence of the daughter of an Earl, in consequence of the accession of their brother to the family honors. (1846-01-17, 1:1)

3404. Suicide of Captain Baker of the 5th Fusiliers.—Enniskillen, 9th Jan., 1846.—I hasten by the first post to announce the death of H.P. Baker, Esq., captain of the 5th Fusiliers, stationed in this town. The fatal occurrence took place in his room in the barracks. Between six and seven o'clock last night, he sent his servant up to the town for some medicine, and on his return up stairs, he heard the report of his musket. On entering, he got his unhappy master lying on the floor, and the top of his skull blown off—he having placed the fire-lock under his chin, and pulled the trigger with his toes.

The reports are various as to the cause that led to this calamity. The most prevalent is, that the deceased made application to his commanding officer to restore a colour sergeant who was reduced yesterday. The colonel gave him some uncourteous reply, and would not. The deceased was observed to be greatly agitated during the evening.

The coroner's inquest was going on in the barrack at present (three o'clock.)

The deceased was gazetted to a company, by purchase, on the 30th of December. Captain Baker was a native of England.

Enniskillen, Jan. 10.—Mr. Collum, the coroner, held an inquest on the body yesterday, at one o'clock, in the barrack, and, after the examination of Captain Baker's servant, Doctor Mackey, Adjutant Lyons, and Captain Kennedy, the respectable jury, brought in a verdict of temporary insanity. Captain Baker was a young man, much esteemed and greatly beloved by both men and officers; he was a native of Cork. It did not appear in his papers, &c., that he was embarrassed, but the contrary. He was observed to be greatly depressed and dejected at the courtmartial held that day; and was spoken to on the subject by Captain Kennedy and Mr. Lyons. The colonel and all the officers examined spoke of the deceased in the very highest terms, as an officer and a gentleman.—He will be interred here on Wednesday next. He was son to Colonel Baker, and has a brother, Captain Baker, in the 51st light infantry. (1846-01-17, 1:3)

3405. Shocking Suicide.—On Saturday last, a comfortable farmer named Millea, residing at Talbot's-hill near Gowran, committed suicide by hanging himself from the rafters in the upper story of the house. It appears that the deceased had been quarrelling all day with his wife, and actuated, as is supposed by jealousy, followed her to her room, whither she had retired at seven o'clock, and beat her with a spade handle in a most inhuman manner, breaking one of her arms, and leaving her in a state of insensibility. The unfortunate wretch, probably supposing that he had entirely deprived the victim of his fury of life, then committed suicide in the manner above stated. An inquest was, we understand, held on yesterday by Mr. Maher, coroner, but the nature of the verdict has not yet reached us.—*Kilkenny Moderator*. (1846-01-17, 2:1)

3406. The Suicide of Captain Baker.—Colonel Sutherland, 5th Fusiliers, presents his compliments to the Editor of the *Dublin Evening Mail*, and will feel extremely obliged if he will do him the favour, without delay, to publish in his highly respectable paper, the enclosed copy of a letter, which the Colonel has, this day, found himself under the necessity of addressing to the Editor of the *Dublin Weekly Freeman's Journal*:—

"To the Editor of the *Freeman's Journal*.

"Enniskillen, 12th Jan., 1846.

"Sir—A friend having directed my attention to a paragraph in the *Weekly Freeman's Journal* of the 10th instant, headed 'second edition,' and stating, in reference to the recent lamentable and much-deplored suicide of the late Captain Baker, that the most prevalent report as to the cause that led to this calamity is, that the deceased made application to his commanding officer to restore a colour sergeant, who was reduced yesterday, 'and received some uncourteous reply,' refusing it, I take leave to request that you will be pleased to contradict 'the report' without delay, as utterly destitute of even the slightest foundation in truth. Captain Baker preferred no request or application on the subject alluded to, or any other, to me since his promotion, and could not, consequently, have received an uncourteous reply on the occasion—nor did he from me, or any other that I am aware of, as during the eight years that the late lamented officer has been under my command, I do not recollect that we ever had a word of difference.

"As 'the report' in question, as well as several others equally baseless and absurd, was publicly contradicted at the coroner's inquest, before the hour (3 p.m.,) cited by your correspondent, I fear that in giving it currency, he has been guilty of wilful misrepresentation, calumny, and falsehood.

"I am, Sir,
"Your obedient servant,
(Signed) "Wm. Sutherland.
Col. and Lieut.-Col. Commanding 5th Fusiliers."
(1846-01-17, 2:3)

3407. Hydrophobia.—Dr. Allnatt recommends the instant adoption of the following simple process in all cases where a wound has been inflicted by a rabid or suspected animal:—A ligature (consisting of a piece of tape or pocket handkerchief) is to be immediately applied round the limb, a few inches above the point of laceration, and drawn sufficiently tight to arrest the circulation, and thus prevent the absorption of the poison into the system, whence the subsequent danger arises. The wound is then to be diligently and perseveringly washed with soap and warm water, and the ablution continued until medical aid be procured. In proportion as the virus has, at the outset, been more or less effectually interrupted from entering the circulation, and the wound cleansed, the danger of subsequent constitutional effects will be augmented or diminished. (1846-01-17, 2:3)

3408. Lines,—In Memory of the Rev. Andrew Bell.
(For the *Tralee Chronicle*.)

The light of youth lit up his blooming face,
And health's bright glow seemed mantling on his cheek;
Bright beamed his eye, ah! sure there was no trace
Of sickness, or of sorrow there to speak.

And manhood's strength seemed in that active frame,
And future years seemed destined long for him;
But false the presage, sudden sickness came,
To pain that brow and bid that eye grow dim.

Severe, exceeding, even unto death,
That wasting fever, youth and strength laid low,
And seized that frame, and caught that struggling breath,
Till the last silence came o'er heart and brow.

And then he passed away for ever!—left
His home beside the wild wave of the deep;
One lonely one was there—of him bereft,
She bows her head a widow's tear to weep.

A solemn thing to see his vacant place,
When in the church stands forth the white-robed Priest;
When speaks the preacher, then we miss the fate,
Missd in the church and at the social feast.

No! we may not forget that stranger young,
Who died amongst us in his early day;
But while the dark graves shade is o'er him flung,
We trust he speeds to happier climes away.

For we have heard him speak with solemn word,
Instructive, warning, while this earth he trod;
Reading that book, the message of his Lord,
Whose blessed rules point up to Heaven and God.

And in that last sad hour of mortal strife,
When at the gates of death he stood alone,
In Jesus was his trust for deathless life,
Jesus the Lord, the Mighty, to atone.

Geraldine.
(1846-01-17, 3:4)

3409. The Dying Child.

"What should it know of death?"

Come closer, closer, dear mamma,
My heart is filled with fears,
My eyes are dark—I hear your sobs
But cannot see your tears.

I feel your warm breath on my lips,
That are so icy cold
Come closer, closer, dear mamma,
Give me your hand to hold.

I quite forgot my little hymn
How doth the little busy bee
Which every day I used to say
When smiling on your knee.

Nor can I recollect my prayers;
And, dear mamma, you know
That the great God will angry be
If I forget them too.

And dear papa, when he comes home,
Oh, will he not be vexed?
Give us this day our daily bread
What is it that comes next?

Thine is the kingdom and the power
I cannot think of more;
It comes and goes away so quick,
It never did before.

"Hush, darling! you are going to
The bright and blessed sky,
Where all God's holy children go,
To live with him on high."

But will he love me, dear mamma,
As tenderly as you,
And will my own papa, one day,
Come and live with me too?

But you must first lay me to sleep
Where grandpapa is laid;
Is not the churchyard cold and dark,
And shan't I feel afraid?

And will you every evening come,
And say my pretty prayer, (*continued…*)

3409, continued:

Over poor Lucy's little grave,
And see that no one's there

And promise me that when you die,
That they your grave shall make
The next to mine, that I may be
Close to you when I awake.

Nay, do not leave me, dear mamma,
Your watch beside me keep,
My heart feels cold—the room's all dark
Now lay me down to sleep.

And should I sleep to wake no more,
Dear—dear mamma, good bye;
Poor nurse is kind, but, oh, do you
Be with me when I die!
(1846-01-17, 4:1)

3410. Last Lines of the Late T. Hood.
Written a few hours before his death.

Farewell life! my senses swim,
And the world is growing dim;
Thronging shadows cloud the light,
Like the advent of the night—
Colder, colder, colder still,
Upward steals a vapor chill;
Strong the earthy odor grows—
I smell the mould above the rose.

Welcome Life! the Spirit strives!
Strength returns and hope revives;
Cloudy fears and shapes forlorn
Fly like shadows at the morn-—
O'er the earth there comes a bloom;
Sunny light for sullen gloom,
Warm perfume for vapor cold—
I smell the roses above the mould.
(1846-01-17, 4:6)

3411. A fatal accident occurred on Monday arising from the dangerous practice of cleaning windows by going out upon the window sill. A poor man named Doherty, whilst engaged in cleaning the windows of the house No. 75, Marlbourgh [sic] street, Dublin, fell from the upper story into the area, and was killed upon the spot. (1846-01-24, 2:3)

3412. Awfully Sudden Death.—(From our Tullamoore Correspondent.)—On Wednesday morning last, a pig-jobber, of the name of James Darcy, residing in Phoenix-street, Dublin, returning from the Athlone fair with about 150*l.* worth of pigs, and while waiting for the fly-boat at the Edenderry Canal, fell down suddenly dead, amongst a number of persons who were standing with him; he has left a wife and large family to deplore his loss. A similar calamity happened to a man a short time before on the same spot.
(1846-01-24, 3:3)

3413. The Executors of the late Earl Belmore have appointed W.A. Dane, Esq., their Law Agent.
(1846-01-24, 3:3)

3414. A melancholy, and, to one person, fatal accident occurred on the Dundalk and Enniskillen railway, on Friday, the 18th instant. Some men were felling trees on an angle of Lord Blayney's demesne, in the neighbourhood of the town of Castleblayney, when one tree being cut, had its top entangled in that of another, which being also cut, and sufficient attention not being paid to the falling of both, one of them struck two of the men engaged in the work, killing one of them instantaneously and breaking the leg of another in two places, besides otherwise injuring him. The person killed, whose name, however, we have not heard, has left a wife and nine children to lament his loss. The poor woman and her family came to Castleblayney to reside on the very evening the melancholy accident took place, but are thus fatally deprived of their natural protection and support.
(1846-01-24, 3:3)

3415. The Death Bed.—By Thomas Hood.

We watch'd her breathing through the night,
Her breathing soft and low,
As in her breast the wave of life
Kept heaving to and fro.

So silently we seem'd to speak,
So slowly mov'd about,
As we had lent her half our powers
To eke her living out.

Our very hopes belied our fears,
Our fears our hopes belied—
We thought her dying when she slept,
And sleeping when she died.

For when the morn came dim and sad,
And chill with early showers,
Her quiet eyelids closed—she had
Another morn than ours.
(1846-01-24, 4:4)

3416. There were great rejoicings in the neighborhood of Carrig-o'Gunniel Castle on Thursday last, on the marriage of Miss Maria F. Dickson, daughter of the respected Rector of Kilkeedy. Tar-barrels blazed on the summit of the old ruin; bonfires and fireworks enlivened the scene, and the peasantry feasted and danced merrily until a late hour. The laborers, decorated with white ribbons, lined the passage to the church, and almost the whole parish were assembled to testify their good will and attachment. (1846-01-31, 3:4)

3417. The remains of the late Captain Baker, 5th Fusileers, were interred in Enniskillen churchyard with military honors, by the Regt. The officers wore black shoulder scarfs and hat bands. (1846-01-31, 4:4)

3418. Consistorial Court of Clogher.—Before the Rev. R.L. Tottenham, Surrogate.—John Irwin and others, Executors to James Irwin, deceased, against Anne Jane Irwin, deceased's wife.

Mr. John Mitchell, Proctor for the Executor, stated the ground of action, which was, that the widow held over a sum of £30, which was in the house of the deceased, at the time of his death, which she should have handed over to the executors, but which she refused to do, alleging, that as she helped to earn it, she had a right to hold it. The said Anne Jane Irwin was left a sum of £60, in the will of the deceased, which was duly paid to her; the executors now pray that she might be compelled to hand this money over to them, for the use of the child of the deceased, allowing her credit for whatever sums she might have paid away for debts due by deceased.

Mr. Mitchell quoted several authorities, by which the admission of a person, as to have money or other property of a person deceased, was sufficient evidence to empower a judge to order same, to be paid to the regularly appointed executors. He contended that she admitted, that she had the money in question, when she said, that she had helped to earn it, and would keep it. This allegation, would be supported by Mr. Patrick Mitchell, to whom it was alleged she made this admission.

Mr. William Jebb (who appeared as Proctor in behalf of the Impugnant) contended that tho' Mr. Mitchell had dwelt at considerable length upon a presumption, that his client had received a certain sum of money, alleged to be the property of her late husband; yet that not a tittle of evidence had been given to sustain his statement, on the contrary; the witnesses produced in behalf of the Promovent, directly and positively deny any knowledge of the transaction, as would appear on reading their depositions (Mr. Jebb here read the articles and the depositions of the witnesses produced to support them) and submitted that Mr. Mitchell, the Promovent, had totally failed in establishing his case, and also urged upon the court, as a strong circumstance in favour of the innocence of his client; the fact of two out of three Executors, named in the will of deceased, refusing to join in the present proceedings and actually being, at the time, in court, to protest against the injustice of the course taken by Mr. Irwin. In conclusion, Mr. Jebb, after having referred to several authorities to support the view he had taken, called upon the court to weigh well the evidence produced on behalf of the Promovent, which he submitted had totally failed, and prayed that the case might be dismissed with costs. The judge deferred giving his judgment till Thursday the 5th inst, when he dismissed the case with full costs. (1846-02-07, 3:4)

3419. Awful Effects of Intemperance.—On Tuesday last, an inquest was held before George Henry, Esq., on the body of a man named John Craig, who, on the previous evening, was found drowned in the Callen river, a few perches from the Asylum. On Saturday night, he was seen drunk in this city [Armagh], strolling down English-street, and went on towards the Asylum, instead of having gone [down?] the road leading to Markethill, beside which he resided. There were nine shillings of silver and fivepence in his trowsers pocket. The verdict was "drowned accidentally in the river Callen, he being in a state of intoxication." (1846-02-07, 4:3)

3420. Mourning.—The universal costume of mourning was white over the world, until about the year 1440. (1846-02-14, 2:4)

3421. Frightful Accident in the Cavan Workhouse.—A dreadful accident occurred in the workhouse on Wednesday last. The windlass, by which the potatoes for the paupers are let down into the kitchen boiler, stands upon a platform, so that the person working it is on a level with the mouth of the boiler. A poor woman, whose turn it was to boil the potatoes on that day, after having drawn up the bucket from the boiler, misjudging the distance from the platform to the ground, let go the windlass before the bucket reached the floor, in consequence of which, the rope ran out with great velocity, and the handle struck her with such violence that she fell backwards into the boiler. Though instantly pulled out by another pauper who was on the spot, the wretched creature was so fearfully scalded that, as we were told by an eye-witness, the whole skin of her body peeled off, and actually fell in large pieces on the floor. Dr. Coyne was sent for on the moment, and was with her within a quarter of an hour of the accident, but collapse had already set in, and death was inevitable. The poor woman lingered for about four hours, aware of her fate, and seemingly resigned to it; she said that she felt no pain whatever, but complained a little of the cold.—After her death, an inquest sat upon her body.—Verdict—Accidental Death.—*Anglo Celt.* (1846-02-21, 1:2)

3422. Supposed Shipwreck off Skerries.—A note, of which the following is a copy, was found enclosed in a bottle picked up by the artilleryman in charge of the fort on Dalky [sic] Island, and brought to Lieutenant Hutchinson, harbour master of Kingstown, on Sunday evening:—

"Brig Spey (or Issey), Feb. 4, 1846.

"Six feet water in the hold—we expect to be soon all lost unless some help arrives—we are about 37 deg. 40 seconds off Skerries—the captain was lost two days ago, and the mate is dead—he died of yellow fever about a week ago.

"John Igo, Seaman."

(1846-02-21, 1:2)

3423. Monaghan Staff District.—Pensioners' Fund.—The frequent occurrence of absolute want in which the Widows and Families of Pensioners are suddenly placed on the death of the Pensioner, has induced the Staff Officer to submit to them the propriety of raising a Fund, by a small quarterly subscription of one shilling from each man belonging to the District, which amount would enable relief to be afforded to the Widow for the support of herself and family for some time.

It is calculated that £28 8s. per quarter will, by this measure, be collected, or an income of £113 12s. per annum, and it is found that 15 Pensioners die annually in the District. (*continued...*)

3423, continued: ...For the purpose of creating a fund, as recommended by the Staff Officer, for affording temporary relief to Widows and Families of deceased Pensioners, it is agreed on by the Pensioners of the Monaghan District, that one shilling shall be paid quarterly by each man, who may be willing, to subscribe to the Fund. That each subscriber's name shall be entered in a book, to be kept for the purpose, with the date of his becoming a subscriber, and that for the purpose of simplifying proceedings, the names of intending subscribers can only be entered as such at the periods of paying Pensioners, at the different stations, in June, September, December and March of each year.

That a Committee shall be annually appointed at head quarters, in the month of June, for the purpose of receiving subscriptions and managing all matters connected with the Fund, and that it shall consist of the Staff Sergeant Major, two Sergeants, two Corporals and two Privates; that a Committee shall be annually appointed in the month of June, at each out-station, to consist of one Sergeant, one Corporal, and one Private, to receive subscriptions at the appointed periods, the amount of which is to be immediately placed in the Bank at Monaghan to the credit of the Pensioners' Fund, and the receipt for which is to be lodged forthwith with the Committee, at head-quarters.

That the amount of relief to be afforded in each case, together with the donation of such relief, shall be decided by the Committee, and that no order on the Fund shall be paid at the Bank until it is signed by the Staff Sergeant Major, one Sergeant, one Corporal, one Private of the Committee, and also till approved of and signed by the Staff Officer.

The Funeral expenses shall be paid out of the allowance granted to the Friends of the deceased Pensioner, and that if, at any time, it can be proved that a Pensioner has been neglected during his illness by his Wife or Family, the Committee shall have the power of withholding the grant, which otherwise they may be entitled to; and that in such case, Funeral Expenses only will be paid.

That when a Pensioner's Widow is known to be improvident, the Committee shall become the Guardians of the Children and give a weekly or monthly allowance for their support, until the whole amount which they are entitled to receive is paid; and that when a Pensioners Widow is notoriously immoral in her conduct, she shall not be entitled to any relief whatever.

That the Wife of a deceased Pensioner shall be obliged to produce her Certificate of Marriage before she can receive any allowance from the Fund.

That should a Pensioner not be married, he shall have the liberty of leaving his share of the Fund to his Mother, Father, Brother or Sister or to those who have taken care of him during his illness, provided the Committee are satisfied that the Pensioner was well taken care of in such cases; however, the Pensioner must nominate the person to whom he may wish the money paid, in presence of at least three witnesses (Pensioners) or some of those in the Committee of Management.

That whenever a Pensioner may leave the District, the amount of subscription paid by him shall be returned, and that, on joining from another district, he must be a member twelve months to entitle his Family, in case of his death, to the full benefit of the Fund, but should he die within the twelve months after joining the Fund, his Family shall only be entitled to such share as the Committee may award. (1846-02-21, 3:1)

3424. My Child's Grave.

My little one! the world looks cold,
My saddend heart doth turn to thee,
And now again my eyes behold,
Thy mould beneath the alder tree!
Once more I tend the flowers that bloom
Beside thine unpretending tomb!

Sweet innocent! they sanctify
Thy place of throbless rest awhile,
With dew drops borrowed from on high,
And many a joyous summer smile!
The rudest winds that o'er thee move
Are softened to a breath of love!

A meditative beauty here
Doth linger on the quiet scene,
And, wakend to a sense of pray'r,
The mind looks forth unveil'd—serene;
While thoughts are rife of those beneath,
Amidst the solitude of Death!

And lovingly we trace again
Each unforgotten semblance o'er—
The fond caress—the playful vein,
The tenderness endear'd of yore!
They steal upon us in that hour
When Memory resumes her power.

And thou, my child, I shadow forth,
In all thy artless infant grace,
That made me prize thee first of earth,
And bless thy bright and winsome face;
Though fleetly closed the dawn of life—
At least it knows no taint of strife!

I fondly thought thou wouldst become
My stay, my hope, in years decline;
But comfortless is now my home,
And dimly doth its taper shine:
And what have I to do with joy,
When thou hast wander'd hence my boy?

I know thou art in yonger heaven,
With rays of fadeless glory crown'd,
But still my steps each quiet even
Bend thither to this holy ground.
Strange sympathy my feelings have
With that secluded moss-clad grave!

There, seated by thy little stone,
My thoughts to other days allied.
I count the weary seasons gone
Since thou wert at thy father's side
And lisping out, as day grew dim,
Thy mother's own loved vesper hymn!

The streamlet murm'ring by doth deem
To wake familiar tones to me;
The passing wind, too, stirs a theme
That brings me nearer still to thee:
And thus in sweet commune of love
I seek my long-lost child above!

I cannot weep—my tears are spent—
But not the less my heart doth mourn,
When upward these weak eyes are bent,
Then desolate—to earth return:
But soon the conflict will be o'er,
And, angel! we shall part no more.

—*Bentley's Miscellany*.
(1846-02-21, 4:1)

3425. Death by Eating a Poisonous Root.—A man named William Woods, who resided in the neighbourhood of Fintona, accidentally poisoned himself by chewing some of the root of the blue rocket, which he imagined to have been ginger. The deceased was a dealer in horses, and was in the habit of carrying ginger and the root of the blue rocket in his pocket. He drank a quantity of water in Finton but could not get rid of the irritation on his tongue and throat, and soon after he had reached his own house, he became very ill, was seized with vomiting, and died in a few hours. (1846-02-21, 4:1)

3426. Married and Single.—I have observed that a married man falling into misfortune is more apt to retrieve his situation in the world than a single one; partly because he is more stimulated to exertion by the necessities of the helpless and beloved beings who depend upon him for subsistence; but chiefly because his spirits soothed and relieved by domestic endearments, and his self-respect kept alive by finding that, though all abroad is darkness and humiliation, yet there is still a world of love at home, of which he is the monarch.—Whereas, a single man is apt to run to waste and self-neglect, to fancy himself lonely and abandoned, and his heart to fall in ruin like some deserted mansion for want of an inhabitant.
(1846-02-21, 4:6)

3427. Fatal Accident.—On Monday the 16th, one of the cart-horses of the Earl of Caledon, while drawing a load of timber down a hill, towards the farm-yard, and the lad in charge of him imagining the animal might make a rush to the gate, called to an old man, named Kowen, to close it. The poor old man, upwards of sixty years of age, with all the promptitude possible, endeavoured to respond to the call; but the horse making a sudden rush, forced the gate back with violence, which struck the old man, knocking out two of his teeth, and inflicting serious injuries of which the old man died almost immediately after. The poor fellow is much regretted, being long in the service of the Caledon family, and was latterly employed in merely sweeping the yards, to give him employment on account of his age. Through the characteristic kindness of the noble Earl, the poor fellow was respectably buried, and the funeral was numerously and respectably attended. This instance of sympathy and benevolence is but another instance of the Earl of Caledon's solicitude and anxiety for the comfort, respectability and best interests, generally, of his tenants and retainers.—*Armagh Gazette*. (1846-02-21, 4:6)

3428. Fatal Accident on the Drogheda Railway.—On Saturday morning, a fatal accident occurred on this line, by which Richard Coleman, stoker, who was attached to the *Alice* engine, met with a sudden and melancholy death—the more melancholy, as it was solely owing to his own carelessness. He left the Drogheda terminus, with the first down train, and on approaching the Killester station, he was standing on the side steps of the engine. The engine driver told him to come up, and the people at the station called to him, but before he could be made sensible of his danger, the engine passed the outside of the platform which struck him on the hip, and he was knocked down, the tender and carriages passing over him.—Every attention was paid to the unfortunate man, but he died very shortly after. In the course of the day, a coroner's inquest was held when the above facts having been proved in evidence, the jury returned a verdict accordingly, with a deodand of one shilling against the engine. No blame whatever attached to the company or any of their officers. (1846-02-28, 4:5)

3429. Epitaph.—In a churchyard in the Isle of Wight, is the following epitaph on a lawyer of the name of Strange:— "Here lies an honest lawyer, and
That's Strange!!!"
(1846-03-14, 1:6)

3430. Life of a Bachelor.—"A bachelor leads an easy life," so says the song; but there is a great deal of misery as well as happiness among bachelors, and it by no means follows that a man must be happy because he is single. There is no doubt, however, that the bachelors enjoy greater freedom than married men, and are less liable to be burdened with anxieties, and this is all that can be said in favour of bachelorhood. I am by no means inclined to consider it either an enviable or commendable state of life, chiefly because it is unsympathising and selfish, and leaves a void in the affections. In short, I believe that a married man, with a moderate competence, and a wife wisely chosen, must necessarily be not only happier, but a better man, than one who, with a similar pecuniary advantage, leads the life of easy bachelorhood. A poor bachelor, however, acts wisely in remaining single. (1846-03-14, 2:1)

3431. Stanzas on the Death of Mr. James A. Lewers. By an Intimate Friend of the Deceased.

"Oh, what a noble heart was here undone,
When science self destroy'd her favorite son,
Yes! she too much indulged thy fond pursuit,
She sow'd the seeds, but death has reap'd the fruit;
'Twas thine own genius gave the final blow,
And help'd to plant the wound that laid thee low."
—Byron.

And art thou fled away from earth,
Thou noblest spirit, my dear friend?
Quench'd in death's gloom is all thy worth,
Our converse here has had an end.

I little thought when last we met,
We never more should meet again,
We ne'er could part without regret,
But then what should have been my pain?

Science has lost a darling child—
The Muses weep thine early flight;
Genius, too, shrieks in accents wild,
Since thy bright sun is lost in night.

But Death, fell tyrant of our race,
Could not destroy thy giant mind;
It hath not died but changed its place—
To heav'nward soarings, 'twas inclined.

Its ardent breathings were too strong
For any form of human mould—
Its flights were far too high—too long
For that weak heart, which now is cold.

Cold now it is, but when in life,
A frigid throb it never gave
The warmest feelings there were rife,
For friend—for country—for the slave.

Oh! that the grave so soon should close,
Upon that sage, though boyish brow,
Where flow'ry bays, in graceful rows,
Should have been placed, long, long, ere now.

But no—e'en they must fade full soon,
And earthly fame shall, too, decay—
The Crown of Life's a nobler boon,
That he shall wear through endless day.

The Book of Truth his ardent mind
Oft studied with a wild delight,
And to its precepts he inclin'd—
A Saviour's love he could not slight.

Then wherefore mourn, since he is gone
To bright and glorious realms above,
To join the tuneful ransom'd throng,
Who ever praise Redeeming love.

Monaghan, March 6, 1846.

(1846-03-14, 2:6)

3432. A young girl about fifteen years of age, of the name of M'Vey, engaged a few days ago in washing a bag in the Foyle, accidentally fell into the water, and before any assistance could be rendered her, she was unfortunately drowned. The body was found some hours after near the place at which the accident happened.
(1846-03-14, 4:3)

3433. Disease (Ireland.)—The following Parliamentary document has been just issued:—

Abstract of the most serious representations made by the several medical superintendents of public institutions (fever hospitals, infirmaries, dispensaries, &c.) in the provinces of Ulster, Munster, Leinster, and Connaught.

(Presented by Command of her Majesty.)

Castle, Dublin, 7th March, 1846.

Sir—The commission having given their deep and serious consideration in the last reports from medical dispensaries, &c., in confirmation of the increase of fever and dysentery throughout the country, respectfully lay before his Excellency the accompanying abstract taken from those statements, and solicit his Excellency's attention to this alarming exigency.

The commission do not venture to propose any distinct measure, but merely to urge the general necessity that his Excellency should have the means of directing medical inspection or attendance immediately as the localities require it, so as to avert the progress of disease, and adopt such other sanatory regulations as may secure the public health.

I have the honour to be, Sir, your obedient servant,
(Signed,)
J.P. Kennedy, Secretary.
Richard Pennefather, Esq., Under Secretary.
&c. &c. &c.

ULSTER.

Antrim—Randalstown, H. Veeson, Medical Officer—"Jaundice and diarrhoea exists from unsoundness and insufficiency of food. Breaking out of disease apprehended where destitution exists."

Armagh—Verner's Bridge, Arthur Ardagh, medical officer—"Diarrhoea to a considerable extent exists in this district, produced from constant use of diseased potatoes. If provisions keep high, fever and other diseases are feared to break out."

Poyntz Pass, William Moorhead, M.D.—"Fever and influenza have increased in the proportion of four to one within last two months; but not only entirely attributable to insufficiency and unsoundness of food."

Markethill, Joseph M. Lynn, M.D.—"Fever, Diarrhoea and dyspepsia have increased considerably, and are in many cases traceable to the use of unsound potatoes. It is very probable that fever will break out and spread, especially among the lower orders. It would be of the utmost importance for every dispensary to have a small fever hospital attached. District is six miles from the hospital of union workhouse."

Cavan—Belturbet, W.M. Wade, M.D.—"Dyspepsia, diseases of alimentary canal, dysentery and diarrhoea are caused by unsound food. Many unemployed poor of district are in a starving condition. Breaking out of disease apprehended with certainty from destitution arising from scarcity of food; it cannot be otherwise. Suggests employment and the erection of a fever hospital to diminish the probability of disease. District is seven Irish miles from Cavan Hospital."

Arvagh, William Myles, Medical Officer—"Apprehends breaking out of disease from destitution, arising from want of food. Bowel complaints, painful and violent griping, with other violent symptoms, continuing eight or ten hours; caused by the use of unsound potatoes. Suggests employment of the poor, and formation of storehouses for oatmeal to be sold at reasonable prices."

Ballyjamesduff, George Nixon, M.D.—"Apprehends fever in districts; strongly recommends establishment of a fever hospital, and the placing of funds in the hands of the clergy and district medical officers for the relief of the poor, who cannot obtain admission into the poor house."

Mullagh, Edward Kellett, M.D.—"Five hundred able-bodied men and an equal number of women, besides many small farmers, are seeking employment. Apprehends breaking out of disease where scarcity exists; the people, being unemployed, are unable to purchase food. Outbreak of fever frequent in summer months, and spreads rapidly for want of an hospital, the want of which is keenly felt by the labouring population. Suggests employment for the poor."

Kingscourt, R. Malcomson, M.D. and Surgeon—"Three thousand and sixty persons relieved at dispensary within five months past. Five or six thousand poor unemployed. Breaking out of disease apprehended in the spring and summer. Suggests the erection of a fever hospital in district where destitution is heavily felt, and is the only available means of preventing the spread of contagion. Medical district of officer embraces a diameter of twelve miles from his residence."

Shercock, James Adams, Medical Officer—"Inflammation of stomach and diarrhoea are frequent, and attributable to the use of bad potatoes. Influenza now epidemic, but will not say it is from insufficiency of food. Increase of fever is expected in April, or sooner. Suggests that fever hospitals be erected on every three square miles of district."

Swanlinbar, Winslow Finlay, Medical Officer—"Several cases of typhus fever have recently appeared; insufficiency of food the cause in some instances. Fever will break out to a frightful extent in the event of scarcity of food. Suggests local fever hospitals to be established for the removal of cases as they occur."

Donegall—Donaghmore, R.M. Tagard, M.D.—"Influenza, scarlatina, small-pox, and, much above all, stomach and bowel disease exist, varying to fatal inflammation. Diseased potatoes may be the existing cause. Apprehends the spread of disease, particularly fever; provisions being likely to be dear and scarce, and the supply of fuel scanty. Suggests temporary hospital relief, and that non contagious medical and surgical cases be admitted to workhouse hospital without the workhouse test."

Moville, John Irvine, surgeon, R.N.—"Typhus fever prevails, but not as an epidemic. Apprehends the breaking out of fever from destitution, arising from failure of potato crop." (1846-03-21, 2:3)

3434. Destructive Fire.—About eleven o'clock on Monday night, the house of Patt Ruan, a hatter, residing in Chapel Lane in this town, was discovered to be on fire, occasioned by the snuff of a candle falling on some straw on the loft. The family were in bed, and, so rapid was the progress of the fire, that it was with much difficulty they escaped with their lives; one of the children was so severely burned, as to leave her recovery very doubtful.—*Tuam Herald*. (1846-03-21, 2:4)

3435. Recent Wills.—The Late Marquis of Ely.—Probate of the will and codicil of the Most Honourable John Marquis of Ely, of Ely Lodge, Fermanagh, Ireland, has just been granted by the Prerogative Court of Canterbury to his son, the present Marquis, late Viscount Loftus, who is the sole executor. The late Marquis, possessing a power of appointment over the estates and properties, manors, town lands, &c., in the counties of Wexford and Fermanagh and in the city of Dublin, in the event of the present Marquis dying without issue male, has made a strict provision in such case, by way of annuity for the life of his son, Lord George William Loftus, and the remainder during his life for his other children, according to the trusts of the settlement. The estates were entailed on a male issue, to sons, and on failure, to daughters. By virtue also of another power of appointment over a sum of 20,000*l*., he leaves the same, with a like provision in seven parts, among his younger sons and daughters—Lord George William Loftus, Lord Adair, Robert Charles Loftus, Lord Augustus William Frederick Spencer Loftus, Lord Henry York Astley Loftus, Lady Charlotte Egerton, Lady Ann Maria Helen Loftus, Lady Catherine Henrietta Mary Loftus. Directed 2,000*l*. to be paid to his wife, the Marchioness, for immediate use, and that she might select a carriage and pair of horses; and has secured for the annual payment of no less than seven policies of insurance which have been effected on her life. The residue to the present Marquis.—The will is dated in December, 1844, and the codicil in August, 1845. His lordship was in his seventy-sixth year, and died on the 26th of September last. (1846-03-21, 2:4)

3436. Recent Wills.—The Earl of Portarlington's Will. —The will of the late Right Honourable John Earl of Portarlington, of Emo Park, Queen's County, Ireland, a colonel in the army, was proved in London on the 23d ult., by his brother, the Right Hon. Lieutenant Colonel George Lionel Dawson Damer, M.P., the sole executor, and a trustee, with Matthew Sheffield Cassan, Esq., to whom is left a legacy of 2,000*l.* if acting. The will was executed in London, on the 11th of April, 1844. He devises his freehold, known as Roscrea, in Tipperary, consisting of 2,243 acres, producing a rental of 3,332*l.* per annum, to the Right Honourable George Lionel Dawson Damer, and to his heirs male for ever, charged with an annuity of 500*l.* to his brother, William Mackenzie Dawson, and 200*l.* a year to John Dawson Hill, and makes certain conditional charges of annuities on residue for others of his family. Beqeaths to Mrs. Blakeney £10,000 beyond all money due to her on mortgage, in trust for her three daughters £5,000 to each, free of legacy duty and bearing interest at 5 per cent till the same can be raised. Devises to trustees all the residue of freehold, copyhold, and leasehold estates, and the manors, townlands, &c., of which he may be seized or possessed, or entitled in expectancy, subject to charges, to dispose thereof, and to invest all moneys in government or real securities in England, Wales, or Ireland, the residue being made a primary fund for the payment of all debts; and after making the respective payments, to stand seized and possessed of the several manors and lords not sold, and the trust moneys and all the personal estate and convey and assign same respectively to his nephew the present Earl, the only son of his late brother, the Honourable Captain W. Henry Dawson Damer, R.N.; but if he dies without male issue, then to the said Right Honourable G.L.D. Damer absolutely, or to the person succeeding to the title. The trustees to keep in good repair the mansion of Emo Park, and not to allow any timber or trees to be cut down on any part of the demesne lands of Emo unless for improvement. The late Earl was in his 65th year, and died in London on the 28th of December, 1845. (1846-03-21, 2:4)

3437. Awful Accident with a Gun.—On Saturday evening, two men were returning from near Saintfield. The person who had the gun in his hand was crossing a ditch, when it went off, and shot his companion through the side. We have been informed that the poor fellow died shortly after the accident. Medical aid was procured, but proved of no avail. (1846-03-21, 3:3)

3438. Omagh Assizes.—Omagh, Friday, March 13.—Samuel Galbraith M'Whinney was indicted for having, on 1st Nov. last, at Castlederg, celebrated a marriage between R. Forest and Sarah Smyth, against the statute.

Mr. Lowry, counsel for the prisoner, was not in a position to defend him, and would adopt the course of throwing him on the mercy of the Court. He is a clergyman of the Established Church.

Mr. Smyly, Q.C., said he would only require security for his appearance when called upon by the Crown.

Judge Torrens—You have, sir, heard what the counsel for the crown has said, that, as you were not aware of the provisions of the act, he will not press the Court for punishment upon you. I am sorry, sir, to see a person of your cloth placed in the position you now occupy, and, as you have pleaded ignorance of the law, I am sorry you were so negligent in not inquiring into the nature of the change in that law. If such a course as you have adopted were suffered to proceed, it would lead to many bad consequences—illegitimacy and forfeiture of property. You are now ordered by court to enter into your own recognizance, for your appearance (if there be a repetition of the offence) in the sum of £500, and find two securities in £100 each, to receive the sentence of the court. (1846-03-21, 4:4)

3439. Down.—Saturday, March, 14.—The Hon. Justice Burton took his seat on the Bench at half-past nine o'clock.—Illegal Marriage—Priest Taggart's Case.

Mr. O'Hagan, addressing his lordship, said that in the case of the *Queen v. Taggart*, there was some peculiarity, but he expected to save time by the course which he would suggest. It was the case of a prosecution instituted under the *7th and 8th Vict., chap. 81*, against the Rev. Mr. Taggart, a Roman Catholic priest, for celebrating a marriage between two Protestants. Under the old law, such a marriage was null and void, and the person celebrating it was liable to a penalty of one hundred pounds and capital punishment. By a late act, the penalties were removed, but the marriage remained null. By the late Marriage Act, all marriages, except those celebrated in certain times and places, were null, and the person celebrating them guilty of felony, except those celebrated by a Roman Catholic Priest. There was no doubt Mr. Taggart had celebrated a marriage between two Protestants; the question was, was it legal or not? He (Mr. O'Hagan) was prepared to argue that it was not unlawful, but as the question was one of great importance, he had come to the conclusion that it was better to have the matter put on record, and have the decision of the Court of Queen's Bench on the subject. He was, therefore, to consent to a special verdict, if the Crown would agree to have the case brought by *certiorari* into the Court of Queen's Bench.

Sir Thomas Stables [sic] consented to the proposition. It would be necessary, however, to have the party arraigned and plead.

Mr. O'Hagan said, that Mr. Taggart should be set at liberty, after entering into the proper recognizance. The following jury were sworn:—Messrs. Wm. Seed, Robert Denvir, James Greer, Denis Breen, William M'Burney, William Carson, Savage Osborne, Andrew

Ringland, Adam Kenning, John Boyd, James Wilson, and Samuel M'Bride.

John Taggart was then arraigned for celebrating an unlawful marriage, between two Protestants, at Downpatrick, and having entered into his recognizances, was discharged. (1846-03-21, 4:6)

3440. A Paragraph for the Ladies.—One of our correspondents seals his letter to us, announcing his marriage with the following motto:—

"The house in which no woman's found,
Will quickly tumble to the ground."

(1846-03-28, 1:4)

3441. Accidental Death of Rev. Dr. Moore, Rockcorry. —On Friday night the 20th inst., Mr. Moore was called upon to visit, in a professional capacity, a woman named Boyd, residing on the Old Ballybay road, near to Bushford. It appears that with the first two or three messengers, he refused to go, being in a very debilitated stated of health and having but lately recovered from a severe attack of inflammation of the lungs. To the entreaties of the last messenger, however, he yielded; and after having performed his duty, he was allowed to leave the house alone, about twelve or one o'clock in a night of unusual roughness. Upon entering the bog which lies between it and Bushford bridge, his hat was blown off, which it seems he did not recover; without it, he had nearly reached the end of the bog, when, unfortunately in his endeavours, it is supposed, to shield his head by his cloak, from the pelting of the sleet storm, he walked off the road and was precipitated into the water, which laves [sic] the road on both sides. He was found next morning, by a man named Crossen, quite dead, leaning against the opposite bank, better than half immersed in the water, after having left traces of a vain effort to extricate himself.—The case is more particularly afflicting as having been engaged upon an errand of mercy, and a promise being given to the family of his protection. He was in the 64th year of his age. (1846-03-28, 2:5)

3442. In Chancery.—Jane Harpur, Administratrix of Henry Kidd, deceased, Plaintiff.—Henry Boyd and Hugh Swanzy, Executors of Josiah Kidd, deceased, Defendants.—Pursuant to the Decree made in this Cause, bearing date the 20th day of January, 1845, I require all Creditors and Legatees of Josiah Kidd, the testator in the pleadings in this cause named, to come in before me, at my office on the Inns Quay, in the City of Dublin, on or before the 1st day of June next, and prove their debts and claim their legacies; otherwise, they will be precluded from the benefit of the said Decree.

Dated this 1st day of April, 1846.
Thomas Goold.
John Bates, Plaintiff's Solicitor,
38, Lower Ormond Quay, Dublin.

(1846-04-04, 3:5)

3443. May You Die Among Your Kindred! —An Original Benediction.

May you die among your kindred!
May you rest your parting gaze
On the loved familiar faces
Of your young and happy days;
May the voices whose kind greeting
To your infancy was dear,
Pour lovingly while life declines,
Their music on your ear.

May you die among your kindred!
May the friends you love the best,
List to your falling accents,
And receive your last request;
Read your unuttered wishes,
On your changeful features dwell,
And mingle sighs of sorrow
With your falt'ring faint farewell.

May you die among your kindred!
May your peaceful grave be made,
In the quiet cool recesses
Of the graveyard's hallowed shade
There may your loved ones wander
At the close of silent day,
Fair buds and fragrant blossoms
On the verdant turf to lay.

'Tis a tender benediction;
Yet methinks it lacks the power
To cast a true serenity
On life's last solemn hour.
Ye whom I love, I may not thus
Love's Christian part fulfil,
List while I ask for you a boon
More dear, more precious still.

So may you die, that though afar
From all your cherished ties,
Though strangers hear your dying words,
And close your dying eyes,
Ye shall not know desertion since
Your saviour shall be near,
To fill your fainting spirit with
The love that casts our fear.

So may you die, so willingly
Submit your soul to God,
That evermore your kindred,
As they tread the path you trod,
May picture your existence
On a far off heavenly shore,
And speak of you as one not lost,
But only gone before.

So may you die that when your death
To pious friends is known,
Each shall devoutly meekly wish
Such lot to be their own;
Not heeding if you died in want,
In exile or in pain,
But feeling that you died in faith
For thus to die is gain.

(1846-04-04, 4:1)

3444. Death of Mr. John Langan.—Tuesday, Mr. John Langan, more familiarly styled and better known as Jack Langan, the pugilist, breathed his last at the house of Mrs. Lewis, Five lane-ends, near Neston, Cheshire. (1846-04-04, 4:3)

3445. Death of James Evatt, Esq.—It is our painful duty to announce the death of one of the best, the most upright, humane, and efficient magistrates that Ireland could boast of—James Evatt, Esq., of Carrickmacross, agent over the extensive estates of the Marquess of Bath, in the county of Monaghan. The sad event, which we record with intense sorrow, took place suddenly, at the residence of the deceased, at Carrickmacross, on Wednesday. Our correspondent states that Mr. Evatt was in perfect health yesterday morning, and that on sitting down to breakfast, he was attacked by apoplexy, which caused the rupture of a blood vessel, and ended in death a few hours after the attack. The sad intelligence was spread through the village at four o'clock in the afternoon, and diffused a universal gloom over the neighbourhood. Every shop was instantly closed, and a complete stop was put to all kinds of business.

The deceased was universally beloved and respected for his endearing qualities of head and heart, in all the relations of life, domestic and public. His management of the 28,000 acres over which he was placed for seventeen years, gave the utmost satisfaction to his noble employer, and in every individual of his large tenantry, who are plunged in the deepest sorrow. Everything that could be done to avert the sad catastrophe was performed, without effect, by Doctors McEffer, Brunker, Montgomery, Walsh, and O'Reilly, who did not quit the side of their patient until he drew his last breath. (1846-04-11, 3:3)

3446. Poor Man's Grave.—By Eliza Cook.

No sable pall, no waving plume,
No thousand torch-lights to illume;
No parting glance, no heavy tear,
Is seen to fall upon the bier.
There is not one of kindred clay
To watch the coffin on its way;
No mortal form, no human breast,
Cares where the pauper's bones may rest.

But one deep mourner follows there,
Whose grief outlives the funeral prayer,
He does not sigh, he does not weep,
But will not leave the sodless heap.
'Tis he who was the poor man's mate,
And made him more content with fate;—
The mongrel dog that shared his crust
Is all that stands beside his dust.

He bends his listening head, as though
He thought to hear a voice below;
He pines to miss that voice so kind,
And wonders why he's left behind.
The sun goes down, the night is come,
He needs no food—he seeks no home;
But stretched upon the dreamless bed,
With doleful howl calls back the dead.

The passing gaze may coldly dwell
On all that polished marbles tell;
For temples built on churchyard earth
Are claimed by riches more than worth;
But who would mark with undimmed eyes
The mourning dog that starves and dies?
Who would not ask, who would not crave,
Such love and faith to guard his grave?
(1846-04-11, 3:6)

3447. Law Intelligence.—Commission Court—Saturday, April 11.—Trial of Mr. Browne for Bigamy.

The Right Hon. Baron Richards and the Hon. Mr. Justice Ball took their seats upon the bench this morning at a quarter-past eleven o'clock, at which hour every part of the court was crowded to excess by those who were fortunate enough to obtain admission to hear the extraordinary bigamy case of

Copeland v. Browne,

which was specially fixed for trial.

Immediately after the sitting of their lordships, the prisoner, who is a barrister, Mr. Henry Augustus Browne, was placed at the bar, and called upon to challenge twenty jurors peremptorily, and as many more as he could show cause for excluding from the jury. The full number of challenges were accordingly put by his solicitor, and the following gentlemen empannelled:—

John Brophy, foreman; Patrick Wm. Brady, T. Carroll, John Rooney, P. Brennan, Christopher Cummings, Joseph Doyle, James Lidley, H. Reilly, Edward Sherry, Michael Whelan, and Palmer Bacon.

Messrs. Hatchell, Q.C.; Butt; and Brereton, appeared as counsel for the prosecution, with Mr. C. Johnston as solicitor; and Messrs. Macdonogh, Q.C.; O'Hea, and Concannon, acted for the prisoner, with Mr. A. O'Sullivan as agent.

Mr. Browne, who was accommodated with a chair in the dock, appeared to have suffered considerably by his incarceration, and was manifestly very much affected by the proceedings. His father and brothers, and several of his friends, were provided with seats in court.

When the jury was sworn, and the city petit jury discharged, the prisoner was given in charge for having, upon the 5th day of November, 1844, married Isabella Copeland, daughter of Charles Copeland, Esq., his former wife, Mary Downs, whom he married upon the 3d of June, 1842, in the parish church of St. Mark, in this city, being alive.

Mr. Browne pleaded not guilty.

The Right Hon. the Earl of Charlemont occupied a seat on the bench with their lordships for the greater part of the day.

Mr. Hatchell, Q.C, then addressed the Court and jury as counsel for the prosecution. He said that in that case he was counsel for the prosecution, and it became his duty to open the facts upon which it had been founded. They had heard from the indictment the nature of the offence with which the prisoner stood charged. The charge against the prisoner was for having upon a second occasion married a lady, his former wife being then alive. He thought he need scarcely state to the jury the nature of that offence, when every one of them should feel that such a crime struck at the very root of civil society, and affected some of the dearest relations of life. Under even ordinary circumstances, the offence was enormous, but there were circumstances connected with that crime which made it a case of considerable aggravation when a prisoner stood in a particular position.—He could not forget that in that case he was counsel for the prosecution. It was not his duty, and it certainly was not his inclination, to endeavour to inflame the passions or bespake the prejudices of a jury against any man who was charged with a criminal offence. He would, therefore, endeavor to confine himself as much as possible to the detail of the facts, without giving utterance to any feelings that might naturally influence the mind of every member of society, in stating a case of that character and description. The prisoner, he regretted to state, was a member of a most respectable family, perhaps one of the best in the west of Ireland, a young gentleman of education and endowments qualifying him to fill, perhaps with success, the profession to which he (Mr. Hatchell) belonged; it was therefore a painful duty to state the circumstances under which the prisoner stood committed for trial. The facts, which would be distinctly and clearly proved, (if he were not greatly misinstructed,) were these: The prosecutor in the case was Mr. Charles Copeland, the manager of the Royal Bank of Ireland. He was placed in such a position by the injury done to his family that he could not avoid proceeding. He was a gentleman of the highest respectability—a native of Scotland—highly connected there. He came to this country some time about twenty years since, where he settled, and resided with his family, honored and respected by those with whom he and they were acquainted. Mr. Copeland had, upon a former occasion, in the discharge of important duties, proceeded to Galway, in the province of Connaught, where he resided and formed a circle of acquaintances. In the summer of 1844, he, with his lady and daugther, was invited to spend some time at the house of a highly-respectable gentleman, Mr. O'Flahertie, who resided in the neighborhood of Galway. At that time, the prisoner at the bar was going the Connaught circuit. The assizes of Galway took place while Mr. Copeland, his wife, and daughter were stopping with Mr. O'Flahertie, and prisoner, who knew one of Mr. O'Flahertie's sons, was also invited to the house. He was introduced there as a barrister highly connected, and his attentions to Miss Copeland became marked. It was not suspected that he had been previously married; and when Mr. Copeland returned to Dublin, it was communicated to him that he had made proposals of marriage to his daughter. Mr. Copeland, upon receiving that communication, stated that his acquiescence in the marriage would depend upon the approval of the prisoner's family. He was a young gentleman entering upon an honorable profession with every prospect of success; in personal appearance unexceptionable, and in every particular apparently a desirable person to contract a marriage with Miss Copeland. The prosecutor came to Dublin to reside at Longford-terrace, near Kingstown, and when the prisoner returned from circuit, he was allowed to visit the family. Nearly six months elapsed from the first proposals of marriage by the prisoner till its solemnisation; and upon the 5th of November, 1844, all the preliminary arrangements having been settled, the marriage took place in the parish church of Monkstown, in the presence of the mutual friends of the parties, the highly respectable rector of that parish (Archdeacon Lindsay) being the officiating clergyman. This marriage—this fatal marriage—was thus celebrated. No suspicion was attached to the prisoner, and could it be possible that, under these circumstances, the slightest suspicion, the most distant surmise, could have suggested itself to the prosecutor that there was any impediment to the legal solemnisation of the marriage? The position of the prisoner was respectable; he was a member of an honorable profession, well connected, and in every respect, to all appearances, it was a desirable match. He was but twenty-three or twenty-four years of age; and could there have been any suspicion, any surmise, that the marriage could not legally take place, or prosper? Therefore, upon the part of Mr. Copeland or any member of his family, there could not be the slightest intimation, or anything like inadvertence, mistake, or want of vigilance with respect to the care and protection of Miss Copeland, laid at the door of her parents. The marriage having been celebrated, under these circumstances, a house was taken in North Frederick-street, and Miss Copeland went to reside there with her supposed husband. They were domesticated there for a period of nearly a year, when the circumstances which he would communicate led to their going abroad. Mr. Browne had a sister, who, it appeared, was in delicate health. He was the son of a gentleman of high position, character, and property in Galway, (Colonel Browne, of Browne Hall, in that county,) and on its being proposed that Miss Browne should go to the Continent for the benefit of her health, Colonel Browne suggested that the prisoner and his supposed wife should accompany her to Rome or Italy, as he could not do so, and thus afford her protection and society. It was also arranged that Colonel Browne should follow them to the Continent, and afford his son an opportunity of (*continued...*)

3447, continued: ...returning to Ireland and pursuing his profession.—Accordingly, in October last, after a year's cohabitation in North Frederick-street, without anything occurring to excite suspicion or alarm, or any one connected with these families, Mr. Browne and Miss Copeland went abroad, and remained with Miss Browne for sometime at Rome. Sometime after Mr. Browne had thus left Ireland, a female called frequently at the house, and inquired of the servants who were left in charge of it, where he was. She called so often, and her manner was so earnest, that conversations took place between her and the servants, and then, for the first time, was it discovered that Mr. Browne had been married before to this female, whose maiden name was Mary Downes [sic]. She announced herself as his legitimate wife, and her object in coming to his house was to demand the rights, support, and protection of him as her husband—of course, this statement was immediately communicated to some friends of the Copeland family, and it soon reached the ear of the family themselves.—He need not tell them the consternation, dismay, and misery, that the allegation caused in the family; but it was considered prudent not to take any course precipitately. There might be mistake—there might be misrepresentation—there might be fraud and imposition—and as it was important to be caution and circumspect. Mrs. Copeland sent for a very respectable connection and professional friend, Mr. Johnson, stated the circumstances to him, and had an inquiry into it instituted. Upon inquiry, it was found that the statement was too fatally true. It was discovered, and he was instructed it would be distinctly proved beyond all question or doubt, that the prisoner had contracted a legal marriage with Mary Downes. He believed that this person was not his equal in rank, as she filled some subordinate situation in some of the families in Dublin. It was ascertained that he had contracted a marriage with this person, which was celebrated in the year 1842, in St. Mark's church, by the Protestant clergyman of the parish—a marriage solemnised under a license, which had been verified by affidavit, and sanctioned by the usual bond given upon those occasions, setting forth there was no impediment to this marriage taking place. He would not suggest to the jury what must have been the sensations of the Copeland family at this juncture. Miss Copeland was but nineteen years of age when she was married, and she was at this time many miles from home. Her father saw her in the position of a person who was not the lawful wife of the prisoner; and he had no course to take but to recover what he considered her then—his lost child. The learned counsel then described the manner in which the prisoner had been arrested, and concluded by stating that he would prove that to be a case of deliberate and unmitigated criminality upon the part of the prisoner.

Richard M'Cartney, examined by Mr. Butt—I know the prisoner since June, 1842; I am a servant in Merrion-square; I saw him on the 2d of June in his lodgings in Nassau-street; and on the following day, I again saw him in St. Mark's church; I saw him married to Mary Downes by the Rev. Mr. Franklin; he was, I believe, the rector; Mary Downes is my wife's sister; and I saw her married to the prisoner on that day; she is now alive; I saw her to-day; book produced; I saw Browne sign his name to that book on the 3d of June, 1842; my name is signed also in it, and also Mary Downes; I was the witness to the marriage.

Cross-examined by Mr. Macdonagh—I first saw Mr. Browne, to know him, on the day before the marriage; my wife, the sexton, and myself were present; Mr. Browne had no friend with him; he then looked a very young man, but I could not tell his age; Mary Downes was a servant at that time in Mr. Browne's father's employment, Colonel Browne; she went there in 1839, or about that time; she was in other services in Dublin before; she was then about eight or nine and twenty; she was, I think, older than my wife; I have five children; I was married on the 12th of July, 1835; I can't say if Colonel Browne's family was then in town; I heard Mary Downes say there was a proposal of marriage made to her in 1841, by a person named Fitzgerald; I heard of her marriage to this Fitzgerald long since, and I did not believe it; I believe it now; she told me of it herself, and I have no doubt about it; when I heard of it first in 1841—I mean the marriage with Fitzgerald—she was in Colonel Browne's service; I had a conversation with her in May, 1842, about this marriage, and she denied it; I spoke to her about it, and asked her if she was married to this Jas. or Wm. Fitzgerald; I don't know which, and she denied it; before November, 1844, I can't say if I heard her say she was married to Fitzgerald; Mary Downes' marriage with Mr. Browne took place about nine o'clock in the morning; I was then in the service of his Grace the Archbishop of Dublin, and I am now in the employment of Mr. John Radcliff, of Merrion-square.

Lorenzo Trigged, examined by Mr. Brereton.—I was parish clerk of St. Mark's in 1842; I know the prisoner at the bar; I saw him in St. Mark's church in June, 1842.—(Book produced); this is the registry marriage book of the parish, and I kept it; I saw the prisoner married to Mary Downes, by the Rev. Alexander Franklin, the senior curate; I made the entry of the marriage which I saw solemnised; and I also saw Mr. Browne and her sign their names; I never saw Mary Downes before that day, but I saw her since, and know her to be the person who was married to Mr. Browne; I see the prisoner; he is the same person I saw married to Mary Downes; the parish of St. Mark is, I believe, in the borough of Dublin.

Cross-examined by Mr. O'Hea—There was no one present at the marriage on the part of Mr. Browne.

John Samuels, examined by Mr. Hatchell.—I am deputy registrar of the Consistorial Court of Dublin, and the archbishop; It is part of my duty to issue marriage licenses from my office; at that time in June, 1842, it was necessary for persons to enter into a bond, upon getting a license; bond produced; this is a bond executed between Henry Browne and Richard M'Cartney; the usual oath was administered to the proper parties by the late Dr. Radcliffe, whose name and handwriting appears to these documents.

Cross-examined by Mr. Concannon.—I cannot tell the hour of the day this license was granted, or the hour it was applied for; I keep no account of those things.

Denis Monks, examined by Mr. Butt.—I fill the situation of clerk in the Consistorial Court.—Bond produced; I am a witness to that bond; I saw it executed by Henry Browne and Richard M'Cartney; I would not know either of them. (Second bond between the prisoner and Mr. Copeland produced.) I witnessed that bond, but I don't know that the prisoner signed it.

Thomas Eustace, examined by Mr. Brereton.—I know the prisoner, and have seen him write.—(Second bond produced.) I cannot swear to his handwriting; I am parish clerk of Monkstown, and was so on the 15th of November, 1845 [sic]; on that day, I saw the prisoner married to Miss Isabella Copeland; the archdeacon of Kildare married them,—(Book produced.) This is the parish registry book; and I find the entry of the marriage in Archdeacon Lindsay's handwriting; he is rector of the parish; I myself saw the prisoner married to Miss Copeland.

The entries of the two marriages having been read, the next witness called was

Mr. Robert Murray.—I am acquainted with Mr. Charles Copeland since 1817; I know his family; I know his daughter, Miss Arabella Copeland; she is his eldest daughter; I saw her married to the prisoner on the 5th of November, 1844, by Archdeacon Lindsay, in Monkstown church; there was a brother of Mr. Browne present; I saw them afterwards as man and wife in company.

Mr. Charles Frazer Johnston, examined by Mr. Hatchell—I know the prisoner, and I have seen him write. —(Bond to first marriage produced.) I see his name to that bond, and it is his hand-writing.—(Second bond produced.) I saw him sign that bond; this is dated the 29th of October, 1844.

Cross-examined by Mr. Macdonagh—I am solicitor for the prosecution; I wrote to the prisoner to Rome. (Letter produced.) That is my original letter, I have no copy of it; the erased parts, I think, relate to private matters.

To Mr. Butt—I was present at Mr. Browne's marriage with Miss Copeland; they lived together as man and wife until he was arrested.

Mr. Allison, the Governor of Kilmainham, having proved that the prisoner was in his custody since the 31st of July last, and the several documents referred to in the case having been entered as read, prosecution closed.

Mr. Macdonogh proceeded to address the jury for the defence. He said he would, in the first place, dispute the harsh statement of his learned friend, Mr. Hatchell, who termed the case one of unmitigated criminality, and called upon the jury to consider the prisoner guilty if it was proved that he had married a second time, his first wife being alive. Such was not the law, as he (Mr. Macdonagh) would satisfy them of his authority, which would show, that unless it was proved that Mr. Browne had feloniously married his second wife, his former wife being alive, the crime was not completed. Mr. Johnston had written to Rome to bring the prisoners, as Mr. Copeland's counsel stated within the pale of English justice, and he had, by it, succeeded in bringing him within that pale—and justice would be done—and to do justice, the jury would have to consider the intent of the party on trial—whether it was felonious or not? This would be seen to be the true state of the law as laid down in the 1st vol. of the "State Trials," which detailed the duties of a juror, and cautioned juries against finding a party guilty on such a charge without full proof on this point. Counsel was reading a long passage from the book in question, when he was interrupted by

Baron Richards, who said he could not permit the law to be misstated. It was not the law that Mr. Macdonagh had laid down; and it was not right to refer to elementary books, and read them for a jury in explanation of the law. The law was this—that if a man married a second time, his first wife being alive, with his knowledge, he was guilty of the crime of bigamy.

Mr. Macdonogh regretted that anything he stated could have called for his lordship's observation, and went on to argue that when it was proved that the prisoner had feloniously married the second time, he should be acquitted, and referred to the case of the *King a. Prosser*, and other cases, in support of the argument.

Baron Richards—I will put the law to the jury as I have told you. What I state is the law, and I shall read it to them from the act of Parliament.

Mr. Macdonogh then resumed his address to the jury, observing that the question of intent was, as he believed, for their consideration, and also informing them that they were not to take the law from him, but from the Court. He said that the statement of his lordship had shortened his speech very much, and it would now be only necessary for him to call upon them to consider the facts of the case. It should be remembered that the prisoner, when he was married in 1842, was under age, and was married to a knowing servant-woman of twenty-nine, who (*continued...*)

3447, continued: ...evidently had entrapped him into bed, a cook, and who, had been, as was stated, married before to a person named Fitzgerald. He was not much more than a boy, and by the *9th of Geo. II.* that marriage could have been broken within twelve months if he chose to take the proper proceedings; but he did not do so, as he considered when he heard of her prior marriage with Fitzgerald, that she was not his wife, and that therefore, he was at liberty to marry any one. This was the exact and true state of the case, and he (Mr. Macdonagh) felt convinced that no jury would, under the circumstances, find a verdict of conviction. They would be proved, and the prisoner would receive the highest possible character, and then it would be their pleasing duty to set him at large, after his lengthened and painful imprisonment.

Colonel Dominick Browne examined by Mr. O'Hea. —I am father to the prisoner. He was not of age in 1842; he took a house in North Frederick-street, and I purchased a library for him when he got married. He was then called to the bar; I lived some time after in his house; I don't think I ever saw greater affection between man and wife than I saw between him and Miss Copeland; I am sure he feels more for her situation than his own at the moment.—(This witness was deeply affected when giving his evidence.)

To Mr. Hatchell—I am quite certain my son was not of age when the first marriage took place.

Mr. Monaghan, Q.C, examined by Mr. Concannon.—I am a Queen's Counsel on the Connaught circuit,—I know the prisoner as a barrister and a gentleman, and I know no one who possessed a higher character.

Mr. G. Fitzgibbon, Q.C., examined by Mr. Macdonogh —I know the prisoner as a barrister and gentleman on the Connaught circuit. From my knowledge of him, no man held a higher character.

Mathew Baker, Esq., examined—He was a member of the Connaught bar. He was acquainted with the prisoner. He always regarded him as a gentleman of respectability and integrity, and he had heard of the present charge against him with surprise and regret.

Walter Bourke, Esq., examined—Knew the prisoner at the bar as a barrister and a private gentleman. He belonged to the same county that he did; and before he came to the bar, and while at the bar, he knew him to be a gentleman of integrity and honor. With the exception of that charge, he never knew anything that was not creditable to him, and he heard of the charge with the greatest regret.

Thomas Warren White, Esq., examined—He had known the prisoner upon circuit. His character was very good; and no one could be more esteemed and regarded by every one that knew him, than he was.

John G. Holmes, Esq., examined—He was also a member of the same circuit with the prisoner; he had the very highest character of him; there was not a gentleman upon the circuit—and he had every opportunity of judging of his character, for he was very intimate with him—who bore a higher character.

Mr. Butt, Q.C, then addressed the jury in reply. He said he felt it necessary to say a few words in reply. He was compelled to do so in consequence of the learned counsel, who had addressed the Court for the prisoner, having complained of harshness and severity on the institution of the prosecution. The learned gentleman then dwelt upon the very heart-rending case which had that day been brought before the jury, and vindicated the course taken by Mr. Copeland, who, as a father, could not have acted otherwise than he had done. Mr. Hatchell had denominated that a case of unmitigated criminality, and in this opinion, he was coerced to concur.

Baron Richards then charged the jury. His lordship read the section of the act of Parliament, (the 10th of George IV., c. 3[*illegible*], section 26,) which enacted that every person who married a party during the lifetime of one to whom he or she had been previously married, was guilty of felony. The case was a most painful one; nevertheless, they were governed by the law, and according to it, their verdict should be found. With regard to the statement, that the female to whom the prisoner had been previously married had been herself married at the time, they could not act upon such a supposition, as it had not been proved by witnesses. He allowed the circumstance to be introduced into the case, because a large discretion as to the admeasuring of punishment was vested in the Court, and he was unwilling to shut out any matter which would have its influence upon his mind in adjudicating upon the case; and if it had turned out that the prisoner, in marrying a second time, had acted under the delusion that the woman whom he had previously married had herself been married at the time, it would have had a moral influence upon him in mitigating the amount of punishment to be inflicted upon the prisoner.

The jury retired, and in about ten minutes, returned with a verdict of guilty.

Mr. Macdonagh, Q.C, stated that his client had made an affidavit, which, by permission of the Court, he would then have sworn by him and read.

The prisoner then swore the affidavit, and our reporters here left the court.

Monday, April 13.

The Queen v. Henry A. Browne.

A Juror, addressing the Court from the county jury box, said that, in the prosecution against Mr. Browne, for bigamy, which had been tried on the previous day, they desired to recommend him to mercy.

Baron Richards—Were you the foreman?

Juror—I was not.

Baron Richards—Then your notification is irregular, and in any event, the proper course would have been to accompany the verdict with the recommendation, if such were intended to be given.

Juror—I believe the foreman is in the box, my lord.

Baron Richards—Then that makes your proceedings more irregular.

Mr. Macdonagh, Q.C, at a subsequent part of the day, applied to their lordships to reserve for the consideration of the twelve judges a question which he wanted to have put to the jury, with regard to the intent of the prisoner when contracting the second marriage. He then proceeded to cite the case of the *King v. Eliza Greenwood*, reported in the supplement to Deacon's *Criminal Law*, where, on an indictment for bigamy, Chief Justice Tyndall left it to the jury to find the intent as Independent of the mere fact of the second marriage celebrated in the life-time of the first husband.

The learned judges intimated that, if they on consideration felt any doubt upon the subject, they would consult the other members of the bench. (1846-04-18, 1:1)

3448. Melancholy Accident—Four Lives Lost.—We regret to be obliged to record an accident attended with serious loss of life, which occurred at Castleblayney on Monday last. A number of young men, among whom was a sailor, who had just returned from a voyage, on a visit to his friends, called on Mr. John Tate, Lord Blayney's head boatman, and requested the use of a boat to have a row on the beautiful lake that spreads itself through his Lordship's demesne. Unfortunately, their importunity was successful, and poor Tate himself accompanied them. After spending some time on the water, and when about a hundred perches from land on their return, the boat was upset by some mismanagement, and the whole party, consisting of five persons, were precipitated into the water. They were all good swimmers, save one, named Maguire, and he grasped at the boat, while the others stretched out for shore.—Fortunately, he succeeded in getting astride upon the keel, where he remained for some minutes until a wave again struck the vessel and turned it up. With desperate energy, he maintained his grasp, and held on until he was rescued. But his less fortunate companions, one after another,sunk to rise no more. Mr. Sheil of Castleblayney proceeded instantly to the place, and, with the aid of drags, got the bodies of three of the unfortunate men—but the remains of poor Tate were not found until next day. Tate has left a wife and five children to deplore his loss. None of the others was married. Their names were Charles Stewart, Robert Stewart, and Robert Keating. (1846-04-18, 3:2)

3449. The Magistracy.—The Lord Lieutenant has been pleased to appoint, under the *act 6, Wm. IV., chap. 13*, Gerard Barry, Esq., a resident magistrate, vice E.A. Douglas, deceased, and to take charge of the district of Athlone, in the county of Roscommon.

The Lord Lieutenant has been pleased to approve of the following changes of stations of the undermentioned resident magistrates, appointed under the *act 6 Wm. IV., chap. 13*:—

John D. Ellard, Esq., from the county of Roscommon, to take charge of the district of Portadown, county of Armagh, vice William Cooke, Esq., R.M., who returns to his station in the county of Kilkenny.

Gerard Fitzgerald, Esq., from the county of Waterford, to take charge of the district of Ballinasloe, county of Galway, vice E.A. Douglas, Esq., deceased.

Patrick C. Howley, Esq., from the county of Longford, to take charge of the district of Dungarvan, county of Waterford, vice G. Fitzgerald, Esq. (1846-04-18, 4:5)

3450. Distress of the People.—Cootehill, April 18.—We are threatened with an awful visitation of both famine and fever. The potatoes are run out with many families, and there is no means of procuring meal; each farmer being able to do more than the work of his own farm, leaves no employment for the poor. Fever is raging to an alarming extent; it commences with the poor, but has extended its ravages to persons in more comfortable circumstances. I have buried a man on yesterday on whose exertions fifteen or sixteen persons depended for support. His widow, with eleven of his family, may enter the poor-house as soon as they are able, if admitted, for the guardians are unwilling to admit persons rising out of fever.—*Evening Post*. (1846-04-25, 2:1)

3451. We deeply regret the painful task which has devolved upon us of recording the demise of the Rev. Thomas Gregg, senior Curate of St. Catherine's, Dublin, who expired this morning at his residence in Blackhall-street. This lamentable event is ascribed to a feverish cold taken about three weeks ago, while attending to his laborious duties as a parish minister, and which has thus bereft the numerous poor of St. Catherines parish, and the many charitable societies with which he was connected, of a most zealous friend, who was never wearied of well-doing on their behalf. To the Association for the relief of Distressed Protestants, and the Protestant Orphans' Society, of which the Reverend Gentleman was an honorary secretary, his loss may be said to be irreparable. Loved and respected by all who had the happiness of knowing him, his name will retain a lasting freshness in the tears of the widow and orphan, and the survivors of the humble and pious. (1846-04-25, 2:1)

3452. Melancholy Accident.—(From a Correspondent.)—Cashel, Monday Evening.—A most melancholy accident has just occurred in this city. A large number of men have been employed by the Commissioners, in order to relieve their distress, and upwards of one hundred of them were assembled this evening in the market house, at six o'clock, in order to receive their day's pay, when the loft gave way, and the (*continued...*)

3452, continued: ...whole of the poor people were precipitated to the floor beneath, and, I regret to state, two of them were killed, and a large number severely injured. It was as deplorable a sight as you could well imagine, to behold the shrieking and groaning mass huddled upon one another amongst the rubbish, with clouds of dust rising as they worked in their agony to extricate themselves. Poor fellows! many a destitute family was waiting in anxious longing for their return with their scanty wages. (1846-04-25, 2:2)

3453. Fatal Accident on the Cashel Railway.—On Tuesday, Sir John Macneil and some other gentlemen had been up towards the end of the works (so far as such have progressed in a direct line from Dublin,) and on their return by a special train, they arrived at a place called Rhandhoon, about eleven miles from Dublin, in the county of Kildare. Here the road was flat, and some bullocks, belonging to Mr. James Mitchell, of Borehead, were grazing in a field.

It is supposed that the noise of the engine frightened the animals, and several of them ran across the line. One of the beasts came in contact with the engine on the rail, and was cut in two, the engine passing over it. This caused the engine to diverge off the rail, and the link which attached the carriages to the engine was broken, and the carriages remained stationary on the line. The engine, by its own impetus, dashed forward and was thrown into an adjoining field. The unfortunate fellow was killed on the spot, and his body was mangled in a fearful manner. He was married only on the previous day.—*Freeman.* (1846-04-25, 2:3)

3454. We perceive by the *Cork Reporter*, received this morning, that an accident, of a fearful nature, occurred at Cashel, on Monday. The floor of a room, in which a lecture was being delivered, gave way, and the whole audience were precipitated to the ground. Forty-seven had been removed to hospital, some of them seriously injured. (1846-04-25, 2:4)

3455. The trial of Mrs. Scott, for bigamy, occupied the Commission Court, Dublin, the whole of last week, terminating in the acquittal of the traverser, in consequence of an informality in her marriage with Mr. Galway. Thus has this extraordinary woman, sprung as she was from the lowest class of society, and elevated to the level of the aristocracy, by the combined influence of her own attractions and the infatuation of her admirers, twice escaped the punishment of bigamy. (1846-04-25, 2:4)

3456. Close of the Commission—Sentence on the Prisoners.—Thursday Morning.—Mr. Browne's Case.

It having been understood that sentence would be this day passed on Mr. Browne, the greatest anxiety prevailed in court.

Precisely at twelve o'clock, the Hon. Mr. Baron Richards and the Hon. Mr. Justice Ball took their seats on the bench, when, on the direction of the former learned judge, the Clerk of the Crown, amid the most solemn stillness, said "Put forward Henry Browne."

Mr. Browne, who seemed greatly altered and careworn, then stood forward; and

Baron Richards addressed the unfortunate young man in a most affecting and truly eloquent strain, closely reviewing the circumstances and progress of his case. However, unwilling to add to the misery of the prisoner, it was his duty to make known to him the position in which he stood. The crime of which he had been found guilty was one of a very heavy—indeed, he would say, a very heinous—character.He was of respectable station in life, a barrister; and, under such circumstances, had no difficulty in getting an introduction to the respectable family of Mr. Copeland, to whose daughter he paid his addresses, under the guise of an unmarried man. The parents of the young lady, not doubting, and having no reason to suppose that they would be deceived, gave their consent. He thus cheated—he must use the expression—this young lady into the belief that she could go through this unholy ceremony. They (the learned judges) were most anxious to ascertain if there were any mitigating circumstances in the case of the prisoner; they even allowed his council to interrogate a witness respecting certain conversations, alleged to have taken place relative to the first marriage; although such was not in fact evidence; but they were unwilling to shut out anything which might be in favor of the prisoner. They also allowed his venerable father—for whom they felt the deepest commiseration—to be examined. They could not believe that the prisoner was under the conviction that the first marriage was invalid; he had made an affidavit, in which he made such an averment; but how could he reconcile that with the fact of his going, previous to the first marriage, to the Consistorial Court, and swearing that he was the full age of 21 years, the reverse of which he now swore as evidence of his considering the first marriage void? But he would not pursue the criticism further. Yielding to the wishes of his counsel, they had submitted the points raised in his favor to the twelve judges; and those learned personages quite agreed with him (Baron Richards) that the conviction was perfectly just and legal. The learned baron concluded by sentencing the prisoner to be transported for seven years.—On the sentence being passed, the unhappy young man bowed in a most firm and determined manner; and there were few persons who witnessed the scene that were not deeply affected. (1846-04-25, 2:5)

3457. By the demise of Mr. Arthur Pollock, one of the Clerkships of the Peace, and thirteen Clerkships of [the] Crown, of which that gentleman, as the reversionary survivor in a patent, held the monopoly, are placed at the disposal of the Lord Lieutenant. It is understood that it is the intention of the government to divide them; and we think such a course will receive general approval; but we equally hope that the selections will be made from amongst the respectable and competent class of professional practitioners, without a seeking out for that spurious and [*illegible*] grasping at popularity which directs the stream of patronage into the ranks of the enemy. Justice to all—favour to friends—should be the guiding principle in making every official appointment. We subjoin a list of the vacancies made, with the salaries attached to each, dividing them into classes:

Carlow...	4th Class...	Salary £185
Dublin, County...	2d Class...	£354
Kildare...	4th Class...	£185
Kilkenny...	3d Class...	£230
Kilkenny, City...	5th Class...	£74
Kings County...	3d Class...	£250
Longford...	4th Class...	£185
Louth...	Ditto...	£185
Meath...	2d Class...	£384
Queens County...	3d Class...	£230
Westmeath...	Ditto...	£230
Wexford...	Ditto...	£230
Wicklow...	4th Class...	£185

... Besides the Clerkship of the Peace for the County Dublin. (1846-04-25, 2:6) *Note: The figures were very blurred in the original text.*

3458. The Late James Evatt, Esq.—We understand that it is the intention of some of the friends of the late Mr. Evatt to erect a Tablet to his memory at the place where he is buried; and in order that the Tenantry of Lord Bath's Estate, over whom he was so long Agent, and others may have an opportunity of testifying their respect and regard for him, a subscription list, restricted to sums between £1 and 1s., now lies at the office of Mr. Gibson in Carrickmacross, where those wishing to do so, may pay their subscriptions.
(1846-04-25, 3:3)

3459. Coronership—County Monaghan.—This day (Friday), Charles Waddel, Esq., of Lisnavane, was elected, without opposition, a coroner for this county. Mr. Waddel was proposed by J. Nunn, Esq., and seconded by William Temple, Esq., M.D., and declared by the Sheriff duly elected. (1846-04-25, 3:3)

3460. Report of the Ballytrain Dispensary.—For the Year ending the 17th April, 1846.

Patients under care the 27th April, 1845, ...	53
Admitted since, ...	1230
	1,283
Of whom were visited, ...	173
Visits paid to them, ...	519
Died, ...	5
Relieved, ...	12
Result unknown, ...	22
Cured, ...	988
On the Book this day, ...	83

1st Case, died, a child of Hooping Cough; 2nd, A man of a vomiting of blood; 3rd, A boy of disease of the heart; 4th, An aged woman, of mortification of the extremities, depending on disease of the heart; 5th, A boy of Emphysema. The most prevalent diseases of the year, were affections of the Chest, Bowel Complaints, and Fever. The Chest affections were induced from the moist season, insufficient clothing, and cold. The numerous bowel complaints were caused from bad food, and cold, fever, was of the mildest type, and all successful.

Samuel Stephenson, Surgeon.
Ballytrain, 2nd April, 1846.
(1846-04-25, 3:3)

3461. Famine and Fever.—(From the *Mail.*)—We now proceed to fulfil our promise of furnishing facts for discussion in the House of Commons on both branches of the POTATO-PEEL-PANIC, or Irish BOBBERY.

And first, of the famine:

Lord Bentinck tells of many farmers in England, who, having in the months of November and December, refused 11s. a sack for potatoes, are now constrained to sell them at less than half price. It is exactly the same in Ireland. Potatoes are growing cheaper every day; at least, so says the *Newry Telegraph* of its district:—"Famine is still, we are glad to say, far from the doors of the community here. As the season advances, food, so far from becoming dearer, is cheapening. Potatoes are to be had, in abundance at reduced prices. [*Another citation, from the Sligo Journal, with mentions of: large quantities of oats and oatmeal; conversion of potatoes into meal; farmers, in hope of higher prices, have withheld the customary supply of potatoes from the markets; Indian meal will soon pour in, by which hoarders will be damaged.*]

From the county of Cavan, a correspondent writes, dating his letter yesterday, the 26th inst.:—"Potatoes are this week very cheap all around us. At Bailieborough, they are selling from 3d. to 4d.; at Killesandra, the same; at Ballinagh, the same in their last respective markets. They are excellent and sound potatoes. In the market of Cavan, on Tuesday, potatoes of the best description were sold from 4d. to 5d. a stone. This is very curious." [*Editorial comments follow.*]

And now for the fever.

The same correspondent informs us that—"There is a good deal of fever in Bailieborough—upwards of forty cases—but not caused by the quality of the potatoes; nor can it be attributed to want of food, as it has attacked the *middle* and *higher classes* there, while the poor are exempt from it. There is very little fever in any other part of the county."

From the *Newry Telegraph*, we copy the following satisfactory intelligence:—

"Neither are we threatened with the epidemic, of an immediate visitation from which certain prophets of evil forewarned the town, at the meeting (*continued...*)

3461, continued: ...on last Saturday. In compliance with our request, and for the satisfaction and comfort of such of the inhabitants as may have been frightened by idle babbling, the following special report has been presented by the medical superintendent of our fever hospital and dispensary, whose sphere of labour, in his public capacity, is confined to that which are to be found the classes more liable, from their circumstances in life, to contagious diseases:—

"My Dear Sir—In answer to your note, relative to the quantum of fever amongst the poor of Newry and its neighbourhood, I beg to state that there are at present, under my care, fifteen fever patients in our hospital, and seven out of hospital, five of whom are of one family and convalescent. These are the only cases of fever in the town and neighbourhood that I am aware of, and there has been no increase of the disease during the week. Indeed, I should say the health of this locality is at present above par. Compared with the corresponding period of last year, fever has been less prevalent this season, among the poorer classes, as is shown by the facts that, according to my books, from the 1st January to 24th April, 1845, I attended 98 cases of fever; and from 1st January to 24th April, 1846, I have attended but 79 cases.—I am, dear Sir, truly yours,

"J. Morison, M.D.,
"Physician to the Newry Fever Hospital and Surgeon to the Newry Dispensary.
"April 24, 1846."

We copy the following extract from the annual medical report of the Physician and Surgeon attached to the Sligo Dispensary:—

"Ladies and Gentlemen—We have again, with thankfulness, to repeat to you, that during the past year, our town and neighbourhood have been remarkably exempt from fever or other contagious diseases; of true typhus fever, we had scarcely any, and indeed, the season seems to have been unfavourable to the spreading of any contagious disease. Thus, on one occasion, there was a remarkable outbreak of measles in the poor house, but the disease extended comparatively little beyond the walls of the institution. On another occasion, in a limited locality, we saw many bad and fatal cases of scarletina, and reason to dread its becoming general, but in three or four weeks, the disease had subsided; on the whole, we can decidedly state, that the amount of sickness has been rather below the average of other years, although during the present month, influenza, chest affections, bowel complaints in children, and in the Drumiskabole district, fever also, have prevailed extensively.

"Although not strictly in the line of our duty, we cannot avoid expressing a hope that some means will be devised of getting employment to the poor during the summer months—employment not concentrated in one or two situations, but if possible, portioned out according to the want of the different localities; if this can be accomplished, we cannot say that we would have much fear for the health of our district.

"Thomas Burrows, M.D., Surgeon.
"Robert Lynn, A.B., M.D., T.C.D.,
"Fellow of the College of Surgeons."

Meanwhile, the Commissioners "appointed in reference to the *apprehended* scarcity," are hounding on the peasantry against their landlords, by such instructions as the following, printed and circulated by the Government:—[*paragraphs based on the premise that the landholders and other rate-payers are the parties both legally and morally answerable for affording due relief to the destitute poor, concluding with:*]

"That where notwithstanding such subscriptions, some assistance is likely to be required from the government, a list of the sums subscribed, together with a list of the landlords who do not contribute, should be confidentially brought under the notice of the Lord Lieutenant, who, after due consideration of the case, will determine on the sum to be contributed from the funds at his disposal in aid of the local subscription."

Surely, those "instructions" gave the people an idea that the landowners *must* support them when they want food; that they *ought*, and *do not*.

No wonder that we have riots and outrages on stores, granaries, and everything else. The people are only following the suggestions of Government.

The Relief Committees are ordered (as we have seen) to "report on the conduct of our landlords."

Why, Cobden and Co. never attempted such a *Jack Cade* system as this. The tender mercies of the Conciliation Hall are now transferred to the Castle of Dublin; and Captain Pitt Kennedy is invested with the office of public accuser, *vice* Tom Steele—superseded. (1846-05-02, 1:1)

3462. Sir Compton Domville, Baronet, Custos Rotulorum of the county of Dublin, has appointed George Wade, Esq., Clerk of the Peace for the county, in the room of A.H.C. Pollock, Esq., deceased. (1846-05-02, 1:4)

3463. The Church.—Deceased.

Diocese of Meath.—The Rev. A. Ardagh, vicar of Moyglad, county of Meath; patron, George Woods, Esq.—Diocese of Cloyne.—The Rev. W. Chatterton, rector of Bohillane, county of Cork.—*Irish Ecclesiastical Journal.* (1846-05-02, 1:5)

3464. Sudden Death of the Rev. Hercules Langrishe.—It is our painful duty to announce the death of the Rev. H. Langrishe, which sad and unexpected event took place at his residence [at] Ballybay on Wednesday morning, at eleven o'clock. The much beloved and respected gentleman entertained some friends at dinner on Tuesday, and promised to dine with his neighbour, the Resident Magistrate, on the next day; but, alas, ere the noon of that day, he drew his last breath. His sister, Mrs. Gore, had been for some days on a visit with the deceased, and she witnessed the sad catastrophe, which has plunged the town and neighborhood in the most melancholy state of affliction. He was a most exemplary and charitable minister of the gospel, and will be long mourned by the poor, to whom he was a most bountiful friend. (1846-05-02, 3:3)

3465. Aughnacloy Fever Hospital.—From the second annual report of the Fever Hospital, it appears that the receipt of that institution during the past year have amounted to £92 11s. 6-1/4. The expenditure has been £33 7s. 10d. above the receipts, owing to the county grant having not yet been received. Out of thirty-eight cases of fever, twenty-eight cures have been effected —five have died, and five still remain in hospital. Three of the five deaths were occasioned by a complication of diseases, two only having perished of fever during the entire year. Such results bear powerful evidence to the beneficial effects derivable from such institutions; and the fact that only five persons suffering under fever are at present remaining in hospital, gives cheering testimony that the unusual amount of Fever, so much apprehended by government, has not yet exhibited itself, at least in this district. We feel satisfied that the inhabitants of Aughnacloy and its vicinity will duly appreciate the unremitting attention of Dr. Scott, the medical attendant of the institution, in discharging the laborious and critical duties of his office. (1846-05-02, 3:3)

3466. Notice—Is hereby given, that a separate building named First Ballybay Presbyterian Church, situated in the townland of Derrivalley, in the parish of Ballybay, in the county of Monaghan, in the district of Castleblayney, being a Building certified according to Law, as a place of religious worship, was on the 9th day of April 1846, duly registered for solemnizing Marriages therein, pursuant to the Act of seventh and eighth Victoria, chap. 81. Witness my hand, this 24th day of April, 1846,

William Rule, Registrar of Marriages
for the District of Castleblayney.
(1846-05-02, 3:5)

3467. The court of Delegates on Saturday, refused to reverse the decision of the Rev. Dr. Millar, Vicar General of the Armagh Consistorial Court, in the suit of *Cope v. Heath*, where the wife was decreed to return to the husband, Mr. Heath. (1846-05-09, 1:5)

3468. Lieut. Hercules Robinson, 87th Fusiliers, eloped with the Hon. Ada Annesley, daughter of Lord Valentia, on Friday week, from Bletchington-park. They were married in London on last Saturday. (1846-05-09, 1:5)

3469. Mr. William Foley, of Wicklow-street, Dublin, cut his throat on Monday, and died soon after. (1846-05-09, 1:5)

3470. At a meeting of the friends of the late Rev. Thos. Gregg, curate of St. Catherine's, Dublin, Judge Keating in the chair, it was agreed to raise a charitable fund, entitled the "Gregg testimonial," to cheer the poor widow and orphan, and as being the most acceptable tribute to the memory of the deceased. (1846-05-09, 1:5)

3471. On Saturday, the 2d of May, the Viscountess Powerscourt was married to Viscount Castlereagh, at the British Embassy, at Paris. The ceremony was performed by Bishop Luscombe in the presence of a few members and friends of the families of the bride and bridegroom. The bride was superbly dressed in white point lace, and looked most beautiful. She was given away by her father, the Earl of Roden. His Excellency Lord Cowly, and Lady Cowly, and Miss Wellesley, were present, as also the Marquis and Marchioness of Londonderry, Lord Seaham, and Lady A. Vane, the Earl and Countess of Roden, and Lady M. Jocelyn, Viscount Jocelyn, and the Hon. Strange Jocelyn, the Countess of Gainsborough, and Lady Victoria Noel, Countess of Tankerville, &c., &c. The happy pair, together with other members of the family, retired after the ceremony in the apartments of the Earl and Countess of Roden, at Maurices Hotel, where they partook of a *dejeune*; and at three o'clock, Lord and Lady Castlereagh set off for Fontainebleau; from thence they proceed, for a few weeks, to Switzerland. The Marquess and Marchioness of Londonderry and suite, as also the Earl and Countess of Roden, &c., will leave Paris in the course of the next week, for London. (1846-05-09, 2:3)

3472. Funeral of the Late Rev. H. Langrishe.—The late Rev. Hercules Langrishe, Rector of Ballibay was, in accordance with a desire he had frequently expressed, interred on Sunday, the 3d instant, in the churchyard of that parish, of which for nineteen years, he had been the kind and faithful pastor.

The funeral, which took place at an early hour, was attended by all the rank and respectability of the neighbourhood, as well as by his more humble and sorrowing parishioners.—At noon service, his curate, the Rev. W.H. Woodwright, who was himself deeply affected, preached a beautiful and appropriate sermon to a large and attentive congregation, taking his text from *Psalm xiii., verse 2*, "When shall I come to appear before the presence of God?"

When directly alluding to the sudden bereavement the parish had sustained in the death of their beloved Rector, and commenting on his exalted character, there was not a dry eye in the church, nor one who did not deeply feel the force of the pathetic and admonitory address, which, from so youthful and recently ordained a minister, gives the fairest promise of a faithful and zealous laborer in his Master's vineyard. (1846-05-09, 3:4)

3473. Auction.—J.E. Jones,—Takes leave to inform the Public, he has received Instructions from the Executor of the late Mr. William Quinn, deceased, to submit to Public Competition at his late residence Rooskey, Toll-Bar, Monaghan, (*continued...*)

3473, continued: ...On Thursday next, the 14th day of May, instant, and following days at 11 o'clock,

All his Household Furniture, Farm Implements, an Outside Jaunting Car and Harness; Two Horses; Two Milch Cows; a well-bred two-year-old Heifer in Calf; two Store Pigs; two Stacks Oats; a large Stack of Hay, Straw, and a good quantity of good Potatoes; two excellent Iron Ploughs and Harness; Break Harrow; three Carts, one quite new, (never used,) Cart Harness; a new double Roller and its carriage, on metal wheels; a Winnow Machine; riddles, Sacks, and Winnow-Cloth; an excellent Ladder 30 feet long; Eight Cat Stoke Pillars, Stands and Cap for a Shed; a Triangle, Beams, Seales, and Metal Weights, &c., &c.

The Furniture comprises a Mahogany Sideboard, Dining and Breakfast Tables, on Castors; Mahogany Chairs, Cane-seat, Painted do.; a Mahogany Square Settee on Castors; a Mahogany Bureau; an Eight-day Clock; a Dial Barometer; two Dublin made Fiddles in a Mahogany Case; a Gold Watch and some Silver Tea-spoons; a large House Clothes Press; Carpets and Hearth Rugs; Brass Fenders and Fire Irons; Bedsteads and Hangings; Feather Beds and Bedding; Mahogany Dressing Tables; Toilet do.; Toilet Glasses; Mahogany Basin Stands, and Painted do.; a Bamboo Dressing Commode; Dressing Table, and Cloths-airer in suit; Bedroom Carpets, Stair do., and Brass Rods; China, Delph, and glass; Dairy and Kitchen Requisites, strong Deal and Elm Tables, and Chairs; Spirit Casks with Cocks; a set of Copper and Pewter Measures; Shop Lamps, Carpenters, Masons, and Garden Tools, with a variety of good and useful articles.

Terms Cash.

J.E. Jones, Auctioneer.

Rooskey Tollbar, May 8th, 1846.

(1846-05-09, 3:5)

3474. Suicide.—On Monday, a private of the Royal Horse Artillery, and servant of Colonel Carter, named John Montgomery, in this garrison, put an end to his existence by cutting his throat. In the morning, the men sleeping in the same room with him turned out for stable duty, and one of them had occasion to return in five or six minutes, when he discovered the unfortunate man dead, with a razor in his hand.—*Limerick Reporter*. (1846-05-09, 4:5)

3475. Extraordinary Birth.—The fruitful wife of Mr. James Mullen, Feeny, near Dungiven, on the 23d inst., presented her husband with three children, two sons and one daughter; the mother is doing well, and the babies are all [*illegible*], strong, and healthy. (1846-05-16, 1:2)

3476. Yesterday sen., an old man named Maginnis, a quack doctor, died in Ballymena, from the effects of an accident received by him while he was being expelled from a shop in the town, which he would not voluntarily leave when ordered to get out. (1846-05-16, 1:4)

3477. A Sweep Roasted Alive.—An inquest was held on Sunday, at Barrington's Hospital, on the body of Michael O'Brien, a chimney-sweep, aged eight years, who was burned to death, in the flue of a chimney in Patrick-street, on Saturday evening, which he was forced to descend by his master, Michael Sullivan, although the chimney had been on fire since early in the afternoon. The body of the unfortunate creature presented an awful appearance, being literally roasted and mangled. The jury returned the following verdict:—Michael O'Brien came by his death from the effects of heat and suffocation, in consequence of having been forced to descend a chimney in Mr. Ryan's house, Patrick-street, by Michael Sullivan. The monster, who was the cause of the boy's death, has absconded.—*Limerick Chron*. (1846-05-16, 1:4)

3478. Marriage in High Life.—(From a Correspondent of the *Packet*.)—We have been informed, on good authority, that the marriage of the Right Hon. Lord Rossmore with the youthful and accomplished Miss Lloyd, of Kilkenny, will shortly be solemnised. The special license for this purpose has already been issued. The age of his lordship is 54, while that of the embryo bride is only 18 years. (1846-05-16, 3:1)

3479. Death by Lightning.—On Tuesday, the 5th instant, about two o'clock, p.m., a boy named Patrick Boylan was herding his master's cattle on the lands of Drummond, near Carrickmacross, during the violent thunderstorm of that day, and in about a quarter of an hour after, was found lying on his face and quite dead! Surgeon Fleming made a post mortem examination of the body, and deposed that he found the cap, clothes, and shirt on the deceased's back, burned to a considerable extent; the back of the neck, shoulder, along the hip, thigh, and half of the left side completely charred and blackened—altogether presenting the appearance of a person who had been greatly injured by an explosion of gunpowder. A verdict of "killed by lightning," was returned by the coroner's jury. (1846-05-16, 3:2)

3480. On Saturday night, four persons were drowned at Waterford by the upsetting of a boat. (1846-05-16, 3:2)

3481. The Church.—The Rev. Lord Adam Loftus, has been appointed to the living of Ballybay, vacant by the death of the late Rev. Hercules Langrishe. (1846-05-16, 3:3)

3482. Join yourself in union with no woman who is selfish, for she will sacrifice you; with no one who is fickle, for she will become a stranger; have nothing to do with a proud one, for she will despise you; and leave a coquette to the fools that flutter around her. (1846-05-16, 3:3)

3483. Accident.—On Wednesday, 6th inst., as Corporal Arthurs, of the 26th Cameronian Regt., quartered in Belleek, was crossing the kitchen floor, he slipped and, attempting to recover his footing, twisted his leg and broke it. Arthurs was a man much beloved by his superiors and comrades, has a wife and family. (1846-05-16, 3:3)

3484. Memorials are being extensively forwarded to the Lord Lieutenant from the Registrars of Marriages in the different counties in Ireland, representing the onerous duties they fulfil in carrying out the provisions of the recent important act, and setting forth that a year of office has now expired without salaries or remuneration for their services. (1846-05-16, 4:4)

3485. Justice Burton has been for several days labouring under a severe attack of diarrhoea, which has caused serious apprehensions amongst his lordship's friends. He is now 87 years of age. (1846-05-16, 4:4)

3486. In the town of Tipperary, fever of the most alarming kind continues to increase. From the report of the relief committee at their last meeting, there are 68 patients suffering from fever in the hospital. Men have been appointed to whitewash the houses, and otherwise cleanse the town, as a preventative to the spread of disease. (1846-05-16, 4:4)

3487. Death from Starvation.—On Tuesday night last, a woman named Mary Ann Fitzpatrick, mother of two children, who resided in Balmer's-Court in this town, died from starvation. It appears that her husband, who was a servant, had been out of place for some time, and that delicacy had prevented him from making the wants of himself and family known, even to his neighbours, until after the unfortunate occurrence took place. —*Belfast Whig*. (1846-05-16, 4:4)

3488. Of 100,000 persons born in England in 1841, only 50,301 will reach forty-five years of age, but of this last number, 9,398 will be alive in 1921. (1846-05-16, 4:4)

3489. Fatal Accident.—On Wednesday last, an accident, which terminated fatally, occurred to Mrs. Morgan, wife of Mr. Morgan, owner of a flax-mill at Ballycrommey near Armagh. The poor woman went to visit the mill, and having incautiously placed her foot on a part of the machinery, while some person was setting it in motion, she was dragged in by the wheel and dreadfully lacerated, so much so that she died of the injuries in about three hours later. Dr. Lavery was in attendance shortly after the accident, and, with his usual skill and promptitude, rendered every professional assistance possible, but, from the serious nature of the injuries, without effect. An inquest was held on the body by Mr. Henry, one of our county coroners, and a verdict of accidental death returned.—*Ulster Gazette*. (1846-05-23, 1:5)

3490. Marriage of Lord Rossmore.—Rejoicings in Monaghan.—On Tuesday evening last, at Ten o'clock, the nuptial ceremony was performed by the Rev. William L. Roper, Rector of Monaghan, by special license, between the Right Hon. Henry Lord Baron Rossmore, and Julia Ellen Josephine Lloyd, the beautiful and accomplished daughter of Henry Lloyd, Esq., of Butler House, Kilkenny, and Harriet, daughter of the late Sir John Carden, Bart., of Templemore House, and The Priory, County of Tipperary.—The ceremony was performed at Camla Vale, the beautiful residence of Colonel Henry Westenra, uncle to the noble Bridegroom and lovely Bride, in the presence of a small and select family party, consisting of the Gallant Colonel, Henry Lloyd, Esq., Mrs. Lloyd, and J. Lloyd, Esq., the parents and brother of the youthful bride, Charles Cambie, Esq., cousin-german to the Noble Lord, and Mrs. Cambie, Miss Lloyd, and Miss Cambie, bridesmaids, and Lieut. Colonel Lewis.

When the ceremony was completed, the joyful event was announced by the ascent of a rocket, and in a few minutes, the town of Monaghan was brilliantly illuminated. Tar-barrels blazed in every street and square, and beer barrels were broached in which the thirsty crowd slacked their throats, hoarse with vociferous cheering for the new married couple. There was not a window that did not exhibit the esteem of the inmates for the Lord of the soil—there was not a group of the well pleased people that did not shower blessings upon their future life. Old political differences were forgotten—electioneering prejudices were buried deep beneath the congratulations of the moment. The sturdy Orangeman, the staunch Repealer, the moderate Conservative and the Whig, all joined in doing honor to a nobleman whose character as a landlord and a private gentleman is *sans peur et sans reproche*. A salute of artillery was the signal for a display of fire works, and amidst the joyous uproar, we never witnessed a more pleasing scene, nor one which displayed more unanimity. We have often witnessed illuminations in Monaghan, but never before without considerable opposition, when the intervals of light and darkness, made the town wear a piebald look, as if clad in motly—but in this instance, the blaze from every house was as creditable to the inhabitants, as to him whose happy nuptials called forth the general outburst of good feeling. In several windows, transparencies, apt and appropriate, were displayed, amongst which we were particularly struck by the beauty and taste evinced in those exhibited at the house of our enterprising neighbour, Mr. M'Coy.—The centre window of his first floor was adorned by a beautiful Irish Harp, illuminated with variegated lamps, and relieved by a background picture of agriculture and a teeming farm yard, indicative of a happy resolution we understand the noble Bridegroom has come to, of becoming a resident amongst us. The adjoining windows bore transparencies of the quartered arms of the houses of Rossmore and Lloyd, with the words "May the Houses of Rossmore and Lloyd prosper," imprinted upon a wreath or scroll held by Cupid and Hymen.

About eleven o'clock, it was announced that one of Lord Rossmore's carriages was entering (*continued...*)

3490, continued: ...the town, when a general rush took place, and in a moment the carriage was surrounded by a dense crowd, whose cheers made the welkin ring. In the carriage was Mr. Cambie, who has lately assumed the management of the Monaghan estates, and, whose affable manners and courteous demeanor have already gained him the esteem and respect of the community—Mr. Cambie rode through the town and was greeted on every side with the hearty welcome of the populace, and with cheers for Lord and Lady Rossmore. Mr. Cambie thanked the populace for their kindness, and said, that Lord and Lady Rossmore deeply felt the compliment paid them by the inhabitants, a compliment as creditable to the good feeling of the people as it was gratifying to the noble pair.

Next day (Wednesday,) his Lordship and his blooming bride left Camla, for his Lordship's picturesque lodge, on the island of Arran, where they will remain for a few days previous to the embarkation for a pleasure trip down the Mediterranean, in his Lordship's splendid yacht. We heartily wish the noble Lord and gentle Lady a fresh breeze, and flowing sail, a happy voyage, and a safe return to their native land and their attached tenantry.

On Tuesday, the paupers in the workhouse were entertained with a capital dinner, at the expense of Lady Rossmore, so that even in the house of despair and poverty, this happy union cast a ray of sunshine.

We also understand, from good authority, that his Lordship, in addition to his supplying the inmates of the Poor-house with an excellent dinner, has left with the respected clergyman of this parish, a liberal contribution for the following humane and charitable purposes, viz.:—Procuring the release of poor debtors from our county prison; clothing the poorer children in our town schools; and lastly, for presenting a handsome gift to 30 poor widows connected with the charitable institutions of this parish. (1846-05-23, 2:6)

3491. Death of a Centenarian.—An inquest, was held at Loughrea, on Wednesday last, by Thomas Welsh, Esq., coroner, on view of the body of a man named Geraghty, who had attained the patriarchal age of 106 years. In early age, he was an architect of some eminence, having been the builder of Mornington House, Dunsandle, &c., but of late years, he endured much privation, being recently an inmate of the workhouse. He was accidentally knocked down by a dray and killed. A verdict was returned accordingly.—*Ballinasloe Star*. (1846-05-23, 3:2)

3492. A Benedict to a Bachelor.

Don't tell me "you haven't got time"—
That other things claim your attention;
There's not the least reason or rhyme
In the wisest excuse you can mention.
Don't tell me about "other fish,"
Your duty is done when you buy 'em;
And you never will relish the dish,
Unless you've a woman to "fry 'em."

You may dream of poetical fame,
But the story may chance to miscarry;
The best way of sending one's name
To posterity, Tom, is to marry.
And here I am willing to own—
After soberly thinking upon it—
I'd very much rather be known
Through a beautiful son than a sonnet.

Don't be frighten'd at querlous stories,
By gossiping grumblers related,
Who argue that marriage a bore is,
Because they've known people mis-mated.
Such fellows, if they had their pleasure,
Because some "bad bargains" are made,
Would propose, as a sensible measure,
To lay an embargo on trade!

When Tom bid your doubting good bye,
And dismiss all fantastic alarms;
Ill be sworn you've a girl in your eye
That you ought to have had in your arms;
Some beautiful maiden—God bless her!
Unencumbered with pride or with palf;
Of every true charm the possessor,
And give to now fault—but yourself.

To procrastination be deaf;
(A caution which came from above;)
The scoundrel's not only "the thief
Of time," but of beauty and love.
Then delay not a moment to win
A prize that is truly worth winning;
Celibacy, Tom, is a sin,
And sadly prolific of sinning.

I could give you a bushel of reasons
For choosing the "double estate;"
It agrees with all climates and seasons,
Though it may be adopted too late.
To one's parents 'tis (gracefully) due;
Just think what a terrible thing
Twould have been, sir, for me and for you,
If ours had neglected the ring.

Don't search for an "angel" a minute;
For suppose you succeed in the sequel,
After all, the deuce would be in it,
For the match would be mighty unequal.
The angels, it must be confessd
In this world are rather uncommon;
And allow me, dear Tom, to suggest,
You'll be better content with a woman.

(1846-05-23, 4:1)

3493. Archdeacon Beresford's wife having recently died at Rome, the Archdeacon was erecting a monument to her memory. The Censor would not permit the inscription, because it concluded with a quotation from Scripture—"Blessed are the dead that die in the Lord"—heretics being excluded from salvation. (1846-05-23, 4:4)

3494. Coroner's Inquest.—An inquest was held on Monday last, before Charles Waddell, Esq., coroner, for this county, upon the body of a young man named James Connolly, of Corlatt, in the parish of Aughnamullen, aged 20 years. It appeared that deceased had shot a water fowl on Saturday evening, and on Sunday, swam into the lake to get the bird which was floating, dead. Upon reaching his object, however, he sank from some unknown cause, perhaps having got entangled in weeds and was drowned.—Verdict, accidental death. (1846-05-30, 3:3)

3495. Death of Major Hamilton Irvine, D.L., Provost of Enniskillen.—This venerable gentleman died at his residence, Greenhill, on Tuesday last, at the age of 77. He was senior Major of the Fermanagh Militia, (which corps he joined when organised) deputy lieutenant, the oldest grand juror and magistrate of Fermanagh, Provost of Enniskillen, and Barrack Master for many years. The Major was one of those active and useful, quiet and beloved class, whom every man respects and delights to honour. Respected by his peers, beloved by the poor, few men have sunk to rest more regretted than did the Major.—*Fermanagh Reporter*. (1846-05-30, 3:4)

3496. Melancholy and Fatal Accident—Four Persons Drowned.—It is our painful duty to state that a very lamentable and fatal accident occurred in Belfast Lough on Sunday last, by which the lives of four of our fellow-townspeople were lost, under the following circumstances. A pleasure party, consisting of Richard Maguire, John Craig, John Hamilton, Sarah Jane M'Allister, Isabella M'Cluskey, Margaret O'Neal, and Margaret M'Allister, proceeded from this town in a small sail boat on a pleasure trip down the Lough. The party intended to land at Carrickfergus to let out one of their number, and were within about a mile of that place when Craig, the person who wished to stop at Carrickfergus, being, as we are informed, slightly the worse of liquor, began rocking the boat, with the object of scaring the ladies, as he said himself. Not satisfied with this, although remonstrated with by Hamilton, he climbed up the mast of the little boat, and ultimately capsized her. The whole party were, of course, immediately plunged into deep water, at a considerable distance from the shore; and, melancholy to relate, four of them were drowned—namely, Craig the author of the calamity, Isabella M'Cluskey, Margaret O'Neill [sic], and Margaret M'Allister. The bodies of the unfortunate deceased not having been found during yesterday, the case has not come before the Coroner or Magistrates. We need hardly remark that this awful calamity is fraught with a solemn warning to all in the habit of partaking in idle, and intemperate, scenes on the Lord's Day.—*Belfast News-letter*. (1846-05-30, 3:4)

3497. A prisoner in Downpatrick gaol, named Gillis, died on Saturday last, from voluntarily abstaining from food, being determined on self-destruction. (1846-06-06, 1:3)

3498. On Monday last, a young lad, son to widow Robinson of Legg, near Churchill, whilst digging in a field, dropped dead. On same day, a heifer and a goat of hers, fell down from the top of a rock and were also killed. This is the third of Mrs. Robinson's sons who died suddenly. (1846-06-06, 1:3)

3499. Canal Accident—A Man Drowned.—On Saturday last, John Stapleton, a boatman from Ticknevin in the county of Kildare, accompanied with his son, about sixteen years, in an empty boat, which he was bringing to this neighbourhood for bricks. While raising the rack of one of the locks at this town, [he] lost his balance and fell into the canal, where he got so entangled at the bottom with the racks and sluices, which were partly up, that he was not got out for half an hour. Several medical men attended, and used their best skill, but to no effect, as life was extinct. There was a man in the boat of the name of Laughran, lying drunk, with whom it appears Stapleton was drinking, and who is supposed to have been inebriated.—Mr. Dillon, the (only) coroner for this county, having been sent for, was in prompt attendance, who held an inquest over the body, the jurors' verdict being—accidentally drowned. The unfortunate deceased, who was a very able-bodied man, has left a wife and six children to deplore his untimely end. (1846-06-06, 2:2)

3500. Death of Andrew Ker, Esq., M.D., of Newbliss.—It is our duty this week to record the death of this gentleman, which took place at his residence, Newbliss House, on Saturday last, in the 80th year of his age. Dr. Ker for some years was in very delicate health, and by his death, the poor have lost a kind friend, and society in general, a charitable and useful member. With a large fortune at his command, it was his pleasure and delight to reward honest industry and real merit, and with no niggard hand did he dispence those blessings which Providence placed at his disposal.

At an early hour, on Wednesday morning, his sorrowing tenantry began to assemble to pay their last tribute of respect to their lamented landlord; and at a few minutes after one o'clock, the procession began to move from the house—scarfs and hat-bands being distributed to every person in attendance. The procession was exceedingly well-ordered, each man falling into his place, as the body passed through the serried line, with military exactness. The coffin was borne by six of his labourers—in the front walked the clergymen of the neighborhood, and immediately following came the relations of the deceased, and the gentry who were in attendance; after them came the day-labourers, amounting to upwards of sixty, and the tenantry; the whole procession numbered close on one thousand persons, and presented an exceedingly picturesque prospect, as it swept through the domain, and beneath the shades of the fine old trees with which it abounds. (*continued...*)

3500, continued: ...The procession reached the church a few minutes before two o'clock, and after the usual burial service being read, the body was placed in the vault beneath the church which the charity, piety, and benevolence of Dr. Ker, erected for the accommodation of the people in and about Newbliss.
(1846-06-06, 3:3)

3501. Sudden Death.—As William Young, an old and respectable tenant of the late Dr. Ker, was returning home after accompanying the remains of his late landlord to his resting place, he was observed to fall off his pony, and, lamentable to relate, when assistance reached him, life was extinct. Surgeon Henry's attendance was immediately procured, who used all the remedies that medical skill could devise, but without effect. He had been in a poor state of health, but could not think of his landlord being interred without being present. Dr. Henry is of opinion [that] apoplexy was the cause of his death. (1846-06-06, 3:3)

3502. On Tuesday last, a boy named Mohan was drowned, while bathing in a lake immediately adjacent to this town, just behind Beechill. He was only a few minutes in the water when he was taken out, and brought to the infirmary, where Doctor Young was in immediate attendance, but life was extinct. An inquest was held on the body before Robert Murray, Esq., M.D., coroner, and a verdict of accidental death returned. (1846-06-06, 3:3)

3503. On Monday last, a respectable man named Thompson, residing at Castleshane, in this county, fell off his horse on his way home from this town, and fractured his skull in such a dreadful manner, that his brains protruded through his ears—death was, of course, the consequence, and a coroner's jury returned a verdict of accidental death. (1846-06-06, 3:3)

3504. Serious Illness of W.D. Freeman, Esq., Q.C.—We regret to state that this learned gentleman, while addressing the Court of Queen's Bench yesterday, was seized with apoplexy. He was borne out from the Queen's Bench to the chamber of the Chief Justice, and shortly after, the Surgeon-General was sent for, and arrived almost immediately. The learned gentleman remained in a state of insensibility, and was thus conveyed in a carriage to his residence, accompanied by Sir Philip Crampton, Mr. Heen, Q.C., and Mr. Smyly. The circumstance created considerable sensation in and about the court, and the entrance to the chamber of the Chief Justice was thronged to excess, immediately after the melancholy occurrence.

The answer to the inquiries this morning were, we regret to state, to the effect that no change has taken place for the better.—*Packet.* (1846-06-06, 4:5)

3505. Miss Reilly, of Enniskillen, who was proceeding on the Bundoran car, on Monday last, to that beautiful bathing place, suddenly dropped dead, and fell off the car, near Carrickreagh. (1846-06-06, 4:5)

3506. Extraordinary Birth.—A female who resides at Feeny in this county, was lately delivered of two girls and a boy at birth. The mother and children are doing well. The former was going about in her accustomed state of health on the last fair day of Feeny.—*Derry Sentinel.* (1846-06-06, 4:5)

3507. Funeral of Peter Purcell, Esq.—Shortly after eight o'clock yesterday morning, the mournful procession moved from Mr. Purcell's late residence in Rutland-square, and proceeded slowly down Sackville-street, to the metropolitan chapel in Marlborough-street, in which the mortal remains of this great and good man were deposited. The numerous workmen in his employment preceded the coffin and, with tearful eyes and heavy hearts, led the way for their kind employer to his grave. Immediately after the hearse came the relatives of the deceased, and among the rest, his eldest brother, John Fitzgerald, Esq., of London, well known in this city for his classical and literary attainments, and as having obtained the first gold medal ever given in Trinity College, in the year 1752. Following his near relations, the council and members of the Royal Agricultural Improvement Society of Ireland walked in procession, having previously assembled at the memory of their founder—then came the Directors of the great Southern Railway in a body, also anxious to testify their respect for a man whose integrity, energy, and judgement their present success and advanced position it is to be mainly attributed—the members of many of the leading public institutions in Dublin followed, to some of which he was a munificent friend, and to others he was an able auxiliary. But the leading feature of the entire ceremony evidently appeared to be the extraordinary unanimity of all creeds and classes to pay a solemn tribute of respect to one whose life was a model, and whose death was a national affliction. On no former occasion did we ever see such a unity of feeling and of sentiments—such a unanimous desire to pay an impressive compliment to the virtues of the man, and the principles of universal benevolence with which his name is identified. Peter Purcell is now gone for ever; may his memory remain to guide and stimulate his friends in that career of utility and good for which he was so distinguished, and may his family learn to bear his loss with that christian spirit which can alone console them in their deep affliction. (1846-06-06, 4:6)

3508. Representation of Carlow.—(From the *Packet.*) —On reference to our report of a numerous and highly respectable meeting at Carlow yesterday, it will be seen that the late worthy representative of that county, Mr. Bunbury, will be succeeded in Parliament by one of his gallant nephews, Captain M'Clintock Bunbury, R.N., son of that excellent country gentleman of the old school, John M'Clintock, Esq., of Drumcar, county Louth, a representative of one of the most ancient houses of our Irish gentry. The captain, and his brother, the

Major, have taken the name of Bunbury, in compliance with the will of their uncle. A better successor than the gallant captain could not be chosen by the gentry and freeholders of that truly independent county, which resisted the assaults of the enemies of order and the law in the worst of times. (1846-06-13, 3:5)

3509. The *Evening Mail* has erroneously stated that Lord Gough is the heir of the late lamented Thomas Bunbury, Esq., M.P., for Carlow. The late hon. gentleman's estates, which are of great magnitude, together with his personal property, which exceeds a quarter of a million sterling, have been devised to his nephews, (Major and Captain M'Clintock,) sons of John M'Clintock, Esq., of Drumcar, subject to a life estate in a portion of the property of Colonel Bunbury, of Bath. (1846-06-13, 3:5)

3510. In Chancery.—In the matter of Rosalinda Elizabeth Johnston, a Minor.—Pursuant to the Order in this Matter bearing Date the 1st of June 1846, I require all Creditors of Thomas Johnston, late of Fortjohnston, in the county of Monaghan, Esq., deceased, who died Intestate, and all Persons having Claims, Charges, or Demands upon the personal Estate of the said Thomas Johnston, to come in before me, at my Chambers on the Inns Quay in the City of Dublin, on or before the 27th day of June, inst., and proceed to prove the same; otherwise, they will be precluded from the benefit of said Order.

Dated, this 13th day of June, 1846.
Thomas Goold.
Thomas Reilly, Solicitor for Henry George Johnston, the Administrator of the said Thomas Johnston, deceased,
10, Lower Ormond Quay, Dublin.
(1846-06-20, 3:5)

3511. Progress of the Cholera.—It is confidently rumored in the best informed medical circles, that the labors of the commission of sanity inquiry will be rendered permanent by the appointment of a board of health to suggest and enforce precautionary measures against the visitation of the Asiatic cholera. (1846-06-27, 1:3)

3512. A man named Loughran died the other day near Dungannon, from glanders, imparted to him by cutting his finger whilst engaged in skinning a horse which had been infected by that disease. (1846-06-27, 1:3)

3513. Runaway Husbands.—On Tuesday, no fewer than seven women were brought to the mayor's office by the master of the Kilkenny Union Poor-house, to swear informations against their husbands for desertion. (1846-06-27, 2:1)

3514. Stanzas for the *Northern Standard.*

I little thought, oh, dearest one,
When first my life was blest in thee,
When fondly link'd our spirits were,
There was a time when one should flee;
So deep my joy in owing thee,
I languished in affection's dream,
And, as the flower, 'neath thy smile
I revell'd in the sunny beam.

My boyish heart had lov'd thy form,
Thy witching glance my soul had fired,
Thy voice awaken'd thoughts more pure
Than heathen sage had e'er inspired;
And while entranced in matchless bliss,
My circling arm was twined in thine,
The future no existence had,
The present hour had made thee mine.

And years rolled on—the virgin girl
Had ripened to the woman fair,
The childish jest had changed been,
To words of solace in my care;
And when perchance in passing grief
The lustre from my eye would fade,
As spirits sent from purer worlds,
Two little children round me played.

And I was happy—oh! how blest
In them and thee—how dear my lot!
Perchance estranged by earthly love,
Heaven's love divine I had forgot;
But how I know not; for their weal
And thine was all my earthly pride,
And yet as slumber-sinking babes,
My little darlings gently died.

Oh! bitter was the burning tear
That fell upon their tiny grave;
Yet, when I gazed upon thy face,
Heaven bade me still some comfort have,
I still had thee;—the iron hand
Of woe could not its acme reach;
And yet one year—one little year
Oh, God! my sobbings choke my speech.

My rugged soul thy precept mild,
Thy gentle piety improved,
Pointing by each example bright,
Toward that Heaven you dearly loved.
Why urge these vain complaints my heart?
Why urge her from a home so fair?
Pray that thy soul, subdued by hers,
In future time may meet her there.

Outis.
June, 1846.
(1846-06-27, 2:4)

3515. The Rev. Lord Adam Loftus and his accomplished bride arrived at Ely Lodge last week. The shores of our romantic and beautiful Erne are becoming quite fashionable for the passing the honeymoon. (1846-06-27, 2:6)

3516. Miss Martineau on the Cholera.—Another fact of the times is, that the cholera is again approaching us. It is spreading from Asia and has already crossed the Russian boundary. There is time to (*continued...*)

3516, continued: ...consider what we can do to make it as little mischievous as possible, if it should visit us—probably in a few months. It will be wiser to begin now to keep our persons and houses clean, to preserve our general health by wholesome and temperate food and exercise, and by encouraging in our houses a cheerful tranquillity of mind; than to be making a fuss when the time comes with white wash and flannel petticoats, and drugs and new diet, all tried in hurry and panic. (1846-06-27, 3:3)

3517. Dungannon Petty Sessions.—Illegal Marriages by a Roman Catholic Priest.—The Rev. Daniel Hughes, Catholic curate of the parish of Donoghmore, in this county (Tyrone), was called up on the charge of illegally celebrating a marriage between one John Sharkey, a Roman Catholic, and Martha M'Niece, a Presbyterian, on the 7th day of February last, in the house of Bernard Mooney, who keeps a public-house in Irish-street in this town.

This case had been fully heard the last petit sessions day, and informations taken, which were submitted at the request of both parties, to government by the magistrates then present (R.D. Coulson, R.M., and Robert Wray, Esq.,) in hopes the government would not proceed further in the prosecution, which it appears the executive would not consent to.

The complainants, Robert Whan and Martha M'Niece, were called this day and perfected their informations, and were bound in a penalty to prosecute at the next Quarter Sessions, to be held in this town on the 30th instant.

The Rev. Mr. Hughes being present, was held to bail, himself in the sum of 50*l*., and two sureties in the sum of 25*l*. each.—*Derry Sentinel.* (1846-07-04, 1:3)

3518. Orange Funeral.—So grand, solemn, and imposing a sight, as the funeral procession of a respectable Orangeman, named Abraham Stinson, who lived midway between Newtownbutler and Clones, and who was interred in the latter town on Friday, 3d instant, had not been seen in this county during the last twenty years. Being, we understand, upwards of eighty years old, and having become a member of the Orange community at a very early age, he was one of the oldest Orangemen in Ireland. And the tenacity with which he adhered, under every vicissitude, to the principles of Orangeism, rendered him much endeared, and highly popular, among his own party, while his sociable disposition and excellent moral character, gained him the friendship and esteem of his Roman Catholic neighbours, also. But it is to his funeral procession we desire to call attention. It extended a full mile, the brethren marching slowly in a column of two deep, all having white scarfs round their hats, and orange sashes round their collars, while about twenty-five stands of colours—all reversed—were carried in front; and no fewer than forty men with fifes and drums continued to play, at intervals, the national anthem, and some beautifully solemn elegaic tunes, until they arrived at the Church-yard. (1846-07-11, 3:1)

3519. County Monaghan.—Auction, at Newbliss House. —John E. Jones Being favoured with instructions by the Trustees of the late Andrew Ker, Esq., Deceased, to submit to public competition at Newbliss House, on Wednesday, the 22d day of July inst., and following days, at eleven o'clock precisely, all his Household Furniture,

Wines, House Linens, Library of Books, Carriages, Carriage and Farm Horses, Stock of In-calf Dairy Cows, Two and Three years old Heifers and Bullocks, Wainling Calves, a famous Three Year Old Durham Bull, an extraordinary fine yearling Bull, got by Mr. Foster's superior Bull (of Ballinure), 23 Ewes, a Ham, 6 Wedders, 19 Lambs and 30 Fleeces of Wool, a large Stock of well saved Upland Old Hay, a large quantity of old Turf, Housed, Threshed Old Oats, Farming Implements, Iron Ploughs, Harrows, a Clover Sewing Machine on the most improved principle, a Winnowing Machine, a Straw Cutter, Farm Carts and Harness, a new Water Cart and Vessel, a Patent Mangle, a Patent Churn.

For a Description of the Furniture
see handbills.

About Forty Dozen
Sherry, Madeira, Port, Claret, &c.,
and twenty dozen empty bottles.

About 200 Volume of Books including the Ordnance Survey of Monaghan, in 34 Maps on Cambrick, Encased in Russia Leather, and Six Volumes of Lewis's Topography of England and Wales, and two Volumes of Ireland.

Terms Cash.

Programme of Sale.

Wednesday, 22d—The Kitchen, Parlours, Drawing Room and Pantry. Thursday, 23d—The Carriages, Horses, Farming Implements and Wines. Friday and Saturday, 24th & 25th—The Bed-Rooms, the House-linens, Books, &c., &c.

Newbliss House, 2d July, 1846.
(1846-07-11, 3:5)

3520. The Widow.—By G. Linnaeus Banks, Esq., Author of *Spring Gatherings*, &c.

Who does not love the widow
With her brow of silent care,
And deem some gentle memory
Of the past is lurking there?
Tho' a lightness like the sunshine
O'er her placid features play,
There's a grief within her bosom
That can never wear away.

Her spirit may be joyous,
As the spirit oft will be,
Tho' tossed upon the stormy wave
Of life's tempestuous sea;
Her eye may be as summer bright
And music in its tone,
But little can she reck of life
When passion's hope is gone.

Go, enter yon lone chamber
Where the dying sufferer lay,
Ere death had touched its victim
With the finger of decay—
And oh, how many agonies
Around the heart will cling,
While bitter streams of memory
From disappointment spring.

Speak kindly of the widow then,
And smooth her brow of care,
Remember her with gentle words
When bowing low in prayer—
For God, whose care is over all,
Loves not the widow less.
And he will bless the hearts of those
Whose hearts the widow bless.

(1846-07-11, 4:1)

3521. Glorious Time for Ladies.—In the reign of Queen Margaret of Scotland, the parliament passed an act, that any maiden lady, of high or low degree, should have the liberty to choose for a husband the man on whom she set her fancy. If a man refused to marry her, he was heavily fined, according to the value of his worldly possessions. The only ground of exemption was previous betrothal. (1846-07-11, 4:5)

3522. Longevity.—A man named John Corr, of Moneyhill, near Kilmore, in this county, died on Sunday, at the advanced age of 102 years. During his whole life, he never was an hour in bed by sickness, and was in perfect health up to the day before his death. There are, at present, in the same neighbourhood, three persons whose united ages about to 291 years. (1846-07-25, 1:3)

3523. Death of the Earl of Kilkenny.—Died, at Ballyconra, at six o'clock on the evening of Thursday, the 16th instant, the Right Hon. Edmond Earl of Kilkenny, in the 76th year of his age. The deceased nobleman had labored many years under mental indisposition, but the illness which caused his death was only of a few days' duration, dying without issue. (1846-07-25, 3:3)

3524. Courtship.—When a young man admires a lady, and thinks her society necessary to his happiness, it is proper before committing himself, or inducing the object of his admiration to do so, to apply to her parents or guardians for permission to address her; this is a becoming mark of respect, and the circumstances must be very peculiar, which would justify deviation from this course. Everything secret and unacknowledged is to be avoided, as the reputation of clandestine intercourse is always more or less injurious through life. The romance evaporates, but the memory of indiscretion survives. Young men frequently amuse themselves by playing with the feelings of young women. They visit them often, they walk with them, they pay them divers attentions, and giving them an idea that they are exclusively attached to them, they either leave them, or what is worse, never come to an explanation of their sentiments. This is to act the character of a dangler, a character truly dastardly and infamous. There is no reason why the passion of love should be wrapped up in mystery. It would prevent much and complicated mystery in the world, if all young persons understood it truly. According to the usages of society, it is the custom for the man to propose marriage, and for the female to refuse or accept the offer as she may think fit. There ought to be a perfect freedom of the will in both parties. A young woman should not be in haste to accept a lover. Let her know him a sufficient time to judge of his qualities of mind, temper, habits, &c., before she allows herself to be inveigled into a marriage. Far better for her to remain single, than to run the risk of a wretched, ill-assorted match. She should consider it no loss if she never married. No man ought to marry who cannot foresee that he will be able to support the additional expenses of a wife and family, and at the same time, fulfil his other necessary obligations. We believe that every industrious, active and sober man will find no serious obstacle in this respect. The opposition of parents should have all reasonable weight with the young of both sexes. If you are under age, by all means, wait until you are legally qualified to decide for yourself; but never, under any circumstances, marry against your inclinations. Our rule is comprehensive. The circumstances cannot be imagined, which would justify male and female in making a repugnant marriage. To save the lives, fortunes, or reputations of ourselves, our parents and friends, we are not justified in making a mockery of the marriage vow by swearing to love her or him, to whom we are at heart indifferent. As well might we undertake to justify murder, theft, or any other crime, under the plea of subserving our own or another's interests. The demeanour of a suitor towards the object of his addresses, in company, should be very circumspect. Nothing is more easy than to make both himself and her ridiculous. He should neither neglect nor pay her too marked attention. His manners towards her should be studiously respectful without being formal. Courting in society is equally indelicate and offensive, and brings both the understandings and the principles into question, if not into actual suspicion; it is, besides, a display of selfishness and vulgarity which is insulting. Lovers would do well to remember that while courtship is the most absorbing and interesting of all occupations to them, it is the most insipid, and when too manifest, the most distasteful, to others. When a wedding takes place in a family, the cards of the newly married pair are sent round to all their acquaintances to apprise them of the event. The cards are sent out by the bridegroom to his acquaintances, and by the bride, or her parents, to hers. In some instances, the cards have been united by (*continued...*)

3524, continued: ...silken or silver cords, but this mode has not been adopted by people of fashion. To those who leave cards at the residence of the bride and bridegroom during their absence in the honey moon, cards are sent to inform them of their return. (1846-07-25, 4:5)

3525. We understand, that the Mastership, vacant by the death of the late Master Goold, has been given to Mr. J. Murphy. (1846-08-01, 2:6)

3526. On the Death of a Mother.

The scene has then closed, and the vision has faded
We have seen thee but here we shall see thee no more,
Thy spirit has gone to the God who has made it,
And the days of thy pilgrimage early are o'er.

We loved thee, and well might we love thee, our mother;
You loved us, and taught us, and toiled for us too;
And now that thou'rt gone, we can ne'er meet another
So kind, or affectionate, faithful as you.

Still, still thou are gone where no want can assail thee,
Nor pain nor affliction disquiet thee more;
Where thousands, ten thousands of angels now hail thee
And welcome thy bark to eternity's shore.

Oh blest be the thought—there the breath of commotion
Ne'er ruffles the calm or the peace of thy soul,
Nor the billows of sorrow, from earth's troubled ocean,
O'er the scenes of thy heavenly happiness roll.

Night darkens our joy, but thy night is now ended—
Day fades from our view, now thy day is begun;
Contracted our sphere, thine immensely distended—
Unnumber'd the joys, and unfaded thy sun.

On Jesus you leaned, as the dark surging billow
Of Jordan came rolling, both fearful and strong,
His hand was thy stay, and his bosom thy pillow,
And the ark of his love bore there lightly along.

Thou are gone, then, our mother, thus early before us;
We have seen your last tear shed—have heard your last sigh—
We have knelt by your side, oh, you loved one, who bore us,
And watched the last gleam of your fast-fading eye.

Thou art gone—thou art gone—with the dead thou art number'd—
Bereft of thy counsel and love we remain,
To weep, but not hopeless; thou only hast slumber'd—
Soon, soon, from that slumber to waken again.

Then the trump of Jehovah, creation awaking,
With the voice of the angel sounds startling and dread,
And the sepulchred saints from their sacred sleep breaking,
Come forth at the call from the vaults of the dead.

Then, then, shalt thou rise up to life and to glory,
And bright as the sun shall immortally shine;
Through ages unending proclaiming the glory
Of love, inexpressible, matchless, divine.

May our lot, then, with thine be for ever united—
Our life be as perfect, our death as serene;
When we pass the dark vale, may the same radiance light it,
And then may we meet thee in Eden's bright scene.

(1846-08-01, 4:1)

3527. Husband's Right of Chastisement.—An unguarded saying which escaped from Justice Buller, unpremeditatedly, excited general animadversion, namely that a husband had a right to chastise his wife with a stick no thicker than his thumb. The subject offered too fair an opportunity to the caricaturist not to be eagerly grasped at. His portrait, as Judge Thumb, speedily adorned the print shops, and the women enjoyed a hearty laugh at the expense of this ungallant champion of club law. A similar ungallant doctrine had been mooted in the preceding century by a Dr. Marmaduke Coghill, judge of the Prerogative Court for Ireland, and with still more detriment to himself.—Having been called to decide the grounds of a divorce sued for by a wife against her husband, who had given her a good beating, the venerable civilian delivered a solemn opinion that, with such a switch as the one he held in his hand, moderate chastisement was within the husband's matrimonial privilege. This legal maxim occasioned so much offence or alarm to a lady to whom the Doctor had been for some time paying his addresses, with a fair prospect of success, that she peremptorily dismissed the assertor of so ungallant a doctrine. Dr. Coghill, as may be guessed from his opinions, died unmarried. The civil law, says the more courtly Blackstone, allowed the husband, for some misdemeanors, *flagellis et fustibus acriter verber are uxorem*, with whips and clubs sharply to strike a wife; but with us, in the politer reign of Charles the Second, this power of correction began to be doubted, and may be now positively denied. The sly remark of the commentator is still too true, that the lower rank of people, who were always fond of the old common law, claim and exert their ancient privilege.—*Townsend's Lives of the Twelve Judges.* (1846-08-01, 4:5)

3528. Fatal Accident.—Yesterday, the Magistrates of this town held an investigation on the body of a man named James Mullan, who was killed under the following circumstances:—The deceased was employed as a labourer on a mill, which is now in the course of erection at Dunmurry, and, on the 28th inst., was on a scaffold used for the building, with a plank in his hand. It would seem that the weight of the plank, or the awkward position in which it was held, overbalanced him, and he, with the timber, fell to the ground from a height of about thirty feet. His head struck upon the metal plate of one of the beams and was severely cut. He never spoke afterwards. Drs. Plane and Blizzard attended him, but their professional efforts were unavailing.—*Banner of Ulster*. (1846-08-08, 1:3)

3529. The English Cholera.—Within the last few days, there has been an enormous increase, at the various metropolitan hospitals and dispensaries, of English cholera, in a very acute form. It is attributable more to atmospheric influences than the use of fruit, to which it is generally ascribed.—*Globe*. (1846-08-08, 1:4)

3530. Death of Grace Berachree.—Grace Berachree, the eldest daughter of the unhappy woman sentenced to transportation for life, for being accessory to the murder of her husband—died on Monday morning last, of fever, in the Nenagh hospital. She was a very handsome girl aged eighteen years, and should have come forward as a prosecutrix with her brothers and sister, against her unnatural parent, but that during the trial, she was sinking fast under a malady which has now, happily for herself, terminated a life which could but prove one scene of agony and corroding grief, to behold her mother banished by criminally acquiescing in her husband's brutal murder. Walsh, the paramour of Mrs. Berachree, and the principal in the murder, sentenced for execution on Saturday, the 22d of August last. What a warning against crime! What a multitude of calamities have befallen this family within a brief period of time—a father murdered! and with the connivance of one who should have loved, cherished, and protected him—one whose natural instinct should have been to shield him from the assassin's blow—a wife expatriated for ever from her offspring and her home—and the children of that lamentable alliance, compelled, by circumstances, to be instruments in the vindication of the law, and the means of their mother's degradation.—*Nenagh Guardian*. (1846-08-08, 2:1)

3531. Marriage in High Life.—On Monday, the marriage of Viscount Seaham, son of the Marquis and Marchioness of Londonderry, and Miss Mary Cornelia Edwards, only daughter and heiress of Sir John Edwards, Montgomeryshire, was solemnised at St. George's Church, Hanover-square.

A very numerous circle of friends of both families were present as spectators of the ceremony, among them we observed, the Duke and Duchess of Cleveland and Lady Augusta Paulett, the Duchess of Northumberland, his Excellence the Russian Minister and Baroness Brunow, the Marquis and Marchioness of Londonderry, the Marquis and Marchioness of Blandford, the Earl and Countess of Powis [sic] and Lady Lucy and Charlotte Herbert, Viscount and Viscountess Castlereagh, Viscount Canterbury, Lady Brindkman, Lord Sudeley, Sir Charles Morgan, Sir Frederick Fitzclarence, Sir Benjamin Hall, &c.

The bride was attired in a superb dress of Brussels lace over white satin, confined at the waist by a splendid Stomacher act with diamonds and sapphires. A wreath of orange blossoms, with a tiara of brilliants, completed the costume.

In the bridal train, the youthful bridesmaids formed a conspicuous group, from the taste displayed in the costumes they respectively wore, all being similarly attired. We believe the ladies Alexandrina and Adelaide Vane, Lady Elizabeth Grosvenor, the Misses Rice Trevor, Miss Wescomb, and Miss Long, were the fair attendants on the bride.

The Bishop of Durham performed the marriage ceremony in a deeply impressive manner, the bride being given away by her father, Sir John Edwards.

Sir John and Lady Edwards gave a splendid entertainment to celebrate the auspicious event, at their own mansion in Portman-square, to which rendezvous the wedding party repaired on departing from the church.

At half past two o'clock, the noble bridegroom and his fair bride left London for Rosebank, the Marquis of Londonderry's villa, near Fulham to pass the honeymoon.

In the evening, the Marchioness of Londonderry had a *soiree dansante* at Holderness House, in honor of the marriage of her son. (1846-08-08, 2:2)

3532. Funeral of an Orangeman.—On Wednesday last, a deceased Orangeman was interred at Seskanore, with all the rites, honours, and ceremonies due to a loyal member of considerable standing in the Orange association. The deceased was Mr. James Mitchell, of Raveagh, aged about 38 years, who had been a tried and zealous member of the Orange society for several years, and who had been among the foremost, on every suitable occasion, to evidence his loyalty and attachment to the cause. The funeral was attended by upwards of sixteen hundred persons, all the men wearing white hat scarfs, which gave an exceedingly picturesque appearance to the solemn scene. There were nine beautiful flags, which, with the hearse, were placed in the front, the drums being muffled: the masters of lodges marched close to the flags, and the Orangemen marched behind the masters and before the hearse; and the Aughnaronan lodge, of which the deceased was deputy-master, brought up the rear. On arriving at the grave yard, the body was committed to the dust, with the secret rites and ceremonies pertaining to the interment of a member of the Orange association. (1846-08-08, 2:1)

3533. Dublin Police—Tuesday.—The Bigamy Case. —Mary Downes, whose case is already before the public, was brought up on Monday for final examination. Mr. Holmes and Mr. Humphreys appeared for the prosecution on behalf of Mr. Brown, Mr. John A. Curran, and Mr. C.F. Johnston, as agent, attended for Mr. Copeland. Mr. Stanley appeared for the prisoner. A discussion took place as to whether Mr. Curran should have the power of cross-examining the witnesses or not, and the magistrates decided unless he appeared for the prisoner, they could not permit him to adopt the course he sought for.

Mr. Curran argues that it was in the discretion of the bench, and that for the sake of public justice alone, he ought to have the liberty of examining the witnesses when he should show such a case as would at once compel the bench to refuse the informations. He stigmatised the whole proceeding as a gross conspiracy got up to convict the prisoner.

This assertion was strongly repudiated by Mr. Holmes and Mr. Humphreys, who contended that Mr. Curran had no right to make such observations, which was done, as they said, in order to get into the newspapers.

Mr. Curran did not charge Mr. Humphreys with getting up the case, or having anything to do with the conspiracy, as he was sure that gentleman was instructed to act by the advice he received. He (Mr. Curran)was acting by his instructions also.

Mr. Humphreys said that the learned gentleman was misinstructed, when he called it a case of conspiracy, and got up for a purpose—such was not the case.

Mr. Holmes said Mr. Curran had no right to be heard there, nor had he a right to use such observations.

Mr. Johnston said he was prepared to prove every word of what was said.

A long discussion of the above nature followed. Mr. Curran urging the necessity of being allowed to interfere on the part of Mr. Copeland, but the court refused unless he appeared for the prisoner, which he did not. He proposed to show the falsehood of the present case, if permitted to enter on it. For the love of justice alone, the other side ought to allow him, but it showed what bad case they had.

Mr. Hitchcock—Since I left off practice in the hall of the courts, I have no love for Justice at all—(laughter.) I used to get valuable consideration for it then.

After a considerable time had been spent in discussing Mr. Curran's proposition, he finally sat down, saying he would prophecy that the prisoner at her trial would plead guilty.

Mr. Stanley said he would keep his defence for the trial, and he had no doubt that his client could establish her innocence. If there was a conspiracy, he knew nothing of it. The witnesses were then produced and re-sworn, when—Mr. Williams, the clerk, read the informations already lodged by them, on which a warrant was granted for the arrest of the prisoner. The first (they are all voluminous documents) was made by John Barry, of Listowel, who stated that he knew William Fitzgerald, who was a dealer in cattle, and a relation of witness's wife. In May, 1839, Fitzgerald asked him to come to Dublin, as he was about to get married; they came to Dublin, and met the prisoner at a house in Fleet-street, kept by a person named Connor. The information went on to give a long history in detail of all that occurred, the principal feature being the marriage of the parties in the Straw Market, by a person named Maguire, who is since dead. The parties lived as man and wife; he saw Fitzgerald in the country after that, and he said he left his wife in service in Dublin, and that she had not as much money as it was thought she had; he heard Fitzgerald say after that his wife was in Mayo at service, and that he heard something of her conduct which he did not like; Fitzgerald died in December, 1843.

Anne Maguire, wife of the deceased person who performed the marriage ceremony, proved an entry in her late husband's book of the marriage.

Mr. Curran repudiated the entry, and another discussion followed.

Lorenzo Trigger and the Rev. Mr. Franklin proved the marriage of the prisoner with Mr. Brown [sic].

A very long information, taken at Kilmainham from Mr. Brown with Mr. Tyndall, was then read. It was a history of the facts that are already before the public. The magistrates decided that there was a *prima facie* case made out against the prisoner, and as they (the magistrates) were merely acting ministerially, they would send the case for trial.—She was accordingly committed. (1846-08-08, 2:3)

3534. Advantage of Wedlock.—None but the married man has a home in his old age. None has friends, then, but he; none but he knows and feels the solace of the domestic hearth; none but he lives and freshens in his green old age, amid the affections of his children. There is no tears shed for the old bachelor; there is no ready hand and kind heart to cheer him in his loneliness and bereavement! there is none in whose eyes he can see himself reflected, and from whose lips he can receive the unfailing assurance of care and love. No. The old bachelor may be courted for his money. He may eat, and drink, and revel, as such things do; and he may sicken and die in a hotel or garret, with plenty of attendants about him, like so many cormorants waiting for their prey. But he will never know what it is to be loved, and to live and to die amid a beloved circle. He can never know the comforts of the domestic fire-side. (1846-08-08, 2:3)

3535. The New Master in Chancery.—Jeremiah J. Murphy, Esq., Q.C., whose appointment we had the gratification of announcing last week, was on Monday sworn in as Master in Chancery, in the room of the late Thomas Goold, Esq. (1846-08-15, 1:4)

3536. Coroners—Fermanagh.—We have had a peep at the new act regulating the office of Coroner which will take effect on the 1st January, 1847. Counties are to be divided into districts, by the magistrates, and Fermanagh will have three—Coroners in office to have the districts in which they reside. £1 10s. for each inquest, but the gross sum at any assizes must not exceed £50. In addition, 6d. per mile travelled will be allowed for expences incurred.—*Fermanagh Reporter.* (1846-08-15, 2:4)

3537. On Sunday, the Rev. Mr. M'Mahon, parish priest at Newtownbutler, after having served mass went to attend a sick cab [sic], and died of apoplexy. He was immediately attended by Doctors Thompson and Fitzgerald, but they could render no assistance.—*Fermanagh Reporter.* (1846-08-15, 2:4)

3538. Wills.—Thomas Bunbury, Esq., late one of the representatives for the county of Carlow, of Lisnevagh and Moyle, in Ireland, has left all his real, freehold and copyhold, and leasehold estates, to his brother, Kane Bunbury, Esq., for life, and after his decease to his nephew, William Bunbury M'Clintock, and his heirs, for ever, upon condition that he shall apply for the necessary license under her Majesty's sign manual to use and bear the surname and arms of Bunbury; and bequeathe to his brother, for his own absolute use, the furniture, books, farming stock and implements, and other effects at Moyle—the plate for his life only, and then to his nephew, John M'Clintock, absolutely, to whom he leaves all his furniture and effects at Bath, and at the St. James' Hotel—and also bequeaths to his nephew, John M'Clintock, a legacy of 50,000*l.* sterling, and 10,000*l.* Irish currency, secured on mortgage; and to his nephew, William B. M'Clintock (to whom he leaves the reversion of his real estates) a legacy of 20,000*l.* To his cousin, Thos. Bunbury, 2,000*l.* To Mrs. C. Elmore, an annuity of 400*l.*, or a sum equivalent, and an immediate bequest of 200*l.* A few other legacies, including his bailiff and household servants; and hopes that his brother Kane, on his succeeding to Moyle, will follow his example and give to each of the laborers and others employed on the estate a suit of clothes, as he had done when he took possession. All legacies to be free of duty. The residue of his personal estate, he leaves in trust, to pay the interest, dividends, and annual proceeds, to his brother Kane for life, and at his demise, to divide the said residue into three parts, giving two thirds to his said nephew, W.B. M'Clintock, and the remaining third to his said nephew, John M'Clintock, absolutely. The executors are his two nephews, W.B. M'Clintock, Esq., of Manor House, Highgate, near Clones, Fermanagh, and John M'Clintock, Esq., of Dromeskin House, near Castlebellingham, Louth, and William Elliott, Esq., of Harcourt Street, Dublin. The deceased died at the age of 71, and executed his will only two days before his death.—Morning Post. (1846-08-22, 1:5)

3539. Death of Rear-Admiral the Hon. William Le Poer Trench.—Ballinasloe, Aug. 16.—This morning, the Hon. William Le Poer Trench, Rear-Admiral, breathed his last. He was in his 76th year, and retained his faculties unimpaired to the moment of dissolution. He possessed a strong and vigorous intellect, combined with sound common sense, which he exercised unceasingly in all the affairs connected with this town and neighbourhood, in which he was deeply interested, and which his position, as agent to the Earl of Clancarty, to whom he stood in the close relationship of uncle, gave him abundant opportunities. He was a fine old man in every sense of the word, blessed with many virtues. He was a junior Commissioner of Customs, and, I believe, received, up to the moment of his demise, a considerable pension from the crown. He was a Rear-Admiral in the Navy, and, though not engaged in any of Nelson's victories, accompanied the fleet of that distinguished hero. There was a stern bravery in the man that well became a sailor—an uncompromising, unselfish daring, that would have prompted him to face the greatest danger when he felt the righteousness of acting. In his everyday life, he gave evidence of this; and I believe that if circumstances during his sojourn in the navy called for it, a more determined, a more courageous, or a braver man was not in the service. He was twice married—his first was a Miss Cuppaidge, of Athlone, sister, I understand, to Major Cuppaidge. By this lady, he had four children. Two of his sons are in the church—Dr. William Le Poer Trench, Rector of Killereran, in this county; and the Rev. John Trench, Rector of Longford. His daughter was married to the Rev. William Guinness, but died at a very early period. His second wife was the widow of Arthur Handcock, Esq., one of the Castlemaine family, by whom he had two children. He will be interred on Tuesday morning in the family vault, at Creagh, near this town.—*Saunders.* (1846-08-22, 2:3)

3540. The Most Rev. Charles Dickinson, D.D.,—Late Lord Bishop of Meath.—(*From the Church of England Magazine.*)—The subject of the following memoir is one whose loss has scarcely ceased to be even outwardly mourned by his clerical brethren, and many private friends, in that portion of the united church of these realms of which he was distinguished, though a short-lived ornament. ... Never perhaps, says his biographer, Dr. West, was there a man less affected with the flush which so commonly attends upon sudden promotion. Though receiving from every quarter congratulations on his advancement, his equable mind and strong Christian sentiment too justly appreciated the value of temporal distinctions to allow room to him for any elation of spirit. On one occasion, while these greetings were still new, in his usual strain of calm cheerfulness, he expressed his indifference to all worldly honours or (*continued...*)

3540, continued: …advantages, and how readily he would at once relinquish all, and even life itself, were it the divine will. [*The foregoing are the opening and closing paragraphs of a two-column biographical sketch. The sketch includes mentions of:* a native of Cork; son of an English gentleman from Cumberland; born in August, 1792, youngest of seventeen children; mother's maiden name was Austen; received the first rudiments at the best English school at that time in Cork, conducted by Mr. Finney; in 1805, commenced more advanced studies under the Rev. Mr. Dwyer, at Kinsale; next, placed at Cork, under the care of the Rev. T.D. Hincks, by whose removal to Belfast, young Dickinson was deprived of the advantages which he had for two years enjoyed; in 1810, entered Trinity college as a pensioner, under Dr. Meredith; competed with Hercules Henry Graves, son of Dr. Graves, senior fellow of the college, and J.T. O'Brien, afterwards a fellow, and now bishop of Ossory and Ferns; enjoyed intimacies with, among others, Charles Wolfe, who was memorialised by the present archdeacon of Clogher, the ven. J.A. Russell; his mathematical ability drew towards him the interest of Dr. Magee, the late archbishop of Dublin; in 1813, obtained a scholarship; took a distinguished part as a member of the College Historical Society; took his degree of bachelor of arts in the spring commencements of 1815; in 1819, was appointed to the assistant chaplaincy of the Magdalen asylum; in 1820, married to Elizabeth, daughter of Abraham Russell, Esq., of Limerick, and sister of J.A. Russell; in 1821, resigned the office he held at the Magdalen asylum; offered a similar post at the Female Orphan House, in which post he continued for the next nine years to enjoy a competent income; among the friends with whom he had long enjoyed constant intercourse was Alexander Knox, and the present archbishop of Dublin; was appointed chaplain to the archbishop; on the death of Dr. Hinks [sic] in 1833, the whole duty of the chaplaincy and secretaryship; appointed to the living of St. Anns, Dublin in 1833; in his office as examining-chaplain, promoted the establishment of the Parochial Visitors' Society, an institution designed to remedy the growing evils arising from the inadequacy of the clerical department of the Established Church to the quantity of work it was expected to perform; in 1840, the see of Meath became vacant by the death of bishop Alexander, and rumour pointed to Dr. Dickinson as the probable successor—however, in a letter to his sister at Kinsale, he indicated how unambitious he was in the prospect of a possible elevation; his consecration took place on the 27th December, 1840, in the cathedral Christ-church, Dublin. Reference was made to *Remains of the most Rev. C. Dickenson,* D.D.*: being a selection from his sermons and tracts, with a biographical sketch,* by the Rev. John West, D.D., London: Fellowes, Grant and Bolton, Dublin, 1845.] (1846-08-22, 4:4)

3541. Pat Welsh, a native of Dublin, one of the crew of the *Clyde* mail steamer, fell from the fore top on Sunday, and was killed. (1846-08-29, 1:3)

3542. Inquest.—Charles Waddel, Esq., held an inquest on Thursday last, the 20th inst., on view of the body of George Hughes, a labouring man, resident in the townland of Annahagh, near Scottstown, in this county. From certain symptoms which exhibited themselves before his death, it was conjectured that he had taken poison; but on the examination of the contents of the stomach by Dr. Reed, it was ascertained that the cause of death was from the deceased having eaten inordinately of bacon and cabbage, and afterwards drinking largely of buttermilk. (1846-08-29, 3:1)

3543. Funeral of the Late Lord Bloomfield.—The remains of the late gallant General, Lord Bloomfield, arrived on Saturday last, at Loughton, accompanied by the present noble lord, the second of that distinguished name. The funeral was attended by the principal gentry of the country, and a vast concourse of the tenantry, on the estates in this and the King's County, of that noble family—and in the family vault at Ballycormack Church, close to the demesne of Laughton [sic], was deposited the body of one of Ireland's best landlords.—*Nenagh Guardian.* (1846-08-29, 3:3)

3544. The Queen has been pleased, by warrant under the Royal Signet and Sign Manual, to give and grant to William Bunbury M'Clintock, of Manor Highgate, in the county of Fermanagh, Esq., Commander in the Royal Navy, Her Majesty's Royal licence and authority, that he and his issue may take and use the surname of Bunbury, in addition to and after that of M'Clintock, and bear the arms of Bunbury quarterly with those of M'Clintock, in compliance with the will of his maternal uncle, Thomas Bunbury, late of Lisnevagh and Moyle, in the county of Carlow, Esq., deceased. (1846-08-29, 3:4)

3545. Death of the Rev. Thomas Ovenden.—We regret to announce the death of Rev. Thos. Ovenden, rector of Magheracross, in this county. The Rev. Gentleman had been complaining for some time and died yesterday at his residence, Crocknacriev, from, it is believed, the bursting of a blood-vessel. He was unmarried, but had many dependent upon him; for he gave a great number employment who will keenly feel his loss in these distressing times.—*Fermanagh Reporter.* (1846-09-05, 3:2)

3546. The Earl of Bandon has been appointed to the colonelcy of the City of Cork Regiment of Militia, vacant by the death of the Marquis of Thomond. (1846-09-05, 4:3)

3547. Hyrdophobia.—As to the existence of a remedy for this awful disease, Dr. O'Reilly, of Belturbet, writes as follows: "A number of the medical profession naturally unwilling to maintain that there exists a specific for any disease whatsoever; still I must confess my belief—a belief entertained by the gentry, the professional men, and all the people of the counties of Cavan, Leitrim, and Fermanagh—that a family named M'Gaurin, residing near to Swanlinbar, possess a perfect remedy for this horrible disease. Persons have gone to M'Gaurin tied on a car, and returned free of all illness. He also cures cattle of this disease, a proof that it is not merely a work of imagination. (1846-09-05, 4:5)

3548. Fever is very prevalent in town at present, especially among the poorer inhabitants residing in narrow filthy streets, and living upon unwholesome and scantily supplied food. We recommend, as speedily as possible, the establishment of a board of health, to inspect the house of the poor; and, by suitable directions concerning cleanliness and food, to arrest, under Providence, the progress of this fearful malady.—*Belfast News-Letter*. (1846-09-12, 4:3)

3549. More girls than boys commit suicide. With men, self-destruction is most prevalent between the ages of 35 to 40; with women, from 25 to 35. (1846-09-12, 4:3)

3550. Sudden Death.—An awfully sudden death occurred on Sunday in Summer-hill, under the following circumstances:—A gentleman, undoubtedly of great respectability, took a car at Summer-hill, and desired to be driven to Marlborough-street. On his way there, he complained of illness, and told the driver to proceed as quickly as he could; but before the car had reached the place to which he wished to be driven, it was found that he was dead. The body was taken to Jervis-street Hospital, where it now lies. We heard that, at a late hour in the evening, the deceased was identified by a servant of Mr. Kane, of Talbot-street, who stated his name to be Caniffery.—We understand the deceased gentleman was nearly connected with Mr. Kane. (1846-09-19, 2:1)

3551. There are at this moment no less than 2,000 souls in Enniskillen in a state of starvation. (1846-09-19, 2:2)

3552. Death of Lord Templeton.—We regret to announce the death of the Hon. John Henry Upton, Lord Viscount Templeton, who departed this life at his residence, Castle Upton, county Antrim, in the 74th year of his age, on Monday the 21s inst. Lord Templeton was one of the best landlords in the county Monaghan, and was engaged, during the week previous to his death, in inspecting his estates in the neighbourhood of Castleblayney, for the purpose of assisting his tenantry in the ensuing season of adversity. He gave directions to have the potato ground of all his tenantry surveyed, and a return made to him, it was supposed, with a view of abating the rent where the crop was lost, when it pleased Providence to call him away. He purchased a large quantity of meal last spring, which has since been distributed to his poor tenants at 14*s*. per cwt., and he gave employment to all the laborers upon his estate at 1*s*. a-day. His Lordship contemplated works of deep and thorough draining upon his estates.

The death of Lord Templeton, who was a Whig in Politics, will make a great alteration in the political aspect of this county. He is succeeded in his titles and estates by his eldest son, who is a staunch Conservative, and upon the Templeton estates, between two and three hundred Conservative votes can be registered. (1846-09-26, 2:5)

3553. Accidental Death of a Centenarian.—On Sunday last, Robert Murray, Esq., coroner, held an inquest on view of the body of James Cummiskey, of Ballinode, aged 106 years, who was run over by a cart, and died in consequence of the injuries then received. Though arrived at the patriarchal age of 106 years, Cummiskey was in the enjoyment of good health and a sound constitution, and up to the day of his death, he was as actively engaged on his farm as he was 60 years ago. A verdict of accidental death was returned. (1846-09-26, 2:5)

3554. Melancholy and Fatal Accident—Death of Amos Palmer Doolan, Esq., J.P.—One of the most distressing events which we have ever been called upon to record, occurred on the afternoon of Monday last, when this and the surrounding towns were thrown into a state of considerable excitement by a report that Amos P. Doolan, Esq., J.P., Derry House, Shinrone, had been accidentally shot. On enquiry, we regret exceedingly to state that the report was found to be true. The painful accident took place at Newhall, a short distance from Sharnavogue House. Mr. Dooland, and the Hon. Colonel Westenra, M.P., were partridge shooting; after Mr. Doolan had crossed a ditch, and proceeded several yards in advance to the left, the Colonel ascended the top of the ditch, and was about to descend, when his feet became entangled in a briar that was fastened across the fence, and he was thrown forward with considerable violence on his face. At the same moment, the gun, which he carried in his right hand, by some unaccountable accident discharged, and the contents entered between Mr. Doolan's shoulders, when he cried out he was shot and then fell to the ground. Colonel Westenra instantly had messengers dispatched to this town, Roscrea, and Shinrone, for any or all the medical assistance that could be procured; and, in the shortest space of time possible, surgeons arrived with all the messengers. A door and a bed were procured, and Mr. Doolan was conveyed to a neighbouring house, where he expired in less than three hours. The shot with which the gun was charged penetrated the lungs and caused internal hoemorrhage, which produced death. James Dillon, Esq., senior coroner, on his arrival in this town, from Shinrone, was called to hold the inquest. He immediately proceeded thither and (*continued...*)

3554, continued: ...empanelled a jury. The persons who were present having detailed the facts, the jury at once returned a verdict of "Accidental Death," after which Mr. Doolan's remains were conveyed to his late residence.

Mr. Doolan has left a widow and three children to deplore his loss. The intelligence of this melancholy catastrophe has created the deepest feelings of regret and sympathy in the minds of all classes, as Mr. Doolan was very much beloved and respected; and, we believe, by none more so than by him who was unfortunately the cause of his sudden death.—Colonel Westenra, in consequence of the unhappy event, which did not arise from any carelessness or want of caution on his part. Indeed, the Colonel has always been remarked for his extreme care and watchfulness when out shooting; and the awful accident must be regarded more as one of the mysterious workings of Providence than the consequence of any instrumentality of human agency. Mr. Doolan was Colonel Westenra's most intimate and loved friend and constant companion. He was bound to him by all the ties that a frank and gentlemanly disposition and a free and amiable nature could give rise to; and such a termination to their intercourse cannot be thought of without the deepest and most painful feelings of regret. Dr. Kingsly, of Roscrea, was obliged to remain with Colonel Westenra, during the night of the day of the disastrous occurrence, the state of his feelings being such as to require both friendly and medical support. We are sorry that such should be the Colonel's unhappy state, and in common with all who have heard of the accident, we offer him our sincere and respectful sympathy.—*King's County Chronicle*. (1846-09-26, 2:6)

3555. The Late Marquis of Downshire.—The tenantry of this late much-respected and highly popular nobleman, who resides upon the King's County part of the extensive family estates, have employed Mr. Joseph R. Kirk, the sculptor, to erect a colossal statue, to be placed upon a pedestal in the most central part of the rising town of Edenderry, adjoining the great market hall erected by the late Marquis. The statue is of Portland stone, white and fine in grain, as if of marble, and represents the subject in his senatorial attire, with a scroll in one hand. It is admirably executed, with vigour and character, and fully proves that the talent of the distinguished parent of Mr. Kirk, as a sculptor, has descended to his son. (1846-10-03, 1:3)

3556. Death of Sir Edward Smith Lees.—We regret to state that Sir Edward Lees, late Secretary to the General Post-office in Scotland, died very suddenly on the morning of the 24th instant, at his cottage at Broughty Ferry, near Dundee. Sir Edward has suffered for years from a complaint of the heart; and it is supposed that he died in his sleep, without a struggle. —*Globe*.

This lamented public officer, for many years, filled a similar situation in Ireland with the utmost advantage to the public service, and with a degree of urbanity and courtesy that deservedly gained for him the respect of all parties. (1846-10-03, 1:4)

3557. Longevity.—Mr. James Taggart, farmer, Baronscourt, has now arrived at the wonderful age of one hundred and twenty one, (which, according to *Keating's history of Ireland*, is within one year of the age of St. Patrick when he died.) More extraordinary still, in the month of August last, he built his own turf-stack; and on the 10th instant, his eldest son, Mr. M. Taggart, who resides at Omagh, was in this town, as a commercial traveller, in which capacity he has acted for seventy years, and is now in the ninety-ninth year of his age. He has a beautiful head of hair—not a white one appearing—and his sight is [so] strong that he can read the smallest print with as much ease as when he was twenty-five. He is, indeed, a wonder.—*Fermanagh Reporter*. (1846-10-03, 1:5)

3558. Auction.—J.E. Jones Being favored with instructions by the Executrix of the late Mr. David Horner, deceased, will submit to public competition,

On Monday the 19th Oct., inst., and following days, at Eleven o'Clock at his late dwelling house, in the Diamond of Monaghan.

His Household Furniture, Shop Goods, Shop and Wareroom Fixtures, Tobacco Presses, Chandling utensils, &c., &c.

Also his interest in Four Fields, (town Parks) in Skehul the Brook, containing eleven Acres for one good life in being.

Terms:—Cash.

All persons to whom Mr. D. Horner stood indebted are requested to furnish their accounts to Mrs. Anne Horner, his Executrix, and all persons who stand indebted to his Estate will pay the same to her, to enable her to discharge all legal demands on his estate.

Monaghan, October 8th, 1846.

(1846-10-10, 2:5)

3559. Fatal Accident at Sea.—On Thursday morning, the 18th instant, two men from Dunfanaghy, named James Hogg and John Warden, went to fish off Tirmore [Tormore?], within two miles of the town, and not returning at the usual time, as the sea was known to be heavy all day, their friends became uneasy, and went to look out for them along the shore, when they found their little boat, or curragh, as it is called, wrecked on the beach near the place from which they set out in the morning. They are supposed to have been lost about two o'clock, p.m., by a wave from a rock known by the name of "The Little Leenan." Hogg has left four small orphans on the world for support; Warden, who was eighty years of age, has left a wife also destitute. Their bodies have not yet been found.—*Derry Sentinel*. (1846-10-17, 2:2)

3560. Marriage in High Life.—On the 8th inst., at Monkstown Church, by the Rev. R. Mauleverer, Alexander Montgomery, Esq., of Clonmannon, County of Wicklow, eldest son of the late Alexander Nixon Montgomery, of Beaumont-Park, county Monaghan, Esq., to Henrietta, daughter of Major Stafford, of Tully, County Cavan. (1846-10-17, 3:1)

3561. On Sunday the fourth inst., at Cavancaragh near Lisbellaw, a boy four years of age, son of Hugh Savage, went into a neighbour's house, when the woman of the house went out, leaving him with another boy behind her. It appears that while the other was stirring the fire, it caught Savage's clothes, and though both had the presence of mind to run out to a stream where one threw the other (Savage) in; yet he had been so much burned, that he died the following day. (1846-10-17, 3:4)

3562. On Tuesday night, in the churchyard at Ballymacin, the vault or tomb of the late Thomas Bell Booth, of Drumcarbin, late Grandmaster of the Orangemen of Cavan, was destroyed; the iron railing and metal chains which enclosed the tomb were carried off. Mr. Booth was shot upon the 22d of June, 1845, at Crossdoney. (1846-10-24, 2:2)

3563. The *Cork Examiner* reports deaths at Castlehaven, in that county, from starvation. Upwards of eight hundred starving creatures daily receive breakfast at Macroom union workhouse—their only sustenance. (1846-10-24, 3:5)

3564. The Life-Clock.—Translated from the German.

There is a little mystic clock
No human eye hath seen;
That beateth on—and beateth on,
From morning until e'en.

And when the soul is wrapped in sleep,
And heareth not a sound,
It ticks and ticks the livelong night,
And never runneth down.

Oh, wondrous is that work of art
Which knells the passing hour;
But are ne'er formed, nor mind conceived,
The life-clock's magic power.

Nor set in gold, nor decked with gems,
By wealth and pride possessed;
But rich or poor, or high or low,
Each bears it in his breast.

When life's deep stream mid beds of flowers
All still and softly glides,
Like the wavelets step with a gentle heats;
It warns of passing tides.

When passion nerves the warrior's arm,
For deeds of haste and wrong,
Though heeded not the dreadful sound,
The knell is deep and strong,

When eyes to eyes are gazing soft,
And tender words are spoken
Then fast and wild it rattles on,
As if with love 'twere broken.

Such is the clock that measures life,
Of flesh and spirit blended;
And thus 'twill run within the breast
Till that strange life is ended.

(1846-10-24, 4:1)

3565. The Late Storm.—Melancholy Accident and Loss of Life.—On Monday last, an accident of a serious and fatal nature took place near Kilgobbin, at the residence of Emanuel Bailey, Esq. It will be remembered that on the previous Sunday evening, there was a very severe thunder storm, which played so violently upon the garden wall of Mr. Bailey's house, that it was almost thrown down—so much so, that it was found necessary to remove it the following day; and it was during its removal, that the unfortunate accident, about to be detailed, took place. Two men were engaged to take it down, and while doing so, Mrs. Bailey, who happened to be present at the moment, called out to them, that the wall was falling, upon which they both endeavoured to get away from under it; but before they had time to do so, it fell upon them, and killed one of them on the spot; the other was sent to the hospital, and lingered for a few hours, when death also put an end to his sufferings. An inquest was held on the bodies of the deceased the day following, when a verdict of "accidental death" was returned by the jury. (1846-10-31, 1:4)

3566. The Late Storm.—The late Gale—Disasters at Sea.—We are sorry to hear that a large quantity of timber, apparently the cargo and wreck of an American vessel, was on Saturday thrown upon the coast between Portrush and Banmouth. A piece of wreck, apparently the cabin door of a vessel, was found at Port Vantage, and, it is said, some casks of salted provisions have also been found. We have not been able to learn any particulars respecting the crew, but it is supposed all must have perished. (1846-10-31, 1:4)

3567. The Late Storm.—Island of Arran—The late Gale.—We are just informed by our correspondent that it was an awful and heartrending sight to view the harbour of Killiney on the morning of the 21st. A smack, laden with slates from Kilrush, which had taken shelter there, is broken to pieces, and no account had of her crew. Sixteen hookers belonging to the island are more or less injured; some of them varying in value from £30 to £50, are beyond repairing.—Killiney may be called a fishing village, because there are more than one hundred families whose sole support is the sea, several of whom are now bereft of all means by the loss of their boats, and any casualty coming at such a period of real distress, is doubly lamentable.—*Galway Mercury*. (1846-10-31, 1:4)

3568. Chancery.—John Jackson, Plaintiff; Anne Hamilton, widow, James M'Watty, Thomas Hamilton the elder, Thomas Hamilton the younger, and others, Defendants.—Anne Hamilton, widow, Plaintiff; John Jackson, James M'Watty, Thomas Hamilton, senior, Thomas Hamilton, junior, and others, Defendants.

Pursuant to the Decree in these Causes, bearing date the 20th day of June, 1846, I hereby require all persons having Incumbrances affecting the respective shares of the Defendants, Thomas Hamilton the younger, and Campbell Hamilton, in the residuary Estates under the Will of William Hamilton, deceased, the Testator in the pleadings in these Causes named, to come in before me at my Chambers, on the Inns Quay, in the City of Dublin, on or before Monday, the 23d day of November next, and proceed to prove same; otherwise they will be precluded the benefit of said decree.

Dated this 20th day of October, 1846.

Jeremiah John Murphy.

Robert Murdock, Solicitor, for Plaintiff,
Chambers, 31 College Green, Dublin.

(1846-10-31, 3:4)

3569. Many years have elapsed since so much sickness was known in Dublin as at present. English cholera, typhus, and cold are the prevailing complaints. (1846-10-31, 4:6)

3570. Very bad cases of fever, from a deficiency of food, damaged potatoes and other deleterious diet, are spreading though the country. (1846-10-31, 4:6)

3571. Two men are now in Cork, who were taken off the mast of a vessel named the *Rose*, wrecked in the late gale. They were taken off by the crew of one of Mr. Scott's boats of Cove. They state the horrible fact that a third man, who was with them on the spar, was eaten by them, they being driven to that frightful extremity by excess of hunger. (1846-10-31, 4:6)

3572. Commission Court—Wednesday, Oct. 27. Bigamy.—*The Queen v. Mary Downes.*

Mary Downes, alias Fitzgerald, alias Browne, a respectable looking young woman, about 30 years of age, was placed at the bar, and indicted for having intermarried with Henry Augustus Browne, in the month of June, 1842, her former husband, Wm. Fitzgerald, being alive.

Considerable interest was attached to the proceedings in this case from the fact that Mr. Browne, who is a barrister, and the prisoner's second husband, was himself tried and convicted of bigamy a few months since, and sentenced to seven years' transportation, for marrying Miss Copeland, daughter of Charles Copeland, Esq., the manager of the Royal Bank in this city, having previously married the prisoner. The court was crowded to excess at an early hour, and particularly by members of the bar.

Counsel for the Crown—Messrs. Plunket, Q.C.; Smyly, and J. Pennefather.

For the prisoner—Messrs. Power and Levy; agent, Mr. Stanley.

For Mr. Copeland—Messrs. Tomb, Q.C., and Rolleston. Solicitor, Mr. Johnston.

For Mr. Brown [sic]—Messrs. Fitzgibbon, Q.C., and Corballis; agent, Mr. Humfreys.

Mr. Brown was in court, seated beside his counsel, having been brought up on a *habeas corpus*.

When the prisoner was called on to plead, she declared that she was "guilty."

Mr. Power said, that as her counsel, he wished, before the plea was received, to say that she was adopting this course contrary to his advice, for he believed she had a very fair chance of an acquittal, if she let the case be investigated. He could not tell why she was so determined on the subject, and he wished to let her know, that she ought not to persist in her plea under any impressions that she would escape punishment by it, for he was afraid that she was influenced by some false feeling.

Mr. Justice Burton, addressing the prisoner, informed her that she was indicted for an offence of a very serious description, and one which might be very much mitigated by circumstances if she allowed the case to go to trial, by pleading "not guilty," which would not involve her in any additional punishment; he would, therefore, give her some time to reflect upon what she had said, and allow her to consult with her professional advisers, in order to see if, by any possibility, she might think proper to change her mind.

Mr. Tomb, Q.C., said he appeared for parties very much interested in the result of the proceedings, and he considered it his duty to state that there was evidence in the possession of his client, and of the crown, which would not be considered matter for mitigation.

Mr. Corballis—I must object to any statement at this stage of the proceeding.

Mr. Smyly—The observations of Mr. Tomb should certainly be postponed until the prisoner has an opportunity of consulting with her counsel.

Mr. Tomb—I know all the facts, and I also know it is most desirable that there should be a full investigation.

Judge Burton—But we cannot now enter upon it.

Mr. Tomb—Perhaps your Lordship would suggest to the prisoner—

Judge Burton—I can't do anything of the kind.

Mr. Smyley [sic]—Suppose your Lordships take up some other business, to give the prisoner an opportunity of recording her plea?

The Court, having approved of this suggestion, proceeded to rule the books; and when they had disposed of all the business remaining, the prisoner was again placed at the bar, and presented in her former plea of guilty, handing in an affidavit in mitigation, which she swore in open court.

Their Lordships having directed it to be read,

The Clerk of the Peace proceeded to read the following document: —

"The Queen at the prosecution of *Henry Augustus Browne and others v. Mary Fitzgerald, alias Downes*, the prisoner in this case, maketh oath and saith, that when she was very young, her parents, who were very respectable persons, residing in the town of Tralee, in the county of Kerry, died, leaving deponent utterly destitute and unprovided for, and that, consequently, to earn a livelihood, this deponent was obliged to go service in the capacity of lady's maid. Deponent said she continued in the same capacity up to the end of the year 1838. This deponent saith, that early in life, she formed an acquaintance, in the county of Kerry, with one William Fitzgerald, son of a farmer, residing near Tralee, and that deponent, at different times, received from the said Fitzgerald proposals of Marriage. Deponent further saith, that in the year 1839, the said William Fitzgerald again entreated this deponent to consent to marry him, and this deponent was married to him in the month of February, 1839, by a clergyman named James Maginn, in the Straw-market, in the city of Dublin, without the knowledge of his family.—This deponent further saith, that she and the said Fitzgerald thenceforward lived together in the city of Dublin, about two months, when deponent and her said husband finding their circumstances such as did not enable them to live comfortably, agreed to separate for a time. This deponent having experience that said Fitzgerald was unable to support her, this deponent determined to return to service to obtain a livelihood, deponent being then destitute of the means of subsistence. Deponent further saith, that about the month of September, 1839, this deponent entered the service of Colonel Dominick Browne, of Browne Hall, in the county of Mayo, as lady's maid, and continued to live in the said service until the month of June, 1842. Deponent further saith that said Fitzgerald, after his marriage with deponent, and after their separation as aforesaid, never lived with deponent, except on two occasions for some days, at different intervals of time. Deponent further saith, that from the neglectful treatment of the said Fitzgerald towards deponent, she believed the said Fitzgerald had deserted her. Deponent further saith, that while in the service of said Colonel Browne, Mr. Henry Augustus Browne, son of said Colonel Brown [sic], paid this deponent attentions, which this deponent foolishly, and as she now bitterly regrets, acquiesced in. This deponent further saith, that blinded by the nature of the said Mr. Henry Augustus Browne's attention to her, and believing then, and long after, that her marriage with the said William Fitzgerald was invalid, and not binding in law, she and the said Fitzgerald having been Roman Catholics, and the marriage having been performed by a Protestant clergyman, whom she heard was a degraded clergyman, not qualified to perform said marriage; and the said Fitzgerald having ceased to live and hold any intercourse with deponent for a long time previous, she, the said deponent, believed she was free to marry again, and under such impression, did marry the said Henry Augustus Browne, in the month of June, 1842, and from whom she secreted the fact of her said marriage, with the said Fitzgerald. Deponent further saith that, although she is not aware of the grievous error she has committed, she never would have been induced to do so, had she not formerly entertained the belief that, when she married the said Henry Augustus Browne, her former marriage with said William Fitzgerald was invalid in law. Deponent further saith, that on the 11th of August last, this hon. court was pleased to make an order, on the application of counsel for the crown, to postpone her trial, and to admit her to bail, herself in 100*l*., and two sureties in 25*l*. each; and saith that, the bail having been excessive, this deponent was unable to procure such bail, in consequence of which, this deponent has been a close prisoner every since she was confined in Newgate.

"Sworn in open court, before the Chief Baron and Mr. Justice Burton."

Mr. Power said, that as his client persisted in her plea, and made this affidavit, he felt it was his duty to state that it was borne out by the information, and he expressed a hope that the court would deal with her case as lightly as possible.

Mr. Justice Burton then proceeded to address the prisoner, and observed that, from the facts disclosed on her affidavit, and considering her age at the time of her first marriage, her sex, and that the crown put forward nothing in aggravation, he thought the ends of justice would be satisfied by sentencing her to two months' imprisonment, in addition to what she had already suffered. (1846-11-07, 1:3)

3573. Death from Glanders.—A smart, active, and intelligent man, named Michael Connolly, and about 50, a carrier, who lived on the borders of Clara, and who drove two horses in the employment of Messrs. Goodby and Sons, took suddenly and alarmingly ill a few days back, when he presented himself to Dr. Walsh, Dispensary House, Clara, who, on examination, interrogated him as to whether he had or had not a sick beast in his establishment, at which he replied that one of his horses had lately the button farcy—he was now well, although he had a little running at the nose, from cold. These, with the symptoms appearing, convinced the doctor that he had contracted that dreadful malady; still he was unable to convince either Connolly or his family of the perilous situation in which he was then placed. Next day, he got worse, became delirious, and ultimately died, a deplorable and pitiable object in a short space of time. The melancholy fate of poor Connolly should prove a sufficient warning to all those who (*continued...*)

3573, continued: ...follow old and hard-wrought horses, that are constantly entering public stables, where all kinds of diseases attending horses are to be found, that they cannot be too cautious of the fearful and calamitous consequences that may ensue.—*King's County Chronicle*. (1846-11-07, 2:3)

3574. On Friday, a young woman, named Mary Corrigan, was killed at the Marsh mills, Drogheda. The deceased, with three or four other young girls, were amusing themselves by clinging to the hoister then at work, and in this way, passing up and down through the trap doors, getting off and on occasionally, as caprice might move them. The deceased, in attempting to stop on the floor on which she worked, was struck by the trap door, and so much injured, that she died whilst being removed to the hospital. (1846-11-14, 1:3)

3575. Awful Suicide.—On Thursday night, an awful suicide took place at the Wicklow Hotel, Wicklow-street. Surgeon Edward Ellis of Longford, a gentleman most respectably connected, while labouring under temporary derangement, inflicted a wound upon his throat with a razor, from the effects of which he died in Mercer's Hospital, whither he was conveyed, at seven o'clock on Friday night. An inquest was held on the body on Saturday, and a verdict in accordance with the above facts returned. (1846-11-14, 1:5)

3576. A man named Cunningham, residing at Boyle, died last week from want; he had to go three miles every day to his work on the public roads, three more back, for eightpence a day, and had seven of a family to support. (1846-11-14, 2:1)

3577. The Magistracy.—His Excellency the Lord Lieutenant has approved of Robert W. Cope, Esq., of Loughgall, being appointed a Deputy Lieutenant of the county of Armagh, in the room of Leonard Dobbin, Esq., deceased. (1846-11-14, 2:4)

3578. The *Louth Advertiser* states, that fever is on the increase in Dundalk. (1846-11-14, 2:4)

3579. The Church.—The Rev. George Truelock, A.M., Vicar General of Killala, has been appointed by the Lord Bishop of Tuam, to the Archdeacon of Killala, vacant by the death of the late venerable Thomas Kingsbury, the ecclesiastical commissioners and privy council having recommended the continuance of this appointment of his excellency the Lord Lieutenant. ...

The Rev. Joseph Morton, A.M., Surrogate of Elphin, has been nominated to the vicarages of Creeve, Shankhill, and Kilmacumsy, by the Lord Bishop of Kilmore, &c., vacant by the demise of the Rev. Oliver Carey. (1846-11-14, 4:5)

3580. Illness of the Poet Moore.—We have received from London a private letter, dated Thursday last, from which, with much regret, we give the following paragraph:—I lament to have to tell you of the rapidly declining health of Ireland's most honoured poet. The sun of life is fast setting, and it is feared that his dissolution is near at hand. His career, until within these few years, has been a glorious one; and when he departs from amongst us, let us hope that it will be for that place where only his melodies can be excelled.—*Western Star*.—(The English papers are silent on this subject.—We sincerely hope our contemporary has been misinformed.) (1846-11-21, 1:4)

3581. The Church.—The Lord Lieutenant has been pleased to appoint the Rev. Ralph Sadler [sic], A.M., Curate of St. Anne's, and Chaplain to his Excellency, to the valuable living of Rincurren, in the diocese of Cork, vacant by the death of the Rev. Benjamin Morris. (1846-11-21, 1:5)

3582. Monaghan Fever Hospital.—Last week, we drew the attention of our readers to this institution, in which a large number of inmates are at present under medical treatment. If the number of applicants continue[s] to increase, the institution will, in a very short time, be without funds, and it is, therefore, necessary to adopt measures to increase the support hitherto afforded it. It occurs to us that, if charity sermons were preached in all the Churches, Meeting Houses, and Chapels in the barony, that a sum would be made up sufficient to meet the emergency. It has become too much the fashion in asking private subscriptions to expect a guinea, and by many it is thought derogatory to give less—and hence, persons either give a guinea or nothing. By means of sermons, small sums could be got, and the aggregate would, perhaps, be greater than what could accrue from guinea subscriptions.

We throw out the hint to the committee of management, who, if they approve of it, should put themselves in communion with the clergy of the various parishes. (1846-11-21, 2:5)

3583. Court of Delegates—Nov. 24.—The Late Bigamy Case.—*Augustus Henry Browne v. Charles Copeland*—Mr. Justice Perrin, Sir Henry Meredyth, Bar., Dr. Longfield, Q.C., and Dr. Finlay, Q.C., sat in his lordship's chamber yesterday morning, to make arrangements for hearing an appeal brought by Mr. Browne, who is at present under sentence of transportation for bigamy, and whose case is so well known to the public, against the decision of Dr. Radcliffe, the judge of the Ecclesiastical Court, which decreed a divorce between him and Miss Elsey Isabella Copeland, daughter of Mr. Charles Copland [sic], the manager of the National Bank. The appeal arises out of the late trial of Mary Downes in the Commission Court, who was charged with bigamy, and who pleaded guilty to the indictment, which alleged that she had married Mr. Browne, her first husband being alive, and the fact of her guilt is relied on as the ground of Mr. Browne's application to be discharged, and for a reversal of the decree of Dr. Radcliffe.

Their Lordships fixed the 14th of December for hearing the appeal, and then adjourned. (1846-11-28, 2:2)

3584. Fatal Accident.—A dreadful accident occurred on Monday morning, at the extensive flax-spinning and thread works, belonging to Mr. Barbour, of Hilden, in consequence of the bursting of the steam boiler. Such was the force of the explosion, that one man named Hugh Fleming, an engineer, was blown into a corner of the House, and so shockingly injured that he died in a short time afterwards. A loft above the boiler was torn up, and a number of girls who were there at work, severely scalded; several of them were immediately removed to the Infirmary at Lisburn, where, of course, every possible exertion will be used for their recovery. Since the above was written, the body of another of the workers, a lad about fifteen years of age, was discovered in the water that runs near the factory; it is supposed that he had been warming himself at the engine-house fire, when the accident took place, from whence he had been driven by the bursting of the boiler into the place in which he was found.—*Banner of Ulster*. (1846-11-28, 2:2)

3585. More Deaths from Starvation.—The Rev. B. Duncan, P.P., of Swineford, in the county of Mayo, communicates the following ghastly fact to the *Freeman's Journal*:—No later than Friday morning last, a man named Thomas Philbion, from the parish of Bohala, died in town of actual starvation. He held out as long as he could, in the vain hope of getting work. That failing, he came for the purpose of being received into the poor-house, the last extremity. But, alas! it was too late for him to seek any relief this side the grave. Before he reached the place of his destination, he died from weakness and inanition.

We learn from the *Cork Examiner* that at an inquest held on the body of Ellen Allen, in Ballinhassig, on Saturday, a verdict was returned that deceased had died of disease of the lungs, and the doctor deposed that her death was accelerated by the want of food.

On Thursday last, Mr. Atkinson, coroner, held an inquest on the body of Thomas Hopkins at Rathnamagh, near Crossmolina. Patrick Langan, son-in-law to the deceased, deposed that the family consisted of five children, himself, his wife, and deceased, and that they had been for the last six weeks subsisting on a scanty morsel on some days, and on others, were obliged to remain without it. Witness is certain that want of food was the cause of death. Dr. M'Nair examined the body, and corroborated the testimony of the witness, and the jury returned a verdict accordingly.—*Mayo Constitution*. (1846-11-28, 2:3)

3586. Melancholy and Fatal Accident.—On the night of Saturday, the 21st, inst., Mr. Joseph Knox, jun., of Shanemulla, near Tullycorbet Church, in this county, was found dead by the side of the road leading from Ballybay to his own residence. Deceased had been in the fair of Ballybay, and was on his way home when the melancholy event occurred; he was discovered by a man of the name of Harkness, who was also returning from the fair. An inquest was held on the body of the deceased, on Monday the 23rd inst., by William Charles Waddell, Esq., of Lisnavane House, coroner. It appeared, by the depositions of witnesses, that there were marks on the road of the horse, on which the deceased was riding, having stumbled and fallen; the forehead of the horse and his side was [sic] dirty; deceased was known to have been a man of temperate habits, and it was deposed by the witnesses, who saw him last alive, that he was in a state of sobriety. The jury returned a verdict, "that Joseph Knox came to his death in consequence of a fall from his horse, producing a concussion on the left temporal bone, causing congestion on the brain." Deceased was an intelligent and respectable farmer; he was universally beloved, and is very much lamented by all classes in the neighbourhood in which he resided. He gave employment to a large number of labourers—to the poor he was most kind and liberal, and in the present circumstances of the country, they particularly feel that they have lost a friend who had a heart to sympathise with them, and was forward to render them assistance. (1846-11-28, 2:6)

3587. Awful Calamity at Sea.—Clonakilty, Nov. 21st, 1846.—Two shipwrecks have occurred off the coast in Danny Cove Bay—one vessel, the *Chester*, from Quebec for Liverpool, completely lost, all hands perished; the other, the *Jessie Torrens*. There were on board twenty-one hands, including a gentleman's son on his return home to Edinburgh. The captain's wife, a young woman of eighteen years, was washed overboard, and not as yet found. More would have been lost but for the courageous attempt of Mr. E.C. Croker, of Ballyva-house, aided by his son George, who, at the risk of their own lives, were let by a rope down a cliff, at least one hundred feet, and rescued one of the crew from destruction. Two lives have been preserved in one week by these gentlemen.—*Cork Constitution*. (1846-11-28, 3:3)

3588. Life—If we consider things impartially, this world is our grave; nor do we really live till we burst the flesh prison, and get beyond the visible skies. (1846-12-05, 1:3)

3589. More Deaths by Starvation.—County of Cork. The Deaths from Starvation at Skibberene.—The Inquests.—The inquests on the bodies of the three persons, reported to have died of starvation, was held in the Court-house of Skibbereen, on Thursday, before Franklin Baldwin, Esq., coroner.

The first inquest was on the body of Michael M'Carthy, of Litter, who died on the 16th of November.

John M'Carthy sworn and examined by Mr. T. M'C. Doowning [sic], on behalf and as one of the relief committee. I live at Litter. My father, Michael M'Carthy, died last Monday week in his house at Litter. Previous to that he was a healthy man, and was working on the Adrigole road. I worked on (*continued...*)

3589, continued: ...the same road, which was about two miles from our house. We were four weeks at work before he died. We got no wages for a fortnight, before he died. It was on the road we used to be paid. On the Thursday before he died, he ate some bread on the road. There were three pints of flour in a cake for me and my father. He did not come home that night, having taken a lodging near the road at 3d. a week. Neither he nor I ate anything that night. We went to work on Friday without breakfast, not having anything to eat. In the evening, I went and bought a 1-1/2d. cake, which I divided with my father. I paid for it. My father had the money in his pocket. I pledged my jacket for 6d. on Saturday, having left the road at 12 o'clock to come into town to do so. I left the road because my father fell on the work from hunger, having eaten nothing since two o'clock the day before, and then I came and pledged my jacket. I was hungry myself, bought but a halfpenny cake for myself, and carried the 5-1/2d. to the road to buy some bread for my two sisters; my father was sitting near a fire where he was put by Mr. Corcoran, the steward, and eating some bread the check clerk gave him. He then recovered a little, and walked home with me. He was weak when going home. Up to that time, my father was always a strong, working man, and never had a cough. Never heard him complain of a pain in his side. It was Mr. Hungerford paid the men on that road.When he got home, he went into a neighbour's house, and said that a fire and something to eat was a good thing. When we came home that night, he had nothing in the world in the way of food. I came to town that night and could get no meal to buy.

Mr. Downing—And a government store groaning here under it.

Witness—I bought no bread in the town, as I thought I would get it better in the country for my money. I thought it better to buy meal than bread.—I bought a penny cake for the little girl. On Sunday, we had nothing in the house. My father and the youngest of the girls were in bed all Sunday. On Monday morning, my father sent me to town to the Court-house, to see would we get any of our hire. It was a very wet day, and I watched the Court-house all day, but no one appeared, and I got no money. My sister came with me, her father telling her if I did not get the hire, for her to beg some food about the town. My sister begged and got a small jug of broth at Mr. Whelpy's.—On Sunday night, my sister came into Skibbereen and purchased 2-1/2d. worth of one-way flour, and we made gruel of it that night. My father drank about a pint and a half of it. When my sister and I came home on Monday night, we were very wet. My father and the little girl were in bed all day on Monday. When I went into the house, I called my father, who appeared to be snoring. There was no fire in the hearth, and I put a sod of turf behind it. We poured a little of the broth in a basin, and I lit a wisp of straw, and went to my father who I thought was asleep. I took up his head and shook him, and I called him five or six times, but he did not answer. He never spoke after, having died in about an hour and a half after. The little girl was in bed, although having eaten nothing.—My other sister came on Sunday into the town to buy meal, but could not get it. I know that if my father had money to purchase food, he would be alive today. My sisters are in the workhouse since. I had no means of getting a coffin for my father, or a sheet to lay over him, nor a candle to light. The bed was some dirty straw. The bed clothes were pawned, and my sister's petticoat.

Mr. Downing.—There's misery for you.

To a Juror.—My father held a farm, but the potatoes having failed, the landlord, Tom Dunston, seized our horse and corn, and we had to leave. Tom Dunston was broken himself since.

To the Coroner.—I have since then been paid the wages due to myself and father.

To Mr. Downing.—I have not since been on the road, as I had no place.

Patrick Dore, Esq., M.D., surgeon, sworn—I think the immediate cause of death was inflammation of the lungs. I am of opinion that the disease was brought on from cold and exposure, and the want of sufficient food would make a person less capable of resisting cold.

John Sullivan sworn—I am clerk on the Adrigole road. I knew Michael M'Carthy. On the Saturday before he died, I saw him stretched across a bank, with a few coals of fire before him. I asked him what was the matter with him, when he made a weak answer that he did not know. My dinner having come up at the time, I gave him part of it, and it recovered him a little, and the overseer sent him home with his son. It struck me that he wanted food. The people on the road were a fortnight on that Saturday without being paid. They were not paid until the Saturday after the Tuesday the man died. Mr. Gaynor, the assistant-engineer, advanced the son 8s. out of his own pocket.

The jury retired, and after half an hour's absence, returned the following verdict:—"We find that the deceased, Michael M'Carthy, died of disease of the lungs, accelerated by cold and want of food."

The next inquest was on the body of James Purcell of Litter, who died on the 18th of November.

Ellen Purcell sworn—I am daughter to deceased.—He died on Wednesday week. He had a wife and three children. He was a farmer, but was lately a labourer. He worked on the Adrigole road. There was a fortnight's wages due to him. He sometimes had food and sometimes not. They got it sometimes by pawning their clothes. He was at work the Saturday before he died. I do not think we ate anything on Friday, but on Saturday he had a pound of bread between himself and his son. He got weak on the road on Saturday. On Sunday, we had no food in the house. He remained in bed from Saturday until he died. I got no food for him on Monday, as all our things were pawned. He drank water on Monday. He asked a woman on Saturday night to give him a pint of milk until he got wages, and she refused him. We had no food on Thursday until that night, when the priest came, who gave him 6d., and Mr. Downing another 6d. We bought some milk and coffee, and a glass of wine. I was running that day to try to get something for him. I got nothing myself, as I did not care for myself, if I could get it for him (here the witness wept bitterly.) He took a little of the wine and coffee. I put some bread in the coffee and gave him a couple of spoonfuls of it, but he was hardly able to swallow it. He died the next day. He couldn't take any more from the time he took the couple of spoonfuls. He didn't send me to get anything for him. He said there was money due to him on the road, but he could not get it to buy something for them to eat.—That was on Monday. Mr. Warner, the saddler, in Skibbereen, got a coffin for him on Friday.

Mr. Downing—The jury and police made up a collection for them as well as Mr. Warner.

Witness.—We had neither fire nor candles when he died. We got the hire on the Friday after he died.—If my father was paid his hire, I know he would be alive to-day.

Dr. Dore examined—I am certain the cause of his death was want of food.

Rev. James Freke—I know a lady who found two interesting females at her door, quite emaciated and weak and, after giving them a table spoonful of soup, she fainted.

Rev. R.F. Webb—I have met frequent instances of the same.

The jury retired and found the following verdict:—"We find that the deceased, James Purcell, died at Litter, for want of food, occasioned by his not having received the fortnight's wages due to him on the Adrigole road under the board of works."

Mr. Downing—Two of the jury were for finding wilful murder against the board of works.

The next inquest was on the body of Denis Bohane, of Kiladerry, who died on the 11th November.

Judith Donovan sworn—I am sister to deceased, who died coming home from the Tragumina road, where he was at work. He was a young man, unmarried. There were in the family my father, mother, my husband, four other children and myself. There were 10s. due to him for the fortnight and three days, and that's what killed him. I declare, as well as if I were at confession, we had not a quart of meal in the house the day before he died, and that I bought that night. The road was two miles from our house. I made a cake of meal, and gave it to deceased and her husband to carry on the road, but they ate but a little of it, and left the rest to the children. This was the day before he died. We got the amount of the wages of my husband, who had 10d. a day, from Madam Townsend, who was paid every week.

Mr. Dore examined—I never in all my life opened a healthier body. I have no doubt he died from want of food. He decidedly died of starvation.

The jury returned the following verdict:—"We find that deceased, Denis Bohane, died on the 11th inst., on the road at Drishane, from want of food, occasioned by his not having received the fortnight's wages due to him on the Tragumina road."

In the absence of the jury, the following conversation took place:—

Father Fitzpatrick wished to know what was to be done for 110 people, who were starving about the streets, having been dismissed from the works ten days ago?

Mr. Downing—And plenty of works have been presented.

Father Fitzpatrick—I applied to Mr. Gaynor, telling him that all had pledged whatever they possessed; but he said he had room on roads, but could not put them on, owing to a late regulation, which required that their names should be returned by Captain Gordon.

Rev. R.F. Webb—The state of the town is frightful.

Father Fitzpatrick—It is really horrifying.

The jury having signed the inquisitions, the Court separated.—*Cork Constitution*. (1846-12-05, 1:4)

3590. Case in Chancery.—The Lord Chancellor gave judgment in the case of the Misses M'Carthy, claiming against the legatees of their father's property. The Misses M'Carthy are nuns, and had signed deeds in favour of the community, under which deeds the present claim was urged. The Lord Chancellor gave his decision at considerable length, dismissing the bill with costs, on the ground that compulsion had been used in the procuring the execution of the deeds under which the plaintiffs claimed. This was the sole ground upon which his lordship pronounced a decision; on the other points, he avoided offering an opinion. (1846-12-05, 1:5)

3591. Melancholy Accident.—On Monday morning, a very melancholy and fatal accident occurred at Hilliden, near Lisburn. Two individuals were killed, and five others seriously wounded, by the bursting of the flue of the steam boiler in the works belonging to Mr. Barber's mill. (1846-12-05, 1:5)

3592. The Church.—On the 25th instant, the Lord Bishop of Kilmore, Elphin, and Ardagh collated the Rev. William Digby to the united rectory and vicarages of Clongish and Clongish-Killoe, vacant by the death of the Rev. Dr. Crawford; the Rev. Alexander Hudson to the united rectories and vicarages of Killashee and Clonodonel, vacant by the resignation of the Rev. William Digby; and the Rev. Theodore Octavius Moore to the vicarage of Clonbrony, vacant by the death of the Rev. Dr. Crawford. (1846-12-05, 2:3)

3593. The Church.—Clergymen Deceased.

Diocess of Down—The Rev. Joshua Free, prebend of Dunsford, county of Down; patron, the Bishop.

Diocess of Elphin—The Rev. John Yates, vicar of Drumcliffe, county of Sligo; patron, the Bishop.

Diocess of Derry—The Rev. J. Christie, perpetual curate of Faughanville, in the county of Derry; patron, the Dean.

Diocess of Cork—The Rev. B. Morris, rector of Rincurran, county of Cork; patron, the Crown.

Diocess of Emly—The Rev. J. Whitly, Rector of the Union of Duntrileage, county Tipperary; patron, the Bishop. (1846-12-05, 2:3)

3594. More Deaths from Starvation.—On last Saturday, a labouring man, named William Fitzpatrick, died at Tea-lane, Maryborough. From the evidence given at the Inquest, an intelligent jury found for their verdict, that the deceased died of want and destitution. Language is inadequate to describe the horrifying misery with which the deceased was encompassed. The night he died, we understand, there was neither fire nor candle-light in the wretched hovel; no drink to allay the death-thirst of his parched lips but cold water; while his bed was a wisp of straw, on a damp floor, with little or no covering—*Leinster Express*.

At the last meeting of the Sligo relief committee, reported accurately in the *Sligo Journal*, the Rev. Malachi Brennan, P.P., stated that two of his parishioners had just died of absolute starvation; and that one family, eight in number, were living for ten days on two stone of oatmeal!

We regret to state, on the authority of Mr. Nimmo, C.E., that two men named Thomas Carter, and James Davin, of the village of Pullbough, have died this week from starvation, having been unable to procure food or employment.—*Galway Mercury*. (1846-12-12, 2:1)

3595. On Wednesday morning last, at the kitchen gate-house of James Ivers, Esq., Glenfield, near Kilmal[lock], county Limerick, John O'Donnell, wife and son—the latter a very fine young man, were found dead; the wife and son lying on the floor, and the father, an [old?] man, dead in bed. Doctor O'Connell, was called [*illegible*] early that morning, and on his arrival, found life extinct in them all, and apparently so for some hours. An inquest was held on Thursday by Charles Ben[net], Esq., coroner, and a post mortem examination [*illegible*] by Doctor Swyny, of Bruff, and it being deposed [in] the medical evidence that death was caused by [*illegible*] respiration and poisonous effects of carbonic acid, produced by combustion in a very small and conf[ined] bed-room. A verdict was returned accordingly. (1846-12-12, 2:6) *Note: A fold in the right-hand margin rendered some of the words illegible.*

3596. Appalling Destitution—Famine, Disease, Death. —We extract the following letter from the *Cork Constitution* of Saturday:—

To His Grace Field-Marshal the Duke of Wellington.—My Lord Duke.—Without apology to preface, I presume so far to trespass on your grace as to state to you, and by the use of your illustrious name, to present to the public the following statement of what I have myself [witnessed] within the last three days:—

Having for many years been intimately connected with the western portion of the county of Cork, and possessing some small property there, I thought it right personally to investigate the truth of the several lamentable accounts which had reached me, of the appalling state of misery to which that part of the country was reduced.

I accordingly went on the 15th inst. to Skibbereen, and to give the instance of one townland which I visited, as an example of the state of the entire coast district, I shall state simply what I saw there. It is situate on the eastern side of Castlehaven harbour, and is named South Reen, in the parish of Myross. Being aware that I should have to witness scenes of hunger, I provided myself with as much bread as five men could carry, and on reaching the spot, I was surprised to find the wretched hamlet apparently deserted. I entered some of the hovels to ascertain the cause, and the scenes which presented themselves were such as no tongue or pen can convey the slightest idea of. In the first, six famished and ghastly skeletons, to all appearance dead, were huddled in a corner on some filthy straw, their sole covering what seemed a ragged horsecloth; their wretched legs hanging about, naked above the knees. I approached in horror, and found by a low moaning they were alive—they were in fever—four children, a woman, and what had once been a man. It is impossible to go through the detail—suffice it to say that in a few minutes, I was surrounded by at least 200 of such phantoms, such frightful spectres, as no words can describe. By far, the greatest number were delirious, either from famine or from fever. Their demoniac yells are still ringing in my ears, and their horrible images are fixed upon my brain. My heart sickens at the recital, but I must go on.

In another case, decency would forbid what follows, but it must be told. My clothes were nearly torn off in my endeavour to escape from the throng of pestilence around, when my neckcloth was seized from behind by a gripe which compelled me to turn. I found myself grasped by a woman with an infant apparently just born in her arms, and the remains of a filthy sack across her loins—the sole covering of herself and babe. The same morning, the police opened a house on the adjoining lands, which was observed shut for many days, and two frozen corpses were found lying upon the mud floor, half devoured by cats.

A mother, herself in fever, was seen the same day to drag out the corpse of her child, a girl about twelve, perfectly naked, and leave it half covered with stones. In another house, within 500 yards of the cavalry station of Skibbereen, the dispensary doctor found seven wretches lying unable to move under the same cloak. One had been dead many hours, but the others were unable to move either themselves or the corpse.

To what purpose should I multiply such cases? If these be not sufficient, neither would they hear who have the power to send relief and do not, even though one came from the dead. Let them, however, believe and tremble, that they shall one day hear the Judge of all the earth pronounce their tremendous doom, with the addition, "I was an hungred and ye gave me no meat; thirsty, and ye gave me no drink; naked, and ye clothed me not."

But I forgot to whom this is addressed. My lord, you are an old and justly honoured man. It is yet to your power to add another honor to your age, to fix another star, and that the brightest, in your galaxy of glory. You have access to our young and gracious Queen. Lay these things before her. She is a woman. She will not allow decency to be outraged.—She has at her command the means of at least mitigating the sufferings of the wretched survivors of this tragedy. They will soon be few, indeed in the district I speak of, if help be longer withheld.

Once more, my lord duke, in the name of starving thousands, I implore you to break the frigid and flimsy chain of official etiquette, and save the land of your birth, the kindred of that gallant Irish blood which you have so often seen lavished to support the honour of the British name, and let there be inscribed upon your tomb, "*Servata Hibernia.*"—I have the honour to be, my lord duke, your grace's obedient humble servant.

N.M. Cummins, J.P.

Ann-Mount, Cork, Dec. 17, 1846.

(1846-12-26, 2:3)

3597. County of Leitrim.—A few days since, a labouring man was found dead, near Clones, with a bag of meal under his arm. He was employed at the public works, was going home with his scanty store, after receiving his payment, when he dropped, never to rise. This is another case of death, by starvation.—*Ballinasloe Star*. (1847-01-02, 1:5)

3598. In Cork workhouse, seventy-four paupers died [last] week. The profit to the union in baking bread [*illegible*] the paupers averages £25 a week. (1847-01-02, 2:6) *Note: A fold in the margin renders some of the words illegible.*

3599. Starvation—Inquest in Tralee.—An inquest was held on Thursday, in Brogue-lane, before Justin Sapple, Esq., coroner, on the body of a man named Connell, a weaver. It appeared in evidence that the poor man had three children, the youngest four, and the eldest thirteen, whom, with a mother-in-law, aged 70, he was endeavouring to support. Sickness seized on all, and for the last few weeks, it appeared they continued to live daily on something about a penny worth of bread. At length, nature sunk under the pressure, and the poor creature was found in a miserable room, six feet in circumference, dead, unwashed, and unshaven, beside his two helpless children, and the old woman in a wad of straw, they being unable to crawl. The eldest child crept out yesterday to beg something for the rest, but even if she could bring anything, it was too late. The two children and old woman must die from exhaustion. It was a picture too harrowing to contemplate, and too appalling to describe. The coroner and jury made up the price of a coffin, and the verdict was, "death by starvation."—*Cork Examiner*. (1847-01-02, 3:1)

3600. On Monday, at Newtownbutler, a respectable lad named Clarke, was driving a horse, sitting in the cart, which, passing through a rut, upturned, and falling on the young man's head, smashed his skull into pieces. (1847-01-02, 3:1)

3601. On Wednesday, a poor man, at the public works near Wattlebridge, fell down and expired. Privation and want, it is thought, caused his death. His name was George Graham. (1847-01-02, 3:1)

3602. It is said that there is a great probability of the Quakers becoming extinct, their marriages having decreased considerably. (1847-01-02, 3:3)

3603. There were 15 deaths on Sunday se'nnight at the Cork Work-house, which is now over filled. (1847-01-02, 4:5)

3604. There is a fearful mortality raging in the poorhouse of Mohill, county of Leitrim, the number of deaths amounting to 15 a week. (1847-01-02, 4:5)

3605. Fire and Loss of Three Lives.—This morning, about half-past two o'clock, a fire broke out in the shop of Mr. Meares, bootmaker, Dame-street, opposite the Lower Castle-gate, from what cause we could not ascertain, which spread with such alarming rapidity that, in less than twenty minutes and before a supply of water was obtained, the entire building was enveloped in flames. The engines belonging to the office of the West of England, Sun, Royal Exchange, National, and Police, were, by the aid of Alderman Gavin's fire-plug, under the direction of Mr. Laurance, speedily at work; and, from the plentiful supply of water afforded, the fire was providentially prevented from extending to the Italian warehouse of Mr. Clarke, next door. The parish engines of St. Mary and St. Andrew were also present. Mr. Meare's children, and a niece, who was on a visit to him, unhappily perished in the flames. (1847-01-09, 1:3)

3606. Deaths by Starvation.—A very lamentable thing has occurred in the vicinage of this town during the course of the current week. Two females, in one house, died of fever, their sad condition being aggravated by extreme want. It was really a heart-rending spectacle to see two corpses lying together, their countenances all pallid and emaciated, bearing testimony to the manner of their death. Relief was (*continued...*)

3606, continued: ...afforded by Mr. Eyre, of the Castle, and other charitable gentlemen, but it came too late—fever-fed famine had already claimed them as his own.—Where, good Heavens, or when, shall these horrors cease.—*Ballinasloe Star*.
(1847-01-09, 2:3)

3607. Notice.—The Meeting-House of Second Monaghan, which was advertised in the *Northern Standard* of the 26th April 1845, and in the *Dublin Gazette*, of the 6th May, 1845, as registered for the celebration of Marriages therein, under the provisions of the *Act 7 and 8 Vic. chap. 81*, is situated in the Townland of Derrynacrew and not in that of Mullaghmore, as stated in the advertisement above mentioned.

Dated this 6th day of January, 1847.

John Goudy, Registrar,
Monaghan District.
(1847-01-09, 3:4)

3608. Mallon, one of the two men that were scalded by the bursting of a boiler in Mulholland and Hinds flax mill, Belfast, a few days ago, died from the effect of the injury he sustained. (1847-01-09, 4:5)

3609. It is the sober belief of many competent judges that the famine, this year, in Ireland, will prove more destructive to human life than the cholera, and that probably a million of persons will be sent away by it.
(1847-01-09, 4:5)

3610. Court of Delegates.—Saturday, Jan. 9.—*Henry A. Browne v. Charles Copeland.*—The examination of witnesses in this case was concluded on Saturday, and the evidence on both sides having closed,

The court intimated that, when they had read over the shorthand writer's notes, they would announce when judgment would be given. (1847-01-16, 1:4)

3611. Notice.—The Meeting-Houses of First Castleblayney and Broomfield, which were advertised in the *Dublin Gazette* and *Northern Standard* in the Month of April, 1845, as registered for the Celebration of Marriages therein, under the provisions of the *Act of 7th and 8th Victoria, chap. 81*, are situated, the former in the townland of Drummillard-B, and not in that of Derrykip, the latter in the townland of Brackagh and not in that of Broomfield, as stated in the advertisement above referred to.

William Rule, Registrar of Marriages
for the District of Castleblayney.
(1847-01-16, 3:6)

3612. The Rev. E. Condon, P.P., of Tallow, Waterford, has been summoned to petty sessions for celebrating a marriage between a recruiting sergeant, a Protestant, and a Catholic. (1847-01-16, 4:5)

3613. No less than eight deaths have occurred within the last week, in Tralee, half of which have been attributed to the effects of destitution. (1847-01-16, 4:5)

3614. State of the Country.—Progress of the Famine.

The accounts from the country still continue to present the same melancholy picture of suffering, disease, and death—suffering and disease borne with astonishing patience, and death welcomed as a happy release! The Rev. J. Molony, P.P., of Rosscarberry, writing to the *Cork Examiner*, declares that famine is slaying hundreds of victims in that locality. He says—"My assistant and I are administering the last rites of religion both day and night, and are called upon to attend several who have no apparent sickness of any kind, save exhaustion for want of food—and upon these occasions, we find many literally naked, even modest females who were obliged to pawn everything they had in shape of dress, to prolong existence."

A correspondent of the same journal, writing from Ballydehob, says deaths from hunger are fearfully on the increase; and in the mountain districts, they die unknown, unpitied, and, in most instances, are unburied for weeks.

In Dingle, where, we understand, some slight relief has been afforded by the government officer, the people are dying with such rapidity that it is deemed an impossibility to hold inquests, while deaths by starvation are looked on so much as a matter of course, that the police no longer deem it necessary to report them.

One of the male paupers admitted into the Tralee work-house on Tuesday, died next day, being unable to eat from intense exhaustion. On the *post mortem* examination, not a trace of food could be found in his stomach.

The Protestant clergyman of the parish of Killysherdiney, near Cootehill, writes to us that—"Within the last three days, three individuals have died of starvation in this parish, making in all seven persons in the last fortnight."

The work of death by starvation is progressing with fearful strides in every part of our country, and yet the government depot at Tarbert, in which we are told, in the language of official insolence, the Indian meal and biscuit are perfectly sweet,remain hermetically sealed.
(1847-01-23, 1:5)

3615. There were ten deaths in Dungarvan workhouse on Tuesday, and hundreds of paupers besiege the doors, claiming relief and admission, but the workhouse is crowded to excess. (1847-01-23, 3:3)

3616. Last week, Mr. Dowell, of Castlecoote, three miles from Athlone, died of glanders, which melancholy distemper he took from his horse a few days previous to his death. (1847-01-23, 4:4)

3617. It is stated that the wealthiest widow in Ireland is about to bring an action for breach of promise of marriage against a Duke lately wedded to love without money. (1847-01-23, 4:5)

3618. A child, about four years old, belonging to Mr. Waddle, Watchmaker, Aughnacloy, was burned to death on Thursday last, by its clothes having caught fire. (1847-01-30, 1:4)

3619. The chairmanship of the Primitive Wesleyan Methodist Society of Ireland is vacant by the lamented death of the venerable Adam Averill, cotemporary of the celebrated John Wesley, at the patriarchal age of 93 years. (1847-01-30, 1:5)

3620. The rectory of Ardstraw, in the diocese of Derry, has become vacant by the death of the Rev. Richard Herbert Nash, D.D., for some time senior fellow of Trinity College, Dublin. This rectory is in the patronage of the college. (1847-01-30, 1:5)

3621. The Famine.—The state of distress is becoming frightful in this county. The poor houses, with the exception of Monaghan, are crammed choke full. In Clones, the guardians have taken tenements in the town, where the miserable victims are stowed away in hundreds, and of course, in such masses of misery, death and disease are rife—daily victims leave those last resources of the wretched, for the cold tomb where their troubles are at rest; and the eyes of the survivors look with gloom foreboding of a similar and hasty fate, upon the sad processions that bear their comrades to the grave. Want and woe are in every home—and it is not only the lack of food that appalls the charitable visitor to those haunts of famine—but the sight of shivering wretches without rags enough to protect [*illegible*]buat modesty, for every article has gone to the pawnbroker, to appease the unquenchable cries of hunger. There is an utter demoralization in the land—honesty, virtue, decency fall down before the insatiable moloch of want—men starved on in silence, while women and children begged—then strong men begged—then they became degraded in their own eyes, and they demanded—now they rob, in open day—in the light of Heaven's own sun—men who boasted that not one of their generation was ever accused of crime,—that they were poor but honest—those men rob, plunder, and with greedy jaws, like ravenous beasts, devour that which they got with crime—to them, crime no more. The moral defences of the nation are breaking down before leviathan misery, which crushes beneath its weight, and into chaos, the demarcation between good and evil—between right and wrong. Where will this mischief end?—what will become of us if we lose our moral code?—if not the horror of evil in itself, but the fear of punishment alone, keeps men from crime—then farewell to virtue—farewell the big hopes that swelled men's hearts for fatherland, and roused to virtuous exertion the patriot philosopher, who would regenerate a people. Demoralization brings degradation, apathy, forgetting of God, and infidelity in its train, and then rude crime, barefaced and vaunting atrocity, hatred of social laws, and blood remorseless revolution, to "purge the floor" of all the vile, that the nation may live again.

Oh, what a picture to draw of this fair land, where nature has lavished her richest treasures, where the earth for centuries teemed with unrivalled fertility—so rich, indeed, that men sunk down in slothfulness, and the poor contentment of a plentiful poverty.—Yet gloomy as is the prospect, we fear it is too true—and as men meet and shake their heads, and ask what will be done, the spectre now before us, rises impalpable as an air-drawn dagger, but yet distinct enough to point an end they fear. They stand like those

Who mark the waxing tide grow wave by wave,
Expecting ever, when some envious surge,
Will in its brinish bowels swallow them.

Midst all this suffering, charity hath done her best, but in such an aggregate of woe, that best is little. A nation is in want—and though soft hearts melt in sympathy for fellow creatures dying, the frequency of distress is making soft hearts callous.—A case of destitution meets the eye—it is relieved—and another and another—a score worse than the first, yet each with an accumulated load of misery on its back enough to make the heart weep; and then as soldiers in battle, who shudder to see the first comrade fall at morn, tramp careless over wounded hosts at eve, we look with pitiless eye, upon that which, in other times, would cause us bitter grief. And this will still progress until the times create a crisis, where those who here won't feel, and those who want will take. Sympathy, friendship, love will be forgotten—civilization will be as an old almanac, and crime will be a boast—virtue a folly.

Forbid it Heaven, and make the men in power
—to feel what wretches feel,
That they may shake the superflux to them,
And shew the Heavens more great.

(1847-01-30, 3:1) *Note: A fold in the left-hand margin rendered some of the words illegible.*

3622. State of the Country.—Distress.—The *Cork Reporter* of Tuesday says—This day again, our columns are crowded with details more awful, and examples of mortal suffering, frenzy, famine, despair, and hideous death more terrible than we thought could be collected within so brief a space from the worst scenes of pestilence and famine.—Death—death—nothing but death, to wind up the paragraphs of every letter we receive, and to meet the reader's view in every passage of the documents and reports we publish. They are now perishing, not in twos and threes, but in twenties in each parish, in hundreds in every barony. The earth is red from the fresh graves, and the pestilence is mowing down the people faster than grass fell before the once strong and cheerful labourer. In the parish of Kilmoe, twenty bodies are consigned to the earth every day. (1847-01-30, 3:4)

3623. State of the Country.—Distress.—Castlebar.—The *Mayo Constitution* contains an account of sixteen inquests held in that locality since the 10th instant, in each of which the verdict was died of starvation. The same journal states that numbers of deaths from starvation are occurring, in various parts of that country without any inquests being held. (1847-01-30, 3:4)

3624. An old man named Walter Furlong, an Irishman, who had been living for fifteen years in the Rue Bailluel [sic], was remarkable for his extraordinary passion for books. No person ever came to see him, and he wore, winter and summer, the same dress of short breeches and white stockings. He lived very economically, in order to buy books, which he did not always read. He had a few pupils, which enabled him to indulge in his bibliomania. Two days back, as the porter found that he had been twenty-four hours without making his appearance, he sent word to the commissary of police. The apartment being broken open, Mr. Furlong was found lying on the floor dead. The place was littered with books of every description.—*Galignani*. (1847-01-30, 4:4)

3625. Deaths from Starvation.—Still must we continue this afflicting heading, and record the fearful catalogue. From every quarter of the country, we are literally besieged with the heart rending particulars of the progress of famine. A respectable correspondent in the neighbourhood of Kilconly, has communicated to us, the loss of no less than eighteen lives, from want and destitution. And this occurring in a few short days.—*Tuam Herald*. (1847-02-06, 1:4)

3626. O! pity the object of famine and dearth,
There's scant in his home, there's cold on his hearth,
His prospects are blasted, relief is denied,
T'were a thousand times better when born he had died.

He would have known nothing of cares or of sorrows,
Of promised reliefs on a hundred to-morrows,
Of misery, of grief, of the chains of a slave,
All, all would be buried, hid out by the grave.

But, oh! he was doomed to submit to a fate,
Whose sorrows are countless, whose hardships are great,
That words can't express half the tolls and distresses,
That thicken around, and each day harder presses.

But what of himself—'tis a mere afterthought—
When compared to his wife's and his children's lot:
He sees them lie huddled in hunger and cold,
In the last shred of covering remaining unsold.

For their savings, their goods, even blanket and bed,
All went to assuage the loud cravings for bread;
Now their stock is exhausted and nothing remains,
But the cravings of hunger, its gnawing, its pains.

Oh, God, must they die, must they die by that death,
Is there none to assist, to preserve their life's breath;
Must they haste to that bourne, when perhaps ill prepared,
When a little relief would have saved, would have spared.

Then, oh, let all join, every grade, every man,
Consult and assist, and do all that ye can,
Let each one suppose on his efforts depend,
The lives of a parent, a brother, a friend.

G.

Monaghan, 27th January, 1847.

(1847-02-06, 4:1)

3627. Loss of a Vessel with Provisions.—Portsmouth, Jan. 25.—A brig called the *Gipsey* was unfortunately wrecked on the Wolseners shoal yesterday, and one of the crew, a boy, drowned. The calamity is more to be lamented, as this vessel was loaded with provisions of various sorts for Ireland from Hull, the cargo having been purchased by the subscribers to the fund raised in that port for the relief of the Irish. Finding all hope of saving the brig gone, the master, and the rest of his crew, took to the long boat, and made for Hayling island, but from the fury of the gale and the heavy sea, it upset, and with great difficulty, they got on shore; one man was nearly exhausted. The exertions of the officer and men of the coast guard were highly praiseworthy in rescuing them. The *Gipsey* is a total wreck, and her cargo quite lost. (1847-02-06, 4:3)

3628. An inquest was held on Monday, the 11th Inst., before William C. Waddell, Esq., our efficient coroner, and a respectable jury, on the body of Patrick Murphy, in the townland of Drumacrowir, in the immediate neighbourhood of Castleblayney, who died suddenly. Several witnesses were examined, amongst others that of Dr. Reed who examined the body of deceased, and stated that he (Patrick Murphy,) came to his death from dysentery, terminating in inflammation of the peritoneum and bowels, brought on from insufficient and injudicious diet.—Verdict accordingly. (1847-02-13, 3:1)

3629. There are 28 patients in our fever Hospital, eleven of whom came from the Work-house. (1847-02-13, 3:1)

3630. An elderly man was sentenced to seven years transportation for sheep stealing at the quarter sessions of Roscommon last week. His appearance in the dock was that of a man reduced to the last agonies of hunger. He died in an hour after he received his sentence. (1847-02-13, 4:5)

3631. Starvation—Inquests.—(From the *Mayo Constitution.*)—On Thursday last, Mr. Atkinson, coroner, held an inquest on the body of Bridget Gilboy, at Bunnafinglass. After the examination of Dr. Whitaker and other witnesses, the jury returned a verdict of—Death from starvation.

On the same day at Mullahowny, Dr. Atkinson held an inquest on the body of Patrick Foy, and a verdict of died from starvation was returned.

On Wednesday, the same coroner held inquests on the bodies of Michael M'Namara and Anne Loftus, at Ballina. In each case, a verdict of "death from starvation" was returned.

On Thursday, the same coroner held an inquest at Shanway, near Foxford, on the body of Bridget Filban, the daughter of a widow with eight children. "No pen," says our correspondent, "could describe the misery I witnessed here. The mother and her other seven children are withering fast, and they must eventually die unless speedily relieved." Dr. Gawley and other witnesses having been examined, the jury returned a verdict of "death from starvation."

On Saturday, the same coroner held an inquest at Ballina, on the bodies of Patrick Price, Bridget Hevran, Michael Walsh, Hugh M'Guire, Mary Dougher, and on Sunday, on the body of Edmond Madden, at Rathball. In each case, a verdict of "death from starvation" was returned. (1847-02-13, 4:6)

3632. More Deaths from Starvation.—(From the *Sligo Champion.*)—The coroner is still busily engaged in this county; the people are still dying of hunger, while the stores of the commissary general are full of corn; but political economy prohibits it being touched. The following inquests were held during the week:—

On the 23d inst., at Shancough, on the body of Francis Kelly.

Same day, at Ballymahon, on the body of Catherine Hoy.

On the 24th, at Ballysodare, on the body of Maurice Conroy.

On the 26th instant, at Killery, on the body of John Caucurn [Cancurn?].

On the 27th, at Kilncallon, on the body of James Kilmartin.

Same day, on the body of Michael Tighe.

Same day, at Rossmore, on the body of Patrick Conolan.

Same day, at Ballinacarrow, on the body of Michael Hart.

The verdict, in every instance, was—died of starvation. (1847-02-13, 4:6)

3633. There died in the Cork workhouse last week 104 paupers. (1847-02-13, 4:6)

3634. Our respected coroner has a busy time, holding inquests daily, and on some days, holding from five to seven. The verdict returned is a general one, died for want of food! We are glad to find that the coroners have now the power to advance money to purchase coffins—in many instances, the people were interred in bull rush mats, and in other instances, without any covering. Within the last six weeks, Mr. Peyton has holden upwards of 50 inquests.—*Boyle Gazette.* (1847-02-13, 4:6)

3635. Death of an Old Orangeman.—On Sunday, the 24th instant, Mr. G. M'Cleary, of Comber, near Dyan, died at the advanced age of 113 years. He was the oldest Orangeman in Ireland, having joined that society previous to the battle of the Diamond, and being the fourth man initiated in lodge No. 1, (the Dyan.) His remains were interred in Caledon Churchyard, on Tuesday, attended by about 300 of the brethren. (1847-02-13, 4:6)

3636. Appointment of Coroners.—At a meeting of magistrates held on Tuesday last, the county Monaghan was divided into two coroners' districts—one comprising the baronies of Monaghan, Trough and Dartree, with a part of the parish of Tullycorbet. The other comprising the baronies of Cremorne and Farney, save that part of Tullycorbet in the first division.

In consequence of this division, there will be one vacancy in the county, as Robert Murray, Esq., M.D., has resigned office, and his resignation has been accepted by the Lord Chancellor. (1847-02-20, 3:1)

3637. Inquest.—On Monday last, an inquest was held before Charles Waddel, Esq., coroner, upon view of the body of a child, aged about five years, which was found in a ditch in the townland of Carne, near this town. The body was terribly mutilated by dogs which had been feeding upon the carcass, and it would appear from the circumstances, as there was no evidence in facts, that the body had been placed there before the snow storm by the unfortunate parents, had remained under the snow during its continuance, and the thaw came, was discovered by the dogs. It was at first supposed that the child perished in the snow, but the fact of the legs and body being swathed in linen would lead to the contrary opinion. There was no medical examination of the body, which is an affair shrouded in mystery (as no person claimed its remains or recognised the body) as this was, we would deem, essentially necessary. (1847-02-20, 3:1)

3638. Coronership.—Mr. Luke Knight, of Comber, has requested to state in this week's number, that he will be a candidate for the vacant coronership for this county. His address to the electors will appear in our next.—There are several other candidates in the field, but we have not yet received their addresses to the constituencies, nor any authority to mention their names. (1847-02-20, 3:1)

3639. Deaths in Cork Workhouse.—There were 174 deaths in this house from Monday to Sunday inclusive, Monday, 25; Tuesday, 25; Wednesday, 26; Thursday, 28; Friday, 22; Saturday, 21; Sunday, 27. Dr. Stephens was ordered down by the Board of (*continued...*)

3639, continued: ...Health, to investigate the cause of the immense increase of deaths in the house. He was occupied yesterday in inquiring into the medical and sanatory condition of the workhouse. (1847-02-20, 3:3)

3640. Bantry.—Mr. T.A. Tisdall, M.D., in a letter to the *Cork Constitution*, dated Bantry, Feb. 13, says—"The workhouse, originally built for the accommodation of 600 persons, has become a perfect pest house, upwards of 200 persons being at present in hospital out of 730, to which number it has been thought prudent to restrict the admissions. The number of deaths for the week ending Saturday, the 6th, was 56. Indeed, sudden deaths have latterly been of such frequent occurrence here, that they have almost ceased to attract attention. (1847-02-20, 3:3)

3641. Castlebar, Feb. 16.—The *Mayo Constitution*, after giving the names of twenty-one persons who had died from starvation during the previous week, and upon several of whom inquests had been held, says—"Mr. Atkinson, Coroner, states that there are twelve more inquests reported in his district, but which, from indiposition, he has been unable to attend." (1847-02-20, 3:3)

3642. In the workhouse of Lurgan, the deaths have increased to an alarming extent. In the first week of January, they amounted to 35, but last week there were 95. (1847-02-20, 4:5)

3643. Peasmeal soup, or porridge, is a cure for dysentery, now so prevalent with the poor. (1847-02-20, 4:5)

3644. The *Ballinasloe Star* contains several deaths from starvation. (1847-02-27, 1:4)

3645. Richard Notter, Esq., J.P., writing from Rock Island, Crookhaven, county of Cork, under the date 17th Feb., says—"Fever is sweeping away whole multitudes. Entire families are lying crowded together, in their wretched hovels, stretched on a sop of straw, without any covering whatsoever; the dead and the dying lie there together; their neighbours will not go near them; all they can be induced to do is to leave a jug of drink at the door of the cabin, and one of the wretched inmates will crawl to take it in."

Our Relief Committee have two coffins with sliding bottoms, in which the corpses are carried to the graveyard, and there deposited in the mother earth.

Mr. Notter adds—"I have just heard that there were thirty-four deaths in the parish this day. Indian meal is 2s. 6d. per stone at Rock Island!" (1847-02-27, 1:4)

3646. The Rev. Robert Thraill [sic], writing from Schull, county of Cork, under the date February 18, gives this fearful statement:—"I may say of a truth that the plague has begun. I am informed that they could not count the bodies which were brought for interment yesterday. One cart alone conveyed three, another two—all without coffins. Every house is filled with famine and its attendants—fever, dysentery, dropsy, death!" (1847-02-27, 1:4)

3647. In the city of Cork, fever is spreading with frightful rapidity, sparing neither rich nor poor. (1847-02-27, 1:4)

3648. The rector of Ballyvourney, Macroom, writes thus to a Cork contemporary—"Funerals 8, 9, and 10, daily pass our door, and the wail of the widow and orphan is ringing in our ears from morning till night. The funerals are not, indeed, large; some may go by unobserved. Last Sunday, on coming out of church, we saw an old man and a young girl attempting to bury a corpse between them!" (1847-02-27, 1:4)

3649. We are informed by a gentleman from Attymass, a parish within three or four miles of this town, that between Friday and Tuesday last, no fewer than eleven persons died from starvation in that locality.—*Tyrawly Herald*. (1847-02-27, 1:4)

3650. From Kerry, the accounts are most pitiful. The *Tralee Chronicle*—"In every street, at every step, the gaunt hand of famishing wretches is stretched out for 'food, food, food,' and the first wound which smites the ear in the morning and the last at night when we close our doors, is the plaintive wail of children. Deaths from starvation have occurred in our streets, within the week—not those of feeble womanhood, but of men who but a month past could boast of stalwart frames." (1847-02-27, 1:4)

3651. A letter from Ventry describes the famine in that district as fearful. It says—"Out of the truly unfortunate village of Ballintlea, there has been a young woman five days dead, taken to the churchyard on Friday last by only two women, and there are at this moment two more dead in it, making in all twenty out of that ill-fated village within the last six weeks. Surely, the angel of death hath visited it, and God only can tell how many more he may mark for himself before his work of destruction is finished." (1847-02-27, 1:4)

3652. In the barony of Corkaguiny generally, the utmost destitution exists, but it is impossible for imagination to form images so truly horrifying, so grave-like, so unearthly, as the starved, spectre like beings that can scarcely be said to live in Dingle and Ventry. —*Kerry Post*. (1847-02-27, 1:4)

3653. Killarney—Some idea may be formed of the state of this district—proverbial as it is for its charities, from the fact that no less than thirteen funerals passed through the town on Sunday last.

Kenmare—Our accounts from Kenmare district continue to be most gloomy, and more particularly from Tousist, which we have already described as a second Skibbereen. In a word, the people are dying in scores every day in the baronies of Glanerough and South Dunkerron.

The Roman Catholic curate says that twelve persons die daily in Tousist of starvation. He expresses it as his opinion that, before the 1st of July, half the population will be lost.

The people now look at death as a blessing, and hence, the secret of their patience. (1847-02-27, 1:4)

3654. Deaths from Starvation.—We, with much regret and feelings of horrors, have to lay before our readers the details of the deaths of so many of our fellow-creatures, who have been the victims of disease and hunger in the past week.

In the neighbourhood of Newport, on Sunday morning last, a poor man named Mulloy, was got on the road side—his emaciated frame betokened that his death was the result of want. He was a native of Burrishoole.

On Friday last, a poor man died at Derradda, near Newport, of actual hunger, leaving a family to follow in rapid succession.

On Saturday, a poor man was also found expiring from exhaustion at Rooskeen, and, notwithstanding relief being brought, the poor man died, food having come too late!

In the neighbourhood of Breaffy, near this town, the following deaths have occurred from starvation and disease:—Michael M'Enally, of Roemon, on the 12th—Peter Swords, of Derranacrishan, on the 12th—his wife, on the 13th—James Gaven, of Ballyshawn, on the 8th—his wife, on the 12th. All these cases proceeded from dysentery and exhaustion.

On Sunday, the 7th instant, Mr. Atkinson, coroner, held an inquest on the body of Patrick Manghan, at Doonanarrow. The deceased has a family who are in the most indigent state. The jury's verdict was—death by starvation. In this village, there is not a family that do not appear likely to fall victims to famine.

On same day, on the body of James Brislan, at Kilcrimmin. The deceased was put on the public works, a few days previous to his death, and was hastening on Saturday to the office of the pay-clerk, but being weak from the want of food, he fell on the way, and was found dead next morning. Verdict—death by starvation.

On Monday, the 8th, on the body of Patrick Howley, at Saltfield. The deceased was employed on the public works, and was found lying on the road where he had fallen, by a person passing; when removed to the nearest habitation, he died immediately. Verdict—death by starvation.

On the same day, on the body of William Sheriden, at Cloonta. The deceased had been in a great state of destitution, and going from one village to another, he fell into a small rivulet which he attempted to cross, and from debility, was unable to extricate himself! Verdict–death by drowning, but attributed to starvation.

This coroner states that there are twelve more inquests reported in his district, which, from indiposition, he has been unable to attend.

During the past week, Mr. O'Grady, coroner, held inquests on the following persons:—Anne Philbin, Pat. Hannon, Francis Gannon, Jordan Morrisroe, Anne Teatum, Patrick Carey, Thomas Costello, Constantine Muller, John Mulloy, Bridget Mulloy. In each of these cases, the verdict was—death from starvation.—*Mayo Constitution.* (1847-02-27, 1:5)

3655. Distress in Mohill.—The most appalling distress prevails in this town and the surrounding neighbourhood. Men, women, and children stalk abroad like spectres, starvation being depicted in their every feature and movement. Within a few days, inquests have been held by Alex. Percy and Doctor Duke on ten persons, the verdict in each case being, "died of hunger and cold." In reply to an application from the secretary of the Mohill relief committee, the Rev. S.E. Hoops, the central relief committee, College-green, Dublin, sent to their aid 25*l.* worth of meal, which was distributed among hundreds who would have been numbered with the dead but for this timely relief. (1847-02-27, 1:6)

3656. Death of Colonel Cairnes–We this day announce, with sincere regret, the death of Colonel Cairnes. In early life, he had served with much distinction under the late gallant Gen. Gillespie, by whom he was appointed one of his Aides de Camp, a post none but a thoroughly brave man could hold; and his services were also recognised by the government, who conferred upon him the Order of Knight of Hanover. For many years, however, he had retired from the service, and resided at Portstewart, where his benevolent exertions on behalf of The Shipwrecked Mariners and Fishermen's Benevolent Society, will long be remembered. —*Coleraine Chronicle.* (1847-02-27, 1:6)

3657. The very latest accounts from Cork continue to be most distressing—disease, famine, and death are sweeping away the poor at a fearful rate. (1847-02-27, 2:5)

3658. A policeman, named Jacob Webb, has signalised himself this week by running off with Miss Honora Macmahon, an heiress possessed of £2,000, per annum, and a native of Newcastle, county of Limerick. Having overcome all obstacles and evaded an active pursuit, and married the lady, he has now retired from the constabulary. (1847-02-27, 2:5)

3659. We regret to state, that Mr. Gervase Parker Bushe, attache to the British embassy, at Vienna, died in that capital, on the 4th instant, of fever. He was the only son of Gervase Bushe, Esq., of Kilkenny, Ireland, and was a member of the same family to which the late Chief Justice Bushe belonged. (1847-02-27, 3:2)

3660. Our readers will remember our predictions, some weeks back, regarding the evident result of the condition of this house. See how they have been verified. We give the mortality of the last three weeks:— (.../)

3660, continued:

First week...	104
Second week...	128
Last week...	164
Total...	396 in 3 weeks.

Thirty six this week over last week; sixty over the week before—about one hundred over any week a month since!—*Cork Examiner.* (1847-02-27, 4:2)

3661. O'Connell.—We copy from the contemporary press, various paragraphs relative to the health of the Hon. Member for Cork:—

"Health of Mr. O'Connell.—A report of the death of Mr. O'Connell was very current about the houses of parliament and at the west end this morning. On making inquiry, however, at the British Hotel, Jermyn street, we are happy to state that the rumour is without foundation. The answer given by the servants of the hotel, to persons calling, was that Mr. O'Connell was quite well."—*Standard of Thursday.*

"A rumour was prevalent yesterday that Mr. O'Connell had been seized with a dangerous illness. On inquiry at the British Hotel, Jermyn street, last night, our informant learned that the hon. gentleman was seriously indisposed, and that it was his intention, if possible, to leave for Ireland immediately.—*Herald of Friday.*

The following appeared in the *D.E. Post* of Saturday:—"'By special command of his Grace Archbishop Murray, the Rev. Dr. Miley left for London, this morning, upon business of extreme urgency and importance.'

"We deeply regret to state that the above paragraph has reference to Mr. O'Connell, who, we learn, is seriously ill."

We have just received the *Limerick Examiner* of Saturday, with its columns in deep mourning for the supposed "Death of the Liberator," which that journal announces on the authority of a letter from Mr. F.W. Russell to his father, Mr. John Norris Russell, an eminent merchant in Limerick, viz.:—

"London, 17th February.

"I have to announce the death of Daniel O'Connell to day—a man whose name must fill a conspicuous place among the most illustrious.

"F.W. Russell."

The latest rumour is that of the *Freeman* of this morning:—"We are happy to be able to add to day that the accounts received yesterday (Sunday) are very cheering. Mr. O'Connell's indisposition is not such as to affect his constitution. The worst of it is that it sometimes interferes with his rest, and then he has to forego his usual carriage exercise, and to stay within by day in order to catch the repose he has lost by night." (1847-02-27, 4:5)

3662. Intermarriage of a Protestant and Roman Catholic. —At the sessions of Tulluw [sic], county of Cork, on Tuesday last, the Rev. Mr. Condon was summoned to answer a charge of having married John Broadbrook, a sergeant of one of her Majesty's regiments, he being a member of the Established Church, and a female of the Roman Catholic religion.

The case had been previously diposed of by the refusal of the magistrates to take an information, and it came before the Court the second time on a summons issued by the chairman, at the instance of the Rev. Alexander M'Loughlin, Protestant curate of Tullow, as it is said. The case had been argued by lawyers on this and the former occasion.

Mr. Kelly begged leave to say with respect to the government sanctioning the proceedings, that he thought himself bound to apply to the government of the country to know for his future conduct. He held in his hand the answer which stated that the law advisers of the Crown, as no case was then pending, did not think it expedient to give him any opinion.—(Applause.)

Mr. Howley, R.M., stated that a case of a similar nature had come before him, in which the magistrates, seven in number—the Marquis of Westmeath, Chairman—doubted their jurisdiction, and the decision upon the books was that it was dismissed. It went before the attorney-general, and he (Mr. Howley) was directed to go down immediately and summon the bench and take informations. The bills went before the quarter sessions, where they were thrown out; and he was directed a second time to take informations and have them sent to the assizes. In any case where the magistrates did not go upon the merits, it was quite open to a party to come again before the Court and ask informations. Let the magistrates, however, in the present situation, dispose of the matter as they pleased. If they were disposed not to take informations in any case, his hands were bound, and he would not oppose them without being expressly directed to do so by the government, or by a mandamus.

Major Croker gave it as his opinion that the question should not be re-opened. He said then, as he had said before, that he considered the case as very ill-timed, unwise, and fraught with the most mischievous consequences—as likely to distract the feelings of thousands already married under the same circumstances, and living in a state of perfect harmony and happiness—as likely, *in fine*, to disturb and convulse this part of the country, and plunge it into discord and disunion.

Mr. Kelly.—No, no.

Major Croker.—Yes, by exciting a spirit of party and schism—by bringing forward such a question before us, where the minds of the people are maddened with want and famine staring them in the face—where every exertion should be made, and Christian charity and Christian feeling should prevail in every instance to alleviate the distress before the public mind.

Mr. Kelly said he should interrupt him—the question before the Court was, whether or not the case was to be gone on with.

Major Croker—I beg leave also to state that I questioned the man (Broadbrook) as to whether it was at his instigation, having heard that a summons had been issued on his complaint; and he positively asserted to me, that he had no hand, act, or interference whatever in the prosecution, and that it was directly against his inclination such a proceeding should be taken at all. I deem it right to make this statement publicly that the man may be able to join his regiment without the slur of such a base and treacherous act resting upon his character before his comrades.—(suppressed cheers.)

The case was formally dismissed by a majority of 3 against 2 of the bench.—*Cork Examiner.*
(1847-02-27, 4:6)

3663. The Church.—We are most happy to announce the appointment of the Rev. Cuthbert T. Hacket to the Rectory of Kilmore, in this diocess, vacant by the death of the Rev. G.H. Schomberg. The appointment rested in the Lord Bishop, who has displayed his usual discrimination in the selection of a gentleman so deserving of promotion in the church, and calculated to give so much satisfaction to the congregation. Mr. Hacket had been for some years curate of the parish, during which, his mild and christian deportment gained the affection and esteem of the congregation.

This is the second appointment of curates of long standing made by the Lord Bishop within the diocess during the last month. (1847-03-06, 2:5)

3664. Any Persons having demands on the late Rev. G.H. Schomberg, Rector of Kilmore, are requested to send them in to Captain Schomberg, R.N., at Kilmore Glebe, forthwith.

Monaghan, March 5, 1847.
(1847-03-06, 3:5)

3665. Late David Smyth, Esq., M.D.—Middletown, March 5.—The remains of this much lamented gentleman, who died on the previous Saturday, of fever, caught in the discharge of his professional duties, were this day interred in the burial ground attached to the Chapelcy of St. John, and were followed to the grave by many of rank and influence; by the Clergy of the several religious denominations, and a large concourse of country people from adjoining parishes. After the funeral, a meeting of the friends of deceased took place in the Market-house.

The Rev. William Maclean, being called upon to preside, stated, that the Meeting was convened for the purpose of raising a subscription in order to testify the public gratitude to the late Doctor Smyth, by the erection of a Monument to his memory; and concluded by suggesting that the Rev. Swithen Williams, Curate of Middletown, and Mr. James Johnston, be requested to act as Secretary and Treasurer, the duties of which were immediately undertaken by these gentlemen.

Mr. H.L. Prentice, whose observations were marked by deep feeling, expressed his entire concurrence in the object of the Meeting, and proposed:—

"That a Testimonial be erected to the memory of the late Dr. Smyth," which proposition was seconded by Mr. Wm. Cochrane, of Annaroe.

The Rev. Mr. Borland, after a forcible and feeling comment on the character and career of the deceased, cut off in the prime of a life which had been employed in dispensing advice and assistance to his needy neighbours, proposed:—

"That a subscription be immediately entered into, and that it be limited to one pound from each individual."

Seconded by the Rev. Mr. Pratt.

Counsellor Tenison said, that as the object of the Meeting was to express the universal respect for the memory of a man, who had been a humane and attentive benefactor to the poor, and endeared to his friends by his high moral worth, and by the practice of the purest benevolence, he thought that it should be mentioned, that the very smallest sum would be received, as many poor people were anxious to subscribe, in order to show that their gratitude was as lasting as their sorrow was sincere.

This suggestion being adopted, a large amount was immediately deposited with the Treasurer, Mr. Johnston, in which were included some contributions from persons in humble circumstances.

It was then moved by Mr. G.R. Clark, of Coolkill, and seconded by Mr. Robt. Waters, M.R.C.S. London —"That the following individuals, with the Secretary and Treasurer, be selected as a Committee, for the purpose of collecting subscriptions, and with full power to put into execution the objects of this meeting, with all practicable dispatch, five members to form a quorum for the transaction of business:—

The Rev. William Maclean, A.M., Prebendary of Tynan.
The Rev. William H. Pratt, A.M., Prebendary of Donagh.
Henry Leslie Prentice, Esq., J.P.
Thomas J. Tenison, Esq., J.P.
Rev. Wm. Quinn, P.P., of Tynan.
William Cochrane, Esq., of Annaroe.
Rev. James Mauleverer, A.M., Incument of Middletown.
Rev. R.P. Borland, P.M. of Lislooney.
Rev. William Smyth, P.M. of Emyvale.
William J. Knox, Esq., of Caledon.
Rev. Peter MMahon, P.P. of Tyholland.
Rev. Samuel Henderson, P.M. of Middletown.
Mr. Wilson Cargill, of Glasslough.
Mr. John Bryants, of Killineal.

The Rev. Mr. Mauleverer moved "That the Committee do meet, and commence its preliminary operations in Middletown, on Thursday, the 25th day of March next, at the hour of 12 o'clock, and that (*continued...*)

3665, continued: ...the subscription list shall not be closed until the 12 of April next."

After the above resolutions had been seconded by Mr. Robert Vogan of Anagola, Mr. Maclean vacated the chair, and the Rev. Wm. Quinn having been called thereto, Mr. Clarke moved and Mr. Knox seconded a vote of thanks to the former, for the dignity and urbanity which characterized his conduct as chairman. (1847-03-06, 3:5)

3666. Mr. O'Connell's Health.—(From the *Freeman's Journal* of Saturday.)—We received a private letter last night from our special correspondent in London, an extract from which, though not written for publication, we place before our readers, as it contains some particulars about the real condition of Mr. O'Connell's health that may be relied upon as accurate. We deeply regret to have this painful corroboration of the general impression that prevails, that the Liberator's health has been so far impaired as to render total and continued cessation from public business essential to its restoration.

"London, Thursday Evening.—It is too true that the Liberator has suffered much for the past few weeks, and that even now he is unable to attend to his wonted duties. I cannot say that he had any distinct attack. His ailment was of that class which may be designated general prostration, and his physicians look to rest, abstinence from business, and strict attention to regime, rather than medicine, for the restoration of the physical and mental energy which formed so permanent a characteristic of O'Connell's nature. All sorts of rumours are afloat as to the real state of Mr. O'Connell's health. I have no hesitation in assuring you that his physicians feel confident that there is no organic disease, and that though a considerable period of time, probably many weeks, or even as many as three or four months, must elapse before he can again venture to take an active part in public life; repose and care will not only restore his health, but restore his energy and vigour. Even the restoration of health must, however, be the work of time; and while I think I may, with certainty, calm the alarm that you express, I would be but exciting false hopes were I to say that Mr. O'Connell can be permitted to take an active part in politics for some months to come.

"I may add that every day during the week, he has taken a carriage drive. I have been speaking with him within the last hour—he had just returned from taking a drive, in which he was accompanied by the Rev. Doctor Miley, and was preparing to take another. Though not looking well, he was certainly better than when I saw him yesterday—more cheerful and more elastic. The temporary attack, which for some days confined Mr. O'Connell to the recumbent posture, has given way, and with it, the irritation which prevented the enjoyment of his accustomed rest. No important alteration in his health can occur for some weeks—his restoration must be very gradual; but, thank God, it has commenced, and its progress may be looked to as slow, but with God's blessing, as certain."

Subjoined is an extract of a letter from London, dated Saturday:—"I have just seen O'Connell, and his kind and considerate friend, Dr. Miley. I do not use words of course when I tell you that I seldom experienced more satisfaction than in my interview to-day. O'Connell, though still far from being well, is decidedly improved; and the alteration, which I have observed since yesterday, leaves no doubt on my mind that a few weeks' rest, and careful attention to his health, will restore him to his wonted energy. I do not speak over-sanguinely—I give you my own decided opinion." (1847-03-06, 4:3)

3667. Progress of the Pestilence and Famine.—On Monday last, Mr. Atkinson held an inquest at Crossmolina, on the body of John Peaton. Verdict—Death from starvation.

On Tuesday, he held an inquest at Carrack, on the body of Anna Conmy; on the same day at Carrack-castle, on the body of Owen Calpin, and at Carrack, on the body of Mary Henegan, and in each case, a verdict of death from starvation was returned.

On yesterday, he held an inquest at Rathdowen on the body of Ellen Langan. Verdict—Death from starvation.—*Tralee Chronicle.*

An inquest was held on Saturday, on the body of a man named Daniel Leahy, who was found lying dead near an archway in Castle-street. Verdict—Death from starvation.—*Tralee Chronicle.*

The Famine.—The ravages that disease and famine are making amongst our population, may be gleaned from the fact, that 292 persons died in our workhouse, and the fever hospital attached, from the 1st of January to the 28 of February, inclusive.—*Longford Journal.*

On Wednesday, a poor woman and two children were discovered in a hopeless condition, brought on by want of nourishment, on the road side near Glasson. Before evening, the unfortunate mother expired.

Kenmare, March 4.—Distress prevails to an alarming extent—the people dying innumerably; bodies, when found, unclaimed or uncalled for by the relatives, if any survive. On this day, I passed a cabin where the mother of six children has been dead for eight days, and two of her children were then lying in fever with the corpse of their parent. It is not known whether they have shared the same fate or not; but certain the mother is dead, and no person would venture into the abode of famine and fever.—*Tralee Chronicle.*

State of Athlone Poorhouse.—Within a fortnight, the master and matron have fallen victims to the fatal malady. Every day furnishes us with at least five or six deaths, and on last Monday morning, no less than thirteen bodies were waiting interment.

Fever and dysentery still prevail in the workhouse, particularly at the female side. The deaths for the last five days were twenty-four. Remaining in the house, 1,191.—*Waterford Mail.* (1847-03-13, 2:3)

3668. In Roscommon, deaths by famine are so prevalent that whole families who retire to rest at night are dead in the morning, and frequently left unburied for days, for want of a coffin. (1847-03-13, 2:4)

3669. There is terrible calamity in the population of Killmurry Ibrickane, who have not only lost the trade in seaweed, but the potato crop, and they are dying in scores daily of famine and pestilence. (1847-03-13, 2:5)

3670. There is much abuse and injury to the farmers of the country by the employment of the able-bodied upon public works—this evil is rendered worse by the system of task work now being introduced into those operations, which, while as with a screw, it drives the old and feeble into open beggary, offers a premium to the able bodied who could be employed in the fields. It is almost impossible to procure a good laborer for farm work, for with less exertion, he can earn more on the roads. If you speak of this to the officials, they tell you, that you can take any men you choose off the works; but the farmers tell you, they will not do a day's work if they are taken off, and they would sooner have one of last year's laborers than half a dozen of them—for the fellows have got into such a system of work-a-day laziness, that they are constantly doing—nothing. You now pay from 7s. to 8s. 6d. a-day for a pair of horses to do the ploughing—but those horses are so attenuated, so miserable, so weak, that they cannot do one day's work in two days, yet you are compelled to pay more for them, by double, than you ever did before. Some of our neighbours have tried spade labour, and have selected from the works a parcel of the ablest men—but the quantity of work done, and the rate of wage paid, would altogether destroy the profit of the crop.

Such is the general state of debility, apathy, and demoralization. The horses are not able to work, the men have not heart to work. Deaths have become so frequent, disease so prevalent, that a mother tells you, with a nonchalance unparalelled, that she wants some aid to buy a coffin for a dead husband.—You give it, and the next moment, another walking skeleton asks for a halfpenny to help to bury a dead child—the craving face is familiar, and you tax her with importuning you with the same demand last week—she admits the fact, but tells you that that was the husband she buried then—a child had gone since, and she did not ask you—that a third would be dead to morrow, when she should make the weary round of those who buried the second—it is a strange kind of "Rule of Three"—those who buried the first will bury the third, and relatively, the second to the fourth. The burying ground laid out in 1832 and enclosed for cholera dead—since untenanted, and lying in solitary blakeness [sic], as if a curse hung over it, now wears a stirring, business-like appearance; the very workhouse keeps it going with a brisk trade and lots of customers. The workhouse hearse which rumbled through the town with many a "God have mercy," and "Lord save us," from the frighted spectators, now bears its three or four bodies to be buried *en groupe*, without causing even a passing remark—so do we get accustomed to great calamities, that we are less astonished by them than by small emergencies.—There is a killing of the people going on that may decimate the nation—but what matters it—they are killed to prove the principle of political economy. Let thousands die, rather than Sir Randolph Routh be mistaken—a million perish, rather than that trade should not be free.

Well, in truth, we are a patient people—we of Ulster—day after day, we see droves of bullocks—herds of heifers and beef cows, wending their weary way to some port to be shipped for Liverpool. This week, the dead cart of the work house, most impertinently intercepted a drove of those bloated natives in a narrow street of our town, and the dead cart stopped, that the living luxuries walking into the maw of England, might pass on. There was life for a thousand in that drove; however, it went to sea, and the people died. This was England's opportunity—it was Ireland's adversity—they have the food out of a starving country—the best of food—they send us in return scant grain, and starve us into a price of their own naming. This is England's opportunity to make great wealth out of Ireland.—England may have an adversity when Irish thews and sinews, gold and produce would be of service. If we then give them with as niggard hand and at such usury, would we deserve the name of sister.

This is a subject we will return to; we have no heart for it just now—we can think of nothing but the present calamity, its effects and its remedies—generosity, nationhood, liberty and action are all paralysed by the one overwhelming catastrophe—starvation. (1847-03-13, 3:2)

3671. An inquest was held a few days since, in the gate-house of the Rev. J. Hurst, parish of Errigle Trough, upon a man, name unknown, before C. Waddell, Esq., Coroner, and a respectable jury. The circumstances are as follows:—Deceased had been inquiring for lodgings in several houses, which he could not obtain; in the course of the evening, he retired into the churchyard, where he sauntered around the graves and tombs until night, when he got over to the Church steps, where he fell and bled profusely, and there remained until early next morning, when he was discovered by some men going to the public works, who removed him to the gate-house of the Rev. Mr. Hurst—Mrs. Hurst was in immediate attendance, ready to extend the right kind of charity, but all to no effect, as death was about to close the tragic scene. Several witnesses were examined, amongst others, Doctor Reed, who examined the body, and stated, that deceased came to his death from starvation—verdict accordingly.

Two other cases of starvation occurred not many days since, one in the neighbourhood of Ballybay, and another in the neighbourhood of Castleblayney. (1847-03-13, 3:3)

3672. Parish of Tydavnet.—Sir George Foster, finding in these times of death, that the parish grave-yards are not capacious enough, has, in a handsome manner, granted to the Rev. James Duffy, P.P., an acre of land, Irish Plantation Measure, adjoining the Chapel of Urbleshany, for a grave-yard, with £5 subscription, towards the enclosure of the ground. This is in accordance with the hereditary benevolence of his family. His father, Rev. Sir Thomas Foster, and his grandfather, Sir Nicholas Foster, made grants of land for churches, chapels, and grave-yards, when such acts of liberality were rare. The parishioners of Tydavnet, in public meeting assembled, have voted an address of thanks to Sir George Foster. (1847-03-13, 3:3)

3673. Cork Jail.—There are nearly 1,000 prisoners in the county jail, and of these, about one-tenth are in fever—the famine fever. The extraordinary number of prisoners is principally owing to the existing distress, the charge being generally for larceny and sheep stealing. (1847-03-13, 3:3)

3674. Thomas Battley, Esq., of the Rolls Office, has been appointed to one of the registrarships of the Bankrupt Court, vacant by the death of John O'Donohoe, Esq., Barrister-at-Law. Mr. Battely [sic] was nominated by the Lord Chancellor. (1847-03-13, 3:5)

3675. There were seventy dead bodies, confined and awaiting interment one day last week, at a burial ground in Cork! (1847-03-13, 4:6)

3676. Sudden Death of a Railway Horse.—Novel Inquest. —A few days ago, a draft horse, first in tandem in a drag on the works of the Ulster extension Railway to this city, dropt dead suddenly, without any previous indications of dissolution. The circumstance was so unexpected, and came so suddenly on those working immediately on that part of the line, that the head ganger, a wag, thought it right to hold an inquest on the body of the animal. Accordingly, a jury of the under gangers was impannelled, when after grave consideration and due examination, a verdict was returned to the effect that the animal died of exhaustion, as man and beast are now doing in this country, in the absence of that skilful prolonger of life, Doctor Murphy—*alias* potato. As soon as the inquest ended, at a signal from the Coroner and head ganger, the works were resumed by all engaged thereon with the usual alacrity and good order. (1847-03-20, 1:5)

3677. We have learned, with pleasure, that Lady Rossmore has given birth to a daughter, and that her ladyship and baby are in good health. (1847-03-20, 3:2)

3678. A daughter of the Lord Lieutenant is to be married to Captain Bernard, 12th Lancers. (1847-03-20, 3:4)

3679. The deaths in the Dunmanway poor house for the week ending on Saturday last were 60. This was out of a house containing little more than 700, and there are over 100 in dysentery. (1847-03-20, 3:5)

3680. No fewer than 190 persons died in the Cork workhouse during the past week. (1847-03-20, 4:3)

3681. In the court of Exchequer, it has been decided that husbands are not answerable for debts contracted by their wives, living separately on a sufficient allowance, even though creditors have no notice. (1847-03-20, 4:3)

3682. Tyrone Assizes.—William Allen, for having on the 12th of August, at Newtownards, married Margaret Mawhinney, having another wife, Mary Willis, alive. Prisoner was discharged. (1847-03-20, 4:5)

3683. The guardians of the Monaghan Union have taken the house formerly occupied as a Cholera Hospital, situate adjacent to the workhouse, and are about to fit it up as a fever hospital. (1847-03-27, 2:5)

3684. There are 36 cases of fever in the Monaghan fever hospital. (1847-03-27, 2:5)

3685. Extract of a letter written by a gentleman of fortune in the county of Cork, to a friend in Dublin:— "I am here surrounded by plague, pestilence, and famine. Except Portugal, on Massena's retreat, I never saw anything like it. The poor are burying their dead on the road side, between this place and Cork. Those who die in the workhouse are brought to be interred in coffins a quarter of an inch thick. I saw the sixth waggon load come out on Friday last, and interred in a ploughed field in a hole like a potato pit, scarcely covered with earth. I fear the warm weather will breed a plague. (1847-03-27, 2:6)

3686. On Friday last, two women were crushed to death in the crowds seeking relief at the Dungarvan workhouse. (1847-03-27, 3:1)

3687. Seven inquests were held during the last few days in the county Tyrone, before Joseph Orr, Esq., coroner, furnishing the most melancholy proof of the rapid progress which destitution and consequent disease is making. (1847-03-27, 3:2)

3688. Fever Hospital.—There are at present, in this Fever hospital, one hundred and two cases, some of them of a malignant character. The patients are, for the most part, all from the country, there being but ten from the town.—*Downpatrick Recorder.* (1847-03-27, 3:2)

3689. Middletown, March 17.—This day, an inquest was held on the body of Philip Galushe, a native of Fermanagh. He was found in a dying state on the road that leads from Middletown to Armagh, and was conveyed, on the 15th, to the hospital, at Middletown, where he died, of disease by destitution and want of the necessaries of life, the morning after. Another inquest was held in the neighbourhood this day, on the body of a female, and the verdict ascribed death to "Extreme destitution." (1847-03-27, 3:2)

3690. Death of the MacDermott Roe, of Alderford.—Cut off suddenly, in the prime of life, while engaged in the most unwearied exertions on behalf of the destitute of the locality in which he lived, The MacDermott Roe, of Alderford. Many are the sorrowing friends and relatives he has left to deplore his untimely death in the 35th year of his age. His mortal remains were entombed within the ancient vault of his family, drawn to the grave and mourned over by a people by whom (it is scarce too much to say) he was adored. (1847-03-27, 3:5)

3691. Recipe for Dysentery.—Boil a large quantity of leaves of the herb rue in water, until a strong bitter decoction is formed; then strain, and to every pint of liquid, add one pound of sugar. Boil both well, and when cold, bottle for use.

A wine glass full forms a dose for an adult, and frequently proves sufficient to stay the complaint. If not, it should be repeated. It will be rendered still more effective in any extreme case by the addition of a few drops of laudanum or chalk mixture. (1847-03-27, 4:6) *Note: The herb rue is toxic. This transcription is provided only for historical interest.*

3692. Starvation.—A poor man was found dead on Monday morning last within a mile of Newbliss. Upon examination, it was found that he died from the effects of want.

On Tuesday last, a poor woman, while waiting for the distribution of soup at the Newbliss soup kitchen, entered the inn yard, where she sat down a few minutes to rest, and fainted away from sheer exhaustion.—Mrs. Ker, the wife of the humane proprietor, having observed the wretched being passing, as it were, from a world of want, immediately administered restoratives, and having poured a little wine down the sufferer's throat, animation was restored. We never saw a more deplorable picture of the effects of starvation than this woman presented; her hands and arms had lost all appearance of humanity, and resembled more the fleshless legs and claws of a bird of prey, than the hands of a woman—the skin of her neck and breast exposed from want of clothing appeared as if a damp parchment had been drawn tightly over a bundle of wires, which protruded through without breaking the skin—and this is the state of hundreds of thousands sacrificed to the principle of political economy, called non-interference with trade. (1847-04-03, 3:3)

3693. Within the last week, there were 215 deaths in the Cork workhouse. (1847-04-03, 4:5)

3694. Special instructions have been issued by the Commissary General to relief committees, to defray the expenses of the burial of dead bodies from relief funds. (1847-04-03, 4:5)

3695. Fever and dysentery are so prevalent in Carrick-on-Shannon workhouse, that the guardians hold their meetings in the Court House. (1847-04-10, 2:1)

3696. Death of the Rev. P. Pounden.—With unaffected sorrow—a sorrow in which the public, to a very large extent, will share—we have to announce the demise of the Rev. Patrick Pounden, Rector of Westport. This excellent and devoted servant of God died, on Saturday last, of fever, caught in the discharge of his sacred duties, and rendered fatal by the exhaustion of mind and body in the course of his unremitting labours for the relief of the poor and needy—the famishing and the dying—in his extensive district. Indeed, he may be said to have mortgaged his life for the benefit of his fellow-creatures; for having guaranteed to the relief funds of his neighbourhood no less a supply than seventy pounds a week, to be raised partly out of his own means, and partly by the subscriptions of the benevolent—it is little to be wondered at that the requisite exertion, united to the discharge of his ministerial functions, visiting from house to house, giving food to the hungry, and spiritual advice to the sick and dying, should have proved too much for his strength, and that he fell a victim to the calamity which affects the country.

Mr. Pounden was a man distinguished through life for the accomplishments of a scholar and the virtues of a Christian. He was well known and beloved in the religious world; and was highly esteemed, not only as an able advocate of the Established Church, but as a profitable example of what a Christian pastor should be. By a dispensation of Providence, which, however mysterious to us, was doubtless to him acceptable and welcome, he has been taken away from the scene of his earthly labours. His end appears to have been what he would have chosen for himself—death in the service of God, and in the case of his fellow-creatures.—*Evening Mail.* (1847-04-10, 3:1)

3697. Fever.—Ballinrobe.—With much pleasure, we have heard that this frightful disease has stayed its ravages in the poorhouse of the above town, insomuch that there are but a few cases at present in the house. But this dire disease has swept away the most efficient officers connected with the establishment. We shall be much astonished if the guardians do not, by some penuniary recompence, endeavour to mitigate the misfortunes which have befallen the survivors of some of those officers, who have been the victims of their assiduity and attention. We refer to those who have left families to deplore their loss.

Clare.—In the neighbourhood of this town and about Ballindine, fever rages fearfully among the peasantry. We have heard that contagion has been spread by persons who, having recovered from the disease, left the workhouse, and returning to those localities, carried the infection with them.—*Mayo Constitution.* (1847-04-10, 3:2)

3698. On Friday last, a labouring man named John Brien, having been dismissed off the public works a few days previous, went into a farmer's (*continued...*)

3698, continued: ...house near Ballyduff, between Lismore and Fermoy, to ask a night's lodging, which he did not obtain—the following day, he was found dead in a pig stye convenient; and was buried the next day without a coffin. (1847-04-10, 3:2)

3699. A man, named George Mulhern, was killed on last Tuesday, 6th instant, while working on the Public Works at Market hill, by a bank falling on him. He has left a wife and three children in helplessness and destitution. (1847-04-10, 3:2)

3700. At Carlow assizes, Miss Galvin, a farmer's daughter, obtained a verdict of 300*l*. damages against Mr. T. Miles, of Saint Mullins, for breach of promise of marriage. (1847-04-10, 4:2)

3701. Cure for a Cold.—The following prescription has been taken from an old black letter book, A.D., 1403. We print it for the benefit of those medical antiquaries who are fond of tracing the progress of medicine:—

Putt your fette in hott water,
As high as your thighes,
Wrappe your head up in flanelle
As low as your eyes.

Take a quart of rum'd gruelle,
When in bed as a dose,
With a number of four dippe
Well tallowe your nose.

(1847-04-10, 4:3)

3702. Mr. O'Connell's Health.—Mr. O'Connell is proceeding towards the holy city with all the expedition which his medical attendants and companions consider advisable for one in his state of health. We announced some days ago the hon. gentleman's departure from Paris en route to Lyons. On Wednesday week, he arrived at La Charite, department de la Nievre. Private letters, received yesterday in London, from a gentleman who saw Mr. O'Connell at Neuvy-sur-Loire, convey the intelligence that, during the period of the patient's brief sojourn in this district, he appeared in cheering spirits, conversed rather freely with those who were permitted the privilege of interviews, and spoke in a more confident tone than he had done for some weeks of his permanent recovery. In the course of conversation with the gentleman alluded to, he said, "I am indeed anxious to visit Rome, the seat of Catholicity; but my anxious hopes are centered on returning to Ireland, and I trust that I may be able once again to labour in her service."—*Globe*. (1847-04-17, 4:4)

3703. It is incumbent on the mistress of a family to remember that the welfare of the house depends mainly on the eye of the superior; and, consequently, that nothing is too trifling for notice, whereby waste may be avoided; and this attention is of more importance now that the price of every necessary of life is so greatly augmented. (1847-04-17, 4:4)

3704. Third Annual Report of the Monaghan Dispensary, From the 18th of May, 1844, till the 18th of May, 1847.—At a Meeting of the Subscribers of the Monaghan Dispensary, Rev. W.L. Roper in the Chair—the following Resolutions were proposed:—

Proposed by the Rev. F. Maguire, and seconded by J. Hatchell, Esq., J.P., "That the best thanks of the Subscribers be given to Dr. Wm. Murray, for the very efficient manner in which he has discharged the duties of the Monaghan Dispensary for the last three years,"—carried unanimously.

Proposed by Mr. Ross and seconded by Mr. H.P. Lennon, "That this Report be printed,"

W.L. Roper, Chairman.
April 9, 1847.

LIST OF SUBSCRIBERS,
For the Year 1846, Ending 1847.

Lord Rossmore, ...	£3	3	0
Rev. H. Maffett, ...	1	1	0
Charles G. Duffey, Esq., ...	1	0	0
James Warren, ...	1	0	0
A. Fleming, ...	1	0	0
Mr. John O'Hanlon, ...	1	0	0
Rev. W.L. Roper, ...	1	0	0
John Hatchell, Esq., ...	1	1	0
James Hamilton, Esq., ...	1	0	0
Henry Rogers, Esq., ...	1	0	0
Hon. Mrs. Winfield, ...	2	2	0
William Anketell, ...	2	2	0
A.K. Young, Esq., ...	1	1	0
Rev. Mr. Moyna, ...	1	0	0
Mr. Francis Fleming, ...	1	0	0
Mr. Henry Lennon, ...	1	1	0
Mr. Patrick Sullivan, ...	1	1	0
Mr. James A. Ross, ...	1	1	0
Mr. Michael M'Quaid, ...	1	1	0
Very Rev. Dean Bellew, ...	2	2	0
Mr. Henry Connell, ...	1	1	0
Peter M'Phillips, ...	1	1	0
Thomas Reilly, Esq., ...	1	1	0
Mr. Peter M'Quaid, ...	1	1	0
E.P. Morphy, Esq., ...	1	1	0
Mr. James Quigley, ...	1	0	0
Mrs. Lucas, Raconnell, ...	1	0	0
Mrs. Cole, ...	1	0	0
Mrs. Phibbs, ...	1	0	0
Rev. P. Duffey, ...	1	0	0
Mr. John Murray, ...	1	0	0
J. Nunn, Esq., ...	1	1	0
R.G. Warren, Esq., ...	1	1	0
Mr. John Mitchell, Proctor, ...	1	1	0
Mr. Francis Adams, ...	1	1	0
Rev. John Blakely, ...	1	0	0
Most Rev. Dr. M'Nally, ...	1	0	0
Colonel Henry Westenra, ...	2	2	0
Mr. Peter MCullagh, ...	1	0	0
William Slate, Esq., ...	1	0	0
Leslie and Company, ...	2	2	0

James Warner, ...		1 1 0
Lord Cremorne, ...		2 2 0

Treasurer's Account, Year ending, May 1845,

Dr.

Balance over, ...	£	9 12 10
Private Subscriptions, ...		51 3 0
County, ...		51 3 0
	£	111 18 10

Cr.

Surgeon's Salary, ...	£	50 0 0
Rent, ...		10 0 0
Medicine and Carriage, ...		46 17 1
Printing, ...		2 0 0
Stamp, 1s. 6d. Form for report, 1s., ...		0 2 6
Balance, ...		2 19 3
	£	111 18 10

Year ending, May 1846.

Dr.

Balance on hands, ...	£	2 19 3
Amount of Private Subscriptions, ...		49 17 0
County Presentment, ...		49 17 0
	£	102 13 3

Cr.

Surgeon's Salary, ...	£	50 0 0
Rent, ...		10 0 0
Medicine and Carriage, ...		28 17 0
Printing, as per account, ...		3 10 0
Stamp, 1s. 6d. form for report, 1s., ...		0 2 6
Balance on hands, ...		13 3 9
	£	102 13 3

Year ending, May, 1847.

Dr.

Balance in Treasurer's hands, ...	£	13 3 9
Amount of private Subscriptions, ...		52 16 0
County Presentment, ...		52 16 0
Balance due Treasurer, ...		1 15 10
	£	120 11 7

Cr.

Surgeon's Salary, ...	£	50 0 0
Rent, ...		10 0 0
Medicine and carriage, ...		57 9 1
Printing per account, ...		3 0 0
Stamp, 1s. 6. Form, 1s., ...		0 2 6
	£	120 11 7

MEDICAL ATTENDANT'S REPORT.

From 15th of May, 1844, till 15th of May, 1845.

Received Advice and Medicine, ...	5193
Visited, ...	640
Parturition, ...	64

From 15th of May, 1845, till 15th of May, 1846.

Received Advice and Medicine, ...	4040
Visited, ...	589
Parturition, ...	45

From 15th of May, 1846, till 8th of April, 1847.

Received Advice and Medicine, ...	5054
Visited, ...	1080
Parturition, ...	36

As there occurred here, in the character of disease, no extraordinary feature during the two years preceding the present, many of the subscribers whom I consulted did not think it necessary to publish a Dispensary Report for those two years. The Treasurer's Account and the numbers receiving advice and medicine at the Institution were published every year in the public order, and the full and rather increasing amount of the subscription list last year afforded safe grounds to conclude that the supporters of the Dispensary have not been dissatisfied with its management.

But the epidemic which prevails in the present year renders a report necessary, and I have the uninterrupted space for two past years to trace without repetition its first appearance and subsequent progress.

I do not think it necessary to specify the names of the various diseases, nor their result which occurred in my Dispensary practise for the two first years specified in this report, further than what is connected with the present epidemic. They were such as are of every day occurrence, viz.: diseases of the skin, acute and chronic rheumatism, acute and chronic diseases of the chest, abdominal vicera [sic], &c. In these years, the mortality was not great, nor the continued diseases of a fatal nor unmanageable character.

But the epidemics of those years, I think it necessary to notice. Some time previous to May '44, the period when this report commences, Scarletina had prevailed in Monaghan and its neighbourhood. Epidemic affections, participating of the character of Scarletina, viz.: soreness of the throat, with and without fever, accompanied in many instances with griping and dysenteric symptoms, were frequent during the remainder of '44 and the beginning of '45. In the latter end of Spring and beginning of Summer, '45, measles and Hooping Cough were prevalent. Irriation of the bowels was increasing. There were some cases of Small pox occurred in this town and district, but the disease was not epidemic. In '46, Stomatitis, or Inflammation of the mouth, prevailed in both town and country; and this affection has not as yet disappeared. Dysentery still continues in frequency (*continued...*)

3704, continued: ...and severity. Continued fevers, most, if not all, of a dysenteric or gastric type, prevailed in the districts round the town and in the suburbs. In October, there was scarcely a house on the Barrack hill where the inmates were not affected with fever. Only one death occurred, the mother of a large family. It is worthy of remark, that since that period, neither fever nor dysentery has prevailed in that locality. In High-street and Glasslough-street, there were many cases of Fever and Dysentery during the winter of '46.—Applications for Dysentery still continued to increase at the Dispensary, during the winter of '46 and spring of '47. In the latter end of February and the beginning of March, Fever with Dysentery, which had partly quitted the localities first infected, broke out in the lanes connected with Dublin-street, in the Shambles-square and adjoining lanes, on the Pound-hill, and among some families round the town. In the Diamond, Park-street, the New Diamond, or Mill-street, there has occurred scarcely any case of Fever, and few cases of Dysentery.

Since the beginning of March, till the 7th of April, '47,666 patients, personally, and by proxy, applied for medicine and advice at the Monaghan Dispensary. Of these, 220 were affected with Dysentery; 70 were attended at their own places of residence; visits, 327; died, 7, mostly children, and persons previously emaciated; under treatment and requiring to be visited, 20. Patients who have been affected with Dysentery, are often subsequently affected with Anasarca, or Dropsical effusion; this is extremely common. Though cases of continued Fever have decreased greatly in the town, applications for the cure of Dysentery from both town and country are increasing; and as the subscribers sanction the liberty, all applicants, in the present trying emergency, who are generally the ill fed and starving poor, without reference to their residence, or other objections, are attended to whenever they apply.

But it is quite clear from the history of the present epidemic, given in this Report, that it has not originated, as has been stated, in the use of Indian meal, as it prevailed before the general use of that diet. I am of opinion that it is of epidemic origin, and that the use of Indian meal, which in general comes to market in a coarsely ground state, and which the poor use hastily and without due preparation, may irritate the bowels, and predispose them to Dysentery.

Attending females in difficult labour;—and here I take the liberty of stating, that in all the cases of that description stated in this Report, which I attended, almost all of whom required instrumental delivery, not one patient died; neither were there more than three children still-born;—attending, as I have said, the poor, under such circumstances—prescribing for diseases in their first stages, when they may be most successfully treated—visiting and deciding on the nature of the disease, when servants or persons employed in private families are suspected to be seized with contagion—visiting in every lane and room, and under every circumstance of wretchedness and distress the poor labouring under contagious diseases—in a word, acting as a guardian of public health, and prescribing every day in the week for Dispensary patients and every hour in the day; a few hours two days in the week being the attendance usually given in other dispensaries, are some of the duties connected with this Institution. It will be seen that these duties, if duly performed, are not of subordinate importance, and consequently have no subordinate claim on public support.

With regard to the supply of medicine furnished to the Monaghan Dispensary, though previously to its being renewed, it may be occasionally reduced, I beg leave to assert that it [is?] as ample as in any other similar Institution in the county; and that the accommodations can be demonstrated to be quite sufficient for their purpose. But be it remembered, that it is not in piles of medicine, nor in external machinery, that the utility of public Institutions of this kind consists; but in the professional intelligence and experience of the superintendent who can make a few remedial materials, available in almost every emergency; but the refined and educated alone are capable of making these distinctions—those of the opposite class, if it may be called reasoning, reason otherwise. But if I have succeeded in rendering substantial services to the poor, and that the clergy and subscribers are satisfied with the manner in which I have discharged my duties, I am most happy that my professional exertions have been useful in carrying out the charitable intentions of the subscribers, whose individual kindness to myself I shall every gratefully remember.

The Patrons of the Monaghan Dispensary are most respectable and numerous, and the Medical Officer, whoever he may be, who merits their confidence and protection, may rest secure that his reputation shall be safe in their hands; and this, to every honourable man, is more dear than life.

William Murray, M.D.,
Medical Attendant.
(1847-04-17, 4:5)

3705. Notice.—Stoppage of Credit.—I Hereby Give Notice, that I will not, after the date hereof, be accountable for any Debt or Debts incurred by my wife, Mary Rankin (formerly Weir) as she has left my house and home without just or legal cause.

James Rankin.
Dated Coravally, County of Monaghan,
this 27th day of March, 1847.
(1847-04-24, 1:3)

3706. Large quantities of human bones have been dug up by the men employed on the public works in the neighbourhood of St. John's Abbey, Tuam.
(1847-04-24, 2:2)

3707. Clonmel.—We regret to state that our respected townsman, James Burke, Esq., Johnson-street, and Mr. John Power, of Priorstown, caught fever whilst attending their duties as poor law guardians, in the workhouse of this union, on Thursday week. The latter gentleman has since died. Notwithstanding the praiseworthy efforts of the officers of health, who are sedulously attending to the enormous duties of their important office, we regret to say that fever and dysentery are rather spreading.—*Tipperary Constitution*. (1847-04-24, 2:3)

3708. Fever.—Our returns from the union fever wards of the workhouse, last night at half-past nine, present the following appalling amount, which the physician anticipates will be augmented this morning by twenty additional patients. The present is the state of the Union Fever Hospital:—Males, 174; Females, 251; Total, 425. —*Belfast Chronicle*. (1847-04-24, 2:3)

3709. Kilkenny.—The medical profession estimate the number of weekly deaths in the electoral divisions of Kilkenny, being the ancient city and liberties, at one hundred and sixty. Now, supposing the continuance of this mortality, let us see how soon would the present population of Kilkenny be entirely cleared away by the great destroyer. The population of Kilkenny electoral division, according to the census of 1841, was 23,000. Upon this calculation, the period it would take to do the work of extermination would be exactly two years, nine months, three weeks, and five days! But then, allowance should be made for the number of births which recruit the population. On the same data, the medical men of Kilkenny calculate the average number of births in the Kilkenny electoral division to be twenty weekly. With this auxiliary to the strength of the inhabitants, Kilkenny would yet be left entirely depopulated, at the same amount of mortality, in the space of three years, two months, and one day.—*Kilkenny Moderator*. (1847-04-24, 2:3)

3710. Fever continues to spread rapidly throughout Sligo. The old and new fever hospitals are crammed full. There is scarcely a single cabin free from the contagion. (1847-04-24, 2:4)

3711. One hundred and thirty-eight paupers died in the Limerick workhouse since Monday se'nnight. In the house, 2,050. (1847-04-24, 2:4)

3712. A dreadful fever has broken out in Oranmore convent. (1847-04-24, 2:4)

3713. Captain Drury, R.N., government relief officer at Kinsale, has fallen a victim to contagious fever, and left a widow and a dozen orphans. (1847-04-24, 2:4)

3714. Suicide in Dublin.—On Saturday, an inquest was held in the Northumberland Hotel, Dublin, by S. Kirwan, on the body of a gentleman named Falloon, 27 years of age, who had committed suicide by taking a large quantity of prussic acid. It appeared that the deceased was a medical student, and that he had lately arrived from Paris, with the view of marrying a young lady to whom he had been paying his addresses. However, the lady's family and herself were quite averse to his advances, and on Saturday, the unfortunate young man learned that it was impossible an alliance could take place. He appeared much depressed, and went to his hotel, when he took over two ounces of prussic acid, and died in a few minutes.
(1847-04-24, 2:5)

3715. Death of the Very Rev. Dean Roper.—It is with unfeigned sorrow we have to announce the demise of the Very Rev. Henry Roper, D.D., Dean of Clonmacnoise, and Rector of Clones, in the fullness of a green old age, having attained his 86th year. He was distinguished in his early days as one of the most courtly and elegant gentlemen in Ireland, and during his long life, he was an ornament to his sacred profession and a distinguished member of the national literati. To say that he was charitable and benevolent would be to speak of things of course, but his affability and courtesy always rendered his gifts of double value to the recipient.

His powerful mind held its perfect dominion to the last hours of his existence, and as words of wisdom fell from his lips, they were listened to by those who heard them as almost oracular. (1847-04-24, 3:5)

3716. A Lament.

Oh, mother! thou art lowly laid
In this thy last sad sleep,
And I, here trembling and afraid,
Can only kneel and weep.

Many a pleasant day has sped,
In my girlhood's wild hours,
Whilst thou my gladsome footsteps led
Through youth's mazy bowers.

But now, alas! those flowing tears,
Outgushing o'er thy grave,
Bespeak a bitter waste of years,
On gliding as a wave.

My future fate is briefly told—
For short's the tale and sad;
No trust have I in man or gold,
But resting on my God.

A Mourner.
Cavan, April 6, 1847.

(1847-04-24, 4:1)

3717. She's Gane to Dwell in Heaven.
—By Allan Cunningham.

She's gane to dwell in Heaven, my lassie,
She's gane to dwell in Heaven:
"Ye're owre pure," quo' the voice o' God,
"For dwelling out o' Heaven." (*continued...*)

3717, continued:

O what'll she do in Heaven, my lassie?
O what'll she do in Heaven;
She'll mix her ain thoughts wi' angels' sangs,
An' make them mair meet for Heaven.

She was beloved by a' my lassie,
She was beloved by a';
But an angel fell in love wi' her,
An' took her frae us a'.

Lowly there thou lies, my lassie,
Lowly there thou lies:
A bonnier form ne'er went to the yird,
For frae it will arise.

Fu' soon I'll follow thee, my lassie,
Fu' soon I'll follow thee;
Thou left me nought to covet ahin',
But tuke gudeness sel' wi' thee.

I looked on thy death-cold face, my lassie,
I looked on thy death-cold face;
Thou seemed a lily new cut I' the bud,
An' fading in its place.

I looked on thy death-shut eye, my lassie,
I looked on thy death-shut eye:
An a lovelier light in the brow of Heaven
Fell time shall neer destroy.

Thy lips were ruddy and calm, my lassie,
Thy lips were ruddy and calm;
But gane was the holy breath o' Heaven
That sang the evening psalm.

There's nought but dust now mine, lassie,
There's nought but dust now mine;
My soul's wi' thee i' the cauld grave,
An' why should I stay behin'!

(1847-04-24, 4:1)

3718. Lyons, April 12.—Mr. O'Connell.—After having been expected for several days, Mr. O'Connell arrived yesterday at the Hotel de l'Univers, where he will probably remain a few days, before he resumes his journey to Italy. (1847-04-24, 4:5)

3719. Mr. O'Connell's Health.- Our illustrious countryman still remains at Lyons, where the weather is represented as of the most disagreeable character. Amid torrents of rain on Thursday afternoon, a deputation from Roman Catholics called at the Hotel de l'Univers, for the purpose of fixing a day on which to present the Liberator with an address. They were courteously received by the member for Dundalk, who promised to convey their wishes to his father, and communicate to them, with as little delay as possible, the result of his determination. On the following morning, the head of the deputation received the following letter from Mr. D. O'Connell, jun.:

"Sir—I am directed by my father to express to you his deep and unaffected regret that his medical attendants having recommended him the greatest possible amount of quietude and absence from excitement, it will be impossible for him to have the honour of receiving the deputation from the Catholics of Lyons. —I have the honour to be, Sir, your obedient servant,

"Daniel O'Connell, jun."

The Roman Catholics of Lyons naturally felt disappointed at being denied the opportunity of paying their tribute of respect to the champion of civil and religious liberty, and sympathising with him in his hour of affliction. Unhappily, however, Mr. O'Connell's malady is of such a character, that the slightest excitement has an exceedingly deteriorating effect both on his health and spirits; and gratifying though the demonstration on the part of the Roman Catholics of Lyons, would have proved to the man by whom catholicity has been so proudly and faithfully served, it was deemed the more prudent course to decline the complaint.—*Freeman*. (1847-05-01, 1:5)

3720. There has been another ornament added to the many which already adorned the beautiful church of Monaghan, in the shape of a monument erected by the inhabitants of this county, to commemorate the glorious death of Captain John Owen Lucas, 29th regiment, son of the late Colonel Lucas of Raconnell, who was killed while leading on his regiment to victory on the hard fought field of Ferozeshah. In tasteful design and beautiful and minute execution, this entablature is second to none that we have ever seen, and we are proud to say that it is altogether the conception and workmanship of Irishmen—the design by our gifted townsman, A.K. Young, Esq., and the execution by Joseph H. Kirk, Esq., of Dublin.

This monument, consisting of a military trophy and sarcophagus cut out of white marble, and projecting in bold relief from a black polished slab, is upwards of seven feet in height, and beautifully proportioned. The trophy is pyramidal in form; the base being composed of cannons, culrass, drum, &c., and flanked by elephants, (emblems of the country in which the action was fought) convey the idea of solidity and strength to the eye of the observer. These are surmounted by helmet, sword, battle axe and guns, with flags (bearing the number of the regiment) gracefully falling from their staves, and tastefully distributed among the emblems underneath, whilst the whole is carried upwards by such imperceptible degrees, that we are not surprised at finding the apex of the pyramid terminated by a single spear head. The entire is resting on the upper slab of the sarcophagus, and the torch broken by a ball emblematic of the sad event it commemorates, is so arranged that the connection of the design is admirably carried out. The sarcophagus itself (which in general we find so heavy when surmounted by other arrangements) is in this instance of an unusual shape-light and finished in appearance, it neither offends the eye by its size or solidity, nor is it at all out of keeping with the trophy which surmounts it. It rests on cannon balls, and bears the following inscription, the good taste of which we admire, and to every sentiment of which we give our most hearty concurrence:—

In memory of
Captain John Owen Lucas, of H.M. 29th Regiment,
Major of Brigade,
And late of Raconnel, in this neighbourhood;
Who was killed whilst in the act of cheering on his men to the attack of the enemy's batteries at Ferozeshah,
On the 22d day of December, 1845,
Aged 35 Years,
THIS MONUMENT
is erected by the Inhabitants of the Co. of Monaghan, as a memorial of esteem for their gallant countryman, as a tribute of respect to his sorrowing family, and as an incentive to the rising generation to elicit, as he has done, the grateful remembrance of their country.

The arms of the family are raised in white marble upon the centre block, which has been judiciously chiselled in the form of a shield, for the purpose of bearing them. The position in which it has been placed in the Church, we find ourselves again called upon to praise. This is so chosen that each part is shown in perfection. The light falling on one side, by increasing the effect of the relief, exhibits the beauty of the design; whilst the minute chiselling and exquisite finish are made perceptible at a considerable distance. The committee and subscribers, we are sure, feel much indebted to our revered Rector, for having given his permission to place the monument in such a position as will best carry out their views, so well expressed in the inscription; and the public will feel grateful that so beautiful a specimen of native talent is so situated that its perfection can be seen and appreciated. (1847-05-01, 3:2)

3721. Alarming Illness of the Lord Lieutenant.—*(From the D.E. Mail.)*—The few lines, in which our publication of Monday announced the severe illness of his Excellency, were briefly strung together, not five minutes before our broad sheet was put to press, with a view of preparing the public mind for a melancholy event, which, at the time we received the intelligence, appeared likely to anticipate another sunrise. There was no room for details; nor could we pause to inquire why the indisposition under which his Excellency was known to have been suffering for some weeks have been made so light of, that its proximate result should be allowed to strike suddenly and unexpectedly upon the chords of public sympathy. It is now, however, generally understood that his Excellency has, for the last six months, been under treatment for aneurism, and that more recent symptoms of hydro-thorax have precipitated the event which, from the bulletin issued this morning (Wednesday,) at the Castle, we fear there is but too much reason to apprehend.—Our announcement on Monday was succeeded by a night of comparative ease, and we hoped that his Excellency might have rallied; but, as the hours of Tuesday crept on without any decided improvement of the symptoms, the prospect of recovery decreased; and we are unaffectedly sorry to add that the bulletin issued this morning (Wednesday,) at nine o'clock, ran in the following terms:—

"April 28, 1847.

"His Excellency continues in a very precarious state."

Should any other bulletin be issued, or further intelligence be received before the hour of our going to press, we shall communicate it to the public.

Mail Office, Wednesday, Three o'clock.

The following is the present bulletin with its date:— "His Excellency continues in a very precarious state up to half-past two o'clock."

(From the *Post* of Thursday Evening.)

The following bulletin was issued at the Castle yesterday:—"Nine o'clock, a.m. His Excellency continues in a very precarious state."

At an advanced hour in the evening, we were informed that no improvement had taken place in the course of the day.

When the illustrious patient's illness had assumed alarming symptoms, Captain Henry Ponsonby proceeded to England to communicate the afflicting intelligence to the members of his Excellency's family resident there; and on the gallant captain's return, he was accompanied by the Rev. Mr. Bourke, Rector of Hatherop, in Gloucestershire, and by Lady Georgina Bourke, the Hon. Charles Gore, and the Countess of Kerry, the Hon. Charles and Lady Mary Ponsonby, all of whom arrived at the Castle yesterday evening. Lord Duncannon and the Hon. Gerald Ponsonby have been in constant attendance upon their noble father, almost from the first day of his illness, and Ladies Emily, Harriet, and Kathleen are never absent from his bedside. The tender solicitude which those affectionate children exercise with unwearied zeal, at the couch of their beloved father, is deeply sympathised in every person of every rank and degree, and their pious resignation to the Divine Will is a subject of admiration to every one who is permitted to know the course of events in the domestic circle.

This Day.

The following bulletin was issued by Sir Philip Crampton and Doctor Purcell, of Carrick-on-Suir, this morning:—"His Excellency passed a tranquil night, and his breathing is much relieved this morning. The general symptoms, however, are much the same as yesterday."

Three o'Clock.—The answer to our inquiry is, that his Excellency's breathing is a little better, but that, in other respects, the symptoms continue without change.

From an early hour yesterday morning, and during this day, a continuous concourse of persons called at the Castle to make anxious inquiry about his Excellency. (1847-05-01, 3:2)

3722. Progress of Fever amongst the Upper Classes.—The death of the late Mr. Martin, M.P., for the county Galway, has given birth to many alarming rumours—particularly with reference to a member of his own family. But we are happy to state that they are entirely destitute of truth. Miss Martin was undoubtedly overwhelmed with affliction on the death of a beloved parent; but further than this, the health of the amiable young lady remains unimpaired.

It is, however, melancholy to state the numbers of the gentry who, in consequence of their devotion to the works of charity, are suffering under the prevailing epidemic. A correspondent, resident on the spot, has furnished us with the names of J. Nolan, Esq. of Ballinderry, a grand juror of the county; J. Kelly, Newton [sic], Esq., J.P.; Mr. Kelly, of Kinclare; Mr. O'Hara, sub-sheriff; Mr. Bate, Clerk of the Crown, and several others connected with the country, who are now suffering under fever.

We learn, with deep regret, that Lord Lurgan is suffering from typhus fever, said to have been contracted in the course of his benevolent exertions for the relief of distress. His Lordship, says the *Northern Whig* of yesterday, "felt slightly unwell on Tuesday last; but it was not until near the end of the week that the symptoms of fever had distinctly developed themselves. On Sunday, there was in Belfast a rumour of his death; and, as may well be supposed, the report caused great uneasiness. Yesterday, he continued in the condition usual in the ordinary course of illness under which he is suffering; and there was not, we are happy to say, any symptoms to excite particular attention."

Our columns elsewhere bear melancholy record of the unabated violence of the diseases under which so many of the poor and rich have already fallen victims. (1847-05-01, 3:3)

3723. Death of T.B. Martin, Esq., M.P.—We regret to state, that accurate accounts have reached town this morning, announcing the death of the above named gentleman, at his seat, Ballinahinch Castle, in this county, which latter he represented in Parliament for many years.—*Galway Mercury*. (1847-05-01, 3:4)

3724. Equity Exchequer.—William Rutherford, Esq., Plaintiff.—Grace Cottnam, Widow, Anne Jane Giles, and others, Defendants.

Pursuant to the Decree made in this Cause, bearing date the 2nd day of Dec., 1845; I will, on Monday, the 31st of May next, at the hour of 1 o'clock in the afternoon, at my Chambers, on the Inns Quay, in the city of Dublin, set up and sell to the highest and fairest bidder, All That and Those the Town and Lands of Bunore, otherwise Bunoe, commonly called Manore, with the Mansion-house thereon; also the Town and Lands of Cortubber, Toneygemryson, otherwise called Tunneygemsey, and party of the Lands of Drum, all situate in the Barony of Dartrey, and County of Monaghan, in the pleadings in this Cause mentioned, or a competent part thereof, for the purposes in said Decree also mentioned.

Dated this 26th day of April, 1847.

Acheson Lyle, A.B.

The above Mansion-house stands on a lawn of about 20 acres, handsomely planted, with an extensive lake in front; situate half a mile from Drum, 3 from Cootehill, 2 of Newbliss, and 5 from Clones; all Post towns; the Parish Church is in the Demesne.

For particulars, apply to
Alex. Dudgeon, Plaintiff's Solicitor,
86, Talbot-Street, Dublin.
(1847-05-01, 3:6)

3725. The Rectory of Clones, vacant by the death of Dean Roper, is value £800 a-year, and in the gift of Sir T.B. Lenard; his right of presentation is disputed by the Bishop of Clogher. (1847-05-01, 4:5)

3726. Death of Lord Rokeby.—This highly respectable nobleman expired on the 7th inst. at Naples, after a short illness. The deceased, Edward Robinson Montagu, was Baron Rekeby [sic] of Armagh, in the peerage of Ireland, and a baronet of Great Britain. He never married, and the honours devolve on his next brother, the Hon. Lieutenant-Colonel John Montagu. (1847-05-01, 4:5)

3727. Typhus Fever.—A gentleman has handed us the following remedy for typhus fever, taken from a newspaper a few years ago:—

"Put one table spoonful of [brewers?] yeast in a gill of warm porter; stir it well, and while warm, give it to the patient, repeating it every six hours, while any symptoms of fever remain; then reduce it to ten hours, and as the patient gets better, increase the distance of time till it becomes once in twenty four hours.

"This remedy has been used by Lady O'Brien. In seventy two cases on her estates, seventy recovered. It has since been introduced into the fever hospital at Parsonstown, with great success."—*Cork Constitution*. (1847-05-01, 4:6)

3728. Death of Lord Lurgan.—With sincere, but unavailing regret, we have to record the death of one of the most estimable noblemen of the north of Ireland. One of the first victims, among the higher classes, to the awful calamity which now threatens the entire population of this country, has been the benevolent nobleman whose name heads this announcement. Lord Lurgan, whose illness our readers have been made aware of from its commencement, thirteen days ago, expired, at Brownlow House, Lurgan, at a quarter-past one on Friday evening, the 30th April, in the fifty-third year of his age. The fatal malady, typhus fever, which, within so short a period, hurried this exemplary nobleman—this excellent landlord—to his premature grave, was contracted, as is supposed, at the Lurgan Union Workhouse, where his zealous attention to the wants of the destitute and the sick exposed him to the contagion which has been long prevalent in that establishment. Lord Lurgan's demise has excited a very deep and painful sympathy among all classes of the community. Among the landlords, he was distinguished for his liberality and his efforts to promote the happiness and comfort of his tenantry; as a member of society, his manners were kind, affectionate, and attractive; and, as a promoter of the various charitable institutions in the town from which he derived his title, and in Belfast, few have more deservedly earned the gratitude and respect of the community. As soon as the melancholy event became known, the shops were shut in Lurgan, and no evidence was wanting of the extreme sorrow felt for his loss by the inhabitants, and by the whole of the surrounding population, to whom he was endeared by many public and private associations.

Lord Lurgan was born on the 17th of April, 1795; he was the second son of the Hon. Charles Brownlow, and succeeded his uncle, the Right Hon. William Brownlow, in the Lurgan estates, worth nearly twenty thousand a year. His lordship was married on the 1st June, 1822, to his cousin, Mary Bligh, second daughter of the Earl of Darnley, and by her, who died the year after her marriage, he had issue, one daughter. He was again married, in 1828, to Jane, fourth daughter of Roderick MacNeil, Esq., of Barra, Invernesshire, Scotland, by whom he had three children —two sons and a daughter. He is succeeded in his title and estates by the eldest of this latter union, the Hon. Charles Brownlow, who was born in April, 1831, and is now in his 17th year—a young man of the best promise, and likely to emulate the virtues of his deceased parent.

Lord Lurgan, in early life, was of ultra Conservative principles, but afterwards, became partial to liberal opinions; and in 1826, he, when the Hon. Charles Brownlow, with the Hon. Henry Caulfield, contested his native county, Armagh, against James Y. Burges, Esq. and Colonel Verner, and succeeded. He was raised, in May 1839, to the peerage, under the title of Baron Lurgan, Lord Lurgan, in the county of Armagh.

To the principles to which he had become a convert, he constantly adhered during his career in parliament, but was never an advocate of the more sweeping measures which the adherents of the liberal party proposed to carry out. Not only in his place in the House of Commons and House of Lords, but as Deputy-Lieutenant of Armagh, and Justice of the Peace for Antrim, Down and Armagh, he paid more than ordinary attention to his public duties, gained the confidence of all, and the respect [and] esteem of his political opponents. He contributed to the charities of all religious denominations with an equally open hand. Among the institutions in which he was more particularly interested, was the Ulster Institution for the Deaf and Dumb and the Blind.

By the death of this nobleman, many of the principal families in the counties of Down and Armagh—the Closes—the Halls—the Fordes—are placed in mourning; but the truest tribute to his public and private worth must be looked for in the universal sorrow which has pervaded all classes of society since the melancholy event became known. (1847-05-08, 1:4)

3729. Deaths from Starvation.—When passing through Clones a few days since, we learned among other particulars that, two women named Catherine Daltan, and Bridget Goodwin, were dead of starvation in that locality, and those in whose houses they died, wanting either the means or the inclination to inter them, they were being left unremoved until the authorities would chance to hear the circumstances, and choose to have them interred. One of them (Catherine Daltan) had been dead four days at this time, and though the corps was already emitting a very offensive odour, and it seemed likely that decomposition would immediately set in, yet so callous have the people grown, that the least effort was not being made to have her removed; and what is infinitely stranger than even this, the friends of the deceased—many of whom are very opulent—live in the immediate neighbourhood, and have refused to take any notice of the unfortunate occurrence! Would that there was some law in existence, which would compel such inhuman wretches, as the relatives of this ill fated woman—who are lost to every good feeling of our nature—to aid their perishing friends and, above all, to defray the expenses of their burial! such a love would particularly in those unhappy times be a desideratum, and one for which there were precedents both in Greece and Rome.

The number of deaths from starvation in the above neighbourhood, during the last six months, notwithstanding all the relief that has been given by public and private charities, has been, considering the number of inhabitants, inconceivably great. There is scarcely a day but there are wretches found dead, or dying, either in Clones town or on some of the roads that lead to it, and not to mention those who die in their huts and in the country. The Town-hall has scarce been without a starving man or woman a single day or night these two months. No sooner is one dead or brought to the poorhouse but another, or two, take his place, though except over head they have little shelter in it more than in the open field. These facts appear strange when it is considered what number are relieved at the soup kitchen, and the union workhouse; but they are not the less true. That crowds get soup at the former place, every day, is quite certain; but all or one third, of those who want cannot get it; and the generality of those who are getting it are merely enabled to sustain life. What is one little pint, of but tolerable soup, to any full grown person when obliged to subsist on it for 24 hours? But the head of the family, however old or feeble, is allowed nothing! —*Fermanagh Reporter*. (1847-05-08, 2:4)

3730. The following is the report of the Ballytrain Dispensary, for the year ending 12th April 1847:—

Patients under care 17th April, 1847 ...	83
Admitted since ...	1,094
Total ...	1,177
Of whom were visited ...	176
Visits paid to them ...	528
Died ...	12
Results unknown ...	28
Cured or relieved ...	865
On the books this day ...	96
Total ...	1,177

(1847-05-08, 3:4)

3731. We have just learned that the Rev. Dr. Maginnis, P.P. of Clones, died of fever, at his residence on Wednesday last. (1847-05-08, 3:5)

3732. Illness of the Lord Lieutenant.—Thursday.—The following bulletin was issued this day:—"His Excellency passed a good night, and the cough which, for some days past, had been troublesome, has abated."

Three O'clock.—The indications of improvement still continue. His Excellency is better and cheerful. (1847-05-08, 3:5)

3733. The Lord Bishop of Cork has appointed the Rev. J. Triphoop to the rectory of Schull, vacant by the death of the regretted Dr. Traill. (1847-05-08, 3:5)

3734. His Excellency the Lord Lieutenant has presented the Rev. Charles Peter Thomas, late Curate of Kenmare, in the diocess of Ardfert, to the union of Kenmare, vacant by the demise of the Rev. William Godfrey, late incumbent thereof. (1847-05-08, 3:5)

3735. A pauper named Terence Sherry, from Liscumasky, was admitted in the Board-room [Monaghan workhouse] at six o'clock on the 5th, and expired at eight same evening, from want of food. (1847-05-08, 3:5)

3736. The Unknown Grave.

Who sleeps below?—who sleeps below?
It is a question idle all,
Ask of the breezes as they blow,
Say, do they heed, or hear thy call?
They murmur in the trees around,
And mock thy voice—an empty sound!

A hundred summer-suns have shower'd
Their fostering warmth, and radiance bright;
A hundred winter storms have lower'd
With piercing floods, and hues of night,
Since first the remnant of his race
Did tenant this lone dwelling-place.

Was he of high or low degree?
Did grandeur smile upon his lot?
Or, born to dark obscurity,
Dwelt he within some lowly cot,
And, from his youth to labour wed,
From toil-strong limbs wrung daily bread?

Say, died he ripe, and full of years,
Bow'd down, and bent by hoary eld,
When sound was silence to his ears,
And the dim eyeball sight withheld;
Like a ripe apple falling down,
Unshaken, 'mid the orchard brown?

When all the friends that blest his prime,
Were vanish'd like a morning dream;
Pluck'd one by one by spareless time,
And scatter'd in oblivion's stream;
Passing away all silently,
Like snow-flakes melting in the sea?

Or, 'mid the summer of his years,
When round him throng'd his children young,
When bright eyes gush'd with balmy tears,
And anguish dwelt on every tongue,
Was he cut off, and left behind
A widow'd wife scarce half resign'd.

Perhaps he perished for the faith
One of that persecuted band
Who suffer'd tortures, bonds, and death,
To free from mental thrall the land,
And, toiling for the martyr's fame,
Espoused his fate, nor found a name!

Say, was he to science blind,
A groper in earth's dungeon dark?
Or one, whose bold aspiring mind
Did in the fair creation mark
The Maker's hand, and kept his soul
Free from this grovelling world's control?

Hush, wild surmise!—'tis vain, 'tis vain,
The summer flowers in beauty blow,
And sighs the wind, and floods the rain,
O'er some old bones that rot below;
No other record can we trace
Of fame or fortune, rank or race!

Then what is life, when thus we see
No trace remains of life's career?
Mortal! whoe'er thou art, for thee
A moral lesson gloweth here;
Putt'st thou in aught of earth thy trust?
Tis doom'd that dust shall mix with dust.

What doth it matter, then, if thus,
Without a stone, without a name,
To impotently herald us,
We float not on the breath of fame;
But, like the dew-drop from the flower,
Pass, after glittering for an hour.

Since soul decays not, freed from earth,
And earthly coils, it bursts away;
Receiving a celestial birth,
And spurning off its bonds of clay,
It soars, and seeks another sphere,
And blooms through heaven's sternal year!

Do good: shun evil: live not thou
As if at death thy being died;
Nor error's syren voice allow

To draw thy steps from truth aside;
Look to thy journey's end—the grave!
And trust in Him whose arm can save.

Moir.

(1847-05-08, 4:1)

3737. Suicide.—Yesterday, Dr. Kirwan, one of the city coroners, held an inquest at Mercer's Hospital, on the body of a man named John Connolly, who died in consequence of wounds inflicted by himself on his throat with a knife on the 22d instant. It appeared from the evidence that deceased was a cane-worker, and resided at Maiden-lane. He was about sixty years of age, and had five children. Some three weeks ago, he became apprehensive that his family would die of starvation, and he became greatly depressed in consequence. On Thursday morning about four o'clock, he got up and cut his throat in three different places with a knife, from the effects of which he died yesterday in hospital. The jury found the following verdict:—"That John Connolly's death was caused by wounds inflicted by himself on his throat, at his own residence, Maiden-lane, on the 23d [sic] instant, whilst labouring under temporary insanity.—*Evening Packet.* (1847-05-08, 4:3)

3738. Illness of the Lord Lieutenant.—His Excellency has, since last we addressed the public, experienced considerable relief from the immediate pressure of his symptoms—but not, as far as we can learn, of so decisive a character as to enable his friends to expect or his physicians to prognosticate his ultimate recovery. The series of bulletins issued since Friday last, indicates, we fear, rather an abatement of personal suffering than any improvement of general health:—

"Saturday.—His Excellency passed a perfect tranquil night, and his breathing is much relieved this morning.

"P. Crampton."

Sunday morning, Twelve o'clock.—At half-past nine to day, the subjoined bulletin was issued: —

"May 2.—His Excellency has passed another good night, and feels somewhat better this morning.

"P. Crampton."

We are glad to perceive by the following, that up to a late hour last night, his Excellency was not worse, but was rather in an improving condition:—

"Eleven o'Clock, Sunday night.—Sir P. Crampton has just left, and the answer was—'His Excellency is nothing worse, but was in an improving condition.'"

The following is the bulletin issued this morning at nine o'clock:—

"May 3.—His Excellency passed another good night, and feels much refreshed this morning."

"P. Crampton.
"W. Stokes.
"P.F. Purcell."

Half past three o'clock, p.m.—"His Excellency continues without any change since the morning."

The following bulletin was issued this morning, (Wednesday):—"His Excellency had more cough than usual last night, and does not feel quite as well as he was yesterday."

"P. Crampton.
"W. Stokes.
"P.F. Purcell."

(1847-05-08, 4:4)

3739. Fever in Limerick.—In the workhouse hospital of Limerick at present, there are no less than 273 cases of fever. (1847-05-08, 4:5)

3740. Fever in Fermanagh.—Fever still continues to rage with unabated malignity in this town and neighbourhood. Several respectable persons are suffering from the epidemic at present. Scarcely a day passes but we hear of some friend or acquaintance being stricken down, who, a few days previously, were in the enjoyment of excellent health. We greatly fear that, without Providential interposition, the ensuing summer will be fraught with evil consequences to this unfortunate country.—*Erne Packet.* (1847-05-08, 4:6)

3741. The Late Thomas Barnwell Martin, M.P. for the County of Galway.—In Lieutenant Grattan's interesting work on the exploits of the 88th, or Connaught Rangers, he has fallen into an error, whilst paying a just tribute to the courage of Mr. Martin; he states that Richard Martin was the gentleman who volunteered with that regiment at the Siege of Badajos; but it was the much regretted person whose name heads this article, the eldest son of Richard Martin, long M.P. for Galway, who thus distinguished himself.

Mr. T.B. Martin also represented the county for many years, and would probably have remained in undisturbed possession of his seat, as a man of any part never had a doubt of his independence of mind, or integrity of principle.

In a publication entitled the *Wars of Europe*, edited (it is described) by an officer of rank, honorable testimony is also borne to the bravery of Mr. Martin, but the same mistake is made as to the Chieftain's name.

The Writer having, from his youth, enjoyed the intimacy and friendship of the late T.B. Martin, and having, not many months since, at his (the writer's) table, again discussed with Mr. Martin the affair of his going to Spain, and serving at Badajos, the version now given may be relied on. Various causes having been assigned for the step taken by Mr. Martin—as a family quarrel, &c., &c. There was, however, nothing very extraordinary necessary to lead a young man of high spirit to take such a step. The simple fact was, that Mr. Martin's brother-in-law was a captain in the 88th, and Mr. Martin's sister (the present Lady P.) to whom Mr. Martin was much attached, was then with her husband in Spain. Many young men of fortune went to Spain as travellers during the war. Mr. Martin, when a mere (*continued...*)

3741, continued: ...boy, had commanded a corps of cavalry, (composed of his father's tenantry,) and raised during the disturbances in Ireland, and was, from his youth, a person of fearless disposition. When he went to Spain, he at once attached himself a volunteer to the 88th, in which were many Galwaymen, (almost all were Connaught-men,) and had not the extreme severity of his wound obliged him to return and remain at home, there is little doubt that he would have done as volunteer Thomas Graham did, raise a regiment, and rivalled in fame that hero, afterwards Lord Lynedoch. It is said Mr. Martin was offered a commission. The only one he would have accepted would have been one of Colonel of a regiment raised by himself; but his wound was most severe; he was shot from an embrasure quite through across the shoulders and back, as he was planting a ladder, and again hit in the head by the fragment of a shell, as the soldiers who loved him for his chivalrous daring, were carrying him off, after he had become insensible from loss of blood.

Mr. Martin could have raised half a dozen regiments of Connaught Rangers on his own estate, and his men would have followed him to the field as readily as they did to the hustings, with fidelity, confidence, and affection. He was loved, respected, and feared—loved for his benevolence, respected for his probity, feared for his rigid administration of justice as a magistrate.

Allusions having been made in print to Mr. Martin's property, and to encumbrances on it, it is due to him to state that he contracted no debts. The length and breadth of his estates are somewhat exaggerated; at a guess, his acres might be estimated from 160,000 to 200,000, with a population from 17,000 to 20,000. He had just raised a large sum at a low interest, and paid off all charges on the property, leaving him a splendid surplus income.

His loss would be deplored as irreparable in Connemara, were it not that his amiable daughter is known to inherit his sentiments and his virtues as well as his property—Miss Martin, brought up under exemplary parents, does not possess the attachment of her tenantry from mere feudal and hereditary claims. Hers are of much higher order; and in the midst of profound affliction, Mrs. and Miss Martin have a consolation in knowing that he whom they mourn for lived as became a man—beloved and respected, and died in a Christian's hope, sincerely and regretted.

J.A. O'N.

(1847-05-15, 1:2)

3742. Death from Fever of the Female Sailor, Jane Gallagher.—On Monday, the 3d inst., the remains of this remarkable female were attended to the burial-ground at the Abbey, near the town of Donegal. She caught the fatal malady whilst attending on her husband, who had been for a length of time confined with the disease which took her life. It may probably be within the recollection of most our readers, that some years ago, and during the time of his Majesty William the 4th, she had been discovered on board a ship in London, disguised in the dress of a sailor boy, having at the time her apprenticeship nearly served. It was thought she went in pursuit of her lover, as she first emigrated to America, missed her passage, then went on board a ship as a boy, expecting to make good her design. The novel circumstance excited so much wonder and amusement, that it at once reached the royal ear. She was introduced to his Majesty, had the honor to have wine and cake in his Royal company, with them, an assurance of his future protection and support. A pension was then granted her during life of £10 a-year, which she enjoyed up to her death; she has left to mourn her premature demise a large family of very young Tars, all of whom bear the names of the family of her Royal mistress and present Queen. It is anxiously hoped that the pension will be continued till they are able to appear in our navy, in the dress in which their poor mother was discovered. During her peregrinations, she has been frequently in company with ladies and gentlemen, has used snuff, smoked her pipe, drank punch, never was seen in the least intoxicated, and was not discovered till London. (1847-05-15, 1:5)

3743. Death of the Rev. S. Nelson, of Pettigo.—The Rev. Simon Nelson, Presbyterian minister of Pettigo, has fallen a victim to fever, after a short but severe illness. His loss will be severely felt in the neighbourhood in which he lived and laboured, as a devoted, successful minister. The home mission of the General Assembly, also, has suffered severely by his death, as for several years, he superintended, very efficiently, the Irish schools in the surrounding districts.
(1847-05-15, 2:4)

3744. Fever.—Fever is rapidly compassing us about. Our Poor house is crammed with a sickly and dying mass of wretches, huddled together for want of accommodation, there being above 200 in the house more than it can properly accommodate. In the gaol, six unfortunates are crammed into a cell six feet by nine—the Fever Hospital has triple its number of patients, and the town is infested with crowds of mendicant vagrants from every quarter of the island, steeped in the lowest depths of filth and destitution. Yet in all this position of danger, it is found impracticable to form a Board of Health, although the Government have expressly provided an act of Parliament for the purpose. A meeting of the Town Commissioners was held on Tuesday for this purpose, and, as it was ascertained that the powers were vested, under the new *Fever Act*, in the Relief Committee of the electoral division, which was then sitting, a deputation of the principal inhabitants waited on the committee in their room, but that body were too busy to attend to a matter in which the lives of the whole community are involved,—and the deputation left the room impressed with anything but a favorable opinion of the courtesy with which their application was treated.—Upon looking over the new act, we do not see that it repeals the power of the *58th Geo. III.*, by which a Board of Health may be formed by the parishioners at vestry, and if we are right in our opinion, the inhabitants should at once have recourse to the old law, by which funds can be advanced from the Treasury upon security of an imperative county presentment, if the Relief Committee do not instanter [sic] avail themselves of the provisions of the new *Fever Act* which we this day print for their guidance. (1847-05-15, 2:6)

3745. Illness of the Lord Lieutenant.—The following bulletin was issued on Wednesday morning:—"The Lord Lieutenant has had a quiet night, but his strength has not improved."

"Philip Crampton.
"Wm. Stokes.
"John F. Purcell."

Eleven o'Clock, p.m.—The answer to inquiries at the Castle at this hour was, that his Excellency underwent no change since morning.

Thursday.—"The Lord Lieutenant passed a quiet night, and feels somewhat stronger this morning."

"Philip Crampton.
"Wm. Stokes.
"J.F. Purcell."

Quarter past Four.—To inquiries at this hour, the answer was that no change had taken place in his Excellency's condition since morning.—*Packet.* (1847-05-15, 3:1)

3746. The Irish Steamers—Quarantine.—The following letter has been addressed to Lloyd's agent at Falmouth:

"Sir—I am directed by the Lords of Council to state to you, for the information of the Commissioners of the Customs, the desire of their lordships, that instructions may be given to the tide surveyors or other officers employed in visiting steam vessels arriving from Ireland (having deck passengers) before entering the docks, to hoist a yellow flag, and place such vessel under quarantine, until visited by a medical officer, so that it may be ascertained whether there be amongst the passengers any individuals suffering from fever; and in the event of its being ascertained by the medical officer that there are one or more cases of fever on board, the officers of customs will direct such steamer to be moved alongside one of the lazarettos in use as an hospital ship, into which the sick persons must be removed, after which the yellow flag is to be hauled down, the vessel admitted to pratique, and the healthy portion of the passengers to land; and it must be particularly notified to the masters of all steamers so released from quarantine, that after the first indulgence, if they should, in any future voyage, bring any passenger suffering from fever, the ship and crew with the sick on board, will be placed under the restraint of quarantine for a limited number of days, according to the state of health of the passengers on board, agreeably to *act 6 Geo. IV., cap. 78.*

"I am, Sir, your obedient servant,
"W.T. Bathurst.
"Council Office, Whitehall, May 5, 1947."
1847-05-15, 3:3)

3747. The Liberator's Health.—We have received a letter from Marseilles, by this evening's post, on the above important subject. It is dated Wednesday, the 5th. The Liberator was about to start from Civita Vecchia by the Sardinian steamer, *Lombardo.*

After visiting the Holy City for a short time, it was the intention of the Liberator to reside for a time at Florence.

The writer of the letter is full of hopefulness, and says the illustrious invalid exhibits every symptom of rapid improvement. (1847-05-15, 3:3)

3748. Death of William Mulholland, Esq.—Amongst the numerous deaths of the mercantile men of Belfast, which we have had the misfortune for some time past to record, we know of scarcely one which has given us more heartfelt sorrow than of Mr. Mulholland. He had been but a few days ill of typhus fever, contracted, we have reason to fear, in the institution which he was the chief means of bringing into existence, and fostering into usefulness—the Day Asylum. He took ill in the early part of last week, and notwithstanding all the appliances of medical skill, and the attentions of his many attached relations, he expired on Tuesday afternoon, in the prime and vigour of life.—*Belfast Chronicle.* (1847-05-15, 3:3)

3749. Monaghan Dispensary District.—Visited Twenty-two cases of fever in my Dispensary district, during the course of the past week.

Wm. Murray, M.D.
April 14, 1847.
(1847-05-15, 3:3)

3750. Newtownbutler Dispensary.—At a meeting of subscribers held on Tuesday, Doctor West of Ballyshannon was appointed medical attendant to the Newtonbutler Dispensary, in the room of the late Doctor Thompson. (1847-05-15, 3:6)

3751. The estate of the late Mr. Martin, M.P., was, in regard to extent, a principality. It extended from the bridge of Galway, in a tolerably straight line of sixty miles, by about thirty in breadth. The length of his avenue has often been the subject of dispute. From the gate-house on the high road to his house is upwards of 2 miles in length, and his tenantry number about ten thousand souls. (1847-05-15, 4:4)

3752. We hear vague rumours every day of deaths from destitution; but as the particulars have not reached us from well authenticated sources, we refrain from mentioning names or places at present. We have heard of one man who preferred dying of starvation, to seeking an asylum in our poorhouse; his principal dread being, that they would throw his corpse into a hole at the back of the house.—*Erne Packet.*
(1847-05-15, 4:5)

3753. Demise of the Lord Lieutenant.—Mr. Redington, Under-Secretary of State, has addressed the following official announcement to the Rt. Hon. the Lord Mayor of Dublin:—

"Dublin Castle, half-past 11, p.m., May 16.

"My Lord—It becomes my painful duty to inform you that his Excellency the Earl of Besborough departed this life at the hour of eleven o'clock, p.m., at the Castle of Dublin.—I have the honour to be your obedient servant,

"T.N. Redington.

"The Right Hon. the Lord Mayor."

The melancholy event so long anticipated has arrived, and the Earl of Besborough is no more.

The recent bulletins issued at the Castle have fully prepared the public mind for the fatal termination of his Excellency's illness. On Saturday morning, the announcement was that "his Excellency's strength was much reduced from the previous day." On Sunday morning, it should appear that the decisive symptoms of a speedy decease had manifested themselves. "His Excellency" (said the bulletin of Sunday) "is somewhat weaker this morning, but makes no complaint of pain." In the evening, the answer to enquiries at the Porter's Lodge was, that "his Excellency's physicians had no hopes of him;" and at eleven o'clock, p.m., on Sunday, the 16th day of May, 1847, his Excellency breathed his last, peacefully and without a struggle.

It was generally supposed, from the language of the bulletin of Sunday morning, that mortification had set in; but we have reason to believe that the immediate cause of the fatal result was an effusion of fluid into the air-cells of the lungs—the consequence of aneurism of the aorta, or great artery proceeding from the heart—a fact which corroborates our original statement of the nature of his Excellency's illness.

His Excellency is said to have been supported throughout his long and painful sufferings by a spirit of fortitude and patience truly admirable, and to have envinced those feelings of Christian resignation to the will of God—that blessed hope of everlasting life—through the merits of a Great Redeemer, which must have been most soothing to the closing hours of his life, and most consoling to his surviving and sorrowing friends. Never, we believe, had any man, in any rank of life, more sympathy and more comforts to sweeten his trial than his Lordship was blessed with in the unremitting love and attentions of his amiable and devoted children, and the other members of his family, who had assembled around him to watch, to soothe, and to alleviate the progress of his malady. He remained—to their great comfort—perfectly conscious and sensible up to the moment of decease, and had the satisfaction of pouring out a farewell blessing upon them all with his parting breath.

"A special messenger (says *Saunders's News-Letter*) was despatched this morning, with the sad intelligence, to London. A Queen's letter will be forthwith issued, nominating Lords Justice to sit until his Excellency's successor be finally nominated. Letters were despatched last night to the Right Hon. the Lord Mayor, the Lieutenant-General commanding, Sir Edward Blakeney; the Lord Chancellor, and other high official personages, announcing the sorrowful event."

It were premature to anticpate what the arrangements for his Excellency's funeral may be. We have, indeed, but few precedents for such a ceremonial. The latest is that of the Duke of Rutland, whose demise took place in 1787, since which time until the present, no Lord Lieutenant died in the administration of the government of Ireland.

His Excellency was in the 66th year of his age, and is succeeded in his titles and estates by his eldest son, John, Viscount Duncannon, M.P.

The late Earl of Besborough was Viscount Duncannon, and Baron of Besborough, Baron Ponsonby, of Sysonby and Duncannon, in Great Britain, P.C., Lt-[*illegible*] and Custos Rotulorum of the Co. Kilkenny, was born 31st August, 1781, succeeded to the title 3d Feb., 1844; married 16th November, 1805, Lady Maria Fane, third daughter of the Earl of Westmoreland.

His Excellency's family consists of Lady Georgiana Sarah, married to the Rev. Sackville Gardiner Bourke, Rector of Hatherop; Lady Augusta Lavinia Priscilla, married first to the late Earl of Kerry, afterwards to the Hon. C.A. Gore; the Hon. F.G. Brabazon, Lady Emily Charlotte Mary, Lady Maria Jane Elizabeth, married to her cousin, the Hon. C.F.A. Cooper Ponsonby, eldest son of Baron de Mauley; Hon. and Rev. W.W. Brabazon, Hon. S.C. Brabazon, Lady Harriet Frederica Anne, Lady Kathleen Louisa Georgina, Hon. G.H. Brabazon.

We understand that the funeral, which is to be a public one, will take place on Friday next.

PREPARATIONS FOR THE FUNERAL.

At an early hour yesterday, Sir William Betham, Ulster King at Arms, sent for Mr. Williams, the eminent undertaker of Stafford street, in order to make the necessary arrangements for the funeral of his Excellency. A programme of the procession and other matters were drawn up, and will be offically issued this day by the authorities.

The funeral is intended to leave the Lower Castle Yard on Friday evening, with a train of carriages, and will arrive at the terminus of the Great Western Railway, Islandbridge, about five o'clock, where special trains will be in attendance to convey the remains and the procession to Carlow, where carriages will be in attendance, to convey the body to the family burying-place, at Besborough, near Kilkenny, where it is expected the melancholy cortege will reach on Saturday evening.

The guns in the Park, by order of Town-Major White, commenced to fire at intervals of one minute, at eight o'clock in the morning, and discharged sixty-six rounds, that being the number of years of his Excellency's life. This is the usual custom when royalty or its representative departs from this life. Town Major White also ordered the bands on the different parades, when mounting guard, to be muffled, &c., and parade is to be carried on in solemn silence until after the interment.

All the vessels in the river had their flags floating half-mast high, which is the sign for mourning on such occasions, and the flags at the Castle, barracks, and magazines, were hoisted in like manner.

It is understood that the Ladies Ponsonby will leave the Castle on Wednesday, en route for Besborough Castle, Kilkenny.

Several noble famiies will be put in mourning by the sad event, which has deprived them of an affectionate relative and friend.

The several tradesmen belonging to his Excellency had their shops closed yesterday in respect to the memory of his lordship, and indeed all classes of citizens seem to be deeply affected at the loss the country has sustained.

The following official communication, relative to the funeral and lying in state, has been received by the Right Hon. the Lord Mayor.

"Dublin Castle, May 17, 1847.

"My Lord—I have to acquaint your lordship that the remains of the late Lord Lieutenant of Ireland are to be removed from the Chapel Royal, on next Friday afternoon, the 21st inst., to the terminus of the Cashel Railway, at King's Bridge, and from thence, privately conveyed to the family vault at Besborough.

"I have the honour to be, my lord,
"Your lordship's obedient servant,
"T.N. Redington.
"The Right Hon. the Lord Mayor of Dublin."

This Day—Monday.

The following was issued at half-past 4 o'clock:

PROGRAMME OF THE CEREMONIAL
AT THE FUNERAL OF HIS LATE EXCELLENCY
JOHN WILLIAM, EARL OF BESSBOROUGH, &C., &C.,
LORD LIEUTENANT GENERAL
AND GENERAL GOVERNOR OF IRELAND,
ON FRIDAY, THE 21ST OF MAY, 1847.

The streets to be lined from the Upper Castle yard, down Cork-hill, Parliament-street, and the Quays, to the Terminus of the Cashel Railway.

The Household and State to be in full dress.

The Knights of St. Patrick in full Dress, with their Collars; and the officers of the order in ribands and badges.

The procession will proceed from the Castle as follows:—

The Town Major on Horseback.
Troop of Cavalry.
Minister and Curate of St. Werburgh's Church.
Standard of Order of St. Patrick.
Servants of the Household.
Medical Staff.
Gentlemen at Large.
with
Master of the Horse.
Banneroll.
Chaplains and Dean of the Chapel Royal.
Great Banner of his Excellency's Arms.

Usher on Horseback.	The Coronet, on a Crimson Velvet Cushion, borne on Horseback, uncovered.	Usher on Horseback.

Steward and Comptrollers, with their white Wands.
Private Secretary.
The Coffin.

Gentleman Usher.	Ulster King of Arms.	Gentleman Usher.

Chief Mourners:—(Lords Justices.)
His Excellency's Family.
The Lord Lieutenants carriage, with the blinds up.
Lord Mayor.
Lord Chancellor.
Knights of St. Patrick.
Nobility according to rank—highest first.
Eldest Sons in Order.
Chief Secretary.
Privy Councillors.
Chief Justice of the Queen's Bench.
Master of the Rolls.
Chief Justice of the Common Pleas.
Lord Chief Baron.
Judges according to Seniority.
Younger Sons of Viscounts.
Younger Sons of Barons.
Baronets.
Knights.
High Sheriff of the City of Dublin.
Officers of the Order of St. Patrick, in their Ribands and Badges.
Solictor General.
Under Secretary to the Lord Lieutenant.
Eldest Sons of Baronets.
Judge of the Admiralty.
Masters in Chancery.
Commissioners of Public Works.
Commissioners of Bankruptcy.
Commissioners of Insolvency.
Commissioners of Police.
The Rev. The Provost, T.C.D.

(continued...)

3753, continued:

Adjutant General.
Deputy Adjutant General.
Deputy Quarter Master General.
Commandant of Artillery.
Inspector-General of Constabulary.
Commandant of Engineers.
Respective Officers of the Ordnance.
Commandant of the Garrison.
Inspecting Field Officer.
Commandant of Hibernian School.
Director General of Medical Department.
Inspector General of Coast Guard.
Inspector General of Prisons.
Secretary of Post Office.
Chief Clerk of the Chief Secretary.
President of Royal Irish Academy.
President of Royal Hibernian Academy.
Governor of the Bank,
&c., &c., &c.

The Carriages of the above will enter the Castle Yard by Ship Street Gate, and be arranged there. All other Carriages will draw up in Dame-street, with their Heads to the West, according to the directions which will be issued by the Commissioners of Police respecting these and other necessary arrangements.

W. Betham, Ulster.
Office of Arms, May 18.
(1847-05-22, 1:1)

3754. Awful and true.—In the parish of Kilglas, this week, the skeleton bodies of seven wretches were found inside a bridge.—The dogs of the surrounding villages had the flesh almost eaten off. The police stationed in the place were called out, and shot seven dogs, in the mouth of one of which was a heart and a portion of the liver.—*Roscommon Journal.* (1847-05-22, 1:3)

3755. At an early hour on Saturday last, as two men were going to the fair of Ballybay, they saw something lying on the edge of the road, between Clementstown and the Drum road, and on nearer approach, found it to be a man with his feet on the water-table and life all but extinct; they carried him up to where a number of houses were, but were refused admittance and, were obliged again to make the side of the road his bed, until one or two humane persons got the key of an empty house, and there he breathed his last. In about three hours after he was found, Mr. Boyd, one of the church-wardens, gave a coffin, and he was interred on Sunday. No inquest was held—he was a complete stranger—a glass tumbler and teaspoon were found in his pocket. (1847-05-22, 3:1)

3756. Accident.—On Friday the 14th inst., a melancholy and fatal accident occurred on the line of the Dundalk and Enniskillen railway, close to the town of Castleblayney. As a man of the name of William Harker was driving a number of loaded waggons up the inclined plain, when he had arrived at the summit, it was necessary to disengage the horse from the foremost waggon; he failed in accomplishing this and was dragged between the wheels of the first and second waggons, the wheels of the second passing over his body in two places, one over the lower part of the abdomen, causing extensive internal injury, which occasioned his death; the other over the lower part of the thigh, breaking the bone close to the knee joint and inflicting two severe wounds. He lingered till two o'clock on the morning of the 18th, in the county infirmary, where he died. An inquest was held this day, the 21st, on the body, and a verdict in accordance with the facts of the case recorded, "That deceased came by his death in consequence of injuries received from a loaded waggon having passed over his body on the Dundalk and Enniskillen railway. (1847-05-22, 3:3)

3757. Victims of the Prevailing Fever—The Rev. Alexander Patterson, of Ballymena, and the Rev. James Patterson, of Rich-hill.—It is with the deepest regret that we announce the death of the Rev. Alexander Patterson, of Ballymena. This most amiable and excellent minister breathed his last on Monday, about half-past twelve o'clock at noon. The disease which cut him off so prematurely was typhus fever. He fell a victim on the eleventh day from the commencement of the attack. We believe he was in the 46th year of his age.

We believe that Mr. Patterson, of Ballymena, is the fifth minister of the Irish Assembly who, within the last two months, has fallen a victim to the prevailing epidemic. In our paper of Saturday, it was our melancholy duty to announce the death of the Rev. James Patterson, of Rich-hill, who expired on the 7th inst. Mr. Patterson, of Rich-hill, was by birth a Scotchman, and was cut down in the prime of life. (1847-05-22, 3:3)

3758. I attended during the past week 17 new cases of fever in my Dispensary district.

Wm. Murray, M.D.
May 21st, 1847.
(1847-05-22, 3:3)

3759. A woman named O'Neill, who lived on Michael's-hill, dropped dead on Monday evening whilst passing through the Castle-yard. (1847-05-22, 3:6)

3760. Cahirciveen.—In this district, the greatest destitution prevails—wretched creatures dropping down in the streets, their remains exposed for days, and often interred without the least covering, save only their mother earth, and two or three inches is considered sufficient. I witnessed a most heart-rending scene on last Monday, which occurred in one of the neighbouring church-yards of this town. A few days ago, the body of one of those poor people, whose death was brought from actual starvation, was found over the surface of the earth, and torn up by a dog, which was found feeding on its putrid remains. Several particles of the bowels were strewed at a distance from the miserable place of his interment. Gracious heaven, is not this horrifying in a Christian country! Is this to be continued? What more could be expected from the bushmen of New Zealand? I will leave you to add the remainder.—*Cor. of the Tralee Chronicle.* (1847-05-22, 4:3)

3761. The following fact furnishes incontestible proof of the frightful amount of mortality in the Bandon Union. Within six days, the number of coffins sent out of one deal yard (the Messrs. Popes) in Bandon, amounted to 136. (1847-05-22, 4:4)

3762. Death of Mr. O'Connell.—*Freeman's Journal* Office, Tuesday, Seven o'Clock.—The worst anticipations of O'Connell's most sanguine friends have been realised. A special messenger from our London Correspondent has just reached our office with the French papers of Saturday night, which contain painful confirmation of the melancholy and afflicting rumours with which the public mind has been especially agitated since Saturday last. The Liberator expired at Genoa on the night of Saturday, May the 15th, at half-past nine o'Clock. *Galignani's Messenger* publishes the following letter from Doctor Duff, the English physician, who attended him at Genoa, dated the 16th instant.

"Some account of the closing scenes of the life of an individual who has filled so remarkable a position in the world as Daniel O'Connell, must prove interesting to the generality of the readers of the *Messenger*, and I, therefore, as an English physician called to attend him, take leave to lay before you the following statement. On Monday, May 10, I saw Mr. O'Connell for the first time, and he was then suffering from profuse and involuntary diarrhea, with great pain of the abdomen under pressure, strong and rapid pulse, flushed face, etc. Mr. O'Connell had also chronic bronchitis of some years standing. From the remedies employed, these symptoms were much ameliorated, and on the morrow he seemed convalescent. But, from Mr. O'Connell's great repugnance to swallow even the simplest medicine, this state of improvement could not be followed up. On the evening of Tuesday (11th), the new symptom of congestion of the brain presented itself. Active measures were immediately had recourse to, and from them, there was a decided improvement. Again, the aid of interal remedies was denied, Mr. O'Connell refusing to take any medicine. Towards the evening of Wednesday (12th), the symptoms increased, Mr. O'Connell was restless, and sometimes slightly incoherent. Our former measures were again employed, but with slight success. During Thursday, all the symptoms increased with great tendency to sleep, from which, however, he could easily be roused; the breathing was much embarrassed; circulation became difficult and in some degree indistinct, and the mind wavered. Thursday night was passed in a state of profound heavy sleep, with increased difficulty of breathing, and, in addressing those about him, he imagined himself in London, and spoke to them as if there. On Friday, he was much worse, the breathing very laborious, the voice scarcely audible and the words half formed; all the symptoms have increased. In this state, he lingered on till Saturday night, seemingly conscious of the presence of those about him, but neither attempting to move nor speak. My treatment of Mr. O'Connell was always in conjunction with Dr. Beretta, of this place, and a young French physician, who had accompanied him from Lyons, and, on the day preceding his demise, we had the advantage of consulting with Dr. Viviani, the oldest practitioner of Genoa, and of high repute. By his advice, and as a last resource, a further application of leeches to the temples, was advised, but all was in vain; he expired last night, at half-past nine o'clock (p.m.), apparently suffering little pain. During the whole period of our attendance upon Mr. O'Connell, it was with the greatest difficulty he could be induced to take medicine, or even necessary food, and he perseveringly abstained from drink for fully forty hours. Had this been otherwise, the period of death might have been procrastinated, but his failing health and spirits, with constant tendency to cerebral congestion, rendered certain his death at no very distant period."

The *Gallignani* says—

A few of our Paris contemporaries have articles on the death of Mr. O'Connell. We begin with the *Univers*, the chief organ of the Roman Catholics in this country. This journal, in respect to the memory of the eminent man who has just expired, is surrounded by a black border. It says—

"Ireland, has experienced so many evils, has just been struck with a misfortune greater to her than all the others, and irreparable—she has lost her Liberator. Mr. O'Connell is dead. This sad news reached Paris yesterday, and although we wish to doubt its correctness, to-day it is certain. He expired at Genoa, disappointing his last wish, and last hope, that yet remained to his friends. The amelioration visible since he left Lyons deceived no person: it was the flicker of an expiring flame; but his friends flattered themselves, in commune with himself, that at least he would be able to reach Rome, and that Daniel O'Connell would die at the feet of Pius IX.—Such was the majesty of the man, and such the place he filled in the world, that Rome alone could provide a tomb worthy of him. Rome was his true country, in effect.

Rome will not have his ashes. It will not be able to point with pride to his footsteps, which would be illustrious among those of so many others who have honoured that immortal soil; but Rome will guard, she will honour his memory, and perhaps one day will raise a statue to the father of a people—to the pacific conqueror of the greatest, of the only benefit that the church demands in this world for her children and for herself—liberty. O'Connell was born under the pontificate of Ganganelli—an unfortunate (*continued...*)

3762, continued: ...epoch, when all Europe, corrupted by its kings and by its writings, raised against the church a parricidal hand. When her children were on all sides torn from the church, O'Connell preserved to it a faithful daughter, and in dying, bequeathed her to it more beautiful than it had ever known her. Ireland was a slave to the despotism of England.—Ireland is now free! O'Connell alone has done the great work: he took the nation between his arms, and, sustained by the strength of his genius, carried her into the salubrious regions of liberty, as a father sustained by love carries to the summit of the mountain his dying son, that he may breathe a free and better air. O'Connell has been threatened, abused, combatted, and betrayed a hundred times; but he accomplished his sublime mission without the shredding of a drop of blood! Who can now say what amount of misfortunes and massacres all Europe will be saved by this example—one of the finest that man ever gave to man, of so extensive a revolution effected through such legitimate means."

In looking at this judgment of God, so fearful for all, we less lament the hero of Ireland. The bitterness which filled his last days, was notwithstanding accompanied with great repose. He was able to review, by the light of faith, all the events of his life. Christian as he was, he knew how to turn to his profit, this pause granted him on the threshold of eternity. He has accepted without a murmur, with joy, perhaps, the supreme anguish in the midst of which he has expired. The greatest of the privileges that God can grant to just men, Christians, is it not to die on the cross.

(*From the Ami de le Religeon.*)

To her deplorable calamities, to her mourning and inexpressible distress, unfortunate but faithful Ireland has to-day, alas, to add the most cruel loss that could fall upon her. The soul so Catholic of the Liberator of Ireland has gone to repose herself in a better life.—Mr. O'Connell died at Genoa, where he had hardly arrived under the fine sky of Italy, to which he had gone to demand health, that he might be able to recommence the great struggle for religious liberty. The Catholics of every country will join in the bitter regret that this irreparable loss causes to their brethren in Ireland and England.

Until we are able to return to the subject, and notice the life of this personage, so celebrated, and so gloriously connected with the religious greatness of our age, we shall borrow from our cotemporaries some observations which give a just idea of the conduct and merit of the great man.

We read in the *Constitutionnel*,

"The hopes which had been conceived of the recovery of Mr. O'Connell have been cruelly disappointed. The great orator had scarcely arrived at Genoa when he felt himself mortally attacked, and was the first to declare that he had only three days to live. His malady was complicated with an inflammation of the intestines, and nothing could stop the progress of the illness. The death of such a man would have been an important event at any period: but in the present difficult situation of England, and with the famine which desolates Ireland, the disappearance of the Liberator acquries extreme importance. Nobody can foresee the consequences of such an event, or the influence that it will exercise over the fate, not merely of the English cabinet, but also that of the three kingdoms."

The following is from the *Courrier Francais*:—

Daniel O'Connell died on arriving at Genoa.—Perhaps this patriarch of the accursed tribe thought the isolated mountain on which he could die far from his own. If he did not despair of his people, it is certain that his people began to despair of him. O'Connell had the soul of a prophet, but he had the mind of a lawyer. It was in the paths of legality that he desired the agitation to move; to the encroachments of England, he always opposed legality, and England often retreated before that respected buckler. But has Ireland made a step? Look where she now is after these thirty years of sterile agitation. If Ireland be bound to pay a tribute of tears and grief to him who announced himself as her Liberator, it is to that magic and inspired voice which it will hear no more, it is to that ardent soul which inspired a whole people with its breathing; it is to that eloquence, winged like a canticle, sad as a psalm, varied as a drama, and in which appeared at times, the disordered inspiration of the ancient prophets—it is, in a word, to the consoler of the afflicted that Ireland owes its regrets, and in no wise to the avenger of the opposed. Let her weep for this great soul which expires, but it is for England especially to regret in O'Connell the conciliator, who by his oratory, effected so long a truce between the oppressed and the oppressor. Perhaps the voyage of O'Connell in Italy was a voluntary exile; perhaps he felt before he died all the vanity of the task he had undertaken. In the last years of his life, he might have seen Ireland, if not separating herself from him, and taking from him the popularity she had given, at least demanding a more powerful and more resolute action, seeking, in short, in Young Ireland more active and more decided instruments of agitation. O'Connell never employed against O'Brien and the other agitators who lately came forward to dispute with him the direction of Ireland, those bitter sarcasms, those crushing bursts of wrath, with which he armed himself against his adversaries. If the great agitator did not confess that he deceived himself in submitting the cause of Ireland to the justice of a Saxon parliament, his noble heart, so loving and so devoted, did not at least desire to show those who thought of the salvation of Ireland by more energetic means that they were wrong. When he saw O'Brien and his friends appeal resolutely from Ireland oppressed to Ireland armed for the combat, the old champion exclaimed, "May they accomplish a work which I have not dared to attempt!" and he retired from the arena to die. (1847-05-29, 2:2)

3763. Belfast.—We regret to say that, in consequence of the almost incessant arrival of strangers from all parts of the country into Belfast, there is no abatement of fever here, but, on the contrary, it would appear to be increasing. All that can be done under our peculiar circumstances—our town turned, as it were, into a receptacle for the diseased of other quarters—is doing by the Board of health, who are making every effort to arrest the epidemic in its course. Among the latest acts of the board is that of turning the old barracks in Barrack-street into an hospital, which will be opened to-day for receiving patients. Dr. Lamont, assisted by a qualified apothecary, has taken charge of this hospital, resigning his office of district medical attendant.—*Banner of Ulster*. (1847-05-29, 2:3)

3764. Castlebar.—The rapid strides of this fearful epidemic are becoming every day more terrific. This country has been fearfully scourged. In the neighbouring towns, we hear of deaths without number from typhus fever, while we regret to observe a want of precautionary measures being adopted to check the spread of this malady. The want of cleanliness among the lower classes, and the filthy condition of the dwellings, must be productive of the worst consequences; and we regret some measures are not taken to remedy so crying an evil. We heard of several deaths from fever in Ballinrobe, during the past week, and also that this disease is raging in Westport. In this town, our institutions are visited, and to prevent its spread, something ought to be done. The Castlebar guardians have resolved on building sheds and erecting a fever hospital.—*Mayo Constitution*. (1847-05-29, 2:3)

3765. Death of the Rev. George Lewis.—Of late, we have been called upon to deplore the loss of many well known, and valued characters in our country—persons of high station and inestimable worth; but it has seldom fallen to our lot to record the death of one more universally beloved than the Rev. George Lewis, the humble and unostentatious, but the faithful, kind, laborious and intelligent curate of Clontibret, in this county. By the inscrutable will of an all-wise God, another of the most promising men of his day, has been cut off in the prime of a useful life by Fever. He died on the 26th instant, after a few days' illness, and was followed to the grave on Thursday by several of his brethren, and the sorrowing flock amongst whom he had so assiduously labored. During the address of the Rev. C. Wolfe, who expatiated warmly on the worth of this devoted man of God, the bursts of grief were audible around. We re-echo the sentiment expressed in our hearing, that the impression made by his life and doctrine may be more firmly rooted in their minds by the sad and unexpected event! We need say no more—this faithful shepherd has fallen asleep in Jesus—he has entered into rest, his name is written in heaven, and his record is on high.

In another part of our paper will be found some lines upon the melancholy event, as touching as they are true. (1847-05-29, 3:2)

3766. Death from Starvation.—Yesterday, an unfortunate being breathed his last in the diamond of our town; he was being conveyed to the poor house, and had he survived a few minutes longer, he would have helped to increase the bills of mortality of that establishment. Cadaverous, emaciated, hideous in filth and rags, this human being, though an object of pity, was still a greater object of disgust. Such a circumstance, a few years ago, nay, months ago, would have created an awful sensation; but now all the finer feelings of humanity have become completely suspended—private charity has all but ceased to exist, and in its place is created the degrading, injurious, ruinous, and almost useless system of outdoor relief. (1847-05-29, 3:2)

3767. It gives us great concern to state, that fever not only continues unabated in this town, but is somewhat on the increase, chiefly among the poorer portion of the inhabitants, though it by no means spares the more respectable classes, in its rapid and fatal course. We learn that the number of fever patients in both the general hospital and the workhouse fever wards, is at present about 900; and that the number of cases reported by the district inspectors of the Board of Health, scattered throughout the town, is not less than 300, exclusive of the patients conveyed to the newly provided hospital, in Barrack-street, from the Night Asylum. The whole number of fever patients, as yet ascertained, in this town may, therefore, be safely set down at nearly 1,300—a sad proof of the alarming extent to which the epidemic has already progressed. —*Belfast News-Letter*. (1847-05-29, 3:3)

3768. On Saturday last, a labourer on the Dublin and Drogheda Railway was engaged in loading some waggons with stone near Rogerstown, when, two waggons being in motion, he accidentally fell between them, and, in endeavouring to get up, he crept between the wheels, one of which passed over his head, and instantly killed him. (1847-05-29, 3:3)

3769. Notice.—I Hereby Caution all Persons against Paying over any Sum of Money, (which they may be indebted to me personally, or as Executrix of the late Mr. Robert Killen,) to any person except to myself, or my Solicitor, Mr. Edmond Morphy. If paid after this Notice, such Amount will not be credited by me.

Rooskey Lodge, 22d May, 1847.

Mary Campbell.

(1847-05-29, 3:5)

3770. The Vacant Coronership of Fermanagh.—We understand that it is the intention of Captain Fausset, Hazelett Beatty, Charles Jones, and Thomas Irwine, Esqrs., to solicit the suffrages of the electors for the Coronership, vacant by the death of Hugh Collum, Esq. If they all go to the poll, we may expect a smart contest. (1847-05-29, 3:5)

3771. Alarming Spread of Fever.—It is with deep regret we learn, that fever is rapidly on the increase throughout all the country. We believe it may be said, with perfect truth, that there is not a single county in Ireland exempt from its ravages. Our remarks apply to those in the upper ranks of life, who are daily falling victims to the fatal pestilence, which spares neither sex nor age. It is our painful duty to notice the following deaths, which have appeared in the provincial journals, since our last publication:—Stepney St. George, Esq., of Headford Castle, Galway; Dr. Collum, Enniskillen; the Rev. Robert Potter, perpetual Curate of Louisburgh, Mayo; Mr. Babington, Apothecary to the Workhouse, Cavan; John Loftus Griffin, Esq., Sub-Inspector of Constabulary, Sligo; Miss Anderson, daughter of the Rev. Mr. Anderson, Rector, of Ballinrobe; the Rev. Mr. Reordan, P.P., Castlelackner; and the Rev. Mr. Duane, C.C., Mitchelstown.—*Dublin Evening Packet.* (1847-05-29, 3:5)

3772. Death of Sir Arthur Chichester, Bart.—We regret to have to announce the death of Sir Arthur Chichester, Bart., which took place, on Tuesday, at his residence, Adelaide Place, in this town. He was created a Baronet in 1821, and was nearly allied to the Donegal and O'Neill families. Sir Arthur represented the Borough of Carrickfergus, on the Conservative interest, for many years. His family seat was at Greencastle, county Donegal; but, owing to the delicate state of his health, he resided, for some time past, continually in this town. From the commencement of the present distress, up to the period at which he was prevented from taking an active part, by illness, Sir Arthur largely evinced the benevolence of his disposition, not only by the generous liberality with which he contributed to the several local relief funds, but by the personal exertions he made in the cause. Deceased was a Deputy-Lieutenant of the County of Antrim, and filled the office of Weighmaster of Belfast. His remains, we understand, will be removed from his late residence, 2, Adelaide-place, on to-morrow morning, at nine o'clock. (1847-05-29, 3:5)

3773. Death of the Rev. R. Matthews.—Another faithful and earnest minister of the Gospel of our Lord Jesus Christ has been added to that devoted band who have sacrificed their lives in this awful crisis, of administering comfort and spiritual aid to those laid low in sickness. The Rev. Robert Mathews, of the Diocesan School of Ballymena, has been carried off by fever. He had the charge of the parish of Ahogill [sic], and caught the prevailing fever in attending the bedside of two of his parishioners; disease made rapid progress, and in a few days, he breathed his last. Than him, there was not a more simple-minded, faithful, and intelligent minister. He was universally respected and beloved, and has left a young and numerous family to deplore his premature loss. Blessed are the dead which die in the Lord. (1847-05-29, 4:4)

3774. Nenagh.—The mortality in and about the vicinity of Nenagh is daily augmenting. The deaths in the workhouse for the last week number 36. There are no fewer than ten coffin making establishments in our town, in which three or four men are daily and often nightly employed. It frequently occurs that one man, with tottering steps, might be seen bearing a coffin, in which is deposited the body of his child, to the grave without no mourner but himself. The patients in Nenagh Fever Hospital this evening, amount to 207, by which the establishment is quite over crowded. The great Majority are from distant parts of the surrounding country.—*Nenagh Guardian.* (1847-05-29, 4:4)

3775. Kilkenny.—We regret to say that fever is alarmingly on the increase, in both the county and city of Kilkenny. This fact has been peculiarly manifested within the last five or six days, by the number of admissions into the fever hospitals.—*Kilkenny Journal.* (1847-05-29, 4:4)

3776. Belfast.—This awful malady is still extending in this locality. At present, there are 415 fever patients in hospital, and numerous applications are daily being made for admission, where it is impossible to comply with, notwithstanding the recent alterations. The old military barrack is not yet in a proper state for the admission of patients, but we believe that every exertion has been made to make it available. As soon as possible, this place will be opened, when those who are at present confined in their ill ventilated habitations will be accommodated with better apartments in the old barrack. The sheds that are in course of erection, in connexion with the Frederick-street hospital, will, it is expected, be fit for the reception of patients in the course of a week. They will afford accommodation for nearly 200 patients. Notwithstanding the numbers who have been seized with this disease, the mortality has not been great.—*News-Letter.* (1847-05-29, 4:4)

3777. Sligo.—Fever continues its malignant sway in this town and vicinity—it is indeed a season of anguish and of bitter trial to vast numbers; those who are this day apparently secure from the pestilence cannot look to the dawn of the coming one with apprehension—but few families can claim exemption from being encompassed with clouds of distress; since our last publication, three of four respectable members of society have been cut off by fever, and from the effects of the prevailing epidemic, many of the humbler classes are being hourly interred. On the morning of the 10th instant, the constable in charge of Arigna Valley station, on the confines of this county, observed the house of a poor woman named Gaffney on fire. The police immediately ran to the place, and, at much risk and considerable personal daring, succeeded in rescuing three children who were lying in one bed with typhus fever, and carried out a coffin, containing the remains of their unfortunate parent, from the flames that encompassed the entire household. The poor mother was not at home during this fearful scene; but we are happy to state that no criminality was discoverable in the transaction, and that the fire was purely accidental. Five persons, including the father, have died in that house from destitution during the last two months; and but for the intrepid conduct of the police, three others would have been added to the number of victims. This is only one out of the innumerable sad instances of the awful ravages consequent on famine and disease in this town and county.—*Sligo Journal*. (1847-05-29, 4:4)

3778. Cavan, Sunday, May 23.—Fever is on the increase here. On Saturday, Mr. Babington, the apothecary of our union workhouse, died of fever, contracted in the discharge of his arduous duties. (1847-05-29, 4:5)

3779. Galway.—We have heard so much of the spread of fever in this locality, that it became our duty to make ourselves acquainted with the facts, and to communicate them to the public. It is quite true, as stated by the medical officer of the poor law union, that in point of numbers, there has existed, and still does exist, a very considerable amount of this form of disease in Galway. But its character is of so mild a nature, it can scarcely be called fever, unless of that kind which accompanies illness of any description. The spotted fever conveys the idea of some awfully malignant disease, at which most people shudder, but it certainly would be an exaggeration of the truth to say, that for some time past, there has been more than what medical men term the Petechial form of the complaint, except in some very rare instances, and this is borne out by the circumstances, that so few, amidst a dense population, have fallen victims to it. No doubt, the deaths in this neighbourhood have been, of late, exceedingly numerous, but the people are carried away not by fever, but by dysentery, dropsy, and other complaints, arising from the want of the common necessaries of life. We have deemed it right to place the truth before the public, so that no false alarm shall go abroad respecting the sanatory condition of Galway.—*Galway Mercury*. (1847-05-29, 4:5)

3780. Dread of Fever.—The great dread which the people entertain of this frightful malady may be said to be unconquerable. In illustration of this, we will mention one instance. On Saturday morning last, as a corpse that had been a victim to fever was about to be removed from one of the almost pestilential courts off North Queen-street, for interment, there was not a single individual to lend a helping hand, to have it carried to the hearse waiting on the street. The neighbours would not approach the precincts of the place at all.—One solitary individual alone was there: it was a woman; and she appeared to be deeply stricken with sorrow. The husband of the deceased was lying, at the time, ill of fever in the hospital. After a considerable lapse of time, the corpse was carried out by two men, and the funeral procession, consisting of three individuals, moved slowly away.—*Belfast Vindicator*. (1847-05-29, 4:6)

3781. Fever in Belfast.—This malady is still progressing, and notwithstanding every increase of accommodation by extending the old hospitals, and renting a new one, the numerous wards thus supplied are immediately filled to overflowing with persons afflicted with fever. In the Frederick-street hospital alone, there were, on last night, no less than 490 fever patients: and in all the hospitals in town, there cannot be less than about 1,200 suffering from this malady. There is still a large number of applicants, for whom there is no room; but as a portion of the sheds adjoining the Frederick-street hospital will be opened to-day, at twelve o'clock, we hope the evil will be remedied.—*News Letter*. (1847-06-05, 1:3)

3782. Solemn Warning.—On Sunday, during the awful thunderstorm with which we were visited, a poor man, named Ritchie, who lived in the neighbourhood of Newtownards, was struck with lightning, which caused his immediate death. He was sitting in his house at the time, when the electric fluid struck a handsaw, hanging upon the wall, thence passing over the man in a moment, in the twinkling of an eye, quenched his existence; also severely injuring a woman in its rapid flight. He has left a wife and two children, who were likewise in the house but escaped unhurt, to deplore their heavy loss.—*Belfast Chronicle*. (1847-06-05, 1:3)

3783. Inquest.—An inquest was held on the 31st ultimo, at Castleshane, on the body of James Devlin, a car driver from Armagh, who fell dead on Sunday evening at that place. It appeared from the evidence that the man had been in good circumstances, but had been suffering from disease in his chest for some time past. He ate a hearty dinner, took half a glass of punch after, and sat for some time out of doors in conversation with another man. He suddenly, without complaining, fell and expired. Verdict, died by the visitation of God. (1847-06-05, 3:1)

3784. To the Editor of the *Northern Standard*.—Sir—A few days since, an inquest was held by W.C. Waddell, Esq., Coroner for this county, in the townland of Drumgavney, on the leading road from Ballibay to Rosslea, on the body of Eliza Grimes, who had met her death on the preceding evening, from having, owing to the darkness of the night, and the unprotected state of the road, fallen into the deep and narrow channel of the small stream which crosses the road there. (1847-06-05, 3:1)

3785. Accidental Death on the Dundalk and Enniskillen Railway, at Castleblayney.—A Coroner's inquest was held on Friday last, the 28th inst., on view of the body of Thomas Hughes, who was killed by a loaded waggon passing over his body; a verdict was returned accordingly. The jury not considering that competent persons were employed to attend the movement of the waggons, or a sufficient motive given of their approach, requested the contractors to (*continued...*)

3785, continued: ...adopt such precautions as would prevent the recurrence of such accidents. We hope this caution will be attended to, as this has been the second death from the same cause, within a very short period. The horse which Hughes was attending was also killed. (1847-06-05, 3:1)

3786. Fever in Monaghan.—There are 119 cases of fever in the Workhouse Hospital, and in the sheds, which are constructed of canvas cloths thrown over the walls and tightened like tents to the ground. There are 40 fever patients in the Baronial Fever Hospital, and the medical attendant of the Monaghan Dispensary District reports 40 out-door new cases of fever since his last report (this day fortnight). (1847-06-05, 3:3)

3787. Christopher Gamble, Esq., of Enniskillen, has been appointed by the Lord Lieutenant to the office of Registrar of Marriages for this district, vice Stewart Betty, Esq., deceased.—*Fermanagh Reporter.* (1847-06-05, 3:3)

3788. Cure for Dysentery.—The following recipe for the cure of this prevalent complaint, had been placed in our hands by a highly respectable gentleman, who assures us of its perfect success in every instance in which it has been given:—Take of carpenter's glue about one inch square; pour as much boiling water on it as will melt it; then put it into a pint of new milk; and add four or five lumps of white sugar; boil them well, and, when cool, take two table spoonsful three times a-day.—*Belfast Chronicle.* (1847-06-05, 3:3) *Note: This is an antiquated treatment. This transcription is provided only to inform for historical interest.*

3789. The Dying Mother to her Daughter.

Bend closer, love, and do not weep
So bitterly for me,
But listen to my words while I
Have power to speak to thee;
The dew of death is on my brow,
Life's pulse is quickly ebbing now,

And thou will soon be left alone
Without a mother's care,
In the wide world which may appear
To thee all bright and fair;
For little does my Emma know
Its sins, its trials, and its woe.

Pleasure, with all its pomp and show,
May for awhile delight,
But never let its votries lure
Thy heart from what is right;
Let virtue be thy constant guide,
A spotless name my Emma's pride.

Remember there is One above
Who knows thy every care,
Oh! may He grant thee fortitude
Thy ev'ry ill to bear:
He will be thy friend and guardian be,
And that sweet thought shall comfort me.

Oh! never, never, love, forget
Thy dying mother's prayer,
Lift up thy heart to heaven, my child,
And pray to meet me there,
How much I love thee, none can tell,
But we must part—farewell, farewell!

(1847-06-05, 4:1)

3790. The Water Cure as applied to Fever.—At the present period, when fever is so rife and its victims daily on the increase, we deem it our duty to call the attention of medical men, boards of guardians, hospital committees, and the public at large, to the water cure, as a most efficacious means of checking the malady, and preventing the spread of infection. We have for some time been impressed with the belief that this system, which has been unfairly cried down, had not received the consideration to which its importance entitled it; and we feel satisfied now that, if its merits be fairly tested and honestly investigated, it will be found, under God, a powerful instrument in the speedy removal of the fever now afflicting our town, as well as all other febrile diseases of what class soever. We can state positively that, in numbers of cases in Belfast, its effects have been of the most decided and successful character—that many respectable inhabitants have been cured of fever by it, in an almost incredibly short time, when apparently all other means were hopeless—and that very many of whom the symptom of the malady were strong [sic] have been altogether restored by the timely application of this system. It possesses this great advantage too, that it is most simple in practice, giving the least possible inconvenience to the patient, and acting upon the hot and parched skin with a refreshing and invigorating power impossible to be appreciated by those labouring under the disease. (1847-06-05, 4:5)

3791. Mortality in the City of Cork.—So great has been the number of deaths in this city since the commencement of autumn, that the cemetery belonging to the Very Rev. Theobald Mathew has received the bodies of over 10,000 persons, exclusive of those buried from the workhouse, within that time. The cemetery is now so completely filled, that the Rev. Mr. Mathew has been compelled, in order to prevent the spread of contagion and disease in the vicinity, to give notice at the health committee that he cannot allow any more burials to take place there, and he has himself declared that he will station two or three men at the end of the lane leading to the cemetery, to see that this shall not be transgressed. He will also be compelled to have the whole surface of the burial-ground covered with several layers of slacked lime and fresh earth, in order to guard against the danger to the neighbourhood from the effluvia arising from the almost putrified ground. It will now be necessary for the relief committee to provide at least two additional burial-places for the city.—*Cork Examiner.* (1847-06-12, 1:5)

3792. The Death Bell.

I. Listen, you can hear it,
'Tis a saddening peal,
If you've heart, 'twill sear it,
As with flaming steel;
'Tis the death bell ringing,
For departed life,
'Tis a spirit singing
Of release from strife.
Hark!!

II. It hath not been idle
In these latter times,
She who at a bridal
Listened to its chimes,
Now indeed is sleeping
Not with him she loved,
See him in his weeping,
To the Soul he's moved.
See.

III. He who was the nearest
Of our friends among,
He who was the dearest,
Kind and true and young,
He has left thee lonely,
Plunged in grief and pain,
With no hope, save only
Ye may meet again.
Weep!

IV. Even the humble peasant,
He whose rugged hand
Worked to feed the Present
From a sterile land,
Now is but a spirit,
And the Present Past,
What shall be his future,
What shall be his last?
Pause.

V. If thy soul to-morrow
Be required of thee,
If life's parting sorrow
Shall thy portion be,
Can'st thou calmly meet it
As the sage of old,
Can'st thou gladly greet it,
Can'st thou Death behold?
Think.

VI. Worthless thy endeavour
Must be at the best,
Now if thou would'st ever
Gain a happy rest,
Fling aside the bubbles
Of a world like this,
Freed from earthly troubles
Pray for Heavenly bliss.
Pray.

Outis.
7th June, 1847. (1847-06-12, 1:6)

3793. (From the *Sligo Champion.*)—The present state of Sligo is truly awful; fever is spreading with the rapidity of wildfire, and, as the hot weather has now set in, there is no rational hope of the disease being checked. The Rev. Mr. Thackerberry, Methodist preacher, died of typhus fever on Thursday morning, and Mr. Patrick Dunnigan, a respectable merchant, also fell a victim to the same malignant disease during the week. Every street is full of infection, and a man would have a better chance of escaping with his life in a battle than in Sligo at present. The mortality at Waterloo was not so great as it is here just now. Every night, from ten to fifteen persons, far gone in fever, are left by their friends outside the fever hospital, and are forced to remain in the open air for want of accommodation! Upon Thursday night last, at the hour of twelve o'clock, we counted sixty human creatures lying upon the flags in the streets. We are quite convinced that one-third of that number were infected with fever. All of them are sickly and famine stricken. Can nothing be done for those houseless wanderers? They are carrying infection about with them and, if it were only for our own sakes, we should adopt some plan to keep them off the streets, and thus prevent the spread of contagion.
(1847-06-12, 2:4)

3794. Prevention of Infection from Typhus Fever.—Dr. J.C. Smith obtained £5,000 from Parliament for the following recipe:—"Take six drachms of powdered nitre (saltpetre), and six drachms of sulphuric acid (oil of vitriol), mix them in a teacup. By adding one drachm of the oil at a time, a copious discharge of nitrous acid gas will take place; the cup to be placed during the preparation on a hot hearth or plate or heated iron, and the mixture stirred with a tobacco pipe. The quantity of gas may be regulated by lessening or increasing the quantity of ingredients. The above is for a moderate-sized room; half the quantity would be sufficient for a small room. Avoid as much as possible breathing the gas, when it first rises from the vessel." No injury to the lungs will happen when the air is impregnated with the gas which is called nitrous acid gas; and it cannot be too widely known that it possesses the property of preventing the spread of fever.—*Dumfries Courier.* (1847-06-12, 2:5) *Note: This article contains antiquated advice. This transcription is provided for historical interest, only.*

3795. Progress of Mortality.—Our burial grounds are full. Mr. Mathew, who has allowed the liberal—the too liberal use of his [burial-ground], is obliged to refuse the paupers sent to him in shoals. Two hundred and forty—sometimes four hundred—a week have been freely admitted by him; but the ground is full, the graves are choked, and, to prevent pestilence, he is compelled to close the gates, and cover the coffins with lime.—*Cork Constitution.* (1847-06-12, 2:5)

3796. Election of Coroner.—On Monday last, pursuant to advertisement, W.A. Dane, Esq., under sheriff, accompanied by the Clerk of the Peace, proceeded to Newtownbutler for the purpose of electing a Coroner for that district. The Court-house having been opened precisely at ten o'clock, the sheriff and the writ of election, also the high sheriff's proclamation. James Moore, Esq., of Drumbad, proposed Mr. J. Armstrong, of Brookboro', as a fit and proper person to fill the office of Coroner, which being seconded by Wm. Betty, Esq., Hill house, Maguire's bridge, the sheriff inquired if any freeholder present wished to put another candidate in nomination. No reply being made, and the necessary qualification having been handed in—he declared James Armstrong, Esq., to be duly elected a Coroner for the County Fermanagh, and administered the usual oaths accordingly. A few minutes after ten, John Edward Taylor, Esq., J.P., Cranbrooke; John P. Hamilton, Esq., J.P., Oakfield; Rev. Wm. Watkins Deering, Aughavea Glebe, &c., were in attendance. The business having terminated, the court was then adjourned. (1847-06-12, 2:5)

3797. Spread of Fever.—We are in a fearful state of fever. One fifth of the inmates of the poorhouse (upwards of 200,) are in hospital; of these, 140 are in fever. Every bed and blanket in the fever hospital is occupied, and in many instances, there are two and three patients in one bed. There are upwards of 40 cases in town and immediate vicinity without proper medical aid, or any nourishment, not that the medical men are not willing to give every assistance in their power, but from the multiplicity of disease they cannot attend all. This week, nine persons were refused admittance to the fever hospital from want of room—and in one case, where a woman and her two children were brought into town in a cart, the carman, being refused admittance for his charge, trundled them off his cart and left them on the high road, where they lay in the open air, in the middle of the community for two days, without any shelter, save that of an egg-crate, which some charitable person placed beside them. (1847-06-12, 2:6)

3798. Monaghan Fever Hospital.—Medical officer's report of the Fever Hospital for the last week, 11th June, 1847.

Admitted, ...	26
Discharged, ...	20
Died, ...	1
In Hospital, ...	45

Fever is greatly on the increase in the town and neighbourhood of Monaghan. The Fever Hospital is crowded far above the number it is capable of accommodating with its present fittings; many very urgent cases have been refused admission.

With some alterations, the hospital could be made to contain 40 beds; at present, it contains only 28. The 45 at present in hospital are lying some two, and even three, in a bed.

Wm. Temple, M.D. (1847-06-12, 2:6)

3799. A young man, named Philip Treanor, son to a respectable farmer in the neighbourhood of Glasslough, died last week of glanders. He caught the disease from an old horse they had in their possession; he suffered severely from the effects of the disease for ten days previous to his death. (1847-06-12, 3:1)

3800. Fever is spreading greatly in and about the neighbourhood of Emyvale. The fever hospital of that town is full, in consequence of which, many poor creatures would be compelled to remain in their own houses amidst filth and wretchedness, but for the extreme kindness of that worthy gentleman, Doctor M'Kinstry, whose unwearied exertions deserve the greatest praise; he has been most successful in every case since he went there; out of 130 cases of fever, not one death has occurred. (1847-06-12, 3:1)

3801. The schoolmaster and schoolmistress of the Workhouse of this Union are both ill of fever, and the nurse at the county infirmary died of fever this week. (1847-06-12, 3:1)

3802. The Rev. F. Thackaberry, Wesleyan minister, has, we lament to announce, fallen a sacrifice to the destructive pestilence.—*Sligo Journal.* (1847-06-12, 3:1)

3803. Clones.—We regret to learn that fever in all its malignity, does not only still continue sadly prevalent in the above town, but has been for some time past, fearfully on the increase. It need not be said now that many respectable as well as poor families had been attacked with it, but very few of either, whether in town or neighbourhood, are at this moment exempt from it.—Very many of the shop keepers and dealing people, in particular, have numbers of their families suffering from it—but owing to a cause which is so obvious that it need scarcely be mentioned:—Diseased people and people just rising from the bed of contagion think nothing of mixing with the healthy, in shops and other places, and the latter, not being sufficiently cautious, catch the disease and thus does it spread among the middle classes.

It is to be hoped, however, that the exertions which the officers of the Board of Health are at present making in that town, in causing the streets, yards, &c., to be thoroughly cleaned, and the houses of the poor, and of those who have been recently afflicted with the malady, to be white-washed and fumigated, will be attended with salutary effects, and will tend in a great measure to check the further progress of the fearful epidemic. (1847-06-12, 3:2)

3804. Death by Starvation.—On Saturday last, 5th inst., a shockingly emaciated old man, who, from his ragged and squalid appearance, and his being not known in the neighbourhood, must have been one of the itinerant beggars, was found dead in a pig-sty belonging to a farmer named M'Ginniss, at Clonfad, near Clones, adjoining this county. Decomposition having set in when the body was found, there exists no doubt but it must have lain there for at least seven or eight days previously, particularly as M'Ginniss had been from home during the time and the house unoccupied.—It appeared so obvious that starvation was the cause of his death, the authorities did not deem it necessary to have an inquest held on the body. (1847-06-12, 3:2)

3805. Monaghan Dispensary.—During the week ending Friday the 11th, 42 cases of fever were prescribed for and attended. (1847-06-12, 3:5)

3806. In Enniskillen, six men are employed as beadles to keep strange paupers from entering the town, and the houses in which there is fever are marked; nearly 2,000 were relieved on Tuesday the first instant. (1847-06-12, 4:4)

3807. We regret to announce the decease of the Rev. Richard Butler Bryan, rector of the parish of Kilkenny, West, in this county, for upwards of thirty years. Mr. Bryan expired on Friday at his residence, Glasson, from the effects of contagious disease, caught while attending a meeting of the local relief committee a few days since.—*Westmeath Independent.* (1847-06-12, 4:5)

3808. Advice to Prevent Fever, and Other Infectious Diseases Amongst the Poor.

"Admit pure air, 'twill aid your health;
In that, you know consists your wealth;
When Fever lurks, delay not cure,
But haste, some medicine to procure."
Martin Doyle.

No. 1. Let your doors and windows be kept open in the day; if you have not a window in the back part of your house, make one; have them so hung as to be easily opened; have a chimney with a good draught, so as to encourage a free current of air through your house.

No. 2. Remove dung and putrid matter of every kind from before, and from behind your house, as the vapour and smell proceeding from them (called *malaria*) has been found by physicians to generate infectious fever.

No. 3. Scrape your floors with a spade, and sweep them every day; also the yards before and behind your houses, as often as you can; keep your hair cut short and combed every day; wash your hands and face; keep your clothes, furniture, and utensils neat and clean.

No. 4. Don't, by any means, indulge in the use of spirituous or other fermented liquors, as intemperance in their use will, to a certainty, render you more susceptible of contagion.

No. 5. All kinds of food badly cooked, or half-boiled, as is a prevailing custom amongst the poor, are most unwholesome.

No. 6. Lying on beds placed on the ground is very injurious to the health. Every family is recommended to be provided with bedsteads, be they ever so homely.

No. 7. Attention should be paid to have the bowels kept daily open, but not too free, and, if necessary, some gentle aperient medicine should be occasionally made use of for this purpose.

No. 8. Don't go into any house where a person is sick, or has been ill, of fever; don't attend the wake of any person who has died of fever; if you do, you will be infected yourself, and will communicate fever to your family.

No. 9. Don't let strolling beggars enter your houses, as they frequently carry infection from one house to another.

No. 10. Whitewash your walls, inside and outside, with lime slacked in the house, and while it continues hot and bubbling; let this be done once a month while fever is prevalent.

No. 11. If fever attacks your family, as soon as the calamity is removed by recovery, or by death, employ the above means as soon as possible; burn the straw of the beds; put all the clothes of the house into cold water, or into a strong solution of chloride of lime—one ounce to a quart of water—wring them out and wash them in hot water, soap, and potashes; let every box, drawer, chest, &c. be emptied and washed, and let the floor under the patient's bed be strewed, with lime fresh slacked and hot. Let no person, upon recovery, go into a neighbour's house, nor into any public place of worship for fourteen days.

No. 12. Heads of families are strongly recommended to have a printed copy of this advice pasted up in their houses, and to enforce a strict observance of its instructions.

No. 13. The gentry are advised to give employment to such persons only as carefully attend to the rules herein contained.

No. 14. A strict adherence to this plan constitutes the sole means of removing the chief cause which generated typhus fever in Ireland, viz., the foetid smell (called *malaria*) exhaled from animal and vegetable substances in a state of putrid fermentation.

No. 15. It is reasonable to hope, that every other cause will be eradicated by comfortable clothing, wholesome food, and good lodgings, which comforts can only be obtained through the medium of constant employment given to the poor.

No. 16. Remember!!!—That cleanliness and good air will improve your health and strength, will check disease, and, under God, will preserve you from all the variety of wretchedness and misery occasioned by infectious fever.

William Kingsley,
Physician to the Fever Hospital, Rosscrea.
(1847-06-19, 1:1)

3809. Fever.—Cork, Saturday.—Fever, we are happy to learn, is diminishing in this city; in three of the parishes—St. Peter's, the North, and South—the number of patients has materially decreased.—*Cork Reporter*. (1847-06-19, 1:3)

3810. Fever.—Belfast, June 12.—It is now, alas! a painfully notorious fact that this fearful epidemic is rapidly on the increase in this town. Its progress is so alarmingly great, that both the hospitals, Frederick-street and Barrack-street, were yesterday obliged to be closed against the admission of any more patients. This is a most lamentable course that necessity dictates to be pursued. The number of cases in the Barrack-street Hospital is 379. A great many applications were made at the hospital yesterday, but they could not be entertained. Though fever patients were stretched at the gates, and piteously imploring commiseration, they could not be received. The sheds that were lately erected at the rere of Frederick-street Hospital are filled with the sick. This Hospital, with all its increased accommodation, contains one hundred cases more than what was designed to be put in it. Yesterday evening, there were no less than 614 patients lying in it. In the Workhouse Fever Hospital, there were about 500 patients; so that, in the three hospitals last night, the aggregate number may be set down as 1,500. With these glaring facts staring us in the face, the public may judge of the extent to which the terrible epidemic has spread in Belfast. The exact number of beings that are afflicted with fever throughout the town cannot rightly be ascertained.—*Belfast Vindicator*. (1847-06-19, 1:3)

3811. Fever.—Waterford.—The majority of the applicants for admission to the workhouse on Friday were fever patients; whole families in fever presented themselves, who, on investigation, invariably appeared to be strangers in this union; nevertheless, from their extreme misery and feebleness, the guardians were induced to admit them temporarily. Few appeared before the board who were not either candidates for the fever hospital or convalescent patients.—*Waterford Chronicle*. (1847-06-19, 1:3)

3812. Fever.—Drogheda.—We have the painful duty to perform of announcing that fever has very much increased in the town and neighbourhood during the week. Several persons in the middle class are, at this moment, suffering under it, and a still larger number of those who reside in the less cleanly parts of this town. It is, however, consolatory to know that it is generally of a mild character, and, if remedies are taken early, not very dangerous.—*Drogheda Argus*. (1847-06-19, 1:3)

3813. Fever.—Ballinasloe.—We lament to say that, in this town—heretofore so healthful—fever is rapidly spreading; and, it is greatly to be feared, unless some immediate steps be taken to check the progress of this terrible disease, that its ravages will be fearfully increased. The hospital is now crowded—so completely so, that several unfortunate creatures, in the height of the disease, cannot get admission, of course, spreading infection through the neighbourhood. Dr. James Colahad represented to the relief commissioners in Dublin, the frightful spread of fever in this district, and applied to have a temporary hospital erected, but it appears the relief committee here had not sufficient money for the purpose. This certainty does not excuse them, as the cost of a temporary hospital or a few sheds would be trifling in comparison with the importance of the necessity which exists; but, even were it far greater, the expense should not, for one moment, be considered, when the lives of thousands are at stake. We feel much gratification now in announcing that the committee, on yesterday (Friday), came to the determination of erecting a number of sheds at the back of the fever hospital.—*Ballinasloe Star*. (1847-06-19, 1:3)

3814. Death of Richard Albert Fitzgerald, Esq., M.P. for Tipperary.—With deep pain, we have learned that letters were received in town yesterday, announcing the death of this estimable gentleman. We understand that he caught fever while attending to the relief of the destitute poor in his locality, and died after four days' illness. A purer patriot, or a more upright and honourable man, did not exist. The death of such a man, at such a time, will be generally and sincerely regretted.—*Freeman*. (1847-06-19, 2:4)

3815. Ballyshannon, June 12.—We are happy in being enabled to state that the fever and dysentery, which have been so prevalent throughout this town and vicinity for some time, have moderated considerably during the past week. We have not had a single death; and all those who have been affected are convalescent. We trust the Lord in his mercy will put a stop to those devastating scourges, and that health and abundance of food will be again restored to our afflicted country.—*Ballyshannon Herald*. (1847-06-19, 2:4)

3816. Dr. Sharpe, of Cootehill, has been appointed medical attendant to the Ashfield and Tullyvin Electoral Divisions, under the new fever act. This appointment has given universal satisfaction, and ensured the greatest confidence amongst the poor. (1847-06-19, 3:1)

3817. Orange Funeral.—One of the largest and most respectable Funeral processions ever witnessed in this neighbourhood, accompanied the mortal remains of our late worthy brother, Mr. John Miller, Derry-creevy, Master of the Benburb, No. 1. District, to his last resting place, in Benburb, on Friday, the 18th inst.—From the dense crowds that accompanied, it would be impossible to give an accurate number of those in procession, but it was calculated as close as possible to be between six and seven hundred; they were composed of the Benburb, Killylea, and Charlemont Districts.—*Armagh Guardian*. (1847-06-26, 1:3)

3818. Progress of Fever.—This epidemic is still progressing with fearful destruction. The poor are dying in the hospitals and in their hovels—and the rich, and the great, are not escaping from the ravages of the pestilence. Age and youth are alike prostrated, and beauty and deformity both made a prey to wretchedness. The following table of disease presents a frightful picture of distress and suffering for one short week only, and let it be remembered that there are many more in private dwellings whose debility, or death, would be still greater loss to the world: [*The table was omitted from article in the original text.*] (1847-06-26, 2:3)

3819. Mr. O'Connell's Remains.—The Oriental Steam Packet Company, through their respected and public-spirited Secretary, Mr. Hartley, have made arrangements, on the most liberal scale, for the conveyance of the remains of Mr. O'Connell from Genoa to Southampton, free of charge. The steamer destined to convey the body of the illustrious deceased is expected at Southampton about the 17th of July. Mr. Hartley has undertaken to convey the body in one of his own vessels, and solely at his own cost, from Southampton to Dublin or Kingstown, as the Dublin Cemetery Committee may select, and has given directions that the *Queen* steamer should be suitably fitted up for this purpose. It is calculated that the remains of Mr. O'Connell will arrive in this City about the 20th of July. (1847-06-26, 3:4)

3820. Cork Election.—The High Sheriff has fixed Monday, June 28, for the election of a representative in the room of the late Daniel O'Connell, Esq. (1847-06-26, 3:4)

3821. Pope Pius and O'Connell.—The Pope, in return for the bequest of O'Connell's heart, has ordered collections to be made, in all the churches under his control, for the starving Irish. (1847-07-03, 2:4)

3822. Fever.—Fever is decidedly on the increase in this neighbourhood, in spite of every exertion to check its progress. The Central Board of Health have sanctioned the erection of a temporary Central Hospital near Monaghan, for the thirteen Electoral divisions within Monaghan Barony, said Hospital to contain 200 beds and have two medical officers. (1847-07-03, 3:1)

3823. Fever.—We regret to learn that dysentery and diarrhoea are decidedly on the increase in the vicinities of Glasslough and Emyvale. We have heard this attributed to the distribution of uncooked India Meal by some of the Relief Committees in the district. (1847-07-03, 3:1)

3824. The Obsequies of the Liberator.—It appears, by a letter received from the Rev. Dr. Miley, that the obsequies of the Liberator at Rome have been postponed from the 25th instant to the 28th. A desire to have every preparation complete to give due effect to the imposing ceremony, is, we believe, the cause of the postponement. (1847-07-03, 3:6)

3825. Marriages goes by Destiny.—There is one circumstance, one event of human life, and that by no means of a trivial nature, over which the influence of Fortune's pipe is considered supreme. It is agreed that "marriage goes by destiny." Here luck reigns paramount, and "good guidance" is useless. No precaution can assure a termagant wife, or a woman against a faithless husband; while unions contracted under the most apparently unfavorable auspices, sometimes afford very edifying examples of conjugal felicity. A ten year courtship will not prevent quarrels in the honeymoon, while an affection sown suddenly at a ball, and of which the harvest follows in six weeks, shall endure unchangeably all the buffetings of life.—Couples arrived at years of discretion have proceeded gradually and steadily through the grammar of Love, and when duly qualified for a matrimonial degree, have advanced in the most decorous manner, and after the most approved method, to the altar of Hymen, Cupid and Minerva preceding them hand in hand, and plenty of congratulating relations following in bridal attire, and a life *a la* cat and dog had been the result; while boys and girls scarcely half way in teens have fallen in love at battledore and shuttlecock, galloped off next morning to Gretna Green, been married by a blacksmith, and thrown two whole families into hysterics, who have afterwards passed their youth like turtle-doves, their maturer years like the tenderest of friends, and their age like Darby and Joan. These strange anomalies are not to be denied, but afford little encouragement to imprudence, since misery may and often does follow it, and there is, undoubtedly, no misery equal to self reproach. If we cannot ensure success, we may at least deserve it. (1847-07-03, 4:6)

3826. Dreadful Death by Dogs.—One of the most horrible occurrences it has been our lot to announce, took place on Tuesday morning, within a short distance from this town. A poor man, from Ballaghadenin, county Mayo, named Hugh Lynch, on his way to England to reap the harvest, arrived within a few miles of this town on Monday evening, and the night being remarkably fine, he entered a field belonging to Mr. Carroll on the Mornington road, in order to pass the night. Mr. Carroll proceeded on Tuesday morning, as was his custom, accompanied by three watch-dogs to see if his cattle were all safe; when on entering the field where poor Lynch was lying, the dogs attacked him in a most savage manner, and notwithstanding the exertions of Mr. Carroll, who endeavoured to save him, they tore the unfortunate creature's flesh from his face, back, &c. Assistance having arrived, the dogs were secured, and the poor man attended by Dr. Calvert, who ordered him to the hospital, where death put an end to his sufferings. The dogs were, we understand, destroyed immediately after. An inquest was held on Wedesday, (the body have been interred the previous day in the Chord,) before his worship the Mayor, and H.B. Fairtlough, Esq., when, (*continued...*)

3826, continued: ...after hearing evidence to the above effect, the inquest was adjourned. The second inquest, in consequence of the occurrence having taken place in the county of Meath, was held on Friday, before Hugh Martin, Esq., Coroner, and a verdict returned in accordance with the facts, several censuring Carrol for keeping such ferocious animals.—*Drogheda Conservative.* (1847-07-10, 1:2)

3827. The Magistracy.—His Excellency, the Earl of Clarendon, Lord Lieutenant of Ireland, has been pleased to appoint Sir Thomas E. Blake, Bart., of Menio Castle, in the county of Galway, to the situation of Stipendiary Magistrate, in the room of Sylvanus Jones, Esq., deceased, and to be stationed at Donegal. (1847-07-10, 1:2)

3828. Eight Roman Catholic Clergy men have recently fallen victims to the pestilence so prevalent in Liverpool among the lower order of the Irish. So great is the mortality there, that it has interfered with the performance of Divine Service. (1847-07-10, 1:6)

3829. Suicide.—On Saturday, John E. Hyndman, Esq., held an inquest at Clarke's bridge, Royal Canal, on the body of a respectable tradesman named Patrick Bryan, who resided in Britain-street. It appeared that between six and seven o'clock in the morning, a police constable who was on duty between Russell-street and Clarke's bridge, observed the hands of a man over water: he called assistance, and after great exertion, the body was got out, but the unfortunate man was quite dead. Every means was resorted to, to produce reanimation, but in vain. The deceased had a son who caused him much annoyance, and this preyed very much on his mind. The jury, after the examination of some witnesses to the above effect, found that deceased drowned himself while labouring under temporary derangement of mind, brought on apparently by the conduct of his son. (1847-07-10, 2:1)

3830. Melancholy Accident.—On Friday, a most melancholy occurrence took place under the following circumstances: Mr. Antony Mathews and Mr. Francis Barlow, second eldest son of J.T. Barlow, Esq., of Moate, were induced to bathe in the Lake of Ballinderry, within about half a-mile of that town. When, some distance from the shore, Mr. Barlow, from some unaccountable cause, became exhausted, and, after a short and uneffectual struggle, sunk to rise no more. The body has not yet been found.—*Westmeath Independent.* (1847-07-10, 2:1)

3831. Fever in Fermanagh.—(From the *Erne Packet.*) —We will be always happy to receive information from correspondents in the rural districts, regarding disease, or any other subject that will be likely to interest our readers. The following letter, from an eminent medical gentleman, will give some idea of the extent of disease in the neighbourhood of Brookeborough:—

To the Editor of the *Erne Packet.*—Sir—In your paper of Thursday, in the paragraph headed fever, you state tht deaths from this disease to a frightful extent, have occurred in Brookeborough. I think it right to mention, that on this point, you are misinformed. In the town of Brookeborough, no deaths from fever have occurred for several months past, I think but three, for a year and a half. It is true that, in the surrounding districts, fever has prevailed and still does so, but not to an alarming extent, nor much beyond what is usual at this season of the year, and the deaths have not been out of proportion numerous. They have more generally happened in the low fever that followed on protracted dysentery, and swellings, than as the consequence of continued or typhus fever.

We have rather reason to be thankful for our comparative immunity hitherto, than to complain of being frightfully visited by this scourge, so widely prevailing through our land.

I am, Sir,
Yours faithfully,
J. Houghton, M.D.
Brookeborough, July 10, 1847. (1847-07-17, 1:6)

3832. Death of the Rev. Allen Mitchell.—It is not with editorial regret, nor every-day-journalist sorrow, that we announce the death of our dearly beloved friend, the Rev. Allen Mitchell, for many years Vicar of Drumsnatt in this county, and lately Rector of Rossory parish, county Fermanagh, nor is it newspaper eulogium to say that a man more beloved, nor more respected, did not exist. If ever human being was created without guile—a genuine philanthropist—a meek and lowly follower of his Divine master—religious without pretence, and charitable without ostentation, Mr. Mitchell was that being. He was not only the pastor of his flock and their spiritual adviser, but the dear friend of every member of his congregation. It is only a few months since we published the farewell address of the people of Drumsnatt to this estimable gentleman upon his removal to Rossory, in which were faintly pictured their deep feelings of attachment, and his reply, in which were shadowed forth the loving propensities of his nature. Alas! he has gone to a better world, and "take him for all in all we neer shall look upon his like again." He died of fever on Monday last, contracted in his ministerings to the afflicted in the new sphere of his duties, and his remains were interred on Wednesday in the family vault at Ballinode, attended to their last home by a large assemblage of those who loved him in life.

Mr. Mitchell was grand chaplain to the Orange society in this county, and his memory, bedewed with heartfelt tears, will live long in the hearts of its members. (1847-07-17, 3:3)

3833. Notice.—I Hereby Caution all persons against giving my wife, Martha Black, any Credit, as I will not be accountable after this date for any debt or debts contracted by her.

Thomas Stewart Black, Corlea.

July 18, 1847.

(1847-07-17, 3:5)

3834. To be Sold—By Private Contract,—Under powers of Sale contained in a certain Deed of Mortgage All That Farm and parcel of Land in the Townland of Corbofin alias Corbyfin,—Containing Ten Acres, Irish Plantation Measure or thereabouts, situate within a mile and a half of the town of Ballybay, on the road to Keady, and being in the Barony and county of Monaghan, as lately in the possession of Samuel Anderson, deceased, and as now in the actual occupation of James Anderson, of Ballybay, Innkeeper.—A good Two Story House with suitable Offices, are standing on the Premises, which are held for Lives renewable for ever, subject to the Rent of 15s. 2d. per Annum, and a renewal fine of 5s. on the fall of each life.

For further particulars and information as to title, apply to Messrs. H.J. & T. Garrett, Solicitors, 16, Castle Lane, Belfast, and 17, North Frederick-street, Dublin. (1847-07-17, 3:5)

3835. The Mother's Grave.

My mother rests beneath yon spot
Where droops the lonely willow tree:
Her memory is now forgot—
Forgot by all but me.
Ah! who can speak the grief I feel
When to a parent's grave we go;
And who the painful sadness heal,
Or ease the soul from woe?

When day declines, and gleaming soft,
The pale star lights my way,
I seek within the churchyard oft
My mother's grave to pray.
The tears that fall relieve a heart
Oppressed with mournful care;
And when I from the spot depart,
I leave my sorrow there.

For, in the deep afflictive hour,
'Tis then our sighings cease,
Upborne by an immortal power,
And filled with sacred peace.
Mother! a few short vigils o'er,
In radiant realms of Love
We'll meet, and separate no more,
Crown'd with the bliss above.

T.F.C.

(1847-07-17, 4:1)

3836. Death of the O'Connor Don.—With profound regret, we have to announce the decease of the Right Hon. Dennis O'Connor, commonly called the O'Connor Don, one of her Majesty's Lords of the Treasury. His death occurred on Thursday morning at seven o'clock, at his residence, 51, Pall-mall, West, where the right hon. the deceased gentleman was attended by two members of the Roman Catholic priesthood, Monsigniore the Rev. Dr. Magee, of Westminster, and the Rev. Mr. Lee, of Warwick street. The O'Connor Don was a man eminently respected in his public character, and more than esteemed by those admitted to his friendship. His dissolution is described to have been serene, and consolatory to those who witnessed it. The deceased was born in 1794, so that he was in his 53d year. In 1824, he was married to Mary Ann, daughter of Major Blake, since deceased. He has occupied his seat in the House of Commons, as representative of the county of Roscommon since 1831, so that he has been sixteen years a member of the British Parliament.—As a politician, the O'Connor Don was an ardent and consistent Liberal; the moral and social advancement of Ireland was among his most fervent and perpetual aspirations; as a Roman Catholic, he was an advocate for a more generalised system of Church endowment; as a philanthropist, he was solicitous for the removal of the more rigorous enactments from our criminal jurisprudence; as an Irishman, he was a Repealer. The O'Connor Don was regarded as the chief of the ancient family of the O'Connors, as his title indicated. (1847-07-31, 1:3)

3837. Death of William Irwine, Esq., Clerk of the Crown.—Died, at his residence, Prospect Hill, Enniskillen, William Irwine, Esq., Clerk of the Crown, and Secretary to the Grand Jury of the county Fermanagh, to the inconsolable regret of his family and numerous friends, by whom he was beloved and respected for his many Christian virtues. In all the relations of life, as a husband, father, friend, and citizen, Mr. Irwine was a pattern of excellence. His loss will be long felt by the poor, to whom he was a kind benefactor. (1847-07-31, 1:5)

3838. Death of Doctor Hurst of Clones.—We regret to be obliged to announce the death of this lamented gentleman and able physician, caused by the fatal epidemic of the day—fever—caught in the discharge of his medical duties. Doctor Hurst's constitution was worn out by his unremitting labour, and when himself attacked, he sunk under the fatal scourge. It is needless to say that he is deeply regretted, for he was not only the professional but the private friend of the great majority of the people of Clones, all of whom will deplore his loss. (1847-08-07, 2:6)

3839. The Rev. Robert Johnston has been appointed to the living of Rossory, vacant by the death of the late lamented Rev. Allen Mitchell. (1847-08-07, 2:6)

3840. Arrival of Mr. O'Connell's Remains.—The *Duchess of Kent* steamer, belonging to the City of Dublin Steam-packet Company, arrived at the North Wall on Monday, about four o'clock, conveying the remains of the late Mr. O'Connell to (*continued...*)

3840, continued: ...their last resting place. There were great numbers of people congregated along the quays on both sides in expectation of the steam-boat; and as she passed down the river on the top of the tide, the crowd increased considerably in the area opposite the Custom-house, where an open hearse, drawn by six horses, awaited the arrival of the remains. There was a large party of police on the spot to keep order, and nothing could be more admirable than the cool and quiet temper exhibited by them, pressed on all sides by a curious crowd. The coffin, covered with crimson Genoa velvet, and handsomely ornamented with gilt escutcheons, handles, &c., and bearing a tablet, inscribed with the name, age, &c., of the deceased, was carried on shore and placed on the hearse. When several members of the family, Messrs. Maurice, John, and Daniel O'Connell, with the Rev. Doctor Miley, and several other Roman Catholic clergymen took their places to join in procession to Marlborough-street Chapel, one of the horses became restive, and kicked and plunged violently, to the great danger of the crowd, which forced its way upon the hearse. The pressure seemed to be from a desire to touch the coffin, and as one touched, he left and was replaced by another. The restiveness of the horse was, after some minutes, subdued, and the procession advanced gently. The crowd of people accumulated upon the hearse to that degree that the family and friends were left some distance behind. The funeral procession went along the quays to Marlborough-street, and the coffin was deposited upon the catafalque prepared for its reception in the chapel, to await the obsequies appointed upon the occasion.

When the vessel arrived, several females singled themselves out of the crowd, and knelt to pray.

The *Isle of Bute* and *Arran Castle*, river steamers, filled with passengers, proceeded down the river to meet the *Duchess of Kent* off Howth, where she awaited the tide, and accompany her to the North Wall.

Crowds of people loitered about Marlborough-street to a late hour of the evening.

THURSDAY.

From an early hour this morning, all the thoroughfares leading to the chapel in Marlborough-street, from whence the funeral cortege was to issue, were crowded with people, and the windows along the line of route were also filled with spectators.

The various bodies and societies—political and religious—appointed to take part in the ceremonial, assembled at different localities near the place from whence the funeral set out, and joined the line of procession as it proceeded.

The Associated Trades walked at the head of the procession, which started about 12 o'clock, after which followed Mr. O'Connell's Triumphal Car, covered with emblems of mourning. It was drawn by six horses, led by mutes. Various confraternities and societies came next, and after them the hearse, drawn by six horses, in which the coffin, richly mounted, and covered with crimson Genoa velvet, was visible to all. A number of mourning coaches followed, after which came the Lord Mayor in his state coach, the Alderman and Town Councillors, &c., and a long string of carriages. Notwithstanding the vast crowds that assembled, the greatest order and decorum were preserved. (1847-08-07, 3:3)

3841. Death of James Young, Esq., Ballymena.—We have to-day the melancholy task of announcing the death, from typhus fever, of James Young, Esq., linen merchant, Ballymena. He took ill on Wednesday, the 21st instant, and died at nine o'clock, p.m., on that day week. Mr. Young was an elder in the Third Presbyterian congregation of Ballymena, the lamented pastor of which has been so lately removed by the same fatal epidemic.—*Banner of Ulster*. (1847-08-07, 3:3)

3842. The Bridal in Paradise.—By Digby T. Starkey.

It was a night of glorious light, magnificent with stars
Which flashed along the firmament in their triumphant cars;
The over arching dome of heaven was blazing far and wide,
For Adam, sinless and sublime, that day had wed his bride.

Within a garden slept the pair, enfolded arm with arm,
Their pulses thrilling as they welled from life's young fountains warm;
Soft went their sighings to and fro, and round each breath there fluttered
Ten thousand words of love, half-winged, and struggling to be uttered.

And one was powerful in sleep, with brow intently wrought—
A solemn calm, as though a spell had fixed some mighty thought;
His length of limb lay still as stone, for the moon's broad beam to carve.
Yet not in marble death, but all electric with life's nerve.

The other lay all loveliness, defencelessly reposing
Within the arm that twined her round; and her sweet lips, unclosing,
Poured murmurs, half in prayer, half dream, yet more of song than word,
As the breath of innocence swept by, and the fresh-strung feelings stirred.

Each lustrous eye, in love's eclipse, was shrouded o'er with fringe,
Which lay like shade, and lent her cheek the glow of contrast's tinge;
And marble carving of her brow shone while 'twixt tress and tress,
Like thoughts pure temple reared amidst a fragrant wilderness.

Hush, hush, earth, air! glide softly, streams! steal, gently, waves, to shore!
Back, echoes, to your inmost grots! repress, O winds, your roar!
Nature, with finger on her lip, looked breathlessly around,
Lest one of her new-fledged brood should break the trance profound.

The shadows plunged amidst the woods, and down in caverns lay,
Which wild beasts haunt, before a tread was planted in their clay;
And orbs unnamed upon the breast of glancing streams were caught,
Unnamed as they, and rolling down through golden sands unsought.

One silver link of harmony stretched between heaven and earth,
Too ravishing for sense to say from which it had its birth;
A nightingale's lone note arose but trembled in the ether,
So slender was the thread that hung silence and song together.

Oh, wherefore was the trance not death? Why did the morning break?
Why, why must they who slept in peace, to sin and sorrow wake
Too long, or far too short that sleep—for, on the morning, Death
Will breathe the lying hope of life, and blast them with his breath!

Peace dreamer! Slumber on, blest pair; ye needs must sin and die.
To him that disobeyeth, Death is Nature's sole reply.
Ye die, but for your life—behold!—a God shall leave the skies!
To murmur o'er each earth's sepulchres the magic word—Arise!

(1847-08-07, 4:1)

3843. Death of Lord Dunsandle.—We regret to announce the death of this nobleman, which took place at his residence in the county of Galway, at two o'clock on Saturday last. Lord Dunsandle was attacked with malignant fever, caught in the discharge of his duties as poor law guardian; and, although the best medical advice was speedily obtained, he died on the fourth day. Sir H. Marsh returned to Dublin on Sunday. (1847-08-14, 1:2)

3844. Fever in the Squadron.—In consequence of the reports of fever prevailing on board the *Andromeda*, store and provision depot, stationed at Killybegs, Deputy Inspector of hospitals, Dr. Lindsay, has proceeded from Cork thither in the *Swallow*, steam vessel, to inquire into the state of the ship's company. (1847-08-14, 1:2)

3845. County Monaghan.—To be Sold—The House and Farm of Sallymount,—the Property of the Late Thomas Robinson, Esq., Deceased.

The Farm consists of Forty-five Acres of Land, Statute Measure, in high cultivation and well Fenced, beautifully situated, about one-mile-and-a-half from Monaghan, on the road leading from thence to Armagh.

The House and Offices are in perfect repair, and will not require any money to be expended thereon for a considerable time; in fact, there cannot be selected a more healthful, more comfortable, or more desirable residence for a family in any part of the County.

The Lease is for one Life at 8s. an Acre, held under the Representatives of the late Doctor Maxwell.

The Purchaser can be accommodated with any quantity of Turbary.

If the above property is not Sold by private Contract, on or before the 28th day of August inst., it will then be Sold by Public Auction, without reserve, together with the Furniture, Crop, Stock, &c.

For further particulars, apply to Mrs. Robinson, Sallymount, or to her Solicitor, Richard Mitchell, Esq., Monaghan. (1847-08-14, 3:5)

3846. Death at Sea.—by Mrs. Ardy.

Slowly we gathered on the deck—what bitter tears we shed,
As we sorrowed for the shipmate who was numbered with the dead;
We could not, like the landsmen, o'er his cherished gravestone weep
No vestige marked his resting place beneath the briny deep.

When mourners go about the streets, when funeral banners wave,
When dewy flowers are scattered on the green and quiet grave,
The mind may cling to outward signs—there may not, cannot, be
The sense of total vacancy attending Death at Sea.

No changeful and inviting scenes there cheer the languid view,
No face supplies the well-known one departed from our crew;
We miss him at the night-watch, at the time of social mirth,
And sigh, when on the forecastle we pass his vacant berth.

Yet, from these hours of dreariness may lasting good arise;
We are drawn to one another by more kind and friendly ties;
Often we speak on holy themes, light jesting is suppressed
Death still among us seems to stand, a dark and awful guest,
And when the cry of land is heard, when grief and gloom are o'er, (*continued...*)

3846, continued:

And friends and kindred gladly throng to greet us on the shore,
Let not the sailor's heart forget, mid scenes of festal glee,
The time of deep and solemn thought—the time of Death at Sea. (1847-08-14, 4:1)

3847. Paying for Soup.—This week, a miserable looking creature named Michael Langan, who has been on the relief list, and constantly got his rations at the soup kitchen of Bohermore, took ill and died; but before his death, he disclosed he had £50 4s. 6d. in his possession. He willed a portion of it for masses for his soul's repose, another sum to be expended on his decent interment, and the remainder to be given in aid of the soup kitchen!! This was a conscientious fellow, and deserved his soup, which is more than can be said of many others, who were in as little want of it, but who, at their death, will be apt to forget the honest example of Langan in bequeathing as liberal a *quid pro quo*. (1847-08-14, 4:6)

3848. Fever.—The malady has happily abated in this town and precincts; there were more deaths a month ago by typhus fever, in one day, than are now heard of in a week; many are still attacked by the epidemic, but it is not of a virulent nature. We much regret to hear that a deservedly popular clergyman, Priest Dwyer, who has done a vast deal of good in the awful time of tribulation, is in a precarious state of fever. The loss of such valuable pastors is indeed deplorable; half of our population would have perished but for the surprising exertions of clergymen of every sect. We lament to hear of this worthy man's demise this morning.—*Sligo Journal*. (1847-08-14, 4:6)

3849. The Church.—The Lord Bishop of Killaloe has presented the Rev. Robert W. Nesbitt, of Ogonelloe, to the Vicarage of Monsea, void by the death of the Rev. H. Trousdell.

Achill Rectory, Mayo, vacant by the death of Rev. C. Willson, is only worth £100 a year, and in the gift of the Bishop of Tuam. (1847-08-21, 1:3)

3850. State of Fever in Belfast.—We have reason to believe that fever is on the decline in this town, owing alike to the exertions of the medical authorities, the active zeal of the Board of Health, in attending to the sanitary improvement of the borough, and preventing the influx of strangers, and the increasing plenty and cheapness of articles of food. The admissions during the week have been, in the three hospitals, fewer than those of any corresponding week for some time past, and from all we can learn, we are inclined to hope that this favourable change will continue to progress. We have given in another place the reports from the three medical institutions, which are now anxiously looked to as the most correct indication of the sanitary condition of the town.—*Belfast Chronicle*. (1847-08-21, 2:2)

3851. Charles Faussett, Esq., has been elected coroner, of the Enniskillen district of the County Fermanagh. (1847-08-21, 3:1)

3852. Supposed Death from Destitution.—On Wednesday last, a poor man, apparently about seventy years of age, was observed leaning against the railing of the Royal Hotel in this town, evidently reduced to a state of extreme destitution and weakness. Wine was administered to him, but without effect, for in a few minutes, after he had been removed to Linen Hall, he expired. The body, which is as yet unclaimed, lies in the Police office, where an investigation will take place to-day.—*Banner of Ulster*. (1847-08-21, 4:4)

3853. Determined Suicide.—On Monday, a poor man named Jos. Douglass, who formerly belonged to Clough, but who was, until Thursday last, an inmate of the Ballymena Poor-House, took a quantity of poison, but not finding it sufficient to take away his life, walked coolly off to the mill-dam, in the neighbourhood of the town, and threw himself into the water, and in a few minutes, sank to rise no more. When he was got out, life was scarcely gone, but all efforts to restore it proved in vain. (1847-08-21, 4:4)

3854. Fatal Accident.—On Friday last, one of Mr. Dargan's labourers, named Hayes, employed in excavating on the Ulster Extension Railway near Portadown, was caught by a falling mass of earth of many tons weight, that gave away sooner than expected; the poor man literally buried alive, and though he was promptly extricated by his fellow-workmen, he died in less than an hour from the injuries he received. Several other labourers at work on the same spot as deceased escaped almost by a miracle.—*Armagh Gazette*. (1847-08-21, 4:6)

3855. Singular Marriage Case.—One of the most extraordinary marriage cases ever, perhaps, brought into a court of justice in this county, was tried a few days back, by Chief Baron Pigott, in the Criminal Court of Downpatrick. In order to understand the nature of the proceedings, it may be necessary to allude to the law of marriages in this country. Parties can be married by a clergyman of the Established Church, either by license from the proper officer of the bishop, or by have their names 'called in church' three successive Sundays. This is law with regard to all sects, and embraces all communions. There is another mode, which may be called a 'civil rite.' Each county is divided into a number of districts containing a registrar of marriages and a licenser, those being invariably Dissenters, as the law was passed to meet their views. When the licenser issues his license, it is taken to the Presbyterian clergyman by whom the ceremony is to be performed, and, after a certain period has elapsed, he celebrates the office. In case parties desire to be married by the registrar in his office, he being always a layman, they give him notice of intention. That notice he forwards to the board of guardians of the poor, by whose clerk it is read at three consecutive meetings of the board, immediately after which the registrar joins the applicants together. In every case, however, the parties must each take an oath that there is no just cause or impediment to their being united, so that if there do exist any legal impediment, they commit perjury. The singular case to which I refer is this:—In the year 1845, a man named Beadness was married in Tullylish Church, to a girl named Anne Bright. This wife died in May 1846, and in the November of that year, he was married by the Banbridge district registrar, upon notice, to Sarah Anne Bright, *the mother of his first wife*! Inasmuch as the Ecclesiastical Court would go no furthern than rendering the marriage void, it was deemed advisable by the Crown lawyers to try Beadness and Sarah Anne Bright for perjury, in swearing before Mr. Scott, the registrar, that there was 'no cause of impediment' to the marriage. Evidence was given to the oath having been administered by Mr. Scott. Mr. Yeates proved the first marriage in church, and Mr. M'Clelland, of the board of guardians, proved the supplication of the notice by reading. The argument of counsel for the defenders at the bar went to this, that, in the first place, evidence should be produced to show that the accused knew of the marriage being within the prohibited degrees when they took the oath before Mr. Scott; and in the second, that those prohibited degrees should be proved to be a part of the law of the land. Sir Thomas Staples, for the Crown, urged that they were part and parcel of the canon law, which was of itself a section of the law generally, and therefore supposed to be known to every subject; and contended that perjury being a crime of fact, knowledge on behalf on the part [sic] of the criminal was not necessary to uphold the guilt. It was then endeavoured to be proven that the male prisoner was an attendant at church, in which he would know the degrees of affinity from the Prayer Book, but the proof failed, as it appeared he attended no place of worship. The Crown failed also to produce any statute in which the prohibitions were set out. His lordship, in charging the jury, agreed with the prisoner's counsel, that, to constitute perjury, the person charged must know that he is taking a false oath, as it would be a dangerous precedent to convict of such a crime on a matter of opinion. There was no doubt a false oath had been taken; but was it taken wilfully and corruptly? His lordship thought not. The jury, after deliberating three hours, could not agree to a verdict, and were discharged—the prisoners being held to bail, to appear again when called upon to answer the arraignment. Beadness has one daughter by his first wife, and another by the present, and it is odd enough to look at the relationship. The grandmother of the first girl is mother to her sister. It is rather a repulsive case; but it has caused great excitement in the county Down.—*Ulster Correspondent of the North British Mail.* (1847-08-28, 1:4)

3856. Fever in Fermanagh.—We regret being obliged to announce again that fever (which for the last few [*illegible*] was on the decline in this county) is again in[—]ng. We have received a number of communi[—]s within the last four or five days from highly [—]ctable quarters, calculated to confirm us in the [—]cy of this unwelcome intelligence. We had [—] that this awful follower of famine had nearly [—]d its onward course of death and suffering; [—]d fondly cherished a hope that[,] with a plentiful [—]t, the hand of death would be stayed, and in [—]ce we would have had a renewal of robust [—], so that we could enjoy the blessings so plenti[—] [—]owered on us by an All-merciful Hand; but it [—]rs our wishes are in vain. An all-wise Pro[—]ce is not yet satisfied; he has not yet sufficiently [—]ched us; his hand is still stretched out to chasten [the] [—] nhabitants of this country. Let us take warning—let each of us recollect that we may be the [—] selected for destruction.—*Erne Packet.* (1847-08-28, 3:1) *Note: Due to a fold in the left-hand margin, a number of characters were illegible.*

3857. Important Sale of a Handsome Residence, Three Farms, Farming Stock, Crop, Farm Implements, and Household Furniture.

To be Sold by Auction,—on Wednesday, the 8th September next, at Sallymount, near Monaghan,—the Residence of the Late Thomas Robinson, Esq.,—The Houses, Offices, and Farm of Sallymount, otherwise Gullree,—Situate within a mile-and-a-half of Monaghan, on the Armagh Road.

The Farm Contains 45 Statute Acres of prime land in first rate condition, held under a Lease for one Life, at 8s. per acre. The purchaser can be accommodated with turbary.

The House and Offices are in perfect repair.

Also a Farm of about Seven Irish Acres of Land, in the townland of Mullaghmore, and Four Acres in the townland of Derry, both held under the Rev. Edward Brook, at the yearly rent of 16 10s. 3d., and adjoining the Farm of Sallymount.

The Stock Comprises three well bred Milch Cows, two two year old Heifers, two weanling Calves, and two good Farm Horses.

The Crop Comprises Five Acres of excellent Potatoes, perfectly free from disease; the produce of 20 Acres of Oats, an Acre of Turnips; a large quantity of prime upland Hay, and a quantity of Turf.

The Crop will be Sold in Lots to suit purchasers.

The Farm Implements Comprise Three Carts and Harness, Two Iron Ploughs, a Drill Harrow, a set of Fans, two Harrows, Wheel Barrows, &c.

The Household Furniture Comprises Mahogany Bedsteads and Feather Beds; Mahogany and Rosewood Tables and Chairs; Presses; Wardrobes; an Eight-day Clock; Sofas; a Sideboard; Guard-de-Vin; a Mahogany Secretary and Book Case; Carpets, (*continued...*)

3857, continued: ...Fenders, and Fire Irons, with Kitchen and Dairy Utensils, and a Patent Churn.

Terms of Sale—Cash. Sale to Commence at Eleven o'clock, a.m.

The Farm and Residence will be put up for Sale precisely at Twelve o'clock.

John Holmes, Auctioneer.

Dated, August 28, 1847. (1847-08-28, 3:2)

3858. County of Monaghan.—Unreserved Auction, at the Rectory, Clones,—(Consequent on the demise of the late Very Rev. Dean Roper), of the Entire Establishment, on Tuesday, the 14th September, 1847, and following day,

The Subscriber is favoured with Instructions to Sell without Reserve, as above, the Furniture, Cattle, Horses, Vehicles, Crops, Farming Utensils, &c., &c.

The Furniture Comprises a superior toned Pianoforte; a single actioned Harp, by Egan, of Dawson-street, Dublin; Feather Beds; Bedding; Bedsteads and Hangings; Mattresses; Wardrobes; Clothes Presses; Dingin; Loo; Card; Sofa; Work and other Tables; Sofas; Loungers; Couches; Ottomans; Chairs in Hair and Damask; Arm Do.; Carpets; Rugs; Fenders, and Fire Irons; Dumb Waiters; China; Glass; Delph; Eight-day Clock; Lamps; Book-cases; &c., &c.; together with extensive Culinary and Dairy Utensils.

The Out Door Establishment Consists of Carriages; Cars; Poney Phaeton; Single and Double Harness; Bridles; Saddles; Farming Utensils; Tumbrels; Water Cart; Cart Harness; Ploughs; Drill, Do.; Scuffles; Harrows; Metal, and other Rollers; Three Horse Threshing Machine, by Lestrange; Oat Bruiser, and Turnip-Cutter, Do.; Steaming Apparatus, by Robinson, of Lisburn; Iron Gates; Barrows, &c., &c.

Horses.—A pair of Superior Bay Carriage Horses; Family Horse; Four Farm, do.; One-High-Bred Mare; One do., Filly; Two do., Colts; Poney; Male, and Cart; Donkey, and do., &c., &c.

Stock.—One Durham Bull, three years [sic] old; Six dairy Cows, in calf, to do.; Four two years old Heifers; Three yearling Bullocks; Seven weaning Calves; Three old Wethers, &c.

Crop.—About twenty Acres of Oats; Seven Acres of Barley; Five Acres of Rye; Four Acres of Bere; Fifty Cocks of Hay; Two-and-a-half Acres of Swedish Turnips; Three roods of Parsnips, and Carrots, &c., &c.

Sale to commence each day at 12 o'Clock.—Terms Cash, and Purchasers to pay Five per Cent Auction Fees.

James Ganley, Auctioneer,

Usher Quay, Dublin, and Bridge-street, Longford.

N.B.—Pedigree of Horses, &c., at time of Sale. (1847-08-28, 3:4)

3859. Death by Drowning.—On Friday last, a melancholy accident, involving the loss of life to a young man named Osbourne Elliott, occurred a short distance from Enniskillen. The deceased, in company with three other persons, went in a boat to have a pleasure excursion on Lough Erne. When about a mile and a half from town, at a place called Tully Point, near Devenish Island, it appears a cap belonging to one of the party fell overboard, and in the effort to save it, the boat capsized, precipitating the whole party into the water. Elliott immediately made for the shore, in order to procure assistance for his companions, but he failed in his effort, having got entangled in weeds, by which means he was drowned. The other three clung to the boat until providentially, a second boat came to their relief. Intelligence of the disaster was then speedily conveyed to Enniskillen, and in a short time after, crowds of people were at the spot, using every means to find the body. Seeing their exertions useless, a man named M'Donald, at great personal risk, dived and found it in an erect position with the hands pressed on the ears. It was immediately conveyed to his sorrowing parents house, where Drs. West and Rogers were in attendance to render medical aid, but their skill was unable to restore animation. The deceased was a young man in the prime and vigour of life, very respectively [sic] connected, and universally lamented. On Sunday evening, his remains were conveyed to their last resting place, attended by a large concourse of sorrowing friends. (1847-09-04, 2:3)

3860. Melancholy Accident.—On last Saturday, the quiet hamlet of Stabannon, near Ardee, was thrown into a state of the greatest excitement on account of the following melancholy circumstance. It appears that about four o'clock on the above evening, a young man, named Maginn, master of the national school, went into the house of a person named Byrne, whose children he was attending. Mr. Byrne had some time previous charged a gun for the purpose of shooting crows; he had just gone out for the purpose of superintending some harvest operations. Maginn took up the gun and tried was it charged—it appears an accident had happened [to] the ramrod, it being rather short, which led Maginn to imagine it was not charged; in consequence, he snapped it at a fine young woman, Mr. Byrne's daughter, when the piece exploded, and the entire charge lodged in her breast, causing instant death.—Maginn immediately absconded, but was taken by the police in the night. An inquest was held the following day before H.M. Blackwell, Esq., and a verdict of accidental death recorded. (1847-09-11, 2:6)

3861. Deputy Lieutenants.—His Excellency the Lord Lieutenant has approved of the following noblemen and gentlemen being appointed Deputy Lieutenants for the Queen's county, viz.:—

The Earl of Portarlington, vice the Earl of Portarlington, deceased.

Richard W. Fitzpatrick, Esq., vice Colonel Rochfort, deceased.

Edmund Staples, Esq., vice M'Cosby, deceased. (1847-09-11, 3:3)

3862. Extent of Mortality.—Some idea may be formed of the amount of destitution and the prevalence of mortality in the districts of Galway, Oranmore and Ballinacourty, from the fact that, in the workhouse of the union alone, there have been, during the last twelve months, over one thousand deaths, while in Oranmore and Ballinacourty, out of a comparatively small population, there have been no less than nine hundred and thirty seven human victims to the starvation policy of the Whigs.—*Galway Mercury*. (1847-09-11, 4:4)

3863. Fatal Accident.—On Tuesday last, a most distressing accident took place at Smithboro' in this county, by which a fine lad of 16 years of age lost his life by the incautious use of fire arms. It appeared by the evidence at the inquest held by Charles Waddel, Esq., on Wednesday, that two of Mrs. Lowry's shop assistants were engaged in cleaning the lock of a flint gun, the barrel of which was loaded without their knowledge. After oiling the lock, one, the elder named Dudgeon, began to screw it on, and then tried the trigger action. There was no powder in the pan, but unfortunately, the spark communicated through the touch-hole, the charge exploded and the shot struck the younger lad in the groin, passing through the intestines and causing almost immediate death. The poor boy exclaimed, "Oh, John, I am shot" and never spoke more, his sufferings having terminated in about twenty minutes. The unfortunate lad, through whose innocent instrumentality the melancholy event took place, is suffering the most acute mental anguish, and the friends of both parties are plunged in the deepest grief. The verdict of the coroner's jury was "Accidental death." (1847-09-18, 3:1)

3864. Fever.—This dreadful disease still increases in its virulence throughout the country. In Westport, its ravages are most fearful, insomuch that the sick are, in many cases, lying by the ditch side in the neighbourhood of the town. In this town, fever is also very prevalent, and continues to increase. We have witnessed creatures lying by the road side, suffering from the epidemic, without any one to look after them or prevent the continuance of this nuisance, which is calculated to spread the disease still more.—*Mayo Constitution*. (1847-09-18, 3:2)

3865. Awful Death.—A young man named Flanigan, near Annaduff, county Leitrim, having taken ill of fever, the kind people there entered into a subscription, and employed the aunt of Flanigan to nurse-tend him. The poor fellow was placed in a hut, but his unnatural aunt having received the sum agreed upon for attending him during his illness, went about her business, leaving the young man stretched alongside the fire. During the night, the straw on which he lay ignited, and, although the unfortunate sufferer endeavoured to make towards the door, yet his strength was not sufficient. His remains were found the following morning near the entrance of the hut, burned to a cinder! A correspondent assures us that it is impossible to form an idea of the number of deaths from fever which weekly occur in the parish of Annaduff.—*Boyle Gazette*. (1847-09-25, 1:6)

3866. (From the *Ballyshannon Herald*.)—John Welsh, Esq., M.D.—This excellent gentleman, who has resided in this town for some years, has removed to Clones, in the county Monaghan, having obtained the unsolicited situation of physician to the fever hospital and other establishments in that town, vacant by the death of the former physician.—His removal is very generally regretted by the inhabitants of this town and neighbourhood, as his professional skill and fortunate treatment of almost all cases which he took in hands, obtained the approbation of his patients. He has (under Providence) been instrumental in restoring many persons to health, of whom little hopes existed before his attendance. We almost envy the inhabitants of Clones the happiness of having such a physician; but on Doctor Welsh's account, we hope he may prove as successful in his practice there as he did here. We wish Doctor Walsh [sic] and his amiable lady long life and prosperity. (1847-09-25, 3:1)

3867. One of the two physicians, M. de Mussy, sent over to this country by the French Government, to report upon the epidemic now prevailing, is ill of fever, at his residence in Stephen's-green, Dublin. (1847-09-25, 4:3)

3868. Melancholy Suicide.—We regret to announce the suicide of a respectable inhabitant of this city [Dublin], named A.W. Niblett, residing at No. 62, Lower Sackville-street, who, about ten o'clock this morning, flung himself into the Royal Canal, near Clarke's-bridge, Summer-hill, and was drowned before any assistance could be procured.

The unfortunate man, who did not return to his home during the night, drove this morning in a covered car to the canal banks, near the place of his suicide, and having paid and dismissed the carman, walked leisurely along the bank. Suddenly, in the view of a woman and boy, who were close to him, he ran forward, jumped into the centre of the deep part of the canal, and sunk. Drags were immediately procured, but his body was not taken out for fully an hour, when life was, of course, extinct. (1847-10-09, 1:1)

3869. The library of the late Rev. Dr. Murphy, Roman Catholic Bishop of Cork, has been valued, by a competent judge from London, at £25,000. (1847-10-09, 1:1)

3870. We have much pleasure in stating that the Lord Bishop of Clogher has been pleased to appoint the Rev. John T. Whitestone, late Rector of Castleblayney, to the living of Killevan [sic], vacant by the death of the Rev. John Wright. His Lordship, in this selection, has displayed that acumen, and knowledge of character, which has distinguished all (*continued...*)

3870, continued: ...his appointments, and we congratulate the inhabitants of Killevan upon their getting one of the most distinguished, energetic, and talented gentlemen in the diocese as their pastor, while we feel that the inhabitants of Castleblayney will deeply deplore the loss of such a man as Mr. Whitestone. (1847-10-09, 2:6)

3871. Elopement Extraordinary.–Aughnacloy.–A young lady, only 14 years of age—young in years and young in experience, an only child—generally a spoiled one—and faultless in person—has eloped, ran off, with one unworthy of her—one beneath her in every respect—a labourer, an hireling, a clod-plodding clown, devoid of everything, without any quality to recommendation—a person anything but prepossessing, almost disgusting; in pocket pennyless, low, mean, and unprincipled in the extreme; and to further add to her moral guilt, the silly infatuated girl, before leaving, broke into her father's cabinet, and extracted therefrom a considerable sum in cash, besides making a bold attempt upon a drawer containing a larger sum, which, however, proved unsuccessful. Nothing daunted by the failure, she stealthily made off with what had been acquired, and being joined by the worthy swain, the ill-directed pair made good their escape. A most vigilant and active search was immediately set on foot, and messengers despatched in every direction, all of which, however, they contrived to elude for some days. Every enquiry proved unsuccessful, until at length, on the fourth day from their departure, they were discovered pursuing their course with accelerating locomotion, in the direction of a western seaport. Here, their further transit was prematurely impeded by their joint capture. Some of the stolen property being found in his possession, and duly recognized and sworn to by the owner, (the ill-abused father,) he was immediately placed under arrest and conveyed to gaol, where the cold stone jug encircles him, instead of the arm of the erring fair one, who has again been brought under the parental care beneath her father's roof. Such has been the unfortunate race run by this fine, promising young girl, with bright prospects before her, and a certain fortune of not less than £2,000. It is thought that if the charge of robbery connected with this nefarious affair can be clearly brought home against the principal actor, that at least the delinquent, now spending the honeymoon in limbo, will be there allowed to remain in glorious confinement for some time to come.—*Erne Packet.* (1847-10-09, 4:4)

3872. Deaths on Board the *Duchess of Kent.*—On Thursday, Friday, and the whole of Saturday last, Mr. Austin, one of the assistant poor law commissioners, was engaged in the large room of the Wardlesworth Workhouse, Rochdale, in taking the depositions of the overseers, relieving officers, magistrates, clerks, and others, relative to the removal of Irish paupers, but more particularly the circumstances attending the removal of the boy, Michael Duigenan, aged twelve, his brother, fourteen, and sister, four years, who were conveyed from the fever hospital at Rochdale, on the 1st September, per railway, to Liverpool, and then on board the *Duchess of Kent* steamer to Dublin. The boy, Michael Duigenan, died as soon as the ship arrived at Dublin, and an inquest was held on the body. The Irish jury censured the conduct of the Rochdale authorities for having removed the children in so weak a state, and attributed the death of the boy to exposure to cold. The depositions from Ireland were read over, and Mr. Austin took great pains in examining the various witnesses. Several magistrates were present during the inquiry, as well as most of the guardians and many of the inhabitants of the town. One of the Catholic priests was also present the whole of the three days, watching the proceedings on behalf of his friends and several Irish members of Parliament. The certificate signed by Mr. Callingwood, surgeon to the fever hospital at Rochdale, as to the boy being fit to be removed to Ireland, could not be found. The magistrate's clerks could give no account of it. The boy was not taken before the magistrates previous to the warrant for his removal. The affair, no doubt, will be brought before Parliament early next session.—*Liverpool Mercury.* (1847-10-09, 4:5)

3873. The Prebend of Annaculla, and the Rectory of Kilmalinoge, in the gift of the Hon. the Lord Bishop of Killaloe, was vacant by the death of the Rev. James Hannagan, who fell a victim to fever. (1847-10-23, 2:2)

3874. Another Railway Accident.—Inquest.—An inquest was held on Wednesday, in the Whitehouse national school, before the coroner, J.K. Jackson, Esq., on the body of a young man about seventeen years of age, named John Moran, who was killed on the previous day, being pressed between two waggons on the Belfast and Ballymena Railway. It appeared from the evidence, that deceased had been engaged oiling the axle of an empty waggon, and that before he could change his position, a loaded one, that had been passing on the line, came into collision with the other, and crushed him almost to death. The poor fellow died an hour or two afterwards. The jury returned a verdict of accidental death. (1847-10-23, 3:2)

3875. Another Railway Accident.—Early on Friday morning, as a porter, named Boyle, employed on the Ulster Railway, was engaged in connecting two luggage trucks, he stepped aside for a moment to avoid the contact with some other carriages, including a horse box, which were being brought up. Unfortunately, he took up a position between the railway and a boundary wall, and, when the train was put in motion, he was so seriously crushed by the horse box, which is a little wider than the other carriages, that little hope is entertained of his recovery. He was at once conveyed to the Surgical Hospital, where every attention was paid to him. No blame whatever attaches to any one of the persons in charge of the train.—*Belfast Chronicle.* (1847-10-23, 3:2)

3876. Fatal Accident on the Ulster Railway.—On Wednesday last, an accident occurred at the Lisburn terminus of the Ulster line of railway, by which one person has, unhappily, lost his life, and another has been very seriously injured. It appears that some carters were engaged in transferring goods from the vehicle into a lurry, the ten o'clock up luggage train, at full speed, appeared in sight; and, before the persons in charge of the horses could get them out of the way, the train was upon them, despite the efforts of the conductor to check its speed by turning off the steam and applying the brake. One of the carters, named Dunlop, was crushed to death upon the spot, and an assistant was carried a considerable distance in front of the advancing train, and so seriously injured, that his life is despaired of. An inquest was held on Friday, on the body of Dunlop, before J.K. Jackson, Esq., and a respectable jury, when, after several witnesses had been examined, the jury returned a verdict of "Accidental death," accompanied by a recommendation to the Ulster Railway Company, to relieve the destitute relatives of the deceased. (1847-10-23, 4:3)

3877. Death of Professor M'Cullagh.—With inexpressible pain and sorrow, we have to communicate the death of Professor M'Cullagh, of Trinity College, Dublin, under circumstances the most afflicting to all his friends, and most deeply to be deplored throughout the civilized world, to no part of which his celebrity had not reached. The fatal event took place yesterday evening, at his chambers in College. The nature of his decease required the intervention of the Coroner; but at the moment we write, the inquest has not been brought to a conclusion. Should our Reporter return in time for this night's post, we shall communicate the details to our readers. In the absence of the particular facts, which, doubtless, have appeared in the course of investigation, no cause can be assigned for the rash act. We understand, however, that for some weeks, at least, he had been depressed in spirits, and was, at the time, under medical treatment. How melancholy is the reflection, that the noblest intellect with which man can be endowed, may thus, in a moment, be overturned beneath the infirmities of its earthly tabernacle.—*Mail.*

Since the foregoing was in type, our Reporter has returned, and we now proceed to lay before our readers, the following report of

THE INQUEST.

At two o'clock, Dr. Kirwan, one of the city coroners, proceeded to hold an inquest upon the body, which was lying in the bed occupied by the deceased, in his rooms in the College.

The following jury were empanelled by Dr. Kirwan: —George M'Dowell, Charles Miller, Garrett Nugent, Donald M'Donald, Frederick Ringwood, W. Nelson Handcock, John Kells Ingram, James Roger North, John A. Byrne, Robert Holmes Orr, and W. Maguire Brady, Esqrs.

The first witness examined was an old woman named Margaret Healy.—I was in the service of the deceased; saw him last about half-past eight o'clock yesterday evening; he was lying on his side upon the bed; he did not dine at home; I was not in the room; I only opened a little of the door; when I opened the door, he asked me what I wanted; I said, I begged his pardon, I did not know he was there; he told me that would do, and desired me to go away; he came in at six o'clock in the evening; I left his tea for him, but I believe he did not take any; I brought him his tea about seven o'clock, with a mutton chop; I thought he looked unwell; I thought his eyes looked full and large, and that he stared [at] me with a wild look; I thought this; I saw him afterwards upon the bed; I saw him again at ten o'clock; it was my business to go to him at half-past nine; he allowed me to go to bed then, and call him at an early hour; I waited in the drawing-room to see if he would call, but he did not ring the bell; I waited for half an hour, and then I went up stairs; I heard him going through the house after I left him first; I heard him slapping the doors and prancing from one room into another; his slapping the doors was nothing remarkable; about ten o'clock, I went to the bed room—this was a second time that I had gone—I called at the door, got no answer; he was lying behind the bed, but I did not see him; I then went to search the house for him. I went up stairs to the closet, and I called at a distance, thinking that he might be there, but I got no answer; I ventured further, and went into the closet; he was not there; I returned to the bed room and saw a black thing (the skirt of his coat) near the bed; I thought he was in a fit, and ran down stairs; his hat, cap, coat, and boots were there, so I knew he could not have gone out; I ran for Mr. Butcher; I thought he was a doctor, as he sent for him one night when he could not get Dr. Stokes; he was not subject to fits; I had no notion that he had committed suicide; I thought he was in a fit, and that Mr. Butcher would bleed him; I thought also, that he would lift him as he was too heavy for me; Mr. Butcher came with me; I did not even know that he had committed the melancholy deed; a porter and Mr. Butcher had raised him before I got in; it was the porter who had put him into the bed.

To a Juror—I could not tell whether he was excited when he asked me why I came into the room, as he was a hasty gentleman; he went out at twelve o'clock; as soon as he came out of church, he prepared, and sent me for a car; I dont know where he went between twelve and six.

Rev. Samuel Butcher, examined.—I live in college; I was a particular friend of the deceased; a few minutes before eleven o'clock, I was going to bed, when I was called and desired to come over instantly to see Mr. M'Cullagh, who had fallen off the bed; that was the message that was given to me; I asked what the matter was, and they seemed unable to (*continued...*)

3876, continued: ...say; the late witness and my servant came together; I do not know which of them spoke to me first; I came over with great haste; I came into the bedroom, and saw the body lying between the bed and the wall, the head towards the top of the bed; I raised him; there was a pool of blood in the corner; he was quite dead; the razor was on the floor; the porter came in; looked for the instrument, and found the razor in the blood; he was quite dead, nearly cold; this was at eleven o'clock; I am not aware that it was one of the razors he was in the habit of using; with the assistance of one of the porters, I raised him and put him into the bed in the position in which the body now lies; the razor was farther from the wall than the body; I saw him last alive upon Saturday at eleven o'clock; he has been in low spirits for the last week, at least, since Monday; he was not more desponding and low spirited on Saturday than on the previous days; I don't know that I can use the word desponding; I will say low spirits; he appeared to be somewhat excited in his mind; he was often low spirited; I do not know of any reason of his low spirits; I cannot tell that the late College election had any effect upon him; he had a constitutional tendency to melancholy; it was generally remarked in College that he was gloomy the last week; he was subject to gloom; I do not think the bed was tossed as if it had been lain in; had a conversation with him, and he laboured under an impression that there were statements in circulation respecting him; he thought there was some charge against him.

Dr. Stokes examined.—Deceased was one of my oldest and dearest friends; I think I never had occasion to prescribe for him till Monday last; he generally enjoyed better health than most men who lead a sedentary life; he called upon me in company with a friend; the friend said to me that he was not very well; that his breath was heavy, and he was depressed; did not prescribe for him then; upon Tuesday morning, I received a note from him; he said he was not well though not in pain, but was afraid that something in his manner had excited the suspicion of his friends, and that persons might suppose he was ill; he did not say mental illness, but he wished it to be inferred; I told him that he was labouring under dyspepsia, derangement of the stomach; he had a fullness of tongue, and heavy breath; but he was not feverish, though he looked like a man who might get fever; he was melancholy; he said he had been working very hard at a difficult mathematical problem. Upon Monday, I gave him a blue pill and a rhubarb draught. He mentioned to me that he had been drinking green tea, which evidently had deranged his stomach very much. He was a man of strictly temperate habits; I saw him three times on Wednesday and Thursday; I told him to give up his mathematical studies and go out; he arranged to go to a friend in the country; he was wonderfully better on Thursday, and still better on Friday, when he promised to come and dine with me; what he chiefly complained of was, lest during his illness, persons might conceive that his mind was not all right—"Even you," said he, "are looking at me;" "Why," said I, "one cannot look cheerful to see you ill;" he did not dine with me on Friday; I saw him on Saturday; he was better, and his natural manner had returned; he was then apparently much better; his tongue was cleaner; he steadily improved since Wednesday; he spent Saturday evening with me at my own house; he was perfectly well to all appearance; he showed no aberration of mind more than as to natural despondency; he asked me would I go to the College Chapel on Sunday; said yes, "then you had better come and breakfast with me, and we will go together. I did so; the only thing remarkable was that when I came, he had breakfasted; he had breakfast prepared for me; his habit, he said, was to breakfast when getting up; there was nothing about him then to draw the attention of any person who had known that he was ill. He acknowledged that he had been ill—that he had been in a dreamy state, but he felt the illness was passing or had passed away; as far as I could ascertain about the depression, it was that his manner had excited suspicion that he was not right in his mind, and that this would go out and damage his character and prospects; I assured him that this illusion arose from physical causes, he said that medical men might think as I did, but that others would misinterpret it into mental illness; there was nothing extraordinary in his state; the only thing unusual in his case was that he had improved so much, and then relapsed: I think that his former hallucination returned stronger than it had been; upon Thursday, he said to me that my servant thinks me very ill, and that she watches me; upon one occasion, he went to the door and shut it, and said that she was listening; I think his disease was melancholia, arising from dyspepsia, which originated from over application of the mind to a difficult mathematical problem, while he neglected his bowels, and was drinking strong tea; I believe him to have been a very religious man; on Sunday morning, I found him reading *Butler's Sermons*, which he said it was his habit to read; he asked me if I had ever read them; I said I had not, and he said, tapping me on the shoulder—My dear friend, I could not recommend you a better book; he often seemed labouring under some despondency; but I never saw him in such health and spirits as he was in, since he left the College election; I heard that, two years ago, he was in excellent health; he stated in his conversation that his object was to bring a still stronger bearing between sacred and revealed religion.

Henry West, Barrister-at-law, examined.—I was a very particular friend of the deceased; on Saturday week last, I came to his room here; some time previous, he had paid me a visit at my father's house [in] Loughlinstown; I came to him to fix a day to come down; he told me he had been working very hard, and with great satisfaction; I remarked that his breath was heavy, and his manner was not so joyous as it used to be when meeting his friends; he appeared to be ill; he agreed to come with me; he walked along Killiney hill; I pointed out objects to him which he did not appear to see; on Sunday, he went to church, and his manner was very abstracted; in the evening, we retired early to the drawing-room, and he said, you know I am no good until I get my tea; met him in town upon Monday; he said to me, did it ever occur to you that persons have some particular formula to test if you have committed any crime, you get read and they get red; I told him that nothing of the kind could be; I thought, as he used the word formula, his mind had been deranged by scientific pursuits; he was wandering and incoherent, like a person in a fever; I thought, upon one or two points, that he was peculiarly minded, that was when he had dyspeptic symptoms; he placed great reliance in Dr. Stokes; the peculiar views I speak of had reference to his College studies; went with him to Dr. Stolkes [sic], and I told him I did not think he was well; Dr. Stokes told him not to study so much.

Doctor Leeson examined.—I found on the neck of deceased a large gash, about six inches in length, and three in breadth, cutting deeply; In fact, as far as the spine, through the carotid artery and jugular vein at the right side; the wound also opens into the mouth, just above the trachea; there was one gash, but visibly three incisions; I think the wounds were inflicted by a razor, which was found in the room, clotted with blood and hair; there cannot be the least question that the wounds were the cause of death; I think that, after he had received the wound across the carotid and jugular veins, that his death was instantaneous.

The Coroner then said, after the admirable testimony which had been given by Dr. Stokes, there could not be any doubt but that the deceased had committed the act while labouring under melancholia, produced by dyspepsia; every one should deplore that the melancholy event had taken place; there could be no doubt that persons who pursued mathematical and abstruse studies were subject to melancholia; and the cases of insanity and melancholy resembled each other so much in many instances, that no one can tell when one began and the other terminated; and Dr. Stokes had known persons commit suicide while affected with melancholia. That being the case, it was quite clear that the deceased had committed the rash and most deplorable act arising from melancholia, brought on by dyspepsia, which had been caused by an over-worked mind. If the jury agreed in this opinion, he would record it as their verdict.

The Jury expressed a wish to retire, and draw up their verdict in their own words, which they did accordingly. They returned in a few minutes with the following verdict:—We find that Professor James M'Cullagh died of wounds inflicted upon himself while labouring under temporary insanity.(1847-10-30, 1:3)

3878. The Church.—The Rev. William West, curate of Delgany, has been promoted to the Rectory of same, vacant by the death of the Rev. Wm. Cleaver.
(1847-11-06, 1:4)

3879. Death of a Lady by Drowning in Dublin.—At seven o'clock on Friday evening, as police-sergeant Hickey was walking along the Royal Canal bank, between Blackquire's bridge and Westmorland bridge, he heard a scream of distress, and on running along the bank a short way, he saw a person struggling in the water; Hickey at once plunged in, and attempted to get a grasp of the clothes of the drowning person—but in vain, as the strength of the wind, then very high, had blown her out into the deep water. Sub-constable Lee came up immediately after, and at once plunged in, and succeeded in getting hold of the body when completely under water. The bystanders, by means of a rope, hauled Lee and his burthen to the land. The appearance of the drowned person was that of an elderly lady of about fifty-six years of age. The usual means for restoring suspended animation were put into operation, but without effect. The deceased's under garments were marked with the name, Catherine Morris. On her person was a plain and rather old gold watch. In her pocket was found some money, two one pound notes, and some silver, besides some few other matters. It is supposed that the deceased was blown into the canal when walking near the brink, by a sudden gust of wind. An inquest was held on Saturday on the body, when it appeared that deceased was a maiden lady, named Catherine Morris, and resided at Athy. She was a person possessing large property. The verdict was "accidental death." (1847-11-06, 1:6)

3880. Dr. S. Gordon has been elected Professor of Medicine to the Apothecaries Hall, Dublin, in place of the late Dr. Curran. (1847-11-06, 2:2)

3881. Last week, an antique tomb was discovered at Coolstuffe, county Wexford, in which the skeleton of a female with an infant in her arms was found.
(1847-11-06, 3:3)

3882. Death of William Mayne, Esq.—It is with the deepest regret we have to announce the death of this excellent man—this sincere friend and estimable country gentleman. The melancholy event took place at Westport House, County of Mayo, the residence of Lord Sligo, on the evening of Sunday last, and was caused by fever caught while discharging his duties as Assistant Barrister for that County. Mr. Mayne had, for many years, managed the extensive estates of Lord Cremorne in this county, and was almost adored by the tenantry, whose friend and advocate he always was. As a magistrate and grand juror, he was a most useful man, and he left a vacant seat in society that will not be easily filled. Mr. Mayne was in his 59th year.
(1847-11-13, 3:1)

3883. In Chancery—Mary Campbell, Widow, Executrix of Robert Killen, Deceased, Plaintiff.—Patrick Frame, and Rachael, his Wife, William Hall, and James Scott Molloy, Defendants.

Pursuant to the Decree in this cause bearing date, the 1st day of July, in the Year 1847—I hereby require all Persons having Charges of Incumbrances affecting all that Tenement in Petticoat Lane, in the Town of Castleblayney, in the County of Monaghan, containing in front, 31 feet, bounded on the north by Terence Duffy's holding, on the east by Mr. Dixon's holding, on the south by John Brannigan's concerns, and on the west by Petticoat Lane; also, all That and Those two Plots of Ground, on the north side of Ballybay-street, together with a Plot of Ground on the east side of York-street, all in the said Town of Castleblayney. Also, all that Tenement or Plot of Ground, situate on the east side of Church-street, in the said Town of Castleblayney, containing in front, 27 feet, and the same in rere, being the Tenement formerly held by John Branagan, and afterwards in the possession of William Branagan; also, All That and Those, that House and Tenement in the Diamond of the said Town of Castleblayney, containing in front, 40 feet, bounded on the north by Mary Whitby's House and Tenement, on the east by the Street, on the south by Robert Ross's House, and William Steel's Concerns, and on the west by Robert Ross's Back Yard and Stable, all which Tenements and Premises are held under the Right Honorable Lord Blayney, by virtue of 4 several Indentures of Lease for Lives renewable for ever, being the Lands and Premises in the Pleadings in this Cause mentioned, to come in before me, at my Chambers, on the Inns Quay, in the City of Dublin, on or before the 14th day of December next, and proceed to prove the same; otherwise, they will be precluded from the benefit of said Decree.

Dated this 10th day of November, 1847.

Jeremiah John Murphy.

Edmond P. Morphy,
Solicitor for the Plaintiff,
43, Dame-street, Dublin.
(1847-11-13, 3:2)

3884. A Dead Subscriber.

A subscriber for years being sad in arrears,
Still neglecting his bills for to pay,
To the Editor said—Unless I am dead,
I shall pay on Christmas day;
The time flew by and the debtor was shy,
But the Editor thought what he said;
In his paper next week the truth he did speak
And announced his subscriber as dead!
(1847-11-13, 4:4)

3885. Lord Dalmeny, son of the Earl of Rosbery, married, about eighty years ago, a widow of Bath, for her beauty. They went abroad, she sickened, and on her death-bed, requested that she might be interred in some particular church-yard, either in Sussex or Suffolk, I forget which. The body was embalmed, but at the custom-house in the port where it was landed, the officers suspected smuggling, and insisted on opening it. They recognised the features of the wife of their clergyman—who having been married to him against her own inclination, had eloped. Both husbands followed the body to the grave. The grandfather of Dr. Smith, of Norwich, knew the lord. (1847-11-13, 4:5)

3886. The University.—We regret to announce the death of the Rev. Doctor Wray, vice Provost of Trinity College, which took place at his house in Merrion-square on Thursday morning last.

The option of accepting the vacant office rests with the Rev. Doctor Wall.

The death of the Vice-Provost will create three vacancies for Fellowships at the next examination.
(1847-11-20, 1:1)

3887. Wreck of an American Packet-Ship—Ninety-Five Lives Lost.—The American packet-ship, *Stephen Whitney*, from New York, bound for Liverpool, was totally lost on Wednesday night last, on the Calves, outside Skull. Nineteen of the passengers and crew were saved, and ninety-five met a watery grave. This intelligence we have received by the *Cork Southern Reporter of Saturday*. The following are the only particulars:—

"Skibbereen, Friday Evening.

"The splendid packet-ship, *Stephen Whitney*, has been wrecked on the coast, near Cape Clear, and, melancholy to relate, ninety-five lives have been lost. She was laden with cotton and cheese, and had a great number of passengers, all of the better class."

"Skibbereen, Nov. 12th.—I am sorry to inform you that, on the night before last, a dreadful shipwreck occurred outside Baltimore harbour, on the rocks called the Calves, ninety-one lives were lost, and nineteen saved. Yesterday, the bodies of a lady and child were thrown on shore. The lady had three gold rings on her fingers, and was very richly dressed. The vessel was an American packet from New York—her name I don't know yet. I am informed Mr. Cleburne's son, of this town, was in the ship, and is one of the parties lost. It is reported, since I began this letter, that there were three vessels lost on the same fatal night."

Reporter Office, Three o'clock.—The Skibbereen coach has just arrived—but we have little additional particulars to communicate. The driver states that the vessel is completely smashed in pieces, and the cargo, which is said to be very valuable, is being carried off by the country people, who flocked in thousands to the scene of the wreck. He states that the number of persons drowned is understood to be ninety-three, and that the captain and his wife were amongst them.
(1847-11-20, 1:2)

3888. Shipwreck.—The brig *Hero*, of London, 145 tons burthen, was wrecked in Cloughey bay, near Portaferry, on Wednesday morning last. She was under ballast from Belfast to Newport, and struck on the Cannon Rock, a little to the north of the North and South light, and soon went to pieces. Four men and a boy, who left the vessel in the long boat, are supposed to have perished. The captain, Charles Herman, and mate, George Bonis, remained in the rigging. After some time, the former could hold no longer, and having dropped into the sea, was drowned. The mate caught him by the breast as he was falling, but his hold gave way, leaving the captain's watch and guard chain in his hand. The Cloughey coast guard, under the command of Chief-boatman M'Bride, after eleven unsuccessful attempts, at the imminent risk of their lives, the boat being nearly swamped twice, succeeded in throwing a line to the mate, who made himself fast to it, and was hauled from the wreck to the boat. The Coast guards deserve great credit for their humane and persevering exertions to rescue the mate from a watery grave. The vessel was the property of Charles Wallace and Co. (1847-11-20, 2:2)

3889. The Church.—The Rev. John Graham, of Loughrea, in the diocese of Clonfert, has been presented by the vicars choral of the cathedral church of St. Patrick's, Dublin, to the vicarage of Strabannon, in the diocese of Armagh, to which his Grace the Lord Primate has added the vicarage of Richardstown, both vacant by the death of the Rev. Thomas Parkinson. (1847-11-20, 2:3)

3890. Important Divorce Case.—At the termination of the long pending case of

Jones v. Smith,

Reported for the *Northern Standard.*

A woman of exceedingly prepossessing appearance came forward, and begged leave to ask the advice of Mr. Tindal, the worthy Magistrate of the College-street Office. Although meanly clad, there was in her manner the evidence of having seen better days, and her deportment throughout, was such as to influence even the most indifferent listener, to consider her case more than a fair one. Constable 184, B, was attempting to prevent her infringing on the legal business of the court, when the presiding Magistrate interfered. She stated that her maiden name was Ireland, and having found that all attempts towards her being rendered comfortable in this life had proved vain, she had taken the liberty of asking the advice of his worship, and by that she would be guided.

His worship here enquired of what nature was her complaint.

The applicant stated that, when comparatively young and inexperienced, she had been joined into an alliance with a gentleman named Bull.

Clerk—Christian name, if you please, madam.

Applicant—John—John Bull.

His Worship—What, the gentleman who labours under such difficulties?

Applicant—The same, your worship—but the report in the *Times* is totally destitute of foundation. (Applicant continued)—She had married the person alluded to. He had held out very many promises as to the great contentment and happiness which would reign amongst her former children—for she had been wedded before to a gentleman named Nationality.

Clerk—Christian name, if your please, madam.

The Applicant said, with some energy, that he had no proper name, but was common to all.

The Clerk remarked it was irregular, and that he would make a note of it.

She (the Applicant,) had been promised for many years a decent sustenance; she had toiled and laboured, but all was in vain. She found that all the money went into his (Bull's) pocket, and the only reward she received was his abuse.

His worship here asked what evidence she had?

Mrs. Ireland replied that a gentleman called Walter, had been paid by Bull to abuse her, and take away the character of a family which was never surpassed in honesty or chivalry in the world.

His worship must interrupt her—If she had anything to say against the gentleman, she must say it without invective.

The applicant replied, that invective was probably the farthest thing from both her heart and speech—for forty-seven years, she had allowed her sons to starve, nay, to murder one amongst the other, rather than offend her husband—but what was she to do? Last year, she could not get as many potatoes as usual, and (for she did not want to take away from his merits, as he was her husband after all,) he had given her a small sum for her children—two or three of them died, but sure that was the will of God—she could not complain of this; but as to the present year, she regretted to say, that while her husband could afford to send (we understood the lady to say) ambassadors to the Court of Rome, (so we caught the words,) he absolutely denied to feed her children, and what was more—

His worship here interrupted her, and said, it was a most scandalous case.

What, then, would your worship have me to do?

His worship—See whether, as my friend Lord Massareene says, your husband will at last do something for you.

The applicant replied, with tears in her eyes, that she feared that day was over.

His worship—Then, madam, your only resource lies in a divorce. Call on the next case.

The conversation created great interest, and should the husband not change his conduct, we believe it may give business to the gentlemen of the long robe. (1847-11-20, 2:5)

3891. Cholera in Sligo.—Three cases of cholera occurred in Sligo during the week. One man, a tailor named Dowd, died after two hours' illness. We entertain strong hopes, however, that the disease which has appeared in this unfortunate town is not that fearful scourge, the Asiatic cholera, but the English cholera. Still, our Board of Health should be vigilant, that in case we should be affected by the former dreadful disorder, every means which human ingenuity can devise may be put in force to check its ravages.—*Champion.* (1847-11-27, 2:4)

3892. Law Appointments.—We have been informed, on what we consider undoubted authority, that the Hon. Mr. Trench, brother of Lord Ashtown, has been appointed to the office of assistant barrister for the county of Westmeath, vacant by the decease of the late Mr. Ellis.—*Freeman.* (1847-11-27, 2:4)

3893. The Gale on Sunday—Loss of a Sloop in the Shannon with Eleven Lives.—On Sunday last, owing to the severity of the weather, it blowing a regular gale, with a spring tide and westerly wind, a sloop belonging to Mr. M'Cloy was forced from its anchorage at Glin, and not being able to gain her position again, she struck, and in a short time, all on board met a watery grave, save one man. The boat was bound for Limerick, and was heavily laden with corn belonging to Doctor Enright, and also butter belonging to several buyers from this city, which had been purchased at the Glin market.—*Limerick Reporter.* (1847-11-27, 3:5)

3894. Court of Prerogative—Nov. 17, 1847, before the Right Hon. Judge Keatinge.—West, Promovant, *v.* Stopford, Impugnant, Foster, Intervenient, *v.* The Same.

Judge Keatinge delivered judgment in this important case, and said—In this case, the executors named in the will of Andrew Ker, Esq., bearing date the 14th of December, 1841, and the codicil to that will, bearing date the 20th of December, 1842, are promovants, and by this suit, these executors seek to establish that will and codicil: The impugnant in this case, Captain Stopford, is a caveator, and does not deny the validity of documents on which the promovants rest their title. He admits the will of the 14th of December, 1841, and he admits the codicil of the 20th of December, 1842, but he says that, in addition to the two testamentary documents on which the promovents rely, there are two other testamentary documents which ought to be examined. He relies on two codicils, dated the 20th of April, 1846, and he contends for their validity. He takes an interest only under the first codicil of the 20th of April, 1846, but he, by pleading, puts both in issue, and relies on both. The second disputed codicil, by which I mean the latter one of the 20th of April, 1846, clearly refers to personal as well as real estate. It professes to annul a power given by the testator to his executors to make a lease of what I believe is freehold property, but it also deals with a legacy of £500 left by the will. [*Continued description of provisions of the codicils, including a forfeiture clause.*] It follows from what I have said, that in my opinion, the court is called upon to pronounce a judgment in this case upon the merits—to decide on the evidence, the question raised in the cause, and to determine upon that evidence, whether the two codicils of the 20th of April, 1846, are or are not a portion of the testamentary acts of the deceased, and as such, entitled to probate. Now, there is a vast deal of evidence in this cause, with the minute particulars of which, I do not intend to deal. They, in my mind, invariably lead to a certain conclusion; and I purpose as I go along, not referring to the particular testimony of the witnesses, except with reference to certain prominent portions of this case.

The deceased was a bachelor, and he lived to the age of from 80 to 82 years. It appears by the evidence, that from time to time, he executed certain wills, and all those wills were prepared with care and attention, and aided by professional advice; and it is impossible to read the undisputed will of the 14th December, 1841, and not to say that upon that occasion, and when making the depositions of property contained in that document, the deceased called to his aid, and had the assistance of very competent professional persons. That will disposed of real and personal estate. The real estate appeared from the evidence to be worth £3,000 a year; the personal property in or about £3,000. Mr. Ker, when he made that will, and three sisters living—he had originally four. One was Mrs. Foster; another sister married a Mr. Hardman, who died, leaving two children, a son and daughter, the latter was Mrs. Stopford, the wife of the impugnant. Captain Stopford married his wife in 1835; she died in 1837, leaving two daughters surviving; and four years after her death, the will of the 14th of December, 1841, was made. By that will, the deceased gave an estate for life to his sisters, with remainders over among them for life, and on the death of his sisters, an estate for life to Miss Foster, his niece; on her death, if she left male issue, to that male issue; but, in the event of her leaving none, the property was to go in thirds, and one of those thirds was to go in certain events to the daughters of the impugnant.—By the same will, the deceased left £7000 to the children of Mr. Hardman, the younger, who had died a short time previous, leaving two children; and £5000 to the children of Captain Stopford, assigning as a reason for giving them a lesser sum, that they had expectations from his sisters, their aunts. By the same will, he made a provision for a lease to be executed at a certain rent of a portion of property on which a house, was to be built for the clergyman of New Bliss, county Monaghan, and he directed £500 to be applied to build that house, unless, in the meantime, he should have expended that sum for the same purpose; and this will contained legacies of several large sums. It appears from the evidence that the testator was a kind-hearted, old gentleman, and the will contained a certain provision, that all the persons who took, not merely the entire estate under the devises, but the thirds into which it might be divided, should assume the name and arms of Ker. The executors and trustees were the Rev. Mr. West, the Rev. J. Richards, and Mr. Lowry, the barrister. By the codicil of the 20th December, 1842, he removed Mr. Richards from the trusteeship, because it would appear, that that gentleman had ceased to be incumbent of the parish of New Bliss, or rather I should say, the Chapel-of-Ease. Mr. Richards, as was a common case with the clergyman of the parish, was a particular friend of the deceased, but having said that he could not act, the deceased made an alteration by the codicil of 1842, when Mr. Richards ceased to be in the possession of the incumbency of New Bliss. I am not aware of any important change in the family from the time of making the will of 1841, down to the making of the disputed codicils. His sister, Bessy, I believe, outlived him.—Mr. Hardman, (Intervenient's Solicitor), observed that she died some years previously.

[*Note: This article proceeds for nine full columns, an outline or extract of which follows*:

[Judge Keatinge described a sum owed by the deceased to Mrs. Foster, as executrix of her husband, and the bequest of the house and demesne of Newbliss, at a certain rent, to Mrs. Foster and, after her death, Miss Foster. The will was executed in duplicate, a copy of which was left in the possession of Mr. Magill, his attorney; the codicil of 1842 was also executed in duplicate. The first codicil of 1846 professes to confirm and ratify a deed of the 6th April, 1846, by which the deceased had assigned to Captain Stopford a portion of his property called Lisalee, which was worth about 200 a year. This court has no power to try any question as to the validity of the deed. Discussion of the deeds, and reference to the court of equity, as intimately connected with the subject of the codicils. Mr. Richard Mayne was employed as the deceased's land agent about ten years ago; description of the transaction of the 10th March, 1846, when Captain Stopford was substituted for Mr. Mayne.

[The case made by the intervenient in this case, Mrs. Foster, is, not that the deceased was totally incapable of making a will, but that he was liable to the influence of contrivance and management, and she calls upon the court to say by its judgment, that upon a mind and capacity weakened, fraudulent influences and control were used, &c., the codicils in dispute were made through the instrumentality of the impugnant, and as he is the person materially benefitted by them, and as deceased was at least a man of bad memory, and weakened capacity, the court would require, in respect of these codicils, more evidence that Captain Stopford has brought forward, and as he has not sufficiently proved the case, that therefore, upon that ground, the court is bound to refuse them probate.

[Discussion of: the testator's capability, the evidence establishes that the deceased was a man of somewhat weakened mind and of defective memory, but not of a mind so weakened, or memory so defective as to render him intestible, &c.; the accounting performed by Mr. Mayne on the testator's estates; the terms on which Captain Stopford and the deceased lived; contrary evidence about the cordiality or lack of same in their relations given by Mrs. H. Burke, who was Mr. Ker's housekeeper for nine years; controversy as to the liking of the deceased for the children of Captain Stopford, with reference to William Ker having witnessed some document; Miss Anne Ker deposed that, on the 9th of March, being out in the carriage with the deceased, he told her to tell Captain Stopford to call upon him on the morning of the following day; the quarrel ends with the impugnant proceeding to the town of Monaghan with a letter to Mr. Jeremiah Nunn, who advised that a power of attorney was essential to be executed to Captain Stopford—description of process, including dismissal of Mr. Mayne.

[Description of the visit of Mr. Mayne and his brother to the deceased upon the morning of the 11th of March, 1846; believed the handwriting to be that of the deceased, but the style of the letter differed from all the previous communications that he had from the deceased; on the 11th, deceased received him in his usual warm and friendly manner, and declared that he had not written such a letter to Mayne, but then stated that he had some recollection of signing a letter that had been prepared by Mr. Wright, or Captain Stopford, or William Ker. Discussion of whether Mr. Mayne and his brother would have committed wilful and corrupt perjury in making these statements. Description of second meeting of Mr. Mayne and his brother with the deceased, with the impugnant who admitted having given the deceased a letter to sign, drafted by William Ker, and having got the deceased to sign a power of attorney, appointing him, the impugnant, sole agent to the deceased; at the request of the deceased, Mayne assented to an arrangement by which the impugnant and Mayne should act jointly, which impugnant immediately refused.

[Letter of Thomas Edmond Wright, 31st March 1846, to Captain Stopford, advising handling of draft leases, an application for a lease by Mayne, and an ejectment against Roper at Newbliss, followed by interpretation of Judge Keatinge.

[Description of memorandum written by Andrew Ker of his intention to give Captain Stopford a deed of conveyance, of the townland of Lisalea, in the parish of Killevan on my own property. Mr. Wright swears that he prepared the deed of conveyance of the 6th of March from the written instructions of the deceased, and that afterwards he received (*continued...*)

3894, continued: ... a letter from a Captain Stopford on the subject—where is that letter? This is a very extraordinary document; and I would have expected that, if it were intended to make a present of a valuable portion of the testator's estate, the written instructions for the purpose would be forthcoming. Dr. Wylie read the evidence of Mr. Wright relative to the verification of the instructions for the deed, followed by Judge Keatinge's commentary. I am to take it, that the deed is prepared in pursuance of the memorandum, which could not have reached Dublin until the 2d of April 1846. The deed is prepared; that deed is brought down to the country by Mr. Wright, and on Monday the 6th, it is executed in the presence of Mr. Wright and a gentleman in the constabulary, Mr. Robinson; and there is a memorial of that deed also executed at the same time, by Mr. Ker, the deceased. Wright had a partner in Monaghan, but he brought down the deed himself. On the following day, the 7th of April, at half-past twelve o'clock, upon the affidavit of Mr. Wright, the memorial is handed in, into the registry-office in Dublin, and there registered. The deed and the memorial are respectively executed on Monday, and on Tuesday the memorial is registered at half-past twelve o'clock. I presume that Mr. Wright came back to town on Monday, by some conveyance of that evening. Now, there is no objection to the immediate registry of deeds. But here the instructions for that deed are not produced, unless this be the paper; but there was a letter from Captain Stopford which is not produced. &c., further discussion of the wills and the codicils, and the manner of execution of these and the deed. Reference to Mrs. Foster having applied to Mr. Lowry upon the subject, and description of Mr. Lowry's meeting with deceased on the 14th April, 1846, and of another meeting, on the same date, with Mr. Wright and his partner, Mr. Nunn. Mr. Lowry had employed Messrs. Nunn and Wright, solicitors, at the Monaghan Assizes to prepare a release of a debt from Mrs. Foster and her daughter to the deceased, in the absence of Mr. Magill, who then lived in the county of Down; in the meeting of the 14th, Mr. Nunn turned to his partner, and said, Thomas, you ought to be very cautious how you interfere in the Doctors affairs. Mr. Lowry swears that Mr. Wright declared that no act should be done affecting the property of the deceased, without being advised by Mr. Lowry professionally, as he had been consulted by the deceased, and was his confidential counsel. Further discussion as to timing and manner of execution of the deed. Judge Keatinge remarked, Mr. Lowry's conduct upon this occasion has been very strongly observed upon. It is said it was most audacious on his part, what right had he to interfere respecting the arrangements of the testator's property? I am not to pronounce my judgment upon the opinion of witnesses, but it appears to me (whether he was right or wrong is a different question) that the result of the conversation of the 14th was to lead Mr. Lowry firmly and conscientiously to believe that the mind of the deceased was gone. He may have been mistaken—perhaps he was, and he might have had wishes, feelings, and prejudices in favour of Mrs. Forster, which may have warped his judgment, but that he entertained that opinion conscientiously, appears to me to be perfectly clear. Mrs. Forster challenges the intelligence of the deceased, and knew a will had been made in her favour, and although she may or may not have had her judgment misled upon the subject, she acted a very perilous part in propagating such a report, unless she was satisfied that it was well founded.

[Description of Mr. Wright's meeting with the deceased on the 15th, with interpretive marks from Judge Keatinge, followed by several columns of evidence, including: letter written by Andrew Ker, at request of Captain Stopford, making a statement of facts about the grant of the townland of Lisalea, including an application to Lord Rossmore, making over the property of Drumskelt, and making Captain Stopford a magistrate; a reference to the London mail reaching Newbliss and Clones; continued analysis of the events of April, 1846.

[Judge Keating: According to the authorities, this court is not to establish any document, as to which, in its conscience, it is not satisfied. No judge has a right to erect a capricious standard, by which to try the credit of parties; but in all cases, and especially where the question is, whether the testamentary act of the party, was the act of a party of sufficient mind; in all questions of that kind, the court, before it grants probate, must be reasonably and morally satisfied, that the instrument in question, had emanated from the mind, free and uncontrolled. Perhaps I have gone too far in saying emanated, for if the mind of the deceased had gone along with the testamentary act although it had been suggested to him, and, if with full knowledge of it, and of its connexion with the various arrangements of his property, he adopted what was suggesed by another, that would be just as good, as if the act originated with himself.

[Discussion of the undisputed will and codicil, which were made in duplicate, and of the codicil in question, which was not, and of conflicting evidence on this matter.

[Reference to the evidence of Mr. Reade and the Rev. Mr. Deering, on the subject of the capacity, that for some years the mind of the deceased was sinking—that a great change had taken place in his memory and recollection. Judge Keatinge: I am relieved from examining the statements on the subject of the gentleman's state of mind, because I have the evidence and admissions to the effect that his mind was weakened (and I do not go beyond that) made by the impugnant himself.

[Discussion of Mrs. H. Burke's evidence on the subject of the feelings of the deceased gentleman towards Captain Stopford.

[Further discussion of the evidence connected with the papers and their execution. Judge Keatinge: The witnesses to the codicil are Mr. Wright and Mr. Williams. I think it is to be regretted, that Mr. Wright did not create and preserve some more evidence than he is now enabled to bring forward. The execution of the codicils depends upon the evidence of Mr. Wright, and of Mr. Williams. Mr. Williams is, I believe, a gentleman of very great respectability. There is a slight contradiction, but not a very important one, between Mr. Williams and Mr. Wright upon this part of the case. Mr. Williams says, that about ten minutes before he was called up, he saw the deceased in the parlour, and, after he saw him in the parlour, he sent for him to go up to witness the instrument. Now, there is something curious, I do not mean to say suspicious, in the fact, that Mr. Williams being there as a witness, is brought there by the impugnant. He wrote a letter requiring him to attend. (Letter reproduced, signed by Thos. Stopford.)

[Another letter connected with the intention to prepare a will, is also in evidence, that is, the letter of the impugnant, Captain Stopford, to William Foster, Esq., of Ballinure, in the county of Monaghan (letter reproduced; references to the Rev. William Roper, William Foster, Esq. of Ballinure, county Monaghan, Robert Evatt, Esq., Mr. Porter, and William Alexander Williams).

[Discussion of the circumstances of the disputed codicil being prepared. The article concludes with the following words spoken by Judge Keatinge:]

Now, if the case were to stand upon the evidence to which I have already referred, some in detail and most of it generally, I am quite prepared to say, that in my opinion, I cannot, unless I violate the authorities, give probate of this first disputed codicil of the 20th of April, 1846, and so with respect to the second codicil in which Captain Stopford has no interest. I am of opinion that the second must share the fate of the first, and it is quite impossible to apply considerations to the one that do not apply to the other. I must be perfectly satisfied, that the testamentary act is the act of a free and competent testator—but I have now to deal with evidence, subsequent to the codicils, which has been the subject of a vast deal of attention, and I presume that those who are acquainted with the evidence in the cause are prepared to hear me announce, that I allude to the testimony of Miss Mary Sterne. That lady is governess of Captain Stopford's children. (Evidence described and interpreted.) The case must stand as if the evidence of Miss Sterne had not been given.

I need not further detain the parties attending the hearing of this case, and I feel myself bound to refuse to grant probate in this case of the two codicils of the 20th of April, 1846.

Then comes another question, and a question of great difficulty. Now, Captain Stopford is a caveator in this case. By his caveat, he has insisted upon his right to have these codicils included in the probate. He has a right to raise that question; and [*illegible*] when I am considering the question of costs, I [—] bear this in mind, that so far as the title of Mr. Stopford is concerned under the deed, that deed relating to freehold, the probate is so much waste paper; and therefore, the validity of the codicil, in relation to the deed, to confirm which it was said to be executed, would still leave the question as to the validity of the deed to be decided before a jury, relating as it does altogether to real estate. This consideration alone would go a great way in my mind towards leading me to a conclusion, if I am right in my judgment, (and my judgment is, I am happy to say, liable to be reviewed.) If I am right, I am bound, without anything further, to award the costs against Captain Stopford, but there is in this case another matter, as to which I have not yet made any observation, and it shall be the last matter. I allude to the letter written by Captain Stopford to Miss Foster in the progress of the cause; and I allude to the evidence connected with that letter, which satisfies my mind, that it was not the work of the moment, but his deliberate act—deliberately written, and deliberately refused to be retracted. It goes [?] some way in showing that Captain Stopford felt in his own breast, that he had at best a doubtful case, but I refer to this, not with reference to the judgment as to the issue between the parties, but as relates to the remaining consideration, the costs of the cause. This letter is addressed to a daughter, informing her that, unless her mother will withdraw her proceeding in this court, and allow him the benefit of the document upon which he now relies, disgrace will be the consequence, and disgrace upon what subject? why, charges of bad temper, and that her ill conduct was the cause of her husband's death. The cause of the death of the father of the young lady he was writing to; that mother being his children's aunt, and the young lady] their cousin. The letter was written to intimidate and terrify, to induce a party upon what now I have a right to call unfounded calumnies, to abandon her legal rights, for as was well put to me—the evidence is closed, and where are the disclosures which the writer threatened? no where!

I do not consider the question of this document would have turned the scale if I had been in doubt, but for the reasons already stated, it strikes me that this court would fall short if it did not award the costs against Captain Stopford, and my decree, which condemns two codicils, will, therefore, award him to pay the costs between party and party, to the intervenient, the executors to have their costs as between proctor and client out of the estate, and the intervenient to have her extra costs also out of the estate. (*continued...*)

3894, continued: ...Counsel for the Promovant—Dr. Darley. Proctor—Mr. J. Stock. Agent—Mr. J. Magill.

Counsel for the Impugnant—Drs. Wilie, Hayes, and Butt. Proctors—Messrs. Tilly, Hamilton, and Co. Agent—Messrs. Wright and Nunn.

Counsel for Intervenient—Drs. Radcliffe and Lloyd, and Mr. Hamilton Smythe. Proctors—Messrs. Moore and Milward. Agents—Messrs. Hardman and Miller. (1847-12-04, 1:1)

3895. Death from Drunkenness.—On Saturday night last, a man named Vance, a carriage spring-maker, was brought to the watch-house of this town by the watchmen and police, in a state of beastly intoxication, and although every attention was paid to him during the night, he died at an early hour on Sunday morning. He had long led a most intemperate life, and his body was attenuated to a skeleton. He seldom ate food for the last year.

An inquest was held on the body on Monday last, by Charles Waddel, Esq., coroner, and a verdict of death from drunkenness recorded. (1847-12-04, 3:5)

3896. In the Queen's Bench on Saturday, Lord Denham decided, in the case of the *Queen v. Chadwick*, that marriage with a deceased wife's sister is void. This decision will destroy the legitimacy of 5,000 children, besides rendering the marriages in the eye of the law incestuous, and against the law of God. (1847-12-04, 4:6)

3897. Correspondence.—To the Editor of the *Northern Standard.*

51, North Great Georges-street.
7th December, 1847.

Dear Sir—I have been forwarded *The Northern Standard* of the 4th inst., containing the judgment, in the case of *West v. Stopford,* (just concluded in the Prerogative Court,) as spoken by the judge.

A report of this case appeared in the Dublin papers, but in yours alone has there been inserted the judgment verbatim.

This may not appear to require any comment, but when I inform you that the decision has been appealed against, and that, even after a further decision upon this part of the case, a trial by a jury of the county of Monaghan may probably take place, you will at once perceive the motives which influenced the publication of such a detailed report in the Monaghan paper, which in *Saunders* occupied less than two columns.

I would not trouble you with this communication but with the hope, that in the spirit of even-handed justice, you will give publicity to the fact, that an appeal has been entered against this judgment, and so remove the impression, that the decision is final or acquiesced in by the defendant.

I am, Dear Sir,
Yours, very truly,
Thos. Edmond Wright.

A.W. Holmes, Esq.,
Editor, *Northern Standard.*

P.S.—In the sixth column of the second page, you have printed, in reference to my answer to the 14th article, the words "a statement which I am quite sure he would *not* now deliberately repeat." The words of the judge were, "a statement which I am quite sure he would now deliberately repeat."

Whether this addition to the judges words is a typographical error or made by design in the copy of the judgment furnished for your insertion, I cannot say, but I think it right to correct it.

T.E.W.

(1847-12-11, 2:4)

3898. To the Editor of the *Northern Standard.*—My Dear Fellow—As you have probably heard that I am on tour, I wish to apprise you, that if I have time, I will pay Monaghan a visit, and as I have been with you before, may I entreat you will stand on no ceremony with me. Should the thoroughfares be dirty, sweep them not on my account. Don't mind ventilating my apartments. I hate persons who raise the wind. To only one thing I object—Camphor; it always disagreed with me, as for my sake, at least, prohibit its importation. In fine, scout editorially, all sanatory measures, and believe me,

My Dear Fellow,
Yours very Fatally,
The Cholera.
Russia, December, 1847.

(1847-12-11, 3:2)

3899. The Lord Chancellor.—We regret much to have no favourable intelligence to report with respect to the health of the Lord Chancellor. We subjoin the bulletins of yesterday and this morning, which are by no means encouraging: —

Tuesday.—"The Chancellor's state has not materially altered since yesterday—he still maintains his ground."

Wednesday.—"The Chancellor had some accession to febrile symptoms last night, which are, this morning, considerably abated."

Henry Marsh.
John Mollan.

(1847-12-18, 1:1)

3900. Dr. Chalmers' Opinion of Marriage with a Deceased Wife's Sister.—In commentating on *Leviticus, xviii. 11, 18,* in his daily Scripture Readings, Dr. Chalmers says:—"It is remarkable that, while there is an express interdict on the marriage of a man with his brother's wife, there is no such prohibition against the marriage with his wife's sister. In verse 18, the prohibition is only against marrying a wife's sister during the life of the first wife, which of itself implies a liberty to marry the sister after her death, besides implying a connivance of polygamy." (1847-12-18, 1:6)

3901. To the Editor of the Northern Standard.

West v. Stopford.

Dublin, 15th December, 1847,
75, Talbot-street.

Dear Sir.—My attention has been directed to a letter from Mr. Wright, which appeared in our publication of the 11th instant, in reference to the report of the Prerogative Court in the above cause.

I am very unwilling to trespass either on your space or the attention of your readers as, however, Mr. Wright has impugned not only the correctness of the report in question, but also the motives which induced the publication of it. I feel called upon—as the party by whom the report was furnished to you—to state, and to pledge myself, that that report is accurately correct, having been taken by the best short-hand writer in this city; and further, that the passage complained of by Mr. Wright, in which the Court is reported—in reference to a portion of Mr. Wright's evidence—to have used the words, a statement which I am quite sure he would not now deliberately repeat, has been correctly reported, and I can add my own testimony to the extreme accuracy not only of that passage in the report, but to the entire of the latter, having been present in Court during the delivery of the judgment; and when Mr. Wright takes upon himself to deny the accuracy of the report, he should bear in mind that he was not present in Court on that day, save for a very few minutes, and certainly was not present when the words alluded to were used; independent, however, of all this, the correctness of the passage in question, as reported, must be apparent to any person who will take the trouble of reading it in connection with the context.

With respect to that part of Mr. Wright's letter, in which he alludes to the motives which influenced the publication of the report and in which he insinuates—as far as prudential motives permitted him to do—that it was done with the object of prejudicing the minds of a Monaghan jury on the merits of the case. I shall not stop here to repudiate such motives either on my own part or that of my client. I would merely observe that, in making such an insinuation, Mr. Wright appears to have forgotten a very recent transaction in which legal proceedings were pending between these very same parties, and were about to come before a Monaghan jury, and on which occasion, circulars were addressed to several, if not to all, the gentlemen composing the special jury panel which had been struck for the trial of the cause. I think your readers will agree with me that, after such an occurrence—from which, however, I entirely exculpate Mr. Wright personally—the insinuations in his letter, above alluded to, were conceived in very bad taste.

As to the merits of this case, I have no intention or desire to enter into them here; they have been already—so far—adjudicated on by a tribunal of competent authority, but should the case come—as it is stated it will—before a jury of the county of Monaghan, I have no fears that the gentlemen composing that jury will allow themselves to be influenced by reports of publications emanating from either party. The insinuation that they could be so influenced comes not from me or my client; it would be an insult to the integrity and understanding of the gentlemen of the county, such as I should be sorry to offer them, and as they would, no doubt, indignantly and fearlessly repudiate.

I am, dear Sir,
Your obedient servant,
Townley W. Hardman.
(1847-12-18, 3:1)

3902. Happy Christmas.—Alas! for the time when neighbour could greet neighbour with "a happy Christmas," when the gratulations of friends were so oft-recurring that new year's gifts and Christmas boxes were bundled together in the expressive "compliments of the season," and these were trundled about with such hearty good will, and joyous hilarity, that while the young laughed merrily, the old smiled pleasantly, as the gambols and pranks of the festive time were enacted before them.

A change, a fearful change, has come over our fated country—a change which is, year after year, deepening the intensity of our sufferings, and plunging us farther into the vortex of misery.

This twelve-day-month, we drew a harrowing picture of the poor man's Christmas—no clothing—no food—no fire—dysentery in the hovel—fever by the ditch side—starvation in the cabin—misery everywhere; yet hope, the last blessing that departs, even from the most abject, whispered of a brighter time coming—hope shadowed forth in dim perspective another and a bounteous harvest—golden corn fields, rich returns for labour, the teeming wealth of the pregnant earth, yielding great store of food for perishing humanity. Hope vaticinated well—hope was a true prophet. The God of Heaven pitied mankind, and vouchsafed that the earth should bring forth her encrease—a horn of plenty was poured upon the land—so great a produce arose from the soil, or grew down in it, that old men with white heads and withered hands wondered, and held up the shrivelled fingers of those hands and blessed God for his mercy. The famine began to be a thing of history—and witlings even cracked jokes upon the horrible past—even the modes and appliances which were at Christmas '46 used to prepare food for the gaunt, starving, dying poor, got nicknames—the very foot itself that the starving mother or tottering father would walk miles and sit in the cold snow for hours and hours to procure, and with which they would stagger home laden, and for which there were craving stomachs and hollow eyes waiting in the fireless hut, aye, even this very food brought here from far countries, has been jeered and scoffed at, so jolly was the plenty that succeeded the famine. (*continued...*)

3902, continued: ...Indian meal was jocularly "yellow buck," and the porridge afforded in charity became in the hearty—(we were going to write *thankfulness*) blithefulness of the present, "the buck soup," of the hard times.

It is at all times a happy disposition of the mind that can forget a great past misfortune, that despite bygone sorrows, can revel in present pleasure, and clothe the future *couleur de rose*. Perhaps we are so disposed ourselves—and if we are, we are thankful for that buoyancy of mind.

But, alas! as journalists, we have no reason to rejoice —as men, we have all in Ireland reason to grieve.

The Christmas of 1847 is the most calamitous for Ireland that he, of the white hair and the withered hands, ever saw.

The Christmas of 1846 saw this land steeped in misfortune, but it was the special visitation of the Omnipotent; no man of the land was to blame—the cause was mystical—the effect, general—the sympathy, universal.

The Christmas of 1847 sees this land steeped in CRIME of the deepest dye—the crime of her children —the crime that the God who released her by his mercies from her sufferings, detests above all others—the crime of shedding the blood of his creatures by his creatures. The men of this land are murderers—they are responsible—the cause is not mystical, the effect is horrible and too general, and the detestation universal. We of Ireland are hideous in the sight of God, even of him whose mercies we are now enjoying.

Last Christmas, sorrow, suffering, and death were in the cabins of the poor, and the rich rushed to the rescue—the landlord mortgaged his estates—the clergyman gave up his spiritual duties to attend to the temporal wants of the people—the merchant gave the fruits of his industry, that they might be fed—all—all underwent a deep security that famine might be driven from the poor man's house, that disease might be remedied, and that the torrent of death that swept the land might be staid—and it was staid.

Is there gratitude for this?

Shame upon Ireland, there is not!

This Christmas, there is wailing and weeping in the landlord's mansion—for he, who worked for the poor, lies a bloody corpse, done to death by some hand that, but for him, would be cold in one of the multitudinous graves that contain the victims of Heaven's vengeance! The fair partner of his exertions, who gave up household duties to minister to the people's wants, stands paralysed over the body of him whose weary hours she solaced after the days working in the cause of charity, wondering, mayhap, if kindness in this fated land begets death.

The minister of God repairing to the sanctity of home, after returning thanks in the Temple of the Most High, that the famine which smote the land had passed, is met on the high road, and instead of grateful thanks for his exertions—for his aid—for his sacrifice of time, labour, and money, in the cause of the people, he gets a bullet in the brain. He dies by the hand he cherished—by one of the people he fed.

There is a wail in the house of the minister!

Brutality goes farther—sex is not spared—even the old Irish chivalry, which boasted the beauty and virtue could go scatheless through our land, is buried beneath this fearful crime of the daymurder. The fair and virtuous lady is met by the ruffian-assassin, who, not content with the horror of the crime he is about to perpetrate, seeks his victim's wife, and, to sink the Irish character deeper, he tells her that her husband is to be murdered—thus, as in the case of Mrs. Beresford, committing a double slaughter.

The friendly agent, intent on carrying out an improvement in the land—he who tells the proprietor that certain sacrifices are necessary for ameliorating the condition of the people—he too is slaughtered. There is no class safe. There is death, or the terror of death, in the house of every man of the higher orders of society, and this, when Providence has restored comfort to the poor man's home.

This is now the rich man's Christmas.

The country is proclaimed—a coercion bill is passed to repress crime in a land just freed from famine. Watch and ward must be on every house—upon one, to detect the murderer—upon another, to protect the victim.

And this is merry Christmas in Ireland. The bayonet is our yule log—the commission court, our Christmas part—the hangman, our head mummer—and the scaffold, our merry mime.

Reader, we are now nine years before you, and we would like to use the old adage, "a merry Christmas to you," but we can't. Our common country lies bleeding beneath a deep and damnable conspiracy—until we get rid of it, no empty compliments—no pleasant jests—and no merry making. We wish you a working Christmas. No "hunt the wren" on St. Stephen's day—"hunt the murderer" be the cry. We would like to see the universal population of Ireland vindicate the justice of the law of God on Christmas day, and drag every murderer from his den, and make him abide the consequence of his crime.

If you do not believe our state to be as hard as we say it is, read Lord Farnham's speech in our sheet, and blush for Ireland. (1847-12-25, 3:1)

3903. Death from Hydrophobia.—On Monday last, a young girl named Tierney, died in the temporary fever hospital of this town, from hydrophobia. About two months since, she was going at an early hour to a neighbour's house to scutch flax, and was met on her way by a dog, in a rabid state, which jumped at her face; she struck him down with her scutching handle, but the brute returned to the charge, and in a second attempt to strike him, the handle flew out of her hand, and he inflicted two ragged wounds on her face. She immediately got the wounds severely cauterised, and adopted every precaution so that the sores healed up, to all appearance, perfectly; but a few days before her death, she was seized with spasms, twitching of the muscles of the throat, and terror of fluids. The poor creature was placed in the fever hospital, where she was attended by Doctor Christian with the greatest care and anxiety, but on Sunday last, the spasms became frequent and, at length, ended in one long paroxysm that terminated in the fearful and agonising death which is always the consequence of this frightful disease. (1847-12-25, 3:3)

:: :: ::

4. SURNAME INDEX

 Reference numbers in indexes refer to article numbers, not to page numbers.

 Reference numbers in indexes refer to article numbers, not to page numbers.

:: :: ::

5. INSTITUTION & PUBLICATION INDEX

:: :: ::

6. SUBJECT INDEX

:: :: ::

7. ARTHUR WELLINGTON HOLMES, PROPRIETOR AND EDITOR

On January 12, 1839, Mr. Arthur Wellington Holmes launched his newspaper, a weekly entitled, *The Northern Standard*, from his office at 26, Mill-street, Monaghan. In that first edition, Mr. Holmes articulated the philosophical and political orientation of the new journal.[1] While the views expressed would be "strictly conservative," Holmes declared that he would be an "impartial advocate" for reform in the face of abuse, and eschew "the shafts of private malice" in his paper. He considered it his "sacred duty" to espouse Conservative views "in the centre of a hitherto undefended district," as the "only defence against anarchy and revolution." Seeking the favour and custom of "every lover of British connection," Holmes pledged to advocate "the cause of the Constitution of Church and State" to the nobility, gentry, and inhabitants of the counties of Monaghan, Cavan, and Armagh.

Holmes was aiming not only to launch the first newspaper in the county Monaghan, but also one of a High Tory character in a staunchly liberal region. In a twist of political irony, not long after *The Northern Standard* commenced publication Holmes fell prey to a debilitating fever. The paper was at risk of not publishing that week, and none other than Charles Gavan Duffy, the editor, and one of the founders, of *The Nation*, came to his rescue. Recalling the incident years later in his memoir, Duffy had met Holmes earlier and liked him. On hearing of Holmes' plight, Duffy "walked down to the office, had all the proofs produced, which [he] carefully revised, called for the latest papers, selected the current Orange news, and the difficulty was overcome. The editor's gratitude spread the story abroad, and it was the subject of endless banter, but it probably did something to mitigate the bitterness of local prejudice."[2]

Grateful though he must have been for this capable assist from a man noted for his work in the cause of nationalism, Holmes employed his newspaper to promote Conservative, High Church, and Orange principles. On at least one occasion, his printed views got him into legal trouble. In 1841, the Rev. James Scott, Roman Catholic Curate, sued Holmes at the Louth Assizes for "having, on the 30th January last, published a certain document purporting to be a remonstrance of the Irish teachers and Scripture readers in the barony of Farney, to the Rev. Mr. Scott, reflecting upon the character of the said plaintiff; and for a prefatory remark of the editor of said paper, containing and repeating the said libelous matter, reflecting upon the said plaintiff's character."[3] The jury returned a verdict of £120, and 6d. costs.

For the remainder of his mortal career, Holmes tended to the advancement of his newspaper. Originally a five-column, four-page publication, the page format of *The Northern Standard* was enlarged to six columns on January 14, 1843. His business interests extended to commercial printing and the letter press; he was also the local agent for the Estate Transfer Office of Ireland. In the community, Arthur Holmes was active in the Monaghan Hunt Club, and in the Orange Society, occupying the post of Grand Secretary in 1846.[4]

On July 13, 1851, Arthur Wellington Holmes died, as noticed by *The Armagh Guardian*, at a "comparatively early age."[5]

---

[1] Refer to the Appendix for a transcript of A.W. Holmes' editorial, transcribed from the inaugural edition of *The Northern Standard*, published January 12, 1839.
[2] *My Life in Two Hemispheres*, Vol. I, by Sir Charles Gavan Duffy (London: T. Fisher Unwin, 1898).
[3] *Dublin Evening Mail*, 6 August 1841.
[4] *Belfast News-Letter*, 14 August 1845, 26 May 1846.
[5] *The Armagh Guardian*, 19 July 1851.

Arthur Wellington Holmes and Family – Biographical Notes:

Arthur Wellington Holmes' father, Arthur H. Holmes, was an officer in Her Majesty's 87th Regiment of Foot, or the Royal Irish Fusiliers.[6] Mr. Holmes obtained his commission not by purchase—but for service rendered. Under the superintendence of Lieutenant-Colonel Charles W. Doyle, Mr. Holmes had, at considerable personal expense, procured Volunteers for the Irish Militia at the formation of the 2nd Battalion for the 87th. After writing several memorials to indicate his desire to serve, and with favourable support, Mr. Holmes was offered a commission as Ensign in September, 1806; he was twenty-six years of age. Precisely one year later, he was promoted to a Lieutenancy.

The Rev. William Lyster married Arthur H. Holmes and Judith Hevy in 1802 at Boyle, county Roscommon; Mr. Holmes was a Sergeant with the Roscommon Militia.[7] Mr. and Mrs. Holmes had three sons, Paul H., born in 1802, Arthur in 1811, and John in 1820. While Lieutenant Holmes served in the Mauritius, India, and the Cape of Good Hope, it appears that his wife and young family remained in Ireland. Arthur, Sr. was placed on half-pay in 1816, for reasons of ill health, a result of service overseas. In 1828, when asked where he had been generally resident for the last five years, Mr. Holmes indicated Boyle. In August 1838, Lieutenant Arthur Holmes was reassigned to the 13th Foot, still on half-pay.

At about this time, one imagines that Arthur, Jr., was either in progress of deciding, or had already decided, that the Town of Monaghan would be the site of his newspaper venture. It may be that he selected this town because it was situated in one of the few Irish counties without a provincial newspaper in the late 1830s.

Arthur Wellington Holmes married, first, Miss Jane Wright, of Monaghan, in August, 1840.[8] Less than two years later, in June 1842, Mrs. Holmes died:

> June 20, after a lingering illness, which she bore with patience and resignation, in her twenty-second year, at her residence, Mill-street, Jane, the beloved wife of A.W. Holmes, Esq., Editor and Proprietor of this paper, and second daughter of the late Henry Wright, Esq., of this town.[9]

Arthur remarried in May 1844:

> On Thursday last, in the Church of Glasslough, by the Rev. William H. Pratt, Vicar of Donagh, Arthur W. Holmes, Esq., proprietor of the Northern Standard, to Jane, second daughter of James George Lepper, Esq., of the Diamond, Monaghan.[10]

In January 1852, six months after the decease of his son Arthur W., Arthur, Sr. died, at the age of seventy-two years[11], then considered to be a good auld age.

Upon Arthur W. Holmes' death in July 1851, his brother, John, assumed the reins of *The Northern Standard.* Before this date, John had made a name for himself as an auctioneer in the county Monaghan. Of his new vocation, William Palmer remarked that he published a "well-conducted paper."[12] John died on September 9, 1870, aged forty-nine years, and unmarried.[13]

---

6 British Army Officer service record, ref. WO 25/762, National Archives, United Kingdom.
7 Church of Ireland marriage record, by subscription to RootsIreland.ie (accessed 2014-02-16).
8 *Smythe-Wood Newspaper Index*, compiled by Roz McCutcheon.
9 *Northern Standard*, 25 June 1842.
10 *Northern Standard*, 4 May 1844.
11 *Northern Standard*, 10 January 1852, per Monaghan County Library Services (2014-02-07).
12 William Palmer, *Recollections of a Visit of Great Britain and Ireland in the Summer of 1862* (Quebec: Hunter, Rose, & Co., 1863).
13 PRONI, *Will Calendars*, online at www.proni.gov.uk (accessed 2014-01-15).

According to a local Rector, the Rev. Canon Augustus Blayney Russell Young, Mrs. Arthur Holmes was a popular and much admired member of the community. In his memoir, the Rev. Young noted that Mrs. Holmes was celebrated as a great beauty even after her husband's demise, that many extolled her aesthetic virtues, and "at a dinner party she always formed the subject of comment."[14] Mrs. Holmes died on September 20, 1870, also at a comparatively early age, and just eleven days after her brother-in-law John's decease.

It appears that Arthur Wellington Holmes had but one son of the marriage, John Paul Holmes.[15]

:: :: ::

In 1870, Mr. William Swan became the new proprietor of *The Northern Standard.*[16] After nearly forty years as the only provincial journal in the county Monaghan, the *Standard* would have to contend with new entrants into the field of competition, in *The Argus* (1875) and *The People's Advocate* (1876) newspapers.

---

[14] A.B.R. Young, *Reminiscences of an Irish Priest* (W. Tempest, Dundalgan Press, 1931).
[15] According to a baptismal record digitised by Roots Ireland (www.rootsireland.ie, accessed 2014-02-18), a child named Arthur Holmes was born on January 2, 1851 in Monaghan, of parents, Arthur Holmes and Mary McKenna. The sponsor was Anne Armstrong; the religious denomination was not recorded. An earlier church record exists, digitised by the same source, for the baptism of Catharina Holmes, in the Roman Catholic parish of Boyle, Diocese of Elphin, on March 4, 1838; parents, Arthur Holmes and Margaret Healy; sponsor, Catharina Keane.
[16] Marie-Louise Legg. *The Irish Provincial Press*, 1850–1892. (Dublin: Four Courts Press, 1999)

APPENDIX

Prospectus of the *Northern Standard, and Cavan, Monaghan, and Armagh Advertiser.*[1]

It is the custom of every candidate for public favor, when presenting himself before his constituents, to make profession of his political faith, and give pledges of the course he intends to pursue, that he may, as it were, "Hold the mirror up to nature," and enable men to judge whether his views accord with reason and their own sentiments. Thus it is, that the establishment of a public Journal requires a precursor to proclaim its creed and views—a Prospectus of its contents to prepare the public for its reception.

In accordance, therefore, with the usage in such cases, the proprietor of the "Northern Standard" hesitates not to declare, that the principles of the Journal he will have the honor to submit to the public, shall be strictly conservative of British connection, and the established institutions of the land; yet, reform, where existing abuses render such necessary, shall, according to the Peel School, meet an impartial advocate. And he conceives that, in introducing a Conservative Journal to the inhabitants of the Interior of the North of Ireland, he is discharging a great and sacred duty to his country, by planting in the centre of a hitherto undefended district, a branch of that might engine of moral warfare, the power of which has been felt and acknowledged in these kingdoms, to be the only defence against anarchy and revolution.

The proprietor has marked through many progressing years of public life, the infringements which bad men have made on the *Palladium* of British independence—our unrivalled constitution—and as their exertions for the cause of evil are unwearied, he conceives that equal vigilance and promptitude are requisite on the part of the friends of of [sic] good order and government:--but without a local press to stimulate to exertion, the best energies of the people sink into apathetic indifference—and yet in the Capitol of Irish Conservatism—the Protestant North—the three rich, commercial, and intelligent counties, the names of which are inserted in the title of this Journal, have not had the advantage of such an organ to echo the voice of the people, or tell the tale of their wrongs, but were wholly dependant on distant publications for intelligence and information respecting their localities.

These considerations have induced the proprietor to present to the Nobility, Gentry, and Inhabitants of the Counties of Monaghan, Cavan, and Armagh, a journal advocating the cause of the Constitution of Church and State, and he pledges himself, that while every exertion is used to forward these principles, no unworthy means shall ever be resorted to, nor shall the columns of the "Standard" ever become the channel through which the domestic feelings of individuals may be wounded by the shafts of private malice; but its remarks and actions will always be guided by the most rigid rules of honor and justice.

Advocating these principles, endeared to us by education, history, and a sense of right, the proprietor of the "Northern Standard" looks confidently to the high-minded and enlightened inhabitants of the North for support and encouragement, equivalent to the expenses and labour attendant on the publication of a news-paper; and he trusts that every lover of British connection will aid him in forwarding the good work he has undertaken.

---

[1] *Northern Standard*, 12 January 1839.

BIBLIOGRAPHY

Adams, Benjamin William. *A Genealogical History of the Family of Adams of Cavan, etc.* London: Mitchell and Hughes, 1903.

Atkinson, A. *Ireland Exhibited to England*, Vol. I. London: Baldwin, Cradock, and Joy, 1823.

Bailey, Thomas. *Records of Longevity, with an Introductory Discourse on Vital Statistics.* London: Darton and Co., 1857.

Bateman, Joseph. *The Excise Officer's Manual*, 2nd ed. London: William Maxwell, 1852.

Bayly, Henry. *Topographical and Historical Account of Lisburn.* Belfast: Thomas Mairs, 1834.

Belfast and Province of Ulster Street Directory for 1852. Belfast: James Alexander Henderson, 1852. Online at Lennon Wylie, www.lennonwylie.co.uk (accessed 13 Oct. 2013).

Belfast and Province of Ulster Street Directory for 1880. Belfast: Belfast News-Letter Office, March 1880. Online at Lennon Wylie, www.lennonwylie.co.uk (accessed 15 February 2014).

Belfast Morning News, 25 March 1880, by subscription to The British Newspaper Archive www.britishnewspaperarchive.co.uk (accessed 2014-02-16).

Belfast News-Letter, 14 August 1845, 26 May 1846, 28 February 1851, by subscription to The British Newspaper Archive www.britishnewspaperarchive.co.uk (accessed 2014-02-16).

Benn, George. *A History of the Town of Belfast*, Vol. II. London: Marcus Ward & Co., and Belfast: Royal Ulster Works, 1880.

Brown, Thomas. *The Union Gazetteer for Great Britain and Ireland*, Vol. I. London: Vernor, Hood, and Sharpe, &c., 1807.

Burke, Bernard. *A Genealogical and Heraldic History of the Landed Gentry of Ireland.* Pall Mall, London: Harrison & Sons, 1875 and 1912 editions.

Burke, John. *A Genealogical and Heraldic Dictionary of the Landed Gentry of Great Britain and Ireland.* London: Henry Colburn, 1847.

Burke, John. *A Genealogical and Heraldic History of The Commoners of Great Britain and Ireland.* London: Henry Colburn, 1835 and 1838 editions.

Burke, John, ed. *The Patrician.* Vol. III. London: E. Churton, 1847.

Burke, John, and John Bernard Burke. *A Genealogical and Heraldic Dictionary of the Landed Gentry of Great Britain and Ireland.* London: Henry Colburn, 1846.

Calder, James Tait. *History of Caithness.* Glasgow: Thomas Murray and Son, 1861.

Carlisle, Nicholas. *A Topographical Dictionary of Ireland.* London: William Savage, 1810.

Cassidy, J.J., ed. *The Canadian Journal of Medicine and Surgery*, Vol. XVIII, July to December, 1905. Toronto: W.A. Young, 1905.

Coote, Charles. *Statistical Survey of the County of Monaghan.* Dublin: Graisberry & Campbell, 1801.

Crozier, John A. *The Life of the Rev. Henry Montgomery*, Vol. I. London: E.T. Whitfield, and Belfast: W.H. Greer, 1875.

Dobson, David. *Scottish-American Heirs, 1683-1883.* Genealogical Publishing Company, 1990.

Dod's Peerage, Baronetage and Knightage of Great Britain and Ireland. London: Simkin, Hamilton, Kent, 1914.

Dublin Almanac, and General Register of Ireland, for 1835. Dublin: Pettigrew and Oulton, 1835.

Dublin Almanac, and General Register of Ireland, for 1847. Dublin: Pettigrew and Oulton, 1847.

Dublin Evening Mail, 6 August 1841, by subscription to The British Newspaper Archive www.britishnewspaperarchive.co.uk (accessed 2014-02-16).

Duffy, Charles Gavan. *My Life in Two Hemispheres*, Vol. I. London: T. Fisher Unwin, 1898.

"Fatal Accident in Hyde Park." *The Annual Register, or a view of the History, and Politics, of the Year 1840*. Vol. VXXXII. London: J.G.F. & J. Rivington, 1841. (pg. 52)

Foster, Joseph. *The Royal Lineage of Our Noble and Gentle Families, together with Their Paternal Ancestry*. London and Aylesbury: Hazell, Watson, and Viney, 1883.

Freeman's Journal, 14 December 1831, 2 June 1840; by subscription to The British Newspaper Archive www.britishnewspaperarchive.co.uk (accessed 2014-02-16).

Gorton, John. *A Topographical Dictionary of Great Britain and Ireland*, Vol. III. London: Chapman and Hall, 1833.

Government of Ireland, Department of Arts, Heritage and the Gaeltacht. *Irish Genealogy: Explore your family history*. Online at www.irishgenealogy.ie (accessed 14, 18 Sept. 2013).

Hayes, John. *Griffiths Valuation of Ireland* (index), online at Fáilte Romhat www.failteromhat.com/griffiths.php.

Hibernian Sunday School Society. *The Eighth Report of the Sunday School Society for Ireland, for the year ending April 22d, 1818*. Dublin: M. Goodwin, 1818.

Historical Record of the Eighty-seventh Regiment, or the Royal Irish Fusiliers. London: George E. Eyre and William Spottiswoode; and, Parker, Furnivall, and Parker, 1853.

House of Commons. *Accounts and Papers: Fifteen Volumes. (7.) relating to Crime; Gaols; Criminals*. Session 31 January – 17 July 1837. HMSO, Vol. XLV, 1837.

House of Commons. *Arms (Ireland); Return to an Order of the Honourable the House of Commons, 18 February 1836*. HMSO, Vol. XLVII, 1836.

House of Commons. *Reports from Commissioners: Sixteen Volumes. (8.) Corporations, Ireland: Appendix, Parts I. & II*. Session 19 February – 10 September 1835. Vol. XXVIII, 1835.

House of Commons. *Reports from Commissioners: Three Volumes. (3.) Bankruptcy and Insolvency; Loan Fund, Ireland; etc*. Session 26 January – 22 June 1841. Vol. XII, 1841.

House of Commons. *Lord Lieutenants and Magistrates (Ireland), Return to an Order of the Honourable the House of Commons*, 27 January 1881. HMSO, Vol. DV, i (1882).

Inland Waterways Association of Ireland. *Guide to the Royal Canal of Ireland*. Online at http://www.iwai.ie/maps/royal/contents.html (accessed 13 Sept. 2013).

Ireland. *Census of Ireland. General Alphabetical Index to the Townlands and Towns, Parishes and Baronies of Ireland*. Dublin: Alexander Thom, 1861. Reprinted by Genealogical Publishing Co., Inc., 2006, with the permission of The Controller, Stationery Office, Dublin.

Irish Council for Research in the Humanities and Social Sciences, and the Programme for Research in Third Level Institutions. *Landed Estates Database*. Database hosted online by the Moore Institute for Research in the Humanities and Social Sciences, at the National University of Ireland, Galway, OÉ Gaillimh. www.landedestates.nuigalway.ie (accessed 2013-07-13).

Irish Family History Foundation. Church of Ireland marriage record (Arthur Holmes, Judith Hevy), by subscription to www.rootsireland.ie (accessed 2014-02-16).

Keane, Deirdre. *A History of Kilkeedy Church and Graveyard*. Article hosted online by the Clare County Library, http://www.clarelibrary.ie/eolas/coclare/history/kilkeedy_church.htm (accessed 2013-09-28).

Kenny, Tom. "Courthouse Square, 1890." *Galway Advertiser*, 11 October 2012. Online at www.advertiser.ie/galway/article/55695/courthouse-square-c1890 (accessed 12 Oct. 2013).

Kilpatrick, Alison, ed. *The Armagh Guardian: Births, Marriages, and Deaths, 1844–1852; Transcripts and Indexes*. Nova Scotia: Quercus Arborealis, 2013.

Lawlor, H.C. *A History of the Family of Cairnes or Cairns and Its Connections*. London: Elliot Stock, 1906.

Leeds Mercury, 23 November 1839 (death notice for the Rev. John Sutcliffe), by subscription to The British Newspaper Archive www.britishnewspaperarchive.co.uk (accessed 2014-02-15).

Legg, Marie-Louise. *The Irish Provincial Press*. Dublin: Four Courts Press, 1999.

Lewis, Samuel. *A Topographical Dictionary of Ireland*, in two volumes. London: S. Lewis & Co., 1837 and 1849 editions.

Lynn, Brendan, and Martin Melaugh. *A Chronology of Key Events in Irish History, 1800–1967*. CAIN Web Service, University of Ulster; www.cain.ulst.ac.uk (accessed 2014-02-10).

M'Clintock, John, and James Strong. *Cyclopaedia of Biblical, Theological, and Ecclesiastical Literature*. New York: Harper & Brothers, 1889.

McCutcheon, Roz, compiler. *Smythe-Wood Newspaper Index*. Online at the Irish Genealogical Research Society, www.igrsoc.org (accessed 2014-02-17).

McGee, Owen, compiler. *Collection List No. 176, Ormonde Papers (Additional), MSS 48,367-377*. Leabharlann Náisiúnta na hÉireann, National Library of Ireland.

Mitchell, C. *The Newspaper Press Directory and Advertisers' Guide, 1847*. London and Provincial Press, March 1847.

Munro, Robert. "On Prehistoric Otter and Beaver Traps. *The Antiquary: A Magazine Devoted to the Study of the Past*. Vol. XXIV. London: Elliot Stock, 1891.

National Archives of Ireland. *Calendars of Wills and Administrations 1858–1920*. Database online www.willcalendars.nationalarchives.ie (accessed 2013-07-13).

National Archives of the United Kingdom. *War Office (WO) 25/762, Services of officers on Full and Half Pay; Returns to the circular letter 27 Oct. 1828*. www.nationalarchives.gov.uk (accessed 2014-02-11).

National Library of Australia. *Trove Digitised Newspapers and More*. Online service, at trove.nla.gov.au.

National Library of Ireland, with OMS Services Ltd. and Eneclann Ltd. *Griffith's Valuation*. Online at Ask about Ireland, askaboutireland.ie/griffith-valuation/ (accessed 14 Sept. 2013).

Palmer, William. *Recollections of a Visit of Great Britain and Ireland in the Summer of 1862*. Quebec: Hunter, Rose, & Co., 1863.

Parishes of Sandford and St Philip's, online at sandford.dublin.anglican.org (accessed 14 September 2013.

"Present State of the Churches throughout Ireland, No. XII." *The Irish Church Advocate*. Vol. XL, No. 476, Dublin, April 2, 1877, pp. 85–86.

Public Record Office of Northern Ireland. *Will Calendars*, online at www.proni.gov.uk (accessed 2014-01-15).

Rivington, F. & J. *The Annual Register or a View of the History and Politics of the Year 1849*. London: George Woodfall and Son, 1850.

Russell, John A. *Remains of the Late Rev. Charles Wolfe, A.B.* Sixth edition. London: Hamilton, Adams, and Co., 1836.

Ruvigny and Raineval, The Marquis of. *The Plantagenet Roll of the Blood Royal*. London: Melville & Company, 1911.

Ruvigny and Raineval, the Marquis of. *The Plantagenet Roll of the Blood Royal*. Mortimer-Percy Volume. London, 1911. Reprinted by Heritage Books, Inc., Maryland, USA, 2001.

Shirley, Evelyn Philip. *The History of the County of Monaghan*. London: Pickering and Company, 1879.

Slater's *National Commercial Directory of Ireland*. London and Manchester: I. Slater, 1846.

Smith, Joseph. *A Descriptive Catalogue of Friends' Books; or Books Written by Members of the Society of Friends, commonly called Quakers*. London: George Rymer, 1863.

Some Characteristics of Irish Lyric Poetry. Catholic World, Vol. XLIV, October 1886 to March 1887 (pp. 484–500). New York: The Catholic Publication Society, 1887.

Stewart, John Watson. *The Gentleman's and Citizen's Almanack*. Dublin: C. Hope, 1837.

The Asiatic Journal, Vol. XXVIII (new series), January – April 1839. London: Wm. H. Allen and Co., 1839.

The Dublin Almanac and General Register of Ireland for the Year of Our Lord 1847. Dublin: Pettigrew and Oulton, 1847.

The Gentleman's Magazine, Vol. XI, new series, January to June inclusive, April 1839 (death notice for Graham Stuart, the "wandering piper", pg. 446).

The Irish Law Times and Solicitors' Journal, Vol. XII. Dublin: John Falconer, 1878.

The Monthly Record of Births, Deaths, & Marriages, for the Month Ending January 1, 1861. London: Alfred Knowler, and Mrs. Janet Taylor, 1861.

The National Archives (UK), Richmond, Surrey. Online at www.nationalarchives.gov.uk. (accessed 23 Sept. 2013).

The Northern Standard, 1839–1847. Monaghan: Arthur Wellington Holmes. Death notices from the 19 July 1851 and 10 January 1852 editions per Monaghan County Library Services.

The Parliamentary Gazetteer of Ireland, 1844–45. Vol. I, II, IV. Dublin, London, and Edinburgh: A. Fullarton, and Co., 1846.

The Spectator Archive. Online service (by subscription), archive.spectator.co.uk. (accessed 11 Sept. 2013).

Thom, Alexander. *Thom's Irish Almanac and Official Directory, with the Post Office Dublin City and County Directory, for the year 1850*. 7th Annual Publication. Dublin: Alexander Thom, Printer and Publisher, 1850.

Thom, Alexander. *Thom's Irish Almanac and Official Directory, with the Post Office Dublin City and County Directory, for the year 1852*. 9th Annual Publication. Dublin: Alexander Thom, Printer and Publisher, 1852; and 1883 ed.

Urban, Sylvanus. *The Gentleman's Magazine*. Volume III, new series. July – December, 1868. London: John Bowyer Nichols and Son, 1848.

Walsh, John E., Edward S. Trevor, John F. Waller, Ross S. Moore, Lewis Morgan, and John Croker Creighton. *Irish Equity Reports of Cases argued and determined in the High Court of Chancery, the Rolls Court, and the Equity Exchequer, during the years 1845 and 1846*. Vol. VIII. Dublin: Hodges and Smith, 1846.

Will & Grant of Probate of Samuel Haslett or Hazlett, Farm at Foyle View, Liberties of Londonderry, 1843. Public Record Office of Northern Ireland, ref. D867/7.

William, Timothy. "The Somerset Estate." *Lord Belmont in Northern Ireland*. Online at lordbelmontinnorthernireland.blogspot.ca (accessed 2013-07-20).

Wilson, W. *The Post-chaise Companion: or, Travellers' Directory through Ireland.* Dublin: Wilson, 1786.

Wright, G.N. *A Guide to the County of Wicklow*. London: Baldwin, Cradock, and Joy, 1822.

Young, Augustus Blayney Russell Young. *Reminiscences of an Irish Priest, 1845–1920*. (Dundalk: W. Tempest, Dundalgan Press, 1931).

Young, Rev. Dr. Edward. *The Works of the Rev. Dr. Edward Young*, in three volumes. Charlestown: C.W.S. & H. Spear, 1811.

Young, Robert M. *Ulster in '98: Episodes and Anecdotes*. Belfast: M. Ward, 1893.

:: :: ::

www.ingramcontent.com/pod-product-compliance
Lightning Source LLC
Chambersburg PA
CBHW060502300426
44112CB00017B/2525
9780986887338